SOCIAL AND POLITICAL PHILOSOPHY

Edited by

John Arthur
State University of New York at Binghamton

William H. Shaw
San Jose State University

Prentice Hall
Upper Saddle River, New Jersey 07458

Library of Congress Cataloging-in-Publication Data

Readings in social and political philosophy / John Arthur, William H.
  Shaw, editors.
    p.   cm.
    ISBN 0–13–753799–9
    1. Civil rights.   2. Democracy.   3. Political obligation.
  4. Political science.   I. Arthur, John   II. Shaw,
  William H.
  JC571.R4353   1991
  320'.01—dc20   91–91927
                                                            CIP

Acquisition Editor: Ted Bolen
Production Editors: Fred Dahl and Rose Kernan
Copy Editor: Rose Kernan
Designer: Fred Dahl
Cover Designer: Karen Salzbach
Prepress Buyer: Herb Klein
Manufacturing Buyer: Patrice Fraccio
Supplements Editor: Ann Knitel

© 1992 by Prentice-Hall, Inc.
A Pearson Education Company
Upper Saddle River, NJ 07458

Printed in the United States of America
10 9 8 7 6 5 4 3 2

ISBN 0-13-753799-9

Prentice-Hall International (UK) Limited, London
Prentice-Hall of Australia Pty. Limited, Sydney
Prentice-Hall Canada Inc., Toronto
Prentice-Hall Hispanoamericana, S.A., Mexico
Prentice-Hall of India Private Limited, New Delhi
Prentice-Hall of Japan, Inc., Tokyo
Pearson Education Asia Pte. Ltd., Singapore
Editoria Prentice-Hall do Brasil, Ltda., Rio De Janeiro

Contents

III. The Nature and Value of Rights

IV. Freedom and the Limits of Liberty

V. Problems of Equality

VI. Justice, Community, and Gender

Introduction

From Socrates' decision to accept the death sentence of the Athenian court to the question of whether burning the American flag is a legitimate act of political protest, philosophy has wrestled with the proper relation between the individual and the state. Many fundamental issues surround that question: the limits of individual freedom, the meaning of patriotism, the nature and importance of rights, the proper functioning of democracy, the requirements of social and economic justice, and the meaning of equality, among many others. More than most areas of philosophy, social and political philosophy brings deep and abstract questions of theory and analysis to bear on issues of practical importance.

Social and Political Philosophy reflects the many faces of philosophical thought about society and politics. Its selections are both historical and contemporary. They include practical applications of philosophy to current political and legal controversies as well as comprehensive visions of the nature of society and the purpose of political organization. In addition, the book's historical selections enable instructors to set contemporary philosophical debates within the larger contours of Western social and political thought. In these ways, *Social and Political Philosophy* endeavors to highlight the immediate relevance of the subject, while at the same time furnishing the theoretical resources needed to address those problems.

A course on social and political philosophy can be taught in a variety of ways. Instructors often have different approaches to the subject, different intellectual and pedagogical goals, and different classroom styles. They therefore emphasize different themes and start at different places. *Social and Political Philosophy* provides teachers with an abundance of philosophical resources, permitting them great flexibility in how they organize their courses. The book is divided into six thematic sections, and while there are important and fruitful connections between the readings of the different sections, the book is structured so that no section presupposes any of the others. In addition, no section need be taught in its entirety. Typically, the first essay of each section provides an overview of that topic and raises a battery of issues, which are then pursued more deeply in the following three or four essays, while the final essay or two and the legal cases that follow address more applied problems. Instructors are thus free to focus on selected parts of the book more intensively, while passing over or treating only lightly other parts, without loss of coherence.

There is more material here than one can cover in a typical semester, and instructors will be able to make choices based on their own interests and their own understanding of the important issues in the field. Fortunately, the quality and the philosophical interest of the various selections—both theoretical and applied, both contemporary and historical—are so high and the interconnections between the various areas of social and political philosophy so rich that almost any starting point and any sequence of readings will lead to fruitful philosophical questions and engaging classroom discussions.

In teaching social and political philosophy, we have often found it effective to begin with the question raised by Plato's dialogue, "Crito"—"Why should I obey the law?"—and then to move on in subsequent readings to questions of democracy, rights, freedom and equality, concluding with the most broad topic of all—namely, competing visions of justice, community, and gender within Western political philosophy. Other instructors may want to start with the more historical material on justice and community gathered together in Section VI, and then turn to selected topics concerning rights, freedom, equality, and so forth. Or they may want to integrate selections from Section VI into the readings they choose from the other five sections.

Another interesting way of organizing a course on social and political philosophy would be to divide the readings according to the approach the author takes, rather than by subject matter. For example, instructors could divide the course among social contract theory, utilitarianism, and communitarianism, tracing the historical roots of each approach and then looking at contemporary philosophers who typify it. There is also ample material to create a unit on feminist thinking by using Mill's classic, *The Subjection of Women*, along with the essays by Wolgast, Richards, Kymlicka, and West. *Social and Political Philosophy* thus permits a variety of thematic emphases. Material has been organized and edited so that each of the six sections stands independently of the others, permitting an instructor to begin with any one of them.

In creating the textbook we have endeavored to strike a balance between philosophical sophistication on the one hand and the needs and interests of students on the other. We have sought material that is philosophically important and intellectually challenging, but also that even those new to philosophy will find provocative and engaging. The readings are edited in a way that avoids recondite issues and spares students needless technicality. Nevertheless, the materials are not easy because the issues they address, even where relevant and topical, are not easy. Editors' introductions to the individual readings are designed to provide sufficient background for introductory students to follow the major arguments, at least in broad outline.

I. POLITICAL OBLIGATION, PATRIOTISM, AND DISSENT

For many people, political philosophy rightly begins with the questions of what obligations, if any, the individual has to the larger community of which he or she is part and why one has those obligations. Perhaps every thinking person has at some time reflected on that question, but rarely has the issue been posed so dramatically as it was for Socrates in Plato's famous dialogue "Crito."

"Crito" is a classic of Western literature and a masterpiece of political philosophy, and for centuries it has captured the imagination of its readers. The Athenian court condemned Socrates to death for asking the awkward questions that are philosophy's hallmark and for exposing the inadequacy of the smug answers of many of Socrates' fellow Athenians. In the "Crito," Socrates' friend Crito visits Socrates in prison, seeking to arrange his escape. In the discussion that follows, Socrates argues that he is obligated to accept the Athenian verdict, and his arguments have resonated in the writings of many political philosophers through the ages and continue to be the subject of vigorous philosophical disputation.

One of these arguments is that by not emigrating and by accepting the benefits of political life, citizens have tacitly consented to obey their government and that this consent is the prime source of our political and legal obligations. John Locke relies on this argument, as have other writers in the social contract tradition. In "Tacit Consent," A. John Simmons vigorously challenges the notion that citizens have consented, tacitly or otherwise, to political rule and, thus, that the state's claim to exercise power legitimately can be said to rest on consent.

Next we include selections from two essays by John Rawls in which he attempts to defend political obligation, though on a different basis than Plato. For Rawls, it is fairness rather than tacit consent that binds individuals to the political order. Rawls does not think, however, that such obligations are absolute, and his famous discussion of the nature and justification of civil disobedience nicely illustrates the importance and complexity of the issues.

Ronald Dworkin concurs with Simmons that political obligation cannot be derived from an alleged, tacit consent of the citizenry, but he also rejects Rawls's account of obligation based on fairness. In "Political Obligation and Community" Dworkin maintains, rather, that legal obligation flows from the fact of membership in a certain sort of political community. Alasdair MacIntyre's "Is Patriotism a Virtue?" likewise emphasizes the deep bonds between the individual and the community. Patriotism draws upon the loyalty those bonds generate, but the local attachments and particular devotion patriotism requires seem hard to square with the universal and impartial perspective that liberal morality demands. The impersonal moral standpoint of modern liberalism and the morality of patriotism are, MacIntyre argues, deeply incompatible, and while liberals view the unconditional loyalty of patriotism as dangerous, MacIntyre delineates the weaknesses and moral hazards of the liberal morality of impartiality.

War poses sharply the question of patriotism and of one's obligations to the political community. In "Collective and Individual Responsibility in War," Michael Walzer discusses first, the responsibility of individual citizens for wars of aggression initiated by their political leaders and, second, the responsibilities of individual soldiers when faced with immoral orders from their superiors. Section I concludes with excerpts from the Supreme Court's discussion of conscientious objection to the draft—in particular whether conscientious objection must be religiously based and whether it must involve a rejection of war as such, rather than opposition to a particular war.

II. DEMOCRATIC VALUES AND CONSTITUTIONAL CONSTRAINTS

This section begins with selections from those responsible for framing the United States Constitution and from their critics who hoped the new plan of government would be rejected. Most of this material is from a series of newspaper articles. Some, known as the Federalist Papers, explained and defended the proposed constitution; others—like the essay we have reprinted by Robert Yates—were written by critics of the newly proposed Constitution. We also include an important exchange of letters between Thomas Jefferson and James Madison in which they debate the nature of democracy and the role of consent in establishing a government's legitimacy. Taken as a whole, this material nicely illustrates the philosophical visions of both those who drafted the Constitution and those who opposed it, along with the strategies the framers used in constructing the new government so it would achieve their objectives.

An oft-heard defense of democratic government is that when decisions are based on majority vote they will reflect the preferences or will of the majority. But the matter is more complicated than this, as Brian Barry argues in "Is Democracy Special?" After discussing the nature of democratic procedure, he argues that voting will not, in fact, identify the will of the majority, if indeed such a will exists. In "Democracy, Fairness, and Compromise," Peter Singer asks whether one has an obligation to obey the law in a democracy that one lacks in other regimes. He argues that because democracy provides a fair compromise by which force is avoided, one has a stronger reason for obedience in a democracy. Fairness, not the will of the people, is the foundation on which democratic government rests.

The two essays by Robert Bork and Ronald Dworkin address a feature of the United States Constitution that has seemed to many an anomaly: Why should unelected judges be allowed to overturn laws enacted by democratically elected representatives in the name of a two hundred year old constitution? Defending radically different styles of constitutional interpretation, each argues that his approach is compatible with the best ideals of democratic government. The legal cases that conclude Section II deal with several intriguing problems that implicate deep issues in democratic theory: legislative reapportionment, voting qualifications, and campaign financing.

III. THE NATURE AND VALUE OF RIGHTS

Questions of political legitimacy, of the value of democracy and of the purpose of constitutional restrains on democratic decision making all involve issues of rights. The readings of Section III offer competing accounts of what fundamental rights we have and rival interpretations of their moral and philosophical bases. We begin with a selection from Joel Feinberg's *Social Philosophy*, in which he discusses a variety of related conceptual and philosophical issues that surround the topic of rights: the differences between rights, on the one hand, and liberties and privileges, on the other; the resolution of conflicting claims and rights; primafacie and absolute rights; the interpretation of constitutional rights; and the nature of moral and human rights.

Most of us are committed to certain basic human rights that are independent of any political or institutional arrangements. We expect any plausible political theory to be able to explain and justify those rights. Utilitarianism is a long-standing and well-developed normative theory with important political implications, but many philosophers believe that it cannot take right seriously and is, therefore, defective. In "Utilitarianism and Rights" Allan Gibbard attempts to meet this criticism, arguing that utilitarians can and should be committed to rights. He contends that rights are an important part of the solution to the utilitarian problem of designing institutions and social practices that maximize social good. Considered in this light, Gibbard argues, accepting, advocating, and fostering a commitment in oneself and others to certain core human rights have great social utility.

In "Utilitarianism Versus Human Rights" James S. Fishkin responds to Gibbard, challenging utilitarianism's ability to provide a basis for respecting human rights. Noting that the rights listed by Gibbard are negative rights, which offer protection from certain kinds of "boundary crossings," Fishkin maintains that even if utilitarianism justifies institutionalizing these rights, the theory would still be unable to guarantee distributional equity. Moreover, Fishkin argues, utilitarianism always remains hostage to empirical considerations that may undermine its commitment to the individual rights Gibbard favors. Even at the level of institutional design, utilitarian calculations might favor alternative social practices that ignore human rights. In "Dignity, Rights, and Self-Control," Michael J. Meyer follows on from Fishkin by developing a non-utilitarian account of human rights which links rights with a conception of human dignity. He argues that human dignity is intimately linked to the capacity for authentic self-control and that rights would have little value to beings that could not exercise self-control.

Natural rights lie at the heart of John Locke's political philosophy, the historical importance of which is hard to exaggerate. Locke's political philosophy rests on his vision of government legitimacy as deriving from the consent of the governed, whose moral and political rights are antecedent to the establishment of a state. Beginning with those assumptions (which are explained in much greater detail in Section VI), Locke's "A Letter Concerning Toleration" states the case for sharply separating the state from religion and defends the right of religious belief and practice. Locke argues that religion and politics belong to distinct spheres; the former is concerned with matters of faith and salvation, the latter with protection of life, liberty, and property.

Like Fishkin and Meyer, Robert Nozick rejects the utilitarian account of rights. In "Rights and the Entitlement Theory," he begins with the Lockean premise that people have certain fundamental moral rights that are prior to the formation of government. These "Lockean rights" are both natural and negative. They are natural in the sense that we possess them independently of any social or political institution. They are negative because they require only that we refrain from interfering with others. Beyond this, we are not obligated to do anything positive for anyone else, nor is anyone else obliged to do anything positive for us. A belief in these rights shapes Nozick's specific theory of economic justice, which he calls the "entitlement theory." Essentially, Nozick argues that as long as you have acquired your goods, money, and property justly, that is, without force, theft or fraud, then you are to entitled to those possessions and may dispose of them however you wish.

After distinguishing three ways of understanding rights—as instruments, as constraints, and as goals—Professor Amartya Sen turns in "Property and Hunger" to questions of economics, in particular the rights to hold, use, and bequeath property. He maintains that famines and starvation result not from absolute lack of food, but from failures of entitlements: Hunger is basically a matter of not owning enough food. This analysis of hunger and famine in terms of property rights rather than availability of food leads Sen to reject Nozick's entitlement view that property rights are morally inviolable regardless of their consequences. He goes on to discuss "the right not to be hungry," the general acceptance of which in India has, he contends, played a substantial role in preventing famines there.

In recent years, many of the U.S. Supreme Court's most controversial decisions, including those concerning abortion and homosexuality, have turned on the meaning of the right to privacy. It is striking, then, that the word *privacy* never occurs in the U.S. Constitution, either in the original text or in the amendments. In "Privacy and the Constitution," John Arthur discusses the constitutional basis of the right to privacy. He then looks critically at two problems: (1) Is this right best understood as protecting individual liberty or protecting information about individuals? (2) Does the right to privacy, as understood by the Court, protect citizens against government efforts to criminalize homosexual sodomy?

We are committed to individual rights, but Professor Elizabeth H. Wolgast argues that our concepts of rights rests on a view of persons as fundamentally independent units, discrete and autonomous. In "Wrong Rights" Wolgast contends that this conception of independent individuals and their rights prevents us from addressing effectively certain injustices. In particular, our model of rights does not take sufficient account of the variety of relationships in which people take responsibility and care for one another. Rights have their place in social and political discourse, Wolgast argues, but their place is limited. The invocation of rights does not solve all the relevant moral and political problems that face us.

The court cases that conclude this section deal with religious rights and privacy rights. *Wisconsin v. Yoder* and *Smith v. Mobile Board of Education* concern, respectively, the right of Amish parents to exempt their children from compulsory education beyond eighth grade on religious grounds and whether school boards, in their efforts to separate education from religion, have in effect established "secular humanism" as an official religion. The next two cases concern a woman's right to get an abortion. *Roe v. Wade* is the 1973 case that first extended the right to privacy to include a woman's right to have an abortion. *Rust v. Sullivan* is one of a series of recent cases in which the Supreme Court has limited that right.

IV. FREEDOM, PATERNALISM, AND THE LIMITS OF LIBERTY

Although John Stuart Mill was a utilitarian, whose fundamental moral and political commitment was therefore to maximizing human well-being, his essay *On Liberty* is perhaps the most absolute and compelling defense of individual liberty in the history of Western political thought. Worried that democracy brings with it conformity and a distrust of individuality, Mill argued that society should interfere with an individual's liberty to think or live as he or she pleases only when the person's conduct risks harm to other people. Though Mill's liberty principle resonates with certain basic values in our political culture, existing societies are far from honoring it in practice. In particular, we frequently pass legislation the purpose of which is to protect individuals from harming themselves or to prevent them from doing what we think is immoral or bad for them.

However, there is no question that our political culture values individual liberty. But what is liberty? In his famous essay, "Two Concepts of Liberty," Isaiah Berlin distinguishes between negative conceptions of liberty—which have connections to the notion of negative rights discussed in the previous section—and positive conceptions of liberty as the freedom that comes from being one's own master and acting in accord with the wishes of one's true self. While Berlin points out the dangers of positive conceptions of freedom, in "Freedom and Society" Frithjof Bergmann exposes some of the shortcomings of the ideal of negative freedom, especially as this ideal is translated into the popular slogan that "the government that governs least governs best." Bergmann argues that it is an error to see the state as being the principle obstacle to freedom.

Janet Radcliffe Richards turns to the feminist goal of liberating women. In "Enquiries for Liberators" she argues that freedom is good in itself and that we are free to the extent that we can control our own destinies and can do as we like. However, she rejects the view of some feminists that a liberated woman must make certain kinds of choices. Richards argues that the fact that women are as they are because of social in-

fluences does not show that their choices are not their own. Her essay explores carefully the relation between freedom and social conditioning and the ways in which feminists ought properly to attack conditioning and enhance the freedom of women.

In "Grounds for Coercion" Joel Feinberg maintains that there is a basic moral presumption in favor of freedom, discusses various possible justifications for state coercion, and examines the harm-to-others principle that Mill defended in *On Liberty*. Feinberg focuses in particular on the important doctrine of legal paternalism—namely, that state coercion may justifiably be used to protect individuals from self-inflicted harm. In the spirit of Mill, Feinberg argues that the state has the right to prevent self-regarding harmful conduct only when it is substantially non-voluntary or when temporary intervention is necessary to determine whether it is voluntary.

Mill's arguments for freedom of expression seem to demand that we tolerate pornography, yet his harm-to-others principle might lend support to the social control of pornography. In "Pornography and the Tyranny of the Majority," Elizabeth H. Wolgast argues that censorship of pornography can be justified on a different basis—because women find it degrading and demeaning. Drawing an analogy with race discrimination, she defends her position against various objections and maintains that Mill himself would have viewed it sympathetically.

The court cases concluding Section IV concern several controversial questions of contemporary political morality, all of which involve issues of freedom and paternalism: whether one has a right for religious reasons to refuse a life-saving blood transfusion (*JFK Memorial Hospital v. Heston*), whether the state is permitted to ban the public exhibition of obscene material in order to maintain a decent society (*Paris Adult Theatre v. Slaton*), whether a city may outlaw the production, sale, exhibition, and distribution of pornographic material because it is degrading to women (*American Booksellers v. Hudnut*); and whether burning the U.S. flag as an act of political protest falls within the scope of the First Amendment's protection of freedom of speech (*Texas v. Johnson*).

V. PROBLEMS OF EQUALITY

"Everyone's created equal": This is a basic principle of our political order, and a belief in human equality is one of our firmest moral and political convictions. But what exactly is equality and what specific policies does a commitment to equality entail? In "Equality and Its Implications," Peter Singer argues that the only way to understand equality is as a principle requiring equal consideration of interests. Although equal consideration does not dictate equal treatment, the principle does have important implications with regard to racial and sexual differences, discrimination, and equality of opportunity.

In his essay "Why Liberals Should Care About Equality," Ronald Dworkin approaches this issue from a different angle. Liberalism as a political theory is committed to social and political equality, but Dworkin distinguishes two versions of liberalism, which differ in the value they place on equality. Dworkin maintains that the preferred version takes as fundamental the idea that government treat its citizens as equals. Because of this commitment, liberalism insists both that the state should not enforce private morality and that it should adjust the workings of the market in a more egalitarian direction.

The essays by Singer and Dworkin reflect the egalitarian temper of our day, in particular the belief that all human beings have equal worth and, therefore, certain fundamental rights, independent of their moral merit. Such a belief, though rarely argued for, is evident in the social policies and programs of the Western liberal democracies. In "Human Worth and Moral Merit," however, John Kekes challenges this widespread belief. He identifies and criticizes three assumptions upon which such a belief rests, upholding the rival conviction that human worth is proportional to moral merit.

A long history of discrimination against women and various ethnic groups has made many Americans sensitive to social and economic inequalities between these groups and white men. In "Why Should We Care About Group Inequality?" Glenn Loury points out that the mere existence of disparities between groups does not show oppressive treatment of individuals, and he raises the hard question of why we find inequality among individuals of the same group acceptable, but not inequality between groups. Loury goes on, however, to argue that superficially color-blind procedures may simply insure that the consequences of past racial bigotry remain a permanent part of the social landscape. For this reason, Loury argues, the state may justifiably adopt preferential policies. At the same time, Loury is alert to the dangers of such policies and urges that they be handled with caution.

In the next essay, "Sexual Equality and Discrimination," Will Kymlicka discusses the traditional approach to sexual equality which sees discrimination as arising when sex-biased distinctions are made arbitrarily or irrationally. Though accepting a few gender differences, the basic goal of the "difference" approach is gender neutrality. The alternative, "dominance" approach argues that genuine equality cannot be achieved merely by elimination of arbitrary discrimination but instead demands an understanding of sexual inequality in terms of male domination.

While most of us are alert to discrimination on racial or sexual grounds, few of us take seriously that fact that unattractive people must regularly contend with discrimination and adverse treatment on the basis of appearance in such diverse areas as housing, employment, and criminal sentencing. The essay "Facial Discrimination" from the *Harvard Law Review* argues that decisions based on appearance are often the result of prejudice and that existing legislation to protect the handicapped should be interpreted to bar employment discrimination on the basis of immutable aspects of one's physical appearance.

The court cases that accompany this section concern several important areas in which fundamental questions about the nature and value of equality have influenced public policy. *Michael M. v. Sonoma County Superior Court* addresses whether statutory rape laws involve sex discrimination; *Dothard v. Rawlinson* deals with whether and when gender can be a "bona fide occupational qualification" and thus figure as a legitimate, nondiscriminatory factor in employment decisions. In *San Antonio School District v. Rodriguez* the question is whether unequal state support to the schools of different districts, and the inequality of opportunity which that entails, violates the "equal protection" clause of the Fourteenth Amendment. Finally, *Regents of the University of California v. Bakke* is the Supreme Court's most famous attempt to grapple with the issue of university affirmative action programs that give preference for admission to racial minorities.

VI. JUSTICE, COMMUNITY, AND GENDER

The readings of this concluding section of *Social and Political Philosophy* offer different and rival perspectives of a more global sort concerning the nature and purpose of political association within the human community—a community composed of two sexes—and the meaning of justice within those political and communal bonds. At stake are not only competing visions of justice and community, but also—at least implicitly—differing accounts of the nature and purpose of political philosophy. Section VI also provides substantial excerpts from some of the classics of political philosophy, thus setting many of the issues of the previous sections in their historical and philosophical context.

Plato's *Republic* is famous for its portrait of his ideal city, governed by philosophers, in which justice consists of each class fulfilling its specific function, and for the parallel Plato draws between the well-governed city and the well-ordered human soul. Plato believed that those with genuine knowledge and a true understanding of the good should be at the helm of the ship of state. His allegory of the cave presents a memorable vision of the proper relation between rulers and the ruled. Remarkably for his time, Plato argued that differences between the sexes are not relevant to politics and that women in the ruling class of guardians should receive the same education and share in the same duties as men.

Aristotle balked at the utopian political construction of his teacher, Plato, which paid too little attention, in Aristotle's view, to the realities of human nature. By contrast, Aristotle sought to root his political theorizing in a more realistic understanding of the purpose of political community. Despite the continuing power of his vision of political association as the necessary framework for the achievement of human excellence, Aristotle seems to have freed himself less successfully than Plato from the prejudices of his era. His *Politics* notoriously defends slavery and upholds the subordination of women to men. In addition to his philosophical account of the nature and purpose of political association, Aristotle's analysis of the strong and weak points of the various forms of political organization make him the founder of political science.

Hobbes's *Leviathan*, arguably the premier work of early modern political philosophy, marks a break with the classical, political perspective of the ancient Greeks. Influenced by the new, Galilean scientific method and faced with the problem of ensuring security and establishing political authority in a world of strife, Hobbes offers a whole philosophical system, in which the recommended form of political organization is rooted in a materialistic account of human nature and motivation. John Locke was strongly influenced by Hobbes's social contract approach, and his own reworking of that vision in his *Second Treatise of Government* has been enormously influential, both philosophically and—via the American revolution—politically.

Marx and Engels blended social and political philosophy with economic, historical, and sociological theorizing. And they prided themselves on offering a comprehensive vision of history, progress, and social organization that was rooted firmly in empirical and historical analysis, rather than philosophical speculation. They stressed the class-divided character of society and the ways in which society's material production shapes its political, legal, and other structures, as well as its ideas of justice and rights. Their comprehensive critique of capitalism has had an influence, for better or worse, that is virtually unique in intellectual history. Their view of the nature and evolution of human society and of the prospects for a more just and egalitarian future offers a perspective with which all contemporary social and political theorists have had to come to grips.

The anarchist thinker Peter Kropotkin advocated "Revolt against all laws!" Anarchy, says Kropotkin in his essay, "Anarchism," means no-government, and he argued that people, being naturally social, need neither government nor law. Only the injustice and repression of government obscures humankind's true cooperative and ethical nature. The anarchist rejection of all political and legal authority stands in sharp contrast both to the theories of Hobbes and Locke and to the Marxist tradition. Anarchism's vision of the human community is a standing challenge to all those who uphold the political legitimacy of government and see the state as necessary for the achievement of social justice.

Utilitarianism is arguably the dominant political philosophy of the day because utilitarian reasoning, at least implicitly, underlies so many government decisions and public policy choices. In this selection from his classic *Utilitarianism*, John Stuart Mill explains and defends the utilitarian theory, elaborating on its account of social justice. In the section from *The Subjection of Women* that follows, Mill criticizes social institutions and legal arrangements that subordinate women to men and upholds the principle of perfect equality between the sexes. Mill's essay is probably the only major feminist writing by a man considered by all to be one of the great political philosophers. *The Subjection of Women* caused more hostile reaction from Mill's contemporaries than anything else he wrote, but it is one of his finest pieces of argument, and it raises a number of issues that continue to be at the center of feminist debate.

John Rawls is the foremost political philosopher of this century, at least in the English language. His major work, *A Theory of Justice*, which develops and refines the social contract approach, is a comprehensive attempt to provide a non-utilitarian account of justice, one which focuses on society's "basic structure." Rawls argues famously that people are to choose the principles to govern their society in the "original position," in ignorance of their social situation and personal characteristics. Forced to choose principles that will govern their choice of a constitution and, eventually of laws in general, people would agree upon two basic principles, he argues. The first would secure basic liberties against the demands of the larger good or utility; the second states in part that social and economic inequalities are to be permitted only insofar as they benefit the least advantaged groups of society.

In "Morality and the Liberal Ideal," Michael Sandel dissents from both utilitarianism and the rights-oriented political theories of contemporary writers like Rawls. He rejects the notion, which he sees as crucial to modern liberalism, that the self is never defined by its aims and attachments but is always capable of standing back to assess and revise them and that the principles of justice and political right can and should be determined independently of any account of the human good. Liberals are reluctant to favor certain individual ends over others or to affirm the superiority of certain ways of living. By contrast, Sandel's communitarianism harkens back to Aristotle. Sandel maintains that we cannot justify political arrangements without reference to our common purposes and aims and supports giving fuller expression to the claim of citizenship and community than the liberal vision allows.

Like Sandel, Robin West is critical of liberalism's individualistic understanding of the self as separate and autonomous. In her essay, "Political Theory and Gender," she outlines the challenge that modern feminist theory poses to the implicitly masculine perspective of traditional political and legal theory, and she explores the nature and possibility of a feminist alternative.

The book ends with an essay by John Rawls, "The Idea of an Overlapping Consensus," that offers a significantly different perspective. Rather than considering specific problems of political philosophy, Rawls weighs the possibilities and limits of political philosophy itself. He is particularly interested in asking how a stable government can be achieved in a society composed of different, often radically opposed religious and cultural groups without sacrificing justice and individual rights. Like Madison in Federalist Number 10, he asks how free, democratic political discourse and decision making can be carried on among people who hold widely different moral, cultural and religious visions. The answer, Rawls argues, lies in seeking an "overlapping consensus" among those with differing comprehensive moral and political perspectives, a consensus that underwrites a conception of justice supporting a liberal political order.

PART I Political Obligation, Patriotism, and Dissent

Crito

Plato

Plato was born into an aristocratic family in Athens around 427 B.C. Socrates (470–399 B.C.) was a friend of Plato's family from the time Plato was a schoolboy. Although a young Athenian of Plato's class would normally have pursued a political career, Plato chose philosophy instead and achieved fames as Socrates' most talented student and one of the world's greatest philosophers.

In 387 B.C., Plato founded the Academy, a school of higher education and research, which existed for over 900 years, and he continued as its head until his death in 347 B.C. at the age of 80. Plato wrote some twenty-five dialogues, including "Crito" and the book-length *Republic* (excerpted in Section VI below).

"Crito" begins after Socrates has been condemned to death for corrupting the youth through his teaching. Friends try to convince Socrates to allow them to save his life by breaking him out of jail, but Socrates will agree only if he can be convinced that violating the law would be just. "Crito" thus sets the stage for centuries of debate over the nature and extent of a citizen's legal obligation. (Socrates, in fact, refused to disobey and was executed.)

SCENE: *The Prison of Socrates*

SOCRATES: Why have you come at this hour, Crito? it must be quite early?

CRITO: Yes, certainly.

SOCRATES: What is the exact time?

CRITO: The dawn is breaking.

SOCRATES: I wonder that the keeper of the prison would let you in.

CRITO: He knows me, because I often come, Socrates; moreover, I have done him a kindness.

SOCRATES: And are you only just come?

CRITO: No, I came some time ago.

SOCRATES: Then why did you sit and say nothing, instead of awakening me at once?

CRITO: Why, indeed, Socrates, I myself would rather not have all this sleeplessness and sorrow. But I have been wondering at your peaceful slumbers, and that was the reason why I did not awaken you, because I wanted you to be out of pain. I have always thought you happy in the calmness of your temperament; but never did I see the like of the easy, cheerful way in which you bear this calamity.

From *The Dialogues of Plato* (3d ed.), trans. Benjamin Jowett (London: Oxford University Press, 1892).

SOCRATES: Why, Crito, when a man has reached my age he ought not to be repining at the prospect of death.

CRITO: And yet other old men find themselves in similar misfortunes and age does not prevent them from repining.

SOCRATES: That may be. But you have not told me why you come at this early hour.

CRITO: I come to bring you a message which is sad and painful; not, as I believe, to yourself, but to all of us who are your friends, and saddest of all to me.

SOCRATES: What! I suppose that the ship has come from Delos, on the arrival of which I am to die?

CRITO: No, the ship has not actually arrived, but she will probably be here today, as persons who have come from Sunium tell me that they left her there; and therefore to-morrow, Socrates, will be the last day of your life.

SOCRATES: Very well, Crito; if such is the will of God, I am willing; but my belief is that there will be a delay of a day.

CRITO: Why do you say this?

SOCRATES: I will tell you. I am to die on the day after the arrival of the ship?

CRITO: Yes; that is what the authorities say.

SOCRATES: But I do not think that the ship will be here until tomorrow; this I gather from a vision which I had last night, or rather only just now, when you fortunately allowed me to sleep.

CRITO: And what was the nature of the vision?

SOCRATES: There came to me the likeness of a woman, fair and comely, clothed in white raiment, who called to me and said: O Socrates,

The third day hence to Phthia shalt thou go.

CRITO: What a singular dream, Socrates!

SOCRATES: There can be no doubt about the meaning, Crito, I think.

CRITO: Yes; the meaning is only too clear. But, Oh! my beloved Socrates, let me entreat you once more to take my advice and escape. For if you die I shall not only lose a friend who can never be replaced, but there is another evil: people who do not know you and me will believe that I might have saved you if I had been willing to give money, but that I did not care. Now, can there be a worse disgrace than this—that I should be thought to value money more than the life of a friend? For the many will not be persuaded that I wanted you to escape, and that you refused.

SOCRATES: But why, my dear Crito, should we care about the opinion of the many? Good men, and they are the only persons who are worth considering, will think of these things truly as they happened.

CRITO: But do you see, Socrates, that the opinion of the many must be regarded, as is evident in your own case, because they can do the very greatest evil to any one who has lost their good opinion.

SOCRATES: I only wish, Crito, that they could; for then they could also do the greatest good, and that would be well. But the truth is, that they can do neither good nor evil: they can not make a man wise or make him foolish; and whatever they do is the result of chance.

CRITO: Well, I will not dispute about that; but please to tell me, Socrates, whether you are not acting out of regard to me and your other friends: are you not afraid that if you escape hence we may get into trouble with the informers for having stolen you away, and lose either the whole or a great part of our property; or that even a worse evil may happen to us? Now, if this is your fear, be at ease; for in order to save you, we ought surely to run this, or even a greater risk; be persuaded, then, and do as I say.

SOCRATES: Yes, Crito, that is one fear which you mention, but by no means the only one.

CRITO: Fear not. There are persons who at no great cost are willing to save you and bring you out of prison; and as for the informers, you may observe that they are far from being exorbitant in their demands; a little money will satisfy them. My means, which, as I am sure, are ample, are at your service, and if you have a scruple about spending all mine, here are strangers who will give you the use of theirs; and one of them, Simmias the Theban, has brought a sum of money for this very purpose; and Cebes and many others are willing to spend their money too. I say therefore, do not on that account hesitate about making your escape, and do not say, as you did in the court, that you will have a difficulty in knowing what to do with yourself if you escape. For men will love you in other places to which you may go, and not in Athens only; there are friends of mine in Thessaly, if you like to go to them, who will value and protect you, and no Thessalian will give you any trouble. Nor can I think that you are justified, Socrates, in betraying your own life when you might be saved; this is playing into the hands of your enemies and destroyers; and moreover I should say that you were betraying your children; for you might bring them up and educate them; instead of which you go away and leave them, and they will have to take their chance; and if they do not meet with the usual fate of orphans, there will be small thanks to you. No man should bring children into the world who is unwilling to persevere to the end in their nurture and education. But you are choosing the easier part, as I think, not the better and manlier, which would rather have become one who professes virtue in all his actions, like yourself. And indeed, I am ashamed not only of you, but of us who are your friends, when I reflect that this entire business of yours will be attributed to our want of courage. The trial need never have come on, or might have been brought to another issue; and the end of all, which is the crowning absurdity, will seem to have been permitted by us, through cowardice and baseness, who might have saved you, as you might have saved yourself, if we had been good for anything (for there was no difficulty in escaping); and we did not see how disgraceful, Socrates, and also miserable all this will be to us as well as to you. Make your mind up then, or rather have your mind already made up, for the time of deliberation is over, and there is only one thing to be done, which must be done, if at all, this very night, and which any delay will render all but impossible; I beseech you therefore, Socrates, to be persuaded by me, and to do as I say.

SOCRATES: Dear Crito, your zeal is invaluable, if a right one; but if wrong, the greater the zeal the greater the evil; and therefore we ought to consider whether these things shall be done or not. For I am and always have been one of those natures who must be guided by reason, whatever the reason may be which upon reflection appears to me to be the best; and now that this fortune has come upon me, I can not put away the reasons which I have before given: the principles which I have hitherto honored and revered I still honor, and unless we can find other and better principles on the instant, I am certain not to agree with you; no, not even if the power of the multitude could inflict many more imprisonments, confiscations, deaths, frightening us like children with hobgoblin terrors. But what will be the fairest way of considering the question? Shall I return to your old argument about the opinions of men some of which are to be regarded, and others, as we were saying, are not to be regarded? Now were we right in maintaining this before I was condemned? And has the argument which was once good now proved to be talk for the sake of talking;—in fact an amusement only, and altogether vanity? That is what I want to consider with your help, Crito:— whether, under my present circumstances, the argument appears to be in any way different or not; and is to be allowed by me or disallowed. That argument, which, as I believe, is maintained by many who assume to be authorities, was to the effect, as I was saying, that the opinions of some men are to be regarded, and of other men not to be regarded. Now you, Crito, are a disinterested person who are not going to die to-morrow—at least, there is no human probability of this, and you are therefore not liable to be deceived by the circumstances in which you are placed. Tell me then, whether I am right in saying that some opinions, and the opinions of some men only, are to be valued, and other opinions and the opinions of other men, are not to be valued. I ask you whether I was right in maintaining this?

CRITO: Certainly.

SOCRATES: Very good; and is not this true, Crito, of other things which we need not separately enumerate? In the matter of just and unjust, fair and foul, good and evil, which are the subjects of our present consultation, ought we to follow the opinion of the many and to fear them; or the opinion of the one man who has understanding, and whom we ought to fear and reverence more than all the rest of the world: and whom deserting we shall destroy and injure that principle in us which may be assumed to be improved by justice and deteriorated by injustice;—is there not such a principle?

CRITO: Certainly there is, Socrates.

SOCRATES: Take a parallel instance:—if, acting under the advice of men who have no understanding, we destroy that which is improvable by health and deteriorated by disease—when that has been destroyed, I say, would life be worth having? And that is—the body?

CRITO: Yes.

SOCRATES: Could we live, having an evil and corrupted body?

CRITO: Certainly not.

SOCRATES: And will life be worth having, if that higher part of man be depraved, which is improved by justice and deteriorated by injustice? Do we suppose that principle, whatever it may be in man, which has to do with justice and injustice, to be inferior to the body?

CRITO: Certainly not.

SOCRATES: More honored, then?

CRITO: Far more honored.

SOCRATES: Then, my friend, we must not regard what the many say of us; but what he, the one man who has understanding of just and unjust, will say, and what the truth will say. And therefore you begin in error when you suggest that we should regard the opinion of the many about just and unjust, good and evil, honorable and dishonorable.—Well, some one will say, "but the many can kill us."

CRITO: Yes, Socrates; that will clearly be the answer.

SOCRATES: That is true: but still I find with surprise that the old argument is, as I conceive, unshaken as ever. And I should like to know whether I may say the same of another proposition—that not life, but a good life, is to be chiefly valued?

CRITO: Yes, that also remains.

SOCRATES: And a good life is equivalent to a just and honorable one—that holds also?

CRITO: Yes, that holds.

SOCRATES: From these premises I proceed to argue the question whether I ought not to try and escape without the consent of the Athenians: and if I am clearly right in escaping, then I will make the attempt; but if not, I will abstain. The other considerations which you mention, of money and loss of character and the duty of educating children, are, as I fear, only the doctrines of the multitude, who would be as ready to call people to life, if they were able, as they are to put them to death—and with as little reason. But now, since the argument has thus far prevailed, the only question which remains to be considered is, whether we shall do rightly either in escaping or in suffering others to aid in our escape and paying them in money and thanks, or whether we shall not do rightly; and if the latter, then death or any other calamity which may ensue on my remaining here must not be allowed to enter into the calculation.

CRITO: I think that you are right, Socrates; how then shall we proceed?

SOCRATES: Let us consider the matter together, and do you either refute me if you can, and I will be convinced; or else cease, my dear friend, from repeating to me that I ought to escape against the wishes of the Athenians: for I am extremely desirous to be persuaded by you, but not against my own better judgment. And now please to consider my first position, and do your best to answer me.

CRITO: I will do my best.

SOCRATES: Are we to say that we are never intentionally to do wrong, or that in one way we ought and in another way we ought not to do wrong, or is doing wrong always evil and dishonorable, as I was just now saying, and as has been already acknowledged by us? Are all our former admissions which were made within a few days to be thrown away? And have we, at our age, been earnestly discoursing with one another all our life long only to discover that we are no better than children? Or are we to rest assured, in spite of the opinion of the many, and in spite of consequences whether better or worse, of the truth of what was then said, that injustice is always an evil and dishonor to him who acts unjustly? Shall we affirm that?

CRITO: Yes.

SOCRATES: Then we must do no wrong?

CRITO: Certainly not.

SOCRATES: Nor when injured injure in return, as the many imagine; for we must injure no one at all?

CRITO: Clearly not.

SOCRATES: Again, Crito, may we do evil?

CRITO: Surely not, Socrates.

SOCRATES: And what of doing evil in return for evil, which is the morality of the many—is that just or not?

CRITO: Not just.

SOCRATES: For doing evil to another is the same as injuring him?

CRITO: Very true.

SOCRATES: Then we ought not to retaliate or render evil for evil to any one, whatever evil we may have suffered from him. But I would have you consider, Crito, whether you really mean what you are saying. For this opinion has never been held, and never will be held, by any considerable number of persons; and those who are agreed and those who are not agreed upon this point have no common ground, and can only despise one another when they see how widely they differ. Tell me, then, whether you agree with and assent to my first principle, that neither injury nor retaliation nor warding off evil by evil is ever right. And shall that be the premiss of our argument? Or do you decline and dissent from this? For this has been of old and is still my opinion; but, if you are of another opinion, let me hear what you have to say. If, however, you remain of the same mind as formerly, I will proceed to the next step.

CRITO: You may proceed, for I have not changed my mind.

SOCRATES: Then I will proceed to the next step, which may be put in the form of a question:—Ought a man to do what he admits to be right, or ought he to betray the right?

CRITO: He ought to do what he thinks right.

SOCRATES: But if this is true, what is the application? In leaving the prison against the will of the Athenians, do I wrong any? or rather do I not wrong those whom I ought least to wrong? Do I not desert the principles which were acknowledged by us to be just? What do you say?

CRITO: I can not tell, Socrates, for I do not know.

SOCRATES: Then consider the matter in this way:—Imagine that I am about to play truant (you may call the proceeding by any name which you like), and the laws and the government come and interrogate me: "Tell us, Socrates," they say;

"what are you about? are you going by an act of yours to overturn us—the laws and the whole state, as far as in you lies? Do you imagine that a state can subsist and not be overthrown, in which the decisions of law have no power, but are set aside and overthrown by individuals?" What will be our answer, Crito, to these and the like words? Any one, and especially a clever rhetorician, will have a good deal to urge about the evil of setting aside the law which requires a sentence to be carried out; and we might reply, "Yes; but the state has injured us and given an unjust sentence." Suppose I say that?

CRITO: Very good, Socrates.

SOCRATES: "And was that our agreement with you?" the law would say; "or were you to abide by the sentence of the state?" And if I were to express astonishment at their saying this, the law would probably add: "Answer, Socrates, instead of opening your eyes: you are in the habit of asking and answering questions. Tell us what complaint you have to make against us which justifies you in attempting to destroy us and the state? In the first place did we not bring you into existence? Your father married your mother by our aid and begat you. Say whether you have any objection to urge against those of us who regulate marriage?" None, I should reply. "Or against those of us who regulate the system of nurture and education of children in which you were trained? Were not the laws, who have the charge of this, right in commanding your father to train you in music and gymnastic?" Right, I should reply, "Well then, since you were brought into the world and nurtured and educated by us, can you deny in the first place that you are our child and slave, as your fathers were before you? And if this is true you are not on equal terms with us; nor can you think that you have a right to do to us what we are doing to you. Would you have any right to strike or revile or do any other evil to a father or to your master, if you

had one, when you have been struck or reviled by him, or received some other evil at his hands?—you would not say this? And because we think right to destroy you, do you think that you have any right to destroy us in return, and your country as far as in you lies? And will you, O professor of true virtue, say that you are justified in this? Has a philosopher like you failed to discover that our country is more to be valued and higher and holier far than mother or father or any ancestor, and more to be regarded in the eyes of the gods and of men of understanding? Also to be soothed, and gently and reverently entreated when angry, even more than a father, and if not persuaded, obeyed? And when we are punished by her, whether with imprisonment or stripes, the punishment is to be endured in silence; and if she lead us to wounds or death in battle, thither we follow as is right; neither may any one yield or retreat or leave his rank, but whether in battle or in a court of law, or in any other place, he must do what his city and his country order him; or he must change their view of what is just: and if he may do no violence to his father or mother, much less may he do violence to his country." What answer shall we make to his, Crito? Do the laws speak truly, or do they not?

CRITO: I think that they do.

SOCRATES: Then the laws will say: "Consider, Socrates, if this is true, that in your present attempt you are going to do us wrong. For, after having brought you into the world, and nurtured and educated you, and given you and every other citizen a share in every good that we had to give, we further proclaim and give the right to every Athenian, that if he does not like us when he has come of age and has seen the ways of the city, and made our acquaintance, he may go where he pleases and take his goods with him; and none of us laws will forbid him or interfere with him. Any of you who does not like us and the city, and who wants to go to a colony or to any other city, may go where he likes, and take his goods with him. But he who has experience of the manner in which we order justice and administer the state, and still remains, has entered into an implied contract that he will do as we command him. And he who disobeys us is, as we maintain, thrice wrong; first, because in disobeying us he is disobeying his parents; secondly, because we are the authors of his education; thirdly, because he has made an agreement with us that he will duly obey our commands; and he neither obeys them nor convinces us that our commands are wrong; and we do not rudely impose them, but give them the alternative of obeying or convincing us;—that is what we offer, and he does neither. These are the sort of accusations to which, as we were saying, you, Socrates, will be exposed if you accomplish your intentions; you, above all other Athenians." Suppose I ask, why is this? they will justly retort upon me that I above all other men have acknowledged the agreement. "There is clear proof," they will say, "Socrates, that we and the city were not displeasing to you. Of all Athenians you have been the most constant resident in the city, which, as you never leave, you may be supposed to love. For you never went out of the city either to see the games, except once when you went to the Isthmus, or to any other place unless you were on military service; nor did you travel as other men do. Nor had you any curiosity to know other states or their laws: your affections did not go beyond us and our state; we were your special favorites, and you acquiesced in our government of you; and this is the state in which you begat your children, which is a proof of your satisfaction. Moreover, you might, if you had liked, have fixed the penalty at banishment in the course of the trial—the state which refuses to let you go now would have let you go then. But you pretended that you preferred death to exile, and that you were not grieved at death. And now you have forgotten these fine sentiments, and pay no respect to us the laws, of whom you are the destroyer; and are doing what only a miserable slave would do, running away and turning your back upon the compacts and agreements which you made as a citizen. And first of all answer this very question: Are we right in saying that you agreed to be governed according to us in deed, and not in word only? Is that true or not?" How shall we answer that, Crito? Must we not agree?

CRITO: There is no help, Socrates.

SOCRATES: Then will they not say: "You, Socrates, are breaking the covenants and agreements which you made with us at your leisure, not in any haste or under any compulsion or deception, but having had seventy years to think of them, during which time you were at liberty to leave the city, if we were not to your mind, or if our covenants appeared to you to be unfair. You had your choice, and might have gone either to Lacedaemon or Crete, which you often praise for their good government, or to some other Hellenic or foreign state. Whereas you, above all other Athenians, seemed to be so fond of the state, or, in other words, of us her laws (for who would like a state that has no laws), that you never stirred out of her; the halt, the blind, the maimed were not more stationary in her than you were. And now you run away and forsake your agreements. Not so, Socrates, if you will take our advice; do not make yourself ridiculous by escaping out of the city."

"For just consider, if you transgress and err in this sort of way, what good will you do either to yourself or to your friends? That your friends will be driven into exile and deprived of citizenship, or will lose their property, is tolerably certain; and you yourself, if you fly to one of the neighboring cities, as, for example,

Thebes or Megara, both of which are well-governed cities, will come to them as an enemy, Socrates, and their government will be against you, and all patriotic citizens will cast an evil eye upon you as a subverter of the laws, and you will confirm in the minds of the judges the justice of their own condemnation of you. For he who is a corruptor of the laws is more than likely to be corruptor of the young and foolish portion of mankind. Will you then flee from well-ordered cities and virtuous men? and is existence worth having on these terms? Or will you go to them without shame, and talk to them, Socrates? And what will you say to them? What you say here about virtue and justice and institutions and laws being the best things among men. Would that be decent of you? Surely not. But if you go away from well-governed states to Crito's friends in Thessaly, where there is a great disorder and license, they will be charmed to have the tale of your escape from prison, set off with ludicrous particulars of the manner in which you were wrapped in a goatskin or some other disguise, and metamorphosed as the fashion of runaways is—that is very likely; but will there be no one to remind you that in your old age you violated the most sacred laws from a miserable desire of a little more life. Perhaps not, if you keep them in a good temper; but if they are out of temper you will hear many degrading things; you will live, but how?—as the flatterer of all men, and the servant of all men; and doing what?—eating and drinking in Thessaly, having gone abroad in order that you may get a dinner. And where will be your fine sentiments about justice and virtue then? Say that you wish to live for the sake of your children, that you may bring them up and educate them—will you take them into Thessaly and deprive them of Athenian citizenship?

Is that the benefit which you would confer upon them? Or are you under the impression that they will be better cared for and educated here if you are still alive, although absent from them; for that your friends will take care of them? Do you fancy that if you are an inhabitant of Thessaly they will take care of them, and if you are an inhabitant of the other world they will not take care of them? Nay; but if they who call themselves friends are truly friends, they surely will.

"Listen, then, Socrates, to us who have brought you up. Think not of life and children first, and of justice afterwards, but of justice first, that you may be justified before the princes of the world below. For neither will you nor any that belong to you be happier or holier or juster in this life, or happier in another, if you do as Crito bids. Now you depart in innocence, a sufferer and not a doer of evil; a victim, not of the laws, but of men. But if you go forth, returning evil for evil, and injury for injury, breaking the covenants and agreements which you have made with us, and wronging those whom you ought least to wrong, that is to say, yourself, your friends, your country, and us, we shall be angry with you while you live, and our brethren, the laws in the world below, will receive you as an enemy; for they will know that you have done your best to destroy us. Listen, then, to us and not to Crito."

This is the voice which I seem to hear murmuring in my ears, like the sound of the flute in the ears of the mystic; that voice, I say, is humming in my ears, and prevents me from hearing any other. And I know that anything more which you may say will be vain. Yet speak, if you have anything to say.

CRITO: I have nothing to say, Socrates.

SOCRATES: Then let me follow the intimations of the will of God.

Tacit Consent

A. John Simmons

The idea that legal obligation is based on consent has deep roots in the Western political tradition, extending from Plato in ancient Greece and John Locke in the seventeenth century to the present. Beginning with a discussion of consent in general and an account of tacit consent in particular, Simmons carefully considers the merits of this approach to legal obligation. He concludes that neither enjoying the benefits of society nor residing within its borders creates a consensual basis for legal obligation.

A. John Simmons teaches social and political philosophy at the University of Virginia. He is the author of numerous works, including *Moral Principles and Political Obligations* (1979).

At least since Locke's impassioned defense of the natural freedom of men born into nonnatural states, the doctrine of personal consent has dominated both ordinary and philosophical thinking on the subject of our political bonds. The heart of this doctrine is the claim that no man is obligated to support or comply with any political power unless he has personally consented to its authority over him; the classic formulation of the doctrine appears in Locke's *Second Treatise of Government*. There is no denying the attractiveness of the doctrine of personal consent (and of the parallel thesis that no government is legitimate which governs without the consent of the governed). It has greatly influenced the political institutions of many modern states and has been a

From A. John Simmons, *Moral Principles and Political Obligations* (Princeton: Princeton University Press, 1979). Copyright © Princeton University Press. Reprinted by permission. Some footnotes omitted.

prime factor in the direction political theory has taken since 1600. . . .

CONSENT DEFINED

. . .Let me begin, then, by considering briefly just what it means to say that a man has "given his consent" to something or someone. In Locke's discussion in his *Second Treatise*, we can distinguish (although Locke himself does not) three sorts of acts which count for him as acts of consent. First, there are promises; second, there are written contracts; and third, there are acts of consent which are essentially authorizations of the actions of others. My own inclination is to say that of the three, only the third sort of act is a genuine act of consent. But there are certainly good reasons for grouping the three together. All are deliberate, voluntary acts whose understood purpose is to change the structure of rights of the parties involved and to generate obligations for the "consentors." In addition, there is a perfectly natural and acceptable sense of the word "consent" which is virtually synonymous with "promise"; thus, when we say that Mr. Smiley has graciously consented to speak at the award dinner, "consented" means here precisely "promised" or "agreed."

My discussion of consent, however, will treat this sense as a secondary one. We will be interested here in a kind of consent that differs from promising in a number of ways. First consent in the strict sense (as Plamenatz rightly notes)[1] is always given to the actions of other persons. Thus, I may consent to my daughter's marriage, to be governed by the decisions of the majority, or to my friend's handling my financial affairs. Promises, on the other hand, cannot, except in very special circumstances, ever be made concerning the actions of another person. Further, while both promises and consent generate special rights and obligations, the emphases in the two cases are different. The primary purpose of a promise is to undertake an obligation; the special rights which arise for the promisee are in a sense secondary. In giving consent to another's actions, however, our primary purpose is to authorize those actions and in so doing create for or accord to another a special right to act; the obligation generated on the consentor not to interfere with the exercise of this right takes, in this case, the secondary role.

Now, I do not wish to appear to be making too much of this distinction. I call attention to it only because in the discussion to follow a number of problems arise which concern consent in this strict sense, but not promising. These problems revolve around the "intentionality" of consent and have caused considerable confusion for political theorists. So while my conclusions concern-

ing the suitability of consent as a ground for political obligation will apply as well to promising or contracting (that is, to all the grounds of "obligations of commitment"), I will hereafter be considering primarily consent in the strict sense, in an effort to approach these confusions as painlessly as possible. When I speak of consenting, then, I will mean the according to another by the consentor of a special right to act within areas within which only the consentor is normally free to act; this is accomplished through a suitable expression of the consentor's intention to enter such a transaction and involves the assuming of a special obligation not to interfere with the exercise of the right accorded.[2]

As with promising, of course, I may give my consent by any number of means. Words, gestures, and lack of response are all suitable methods in appropriate contexts. I propose not to dwell here on the contextual and procedural conditions necessary for consenting. Insofar as these conditions can be specified at all, they are similar to those for promising (which have received considerable attention elsewhere).[3] Rather, I wish to emphasize only two general conditions, which will figure in later discussion. First, consent must be given intentionally and (perhaps this is redundant) knowingly. As with promising, one can consent insincerely, but not unintentionally. Second, consent must be given voluntarily. It is not possible to be very precise about this condition, but there are at least obvious cases on either side of a very fuzzy line; "consent" which is given under the direct threat of serious physical violence is, for instance, not really consent according to this condition. . . .

TACIT CONSENT

Since the earliest consent theories it has of course been recognized that "express con-

---

[1] Plamenatz, *Consent, Freedom, and Political Obligation*, p. 3.

[2] Here I follow, to a certain extent, Hart's discussion in "Are There Any Natural Rights?" p. 184.

[3] See especially J. R. Searle, *Speech Acts*, Cambridge University Press, 1970, chap. 3.

sent" is not a suitably general ground for political obligation. The paucity of express consentors is painfully apparent. Most of us have never been faced with a situation where express consent to a government's authority was even appropriate, let alone actually performed such an act. And while I think that most of us agree that express consent is a ground of political obligation (and certainly this is my view), the real battleground for consent theory is generally admitted to be the notion of tacit consent. It is on this leg that consent theory must lean most heavily if it is to succeed.

Thomas Hobbes noted that "signs of contract are either express or by inference,"[1] but he had little clear to say about this distinction. Discussions of tacit consent since that time have generally added only confusions to Hobbes's lack of clarity. Certainly Locke's discussion of tacit consent has puzzled many political philosophers by stretching the notion of consent far beyond the breaking point. But we must not be led by these confusions to believe that there is no such thing as tacit consent. On the contrary, genuine instances of tacit consent, at least in nonpolitical contexts, are relatively frequent.

Consider: Chairman Jones stands at the close of the company's board meeting and announces, "There will be a meeting of the board at which attendance will be mandatory next Tuesday at 8:00, rather than at our usual Thursday time. Any objections?" The board members remain silent. In remaining silent and inactive, they have all tacitly consented to the chairman's proposal to make a schedule change (assuming, of course, that none of the members is asleep, or failed to hear, etc.). As a result, they have given the chairman the right (which he does not normally have) to reschedule the meeting, and they have undertaken the obligation to attend at the new time.

Now this example should allow us to elaborate more constructively on the conditions

necessary for tacit consent. First, consent here is called "tacit" not because it has a different sort of significance than express consent, nor because it, e.g., binds less completely (as Locke seems to have thought). Consent is called tacit when it is given by remaining silent and inactive; it is not express, explicit, directly and distinctly expressed by action, but rather is expressed by the failure to do certain things. But tacit consent is nonetheless given or expressed. Silence after a call for objections can be just as much an expression of consent as shouting "aye" after a call for ayes and nayes. Calling consent tacit, then, points only to the special mode of its expression.

But under what conditions can silence be taken as a sign of consent? At least three spring quickly to mind.[5] (1) The situation must be such that it is perfectly clear that consent is appropriate and that the individual is aware of this. This includes the requirement that the potential consentor be awake and aware of what is happening. (2) There must be a definite period of reasonable duration when objections or expressions of dissent are invited or clearly appropriate, and the acceptable means of expressing this dissent must be understood by or made known to the potential consentor. (3) The point at which expressions of dissent are no longer acceptable must be obvious or made clear in some way to the potential consentor. These three conditions seem to jointly guarantee that the potential consentor's silence is *significant*. For they show that the silence does not result simply from (1) a failure to grasp the nature of the situation, (2) a lack of understanding of proper procedures, or (3) a misunderstanding about how long one has to decide whether or not to dissent. If any one of the conditions is not satisfied, then silence may indicate a breakdown in communication of

---

[4] *Leviathan*, chap. 14.

[5] Some of the following points are suggested by J. F. M. Hunter's remarks in "The Logic of Social Contracts," *Dialogue* 5 (June 1966).

one of these kinds. In that case, silence could not be taken as a sign of consent.

Our example of the board meeting meets these three conditions, although the time period specified in condition 3 is fairly informally and loosely set. In addition, of course, the example seems to meet the more general conditions for the possibility of consent of any sort. But while in most circumstances these conditions are, I think, sufficient, I want to suggest two additional conditions which will be important to the political applications of theory of tacit consent: (4) the means acceptable for indicating dissent must be reasonable and reasonably easily performed; and (5) the consequences of dissent cannot be extremely detrimental to the potential consentor. The violation of either condition 4 or 5 will mean that silence cannot be taken as a sign of consent, even though the other conditions for consent and tacit consent are satisfied.

We can easily imagine situations which would fail to satisfy our new conditions 4 and 5. For instance, if Chairman Jones had, in our previous example, said, "Anyone with an objection to my proposal will kindly so indicate by lopping off his arm at the elbow," both conditions would be violated, as they would be if dissent could only be expressed by resignation and the forfeit of company benefits, etc. Less dramatically, perhaps, condition 4 alone would be violated if board meeting traditions demanded that dissent could only be indicated by turning a perfect back handspring. And if the invariable consequence of objecting at a board meeting was dismissal and imprisonment (Chairman Jones happens also to be the local magistrate), our condition 5 would not be satisfied.

In any of these cases, silence cannot be taken as a sign of consent. As with all of the previous conditions, it is not possible to draw lines very clearly here; but if, say, the obstacles to consent were only the board members' nervousness about talking to Chairman Jones, or the fear that he might not give them a lift to the train station after the meeting, the situation would pretty clearly not violate conditions 4 and 5. . . .

LOCKE AND THE FAILURE OF TACIT CONSENT

Now that we have a reasonably clear notion of tacit consent as a tool, we can approach Locke's account of tacit consent somewhat more confidently.[6] Locke's famous discussion of tacit consent begins as follows: "The difficulty is, what ought to be looked upon as a tacit consent, and how far it binds, i.e., how far any one shall be looked on to have consented, and thereby submitted to any government, where he has made no expressions of it at all."[7] It seems that tacit consent need not really be expressed in the strict sense at all for Locke. Tacit consent can be understood or inferred by the observer, quite independent of the consentor's intentions or awareness that he is consenting. This is borne out by Locke's answer to his question: "And to this I say that every man, that hath any possession, or enjoyment, of any part of the dominions of any government, doth thereby give his tacit consent, and is as far forth obliged to obedience to the laws of that government. . . . "[8]

Now I have already suggested that tacit consent should not be taken by the consent theorist to be an "unexpressed" consent; calling consent tacit on my account specifies its mode of expression, not its lack of expression. But this is not the only thing which makes Locke's account of consent seem suspicious. For Locke, owning land in the state, lodging in a house in the state, traveling on a highway in the state, all are ways in which one gives his consent. In fact, signs of consent go "as far as the very being of any one

---

[6] For a thorough discussion of Locke on consent, see J. P. Plamenatz, *Man and Society*, Longmans, Green & Co., 1963, vol. I, 220–241.

[7] *Second Treatise of Government*, sec. 119.

[8] Ibid.

within the territories of that government."[9] Now, it is important to understand that Locke is not just saying that these are ways in which one might give his consent without putting it into words; that, of course, would be quite unobjectionable since nearly any act can, given suitable background conditions including the right sorts of conventions, be one whereby a man expresses his consent. Locke is saying rather that, in modern states at least, these acts necessarily constitute the giving of tacit consent. In other words, such acts are always signs of consent, regardless of the intentions of the actor or his special circumstances.

It is easy to see that this sort of "consent" violates (within modern states) nearly all of the general conditions necessary for an act to be an act of giving consent, tacit or otherwise. Most importantly, of course, Locke's suggestion that binding consent can be given unintentionally is a patent absurdity. The weakness of Locke's notion of consent has even led some to question Locke's traditionally accepted status as a consent theorist (indeed, as the classic consent theorist). The most interesting feature of Hanna Pitkin's "Obligation and Consent" is precisely such a questioning of Locke's devotion to personal consent as the ground of political obligation. I want to summarize her argument briefly, since analyzing it will lead us, I think, to a consideration of one of the fundamental confusions about tacit consent that has plagued discussions of this topic.

Pitkin argues that in widening his definition of consent so as "to make it almost unrecognizable," Locke seems to make a citizen's consent virtually automatic. "Why," she asks, "all the stress on consent if it is to include everything we do?"[10] Among other things, this forces us to conclude that residence within the territory of the worst sort of tyranny would constitute consent to it, which conclusion seems far indeed from Locke's intentions. But, of course, Locke holds that we cannot become bound to such a government even if we try.[11] How then can he reconcile this position with his claim that residence always constitutes consent? Pitkin answers that Locke intends tacit consent to be understood as a special consent given only to "the terms of the original contract which the founders of the commonwealth made."[12] In this manner, residing in or using roads within the territories of a government that is tyrannical or is otherwise acting ultra vires does not constitute tacit consent to the rule of that government. Only when the government acts within its assigned limits do these acts constitute consent.

Regardless of the merits of this argument as an exercise in Locke scholarship, the conclusion Pitkin draws is an interesting one. She maintains that, insofar as consent is virtually automatic in Locke, Locke did not really take personal consent seriously as a ground of political obligation. Rather, she interprets Locke as holding that "you are obligated to obey because of certain characteristics of the government—that it is acting within the bounds of a trusteeship based on an original contract."[13] Further, since she reads Locke as holding that "the terms of the original contract are . . . self-evident truths," Locke can be understood as claiming that our obligations in fact arise from the government's conformity to the only possible terms of a not necessarily actual (i.e., possibly hypothetical) contract.

The interesting aspect of this conclusion is the way in which it ties Locke to two contemporary methods for approaching these political problems. First, it brings Locke closer to what is often called a theory of "hypothetical contract," whereby the quality of government is determined in reference to the limits which would be placed on it by rational and self-interested original contrac-

---

[9] Ibid.

[10] "Obligation and Consent—I," *American Political Science Review* 59 (December 1965), p. 995.

[11] *Second Treatise of Government*, sec. 23.

[12] "Obligation and Consent—I," p. 995.

[13] Ibid., p. 996.

tors. This sort of theory has its most mature formulation in John Rawls's *A Theory of Justice*. Second, Pitkin makes Locke appear more like contemporary writers who deemphasize individuals' histories in a theory of political obligation, to stress instead the quality of the government as the source from which our political obligations arise.

This reading of Locke is obviously inconsistent with the radical individualism and voluntarism so evident throughout the *Second Treatise*. But my belief that Pitkin's reading is mistaken is based on more than a desire to preserve intact the Lockean spirit. I think that the oddity of Pitkin's interpretation can be explained by pointing to a single mistake which she makes in understanding Locke's position. The mistake is made when Pitkin concludes that the obligation to obey the government must derive from the quality of the government in question. This conclusion is essentially drawn from two sound premises: first, residence for Locke always constitutes consent; and second, for Locke we are bound to obey good governments but not bad ones. Pitkin concludes that consent must be essentially irrelevant to our political bonds in Locke's theory, for it seems inconsistent to hold all of the following: (1) By residing within their territories, we give our consent even to bad governments; (2) we are not obligated to bad governments; (3) consent is the ground of political obligation. To preserve consistency in Locke, Pitkin sacrifices (3); but she seems to ignore the possibility that consent might be only a necessary, rather than a sufficient, condition for the generation of political obligations. Let me clarify this observation by again describing a parallel case involving promises.

I make two promises to a friend—one to help him commit murder most foul, the other to give him half my yearly income. It is usually maintained, and it is certainly my belief, that while both promises are real promises, the latter obligates me while the former does not. But following reasoning similar to Pitkin's, we ought to conclude

from this that the obligation I am under to keep this latter promise arises solely from the morally commendable (or at least not morally prohibited) quality of the promised act. But this conclusion would be false. The obligation arises solely from my having promised. The moral quality of the act merely *prevents* one of the promises (the one to commit murder) from obligating me. But in no way is the morally acceptable quality of the other promised act the ground of my obligation to perform it.

Similarly, we might hold that consent to the authority of a tyrannical government does not bind one, just as a promise to act immorally does not bind one. And while I have suggested earlier that I think that consent to a tyranny can sometimes bind one, Locke's position, I maintain, is exactly that described above. Locke holds that our consent only binds us when it is given to good governments. But consent is still the sole ground of the obligation. The quality of the government is, for Locke, merely a feature relevant to the binding force of the consent. This he makes quite clear, I think, in Chapter IV: "For a man, not having the power over his own life, cannot, by compact, or his own consent, enslave himself to any one, nor put himself under the absolute, arbitrary power of another. . . ."[14]

Here Locke asserts that while a man may consent to an arbitrary government's rule, he is never bound to that government, for becoming so bound would involve disposing of rights which he does not possess. This suggests to me that Locke's doctrine of personal consent can with perfect consistency be joined to the claims that residence in any state constitutes consent and that we are only bound to good governments. All that is needed is the additional premise that consent is not always sufficient to obligate. In overlooking Locke's use of this premise, Pitkin has been led to misinterpret Locke's account of political obligation, emphasizing

---

[14] *Second Treatise of Government*, sec. 23.

the quality of the government over the consensual act.

I do not, of course, deny that in saying that a man who gives his tacit consent is "as far forth obliged to obedience," Locke appears to make consent sufficient for obligation. I suggest, however, that we understand him here to be thinking specifically of good governments, or, at worst, to be suffering from momentary carelessness. For when he begins seriously to consider tyrannical and arbitrary forms of government later in the *Second Treatise*, Locke frequently repeats his claim that we cannot bind ourselves to such governments by any means, compact included,[15] although we can certainly consent to such governments. Consent in Locke, then, cannot be sufficient always to generate obligations.

My suggestion is that we can believe Locke when he asserts that he holds personal consent to be the sole ground of political obligation. His claims on this point seem to be consistent, if perhaps mistaken. Still, one cannot help but be suspicious, as Pitkin certainly was, of a consent theory in which consent seems to fade into whatever is necessary to obligate everyone living under a good government. And these suspicions may again lead us to believe that Locke was really only halfhearted in his insistence on personal consent as the source of our political bonds.

I would like to suggest, however, that these suspicions can be allayed somewhat by understanding Locke as having become muddled about a distinction that has been similarly missed by many political theorists down to the present day. That distinction is between acts which are "signs of consent" and acts which "imply consent." In calling an act a "sign of consent," I mean that because of the context in which the act was performed, including the appropriate conventions (linguistic or otherwise), the act counts as an expression of the actor's intention to consent; thus, all genuine consensual acts are the givings of "signs of consent." But in saying that an act "implies consent," we mean neither that the actor intended to consent nor that the act would normally be taken as an attempt to consent. There are three ways in which an act might be said to "imply consent" in the sense I have in mind.

1. An act may be such that it leads us to conclude that the actor was in an appropriate frame of mind to, or had attitudes which would lead him to, consent if suitable conditions arose. This conclusion may be expressed by the conditional: if he had been asked to (or if an appropriate situation had otherwise arisen), he would have consented.

2. An act may be such that it "commits" the actor to consenting. By this I mean that the act would be pointless or hopelessly stupid unless the actor was fully prepared to consent; the act commits the actor "rationally" to giving his consent. Thus, for example, discoursing at great length on how a man would be an idiot not to consent to be governed by the government would, under normal circumstances, imply consent to be so governed, in sense 2 (as well, perhaps, as in sense 1).

3. An act may be such that it binds the actor morally to the same performance to which he would be bound if he had in fact consented. I may do something which is not itself an act of consent, but which nonetheless binds me as if I had consented; after performing the act, it would be wrong (ceteris paribus) for me not to do those things which my actual consent would have bound me to do. Consider a simple case like joining a game of baseball. Many writers have held that although in joining the game I do nothing which could be construed as giving my consent (tacit or otherwise) to be governed by the umpire's decisions, nonetheless, by participating in the activity, I may become bound to be so governed, just as I would be if I had in fact consented. The analysis of the ground of this moral bond, however, would appeal to something other than the performance of a deliberate undertaking, focusing instead on, e.g., the receipt of benefits from or the taking advantage of some established scheme.

All of these are types of acts which I will say "imply consent," though none of them is

---

[15] Ibid., secs. 135, 137, 149, 171, 172.

normally a "sign of consent." Each is closely related to genuine consent in some way without in fact being consent. I believe that in his peculiar notion of tacit consent Locke has actually, but unknowingly, developed a notion of acts which may very well "imply consent" in sense 3. Tacit consent is for Locke, remember, a consent which is not expressed but which is given in the performance of certain acts; in particular, Locke specifies the "enjoyments" of certain benefits granted by the state as being the sorts of acts in which we are interested. These "enjoyments" are seen by Locke to "imply consent" in the sense that it would be morally wrong for us to accept these enjoyments while refusing to accept the government's authority. When we enjoy the public highways, owning land, police protection, etc., our "acts of enjoyment," though not expressions of our consent, nonetheless are thought by Locke to "imply" our consent by binding us to obedience as if we had in fact consented. . . .

My chief purpose here is to examine Locke's *analysis* of this ground of political obligation, and it is in this analysis that the most obvious problems arise. For in his dedication to personal consent as the sole ground of political obligation, Locke confusedly labels the enjoyments of the benefits of government as a special sort of consensual act—"tacit" consent. But we have seen that while Locke's "enjoyments" might "imply consent," and might therefore have "something to do with" personal consent, they are not "signs of consent." Such enjoyments are not normally deliberate undertakings. In trying to rob consent of its intentionality, Locke succeeds only in undermining the appeal of his own consent theory, with its dedication to the thesis that only through deliberate undertakings can we become politically bound.

My suggestion is that none of Locke's "consent-implying enjoyments" is in fact a genuine consensual act. In analyzing any obligations which might arise from such enjoyments, we do not appeal to a principle of consent. Rather, such obligations would

arise, if at all, because of considerations of fairness or gratitude. Locke's primary error, then, seems to lie in his confusion of consent with other grounds which may be sufficient to generate obligations, grounds which may at best be called "consent-implying."

But if Locke was confused about this distinction between "signs of consent" and "consent-implying" acts, he is certainly not alone. Political theorists have remained confused on the same point for the nearly three hundred years since Locke's ground-breaking confusion. Over and over it is claimed that voting in an election, running for political office, applying for a passport, etc. are signs of consent to the political institutions of the state which bind the actor accordingly. . . . Perhaps the best contemporary example of this confusion surfaces in the second edition of J. P. Plamenatz's *Consent, Freedom, and Political Obligation*. Plamenatz, after avoiding many of these confusions in the body of his book, observes in his apologetic "Postscript to the Second Edition" that certain acts "signify" consent without being simple "expressions" of consent. He is concerned particularly with voting:

If Smith were in fact elected, it would be odd to say of anyone who had voted for him that he did not consent to his holding office. . . . Where there is an established process of election to an office, then, provided the election is free, anyone who takes part in the process consents to the authority of whoever is elected to the office.[16]

And beyond just voting, people can be properly said to consent to a political system simply "by taking part in its processes."[17]

But if my account of consent has been correct, all of these observations must be mistaken. For while political participation may "imply consent" (or might under special arrangements be a sign of consent), it is not under current arrangements in most

---

[16] *Consent, Freedom, and Political Obligation*, pp. 168, 170.

[17] Ibid., p. 171.

states a sign of consent. One may, and probably the average man does, register and vote with only minimal awareness that one is participating at all, and with no intention whatsoever of consenting to anything. Talk of consent in such situations can be no more than metaphorical.

It is easy to be misled, as Plamenatz probably was, by what I will call the "attitudinal" sense of "consent"; "consent" in this sense is merely having an attitude of approval or dedication. And certainly it would be odd (though not inconceivable) if a man who ran for public office did not "consent" to the political system in this attitudinal sense, or if the man who voted for him did not "consent" to his holding office. Voting, after all, is normally at least in part a sign of approval. But this sense of "consent" is quite irrelevant to our present discussion, where we are concerned exclusively with consent in the "occurrence" sense, i.e., with consent as an act which may generate obligations. An attitude of approval or dedication is completely irrelevant to the rights and obligations of the citizen who has it. When a man consents, he has consented and may be bound accordingly, regardless of how he feels about what he has consented to. It is my belief that confusions about this attitudinal-occurrence distinction, conjoined with similar failures to distinguish signs of consent from consent-implying acts, are responsible for most of the mistakes made in discussions of consent theory from Locke down to contemporary writers.

All of this has been leading, of course, to the conclusion that tacit consent must meet the same fate as express consent concerning its suitability as a general ground of political obligation. For it seems clear that very few of us have ever tacitly consented to the government's authority in the sense developed in this essay; the situations appropriate for such consent simply do not arise frequently. Without major alterations in modern political processes and conventions, consent theory's big gun turns out to be of woefully small caliber. While consent, be it tacit or express, may still be the firmest ground of political

obligation (in that people who have consented probably have fewer doubts about their obligations than others), it must be admitted that in most modern states consent will only bind the smallest minority of citizens to obedience. Only attempts to expand the notion of tacit consent beyond proper limits will allow consent to appear to be a suitably general ground of political obligation.

And while we have admitted that Locke does attempt such an illegitimate expansion, we can, from another vantage point, see that Locke was not completely confused in this attempt. For Locke's unconscious transition to "consent-implying" acts as grounds of obligation includes the important (though unstated) recognition that deliberate undertakings, such as promises or consensual acts, may *not* be necessary for the generation of political obligations; other sorts of acts may serve as well, in spite of their not being genuine acts of consent. This recognition, however, cannot form a part of a consent theory, with its insistence on consent as the sole ground of political obligation.

But it is nonetheless an important insight. The "enjoyments" of benefits of government (which Locke mistakenly classifies as acts of tacit consenting) may very well generate political obligations, as Locke believed. These obligations would not, however, fall under principles of fidelity or consent. There are, of course, other sorts of obligations than those generated by consent, and Locke seems to rely on them while, as a consent theorist, officially denying their existence. Thus, some of Locke's consent-implying enjoyments might in fact bind us to political communities under a "principle of fair play," as developed by Hart[18] and Rawls;[19] or they might be thought to bind us under a principle of gratitude, as Plamenatz at one point suggests,[20] or under some other

---

[18] "Are There Any Natural Rights?" pp. 185–186.

[19] John Rawls, "Legal Obligation and the Duty of Fair Play," in S. Hook (ed.), *Law and Philosophy*, New York University Press, 1964.

[20] *Consent, Freedom, and Political Obligation*, p. 24.

kind of principle of repayment. If so, then Locke's intuitions about obligation, and those of more recent consent theorists, may be essentially sound. Their mistakes may lie primarily in confusing obligation-generating acts with consensual acts,[21] and in overlooking the fact that the consent-implying status of an act is substantially irrelevant to the obligation it generates. Consent theory, then, while it surely fails to give a suitably general account of our political obligations, seems to point the way toward other avenues of inquiry which may prove more rewarding. . . .

TACIT CONSENT AND RESIDENCE

I have, to this point, said relatively little about a problem of tacit consent that lies at the heart of most contemporary works in consent theory. This is the problem of "tacit consent through residence." Locke, as we have observed, believed that residence was a sign of tacit consent. Similarly, Rousseau maintains that "when the State is instituted, residence constitutes consent; to dwell within its territory is to submit to the Sovereign."[22] And more recently, W. D. Ross has written that an "implicit promise to obey" is involved in permanent residence in a state.[23] We have, of course, argued that residence cannot reasonably be thought to constitute genuine consent (given, at least, the current state of political conventions). For it to do so, continued residence would have to be (among other things) a lack of response to a clearly presented "choice situation" allowing for consent or dissent. And clearly, no such choice is ever made available to most of us.

But Socrates has "the Laws" tell us in the *Crito* that Athens systematically did present such a "choice situation" to its people:

We openly proclaim this principle, that any Athenian, on attaining to manhood and seeing for himself the political organization of the state and us its laws, is permitted, if he is not satisfied with us, to take his property and go away wherever he likes. If any of you chooses to go to one of our colonies, supposing that he should not be satisfied with us and the state, or to emigrate to any other country, not one of the laws hinders or prevents him from going away wherever he likes, without any loss of property. On the other hand, if any one of you stands his ground when he can see how we administer justice and the rest of our public organization, we hold that by doing so he has in fact undertaken to do anything that we tell him.[24]

Socrates, in his remarkably modern dialogue, develops a claim of tacit consent through residence which is much more plausible than the Locke-Rousseau conception (which does not have the benefit of such a choice situation). Our question becomes, then, is it possible through suitable alterations in our political processes to make residence a genuine sign of tacit consent? The answer to this question should be of great importance to contemporary consent theorists like Joseph Tussman and Michael Walzer; for obviously, if one believes that consent is the only ground of political obligation, and that a government's legitimacy depends on the consent of its citizens, then the very possibility of legitimate government and widespread political obligation will turn on the possibility of instituting such a choice situation, to draw out the consent of the masses. But there are also other reasons for believing that a situation in which residence constituted consent would be a desirable one. For in that case, each citizen would know that he had consented to the government's authority, and one aspect of his doubts about how he ought to behave in matters political would be eliminated. Further, not only might the presentation of a choice situation heighten awareness of membership in a community, but presumably a general knowledge that such aware-

---

[21] Hart seems to have this point in mind in "Are There Any Natural Rights?" p. 186.

[22] *Social Contract*, IV.ii.

[23] Ross, *The Right and the Good*, p. 27.

[24] Plato, *Crito*, 51d–e.

ness was shared by one's fellow citizens would reap further benefits of trust and co-operation.

I mention these points only to emphasize the fact that the possibility of making residence a genuine sign of consent is not an idle issue. . . .

Could a choice situation, like the one described by Socrates, make continued residence a sign of consent? Joseph Tussman has answered this question in the affirmative. As long as the situation makes it clear that one who remains a resident is aware of the significance of so remaining, and as long as there remains a genuine alternative to giving one's tacit consent, then residence will be a sign of consent. We should not be concerned. Tussman argues, that the alternative to consent, namely emigration, is such an unpleasant alternative.[25] For "to say that consenting to the status of a member is involuntary because the alternative is not as pleasant or convenient is simply to confuse convenience with necessity"; the unpleasantness of emigration "does not rob a deliberate choice of its voluntary character."[26]

A formal choice procedure, then, seems to satisfy the demands that consent be knowingly given and voluntary. Similarly, such a procedure could easily be structured to satisfy our first three conditions for giving consent through silence—a clear choice situation, a period where dissent is invited, and a limit to time for allowable dissent. But it is not so clear that our conditions 4 and 5 will be satisfied by such a procedure. These conditions state that silence or inactivity cannot be taken as a sign of consent if the means of indicating dissent are unreasonable or very difficult to perform or if the consequences of dissent are extremely detri-

mental to the consentor. Emigration is a difficult course which might well have disastrous consequences. Of course, even if conditions 4 and 5 were not met, we might still want to call the act of remaining in residence a "voluntary act"; but it is not clear that mere voluntariness is sufficient to make such an act a sign of consent, as Tussman apparently believes. One cannot but feel somewhat inclined to agree with Hume on this point:

Can we seriously say, that a poor peasant or partizan has a free choice to leave his country, when he knows no foreign language or manners, and lives from day to day, by the small wages which he acquires. We may as well assert that a man, by remaining in a vessel, freely consents to the dominion of the master; though he was carried on board while asleep, and must leap into the ocean, and perish, the moment he leaves her.[27]

Does a man choose freely to remain in prison because he has a knife with which he can wound himself seriously enough to be removed to a hospital? These are strong metaphors, but it is easy to respond that our choice procedure can make provisions for dealing with such difficult cases. It might include, for instance, provisions for assisting the poor and oppressed (who would most desire and be least able to leave) in emigrating.

Would these sorts of provisions finally render continued residence a sign of tacit consent? There is one other problem which suggests that even with such provisions our choice procedure could not satisfy conditions 4 and 5 for tacit consent; and this problem cannot be circumvented by simply adding new provisions to the choice procedure. The problem is that it is precisely the most valuable "possessions" a man has that are often tied necessarily to his country of residence and cannot be taken from it.

---

[25] There could be, as Pitkin notes ("Obligation and Consent—I," p. 995), no such thing as "tacit dissent," short of emigration. Some contemporary consent theorists, like Michael Walzer, try to incorporate something like "tacit dissent" in their theories. See Walzer, *Obligations*, chaps. 3 and 5.

[26] Tussman, *Obligation and the Body Politic*, p. 38.

[27] David Hume, "Of the Original Contract," in A. MacIntyre (ed.), *Hume's Ethical Writings*, Collier-Macmillan, 1965, p. 263.

Most men will treasure home, family, and friends above all things. But these goods are not moveable property and cannot simply be packed on the boat with one's books and television set. Even if a man's home is in a tyrannical state, home can still be the most important thing in his life. And this places a very heavy weight on the side of continued residence. Emigration cannot be thought of as merely unpleasant or inconvenient for most of us; it may very well constitute a "disaster," if only a small one. And if that is true, it may well be that emigration routinely has consequences sufficiently unpleas-ant to make any formal political choice procedures fail our condition 5. In that case, we would be justified in concluding that no such procedure could ever allow us to take continued residence as a sign of tacit consent to the government's authority. The challenge, then, seems to remain open to the modern-day consent theorist to show us how government by consent can be made a reality. In any event, however, the more plausible alternative is to turn our attention from consent to other possible grounds of political obligation.

Legal Obligation, Fair Play, and Civil Disobedience

John Rawls

In the following section, John Rawls discusses the related questions of legal obligation and civil disobedience, both within the context of social contract theory. Legal obligation, he argues, is based on the duty of fair play. Even assuming the constitution is just, there is no assurance laws enacted in accordance with its procedures will also be just. Nonetheless, Rawls argues, citizens may have an obligation to obey which is based on their having benefited from the (generally) just regime. He concludes with a discussion of the role of civil disobedience in a constitutional democracy including the circumstances in which it would be justified.

John Rawls is a professor of philosophy at Harvard University and is among this century's pre-eminent political philosophers. His major work, *A Theory of Justice*, has won wide acclaim. (Selections from it are reprinted in section VI below.)

INTRODUCTION

I should like to discuss briefly, and in an informal way, the grounds of civil disobedience in a constitutional democracy. Thus,

Reprinted from *Civil Disobedience*, ed. Hugo Bedau (Pegasus, 1969) and *Law and Philosophy*, ed. Sidney Hook (New York: New York University Press, 1968) by permission of the author.

I shall limit my remarks to the conditions under which we may, by civil disobedience, properly oppose legally established democratic authority; I am not concerned with the situation under other kinds of government nor, except incidentally, with other forms of resistance. My thought is that in a reasonably just (though of course not perfectly just) democratic regime, civil disobedience, when it is justified, is normally to be understood as a political action which addresses the sense of justice of the majority in order to urge reconsideration of the measures protested and to warn that in the firm opinion of the dissenters the conditions of social cooperation are not being honored. This characterization of civil disobedience is intended to apply to dissent on fundamental questions of internal policy, a limitation which I shall follow to simplify our question.

THE SOCIAL CONTRACT DOCTRINE

It is obvious that the justification of civil disobedience depends upon the theory of political obligation in general, and so we may appropriately begin with a few comments on this question. The two chief virtues of social institutions are justice and efficiency, where by the efficiency of institutions I understand their effectiveness for certain social conditions and ends the fulfillment of which is to everyone's advantage. We should comply with and do our part in just and efficient social arrangements for at least two reasons: first of all, we have a natural duty not to oppose the establishment of just and efficient institutions (when they do not yet exist) and to uphold and comply with them (when they do exist); and second, assuming that we have knowingly accepted the benefits of these institutions and plan to continue to do so, and that we have encouraged and expect others to do their part, we also have an obligation to do our share when, as the arrangement requires, it comes our turn. Thus, we often have both a natural duty as well as an obligation to support just and efficient institutions, the obligation arising from our voluntary acts while the duty does not.

Now all this is perhaps obvious enough, but it does not take us very far. Any more particular conclusions depend upon the conception of justice which is the basis of a theory of political obligation. I believe that the appropriate conception, at least for an

account of political obligation in a constitutional democracy, is that of the social contract theory from which so much of our political thought derives. If we are careful to interpret it in a suitably general way, I hold that this doctrine provides a satisfactory basis for political theory, indeed even for ethical theory itself, but this is beyond our present concern.[1] The interpretation I suggest is the following: that the principles to which social arrangements must conform, and in particular the principles of justice, are those which free and rational men would agree to in an original position of equal liberty; and similarly, the principles which govern men's relations to institutions and define their natural duties and obligations are the principles to which they would consent when so situated. It should be noted straightway that in this interpretation of the contract theory the principles of justice are understood as the outcome of a hypothetical agreement. They are principles which would be agreed to if the situation of the original position were to arise. There is no mention of an actual agreement nor need such an agreement ever be made. Social arrangements are just or unjust according to whether they accord with the principles for assigning and securing fundamental rights and liberties which would be chosen in the original position. This position is, to be sure, the analytic analogue of the traditional notion of the state of nature, but it must not be mistaken for a historical occasion. Rather it is a hypothetical situation which embodies the basic ideas of the contract doctrine; the description of this situation enables us to work out which principles would be adopted. I must now say something about these matters.

The contract doctrine has always supposed that the persons in the original posi-

---

[1] By the social contract theory I have in mind the doctrine found in Locke, Rousseau, and Kant. I have attempted to give an interpretation of this view in: "Justice as Fairness," *Philosophical Review* (April, 1958); "Justice and Constitutional Liberty," *Nomos*, VI (1963); "The Sense of Justice," *Philosophical Review* (July 1963).

tion have equal powers and rights, that is, that they are symmetrically situated with respect to any arrangements for reaching agreement, and that coalitions and the like are excluded. But it is an essential element (which has not been sufficiently observed although it is implicit in Kant's version of the theory) that there are very strong restrictions on what the contracting parties are presumed to know. In particular, I interpret the theory to hold that the parties do not know their position in society, past, present, or future; nor do they know which institutions exist. Again, they do not know their own place in the distribution of natural talents and abilities, whether they are intelligent or strong, man or woman, and so on. Finally, they do not know their own particular interests and preferences or the system of ends which they wish to advance: they do not know their conception of the good. In all these respects the parties are confronted with a veil of ignorance which prevents any one from being able to take advantage of his good fortune or particular interests or from being disadvantaged by them. What the parties do know (or assume) is that Hume's circumstances of justice obtain: namely, that the bounty of nature is not so generous as to render cooperative schemes superfluous nor so harsh as to make them impossible. Moreover, they assume that the extent of their altruism is limited and that, in general, they do not take an interest in one another's interests. Thus, given the special features of the original position, each man tries to do the best he can for himself by insisting on principles calculated to protect and advance his system of ends whatever it turns out to be.

I believe that as a consequence of the peculiar nature of the original position there would be an agreement on the following two principles for assigning rights and duties and for regulating distributive shares as these are determined by the fundamental institutions of society: first, each person is to have an equal right to the most extensive liberty compatible with a like liberty for all;

second, social and economic inequalities (as defined by the institutional structure or fostered by it) are to be arranged so that they are both to everyone's advantage and attached to positions and offices open to all. In view of the content of these two principles and their application to the main institutions of society, and therefore to the social system as a whole, we may regard them as the two principles of justice. Basic social arrangements are just insofar as they conform to these principles, and we can, if we like, discuss questions of justice directly by reference to them. But a deeper understanding of the justification of civil disobedience requires, I think, an account of the derivation of these principles provided by the doctrine of the social contract. Part of our task is to show why this is so.

THE GROUNDS OF COMPLIANCE WITH AN UNJUST LAW

If we assume that in the original position men would agree both to the principle of doing their part when they have accepted and plan to continue to accept the benefits of just institutions (the principle of fairness), and also to the principle of not preventing the establishment of just institutions and of upholding and complying with them when they do exist, then the contract doctrine easily accounts for our having to conform to just institutions. But how does it account for the fact that we are normally required to comply with unjust laws as well? The injustice of a law is not a sufficient ground for not complying with it any more than the legal validity of legislation is always sufficient to require obedience to it. Sometimes one hears these extremes asserted, but I think that we need not take them seriously.

An answer to our question can be given by elaborating the social contract theory in the following way. I interpret it to hold that one is to envisage a series of agreements as follows: first, men are to agree upon the principles of justice in the original position.

Then they are to move to a constitutional convention in which they choose a constitution that satisfies the principles of justice already chosen. Finally they assume the role of a legislative body and guided by the principles of justice enact laws subject to the constraints and procedures of the just constitution. The decisions reached in any stage are binding in all subsequent stages. Now whereas in the original position the contracting parties have no knowledge of their society or of their own position in it, in both a constitutional convention and a legislature they do know certain general facts about their institutions, for example, the statistics regarding employment and output required for fiscal and economic policy. But no one knows particular facts about his own social class or his place in the distribution of natural assets. On each occasion the contracting parties have the knowledge required to make their agreement rational from the appropriate point of view, but not so much as to make them prejudiced. They are unable to tailor principles and legislation to take advantage of their social or natural position; a veil of ignorance prevents their knowing what this position is. With this series of agreements in mind, we can characterize just laws and policies as those which would be enacted were this whole process correctly carried out.

In choosing a constitution the aim is to find among the just constitutions the one which is most likely, given the general facts about the society in question, to lead to just and effective legislation. The principles of justice provide a criterion for the laws desired; the problem is to find a set of political procedures that will give this outcome. I shall assume that, at least under the normal conditions of a modern state, the best constitution is some form of democratic regime affirming equal political liberty and using some sort of majority (or other plurality) rule. Thus it follows that on the contract theory a constitutional democracy of some sort is required by the principles of justice. At the same time it is essential to observe that the constitutional process is always a case of what we may call imperfect procedural justice: that is, there is no feasible political procedure which guarantees that the enacted legislation is just even though we have (let us suppose) a standard for just legislation. In simple cases, such as games of fair division, there are procedures which always lead to the right outcome (assume that equal shares is fair and let the man who cuts the cake take the last piece). These situations are those of perfect procedural justice. In other cases it does not matter what the outcome is as long as the fair procedure is followed: fairness of the process is transferred to the result (fair gambling is an instance of this). These situations are those of pure procedural justice. The constitutional process, like a criminal trial, resembles neither of these; the result matters and we have a standard for it. The difficulty is that we cannot frame a procedure which guarantees that only just and effective legislation is enacted. Thus even under a just constitution unjust laws may be passed and unjust policies enforced. Some form of the majority principle is necessary but the majority may be mistaken, more or less willfully in what it legislates. . . .

It should be observed that the majority principle has a secondary place as a rule of procedure which is perhaps the most efficient one under usual circumstances for working a democratic constitution. The basis for it rests essentially upon the principles of justice and therefore we may, when conditions allow, appeal to these principles against unjust legislation. . . .

LEGAL OBLIGATION AND THE DUTY OF FAIR PLAY

. . .I shall assume as requiring no argument, that there is, at least in a society such as ours, a moral obligation to obey the law, although it may, of course, be overridden in certain cases by other more stringent obligations. I shall assume also that this obligation must rest on some general moral principle; that is, it must depend on some principle of justice or upon some principle of social utility or the common good, and the like. Now, it may appear to be a truism, and let us suppose it is, that a moral obligation rests on some moral principle. But I mean to exclude the possibility that the obligation to obey the law is based on a special principle of its own. After all, it is not, without further argument, absurd that there is a moral principle such that when we find ourselves subject to an existing system of rules satisfying the definition of a legal system, we have an obligation to obey the law; and such a principle might be final, and not in need of explanation, in the way in which the principles of justice or of promising and the like are final. I do not know of anyone who has said that there is a special principle of legal obligation in this sense. Given a rough agreement, say, on the possible principles as being those of justice, of social utility, and the like, the question has been on which of one or several is the obligation to obey the law founded, and which, if any, has a special importance. I want to give a special place to the principle defining the duty of fair play.

In speaking of one's obligation to obey the law, I am using the term "obligation" in its more limited sense, in which, together with the notion of a duty and of a responsibility, it has a connection with institutional rules. Duties and responsibilities are assigned to certain positions and offices, and obligations are normally the consequence of voluntary acts of persons, and while perhaps most of our obligations are assumed by ourselves, through the making of promises and the accepting of benefits, and so forth, others may put us under obligation to them (as when on some occasion they help us, for example, as children). I should not claim that the moral grounds for our obeying the law is derived from the duty of fair-play except insofar as one is referring to an obligation in this sense. It would be incorrect to say that our duty not to commit any of the legal offenses, specifying crimes of violence, is based on the duty of fair play, at

least entirely. These crimes involve wrongs as such, and with such offenses, as with the vices of cruelty and greed, our doing them is wrong independently of there being a legal system the benefits of which we have voluntarily accepted. . . .

Some have thought that there is ostensibly a paradox of a special kind when a citizen, who votes in accordance with his moral principles (conception of justice), accepts the majority decision when he is in the minority. Let us suppose the vote is between two bills, A and B each establishing an income tax procedure, rates of progression, or the like, which are contrary to one another. Suppose further that one thinks of the constitutional procedure for enacting legislation as a sort of machine that yields a result when the votes are fed into it—the result being that a certain bill is enacted. The question arises as to how a citizen can accept the machine's choice, which (assuming that B gets a majority of the votes) involves thinking that B ought to be enacted when, let us suppose, he is of the declared opinion that A ought to be enacted. For some the paradox seems to be that in a constitutional democracy a citizen is often put in a situation of believing that both A and B should be enacted when A and B are contraries: that A should be enacted because A is the best policy, and that B should be enacted because B has a majority—and moreover, and this is essential, that this conflict is different from the usual sort of conflict between prima facie duties.

There are a number of things that may be said about this supposed paradox, and there are several ways in which it may be resolved, each of which brings out an aspect of the situation. But I think the simplest thing to say is to deny straightway that there is anything different in this situation than in any other situation where there is a conflict of prima facie principles. The essential of the matter seems to be as follows: (1) Should A or B be enacted and implemented, that is, administered? Since it is supposed that everyone accepts the outcome of the vote, within limits, it is appropriate to put the enactment and implementation together. (2) Is A or B the best policy? It is assumed that everyone votes according to his political opinion as to which is the best policy and that the decision as to how to vote is not based on personal interest. There is no special conflict in this situation: the citizen who knows that he will find himself in the minority believes that, taking into account only the relative merits of A and B as prospective statutes, and leaving aside how the vote will go, A should be enacted and implemented. Moreover, on his own principles he should vote for what he thinks is the best policy, and leave aside how the vote will go. On the other hand, given that a majority will vote for B, B should be enacted and implemented, and he may know that a majority will vote for B. These judgments are relative to different principles (different arguments). The first is based on the person's conception of the best social policy; the second is based on the principles on which he accepts the constitution. The real decision, then, is as follows: A person has to decide, in each case where he is in the minority, whether the nature of the statute is such that, given that it will get, or has got, a majority vote, he should oppose its being implemented, engage in civil disobedience, or take equivalent action. In this situation he simply has to balance his obligation to oppose an unjust statute against his obligation to abide by a just constitution. This is, of course, a difficult situation, but not one introducing any deep logical paradox. Normally, it is hoped that the obligation to the constitution is clearly the decisive one.

Although it is obvious, it may be worthwhile mentioning, since a relevant feature of voting will be brought out, that the result of a vote is that a rule of law is enacted, and although given the fact of its enactment, everyone agrees that it should be implemented, no one is required to believe that the statute enacted represents the best policy. It is consistent to say that another statute would have been better. The vote does not

result in a statement to be believed: namely, that B is superior, on its merits, to A. To get this interpretation one would have to suppose that the principles of the constitution specify a device which gathers information as to what citizens think should be done and that the device is so constructed that it always produces from this information the morally correct opinion as to which is the best policy. If in accepting a constitution it was so interpreted, there would, indeed, be a serious paradox: for a citizen would be torn between believing, on his own principles, that A is the best policy, and believing at the same time that B is the best policy as established by the constitutional device, the principles of the design of which he accepts. This conflict could be made a normal one only if one supposed that a person who made his own judgment on the merits was always prepared to revise it given the opinion constructed by the machine. But it is not possible to determine the best policy in this way, nor is it possible for a person to give such an undertaking. . . .

Now to turn to the main problem, that of understanding how a person can properly find himself in a position where, by his own principles, he must grant that, given a majority vote, B should be enacted and implemented even though B is unjust. There is, then, the question as to how it can be morally justifiable to acknowledge a constitutional procedure for making legislative enactments when it is certain (for all practical purposes) that laws will be passed that by one's own principles are unjust. It would be impossible for a person to undertake to change his mind whenever he found himself in the minority; it is not impossible, but entirely reasonable, for him to undertake to abide by the enactments made, whatever they are, provided that they are within certain limits. But what more exactly are the conditions of this undertaking?

First of all, it means, as previously suggested, that the constitutional procedure is misinterpreted as a procedure for making legal rules. It is a process of social decision that does not produce a statement to be believed (that B is the best policy) but a rule to be followed. Such a procedure, say involving some form of majority rule, is necessary because it is certain that there will be disagreement on what is the best policy. This will be true even if we assume, as I shall, that everyone has a similar sense of justice and everyone is able to agree on a certain constitutional procedure as just. There will be disagreement because they will not approach issues with the same stock of information, they will regard different moral features of situations as carrying different weights, and so on. The acceptance of a constitutional procedure is, then, a necessary political device to decide between conflicting legislative proposals. If one thinks of the constitution as a fundamental part of the scheme of social cooperation, then one can say that if the constitution is just, and if one has accepted the benefits of its working and intends to continue doing so, and if the rule enacted is within certain limits, then one has an obligation, based on the principle of fair play, to obey it when it comes one's turn. In accepting the benefits of a just constitution one becomes bound to it, and in particular one becomes bound to one of its fundamental rules: given a majority vote in behalf of a statute, it is to be enacted and properly implemented.

The principle of fair play may be defined as follows. Suppose there is a mutually beneficial and just scheme of social cooperation, and that the advantages it yields can only be obtained if everyone, or nearly everyone, cooperates. Suppose further that cooperation requires a certain sacrifice from each person, or at least involves a certain restriction of his liberty. Suppose finally that the benefits produced by cooperation are, up to a certain point, free: that is, the scheme of cooperation is unstable in the sense that if any one person knows that all (or nearly all) of the others will continue to do their part, he will still be able to share a gain from the scheme even if he does not do his part. Under these conditions a person who has

accepted the benefits of the scheme is bound by a duty of fair play to do his part and not to take advantage of the free benefit by not cooperating. The reason one must abstain from this attempt is that the existence of the benefit is the result of everyone's effort, and prior to some understanding as to how it is to be shared, if it can be shared at all, it belongs in fairness to no one.

Now I want to hold that the obligation to obey the law, as enacted by a constitutional procedure, even when the law seems unjust to us, is a case of the duty of fair play as defined. It is, moreover, an obligation in the more limited sense in that it depends upon our having accepted and our intention to continue accepting the benefits of a just scheme of cooperation that the constitution defines. In this sense it depends on our own voluntary acts. Again, it is an obligation owed to our fellow citizens generally: that is, to those who cooperate with us in the working of the constitution. It is not an obligation owed to public officials, although there may be such obligations. That it is an obligation owed by citizens to one another is shown by the fact that they are entitled to be indignant with one another for failure to comply. Further, an essential condition of the obligation is the justice of the constitution and the general system of law being roughly in accordance with it. Thus the obligation to obey (or not to resist) an unjust law depends strongly on there being a just constitution. Unless one obeys the law enacted under it, the proper equilibrium, or balance, between competing claims defined by the constitution will not be maintained. Finally, while it is true enough to say that the enactment by a majority binds the minority, so that one may be bound by the acts of others, there is no question of their binding them in conscience to certain beliefs as to what is the best policy, and it is a necessary condition of the acts of others binding us that the constitution is just, that we have accepted its benefits, and so forth. . . .

Now recall that the question is this: How is it possible that a person, in accordance with his own conception of justice, should find himself bound by the acts of another to obey an unjust law (not simply a law contrary to his interests)? Put another way: Why, when I am free and still without my chains, should I accept certain a priori conditions to which any social contract must conform, a priori conditions that rule out all constitutional procedures that would decide in accordance with my judgment of justice against everyone else? To explain this, we require two hypotheses: that among the very limited number of procedures that would stand any chance of being established, none would make my decision decisive in this way; and that all such procedures would determine social conditions that I judge to be better than anarchy. Granting the second hypothesis, I want to elaborate on this in the following way: the first step in the explanation is to derive the principles of justice that are to apply to the basic form of the social system and, in particular, to the constitution. Once we have these principles, we see that no just constitutional procedure would make my judgment as to the best policy decisive. It is not simply that, among the limited number of procedures actually possible as things are, no procedure would give me this authority. The point is that even if such were possible, given some extraordinary social circumstances, it would not be just. (Of course it is not possible for everyone to have this authority.) Once we see this, we see how it is possible that within the framework of a just constitutional procedure to which we are obligated, it may nevertheless happen that we are bound to obey what seems to us to be and is an unjust law. Moreover, the possibility is present even though everyone has the same sense of justice (that is, accepts the same principles of justice) and everyone regards the constitutional procedure itself as just. Even the most efficient constitution cannot prevent the enactment of unjust laws if, from the complexity of the social situation and like conditions, the majority decides to enact them. A just constitutional procedure cannot foreclose all injustice; this depends on those who carry out the procedure.

To summarize, I have suggested that . . . our moral obligation to obey the law is a special case of the duty of fair play. This means that the legal order is construed as a system of social cooperation to which we become bound because: first, the scheme is just (that is, it satisfies the two principles of justice), and no just scheme can ensure against our ever being in the minority in a vote; and second, we have accepted, and intend to continue to accept, its benefits. If we failed to obey the law, to act on our duty of fair play, the equilibrium between conflicting claims, as defined by the concept of justice, would be upset. The duty of fair play is not, of course, intended to account for its being wrong for us to commit crimes of violence, but it is intended to account, in part, for the obligation to pay our income tax, to vote, and so on. . . .

THE PLACE OF CIVIL DISOBEDIENCE IN A CONSTITUTIONAL DEMOCRACY

We are now in a position to say a few things about civil disobedience. I shall understand it to be a public, nonviolent, and conscientious act contrary to law usually done with the intent to bring about a change in the policies or laws of the government.[2] Civil disobedience is a political act in the sense that it is an act justified by moral principles which define a conception of civil society and the public good. It rests, then, on political conviction as opposed to a search for self or group interest; and in the case of a constitutional democracy, we may assume that this conviction involves the conception of justice (say that expressed by the contract doctrine) which underlies the constitution itself. That is, in a viable democratic regime there is a

---

[2] Here I follow H. A. Bedau's definition of civil disobedience. See his "On Civil Disobedience," *Journal of Philosophy* (October, 1961).

common conception of justice by reference to which its citizens regulate their political affairs and interpret the constitution. Civil disobedience is a public act which the dissenter believes to be justified by this conception of justice and for this reason it may be understood as addressing the sense of justice of the majority in order to urge reconsideration of the measures protested and to warn that, in the sincere opinion of the dissenters, the conditions of social cooperation are not being honored. For the principles of justice express precisely such conditions, and their persistent and deliberate violation in regard to basic liberties over any extended period of time cuts the ties of community and invites either submission or forceful resistance. By engaging in civil disobedience a minority leads the majority to consider whether it wants to have its acts taken in this way, or whether, in view of the common sense of justice, it wishes to acknowledge the claims of the minority.

Civil disobedience is also civil in another sense. Not only is it the outcome of a sincere conviction based on principles which regulate civil life, but it is public and nonviolent, that is, it is done in a situation where arrest and punishment are expected and accepted without resistance. In this way it manifests a respect for legal procedures. Civil disobedience expresses disobedience to law within the limits of fidelity to law, and this feature of it helps to establish in the eyes of the majority that it is indeed conscientious and sincere, that it really is meant to address their sense of justice.[3] Being completely open about one's acts and being willing to accept the legal consequences of one's conduct is a bond given to make good one's sincerity, for that one's deeds are conscientious is not easy to demonstrate to another or even before oneself. No doubt it is possible to imagine a legal system in which conscientious belief that the law is unjust is ac-

cepted as a defense for noncompliance, and men of great honesty who are confident in one another might make such a system work. But as things are such a scheme would be unstable; we must pay a price in order to establish that we believe our actions have a moral basis in the convictions of the community.

The nonviolent nature of civil disobedience refers to the fact that it is intended to address the sense of justice of the majority and as such it is a form of speech, an expression of conviction. To engage in violent acts likely to injure and to hurt is incompatible with civil disobedience as a mode of address. Indeed, an interference with the basic rights of others tends to obscure the civilly disobedient quality of one's act. Civil disobedience is nonviolent in the further sense that the legal penalty for one's action is accepted and that resistance is not (at least for the moment) contemplated. Nonviolence in this sense is to be distinguished from nonviolence as a religious or pacifist principle. While those engaging in civil disobedience have often held some such principle, there is no necessary connection between it and civil disobedience. For on the interpretation suggested, civil disobedience in a democratic society is best understood as an appeal to the principles of justice, the fundamental conditions of willing social cooperation among free men, which in the view of the community as a whole are expressed in the constitution and guide its interpretation. Being an appeal to the moral basis of public life, civil disobedience is a political and not primarily a religious act. It addresses itself to the common principles of justice which men can require one another to follow and not to the aspirations of love which they cannot. Moreover by taking part in civilly disobedient acts one does not foreswear indefinitely the idea of forceful resistance; for if the appeal against injustice is repeatedly denied, then the majority has declared its intention to invite submission or resistance and the latter may conceivably be justified even in a democratic regime. We are not

---

[3] For a fuller discussion on this point to which I am indebted, see Charles Fried, "Moral Causation," *Harvard Law Review* (1964).

required to acquiesce in the crushing of fundamental liberties by democratic majorities which have shown themselves blind to the principles of justice upon which justification of the constitution depends.

THE JUSTIFICATION OF CIVIL DISOBEDIENCE

So far we have said nothing about the justification of civil disobedience, that is, the conditions under which civil disobedience may be engaged in consistent with the principles of justice that support a democratic regime. Our task is to see how the characterization of civil disobedience as addressed to the sense of justice of the majority (or to the citizens as a body) determines when such action is justified.

First of all, we may suppose that the normal political appeals to the majority have already been made in good faith and have been rejected, and that the standard means of redress have been tried. Thus, for example, existing political parties are indifferent to the claims of the minority and attempts to repeal the laws protested have been met with further repression since legal institutions are in the control of the majority. While civil disobedience should be recognized, I think, as a form of political action within the limits of fidelity to the rule of law, at the same time it is a rather desperate act just within these limits, and therefore it should, in general, be undertaken as a last resort when standard democratic processes have failed. In this sense it is not a normal political action. When it is justified there has been a serious breakdown; not only is there grave injustice in the law but a refusal more or less deliberate to correct it.

Second, since civil disobedience is a political act addressed to the sense of justice of the majority, it should usually be limited to substantial and clear violations of justice and preferably to those which, if rectified, will establish a basis for doing away with remaining injustices. For this reason there is a presumption in favor of restricting civil disobedience to violations of the first principle of justice, the principle of equal liberty, and to barriers which contravene the second principle, the principle of open offices which protects equality of opportunity. It is not, of course, always easy to tell whether these principles are satisfied. But if we think of them as guaranteeing the fundamental equal political and civil liberties (including freedom of conscience and liberty of thought) and equality of opportunity, then it is often relatively clear whether their principles are being honored. After all, the equal liberties are defined by the visible structure of social institutions; they are to be incorporated into the recognized practice, if not the letter, of social arrangements. When minorities are denied the right to vote or to hold certain political offices, when certain religious groups are repressed and others denied equality of opportunity in the economy, this is often obvious and there is no doubt that justice is not being given. However, the first part of the second principle which requires that inequalities be to everyone's advantage is a much more imprecise and controversial matter. Not only is there a problem of assigning it a determinate and precise sense, but even if we do so and agree on what it should be, there is often a wide variety of reasonable opinion as to whether the principle is satisfied. The reason for this is that the principle applies primarily to fundamental economic and social policies. The choice of these depends upon theoretical and speculative beliefs as well as upon a wealth of concrete information, and all of this mixed with judgment and plain hunch, not to mention in actual cases prejudice and self-interest. Thus unless the laws of taxation are clearly designed to attack a basic equal liberty, they should not be protested by civil disobedience; the appeal to justice is not sufficiently clear and its resolution is best left to the political process. But violations of the equal liberties that define the common status of citizenship are another matter. The deliberate denial of these more or less over any extended period of time in the face of normal political protest is, in general, an appropriate object of civil disobedience. We may think of the social system as divided roughly into two parts, one which incorporates the fundamental equal liberties (including equality of opportunity) and another which embodies social and economic policies properly aimed at promoting the advantage of everyone. As a rule civil disobedience is best limited to the former where the appeal to justice is not only more definite and precise, but where, if it is effective, it tends to correct the injustices in the latter.

Third, civil disobedience should be restricted to those cases where the dissenter is willing to affirm that everyone else similarly subjected to the same degree of injustice has the right to protest in a similar way. That is, we must be prepared to authorize others to dissent in similar situations and in the same way, and to accept the consequences of their doing so. Thus, we may hold, for example, that the widespread disposition to disobey civilly clear violations of fundamental liberties more or less deliberate over an extended period of time would raise the degree of justice throughout society and would insure men's self-esteem as well as their respect for one another. Indeed, I believe this to be true, though certainly it is partly a matter of conjecture. As the contract doctrine emphasizes, since the principles of justice are principles which we would agree to in an original position of equality when we do not know our social position and the like, the refusal to grant justice is either the denial of the other as an equal (as one in regard to whom we are prepared to constrain our actions by principles which we would consent to) or the manifestation of a willingness to take advantage of natural contingencies and social fortune at his expense. In either case, injustice invites submission or resistance; but submission arouses the contempt of the oppressor and confirms him in his intention. If straightway, after a decent period of time to make reasonable political appeals in

the normal way, men were in general to dissent by civil disobedience from infractions of the fundamental equal liberties, these liberties would, I believe, be more rather than less secure. Legitimate civil disobedience properly exercised is a stabilizing device in a constitutional regime, tending to make it more firmly just.

Sometimes, however, there may be a complication in connection with this third condition. It is possible, although perhaps unlikely, that there are so many persons or groups with a sound case for resorting to civil disobedience (as judged by the foregoing criteria) that disorder would follow if they all did so. There might be serious injury to the just constitution. Or again, a group might be so large that some extra precaution is necessary in the extent to which its members organize and engage in civil disobedience. Theoretically the case is one in which a number of persons or groups are equally entitled to and all want to resort to civil disobedience, yet if they all do this, grave consequences for everyone may result. The question, then, is who among them may exercise their right, and it falls under the general problem of fairness. I cannot discuss the complexities of the matter here. Often a lottery or a rationing system can be set up to handle the case; but unfortunately the circumstances of civil disobedience rule out this solution. It suffices to note that a problem of fairness may arise and that those who contemplate civil disobedience should take it into account. They may have to reach an understanding as to who can exercise their right in the immediate situation and to recognize the need for special constraint.

The final condition, of a different nature, is the following. We have been considering when one has a right to engage in civil disobedience, and our conclusion is that one has the right should three conditions hold: when one is subject to injustice more or less deliberate over an extended period of time in the face of normal political protests; where the injustice is a clear violation of the liberties of equal citizenship; and provided that the general disposition to protest similarly in similar cases would have acceptable consequences. These conditions are not, I think, exhaustive but they seem to cover the more obvious points; yet even when they are satisfied and one has the right to engage in civil disobedience, there is still the different question of whether one should exercise this right, that is, whether by doing so one is likely to further one's ends. Having established one's right to protest one is then free to consider these tactical questions. We may be acting within our rights but still foolishly if our action only serves to provoke the harsh retaliation of the majority; and it is likely to do so if the majority lacks a sense of justice, or if the action is poorly timed or not well designed to make the appeal to the sense of justice effective. It is easy to think of instances of this sort, and in each case these practical questions have to be faced. From the standpoint of the theory of political obligation we can only say that the exercise of the right should be rational and reasonably designed to advance the protester's aims, and that weighing tactical questions presupposes that one has already established one's right, since tactical advantages in themselves do not support it.

CONCLUSION: SEVERAL OBJECTIONS CONSIDERED

In a reasonably affluent democratic society justice becomes the first virtue of institutions. Social arrangements irrespective of their efficiency must be reformed if they are significantly unjust. No increase in efficiency in the form of greater advantages for many justifies the loss of liberty of a few. That we believe this is shown by the fact that in a democracy the fundamental liberties of citizenship are not understood as the outcome of political bargaining nor are they subject to the calculus of social interests. Rather these liberties are fixed points which serve to limit political transactions and which determine the scope of calculations of social advantage. It is this fundamental

place of the equal liberties which makes their systematic violation over any extended period of time a proper object of civil disobedience. For to deny men these rights is to infringe the conditions of social cooperation among free and rational persons, a fact which is evident to the citizens of a constitutional regime since it follows from the principles of justice which underlie their institutions. The justification of civil disobedience rests on the priority of justice and the equal liberties which it guarantees.

It is natural to object to this view of civil disobedience that it relies to heavily upon the existence of a sense of justice. Some may hold that the feeling for justice is not a vital political force, and that what moves men are various other interests, the desire for wealth, power, prestige, and so on. Now this is a large question the answer to which is highly conjectural and each tends to have his own opinion. But there are two remarks which may clarify what I have said: first, I have assumed that there is in a constitutional regime a common sense of justice the principles of which are recognized to support the constitution and to guide its interpretation. In any given situation particular men may be tempted to violate these principles, but the collective force in their behalf is usually effective since they are seen as the necessary terms of cooperation among free men; and presumably the citizens of a democracy (or sufficiently many of them) want to see justice done. Where these assumptions fail, the justifying conditions for civil disobedience (the first three) are not affected, but the rationality of engaging in it certainly is. In this case, unless the costs of repressing civil dissent injures the economic self-interest (or whatever) of the majority, protest may simply make the position of the minority worse. No doubt as a tactical matter civil disobedience is more effective when its appeal coincides with other interests, but a constitutional regime is not viable in the long run without an attachment to the principles of justice of the sort which we have assumed.

Then, further, there may be a misapprehension about the manner in which a sense of justice manifests itself. There is a tendency to think that it is shown by professions of the relevant principles together with actions of an altruistic nature requiring a considerable degree of self-sacrifice. But these conditions are obviously too strong, for the majority's sense of justice may show itself simply in its being unable to undertake the measures required to suppress the minority and to punish as the law requires the various acts of civil disobedience. The sense of justice undermines the will to uphold unjust institutions, and so a majority despite its superior power may give way. It is unprepared to force the minority to be subject to injustice. Thus, although the majority's action is reluctant and grudging, the role of the sense of justice is nevertheless essential, for without it the majority would have been willing to enforce the law and to defend its position. Once we see the sense of justice as working in this negative way to make established injustices indefensible, then it is recognized as a central element of democratic politics.

Finally, it may be objected against this account that it does not settle the question of who is to say when the situation is such as to justify civil disobedience. And because it does not answer this question, it invites anarchy by encouraging every man to decide the matter for himself. Now the reply to this is that each man must indeed settle this question for himself, although he may, of course, decide wrongly. This is true on any theory of political duty and obligation, at least on any theory compatible with the principles of a democratic constitution. The citizen is responsible for what he does. If we usually think that we should comply with the law, this is because our political principles normally lead to this conclusion. There is a presumption in favor of compliance in the absence of good reasons to the contrary. But because each man is responsible and must decide for himself as best he can whether the circumstances justify civil disobedience, it does not follow that he may

decide as he pleases. It is not by looking to our personal interests or to political allegiances narrowly contrued, that we should make up our mind. The citizen must decide on the basis of the principles of justice that underlie and guide the interpretation of the constitution and in the light of his sincere conviction as to how these principles should be applied in the circumstances. If he concludes that conditions obtain which justify civil disobedience and conducts himself accordingly, he has acted conscientiously and perhaps mistakenly, but not in any case at his convenience.

In a democratic society each man must act as he thinks the principles of political right require him to. We are to follow our understanding of these principles, and we cannot do otherwise. There can be no morally binding legal interpretation of these principles, not even by a supreme court or legislature. Nor is there any infallible procedure for determining what or who is right. In our system the Supreme Court, Congress, and the President often put forward rival interpretations of the Constitution. Although the Court has the final say in settling any particular case, it is not immune from powerful political influence that may change its reading of the law of the land. The Court presents its point of view by reason and argument; its conception of the Constitution must, if it is to endure, persuade men of its soundness. The final court of appeal is not the Court, or Congress, or the President, but the electorate as a whole. The civilly disobedient appeal in effect to this body. There is no danger of anarchy as long as there is a sufficient working agreement in men's conceptions of political justice and what it requires. That men can achieve such an understanding when the essential political liberties are maintained is the assumption implicit in democratic institutions. There is no way to avoid entirely the risk of divisive strife. But if legitimate civil disobedience seems to threaten civil peace, the responsibility falls not so much on those who protest as upon those whose abuse of authority and power justifies such opposition.

Political Obligation and Community

Ronald Dworkin

Ronald Dworkin begins with a critique of tacit consent, the duty to be just, and fair play as potential bases for political legitimacy. Legal obligation, he argues, flows not from individual agreements or private benefits but instead rests on the fact of membership in a certain type of political community, one which resembles the family. But of course not all communities, and certainly not all political systems, can be said to generate such obligations. He then describes the four characteristics which any community must exhibit if it is to achieve the status of an associative community.

Dworkin next considers which of three models of political community might constitute such as associative community, arguing that only a "model of principle" would qualify. Besides seeking virtues of justice, due process, and fairness (that is, to protect individual rights and provide for economic justice, secure a sound criminal justice system, and assure democratic processes) a model of principle seeks a fourth virtue. It demands that its officials treat its citizens with "integrity"—a concept he discusses elsewhere in his work.

Integrity requires a political system to seek the consistent application of its laws, interpreted in the best light, to all of its citizens equally. It demands, that is, that law makers and judges first seek to understand their political practices as embodying the three other virtues of justice, due process, and fairness. It then requires that those principles be extended, consistently, to all its members. Then, but only then, can a political system be said to manifest integrity, which is essential if is to achieve the status of an associative community with the attendant obligations of membership.

Ronald Dworkin is University Professor of Jurisprudence, Oxford University, and Professor of Law, New York University. In addition to many articles, he has written three books: *Taking Rights Seriously* (1978), *A Matter of Principle* (1985), and *Law's Empire* (1986).

THE PUZZLE OF LEGITIMACY

. . . How can *anything* provide [a] general . . . justification for coercion in ordinary politics? What can ever give anyone the kind

33

of authorized power over another that politics supposes governors have over the governed? Why does the fact that a majority elects a particular regime, for example, give that regime legitimate power over those who voted against it?

This is the classical problem of the legitimacy of coercive power. It rides on the back of another classical problem: that of political obligation. Do citizens have genuine moral obligations just in virtue of law? Does the fact that a legislature has enacted some requirement in itself give citizens a moral as well as a practical reason to obey? Does that moral reason hold even for those citizens who disapprove of the legislation or think it wrong in principle? If citizens do not have moral obligations of that character, then the state's warrant for coercion is seriously, perhaps fatally, undermined. These two issues—whether the state is morally legitimate, in the sense that it is justified in using force against its citizens, and whether the state's decisions impose genuine obligations on them—are not identical. No state should enforce all of a citizen's obligations. But though obligation is not a sufficient condition for coercion, it is close to a necessary one. A state may have good grounds in some special circumstances for coercing those who have no duty to obey. But no general policy of upholding the law with steel could be justified if the law were not, in general, a source of genuine obligations.

A state is legitimate if its constitutional structure and practices are such that its citizens have a general obligation to obey political decisions that purport to impose duties on them. . . .

Tacit Consent

Philosophers make several kinds of arguments for the legitimacy of modern democracies. One argument uses the idea of a social contract, but we must not confuse it with arguments that use that idea to establish the character or content of justice. John Rawls, for example, proposes an imaginary social contract as a device for selecting the best conception of justice in the circumstances of utopian political theory He argues that under specified conditions of uncertainty everyone would choose certain principles of justice as in his interests, properly understood, and he says that these principles are therefore the right principles for us. Whatever we may think of his suggestion, it has no direct connection to our present problem of legitimacy in the circumstances of ordinary politics where Rawls's principles of justice are very far from dominion. It would be very different, of course, if every citizen were a party to an actual, historical agreement to accept and obey political decisions taken in the way his community's political decisions are in fact taken. Then the historical fact of agreement would provide at least a good prima facie case for coercion even in ordinary politics. So some political philosophers have been tempted to say that we have in fact agreed to a social contract of that kind tacitly, by just not emigrating when we reach the age of consent. But no one can argue that very long with a straight face. Consent cannot be binding on people, in the way this argument requires, unless it is given more freely, and with more genuine alternate choice, than just by declining to build a life from nothing under a foreign flag. And even if the consent were genuine, the argument would fail as an argument for legitimacy, because a person leaves one sovereign only to join another; he has no choice to be free from sovereigns altogether.

The Duty to Be Just

Rawls argues that people in his original position would recognize a natural duty to support institutions that meet the tests of abstract justice and that they would extend this duty to the support of institutions not perfectly just, at least when the sporadic injustice lay in decisions reached by fair, majoritarian institutions. Even those who reject Rawls's general method might accept the duty to support just or nearly just institutions. That duty, however, does not provide a good explanation of legitimacy, because it does not tie political obligation sufficiently tightly to the particular community to which those who have the obligation belong; it does not show why Britons have any special duty to support the institutions of Britain. We can construct a practical, contingent argument for the special duty. Britons have more opportunity to aid British institutions than those of other nations whose institutions they also think mainly just. But this practical argument fails to capture the intimacy of the special duty. It fails to show how legitimacy flows from and defines citizenship. This objection points away from justice, which is conceptually universalistic, and toward integrity, which is already more personal in its different demands on different communities, as the parent of legitimacy.

Fair Play

The most popular defense of legitimacy is the argument from fair play: if someone has received benefits under a standing political organization, then he has an obligation to bear the burdens of that organization as well, including an obligation to accept its political decisions, whether or not he has solicited these benefits or has in any more active way consented to these burdens. This argument avoids the fantasy of the argument from consent and the universality and other defects of the argument from a natural duty of justice and might therefore seem a stronger rival to my suggestion that legitimacy is best grounded in integrity. But it is vulnerable to two counterarguments that have frequently been noticed. First, the fair play argument assumes that people can incur obligations simply by receiving what they do not seek and would reject if they had the chance. This seems unreasonable. Suppose a philosopher broadcasts a stunning and valuable lecture from a sound truck. Do all those who hear it—even all those who enjoy and profit by it—owe him a lecture fee?*

* This is an adaptation of Robert Nozick's argument against the fair play principle.

Second, the fair play argument is ambiguous in a crucial respect. In what sense does it suppose that people benefit from political organization? The most natural answer is this: someone benefits from a political organization if his overall situation—his "welfare" in the way economists use that phrase—is superior under that organization to what it would otherwise be. But everything then turns on the benchmark to be used, on what "otherwise" means, and when we try to specify the benchmark we reach a dead end. The principle is plainly too strong—it justifies nothing—if it requires showing that each citizen is better off under the standing political system than he would be under any other system that might have developed in its place. For that can never be shown for all the citizens the principle is meant to embrace. And it is plainly too weak—it is too easy to satisfy and therefore justifies too much—if it requires showing only that each citizen is better off under the standing organization than he would be with no social or political organization at all, that is, under a Hobbesian state of nature.

We can deflect this second objection if we reject the "natural" interpretation I described of the crucial idea of benefit. Suppose we understand the argument in a different way: it assumes not that each citizen's welfare, judged in some politically neutral way, has been improved *by* a particular social or political organization, but that each has received the benefits *of* that organization. That is, that he has actually received what is due him according to the standards of justice and fairness on which it is constructed. The principle of fair play, understood that way, states at least a condition necessary to legitimacy. If a community does not aim to treat someone as an equal, even according to its own lights, then its claim to his political obligation is fatally compromised. But it remains unclear how the negative fact that society has not discriminated against someone in this way, according to its own standards, could supply any positive reason why he should accept its laws as obligations. Indeed, the first objection I described becomes more powerful yet if we make this response to the second. For now the argument from fair play must be understood as claiming, not that someone incurs an obligation when his welfare is improved in a way he did not seek, but that he incurs an obligation by being treated in a way that might not even improve his welfare over any appropriate benchmark. For there is nothing in the fact that some individual has been treated fairly by his community according to its own standards that guarantees him any further, more material advantage.

OBLIGATIONS OF COMMUNITY

Circumstances and Conditions

Is it true that no one can be morally affected by being given what he does not ask for or choose to have? We will think so if we consider only cases of benefits thrust upon us by strangers like philosophers in sound trucks. Our convictions are quite different, however, when we have in mind obligations that are often called obligations of role but that I shall call, generically, associative or communal obligations. I mean the special responsibilities social practice attaches to membership in some biological or social group, like the responsibilities of family or friends or neighbors. Most people think that they have associative obligations just by belonging to groups defined by social practice, which is not necessarily a matter of choice or consent, but that they can lose these obligations if other members of the group do not extend them the benefits of belonging to the group. These common assumptions about associative responsibilities suggest that political obligation might be counted among them, in which case the two objections to the argument from fair play would no longer be pertinent. On the whole, however, philosophers have ignored this possibility, I believe for two reasons. First, communal obligations are widely thought to depend upon emotional bonds that presuppose that each

member of the group has personal acquaintance of all others, which of course cannot be true in large political communities. Second, the idea of special communal responsibilities holding within a large, anonymous community smacks of nationalism, or even racism, both of which have been sources of very great suffering and injustice.

We should therefore reflect on the character of familiar associative obligations to see how far these apparent objections actually hold. Associative obligations are complex, and much less studied by philosophers than the kinds of personal obligations we incur through discrete promises and other deliberate acts. But they are an important part of the moral landscape: for most people, responsibilities to family and lovers and friends and union or office colleagues are the most important, the most consequential obligations of all. The history of social practice defines the communal groups to which we belong and the obligations that attach to these. It defines what a family or a neighborhood or a professional colleague is, and what one member of these groups or holder of these titles owes to another. . . . Even associations we consider mainly consensual, like friendship, are not formed in one act of deliberate contractual commitment, the way one joins a club, but instead develop through a series of choices and events that are never seen, one by one, as carrying a commitment of that kind.

We have friends to whom we owe obligations in virtue of a shared history, but it would be perverse to describe this as a history of *assuming* obligations. On the contrary, it is a history of events and acts that *attract* obligations, and we are rarely even aware that we are entering upon any special status as the story unfolds. People become self-conscious about the obligations of friendship in the normal case only when some situation requires them to honor these obligations, or when they have grown weary of or embarrassed by the friendship, and then it is too late to reject them without betrayal. Other forms of association that carry special responsibilities—of academic colleagueship, for example—are even less a matter of free choice: someone can become my colleague even though I voted against his appointment. And the obligations some members of a family owe to others, which many people count among the strongest fraternal obligations of all, are matters of the least choice.

. . .We have a duty to honor our responsibilities under social practices that define groups and attach special responsibilities to membership, but this natural duty holds only when certain other conditions are met or sustained. Reciprocity is prominent among these other conditions. I have special responsibilities to my brother in virtue of our brotherhood, but these are sensitive to the degree to which he accepts such responsibilities toward me; my responsibilities to those who claim that we are friends or lovers or neighbors or colleagues or countrymen are equally contingent on reciprocity. But we must be careful here: if associative concepts are interpretive—if it can be an open question among friends what friendship requires—then the reciprocity we demand cannot be a matter of each doing for the other what the latter thinks friendship concretely requires. Then friendship would be possible only between people who shared a detailed conception of friendship and would become automatically more contractual and deliberative than it is, more a matter of people checking in advance to see whether their conceptions matched well enough to allow them to be friends.

. . . Friends have a responsibility to treat one another as friends, and that means, put subjectively, that each must act out of a conception of friendship he is ready to recognize as vulnerable to an interpretive test, as open to the objection that this is not a plausible account of what friendship means in our culture. Friends or family or neighbors need not agree in detail about the responsibilities attached to these forms of organization. Associative obligations can be sustained among people who share a general and diffuse sense of members' special rights and responsibilities from or toward one an-

other, a sense of what sort and level of sacrifice one may be expected to make for another. I may think friendship, properly understood, requires that I break promises to others to help a friend in need, and I will not refuse to do this for a friend just because he does not share this conviction and would not do it for me. But I will count him a friend and feel this obligation only if I believe he has roughly the same concern for me as I thereby show for him, that he would make important sacrifices for me of some other sort.

Nevertheless, the members of a group must by and large hold certain attitudes about the responsibilities they owe one another if these responsibilities are to count as genuine fraternal obligations. First, they must regard the group's obligations as *special*, holding distinctly within the group, rather than as general duties its members owe equally to persons outside it. Second, they must accept that these responsibilities are *personal*: that they run directly from each member to each other member, not just to the group as a whole in some collective sense. My brother or my colleague may think he has responsibilities to the reputation of the family or the university he best acquits by concentrating on his own career and thus denying me help when I need it or company when I want it. He may be right about the best use of his time overall from the standpoint of the general good of these particular communities. But his conduct does not form the necessary basis for my continuing to recognize fraternal obligations toward him.

Third, members must see these responsibilities as flowing from a more general responsibility each has of *concern* for the well-being of others in the group; they must treat discrete obligations that arise only under special circumstances, like the obligation to help a friend who is in great financial need, as derivative from and expressing a more general responsibility active throughout the association in different ways. A commercial partnership or joint enterprise, conceived as a fraternal association, is in that way different from even a long-standing contractual relationship. The former has a life of its own: each partner is concerned not just to keep explicit agreements hammered out at arm's length but to approach each issue that arises in their joint commercial life in a manner reflecting special concern for his partner as partner. Different forms of association presuppose different kinds of general concern each member is assumed to have for others. The level of concern is different—I need not act toward my partner as if I thought his welfare as important as my son's—and also its range: my concern for my union "brother" is general across the economic and productive life we share but does not extend to his success in social life, as my concern for my biological brother does. (Of course my union colleague may be my friend as well, in which case my overall responsibilities to him will be aggregative and complex.) But within the form or mode of life constituted by a communal practice, the concern must be general and must provide the foundation for the more discrete responsibilities.

Fourth, members must suppose that the group's practices show not only concern but an *equal* concern for all members. Fraternal associations are in that sense conceptually egalitarian. They may be structured, even hierarchical, in the way a family is, but the structure and hierarchy must reflect the group's assumption that its roles and rules are equally in the interests of all, that no one's life is more important than anyone else's. Armies may be fraternal organizations if that condition is met. But caste systems that count some members as inherently less worthy than others are not fraternal and yield no communal responsibilities.

We must be careful to distinguish, then, between a "bare" community, a community that meets the genetic or geographical or other historical conditions identified by social practice as capable of constituting a fraternal community, and a "true" community, a bare community whose practices of group responsibility meet the four conditions just

identified. The responsibilities a true community deploys are special and individualized and display a pervasive mutual concern that fits a plausible conception of equal concern. These are not psychological conditions. Though a group will rarely meet or long sustain them unless its members by and large actually feel some emotional bond with one another, the conditions do not themselves demand this. . . . These must be practices that people with the right level of concern would adopt—not a psychological property of some fixed number of the actual members. So, contrary to the assumption that seemed to argue against assimilating political to associative obligations, associative communities can be larger and more anonymous than they could be if it were a necessary condition that each member love all others, or even that they know them or know who they are.

Nor does anything in the four conditions contradict our initial premise that obligations of fraternity need not be fully voluntary. If the conditions are met, people in the bare community have the obligations of a true community whether or not they want them, though of course the conditions will not be met unless most members recognize and honor these obligations. It is therefore essential to insist that true communities must be bare communities as well. People cannot be made involuntary "honorary" members of a community to which they do not even "barely" belong just because other members are disposed to treat them as such. I would not become a citizen of Fiji if people there decided for some reason to treat me as one of them. Nor am I the friend of a stranger sitting next to me on a plane just because he decides he is a friend of mine.

Conflicts with Justice

An important reservation must be made to the argument so far. Even genuine communities that meet the several conditions just described may be unjust or promote injustice and so produce the conflict we have already noticed in different ways, between the integrity and justice of an institution. Genuine communal obligations may be unjust in two ways. First, they may be unjust to the members of the group: the conception of equal concern they reflect, though sincere, may be defective. It may be a firm tradition of family organization in some community, for example, that equal concern for daughters and sons requires parents to exercise a kind of dominion over one relaxed for the other. Second, they may be unjust to people who are not members of the group. Social practice may define a racial or religious group as associative, and that group may require its members to discriminate against nonmembers socially or in employment or generally. If the consequences for strangers to the group are grave, as they will be if the discriminating group is large or powerful within a larger community, this will be unjust. In many cases, requiring that sort of discrimination will conflict, not just with duties of abstract justice the group's members owe everyone else, but also with associative obligations they have because they belong to larger or different associative communities. For if those who do not belong to my race or religion are my neighbors or colleagues or (now I anticipate the argument to follow) my fellow citizens, the question arises whether I do not have responsibilities to them, flowing from those associations, that I ignore in deferring to the responsibilities claimed by my racial or religious group.

We must not forget, in puzzling about these various conflicts, that associative responsibilities are subject to interpretation, and that justice will play its normal interpretive role in deciding for any person what his associative responsibilities, properly understood, really are. If the bare facts of social practice are indecisive, my belief that it is unjust for parents to exercise absolute dominion over their children will influence my convictions about whether the institution of family really has that feature. . . . Even if the practice of dominion is settled and unquestioned, the interpretive attitude may isolate it as a mistake because it is con-

demned by principles necessary to justify the rest of the institution. There is no guarantee, however, that the interpretive attitude will always justify reading some apparently unjust feature of an associative institution out of it. We may have to concede that unjust dominion lies at the heart of some culture's practices of family, or that indefensible discrimination is at the heart of its practices of racial or religious cohesion. Then we will be aware of another possibility we have also noticed before, in other contexts. The best interpretation may be a deeply skeptical one: that no competent account of the institution can fail to show it as thoroughly and pervasively unjust, and that it should therefore be abandoned. Someone who reaches that conclusion will deny that the practice can impose genuine obligations at all. He thinks the obligations it purports to impose are wholly canceled by competing moral principle.

So our account of associative obligation now has the following rather complex structure. It combines matters of social practice and matters of critical interpretation in the following way. The question of communal obligation does not arise except for groups defined by practice as carrying such obligations: associative communities must be bare communities first. But not every group established by social practice counts as associative: a bare community must meet the four conditions of a true community before the responsibilities it declares become genuine. Interpretation is needed at this stage, because the question whether the practice meets the conditions of genuine community depends on how the practice is properly understood, and that is an interpretive question. Since interpretation is in part a matter of justice, this stage may show that apparently unjust responsibilities are not really part of the practice after all, because they are condemned by principles needed to justify other responsibilities the practice imposes. But we cannot count on this: the best interpretation available may show that its unjust features are compatible with the rest of its structure. Then, though the obligations it imposes are prima facie genuine, the question arises whether the injustice is so severe and deep that these obligations are canceled. That is one possibility, and practices of racial unity and discrimination seem likely examples. But sometimes the injustice will not be that great; dilemmas are then posed because the unjust obligations the practice creates are not entirely erased.

I can illustrate this complex structure by expanding an example already used. Does a daughter have an obligation to defer to her father's wishes in cultures that give parents power to choose spouses for daughters but not sons? We ask first whether the four conditions are met that transform the bare institution of family, in the form this has taken there, into a true community, and that raises a nest of interpretive questions in which our convictions about justice will figure. Does the culture genuinely accept that women are as important as men? Does it see the special parental power over daughters as genuinely in the daughter's interest? If not, if the discriminatory treatment of daughters is grounded in some more general assumption that they are less worthy than sons, the association is not genuine, and not distinctly associative responsibilities, of any character, arise from it. If the culture does accept the equality of the sexes, on the other hand, the discrimination against daughters may be so inconsistent with the rest of the institution of family that it may be seen as a mistake within it and so not a real requirement even if the institution is accepted. Then the conflict disappears for that reason.

But suppose the culture accepts the equality of sexes but in good faith thinks that equality of concern requires paternalistic protection for women in all aspects of family life, and that parental control over a daughter's marriage is consistent with the rest of the institution of family. If that institution is otherwise seriously unjust—if it forces family members to commit crimes in the interest of the family, for example—we will think it cannot be justified in any way that recommends continuing it. Our attitude is fully skeptical, and again we deny

any genuine associative responsibilities and so deny any conflict. Suppose, on the other hand, that the institution's paternalism is the only feature we are disposed to regard as unjust. Now the conflict is genuine. The other responsibilities of family membership thrive as genuine responsibilities. So does the responsibility of a daughter to defer to parental choice in marriage, but this may be overridden by appeal to freedom or some other ground of rights. The difference is important: a daughter who marries against her father's wishes, in this version of the story, has something to regret. She owes him at least an accounting, and perhaps an apology, and should in other ways strive to continue her standing as a member of the community she otherwise has a duty to honor.

I have paid such great attention to the structure of associative obligation, and to the character and occasions of its conflict with other responsibilities and rights, because my aim is to show how political obligation can be seen as associative, and this can be plausible only if the general structure of associative obligations allows us to account for the conditions we feel must be met before political obligation arises, and the circumstances we believe must either defeat it or show it in conflict with other kinds of obligations. . . .

FRATERNITY AND POLITICAL COMMUNITY

We are at last able to consider our hypothesis directly: that the best defense of political legitimacy—the right of a political community to treat its members as having obligations in virtue of collective community decisions—is to be found not in the hard terrain of contracts or duties of justice or obligations of fair play that might hold among strangers, where philosophers have hoped to find it, but in the more fertile ground of fraternity, community, and their attendant obligations. Political association, like family and friendship and other forms of association more local and intimate, is in itself pregnant of obligation. It is no objection to that claim that most people do not choose their political communities but are born into them or brought there in childhood. If we arrange familiar fraternal communities along a spectrum ranging from full choice to no choice in membership, political communities fall somewhere in the center. Political obligations are less involuntary than many obligations of family, because political communities do allow people to emigrate, and though the practical value of this choice is often very small the choice itself is important, as we know when we contemplate tyrannies that deny it. So people who are members of bare political communities have political obligations, provided the other conditions necessary to obligations of fraternity, appropriately defined for a political community, are met.

We must therefore ask what account of these conditions is appropriate for a political community. . . . We have no difficulty finding in political practice the conditions of bare community. People disagree about the boundaries of political communities, particularly in colonial circumstances or when standing divisions among nations ignore important historical or ethnic or religious identities. But these can be treated as problems of interpretation, and anyway they do not arise in the countries of our present main concern. Practice defines the boundaries of Great Britain and of the several states of the United States well enough for these to be eligible as bare political communities. We have noticed this already: we noticed that our most widespread political convictions suppose the officials of these communities to have special responsibilities within and toward their distinct communities. We also have no difficulty in describing the main obligations associated with political communities. The central obligation is that of general fidelity to law, the obligation political philosophy has found so problematic. So our main interest lies in the four conditions we identified. What form would these take in a political community? What must politics be like for a bare political society to become a true fraternal mode of association?

Three Models of Community

We are able to imagine political society as associative only because our ordinary political attitudes seem to satisfy the first of our four conditions. We suppose that we have special interests in and obligations toward other members of our own nation. Americans address their political appeals, their demands, visions, and ideals, in the first instance to other Americans; Britons to other Britons; and so forth. We treat community as prior to justice and fairness in the sense that questions of justice and fairness are regarded as questions of what would be fair or just within a particular political group. In that way we treat political communities as true associative communities. What further assumptions about the obligations and responsibilities that flow from citizenship could justify that attitude by satisfying its other conditions? This is not a question of descriptive sociology, though that discipline may have a part to play in answering it. We are not concerned, that is, with the empirical question of which attitudes or institutions or traditions are needed to create and protect political stability, but with the interpretive question of what character of mutual concern and responsibility our political practices must express in order to justify the assumption of true community we seem to make.

A community's political practices might aim to express one of three general models of political association. Each model describes the attitudes members of a political community would self-consciously take toward one another if they held the view of community the model expresses. The first supposes that members of a community treat their association as only a de facto accident of history and geography, among other things, and so as not a true associative community at all. People who think of their community this way will not necessarily treat others only as means to their own personal ends. That is one possibility: imagine two strangers from nations that despise each other's morals and religion are washed up on a desert island after a naval battle between the two countries. The strangers are thrown together initially by circumstance and nothing more. Each may need the other and may refrain from killing him for that reason. They may work out some division of labor, and each may hold to the agreement so long as he thinks it is to his advantage to do so, but not beyond that point or for any other reason. But there are other possibilities for de facto association. People might regard their political community as merely de facto, not because they are selfish but because they are driven by a passion for justice in the world as a whole and see no distinction between their community and others. A political official who takes that view will think of his constituents as people he is in a position to help because he has special means—those of his office—for helping them that are not, regrettably, available for helping other groups. He will think his responsibilities to his own community special in no other way, and therefore not greater in principle. So when he can improve justice overall by subordinating the interests of his own constituents, he will think it right to do so.

I call the second model of community the "rulebook" model. It supposes that members of a political community accept a general commitment to obey rules established in a certain way that is special to that community. Imagine self-interested but wholly honest people who are competitors in a game with fixed rules or who are parties to a limited and transient commercial arrangement. They obey the rules they have accepted or negotiated as a matter of obligation and not merely strategy, but they assume that the content of these rules exhausts their obligation. They have no sense that the rules were negotiated out of common commitment to underlying principles that are themselves a source of further obligation; on the contrary, they take these rules to represent a compromise between antagonistic interests or points of view. If the rules are the product of special negotiation, as in the contract case, each side has tried to give up as little in return for as much as possible, and it would therefore be unfair and not merely mistaken for either to claim that their agreement embraces anything not explicitly agreed. . . .

The third model of community is the model of principle. It agrees with the rulebook model that political community requires a shared understanding, but it takes a more generous and comprehensive view of what that understanding is. It insists that people are members of a genuine political community only when they accept that their fates are linked in the following strong way: they accept that they are governed by common principles, not just by rules hammered out in political compromise. Politics has a different character for such people. It is a theater of debate about which principles the community should adopt as a system, which view it should take of justice, fairness, and due process,* not the different story, appropriate to the other models, in which each person tries to plant the flag of his convictions over as large a domain of power or rules as possible. Members of a society of principle accept that their political rights and duties are not exhausted by the particular decisions their political institutions have reached, but depend, more generally, on the scheme of principles those decisions presuppose and endorse. So each member accepts that others have rights and that he has duties flowing from that scheme, even though these have never been formally identified or declared. Nor does he suppose that these further rights and duties are conditional on his wholehearted approval of that scheme; these obligations arise from the historical fact that his community has adopted that scheme, which is then special

---

*Justice refers to the distribution of economic income, opportunities and rights; fairness to the distribution of political power; due process to the procedures used to judge law violators. [eds.]

to it, not the assumption that he would have chosen it were the choice entirely his. In short, each accepts political integrity as a distinct political ideal and treats the general acceptance of that ideal, even among people who otherwise disagree about political morality, as constitutive of political community.

Now our stage is properly set (or rather managed) for the crucial question. Each of these three models of community describes a general attitude that members of a political community take toward one another. Would political practices expressing one or another of these attitudes satisfy the conditions of true associative community we identified? We need not pause long over the de facto model of circumstance. It violates even the first condition: it adds nothing, by way of any special attitudes of concern, to the circumstances that define a bare political community. It admits community among people who have no interest in one another except as means to their own selfish ends. Even when this form of community holds among selfless people who act only to secure justice and fairness in the world as they understand these virtues, they have no special concern for justice and fairness toward fellow members of their own community. (Indeed, since their only concern is abstract justice, which is universalistic in its character, they can have no basis for special concern.)

The rulebook model of community might seem more promising. For its members do show a special concern for one another beyond each person's general concern that justice be done according to his lights, a special concern that each other person receive the full benefit of whatever political decisions have in fact been taken under the standing political arrangements. That concern has the necessary individualized character to satisfy the second condition: it runs separately from each person directly to everyone else. But it cannot satisfy the third, for the concern it displays is too shallow and attenuated to count as pervasive, indeed to count as genuine concern at all. People in a rulebook community are free to act in poli-

tics almost as selfishly as people in a community of circumstances can. Each one can use the standing political machinery to advance his own interests or ideals. True, once that machinery has generated a discrete decision in the form of a rule of law or a judicial decision, they will accept a special obligation to secure the enforcement of that decision for everyone whom it happens to benefit. But that commitment is too formal, too disconnected from the actual circumstances it will promote, to count as expressing much by way of genuine concern, and that is why it rings hollow as an expression of fraternity. It takes hold too late in the political process; it permits someone to act at the crucial legislative stage with no sense of responsibility or concern for those whom he pretends, once every possible advantage has been secured at their expense, to count as brothers. The familiar version of the argument from fair play—these are the rules under which you have benefited and you must play by them—is particularly appropriate to a rulebook community, which takes politics, as I said, to be a kind of game. But that is the version of the argument most vulnerable to all the objections we began by noticing.

The model of principle satisfies all our conditions, at least as well as any model could in a morally pluralistic society. It makes the responsibilities of citizenship special: each citizen respects the principles of fairness and justice instinct in the standing political arrangement of his particular community, which may be different from those of other communities, whether or not he thinks these the best principles from a utopian standpoint. It makes these responsibilities fully personal: it commands that no one be left out, that we are all in politics together for better or worse, that no one may be sacrificed, like wounded left on the battlefield, to the crusade for justice overall. The concern it expresses is not shallow, like the crocodile concern of the rulebook model, but genuine and pervasive. It takes hold immediately politics begins and is sustained through legislation to adjudication and enforcement. Everyone's political acts express on every occasion, in arguing about what the rules should be as well as how they should be enforced, a deep and constant commitment commanding sacrifice, not just by losers but also by the powerful who would gain by the kind of logrolling . . . integrity forbids. Its rationale tends toward equality in the way our fourth condition requires: its command of integrity assumes that each person is as worthy as any other, that each must be treated with equal concern according to some coherent conception of what that means. As association of principle is not automatically a just community; its conception of equal concern may be defective or it may violate rights of its citizens or citizens of other nations in the way we just saw any true associative community might.

But the model of principle satisfies the conditions of true community better than any other model of community that it is possible for people who disagree about justice and fairness to adopt.

A community of principle can claim the authority of a genuine associative community and can therefore claim moral legitimacy—that its collective decisions are matters of obligation and not bare power—in the name of fraternity. These claims may be defeated, for even genuine associative obligations may conflict with, and must sometimes yield to, demands of justice. But any other form of community, whose officials rejected that commitment, would from the outset forfeit any claim to legitimacy under a fraternal ideal. . . .

Is Patriotism a Virtue?

Alasdair MacIntyre

Modern "liberal" moral theories, argues MacIntyre, are generally impersonal: they seek to judge actions from an impartial standpoint. But then
patriotism, rather than being a virtue, would seem to be a vice; for it is clear
that patriots are partial to their own nation. MacIntyre seeks to resolve this
conflict by questioning the adequacy of the liberal moral vision, arguing
that it should be replaced by the patriot's willingness to exempt his nation's
projects and practices from criticism. Such an exemption does not mean,
however, that the patriot must support any particular policy or government—only that he or she remains committed to the nation viewed as an
historic project with a distinctive political and moral identity. Only through
such a patriotic stance, he argues, can a satisfactory moral vision be supported, one which maintains the essentially historical connections which
create an identity and provide a life with meaning.

Alasdair MacIntyre teaches philosophy at Notre Dame University. He is
the author of many books and articles including *Against the Self-Image of the
Age* (1978), *Marxism and Christianity* (1968), *After Virtue* (1981) and *Whose
Justice, Which Rationality?* (1988).

I.

One of the central tasks of the moral philosopher is to articulate the convictions of the
society in which he or she lives so that these
convictions may become available for rational scrutiny. This task is all the more urgent
when a variety of conflicting and incompatible beliefs are held within one and the same
community, either by rival groups who differ on key moral questions or by one and
the same set of individuals who find within
themselves competing moral allegiances. In
either of these types of case the first task of
the moral philosopher is to render explicit
what is at issue in the various disagreements
and it is a task of this kind that I have set
myself in this lecture.

For it is quite clear that there are large
disagreements about patriotism in our society. And although it would be a mistake to
suppose that there are only two clear, simple
and mutually opposed sets of beliefs about
patriotism, it is at least plausible to suggest
that the range of conflicting views can be
placed on a spectrum with two poles. At one
end is the view, taken for granted by almost
everyone in the nineteenth century, a com-

monplace in the literary culture of the McGuffey readers, that 'patriotism' names a virtue. At the other end is the contrasting view, expressed with sometimes shocking clarity in the nineteen sixties, that 'patriotism' names a vice. It would be misleading for me to suggest that I am going to be able to offer good reasons for taking one of these views rather than the other. What I do hope to achieve is a clarification of the issues that divide them.

A necessary first step . . . is to distinguish patriotism properly so-called from two other sets of attitudes that are all too easily assimilated to it. The first is that exhibited by those who are protagonists of their own nation's causes because and only because, so they assert, it is their nation which is *the* champion of some great moral ideal. In the Great War of 1914–18 Max Weber claimed that Imperial Germany should be supported because its was the cause of *Kultur*, while Emile Durkheim claimed with equal vehemence that France should be supported because its was the cause of *civilisation*. And here and now there are those American politicians who claim that the United States deserves our allegiance because it champions the goods of freedom against the evils of communism. What distinguishes their attitude from patriotism is twofold: first it is the ideal and not the nation which is the primary object of their regard; and secondly insofar as their regard for the ideal provides good reasons for allegiance to their country, it provides good reasons for anyone at all to uphold their country's cause, irrespective of their nationality or citizenship.

Patriotism by contrast is defined in terms of a kind of loyalty to a particular nation which only those possessing that particular nationality can exhibit. Only Frenchmen can be patriotic about France, while anyone can make the cause of *civilisation* their own. But it would be all too easy in noticing this to fail to make a second equally important distinction. Patriotism is not to be confused with a mindless loyalty to one's own particular nation which has no regard at all for the

characteristics of that particular nation. Patriotism does generally and characteristically involve a peculiar regard not just for one's own nation, but for the particular characteristics and merits and achievements of one's own nation. These latter are indeed valued *as* merits and achievements and their character as merits and achievements provides reason's supportive of the patriot's attitudes. But the patriot does not value in the same way precisely similar merits and achievements when they are the merits and achievements of some nation other than his or hers. For he or she—at least in the role of patriot—values them not just as merits and achievements, but as the merits and achievements of this particular nation. . . .

The particularity of the relationship is essential and ineliminable, and in identifying it as such we have already specified one central problem. What *is* the relationship between patriotism as such, the regard for this particular nation, and the regard which the patriot has for the merits and achievements of his or her nation and for the benefits which he or she has received? The answer to this question must be delayed for it will turn out to depend upon the answer to an apparently even more fundamental question, one that can best be framed in terms of the thesis that, if patriotism is understood as I have understood it, then 'patriotism' is not merely not the name of a virtue, but must be the name of a vice, since patriotism thus understood and morality are incompatible.

II.

The presupposition of this thesis is an account of morality which has enjoyed high prestige in our culture. According to that account to judge from a moral standpoint is to judge impersonally. It is to judge as any rational person would judge, independently of his or her interests, affections and social position. And to act morally is to act in accordance with such impersonal judgments. Thus to think and to act morally involves moral agent in abstracting him or herself from all social particularity and partiality. The potential conflict between morality so understood and patriotism is at once clear. For patriotism requires me to exhibit peculiar devotion to my nation and you to yours. It requires me to regard such contingent social facts as where I was born and what government ruled over that place at that time, who my parents were, who my great-great-grandparents were and so on, as deciding for me the question of what virtuous action is—at least insofar as it is the virtue of patriotism which is in question. Hence the moral standpoint and the patriotic standpoint are systematically incompatible.

Yet although this is so, it might be argued that the two standpoints need not be in conflict. For patriotism and all other such particular loyalties can be restricted in their scope so that their exercise is always within the confines imposed by morality. Patriotism need be regarded as nothing more than a perfectly proper devotion to one's own nation which must never be allowed to violate the constraints set by the impersonal moral standpoint. This is indeed the kind of patriotism professed by certain liberal moralists who are often indignant when it is suggested by their critics that they are not patriotic. To those critics however patriotism thus limited in its scope appears to be emasculated, and it does so because in some of the most important situations of actual social life either the patriotic standpoint comes into serious conflict with the standpoint of a genuinely impersonal morality or it amounts to no more than a set of practically empty slogans. What kinds of circumstances are these? They are at least twofold.

The first kind arises from scarcity of essential resources, often historically from the scarcity of land suitable for cultivation and pasture, and perhaps in our own time from that of fossil fuels. What your community requires as the material prerequisites for your survival as a distinctive community and your growth into a distinctive nation may be exclusive use of the same or some of the same natural resources as my community requires for its survival and growth into a distinctive nation. When such a conflict arises, the standpoint of impersonal morality requires an allocation of goods such that each individual person counts for one and no more than one, while the patriotic standpoint requires that I strive to further the interests of my community and you strive to further those of yours, and certainly where the survival of one community is at stake, and sometimes perhaps even when only large interests of one community are at stake, patriotism entails a willingness to go to war on one's community's behalf.

The second type of conflict-engendering circumstance arises from differences between communities about the right way for each to live. Not only competition for scarce natural resources, but incompatibilities arising from such conflict-engendering beliefs may lead to situations in which once again the liberal moral standpoint and the patriotic standpoint are radically at odds. The administration of the *pax Romana* from time to time required the Roman *imperium* to set its frontiers at the point at which they could be most easily secured, so that the burden of supporting the legions would be reconcilable with the administration of Roman law. And the British empire was no different in its time. But this required infringing upon the territory and the independence of barbarian border peoples. A variety of such peoples—Scottish Gaels, Iroquois Indians, Bedouin—have regarded raiding the territory of their traditional enemies living within the confines of such large empires as an essential constituent of the good life; whereas the settled urban or agricultural communities which provided the target for their depredations have regarded the subjugation of such peoples and their reeducation into peaceful pursuits as one of their central responsibilities. And on such issues once again the impersonal moral standpoint and that of patriotism cannot be reconciled.

For the impersonal moral standpoint, understood as the philosophical protagonists of modern liberalism have understood it, requires neutrality not only between rival and competing interests, but also between rival and competing sets of beliefs about the best way for human beings to live. Each individual is to be left free to pursue in his or her own way that way of life which he or she judges to be best; while morality by contrast consists of rules which, just because they are such that any rational person, independently of his or her interests or point of view on the best way for human beings to live, would assent to them, are equally binding on all persons. Hence in conflicts between nations or other communities over ways of life, the standpoint of morality will once again be that of an impersonal arbiter, adjudicating in ways that give equal weight to each individual person's needs, desires, beliefs about the good and the like, while the patriot is once again required to be partisan.

Notice that in speaking of the standpoint of liberal impersonal morality in the way in which I have done I have been describing a standpoint whose truth is both presupposed by the political actions and utterances of a great many people in our society and explicitly articulated and defended by most modern moral philosophers; and that it has at the level of moral philosophy a number of distinct versions—some with a Kantian flavour, some utilitarian, some contractarian. I do not mean to suggest that the disagreements between these positions are unimportant. Nonetheless the five central positions that I have ascribed to that standpoint appear in all these various philosophical guises: first, that morality is constituted by rules to which any rational person would under certain ideal conditions give assent; secondly, that those rules impose constraints upon and are neutral between rival and competing interests—morality itself is not the expression of any particular interest; thirdly, that those rules are also neutral between rival and competing sets of beliefs about what the best way for human beings to live is; fourthly, that the units which provide the subject-matter of morality as well as its agents are individual human beings and that in moral evaluations each individual is

to count for one and nobody for more than one; and fifthly, that the standpoint of the moral agent constituted by allegiance to these rules is one and the same for all moral agents and as such is independent of all social particularity. What morality provides are standards by which all actual social structures may be brought to judgment from a standpoint independent of all of them. It is morality so understood allegiance to which is not only incompatible with treating patriotism as a virtue, but which requires that patriotism—at least in any substantial version—be treated as a vice.

But is this the only possible way to understand morality? As a matter of history, the answer is clearly 'No'. This understanding of morality invaded post Renascence Western culture at a particular point in time as the moral counterpart to political liberalism and social individualism and its polemical stances reflect its history of emergence from the conflicts which those movements engendered and themselves presuppose alternatives against which those polemical stances were and are directed. Let me therefore turn to considering one of those alternative accounts of morality, whose peculiar interest lies in the place that it has to assign to patriotism.

III.

According to the liberal account of morality *where* and *from whom* I learn the principles of morality are and must be irrelevant both to the question of what the content of morality is and to that of the nature of my commitment to it, as irrelevant as *where* and *from whom* I learn the principles and precepts of mathematics are to the content of mathematics and the nature of my commitment to mathematical truths. By contrast on the alternative account of morality which I am going to sketch, the questions of *where* and *from whom* I learn my morality turn out to be crucial for both the content and the nature of moral commitment.

On this view it is an essential characteristic of the morality which each of us acquires that it is learned from, in and through the way of life of some particular community. Of course the moral rules elaborated in one particular historical community will often resemble and sometimes be identical with the rules to which allegiance is given in other particular communities, especially in communities with a shared history or which appeal to the same canonical texts. But there will characteristically be *some* distinctive features of the set of rules considered as a whole, and those distinctive features will often arise from the way in which members of that particular community responded to some earlier situation or series of situations in which particular features of difficult cases led to one or more rules being put in question and reformulated or understood in some new way. Moreover the form of the rules of morality as taught and apprehended will be intimately connected with specific institutional arrangements. The moralities of different societies may agree in having a precept enjoining that a child should honor his or her parents, but what it is so to honor and indeed what a father is and what a mother is will vary greatly between different social orders. So that what I learn as a guide to my actions and as a standard for evaluating them is never morality as such, but always the highly specific morality of some highly specific social order.

To this the reply by the protagonists of modern liberal morality might well be: doubtless this is how a comprehension of the rules of morality is first acquired. But what allows such specific rules, framed in terms of particular social institutions, to be accounted moral rules at all is the fact they are nothing other than applications of universal and general moral rules and individuals acquire genuine morality only because and insofar as they progress from particularised socially specific applications of universal and general moral rules to comprehending them as universal and general. To learn to understand oneself as a moral agent just is to learn to free oneself from social particularity and to adopt a standpoint independent of any particular set of social institutions and the fact that everyone or almost everyone has to learn to do this by starting out from a standpoint deeply infected by social particularity and partiality goes no way towards providing an alternative account of morality. But to this reply a threefold rejoinder can be made.

First, it is not just that I first apprehend the rules of morality in some socially specific and particularised form. It is also and correlatively that the goods by reference to which and for the sake of which any set of rules must be justified are also going to be goods that are socially specific and particular. For central to those goods is the enjoyment of one particular kind of social life, lived out through a particular set of social relationships and thus what I enjoy is the good of *this* particular social life inhabited by me and I enjoy *it* as what *it* is. It may well be that it follows that I would enjoy and benefit equally from similar forms of social life in other communities; but this hypothetical truth in no way diminishes the importance of the contention that my goods are as a matter of fact found *here*, among *these* particular people, in *these* particular relationships. Goods are never encountered except as thus particularised. Hence the abstract general claim, that rules of a certain kind are justified by being productive of and constitutive of goods of a certain kind, is true only if these and these and these particular sets of rules incarnated in the practices of these and these and these particular communities are productive of or constitutive of these and these and these particular goods enjoyed at certain particular times and places by certain specifiable individuals.

It follows that *I* find *my* justification for allegiance to these rules of morality in *my* particular community; deprived of the life of that community, *I* would have no reason to be moral. But this is not all. To obey the rules of morality is characteristically and generally a hard task for human beings. Indeed were it not so, our need for morality would not be what it is. It is because we are continually liable to be blinded by immediate desire, to be distracted from our responsibilities, to lapse into backsliding and because even the best of us may at times encounter quite unusual temptations that it is important to morality that *I* can only be a moral agent because *we* are moral agents, that I need those around me to reinforce my moral strengths and assist in remedying my moral weaknesses. It is in general only within a community that individuals become capable of morality, are sustained in their morality and are constituted as moral agents by the way in which other people regard them and what is owed to and by them as well as by the way in which they regard themselves. In requiring much from me morally the other members of my community express a kind of respect for me that has nothing to do with expectations of benefit; and those of whom nothing or little is required in respect of morality are treated with a lack of respect which is, if repeated often enough, damaging to the moral capacities of those individuals. Of course, lonely moral heroism is sometimes required and sometimes achieved. But we must not treat this exceptional type of case as though it were typical. And once we recognize that typically moral agency and continuing moral capacity are engendered and sustained in essential ways by particular institutionalised social ties in particular social groups, it will be difficult to counterpose allegiance to a particular society and allegiance to morality in the way in which the protagonists of liberal morality do.

Indeed the case for treating patriotism as a virtue is now clear. *If* first of all it is the case that I can only apprehend the rules of morality in the version in which they are incarnated in some specific community; and *if* secondly it is the case that the justification of morality must be in terms of particular goods enjoyed within the life of particular communities; and *if* thirdly it is the case that I am characteristically brought into being and maintained as a moral agent only through the particular kinds of moral sustenance afforded by my community, *then* it is clear that deprived of this community, I am

unlikely to flourish as a moral agent. Hence my allegiance to the community and what it requires of me—even to the point of requiring me to die to sustain its life—could not meaningfully be contrasted with or counterposed to what morality required of me. Detached from my community, I will be apt to lose my hold upon all genuine standards of judgment. Loyalty to that community, to the hierarchy of particular kinship, particular local community and particular natural community, is on this view a prerequisite for morality. So patriotism and those loyalties cognate to it are not just virtues but central virtues. Everything however turns on the truth or falsity of the claims advanced in the three preceding if-clauses. And the argument so far affords us no resources for delivering a verdict upon that truth or falsity. Nonetheless some progress has been achieved, and not only because the terms of the debate have become clearer. For it has also become clear that this dispute is not adequately characterised if it is understood simply as a disagreement between two rival accounts of morality, as if there were some independently identifiable phenomenon situated somehow or other in the social world waiting to be described more or less accurately by the contending parties. What we have here are two rival and incompatible moralities, each of which is viewed from within by its adherents as morality-as-such, each of which makes its exclusive claim to our allegiance. How are we to evaluate such claims?

One way to begin is to be learned from Aristotle. Since we possess no stock of clear and distinct first principles or any other such epistemological resource which would provide us with a neutral and independent standard for judging between them, we shall do well to proceed dialectically. And one useful dialectical strategy is to focus attention on those accusations which the adherents of each bring against the rival position which the adherents of that rival position treat as of central importance to rebut. For this will afford at least one indication of the issues about the importance of which both sides agree and about the characterisation of which their very recognition of disagreement suggests that there must also be some shared beliefs. In what areas do such issues arise?

IV.

One such area is defined by a charge which it seems reasonable at least *prima facie* for the protagonists of patriotism to bring against morality. The morality for which patriotism is a virtue offers a form of rational justification for moral rules and precepts whose structure is clear and rationally defensible. The rules of morality are justifiable if and only if they are productive of and partially constitutive of a form of shared social life whose goods are directly enjoyed by those inhabiting the particular communities whose social life is of that kind. Hence *qua* member of this or that particular community I can appreciate the justification for what morality requires of me from within the social roles that I live out in my community. By contrast, it may be argued, liberal morality requires of me to assume an abstract and artificial—perhaps even an impossible—stance, that of a rational being as such, responding to the requirements of morality not *qua* parent or farmer or quarterback, but *qua* rational agent who has abstracted him or herself from all social particularity, who has become not merely Adam Smith's impartial spectator, but a correspondingly impartial actor, and one who in his impartiality is doomed to rootlessness, to be a citizen of nowhere. How can I justify to myself performing this act of abstraction and detachment?

The liberal answer is clear: such abstraction and detachment is defensible, because it is a necessary condition of moral freedom, of emancipation from the bondage of the social, political and economic *status quo*. For unless I can stand back from every and any feature of that *status quo*, including the roles within it which I myself presently inhabit, I will be unable to view it critically and to decide for myself what stance it is rational and right for me to adopt towards it. This does not preclude that the outcome for such a critical evaluation may not be an endorsement of all or some of the existing social order; but even such an endorsement will only be free and rational if I have made it for myself in this way. (Making just such an endorsement of much of the economic *status quo* is the distinguishing mark of the contemporary conservative liberal, such as Milton Friedman, who is as much a liberal as the liberal liberal who finds much of the *status quo* wanting—such as J. K. Galbraith or Edward Kennedy—or the radical liberal.) Thus liberal morality does after all appeal to an overriding good, the good of this particular kind of emancipating freedom. And in the name of this good it is able not only to respond to the question about how the rules of morality are to be justified, but also to frame a plausible and potentially damaging objection to the morality of patriotism.

It is of the essence of the morality of liberalism that no limitations are or can be set upon the criticism of the social *status quo*. No institution, no practice, no loyalty can be immune from being put in question and perhaps rejected. Conversely the morality of patriotism is one which precisely because it is framed in terms of the membership of some particular social community with some particular social, political and economic structure, must exempt at least some fundamental structures of that community's life from criticism. Because patriotism has to be a loyalty that is in some respects unconditional, so in just those respects rational criticism is ruled out. But if so the adherents of the morality of patriotism have condemned themselves to a fundamentally irrational attitude—since to refuse to examine some of one's fundamental beliefs and attitudes is to insist on accepting them, whether they are rationally justifiable or not, which is irrational—and have imprisoned themselves within that irrationality. What answer can the adherents of the morality of patriotism make to this kind of accusation? The reply must be threefold.

When the liberal moralist claims that the patriot is bound to treat his or her nation's projects and practices in some measure uncritically, the claim is not only that at any one time certain of these projects and practices will be being treated uncritically; it is that some at least must be permanently exempted from criticism. The patriot is in no position to deny this; but what is crucial to the patriot's case is to identify clearly precisely what it is that is thus exempted. . . . What then is exempted? The answer is: the nation conceived *as a project*, a project somehow or other brought to birth in the past and carried on so that a morally distinctive community was brought into being which embodied a claim to political autonomy in its various organized and institutionalised expressions. Thus one can be patriotic towards a nation whose political independence is yet to come—as Garibaldi was; or towards a nation which once was and perhaps might be again—like the Polish patriots of the 1860s. What the patriot is committed to is a particular way of linking a past which has conferred a distinctive moral and political identity upon him or her with a future for the project which is his or her nation which it is his or her responsibility to bring into being. Only this allegiance is unconditional and allegiance to particular governments or forms of government or particular leaders will be entirely conditional upon their being devoted to furthering that project rather than frustrating or destroying it. Hence there is nothing inconsistent in a patriot's being deeply opposed to his country's contemporary rulers, as Péguy was, or plotting their overthrow as Adam von Trott did.

Yet although this may go part of the way towards answering the charge of the liberal moralist that the patriot must in certain areas be completely uncritical and therefore irrationalist, it certainly does not go all the way. For everything that I have said on behalf of the morality of patriotism is compatible with it being the case that on occasion patriotism might require me to support and work for the success of some enterprise of my nation as crucial to its overall project, crucial perhaps to its survival, when the success of that enterprise would not be in the best interests of mankind, evaluated from an impartial and an impersonal standpoint. The case of Adam von Trott is very much to the point.

Adam von Trott was a German patriot who was executed after the unsuccessful assassination attempt against Hitler's life in 1944. Trott deliberately chose to work inside Germany with the minuscule, but highly placed, conservative opposition to the Nazis with the aim of replacing Hitler from within, rather than to work for an overthrow of Nazi Germany which would result in the destruction of the Germany brought to birth in 1871. But to do this he had to appear to be identified with the cause of Nazi Germany and so strengthened not only his country's cause, as was his intention, but also as an unavoidable consequence the cause of the Nazis. This kind of example is a particularly telling one, because the claim that such and such a course of action is "to the best interests of mankind" is usually at best disputable, at worst cloudy rhetoric. But there are a very few causes in which so much was at stake—and that this is generally much clearer in retrospect than it was at the time does not alter that fact—that the phrase has clear application: the overthrow of Nazi Germany was one of them.

How ought the patriot then to respond? Perhaps in two ways. The first begins by reemphasising that from the fact that the particularist morality of the patriot is rooted in a particular community and inextricably bound up with the social life of that community, it does not follow that it cannot provide rational grounds for repudiating many features of that country's present organized social life. The conception of justice engendered by the notion of citizenship within a particular community may provide standards by which particular political institutions are found wanting: when Nazi anti-Semitism encountered the phenomena of German Jewish ex-soldiers who had won the Iron Cross, it had to repudiate German particularist standards of excellence (for the award of the Iron Cross symbolised a recognition of devotion to Germany). Moreover the conception of one's own nation having a special mission does not necessitate that this mission may not involve the extension of a justice originally at home only in the particular institutions of the homeland. And clearly particular governments or agencies of government may defect and may be understood to have defected from this mission so radically that the patriot may find that a point comes when he or she has to choose between the claims of the project which constitutes his or her nation and the claims of the morality that he or she has learnt as a member of the community whose life is informed by that project. Yes, the liberal critic of patriotism will respond, this indeed *may* happen; but it may not and it often will not. Patriotism turns out to be a permanent source of moral danger. And this claim, I take it, cannot in fact be successfully rebutted.

A second possible, but very different type of answer on behalf of the patriot would run as follows. I argued earlier that the kind of regard for one's own country which would be compatible with a liberal morality of impersonality and impartiality would be too insubstantial, would be under too many constraints, to be regarded as a version of patriotism in the traditional sense. But it does not follow that some version of traditional patriotism may not be compatible with some other morality of universal moral law, which sets limits to and provides both sanction for and correction of the particularist morality of the patriot. Whether this is so or not is too large and too distinct a question to pursue in this present paper. But we ought to note that even if it is so—and all those who have been both patriots and Christians *or* patriots and believers in Thomistic natural law *or*

patriots and believers in the Rights of Man have been committed to claiming that it is so—this would not diminish in any way the force of the liberal claim that patriotism is a morally dangerous phenomenon.

That the rational protagonist of the morality of patriotism is compelled, if my argument is correct, to concede this does not mean that there is not more to be said in the debate. And what needs to be said is that the liberal morality of impartiality and impersonality turns out also to be a morally dangerous phenomenon in an interestingly corresponding way. For suppose the bonds of patriotism to be dissolved: would liberal morality be able to provide anything adequately substantial in its place? What the morality of patriotism at its best provides is a clear account of and justification for the particular bonds and loyalties which form so much of the substance of the moral life. It does so by underlining the moral importance of the different members of a group acknowledging a shared history. Each one of us to some degree or other understands his or her life as an enacted narrative; and because of our relationships with others we have to understand ourselves as characters in the enacted narratives of other people's lives. Moreover the story of each of our lives is characteristically embedded in the story of one or more larger units. I understand the story of my life in such a way that it is part of the history of my family or of this farm or of this university or of this countryside; and I understand the story of the lives of other individuals around me as embedded in the same larger stories, so that I and they share a common stake in the outcome of that story and in what sort of story it both is and is to be: tragic, heroic, comic.

A central contention of the morality of patriotism is that I will obliterate and lose a central dimension of the moral life if I do not understand the enacted narrative of my own individual life as embedded in the history of my country. For if I do not so understand it I will not understand what I owe to others or what others owe to me, for what crimes of my nation I am bound to make reparation, for what benefits to my nation I am bound to feel gratitude. Understanding what is owed to and by me and understanding the history of the communities of which I am a part is on this view one and the same thing.

It is worth stressing that one consequence of this is that patriotism, in the sense in which I am understanding it in this paper, is only possible in certain types of national community under certain conditions. A national community, for example, which systematically disowned its own true history or substituted a largely fictitious history for it or a national community in which the bonds deriving from history were in no way the real bonds of the community (having been replaced for example by the bonds of reciprocal self-interest) would be one towards which patriotism would be—from any point of view—an irrational attitude. For precisely the same reasons that a family whose members all came to regard membership in that family as governed only by reciprocal self-interest would no longer be a family in the traditional sense, so a nation whose members took up a similar attitude would no longer be a nation and this would provide adequate grounds for holding that the project which constituted that nation had simply collapsed. Since all modern bureaucratic states tend towards reducing national communities to this condition, all such states tend towards a condition in which any genuine morality of patriotism would have no place and what paraded itself as patriotism would be an unjustifiable simulacrum.

Why would this matter? In modern communities in which membership is understood only or primarily in terms of reciprocal self-interest, only two resources are generally available when destructive conflicts of interest threaten such reciprocity. One is the arbitrary imposition of some solution by force; the other is appeal to the neutral, impartial and impersonal standards of liberal morality. The importance of this resource is scarcely to be underrated; but

how much of a resource is it? The problem is that some motivation has to be provided for allegiance to the standards of impartiality and impersonality which both has rational justification and can outweigh the considerations provided by interest. Since any large need for such allegiance arises precisely and only when and insofar as the possibility of appeals to reciprocity in interests has broken down, such reciprocity can no longer provide the relevant kind of motivation. And it is difficult to identify anything that can take its place. The appeal to moral agents *qua* rational beings to place their allegiance to impersonal rationality above that to their interests has, just because it is an appeal to rationality, to furnish an adequate reason for so doing. And this is a point at which liberal accounts of morality are notoriously vulnerable. This vulnerability becomes a manifest practical liability at one key point in the social order.

Every political community except in the most exceptional conditions requires standing armed forces for its minimal security. Of the members of these armed forces it must require both that they be prepared to sacrifice their own lives for the sake of the community's security and that their willingness to do so be not contingent upon their own individual evaluation of the rightness or wrongness of their country's cause on some specific issue, measured by some standard that is neutral and impartial relative to the interests of their own community and the interests of other communities. And, that is to say, good soldiers may not be liberals and must indeed embody in their actions a good deal at least of the morality of patriotism. So the political survival of any polity in which liberal morality had secured large-scale allegiance would depend upon there still being enough young men and women who rejected that liberal morality. And in this sense liberal morality tends towards the dissolution of social bonds.

Hence the charge that the morality of patriotism can successfully bring against liberal morality is the mirror-image of that which liberal morality can successfully urge against the morality of patriotism. For while the liberal moralist was able to conclude that patriotism is a permanent source of moral danger because of the way it places our ties to our nation beyond rational criticism, the moralist who defends patriotism is able to conclude that liberal morality is a permanent source of moral danger because of the way it renders our social and moral ties too open to dissolution by rational criticism. And each party is in fact in the right against the other.

V.

. . . Hegel employs a useful distinction which he marks by his use of words *Sittlichkeit* and *Moralität*. *Sittlichkeit* is the customary morality of each particular society, pretending to be no more than this. *Moralität* reigns in the realm of rational universal, impersonal morality, of liberal morality, as I have defined it. What those immigrants were taught in effect was that they had left behind countries and cultures where *Sittlichkeit* and *Moralität* were certainly distinct and often opposed and arrived in a country and a culture whose *Sittlichkeit* just is *Moralität*. And thus for many Americans the cause of America, understood as the object of patriotic regard, and the cause of morality, understood as the

liberal moralist understands it, came to be identified. The history of this identification could not be other than a history of confusion and incoherence, if the argument which I have constructed in this lecture is correct. For a morality of particularist ties and solidarities has been conflated with a morality of universal, impersonal and impartial principles in a way that can never be carried through without incoherence.

One test therefore of whether the argument that I have constructed has or has not empirical application and practical significance would be to discover whether it is or is not genuinely illuminating to write the political and social history of modern America as in key part the living out of a central conceptual confusion, a confusion perhaps required for the survival of a large-scale modern polity which has to exhibit itself as liberal in many institutional settings, but which also has to be able to engage the patriotic regard of enough of its citizens, if it is to continue functioning effectively. To determine whether that is or is not true would be to risk discovering that we inhabit a kind of polity whose moral order requires systematic incoherence in the form of public allegiance to mutually inconsistent sets of principles. But that is a task which—happily—lies beyond the scope of this lecture.

Collective and Individual Responsibility in War

Michael Walzer

In this selection, Michael Walzer considers the responsibilities of citizens whose governments are engaged in wars of aggression and of individual soldiers ordered to commit war crimes. Drawing on examples from World War II and the Vietnam war, including the My Lai massacre, he discusses the collective responsibility citizens may share for their government's policies as well as the soldier's duty to refuse orders of a superior officer.

Michael Walzer teaches in the Department of Government at Harvard University. In addition to *Just and Unjust Wars*, from which this selection is taken, he has written many articles and several books, including *Spheres of Justice* (1983).

I. THE CRIME OF AGGRESSION: POLITICAL LEADERS AND CITIZENS

Democratic Responsibilities

What about the . . . citizens . . . of a state engaged in an aggressive war? Collective responsibility is a hard notion, though it is worth stressing at once that we have fewer problems with collective punishment. Resistance to aggression is itself "punishing" to the aggressor state and is often described in those terms. With reference to the actual fighting, as I have already argued, civilians on both sides are innocent, equally innocent, and never legitimate military targets. They are, however, political and economic targets once the war is over; that is, they are the victims of military occupation, political reconstruction, and the exaction of reparative payments. We may take the last of these as the clearest and simplest case of collective

From Michael Walzer, *Just and Unjust Wars* (New York: Basic Books, 1977). Reprinted by permission.

punishment. Reparations are surely due the victims of aggressive war, and they can hardly be collected only from those members of the defeated state who were active supporters of the aggression. Instead, the costs are distributed through the tax system, and through the economic system generally, among all the citizens, often over a period of time extending to generations that had nothing to do with the war at all. In this sense, citizenship is a common destiny, and no one, not even its opponents (unless they become political refugees, which has its costs, too) can escape the effects of a bad regime, an ambitious or fanatic leadership, or an overreaching nationalism. But if men and women must accept this destiny, they can sometimes do so with a good conscience, for the acceptance says nothing about their individual responsibility. The distribution of costs is not the distribution of guilt.

At least one writer has tried to argue that political destiny is a kind of guilt: existential, unavoidable, frightening. For the soldier or citizen of a state at war, writes J. Glenn Gray in his philosophical memoir of World War II, is the member of a "coarse, vulgar, heedless, and violent" community and, willy-nilly, a participant in an enterprise "whose spirit is to win at any cost." He cannot cut himself loose.[1]

He is bound to reflect that his nation has given him refuge and sustenance, provided him with whatever education and property he calls his own. He belongs and will always belong to it in some sense no matter where he goes or how hard he seeks to alter his inheritance. The crimes, therefore, that his nation or one of its units commits cannot be indifferent to him. He shares the guilt as he shares the satisfaction in the generous deeds and worthy products of nation or army. Even if he did not consciously will them and was unable to prevent them, he cannot wholly escape responsibility for collective deeds.

Maybe; but it is not an easy move from "the ache of guilt," which Gray almost lovingly describes, to hard talk about responsibility. It might be better to say of loyal citizens who watch their government or army (or their comrades in battle) doing terrible things that they feel or should feel ashamed rather than responsible—unless they actually are responsible by virtue of their particular participation or acquiescence. Shame is the tribute we pay to the inheritance that Gray describes. "A burning sense of shame at the deeds of his government and the acts of horror committed by German soldiers and police was the mark of a conscientious German at the close of the war." That is exactly right, but we won't ourselves blame that conscientious German or call him responsible; nor need he blame himself unless there was something he should have done, and could do, in the face of the horror.

Perhaps it can always be said of such a person that he could have done more than he did do. Certainly conscientious men and women are likely to believe that of themselves; it is a sign of their conscientiousness.[2]

On this or that occasion he has been silent when he should have spoken out. In his own smaller or larger circle of influence he has not made his whole weight felt. Had he brought forth the civil courage to protest in time, some particular act of injustice might have been avoided.

Such reflections are endless and endlessly dispiriting; they lead Gray to argue that behind collective responsibility there lies "metaphysical guilt," which derives from "our failure as human beings to live in accordance with our potentialities and our vision of the good." But some of us, surely, fail more dismally than others; and it is necessary, with all due caution and humility, to mark out standards by which we can measure the respective failures. Gray suggests the right standard, though he goes on very quickly to insist that we can never apply it to anyone but ourselves. But that kind of self-regard is not possible in politics and morality. Judging ourselves, we necessarily judge other people, with whom we share a common life. And how is it possible to criticize and blame our leaders, as we sometimes must do, without involving their enthusiastic followers (our fellow citizens)? Though responsibility is always personal and particular, moral life is always collective in character.

This is Gray's principle, which I mean to adopt and expound: *"The greater the possibility of free action in the communal sphere, the greater the degree of guilt for evil deeds done in the name of everyone."*[3] The principle invites us to focus our attention on democratic rather than authoritarian regimes. Not that free action is impossible even in the worst of authoritarian regimes; at the very least, people can resign, withdraw, flee. But in democracies there are opportunities for positive response, and we need to ask to what extent these opportunities fix our obligations, when evil deeds are committed in our name.

---

[1] *The Warriors*, 196–97.
[2] *The Warriors*, p. 198.

[3] *The Warriors*, p. 199.

The American People and the War in Vietnam

If the argument in chapters 6 and 11 is right, the American war in Vietnam was, first of all, an unjustified intervention, and it was, secondly, carried on in so brutal a manner that even had it initially been defensible, it would have to be condemned, not in this or that aspect but generally. I am not going to re-argue that description, but assume it, so that we can look closely at the responsibility of democratic citizens—and at a particular set of democratic citizens, namely, ourselves.[1]

Democracy is a way of distributing responsibility (just as monarchy is a way of refusing to distribute it). But that doesn't mean that all adult citizens share equally in the blame we assign for aggressive war. Our actual assignments will vary a great deal, depending on the precise nature of the democratic order, the place of a particular person in that order, and the pattern of his own political activities. Even in a perfect democracy, it cannot be said that every citizen is the author of every state policy, though every one of them can rightly be called to account. Imagine, for example, a small community where all the citizens are fully and accurately informed about public business, where all of them participate, argue, vote on matters of communal interest, and where they all take turns holding public office. Now this community, let us say, initiates and wages an unjust war against its neighbors—for the sake of some economic advantage, perhaps, or out of zeal to spread its (admirable) political system. There is no question of self-defense; no one has attacked it or is planning to do so. Who is responsible for this war? Surely all those men and women who voted for it and who cooperated in planning, initiating, and waging it. The soldiers who do the actual fighting are not re-sponsible as soldiers; but as citizens, they are, assuming that they were old enough to have shared in the decision to fight.* All of them are guilty of the crime of aggressive war and of no lesser charge, and we would not hesitate in such a case to blame them publicly. Nor would it make any difference whether their motive was economic selfishness or a political zeal that appeared to them entirely disinterested. Either way, the blood of their victims would complain against them.

Those who voted against the war or who refused to cooperate in the waging of it could not be blamed. But what would we think of a group of citizens that didn't vote? Had they voted, let's say, the war might have been avoided, but they were lazy, didn't care, or were afraid to come down on one side or the other of a hotly disputed issue. The day of the crucial decision was a day off from work; they spent it in their gardens. I am inclined to say that they are blameworthy, though they are not guilty of aggressive war. Surely those of their fellow citizens who went to the assembly and opposed the war can blame them for their indifference and inaction. This seems a clear counter-example to Gray's assertion that "No citizen of a

---

[1] In thinking about these issues, I have been greatly helped by the essays in Joel Feinberg's *Doing and Deserving*.

* Why aren't they responsible as soldiers? If they are morally bound to vote against the war, why aren't they also bound to refuse to fight? The answer is that they vote as individuals, each one deciding for himself, but they fight as members of the political community, the collective decision having already been made, subject to all the moral and material pressures that I described in chapter 3. They act very well if they refuse to fight, and we should honor those—they are likely to be few—who have the self-certainty and courage to stand against their fellows. I have argued elsewhere that democracies ought to respect such people and ought certainly to tolerate their refusals. (See the essay on "Conscientious Objection" in *Obligations.*) That doesn't mean, however, that the others can be called criminals. Patriotism may be the last refuge of scoundrels, but it is also the ordinary refuge of ordinary men and women, and it requires of us another sort of toleration. But we should expect opponents of the war to refuse to become officers or officials, even if they feel bound to share combat risks with their countrymen.

free land can justly accuse his neighbor . . . of not having done as much as he should to prevent the state of war or the commission of this or that state crime. But each can . . . accuse himself . . . "[5] In a perfect democracy, we would know a great deal about one another's duties, and just accusations would not be impossible.

Imagine now that the minority of citizens that was defeated could have won (and prevented the war) if instead of merely voting, they had held meetings outside the assembly, marched and demonstrated, organized for a second vote. Let's assume that none of this would have been terribly dangerous to them, but they chose not to take these measures because their opposition to the war wasn't all that strong; they thought it unjust but were not horrified by the prospect; they hoped for a quick victory; and so on. Then they are blameworthy, too, though to a lesser degree than those slothful citizens who did not even bother to go to the assembly.

These last two examples resemble the good samaritan cases in domestic society, where we commonly say that if it is possible to do good, without risk or great cost, one ought to do good. But when the issue is war, the obligation is stronger, for it is not a question of doing good, but of preventing serious harm, and harm that will be done in the name of my own political community—hence, in some sense, in my own name. Here, assuming still that the community is a perfect democracy, it looks as if a citizen is blameless only if he takes back his name. I don't think this means that he must become a revolutionary or an exile, actually renouncing his citizenship or loyalty. But he must do all he can, short of accepting frightening risks, to prevent or stop the war. He must withdraw his name from this act (the war policy) though not necessarily from every communal action, for he may still value, as he probably should, the democracy he and his fellow citizens have achieved. This,

then, is the meaning of Gray's maxim: the more one can do, the more one has to do.

We can now drop the myth of perfection and paint a more realistic picture. The state that goes to war is, like our own, an enormous state, governed at a great distance from its ordinary citizens by powerful and often arrogant officials. These officials, or at least the leading among them, are chosen through democratic elections, but at the time of the choice very little is known about their programs and commitments. Political participation is occasional, intermittent, limited in its effects, and it is mediated by a system for the distribution of news which is partially controlled by those distant officials and which in any case allows for considerable distortions. It may be that a politics of this sort is the best we can hope for (though I don't believe that) once the political community reaches a certain size. Anyway, it is no longer as easy to impose responsibility as it is in a perfect democracy. One doesn't want to regard those distant officials as if they were kings, but for certain sorts of state action, secretly prepared or suddenly launched, they bear a kind of regal responsibility.

When a state like this commits itself to a campaign of aggression, its citizens (or many of them) are likely to go along, as Americans did during the Vietnam war, arguing that the war may after all be just; that it is not possible for them to be sure whether it is just or not; that their leaders know best and tell them this or that, which sounds plausible enough; and that nothing they can do will make much difference anyway. These are not immoral arguments, though they reflect badly on the society within which they are made. And they can, no doubt, be made too quickly by citizens seeking to avoid the difficulties that might follow if they thought about the war for themselves. These people are or may be blameworthy, not for aggressive war, but for bad faith as citizens. But that is a hard charge to make, for citizenship plays such a small part in their everyday lives. "Free action in the

---

[5] *The Warriors*, p. 199.

communal sphere" is a possibility for men and women in such a state only in the formal sense that serious governmental restraint, actual repression, doesn't exist. Perhaps it should also be said that the "communal sphere" doesn't exist, for it is only the day-by-day assumption of responsibility that creates that sphere and gives it meaning. Even patriotic excitement, war fever, among such people is probably best understood as a reflex of distance, a desperate identification, stimulated, it may be, by a false account of what is gong on. One might say of them what one says of soldiers in combat, that they are not to blame for the war, since it is not their war.*

But as an account of all the citizens, even in such a state, this is certainly exaggerated. For there exists a group of more knowledgeable men and women, members of what political scientists call the foreign policy elites, who are not so radically distanced from the national leadership; and some subset of these people, together with others in touch with them, is likely to form an "opposition" or perhaps even a movement of opposition to the war. It would seem possible to regard the entire group of knowledgeable people as at least potentially blameworthy if that war is aggressive and unless they join the opposition.[6] To say that is to presume upon the knowledge they have and their private sense of political possibility. But if we turn to an actual case of imperfect democracy, like the United States in the late

1960s and early 1970s, the presumption doesn't seem unwarranted. Surely there was knowledge and opportunity enough among the country's elites, the national and local leaders of its political parties, its religious establishments, its corporate hierarchies, and perhaps above all its intellectual teachers and spokesmen—the men and women who Noam Chomsky has named, in tribute to the role they play in contemporary government, "the new mandarins."[7] Surely many of these people were morally complicitous in our Vietnam aggression. I suppose one can also say of them what many of them have said of themselves: that they were simply mistaken in their judgments of the war, failed to realize this or that, thought that was true when it was not, or hoped for this result which never came about. In moral life generally, one makes allowances for false beliefs, misinformation, and honest mistakes. But there comes a time in any tale of aggression and atrocity when such allowances can no longer be made. I cannot mark out that time here; nor am I interested in pointing at particular people or certain that I can do so. I only want to insist that there are responsible people even when, under the conditions of imperfect democracy, moral accounting is difficult and imprecise.

The real moral burden of the American war fell on that subset of men and women whose knowledge and sense of possibility was made manifest by their oppositional activity. They were the ones most likely to reproach themselves and one another, continually asking whether they were doing enough to stop the fighting, devoting enough time and energy, working hard enough, working as effectively as they could. For most of their fellow citizens, anxious, apathetic, and alienated, the war was merely an ugly or an exciting spectacle (until they were forced to join it). For the dissidents, it was a kind of moral torture—self-torture, as Gray describes it, though they also tortured one another, wastefully, in sav-

---

* But see the note in Anne Frank's *Diary:* "I don't believe that only governments and capitalists are guilty of aggression. Oh no, the little man is just as keen on it, for otherwise the people of the world would have risen in revolt long ago." I'm sure she is right about the keenness, and I don't want to excuse it. But we don't, for all that, call the little men war criminals, and I am trying to explain why we don't. (*The Diary of a Young Girl,* trans. B. M. Mooyaart-Doubleday, New York, 1953, p. 201.)

[6] See Richard A. Falk, "The Circle of Responsibility," in *Crimes of War,* ed. Falk, G. Kolko, and R. J. Lifton (New York, 1971), p. 230: "The circle of responsibility is drawn around all who have or should have knowledge of the illegal and immoral character of the war."

[7] *American Power and the New Mandarins* (New York, 1969).

age internecine conflicts over what was to be done. And this self-torture bred a kind of self-righteousness *vis-a-vis* the others, an endemic failing on the Left, though understandable enough under conditions of aggressive war and mass acquiescence. The expression of that self-righteousness, however, is not a useful way to get one's fellow citizens to think seriously about the war or to join the opposition: nor was it useful in this case. It is not easy to know what course of action might serve these purposes. Politics is difficult at such a time. But there is intellectual work to do that is less difficult: one must describe as graphically as one can the moral reality of war, talk about what it means to force people to fight, analyze the nature of democratic responsibilities. These, at least, are encompassable tasks, and they are morally required of the men and women who are trained to perform them. Nor is it dangerous to perform them, in a democratic state, waging war in a distant country. And the citizens of such a state have time to listen and reflect; they, too, are in no immediate danger. War imposes harsher burdens than any these people have to bear—as we shall see when we consider, finally, the moral life of men at arms.

II. WAR CRIMES: SOLDIERS AND THEIR OFFICERS

We are concerned now with the conduct of war and to its overall justice. For soldiers, as I have already argued, are not responsible for the overall justice of the wars they fight; their responsibility is limited by the range of their own activity and authority. Within that range, however, it is real enough, and it frequently comes into question. "There wasn't a single soldier," says an Israeli officer who fought in the Six Day War, "who didn't at some stage have to decide, to choose, to make a moral decision . . . quick and modern though [the war] was, the soldier was not turned into a mere technician. He had to make decisions that were of real

significance."[8] And when faced with decisions of that sort, soldiers have clear obligations. They are bound to apply the criteria of usefulness and proportionality until they come up against the basic rights of the people they are threatening to kill or injure, and then they are bound not to kill or injure them. . . .

The war convention requires soldiers to accept personal risks rather than kill innocent people. This requirements takes different forms in different combat situations . . . my concern now is with the requirement itself. The rule is absolute: self-preservation in the face of the enemy is not an excuse for violations of the rules of war. Soldiers, it might be said, stand to civilians like the crew of a liner to its passengers. They must risk their own lives for the sake of the others. No doubt this is easy to say, less easy to do. But if the rule is absolute, the risks are not; it is a question of degree; the crucial point is that soldiers cannot enhance their own security at the expense of innocent men and women.* This might be called an obligation of

---

[8] *The Seventh Day: Soldiers Talk About the Six Day War* (London, 1970), p. 126.

* Telford Taylor suggests a possible exception to this rule, citing a hypothetical case which has often been discussed in the legal literature. A small detachment of troops on a special mission or cut off from its main force takes prisoners "under such circumstances that men cannot be spared to guard them . . . and that to take them along would greatly endanger the success of the mission or the safety of the unit." The prisoners are likely to be killed, Taylor says, in accordance with the principle of military necessity. (*Nuremberg and Vietnam*, New York, 1970, p. 36.) But if it is only the safety of the unit that is in question (its mission may already have been accomplished), the proper appeal would be to self-preservation. The argument from necessity has not, despite Taylor, been accepted by legal writers; the argument from self-preservation has won greater support. In his military code for the Union Army, for example, Francis Lieber writes that "a commander is permitted to direct his troops to give no quarter . . . when his own salvation makes it impossible to cumber himself with prisoners." (Taylor, p. 36n.) But surely in such a case the prisoners should be disarmed and then released. Even if it is "impossible" to take them along, it is not impossible to set them free. There may be risks in doing that, but these are exactly the sorts of risks soldiers must accept. The risks involved in leaving wounded men behind are of the same sort, but that is not a

soldiering as an office, but it is a hard question whether one can rightly be said to assume such obligations when one comes into the office as unwillingly as most soldiers do. Imagine a liner manned by kidnapped sailors: would the members of such a crew be bound, as the ship was sinking, to see to the safety of the passengers before seeing to their own?

I am not sure how to answer that question, but there is a crucial difference between the work of coerced crew members and that of military conscripts: the first group is not in the business of sinking ships, the second is. Conscripts impose risks on innocent people; they are themselves the immediate source of the danger and they are its effective cause. And so it is not a question of saving themselves, letting others die, but of killing others in order to improve their own odds. Now that they cannot do, because that no man can do. Their obligation isn't in practice mediated by the office of soldiering. It arises directly from the activity in which they are engaged, whether that activity is voluntary or not, or at least it arises so long as we regard soldiers as moral agents and even if we regard them as coerced moral agents.[9] They are not mere instruments; they do not stand to the army as their weapons do to them. It is precisely because they do (sometimes) choose to kill or not, to impose risks or accept them, that we require them to choose in a certain way. That requirement shapes the whole pattern of their rights and duties in combat. And when they break out of that pattern, it is a matter of some significance that they don't by and large deny the requirement. They claim, instead, that they literally were not able to fulfill it; that they were not at the moment of their "crime" moral agents at all. . . .

It is a feature of criminal responsibility that it can be distributed without being divided. We can, that is, blame more than one person for a particular act without splitting up the blame we assign.[10] When soldiers are shot trying to surrender, the men who do the actual shooting are fully responsible for what they do, unless we recognize particular extenuating circumstances; at the same time, the officer who tolerates and encourages the murders is also fully responsible, if it lay within his power to prevent them. Perhaps we blame the officer more, for his coolness, but . . . combat soldiers, too, should be held to high standards in such matters (and they will surely want their enemies held to high standards). The case looks very different, however, when combatants are actually ordered to take no prisoners or to kill the ones they take or to turn their guns on enemy civilians. Then it is not their own murderousness that is at issue but that of their officers; they can act morally only by disobeying their orders. In such a case, we are likely to divide as well as distribute responsibility: we regard soldiers under orders as men whose acts are not entirely their own and whose liability for what they do is somehow diminished.

Superior Orders

The My Lai Massacre. The incident is infamous and hardly needs retelling. A company of American soldiers entered a Vietnamese village where they expected to encounter enemy combatants, found only civilians, old men, women, and children, and began to kill them, shooting them singly or collecting them in groups, ignoring their obvious helplessness and their pleas for mercy, not stopping until they had murdered between four and five hundred people. Now, it has been argued on behalf of these soldiers that they acted, not in the heat

---

satisfactory reason for killing them. For a useful discussion of these issues, see Marshall Cohen, "Morality and the Laws of War," in Held, Morgenbesser, and Nagel, eds., *Philosophy, Morality, and International Affairs*, New York, 1974, pp. 76–78.

[9] I owe this point to Dan Little.

---

[10] See the discussion of this point by Samuel David Resnick, *Moral Responsibility and Democratic Theory*, unpublished Ph.D. dissertation (Harvard University, 1972).

of battle (since there was no battle) but in the context of a brutal and brutalizing war which was in fact, if only unofficially, a war against the Vietnamese people as a whole. In this war, the argument goes on, they had been encouraged to kill without making careful discriminations—encouraged to do so by their own officers and driven to do so by their enemies, who fought and hid among the civilian population.[11] These statements are true, or partly true; and yet massacre is radically different from guerrilla war, even from a guerrilla war brutally fought, and there is considerable evidence that the soldiers at My Lai knew the difference. For while some of them joined in the murders readily enough, as if eager to kill without risk, there were a few who refused to fire their guns and others who had to be ordered to fire two or three times before they could bring themselves to do so. Others simply ran away; one man shot himself in the foot so as to escape the scene; a junior officer tried heroically to stop the massacre, standing between the Vietnamese villagers and his fellow Americans. Many of his fellows, we know, were sick and guilt-ridden in the days that followed. This was not a fearful and frenzied extension of combat, but "free" and systematic slaughter, and those men that participated in it can hardly say that they were caught in the grip of war. They can say, however, that they were following orders, caught in the grip of the United States Army.

The orders of Captain Medina, the company commander, had in fact been ambiguous; at least, the men who heard them could not agree afterwards as to whether or not they had been told to "waste" the inhabitants of My Lai. He is quoted as having told his company to leave nothing living behind them and to take no prisoners: "They're all V.C.'s, now go and get them." But he is also said to have ordered only the killing of "enemies," and when asked, "Who is the enemy?" to have offered the following definition (in the words of one of the soldiers): "anybody that was running from us, hiding from us, or who appeared to us to be the enemy. If a man was running, shoot him; sometimes even if a woman with a rifle was running, shoot her."[12] That is a very bad definition, but it isn't morally insane; barring a loose interpretation of the "appearance" of enmity, it would have excluded most of the people killed at My Lai. Lieutenant Calley, who actually led the unit that entered the village, gave far more specific orders, commanding his men to kill helpless civilians who were neither running nor hiding, let alone carrying rifles, and repeating the command again and again when they hesitated to obey.* The army's judicial system singled him out for blame and punishment, though he claimed he was only doing what Medina had ordered him to do. The enlisted men who did what Calley ordered them to do were never charged.

It must be a great relief to follow orders. "Becoming a soldier," writes J. Glenn Gray, "was like escaping from one's own shadow." The world of war is frightening; decisions are difficult; and it is comforting to slough off responsibility and simply do what one is told. Gray reports soldiers insisting on this special kind of freedom: "When I raised my right hand and took the [army oath], I freed myself of the consequences for what I do. I'll do what they tell me and nobody can blame me."[13] Army training encourages this view, even though soldiers are also in-

---

[12] Hersh, p. 42.

* It may be useful to suggest the sorts of commands that should be issued at such a time. Here is an account of an Israeli unit entering Nablus during the Six Day War: "The battalion CO got on the field telephone to my company and said, 'Don't touch the civilians . . . don't fire until you're fired at and don't touch the civilians. Look, you've been warned. Their blood be on your heads.' In just those words. The boys in the company kept talking about it afterwards . . . They kept repeating the words . . . 'Their blood be on your heads.' " *The Seventh Day: Soldiers Talk About the Six Day War*, London, 1970, p. 132.

[13] *The Warriors*, p. 181.

---

[11] Seymour Hersh, *My Lai 4: A Report on the Massacre and its Aftermath* (New York, 1970); see also David Cooper, "Responsibility and the 'System' " in *Individual and Collective Responsibility: The Massacre at My Lai*, ed. Peter French (Cambridge, Mass., 1972), pp. 83–100.

formed that they must refuse "unlawful" orders. No military force can function effectively without routine obedience, and it is the routine that is stressed. Soldiers are taught to obey even petty and foolish commands. The teaching process has the form of an endless drill, aimed at breaking down their individual thoughtfulness, resistance, hostility, and waywardness. But there is some ultimate humanity that cannot be broken down, the disappearance of which we will not accept. In his play *The Measures Taken*, Bertolt Brecht describes militant communists as "blank pages on which the Revolution writes its instructions."[14] I suppose there are many drill sergeants who dream of a similar blankness. But the description is a false one and the dream a fantasy. It is not that soldiers don't sometimes obey as if they were morally blank. What is crucial is that the rest of us hold them responsible for what they do. Despite their oath, we blame them for the crimes that follow from "unlawful" or immoral obedience.

Soldiers can never be transformed into mere instruments of war. The trigger is always part of the gun, not part of the man. If they are not machines that can just be turned off, they are also not machines that can just be turned on. Trained to obey "without hesitation," they remain nevertheless capable of hesitating. I have already cited examples of refusal, delay, doubt, and anguish at My Lai. These are internal confirmations of our external judgments. No doubt we can make these judgments too quickly, without hesitations and doubts of our own, paying too little attention to the harshness of battle and the discipline of the army. But it is a mistake to treat soldiers as if they were automatons who make no judgments at all. Instead, we must look closely at the particular features of their situation and try to understand what it might mean, in *these* circumstances, at *this* moment, to accept or defy a military command.

The defense of superior orders breaks down into two more specific arguments: the claim of ignorance and the claim of duress. These two are standard legal and moral claims, and they seem to function in war very much as they do in domestic society.[15] It is not the case, then, as has often been argued, that when we judge soldiers we must balance the necessities of military discipline (that obedience be quick and unquestioning) against the requirements of humanity (that innocent people be protected).[16] Rather, we view discipline as one of the conditions of wartime activity, and we take its particular features into account in determining individual responsibility. We do not excuse individuals in order to maintain or strengthen the disciplinary system. The army may cover up the crimes of soldiers or seek to limit liability for them with that end (or that pretended end) in view, but such efforts do not represent the delicate working out of a conception of justice. What justice requires is, first of all, that we commit ourselves to the defense of rights and, second, that we attend carefully to the particular defenses of men who are charged with violating rights.

Ignorance is the common lot of the common soldier, and it makes an easy defense, especially when calculations of usefulness and proportionality are called for. The soldier can plausibly say that he does not know and cannot know whether the campaign in which he is engaged is really required for the sake of victory, or whether it has been designed so as to hold unintended civilian deaths within acceptable limits. From his narrow and confined vantage point, even direct violations of human rights—as in the conduct of a siege, for example, or in the strategy of an anti-guerrilla campaign—may be unseen and unseeable. Nor is he bound to seek out information; the moral life of a

---

[14] *The Measures Taken*, in *The Jewish Wife and Other Short Plays*, trans. Eric Bentley (New York, 1965), p. 82.

[15] The best account of the present legal situation is Yoram Dinstein, *The Defense of Obedience to Superior Orders in International Law* (Leiden, 1965).

[16] McDougal and Feliciano, *Law and Minimum World Public Order*, p. 690.

combat soldier is not a research assignment. We might say that he stands to his campaigns as to his wars: he is not responsible for their overall justice. When war is fought at a distance, he may not be responsible even for the innocent people he himself kills. Artillery men and pilots are often kept in ignorance of the targets at which their fire is directed. If they ask questions, they are routinely assured that the targets are "legitimate military objectives." Perhaps they should always be skeptical, but I don't think we blame them if they accept the assurances of their commanders. We blame instead the far-seeing commanders. As the example of My Lai suggests, however, the ignorance of common soldiers has its limits. The soldiers in the Vietnamese village could hardly have doubted the innocence of the people they were ordered to kill. It is in such a situation that we want them to disobey: when they receive orders which, as the army judge said at the Calley trial, "a man of ordinary sense and understanding would, under the circumstances, know to be unlawful."[17]

Now, this implies an understanding not only of the circumstances but also of the law, and it was argued at Nuremberg and has been argued since that the laws of war are so vague, uncertain, and incoherent that they can never require disobedience.[18] Indeed, the state of the positive law is not very good, especially where it relates to the exigencies of combat. But the prohibition against massacre is plain enough, and I think it is fair to say that common soldiers have been charged and convicted only for the knowing murder of innocent people: shipwrecked survivors struggling in the water, for example, or prisoners of war, or helpless civilians. Nor is it a question here only of the law, for these are acts that not only "violate unchallenged rules of warfare," as the British

field manual of 1944 states, but that also "outrage the general sentiments of humanity."[19] Ordinary *moral* sense and understanding rule out killings like those at My Lai. One of the soldiers there remembers thinking to himself that the slaughter was "just like a Nazi-type thing." That judgment is precisely right, and there is nothing in our conventional morality that renders it doubtful.

But the excuse of duress may hold even in a case like this, if the order to kill is backed up by a threat of execution. I have argued that soldiers in combat cannot plead self-preservation when they violate the rules of war. For the dangers of enemy fire are simply the risks of the activity in which they are engaged, and they have no right to reduce those risks at the expense of other people who are not engaged. But a threat of death directed not at soldiers in general but at a particular solider—a threat, as the lawyers say, "imminent, real, and inevitable"—alters the case, lifting it out of the context of combat and war risk. Now it becomes like those domestic crimes in which one man forces another, under threat of immediate death, to kill a third. The act is clearly murder, but we are likely to think that the man in the middle is not the murderer. Or, if we do think him a murderer, we are likely to accept the excuse of duress. Surely someone who refuses to kill at such a time, and dies instead, is not just doing his duty; he is acting heroically. Gray provides a paradigmatic example:[20]

In the Netherlands, the Dutch tell of a German soldier who was a member of an execution squad ordered to shoot innocent hostages. Suddenly he stepped out of rank and refused to participate in the execution. On the spot he was charged with treason by the officer in charge and was placed with the hostages, where he was promptly executed by his comrades.

Here is a man of extraordinary nobility, but

---

[17] Quoted in Kurt Baier's analysis of the Calley trial, "Guilt and Responsibility," *Individual and Collective Responsibility*, p. 42.

[18] See Wasserstrom, "The Responsibility of the Individual."

[19] Quoted in Telford Taylor, *Nuremberg and Vietnam*, p. 49.

[20] *The Warriors*, pp. 185–86.

what are we to say of his (former) comrades? That they are committing murder when they fire their guns, and that they are not responsible for the murder they commit. The officer in charge is responsible, and those among his superiors who determined on the policy of killing hostages. Responsibility passes over the heads of the members of the firing squad, not because of their oaths, not because of their orders, but because of the direct threat that drives them to act as they do.

War is a world of duress, of threat and counter-threat, so we must be clear about those cases in which duress does, and those in which it does not count as an excuse for conduct we would otherwise condemn. Soldiers are conscripted and forced to fight, but conscription by itself does not force them to kill innocent people. Soldiers are attacked and forced to fight, but neither aggression nor enemy onslaught forces them to kill innocent people. Conscription and attack bring them up against serious risks and hard choices. But constricted and frightening as their situation is, we still say that they choose freely and are responsible for what they do. Only a man with a gun at his head is not responsible.

But superior orders are not always enforced at the point of a gun. Army discipline in the actual context of war is often a great deal more haphazard than the firing squad example suggests. "It is a great boon of frontline positions," writes Gray, "that . . . disobedience is frequently possible, since supervision is not very exact where danger of death is present."[21] And in rear areas as well as at the front, there are ways of responding to an order short of obeying it: postponement, evasion, deliberate misunderstanding, loose construction, overly literal construction, and so on. One can ignore an immoral command or answer it with questions or protests; and sometimes even an overt refusal only invites reprimand, demotion, or detention; there is no risk of death. Whenever these possibilities are open, mor-

al men will seize upon them. The law seems to require a similar readiness, for it is a legal principle that duress excuses only if the harm the individual soldier inflicts is not disproportionate to the harm with which he is threatened.[22] He is not excused for the murder of innocent people by the threat of demotion.

It has to be said, however, that officers are far more capable than enlisted men of weighing the dangers they face. Telford Taylor has described the case of Colonel William Peters, an officer in the Confederate Army during the American Civil War, who refused a direct order to burn the town of Chambersburg, Pennsylvania.[23] Peters was relieved of his command and placed under arrest, but he was never brought before a court martial. We may admire his courage, but if he anticipated that his superiors would ("prudently", as another Confederate officer said) avoid a trial, his decision was relatively easy. The decision of an ordinary soldier, who may well be subject to summary justice and who knows little of the temper of his more distant superiors, is much harder. At My Lai, those men who refused to fire never suffered for their refusal and apparently did not expect to suffer; and that suggests that we must blame the others for their obedience. In more ambiguous cases, the duress of superior orders, though it is not "imminent, real, and inevitable" and cannot count as a defense, is commonly regarded as an extenuating factor. That seems the right attitude to take, but I want to stress once again that when we take it we are not making concessions to the need for discipline, but simply recognizing the plight of the common soldier.

There is another reason for extenuation, unmentioned in the legal literature, but prominent in moral accounts of disobedience. The path that I have marked out as the right one is often a very lonely path. Here, too, the cases of the German soldier who broke ranks with his fellow execu-

---

[21] *The Warriors*, p. 189.

[22] McDougal and Feliciano, pp. 693–94 and notes.

[23] *Nuremberg and Vietnam*, p. 55n.

tioners and was promptly executed by them is unusual and extreme. But even when a soldier's doubts and anxieties are widely shared, they are still the subject of private brooding, not of public discussion. And when he acts, he acts alone, with no assurance that his comrades will support him. Civil protest and disobedience usually arise out of a community of values. But the army is an organization, not a community, and the communion of ordinary soldiers is shaped by the character and purposes of the organization, not by their private commitments. Theirs is the rough solidarity of men who face a common enemy and endure a common discipline. On both sides of a war, unity is reflexive, not intentional or premeditated. To disobey is to breach that elemental accord, to claim a moral separateness (or a moral superiority), to challenge one's fellows, perhaps even to intensify the dangers they face. "This is what is most difficult," wrote a French soldier who went to Algeria and then refused to fight, "being cut off from the fraternity, being locked up in a monologue, being incomprehensible."[24]

Now, *incomprehensible* is perhaps too strong a word, for a man appeals at such a time to common moral standards. But in the context of a military organization, that appeal will often go unheard, and so it involves a risk that may well be greater than that of punishment: the risk of a profound and morally disturbing isolation. This is not to say that one can join in a massacre for the sake of togetherness. But it suggests that moral life is rooted in a kind of association that military discipline precludes or temporarily cuts off, and that fact, too, must be taken into account in the judgments we make. It must be taken into account especially in the case of common soldiers, for officers are more free in their associations and more involved in discussions about policy and strategy. They have a say in the shape and character of the organization over which they preside.

---

[24] Jean Le Meur, "The Story of a Responsible Act," in *Political Man and Social Man*, ed. Robert Paul Wolff (New York, 1964), p 204.

Gillette v. United States and *Negre v. Larsen:* Conscientious Objection

These cases concerned two persons who objected to U.S. involvement in the Vietnam War, neither of whom was granted conscientious objector status. The legal issue was the meaning and constitutionality of the Military Selective Service Act of 1967, which requires that conscientious objectors be opposed to "participation in war in any form."

Mr. Justice Marshall delivered the opinion of the Court. These cases present the question whether conscientious objection to a particular war, rather than objection to war as such, relieves the objector from responsibilities to military training and service. Specifically, we are called upon to decide whether conscientious scruples relating to a particular conflict are within the purview of established provisions relieving conscientious objectors to war from military service. Both petitioners also invoke constitutional principles barring government interference with the exercise of religion and requiring governmental neutrality in matters of religion.

401 U.S. 437 (1971)

In No. 85, petitioner Gillette was convicted of willful failure to report for induction into the armed forces. Gillette defended on the ground that he should have been ruled exempt from induction as a conscientious objector to war. In support of his unsuccessful request for classification as a conscientious objector, this petitioner had stated his willingness to participate in a war of national defense or a war sponsored by the United Nations as a peace-keeping measure, but declared his opposition to American military operations in Vietnam, which he characterized as "unjust." Petitioner concluded that he could not in conscience enter and serve in the armed forces during the period of the Vietnam conflict. Gillette's view of his duty to abstain from any involvement in a war seen as unjust is, in his words, "based on a humanist approach to religion," and his personal decision concerning military service was guided by fundamental principles of conscience and deeply held views about the purpose and obligation of human existence.

The District court determined that there was a basis in fact to support administrative denial of exemption in Gillette's case. The denial of exemption was upheld, and Gillette's defense to the criminal charge rejected, not because of doubt about the sincerity or the religious character of petitioner's objection to military service, but because his objection ran to a particular war. . . .

In No. 325, petitioner Negre, after induction into the Army, completion of basic training, and receipt of orders for Vietnam duty, commenced proceeding looking to his discharge as a conscientious objector to war. Application for discharge was denied, . . . Again, no question is raised as to the sincerity or the religious quality of this petitioner's views. In line with religious counseling and numerous religious texts, Negre, a devout Catholic, believes that it is his duty as a faithful Catholic to discriminate between "just" and "unjust" wars, and to forswear participation in the latter. His assessment of the Vietnam conflict as an unjust war be-

came clear in his mind after completion of infantry training, and Negre is now firmly of the view that any personal involvement in that war would contravene his conscience and "all that I had been taught in my religious training."

. . . We affirm the judgments below in both cases.

Each petitioner claims a nonconstitutional right to be relieved of the duty of military service in virtue of his conscientious scruples. Both claims turn on the proper construction of § 6 (j) of the Military Selective Service Act of 1967. . . .

For purposes of determining the statutory status of conscientious objection to a particular war, the focal language of § 6 (j) is the phrase, "conscientiously opposed to participation in war in any form." This language, on a straightforward reading, can bear but one meaning; that conscientious scruples relating to war and military service must amount to conscientious opposition to participating personally in any war and all war. . . .

Sicurella v. United States, 348 U.S. 385 (1955), presented the only previous occasion for this Court to focus on the "participation in war in any form" language of § 6 (j). In *Sicurella* a Jehovah's Witness who opposed participation in secular wars was held to possess the requisite conscientious scruples concerning war, although he was not opposed to participation in a "theocratic war" commanded by Jehovah. The Court noted that the "theocratic war" reservation was highly abstract—no such war had occurred since biblical times, and none was contemplated. Congress, on the other hand, had in mind "real shooting wars." *id.,* at 391, and Sicurella's abstract reservations did not undercut his conscientious opposition to participating in such wars. Plainly, *Sicurella* cannot be read to support the claims of those, like petitioners, who for a variety of reasons consider one particular "real shooting war" to be unjust, and therefore oppose participation in that war. . . .

. . .The question here is not whether

these petitioners' beliefs concerning war are "religious" in nature. . . . Nor do we decide that conscientious objection to a particular war necessarily falls within § 6 (j)'s expressly excluded class of "essentially political, sociological, or philosophical views, or a merely personal moral code." Rather, we hold that Congress intended to exempt persons who oppose participating in all war—"participation in war in any form"—and that persons who object solely to participation in a particular war are not within the purview of the exempting section, even though the latter objection may have such roots in a claimant's conscience and personality that it is "religious" in character.

A further word may be said to clarify our statutory holding. Apart from abstract theological reservations, two other sorts of reservations concerning use of force have been thought by lower courts not to defeat a conscientious objector claim. Willingness to use force in self-defense against immediate acts of aggressive violence toward other persons in the community, has not been regarded as inconsistent with a claim of conscientious objection to war as such. . . . But surely willingness to use force defensively in the personal situations mentioned is quite different from willingness to fight in some wars but not in others. . . .

Both petitioners argue that § 6 (j), construed to cover only objectors to all war, violates the religious clauses of the First Amendment. The First Amendment provides that "Congress shall make no law respecting an establishment of religion, or prohibiting the free exercise thereof. . . ." Petitioners contend that Congress interferes with free exercise of religion by failing to relieve objectors to a particular war from military service, when the objection is religious or conscientious in nature. . . .

[As] a general matter it is surely true that the Establishment Clause prohibits government from abandoning secular purposes in order to put an imprimatur on one religion, or on religion as such, or to favor the adherents of any sect or religious organization.

The metaphor of a "wall" or impassible barrier between Church and State, taken too literally, may mislead constitutional analysis, but the Establishment Clause stands at least for the proposition that when government activities touch on the religious sphere, they must be secular in purpose, evenhanded in operation, and neutral in primary impact.

The critical weakness of petitioners' establishment claim arises from the fact that § 6 (j), on its face, simply does not discriminate on the basis of religious affiliation or religious belief, apart of course from beliefs concerning war. The section says that anyone who is conscientiously opposed to all war shall be relieved of military service. The specified objection must have a grounding in "religious training and belief," but no particular sectarian affiliation or theological position is required. . . .

Properly phrased, petitioners' contention is that the special statutory status accorded conscientious objection to all war, but not objection to a particular war, works a de facto discrimination among religions. This happens, say petitioners, because some religious faiths themselves distinguish between personal participation in "just" and in "unjust" wars, commending the former and forbidding the latter, and therefore adherents of some religious faiths—and individuals whose personal beliefs of a religious nature include the distinction—cannot object to all wars consistently with what is regarded as the true imperative of conscience. Of course, this contention of de facto religious discrimination, rendering § 6 (j) fatally underinclusive, cannot simply be brushed aside. The question of governmental neutrality is not concluded by the observation that § 6 (j) on its face makes no discrimination between religions, for the Establishment Clause forbids subtle departures from neutrality, "religious gerrymanders," as well as obvious abuses. . . . For the reasons that follow, we believe that petitioners have failed to make the requisite showing with respect to § 6 (j).

Section 6 (j) serves a number of valid

purposes having nothing to do with a design to foster or favor any sect, religion, or cluster of religions. There are considerations of a pragmatic nature, such as the hopelessness of converting a sincere conscientious objector into an effective fighting man, but no doubt the section reflects as well the view that "in the forum of conscience, duty to a moral power higher than the State has always been maintained." *United States v. Macintosh*, 283 U.S. 605, 633 (1973) (HUGHES, C. J., dissenting). We have noted that the legislative materials show congressional concern for the hard choice that conscription would impose on conscientious objectors to war, as well as respect for the value of conscientious action and for the principle of supremacy of conscience.

Naturally the considerations just mentioned are affirmative in character, going to support the existence of an exemption rather than its restriction specifically to persons who object to all war. The point is that these affirmative purposes are neutral in the sense of the Establishment Clause. . . . And while the objection must have roots in conscience and personality that are "religious" in nature, this requirement has never been construed to elevate the conventional piety or religiosity of any kind above the imperatives of a personal faith.

In this state of affairs it is impossible to say that § 6 (j) intrudes upon "voluntarism" in religious life, . . . or that the congressional purpose in enacting § 6 (j) is to promote or foster those religious organizations that traditionally have taught the duty to abstain from participation in any war. A claimant, seeking judicial protection for his own conscientious beliefs, would be hard put to argue that § 6 (j) encourages membership in putatively "favored" religious organizations, for the painful dilemma of the sincere conscientious objector arises precisely because he feels himself bound in conscience not to compromise his beliefs or affiliations.

We conclude not only that the affirmative purposes underlying § 6 (j) are neutral and secular, but also that valid neutral reasons exist for limiting the exemption to objectors

to all war, and that the section therefore cannot be said to reflect a religious preference.

Apart from the Government's need for manpower, perhaps the central interest involved in the administration of conscription laws is the interest in maintaining a fair system for determining "who serves when not all serve." When the Government exacts so much, the importance of fair, evenhanded, and uniform decisionmaking is obviously intensified. The Government argues that the interest in fairness would be jeopardized by expansion of § 6 (j) to include conscientious objection to a particular war. The contention is that the claim to relief on account of such objection is intrinsically a claim of uncertain dimensions, and that granting the claim in theory would involve a real danger of erratic or even discriminatory decisionmaking in administrative practice.

A virtually limitless variety of beliefs are subsumable under the rubric, "objection to a particular war." All the factors that might go into nonconscientious dissent from policy, also might appear as the concrete basis of an objection that has roots as well in conscience and religion. . . . The difficulties of sorting the two, with a sure hand, are considerable. Moreover, the belief that a particular war at a particular time is unjust is by its nature changeable and subject to nullification by changing events. Since objection may fasten on any of an enormous number of variables, the claim is ultimately subjective, depending on the claimant's view of the facts in relation to his judgment that a given factor or congeries of factors colors the character of the war as a whole. In short, it is not at all obvious in theory what sorts of objections should be deemed sufficient to excuse an objector, and there is considerable force in the Government's contention that a program of excusing objectors to particular wars may be "impossible to conduct with any hope of reaching fair and consistent results. . . . "

Mr. Justice Douglas, dissenting (in* Gillette *v. U.S.) Gillette's objection is to combat service in the Vietnam war, not to wars in general, and the basis of his objection is his conscience. His objection does not put him into the statutory exemption which extends to one "who, by reason of religious training and belief, is conscientiously opposed to participation in war in any form."

He stated his views as follows:

"I object to any assignment in the United States Armed Forces while this unnecessary and unjust war is being waged, on the grounds of religious belief specifically 'Humanism.' This essentially means respect and love for man, faith in his inherent goodness and perfectability, and confidence in his capability to improve some of the pains of the human condition."

... There is no doubt that the views of Gillette are sincere, genuine, and profound. . . .

The question, Can a conscientious objector, whether his objection be rooted in "religion" or in moral values, be required to kill? has never been answered by the Court. . . .

It is true that the First Amendment speaks of the free exercise of religion, not of the free exercise of conscience or belief. Yet conscience and belief are the main ingredients of the First Amendment rights. They are the bedrock of free speech as well as religion. . . .

Conscience is often the echo of religious faith. But, as this case illustrates, it may also be the product of travail, meditation, or sudden revelation related to a moral comprehension of the dimensions of a problem, not to a religion in the ordinary sense.

Tolstoy[1] wrote of a man, one Van der Veer, "who, as he himself says, is not a Christian, and who refuses military service, not from religious motives, but from motives of the simplest kind, motives intelligible and common to all men, of whatever religion or nation, whether Catholic, Mohammedan, Buddhist, Confucian, whether Spaniards or Japanese.

"Van der Veer refuses military service, not because he follows the commandment. 'Thou shalt do no murder,' not because he is a Christian, but because he holds murder to be opposed to human nature."

Tolstoy[2] goes on to say:

"Van der Veer says he is not a Christian. But the motives of his refusal and action are Christian. He refuses because he does not wish to kill a brother man; he does not obey, because the commands of his conscience are more binding upon him than the commands of men. . . . Thereby he shows that Christianity is not a sect or creed which some may profess and others reject; but that it is naught else than a life's following of that light of reason which illumines all men. . . .

"Those men who now behave rightly and reasonably do so, not because they follow prescriptions of Christ, but because that line of action which was pointed out eighteen hundred years ago has now become identified with human conscience."

. . .But the constitutional infirmity in the present Act seems obvious once "conscience" is the guide. As Chief Justice Hughes said in the *Macintosh* case:

"But, in the forum of conscience, duty to a moral power higher than the State has always been maintained. The reservation of that supreme obligation, as a matter of principle, would unquestionably be made by many of our conscientious and law-abiding citizens. The essence of religion is belief in a relation to God involving duties superior to those arising from any human relation." 283 U.S., at 633–634.

The law as written is a species of those which show an invidious discrimination in favor of religious persons and against others with like scruples. MR. JUSTICE BLACK once said: "The First Amendment has lost much if the religious follower and the atheist are no longer to be judicially regarded as entitled to equal justice under law." *Zorach v. Clauson*, 343 U.S. 306, 320 (dissenting). We said as much in our recent decision in *Epper-*

---

[1] L. Tolstoy, Writings on Civil Disobedience and Non-Violence 12 (1967).

[2] *Id.*, at 15–16.

son v. Arkansas, 393 U.S. 97, where we struck down as unconstitutional a state law prohibiting the teaching of the doctrine of evolution in the public schools:

"Government in our democracy, state and national, must be neutral in matters of religious theory, doctrine, and practice. It may not be hostile to any religion or to the advocacy of noreligion; and it may not aid, foster, or promote one religion or religious theory against another or even against the militant opposite. The First Amendment mandates governmental neutrality between religion and religion, and between religion and nonreligion." *Id.*, at 103–104.

. . .I would reverse this judgment.

Mr. Justice Douglas, dissenting in Negre v. Larsen. I approach the facts of this case with some diffidence, as they involve doctrines of the Catholic Church in which I was not raised. But we have in one of petitioner's briefs an authoritative lay Catholic scholar, Dr. John T. Noonan, Jr., and from that brief I deduce the following:

Under the doctrines of the Catholic Church a person has a moral duty to take part in wars declared by his government so long as they comply with the tests of his church for just wars. Conversely, a Catholic has a moral duty not to participate in unjust wars.

The Fifth Commandment, "Thou shall not kill," provides a basis for the distinction between just and unjust wars. In the 16th century Francisco Victoria, Dominican master of the University of Salamanca and pioneer in international law, elaborated on the distinction. "If a subject is convinced of the injustice of a war, he ought not to serve in it, even on the command of his prince. This is clear, for no one can authorize the killing of an innocent person." . . . Well over 400 years later, today, the Baltimore Catechism makes an exception to the Fifth Commandment for a "soldier fighting a just war."

No one can tell a Catholic that this or that war is either just or unjust. This is a personal decision that an individual must make on the basis of his own conscience after studying the facts.

Like the distinction between just and unjust wars, the duty to obey conscience is not a new doctrine in the Catholic Church. . . . That duty has not changed. Pope Paul VI has expressed it as follows: "On his part, man perceives and acknowledges the imperatives of the divine law through the mediation of conscience. In all his activity a man is bound to follow his conscience, in order that he may come to God, the end and purpose of life."

. . .Moreover, no conceivable cause could ever be sufficient justification for the evils, the slaughter, the destruction, the moral and religious upheavals which war today entails. *In practice, then, a declaration of war will never be justifiable.*"[3] The full impact of the horrors of modern war were emphasized in the Pastoral Constitution announced by Vatican II:

"The development of armaments by modern science has immeasurably magnified the horrors and wickedness of war. Warfare conducted with these weapons can inflict immense and indiscriminate havoc which goes far beyond the bounds of legitimate defense. Indeed, if the kind of weapons now stocked in the arsenals of the great powers were to be employed to the fullest, the result would be the almost complete reciprocal slaughter of one side by the other, not to speak of the widespread devastation that would follow in the world and the deadly aftereffects resulting from the use of such arms.

"All these factors force us to undertake a completely fresh reappraisal of war. . . . "

"[I]t is one thing to wage a war of self-defense; it is quite another to seek to impose domination on another nation. . . ."

The Pastoral Constitution announced that "[e]very act of war directed to the indiscriminate destruction of whole cities or vast areas with their inhabitants is a crime against God and man which merits firm and unequivocal condemnation."[4]

---

[3] The Future of Offensive War, 30 Blackfriars 415.
[4] Pastoral Constitution ¶ ¶ 79, 80.

Louis Negre is a devout Catholic. In 1951 when he was four, his family immigrated to this country from France.[5] He attended Catholic schools in Bakersfield, California, until graduation from high school. Then he attended Bakersfield Junior College for two years. Following that, he was inducted into the Army.

At the time of his induction he had his own convictions about the Vietnam war and the Army's goals in the war. He wanted, however, to be sure of his convictions. "I agreed to myself that before making any decision or taking any type of stand on the issue, I would permit myself to see and understand the Army's explanation of its reason for violence in Vietnam. For, without getting an insight on the subject, it would be unfair for me to say anything, without really knowing the answer."

_____

[5] Petitioner suggests that one of the reasons his parents left France was their opposition to France's participation in the Indo-China war.

On completion of his advanced infantry training, "I knew that if I would permit myself to go to Vietnam I would be violating my own concepts of natural law and would be going against all that I had been taught in my religious training." Negre applied for a discharge as a conscientious objector. His application was denied. He then refused to comply with an order to proceed for shipment to Vietnam. A general court-martial followed, but he was acquitted. After that he filed this application for discharge as a conscientious objector.

Negre is opposed under his religious training and beliefs to participation in any form in the war in Vietnam. His sincerity is not questioned. His application for a discharge, however, was denied because his religious training and beliefs led him to oppose only a particular war which according to his conscience was unjust.

For the reasons I have stated in my dissent in the *Gillette* case decided this day, I would reverse the judgment.

PART II   Democratic Values and Constitutional Constraints

On Democracy and the U.S. Constitution

James Madison, Alexander Hamilton, Thomas Jefferson, and Robert Yates

Article VII of the U.S. Constitution calls for it to be ratified by the states; at the close of the Constitutional Convention there followed a period of intense debate over the new national government. Best known of the works written during that period are the *Federalist Papers* written by Madison, Hamilton, and Jay.

They began appearing in a New York newspaper a few weeks after the convention adjourned, and set forth in detail the significance of the various provisions of the document and presented the case for adoption. Many, however, were initially skeptical, including Thomas Jefferson, who had not attended the convention. While he was eventually convinced to support adoption, others remained opposed. Prominent among these antifederalist authors was a New York lawyer and delegate to the convention named Robert Yates. Writing under the name of Brutus, he published a series of essays in the *The New York Journal* which appeared at the same time as the *Federalist Papers*. Some of the Constitution's critics shared the federalists' vision of the purposes of government; others like Jefferson and Yates, had deeper philosophical objections to the constitution, particularly its evident distrust of popular democracy and its emphasis on minority rights.

JAMES MADISON,

FEDERALIST NUMBER 10

Among the numerous advantages promised by a well constructed Union, none deserves to be more accurately developed than its tendency to break and control the violence of faction. The friend of popular governments, never finds himself so much alarmed for their character and fate, as when he contemplates their propensity to this dangerous vice. . . .

By a faction I understand a number of citizens, whether amounting to a majority or minority of the whole, who are united and actuated by some common impulse of passion, or of interest, adverse to the rights of other citizens, or to the permanent and aggregate interests of the community.

There are two methods of curing the mischiefs of faction: the one, by removing its causes; the other, by controlling its effects.

There are again two methods of removing the causes of faction: the one by destroying the liberty which is essential to its existence; the other, by giving to every citizen the same opinions, the same passions, and the same interests.

It could never be more truly said than of

the first remedy, that it is worse than the disease. Liberty is to faction, what air is to fire, an aliment without which it instantly expires. But it could not be a less folly to abolish liberty, which is essential to political life, because it nourishes faction, than it would be to wish the annihilation of air, which is essential to animal life, because it imparts to fire its destructive agency.

The second expedient is as impracticable, as the first would be unwise. As long as the reason of man continues fallible, and he is at liberty to exercise it, different opinions will be formed. As long as the connection subsists between his reason and his self-love, his opinions and his passions will have a reciprocal influence on each other; and the former will be objects to which the latter will attach themselves. The diversity in the faculties of men from which the rights of property originate, is not less an insuperable obstacle to the uniformity of interests. The protection of these faculties is the first object of Government. From the protection of different and unequal faculties of acquiring property, the possession of different degrees and kinds of property immediately results: and from the influence of these on the sentiments and views of the respective proprietors, ensues a division of the society into different interests and parties.

The latent causes of faction are thus sown in the nature of man; and we see them everywhere brought into different degrees of activity, according to the different circumstances of civil society. A zeal for different opinions concerning religion, concerning Government and many other points, as well of speculation as of practice; an attachment to different leaders ambitiously contending for pre-eminence and power; or to persons of other descriptions whose fortunes have been interesting to the human passions, have in turn divided mankind into parties, inflamed them with mutual animosity, and rendered them much more disposed to vex and oppress each other, than to co-operate for their common good. So strong is this propensity of mankind to fall into mutual animosities, that where no substantial occasion presents itself, the most frivolous and fanciful distinctions have been sufficient to kindle their unfriendly passions, and excite their most violent conflicts. But the most common and durable source of factions, has been the various and unequal distribution of property. . . .

No man is allowed to be a judge of his own cause; because his interest would certainly bias his judgment, and, not improbably, corrupt his integrity. With equal, nay with greater reason, a body of men, are unfit to be both judges and parties, at the same time; yet, what are many of the most important acts of legislation, but so many judicial determinations, not indeed concerning the rights of single persons, but concerning the rights of large bodies of citizens; and what are the different classes of legislators, but advocates and parties to the causes which they determine? . . .

It is in vain to say, that enlightened statesmen will be able to adjust these clashing interests, and render them all subservient to the public good. Enlightened statesmen will not always be at the helm. . . .

The inference to which we are brought, is, that the *causes* of faction cannot be removed; and that relief is only to be sought in the means of controlling its *effects*.

If a faction consists of less than a majority, relief is supplied by the republican principle, which enables the majority to defeat its sinister views by regular vote: It may clog the administration, it may convulse the society; but it will be unable to execute and mask its violence under the forms of the Constitution. When a majority is included in a faction, the form of popular government on the other hand enables it to sacrifice to its ruling passion or interest, both the public good and the rights of other citizens. To secure the public good, and private rights, against the danger of such a faction, and at the same time to preserve the spirit and the form of popular government, is then the great object to which our enquiries are directed. . . .

From this view of the subject, it may be concluded, that a pure Democracy, by which

I mean, a Society, consisting of a small number of citizens, who assemble and administer the Government in person, can admit of no cure for the mischiefs of faction. . . .

The two great points of difference between a Democracy and a Republic are, first, the delegation of the Government, in the latter, to a small number of citizens elected by the rest: secondly, the greater number of citizens, and greater sphere of country, over which the latter may be extended.

The effect of the first difference is, on the one hand to refine and enlarge the public views, by passing them through the medium of a chosen body of citizens, whose wisdom may best discern the true interest of their country, and whose patriotism and love of justice, will be least likely to sacrifice it to temporary or partial considerations. Under such a regulation, it may well happen that the public voice pronounced by the representatives of the people, will be more consonant to the public good, than if pronounced by the people themselves convened for the purpose. . . .

In the next place, as each Representative will be chosen by a greater number of citizens in the large than in the small Republic, it will be more difficult for unworthy candidates to practise with success the vicious arts, by which elections are too often carried; and the suffrages of the people being more free, will be more likely to centre on men who possess the most attractive merit, and the most diffusive and established characters. . . .

The other point of difference is, the greater number of citizens and extent of territory which may be brought within the compass of Republican, than of Democratic Government; and it is this circumstance principally which renders factious combinations less to be dreaded in the former, than in the latter. The smaller the society, the fewer probably will be the distinct parties and interests composing it; the fewer the distinct parties and interests, the more frequently will a majority be found of the same party; and the smaller the number of individuals composing a majority, and the small-er the compass within which they are placed, the more easily will they concert and execute their plans of oppression. Extend the sphere, and you take in a greater variety of parties and interests; you make it less probable that a majority of the whole will have a common motive to invade the rights of other citizens; or if such a common motive exists, it will be more difficult for all who feel it to discover their own strength, and to act in unison with each other. Besides other impediments, it may be remarked, that where there is a consciousness of unjust or dishonorable purposes, communication is always checked by distrust, in proportion to the number whose concurrence is necessary.

Hence it clearly appears, that the same advantage, which a Republic has over a Democracy, in controlling the effects of faction, is enjoyed by a large over a small Republic—is enjoyed by the Union over the States composing it. Does this advantage consist in the substitution of Representatives, whose enlightened views and virtuous sentiments render them superior to local prejudices, and to schemes of injustice? It will not be denied, that the Representation of the Union will be most likely to possess these requisite endowments. Does it consist in the greater security afforded by a greater variety of parties, against the event of any one party being able to outnumber and oppress the rest? In an equal degree does the increased variety of parties, comprised within the Union, increase this security. Does it, in fine, consist in the greater obstacles opposed to the concert and accomplishment of the secret wishes of an unjust and interested majority? Here, again, the extent of the Union gives it the most palpable advantage.

The influence of factious leaders may kindle a flame within their particular States, but will be unable to spread a general conflagration through the other States: a religious sect, may degenerate into a political faction in a part of the Confederacy; but the variety of sects dispersed over the entire face of it, must secure the national Councils against any danger from that source: a rage for paper money, for an abolition of debts, for an equal division of property, or for any other improper or wicked project, will be less apt to pervade the whole body of the Union, than a particular member of it; in the same proportion as such a malady is more likely to taint a particular country or district, than an entire State.

In the extent and proper structure of the Union, therefore, we behold a Republican remedy for the diseases most incident to Republican Government. And according to the degree of pleasure and pride, we feel in being Republicans, ought to be our zeal in cherishing the spirit, and supporting the character of Federalists.

JAMES MADISON,

FEDERALIST NUMBER 51

To what expedient then shall we finally resort for maintaining in practice the necessary partition of power among the several departments, as laid down in the constitution? The only answer that can be given is, that as all these exterior provisions are found to be inadequate, the defect must be supplied, by so contriving the interior structure of the government, as that its several constituent parts may, by their mutual relations, be the means of keeping each other in their proper places. Without presuming to undertake a full development of this important idea, I will hazard a few general observations, which may perhaps place it in a clearer light, and enable us to form a more correct judgment of the principles and structure of the government planned by the convention.

In order to lay a due foundation for that separate and distinct exercise of the different powers of government, which to a certain extent, is admitted on all hands to be essential to the preservation of liberty, it is evident that each department should have a will of its own; and consequently should be so constituted, that the members of

each should have as little agency as possible in the appointment of the members of the others. . . .

But the great security against a gradual concentration of the several powers in the same department, consists in giving to those who administer each department, the necessary constitutional means, and personal motives, to resist encroachments of the others. The provision for defence must in this, as in all other cases, be made commensurate to the danger of attack. Ambition must be made to counteract ambition. The interest of the man must be connected with the constitutional rights of the place. It may be a reflection on human nature, that such devices should be necessary to control the abuses of government. But what is government itself but the greatest of all reflections on human nature? If men were angels, no government would be necessary. If angels were to govern men, neither external nor internal controls on government would be necessary. In framing a government which is to be administered by men over men, the great difficulty lies in this: You must first enable the government to control the governed; and in the next place, oblige it to control itself. A dependence on the people is no doubt the primary control on the government; but experience has taught mankind the necessity of auxiliary precautions.

This policy of supplying by opposite and rival interests, the defect of better motives, might be traced through the whole system of human affairs, private as well as public. We see it particularly displayed in all the subordinate distributions of power; where the constant aim is to divide and arrange the several offices in such a manner as that each may be a check on the other; that the private interest of every individual, may be a sentinel over the public rights. These inventions of prudence cannot be less requisite in the distribution of the supreme powers of the state.

But it is not possible to give to each department an equal power of self defence. In republican government the legislative authority, necessarily, predominates. The remedy for this inconveniency is, to divide the legislature into different branches; and to render them by different modes of election, and different principles of action, as little connected with each other, as the nature of their common functions, and their common dependence on the society, will admit. . . .

There are moreover two considerations particularly applicable to the federal system of America, which place that system in a very interesting point of view.

First. In a single republic, all the power surrendered by the people, is submitted to the administration of a single government; and usurpations are guarded against by a division of the government into distinct and separate departments. In the compound republic of America, the power surrendered by the people, is first divided between two distinct governments, and then the portion allotted to each, subdivided among distinct and separate departments. Hence a double security arises to the rights of the people. The different governments will control each other; at the same time that each will be controlled by itself.

Second. It is of great importance in a republic, not only to guard the society against the oppression of its rulers; but to guard one part of the society against the injustice of the other part. Different interests necessarily exist in different classes of citizens. If a majority be united by a common interest, the rights of the minority will be insecure. . . . Whilst all authority in it will be derived from and dependent on the society, the society itself will be broken into so many parts, interests and classes of citizens, that the rights of the individuals or of the minority, will be in little danger from interested combinations of the majority. In a free government, the security for civil rights must be the same as for religious rights. It consists in the one case in the multiplicity of interests, and in the other, in the multiplicity of sects. The degree of security in both cases will depend on the number of interests and sects; and this may be presumed to depend on the extent of country and number of people comprehended under the same government. . . .

ALEXANDER HAMILTON,

FEDERALIST NUMBER 78

. . .Whoever attentively considers the different departments of power must perceive that, in a government in which they are separated from each other, the judiciary, from the nature of its functions, will always be the least dangerous to the political rights of the Constitution; because it will be least in capacity to annoy or injure them. The Executive not only dispenses honors, but holds the sword of the community. The legislature not only commands the purse, but prescribes the rules by which the duties and rights of every citizen are to be regulated. The judiciary, on the contrary, has no influence over either the sword or the purse; no direction either of the strength or the wealth of the society; and can take no active resolution whatever. It may truly be said to have neither FORCE nor WILL, but merely judgment; and must ultimately depend upon the aid of the executive arm even for the efficacy of its judgment. . . .

Some perplexity respecting the rights of the courts to pronounce legislative acts void, because contrary to the constitution, has arisen from an imagination that the doctrine would imply a superiority of the judiciary to the legislative power. . . . It is far more rational to suppose, that the courts were designed to be an intermediate body between the people and the legislature, in order, among other things, to keep the latter within the limits assigned to their authority. The interpretation of the laws is the proper and peculiar province of the courts. A constitution is, in fact, and must be regarded by the judges, as a fundamental law. It therefore belongs to them to ascertain its meaning, as well as the meaning of any particular act proceeding from the legislative body. If there should happen to be an irreconcilable variance between the two, that which has the superior obligation and validity ought, of course, to be preferred; or, in other words, the Constitution ought to be preferred to the statute, the intention of the people to the intention of their agents.

Nor does this conclusion by any means suppose a superiority of the judicial to the legislative power. It only supposes a superiority of the people is superior to both; and that where the will of the legislature, declared in its statutes, stands in opposition to that of the people, declared in the Constitution, the judges ought to be governed by the latter rather than the former. They ought to regulate their decisions by the fundamental laws, rather than by those which are not fundamental. . . .

It can be of no weight to say that the courts, on the pretence of a repugnancy, may substitute their own pleasure to the constitutional intentions of the legislature. This might as well happen in the case of two contradictory statutes; or it might as well happen in every adjudication upon any single statute. The courts must declare the sense of the law; and if they should be disposed to exercise WILL instead of JUDGMENT, the consequence would equally be the substitution of their pleasure to that of the legislative body. The observation, if it prove any thing, would prove that there ought to be no judges distinct from that body.

If, then, the courts of justice are to be considered as the bulwarks of a limited Constitution against legislative encroachments, this consideration will afford a strong argument for the permanent tenure of judicial offices, since nothing will contribute so much as this to that independent spirit in the judges which must be essential to the faithful performance of so arduous a duty.

This independence of the judges is equally requisite to guard the Constitution and the rights of individuals from the effects of those ill humors, which the arts of designing men, or the influence of particular conjunctures, sometimes disseminate among the people themselves, and which, though they speedily give place to better information, and more deliberate reflection, have a tendency, in the meantime, to occasion dangerous innovations in the government, and serious oppressions of the minor party in the community. . . . Until the people have, by some solemn and authoritative act, annulled or changed the established form, it is binding upon themselves collectively, as well as individually; and no presumption, or even knowledge, of their sentiments, can warrant their representatives in a departure from it, prior to such an act. But it is easy to see, that it would require an uncommon portion of fortitude in the judges to do their duty as faithful guardians of the Constitution, where legislative invasions of it had been instigated by the major voice of the community. . . .

LETTER FROM THOMAS JEFFERSON TO JAMES MADISON

Paris, September 6, 1789.

DEAR SIR,—I sit down to write to you without knowing by what occasion I shall send my letter. I do it because a subject comes into my head which I would wish to develope a little more than is practicable in the hurry of the moment of making up general despatches.

The question: Whether one generation of man has a right to bind another, seems never to have been started either on this or our side of the water. Yet it is a question of such consequences as not only to merit decision, but place also, among the fundamental principles of every government. The course of reflection in which we are immersed here on the elementary principles of society has presented this question to my mind; and that no such obligation can be transmitted I think very capable of proof. I set out on this ground which I suppose to be self-evident, *"that the earth belongs in usufruct to the living;"*

that the dead have neither powers nor rights over it. The portion occupied by any individual ceases to be his when himself ceases to be, and reverts to the society. If the society has formed no rules for the appropriation of its lands in severalty, it will be taken by the first occupants. These will generally be the wife and children of the decedent. If they have formed rules of appropriation, those rules may give it to the wife and children, or to some one of them, or to the legatee of the deceased. So they may give it to his creditor. But the child, the legatee or creditor takes it, not by any natural right, but by a law of society of which they are members, and to which they are subject. Then no man can by *natural right* oblige the lands he occupied, or the persons who succeed him in that occupation, to the paiment of debts contracted by him. For if he could, he might during his own life, eat up the usufruct of the lands for several generations to come, and then the lands would belong to the dead, and not to the living, which would be reverse of our principle. What is true of every member of the society individually, is true of them all collectively, since the rights of the whole can be no more than the sum of the rights of individuals. . . .

What is true of a generation all arriving to self-government on the same day, and dying all on the same day, is true of those on a constant course of decay and renewal, with this only difference. A generation coming in and going out entire, as in the first case, would have a right in the 1st year of their self dominion to contract a debt for 33. years, in the 10th. for 24. in the 20th. for 14. in the 30th. for 4. whereas generations changing daily, by daily deaths and births, have one constant term beginning at the date of their contract, and ending when a majority of those of full age at that date shall be dead. The length of that term may be estimated from the tables of mortality, corrected by the circumstances of climate, occupation &c. peculiar to the country of the contractors. . . .

I suppose that the received opinion, that the public debts of one generation devolve on the next, has been suggested by our seeing habitually in private life that he who succeeds to lands is required to pay the debts of his ancestor or testator, without considering that this requisition is municipal only, not moral, flowing from the will of the society which has found it convenient to appropriate the lands become vacant by the death of their occupant on the condition of a payment of his debts; but that between society and society, or generation and generation there is no municipal obligation, no umpire but the law of nature. We seem not to have perceived that, by the law of nature, one generation is to another as one independant nation to another. . . .

On similar ground it may be proved that no society can make a perpetual constitution, or even a perpetual law. The earth belongs always to the living generation. They may manage it then, and what proceeds from it, as they please, during their usufruct. They are masters too of their own persons, and consequently may govern them as they please. But persons and property make the sum of the objects of government. The constitution and the laws of their predecessors extinguish them, in their natural course, with those whose will gave them being. This could preserve that being till it ceased to be itself, and no longer. Every constitution, then, and every law, naturally expires at the end of 19. years [because half of the voters will be dead in 19 years]. If it be enforced longer, it is an act of force and not of right.

It may be said that the succeeding generation exercising in fact the power of repeal, this leaves them free as if the constitution or law had been expressly limited to 19. years only. In the first place, this objection admits the right, in proposing an equivalent. But the power of repeal is not an equivalent. It might be indeed if every form of government were so perfectly contrived that the will of the majority could always be obtained fairly and without impediment. But this is true of no form. The people cannot assemble themselves; their representation is unequal and vicious. Various checks are opposed to every legislative proposition. Factions get possession of the public councils. Bribery corrupts them. Personal interests lead them astray from the general interests of their constituents; and other impediments arise so as to prove to every practical man that a law of limited duration is much more manageable than one which needs a repeal. . . .

Turn this subject in your mind, my Dear Sir, and particularly as to the power of contracting debts, and develope it with that perspicuity and cogent logic which is so peculiarly yours. Your station in the councils of our country gives you an opportunity of producing it to public consideration, of forcing it into discussion. At first blush it may be rallied as a theoretical speculation; but examination will prove it to be solid and salutary. It would furnish matter for a fine preamble to our first law for appropriating the public revenue; and it will exclude, at the threshold of our new government the contagious and ruinous errors of this quarter of the globe, which have armed despots with means not sanctioned by nature for binding in chains their fellow-men. . . .

LETTER FROM JAMES MADISON TO THOMAS JEFFERSON

New York, February 4, 1790.

DEAR SIR,—Your favor of January 9, inclosing one of September last, did not get to hand till a few days ago. The idea which the latter evolves is a great one, and suggests many interesting reflections to Legislators, particularly when contracting and providing for public debts. Whether it can be received in the extent to which your reasonings carry it is a question which I ought to turn more in my thoughts than I have yet been able to do before I should be justified in making up a full opinion on it. My first thoughts lead me to view the doctrine as not *in all respects* compatible with the course of human affairs. I will endeavour to sketch

the grounds of my skepticism. "As the Earth belongs to the living, not to the dead, a living generation can bind itself only; in every Society, the will of the majority binds the whole; according to the laws of mortality, a majority of those ripe for the exercise of their will do not live beyond the term of 19 years; to this term, then, is limited the validity of every act of the society, nor can any act be continued beyond this term, without an *express* declaration of the public will." This I understand to be the outline of the argument.

The acts of a political society may be divided into three classes:

1. The fundamental constitution of the Government.
2. Laws involving some stipulation which renders them irrevocable at the will of the Legislature.
3. Laws involving no such irrevocable quality.

1. However applicable in theory the doctrine may be to a Constitution, it seems liable in practice to some weighty objections.

Would not a Government, ceasing of necessity at the end of a given term, unless prolonged by some Constitutional Act previous to its expiration, be too subject to the casualty and consequences of an interregnum?

Would not a Government so often revised become too mutable and novel to retain that share of prejudice in its favor which is a salutary aid to the most rational Government?

Would not such a periodical revision engender pernicious factions that might not otherwise come into existence, and agitate the public mind more frequently and more violently than might be expedient?

2. In the second class, of acts involving stipulations, must not exceptions, at least to the doctrine, be admitted?

If the earth be the gift of *nature* to the living, their title can extend to the earth in its *natural* state only. The *improvements* made by the dead form a debt against the living, who take the benefit of them. This debt cannot be otherwise discharged than by a proportionate obedience to the will of the Authors of the improvements.

But a case less liable to be controverted may, perhaps, be stated. Debts may be incurred with a direct view to the interests of the unborn, as well as of the living. Such are debts for repelling a Conquest, the evils of which descend through many generations. Debts may even be incurred principally for the benefit of posterity. Such, perhaps, is the debt incurred by the United States. In these instances the debt might not be dischargeable within the term of 19 years.

There seems, then, to be some foundation in the nature of things, in the relation which one generation bears to another, for the *descent* of obligations from one to another. Equity may require it. Mutual good may be promoted by it. And all that seems indispensable in stating the account between the dead and the living is, to see that the debts against the latter do not exceed the advances made by the former. Few of the incumbrances entailed on nations by their predecessors would bear a liquidation even on this principle.

3. Objections to the doctrine, as applied to the third class of acts, must be merely practical. But in that view alone they appear to be material.

Unless such temporary laws should be kept in force by acts regularly anticipating their expiration, all the rights depending on positive laws, that is, most of the rights of property, would become absolutely defunct, and the most violent struggles ensue between the parties interested in reviving, and those interested in reforming the antecedent state of property. Nor does it seem improbable that such an event might be suffered to take place. The checks and difficulties opposed to the passage of laws, which render the power of repeal inferior to an opportunity to reject, as a security against oppression, would here render the latter an insecure provision against anarchy. Add to this that the very possibility of an event so hazardous to the rights of property could not but depreciate its value; that the approach of the crisis would increase the effect; that the frequent return of periods superseding all the obligations dependent on antecedent laws and usages must, by weakening the sense of them, co-operate with motives to licenciousness already too powerful; and that the general uncertainty and vicissitudes of such a state of things would, on one side, discourage every useful effort of steady industry pursued under the sanction of existing laws, and, on the other give an immediate advantage to the more sagacious over the less sagacious part of the Society.

I can find no relief from such embarrassments but in the received doctrine that a *tacit* assent may be given to established Governments and laws, and that this assent is to be inferred from the omission of an express revocation. It seems more practicable to remedy by well-constituted Governments the pestilent operation of this doctrine in the unlimited sense in which it is at present received, than it is to find a remedy for the evils necessarily springing from an unlimited admission of the contrary doctrine.

It is not doubtful whether it be possible to exclude wholly the idea of an implied or tacit assent, without subverting the very foundation of Civil Society?

On what principles is it that the voice of the majority binds the minority? It does not result, I conceive, from a law of nature, but from compact founded on utility. A greater proportion might be required by the fundamental Constitution of Society, if under any particular circumstances it were judged eligible. Prior, therefore, to the establishment of this principle, *unanimity* was necessary; and rigid Theory accordingly presupposes the assent of every individual to the rule which subjects the minority to the will of the majority. If this assent cannot be given tacitly, or be not implied where no positive evidence forbids, no person born in Society could, on attaining ripe age, be bound by any acts of the majority, and either a unanimous renewal of every law would be necessary as often as a new member should be added to the Society, or the express consent of every new member be obtained to the rule by which the majority decides for the whole.

If these observations be not misapplied, it follows that a limitation of the validity of all Acts to the computed life of the generation establishing them is in some cases not required by theory, and in others not consistent with practice. They are not meant, however, to impeach either the utility of the principle as applied to the cases you have particularly in view, or the general importance of it in the eye of the Philosophical Legislator. On the contrary, it would give me singular pleasure to see it first announced to the world in a law of the United States, and always kept in view as a salutary restraint on living generations from *unjust and unnecessary* burdens on their successors. This is a pleasure, however, which I have no hope of enjoying. The spirit of Philosophical legislation has not prevailed at all in some parts of America and is by no means the fashion of this part, or of the present Representative Body. The evils suffered or feared from weakness in Government and licenciousness in the people have turned the attention more towards the means of strengthening the powers of the former, than of narrowing their extent in the minds of the latter. Besides this it is so much easier to descry the little difficulties immediately incident to every great plan than to comprehend its general and remote benefits, that further light must be added to the Councils of our Country before many truths which are seen through the medium of Philosophy become visible to the naked eye of the ordinary politician.

ROBERT YATES (BRUTUS) TO THE CITIZENS OF NEW YORK

Let us now proceed to enquire whether it is best the thirteen United States should be reduced to one republic, or not. . . .

If respect is to be paid to the opinion of the greatest and wisest men who have ever thought or wrote on the science of government, we shall be constrained to conclude, that a free republic cannot succeed over a country of such immense extent, containing such a number of inhabitants, and these encreasing in such rapid progression as that of the whole United States. Among the many illustrious authorities which might be produced to this point, quoting only two. The one is the baron de Montesquieu, spirit of laws, chap. xvi. vol. I [book VIII]. "It is natural to a republic to have only a small territory, otherwise it cannot long subsist. In a large republic there are men of large fortunes, and consequently of less moderation; there are trusts too great to be placed in any single subject; he has interest of his own; he soon begins to think that he may be happy, great and glorious, by oppressing his fellow citizens; and that he may raise himself to grandeur on the ruins of his country. In a large republic, the public good is sacrificed to a thousand views; it is subordinate to exceptions, and depends on accidents. In a small one, the interest of the public is easier perceived, better understood, and more within the reach of every citizen; abuses are of less extent, and of course are less protected."

History furnishes no example of a free republic, any thing like the extent of the United States. The Grecian republics were of small extent; so also was that of the Romans. Both of these, it is true, in process of time, extended their conquests over large territories of country; and the consequence was, that their governments were changed from that of free governments to those of the most tyrannical that ever existed in the world.

Not only the opinion of the greatest men, and the experience of mankind, are against the idea of an extensive republic, but a variety of reasons may be drawn from the reason and the nature of things, against it. In every government, the will of the sovereign is the law. In despotic governments, the supreme authority being lodged in one, his will is law, and can be as easily expressed to a large extensive territory as to a small one. In a pure democracy the people are the sovereign, and their will is declared by themselves; for this purpose they must all come together to deliberate, and decide. This kind of government cannot be exercised, therefore, over a country of any considerable extent: it must be confined to a single city, or at least limited to such bounds as that the people can conveniently assemble, be able to debate, understand the subject submitted to them, and declare their opinion concerning it.

In a free republic, although all laws are derived from the consent of the people, yet the people do not declare their consent by themselves in person, but by representatives, chosen by them, who are supposed to know the minds of their constituents, and to be possessed of integrity to declare this mind.

In every free government, the people must give their assent to the laws by which they are governed. This is the true criterion between a free government and an arbitrary one. The former are ruled by the will of the whole, expressed in any manner they may agree upon; the latter by the will of one, or a few. If the people are to give their assent to the laws, by persons chosen and appointed by them, the manner of the choice and the number chosen, must be such, as to possess, be disposed, and consequently qualified to declare the sentiments of the people; for if they do not know, or are not disposed to speak the sentiments of the people, the people do not govern, but the sovereignty is in a few. Now, in a large extended country, it is impossible to have a representation, possessing the sentiments, and of integrity, to declare the minds of the people, without having it so numerous and unwieldly, as to be subject in great measure to the inconveniency of a democratic government.

The territory of the United States is of vast extent; it now contains near three millions of souls, and is capable of containing much more than ten times that number. Is it practicable for a country, so large and so numerous as they will soon become, to elect a representation, that will speak their sentiments, without their becoming so numerous as to be incapable of transacting public business? It certainly is not.

In a republic, the manners, sentiments, and interests of the people should be similar. If this be not the case, there will be a constant clashing of opinions; and the representatives of one part will be continually striving against those of the other. This will retard the operations of government, and prevent such conclusions as will promote the public good. If we apply this remark to the condition of the United States, we shall be convinced that it forbids that we should be one government. The United States includes a variety of climates. The productions of the different parts of the union are very variant, and their interests, of consequence, diverse. Their manners and habits differ as much as their climates and productions; and their sentiments are by no means coincident. The laws and customs of the several states are, in many respects, very diverse, and in some opposite; each would be in favor of its own interests and customs, and, of consequence, a legislature, formed of representatives from the respective parts, would not only be too numerous to act with any care or decision, but would be composed of such heterogenous and discordant

principles, as would constantly be contending with each other. . . .

The confidence which the people have in their rulers, in a free republic, arises from their knowing them, from their being responsible to them for their conduct, and from the power they have of displacing them when they misbehave; but in a republic of the extent of this continent, the people in general would be acquainted with very few of their rulers; the people at large would know little of their proceedings, and it would be extremely difficult to change them. The people in Georgia and New Hampshire would not know one another's mind, and therefore could not act in concert to enable them to effect a general change of representatives. The different parts of so extensive a country could not possibly be made acquainted with the conduct of their representatives, nor be informed of the reasons upon which measures were founded. The consequence will be, they will have no confidence in their legislature, suspect them of ambitious views, be jealous of every measure they adopt, and will not support the laws they pass. Hence the government will be nerveless and inefficient, and no way will be left to render it otherwise, but by establishing an armed force to execute the laws at the point of the bayonet—a government of all others the most to be dreaded.

In a republic of such vast extent as the United States, the legislature cannot attend to the various concerns and wants of its different parts. It cannot be sufficiently numerous to be acquainted with the local condition and wants of the different districts, and if it could, it is impossible it should have sufficient time to attend to and provide for all the variety of cases of this nature, that would be continually arising.

In so extensive a republic, the great officers of government would soon become above the control of the people, and abuse their power to the purpose of aggrandizing themselves, and oppressing them. The trust committed to the executive offices, in a country of the extent of the United States, must be various and of magnitude. The command of all the troops and navy of the republic, the appointment of officers, the power of pardoning offences, the collecting of all the public revenues, and the power of expending them, with a number of other powers, must be lodged and exercised in every state, in the hands of a few. When these are attended with great honor and emolument, as they always will be in large states, so as greatly to interest men to pursue them, and to be proper objects for ambitious and designing men, such men will be ever restless in their pursuit after them. They will use the power, when they have acquired it, to the purposes of gratifying their own interest and ambition, and it is scarcely possible, in a very large republic, to call them to account for their misconduct, or to prevent their abuse of power.

These are some of the reasons by which it appears, that a free republic cannot long subsist over a country of the great extent of these states. If then this new constitution is calculated to consolidate the thirteen states into one, as it evidently is, it ought not to be adopted. . . .

The constitution proposed to your acceptance, is designed not for yourselves alone, but for generations yet unborn. The principles, therefore, upon which the social compact is founded, ought to have been clearly and precisely stated, and the most express and full declaration of rights to have been made—But on this subject there is almost an entire silence.

If we may collect the sentiments of the people of America, from their own most solemn declarations, they hold this truth as self evident, that all men are by nature free. No one man, therefore, or any class of men, have a right, by the law of nature, or of God, to assume or exercise authority over their fellows. The origin of society then is to be sought, not in any natural right which one man has to exercise authority over another, but in the united consent of those who associate. The mutual wants of men, at first dictated the propriety of forming societies; and when they were established, protection and defence pointed out the necessity of insti-

tuting government. In a state of nature every individual pursues his own interest; in this pursuit it frequently happened, that the possessions or enjoyments of one were sacrificed to the views and designs of another; thus the weak were a prey to the strong, the simple and unwary were subject to imposition from those who were more crafty and designing. In this state of things, every individual was insecure; common interest therefore directed, that government should be established, in which the force of the whole community should be collected, and under such directions, as to protect and defend every one who composed it. The common good, therefore, is the end of civil government, and common consent, the foundation on which it was established. To effect this end, it was necessary that a certain portion of natural liberty should be surrendered, in order, that what remained should be preserved; how great a proportion of natural freedom is necessary to be yielded by individuals, when they submit to government, I shall not now enquire. So much, however, must be given up, as will be sufficient to enable those, to whom the administration of the government is committed, to establish laws for the promoting the happiness of the community, and to carry those laws into effect. But it is not necessary, for this purpose, that individuals should relinquish all their natural rights. Some are of such a nature that they cannot be surrendered. Of this kind are the rights of conscience, the right of enjoying and defending life, etc. Others are not necessary to be resigned, in order to attain the end for which government is instituted, these therefore ought not to be given up. To surrender them, would counteract the very end of government, to wit, the common good. . . .

I presume, to an American, then, that this principle is a fundamental one, in all the constitutions of our own states; there is not one of them but what is either founded on a declaration or bill of rights, or has certain express reservation of rights interwoven in the body of them. From this it appears, that at a time when the pulse of liberty beat high and when an appeal was made to the people to form constitutions for the government of themselves, it was their universal sense, that such declarations should make a part of their frames of government. It is therefore the more astonishing, that this grand security, to the rights of the people, is not to be found in this constitution. . . .

The very term, representative, implies, that the person or body chosen for this purpose, should resemble those who appoint them—a representation of the people of America, if it be a true one, must be like the people. It ought to be so constituted, that a person, who is a stranger to the country, might be able to form a just idea of their character, by knowing that of their representatives. They are the sign—the people are the thing signified. It is absurd to speak of one thing being the representative of another, upon any other principle. The ground and reason of representation, in a free government, implies the same thing. Society instituted government to promote the happiness of the whole, and this is the great end always in view in the delegation of powers. It must then have been intended, that those who are placed instead of the people, should possess their sentiments and feelings, and be governed by their interests, or, in other words, should bear the strongest resemblance of those in whose room they are substituted. It is obvious, that for an assembly to be a true likeness of the people of any country, they must be considerably numerous.—One man, or a few men, cannot possibly represent the feelings, opinions, and characters of a great multitude. In this respect, the new constitution is radically defective.—The house of assembly, which is intended as a representation of the people of America, will not, nor cannot, in the nature of things, be a proper one—sixty-five men cannot be found in the United States, who hold the sentiments, possess the feelings, or are acqainted with the wants and interests of this vast country. This extensive continent is made up of a number of different classes of people; and to have a proper representation of them, each class ought to

have an opportunity of choosing their best informed men for the purpose; but this cannot possibly be the case in so small a number. According to the common course of human affairs, the natural aristocracy of the country will be elected. Wealth always creates influence, and this is generally much increased by large family connections; this class in society will for ever have a great number of dependents; besides, they will always favour each other—it is their interest to combine—they will therefore constantly unite their efforts to procure men of their own rank to be elected—they will concenter all their force in every part of the state into one point, and by acting together, will most generally carry their election. . . . The great body of the yeomen of the country cannot expect any of their order in this assembly— the station will be too elevated for them to aspire to—the distance between the people and their representatives, will be so very great, that there is no probability that a farmer, however respectable, will be chosen—the mechanicks of every branch, must expect to be excluded from a seat in this Body—It will and must be esteemed a station too high and exalted to be filled by any but the first men in the state, in point of fortune; so that in reality there will be no part of the people represented, but the rich, even in that branch of the legislature, which is called the democratic.—The well born, and highest orders in life, as they term themselves, will be ignorant of the sentiments of the midling class of citizens, strangers to their ability, wants, and difficulties, and void of sympathy, and fellow feeling. This government is a complete system, not only for making, but for executing laws. And the courts of law, which will be constituted by it, are not only to decide upon the constitution and the laws made in pursuance of it, but by officers subordinate to them to execute all their decisions. The real effect of this system of government, will therefore be brought home to the feelings of the people, through the medium of the judicial power. It is, moreover, of great importance, to examine with care the nature and extent of the judicial power, because those who are to be vested with it, are to be placed in a situation altogether unprecedented in a free country. They are to be rendered totally independent, both of the people and the legislature, both with respect to their offices and salaries. No errors they may commit can be corrected by any power above them, if any such power there be, nor can they be removed from office for making ever so many erroneous adjudications.

The only causes for which they can be displaced, is, conviction of treason, bribery, and high crimes and misdemeanors. . . .

The judicial are not only to decide questions arising upon the meaning of the constitution in law, but also in equity.

By this they are empowered, to explain the constitution according to the reasoning spirit of it, without being confined to the words or letter. . . .

They will give the sense of every article of the constitution, that may from time to time come before them. And in their decisions they will not confine themselves to any fixed or established rules, but will determine, according to what appears to them, the reason and spirit of the constitution. The opinions of the supreme court, whatever they may be, will have the force of law; because there is no power provided in the constitution, that can correct their errors, or controul their adjudications. From this court there is no appeal. And I conceive the legislature themselves, cannot set aside a judgment of this court, because they are authorised by the constitution to decide in the last resort. The legislature must be controuled by the constitution, and not the constitution by them. They have therefore no more right to set aside any judgment pronounced upon the construction of the constitution, than they have to take from the president, the chief command of the army and navy, and commit it to some other person. The reason is plain; the judicial and executive derive their authority from the same source, that the legislature do theirs; and therefore in all cases, where the constitution does not make the one responsible to, or controulable by the other, they are altogether independent of each other.

The judicial power will operate to effect, in the most certain, but yet silent and imperceptible manner, what is evidently the tendency of the constitution:—I mean, an entire subversion of the legislative, executive and judicial powers of the individual states. Every adjudication of the supreme court, on any question that may arise upon the nature and extent of the general government, will affect the limits of the state jurisdiction. In proportion as the former enlarge the exercise of their powers, will that of the latter be restricted. . . .

Considerations On Representative Government

John Stuart Mill

John Stuart Mill (1806–1873) had an unusual life by almost any account. His father, James Mill, who was a friend of the economist David Ricardo and the legal theorist John Austin, was among the most devoted followers of Jeremy Bentham, the utilitarian philosopher. Like Bentham, the senior Mill held that human behavior is best understood in terms of self-interest and that government serves the common good by promoting the happiness of its citizens. Happiness, in turn, was assumed to refer to pleasure and the absence of pain.

James resolved to raise his son John Stuart according to sound utilitarian principles. With Bentham's help, he developed a plan that included a rigorous tutoring program and keeping the boy away from other children. By the age of three, John Stuart had begun learning Greek. At eight he learned Latin and pursued mathematics and history. By the age of twelve, he was studying logic and political economy. At fourteen, he went to France to live with Bentham's brother. A year later he studied law with John Austin, then professor at University College, London. However, when Mill was twenty, he entered a depression that lasted five years, during which he rejected Bentham's narrow hedonism in favor of a more complex conception of human well-being. At twenty-four, he began a lifelong friendship and intellectual collaboration with Harriet Taylor. Although the two were close companions, Harriet remained married to John Taylor for two decades. When John Taylor died, John Stuart Mill and Harriet Taylor were married. The two lived happily together for seven years until her death. Mill served for three years as a member of Parliament. After being defeated for re-election, he retired to France where he died. Mill's works include *On Liberty* (1859), *Utilitarianism* (1863), and *On the Subjection of Woman* (1869); selections from all these are reprinted in later sections.

Democracy (understood as a system in which the ultimate control of government is vested in the majority of people through an electoral process) can be defended in various ways. Some maintain that democratic procedures are intrinsically better than the alternatives since they allow people to share equally in the political decisions which shape their lives. Others, including John Stuart Mill, believe democracy's strength lies in its consequences: It promotes the general welfare and encourages citizens to develop their intellectual and moral capacities. In the selection below Mill discusses the concept of representation and the legitimate role of elected officials, together with the difficult problem of assuring that minorities are given adequate say in the decision-making process.

THAT THE IDEALLY BEST FORM OF GOVERNMENT IS REPRESENTATIVE GOVERNMENT

It has long (perhaps throughout the entire duration of British freedom) been a common saying, that if a good despot could be ensured, despotic monarchy would be the best form of government. I look upon this as a radical and most pernicious misconception of what good government is; which, until it can be got rid of, will fatally vitiate all our speculations on government.

The supposition is, that absolute power, in the hands of an eminent individual, would ensure a virtuous and intelligent performance of all the duties of government. Good laws would be established and enforced, bad laws would be reformed; the best men would be placed in all situations of trust; justice would be as well administered, the public burthens would be as light and as judiciously imposed, every branch of administration would be as purely and as intelligently conducted, as the circumstances of the country and its degree of intellectual and moral cultivation would admit. I am willing, for the sake of the argument, to concede all this; but I must point out how great the concession is; how much more is needed to produce even an approximation to these results than is conveyed in the simple expression, a good despot. Their realisation would in fact imply, not merely a good monarch, but an all-seeing one. He must be at all times informed correctly, in considerable detail, of the conduct and working of every branch of administration, in every district of the country, and must be able, in the

twenty-four hours per day which are all that is granted to a king as to the humblest labourer, to give an effective share of attention and superintendence to all parts of this vast field; or he must at least be capable of discerning and choosing out, from among the mass of his subjects, not only a large abundance of honest and able men, fit to conduct every branch of public administration under supervision and control, but also the small number of men of eminent virtues and talents who can be trusted not only to do without that supervision, but to exercise it themselves over others. So extraordinary are the faculties and energies required for performing this task in any supportable manner, that the good despot whom we are supposing can hardly be imagined as consenting to undertake it, unless as a refuge from intolerable evils, and a transitional preparation for something beyond. But the argument can do without even this immense item in the account. Suppose the difficulty vanquished. What should we then have? One man of superhuman mental activity managing the entire affairs of a mentally passive people. Their passivity is implied in the very idea of absolute power. The nation as a whole and every individual composing it, are without any potential voice in their own destiny. They exercise no will in respect to their collective interests. All is decided for them by a will not their own, which it is legally a crime for them to disobey. What sort of human beings can be formed under such a regimen? What development can wither their thinking or their active faculties attain under it? On matters of pure theory they might perhaps be allowed to speculate, so long as their speculations either did not approach politics, or had not the remotest connection with its practice. On practical affairs they could at most be only suffered to

From John Stuart Mill, *Considerations On Representative Government* (1861).

suggest; and even under the most moderate of despots, none but persons of already admitted or reputed superiority could hope that their suggestions would be known to, much less regarded by, those who had the management of affairs. A person must have a very unusual taste for intellectual exercise in and for itself, who will put himself to the trouble of thought when it is to have no outward effect, or qualify himself for functions which he has no chance of being allowed to exercise. The only sufficient incitement to mental exertion, in any but a few minds in a generation, is the prospect of some practical use to be made of its results. It does not follow that the nation will be wholly destitute of intellectual power. The common business of life, which must necessarily be performed by each individual or family for themselves, will call forth some amount of intelligence and practical ability, within a certain narrow range of ideas. There may be a select class of *savants*, who cultivate science with a view to its physical uses, or for the pleasure of the pursuit. There will be a bureaucracy, and persons in training for the bureaucracy, who will be taught at least some empirical maxims of government and public administration. There may be, and often has been, a systematic organisation of the best mental power in the country in some special direction (commonly military) to promote the grandeur of the despot. But the public at large remains without information and without interest on all the greater matters of practice; or, if they have any knowledge of them, it is but a *dilettante* knowledge, like that which people have of the mechanical arts who have never handled a tool. Nor is it only in their intelligence that they suffer. Their moral capacities are equally stunted. Wherever the sphere of action of human beings is artificially circumscribed, their sentiments are narrowed and dwarfed in the same proportion. The food of feeling is action: even domestic affection lives upon voluntary good offices. Let a person have nothing to do for his country, and he will not care for

it. It has been said of old, that in a despotism there is at most but one patriot, the despot himself; and the saying rests on a just appreciation of the effects of absolute subjection, even to a good and wise master. . . .

Leaving things to the Government, like leaving them to Providence, is synonymous with caring nothing about them, and accepting their results, when disagreeable, as visitations of Nature. With the exception, therefore, of a few studious men who take an intellectual interest in speculation for its own sake, the intelligence and sentiments of the whole people are given up to the material interests, and, when these are provided for, to the amusement and ornamentation, of private life. But to say this is to say, if the whole testimony of history is worth anything, that the era of national decline has arrived: that is, if the nation had ever attained anything to decline from. If it has never risen above the condition of an Oriental people, in that condition it continues to stagnate. But if, like Greece or Rome, it had realised anything higher, through the energy, patriotism, and enlargement of mind, which as national qualities are the fruits solely of freedom, it relapses in a few generations into the Oriental state. And that state does not mean stupid tranquillity, with security against change for the worse; it often means being overrun, conquered, and reduced to domestic slavery, either by a stronger despot, or by the nearest barbarous people who retain along with their savage rudeness the energies of freedom.

Such are not merely the natural tendencies, but the inherent necessities of despotic government; from which there is no outlet, unless in so far as the despotism consents not to be despotism. . . .

There is no difficulty in showing that the ideally best form of government is that in which the sovereignty, or supreme controlling power in the last resort, is vested in the entire aggregate of the community; every citizen not only having a voice in the exercise of that ultimate sovereignty, but being, at least occasionally, called on to take an actual part in the government, by the personal discharge of some public function, local or general.

To test this proposition, it has to be examined in reference to the two branches into which, as pointed out in the last chapter, the inquiry into the goodness of a government conveniently divides itself, namely, how far it promotes the good management of the affairs of society by means of the existing faculties, moral, intellectual, and active, of its various members, and what is its effect in improving or deteriorating those faculties.

The ideally best form of government, it is scarcely necessary to say, does not mean one which is practicable or eligible in all states of civilization, but the one which, in the circumstances in which it is practicable and eligible, is attended with the greatest amount of beneficial consequences, immediate and prospective. A completely popular government is the only polity which can make out any claim to this character. It is pre-eminent in both the departments between which the excellence of a political constitution is divided. It is both more favourable to present good government, and promotes a better and higher form of national character, than any other polity whatsoever.

Its superiority in reference to present well-being rests upon two principles, of as universal truth and applicability as any general propositions which can be laid down respecting human affairs. The first is, that the rights and interests of every or any person are only secure from being disregarded when the person interested is himself able, and habitually disposed, to stand up for them. The second is, that the general prosperity attains a greater height, and is more widely diffused, in proportion to the amount and variety of the personal energies enlisted in promoting it.

Putting these two propositions into a shape more special to their present application; human beings are only secure from evil at the hands of others in proportion as they have the power of being, and are,

self-*protecting*; and they only achieve a high degree of success in their struggle with Nature in proportion as they are self-*dependent*, relying on what they themselves can do, either separately or in concert, rather than on what others do for them.

The former proposition—that each is the only safe guardian of his own rights and interests—is one of those elementary maxims of prudence, which every person, capable of conducting his own affairs, implicitly acts upon, wherever he himself is interested. . . .

It is an adherent condition of human affairs that no intention, however sincere, of protecting the interests of others can make it safe or salutary to tie up their own hands. Still more obviously true is it, that by their own hands only can any positive and durable improvement of their circumstances in life be worked out. Through the joint influence of these two principles, all free communities have both been more exempt from social injustice and crime, and have attained more brilliant prosperity, than any others, or than they themselves after they lost their freedom. Contrast the free states of the world, while their freedom lasted, with the contemporary subjects of monarchical or oligarchical despotism. . . . Their superior prosperity was too obvious ever to have been gainsaid; while their superiority in good government and social relations is proved by the prosperity, and is manifest besides in every page of history. . . .

Thus stands the case as regards present well-being; the good management of the affairs of the existing generation. If we now pass to the influence of the form of government upon character, we shall find the superiority of popular government over every other to be, if possible, still more decided and indisputable.

This question really depends upon a still more fundamental one, viz., which of two common types of character, for the general good of humanity, it is most desirable should predominate—the active, or the passive type; that which struggles against evils, or that which endures them; that which bends to circumstances, or that which endeavours to make circumstances bend to itself.

The commonplace of moralists, and the general sympathies of mankind, are in favour of the passive type. Energetic characters may be admired, but the acquiescent and submissive are those which most men personally prefer. The passiveness of our neighbours increases our sense of security, and plays into the hands of our wilfulness. Passive characters, if we do not happen to need their activity, seem an obstruction the less in our own path. A contented character is not a dangerous rival. Yet nothing is more certain than that the improvement in human affairs is wholly the work of the uncontented characters; and, moreover, that it is much easier for an active mind to acquire the virtues of patience than for a passive one to assume those of energy.

Of the three varieties of mental excellence, intellectual, practical, and moral, there never could be any doubt in regard to the first two which side had the advantage. All intellectual superiority is the fruit of active effort. Enterprise, the desire to keep moving, to be trying and accomplishing new things for our own benefit or that of others, is the parent even of speculative, and much more of practical, talent. The intellectual culture compatible with the other type is of that feeble and vague description which belongs to a mind that stops at amusement, or at simple contemplation. The test of real and vigorous thinking, the thinking which ascertains truths instead of dreaming dreams, is successful application to practice. . . . With respect to practical improvement, the case is still more evident. The character which improves human life is that which struggles with natural powers and tendencies, not that which gives way to them. The self-benefiting qualities are all on the side of the active and energetic character: and the habits and conduct which promote the advantage of each individual member of the community must be at least a part of those which conduce most in the end to the advancement of the community as a whole.

But on the point of moral preferability, there seems at first sight to be room for doubt. I am not referring to the religious feeling which has so generally existed in favour of the inactive character, as being more in harmony with the submission due to the divine will. Christianity as well as other religions has fostered this sentiment; but it is the prerogative of Christianity, as regards this and many other perversions, that it is able to throw them off. Abstractedly from religious considerations, a passive character, which yields to obstacles instead of striving to overcome them, may not indeed be very useful to others, no more than to itself, but it might be expected to be at least inoffensive. Contentment is always counted among the moral virtues. But it is a complete error to suppose that contentment is necessarily or naturally attendant on passivity of character; and useless it is, the moral consequences are mischievous. Where there exists a desire for advantages not possessed, the mind which does not potentially possess them by means of its own energies is apt to look with hatred and malice on those who do. The person bestirring himself with hopeful prospects to improve his circumstances is the one who feels good will towards others engaged in, or who have succeeded in, the same pursuit. And where the majority are so engaged, those who do not attain the object have had the tone given to their feelings by the general habit of the country, and ascribe their failure to want of effort or opportunity, or to their personal ill luck. But those who, while desiring what others possess, put no energy into striving for it, are either incessantly grumbling that fortune does not do for them what they do not attempt to do for themselves, or overflowing with envy and ill-will towards those who posses what they would like to have. . . .

There are, no doubt, in all countries, really contented characters, who not merely do not seek, but do not desire, what they do not already possess, and these naturally bear no ill-will towards such as have apparently a more favoured lot. But the great mass of seeming contentment is real discontent, combined with indolence or self-indulgence, which, while taking no legitimate means of raising itself, delights in bringing other down to its own level. And if we look narrowly even at the cases of innocent contentment, we perceive that they only win our admiration when the indifference is solely to improvement in outward circumstances, and there is a striving for perpetual advancement in spiritual worth, or at least a disinterested zeal to benefit others. The contented man, or the contented family, who have no ambition to make any one else happier, to promote the good of their country or their neighbourhood, or to improve themselves in moral excellence, excite in us neither admiration nor approval. We rightly ascribe this sort of contentment to mere unmanliness and want of spirit. The content which we approve is an ability to do cheerfully without what cannot be had, a just appreciation of the comparative value of different objects of desire, and a willing renunciation of the less when incompatible with the greater. These, however, are excellences more natural to the character, in proportion as it is actively engaged in the attempt to improve its own or some other lot. He who is continually measuring his energy against difficulties learns what are the difficulties insuperable to him, and what are those which, though he might overcome, the success is not worth the cost. He whose thoughts and activities are all needed for, and habitually employed in, practicable and useful enterprises, is the person of all others least likely to let his mind dwell with brooding discontent upon things either not worth attaining, or which are not so to him. Thus the active, self-helping character is not only intrinsically the best, but is the likeliest to acquire all that is really excellent or desirable in the opposite type.

The striving, go-ahead character of England and the United States is only a fit subject of disapproving criticism on account of the very secondary objects on which it commonly expends its strength. In itself it is the foundation of the best hopes for general improvement of mankind. . . .

Now there can be no kind of doubt that the passive type of character is favoured by the government of one or a few, and the active self-helping type by that of the many. Irresponsible rulers need the quiescence of the ruled more than they need any activity but that which they can compel. Submissiveness to the prescription of men as necessities of nature is the lesson inculcated by all governments upon those who are wholly without participation in them. The will of superiors, and the law as the will of superiors, must be passively yielded to. But no men are mere instruments or materials in the hands of their rulers who have will or spirit or a spring of internal activity in the rest of their proceedings: and any manifestation of these qualities, instead of receiving encouragement from despots, has to get itself forgiven by them.

Very different is the state of the human faculties where a human being feels himself under no other external restraint than the necessities of nature, or mandates of society which he has his share in imposing, and which it is open to him, if he thinks them wrong, publicly to dissent from, and exert himself actively to get altered. No doubt, under a government partially popular, this freedom may be exercised even by those who are not partakers in the full privileges of citizenship. But it is a great additional stimulus to any one's self-help and self-reliance when he starts from even ground, and has not to feel that his success depends on the impression he can make upon sentiments and the disposition of a body of whom he is not one. It is a great discouragement to an individual, and a still greater one to a class, to be left out of the constitution; to be reduced to plead from outside the door to the arbiters of their destiny, not taken into consultation within. The maximum of the invigorating effect of freedom upon character is only obtained when the person acted on either is, or is looking forward to becoming, a citizen as fully privileged as any other. What is still more important than even this matter of feeling is the practical discipline which the character obtains from the occasional demand made upon the citizens to exercise, for a time and in their turn, some social function. It is not sufficiently considered how little there is in most men's ordinary life to give any largeness either to their conceptions or to their sentiments. Their work is a routine; not a labour of love, but of self-interest in the most elementary form, the satisfaction of daily wants; neither the thing done, nor the process of doing it, introduces the mind to thoughts or feelings extending beyond individuals; if instructive books are within their reach, there is no stimulus to read them; and in most cases the individual has no access to any person of cultivation much superior to his own. Giving him something to do for the public, supplies, in a measure, all these deficiencies. If circumstances allow the amount of public duty assigned him to be considerable, it makes him an educated man. Notwithstanding the defects of the social system and moral ideas of antiquity, the practice of the dicastery and the ecclesia raised the intellectual standard of an average Athenian citizen far beyond anything of which there is yet an example in any other mass of men, ancient or modern. The proofs of this are apparent in every page of our great historian of Greece; but we need scarcely look further than to the high quality of the addresses which their great orators deemed best calculated to act with effect on their understanding and will. A benefit of the same kind, though far less in degree, is produced on Englishmen of the lower middle class by their liability to be placed on juries and to serve parish offices; which, though it does not occur to so many, nor is so continuous, nor introduces them to so great a variety of elevated considerations, as to admit of comparison with the public education which every citizen of Athens obtained from her democratic institutions, must make them nevertheless very different beings, in range of ideas and development of faculties, from those who have done nothing in their lives but drive a quill, or sell goods over a counter. Still more salutary is the moral part of the instruction afforded by the participation of the private citizen, if even rarely, in public functions. He is called upon, while so engaged, to weigh interests not his own; to be guided, in case of conflicting claims, by another rule than his private partialities; to apply, at every turn, principles and maxims which have for their reason of existence the common good: and he usually finds associated with him in the same work minds more familiarised than his own with these ideas and operations, whose study it will be to supply reasons to his understanding, and stimulation to his feeling for the general interest. He is made to feel himself one of the public, and whatever is for their benefit to be for his benefit. Where this school of public spirit does not exist, scarcely any sense is entertained that private persons, in no eminent social situation, owe any duties to society, except to obey the laws and submit to the government. There is no unselfish sentiment of identification with the public. Every thought or feeling, either of interest or of duty, is absorbed in the individual and in the family. The man never thinks of any collective interest, of any objects to be pursued jointly with others, but only in competition with them, and in some measure at their expense. A neighbour, not being an ally or an associate, since he is never engaged in any common undertaking for joint benefit, is therefore only a rival. Thus even private morality suffers, while public is actually extinct. Were this the universal and only possible state of things, the utmost aspirations of the lawgiver or the moralist could only stretch to make the bulk of the community a flock of sheep innocently nibbling the grass side by side.

From these accumulated considerations it is evident that only government which can fully satisfy all the exigencies of the social state is one in which the whole people participate; that any participation, even in the smallest public function, is useful; that the participation should everywhere be as great as the general degree of improvement of the community will allow; and that nothing less can be ultimately desirable than the admission of all to a share in the sovereign power of the state. But since all cannot, in a community exceeding a single small town, participate personally in any but some very minor portions of the public business, it follows that the ideal type of a perfect government must be representative.

OF THE PROPER FUNCTIONS OF REPRESENTATIVE BODIES

In treating of representative government, it is above all necessary to keep in view the distinctions between its idea or essence, and the particular forms in which the idea has been clothed by accidental historical developments, or by the notions current at some particular period.

The meaning of representative government is, that the whole people, or some numerous portion of them, exercise through deputies periodically elected by themselves the ultimate controlling power, which, in every constitution, must reside somewhere. This ultimate power they must possess in all its completeness. They must be masters, whenever they please, of all the operations of government. There is no need that the constitutional law should itself give them this mastery. It does not in the British Constitution. But what it does give practically amounts to this. . . .

But while it is essential to representative government that the practical supremacy in the state should reside in the representatives of the people, it is an open question what actual functions, what precise part in the machinery of government, shall be directly and personally discharged by the representative body. Great varieties in this respect are compatible with the essence of representative government, provided the functions are such as secure to the representative body the control of everything in the last resort.

There is a radical distinction between controlling the business of government and actually doing it. The same person or body may be able to control everything, but cannot possibly do everything; and in many cases its control over everything will be more perfect the less it personally attempts to do. The commander of any army could not direct its movements effectually if he himself fought in the ranks, or led an assault. It is the same with bodies of men. Some things cannot be done except by bodies; other things cannot be well done by them. It is one questions, therefore, what a popular assembly should control, another what it should itself do. . . . In the first place, it is admitted in all countries in which the representative system is practically understood, that numerous representative bodies ought not to administer. The maxim is grounded not only on the most essential principles of good government, but on those of the successful conduct of business of any description. No body of men, unless organised and under command, is fit for action, in the proper sense. Even a select board, composed of a few members, and these specially conversant with the business to be done, is always an inferior instrument to some one individual who could be found among them, and would be improved in character if that one person were made the chief, and all the others reduced to subordinates. What can be done better by a body than by any individual is deliberation. When it is necessary or important to secure hearing and consideration to many conflicting opinions, a deliberative body is indispensable. . . .

Instead of the function of governing, for which it is radically unfit, the proper office of a representative assembly is to watch and control the government; to throw the light of publicity on its acts; to compel a full exposition and justification of all of them which any one considers questionable; to censure them if found condemnable, and, if the men who compose the government abuse their trust, or fulfil it in a manner which conflicts with the deliberate sense of the nation, to expel them from office, and either expressly or virtually appoint their successors. This is surely ample power, and security enough for the liberty of the nation. In addition to this, the Parliament has an office, not inferior even to this in importance; to be at once the nation's Committee of Grievances, and its Congress of Opinions; an arena in which not only the general opinion of the nation, but that of every section of it, and as far as possible of every eminent individual whom it contains, can produce itself in full light and challenge discussion; where every person in the country may count upon finding somebody who speaks his mind, as well or better than he could speak it himself—not to friends and partisans exclusively, but in the face of opponents, to be tested by adverse controversy; where those whose opinion is overruled, feel satisfied that it is heard, and set aside not by a mere act of will, but for what are thought superior reasons, and commend themselves as such to the representatives of the majority of the nation; where every party or opinion in the country can muster its strength, and be cured of any illusion concerning the number or power of its adherents; where the opinion which prevails in the nation makes itself manifest as prevailing, and marshals its hosts in the presence of the government, which is thus enabled and compelled to give way to it on the mere manifestation, without the actual employment, of its strength; where statesmen can assure themselves, far more certainly than by any other signs, what elements of opinions and power are growing, and what declining, and are enabled to shape their measures with some regard not solely to present exigencies, but to tendencies in progress. Representative assemblies are often taunted by their enemies with being places of mere talk and *bavardage*. There has seldom been more misplaced derision. I know not how a representative assembly can more usefully employ itself than in talk, when the subject of talk is the great public interests of the country, and every sentence of it represents the opinion either of some important body of persons in the nation, or of an individual in whom some such body

have reposed their confidence. A place where every interest and shade of opinion in the country can have its cause even passionately pleaded, in the face of the government and of all other interests and opinions, can compel them to listen, and either comply, or state clearly why they do not, is in itself, if it answered no other purpose, one of the most important political institutions that can exist anywhere, and one of the foremost benefits of free government. Such "talking" would never be looked upon with disparagement if it were not allowed to stop "doing;" which it never would, if assemblies knew and acknowledge that talking and discussion are their proper business, while *doing*, as the result of discussion, is the task not of a miscellaneous body, but of individuals specially trained to it; that the fit office of an assembly is to see that those individuals are honestly and intelligently chosen, and to interfere no further with them, except by unlimited latitude of suggestion and criticism, and by applying or withholding the final seal of national assent. . . . But the very fact which most unfits such bodies for a Council of Legislation qualifies them the more for their other office—namely, that they are not a selection of the greatest political minds in the country, from whose opinions little could with certainty be inferred concerning those of the nation, but are, when properly constituted, a fair sample of every grade of intellect among the people which is at all entitled to a voice in public affairs. Their part is to indicate wants, to be an organ for popular demands, and a place of adverse discussion for all opinions relating to public matters, both great and small; and, along with this, to check by criticism, and eventually by withdrawing their support, those high public officers who really conduct the public business, or who appoint those by whom it is conducted. Nothing but the restriction of the function of representative bodies within these rational limits will enable the benefits of popular control to be enjoyed in conjunction with the no less important requisites (growing ever more important as human affairs increase in scale and in complexity) of skilled legislation and administration. . . .

OF TRUE AND FALSE DEMOCRACY; REPRESENTATION OF ALL AND REPRESENTATION OF THE MAJORITY ONLY

It has been seen that the danger incident to a representative democracy are of two kinds: danger of a low grade of intelligence in the representative body, and in the popular opinion which controls it; and danger of class legislation on the part of the numerical majority, these being all composed of the same class. We have next to consider how far it is possible so to organise the democracy as, without interfering materially with the characteristic benefits of democratic government, to do away with these two great evils, or at least to abate them, in the utmost degree attainable by human contrivance.

The common mode of attempting this is by limiting the democratic character of the representation, through a more or less restricted suffrage. But there is a previous consideration which, duly kept in view, considerably modifies the circumstances which are supposed to render such a restriction necessary. A completely equal democracy, in a nation in which a single class composes the numerical majority, cannot be divested of certain evils; but those evils are greatly aggravated by the fact that the democracies which at present exist are not equal, but systematically unequal in favour of the predominant class. Two very different ideas are usually confounded under the name democracy. The pure idea of democracy, according to its definition, is the government of the whole people by the whole people, equally represented. Democracy as commonly conceived and hitherto practised is the government of the whole people by a mere majority of the people, exclusively represented. The former is synonymous with the equality of all citizens; the latter, strangely confounded with it, is a government of privilege, in favour of the numeri-

cal majority, who alone possess practically any voice in the State. This is the inevitably consequence of the manner in which the votes are now taken, to the complete disfranchisement of minorities. . . .

That the minority must yield to the majority, the smaller number to the greater, is a familiar idea; and accordingly men think there is no necessity for using their minds any further, and it does not occur to them that there is any medium between allowing the smaller number to be equally powerful with the greater, and blotting out the smaller number altogether. In a representative body actually deliberating, the minority must of course be overruled; and in any equal democracy (since the opinions of the constituents, when they insist on them, determine those of the representative body) the majority of the people, through their representatives, will outvote and prevail over the minority and their representatives. But does it follow that the minority should have no representatives at all? Because the majority ought to prevail over the minority, must the majority have all the votes, the minority none? Is it necessary that the minority should not even be heard? Nothing but habit and old association can reconcile any reasonable being to the needless injustice. In a really equal democracy, every or any section would be represented, not disproportionately, but proportionately. A majority of the electors would always have a majority of the representatives; but a minority of the electors would always have a minority of the representatives. Man for man they would be as fully represented as the majority. Unless they are, there is not equal government, but a government of inequality and privilege: one part of the people rule over the rest: there is a part whose fair and equal share of influence in the representation is withheld from them; contrary to all just government, but, above all, contrary to the principle of democracy, which professes equality as its very root and foundation.

The injustice and violation of principles are not less flagrant because those who suffer by them are a minority; for there is not equal suffrage where every single individual does not count for as much as any other single individual in the community. But it is not only a minority who suffer. Democracy, thus constituted, does not even attain its ostensible object, that of giving the powers of government in all cases to the numerical majority. It does something very different; it gives them to a majority of the majority; who may be, and often are, but a minority of the whole. All principles are most effectually tested by extreme cases. Suppose then, that, in a country governed by equal and universal suffrage, there is a contested election in every constituency, and every election is carried by a small majority. The Parliament thus brought together represents little more than a bare majority of the people. This Parliament proceeds to legislate, and adopts important measures by a bare majority of itself. What guarantee is there that these measures accord with the wishes of a majority of the people? Nearly half the electors, having been outvoted at the hustings, have had no influence at all in the decision; and the whole of these may be, a majority of them probably are, hostile to the measures, having voted against those by whom they have been carried. Of the remaining electors, nearly half have chosen representatives who, by supposition, have voted against the measures. It is possible, therefore, and not at all improbable, that the opinion which has prevailed was agreeable only to a minority of the nation, though a majority of that portion of it whom the institutions of the country have erected into a ruling class. If democracy means the certain ascendancy of the majority, there are no means of insuring that but by allowing every individual figure to tell equally in the summing up. Any minority left out, either purposely or by the play of the machinery, gives the power not to the majority, but to a minority in some other part of the scale.

The only answer which can possibly be made to this reasoning is, that as different opinions predominate in different localities, the opinion which is in a minority in some places has a majority in others, and on the whole every opinion which exists in the constituencies obtains its fair share of voices in the representation. . . . This is strikingly exemplified in the United States; where, at the election of President, the strongest party never dares put forward any of its strongest men, because every one of these, from the mere fact that he has been long in the public eye, has made himself objectionable to some portion or other of the party, and is therefore not so sure a card for rallying all their votes as a person who has never been heard of by the public at all until he is produced as the candidate. Thus, the man who is chosen, even by the strongest party, represents perhaps the real wishes only of the narrow margin by which that party outnumbers the other. Any section whose support is necessary to success possesses a veto on the candidate. Any section which holds out more obstinately than the rest can compel all the others to adopts its nominee; and this superior pertinacity is unhappily more likely to be found among those who are holding out for their own interest than for that of the public. The choice of the majority is therefore very likely to be determined by that portion of the body who are the most timid, the most narrow-minded and prejudiced, or who cling most tenaciously to the exclusive class-interest; in which case the electoral rights of the minority, while useless for the purpose for which votes are given, serve only for compelling the majority to accept the candidate of the weakest or worst portion of themselves. . . .

But real equality of representation is not obtained unless any set of electors amounting to the average number of a constituency, wherever in the country they happen in reside, have the power of combining with one another to return a representative. This degree of perfection in representation appeared impracticable until a man of great capacity, fitted alike for large general views and for the contrivance of practical details—Mr. Thomas Hare—had proved its possibility by drawing up a scheme for its accomplishment, embodied in a Draft of an Act of Parliament: a scheme which has the almost unparalleled merit of carrying out a great principle of government in a manner approaching to ideal perfection as regards the special object in view, while it attains incidentally several other ends of scarcely inferior importance.

According to this plan, the unit of representation, the quota of electors who would be entitled to have a member to themselves, would be ascertained by the ordinary process of taking averages, the number of voters being divided by the number of seats in the House: and every candidate who obtained that quota would be returned, from however great a number of local constituencies it might be gathered. The votes would, as at present, be given locally; but any elector would be at liberty to vote for any candidate in whatever part of the country he might offer himself. Those electors, therefore, who did not wish to be represented by any of the local candidates, might aid by their vote in the return of the person they liked best among all those throughout the country who had expressed a willingness to be chosen. This would, so far, give reality to the electoral rights of the otherwise virtually disfranchised minority. But it is important that not those alone who refuse to vote for any of the local candidates, but those also who vote for one of them and are defeated, should be enabled to find elsewhere the representation which they have not succeeded in obtaining in their own district. It is therefore provided that an elector may deliver a voting paper, containing other names in addition to the one which stands foremost in his preference. His vote would only be counted for one candidate; but if the object of his first choice failed to be returned, from not having obtained the quota, his second perhaps might be more fortunate. He may extend his list to a greater number, in the order of his preference, so that if the names which stand near the top of the list either cannot make up the quota, or are able to make it up without his vote, the vote may still be used for some one whom it may assist in returning. To obtain the full number of members required to complete the House,

as well as to prevent very popular candidates from engrossing nearly all the suffrages, it is necessary, however many votes a candidate may obtain, that no more of them than the quota should be counted for his return: the remainder of those who voted for him, would have their votes counted for the next person on their respective lists who needed them, and could by their aid complete the quota. To determine which of a candidate's votes should be used for his return, and which set free for others, several methods are proposed, into which we shall not here enter. He would of course retain the votes of all those who would not otherwise be represented; and for the remainder, drawing lots, in default of better, would be an unobjectionable expedient. The voting papers would be conveyed to a central office, where the votes would be counted, the number of first, second, third, and other votes given for each candidate ascertained, and the quota would be allotted to every one who could make it up, until the number of the House was complete: first votes being preferred to second, second to third, and so forth. . . .

In the first place, it secures a representation, in proportion to numbers, of every division of the electoral body: not two great parties alone, with perhaps a few large sectional minorities in particular places, but every minority in the whole nation, consisting of a sufficiently large number to be, on principles of equal justice, entitled to a representative. Secondly, no elector would, as at present, be nominally represented by some one whom he had not chosen. Every member of the House would be the representative of a unanimous constituency. He would represent a thousand electors, or two thousand, or five thousand, or ten thousand, as the quota might be, every one of whom would have not only voted for him, but selected him from the whole country; not merely from the assortment of two or three perhaps rotten oranges, which may be the only choice offered to him in his local market. Under this relation the tie between the elector and the representative would be of a strength, and a value, of which at present we have no experience. Every one of the electors would be personally identified with his representative, and the representative with his constituents. Every elector who voted for him would have done so either because, among all the candidates for Parliament who are favourably known to a certain number of electors, he is the one who best expresses the voter's own opinions, or because he is one of those whose abilities and character the voter most respects, and whom he most willingly trusts to think for him. The member would represent persons, not the mere bricks and mortar of the town—the voters themselves, not a few vestrymen or parish notabilities merely. All, however, that is worth preserving in the representation of places would be preserved. Though the Parliament of the nation ought to have as little as possible to do with purely local affairs, yet, while it has to do with them, there ought to be members specially commissioned to look after the interests of every important locality: and these there would still be. In every locality which could make up the quota within itself, the majority would generally prefer to be represented by one of themselves; by a person of local knowledge, and residing in the locality, if there is any such person to be found among the candidates, who is otherwise well qualified to be their representative. It would be the minorities chiefly, who being unable to return the local member, would look out elsewhere for a candidate likely to obtain other votes in addition to their own.

Of all modes in which a national representation can possibly be constituted, this one affords the best security for the intellectual qualifications desirable in the representatives. At present, by universal admission, it is becoming more and more difficult for any one who has only talents and character to gain admission into the House of Commons. The only persons who can get elected are those who possess local influence, or make their way by lavish expenditure, or who, on the invitation of three or four tradesmen or attorneys, are sent down by one of the two

great parties from their London clubs, as men whose votes the party can depend on under all circumstances. On Mr. Hare's system, those who did not like the local candidates, or who could not succeed in carrying the local candidate they preferred, would have the power to fill up their voting papers by a selection from all the persons of national reputation, on the list of candidates, with whose general political principles they were in sympathy. Almost every person, therefore, who had made himself in any way honourably distinguished, though devoid of local influence, and having sworn allegiance to no political party, would have a fair chance of making up the quota; and with this encouragement such persons might be expected to offer themselves, in numbers hitherto undreamt of. Hundreds of able men of independent thought, who would have no chance whatever of being chosen by the majority of any existing constituency, have by their writings, or their exertions in some field of public usefulness, made themselves known and approved by a few persons in almost every district of the kingdom; and if every vote that would be given for them in every place could be counted for their election, they might be able to complete the number of the quota. In no other way which it seems possible to suggest would Parliament be so certain of containing the very *élite* of the country.

OF THE EXTENSION OF THE SUFFRAGE

Whoever, in an otherwise popular government, has no vote, and no prospect of obtaining it, will either be a permanent malcontent, or will feel as one whom the general affairs of society do not concern; for whom they are to be managed by others; who 'has no business with the laws except to obey them,' nor with public interests and concerns except as a looker-on. What he will know or care about them from this position, may partly be measured by what an average woman of the middle class knows and cares about politics, compared with her husband or brothers.

Independently of all these considerations, it is a personal injustice to withhold from any one, unless for the prevention of greater evils, the ordinary privilege of having his voice reckoned in the disposal of affairs in which he has the same interest as other people. If he is compelled to pay, if he may be compelled to fight, if he is required implicitly to obey, he should be legally entitled to be told what for; to have his consent asked, and his opinion counted at its worth, though not at more than its worth. There ought to be no pariahs in a full-grown and civilized nation; no persons disqualified, except through their own default. Every one is degraded, whether aware of it or not, when other people, without consulting him, take upon themselves unlimited power to regulate his destiny. And even in a much more improved state than the human mind has ever yet reached, it is not in nature that they who are thus disposed of should meet with as fair play as those who have a voice. Rulers and ruling classes are under a necessity of considering the interests and wishes of those who have the suffrage; but of those who are excluded, it is in their option whether they will do so or not and however honestly disposed, they are in general too fully occupied with things which they *must* attend to, to have much room in their thoughts for anything which they can with impunity disregard. No arrangement of the suffrage, therefore, can be permanently satisfactory, in which any person or class is peremptorily excluded; in which the electoral privilege is not open to all persons of full age who desire to obtain it.

There are, however, certain exclusions, required by positive reasons, which do not conflict with this principle, and which, though an evil in themselves, are only to be got rid of by the cessation of the state of things which requires them. I regard it as wholly inadmissible that any person should participate in the suffrage, without being able to read, write, and, I will add, perform the common operations of arithmetic. Justice demands, even when the suffrage does not depend on it, that the means of attaining these elementary acquirements should be within the reach of every person, either gratuitously, or at an expense not exceeding what the poorest who earn their own living, can afford. If this were really the case, people would no more think of giving the suffrage to a man who could not read, than of giving it to a child who could not speak; and it would not be society that would exclude him, but his own laziness. When society has not performed its duty, by rendering this amount of instruction accessible to all, there is some hardship in the case, but it is a hardship that ought to be borne. If society has neglected to discharge two solemn obligations, the more important and more fundamental of the two must be fulfilled first: universal teaching must precede universal enfranchisement. . . .

It is also important, that the assembly which votes the taxes, either general or local, should be elected exclusively by those who pay something towards the taxes imposed. Those who pay no taxes, disposing by their votes or other people's money, have every motive to be lavish, and none to economize. As far as money matters are concerned, any power of voting possessed by them is a violation of the fundamental principle of free government; a severance of the power of control, from the interest in its beneficial exercise. It amounts to allowing them to put their hands into other people's pockets, for any purpose which they think fit to call a public one; which in some of the great towns of the United States is known to have produced a scale of local taxation onerous beyond example, and wholly borne by the wealthier classes. . . .

However this may be, I regard it as required by first principles, that the receipt of parish relief should be a peremptory disqualification for the franchise. He who cannot by his labour suffice for his own support, has no claim to the privilege of helping himself to the money of others. By becoming dependent on the remaining members of the community for actual subsistence, he abdicates his claim to equal rights with them in other respects. Those to whom he is indebted for the continuance of his very existence, may justly claim the exclusive management of those common concerns, to which he now brings nothing, or less than he takes away. As a condition of the franchise, a term should be fixed, say five years previous to the registry, during which the applicant's name has not been on the parish books as a recipient of relief. . . .

Non-payment of taxes, when so long persisted in that it cannot have arisen from inadvertence should disqualify while it lasts. These exclusions are not in their nature permanent. They exact such conditions only as all are able, or ought to be able, to fulfill if they choose. They leave the suffrage accessible to all whom are in the normal condition of a human being: and if any one has to forego it, he either does not care sufficiently for it, to do for its sake what he is already bound to do, or he is in a general condition of depression and degradation in which this slightly addition, necessary for the security of others, would be unfelt, and on emerging from which, this mark of inferiority would disappear with the rest.

In the long run, therefore (supposing no restrictions to exist but those of which we have now treated), we might expect that all, except that (it is to be hoped) progressively diminishing class, the recipients of parish relief, would be in possession of votes, so that the suffrage would be, with that slight abatement, universal. That it should be thus widely expanded, is, as we have seen, absolutely necessary to an enlarged and elevated conception of good government. Yet in this state of things, the great majority of voters, in most countries, and emphatically in this, would be manual labourers; and the twofold danger, that of too low a standard of political intelligence, and that of class legislation, would still exist, in a very perilous degree. It remains to be seen whether any means exist by which these evils can be obviated.

They are capable of being obviated, if men sincerely wish it; not by any artificial contrivance, but by carrying out the natural order of human life, which recommends itself to every one in things in which he has no interest or traditional opinion running counter to it. In all human affairs, every person directly interested, and not under positive tutelage, has an admitted claim to a voice, and when his exercise of it is not inconsistent with the safety of the whole, cannot justly be excluded from it. But though everyone ought to have a voice—that everyone should have an equal voice is a totally different proposition. When two persons who have a joint interest in any business, differ in opinion, does justice require that both opinions should be held of exactly equal value? If with equal virtue, one is superior to the other in knowledge and intelligence—or if with equal intelligence, one excels the other in virtue— the opinion, the judgment, of the higher moral or intellectual being, is worth more than that of the inferior: and if the institutions of the country virtually assert that they are of the same value, they assert a thing which is not. . . .

Everyone has a right to feel insulted by being made a nobody, and stamped as of no account of all. No one but a fool, and only a fool of a peculiar description, feels offended by the acknowledgment that there are others whose opinion, and even whose wish, is entitled to a greater amount of consideration than his. To have no voice in what are partly his own concerns, is a thing which nobody willingly submits to; but when what is partly his concern is also partly another's, and he feels the other to understand the subject better than himself, that the other's opinion should be counted for more than his own, accords with his expectations, and with the course of things which in all other affairs of life he is accustomed to acquiesce in. It is only necessary that this superior influence should be assigned on grounds which he can comprehend, and of which he is able to perceive the justice. . . .

If there existed such a thing as a really

national education, or a trustworthy system of general examination, education might be tested directly. In the absence of these, the nature of a person's occupation is some test. An employer of labour is on the average more intelligent than a labourer; for he must labour with his head, and not solely with his hands. A foreman is generally more intelligent than an ordinary labourer, and a labourer in the skilled trades than in the unskilled. A banker, merchant, or manufacturer, is likely to be more intelligent than a tradesman, because he has larger and more complicated interests to manage. In all these cases it is not the having merely undertaken the superior function, but the successful performance of it, that tests the qualifications; for which reason, as well as to prevent persons from engaging nominally in an occupation for the sake of the vote, it would be proper to require that the occupation should have been persevered in for some length of time (say three years). Subject to some such condition, two or more votes might be allowed to every person who exercises any of these superior functions. The liberal professions, when really and not nominally practised, imply, of course, a still higher degree of instruction; and wherever a sufficient examination, or any serious conditions of education, are required before entering on a profession, its members could be admitted at once to a plurality of votes. The same rule might be applied to graduates of universities; and even to those who bring satisfactory certificates of having passed through the course of study required by any school at which the higher branches of knowledge are taught, under proper securities that the teaching is real, and not a mere pretence. . . .

Let me add, that I consider it an absolutely necessary part of the plurality scheme, that it be open to the poorest individual in the community to claim its privileges, if he can prove that, in spite of all difficulties and obstacles, he is, in point of intelligence, entitled to them. There ought to be voluntary examinations at which any person whatever might present himself, might prove that he came up to the standard of knowledge and ability laid down as sufficient, and be admitted, in consequence, to the plurality of votes. A privilege which is not refused to any one who can show that he has realized the conditions on which in theory and principle it is dependent, would not necessarily be repugnant to any one's sentiment of justice: but it would certainly be so, if, while conferred on general presumptions not always infallible, it were denied to direct proof.

Is Democracy Special?

Brian Barry

One oft-heard defense of democratic government is that it gives the majority what it wants or, in other words, that when decisions are based on a majority vote, they reflect the majority's preferences. Beginning with a brief discussion of democratic procedure, Barry considers the assumptions which underlie this claim. He concludes that we must look beyond this "majority principle" if democratic procedures are to provide a special justification of legal authority.

Brian Barry teaches at the London School of Economics and Political Science. He is the author of *Political Argument* (1965), *Sociologists, Economists, and Democracy* (1970), *The Liberal Theory of Justice* (1973), and *Theories of Justice* (1989) as well as many articles.

[T]he question I wish to raise is whether or not a law's having been enacted (or not repealed) by a democratic procedure adds a reason for obeying it to whatever reasons exist independently of that. By a democratic procedure I mean a method of determining the content of laws (and other legally binding decisions) such that the preferences of the citizens have some formal connection with the outcome in which each counts equally. Let me make four comments on this definition.

First, I follow here those who insist that 'democracy' is to be understood in procedural terms. That is to say, I reject the notion that one should build into 'democracy' any constraints on the content of the outcomes produced, such as substantive equality, respect for human rights, concern

for the general welfare, personal liberty or the rule of law. The only exceptions (and these are significant) are those required by democracy itself as a procedure. Thus, some degree of freedom of communication and organization is a necessary condition of the formation, expression and aggregation of political preferences. And in a state (as against a small commune, say) the only preferences people can have are preferences for general lines of policy. There are not going to be widely held preferences about whether or not Mr. Jones should be fined £10 for speeding or Mrs. Smith should get supplementary benefit payments of £3.65 per week. At most there can be preferences for a speeding tariff or for general rules about eligibility for supplementary benefit. If magistrates or civil servants are arbitrary or capricious, therefore, they make democracy impossible.

Second, I require that there should be a formal connection between the preferences

From Peter Laslett and James Fishkin, eds. *Philosophy, Politics, and Society*, 5th series (New Haven: Yale University Press, 1979).

of the citizens and the outcomes produced. My intention in specifying a formal connection is to *rule* out cases where the decision-making process is *de facto* affected by the preferences of the citizens but not in virtue of any constitutional rule. Thus, eighteenth century England has been described as 'oligarchy tempered by riot.'[1] But however efficacious the rioters might be I would not say that their ability to coerce the government constituted a democratic procedure. In the concluding word of the judge appointed to enquire into riots in West Pakistan in 1953: 'But if democracy means the subordination of law and order to political ends—then Allah knoweth best and we end the report.'[2]

Third, by 'some formal connection' I intend deliberately to leave open a variety of possible ways in which democratic procedures might be implemented. In particular, I wish to include both *voting on laws* by citizens at large and voting for *representatives* who exercise the law-making function. I shall take either of these to constitute 'some formal connection with the outcome' in the sense required by the definition: in the first case the citizens choose the laws and in the second they choose the law-makers (in both cases, of course, within the limits of the choice presented to them).

Finally, the phrase 'each counts equally' has to be read in conjunction with the preceding phrase 'some formal connection with the outcome.' That is to say, *nothing* is suggested by the definition of democratic procedure about *equality of actual influence on outcomes*. The equality is in the formal aspect: each adult citizen is to have a vote (only minor exceptions covering a tiny proportion of those otherwise eligible being allowed) and there are to be no 'fancy franchises' giving extra votes to some.

What about the notion that each vote should have an 'equal value'? This is valid if we construe it as a formal requirement. If there are two constituencies each of which returns one representative, the value of a vote is obviously unequal if one constituency contains more voters than another.[3] To talk about 'equal value' except in this *a priori* sense is, in my view, sheer muddle. In recent years, for example, supporters of systems of proportional representation in Britain have succeeded in scoring something of a propaganda victory by pressing the idea that the vote for a candidate who comes third (or lower) in a plurality system is 'wasted' and the people who vote for the candidate are 'effectively disfranchised.' But then why stop there? The only way of making sense of this argument is by postulating that anyone who voted for a candidate other than the actual winner—even the runner-up—was 'effectively disfranchised'; and it was not long before some academics stumbled on this amazing theoretical breakthrough.[4] I do not think that anyone of ordinary intelligence would be found saying of an election for, say, the post of president of a club: 'I didn't vote for the winning candidate. In other words my vote didn't help elect anybody. And that means I was effectively disfranchised'. It is a little alarming that such palpably fallacious reasoning should have the power to impose on people when the context is a parliamentary election.

There is one simple, and, *on the face of it*, attractive, reason for giving special weight to laws arrived at by democratic procedures, namely that, on any given question about which opinion is divided, the decision must, as a matter of logic, *accord with either the*

[1] W. J. M. Mackenzie, *Power, Violence, Decision* (Harmondsworth: Penguin, 1975), p. 151.

[2] Quoted in Hugh Tinker, *Ballot Box and Bayonet: People and Government in Emergent Asian Countries* (Chatham House Essays, 5; London: Oxford University Press, 1964), p. 83.

[3] This is, it may be noted, the line taken by the U.S. Supreme Court in its decision requiring redistricting to secure approximately equal constituencies. (The leading case is Reynolds v. Sims, 377 U.S. 533 (1964).)

[4] An analysis with whose general line I concur is Paul E. Meehl, 'The Selfish Voter Paradox and the Thrown-Away Vote Argument', *The American Political Science Review* LXXI (1977): pp. 11–30.

preferences of the majority or the preferences of the minority. And, by something akin to the rule of insufficient reason, it seems difficult to say why the decision should go in the way wanted by the minority rather than in the way wanted by the majority.

Obviously, even if the majority principle were accepted, there would still be a gap between the majority principle and democratic procedures as I have defined them. The implication of the majority principles is, fairly clearly, that the best form of democratic procedure is that which permits a vote on issues by referendum. There is no guarantee that elected representatives will on every issue vote in such a way that the outcome preferred by a majority of citizens will be the one chosen. However much we cry up the effects of electoral competition in keeping representatives in line, there is no theoretical reason for expecting that a party or coalition of parties with a majority will always do what a majority of voters want. (Persistent non-voters will in any case have their preferences disregarded by competitive parties—though it may be noted that this is equally so in a referendum.) Even a purely opportunistic party would not necessarily be well-advised to back the side on every issue that the majority supports, as Anthony Downs pointed out.[5] And in practice no party is purely opportunistic—indeed a purely opportunistic party would be in most circumstances be an electoral failure because it would be too unpredictable. The party or parties with a legislative majority are therefore always able to have a package of policies approved of by a majority and policies opposed by a majority. (On many other issues, there may be no single policy with majority support, but that is a complication in the specification of the majority principle (that I shall discuss below).

All this, however, is not as damaging for democratic procedures as might be supposed. For it may surely be said that no method for selecting law-makers and governments that was *not* democratic (in the sense defined) could provide a better long-run prospect of producing outcomes in accord with the majority principle. However disappointed an adherent of the majority principle might be in the actual working of democratic procedures, it is hard to see what he or she would stand to gain by helping to secure their overthrow. . . .

I have suggested, then, that the majority principle provides fairly strong backing for democratic procedures. What now has to be asked, of course, is whether there is any reason for accepting the majority principle. The view that there is something natural and inevitable about it was expressed forcefully by John Locke in paragraphs 95–9 of the *Second Treatise*. The argument is tied up with Locke's consent theory of political authority but can, I think, be detached from it. The nub is that if there is going to be a body capable of making binding decisions then it 'must move one way' and 'it is necessary the Body should move that way whither the greater force carries it, which is the *consent of the majority*'. Locke adds that 'therefore we see that in Assemblies impowered to act by positive Laws where no number is set by that positive Law which impowers them, the *act of the Majority* passes for the act of the whole, and of course determines, as having by the Law of Nature and Reason, the power of the whole.[6]

In my first book, *Political Argument*, I put forward the example of 'five people in a railway compartment which the railway operator has omitted to label either "smoking" or "no-smoking" each of whom 'either wants to smoke or objects to others smoking in the vicinity'.[7] I should have added that the carriage should be understood as one of the sort that does not have a corridor, so the option of changing compartments is not

---

[5] A. Downs, *An Economic Theory of Democracy* (New York: Harper and Brothers, 1957), pp. 55–60.

[6] John Locke, *Two Treatises of Government*, ed. Peter Laslett (New York: The New American Library, Mentor Book, 1965), pp. 375–6.

[7] B. M. Barry, *Political Argument* (London: Routledge and Kegan Paul, 1965), p. 312.

open.) I still think that the example was a good one. Unless all five can reach agreement on some general substantive principle—that in the absence of positive regulation there is a 'natural right' to smoke or a 'natural right' for any one person to veto smoking—it is difficult to see any plausible alternative to saying that the outcome should correspond to majority preference.

The position of someone who is outvoted but refuses to accept the decision is difficult to maintain. As I have suggested, quite persuasive arguments can be made for saying that the decision should not simply reflect the number of people who want to smoke as against the number who dislike being in the presence of smokers. But, since opposing principles can be advanced, the existence of relevant principles does not seem to offer a sound basis for resistance to a majority decision. Or suppose that one of the travellers happens to be the Archbishop of Canterbury. He might claim the right to decide the smoking question on the basis either of his social position or on the basis of his presumptive expertise in casuistry. If his claim is accepted by all the other passengers, no decision-making problem arises because there is agreement. If not all the fellow-passengers accept his claim, however, it again seems difficult to see how the question can be settled except by a vote. And if he finds himself in the minority it must be because he has failed to convince the others (or more than one of them) of his claim to authority. He may continue to maintain that it should have been accepted, just as a believer in the natural right to smoke may continue to maintain that the others should have accepted that principle. But in the face of actual non-acceptance, the case for bowing to the majority decision looks strong.

On further analysis, however, we have to recognize that the 'naturalness' of the majority principle as a way of settling the dispute rests on several features of the particular example which are not commonly found together. I am therefore now inclined to say that it was a good example in the sense that

it illustrated well the case for the majority principle but that it was in another sense a bad example because of its special features. I shall single out four, the first three of which make the majority principle determinate while the fourth makes it acceptable. First, we implicitly assume that the people in the compartment have to make only this one decision. Second, only two alternatives are envisaged: smoking or non-smoking. Third, the decision-making constituency is not open to doubt. And fourth, nothing has been said to suggest that the outcome on the issue is of vital importance for the long-term well-being of any of those involved.

To begin with, then, let us retain the feature from the original case that the decisions to be made are dichotomous (that is to say, there are only two alternatives to choose between) but now say that several different decisions have to be taken. In addition to the question whether to permit smoking the passengers also have to decide whether to allow the playing of transistor radios. Suppose that a vote is taken on each question and there is a majority against each. It may be that a majority of the passengers would nevertheless prefer permitting both to prohibiting both, if they were given a choice in those terms.

Let us assign the following symbols: W is no smoking, X is smoking allowed; Y is no playing of radios, Z is playing allowed. The preferences of the five passengers (A, B , C, D and E) are in descending order as in Table 1.[8]

TABLE 1

Rank order	A	B	C	D	E
1	WZ	WZ	XY	WY	WY
2	XZ	XZ	XZ	WZ	XY
3	WY	WY	WY	XY	WZ
4	XY	XY	WZ	XZ	XZ

---

[8] Adapted from Appendix, Example 1 (p. 69) of Nicholas R. Miller, 'Logrolling, Vote Trading, and the Paradox of Voting: A Game-Theoretical Overview', *Public Choice* 30 (1977): pp. 49–75.

In a straight vote A, B, D and E all prefer W to X, and C, D and E prefer Y to Z, so the outcome would be W and Y. But the pair WY is less well liked than the opposite pair XZ by A, B and C.

We now ask: what does the majority principle prescribe in a situation like this? Are we committed to the view that neither smoking nor playing radios should be allowed, because there is a majority against each? Or can we take account of the fact that there is a majority in favour of overturning the result of the two separate votes and substituting their opposites?

The case just presented is consistent with each person's preferences on smoking being independent of what is decided about radio playing, and vice versa. But, in most political matters, this assumption of 'separability' does not hold. What we favour on one issue depends on how other issues are settled. Some things are complementary: we don't want to vote for buying the land unless there is going to be a majority for spending money on the building that is proposed to go on the land. Others are competitive: if expensive project X is going to be funded, we don't want to vote for expensive project Y as well, but if project X is going to be defeated, we would favour project Y. In such a case, the whole concept of a majority on a single issue become indeterminate, because each person's preference depends on his or her expectations about the way the other relevant issues are going to be decided. And the outcome if issues are packaged together depends on the way the packaging is done.

A further difficulty is that as soon as we aggregate two or more dichotomous decisions we get a choice between more than two outcomes, and there is then the possibility that no one is capable of getting a majority over each of the others in a pair-wise vote. (In the jargon of collective choice theory, there is no Condorcet winner among the alternatives.) Thus, in the example I set out, I pointed out that A, B and C prefer XZ to WY. But I could have gone on to say that C,

D and E prefer XY to XZ, that A, B and D prefer WZ to XY, and that C, D and E prefer WY to WZ. Since, as we already know, A, B and C prefer XZ to WY, it is clear that we have here a cycle including all four possible combinations. No outcome is capable of getting a majority over each of the others and so the majority principle offers no guidance.

The simplest way of generating a situation in which there are cyclical majorities is to have a choice between three possible outcomes. Suppose that our passengers consider three candidates for a binding rule about smoking: X (no smoking), Y (smoking but only of cigarettes) and Z (smoking of pipes and cigars as well as cigarettes). There may, of course, be an outright majority for one outcome. . . .

The trouble is that there may not be any outcome that is capable of getting majority support against any other (or, in the case of even numbers, two that are equally good. . . . Thus, suppose now that D and E do not like to smoke cigarettes and, if they cannot smoke their pipes, would prefer a smoke-free environment to one contaminated by C's cigarette smoke. Then the preference matrix becomes as in Table 2. We now pit each possible outcome against each other in a series of three pairwise comparisons and get the result that X beats Y (A, B, D and E prefer it), Z beats X (C, D and E prefer it) and Y beats Z (A, B and C prefer it). Thus, a quite plausible distribution of preferences generates a 'paradox of voting' in which the majorities arising from pairwise comparisons form a cycle.

The two sources of indeterminacy in the majority principle that I have so far been pointing out may be considered rather dull

TABLE 2

Rank order	A and B	C	D and E
1	X	Y	Z
2	Y	Z	X
3	Z	X	Y

and technical, incapable of arousing political passions. This is by no means true. Consider, for example, the importance that both sympathizers of President Allende and apologists for the coup that overthrew him and the regime have attached in their polemics to the question whether or not he had majority support for his policies. Given a political setup with three blocs, Allende was able to come into power as President on a bare plurality; and the Popular Unity Coalition that supported him never achieved a majority of votes cast. It was on the basis of these facts that the junta claimed legitimacy in terms of the majority principle for overthrowing the constitutional government. On the other side, however, it may be argued that 'one cannot infer that those who opposed Allende necessarily supported a military coup, especially the bloody one that ensued following his overthrow. Thus there is little evidence that a majority of Chileans wanted Allende overthrown by the military.'[9]

It is not my intention to join in this debate, merely to point out that, where the majority principle is indeterminate, generals find it worth appealing to it and scholars find it worth rebutting that appeal. However, if we measure the importance of a question by the blood spilt over it (and I find it hard to think of a better criterion) the importance of the *third reason* for the *indeterminacy* of the majority principle can hardly be denied. The question is the deceptively innocent one: *majority of what?*

In the railway carriage example this is not a problem. If the decision about permitting or prohibiting smoking is to be made according to majority preference there can be no doubt that the people whose preferences should be taken into account are the five people in the railway carriage who will be affected by the decision. But when the question is the boundaries of political entities—

empires, supranational organizations, federations, nation states, provinces or other sub-divisions—and their respective decision-making powers, the question 'who is included?' is an explosive one.

There is no need to labour the point. The briefest survey is enough. In Western Europe, after centuries of wars between states, civil wars, and heavy-handed centralizing government, Northern Ireland is paralyzed by conflict, Scottish nationalism is a powerful force, the centralized Belgian state has been virtually partitioned, unfinished business from the nineteenth century still hangs over the Swiss Jura and the Alto Adige, while in Spain Basque and Catalan separatism are stirring again after the long freeze. In Eastern Europe almost every state has claims on the territory of at least one other. Order, of a kind, is maintained by the Soviet Union, which is itself a patchwork of nationalities held together by coercion. And nobody is taking bets on the existence of Yugoslavia in ten years time. In North America, Quebec has a separatist government, and the unity of the country is in question. In the Middle East three wars have been fought over the boundaries of Israel and no end is in sight. In Africa, the boundaries bequeathed by the colonial powers, after a period of surprising stability (interrupted only by the Biafran and Katagan secessions) are coming under pressure in the Horn of Africa, and the trouble looks as if it may well spread further in coming years. The Indian subcontinent has seen first the convulsion of the creation of Pakistan and then the almost equally bloody process of its splitting into two; while in India the states have had to be reconstituted, amid a good deal of disorder, in an attempt to satisfy the aspirations of linguistic groups. There are few parts of the world where boundaries are not a potential source of serious conflict, and where we do not hear that they are (e.g. China) this is as likely to reflect our ignorance as the absence of potential conflict.

The only thing that has to be established,

[9] James Petras and Morris Morley, 'Chilean Destabilisation and Its Aftermath', *Politics* XI (1976): pp. 140–8 at p. 145.

beyond the existence of conflicts over boundaries, is that the majority principle has no way of solving them, either in practice or in theory. In practice, the majority principle, so far from alleviating conflicts over boundaries, greatly exacerbates them. It may be tolerable to be ruled over by a cosmopolitan autocracy, like the Austrian empire, or a more or less even-handed colonial power like the British in India. But to be subject to a majority of different language, religion or national identity is far more threatening. In an area where nationalities are intermingled, like the Balkans, every move to satisfy majority aspirations leaves the remaining minorities even more vulnerable.

On a theoretical level, any use of the majority principle in order to establish boundaries must involve begging the question. Locke, to do him credit, saw that the majority principle could come into play only after the constituency has been identified, but he finessed the problem by resorting to the fiction that those who are to form 'one body' all individually agree to do so. This approach obviously fails to provide any guidance in any situation where it is actually needed, that is to say where people are disagreeing about the 'body' they want to be members of. . . .

Meanwhile, it should be noted that the upshot of the discussion is that any attempt to justify boundaries by appealing to the majority principle must be void. You can have as many referenda as you like, and show every time that over half of the people within the existing boundaries approve of them, but you cannot use that to prove to a minority that wants to secede that they ought to acquiesce in the *status quo*. If their loyalty is to be awakened, other and better arguments—backed by deeds rather than votes—are needed.

Suppose, however, that the composition of the group that is to be subject to a common policy is not at issue, and that the two more technical sources of indeterminacy are absent, does that make the majority principle unassailable? Of course not. The *fourth* and last of the special features of the railway carriage case that I singled out was that, as the story had been told, we had no reason to suppose that the question of smoking or not smoking was of vital importance to any of the people involved. (It might be said that smoking is inherently a vital interest in that being smoked at lowers one's expectation of life; but, if we put it as a question of interests, is a few minutes more life a greater interest than the freedom of the addict from withdrawal symptoms?) Suppose, however, that one of the passengers suffers from severe asthma or emphysema, and that being subjected to tobacco smoke is liable to precipitate a dangerous attack. No doubt one would hope that this fact, when explained, would lead the others to agree not to smoke, however many of them would like to. But say that it does not. It seems clear to me that the person at risk would be behaving with an almost insane disregard for his or her interests in accepting a majority decision to allow smoking. The obvious recourse would be, I presume, to pull the communication cord and bring the train to a grinding halt.

It might be argued that nothing said here shows that the majority principle lacks universality; it still applies but in some cases the reason it provides for obedience is overridden by a more pressing consideration, such as self-protection against a risk of substantial harm. However, it does not seem to me that this is a correct representation of the position. Where the decision is sufficiently threatening to the vital interests of (some of) those affected by it, its pedigree is neither here nor there.

Take for example a group of youths like those in *The Clockwork Orange* who beat up strangers for fun. Would we be inclined to say 'Well, at least there's one redeeming feature: they choose their victims by majority vote'? I think not. This example of course raises the question of constituency, since the victim is outside the decision-making group. But if we modify it so that the members of a group decide by majority vote to beat up one of their own number I still do not think that the chosen victim has less reason to resist or escape than he would if the decision were taken by a strong-arm leader. I do not see any significant respect in which my modified example of the railway passengers differs from that. I suppose that someone might adduce the difference between deliberately causing harm and doing something whose known but unintended consequences are harmful, but that is not in my view a morally relevant distinction.

The political parallels hardly need to be filled in. No minority can be, or should be, expected to acquiesce in the majority's trampling on its vital interests. Unfortunately the parallel to pulling the communication cord— bringing the state, or that part of its policy that is objectionable, to a grinding halt—is a much more messy business and carries the risk of incurring costs much higher than a £25 fine. But the principle is clear enough. Nobody but a moral imbecile would really be prepared to deliver himself over body and soul to the majority principle.

This is not to say that no reason can be found for giving weight to the fact that a law arose from a democratic procedure. But it is to say that the majority principle is a broken reed. The attraction of the majority principle lies in the claim that the majority 'naturally' is entitled to act for the whole. If it turns out that this 'naturalness' is contingent on the presence of a number of highly restrictive conditions, we must press our enquiries further and ask whether we can identify some more fundamental basis for saying that democratic procedures matter. . . .

Democracy, Fairness, and Compromise

Peter Singer

Peter Singer begins his essay by distinguishing three models which illustrate different decision-making procedures a group might follow in making a decision as to whether or not to subscribe to a controversial newspaper. He goes on to argue that the third, democratic procedure has special legitimacy because it provides for a fair compromise in the sense that it gives everybody an equal share of influence in the dispute. Singer then reviews recent work by political scientists, asking if modern democratic political systems match the model and are, therefore, a fair compromise.

Peter Singer is Professor of Philosophy and Director for the Centre of Human Bioethics at Monash University in Australia. In addition to many articles, he is also the author of *Animal Liberation* (1975), *Practical Ethics* (1979), *Marx* (1980), and *The Expanding Circle* (1981).

I. DEMOCRATIC AND NON-DEMOCRATIC MODELS COMPARED

A. The Models

I take as my basic model a common-room association of a university college, similar to those at Oxford. At Oxford colleges, the Junior Common Room is the political body of all the undergraduate students. It functions in a manner similar to student unions at many other universities. Because of its small size, however, and because it is easier for members to meet together in a residential college, it suits my purpose slightly better than a students' union at a large, non-residential university would. The accuracy of my account as an account of how Oxford common-room associations function is, of course, immaterial. I will just stipulate that the following facts hold, and the reader can regard the model as a purely hypothetical construct. The relevant facts, then, are these. Membership of the common-room association is automatic for all members of the college. Subscriptions to the association are taken from college fees, so one can withdraw from the association only by withdrawing from the college altogether. This would be highly inconvenient, and to withdraw from one college without joining another is, we shall say, out of the question. Any other college to which one went would have a similar common-room association to which one would also have to belong. The common-room association has been in existence for as long as anyone can remember, and if any records of its origin ever existed, they have

From Peter Singer, *Democracy and Disobedience* (New York: Oxford University Press, 1974). Reprinted by permission.

been lost. So none of the members knows how the association was originally set up, or for what purposes. Every member simply found the association in existence when he joined the college.

This is the basic model. I will now describe three variants of it. Consider first an association in which all the important decisions about what the association shall do, how its money be spent, and so on, are made by one man, known as the Leader. The origin of this particular system is found in the immediate past history of the common-room association. Some time ago, the man who is now the Leader claimed that the decision-procedure then operating had led to stupid decisions, not in the real interests of the association. Henceforth, he would make all the decisions himself, guided by the interests of the members. If anyone objected, they were invited to fight it out with the Leader's friends, who were the best fighters in the association. No one objected. Since taking power, the Leader's decisions have accorded reasonably well with his promise to rule in the interests of all.

One of the tasks which the association has carried out for as long as anyone can remember is the selection of a number of newspapers for the common room, to be paid for from general funds, and read by whoever wants to read them. So that all may read these papers, there is a regulation that no one is to remove papers from the common room until they have been there for a week. One day, the Leader decides that the common room should subscribe to a new paper, which I shall call *The News*. A member of the college, who will be called the Dissenter, objects to the newspaper, not for personal or aesthetic reasons, but because the paper carries out a scurrilous campaign against the minority of black people in the country, implying that blacks are always dirty, lazy, and dishonest, and should not be allowed to mix with the whites. This campaign, we shall say, manages to keep within the bounds of the law. The Dissenter finds the very presence of the paper in the

common-room offensive; he also fears that if other common-room members, less aware than he is of the paper's bias and distortion, read the paper regularly, it will inflame latent prejudices and they will come to discriminate against the two or three black members of the college. (Once again, whether this would really happen is not relevant for our purposes; if the reader finds the example implausible he can substitute one of his own. It would not matter if the Dissenter's objection to *The News* was on the grounds of obscenity, or because it was a propaganda sheet for the armed forces.)

The Dissenter asks the Leader to reconsider his decision, but the leader is unmoved. The Dissenter then decides to take stronger action. He goes into the common-room every morning, before the other members are about, and removes the paper.

For comparison, consider now two common-room associations similar to the above in every respect, except for the methods of taking decisions. Firstly, consider an association in which decisions are still made by one man, but he did not have to seize power, and he does not have to intimidate opponents with threats of violence. In this association there has been a tradition, for as long as can be remembered, that the person who has been a member of the college for the longest time—the Senior Member—makes all the decisions (there is a recognized method for determining who of those who entered in the same year is the most senior). The Senior Member is expected to decide in the interests of all, and it is, again, reasonable to claim that he does so.

As in the first association, the decision to subscribe to *The News* is taken, the Dissenter vainly puts his case to the Senior Member, and finally resorts to removing the paper.

In the final association, the custom is and, so far as is known, always has been, for decisions to be taken by a vote of the whole association at a general meeting, the majority view prevailing. The Dissenter attends these meetings, and votes according to his opinions. Sometimes motions which he favours are carried, sometimes they are lost. When a motion is carried, those who voted against it accept it, and do not hinder its being put into effect, although they may try to get the decision changed at subsequent meetings. At the meetings, all members are free to speak, subject only to some necessary procedural restrictions. The meetings are conducted fairly, and the votes tallied accurately. . . .

B. Fairness and Compromise

[A]lthough the decision-making power in the second model association is unequally distributed, the Senior Member can still contend that it is fairly distributed, because there is adequate reason for him to have complete power. Now in the dispute over *The News*, the Dissenter's action (removing the paper) is an attempt to assume complete power in respect of whether members of the association shall read the paper. Like the Senior Member, the Dissenter can claim that there is good reason for him to exercise more than an equal share of power over this issue—because, say, he is the only member of the association fully aware of the harmful tendencies of the paper. The Dissenter could put forward this justification of his action in all three model associations. In the first two associations, it is a claim against the claims of the Leader and Senior Member. In the third association, where the decision-making power is evenly distributed, the Dissenter's claim is against all the other members. His claim will be challenged by other members who, having voted in favour of subscribing to the paper, will consider him to be mistaken about its harmful tendencies, or perhaps about the importance of these tendencies. The Dissenter, after all, is acting on his own judgement about this. The other members have their own judgements too, which they sincerely believe correct. In claiming that his own judgement entitles him to a greater say in the matter than the others, the Dissenter is making a claim which the others could make, and which, if

many of them did make, would be incompatible with the continued existence of a peaceful decision-procedure. . . .

The decision-procedure of the third association, in which all members have equal say in decisions, and then accept the result, is a paradigm of a fair compromise. It is, obviously, a beneficial compromise, since a peaceful settlement of disputes is better than settlement by force. The benefit of peaceful settlement would, however, also be achieved if everyone accepted any other decision-procedure. The distinction between the associations is that it is only in the third association that the nature of the decision-procedure makes it possible for everyone to refrain from acting on his own judgment about particular issues without giving up more than the theoretical minimum which it is essential for everyone to give up in order to achieve the benefits of a peaceful solution to disputes. It is the fairness of the compromise by which force is avoided that gives rise to the stronger reason for accepting the decision-procedure of the third association. This may seem a strange thing to say, since I have previously argued that abstract discussion cannot prove the third system to be fairer than the second. My point depends upon a distinction between 'absolute fairness' and the kind of fairness which is limited by what can be achieved in a given situation—or as I shall call it, perhaps rather loosely, 'fairness as a compromise.'

When we say that an arrangement is fair, we often mean not that it is absolutely fair, but that it is fair given the conditions under which the arrangement is made. These conditions may include a certain amount of ignorance, or a lack of agreement in a situation in which agreement is essential. For example, if we were called upon to judge between two claimants to a sum of money, and after hearing both sides we were of the opinion that although the claims were incompatible, there was no way of telling which was the better, we might think it fair to divide the money between the two. If the claims were to something which could not be divided, we might toss a coin to decide. Under the circumstances, this would be a fair compromise, although from the point of view of one who had 'absolute' knowledge, and thus knew which of the claimants was entitled to the money, it could be said to be unfair because it gives as much to the party who deserves none as to the party who deserves all.

For a different example, in which a compromise is required not so much because of ignorance as to what is absolutely fair, as because of the need to come to some agreement, we might take a dispute between husband and wife as to who should get up when the baby cries at night. The wife may say that the husband should get up, because she attends to the baby all day, while the husband feels that the wife should get up, since he has worked all day. They both feel, equally strongly, that their own position is correct. Agreement on the merits of the matter cannot be reached, but some agreement is essential, since neither wants the baby to cry unattended. A fair compromise under these circumstances would be for the husband and wife to take it in turns in getting up. This is a compromise because both parties give up some part of what they claim, in order to reach an agreement which is even more important than having their own way on the particular issue. There could, of course, be other compromise solutions. If the husband were, in the last resort, prepared to let the baby cry all night, while the wife were not, she might have to settle for some other arrangement, for instance, that she would get up every week-night, and the husband only at weekends. This would still be a compromise—both parties are still giving up something—but it would no longer be a fair compromise. The unequal arrangement is not based on any recognition that the husband's case is the better one. It is based merely on the greater strength of his position.

I hope that these examples have made the notion of 'fairness as a compromise' rea-

sonably clear. When the merits of incompatible claims cannot be ascertained, or when agreement on the merits of such claims cannot be reached, a procedure like tossing a coin, or dividing what is in dispute equally is the fairest course that can be taken. It is generally to be preferred to allowing superior force to settle the issue.

It should be obvious from what has been said before that a society which disagrees fundamentally over the kind of decision-procedure it should have is in a state appropriate for fair compromise. The various incompatible claims that are being made cannot be settled by rational argument, nor is it likely that they can be settled by any decision-procedure, since it is precisely the decision-procedure that is in dispute. As the Italian anarchist Errico Malatesta once argued:

If you choose 100 partisans of dictatorship, you will discover that each of the hundred believes himself capable of being, if not sole dictator, at least of assisting very materially in the dictatorial government. The dictators would be those who, by one means or another, succeeded in imposing themselves on society. And, in course of time, all their energy would inevitably be employed in defending themselves against the attacks of their adversaries. . . [1]

Malatesta thought that this was a reason against having any government at all; it seems to me that it counts at least as strongly in favour of the obvious compromise solution of giving everyone an equal voice in decisions, and if we think that, men being what they are, some government is preferable to no government, we will prefer a fair compromise solution to the anarchist solution.

As a further illustration of the need for compromise, consider the fate of the proposal made by John Stuart Mill, which I have already mentioned, that while every-

---

[1] E. Malatesta, *Anarchy* (Freedom Press, London, 7th ed., 1942), p. 35.

one should have at least one vote, those with superior education and intelligence should have additional votes. As Mill himself said, later in life, this was a proposal which found favour with no one. The reason, I think, is not that it would obviously be unfair to give more votes to better qualified people, but rather that it would be impossible to get everyone to agree on who was to have the extra votes. Mill seems to have believed that the uneducated would accept the claims of the educated, and agree that education was a proper qualification for having a greater voice in decisions. Yet even now, when everyone has one vote, there are frequent complaints about 'pointy-headed intellectuals' who think they know better than ordinary men how the country should be run. Assuming that we did believe Mill's system of voting to be perfectly fair, it would still be a brave, or rather a foolhardy, man who would put it forward as a serious proposal. In view of the row such a proposal would stir up, it would be wise to put aside beliefs about what is perfectly fair, and settle for the sort of compromise represented by 'one man, one vote'.

The decision procedure of the third association, then, is a fair compromise between the competing claims to determine what the association shall do, because it gives no advantage to any of the parties to the dispute. (It would be more accurate to say: it gives no inbuilt advantages. It may give an advantage to a particularly persuasive speaker, but this is an incidental and probably minor factor. If this were felt to prejudice the fairness of the compromise, however, it would be possible to avoid it, at some cost, by allowing chance to determine who shall take decisions, in rotation. The ancient Greeks used this method. Our disinclination to do so is probably based on the feeling that the incidental unfairness involved in a system like that of the third association does not justify the presumably inferior decisions that would be the result of distributing power by lot.) As a fair compromise, it is greatly preferable to a 'fight to the finish' over each

controversial issue. Fairness as a compromise is all that can be expected because, as we have seen, it is extraordinarily difficult to decide—let alone to reach agreement on—what is a sufficient reason for an unequal distribution of power.

The point I am making can also be seen as a point about the different implications of a resort to force in different situations. The Dissenter, in removing *The News*, is resorting to force against the decision-procedure of his association, no matter what that decision-procedure is. But the position he takes in respect of the use of force is importantly different in the third model. Disobedience to a system which is a fair compromise implies willingness to impose one's own views on the association. It is an attempt to gain, by force, greater say than others have about what should be done (or, in the case of disobedience intended not to affect a particular issue, but to lead to the overthrow of the decision-procedure in operation and its replacement by some other decision-procedure, an attempt to have greater say about what sort of decision-procedure there is to be). This is not necessarily true of disobedience to a decision in which the Dissenter was denied the participation that he would have had under a fair compromise. In the first and second associations, disobedience is compatible with willingness to accept a fair compromise whereby one's own views have no more influence than those of anyone else. When there is no fair compromise, one can disobey in order to obtain a decision-procedure which does represent a fair compromise. To disobey when there already is a fair compromise in operation is necessarily to deprive others of the say they have under such a compromise. To do so is to leave the others with no remedy but the use of force in their turn.

What all this amounts to is that there are strong reasons for playing one's part in supporting and preserving a decision-procedure which represents a fair compromise. To disobey under these circumstances is to reject the compromise and to attempt to use force to impose one's views on others. . . .

II. FROM MODEL TO REALITY

. . .Whatever controversies there may be about the nature of democracy, I think no one will deny that my third model can properly be described as democratic. If the conclusions we have reached by discussing these models are to have any application to the real world, however, we must ask to what extent they apply to existing full-size political communities.

A. Democracy, Direct and Representative

First, to recapitulate those features of the third model association that gave rise to the reasons for obedience applicable to the third model only: the association decided issues by a vote of the assembled members, the majority view prevailing; every member's vote counted equally; the meetings were conducted according to impartial procedural rules, and the votes tallied accurately; any member could propose a motion and there was, within the procedural rules, complete freedom to speak for or against any proposal; the majority did not use its numerical superiority to exploit any minority.

Democracy, as the *Concise Oxford Dictionary* defines it, means '(State practising) government by the people, direct or representative.' My third model is a form of direct democracy. The members themselves take the decisions about how their community is to be organized. Direct democracy can claim to be the basic form of democracy, both historically and conceptually. Historically, Western democratic thought goes back to Athens in the fifth century B.C. In the Athenian city-state at that time, the citizens met in a General Assembly and there, under conditions of political equality and free debate, discussed and voted on the major issues that faced the community. Admittedly,

not all those who lived in Athens were citizens in the legal sense, and it is sometimes said (though just as often denied) that Athenian citizens would not have had the leisure demanded by their political system, were it not for the existence of slavery. I do not know whether there is any truth in this claim. In any case, within the limits of its qualifications for citizenship, the Athenian system was an example of direct democracy like our third model association. Whatever obligations exist in this third model would also exist in a direct democracy.

Conceptually, too, direct democracy is the basic form of democracy. The idea of representative democracy implies representatives who 'take the place of' or 'are present instead of' others. Representative democracy is therefore in virtue of the meaning of the term a substitute for something else, and this something else can only be direct democracy. . . .

One of the most common platitudes in political theory, repeated in all the elementary textbooks, is that while direct democracy might be all very well in a small city-state, it is obviously quite unrealistic in a nation-state of several million people. In fact, this platitude is certainly false. With the communications technology available to us today, an extension of Athenian-style democracy to a modern state would be perfectly feasible. Without going into details, it is easy to envisage vote-recording devices installed in private homes and public places, linked to a central computer and operated by means of some personalized device, like those already in use for obtaining cash from the automatic machines outside banks. Proposals could be debated on radio and television, and the public could contribute by telephone—not everyone, of course, but then not everyone could contribute in Athens. If, then, we have not seized the opportunity provided by technological advances to restore democracy to its purest form, it must be because for one reason or another we are unenthusiastic about such a restoration. Maybe people would find it inconvenient to vote frequently, or consider themselves incompetent to express an opinion on major issues, or perhaps those who are influential in forming opinion on these matters are apprehensive about the decisions that might emerge from direct popular votes on issues relating to racial equality, capital punishment, or foreign policy.

Looking at the matter historically, however, we must concede this much truth to the common platitude: representative systems came into existence at a time when it was impossible for all the citizens of the state to take collective decisions directly. Nation-states cover many more people, and much greater territory, than the Greek city-states. So those who could not go to a central meeting sent others to go in their place. This leads us to the most straightforward of the various theories of representation. It is the theory suggested by taking the term literally. The representative is to speak and vote as those he is representing would have spoken and voted, had they been able to be present. Representation, on this view, is a device for producing a system of government differing from direct democracy only in so far as is inevitable if it is to operate effectively in a large society without a sophisticated communication network.

There are, however, difficulties in this notion of a representative doing as those he represents would have done. If the citizen wants something (say, lower taxes) which the representative knows to be incompatible with other things the citizen wants (more schools) but the citizen does not appreciate this incompatibility, what is the representative to do? The citizen, if he were present, would vote for both lower taxes and more schools, but the representative can hardly do this. Even greater difficulties arise when we consider that the representative is taking the place not of one citizen, but of a considerable number, with a variety of opinions. Quite apart from the minority who did not vote for the candidate who obtained the most votes, there will be differences of opinion among those who did vote for him.

These and related difficulties have led some thinkers, most notably Rousseau, to deny that the people can be represented. Others have insisted that the difficulties arise only on a mistaken view of what a representative should be, and have therefore offered alternative accounts of what a representative should be. While Rousseau rejected representation because he believed 'will cannot be represented'[2] Edmund Burke told his electors: 'If government were a matter of will upon any side, yours without question ought to be superior. But government and legislation are matters of reason and judgement.'[3] Burke's view that the member of parliament, once elected, is free to exercise his own judgement, independently of the desires of his electors, is often cited in defence of parliamentary decisions which are contrary to public opinion. The electors, on this view, are voting for the man they think will make the best decisions, rather than for a man who will express their own opinions or promote their own interests.

Another means of overcoming difficulties in the idea of the representative doing as his constituents would have done is the suggestion that the representative body 'should be an exact portrait, in miniature, of the people at large, as it should think, feel, reason, and act like them'.[1]

Fortunately, we do not have to decide which of these and other possible theories of representation we prefer. . . .

None of the theories of representation mentioned above necessarily involves a departure from fair compromise. If the general meeting is a fair compromise between competing claims to power in a small society, giving no advantage to any individual or faction, these representative systems could all function so as to give no advantage to

---

[2] J.-J. Rousseau, *The Social Contract*, trans. G. Hopkins, in *Social Contract*, ed. E. Barker (O.U.P., London, 1947), Bk. III, ch. 15.

[3] E. Burke, 'Speech to the Electors of Bristol' (1774) in *The Works of Edmund Burke* (Bohn's standard Library, George Bell and Sons, London, 1886), vol. I, p. 447.

[4] John Adams, quoted in H. Pitkin, *The Concept of Representation*, p. 60.

individuals or factions in a larger society.[5] This would clearly be the case if representatives really could vote as those who elected them would have voted, had they been present and properly informed; it would also apply if the assembly of representatives was a genuine microcosm of society as a whole (a result more likely to be produced by proportional representation than by the simple majority systems of voting used in Great Britain and the United States). It is perhaps more doubtful if Burke's view satisfies the fair compromise requirement. It would satisfy it if everyone had the opportunity to vote for a representative in whose judgement he had confidence; if, however, there were some who could find no candidate they trusted, they would be at a disadvantage, and might see no point in voting at all. Burke could reply that one is always free to stand oneself, but practical considerations may make this a purely theoretical freedom. . . .

B. Contemporary Western Democracy

Although differing on many points, those who have written about modern democratic forms of government tend to agree that the traditional theories of representative democracy do not describe any existing national political system. Representatives do not vote as their constituents would have voted; nor do electors choose those whose wise judgement they feel they can trust; nor are representative bodies microcosms of the nation. All these theories, contemporary writers say, unrealistically attribute to ordinary people informed opinions on the major issues of the day, or on the personal characteristics of candidates for electoral office. In no large-scale society do the great mass of people have such opinions. Some

writers would add: it is a good thing that they do not. These writers . . . are not enemies of democracy. They regard themselves as its supporters. The man who did more than anyone else to gain acceptance for this revised view of democracy was Joseph Schumpeter, who served as Minister of Finance in a Social-Democrat Government in Austria after the First World War and quit a professorship in Berlin to go to America when Nazism was beginning to assert itself in Germany. Earlier writers, notably Mosca and Pareto, had criticized classical democratic theory along similar lines, but it was only with Schumpeter's *Capitalism, Socialism, and Democracy* (first published in 1942) that these ideas began to take hold among democrats. The book contains a forthright attack on the 'myths' of democracy, including the belief that ' . . . "the people" hold a definite and rational opinion about every individual question and that they give effect to this opinion—in a democracy—by choosing "representatives" who will see to it that the opinion is carried out.'[6] In place of this myth of classical democratic theory, Schumpeter proposes a more realistic revision:

Voters do not decide issues. But neither do they pick their members of parliament from the eligible population with a perfectly open mind. In all normal cases the initiative lies with the candidate who makes a bid for the office of member of parliament and such local leadership as that may imply. Voters confine themselves to accepting this bid in preference to others or refusing to accept it.[7]

It should be noted that Schumpeter is going beyond what Burke said about the independence of the candidate, once elected. Burke did not deny that voters have a real and unlimited choice as to whom they shall elect; according to Schumpeter, however, the initiative lies with the candidate, not the voters, and the voters' choice is lim-

---

[5] As in the model, 'no advantages' can only mean 'no inbuilt advantages'. Just as, in the model, taking decisions at meetings gave an advantage to the most persuasive speakers, so in a larger society there could be incidental advantages for some, for instance, for those who control the major newspapers and television stations. . . .

[6] 3rd ed. (Allen and Unwin, London, 1961), p. 269.

[7] *Capitalism, Socialism, and Democracy*, p. 282.

ited to accepting one of the small number of 'bids' made to him.

Strong support for the view that it is unrealistic to expect voters to do more than accept one of a very limited number of options has come from studies of how people vote. Surveys of voting behavior have found that very few voters are properly informed about the issues at stake in elections; in particular, the minority who change their vote between elections (and so effectively determine the outcome of elections) are generally less well informed than the average voter, and vote on the basis of actors normally considered trivial or irrelevant.[8] These results could, of course, have been taken as an indication that real democracy is yet to be achieved; instead, most post-war democratic theorists, clinging to the idea that if 'democracy' has any meaning at all, then the United States, Britain, and nations with similar political systems must be democracies, have argued that the voting studies make obsolete traditional ideas about the role of the people in a democracy. It would be tedious to illustrate this with quotations from even a sample of the writers who have taken this position.[9] Instead I shall, in the following discussion, rely mainly on the work of Robert Dahl, a well-known and generally middle-of-the-road representative of modern American writers on democracy. Dahl accepts Schumpeter's criticism of traditional ideas about democracy, in so far as he believes that:

A good deal of democratic theory leads us to expect more from national elections than they can possibly provide. We expect elections to reveal the 'will' or the preferences of a majority on a set of issues. This is one thing elections rarely do, except in an almost trivial fashion . . . Elec-

tions and political competition do not make for government by majorities in any very significant way, but they vastly increase the size, number, and variety of minorities whose preferences must be taken into account by leaders in making policy choices.[10]

I shall accept the consensus of political scientists that these views describe, far better than the traditional theory of democracy, what actually happens in a modern state of the type we know as Western democracy. . . . In this connection we can note that in giving up the notion of effective mass participation the new theories also give up an aim that J. S. Mill thought very important, the aim of self-development through participation in the government of one's community. Against this we must balance, if the revisionists are right, certain advantages: stability, elitist restraint of mass 'stampedes',[11] protection for some (though not all) minorities against majority tyranny,[12] and flexibility.[13] The political systems described by the revisionist writers also save us time and inconvenience, in that less of us have to concern ourselves with political issues. Despite these advantages, there is little doubt in my mind that these writers have made virtues out of necessity. The political system they describe may be better than any other existing political system. It may even be the best workable system a large nation-state could have. This, no doubt, is what the revisionists believe, and so they think it important that we should not be tempted to abandon or alter the system we have for the sake of the ideals of traditional democratic theory. Whether a closer approximation to these ideals would be workable is something about

---

[8] Of these studies, perhaps the best known is that by B. Berelson, P. Lazarsfeld, and W. McPhee, *Voting* (University of Chicago Press, Chicago, 1954).

[9] For an excellent brief analysis of the most notable of these, see P. Bachrach, *The Theory of Democratic Elitism* (Athlone Press, London, 1969) to which the present discussion is indebted.

[10] University of Chicago Press, Chicago, 1956, pp. 131–2.

[11] Schumpeter, *Capitalism, Socialism, and Democracy*, p. 283; G. Sartori, *Democratic Theory* (Praeger, New York, 1965), p. 119.

[12] Dahl, *A Preface to Democratic Theory*, pp. 132, 151.

[13] Berelson, Lazarsfeld, and McPhee, *Voting*, pp. 316–22.

which we cannot be certain. If we think that the system we have is as good a political system as human beings possibly can have, we will see this as a reason for supporting, and therefore obeying the verdict of, this system. If, on the other hand, we believe the ideals of democratic theory both workable and worth striving for, we may take the findings of the voting studies simply as an indication of the distance still to be covered in realizing these ideals. . . .

According to earlier ideas of democracy, fairness is achieved by the institution of elections, in which each member of the society has one vote, which he allots to the candidate who he believes will best represent his views, interests, or social group, or who will make the best decisions on the major issues of the day. We have already seen that Schumpeter and Dahl deny that elections function in any of these ways. It is clear that it does not follow from the fact that everyone has a vote in an election that the election is a fair indication of the preferences of the electorate. It may not be a fair indication if, as Schumpeter suggests, voters are confined to accepting one of a small number of bids. This is the case when voters are, for all practical purposes, limited to a choice between two major parties. The theory of representative democracy developed in a time when there were no political parties in the modern sense, and it has been found difficult to reconcile the existence of parties with democratic presuppositions. As one writer has observed: 'while British political practice is now dominated by the assumption that the Parliamentary parities will behave as disciplined blocks, British political thought still lacks any justification of party discipline that is generally accepted.[14] One might well think that whenever voters are limited to a choice between two or three major parties, views not represented by these parties are unfairly excluded. Before reaching this conclusion, however, it is necessary to consider the nature of political parties and the role they play in the democratic process, for there have been attempts to show that this role is compatible with democratic principles of equality.

In this book *Pluralist Democracy in the United States: Conflict and Consent*,[15] Dahl has a chapter entitled 'Political Parties: Contributions to Democracy'. In the course of this discussion Dahl concedes that 'A voter presented with two rival candidates might prefer neither of them so much as a third possible candidate who failed to win a nomination by either party.[16] Dahl defends the party system by the following argument.

The fact remains, then, that whenever a diversity of viewpoints and desired alternatives exists among the citizens of a democracy, the citizens must, sooner or later, by one process or another, reject all but one alternative (even if the final choice is, in effect, the null alternative of inaction). There is no escaping this process; it is the essence of 'rationality', the only question is where and how it takes place. Much of the process of winnowing out alternatives could take place *before* an election, or *in* the election itself, or in negotiations *after* the election. All party systems do some winnowing *before* an election, making the *election* itself more decisive by reducing the alternatives, thus leaving less winnowing to be done after the election by bargaining and negotiation among members different parties . . .

The notion, then, that parties increase irrationality in making choices by reducing the alternatives is based upon too simple a picture of the processes by which collective political decisions can be made, for all such processes necessarily involve a drastic reduction in the alternatives. Although the question is obviously exceedingly complex, it seems much more reasonable to conclude (as most students of a party do) that on the whole the parties play a beneficial role in this process.[17]

---

[14] A. H. Birch, *Representative and Responsible Government* (Allen and Unwin, London, 1964), p. 121; quoted in A. H. Birch, *Representation*, (Pall Mall, London, 1971), p. 100.

[15] Rand McNally, Chicago, 1967.

[16] Ibid, p. 251.

[17] Ibid., p. 252. Emphasis in original.

Obviously Dahl is right to say that the process of reducing alternative policies to one policy must be done somewhere; what is curious, especially in view of the title of the chapter in which this passage appears, is his apparent indifference whether this reduction takes place before, in, or after an election. Surely if the political system is to operate democratically, it will be best if the reduction of alternatives takes place in the election itself, so that all citizens participate equally in it, instead of being presented with a *fait accompli* that leaves them little meaningful choice in the election. The next best would perhaps be if the reduction of alternatives were done after the election, so that it is done by the elected representatives of the voters. If, however, it is thought that unless a great deal of reduction is done before the election the voters will be faced with too complex and confusing a series of choices, then it would at least be essential that this prior reduction of alternatives is done in a democratic manner. In a modern party system of democracy, this could occur only if political parties were democratically organized. Dahl's indifference to how the reduction of alternatives takes place is made even more puzzling by his views on this matter. Discussing the criticism that parties are 'internally undemocratic and are ruled by oligarchies', Dahl readily concedes:

The charge is in considerable measure true. That the nominations and policies of political parties tend to be controlled by leaders, rather than the rank and file of members or registered supporters, seems undeniable. There is . . . more decentralization and diffusion of control in the two American parties than in many European parties; even so, both the Democratic and Republican parties would be more accurately described as coalitions of oligarchies than as democratic organizations.[18]

The picture that emerges is one of elections which present the citizen with a choice of two, perhaps three or four, alternative policies and candidates, the selection of alternatives to be presented to the citizens being made by oligarchical organizations. It is hard to see how this can satisfy the requirement of fair compromise. Those who have influence in the major political parties possess far more power than fair compromise would allow them.

A democratic process dominated by two or three major parties is unlikely to be fair even when the parties genuinely differ, for the combinations of policies that they present are still 'package deals', and may not be those which the voters would prefer, were they free to select some policies from one party and others from another. When policies of the major parties do not differ at all, or differ only insignificantly, the unfairness created by the dominance of parties becomes greater still. I have already mentioned, in a different context, the 1968 election for the Presidency of the United States. Although a substantial proportion of the population was opposed to the continuation of the war in Vietnam, the election gave this opposition no real opportunity to express itself, or to campaign and attempt to win influence in decision-making. Under these conditions, an election cannot be regarded as a fair compromise, for those in favour of continuing the war had the enormous advantage of controlling both the major political parties. In a less dramatic way, the same sort of thing happens whenever, in a two-party system, both parties agree on an issue.

Schumpeter, with characteristic frankness, acknowledges the unfairness of the party system when he says that his definition of democracy allows ways of competing for the peoples' votes which are 'strikingly analogous to the economic phenomena we label

---

[18] p. 245. This verdict is echoed by many students of political parties in other modern democracies. S. H. Beer, for example, summarizes one of the findings of his *Modern British Politics: A Study of Parties and Pressure Groups* (2nd ed., Faber and Faber, London, 1969) as

follows: 'As has often been observed, the mass party, even if its inspiration is highly democratic, tends to separate leadership from the rank and file and to accumulate influence in the hands of an elite.' (p. 405.)

"unfair" or "fraudulent" competition or restraint of trade'. Schumpeter defends this by saying:

we cannot exclude them because if we did we should be left with a completely unrealistic ideal. Between this ideal case which does not exist and the cases in which all competition with the established leader is prevented by force, there is a continuous range of variation within which the democratic method of government shades off into the autocratic one by imperceptible steps. But if we wish to understand and not to philosophize, this is as it should be.[19]

Schumpeter, of course, is entitled to prefer understanding to philosophizing, but once we ask whether we ought to obey a law, we cannot avoid philosophizing (in the sense in which this whole book is a piece of philosophizing). In answering this question the difference between a fair and unfair system may be more significant than the difference between a dictatorship and what Schumpeter would call a democracy.

In view of these acknowledged shortcomings of elections in many Western democracies, it is not surprising that political theoriest have looked to other aspects of these societies in order to show that the system is not really as unfair as consideration of elections alone might lead us to believe. According to many recent writers, the preferences of ordinary members of the public become politically significant not by means of elections, but only when they are organized into pressure groups. These groups bring their influence to bear on the government, and the course the government takes is, within broad limits, an attempt to satisfy the pressure groups and thus, indirectly, to put into effect the preferences of the members of the groups. This system could be a fair compromise, but only if it worked so as to give any individual the same influence, or at least the same opportunity for having influence, as any other individual.

Dahl thinks the role of minority groups vitally important in the politics of a country such as the United States—so important, in fact, that he sometimes refers to the American system of government as a 'polyarchy'. It is, he thinks, mainly the distinction between rule by a minority and rule by minorities which constitutes the difference between a democracy and a dictatorship:

... if there is anything to be said for the processes that distinguish democracy (or polyarchy) from dictatorship, it is not discoverable in the clear-cut distinction between government by a majority and government by a minority. The distinction comes much closer to being one between government by a minority and government by *minorities*. As compared with the political processes of a dictatorship, the characteristics of polyarchy greatly extend the number, size and diversity of the minorities whose preferences will influence the outcome of governmental decisions.[20]

Later, Dahl defines the 'normal' American political process as one 'in which all the active and legitimate groups in the population can make themselves heard at some crucial stage in the process of decisions.'[21]

Does this mean that the normal American political system, assuming Dahl's description to be accurate, is a fair compromise? Not quite. We must examine the significance of the qualifying phrase 'active and legitimate' in order to see what groups cannot make themselves heard effectively. To take first 'active'. One might think that if a group is inactive, this is an indication that it cannot care very much about having influence on the government. If this were so, the exclusion of inactive groups would not matter much. It might even be desirable, as a means of taking into account not only numbers, but also the intensity with which people want to see their preferences expressed

---

[19] *Capitalism, Socialism, and Democracy*, p. 271.

[20] *A Preface to Democratic Theory*, p. 133. Emphasis in original.

[21] Ibid., pp. 137–8.

in government decisions. So only as every group has the opportunity to be active, the requirements of fair compromise may well be satisfied. Unfortunately, this is not what Dahl means. An inactive group, for him, is not necessarily a group which cannot be bothered to be active. A group may be inactive, he acknowledges, 'by free choice, violence, intimidation, or law.'

The qualification 'legitimate' is just as serious a restriction: 'By "legitimate" I mean those whose activity is accepted as right and proper by a preponderant portion of the active. In the South, Negroes were not until recently an active group. Evidently, Communists are not now a legitimate group.[22] Thus groups may be denied the opportunity of being heard effectively because violence, intimidation, or law prevent them from being active, or because their activity, for some reason or other, is not accepted as right and proper by the active majority. It is clear that no justification, in terms of a fair compromise, can be given for such exclusion. The groups excluded in these ways, therefore, would not have the special reason for obeying the law which exists in a model democracy, based on fair compromise.

There are other ways in which a pressure group system is unlikely to be fair to all members of society. As Dahl readily admits: 'To be "heard" covers a wide range of activities . . . Clearly, it does not mean that every group has equal control over the outcome . . . neither individuals nor groups are political equals.[23] It is indeed obvious to anyone who reflects on the way pressure groups operate that they are anything but equal in influence (I mean by this, as I presume Dahl does, in proportion to their numbers). Some quite small groups, for instance, those representing big business, are in a favourable position. They have the money to contribute significantly to party funds, and to establish full-time public relations bureaux to put their point of view. They are more likely than other groups to have personal contacts with leading politicians, since they will tend to come from the same social strata, to have attended the same schools and colleges, belong to the same golf or social club, have professional contacts, and so on. Much larger groups, such as the consumers, will find it harder to get organized, contribute to party funds, or contact politicians. They may succeed eventually, if they are large enough, by making the issue electorally important. For other groups, however, with neither the influence of the small, highly organized group, nor the size of a group like the consumers, there may be no way in which they can make themselves heard effectively. The poor, for example, cannot organize properly as a pressure group, and are not numerous enough to have national electoral significance. These defects mean that the political system is permanently, or for long periods, biased against certain section of the community. If these section should find themselves faced with a law which they opposed, but was passed because of the disproportionate influence of other groups, they cannot be urged to obey on the grounds that the pressure group system is a fair compromise.

We may conclude that modern democracies, as described by those favourable to this system of government, are not fair compromises between all competing groups and individuals. To say this is not to say that from this point of view there is no difference between a modern democracy and a dictatorship. We must agree with Dahl when he says that the former is ruled by more, larger, and more diverse minority groups than the latter. This means that there will be more groups, and more members of groups, who have had at least the share of influence on decisions that they would receive under a fair compromise. These people will have the same reason for obedience that they would have in a model democracy, in which there was fair compromise, since

---

[22] Ibid, p. 138.

[23] Ibid., p. 145. See also Dahl, *Pluralist Democracy in the United States*, Pt. IV.

they will have had at least as much influence as they would have had in a model democracy. But those people who are deprived of the share of influence on decisions they would have had under a fair compromise

does not have this basic reason for obedience. In respect of this particular reason for obedience, these people are in the same position as they would be if they were living under a dictatorship. . . .

Neutral Principles

Robert Bork

President Reagan's nomination of Robert Bork to the Supreme Court in 1987 provoked an intense debate over the role of the Court as well as over the merits of many recent Court opinions. Bork was rejected by the Senate largely on philosophical grounds: his views on the rights to privacy, speech, and equal protection, senators said, were well outside the mainstream of American politics. In addition to these specific objections, many also attacked his philosophy of constitutional interpretation. The following article, written in 1971, was the basis of much of the resistance to Bork's nomination.

Robert Bork was formerly professor of law at Yale Law School. He also served as a federal judge in the District of Columbia, but is currently working for a Washington, D.C. research group. Besides his interest in constitutional law, Bork is also the author of *The Antitrust Paradox* (1978).

A persistently disturbing aspect of constitutional law is its lack of theory, a lack which is manifest not merely in the work of the courts but in the public, professional and even scholarly discussion of the topic. The result, of course, is that courts are without effective criteria and, therefore we have come to expect that the nature of the Constitution will change, often quite dramatically, as the personnel of the Supreme Court changes. In the present state of af-

fairs that expectation is inevitable, but it is nevertheless deplorable.

The remarks that follow do not, of course, offer a general theory of constitutional law. They are more properly viewed as ranging shots, an attempt to establish the necessity for theory and to take the argument of how constitutional doctrine should be evolved by courts a step or two farther. The first section centers upon the implications of Professor Wechsler's concept of "neutral principles," (and the second attempts to apply those implications to some important and much-debated problems in the interpretation of the first amendment). . . . [Part 2 is omitted . . . Eds.]

From "Neutral Principles and Some First Amendment Problems," *Indiana Law Journal*, Vol. 47, No. 1 (Fall, 1971). Reprinted by permission.

THE SUPREME COURT AND
THE DEMAND FOR PRINCIPLE

The subject of the lengthy and often acrimonious debate about the proper role of the Supreme Court under the Constitution is one that preoccupies many people these days: when is authority legitimate? I find it convenient to discuss that question in the context of the Warren Court and its works simply because the Warren Court posed the issue in acute form. The issue did not disappear along with the era of the Warren Court majorities, however. It arises when any court either exercises or declines to exercise the power to invalidate any act of another branch of government. The Supreme Court is a major power center, and we must ask when its power should be used and when it should be withheld.

Our starting place, inevitably, is Professor Herbert Wechsler's argument that the Court must not be merely a "naked power organ," which means that its decisions must be controlled by principle.[1] "A principled decision," according to Wechsler, "is one that rests on reasons with respect to all the issues in a case, reasons that in their generality and their neutrality transcend any immediate result that is involved."[2]

Wechsler chose the term "neutral principles" to capsulate his argument, though he recognizes that the legal principle to be applied is itself never neutral because it embodies a choice of one value rather than another. Wechsler asked for the neutral application of principles, which is a requirement, as Professor Louis L. Jaffe puts it, that the judge "sincerely believe in the principle upon which he purports to rest his decision." "The judge," says Jaffe, "must believe in the validity of the reasons given for the decision at least in the sense that he is prepared to apply them to a later case which he cannot honestly distinguish."[3] He must not, that is, decide lawlessly. But is the demand for neutrality in judges merely another value choice, one that is no more principled than any other? I think not, but to prove it we must rehearse fundamentals. This is familiar terrain but important and still debated.

The requirement that the Court be principled arises from the resolution of the seeming anomaly of judicial supremacy in a democratic society. If the judiciary really is supreme, able to rule when and as it sees fit, the society is not democratic. The anomaly is dissipated, however, by the model of government embodied in the structure of the Constitution, a model upon which popular consent to limited government by the Supreme Court also rests. This model we may for convenience, though perhaps not with total accuracy, call "Madisonian."[4]

A Madisonian system is not completely democratic, if by "democratic" we mean completely majoritarian. It assumes that in wide areas of life majorities are entitled to rule for no better reason that they are majorities. We need not pause here to examine the philosophical underpinnings of that assumption since it is a "given" in our society; nor need we worry that "majority" is a term of art meaning often no more than the shifting combinations of minorities that add up to temporary majorities in the legislature. That majorities are so constituted is inevitable. In any case, one essential premise of the Madisonian model is majoritarianism. The model has also a counter-majoritarian premise, however, for it assumes there are some areas of life a majority should not control. There are some things a majority should not do to us no matter how democratically it decides to do them. These are areas properly left to individual freedom,

---

[1] H. WECHSLER, *Toward Neutral Principles of Constitutional Law*, in PRINCIPLES, POLITICS, AND FUNDAMENTAL LAW 3, 27 (1961) [hereinafter cited as WECHSLER].

[2] *Id.*

[3] L. JAFFE, ENGLISH AND AMERICAN JUDGES AS LAWMAKERS 38 (1969).

[4] *See* R. DAHL, A PREFACE TO DEMOCRATIC THEORY 4-33 (1956).

and coercion by the majority in these aspects of life is tyranny.

Some see the model as containing an inherent, perhaps an insoluble, dilemma.[5] Majority tyranny occurs if legislation invades the areas properly left to individual freedom. Minority tyranny occurs if the majority is prevented from ruling where its power is legitimate. Yet, quite obviously, neither the majority nor the minority can be trusted to define the freedom of the other. This dilemma is resolved in constitutional theory, and in popular understanding, by the Supreme Court's power to define both majority and minority freedom through the interpretation of the Constitution. Society consents to be ruled undemocratically within defined areas by certain enduring principles believed to be stated in, and placed beyond the reach of majorities by, the Constitution.

But this resolution of the dilemma imposes severe requirements upon the Court. For it follows that the Court's power is legitimate only if it has, and can demonstrate in reasoned opinions that it has, a valid theory, derived from the Constitution, of the respective spheres of majority and minority freedom. If it does not have such a theory but merely imposes its own value choices, or worse if it pretends to have a theory but actually follows its own predilections, the Court violates the postulates of the Madisonian model that alone justifies its power. It then necessarily abets the tyranny either of the majority or of the minority.

This argument is central to the issue of legitimate authority because the Supreme Court's power to govern rests upon popular acceptance of this model. Evidence that this is, in fact, the basis of the Court's power is to be gleaned everywhere in our culture. We need not canvass here such things as high school civics texts and newspaper commentary, for the most telling evidence may be found in the U.S. Reports. The Supreme Court regularly insists that its results, and most particularly its controversial results, do not spring from the mere will of the Justices in the majority but are supported, indeed compelled, by a proper understanding of the Constitution of the United States. Value choices are attributed to the Founding Fathers, not to the Court. The way an institution advertises tells you what it thinks its customers demand.

This is, I think, the ultimate reason the Court must be principled. If it does not have and rigorously adhere to a valid and consistent theory of majority and minority freedoms based upon the Constitution, judicial supremacy, given the axioms of our system, is, precisely to that extent, illegitimate. The root of its illegitimacy is that it opens a chasm between the reality of the Court's performance and the constitutional and popular assumptions that give it power.

I do not mean to rest the argument entirely upon the popular understanding of the Court's function. Even if society generally should ultimately perceive what the Court is in fact doing and, having seen, prove content to have major policies determined by the unguided discretion of judges rather than by elected representatives, a principled judge would, I believe, continue to consider himself bound by an obligation to the document and to the structure of government that it prescribes. At least he would be bound so long as any litigant existed who demanded such adherence of him. I do not understand how, on any other theory of judicial obligation, the Court could, as it does now, protect voting rights if a large majority of the relevant constituency were willing to see some groups or individuals deprived of such rights. But even if I am wrong in that, at the very least an honest judge would owe it to the body politic to cease invoking the authority of the Constitution and to make explicit the imposition of his own will, for only then would we know whether the society understood enough of what is taking place to be said to have consented. . . .

---

[5] *Id.* at 23–24.

The man who understand the issues and nevertheless insists upon the rightness of the Warren Court's performance ought also, if he is candid, to admit that he is prepared to sacrifice democratic process to his own moral views. He claims for the Supreme Court an institutionalized role as perpetrator of limited coups d'etat.

Such a man occupies an impossible philosophic position. What can he say, for instance, of a Court that does not share his politics or his morality? I can think of nothing except the assertion that he will ignore the Court whenever he can get away with it and overthrow it if he can. In his view the Court has no legitimacy, and there is no reason any of us should obey it. And, this being the case, the advocate of a value-choosing Court must answer another difficult question. Why should the Court, a committee of nine lawyers, be the sole agent of change? The man who prefers results to processes has no reason to say that the Court is more legitimate than any other institution. If the Court will not listen, why not argue the case to some other group, say the Joint Chiefs of Staff, a body with rather better means for implementing its decisions?. . .

Recognition of the need for principle is only the first step, but once that step is taken much more follows. Logic has a life of its own, and devotion to principle requires that we follow where logic leads. . . .

We have not carried the idea of neutrality far enough. We have been talking about neutrality in the *application* of principles. If judges are to avoid imposing their own values upon the rest of us, however, they must be neutral as well in the *definition* and the *derivation* of principles.

It is easy enough to meet the requirement of neutral application by stating a principle so narrowly that no embarrassment need arise in applying it to all cases it subsumes, a tactic often urged by proponents of "judicial restraint." But that solves very little. It certainly does not protect the judge from the intrusion of his own values. The problem

may be illustrated by *Griswold v. Connecticut,*[6] in many ways a typical decision of the Warren Court. *Griswold* struck down Connecticut's statute making it a crime, even for married couples, to use contraceptive devices. If we take the principle of the decision to be a statement that government may not interfere with any acts done in private, we need not even ask about the principle's dubious origin for we know at once that the Court will not apply it neutrally. The Court, we may confidently predict, is not going to throw constitutional protection around heroin use or sexual acts with a consenting minor. We can gain the possibility of neutral application by reframing the principle as a statement that government may not prohibit the use of contraceptives by married couples, but that is not enough. The question of neutral definition arises: Why does the principle extend only to married couples? Why, out of all forms of sexual behavior, only to the use of contraceptives? Why, out of all forms of behavior, only to sex? The question of neutral derivation also arises: What justifies any limitation upon legislatures in this area? What is the origin of any principle one may state?

To put the matter another way, if a neutral judge must demonstrate why principle X applies to cases A and B but not to case C (which is, I believe, the requirement laid down by Professors Wechsler and Jaffe), he must, by the same token, also explain why the principle is defined as X rather than as X *minus*, which would cover A but not cases B and C, or a X *plus*, which would cover all cases, A, B and C. Similarly, he must explain why X is a proper principle of limitation on majority power at all. Why should he not choose *non-X*? If he may not choose lawlessly between cases in applying principle X, he may certainly not choose lawlessly in defining X or in choosing X, for principles are after all only organizations of cases into groups. To choose the principle and define it is to decide the cases.

---

[6] 381 U.S. 479 (1965).

It follows that the choice of "fundamental values" by the Court cannot be justified. Where constitutional materials do not clearly specify the value to be preferred, there is no principled way to prefer any claimed human value to any other. The judge must stick close to the text and the history, and their fair implications, and not construct new rights. The case just mentioned illustrates the point. The *Griswold* decision has been acclaimed by legal scholars as a major advance in constitutional law, a salutary demonstration of the Court's ability to protect fundamental human values. I regret to have to disagree, and my regret is all the more sincere because I once took the same position and did so in print.[7] In extenuation I can only say that at the time I thought, quite erroneously, that new basic rights could be derived logically by finding and extrapolating a more general principle of individual autonomy underlying the particular guarantees of the Bill of Rights.

The Court's *Griswold* opinion, by Justice Douglas, and the array of concurring opinions, by Justices Goldberg, White and Harlan, all failed to justify the derivation of any principle used to strike down the Connecticut anti-contraceptive statute or to define the scope of the principle. Justice Douglas, to whose opinion I must confine myself, began by pointing out that "specific guarantees in the Bill of Rights have penumbras, formed by emanations from those guarantees that help give them life and substance."[8] Nothing is exceptional there. In the case Justice Douglas cited, *NAACP v. Alabama*,[9] the State was held unable to force disclosure of membership lists because of the chilling effect upon the rights of assembly and political action of the NAACP's members. The penumbra was created solely to preserve a value central to the first amendment, applied in this case through the fourteenth

amendment. It had no life of its own as a right independent of the value specified by the first amendment.

But Justice Douglas then performed a miracle of transubstantiation. He called the first amendment's penumbra a protection of "privacy" and then asserted that other amendments create "zones of privacy." He had no better reason to use the word "privacy" than that the individual is free within these zones, free to act in public as well as in private. None of these penumbral zones—from the first, third, fourth or fifth amendments, all of which he cited, along with the ninth—covered the case before him. One more leap was required. Justice Douglas asserted that these various "zones of privacy" created an independent right of privacy, a right not lying within the penumbra of any specific amendment. He did not disclose, however, how a series of specified rights combined to create a new and unspecified right.

The *Griswold* opinion fails every test of neutrality. The derivation of the principle was utterly specious, and so was its definition. In fact, we are left with no idea of what the principle really forbids. Derivation and definition are interrelated here. Justice Douglas called the amendments and their penumbras "zones of privacy," though of course they are not that at all. They protect both private and public behavior and so would more properly be labelled "zones of freedom." If we follow Justice Douglas in his next step, these zones would then add up to an independent right of freedom, which is to say, a general constitutional right to be free of legal coercion, a manifest impossibility in any imaginable society.

Griswold, then, is an unprincipled decision, both in the way in which it derives a new constitutional right and in the way it defines that right, or rather fails to define it. We are left with no idea of the sweep of the right of privacy and hence no notion of the cases to which it may or may not be applied in the future. The truth is that the Court could not reach its result in *Griswold* through principle. The reason is obvious.

---

[7] Bork, *The Supreme Court Needs a New Philosophy*, Fortune, Dec., 1968, at 170.

[8] 381 U.S. at 484.

[9] 357 U.S. 449 (1958).

Every clash between a minority claiming freedom and a majority claiming power to regulate involves a choice between the gratifications of the two groups. When the Constitution has not spoken, the Court will be able to find no scale, other than its own value preferences, upon which to weigh the respective claims to pleasure. Compare the facts in *Griswold* with a hypothetical suit by an electric utility company and one of its customers to void a smoke pollution ordinance as unconstitutional. The cases are identical.

In *Griswold* a husband and wife assert that they wish to have sexual relations without fear of unwanted children. The law impairs their sexual gratifications. The State can assert, and at one stage in that litigation did assert, that the majority finds the use of contraceptives immoral. Knowledge that it takes place and that the State makes no effort to inhibit it causes the majority anguish, impairs their gratifications.

The electrical company asserts that it wishes to produce electricity at low cost in order to reach a wide market and make profits. Its customer asserts that he wants a lower cost so that prices can be held low. The smoke pollution regulation impairs his and the company's stockholders' economic gratifications. The State can assert not only that the majority prefer clean air to lower prices, but also that the absence of the regulation impairs the majority's physical and aesthetic gratifications.

Neither case is covered specifically or by obvious implication in the Constitution. Unless we can distinguish forms of gratification, the only course for a principled Court is to let the majority have its way in both cases. It is clear that the Court cannot make the necessary distinction. There is no principled way to decide that one man's gratifications are more deserving of respect than another's or that one form of gratification is more worthy than another.[10] Why is sexual gratification more worthy than moral gratification? Why is sexual gratification nobler than economic gratification? There is no way of deciding these matters other than by reference to some system of moral or ethical values that has no objective or intrinsic validity of its own and about which men can and do differ. Where the Constitution does not embody the moral or ethical choice, the judge has no basis other than his own values upon which to set aside the community judgment embodied in the statute. That, by definition, is an inadequate basis for judicial supremacy. The issue of the community's moral and ethical values, the issue of the degree of pain an activity causes, are matters concluded by the passage and enforcement of the laws in question. The judiciary has no role to play other than that of applying the statutes in a fair and impartial manner.

One of my colleagues refers to this conclusion, not without sarcasm, as the "Equal Gratification Clause." The phrase is apt, and I accept it, though not the sarcasm. Equality of human gratifications, where the document does not impose a hierarchy, is an essential part of constitutional doctrine because of the necessity that judges be principled. To be perfectly clear on the subject, I repeat that the principle is not applicable to legislatures. Legislation requires value choice and cannot be principled in the sense under discussion. Courts must accept any value choice the legislature makes unless it clearly runs contrary to a choice made in the framing of the Constitution.

It follows, of course, that broad areas of constitutional law ought to be reformulated. Most obviously, it follows that substantive due process, revived by the *Griswold* case, is and always has been an improper doctrine. Substantive due process requires the Court to say, without guidance from the Constitution, which liberties or gratifications may be infringed by majorities and which may not. This means that *Griswold's* antecedents

---

[10] The impossibility is related to that of making interpersonal comparisons of utilities. *See* L. ROBBINS, THE NATURE AND SIGNIFICANCE OF ECONOMIC SCIENCE, ch. 4 (2d ed. 1969): P. SAMUELSON, FOUNDATIONS OF ECONOMIC ANALYSIS 243–52 (1965).

were also wrongly decided, *e.g., Meyer v. Nebraska,*[11] which struck down a statute forbidding the teaching of subjects in any language other than English; *Pierce v. Society of Sisters,*[12] which set aside a statute compelling all Oregon school children to attend public schools; *Adkins v. Children's Hospital,*[13] which invalidated a statute of Congress authorizing a board to fix minimum wages for women and children in the District of Columbia; and *Lochner v. New York,*[14] which voided a statute fixing maximum hours of work for bakers. With some of these cases I am in political agreement, and perhaps *Pierce's* result could be reached on acceptable grounds, but there is no justification for the Court's methods. In *Lochner,* Justice Peckham, defending liberty from what he conceived as a mere meddlesome interference, asked, "[A]re we all. . . at the mercy of legislative majorities?"[15] The correct answer, where the Constitution does not speak, must be "yes."

The argument so far also indicates that most of substantive equal protection is also improper. The modern Court, we need hardly be reminded, used the equal protection clause the way the old Court used the due process clause. The only change was in the values chosen for protection and the frequency with which the Court struck down laws.

The equal protection clause has two legitimate meanings. It can require formal procedural equality, and, because of its historical origins, it does require that government not discriminate along racial lines. But much more than that cannot properly be read into the clause. The bare concept of equality provides no guide for courts. All law discriminates and thereby creates inequality. The Supreme Court has no principled way of saying which non-racial inequalities are impermissible. What it has done, therefore, is to appeal to simplistic notions of "fairness' or to what it regards as "fundamental" interests in order to demand equality in some cases but not in others, thus choosing values and producing a line of cases as improper and as intellectually empty as *Griswold v. Connecticut.* Any casebook lists them, and the differing results cannot be explained on any ground other than the Court's preferences for particular values: *Skinner v. Oklahoma*[16] (a forbidden inequality exists when a state undertakes to sterilize robbers but not embezzlers); *Kotch v. Board of River Port Pilot Commissioners*[17] (no right to equality is infringed when a state grants pilots' licenses only to persons related by blood to existing pilots and denies licenses to persons otherwise as well qualified); *Goesaert v. Clearny*[18] (a state does not deny equality when it refuses to license women as bartenders unless they are the wives or daughters of male owners of licensed liquor establishments); *Railway Express Agency v. New York*[19] (a city may forbid truck owners to sell advertising space on their trucks as a distracting hazard to traffic safety though it permits owners to advertise their own business in that way); *Shapiro v. Thompson*[20] (a state denies equality if it pays welfare only to persons who have resided in the state for one year); *Levy v. Louisiana*[21] (a state may not limit actions for a parent's wrongful death to legitimate children and deny it to illegitimate children). The list could be extended, but the point is that the cases cannot be reconciled on any basis other than the Justices' personal beliefs about what interests or gratifications ought to be protected.

Professor Wechsler notes that Justice

---

[11] 262 U.S. 390 (1922).

[12] 268 U.S. 510 (1925).

[13] 261 U.S. 525 (1923).

[14] 198 U.S. 45 (1905).

[15] *Id.* at 59.

[16] 316 U.S. 535 (1942).

[17] 330 U.S. 552 (1947).

[18] 335 U.S. 464 (1948).

[19] 336 U.S. 106 (1949).

[20] 394 U.S. 618 (1969).

[21] 391 U.S. 68 (1968).

Frankfurter expressed "disquietude that the line is often very thin between the cases in which the Court felt compelled to abstain from adjudication because of their 'political' nature, and the cases that so frequently arise in applying the concepts of 'liberty' and 'equality.'"[22] The line is not very thin; it is non-existent. There is no principled way in which anyone can define the spheres in which liberty is required and the spheres in which equality is required. These are matters of morality, of judgment, of prudence. They belong, therefore, to the political community. In the fullest sense, these are political questions.

We may now be in a position to discuss certain of the problems of legitimacy raised by Professor Wechsler. Central to his worries was the Supreme Court's decision in *Brown v. Board of Education*.[23] Wechsler said he had great difficulty framing a neutral principle to support the *Brown* decision, though he thoroughly approved of its result on moral and political grounds. It has long been obvious that the case does not rest upon the grounds advanced in Chief Justice Warren's opinion, the specially harmful effects of enforced school segregation upon black children. That much, as Wechsler and others point out, is made plain by the [later] decisions that followed outlawing segregated public beaches, public golf courses and the like. The principle in operation may be that government may not employ race as a classification. But the genesis of the principle is unclear. . . .

Wechsler notes that *Brown* has to do with freedom to associate and freedom not to associate, and he thinks that a principle must be found that resolves the following dilemma:

[I]f the freedom of association is denied by segregation, integration forces an association upon those for whom it is unpleasant or repugnant. Is this not the heart of the issue involved, a conflict in human claims of high dimension. . . . Given a situation where the state must practically choose between denying the association to those individuals who wish it or imposing it on those who would avoid it, is there a basis in neutral principles for holding that the Constitution demands that the claims for association should prevail? I should like to think there is, but I confess that I have not yet written the opinion. To write it is for me the challenge of the school-segregation cases.[24]

It is extremely unlikely that Professor Wechsler ever will be able to write that opinion to his own satisfaction. He has framed the issue in insoluble terms by calling it a "conflict between human claims of high dimension," which is to say that it requires a judicial choice between rival gratifications in order to find a fundamental human right. So viewed it is the same case as *Griswold v. Connecticut* and not susceptible of principled resolution.

A resolution that seems to me more plausible is supported rather than troubled by the need for neutrality. A court required to decide *Brown* would perceive two crucial facts about the history of the fourteenth amendment. First, the men who put the amendment in the Constitution intended that the Supreme Court should secure against government action some large measure of racial equality. That is certainly the core meaning of the amendment. Second, those same men were not agreed about what the concept of racial equality requires. Many or most of them had not even thought the matter through. Almost certainly, even individuals among them held such views as that blacks were entitled to purchase property from any willing seller but not to attend integrated schools, or that they were entitled to serve on juries but not to intermarry with whites, or that they were entitled to equal physical facilities but that the facilities should be separate, and so on through the

---

[22] WECHSLER, *supra* note 1, at 11, *citing* Frankfurter, *John Marshall and the Judicial Function.* 69 HARV. L. REV. 217, 227–28 (1955).

[23] 347 U.S. 483 (1954).

[24] 35. Id. at 47.

endless anomalies and inconsistencies with which moral positions so frequently abound. The Court cannot conceivably know how these long-dead men would have resolved these issues had they considered, debated and voted on each of them. Perhaps it was precisely because they could not resolve them that they took refuge in the majestic and ambiguous formula: the equal protection of the laws.

But one thing the Court does know: it was intended to enforce a core idea of black equality against governmental discrimination. And the Court, because it must be neutral, cannot pick and choose between competing gratifications and, likewise, cannot write the detailed code the framers omitted, requiring equality in this case but not in another. The Court must, for that reason, choose a general principle of equality that applies to all cases. For the same reason, the Court cannot decide that physical equality is important but psychological equality is not. Thus, the no-state-enforced-discrimination rule of *Brown* must overturn and replace the separate-but-equal doctrine of *Plessy v. Ferguson*. The same result might be reached on an alternative ground. If the Court found that it was incapable as an institution of policing the issue of the physical equality of separate facilities, the variables being insufficiently comparable and the cases too many, it might fashion a no-segregation rule as the only feasible means of assuring even physical equality.

In either case, the value choice (or, perhaps more accurately, the value impulse) of the fourteenth amendment is fleshed out and made into a legal rule—not by moral precept, not by a determination that claims for association prevail over claims for separation as a general matter, still less by consideration of psychological test results, but on purely juridical grounds. . . .

The argument this far claims that, cases of race discrimination aside, it is always a mistake for the Court to try to construct substantive individual rights under the due process or the equal protection clause. Such

rights cannot be constructed without comparing the worth of individual gratifications, and that comparison cannot be principled. Unfortunately, the rhetoric of constitutional adjudication is increasingly a rhetoric about "fundamental" rights that inhere in humans. That focus does more than lead the Court to construct new rights without adequate guidance from constitutional materials. It also distorts the scope and definition of rights that have claim to protection.

There appear to be two proper methods of deriving rights from the Constitution. The first is to take from the document rather specific values that text or history show the framers actually to have intended and which are capable of being translated into principled rules. We may call these specified rights. The second method derives rights from governmental processes established by the Constitution. These are secondary or derived individual rights. This latter category is extraordinarily important. This method of derivation is essential to the interpretation of the first amendment, to voting rights, to criminal procedure and to much else.

Secondary or derivative rights are not possessed by the individual because the Constitution has made a value choice about individuals. Neither are they possessed because the Supreme Court thinks them fundamental to all humans. Rather, these rights are located in the individual for the sake of a governmental process that the Constitution outlines and that the Court should preserve. They are given to the individual because his enjoyment of them will lead him to defend them in court and thereby preserve the governmental process from legislative or executive deformation.

The distinction between rights that are inherent and rights that are derived from some other value is one that our society worked out long ago with respect to the economic market place, and precisely the same distinction holds and will prove an aid to clear thought with respect to the political market place. A right is a form of property, and our thinking about the category of constitutional property might usefully follow the progress of thought about economic property. We now regard it as thoroughly old hat, passe and in fact downright tiresome to hear rhetoric about an inherent right to economic freedom or to economic property. We no longer believe that economic rights inhere in the individual because he is an individual. The modern intellectual argues the proper location and definition of property rights according to judgments of utility—the capacity of such rights to forward some other value. We may, for example, wish to maximize the total wealth of society and define property rights in a way we think will advance that goal by making the economic process run more efficiently. As it is with economic property rights, so it should be with constitutional rights relating to governmental processes.

The derivation of rights from governmental processes is not an easy task, and I do not suggest that a shift in focus will make anything approaching a mechanical jurisprudence possible. I do suggest that, for the reasons already argued, no guidance whatever is available to a court that approaches, say, voting rights or criminal procedures through the concept of substantive equality.

The state legislative reapportionment cases were unsatisfactory precisely because the Court attempted to apply a substantive equal protection approach. Chief Justice Warren's opinions in this series of cases are remarkable for their inability to muster a single respectable supporting argument. The principle of one man, one vote was not neutrally derived: it runs counter to the text of the fourteenth amendment, the history surrounding its adoption and ratification and the political practice of Americans from colonial times up to the day the Court invented the new formula. The principle was not neutrally defined: it presumably rests upon some theory of equal weight for all

votes, and yet we have no explanation of why it does not call into question other devices that defeat the principle, such as the executive veto, the committee system, the filibuster, the requirement on some issues of two-thirds majorities and the practice of districting. . . .

To approach these cases as involving rights derived from the requirements of our form of government is, of course, to say that they involve guarantee clause claims. . . . [But] whether one chooses to use the guarantee of a republican form of government of article IV, § 4 as a peg or to proceed directly to considerations of constitutional structure and political practice probably makes little difference. Madison's writing on the republican form of government specified by the guarantee clause suggests that representative democracy may properly take many forms, so long as the forms do not become "aristocratic or monarchical."[25] That is certainly less easily translated into the rigid one person, one vote requirement, which rests on a concept of the right of the individual to equality, than into the requirement expressed by Justice Stewart in *Lucas v. Forty-Fourth General Assembly*[26] that a legislative apportionment need only be rational and "must be such as not to permit the systematic frustration of the will of a majority of the electorate of the State."[27] The latter is a standard derived from the requirements of a democratic process rather than from the rights of individuals. The topic of governmental processes and the rights that may be derived from them is so large that it is best left at this point. It has been raised only as a reminder that there is a legitimate mode of deriving and defining constitutional rights, however difficult intellectually, that is available to replace the present unsatisfactory focus. . . .

---

[25] THE FEDERALIST No. 43 (J. Madison).

[26] 377 U.S. 713 (1964).

[27] *Id.* at 753–54.

Constitutional Cases

Ronald Dworkin

Few, if any, contemporary thinkers have had more influence on legal theory than Ronald Dworkin. In the following essay, he defends judicial activism against those who argue that judges should allow the decisions of other branches of government to stand whenever there is controversy about a law's constitutionality. The latter view, which he terms *judicial restraint*, could be defended on one of two grounds: skepticism about the existence of moral rights and deference to democratic political institutions. Dworkin considers and rejects each of these defenses of judicial restraint.

1.

When Richard Nixon was running for President he promised that he would appoint to the Supreme Court men who represented his own legal philosophy, that is, who were what he called "strict constructionists.". . .

Nixon claimed that his opposition to the Warren Court's desegregation decisions, and to other decisions it took, were not based simply on a personal or political distaste for the results. He argued that the decisions violated the standards of adjudication that the Court should follow. The Court was usurping, in his views, powers that rightly belong to other institutions, including the legislatures of the various states whose school systems the Court sought to reform. . . .

From *Taking Rights Seriously* by Ronald Dworkin (Cambridge, MA: Harvard University Press, 1978(1). © Copyright 1978 by Ronald Dworkin. Reprinted by permission of the author.

I shall argue that there is in fact no coherent philosophy to which such politicians may consistently appeal. . . .

Nixon is no longer president, and his crimes were so grave that no one is likely to worry very much any more about the details of his own legal philosophy. Nevertheless in what follows I shall use the name "Nixon" to refer, not to Nixon, but to any politician holding the set of attitudes about the Supreme Court that he made explicit in his political campaigns. There was, fortunately, only one real Nixon, but there are, in the special sense in which I use the name, many Nixons.

What can be the basis of this composite Nixon's opposition to the controversial decisions of the Warren Court? He cannot object to these decisions simply because they went beyond prior law, or say that the Supreme Court must never change its mind. Indeed the Burger Court itself seems intent on limiting the liberal decisions of the Warren Court, like *Miranda*. The Constitution's guarantee of "equal protection of the laws," it is true, does not in plain words determine that "separate but equal" school facilities are unconstitutional, or that segregation was so unjust that heroic measures are required to undo its effects. But neither does it provide that as a matter of constitutional law the Court would be wrong to reach these conclusions. It leaves these issues to the Court's judgment. . . .

2.

The constitutional theory on which our government rests is not a simple majoritarian theory. The Constitution, and particularly the Bill of Rights, is designed to protect individual citizens and groups against certain decisions that a majority of citizens might want to make, even when that majority acts in what it takes to be the general or common interest. Some of these constitutional restraints take the form of fairly precise rules, like the rule that requires a jury trial in federal criminal proceedings or, perhaps, the rule that forbids the national Congress to abridge freedom of speech. But other constraints take the form of what are often called "vague" standards, for example, the provision that the government shall not deny men due process of law, or equal protection of the laws.

This interference with democratic practice requires a justification. The draftsmen of the Constitution assumed that these restraints could be justified by appeal to moral rights which individuals possess against the majority, and which the constitutional provisions, both "vague" and precise, might be said to recognize and protect.

The "vague" standards were chosen deliberately, by the men who drafted and adopted them, in place of the more specific and limited rules that they might have enacted. But their decision to use the language they did has caused a great deal of legal and political controversy, because even reasonable men of good will differ when they try to elaborate, for example, the moral rights that the due process clause or the equal protection clause brings into the law. They also differ when they try to apply these rights, however defined, to complex matters of political administration, like the educational practices that were the subject of the segregation cases.

The practice has developed of referring to a "strict" and a "liberal" side to these controversies, so that the Supreme Court might be said to have taken the "liberal" side in the segregation cases and its critics the "strict" side. Nixon has this distinction in mind when he calls himself a "strict constructionist." But the distinction is in fact confusing, because it runs together two different issues that must be separated. Any case that arises under the "vague" constitutional guarantees can be seen as posing two questions: (1) Which decision is required by strict, that is to say faithful, adherence to the text of the Constitution or to the intention of those who adopted that text? (2) Which decision is required by a political philosophy that takes a strict, that is to say narrow, view of the moral rights that individuals have against society? Once these questions are distinguished, it is plain that they may have different answers. The text of the First Amendment, for example, says that Congress shall make *no* law abridging the freedom of speech, but a narrow view of individual rights would permit many such laws, ranging from libel and obscenity laws to the Smith Act.

In the case of the "vague" provisions, however, like the due process and equal protection clauses, lawyers have run the two questions together because they have relied, largely without recognizing it, on a theory of meaning that might be put this way: If the framers of the Constitution used vague language, as they did when they condemned violations of "due process of law," then what they "said" or "meant" is limited to the instances of official action that they had in mind as violations, or, as least, to those instances that they would have thought were violations if they had had them in mind. If those who were responsible for adding the due process clause to the Constitution believed that it was fundamentally unjust to provide separate education for different races, or had detailed views about justice that entailed that conclusion, then the segregation decisions might be defended as an application of the principle they had laid down. Otherwise they could not be defended in this way, but instead would show that the judges had substituted their own ideas of justice for those the constitutional drafters meant to lay down.

This theory makes a strict interpretation of the text yield a narrow view of constitutional rights, because it limits such rights to those recognized by a limited group of people at a fixed date of history. It forces those who favor a more liberal set of rights to concede that they are departing from strict legal authority, a departure they must then seek to justify by appealing only to the desirability of the results they reach.

But the theory of meaning on which this argument depends is far too crude; it ignores a distinction that philosophers have made but lawyers have not yet appreciated. Suppose I tell my children simply that I expect them not to treat others unfairly. I no doubt have in mind examples of the conduct I mean to discourage, but I would not accept that my "meaning" was limited to these examples, for two reasons. First I would expect my children to apply my instructions to situations I had not and could not have thought about. Second, I stand ready to admit that some particular act I had thought was fair when I spoke was in fact unfair, or vice versa, if one of my children is able to convince me of that later; in that case I should want to say that my instructions covered the case he cited, not that I had changed my instructions. I might say that I meant the family to be guided by the *concept* of fairness, not by any specific *conceptions* of fairness I might have had in mind.

This is a crucial distinction which it is worth pausing to explore. Suppose a group believes in common that acts may suffer from a special moral defect which they call unfairness, and which consists in a wrongful division of benefits and burdens, or a wrongful attribution of praise or blame. Suppose also that they agree on a great number of standard cases of unfairness and use these as benchmarks against which to test other, more controversial cases. In that case, the group has a concept of unfairness, and its members may appeal to that concept in moral instruction or argument. But members of that group may nevertheless differ over a large number of these controversial cases, in a way that suggests that each either has or acts on a different theory of *why* the standard cases are acts of unfairness. They may differ, that is, on which more fundamental principles must be relied upon to show that a particular division or attribution is unfair. In that case, the members have different conceptions of fairness.

If so, then members of this community who give instructions or set standards in the name of fairness may be doing two different things. First they may be appealing to the concept of fairness, simply by instructing others to act fairly; in this case they charge those whom they instruct with the responsibility of developing and applying their own conception of fairness as controversial cases arise. That is not the same thing, of course, as granting them a discretion to act as they like; it sets a standard which they must try—and may fail—to meet, because it assumes that one conception is superior to another. The man who appeals to the concept in this way may have his own conception, as I did when I told my children to act fairly; but he holds this conception only as his own theory of how the standard he set must be met, so that when he changes his theory he has not changed that standard.

On the other hand, the members may be laying down a particular conception of fairness; I would have done this, for example, if I had listed my wishes with respect to controversial examples or if, even less likely, I had specified some controversial and explicit theory of fairness, as if I had said to decide hard cases by applying the utilitarian ethics of Jeremy Bentham. The difference is a difference not just in the *detail* of the instructions given but in the *kind* of instructions given. When I appeal to the concept of fairness I appeal to what fairness means, and I give my views on that issue no special standing. When I lay down a conception of fairness, I lay down what I mean by fairness, and my view is therefore the heart of the matter. When I appeal to fairness I pose a moral issue; when I lay down my conception of fairness I try to answer it.

Once this distinction is made it seems obvious that we must take what I have been calling "vague" constitutional clauses as representing appeals to the concepts they employ, like legality, equality, and cruelty. The Supreme Court may soon decide, for example, whether capital punishment is "cruel" within the meaning of the constitutional clause that prohibits "cruel and unusual punishment." It would be a mistake for the Court to be much influenced by the fact that when the clause was adopted capital punishment was standard and unquestioned. That would be decisive if the framers of the clause had meant to lay down a particular conception of cruelty, because it would show that the conception did not extend so far. But it is not decisive of the different question the Court now faces, which is this: Can the Court, responding to the framers' appeal to the concept of cruelty, now defend a conception that does not make death cruel?

Those who ignore the distinction between concepts and conceptions, but who believe that the Court ought to make a fresh determination of whether the death penalty is cruel, are forced to argue in a vulnerable way. They say that ideas of cruelty change over time, and that the Court must be free to reject out-of-date conceptions; this suggests that the Court must change what the Constitution enacted. But in fact the Court can enforce what the Constitution says only by making up its own mind about what is cruel, just as my children, in my example,

can do what I said only by making up their own minds about what is fair. If those who enacted the broad clauses had meant to lay down particular conceptions, they would have found the sort of language conventionally used to do this, that is, they would have offered particular theories of the concepts in question.

Indeed the very practice of calling these clauses "vague," in which I have joined, can now be seen to involve a mistake. The clauses are vague only if we take them to be botched or incomplete or schematic attempts to lay down particular conceptions. If we take them as appeals to moral concepts they could not be made more precise by being more detailed.[1]

The confusion I mentioned between the two senses of "strict" construction is therefore very misleading indeed. If courts try to be faithful to the text of the Constitution, they will for that very reason be forced to decide between competing conceptions of political morality. So it is wrong to attack the Warren Court, for example, on the ground that it failed to treat the Constitution as a binding text. On the contrary, if we wish to treat fidelity to that text as an overriding requirement of constitutional interpretation, then it is the conservative critics of the Warren Court who are at fault, because their philosophy ignores the direction to face issues of moral principle that the logic of the text demands.

I put the matter in a guarded way because we may *not* want to accept fidelity to the spirit of the text as an overriding principle of constitutional adjudication. It may be more important for courts to decide consti-

---

[1] It is less misleading to say that the broad clauses of the Constitution "delegate" power to the Court to enforce its own conceptions of political morality. But even this is inaccurate if is suggests that the Court need not justify its conception by arguments showing the connections between its conception and standard cases, as described in the text. If the Court finds that the death penalty is cruel, it must do so on the basis of some principles or groups of principles that unite the death penalty with the thumbscrew and the rack.

tutional cases in a manner that respects that judgments of other institutions of government, for example. Or it may be more important for courts to protect established legal doctrines, so that citizens and the government can have confidence that the courts will hold to what they have said before. But it is crucial to recognize that these other policies compete with the principle that the Constitution is the fundamental and imperative source of constitutional law. They are not, as the "strict constructionists" suppose, simply consequences of that principle.

3.

Once the matter is put in this light, moreover, we are able to assess these competing claims of policy, free from the confusion imposed by the popular notion of "strict construction." For this purpose I want now to compare and contrast two very general philosophies of how the courts should decide difficult or controversial constitutional issues. I shall call these two philosophies by the names they are given in the legal literature—the programs of "judicial activism" and "judicial restraint"—though it will be plain that these names are in certain ways misleading.

The program of judicial activism holds that courts should accept the directions of the so-called vague constitutional provisions in the spirit I described, in spite of competing reasons of the sort I mentioned. They should work out principles of legality, equality, and the rest, revise these principles from time to time in the light of what seems to the Court fresh moral insight, and judge the acts of Congress, the states, and the President accordingly. (This puts the program in its strongest form; in fact its supporters generally qualify it in ways I shall ignore for the present.)

The program of judicial restraint, on the contrary, argues that courts should allow the decisions of other branches of government to stand, even when they offend the

judges' own sense of the principles required by the broad constitutional doctrines, except when these decisions are so offensive to political morality that they would violate the provisions on any plausible interpretation, or, perhaps, when a contrary decision is required by clear precedent. (Again, this put the program in a stark form; those who profess the policy qualify it in different ways.). . .

We must now . . . notice a distinction between two forms of judicial restraint, for there are two different, and indeed incompatible, grounds on which that policy might be based.

The first is a theory of political *skepticism* that might be described in this way. The policy of judicial activism presupposes a certain objectivity of moral principle; in particular it presupposes that citizens do have certain moral rights against the state, like a moral right to equality of public education or to fair treatment by the police. Only if such moral rights exist in some sense can activism be justified as a program based on something beyond the judge's personal preferences. The skeptical theory attacks activism at its roots; it argues that in fact individuals have no such moral rights against the state. They have only such *legal* rights as the Constitution grants them, and these are limited to the plain and uncontroversial violations or public morality that the framers must have had actually in mind, or that have since been established in a line of precedent.

The alternative ground of a program of restraint is a theory of judicial *deference*. Contrary to the skeptical theory, this assumes that citizens do have moral rights against the state beyond what the law expressly grants them, but it points out that the character and strength of these rights are debatable and argues that political institutions other than courts are responsible for deciding which rights are to be recognized.

This is an important distinction, even though the literature of constitutional law does not draw it with any clarity. The skeptical theory and the theory of deference differ dramatically in the kind of justification they assume, and in their implications for the more general moral theories of the men who profess to hold them. These theories are so different that most American politicians can consistently accept the second, but not the first.

A skeptic takes the view, as I have said, that men have no moral rights against the state and only such legal rights as the law expressly provides. But what does this mean, and what sort of argument might the skeptic make for his view? There is, of course, a very lively dispute in moral philosophy about the nature and standing of moral rights, and considerable disagreement about what they are, if they are anything at all. I shall rely, in trying to answer these questions, on a low-key theory of moral rights against the state. . . . Under that theory, a man has a moral right against the state if for some reason the state would do wrong to treat him in a certain way, even though it would be in the general interest to do so. So a black child has a moral right to an equal education, for example, if it is wrong for the state not to provide that education, even if the community as a whole suffers thereby.

I want to say a word about the virtues of this way of looking at moral rights against the state. A great many lawyers are wary of talking about moral rights, even though they find it easy to talk about what is right or wrong for government to do, because they suppose that rights, if they exist at all, are spooky sorts of things that men and women have in much the same way as they have non-spooky things like tonsils. But the sense of rights I propose to use does not make ontological assumptions of that sort: it simply shows a claim of right to be a special, in the sense of a restricted, sort of judgment about what is right or wrong for governments to do.

Moreover, this way of looking at rights avoids some of the notorious puzzles associated with the concept. It allows us to say, with no sense of strangeness, that rights may vary in strength and character from case to case, and from point to point in history. If

we think of rights as things, these metamorphoses seem strange, but we are used to the idea that moral judgments about what it is right or wrong to do are complex and are affected by considerations that are relative and that change.

The skeptic who wants to argue against the very possibility of rights against the state of this sort has a difficult brief. He must rely, I think, on one of three general positions: (a)He might display a more pervasive moral skepticism, which holds that even to speak of an act being morally right or wrong makes no sense. If no act is morally wrong, then the government of North Carolina cannot be wrong to refuse to bus school children. (b)He might hold a stark form of utilitarianism, which assumes that the only reason we ever have for regarding an act as right or wrong is its impact on the general interest. Under that theory, to say that busing may be morally required even though it does not benefit the community generally would be inconsistent. (c)He might accept some form of totalitarian theory, which merges the interests of the individual in the good of the general community, and so denies that the two can conflict.

Very few American politicians would be able to accept any of these three grounds. Nixon, for example, could not, because he presents himself as a moral fundamentalist who knows in his heart that pornography is wicked and that some of the people of South Vietnam have rights of self-determination in the name of which they and we may properly kill many others.

I do not want to suggest, however, that no one would in fact argue for judicial restraint on grounds of skepticism; on the contrary, some of the best known advocates of restraint have pitched their arguments entirely on skeptical grounds. In 1957, for example, the great judge Learned Hand delivered the Oliver Wendell Holmes lectures at Harvard. Hand was a student of Santayana and a disciple of Holmes, and skepticism in morals was his only religion. He argued for judicial restraint, and said that the Supreme Court had done wrong to declare school segregation illegal in the *Brown* case. It is wrong to suppose, he said, that claims about moral rights express anything more than the speakers' preferences. If the Supreme Court justifies it decisions by making such claims, rather than by relying on positive law, it is usurping the place of the legislature, for the job of the legislature, representing the majority, is to decide whose preferences shall govern.

This simple appeal to democracy is successful if one accepts the skeptical premise. Of course, if men have no rights against the majority, if political decision is simply a matter of whose preferences shall prevail, then democracy does provide a good reason for leaving that decision to more democratic institutions than courts, even when these institutions make choices that the judges themselves hate. But a very different, and much more vulnerable, argument from democracy is needed to support judicial restraint if it is based not on skepticism but on deference, as I shall try to show.

4.

If Nixon holds a coherent constitutional theory, it is a theory of restraint based not on skepticism but on deference. He believes that courts ought not to decide controversial issues of political morality because they ought to leave such decisions to other departments of government. . . .

There is one very popular argument in favor of the policy of deference, which might be called the argument from democracy. It is at least debatable, according to this argument, whether a sound conception of equality forbids segregated education or requires measures like busing to break it down. Who ought to decide these debatable issues of moral and political theory? Should it be a majority of a court in Washington, whose members are appointed for life and are not politically responsible to the public whose lives will be affected by the decision? Or should it be the elected and responsible

state or national legislators? A democrat, so this argument supposes, can accept only the second answer.

But the argument from democracy is weaker than it might first appear. The argument assumes, for one thing, that state legislatures are in fact responsible to the people in the way that democratic theory assumes. But in all the states, though in different degrees and for different reasons, that is not the case. In some states it is very far from the case. I want to pass that point, however, because it does not so much undermine the argument from democracy as call for more democracy, and that is a different matter. I want to fix attention on the issue of whether the appeal to democracy in this respect is even right in principle.

The argument assumes that in a democracy all unsettled issues, including issues of moral and political principle, must be resolved only by institutions that are politically responsible in the way courts are not. Why should we accept that view of democracy? To say that that is what democracy means does no good, because it is wrong to suppose that the word, as a word, has anything like so precise a meaning. Even if it did, we should then have to rephrase our question to ask why we should have democracy, if we assume that is what it means. Nor is it better to say that that view of democracy is established in the American Constitution, or so entrenched in our political tradition that we are committed to it. We cannot argue that the Constitution, which provides no rule limiting juridical review to clear cases, establishes a theory of democracy that excludes wider review, nor can we say that our courts have in fact consistently accepted such a restriction. The burden of Nixon's argument is that they have.

So the argument from democracy is not an argument to which we are committed either by our words or our past. We must accept it, if at all, on the strength of its own logic. In order to examine the arguments more closely, however, we must make a further distinction. The argument as I have set it out might be continued in two different ways: one might argue that judicial deference is required because democratic institutions, like legislatures, are in fact likely to make *sounder* decisions than courts about the underlying issues that constitutional cases raise, that is, about the nature of an individual's moral rights against the state.

Or one might argue that it is for some reason *fairer* that a democratic institution rather than a court should decide such issues, even though there is no reason to believe that the institution will reach a sounder decision. The distinction between these two arguments would make no sense to a skeptic, who would not admit that someone could do a better or worse job at identifying moral rights against the state, any more than someone could do a better or worse job of identifying ghosts. But a lawyer who believes in judicial deference rather than skepticism must acknowledge the distinction, though he can argue both sides if he wishes.

I shall start with the second argument, that legislatures and other democratic institutions have some special title to make constitutional decisions, apart from their ability to make better decisions. One might say that the nature of this title is obvious, because it is always fairer to allow a majority to decide any issue than a minority. But that, as has often been pointed out, ignores the fact that decisions about rights against the majority are not issues that in fairness ought to be left to the majority. Constitutionalism—the theory that the majority must be restrained to protect individual rights—may be a good or bad political theory, but the United States has adopted that theory, and to make the majority judge in its own cause seems inconsistent and unjust. So principles of fairness seem to speak against, not for, the argument from democracy.

Chief Justice Marshall recognized this in his decision in *Marbury v. Madison*, the famous case in which the Supreme Court first claimed the power to review legislative decisions against constitutional standards. He argued that since the Constitution provides that the Constitution shall be the supreme law of the land, the courts in general, and the Supreme Court in the end, must have power to declare statutes void that offend that Constitution. Many legal scholars regard his argument as a *non sequitur*, because, they say, although constitutional constraints are part of the law, the courts, rather than the legislature itself, have not necessarily been given authority to decide whether in particular cases that law has been violated.[2] But the argument is not a *non sequitur* if we take the principle that no man should be judge in his own cause to be so fundamental a part of the idea of legality that Marshall would have been entitled to disregard it only if the Constitution had expressly denied judicial review.

Some might object that it is simpleminded to say that a policy of deference leaves the majority to judge its own cause. Political decisions are made, in the United States, not by one stable majority but by many different political institutions each representing a different constituency which itself changes its composition over time. The decision of one branch of government may well be reviewed by another branch that is also politically responsible, but to a larger or different constituency. The acts of the Arizona police which the Court held unconstitutional in *Miranda*, for example, were in fact subject to review by various executive boards and municipal and state legislatures of Arizona, as well as by the national Con-

---

[2] I distinguish this objection to Marshall's argument from the different objection, not here relevant, that the Constitution should be interpreted to impose a legal *duty* on Congress not, for example, to pass laws abridging freedom of speech, but it should not be interpreted to detract from the legal *power* of Congress to make such a law valid if it breaks its duty. In this view, Congress is in the legal position of a thief who has a legal duty not to sell stolen goods, but retains legal power to make a valid transfer if he does. This interpretation has little to recommend it since Congress, unlike the thief, cannot be disciplined except by denying validity to its wrongful acts, at least in a way that will offer protection to the individuals the Constitution is designed to protect.

gress. It would be naïve to suppose that all of these political institutions are dedicated to the same policies and interests, so it is wrong to suppose that if the Court had not intervened the Arizona police would have been free to judge themselves.

But this objection is itself too glib, because it ignores the special character of disputes about individual moral rights as distinct from other kinds of political disputes. Different institutions do have different constituencies when, for example, labor or trade or welfare issues are involved, and the nation often divides sectionally on such issues. But this is not generally the case when individual constitutional rights, like the rights of accused criminals, are at issue. It has been typical of these disputes that the interests of those in political control of the various institutions of the government have been both homogeneous and hostile. Indeed that is why political theorists have conceived of constitutional rights as rights against the "state" or the "majority" as such, rather than against any particular body or branch of government. . . .

It does seem fair to say, therefore, that the argument from democracy asks that those in political power be invited to be the sole judge of their own decisions, to see whether they have the right to do what they have decided they want to do. That is not a final proof that a policy of judicial activism is superior to a program of deference. Judicial activism involves risks of tyranny; certainly in the stark and simple form I set out. It might even be shown that these risks override the unfairness of asking the majority to be judge in its own cause. But the point does undermine the argument that the majority, in fairness, must be allowed to decide the limits of its own power.

We must therefore turn to the other continuation of the argument from democracy, which holds that democratic institutions, like legislatures, are likely to reach *sounder* results about the moral rights of individuals than would courts. In 1969 the late Professor Alexander Bickel of the Yale Law School delivered his Holmes Lectures at Harvard and argued for the program of judicial restraint in a novel and ingenious way. He allowed himself to suppose, for purposes of argument, that the Warren Court's program of activism could be justified if in fact it produced desirable results.[3] He appeared, therefore, to be testing the policy of activism on its own grounds, because he took activism to be precisely the claim that the courts have the moral right to improve the future, whatever legal theory may say. Learned Hand and other opponents of activism had challenged that claim. Bickel accepted it, at least provisionally, but he argued that activism fails its own test. . . .

What are we to make of Bickel's argument? His account of recent history can be, and has been, challenged. It is by no means plain, certainly not yet, that racial integration will fail as a long-term strategy; and he is wrong if he thinks that black Americans, of whom more still belong to the NAACP than to more militant organizations, have rejected it. No doubt the nation's sense of how to deal with the curse of racism swings back and forth as the complexity and size of the problem become more apparent, but Bickel may have written at a high point of one arc of the pendulum.

He is also wrong to judge the Supreme Court's effect on history as if the Court were the only institution at work, or to suppose that if the Court's goal has not been achieved the country is worse off than if it had not tried. Since 1954, when the Court laid down the principle that equality before the law requires integrated education, we have not had, except for a few years of the Johnson Administration, a national execu-

---

[3] Professor Bickel also argued, with his usual very great skill, that many of the Warren Court's major decisions could not even be justified on conventional grounds, that is, by the arguments the Court advanced in its opinions. His criticism of these opinions is often persuasive, but the Court's failures of craftsmanship do not affect the argument I consider in the text. (His Holmes lectures were amplified in his book *The Supreme Court and the Ideal of Progress*, 1970.)

tive willing to accept that principle as an imperative. For the past several years we have had a national executive that seems determined to undermine it. Nor do we have much basis for supposing that the racial situation in America would now be more satisfactory, on balance, if the Court had not intervened, in 1954 and later, in the way that it did.

But there is a very different, and for my purpose much more important, objective to take to Bickel's theory. His theory is novel because it appears to concede an issue of principle to judicial activism, namely, that the Court is entitled to intervene if its intervention produces socially desirable results. But the concession is an illusion, because his sense of what is socially desirable is inconsistent with the presupposition of activism that individuals have moral rights against the state. In fact, Bickel's argument cannot succeed, even if we grant his facts and his view of history, except on a basis of a skepticism about rights as profound as Learned Hand's. . . .

On this view, the rights of blacks, suspects, and atheists will emerge through the process of political institutions responding to political pressures in the normal way. If a claim of right cannot succeed in this way, then for that reason it is, or in any event it is likely to be, an improper claim of right. But this bizarre proposition is only a disguised form of the skeptical point that there are in fact no rights against the state.

Perhaps, as Burke and his modern followers argue, a society will produce the institutions that best suit it only by evolution and never by radical reform. But rights against the state are claims that, if accepted, require society to settle for institutions that may not suit it so comfortably. The nerve of a claim of right, even on the demythologized analysis of rights I am using, is that an individual is entitled to protection against the majority even at the cost of the general interest. Of course the comfort of the majority will require some accommodation for minorities but only to the extent necessary to preserve order; and that is usually an accommodation that falls short of recognizing their rights.

Indeed the suggestion that rights can be demonstrated by a process of history rather than by an appeal to principle shows either a confusion or no real concern about what rights are. A claim of right presupposes a moral argument and can be established in no other way. Bickel paints the judicial activists (and even some of the heroes of judicial restraint, like Brandeis and Frankfurter, who had their lapses) as eighteenth-century philosophers who appeal to principle because they hold the optimistic view that a blueprint may be cut for progress. But this picture confuses two grounds for the appeal to principle and reform, and two senses of progress.

It is one thing to appeal to moral principle in the silly faith that ethics as well as economics moves by an invisible hand, so that individual rights and the general good will coalesce, and law based on principle will move the nation to a frictionless utopia where everyone is better off than he was before. Bickel attacks that vision by his appeal to history, and by his other arguments against government by principle. But it is quite another matter to appeal to principle *as* principle, to show, for example, that it is unjust to force black children to take their public education in black schools, even if a great many people *will* be worse off if the state adopts the measures needed to prevent this.

This is a different version of progress. It is moral progress, and though history may show how difficult it is to decide where moral progress lies, and how difficult to persuade others once one has decided, it cannot follow from this that those who govern us have no responsibility to face that decision or to attempt that persuasion.

5.

This has been a complex argument, and I want to summarize it. Our constitutional system rests on a particular moral theory, namely, that men have moral rights against the state. The difficult clauses of the Bill of Rights, like the due process and equal protection clauses, must be understood as appealing to moral concepts rather than laying down particular conceptions; therefore a court that undertakes the burden of applying these clauses fully as law must be an activist court, in the sense that it must be prepared to frame and answer questions of political morality. . . .

If we give the decisions of principle that the Constitution requires to the judges, instead of to the people, we act in the spirit of legality, so far as our institutions permit. But we run a risk that the judges may make the wrong decisions. Every lawyer thinks that the Supreme Court has gone wrong, even violently wrong, at some point in its career. If he does not hate the conservative decisions of the early 1930s, which threatened to block the New Deal, he is likely to hate the liberal decisions of the last decade.

We must not exaggerate the danger. Truly unpopular decisions will be eroded because public compliances will be grudging, as it has been in the case of public school prayers, and because old judges will die or retire and be replaced by new judges appointed because they agree with a President who has been elected by the people. The decisions against the New Deal did not stand, and the more daring decisions of recent years are now at the mercy of the Nixon Court. Nor does the danger of wrong

decisions lie entirely on the side of excess; the failure of the Court to act in the McCarthy period, epitomized by its shameful decision upholding the legality of the Smith Act in the *Dennis* case, may be thought to have done more harm to the nation than did the Court's conservative bias in the early Roosevelt period. . . .

Constitutional law can make no genuine advance until it isolates the problem of rights against the state and makes that problem part of its own agenda. That argues for a fusion of constitutional law and moral theory, a connection that, incredibly, has yet to take place. It is perfectly understandable that lawyers dread contamination with moral philosophy, and particularly with those philosophers who talk about rights, because the spooky overtones of that concept threaten the graveyard of reason. But better philosophy is now available than the lawyers may remember. Professor Rawls of Harvard, for example, has published an abstract and complex book about justice which no constitutional lawyer will be able to ignore.[1] There is no need for lawyers to play a passive role in the development of a theory of moral rights against the state, however, any more than they have been passive in the development of legal sociology and legal economics. They must recognize that law is no more independent from philosophy than it is from these other disciplines.

_____
[1] *A Theory of Justice*, 1972. See Chapter 6.

Reynolds v. Sims:
Reapportionment and Voting Power

The original Constitution is almost silent on the question of who should be allowed to vote. The one exception is Article I which provides that everybody who is allowed by their state to vote for members of the largest state legislative body must also be allowed to vote in Congressional elections. Other mention of elections, all found in amendments, is negative, preventing disenfranchisement based on race (fifteenth), gender (nineteenth), age (twenty-sixth), and ability to pay a poll tax (twenty-fourth). So when the Warren Court confronted the failure of state legislatures to reapportion themselves, it did so largely on a clean slate.

In a series of cases, all announced the same day in 1964, the Supreme Court invalidated the apportionment schemes in eight states, including Alabama and Colorado. The leading case is *Reynolds v. Sims*. A group of Alabama citizens challenged their state's scheme for determining the size of election districts, which had not changed since the census of 1900. According to the 1960 census, population in Alabama's senate districts varied from 15,000 to 634,000 and its house districts from 6,700 to 104,000. The district court had rejected several state reapportionment proposals which would still have allowed wide variations in population and ordered implementation of its own reapportionment plan. For different reasons, both the private citizens and the state appealed to the Supreme Court.

Mr. Chief Justice WARREN delivered the opinion of the Court. . . . Undeniably the Constitution of the United States protects the right of all qualified citizens to vote, in state as well as in federal elections. A consistent line of decisions by this Court in cases involving attempts to deny or restrict the right of suffrage has made this indelibly clear. . . . And history has seen a continuing expansion of the scope of the right of suffrage in this country. The right to vote freely for the candidate of one's choice is of the

377 U.S. 533 (1964)

essence of a democratic society, and any restrictions on that right strike at the heart of representative government. And the right of suffrage can be denied by a debasement or dilution of the weight of a citizen's vote just as effectively as by wholly prohibiting the free exercise of the franchise. . . .

A predominant consideration in determining whether a State's legislative apportionment scheme constitutes an invidious discrimination violative of rights asserted under the Equal Protection Clause is that the rights allegedly impaired are individual and personal in nature. . . . Undoubtedly, the right of suffrage is a fundamental matter in a free and democratic society. Especially since the right to exercise the franchise in a free and unimpaired manner is preservative of other basic civil and political rights, any alleged infringement of the right of citizens to vote must be carefully and meticulously scrutinized. . . . [I]n Yick Wo v. Hopkins [1886] the Court referred to "the political franchise of voting" as "a fundamental political right, because preservative of all rights."

Legislators represent people, not trees or acres. Legislators are elected by voters, not farms or cities or economic interests. As long as ours is a representative form of government, and our legislatures are those instruments of government elected directly by and directly representative of the people, the right to elect legislators in a free and unimpaired fashion is a bedrock of our political system. . . . Weighting the votes of citizens differently, by any method or means, merely because of where they happen to reside, hardly seems justifiable. . . .

State legislatures are, historically, the fountainhead of representative government in this country. . . . But representative government is in essence self-government through the medium of elected representatives of the people, and each and every citizen has an inalienable right to full and effective participation in the political processes of his State's legislative bodies. Most citizens can achieve this participation only as qualified voters through the election of legislators to represent them. Full and effective participation by all citizens in state government requires, therefore, that each citizen have an equally effective voice in the election of members of his state legislature. Modern and viable state government needs, and the Constitution demands, no less.

Logically, in a society ostensibly grounded on representative government, it would seem reasonable that a majority of the people of a State could elect a majority of that State's legislators. To conclude differently, and to sanction minority control of state legislative bodies, would appear to deny major-

ity rights in a way that far surpasses any possible denial of minority rights that might otherwise be thought to result. Since legislatures are responsible for enacting laws by which all citizens are to be governed, they should be bodies which are collectively responsive to the popular will. And the concept of equal protection has been traditionally viewed as requiring the uniform treatment of persons standing in the same relation to the governmental action questioned or challenged. With respect to the allocation of legislative representation, all voters, as citizens of a State, stand in the same relation regardless of where they live. Any suggested criteria for the differentiation of citizens are insufficient to justify any discrimination, as to the weight of their votes, unless relevant to the permissible purposes of legislative apportionment. Since the achieving of fair and effective representation for all citizens is concededly the basic aim of legislative apportionment, we conclude that the Equal Protection Clause guarantees the opportunity for equal participation by all voters in the election of state legislators. Diluting the weight of votes because of place of residence impairs basic constitutional rights under the Fourteenth Amendment just as much as invidious discriminations based upon factors such as race. . . .

We hold that, as a basic constitutional standard, the Equal Protection Clause requires that the seats in both houses of a bicameral state legislature must be apportioned on a population basis. Simply stated, an individual's right to vote for state legislators is unconstitutionally impaired when its weight is in a substantial fashion diluted when compared with votes of citizens living in other parts of the State. . . .

[We] find the federal analogy inapposite and irrelevant to state legislative districting schemes. Attempted reliance on the federal analogy appears often to be little more than an after-the-fact rationalization offered in defense of maladjusted state apportionment arrangements. . . .

The system of representation in the two

Houses of the Federal Congress is one ingrained in our Constitution, as part of the law of the land. It is one conceived out of compromise and concession indispensable to the establishment of our federal republic. Arising from unique historical circumstances, it is based on the consideration that in establishing our type of federalism a group of formerly independent States bound themselves together under one national government. . . .

Political subdivisions of States—counties, cities, or whatever—never were and never have been considered as sovereign entities. Rather, they have been traditionally regarded as subordinate governmental instrumentalities created by the State to assist in the carrying out of state governmental functions. . . . The relationship of the States to the Federal Government could hardly be less analogous. . . .

We do not believe that the concept of bicameralism is rendered anachronistic and meaningless when the predominant basis of representation in the two state legislative bodies is required to be the same—population. A prime reason for bicameralism, modernly considered, is to insure mature and deliberate consideration of, and to prevent precipitate action on, proposed legislative measures. Simply because the controlling criterion for apportioning representation is required to be the same in both houses does not mean that there will be no differences in the composition and complexion of the two bodies. Different constituencies can be represented in the two houses. One body could be composed of single-member districts while the other could have at least some multimember districts. The length of terms of the legislators in the separate bodies could differ. The numerical size of the two bodies could be made to differ, even significantly, and the geographical size of districts from which legislators are elected could also be made to differ. And apportionment in one house could be arranged so as to balance off minor inequities in the representation of certain areas in the other house. . . .

[T]he Equal Protection Clause requires that a State make an honest and good faith effort to construct districts, in both houses of its legislature, as nearly of equal population as is practicable. We realize that it is a practical impossibility to arrange legislative districts so that each one has an identical number of residents, or citizens, or voters. Mathematical exactness or precision is hardly a workable constitutional requirement. . . .

So long as the divergences from a strict population standard are based on legitimate considerations incident to the effectuation of a rational state policy, some deviations from the equal-population principle are constitutionally permissible. . . . But neither history alone, nor economic or other sorts of group interests, are permissible factors in attempting to justify disparities from population-based representation. Citizens, not history or economic interests, cast votes. Considerations of area alone provide an insufficient justification for deviations from the equal-population principle. Again, people, not land or trees or pastures, vote. Modern developments and improvements in transportation and communications make rather hollow, in the mid-1960s, most claims that deviations from population-based representation can validly be based solely on geographical considerations. . . .

Lucas v. Forty-fourth General Assembly:
Reapportionment and Voting Power

Lucas was another of the eight reapportionment cases decided along with *Reynolds*. In a 1962 referendum, the people of Colorado chose between two amendments, each of which provided an alternative method for reapportionment of its state legislature. Amendment B called for both the state House of Representatives and the Senate to be apportioned on a "population basis." That Amendment was defeated by a vote of 305,700 to 172,725, while Amendment 7 was approved by an almost identical margin of the Colorado electorate and a majority of voters in every county. Amendment 7 provided for apportionment of the House of Representatives on the basis of population, but maintained the existing apportionment in the Senate, which was based on a combination of population and other factors. A three judge Appeals Court panel had already upheld Amendment 7, but the Supreme Court reversed this decision. Justice Stewart dissented in *Lucas*; Justice Harlan's dissent, also reprinted below, applied to all eight cases.

Warren, C. J. Although the initiative device provides a practicable political remedy to obtain relief against alleged legislative malapportionment, an individual's constitutionally protected right to cast an equally weighted vote cannot be denied even by a vote of a majority of a State's electorate, if the apportionment scheme adopted by the voters fails to measure up to the requirements of the Equal Protection Clause. [A] citizen's constitutional rights can hardly be infringed simply because a majority of the people choose that it be.

Stewart, J. dissenting. First, says the Court, it is 'established that the fundamental principle of representative government in this country is one of equal representation for equal numbers of [people].' [But] this 'was not the colonial system, it was not the system chosen for the national government by the Constitution, it was not the system exclusively or even predominantly practiced by the States at the time of adoption of the Fourteenth Amendment, it is not predominantly practiced by the States today.* Secondly, says the Court, unless legislative districts are equal in population, voters in the more populous districts will suffer a 'debasement' amounting to a constitutional in-

---

* See also Bickel, *The Supreme Court and Reapportionment*, in Reapportionment in the 1970's, 57, 58–59 (Polsby ed. 1971): "[A] rigorous majoritarianism is not what our institutions rest [on]. American government [includes] a Supreme Court which wields political power and [is] not elected at all. Our government includes a Senate [in] which each state, regardless of population, has an equal vote that not even a duly enacted and ratified constitutional amendment can, without its own consent, deprive it of. Our government includes a House of Representatives in which each state has at least one vote, even though the whole state may be (as some are) considerably smaller in population than the average congressional district."

377 U.S. 713 (1964)

jury. [I] find it impossible to understand how or why a voter in California, for instance, either feels or is less a citizen than a voter in Nevada, simply because, despite their population disparities, each of those States is represented by two United States Senators.

[My] own understanding of the various theories of representative government is that no one theory has ever commanded unanimous [assent]. But even if it were thought that the rule announced today by the Court is, as a matter of political theory, the most desirable, [I] could not join in the fabrication of a constitutional mandate which imports and forever freezes one theory of political thought into our Constitution, and forever denies to every State any opportunity for enlightened and progressive innovation. . . .

Representative government is a process of accommodating group interests through democratic institutional arrangements. . . . Appropriate legislative apportionment, therefore, should ideally be designed to insure effective representation in the State's legislature, in cooperation with other organs of political power, of the various groups and interests making up the electorate. In practice, of course, this ideal is approximated in the particular apportionment system of any State by a realistic accommodation of the diverse and often conflicting political forces operating within the State.

[The] fact of geographic districting, the constitutional validity of which the Court does not question, carries with it an acceptance of the idea of legislative representation of regional needs and interests. Yet if geographical residence is irrelevant, as the Court suggests, and the goal is solely that of equally 'weighted' votes, I do not understand why the Court's constitutional rule does not require the abolition of districts and the holding of all elections at large.*

---

* Even with legislative districts of exactly equal voter population, 26% of the electorate (a bare majority of the voters in a bare majority of the districts) can, [by]

The fact is, of course, that population factors must often to some degree be subordinated in devising a legislative apportionment plan which is to achieve the important goal of ensuring a fair, effective, and balanced representation of the regional, social, and economic interests within a State. And the further fact is that throughout our history the apportionments of State Legislatures have reflected the strongly felt American tradition that the public interest is composed of many diverse interests, and that in the long run it can better be expressed by a medley of component voices than by the majority's monolithic command. [I] think the cases should be decided by application of accepted principles of constitutional adjudication under the Equal Protection Clause [and that] demands but two basic attributes of any plan of state legislative apportionment. First, it demands that, in the light of the State's own characteristics and needs, the plan must be a rational one. Secondly, it demands that the plan must be such as not to permit the systematic frustration of the will of a majority of the electorate of the State. . . .

[In] the Colorado House, the majority unquestionably [rules]. It is true that, as a matter of theoretical arithmetic, a minority of 36% of the voters could elect a majority of the Senate, but this percentage has no real meaning in terms of the legislative process. [N]o possible combination of Colorado senators from rural districts, even assuming arguendo that they would vote as a bloc, could control the Senate. To arrive at the 36% figure, one must include [a] substantial number of urban [districts].

the kind of theoretical mathematics embraced by the Court, elect a majority of the legislature under our simple majority electoral system. Thus, the Court's constitutional rule permits minority rule.

Students of the mechanics of voting systems tell us that if all that matters is that votes count equally, the best vote-counting electoral system is proportional representation in statewide elections. [B]ecause electoral systems are intended to serve functions other than satisfying mathematical theories, [however,] proportional representation has not been widely adopted.

[T]he people living in each of [the state's] four regions have interests unifying themselves and differentiating them from those in other regions. Given these underlying facts, certainly it was not irrational to conclude [that] planned departures from a strict per capita standard of representation were a desirable way of assuring [that] districts should be small enough in area, in a mountainous state like Colorado, where accessibility is affected by configuration as well as compactness of districts, to enable each senator to have firsthand knowledge of his entire district and to maintain close contact with his constituents. . . .

"[I]f per capita representation were the rule in both houses of the Colorado Legislature, counties having small populations would have to be merged with larger counties having totally dissimilar interests. Their representatives would not only be unfamiliar with the problems of the smaller county, but the interests of the smaller counties might well be totally submerged to the interests of the larger counties with which they are joined. . . .*

---

* Under *Reynolds*, could Colorado still give such counties "effective representations" by permitting them each to have a representative in the legislature, but granting that legislator only a fractional vote determined on a population basis (or granting him a full vote but giving legislators from larger counties a more heavily weighted vote)? Consider Dixon, *Reapportionment Perspectives: What is Fair Representation?* 51 A.B.A.J. 319, 322 (1965): "[W]eighted voting may be nullified for several reasons. One of the most important reasons would be the consideration that one man casting nineteen votes is not as effective in terms of representation as nineteen separate voices (or lobbyists). Another would be that nineteen men separately elected would provide more opportunity for expression of divergent views. [B]oth of these arguments involve going beyond the simple mathematical tenor of the Supreme Court's 'one-man, one-vote' decisions. They involve putting reapportionment in the context of the actual complexities of representation—and the difficulties in determining what is fair and effective representation." Does this objection go similarly to fractional voting? If not, should fractional voting also extend to committee voting? Assignment to committee? Compensation? What else? See generally Banzhaf, *One Man, ? Votes: Mathematical Analysis of Voting Power and Effective Representa-*

"The present apportionment, adopted overwhelmingly by the people [is] entirely rational, [and] the majority has consciously chosen to protect the minority's interests, and under the liberal initiative provisions of the Colorado Constitution, it retains the power to reverse its decision to do so. Therefore, there can be no question of frustration of the basic principle of majority rule.

***Harlan, J. dissenting in both* Reynolds *and* Lucas.** . . . Stripped of aphorisms, the Court's argument boils down to the assertion that appellees' right to vote has been invidiously "debased" or "diluted" by systems of apportionment which entitle them to vote for fewer legislators than other voters, an assertation which is tied to the Equal Protection Clause only by the constitutionally frail tautology that "equal" means "equal."

Had the Court paused to probe more deeply into the matter, it would have found that the Equal Protection Clause was never intended to inhibit the States in choosing any democratic method they pleased for the apportionment of their legislatures. This is shown by the language of the Fourteenth Amendment taken as a whole, by the understanding of those who proposed and ratified it, and by the political practices of the States

---

tion, 36 Geo. Wash.L.Rev. 808 (1968); Note, *Equal Representation and the Weighted Voting Alternatives,* 79 Yale L.J. 311 (1969).

What about a system of cumulative voting? Consider Note, *Apportionment Problems in Local Government,* 49 Not.D.Law. 671, 683–84 (1974): "[E]ach elector has as many votes as there are representatives to be elected from the area at large, and he may cast his votes in any combination for the candidates on the slate. If there are three candidates to be elected, the voter may cast all three votes for one candidate, or give one candidate two votes and give another candidate one vote, or give one vote to each of three candidates. The three candidates with the highest number of votes are the winners. [Where] there are several positions to be filled minority groups can easily achieve a voice by running only a few candidates (or only one) and then voting in blocs. In this manner cumulative voting becomes very much like proportional representation."

at the time the Amendment was adopted. . . .

Although the Court—necessarily, as I believe—provides only generalities in elaboration of its main thesis, its opinion nevertheless fully demonstrates how far removed these problems are from fields of judicial competence. Recognizing that "indiscriminate districting" is an invitation to "partisan gerrymandering," the Court nevertheless excludes virtually every basis for the formation of electoral districts other than "indiscriminate districting.". . . : (1) history; (2) "economic or other sorts of group interests"; (3) area; (4) geographical considerations; (5) a desire "to insure effective representation for sparsely settled areas"; (6) "availability of access of citizens to their representatives"; (7) theories of bicameralism (except those approved by the Court); (8) occupation; (9) "an attempt to balance urban and rural power"; (10) the preference of a majority of voters in the State.

So far as presently appears, the *only* factor which a State may consider, apart from numbers, is political subdivisions. But even "a clearly rational state policy" recognizing this factor is unconstitutional if "population is submerged as the controlling consideration. . . ."

I know of no principle of logic or practical or theoretical politics, still less any constitutional principle, which establishes all or any of these exclusions. . . . So far as the Court says anything at all on this score, it says only that "legislators represent people, not trees or acres"; that "citizens, not history or economic interests, cast votes"; that "people, not land or trees or pastures, vote." All this may be conceded. But it is surely equally obvious, and, in the context of elections, more meaningful to note that people are not ciphers and that legislators can represent their electors only by speaking for their interests—economic, social, political—many of which do reflect the place where the electors live. The Court does not establish, or indeed even attempt to make a case for the proposition that conflicting interests within a State can only be adjusted by disregarding them when voters are grouped for purposes of representation. . . .

Finally, these decisions give support to a current mistaken view of the Constitution and the constitutional function of this Court. This view, in a nutshell, is that every major social ill in this country can find its cure in some constitutional "principle," and that this Court should "take the lead" in promoting reform when other branches of government fail to act. The Constitution is not a panacea for every blot upon the public welfare, nor should this Court, ordained as a judicial body, be thought of as a general haven for reform movements. The Constitution is an instrument of government, fundamental to which is the premise that in a diffusion of governmental authority lies the greatest promise that this Nation will realize liberty for all its citizens. This Court, limited in function in accordance with that premise, does not serve its high purpose when it exceeds its authority, even to satisfy justified impatience with the slow workings of the political process. For when, in the name of constitutional interpretation, the Court *adds* something to the Constitution that was deliberately excluded from it, the Court in reality substitutes its view of what should be so for the amending process. . . .

Kramer v. Union Free School District: Voting Qualifications

Voting is treated by the Supreme Court as a fundamental interest, so that if a law infringes on it the Court applies the same sort of heightened scrutiny as when laws rely on suspect classifications like race. Prior to this case, the Court had struck down a Virginia poll tax of $1.50, payment of which was a requirement of voting. Wealth, said the Court, is "not germane to one's ability to participate intelligently in the electoral process." (*Harpur v. Virginia Board of Elections*, 1966) In *Kramer*, the Court assessed a New York law which provided that residents could vote in school district elections only if they own or lease taxable property within the district or else have children enrolled in local public schools. (Property taxes were used to finance the district's school system.)

Warren, C. J. In this case we are called on to determine whether §2012 of the New York Education Law is constitutional. The legislation provides that in certain New York school districts residents who are otherwise eligible to vote in state and federal elections may vote in the school district election only if they . . . [are] either (1) . . . the owner or lessee of taxable real property located in the district, (2) . . . the spouse of one who owns or leases qualifying property, or (3) . . . the parent or guardian of a child enrolled for a specified time during the preceding year in a local district school. . . .

In determining whether or not [this] law violates the Equal Protection Clause, . . . we must give the statute a close and exacting examination. . . . Any unjustified discrimination in determining who may participate in political affairs or in the selection of public officials undermines the legitimacy of representative government.

. . . [S]tatutes granting the franchise to residents on a selective basis always pose the danger of denying some citizens any effective voice in the governmental affairs which substantially affect their lives. Therefore, if a challenged state statute grants the right to vote to some bona fide residents of requisite age and citizenship and denies the franchise to others, the Court must determine whether the exclusions are necessary to promote a compelling state interest.

And, for these reasons, the deference usually given to the judgment of legislators does not extend to decisions concerning which resident citizens may participate in the election of legislators and other public officials. Those decisions must be carefully scrutinized by the Court to determine whether each resident citizen has, as far as is possible, an equal voice in the selections. Accordingly, when we are reviewing statutes which deny some residents the right to vote, the general presumption of constitutionality afforded state statutes and the traditional approval given state classifications if the Court can conceive of a "rational basis" for

395 U.S. 621 (1969)

the distinctions made are not applicable. . . . The presumption of constitutionality and the approval given "rational" classifications in other types of enactments are based on an assumption that the institutions of state government are structured so as to represent fairly all the people. However, when the challenge to the statute is in effect a challenge of this basic assumption, the assumption can no longer serve as the basis for presuming constitutionality. And, the assumption is no less under attack because the legislature which decides who may participate at the various levels of political choice is fairly elected. Legislation which delegates decision making to bodies elected by only a portion of those eligible to vote for the legislature can cause unfair representation. Such legislation can exclude a minority of voters from any voice in the decisions just as effectively as if the decisions were made by legislators the minority had no voice in selecting.

The need for exacting judicial scrutiny of statutes distributing the franchise is undiminished simply because, under a different statutory scheme, the offices subject to election might have been filled through appointment. . . .

Besides appellant and others who similarly live in their parent's homes,[1] the statute also disenfranchises the following persons (unless they are parents or guardians of children enrolled in the district public school): senior citizens and others living with children or relatives; clergy, military personnel, and others who live on tax-exempt property; boarders and lodgers; parents who neither own nor lease qualifying property and whose children are too young to attend school; parents who neither own nor lease qualifying property and whose children attend private schools. . . . All members of the community have an interest in the quality and structure of public education, appellant says, and he urges that

"the decisions taken by local boards . . . may have grave consequences to the entire population." Appellant also argues that the level of property taxation affects him, even though he does not own property, as property tax levels affect the price of goods and services in the community.

We turn therefore to question whether the exclusion is necessary to promote a compelling state interest. First, appellees argue that the State has a legitimate interest in limiting the franchise in school district elections to "members of the community of interest"—those "primarily interested in such elections." Second, appellees urge that the State may reasonably and permissibly conclude that "property taxpayers" (including lessees of taxable property who share the tax burden through rent payments) and parents of the children enrolled in the district's schools are those "primarily interested" in school affairs.

We do not understand appellees to argue that the State is attempting to limit the franchise to those "subjectively concerned" about school matters. Rather, they appear to argue that the State's legitimate interest is in restricting a voice in school matters to those "directly affected" by such decisions. The State apparently reasons that since the schools are financed in part by local property taxes, persons whose out-of-pocket expenses are "directly" affected by property tax changes should be allowed to vote. Similarly, parents of children in school are thought to have a "direct" stake in school affairs and are given a vote.

Appellees argue that it is necessary to limit the franchise to those "primarily interested" in school affairs because "the ever increasing complexity of the many interacting phases of the school system and structure make it extremely difficult for the electorate fully to understand the why and wherefores of the detailed operations of the school system." Appellees say that many communications of school boards and school administrations are sent home to the parents through the district pupils and are "not broadcast to the general public"; thus,

---

[1] "Appellant is a 31-year-old college-educated stockbroker who lives in his parents' home. . . . He is a citizen of the United States and has voted in federal and state elections since 1959."

nonparents will be less informed than parents. Further, appellees argue, those who are assessed for local property taxes (either directly or indirectly through rent) will have enough of an interest "through the burden on their pocketbooks, to acquire such information as they may need.". . .

Whether classifications allegedly limiting the franchise to those resident citizens "primarily interested" deny those excluded equal protection of the laws depends, inter alia, on whether all those excluded are in fact substantially less interested or affected than those the statute includes. In other words, the classifications must be tailored so that the exclusion of appellant and members of his class is necessary to achieve the articulated state goal.[2] Section 2012 does not meet the exacting standard of precision we require of statutes which selectively distribute the franchise. The classifications in §2012 permit inclusion of many persons who have, at best, a remote and indirect interest in school affairs and, on the other hand, exclude others who have a distinct and direct interest in the school meeting decisions.[3]

Nor do appellees offer any justification for the exclusion of seemingly interested and informed residents—other than to argue that the §2012 classifications include those "whom the State could understandably deem to be the most intimately interested in actions taken by the school board.". . . The requirements of §2012 are not sufficiently tailored to limiting the franchise to those "primarily interested" in

---

[2] Of course, if the exclusions are necessary to promote the articulated state interest, we must then determine whether the interest promoted by limiting the franchise constitutes a compelling state interest. We do not reach that issue in this case.

[3] For example, appellant resides with his parents in the school district, pays state and federal taxes and is interested in and affected by school board decisions; however, he has no vote. On the other hand, an uninterested unemployed young man pays no state or federal taxes, but who rents an apartment in the district, can participate in the election.

school affairs to justify the denial of the franchise to appellant and members of his class. . . .

Stewart, J., joined by Black and Harlan, JJ., dissenting. . . . [T]he appellant explicitly concedes, as he must, the validity of voting requirements relating to residence, literacy, and age. Yet he argues—and the Court accepts the argument—that the voting qualifications involved here somehow have a different constitutional status. I am unable to see the distinction.

Clearly a State may reasonably assume that its residents have a greater stake in the outcome of elections held within its boundaries than do other persons. Likewise, it is entirely rational for a state legislature to suppose that residents, being generally better informed regarding state affairs than are nonresidents, will be more likely than nonresidents to vote responsibly. And the same may be said of legislative assumptions regarding the electoral competence of adults and literate persons on the one hand, and of minors and illiterates on the other. It is clear, of course, that lines thus drawn cannot infallibly perform their intended legislative function. Just as "[i]lliterate people may be intelligent voters," nonresidents or minors might also in some instances by interested, informed, and intelligent participants in the electoral process. Persons who commute across a state line to work may well have a great stake in the affairs of the State in which they are employed; some college students under 21 may be both better informed and more passionately interested in political affairs than many adults. But such discrepancies are the inevitable concomitant of the line drawing that is essential to law making. So long as the classification is rationally related to a permissible legislative end, therefore—as are residence, literacy, and age requirements imposed with respect to voting—there is no denial of equal protection.

Thus judged, the statutory classification involved here seems to me clearly to be valid. New York has made the judgment that local educational policy is best left to those persons who have certain direct and definable interests in that policy: those who are either immediately involved as parents of school children or who, as owners or lessees of taxable property, are burdened with the local cost of funding school district operations. True, persons outside those classes may be genuinely interested in the conduct of a school district's business—just as commuters from New Jersey may be genuinely interested in the outcome of a New York City election. But . . . I see no way to justify the conclusion that the legislative classification involved here is not rationally related to a legitimate legislative purpose.

With good reason, the Court does not really argue the contrary. Instead, it strikes down New York's statute by asserting that the traditional equal protection standard is inapt in this case, and that a considerably stricter standard—under which classifications relating to "the franchise" are to be subjected to "exacting judicial scrutiny"— should be applied. But the asserted justification for applying such a standard cannot withstand analysis. . . .

The voting qualifications at issue have been promulgated, not by Union Free School District No. 15, but by the New York State Legislature, and the appellant is of course fully able to participate in the election of representatives in that body. There is simply no claim whatever here that the state government is not "structured so as to represent fairly all the people," including the appellant. . . . The appellant is eligible to vote in all state, local and federal elections in which general governmental policy is determined. He is fully able, therefore, to participate not only in the processes by which the requirements for school district voting may be changed, but also in those by which the levels of state and federal financial assistance to the District are determined. He clearly is not locked into any self-perpetuating status of exclusion from the electoral process.

. . . The appellant's status is merely that of a citizen who says he is interested in the affairs of his local public schools. If the Constitution requires that he must be given a decision-making role in the governance of those affairs, then it seems to me that any individual who seeks such a role must be given it. For as I have suggested, there is no persuasive reason for distinguishing constitutionally between the voter qualifications New York has required for its Union Free School District elections and qualifications based on factors such as age, residence, or literacy.

Buckley v. Valeo:
Campaign Financing

This case involves constitutional challenges to the Federal Election Campaign Act of 1971. That act limited the contributions individuals could make on behalf of specific candidates and the campaign expenditures of candidates for certain federal offices. It also established a system of public funding of Presidential campaigns and a reporting procedure for expenditures and contributions above specified levels. Though it upheld the individual contribution limits along with the public financing and reporting provisions, the court overturned the Act's limitations on candidate's campaign expenditures.

Per Curiam. These appeals present constitutional challenges to the key provisions of the Federal Election Campaign Act of 1971 (Act), and related provisions of the Internal Revenue Code of 1954, all as amended in 1974. . . .

[The] statutes at issue [contain] the following provisions: (a) individual political contributions [and expenditures] "relative to a clearly identified candidate" are limited, [and] campaign spending by candidates for various federal offices [are] subject to prescribed limits; (b) contributions and expenditures above certain threshold levels must be reported and publicly disclosed; (c) a system for public funding of Presidential campaign activities is established; [and] (d) a Federal Election Commission is established to administer and enforce the legislation. . . .

CONTRIBUTION AND EXPENDITURE LIMITATIONS

The intricate statutory scheme adopted by Congress to regulate federal election cam-

424 U.S. 1 (1976)

paigns includes restrictions on political contributions and expenditures that apply broadly to all phases of and all participants in the election process. The major contribution and expenditure limitations in the Act prohibit individuals from contributing more than $25,000 in a single year or more than $1,000 to any single candidate for an election campaign and from spending more than $1,000 a year "relative to a clearly identified candidate." Other provisions restrict a candidate's use of personal and family resources in his campaign and limit the overall amount that can be spent by a candidate in campaigning for federal office. . . .

General Principles

The Act's contribution and expenditure limitations operate in an area of the most fundamental First Amendment activities. Discussion of public issues and debate on the qualifications of candidates are integral to the operation of the system of government established by our Constitution. . . .

The interests served by the Act include

restricting the voices of people and interest groups who have money to spend and reducing the overall scope of federal election campaigns. Although the Act does not focus on the ideas expressed by persons or groups subject to its regulations, it is aimed in part at equalizing the relative ability of all voters to affect electoral outcomes by placing a ceiling on expenditures for political expression by citizens and groups. . . .

Nor can the Act's contribution and expenditure limitations be sustained, as some of the parties suggest, by reference to the constitutional principles reflected in . . . [earlier cases that] involved place or manner restrictions on legitimate modes of expression—picketing, parading, demonstrating, and using a soundtruck. The *critical difference* between this case and those time, place, and manner cases is that *the present Act's contribution and expenditure limitations impose direct quantity restrictions on political communication and association by persons, groups, candidates, and political parties* in addition to any reasonable time, place, and manner regulations otherwise imposed.[1]

A restriction on the amount of money a person or group can spend on political communication during a campaign necessarily reduces the quantity of expression by restricting the number of issues discussed, the depth of their exploration, and the size of the audience reached.[2] This is because virtually every means of communicating ideas in today's mass society requires the expenditure of money. . . .

The expenditure limitations contained in the Act represent substantial rather than merely theoretical restraints on the quantity and diversity of political speech. . . .

By contrast with a limitation upon expenditures for political expression, a limitation upon the amount that any one person or group may contribute to a candidate or political committee entails only a marginal restriction upon the contributor's ability to engage in free communication, [for] it permits the symbolic expression of support evidenced by a contribution but does not in any way infringe the contributor's freedom to discuss candidates and issues. . . .

Given the important role of contributions in financing political campaigns, contribution restrictions could have a severe impact on political dialogue if the limitations prevented candidates and political committees from amassing the resources necessary for effective advocacy. There is no indication, however, that the contribution limitations imposed by the Act would have any dramatic adverse effect on the funding of campaigns and political associations.[3] The overall effect of the Act's contribution ceilings is merely to require candidates and political committees to raise funds from a greater number of persons and to compel people who would otherwise contribute amounts greater than the statutory limits to expend such funds on direct political expression, rather than to reduce the total amount of money potentially available to promote political expression. . . .

In sum, although the Act's contribution and expenditure limitations both implicate fundamental First Amendment interests, its expenditure ceilings impose significantly more severe restrictions on protected freedoms of political expression and association

---

[1] The nongovernmental appellees argue that just as the decibels emitted by a sound track can be regulated consistently with the First Amendment, [*Kovacs*], the Act may restrict the volume of dollars in political campaigns without impermissibly restricting freedom of speech. [This] comparison underscores a fundamental misconception. The decibel restriction upheld in *Kovacs* limited the *manner* of operating a soundtrack, but not the *extent* of its proper use. By contrast, the Act's dollar ceilings restrict the extent of the reasonable use of virtually every means of communicating information. . . .

[2] Being free to engage in unlimited political expression subject to a ceiling on expenditures is like being free to drive an automobile as far and as often as one desires on a single tank of gasoline.

[3] Statistical findings agreed to by the parties reveal that approximately 5.1% of the $73,483,613 raised by the 1,161 candidates for Congress in 1974 was obtained in amounts in excess of $1,000. . . .

than do its limitations on financial contributions.

. . . It is unnecessary to look beyond the Act's primary purpose—to limit the actuality and appearance of corruption resulting from large individual financial contributions—in order to find a constitutionally sufficient justification for the $1,000 contribution limitation. [The] increasing importance of the communications media and sophisticated mass-mailing and polling operations to effective campaigning make the raising of large sums of money an ever more essential ingredient of an effective candidacy. To the extent that large contributions are given to secure a political quid pro quo from current and potential office holders, the integrity of our system of representative democracy is undermined. . . .

Of almost equal concern [is] the appearance of corruption stemming from [the] opportunities for abuse inherent in a regime of large individual financial contributions. [Congress] could legitimately conclude that the avoidance of the appearance of improper influence [is] "critical [if] confidence in the system of representative Government is not to be [eroded].". . .

Appellants contend that the contribution limitations must be invalidated because bribery laws and narrowly drawn disclosure requirements constitute a less restrictive means of dealing with "proven and suspected quid pro quo arrangements." But laws making criminal the giving and taking of bribes deal with only the most blatant and specific attempts of those with money to influence governmental action. And while disclosure requirements serve [many salutary purposes] Congress was surely entitled to conclude that disclosure was only a partial measure, and that contribution ceilings were a necessary legislative concomitant to deal with the reality or appearance of corruption. . . .

We find that, under the rigorous standard of review established by our prior decisions, the weighty interests served by restricting the size of financial contributions to political candidates are sufficient to justify the limited effect upon First Amendment freedoms caused by the $1,000 contribution ceiling.

[Appellants argue further, however,] that the contribution limitations work [an] invidious discrimination between incumbents and [challengers].[4] [But] there is [no] evidence [that] contribution limitations [discriminate] against major-party challengers to incumbents, [and although] the charge of discrimination against minor-party and independent candidates is more troubling, [the] record provides no basis for concluding that the Act invidiously disadvantages such candidates. [Indeed, in some circumstances] the restriction would appear to benefit minor-party and independent candidates relative to their major-party opponents because major-party candidates receive far more money in large contributions. . . .

In view of these considerations, we conclude that the impact of the Act's $1,000 contribution limitation on major-party challengers and on minor-party candidates does not render the provision unconstitutional on its face.

[For similar reasons, the Court also upheld the $5,000 limit on contributions by "political committees," the limits on volun-

---

[4] In this discussion, we address only the argument that the contribution limitations alone impermissibly discriminate against nonincumbents. We do not address the more serious argument that these limitations, in combination with the limitation on expenditures [invidiously] discriminate against major-party challengers and minor-party candidates.

Since an incumbent is subject to these limitations to the same degree as his opponent, the Act, on its face, appears to be evenhanded. The appearance of fairness, however, may not reflect political reality. Although some incumbents are defeated in every congressional election, it is axiomatic that an incumbent usually begins the race with significant advantages. [In some circumstances] the overall effect of the contribution and expenditure limitations enacted by Congress could foreclose any fair opportunity of a successful challenge.

However, since we decide, infra, that the ceilings on [expenditures] are unconstitutional under the First Amendment, we need not express any opinion with regard to the alleged invidious discrimination resulting from the full sweep of the legislation as enacted.

teers' incidental expenses, and the $25,000 limit on total political contributions by an individual during a single calendar year.]

Expenditure Limitations

The Act's expenditure ceilings impose direct and substantial restraints [on] the quantity of campaign speech by individuals, groups, and candidates. The restrictions, while neutral as to the ideas expressed, limit political expression "at the core of our electoral process and of the First Amendment freedoms." . . .

We find that the governmental interest in preventing corruption and the appearance of corruption is inadequate to justify §608(e)(1)'s ceiling on independent expenditures. §608(e)(1) prevents only some large expenditures. So long as persons and groups eschew expenditures that in express terms advocate the election or defeat of a clearly identified candidate, they are free to spend as much as they want to promote the candidate and his views. The exacting interpretation of the statutory language necessary to avoid unconstitutional vagueness thus undermines the limitation's effectiveness . . .

It is argued [that] governmental interest in equalizing the relative ability of individuals [to] influence the outcome of elections [justifies the] expenditure ceiling. But the concept that government may restrict the speech of some [in] order to enhance the relative voice of others is wholly foreign to the First Amendment, which was designed "to secure 'the widest possible dissemination of information from diverse and antagonistic sources.' " [The] First Amendment's protection against governmental abridgment of free expression cannot properly be made to depend on a person's financial ability to engage in public discussion. [Section] 608(e)(1)'s [expenditure] limitation is unconstitutional under the First Amendment. . . .

The Act also [limits] expenditures by a candidate "from his personal funds, or the personal funds of his immediate family, in connection with his campaigns during any calendar year." . . .

The ceiling on personal expenditures by candidates on their own [behalf] imposes a substantial restraint on the ability of persons to engage in protected First Amendment expression. The candidate, no less than any other person, has a First Amendment right to engage in the discussion of public issues and [to] advocate his own election. . . .

The [interest] in equalizing the relative financial resources of candidates competing for elective office is clearly not sufficient to justify the provision's infringement of fundamental First Amendment rights . . .

Section 608(c) places limitations on overall campaign expenditures by candidates seeking nomination for election and election to federal office.

No governmental interest that has been suggested is sufficient to justify the restriction on the quantity of political expression imposed by §608(c)'s campaign expenditure limitations. [The] interest in alleviating the corrupting influence of large contributions is served by the Act's contribution limitations and disclosure provisions, [and the] interest in equalizing the financial resources of candidates [is not a] convincing justification for restricting the scope of federal election campaigns. [The] campaign expenditure ceilings appear to be designed primarily to [reduce] the allegedly skyrocketing costs of political campaigns. [But the] First amendment denies government the power to determine that spending to promote one's political views is wasteful, excessive, or unwise. In the free society ordained by our Constitution it is not the government, but the people—individually as citizens and candidates and collectively as associations and political committees—who must retain control over the quantity and range of debate on public issues in a political campaign.

For these reasons we hold that §608(c) is constitutionally invalid.

Mr. Justice White, concurring in part and dissenting in part. . . . I dissent [from] the

Court's view that the expenditure limitations [violate] the First Amendment. . . .

The congressional judgment [was that expenditure limitations are necessary] to counter the corrosive effects of money in federal election campaigns. [The] Court strikes down [§608(e)], strangely enough claiming more [knowledge] as to what may improperly influence candidates that is possessed by the majority of Congress that passed this bill and the President who signed it. [I] would take the word of those who know—that limiting independent expenditures is essential to prevent transparent and widespread evasion of the contribution limits. . . .

The Court also rejects Congress' judgment manifested in §608(c) that the federal interest in limiting total campaign expenditures by individual candidates justifies the incidental effect on their opportunity for effective political speech. I disagree. . . .

[The] argument that money is speech and that limiting the flow of money to the speaker violates the First Amendment proves entirely too much. Compulsory bargaining [has] increased the labor costs of those who publish newspapers, [and] taxation directly removes from company coffers large amounts of money that might be spent on larger and better newspapers. [But] it has not been suggested [that] these laws, and many others, are invalid because they siphon [off] large sums that would otherwise be available for communicative activities.

[The] judgment of Congress was that reasonably effective campaigns could be conducted within the limits established by the Act. [There] is no sound basis for invalidating the expenditure limitations, so long as the purposes they serve are legitimate and sufficiently substantial, which in my view they are.

[Expenditure] ceilings reinforce the contribution limits and help eradicate the hazard of corruption. [Without] limits on total expenditures, campaign costs will [inevitably] escalate, [creating an incentive to accept unlawful contributions. Moreover,] the cor-

rupt use of money by candidates is as much to be feared as the corrosive influence of large contributions. There are many illegal ways of spending money to influence elections. [The] expenditure limits could play a substantial role in preventing unethical practices. There just would not be enough of "that kind of money" to go around. . . .

It is also important to [restore] public confidence in federal elections. It is critical to obviate [the] impression that federal elections are purely and simply a function of money. [The] ceiling on candidate expenditures represents the considered judgment of Congress that elections are to be decided among candidates none of whom has overpowering advantage by reason of a huge campaign war chest. [This] seems an acceptable purpose and the means chosen a common sense way to achieve it. . . .

I also disagree with the Court's judgment that §608(a), which limits the amount of money that a candidate or his family may spend on his campaign, violates the Constitution. [By] limiting the importance of personal wealth, §608(a) helps to assure that only individuals with a modicum of support from others will be viable candidates. [This] would tend to discourage any notion that the outcome of elections is primarily a function of money. Similarly, §608(a) tends to equalize access to the political arena, encouraging the less wealthy [to] run for political office. [Congress] was entitled to determine that personal wealth ought to play a less important role in political campaigns that it has in the past. Nothing in the First Amendment stands in the way of that determination. . . .

Mr. Justice Marshall, concurring in part and dissenting in part. [The Court invalidates §608(a), [which limits the amount a candidate may spend from personal or family funds], as violative of the candidate's First Amendment Rights. [I] disagree.

[The] perception that personal wealth wins elections may not only discourage potential candidates without significant personal wealth from entering the political arena, but also undermine public confidence in the integrity of the electoral process.[5]

The concern that candidacy for public office not become, or appear to become, the exclusive province of the wealthy assumes heightened significance when one considers the impact of §608(b), which the Court today upholds. That provision prohibits contributions from individuals and groups to candidates in excess of $1,000, and contributions from political committees in excess of $5,000. While the limitations on contributions are neutral there can be no question that large contributions generally mean more to the candidate without a substantial personal fortune to spend on his campaign. Large contributions are the less wealthy candidate's only hope of countering the wealthy candidate's immediate access to substantial sums of money. [Section §608(a) thus provides] some symmetry to a regulatory scheme that otherwise enhances the natural advantage of the wealthy. . . .

---

[5] "In the Nation's seven largest States in 1970, 11 of the 15 major senatorial candidates were millionaires. The four who were not millionaires lost their bid for election." . . .

PART III   The Nature and Value of Rights

Legal Rights And Human Rights

Joel Feinberg

Legal rights in the narrow sense are what Feinberg calls "claim-rights." They differ from privileges and other legal benefits because they provide the grounds of other people's duties toward the right-holder, and Feinberg argues that a world without claim-rights, no matter how full of benevolence and devotion to duty, would be morally impoverished. After discussing the problems posed by conflicting legal claims and rights, Feinberg addresses the question of whether institutional rights, especially those guaranteed by the First Amendment, are "absolute." He then turns from legal and institutional rights, which are typically conferred by specific rules, to moral rights and human rights. Human rights, in particular, are fundamentally important rights held by all human beings, unconditionally and unalterably. After arguing that it is important to separate the question of whether there are such rights from the question of whether they are absolute, Feinberg critically examines the 1948 U.N. Declaration of Human Rights. That Declaration is important for going beyond eighteenth-century manifestos of natural rights by endorsing not only the rights of an individual not to be interfered with by others, but also numerous positive rights to receive benefits and be provided with the means to satisfy basic human needs.

Joel Feinberg is Professor of Philosophy at the University of Arizona. He has written extensively in social, political, and legal philosophy. His most recent book, *Harmless Wrongdoing* (1988), is the fourth and final volume of his treatise, *The Moral Limits of the Criminal Law*, published by Oxford University Press.

RIGHTS, LIBERTIES, AND PRIVILEGES

Legal writers commonly distinguish "rights in a strict and narrow sense," usually called *claim-rights,* from "mere liberties," often called *privileges* and sometimes *licenses.* A lib-

erty or privilege in this sense is simply the absence of a duty. To say that Doe is privileged or at liberty to do X is to say that Doe has no duty to refrain from doing X. Normally all citizens are under an obligation to refrain from striking other persons. The criminal law, in forbidding assaults, imposes such a duty on everyone. If Roe nevertheless assaults Doe, then Doe has the legal privilege of striking back in self-defense; he

Reprinted from Joel Feinberg, *Social Philosophy* (Englewood Cliffs, N.J.: Prentice-Hall, 1973).

is free of his usual duty of forbearance. Similarly, if Doe is sworn in as a witness, he acquires the liberty of saying words about other persons that it was "previously his legal duty not to say." Sometimes the law leaves two or more persons in a competitive situation in which each person is privileged to do something at the expense of the other. If Doe and Roe each see a fifty dollar bill on the sidewalk, neither has a duty to let the other have it. Rather, both are privileged to get it if they can, though neither is at liberty to use force or violence in the process. . . .

There is finally a sense of "privilege" which refers to a kind of legal benefit which is less secure than a right and is often described as a "mere privilege." A driver's license gives a person a right to drive an automobile in the sense that it imposes a duty of noninterference on others that is enforced by the state. This valuable benefit differs from some other rights in that one must make application for it. One must assume the burden of demonstrating to state officials that one is worthy of it; it is granted at the discretion of the state, and is very easily forfeitable. The state, in short, is under no duty to confer the benefit on me. It is nothing I can demand as my due. Rather the state grants or withholds it at its pleasure, and since I have no choice but to take it on the state's own terms, it is a *mere* privilege. A privilege in this sense may be either a liberty (privilege in the earlier sense) or a claim-right in the sense to be explained below. What distinguishes a privilege in this sense is its lack of guarantee. It is the basis of no correlative state duty, and can be withheld or withdrawn by the state at its pleasure.

Rights in the strict sense stand in sharp contrast to both liberties and (especially) "mere revocable privileges." Legal claim-rights are necessarily the grounds of other people's duties toward the right-holder. A legal right is a claim to performance, either action or forbearance as the case may be, usually against other private persons. It is also a claim against the state to recognition and enforcement.

What have come to be standard examples of claim-rights were given by Corben.[1] *B* owes *A* one hundred dollars. That is, *B* has a duty to pay *A* that amount, and that duty seen from *A*'s perspective is *A*'s right to receive one hundred dollars. *B* contracts to deliver goods to *A*, hence *A* has a right to receive those goods from *B*, and that right is simply *B*'s contractual duty seen from *A*'s vantage point. *A* has a right that *B* shall not strike him, and that right (unlike a mere liberty) entails a corresponding duty of *B*'s not to strike *A*.

One can have a liberty which is not also a right, but one cannot have a right which is not also a liberty, for rights can be understood to contain liberties as components. If I have a right to do *X*, then I cannot also have a duty to refrain from doing *X*. But to say that I lack a duty to refrain is to say that I have a liberty or privilege to do. Hence, if I have a right to do *X*, I must also be at liberty to do *X*. What the right adds to the liberty is the duty of others not to interfere.

Legal claim-rights are indispensably valuable possessions. A world without claim-rights, no matter how full of benevolence and devotion to duty, would suffer an immense moral impoverishment. Persons would no longer hope for decent treatment from others on the ground of desert or rightful claim. Indeed, they would come to think of themselves as having no special claim to kindness or consideration from others, so that whenever even minimally decent treatment is forthcoming they would think themselves lucky rather than inherently deserving, and their benefactors extraordinarily virtuous and worthy of great gratitude. The harm to individual self-esteem and character development would be incalculable.[2]

A claim-right, on the other hand, can be urged, pressed, or rightly demanded against

---

[1] Corbin, "Legal Analysis and Terminology," pp. 164–66.

[2] The effects of this kind of treatment on Southern Negroes is vividly described by Richard Wasserstrom, "Rights, Human Rights and Racial Discrimination," *Journal of Philosophy*, LXI (1964), 628–41.

other persons. In appropriate circumstances the right-holder can "urgently, peremptorily, or insistently"[3] call for his rights, or assert them authoritatively, confidently, unabashedly. Rights are not mere gifts or favors, motivated by love or pity, for which gratitude is the sole fitting response. A right is something a man can *stand* on, something that can be demanded or insisted upon without embarrassment or shame. When that to which one has a right is not forthcoming, the appropriate reaction is indignation; when it is duly given there is no reason for gratitude, since it is simply one's own or one's due that one received. A world with claim-rights is one in which all persons, as actual or potential claimants, are dignified objects of respect, both in their own eyes and in the view of others. No amount of love and compassion, or obedience to higher authority, or noblesse oblige, can substitute for those values. . . .

CONFLICTS OF CLAIMS

There is no reason why a legal claim possessed by one citizen cannot conflict with a legal claim possessed by another. Having a claim, as we have seen, is something like "having a point," or "having a case," or even "having a complaint." It consists in having relevant reasons of some weight that put one in a position to *make* claim to something. These reasons, were they to be put forward, would tend to support a claim and lend it credence and cogency, even if, in the end, they should fail to *establish* the claim and compel its recognition. Having a case is better than having no case at all, but it can be somewhat less than having a decisive or conclusive case. Claims, then, can differ in degree; some are stronger than others. When Doe and Roe both have claims to X which are such that not both can be granted or

recognized, then their claims can be said to be in conflict. A judge may decide that while both competing claims are plausible enough to deserve a hearing, neither is strong enough to be recognized or declared valid, or he may decide that only one is valid. In either event, the conflict of claims remains but does not grow into anything stronger. The law remains consistent and gives no sanction to socially disruptive combat. It would be otherwise, however, if the court were to declare that *both* conflicting claims were *valid*. . . .

Apparent conflicts between specific valid claims are more serious matters. When both Abel and Baker have a valid claim to exclusive possession of the same object at the same time, their claims cannot be *rights*, for they entail no correlative duties in the other to forbear. Conflict automatically reduces the claims to *liberties*. Each may do his best to exclude the other, and the state will not intervene. When both are prepared to fight, however, the result will be that kind of violent struggle between equally right and equally self-righteous gladiators that no civil society can long tolerate. Conflict between equally valid competencies will have the same unhappy result whenever the right-holders choose to exercise their discretion in the same way.

A legal system cannot very well countenance conflicting specific rights. Normally courts avoid such conflict by redefining the boundaries of the conflicting claims, either by writing express exceptive clauses into the claims to make them mutually consistent, or (more commonly) by "finding" such clauses implicit in the rules that conferred the rights on the contending parties. By virtue of such processes, rights become more complex. The full statement of any legal right, no matter how simple its name or brief its description, will often include numerous exceptive clauses, many of which are themselves qualified by further exceptive clauses, and so on. It may even be that no legal right has its boundaries fixed and stable for all time, that new and unanticipated conflicts with other rights may at any time require

---

[3] G. J. Warnock, "Claims to Knowledge," *Proceedings of the Aristotelian Society*, Supplementary volume 36 (1962), p. 21.

sharper specification of boundary lines via the method of appended exceptive clauses.

Imagine a simple legal system at an early and immature stage that contains a rule granting everybody the right to move his arms through space in whatever direction and velocity he pleases, and also a rule granting everyone the right not to be punched in the nose. Nip then punches Tuck in the nose and claims in court that he was well within his rights, while Tuck claims with equally righteous conviction that his right was violated. If the relevant statutes contain no exceptive clauses and there are no relevant precedents, the court will have to make a decision about how these inconsistent statutes are to be interpreted. The court may turn to records of the deliberations of the legislature that passed the statutes in an effort to divine the original intentions of the lawmakers, or it may unabashedly "make law," that is, further refine and specify existing law on its own. In either case, it is likely to have recourse to the same sort of interest-balancing procedures that often guide the deliberations of legislators. It will find that the defendant was promoting a private interest in the free and vigorous motion of his limbs, but that his victim's private interest in freedom from facial pain and injury was more important to him than the competing interest was to the defendant. Evidence may be adduced to show that most or even all people who have both interests weigh the facial interest more heavily than the limb interest. Moreover, the court may discover a public interest in protecting faces (preventing medical expenses, vendettas, lost man hours) that is heavier than a public interest in promoting vigorous arm motion. Consequently, it may restrict the free motion right by an appropriate exceptive clause protecting faces, and its new rule will be binding on subsequent courts. In such a way, the boundaries between rights, while always in some degree of flux, become relatively fixed and stable; away from the boundaries, within each right's "central core," there will be more and more security.

PRIMA-FACIE RIGHTS

There is no way of drawing the boundaries of all individual legal rights so tightly that we can dispense with the need for judgment when conflicts threaten. Accommodation must often be worked out after the fact of conflict rather than prevented in advance by rules and decrees. This has led some theorists to proclaim that all legal discretionary rights are, in the very nature of the case, *provisional*. On this view, it is tacitly understood that recognition of a right can always be withdrawn or qualified when necessary to permit satisfaction of a conflicting claim. There are no "absolute" rights which always have the right of way when collisions threaten. Put another way, "the right to X" is always to be understood as "the right to X *unless* some stronger claims shows up," the "unless clause" being tacitly understood. According to this theory, since there is no foolproof way of knowing when a stronger claim will turn up, reliance upon our rights should always be tempered with skepticism; a right is no ironclad guarantee. Possession of a discretionary right creates only a *presumption* in a given case at a given time that one also has a specific right normally derivable from it.

Many writers call a merely presumptive right a "prima-facie right," and oppose it, in meaning, to the "absolute " right that a person can possess unconditionally. The right that people have to exchange ideas freely, according to Richard Brandt, is a prima-facie right. The ascription of that right is properly translated thus: "People have a right (in the strong [absolute] sense) to exchange ideas freely if and whenever no conflicting more urgent moral considerations stand in the way."[1] When more urgent conflicting considerations are not present, the prima-facie right becomes an absolute right, that is, the presumption of an absolute right becomes conclusive. However, the presumption is subject to immediate weakening

---

[1] Richard B. Brandt, *Ethical Theory* (Englewood Cliffs, N.J.: Prentice-Hall, Inc., 1959), p. 437.

the moment circumstances change, so that absolute rights lapse back into prima-facie ones, and formerly conclusive presumptions are overturned. What cannot be overturned, on this view, is possession of the prima-facie right as such. One continues to have *a* claim, no matter what happens; no one can take *that* away. The validity of the claim, however, comes and goes with the changing circumstances.

Upon consideration, the theory that all legal rights are prima facie in the sense explained seems highly paradoxical. The basis of the distinction between "having a claim" and "having a valid claim" is that mere claims differ in strength and hence are subject to defeat by rival claims, whereas validity is not a property that can vary in degree. In respect to their validity, all genuine rights are equal. But if *all* valid claims are merely presumptive, their validity does not distinguish them in kind from those "mere claims" that are understood to have a merely presumptive character, and a useful distinction is undermined. Similarly, the basis of the distinction between rights and "mere privileges" is thrown in doubt if all rights are, like revocable privileges, subject to the withdrawal at any time of legal recognition. Yet, for all these misgivings based on the utility of ordinary distinctions, there remains the fact upon which the theory of prima-facie rights is based, namely, the apparent impossibility in a world full of conflict of treating any right as an unconditional guarantee.

Perhaps the way out of this dilemma, at least in respect to legal rights, is to take seriously the distinction between recognition and enforcement. The state's promise of enforcement to any given rightholder cannot be totally unconditional, but perhaps its recognition of the validity of rightholders' claims *can* be totally unconditional (or at least much closer to being so than the promise of enforcement). Unconditional recognition does have some value, after all, even if it does not prevent infringement in every conceivable circumstance, for it certifies a feature that we all take to be essential

to rights, whether in conflict or not—that they are not something that one has only at specific moments, only to lose, regain, and lose again as circumstances shift. Rights are themselves *property*, things we own, and from which we may not even temporarily be dispossessed. Perhaps in some circumstances rights may be rightfully infringed, but that is quite different from their being taken away and then returned.

A less paradoxical alternative to the theory of prima-facie rights is the view that a person can maintain a right to X even when he is not morally justified in its exercise, or others are justified in not according it to him. Lack of moral justification for exercising a right does not entail (even temporary) nonpossession. Moreover, it is possible to have a duty but, because of conflicting duties and other moral considerations, also to have a moral justification for not acting in accordance with it. There is no contradiction in saying of a person that he *ought* not to perform one of his duties. The right correlated with that duty remains a right, even when honored in the breech.

It may seem paradoxical to say that it can sometimes be right not to give a man his due (what he deserves or has a right to), for that is to say that it can be right to treat a man unjustly. But that, in fact, is precisely the final moral of the rejection of the theory of prima-facie rights. The realm of justice is not the whole of morality, and even within its spacious domain, certified injustice is unavoidable. This is an unpleasant fact of life that every moralist must accommodate. To deny that a rightly violated right could have been a real right at all is to deny this fact of life, and to do so in a way that can only encourage injustice, whether necessary or not, and discourage the spirit of reluctance, apology, and respect that should attend even justified or necessary injustice. I cannot forbear, in conclusion, quoting at length from Herbert Morris, who puts this point eloquently:

It may be justifiable not to accord a man his rights; it may be right not to; it may be justifiable infringing his rights. But it is no less a wrong to *him*, no less an infringement. It is seriously misleading to turn all justifiable infringements into non-infringements by saying that the right is only *prima-facie*, as if we have in concluding that we should not accord a man his rights, made out a case that he had none. To use the language of *prima-facie* rights misleads, for it suggests that a presumption of the existence of a right has been overcome in these cases where all that can be said is that the presumption in favor of according a man his rights has been overcome.[5]

Still, the point of the prima-facie right theorists may tell when put in another way. When they speak about prima-facie rights they talk in a manner appropriate to *ideal directives*, not to specific and discretionary rights; mere presumptiveness is not unbecoming in a guiding ideal, though it be fatal to the very existence of an established right.

TRANSCATEGORIAL CONFLICTS

How can conflicts between legal rights, which are intolerable in any legal system aspiring to consistency, be obviated, or, failing that, be resolved? In some cases, relatively clear rules can be formulated for determining the right of way in anticipation of right-collisions. More typically, however, our question calls for the formulation of *policy* for dealing with conflicts in the absence of precise rules. When there are applicable rules for determining the right of way in a given case, the colliding interests cannot both be treated as rights. If the rule states that all cars may proceed carefully through intersections but that red cars always have precedence over blue ones, then the driver of a blue car has a general right to proceed through intersections *unless* a red car is doing the same, and *that* right (so qualified) is not in conflict with the right of the red car driver. (Subordination is not a form of conflict!) The blue car driver simply has no

right against the red car driver in the first place. Many conflict situations, however, are much more complicated than this, and therefore not subject to a priori resolutions via the application of simple right of way rules.

Formulation of policies for dealing with the more complex conflicts necessarily requires assessment of the protected interests involved. The difficulty is that we often cannot say in a general way which interests are the weightiest. It is hard enough balancing types of interests in the abstract, when we speak of "the Interest (with a capital I) in something" as if it were an impersonal entity belonging to no one in particular, but it becomes more difficult still when we must weigh the conflicting interests of particular persons in particular cases without knowing how heavily they sit on the scale. In these cases, we are not out to determine how heavy a given Interest is generally, but how heavy an interest of a given general kind is when it belongs to a particular litigant in a particular case. Insofar as we think that certain kinds of conflict can be obviated by simple "right of way" rules, the formulation of such rules might best be understood as a task for an ideal legislature. When the type of conflict seems to require instead policies for the guidance of interest balancing in particular cases, perhaps the cautious philosopher should think of it as a question for some "ideal court."

Conflicts between personal and property rights are especially controversial examples of transcategorial conflict. It is sometimes said that in a conflict between a property right and a personal (i.e., nonproperty) right, the personal right always has precedence. This generalization, which makes about as much sense as the assertion that red things are always heavier than green things, is usually made by people who have taken category labels far too seriously. It is not difficult to think of circumstances in which a specific personal right belonging to John Doe should be given priority over a specific property right belonging to Richard Roe, but it is equally easy to think of exam-

---

[5] Herbert Morris, "Persons and Punishment," *The Monist* (October 1968), p. 499.

ples where the priority relation is reversed. Doc's ownership of a lot and house confers on him the right to possess, enjoy, use, or dispose of it as he sees fit; but if he sees fit to use it in such a way as to cause a widespread and nauseating stench, nerve-shattering noise, or dangerous pitfalls on the adjacent public streets, his property rights are subject to justifiable delimitation in order to protect what may be more important personal (and property) rights of neighbors and passersby. On the other hand, it is perfectly clear that Mr. and Mrs. Doe have the right to make love to one another. Yet, if they choose to exercise this right in Mr. Roe's flower beds, their neighbor's property rights take precedence.

Can it not be said that rights of the one category are "on the whole" more important than rights of the other? Even this is probably too broad a generalization to sustain, and in any case it is insufficiently precise to have any utility. Suppose we could give every specific property right and every specific personal right a "score" and place it in a ranking order on some common scale of "importance." What could we expect to find? Our examples suggest that specific instances of each type of right would be interspersed throughout with instances of the other kind. It would be very much like ranking human beings of different races, sexes, or classes in respect to scores on an objective test of intelligence, strength, or resistance to disease. Even if one group should have a heavier concentration of scores at the top end of the scale and a sparser concentration at the lower end, making its average score or position higher, we could still expect a large degree of overlap in the distribution. For example, it might even be possible that the poorer group "on the whole" contributed the individual with the single highest score, and the better group "on the whole" contributed the individual with the single lowest score. It would be otherwise if we were comparing all human beings with (say) all chimpanzees. In that case we would expect to find that the poorest human score would still be above the highest chimp score, and

that a substantial gap would separate the two. If the grading of rights came out that way, so that the most trivial personal right was still more important than the most serious property right, or if there were only a tiny amount of overlap rather than general interdispersion, then the results would be of considerable utility, and transcategorial conflicts, with only a few well-known exceptions, could all be resolved in the same way. But nobody's ranking of rights, either his own or others', comes out that simply.

Still, it is possible for like-minded persons to agree that particular narrowly described subclasses of rights in one category are *always* to be treated as more important than certain precisely described subclasses of rights in another category. Legislators, for example, may agree that everyone has a right to do X except when doing X would infringe someone else's right to do Y. This is, in effect, to direct that all conflicts in the future between rights to X and rights to Y are to be resolved uniformly in favor of Y. More precisely, since this is achieved by a new *law*, the rights themselves have been redefined so that they no longer *can* conflict. There no longer is such a thing as a right to do X simply, for it has been replaced by a "right to do X except when it would prevent others from doing Y," and that new right obviously cannot be in conflict with anyone's right to do Y.

Before the passage of the Civil Rights Act of 1965, any American Negro who wished to drive his family from (say) Washington, D.C., to Jackson, Mississippi, ran the risk of severe inconvenience and even danger. Because highway facilities were by local custom segregated, he could not anticipate when it would be necessary to drive miles out of his way to find a "public" rest room, a place to eat, or, more importantly, lodgings for the night. Owners of gas stations, restaurants, and motels had the legal right to solicit, accept, or exclude customers as they saw fit, and most of them saw fit to exercise their property rights by excluding all Negroes. Since passage of the Civil Rights Law, things must be described differently. Southern homeowners still have the right (derived from their ownership) to exclude anyone from their property, but those who are permitted to serve the public by providing food and lodgings in exchange for money must serve *all* the public or none at all. (More exactly, their exclusions cannot be merely arbitrary.) Their former right to exclude anyone at all from their property has now been replaced by the right to exclude anyone *except* those applying for licensed and advertised services (and who are not drunk, disorderly, and so on). Congress decided that a motorist's right not to be excluded on arbitrary grounds from hotels and restaurants along public highways is *always* more important than the innkeeper's right to serve whomever he pleases. Hence the latter right was changed in such a way that it can never conflict with the former.

This sort of legislative carving of an exception out of a previously existing right bears some resemblance to what is often done by private rightholders themselves through contracts and other special legal devices. "Thus the right of a landowner may be subject to, and limited by, that of a tenant to the temporary use of the property; or to the right of a mortgagee to sell or take possession; or to the right of a neighboring landowner to the use of a way or other easement; or to the right of the vendor of land in respect of restrictive covenants entered into by the purchaser as to the use of it; for example, a covenant not to build upon it."[6] The right in these examples that "limits or derogates from some more general right belonging to some other person"[7] is called by lawyers an *encumbrance*, or "right over the property of someone else." An encumbrance upon another person's right may be itself subject to another encumbrance, as when a tenant sublets; in principle there is no reason why the process cannot go on indefinitely. What is important for present

purposes is that an encumbrance on a right is not a conflict between the rights of different parties, but an agreed method for redrawing right-boundaries, at least temporarily, so as to prevent conflict.

Legislatively restricted rights and encumbranced rights, even though they can be described as rights with exceptive clauses, are not the same as so-called "prima-facie" rights, and are not vulnerable to the same objections. A restricted or encumbranced right is a right to do X except in certain definitely and exhaustively described circumstances, whereas a prima-facie right is a right to do X except when there is "some more urgent moral consideration," its nature unspecified and open-ended, that stands in the way.

THE CONCEPT OF AN ABSOLUTE CONSTITUTIONAL RIGHT

A controversy has raged in recent years over whether constitutional rights, especially those guaranteed by the First Amendment, should be interpreted by the courts as "absolute." Many First Amendment cases were decided by the U.S. Supreme Court in the period from 1959–1962 over the eloquent dissents of Justice Hugo Black, the leading spokesman for the "absolutist" position. Justice Black in one case insisted that "the First Amendment means what it says."[8] What the First Amendment *says* is:

Congress shall make no law respecting an establishment of religion, or prohibiting the free exercise thereof; or abridging the freedom of speech, or of the press; or the right of the people peaceably to assemble, and to petition the Government for a redress of grievances.

"I read 'no law . . . abridging,' " said Justice Black, "to mean *no law abridging*,"[9] which

----

[6] John Salmond, *Jurisprudence*, 11th ed., ed. Glanville Williams (London: Sweet & Maxwell Ltd., 1957), p. 294.

[7] Salmond, *Jurisprudence*, p. 294.

[8] Barenblatt v. United States, 360 U.S. 109, 143–44 (1959). Dissenting opinion.

[9] Smith v. California, 361 U.S. 147, 157 (1959). Concurring opinion.

is to say (he makes clear) that the First Amendment prohibition is complete, exceptionless, and unconditional: ". . . the principles of the First Amendment are stated in precise and mandatory terms and unless they are applied in those terms, the freedoms of religion, speech, press, assembly, and petition will have no effective protection."[10]

The opposing position, and the one that actually prevailed in the early 1960's, is most frequently associated with the late Justice Felix Frankfurter. In this view, there are no absolute rights, even in the First Amendment, and when the interest protected by a constitutional right conflicts with a weightier interest in public safety or public order, the courts must permit infringement of the right. In one free speech case, Frankfurter declared that "The demands of free speech in a democratic society as well as the interest in national security are better served by candid and informed weighing of the competing interests, within the confines of the judicial process, than by announcing dogmas too inflexible for the . . . problems to be solved."[11] The alternative to inflexible dogmas is the method of ad hoc "interest-balancing." Even when a judicially recognized constitutional right is on one side of the balance, it might be invaded or even "infringed" when the interest on the other side more than balances it:

We agree that compulsory disclosure of the names of an organization's members may in certain instances infringe constitutionally protected rights of association. . . . But to say this much is only to recognize one of the points of reference from which analysis must begin. . . . Against the impediments which particular governmental regulation causes to entire freedom of individual action, there must be weighed the value to the public of the end which the regulation may achieve.[12]

It is of course beyond the scope of this work to decide whether any American constitutional rights *are* absolute. The philosophically prior question is: How *could* a right be "absolute?" What can it *mean* to say of a right that it is absolute? One source of confusion can be eliminated by a distinction between a right's *scope* and its degree of *incumbency* within that scope. It is plain that such First Amendment rights as free speech cannot be unlimited in scope; no one can expect the courts to guarantee his "right" to say anything, any time, any place. If there were such a right there could be no law of defamation, no protection against fraud, no penalty for solicitation to crime, and, in short, no protection of other rights as vital to private and public interests as free speech itself. Consequently, various implicit exceptive clauses must be understood as part of the rule that spells out the right to free speech. Some of these clauses presumably were understood at the time the First Amendment was adopted, for there was even then a well-developed body of law on defamation, fraud, incitement, and solicitation. Other exceptions have no doubt developed slowly through the piece-meal evolution of the common law and forced judicial clarifications of borderline cases. As a result, the boundaries of the right's domain have become reasonably clear and stable, though there may still be occasional waverings, and controversial marginal cases on both sides of the boundaries may always exist.

First Amendment rights, then, are not "absolute" in the sense of "unlimited in scope": the scope of free speech must necessarily be narrower than the range of all possible speech. But that is no reason why these rights, as qualified by exceptive clauses, cannot be absolute in the sense of laying *unconditionally incumbent* duties of respect and enforcement upon the courts. A rule with exceptive clauses may itself have no exceptions. A First Amendment right, in short, may be limited in extent by the definitions of established judicial rules, yet be unconditionally obligatory within its proper domain. The courts would decide whether a given

---

[10] Wilkinson v. United States, 365 U.S. 399, 422–23 (1961). Dissenting opinion.

[11] Dennis v. United States, 341 U.S. 524–25 (1951).

[12] Communist Party v. Subversive Activities Control Board, 367 U.S. 190–91 (1961).

exercise of free speech, for example, falls *clearly* within the boundaries of First Amendment protection; if it does, then any statute that prohibits it, or any governmental action that restricts it, must be declared unconstitutional. If the speech in question falls in the vague no man's land near the right's wavering boundaries, the court must further clarify the law and fix its boundaries by whatever procedures of constitutional interpretation (perhaps including "interest-balancing") are open to it. But once having pronounced the act in question to be within the area of constitutional protection, on the intelligible "absolutistic" view we are considering, it is no longer open to the court to "weigh" that protection against other considerations, for the constitution says that its guaranteed rights, once correctly determined, always have more weight than any possible combination of opposing interests, private or public.

The "defining of absolutes" method is possible only in a legal system of sufficient maturity to have reasonably settled boundary lines, established after much conflict and redefinition through explicit and implicitly understood exceptive clauses, between the various rights it confers. The method presupposes that each right, no matter how vague its boundaries at the periphery, has a central core of clear and certain cases that are (unless resort is made to constitutional amendment) permanently and unconditionally established. Thus, it is always open to an American citizen, without any question, to express in speech or writing his opinion that a policy of his government is unwise, unjust, or otherwise mistaken, or his opinion as to "what the public welfare requires."[13] It is unconditionally open to an American to receive without interference the sacraments of his church, or to have some time and place to engage in prayer or worship, or simply to be a member of a church. These activities are at the "hard core" of the free exercise of religion right,

well away from the boundaries with other rights, unrestricted by legislated exceptive clauses, and unemcumbranced.

Laurent Frantz has pointed out that some constitutional rights other than those in the First Amendment were universally accepted as absolutely unconditional in their central core cases. If an accused person is to be denied the right to counsel, the Constitution will have to be amended first, for its guarantee is not subject to judicial overruling as a result of "interest-balancing" in a given case. It is simply not open to courts to balance a clearly defined and acknowledged right against *any* interests, even those in public safety and public welfare. If, on the other hand, a court could weigh interests against acknowledged core cases of constitutional rights, case by case, then the results might be contrary to everyone's present understanding:

> Defendants in criminal cases can be tried in secret, or held incommunicado without trial, can be denied knowledge of the accusation against them, and the right to counsel, and the right to call witnesses in their own defense, and the right to trial by jury. Ex post facto laws and bills of attainder can be passed. Habeas corpus can be suspended, though there is neither rebellion nor invasion. Private property can be taken for public use without just, or any, compensation. Suffrage qualifications based on sex or race can be reinstituted. Anything which the Constitution says *cannot* be done *can* be done, if Congress thinks and the Court agrees (or is unwilling to set aside the congressional judgment) that the interests thereby served outweighed those which were sacrificed. Thus the whole idea of a government of limited powers, and of a written constitution as a device for attaining that end, is at least potentially at stake.[14]

Are these hard core rights *never*, under any conceivable circumstances, abridgeable? (They are of course subject to change by constitutional amendment, but that is another matter.) Is an individual to be given his rights even if the whole public safety or

---

[13] Laurent B. Frantz, "The First Amendment in the Balance," *Yale Law Journal*, LXXI (1962), 1438.

[14] Frantz, "The First Amendment in the Balance," 1445.

welfare must be sacrificed in the process, or national independence lost as a consequence? Would it not be better in extreme emergencies, where all that is precious rides on what we do, to deny a given individual his opinion, his sacrament, his trial by jury? *Better,* perhaps, or wiser, or more prudent, or even more justifiable on the whole, but still a desperate emergency measure, like the amputation of a limb. It would be the sacrifice of legality itself, of justice, of an undenied right, for the sake of something held even more important. Perhaps courts *ought* to infringe rights in desperate circumstances, but that can never be their understood legal function. If or when judges take such desperate extralegal steps, their actions are special, ad hoc, and presumably sorrowful infringements or suspensions of rights, not the authoritative redefining of right-boundaries, or the official denial that a right existed in the first place. "One's need for a new car," wrote Frantz, "may be balanced against the other uses to which the same money might be put but not against 'Thou shalt not steal.' "[15] In truly extraordinary circumstances, one might conceivably be justified, in one's own conscience, in stealing another's car, but that justification doesn't affect the shape of the other's property rights. A justified violation of another's legal rights is still a violation of his rights, which one can never have a legal right to do. The point applies even to violations by courts of law.

A guaranteed *right,* "absolute" within its established sphere, adds something of great importance to a liberty, or a "mere privilege," or a "right" that is vulnerable to overturning by interest-balancing procedures. When the government leaves me at liberty (merely) to do X, it tells me in effect that I may do X if I can, but it will not protect me by imposing a duty of noninterference upon others. A liberty is a permission without a protection. A "mere privilege" may or may not add protection to the permission. When

it does, the privilege looks more like a right than like a mere liberty. Unlike rights, however, neither the permission nor the continued protection are assured; either can be withdrawn at any time at the state's pleasure, although the holder of a privilege will be warned in advance that withdrawal is coming. It would be otherwise with a so-called "nonabsolute right." When the government grants me a "right" that is vulnerable to interest-balancing tests even at its core, it tells me, in effect, that I may do X and others may not interfere, *but* that this permission cum protection does not apply whenever the state finds it useful to withdraw it, without prior warning, in a given case. "When you speak quietly at a private gathering," says the state, "you may say anything you please about the wisdom of a government policy *unless* a court later determines that interfering with your right at the time was more conducive to the public interest than protecting it." Such a right begins to resemble a so-called prima-facie right in that its exceptive clause is virtually unspecified and unlimited. It is only a small parody to interpret the prima-facie right as permission to do anything except what one shouldn't, and to interpret the nonabsolute "right" as permission to do anything for which permission is not subsequently withdrawn. These are hardly "rights" that one can stand upon, demand, fight for, or treasure. They are "rights" that make men humble, not claims that make men bold.

MORAL RIGHTS

Legal and institutional rights are typically conferred by specific rules recorded in handbooks of regulations that can be observed and studied by the citizens or members subject to the rules. But not all rights are derived from such clearly visible laws and institutional regulations. On many occasions we assert that someone has a right to something even though we know there are no regulations or laws conferring such a right. Such talk clearly makes sense, so any

---

[15] Frantz, "The First Amendment in the Balance,' 1440.

theory of the nature of rights that cannot account for it is radically defective.

The term "moral rights" can be applied to all rights that are held to exist prior to, or independently of, any legal or institutional rules. Moral rights so conceived form a genus divisible into various species of rights having little in common except that they are not (necessarily) legal or institutional. The following are the main specific senses of "moral right": (1) A *conventional right* is one derived from established customs and expectations, whether or not recognized by law (e.g., an old woman's right to a young man's seat on a subway train). (2) An *ideal right* is not necessarily an actual right of any kind, but is rather what *ought* to be a positive (institutional or conventional) right, and would be so in a better or ideal legal system or conventional code. (3) A *conscientious right* is a claim the recognition of which as valid is called for, not (necessarily) by actual or ideal rules or conventions, but rather by the principles of an enlightened individual conscience. (4) An *exercise right* is not, strictly speaking, a right at all, though it is so-called in popular usage; it is simply moral justification in the exercise of a right of some other kind, the latter right remaining in one's possession and unaffected by considerations bearing on the rightness or wrongness of its exercising. When a person speaks of a moral right, he may be referring to a generically moral right not further specified, or to a right in one of these four specific senses; sometimes the context does not reveal which sense of "moral" is employed, and the possibility of equivocation is always present.

HUMAN RIGHTS

Among the rights that are commonly said to be moral in the generic sense (that is, independent of legal or other institutional recognition) are some also called "human rights." Human rights are sometimes understood to be ideal rights, sometimes conscientious rights, and sometimes both. In any case, they are held to be closely associated with actual claims. If a given human right is an ideal right, then human rightholders do or will have a claim against political legislators to convert (eventually) their "moral right" into a positive legal one. If the human right in question is a conscientious right, then it is an actual claim against private individuals for a certain kind of treatment—a claim that holds *now,* whatever the positive law may say about it.

I shall define "human rights" to be generically moral rights of a fundamentally important kind held equally by all human beings, unconditionally and unalterably. Whether these rights are "moral" in any of the more precise senses, I shall leave an open question to be settled by argument, not definition. Of course, it is also an open question whether there *are* any human rights and, if so, just what those rights are. All of the rights that have been characterized as "natural rights" in the leading manifestoes[16] can also be called human rights, but, as I shall be using the terms, not all human rights are also by definition natural rights. The theory of natural rights asserts not only that there are certain human rights, but also that these rights have certain further epistemic properties and a certain metaphysical status. In respect to questions of moral ontology and moral epistemology, the theory of human rights is neutral. Finally, it should be noticed that our definition includes the phrase "*all* human beings" but does not say "*only* human beings," so that a human right held by animals is not excluded by definition.

In addition to the characteristics mentioned in our definition, human rights have also been said to be "absolute." Sometimes this is simply a redundancy, another way of referring to the properties of universality and inalienability; but sometimes "absoluteness" is meant to refer to an additional characteristic, which in turn is subject to at least three

---

[16] E.g., the American Declaration of Independence (1776), the Virginia Bill of Rights (1775), and the French Declaration of the Rights of Man and of Citizens (1789).

interpretations. Human rights can be absolute, first, only in the sense that all rights are absolute, namely, unconditionally incumbent within the limits of their well-defined scope. Second, a human right might be held to be absolute in the sense that the rights to life, liberty, and the pursuit of happiness, as proclaimed in the Declaration of Independence, are most plausibly interpreted as absolute, namely, as "ideal directives" to relevant parties to "do their best" for the values involved. If the state has seriously considered Doe's right to his land, done its best to find alternative routes for a public road, and compensated Doe as generously as possible before expropriating him by eminent domain, it has faithfully discharged its duty of "due consideration" that is the correlative of his "right to property" conceived simply as an ideal directive. If a human right is absolute only in the sense in which an ideal directive is absolute, then it is satisfied whenever it is given the serious and respectful consideration it always deserves, even when that consideration is followed by a reluctant invasion of its corresponding interest.

The strongest and most interesting sense of "absolute" attributed to rights is that of being "absolutely exceptionless" not only within a limited scope but throughout a scope *itself* unlimited. The right to free speech would be absolute in this sense *if* it protected all speech without exception in all circumstances. In that case, the limits of the right would correspond with the limit of the form of conduct specified, and once these wide boundaries had been defined, no further boundary adjustments, incursions or encumbrances, legislative restrictions, or conditions for emergency suspensions would be permitted. For a human right to have this character it would have to be such that no conflicts with other human rights, either of the same or another type, would be possible.

Some formulations of human rights might be passed off as absolute in the strongest sense merely because they are so vaguely put. Some are formulated in conditional language ("a right to adequate nutrition *if* or *when* food is available") and then held to be absolute qua

conditional. Other rights, put in glittering and general language ("a right to be treated like a human being," "a right to be treated like a person, not a thing") are safely held to be absolute because without detailed specification they yield few clear and uncontroversial injunctions. Others are formulated in language containing "standard-bearing terms" such as "reasonable," "proper," or "worthy," without any clue to the standards to be employed in applying these terms. Thus it is said that all men (like all animals) have a right not to be treated cruelly. So far, so good; there can be no exceptions to that right. But its "absoluteness" can be seen to be merely formal when one considers that cruel treatment is treatment that inflicts *unnecessary, unreasonable,* or *improper* suffering on its victim. The air of self-evidence and security beyond all controversy immediately disappears from this human right when men come to propose and debate precise standards of necessity, reasonableness, and propriety.

We should not despair, however, of finding explicit standards of (say) cruelty that will give human rights content and yet leave them plausible candidates for absoluteness in the strong sense. The right not to be *tortured,* for example, comes close to exhaustive definability in nonstandard-bearing terms, and may be such that it cannot conflict with other rights, including other human rights, and can therefore be treated as categorical and exceptionless. If torture is still too vague a term, we can give exact empirical descriptions of the Chinese Water Torture, the Bamboo Fingernail Torture, and so on, and then claim that everyone has an absolutely exceptionless right in every conceivable circumstance not to be treated in any of those precisely described ways. Does this right pass the test of nonconflict with other rights?

Suppose a foreign tyrant of Caligulan character demands of our government that it seize certain political critics, imprison them, and slowly torture them to death, and threatens that unless that is done, his police will seize the members of our diplomatic staff in his country and torture *them* to death. At first sight this appears to be an authentic case of conflict between human rights, in that it would be impossible to do anything that would have as its consequence the fulfillment of everyone's right not to be tortured. What we should say about this blackmail situation if we wish to maintain that the right not to be tortured is nevertheless absolute (exceptionless and nonconflictable) is as follows. If the political critics in our grasp have a human right never to be tortured, then we have a categorical duty not to torture them. Thus, we ought not and will not torture them. We know, however, that this is likely to lead to the torture of the diplomatic hostages. We should therefore make every effort to dissuade Caligula, perhaps even through military pressure, not to carry out his threat. If Caligula nevertheless tortures his hostages, their rights have been infringed, but by Caligula, *not by us*.

All cases of apparent conflict of rights not to be tortured can be treated in this way. Whenever it is impossible to honor all of them, the situation causing that impossibility is itself voluntary creation of human beings. Nothing in nature itself can ever bring such a conflict into existence. A tyrant's threat is in this respect unlike a plague that renders it impossible for everybody to get enough to eat. It would be idle to claim that the right to enough food is an absolute, categorical right, exceptionless in every conceivable circumstance, because we cannot legislate over nature. But we can legislate for man (the argument continues), and this is a plausible way to do it: *No acts of torture anywhere at any time are ever to be permitted.* All human beings can thus be possessed of a right that is absolutely exceptionless. That we have no guarantee that some people somewhere won't violate it or try to force us to violate it is no argument against the "legislation" itself.

There is therefore no objection in principle to the idea of human rights that are absolute in the sense of being categorically exceptionless. It is another question as to whether there are such rights, and what they might be. The most plausible candidates, like the right not to be tortured, will be passive negative rights, that is, rights not to be done to by others in certain ways. It is more difficult to think of active negative rights (rights not to be interfered with) or positive rights (rights to be done to in certain ways) as absolutely exceptionless. The positive rights to be given certain essentials—food, shelter, security, education—clearly depend upon the existence of an adequate supply, something that cannot be guaranteed categorically and universally.

If absoluteness in this strong sense is made part of the very meaning of the expression "human right," then it would seem that there is a lamentable paucity of human rights, if any at all. Clarity will best be served, I think, if we keep "absoluteness" out of the definition of "human right." Two questions can then be kept separate: (1) Are there any human rights, i.e., generically moral, unforfeitable, irrevocable rights held equally and universally by human beings (at least)? (2) If so, are any of these rights absolute? . . .

ABSOLUTE AND NONABSOLUTE HUMAN RIGHTS

In December 1948, the General Assembly of the United Nations adopted a Universal Declaration of Human Rights. Unlike the eighteenth-century manifestoes of natural rights, which were concerned almost exclusively with the individual's rights not to be interfered with by others, the U.N. Declaration endorses numerous basic positive rights to receive benefits and be provided with the means to satisfy basic human needs. Even the conception in the U.N. document of a basic need (in contrast to an unneeded but valuable commodity) reflected changes in the world's outlook and hopes since the eighteenth century. The U.N. Declaration contains the old-style negative rights, mostly pertaining to civic and political activities and criminal procedures as well as the new "social and economic rights" that are correlated with the positive duties of others (usually of the state). Rights of the former kind impose duties upon private citizens and the state alike to keep hands off individuals in certain respects, to leave them alone.

Other articles, however, impose duties upon others that are so difficult that they may, under widely prevalent conditions of scarcity and conflict, be impossible for *anyone* to discharge. Articles 22–27, for example, state that "everyone, as a member of society . . . has the right to work, to free choice of employment . . . to protection against unemployment . . . to just and favorable remuneration . . . to rest and leisure . . . and periodic holidays with pay . . . to food, clothing, housing, and medical care . . . to education . . . to enjoy the arts and to share in scientific advancement and its benefits."[17] Now as we have seen,[18] these positive (as opposed to negative) human rights are rights in an unusual new "manifesto sense," for, unlike all other claim-rights, they are not necessarily correlated with the duties of any assignable persons. The Declaration must therefore be interpreted to say that all men as such have a claim (that is, are in a position to make claim) to the goods therein mentioned, even if there should temporarily be no one in the corresponding position to be claimed against.

These social and economic human rights, therefore, are certainly not *absolute* rights, since easily imaginable and commonly actual circumstances can reduce them to mere claims. Moreover, these rights are clearly not nonconflictable. For example, where there are two persons for every job, there must be conflict between the claims of some workers to "free choice of employment," in the sense that if one worker's claim is recognized as valid, another's *must* be rejected.

Can any human rights plausibly be construed as absolutely exceptionless and there-

fore nonconflictable in principle, or must all rights in their very natures be vulnerable to legitimate invasion in some circumstances? The most plausible candidates for absoluteness are (some) *negative rights;* since they require no positive actions or contributions from others, they are less likely to be affected by conditions of scarcity. To say of a given negative right that it is nonconflictable is to say: (1) if conflicts occur with rights of others kinds, it must always win, and (2) no conflict is possible with other rights of its own kind. The right to speak freely is a plausible human right and is conferred by Article 19 of the U.N. Declaration, but is certainly not nonconflictable in the sense defined above, for it cannot plausibly be said always and necessarily to win out whenever it conflicts with another's right to reputation, privacy, or safety. In theory, of course, we could consistently hold that the free expression right always overrides rights of other kinds, but then that right would fail to satisfy the second condition for nonconflictability, no matter how stubbornly we back it. The requirement that the right in question be incapable in principle of conflicting with another person's right of the *same* kind is the real stumbling block in the path of absoluteness. Consider an audience of hecklers exercising *their* "free speech" to shout down a speaker, or some scoundrel using his "free speech" to persuade others to cut out the tongue of his hated rival. In these cases, free speech must be limited in its *own* interest. Similar examples can be provided, *mutatis mutandis,* for freedom of movement, free exercise of religion, the right to property, and to virtually all of the characteristically eighteenth-century rights of noninterference.

There remain at least three kinds of human rights that may very well be understood (without obvious absurdity) to be absolute and nonconflictable. Positive rights to "goods" that cannot ever, in the very nature of the case, be in scarce supply, are one possibility. Perhaps the right to a fair trial (really a package of positive and negative rights) or the right to equal protection of the

---

[17] UNESCO, *Human Rights, a symposium* (London and New York: Allan Wingate, 1949).

[18] *Supra,* pp. 177–78.

law, or "the right to equal consideration,"[19] fall into this category.

A second possibility is the negative right not to be treated inhumanely or cruelly, not to be tortured or treated barbarously. Whether we as legislators (actual or ideal) should confer such an absolute right on everyone is entirely up to us. There may be good policy reasons against it, but if we are convinced by the powerful policy and moral reasons in favor of it, we needn't be deterred by the fear of conflictability. As I argued in the previous section, we can *decide* without absurdity to let this right override rights of all *other* kinds, and there is nothing in nature to bring this right into conflict with other persons' rights of the *same* kind. Article 5 of the U.N. Declaration, which forbids "torture or . . . cruel, inhuman . . . treatment," may be conceived as conferring a human right in a very strong sense, namely one which is not only universal and inalienable, but also absolute. It is still not a human right in the very strongest sense—one that applies absolutely and unalterably to all and *only* humans—for it is presumably the one right that the higher animals have, if they have any rights at all.

A third possibility is the right not to be subjected to exploitation or degradation

even when such subjection is utterly painless and therefore not cruel. It is possible to treat human beings with drugs, hypnosis, or other brainwashing techniques so that they become compliant tools in the hands of their manipulators, useful as means to their manipulators' ends, but with all serious purposes of their own totally obliterated. Once human beings are in this condition, they may have no notion that they are being exploited or degraded, having come to accept and internalize their exploiters' image of themselves as their own. In this state, human beings might be raised, as Swift suggested, for food, fattened up for a few years, and then slaughtered (humanely, of course); or they might be harnessed, like donkeys, to wagons or millstones. It would be good business as well as good morals to treat them kindly (so long as they are obedient), for that way one can get more labor out of them in the long run. Clearly, kindness and "humanity," while sufficient to satisfy the rights of animals, are not sufficient for human beings, who must therefore have ascribed to them another kind of right that we deliberately withhold from animals. That is a right to a higher kind of respect, an inviolate dignity, which as a broad category includes the negative rights not to be brainwashed, not to be made into a docile instrument for the purposes of others, and not to be converted into a domesticated animal. Rights in this category are probably the only ones that are human rights in the strongest sense: unalterable, "absolute" (exceptionless and nonconflictable), and universally and *peculiarly* human.

---

[19] "Notice . . . that there is one ['natural'] right which . . . is to all intents and purposes an absolute right. That is the right to equal consideration—the right to be treated as the formula for justice provides. For this right is one which is the most basic of all, one which is under no conditions to be violated." Lucius Garvin, *A Modern Introduction to Ethics* (Boston: Houghton Mifflin Company, 1953), p. 491.

Utilitarianism and Rights

Allan Gibbard

Because most of us are committed to certain basic human rights, we expect any plausible moral and political theory to be able to explain and justify those rights. Utilitarianism is a longstanding and well-developed normative theory, but many philosophers believe that it cannot take rights seriously and is, therefore, defective. In this essay, Allan Gibbard, Professor of Philosophy at the University of Michigan, argues that utilitarians can and should be committed to rights. He contends that rights are an important part of the solution to the utilitarian problem of designing institutions and social practices that maximize social good. Considered in this light, Gibbard argues, accepting, advocating, and fostering a commitment in oneself and others to basic human rights have great social utility.

Professor Gibbard has written extensively on issues in social and political philosophy. He is the author of *Wise Choices, Apt Feelings* (Harvard University Press, 1990).

INTRODUCTION

We look to rights for protection. The hope of advocates of "human rights" has been that certain protections might be accorded to all of humanity. Even in a world only a minority of whose inhabitants live under liberal democratic regimes, the hope is, certain standards accepted in the liberal democracies will gain universal recognition and respect. These include liberty of persons as opposed to enslavement, freedom from cruelty, freedom from arbitrary execution, from arbitrary imprisonment, and from arbitrary deprivation of property or livelihood, freedom of religion, and freedom of inquiry and expression.

Philosophers, of course, concern themselves with the theory of rights, and that is partly because of the ways questions of rights bear on fundamental normative theory. By far the most highly developed general normative theory has been utilitarianism. Now many opponents of utilitarianism argue that considerations of rights discredit utilitarianism, that utilitarianism yields conclusions about rights that we would normally regard as faulty, and that moreover, the reasons for regarding those conclusions as faulty turn out, upon examination, to be stronger than the reasons for regarding utilitarianism as valid. A valid theory cannot have faulty conclusions, and so thinking about rights shows utilitarianism not to be a valid normative theory.

Jeremy Bentham, the founder of the utilitarian movement in nineteenth century England, accepted the incompatibility of utilitarianism and "the rights of man," and

Reprinted by permission from *Social Philosophy and Policy*, Vol. 2, No. 1, 1984, pp. 92–102.

rejected talk of the latter as "anarchical fallacies." His great successor John Stuart Mill, however, argued that a perceptive and far-sighted utilitarianism supports strong rights both of democratic participation and of individual freedom of action. Here, I want to examine utilitarian arguments for rights in general, with an eye toward the commonly recognized core of human rights.

On a utilitarian view of rights, the problem to be addressed is one of institutional design, and more broadly, of the design of social practices. Rights are not part of this problem, but part of its solution. At the most fundamental level, that is to say, institutions and practices are to be evaluated by their performance, and the standards by which performance is to be judged do not themselves involve rights. Rights, utilitarian liberals claim, are an important part of the best solution to this problem of design. In the case of the core "human rights," the social practices in question are of two kinds, national and world. The ultimate hope is that protection of these rights may become a part of the effective constitution of every nation. The more immediate hope is that respect for human rights may be promoted and buttressed by the power of world opinion. A commonly recognized core of human rights, the hope is, can provide standards for worldwide public criticism of the ways governments treat those subject to their power.

It is notorious, though, that any utilitarian defense of rights threatens paradox. If I, a government official, am committed not to violate a commonly recognized core of human rights, then either I must think that violating those rights is never what is best calculated to promote the general good, or I must be prepared to sacrifice the general good in order not to violate those rights. Now it may seem implausible that the violation of commonly recognized human rights is never what is best calculated to promote the general good. In any case, it affords us little protection if rulers around the world are committed merely to respect human rights whenever doing so seems to them to fit the principle of utility. The situations in which commonly recognized human rights are violated are often ones of serious conflict and high passion, where the violators of human rights will almost always take their actions to be promoting the general good. Can a utilitarian, then, have a commitment to rights that is effective? Can he be genuinely committed not to violate certain rights, even if cases arise in which the course of action best calculated to promote the general good involves violating those rights? Or is that simply to renounce utilitarianism?

A main reason for treasuring these rights is the protection they offer: the prospect that their recognition will enhance human thriving and human happiness. If that hope is warranted, then utilitarians have strong reason to advocate respect for human rights, and cannot rightly renounce them. That, then, is the threatened paradox: utilitarians have strong reason to want the commonly respected core of human rights to be respected universally, even when respect for these rights appears to conflict with the demands of the general good. "Utilitarianism," though, whatever we take the term to mean precisely, is the doctrine that in some sense, the ultimate moral standard is the promotion of the general good. How can concern with the general good dictate that respect for rights takes precedence over considerations of the general good?

This challenge is sometimes met by formulating a "rule utilitarianism" that deviates from the prescriptions of standard "act-utilitarianism" when the principles it would be good to have recognized do not prescribe the act that would most promote the general good. The move to rule utilitarianism, though, may appear *ad hoc*, or a concession to irrational rule-worship. In this paper, I want to approach this perennial controversy by starting with the root idea of utilitarianism: that morality is a matter of the rational pursuit of the general good. What kind of utilitarianism emerges from this root precept?

PRAGMATIC INSTITUTIONAL DESIGN

Rights, I have said, on the view of a utilitarian liberal, are solutions to problems of institutional design, and are not, at the most fundamental level, part of the problem. They are good solutions in virtue of facts of human motivational psychology. What I now want to do is to back up from this claim about the moral status of rights, and examine the problem that faces a pragmatic designer of institutions. In doing so, I obliquely address standard problems of utilitarianism, but I do so by placing responses to them within the framework of a kind of problem that faces anyone trying to develop a theory of institutional design on a pragmatic basis. I want in this section to take up the project of pragmatic institutional design on its own terms and see where it leads, without regard, for the moment, to whether it leads to anything recognizable as principled political advocacy.

What is the problem of pragmatic institutional design? Here are some caricatures. The problem might be one of *scriptwriting*. The script would prescribe what each member of the institution should do, and be judged by the total amount of happiness that would be produced were those prescriptions followed. Imagine a script for a marionette show with the following novel features: the script is general, the happiness of the marionettes is affected by what the script has them do, and the test of quality is not aesthetic and not a matter of how the show affects an audience, but a matter of how happy the marionettes are as the performance proceeds.

Now, of course, one problem with the scriptwriting caricature is that it is hard to imagine people as marionettes without ignoring some of the central sources of happiness in life: the active pursuit of purposes. Another central problem is that no one has the power to get his script produced. The scriptwriting account ignores all matters of causation within a society: all design of systems of communication, coordination, and incentive. If we can write the script, why waste our puppets' efforts on getting each other to follow it? Either we choose among scripts on the assumption that the one we choose will be followed, or the scriptwriting account sets no well-defined problems to the designer of institutions.

Perhaps, then, the problem of institutional design is this: to design people and their relationships in such a way that the resulting mechanism produces good without further intervention of the designer. It is, in effect, an idealized problem of institutional engineering. The caricature of *institutional engineering* goes like this: an engineer designing a machine must know what his materials can do and how they would interact in various possible designs. He can deduce how machines of various possible designs could be expected to perform, and how reliably. He is given standards of cost and effectiveness for judging the expected performance of alternative mechanisms, including the costs of breakdowns, and he chooses the design that is the best, by these standards, of the alternatives he has analyzed. The institutional engineer is special in that he works primarily with people as his materials, and chooses a design on the basis of how much happiness it would produce.

As a caricature of mechanical engineering, what I have said abstracts from the problem of how to convince anyone to build the machine, and how to get people to use the machine as it was designed to be used. Institutional design involves the same problems. One cannot simply put properly designed people in their proper places and let the institutional machine work. Institutions depend on habits, accepted norms, and all the other aspects of human psychology that go to determine how people will act. Norms and habits can be affected by education and indoctrination, by discussion, praise, and criticism, by rewards and penalties—but hardly to industrial levels of precision.

Where institutions are to be designed, moreover, the designer is part of the design, or at least must speak to those who are part of the design as person to person. Rousseau (*Social Contract*, 1762, Bk. 2 Ch. 7), in contemplating the problem of institutional design, resorts to a *legislateur* of wisdom far greater than that of the people for whom he legislates, who wins the people to his laws not by reason, but by claiming to speak for the gods. The institutional designer's problem is how to proceed if no such claim will be believed.

Perhaps, then, the institutional designer must be benevolent Machiavellian. A utilitarian, after all, acts to maximize expected utility—that is, the expected value of the consequence of what he does, where the evaluation counts equally the happiness of everyone. Now, writing and speaking about rights constitutes action, of a kind, and the rational utilitarian will judge what to say about rights, or what to do instead of talking about rights, by expected utility. If he affirms a right or denies one, he does so, and does so in the way he does, not because he believes what he is saying, but because doing so in that way has the highest expected utility of all the things he might have done at the time. On a given occasion, the benevolent Machiavellian may propagandize and manipulate, in the sense that he puts forth as his own, reasons he does not in fact accept for doing what he does think ought to be done. He may even advocate something he thinks ought not to be done—say to win favor, and thereby put himself in a position of more power to do good than he otherwise would be. The choice hinges on expected utility. He may, of course, speak honestly, giving his own reasons for conclusions he accepts—but only when honesty is the best policy on benevolent grounds.

This benevolent Machiavellian is no doubt not someone we would respect, much less trust, but that is not the point now, which is to apply the utilitarian standard to what the benevolent Machiavellian does. Does utilitarianism prescribe a benevolent Machiavellianism? For a person with perfect self-control in the service of benevolence and perfect power to weigh evidence and ascribe expected utility to policies open to him, whose own good is not substantially dependent on a non-manipulative approach to human relations, the answer must undoubtedly be yes. A benevolent god will not have an admirable character by human standards. If this account of a benevolent Machiavellianism is, indeed, a caricature of utilitarian political advocacy, and a utilitarian morality of advocacy turns out to look at all like familiar morality, that will be because of human imperfection. That, alas, need not be a shaky foundation.

What goes wrong, from a purely utilitarian standpoint, when we drop the assumption of human perfection? In the first place, much of a person's happiness will depend on interpersonal relations that he experiences as reciprocally non-manipulative. This effect on his own happiness may, to be sure, be outweighed by his effect on others: perhaps kings, diplomats, and leaders of movements must sacrifice intimacy and plain dealing for the sake of others; but it could well be self-delusion to suppose that the rest of us face that choice. Consider also, though, matters of self-control. Is it not likely that starvation from human fellowship produces needs that cloud judgment, so that the benevolent Machiavellian risks becoming a Stalin? Most important of all, though, the benevolent Machiavellian with persuasive power needs some way of judging the expected utility of his words. The expected utility of his words will depend on considerations of great difficulty: on matters of evidence that can only be well judged with interpersonal support in an atmosphere of reciprocal honesty. The benevolent Machiavellian, then, seems caught on the horns of a dilemma. On the one horn, if he has little power to affect events with his social theorizing, then his own happiness and that of his intimates is of prime concern, and those are fostered by honesty. On the other horn, if he has any substantial power to influence events by his action or persuasion, then the fixity of his benevolence and the stability of the judgment that guides it are of prime concern, and those are fostered by honesty. Pure Machiavellian benevolence has poor utilitarian backing as a standard for a person of anything close to human possibilities and limitations.

What are the alternatives to Machiavellian benevolence as ways of working to bring institutions into existence? The achievement of consensus is one, institution by agreement is another, and using one's powers within existing institutions, such as the legal system, is another. Persuasion is important for all of these: persuasion to accept a principle, persuasion to enter into an agreement, and persuasion to exercise one's institutional powers in a given way. Now, persuasion itself draws on existing institutions, in which people play roles governed by norms: particularly on the institution we might call *dialogue*. The norms of dialogue are to be open about what one finds persuasive and to give serious attention to what the other side puts forth as possible considerations. The political advocate acts within an existing institution of dialogue, and the problem of how utilitarian advocacy is to proceed is a part of the general problem of how a utilitarian is to act within institutions.

THE RATIONAL PURSUIT OF AN END

J. S. Mill and Henry Sidgwick differed from many ethical theorists of today in that both took the fundamental problem of ethics to be the choice of an ultimate end. Utilitarianism as they conceived it is the thesis that the proper ultimate end is the same for each person, that that end is the "general good" or "good from the point of view of the universe," which is the sum of the goods of individuals, and that the good of each person is his happiness. How utilitarianism in this sense bears on conduct is a matter of what constitutes the rational pursuit of its end: what, the question is, would it be rationally to pursue the general happiness as one's ultimate end?

Consider, then, the general question of what constitutes the rational pursuit of an end. Sidgwick tackles this question first in his discussion of egoism, in the course of which he discusses whether the pursuit of pleasure can bring as much pleasure as can other pursuits. (*Methods of Ethics*, 1901, I. iv.2 and II.iii.2) If it cannot, the pursuit of pleasure is self-defeating; that, he calls the "Fundamental Paradox of Egoistic Hedonism." The argument for the paradox stems from Butler. Most pleasure, Sidgwick says, comes from the pursuit and attainment of goals that are distinct from the egoist's goal of his own happiness. A prime example is the pleasure of scoring a point in a competitive game. A player would get no great pleasure from scoring if he were not trying so hard to score, and although he plays the game for pleasure, in the heat of the competition he is not trying to score merely for the sake of the pleasure he thinks that will bring. He simply wants to score.

The "paradox" for egoism is this. A pure egoist is someone who desires nothing but happiness, a high balance of pleasure over pain in his life. Such a person, though, lacks the very kinds of desires from which most pleasures come. From the rational pursuit of happiness, then, will come a life of little pleasure, whereas having non-egoistic goals could lead to a life with much more pleasure and not much more pain. The rational pursuit of happiness is self-defeating.

Sidgwick dismisses this as no serious problem for egoism.

It is an experience only too common among men, in whatever pursuit they may be engaged, that they let the original object and goal of their efforts pass out of view, and come to regard the means to this end as ends to themselves . . . And if it be thus easy and common to forget the end in the means overmuch, there seems no reason why it should be difficult to do it to the extent that Rational Egoism prescribes: and, in fact, it seems to be continually done by ordinary persons in the case of amusements and pastimes of all kinds. (II. iii. 2, p. 137)

Now, perhaps this reply concedes the objection. By definition, after all, an egoist's sole goals are pleasure and the absence of pain in his life, and Sidgwick concedes that a person who had only those goals would find little pleasure in life. All Sidgwick has done, then, is to note what incorrigible non-egoists we are: that even if we set out to be egoists, we would not keep at it, but would soon be pursuing non-egoistic goals. What this shows is not that anyone can enjoy life while remaining an egoist, but that no one will long remain an egoist.

The problem with this reply to Sidgwick is that it bypasses the kind of egoism that matters. Suppose a man loves his wife and children, and finds life fulfilling in ways that depend on his concern for their happiness. Suppose also, though, that he would set out to wean himself of his love for them, and leave them miserable and destitute if, on reflection, he thought he would find life somewhat more fulfilling that way. Such a man, to be sure, will have many desires that are not simply desires for his own happiness, and are not desires for things simply as instrumental to his own happiness. He wants his family to love him and to be happy. If on that account, though, we say he is not an egoist, then we need a new name for the kind of person he is. What shall we call him? His own happiness is, in an important sense, what he takes as the ultimate goal of his conduct, for he fosters intrinsic desires when he thinks on reflection that having them promotes his own happiness, and takes steps to rid himself of desires when he thinks that doing so would foster his happiness. Indeed, that, it seems, is what is involved in the rational pursuit of any long-range goal, be it money, fame, pedagogical success, a winning season, one's own happiness, or anything else. If that is not "egoism" in the strictest sense, we ought to change the sense, so that we can apply the term 'egoism' to a theory that is worth taking seriously.

What does all this tell us about the rational pursuit of the general happiness? Clearly, the rational utilitarian, in the sense of the term that matters, will not keep his attention fixed on the goal of the general business. He will take the general happiness as his ultimate goal in the same way as a rational egoist takes his own happiness as his ultimate goal. He will reflect from time to time on himself and his situation, and consider the desires which in the ordinary course of life he experiences as intrinsic. Those desires may well be ones that stem from regarding actions as morally legitimate or illegitimate, equitable or inequitable, proper or improper. They may well include the desires that constitute commitment to a principle. A rational utilitarian will foster in himself and others those attitudes, habits, and ways of deliberating the fostering of which he thinks conducive to the general happiness, and work to rid himself and others of moral attitudes, habits, and ways of deliberating when he sees that that has utility.

UTILITARIAN POLITICAL ADVOCACY

If what I have been saying is right, the puzzle of a utilitarian theory of rights hinges on a general question: What constitutes the rational pursuit of the general happiness within institutions? How should a utilitarian treat the accepted norms of dialogue? Now, in his participation in institutions, it follows from what I have said, a rational utilitarian will reflect from time to time about which tendencies of character and personal make-up work on the whole toward the general happiness in those institutions. The answer, of course, will depend on the nature of the institutions and the distribution of ways in which others are disposed to act in their institutional roles. Clearly in some cases, a rational utilitarian will violate institutional norms, whereas in other cases he will conform to them.

What utilitarian support, then, can be given for respect for human rights? In the first place, they may have a kind of "log-rolling" rationale. The utilitarian's reason for wanting human rights to be respected is his conviction that in most cases their violation detracts from the general happiness, that human judgment of what the exceptions are is notoriously unreliable, and that criticism that appeals to the promotion of the general good is ineffective compared to criticism that appeals to commonly recognized standards of human rights, because it is so highly debatable what best promotes the general good. The problem for a utilitarian advocate of rights is that he recognizes that anyone who investigates carefully would find a case, from time to time, that was exceptional, in that as far as he could see, it would further the general good on balance to violate one of the widely recognized human rights in that case. Suppose, though, that even careful investigators would come to little agreement with each other on which cases are the exceptions, and those who had not investigated with the care of experts would not agree on which of the experts to believe. Thus, although someone who investigated carefully might conclude that the ideal policy involves violation of a widely accepted human right, he might also conclude that no institution for deciding when that is so would do better than an institution of automatic condemnation of violations of certain recognized rights.

What, though, if the experts agree. Then the "log-rolling" rationale that I have been giving does not apply, and there is a case for refining our public understanding of what the universal human rights are. There is danger, though, in too much refinement. In human affairs, there is ordinarily no way to impose a rule unless the importance of keeping to the rule can be securely made to carry conviction. Even the clauses of a written constitution with a bill of rights work through human adherence: through legislative self-restraint, judicial review, or refusal of individual citizens to regard themselves as bound by purported laws they think unconstitutional. Even when legislators or judges adhere to the constitution itself, they can often talk themselves around provisions for which they find no satisfying rationale, and the aura of legitimacy on which legislators and judges depend requires that they act to a considerable degree on norms that they share with the rest of the community. If, on the other hand, the principle is to

govern not through the provisions of a written constitution but by consensus, as is the hope for human rights secured by the power of world opinion, the point is apparent: a principle that applies to important matters will be followed only if the importance of keeping to it can draw conviction.

In this respect, there is a special virtue in principles that carry with them a strong non-utilitarian rationale. Principles like freedom from arbitrary arrest have a direct rationale in the dignity and security of each person protected. To qualify the principle with exceptions would be to undermine that rationale. "Why except this case?" it would then be asked, "and to what else does the same kind of reasoning apply?" Some principles, then, make more effective taboos than others.

What place does a non-utilitarian rationale have in utilitarian argument? Just this: People in general, utilitarians and non-utilitarians, can be strongly moved by a principle with a coherent rationale, and especially one that seems to fill in the dictum "To each his own." Utilitarians, to be sure, argue that being strongly moved is not enough for rational moral conviction. They claim that when we look at the principles that have such strong appeal and test them carefully against our more specific moral convictions, we find no coherent whole. With that, of course, intuitionistic opponents of utilitarianism agree, but whereas the intuitionists try to construct a coherent whole by a strategy of piecemeal adjustments, utilitarians look for a standard by which conflicts may be resolved. The utilitarian, though, is not a person unmoved by principles, but a person who has learned to distrust the principles he finds moving until he has tested them by the standard of utility.

A principle with a rationale that carries conviction may be of great utility. Suppose two alternative principles both have a high *acceptance-utility:* for each, its being adopted and followed by most people would have high utility. If one has much more natural appeal as a principle than does the other, there will be greater utility in supporting it even if it has slightly less acceptance-utility. It will not only be more convincing to others; it will command the utilitarian's own principled adherence more securely.

What bearing does this have on political advocacy and political commitment? Advocacy often at least purports to be governed by the norms of dialogue: sincerity and willingness to consider what others say. Sincerity in the advocacy of principles consists in advocating principles by which one is willing to be bound, either unconditionally or if enough others are. The questions to ask, then, are whether a utilitarian should abide by the norm of sincerity, and if so, what principle he should advocate under the constraint of this norm. The issue, here, is not whether to be sincere in all circumstances, actual or possible, but whether to be sincere in a discussion of political institutions when others, for the most part, are.

Now deception, as we know, has various psychological costs: it cuts a person off from some of the emotional rewards of human company, and it is likely to give him an artificial manner which makes him at once less convincing and less rewarding as a conversationalist. Insincerity in writing may be less costly psychologically, but it is hard to write insincerely and speak sincerely: the secret will out.

Perhaps the most important consideration, though, is the way insincere advocacy is likely to affect the advocate's judgment. If matters are easy to think through, this consideration will not apply, but then in most such cases, the greatest utility lies in advocating the clear basis of one's own conviction. In difficult matters, the thinker needs the exercise of sincere participation in dialogue, for sincere dialogue can help thinking in a way that delivering a sales talk cannot. Cultivating habits of sincerity will normally foster good habits of thought.

Now, whereas in matters of fact and evidence, sincerity is not achieved by adjusting one's beliefs to what one wants to assert, in matters of commitment to principle, it can be. That is to say, one can adopt a principle on the basis of the utility of advocating it. Of

course, one cannot adopt a principle at will: commitment must be fostered and practiced. How well one can expect to be able to cultivate the various alternative commitments one might now choose to foster bears also on a utilitarian choice of principles: if commitment to either of two principles would have high utility, but one of the principles is felt as more compelling, that may be a strong point in its favor from a utilitarian point of view.

If, then, you are a utilitarian who thinks the facts of social psychology are as I have been supposing, here is why you should accept certain principles of individual human rights, advocate them, and foster your own commitment to them. The facts I have been supposing are these: for the most part, violations of the commonly recognized core of human rights detract from the general good. There may well be exceptions, but even with careful investigation, there will be much disagreement on what those exceptions are. Moreover, even if we can agree on a few exceptions, a principle without qualifications to provide for those exceptional cases may have a much stronger natural appeal than a principle meticulously qualified. Suppose, then, you have a choice between the following: (1) A simple principle of great natural appeal—say, the principle of freedom from arrest without probable cause and a speedy trial; (2) That principle with provisos for the rare kinds of cases where detention without trial, we all now agree, seems best calculated to promote the general good; and (3) No principle at all other than the principle of acting in the way best calculated to promote the general good. Questions of sincerity aside, advocacy of the simple principle may well have the greatest expected utility. For commitment to it is likely to be especially easy and firm, because of its compelling non-utilitarian rationale.

Now reintroduce considerations of sincerity. Should you (a) advocate the simple principle and accept it, (b) advocate the simple principle and accept an alternative, or (c) both advocate and accept an alternative? Recall that if you accept an alternative, you will in some ways have a more difficult time fostering your own commitment to it than you would have in fostering a commitment to a principle with strong natural appeal. If you both accept and advocate an alternative to the simple principle, you lose the advantage of natural appeal of the simple principle. If you advocate the simple principle but secretly accept an alternative, you lose the utility of sincerity, and gain little or nothing in utility from your commitment to the principle you think ideal. It is ideal, after all, only in that so far as you can determine, widespread, firm commitment to it would have greater expected utility than would widespread, firm commitment to any alternative. If you cannot even secure your own firm commitment to it, that is a poor utilitarian recommendation for the principle.

Principles are often rejected as dangerous, and courses of action are often rejected as violating principles it is important to maintain and foster. These lines of argument often seem to embody wisdom, but they seem available to the utilitarian only at the price of making him crafty and manipulative rather than wise. I have tried to explore what happens if we think of utilitarianism not as taking the form, "An act is right if and only if . . .," but as saying that everyone should take as his ultimate end the greatest total good of all sentient beings, and pursue that end rationally.

Utilitarians think that the justification of moral principles often requires sagacity: understanding of important aspects of human psychology, of social and institutional dynamics, and of the consequences of these for the rational pursuit of the general happiness. Here, what I have tried to do is not to provide utilitarianism with the social theory it needs, but to sketch the kind of argument a utilitarian might give for a commitment to human rights. There is nothing incoherent, I maintain, in the general form of a utilitarian argument for rights.

Utilitarianism Versus Human Rights

James S. Fishkin

In this response to Gibbard, James S. Fishkin challenges utilitarianism's ability to provide a basis for respecting human rights. Noting that the rights listed by Gibbard are negative rights, which offer protection from certain kinds of "boundary crossings," Fishkin maintains that even if utilitarianism justifies institutionalizing these rights, the theory would still be unable to guarantee distributional equity. Moreover, Fishkin argues, utilitarianism always remains hostage to empirical considerations that may undermine its commitment to the individual rights Gibbard favors. Even at the level of institutional design, utilitarian calculations might favor alternative social practices that ignore human rights.

James S. Fishkin is Professor of Government and Philosophy at the University of Texas at Austin. He is the author of several books on moral and political philosophy, including *Tyranny and Legitimacy* (1979), *The Limits of Obligation* (1982), *Justice, Equal Opportunity, and the Family* (1983), and *Beyond Subjective Morality* (1984).

Rather than respond to Gibbard, point by point, I will comment on what I take to be the general spirit of his argument. The old consensus on some form or another of utilitarianism, a consensus that dominated discussions in moral and political theory only a few years ago, has now largely evaporated before the heat of distributional objections founded on justice, the "separateness of persons," and other concerns for the severe sacrifices that utilitarianism might require of some for the sake of greater gains to others (or for the sake of gains to a greater number of others.)[1]

By attempting to develop a utilitarian basis for adherence to "core human rights," Gibbard is offering a variant of utilitarianism that holds out the promise of withstanding some of these distributional objections and, perhaps, of rehabilitating some form of the theory in a thorough-going way. After all, many of the standard anti-utilitarian arguments focus on the theory's ability to legitimate deprivations of what Gibbard calls core human rights.

Liberty of person as opposed to enslavement, freedom from cruelty, freedom from arbitrary execution, from arbitrary imprisonment, and

---

Reprinted by permission from *Social Philosophy and Policy*, Vol. 2, No. 1, 1984, pp. 103–107.

[1] For some insightful remarks on this general transition see H. L. A. Hart "Between Utility and Rights" in Alan Ryan (ed.) *The Idea of Freedom: Essays in Honour of*

Isaiah Berlin (Oxford: Oxford University Press, 1979).

For one attempt to formulate distributional objections to utilitarianism and other key principles see my *Tyranny and Legitimacy: A Critique of Political Theories* (Baltimore: Johns Hopkins, 1979).

from arbitrary deprivation of property or livelihood, freedom of religion and freedom of inquiry and expression.

If adherence to these core human rights can be given a utilitarian basis, then many anti-utilitarian arguments can be dismissed.

I wish to argue that this strategy faces three basic difficulties. First, it takes more than Gibbard's list of core human rights to protect utilitarianism from strong distributional objections. Second, if the ultimate basis for institutionalizing one set of rights-defining practices rather than another is utilitarian, then those core human rights have a most uncertain basis. It is an open, quasi-empirical question whether other practices, abhorrent to rights advocates, might not produce greater aggregate utility. Third, the core rights on his list may constitute major impediments, in themselves, to the manipulation of preferences and practices required by the rest of his argument. If one relies, as Gibbard advocates, on "the facts of social psychology" one will have to choose, under realistic conditions between utilitarianism and human rights. This is a choice Gibbard's paper has not equipped us to make.

1. Let us begin by imagining a society in which the practices on Gibbard's list of core human rights have been institutionalized— freedom from arbitrary execution and imprisonment, freedom from arbitrary deprivation of property or livelihood, freedom of religion, inquiry, and expression. The first thing to notice about these "core human rights" is that they are all formulated as freedom "from" certain kinds of coercive interference. They are forms of "negative liberty" if you will, or in Nozick's terms, they offer protection from certain kinds of "boundary crossings."

I believe that a consistent utilitarianism— even when applied within the confines of such core rights—is subject to some disturbing distributional objections. For example, let us suppose that the society institutionalizing these core human rights has no developed welfare state apparatus. Nothing on Gibbard's list would require such an apparatus. The basic structure of this state, let us assume, is more or less that of a Nozickian minimal state. Now, let us also assume that this state faces an economic situation rather like our own at present and that the state tolerates increasing unemployment, concentrated among the poor and unskilled and the members of various minority groups, in the interests of moderating inflation.

Nothing on Gibbard's list would mandate even the meager "safety net" tolerated by the Reagan administration. We might assume, however, that Gibbard means for utilitarianism to determine not only institutional design but also particular policies. However, if Gibbard's policymakers are consistent utilitarians, then whether anything at all is done for the poor, starving, and unemployed depends on a series of empirical issues. One factor supporting at least some redistribution is the degree to which there is declining marginal utility of income. But there are also weighty factors on the other side. Incentive effects may require substantial inequalities and they may sharply limit how much is available for redistribution. Furthermore, we can tip the balance of purely utilitarian calculations against potential welfare recipients (or job program recipients) by imagining strong patterns of racial or ethnic hatred such that large numbers of the better off would intensely resent any give-aways to the poor. Nothing in Gibbard's paper would rule out counting such "external" or "public-regarding" preferences.[2] Indeed, once a utilitarian begins choosing among the preferences that are to count as utility, there are serious questions to be raised about whether he is still a utilitarian at all. But once such external preferences are included, severe deprivations and blighted life chances to the poor and the black may be balanced out, in utilitarian calculations, by the resentment and smug satis-

---

[2] For efforts to draw this distinction more precisely see *Tyranny and Legitimacy* 26–9 and Ronald Dworkin *Taking Rights Seriously* (Cambridge, Mass.: Harvard University Press, 1978) 234–5.

faction of the rest of the population—particularly when the latter may also directly benefit from some moderation in inflation. The issue is quasi-empirical. However, we may easily imagine a world—not too distant from our own—in which strictly utilitarian calculations would support such disturbing distributional results—even when Gibbard's core human rights are fully institutionalized. His rights would protect people from arbitrary *deprivations* of property but they would not require adequate opportunities to acquire property or a means of livelihood in the first place. There is no one to single out for a rights violation if the "hidden hand" does not provide.

2. Now, let me turn to a somewhat stylized example of the kind of case for which Gibbard's proposal would seem perfectly adequate. My point will be that if utilitarianism is the ultimate criterion for determining which rights-defining practices are to be institutionalized in the first place, then the strategy may not even hold for such obvious cases—because one might imagine alternative practices outside Gibbard's proposed list which would, under some empirical conditions, produce greater aggregate utility. If Gibbard is ultimately a utilitarian, then he must face the prospect that some utilitarian calculations about which practices to institutionalize will, in some empirical contexts, yield practices that run counter to his core list of rights.

I borrow this stock anti-utilitarian example from Gilbert Harman.[3] Let us first imagine a doctor who must choose between concentrating on one patient to the exclusion of five others in an emergency situation or saving the five others. In this simplified situation, if we must choose between saving one life and saving five, many of us would support the utilitarian calculation that the five be saved. I say "utilitarian" because in introducing no further facts about the six patients, I am making it easy for a utilitarian to count them equally and to treat the saving

of life as a place-holder for the production of a future stream of utility. Furthermore, this calculation would appear quite favorable to utilitarianism because by counting lives rather than utilities or dollars, I am permitting the utilitarian to avoid the well-known Paretian difficulties with interpersonal comparisons.

The second step in the example is to imagine the same doctor with five patients, each of whom requires a different organ (one a kidney, another a lung, another a heart, etc.). Without the required transplants, they will each die in the immediate future. The difficulty is that there is no available donor. There is, however, a patient in room 306 who has all the required characteristics and organs in good condition. He has checked in for a routine set of physical exams. If he were killed and the required organs redistributed, five lives could be saved at the cost of one lost.

Now, this is the point in anti-utilitarian horror stories when the rejoinders focus on the dangers of exceptions, the value of maintaining ongoing practices, and the disutility of a climate of fear that might be created if exceptions to an on-going practice—such as those defining the routine physical exam—were permitted. Much that Gibbard says along these lines is persuasive. Furthermore, his proposed right to protection from arbitrary loss of life or liberty might be held to protect the patient in room 306—even when the utilitarian calculations might support taking his life in the interests of saving five others (and even when secrecy and deception might be employed to prevent fear and other forms of disutility from entering the calculation).

However, what is the criterion for deciding, in the first place, that one set of rights-defining practices rather than another is to be institutionalized? If it is utilitarian, as Gibbard implies, then he must face the difficulty that under some empirical conditions, alternative *practices*, even those antithetical to the concerns motivating his list, may yield greater aggregate utility.

For example, if the calculation takes

---

[3] Gilbert Harman *The Nature of Morality* (New York: Oxford University Press, 1977) 3–4.

place at the level of institutional design, it may very well turn out to be the case that a forced practice of involuntary organ donation may lead to more lives saved. Only a consistent consequentialism, insensitive to all distinctions between omissions and commissions, could lead us to consider such a horrendous practice. But utilitarian calculations might favor such a practice: (a) if the bulk of the population viewed themselves as potential beneficiaries; (b) if a substantial number of lives could be saved as a result; (c) if there were some reason why the bulk of the population could neglect or discount the possibility that they might turn out to be organ donors. This third condition might be satisfied if organ donation was concentrated unfairly upon some particular sector or group or if it were spread so widely by a lottery system that each person's chances of sacrifice were negligible (or about like those we face in auto accidents). Deception about the risks, per capita, of the practice is another possibility. Under such conditions, purely utilitarian calculations might very well support institutionalization of a practice requiring arbitrary deprivations of life quite as abhorrent as that demanded from the patient in room 306. Even if the donor were picked by a lottery rather than plucked from his routine physical, many of us would strongly object to his involuntary sacrifice—although that objection would have to be non-utilitarian under the conditions I have described.

3. Lastly, it is worth emphasizing that the results of utilitarian calculation—even at the level of institutional design of alternative social practices—will depend crucially upon the preferences and characters of the people whose utilities are being calculated. Some of my objections could be set aside if people were imagined to be far less nasty, selfish, and resentful than I hypothesized. My point, however, is that if the preferences are as I imagined, then what Gibbard calls the "facts of social psychology" support utilitarian calculations that are distributionally objectionable.

One strategy of response might be to attempt a thorough-going reform of human psychology. If we simply assume universally benign preferences, then many of my objections will have to be set aside. But if we make sufficiently counter-factual assumptions, utilitarianism like most any other theory, can be made to yield almost any results. (I am reminded here of the Yiddish proverb, "if my grandmother had wheels, she'd be a trolley car"). The real issue is what utilitarianism will yield given a *realistic* consideration of the problem of institutional design. And, here, the very core rights Gibbard proposes to implement stand as a stark impediment to the manipulability of preferences in any on-going system. Freedom of thought, freedom of inquiry and expression, freedom from arbitrary deprivations, freedom of association[4] all of these freedoms make the process of preference and character formation difficult to control by "institutional engineers," "scriptwriters" or "Machiavellian" leaders. Free speech, for example, must protect the Nazis marching in Skokie, the Klan rallies in Connecticut, the distribution of pornography victimizing women and children, and hate campaigns against homosexuals, to mention only a few examples. As attached as I am to free speech, it must be admitted that in some empirical contexts it may foster and nurture precisely the preferences that support the most perverse utilitarian calculations. At the very least, institutionalization of these core rights (along with some related customary assumptions about the family—in particular the right of parents to influence their children[5]) renders the process of preference formation insensitive to centralized manipulation. Hence, a defender of Gibbard's position could not defend a pro-rights utilitarian calculation through a continuing manipulation of the preferences fed into the calculation—without also having to sacrifice the very

---

[4] This last right is not on his list but I assume it is an oversight.

[5] For a discussion of this latter right and related issues of liberty see my *Justice, Equal Opportunity, and the Family* (New Haven: Yale University Press, 1983).

rights whose protection was the point of the exercise. Once more, the choice comes down to utilitarianism *versus* human rights. It seems hopelessly unrealistic to imagine that the latter will always support calculations institutionalizing the former. I can

only conclude that taking account of the "facts" of human psychology—the imperfections of human nature—leads us to a hard choice between ultimate principles rather than to their easy reconciliation.

Dignity, Rights, and Self-Control

Michael J. Meyer

Why do we value individual rights? Although, as the previous essays in this section have made evident, philosophers disagree about the nature and theoretical basis of rights, there is, nonetheless, a strong tendency in contemporary discussions of political theory to link talk of human rights with a conception of human dignity. In this essay, Michael J. Meyer discusses what it is about rights that make them particularly important to human dignity. He argues that human dignity is intimately linked to the capacity for authentic self-control and that rights would have little value to beings that could not exercise self-control.

Professor Meyer writes on ethics and political philosophy; he teaches philosophy at the University of Santa Clara.

I

One outstanding feature of both contemporary discussions of political theory and modern political rhetoric is the strong tendency to link talk of human rights with a conception of human dignity.[1] In recent his-

tory some have seen a direct relationship between human dignity and the "rights of man." Kant for one leads us in this direction. He observes that "the dignity of humanity in us" provides us with a duty that we not "suffer [our] rights to be tram-

From *Ethics*, Vol. 99, No. 3 (April 1989). Copyright © 1989 by the University of Chicago Press. Reprinted with the permission of the University of Chicago Press.

[1] Rhetorical recognition of a connection between human rights and human dignity includes (1) *The Charter of the United Nations* (1946) which "reaffirm[s] faith in fundamental human rights, in the dignity and worth of the human person." *Everyman's United Nations* (New York, 1948), p. 553. (2) "The Universal Declaration of Human Rights" (1948) which begins with "recognition of the inherent dignity and . . . the equal and inalienable rights of all members of the human family." See also arts. 1, 22, 23, in *Everyman's United Nations*, pp.

586–90. (3) Pope John XXIII's encyclical "Peace on Earth" (1958) in *Papal Encyclicals, 1958–1981* (Wilmington, N.C.: McGrath, 1981). (4) American Hospital Association, "A Patient's Bill of Rights," *American Medical News* (August 1980), p. 9. More theoretical discussions of a connection between rights and dignity include Peter Berger, *The Homeless Mind* (New York: Random House, 1973), pp. 85–96; Bernard Boxill, *Blacks and Social Justice* (Totowa, N.J.: Rowman & Allanheld, 1984), pp. 195–99; Ronald Dworkin, *Taking Rights Seriously* (Cambridge, Mass.: Harvard University Press, 1977), pp. 198–205; A. I. Melden, *Rights and Persons* (Berkeley: University of California Press, 1977), pp. 194–95; Henry Shue, *Basic Rights* (Princeton, N.J.: Princeton University Press, 1980), pp. 188 ff.

pled underfoot by others with impunity."[2] Though such assertions are not particularly startling these days, the alleged connection between human rights and human dignity remains largely unanalyzed. Most of those who claim human dignity is fundamentally associated with some set of rights do not explain just how they are linked. Is it necessary that a person have rights to have dignity? Is the possession of rights alone enough to guarantee one's dignity?

Though human dignity has come to be closely associated with the idea of human rights, a discussion of rights alone will not provide a full account of human dignity. In short, having human rights—though they are at times well suited to the expression of our dignity—does not capture everything that is significant about human dignity. While having and exercising certain rights is important to our dignity as human beings, what we commonly regard as essential to human dignity would not be explained even if we were able to delineate all of the relevant rights and the particular ways in which each of them expresses or protects human dignity. By "human rights" I simply refer to whatever set of fundamental rights are taken to be linked to human dignity. Such rights might be called basic rights or natural rights, but present purposes allow us to set aside these labels. An enumeration of such rights is not necessary, because I do not wish to discuss the question of why any particular rights are important. I plan, rather, to investigate the underlying question, What is it about rights themselves that is deemed particularly important to human dignity?

II

One suggestive account of this connection between dignity and rights has been offered by Joel Feinberg.[3] To help us determine the value of rights he instructs us to imagine a world without rights. The hope is that in so doing we will understand what is valuable about rights, since it is precisely this which will be lacking in a world without them. Feinberg is, however, quick to fix this world sans rights (which he calls "Nowheresville") by including in it as much moral behavior as is consistent with an absence of rights. Nowheresville may be chock full of "benevolence, compassion, sympathy and pity," and in addition "the sense of duty [can] be a sufficient motive for many beneficent and honorable actions."[4] The only real restriction in Nowheresville is that here, strictly speaking, no one owes any duties to fellow Nowheresvillians.[5] Nowheresville is totally devoid of rights held by individuals, and even though the breach of a contract to which you are a party can be punished, nobody owes any contractual duties to you.[6] As a result you cannot properly claim any rights as your due; even if you are in a position to point out the transgression of such agreements, you are not in a unique

---

[2] Immanuel Kant, *The Metaphysical Principles of Virtue* (1797), trans. J. W. Ellington (Indianapolis: Hackett, 1983), pp. 98–99, Prussian Academy edition (Berlin, 1902), p. 436. For an account of other Enlightenment figures who connect human rights with human dignity, see Michael J. Meyer, "Kantian Dignity and Modern Political Thought," *History of European Ideas* 8 (1987): 319–32.

[3] Joel Feinberg, "The Nature and Value of Rights," *Journal of Value Inquiry* 4 (1970): 243–57.

[4] Ibid., p. 243.

[5] There is also room for the concept of personal desert in Nowheresville. The connection between a good performance and the justly deserved applause has not been erased with the departure of rights. Though it does seem true that, as Feinberg points out, this is just the kind of desert we typically do not claim as our due, all of Feinberg's examples do not ring true. Do students have no rights to the grades they receive? Clearly they at least have the right not to receive poor grades if they perform well.

[6] Feinberg focuses on the elimination of individual rights. He allows into Nowheresville many practices important to the regulation of society as we know it. Nowheresville has "property ownership, bargains and deals, promises and contracts, appointments and loans, marriages and partnerships" (Feinberg, p. 247). It is possible to have these practices in Nowheresville without introducing individual rights by way of what Feinberg calls a "sovereign right monopoly." Whatever obligations arise from such transactions are all owed to some "outside authority." The point here is simple enough: though not totally devoid of rights, Nowheresville lacks individual liberties, powers, and privileges.

position to do so. Now, this consequence is just the characteristic of Nowheresville Feinberg finds worrisome. This difference, believes Feinberg, makes all the difference, especially for the dignity of Nowheresvillians. Since both the activity of claiming rights and the capacity for claiming rights are absent in a world without individual rights, I will in turn focus on how each might affect human dignity.

It is reasonable to suppose that the disappearance of the activity of claiming rights is a real loss to those living in a world without rights. Feinberg states that "the activity of claiming, finally, as much as any other thing . . . gives a sense to the notion of personal dignity."[7] Perhaps the clearest way to put this point is to say that by failing to engage in the activity of claiming, what is most clearly forfeited is one very important way of expressing dignity. The loss of rights leaves Nowheresvillians in a state of rhetorical deficit. Since claiming their rights is sometimes an especially appropriate way for human beings to express their dignity, one fundamental problem with Nowheresville is that its inhabitants are significantly hampered in expressing their dignity.

Why is the activity of claiming individual rights so appropriate to the expression of human dignity? First, we must recognize that it does make sense to talk about expressing dignity. This is clear enough from a look at the ways we commonly use 'dignity'. It is familiar to hear it said that someone "speaks with dignity" or "presents himself with dignity." To "carry oneself with dignity" or to "walk with dignity" are forms of expression, a style of presenting oneself to others. On the other hand, we do not say that someone speaks with "worth," or carries himself with "value." We might say that the worth of a person represented by his dignity has a public availability. Dignity has a presentational aspect that not all terms of value possess, and it seems this presentational feature of the dignity of human be-

ings is especially apparent when they engage in the activity of claiming their rights.

The observation that the very activity of claiming rights bespeaks a person's dignity raises questions. Is the activity of claiming rights always expressive of dignity? If not, when does claiming rights typically fail to be expressive of human dignity? First of all, claiming rights is especially expressive of a person's dignity when he is under the pressure of an external challenge. Suppose a group of bigots tells a black man, in no uncertain terms, that they believe he is no better than a dog, and add that they plan to treat or at least regard him as such. Here, claiming one's rights not to be regarded or treated in this manner is a meaningful, personal way of expressing one's dignity to one's oppressors. At least when under the pressure of belittlement, expressing dignity seems to require a forceful, though perhaps calm, assertion.[8] Indignation is perhaps the most direct feeling aroused by such a pointed affront, and claiming rights is no doubt one particularly effective way for individuals to express their dignity and give vent to their indignation. There are, in fact, two aspects of an expression relevant to the present point: (1) the manner or style of the expression—standing tall and speaking without hesitation, and (2) the content of the expression—the apposite (though perhaps unspoken) claim that you should not treat me like a dog for I am a person just like you.

In the face of such a challenge it is particularly difficult to imagine someone expressing dignity (with respect to the style or the content) with a deferential expression. Suppose the man in my example risks no serious repercussions to himself or his loved ones for his response to the bigots' insult. Given this, imagine the man says (without the touch of sarcasm that might well lend dignity to the content of his expression) "Would

---

[7] Ibid., p. 257.

[8] See Boxill, p. 198. Boxill is also right to claim that all insults offensive to human dignity as well as those which tend to undermine one's sense of dignity do not necessarily involve any violation of human rights.

you *please* take that back." Suppose this is all the man ever says, even in the face of additional abuse this meek response brings forth. As we will see below, it is not my point that such a response is meek in every context. And, while asking favors or making requests is not always antithetical to expressing dignity, they are surely not paradigm cases of expressing oneself in a dignified fashion in the face of such ridicule.[9]

Continuing with this case, imagine that the man resorted to begging that the ridicule stop. Here the individual's failure to express his dignity is even clearer, because it seems that begging—in both style and content—is an activity that usually puts one on such a low footing with one's perceived benefactor as to destroy the possibility of a dignified expression.[10] As Richard Wasserstrom notes about acquiring anything by claiming it as your right, "[it] is crucially different from seeking or obtaining it through the grant of a privilege, the receipt of a favor or the presence of a permission."[11] One thing that Wasserstrom is noticing about rights is how claiming them can ex-

press that you feel worthy to preempt the powers of others over you—that on your own behalf you press a legitimate claim. One's human dignity, if it is a mark of anything, is a mark of one's equality on some fundamental level with other human beings. It is the very fact of this equality that usually makes deferential behavior a particularly inappropriate way of expressing one's dignity and, at times, makes claiming rights such a dignified expression.

However, every time a person claims his rights this activity is not expressive of his dignity. Claiming one's rights might be unrelated to expressing dignity or even, in extreme cases, antithetical to the expression of human dignity. Someone might conceivably claim his rights in a very undignified way. He might be too pushy about his rights or he might claim some rights insincerely, not really believing that they were his but still hoping to receive the benefit of the display. Envision an impatient child who knows that if he persists in some claim his beleaguered parent will give in. In claiming their rights people might be reckless or rash, presumptuous or even unfair. Such attitudes affect the manner in which people go about securing what their rights guarantee, and consequently not all circumstances that lead people to claim their rights will lead them directly to an expression of their dignity as human beings.

First, consider a case where claiming rights is, if not undignified—that is, where a certain expected minimum expression of dignity is absent—at least unrelated to the expression of dignity. Imagine a situation where an individual is under no particular threat, and no affront has been directed his way. He just claims his rights in order to complete some task. Picture a barricade across a road that anyone is free to pass, if he only claims his right to do so. Since everyone has the right to pass, the gate opens and closes with regularity. Claiming rights like these is a kind of social ritual, a bureaucratic ritual, if you will. Just claim the right and continue on your way. Suppose that for those who do claim their rights in this situa-

---

[9] As I will explain, in some circumstances not claiming one's rights is a perfectly recognizable expression of dignity. Part of what is important in my example is not only the recognition of whom we have rights against—we do not have rights against those without the capacity to respect them or the mute and implacable natural world—but also the recognition of just when claiming rights might be fatuous. By analogy we might come to understand why uncomplaining self-restraint is thought by many to be a characteristically dignified way to face a natural disaster like drought.

[10] Begging is actually a very complex social activity. Asking for something you need is not necessarily begging; to beg is to ask for something as charity, to ask knowing that you must rely on others' compassion alone to secure your needs. There are more and less dignified ways to beg, and these differ from one culture to another. For example, in Islamic societies begging is not always as deferential or demeaning as it is in the United States. This is perhaps because of the existence of some more or less formal protocol for begging which is linked to the existence of traditional hierarchies and the Koranic duty to give alms; see *The Koran*, 107:1–7 (Suffolk: Penguin Classics, 1983), p. 28.

[11] Richard Wasserstrom, "Rights, Human Rights and Racial Discrimination," *Journal of Philosophy* 61 (1964):630.

tion the activity is purely a rote affair. It seems clear enough that when claiming rights becomes perfunctory, doing so is not related to the expression of human dignity.[12]

One might object that this scenario is not an adequate case for our general discussion of human rights. Human rights are presumably fundamental to our opportunity to live decent, meaningful lives, and hence any case of their abridgment is a serious affair. However, we are not only called upon to claim our rights when they are challenged or abridged. Take a right that seems fundamental to many: an individual's right to political self-determination. Take as a specific case of this right the right to vote for the leaders of one's country. A black man claiming his right to vote in the U.S. presidential election of 1900 may well have been expressing his dignity. The same cannot so easily be said of a white male claiming his established right to vote in 1988, even though he might still regard his right to vote as a fundamental and valuable right. When rights are so well protected as to make claiming them a bureaucratic affair, marked principally by officialism and perhaps red tape, even the activity of claiming basic rights might be unrelated to an expression of human dignity.

Cases like the previous one are perhaps not surprising—since for the activity of claiming rights to be fundamentally linked to expressing human dignity it need not be true that every case is expressive of such dignity. But what of situations where claiming one's rights is not simply unrelated to the expression of dignity but actually undignified? Interestingly, there has been little notice of such cases, even though no one, including Feinberg, seems to deny their pos-

sibility. I will examine two cases. The first I call the case of the bumptious man. From the start let us leave aside the possibility that his claims are insincere. Each time the bumptious man claims his rights his particular failing is not that he believes these are not really his rights. When he claims his rights he is perfectly sure that these are in fact his proper due, and let us suppose further that he is correct. In spite of his sincerity, though, the bumptious man is impatient about his rights. He often claims them out of turn, insensitive to others' claims in his headlong rush to make sure his are not ignored. He also has a strong tendency to claim his rights too vehemently and at all the wrong times, seemingly asserting that people are always on the verge of denying him his rights. Not only is the bumptious man rudely impatient, but he is unreasonably worried that others do not really respect him as a person.

In fact, it is this deep apprehension that drives him to be so presumptuous, so offensively self-assertive. As he sees the world, others take him for granted. He is noisy and obtrusive about his rights because he is gripped by the unfounded, but for him very powerful, fear that others pay him no heed. And it is when he is overcome by this fear—which is quite often—that he is most strident and shrill. This is when his offensive self-assertiveness is most undignified. At times like these, claiming his rights surely does not display the bumptious man's dignity; instead it reveals his ungoverned rage at what he sees as a damnably insensitive, confrontational world. It may be that he creates many enemies with his bitterly defiant style, and that his own fear is one of his greatest enemies. He may or may not recognize this. What is important is how, for him, the activity of claiming his rights is directly opposed to the expression of his dignity.[13]

---

[12] It might, however, express something if one day I fail to claim rights that are so well worn. It might be expressive of some overwhelming sense of inferiority; it might just as well express protest against a meaningless bureaucratic ritual. Also, of course, if I do claim such a right in spite of an overwhelming sense of inferiority, it might serve to reinforce my own sense of dignity.

[13] Though the bumptious man may see that in such cases his style is "rough," from his point of view he may think the content of his expression does display his dignity. He may believe all claims of rights are, at least in content, an expression of dignity. However, even the

Look for a moment at a related scenario—the case of the hopeless dependent. He might depend on another person, on a supporting institution, or both. Once again, when he presses his rights he is neither insincere nor in the habit of misidentifying them. But he, too, presses his claims too strongly, always imagining that the person who owes him the obligation in question is ready to renege. His particular stridency is born out of his disproportionate fear that without constant clamor he will be deprived of any of the nurturing assistance so important to human life and so seemingly fleeting in his own. He too is uncontrollably worried, impatient, at times rude, always claiming his rights in that unmistakably quavering voice that indicates he is haunted by the fear of being left by the wayside.

From the point of view of those who bear the brunt of their onslaughts, the hopeless dependent and the bumptious man might seem indistinguishable. Yet the bumptious man is offensive and pushy because of his incessant worry that others do not respect him as a person, whereas the hopeless dependent just cannot get it off his mind that others, though they may respect him, are just about to leave him in the lurch, or that the institution he depends on for succor is ready to close up shop. However, in spite of their differences, their important similarity lies in the fact that each of them harbors the deep and uncontrolled fear that the world is hard and uncaring. They both believe that the only way to get the attention of others is to announce your presence in no uncertain terms and thereby let them know ahead of time that they cannot go backsliding on the duties they owe you. Though the bumptious man and the hopeless dependent have different fears, there *is* something in the character of their fear that is interestingly alike, something which leads the assertion of their rights to be undignified.

Both cases point to the fact that there is something to the expression of dignity beyond the mere claiming of rights, or for that matter, the activity of claiming rights in protest. It may seem that what the bumptious man and the hopeless dependent lack are clear cases of genuine protest, but this observation misses the real point. Both are protesting; they are protesting potential— even imminent—repudiations of their rights. However, in the end their protests are undignified because their incessant worries, their near-paranoid fears, betray how they fail to express their dignity on an even deeper level. In both cases what seems particularly undignified is their near total lack of self-control—their continuing failure to quell their own ungoverned fears. The greatest challenge to their dignity comes not from without but from within. Remarkably enough, it is just this way of expressing dignity—through some form of self-control—that Feinberg, among others, seems to ignore. It is also inadequate to see such a failure of self-control only as a symptom of some internal diminishment of dignity. This is to confuse one's expression of dignity with one's sense of dignity. The former, as described above, is a public event. The latter is a psychological condition akin to, but not identical with, self-respect and the related notion of self-esteem. And while one's loss of a sense of dignity may indeed be one psychological condition leading to one's failure to express dignity, this psychological story is no reason to conflate a sense of dignity with an expression of that sense.

If in fact an expression of our human dignity is related in some important way to an expression of self-control, let us see if

---

content of a dignified expression—i.e., that as a human being one should not be denied one's proper standing—is inextricably related to the context of the claim. While the content of an expression of dignity does not reduce to the manner of the expression, the very content of the expression can be undermined by bad timing. For example, for the bumptious man to claim some basic right, thereby ostensibly asserting "I am indeed your equal" in a situation where it is simply outrageous to suppose that this was ever in doubt, provides his expression with ambiguous content. In cases like this the content that would make the statement expressive of dignity is possibly overwhelmed—at least from the point of view of the audience—by the second message that in fact the bumptious man feels, without real justification, that others regard him as an inferior.

there is a case where the dignified expression of self-control might even persuade one to refrain from claiming one's legitimate rights. Return to the example of the black man once again. Suppose this time he is insulted in the same fashion, but in this instance the offender is not a group of the town's bigots, but the town idiot. This sorry fellow meanders through life insulting everybody—perhaps especially blacks—and for the most part people try to ignore him. For a black person to meet him on the street is to expect a disconnected and offensive outburst liberally spiced with invectives. For one reason or another many communities do tolerate such individuals. No matter why, the idiot is allowed to roam the streets; even the blacks put up with him. Now, when confronted by the simpleton the black man might deem it wise to choose to control his anger and refrain from protesting in the face of this insult.

It is not quite right to say that the black man feels no anger, because he may see the idiot as a classic, if pitiful, upshot of a hateful and racist society. He still burns inside at the catcalls and the rude cry of "nigger." But it is quite possible that he chooses what he sees as the dignified expression: to control his anger and ignore the dolt. The black man expresses his dignity by calmly telling his children that this man is not like the others—that here you must refuse to dignify such insults with a response. He teaches his children that there is not always a point to impassioned protest, that sometimes by silent self-control you can better express your dignity. Of course, he might even have tried this same tactic with the bigots (and been successful), though in this case it may have been both more difficult and less appropriate to do so.

It is crucially important here to point out that self-control should not be equated with self-repression. To do so is to trivialize the conception of self-control significant to human dignity. To be sure, self-control may sometimes require the repression of certain outbursts or even, as in the previous case, the repression of justified claims of right.

Yet self-control may equally well require that one stand up and protest with impassioned vigor. The shy man may suffer from an unrestrained fear of even a casual talk with strangers, let alone a public declaration of his rights. For him it may well take an act of great self-control to quiet the inevitable fear of embarrassment associated with the situation where he stands up and claims his rights. In this case controlling one's apprehensions long enough to claim one's rights is a genuine manifestation of dignified self-control. It is clear that what recommends the particular form of self-restraint to the black man faced with the abusive town idiot is not a weak-kneed feeling of deference (which is rather evidence of a morally significant lack of self-control) but his deeper understanding of the situation. His realization is that some restraint (in this case of his indignation) is a more dignified manifestation than any flurry of claiming rights.

So far I have outlined the following points. First, the activity of claiming one's rights is sometimes, but not always, expressive of dignity; at times it might be unrelated to an expression of dignity or even be undignified. Second, in some cases, lacking self-control might well lead one to an undignified expression; such a loss of self-control can even render the activity of claiming rights undignified. However, we must refrain from simply identifying the idea of self-control with the restraint of one's outward expression. Expressing human dignity is a complex affair, composed of at least two components: (1) standing forth and protesting when one's oppressors threaten from without, a task for which the activity of claiming rights is particularly well suited; and (2) conducting oneself with some self-control, neither claiming one's rights out of blind and uncontrolled passion nor failing to do so for the same reason. Dignified protest requires some self-restraint; dignified self-control may well require vehement (albeit not uncontrolled) protest.[14]

---

[14] It is worth noting that the perception that such unself-controlled outbursts are undignified expres-

III

So far we have only examined what it is for human beings to express their dignity. We have done so without yet investigating what it is for an individual to have human dignity. In fact a person may be said to have human dignity even if he fails to express his dignity, indeed even if he has been proven to be prone to quite undignified outbursts. One important example of this belief is manifest in our attitudes, as well as our legislation, regarding criminals. Criminals (perhaps not the criminally insane) may be said to have dignity even if they constantly express their feelings of humiliation. It is an important moral realization that their undignified outbursts do not free us to treat them as if they had no dignity—that is, to treat them like animals and not responsible, though reprehensible, human beings.

A. I. Melden suggests a conception of having dignity that falters on this very point. Melden claims, "What we label the dignity of a person is not a matter pertaining to some precious internal quality of his . . . but that sense he displays of his own status as a being who is authorized by his rights to conduct himself in the expectation that his rights will be honored by others."[15] The problem here is that Melden conflates having human dignity with having a proper sense of dignity. This is an unacceptable conclusion. As was noted earlier, both the bumptious man and the hopeless dependent may lack a proper sense of dignity. Yet while we may recognize this as one of their

shortcomings, such an observation is clearly about their psychological state and not about their ultimate worth as human beings. The problem with equating having dignity and having a sense of dignity is that to say a person has dignity goes beyond an observation about his sense of self-worth to an observation about his ultimate value as a human being. Lacking an adequate sense of self-worth is a serious enough moral complication for the bumptious man without the conceptual confusion Melden seems to promote, that we are to gauge someone's worth strictly by his own sense of his worth or status. Melden's observation notwithstanding, we are clearly not free to use as mere objects those who have internalized the oppression of others or otherwise arrived at an unacceptably low estimation of their own value. The bumptious man's self-doubts or a criminal's powerful urge to degrade himself free no one to disregard his humanity with impunity.

The fact that anyone engages in undignified behavior or fails to have an appropriate sense of dignity gives no individual moral license to treat him—even while he is doing so—as if he has no dignity. While we might say of someone who degrades himself that he has "lost his dignity," we nonetheless recognize that this "loss" is not complete in this important sense: it does not provide others with the privilege to treat him like an object or deprive him of the status of a human being. This observation leads directly to a second worry about Feinberg's Nowheresville: since individuals there do not have rights, they also lack the capacity to claim them. The capacity to claim rights is different from the activity of claiming them and different again from the appropriate sense one has that in having rights one has a value equal to others.

Feinberg suggests that having dignity is tantamount to having the capacity to claim rights: "What is called 'human dignity' may simply be the recognizable *capacity* to assert claims. To respect a person then, or to think of him as possessed of human dignity, simply *is* to think of him a *potential maker of*

---

sions does not necessarily fall prey to some simple cultural relativism of judgment about such matters. It is not only that the undignified tirades of the bumptious man are undignified because of his transgression of certain narrowly defined codes of propriety. This is true because such a loss of self-control would lead to unique outbursts in different cultural contexts. What is undignified is not just the particular form of the outburst but the very lack of control that leads to it. Though the forms of undignified behavior do vary from culture to culture, the lack of self-control that can give rise to them is a cross-cultural phenomenon.

[15] Melden, p. 194.

claims" (my emphasis).[16] As I have just suggested, it is correct to focus on the capacity to claim rights and not simply the activity of claiming rights (or one's sense of self-worth) as one mark of the possession of human dignity. This is so because one might not actively claim rights (or for that matter, express dignity in any other way) but still retain the capacity to do so, thereby retaining a special status associated with human dignity. It seems as evident as it is important that one undignified expression, or even a series of such expressions, does not destroy an individual's dignity—that is, it does not make him into an object to be used at the discretion of others—unless, of course, it is an action or a series of actions that results in the elimination of the capacity itself. Yet, Feinberg's identification of having human dignity and having the capacity to claim rights raises this important question: does someone who has the capacity to claim rights thereby have all the characteristics essential to human dignity?

In answer to this question try one further thought experiment. Let us restore to Nowheresville all of the personal rights held against others that Feinberg first denied it. (According to Feinberg, doing so should restore the lost dignity of Nowheresvillians; and I do agree that in such a world their dignity has been greatly augmented. When they find themselves challenged by others the range of significant ways to express their dignity has increased in an important way. And, even if they are not actively expressing their dignity, there is the further sense in which they still retain their dignity; their rights are still protecting them from the depredation of others.) In this second thought experiment, however, imagine a new breed of Nowheresvillian, bristling with individual rights but denied some form of the capacity for self-control. Denying even a single Nowheresvillian the capacity to exercise some kinds of self-control will put him in an even

worse position—with respect to his human dignity—than he was before.

Looking at some of the lives available in this revisitation of Nowheresville, it will become evident how the capacity to claim rights is not the only or even the principal capacity relevant to the possession of human dignity. Those inhabitants of Nowheresville II who lack the capacity for some kinds of self-control lack the most fundamental characteristic of the possession of human dignity. Let us suppose, for just one example, that some of them totally lose the ability to control their appetites. Though it may be true that this new breed of Nowheresvillian is not used by others—perhaps because now they stand up for themselves in light of their newly reinstated rights—they do, however, face an equally daunting foe from within.

Though well armed with individual rights, the new Nowheresvillian may easily fight and lose an even more important battle for the possession of his human dignity (a battle in which rights against others are of little use). Imagine the uncontrollably compulsive gambler of Nowheresville II. He bets on anything he can: on the horses or on college basketball, on pro wrestling or even on his children's grades at school. The real purpose of winning any bet is the opportunity this provides to bet again. It is not that he just likes to place a bet, like the more familiar compulsive gamblers of our world who do have the capacity to control their betting but just repeatedly fail to do so. All he can think about is betting. Every event in his world, even those which animate his most intimate relationships, is the possible object of a wager. This compulsive gambler is ruled by his desire to bet; he has become a slave to his own uncontrollable drive to tempt fortune. This fact no doubt affects the quality of the rest of his life; indeed, he has no time or emotional energy for anything or anyone else.

But in reality his plight is far worse than a loss of time and emotional energy. The man who must always make a bet—or always have food, drink, sex, or affection—is in a

---

[16] Feinberg, p. 252.

true sense not in control of his own life. He might recognize this total loss of self-control as his own perverse path to self-destruction; he might not. The point is that the glutton of Nowheresville II (who has lost the very capacity for self-control) does not always want to want food. It is just his peculiar makeup which drives him without mercy toward food. For him food is not just sustenance or nourishment but the overwhelming subject of his conscious life.

Malcolm Lowry's vivid portrait of a day in the life of the alcoholic British consul Geoffrey Firmin might be taken as one further example:

No angels nor Yvonne nor Hugh could help him here. As for the demons, they were inside him as well as outside; quiet at the moment—taking their siesta perhaps—he was nonetheless surrounded by them and occupied; they were in possession. . . . "Yet I shall face [the truth]." How? When he not only lied to himself, but himself believed the lie and lied back again to those lying factions. . . . There was not even a consistent basis to his self-deceptions. How should there be then to his attempts at honesty? "Horror," he said. "Yet I will not give in." But who was I, how find that I, where had "I" gone?[17]

Now, your ordinary drunk or compulsive gambler typically does not experience such "horror." But in Nowheresville II the man lacking the capacity for self-control is truly a defenseless menial at the service of his own inner impulses. He is so, even though he may at times disavow that this is his desire to eat or to drink or to gamble. Since he is not able to exercise any direction over his appetites, he loses himself to them, and none of his newly restored rights can protect him from this inevitable decline. Unable to regulate them, he is controlled by them. He may see, in glimpses, other possibilities for his life—when his passions "take their siesta"—but he is ultimately not capable of any self-realization independent of these appetites.

One might suppose that in Nowheresville II the uncontrollably compulsive alcoholic's loss of dignity is not a function of his lost capacity to control his appetite but, rather, a consequence of the fact that the particular appetite he cannot control promotes unlimited undignified behavior (drunken stupors, sloppy speech, etc.). Suppose, this objection goes, we have an equally compulsive fellow with a passion for decorum. This guy has lost the capacity for uncouth behavior. Even if he wanted to, he could never bring himself to use his salad fork for his fish—his social forms are unalterably perfect. The suggestion here is: having dignity is simply a matter of how one acts (i.e., the social forms one's behavior instantiates) and has nothing to do with the existence of one's capacity to choose such actions (i.e., the capacity to choose to engage in a particular social form).

One consequence of accepting this suggestion is the result that any trained animal might thereby be thought to have a dignity equal to that of a human being. And, while animals may express something akin to dignity (perhaps grace?), the possession of human dignity depends not on the display of certain social forms, but what has given rise to such social forms in the first place, human choices. Actually, the uncontrollably proper man—the one who just cannot put his decorum to rest—would not always be able to express his dignity. At an informal gathering his polished behavior would be priggish, not dignified. The problem with this objection is that the loss of the capacity for self-control, in this case control over one's impulse to be proper, cannot legitimately be seen as a covert commitment to the principle that sloppy behavior is uncalled for. Having lost the capacity to set decorum aside, his loss is ultimately the loss of the ability to exercise genuine judgment about such matters.

Now, in spite of the suggestion that by restoring rights to Nowheresville we would restore everything essential to human dignity, the man without the capacity for self-

---

[17] Malcolm Lowry, *Under the Volcano* (New York: Signet, 1965), p. 205.

control is not in possession of his human dignity. Even though the new Nowheres-villian has all the rights against others he might want, his uncontrollable compulsion, whatever it may be, is a roadblock to his possession of human dignity. This is the case because at present all that his capacity to claim rights serves is the demands of the demons within. In this state even the value of these rights is diminished, because he cannot use them to guarantee the possibility of an authentic self-expression. No doubt his rights still do protect him from some quite serious challenges—others may not legitimately use him solely as a means to their ends. However, losing the capacity to battle with his own appetites or other desires, the gambler or the glutton of Nowheresville II suffers a deeply significant loss of human dignity.[18]

Some self-control is necessary for expressing human dignity; equally so, the capacity to exercise self-control is necessary if one is to be said to have dignity. Though we might believe that the capacity to claim one's rights and the capacity to control one's own life from within are importantly related, they are not, at least prima facie, the same capacity. In Nowheresville II having the capacity to claim rights does not necessarily entail having the capacity to claim them in the defense of some previously controlled or integrated self. A person who has human

dignity is fundamentally a person who is self-possessed; he at least has the capacity to give direction to his own life. The fact that he is self-possessed implies that he is not possessed by either of two potential enemies to his dignity: other people or random, uncontrolled desires from within. Having human dignity—that special office or rank had by most all human beings—is necessarily related to the possession of not only the capacity to claim rights but at least the further capacity to exercise self-control.

The observation that the capacity for self-control has a deep importance for human dignity stands forth as a crucial counterpoint to the pictures offered by Feinberg or Melden. In a person possessed of human dignity, his rights and his ability to exercise self-control may be intimately intertwined. However, it is worth noting that the capacity for self-control has significant value even in a world without rights. Clearly, Feinberg's Nowheresville is vastly improved by the presence of the capacity for self-control. It is this very capacity that underwrites many of the moral practices Feinberg left in Nowheresville to make it more acceptable. No matter how blighted by the loss of individual rights, depriving some of the inhabitants of Nowheresville of their capacity for self-control would worsen their plight. Most significant, it would further undermine their human dignity. The fact that the loss of the capacity for self-control would deprive Nowheresvillians—already deprived of their rights—of their dignity, is indicative of the independent and fundamental value of this capacity for the possession of human dignity.

Finally, even though in a world without rights the capacity for self-control would have significant value, the converse is not so obviously true. What is the value of the unself-controllable gambler's capacity to claim rights? In Nowheresville II this gambler's rights not only fail to reinstate his dignity, but in fact without some disposition to self-control the basic purpose of these rights becomes obscured. The value of our capacity to claim rights relies on our capaci-

---

[18] Or, in a related scenario we have touched on already, even though restored to his full rights, the uncontrollably shy man of Nowheresville II (having lost the capacity to control his shyness) would be unable to use these rights to express his dignity. Lacking the capacity for self-control is a more significant blow to the possession of human dignity than having the capacity and just repeatedly choosing to be unself-controlled. This is so because the loss of the capacity—even if it were somehow restorable—deprives one of the ability to regulate such impulses, whereas the continued choice to be unself-controlled still leaves one morally significant options for action. For example, we feel perfectly justified in treating those who have lost the capacity for self-control, and Herbert Morris has argued quite ably that this is tantamount to a denial of their basic humanity; see his "Persons and Punishment." *Monist* 52 (1968): 475–501.

ty to control ourselves, to direct our own lives. The value of human rights relies fundamentally on our ability to make these rights serve our own ends. What would be the value of rights for an entity which by its very constitution cannot exercise self-control? Rivers, lawn mowers, and the New York Stock Exchange do not have rights, not because they cannot be thought of as having purposes, but because it makes no sense to say they have purposes of their own. They are not ultimately self-controllable. The fact that rights have some value presumes, at bare minimum, the existence of beings who are self-directed; it presupposes the actuality of beings who are able to take genuine advantage of these rights. Though human rights do perform a moral function (the moral function of obliging others to respect us by way of respecting some of our most basic claims), what makes their function moral is the fact of the human capacity for authentic self-control.

A Letter Concerning Toleration

John Locke

John Locke was born in 1632, the son of a Puritan attorney who fought on the side of Parliament against King Charles I. After attending Oxford, Locke briefly pursued a diplomatic career before becoming physician and secretary to the Earl of Shaftesbury. Shaftesbury plotted against the Stuarts, and when he was forced to flee to Holland in 1683, Locke followed him. After the Glorious Revolution in 1688, Locke returned to England.

Few, if any, philosophers had as much influence on the thinking of the American framers as John Locke. Although today we focus on his *Second Treatise On Government*, excerpted in section VI, *A Letter Concerning Toleration* was much more influential at the time. In his *Letter*, Locke begins with a brief indication of his general theory of the powers of government. Legitimate government, he thinks, derives its powers from the consent of the governed, but such consent can best be understood by first imagining people in a pre-political "state of nature." There, Locke thinks, people would give up their natural right to life and property in order to gain greater protection of those rights by the state. The powers of the state, however, are limited by the original reasons that would motivate people to join and accept its authority. With this as background, Locke considers freedom of religion and conscience, an issue of central importance to the American framers as well. No government, he argues, should exercise force to promote or prohibit religious beliefs and practices.

Honored sir, . . . I esteem it above all things necessary to distinguish exactly the business of civil government from that of religion, and to settle the just bound that lie between the one and the other. If this be not done, there can be no end put to the controversies that will be always arising between those that have, or at least pretend to have, on the one

From John Locke, *A Letter Concerning Toleration* in *John Locke on Politics and Education*, ed. Howard R. Penniman (New York: Van Norstrand Company, 1947).

side, a concernment for the interest of men's souls, and, on the other side, a care of the commonwealth.

The commonwealth seems to me to be a society of men constituted only for the procuring, preserving, and advancing their own civil interests.

Civil interests I call life, liberty, health, and indolency of body; and the possession of outward things, such as money, lands, houses, furniture, and the like.

It is the duty of the civil magistrate, by the impartial execution of equal laws, to secure unto all the people in general, and to every one of his subjects in particular, the just possession of these things belonging to this life. If any one presume to violate the laws of public justice and equity, established for the preservation of those things, his presumption is to be checked by the fear of punishment, consisting of the deprivation or diminution of those civil interests, or goods, which otherwise he might and ought to enjoy. But seeing no man does willingly suffer himself to be punished by the deprivation of any part of his goods, and much less of his liberty or life, therefore is the magistrate armed with the force and strength of all his subjects, in order to the punishment of those that violate any other man's rights.

Now that the whole jurisdiction of the magistrate reaches only to these civil concernments, and that all civil power, right, and dominion, is bounded and confined to the only care of promoting these things; and that it neither can nor ought in any manner to be extended to the salvation of souls, these following considerations seem unto me abundantly to demonstrate.

First, because the care of souls is not committed to the civil magistrate, any more than to other men. It is not committed unto him, I say, by God; because it appears not that God has ever given any such authority to one man over another, as to compel any one to his religion. Nor can any such power be vested in the magistrate by the consent of the people, because no man can so far abandon the care of his own salvation as blindly to leave to the choice of any other, whether prince or subject, to prescribe to him what faith or worship he shall embrace. For no man can, if he would, conform his faith to the dictates of another. All the life and power of true religion consist in the inward and full persuasion of the mind; and faith is not faith without believing. Whatever profession we make, to whatever outward worship we conform, if we are not fully satisfied in our own mind that the one is true, and the other well pleasing unto God, such profession and such practice, far from being any furtherance, are indeed great obstacles to our salvation. For in this manner, instead of expiating other sins by the exercise of religion, I say, in offering thus unto God Almighty such a worship as we esteem to be displeasing unto him, we add unto the number of our other sins those also of hypocrisy, and contempt of his Divine Majesty.

In the second place, the care of souls cannot belong to the civil magistrate, because his power consists only in outward force; but true and saving religion consists in the inward persuasion of the mind, without which nothing can be acceptable to God. And such is the nature of the understanding, that it cannot be compelled to the belief of anything by outward force. Confiscation of estate, imprisonment, torments, nothing of that nature can have any such efficacy as to make men change the inward judgment that they have framed of things.

It may indeed be alleged that the magistrate may make use of arguments, and thereby draw the heterodox into the way of truth, and procure their salvation. I grant it; but this is common to him with other men. In teaching, instructing, and redressing the erroneous by reason, he may certainly do what becomes any good man to do. Magistracy does not oblige him to put off either humanity or Christianity; but it is one thing to persuade, another to command; one thing to press with arguments, another with penalties. This civil power alone has a right to do; to the other good-will is authority enough. Every man has commission to admonish, exhort, convince another of error, and, by reasoning, to draw him into truth; but to give laws, receive obedience, and compel with the sword, belongs to none but the magistrate. And upon this ground, I affirm that the magistrate's power extends not to the establishing of any articles of faith, or forms of worship, by the force of his laws. For laws are of no force at all without penalties, and penalties in this case are absolutely impertinent, because they are not proper to convince the mind. Neither the profession of any articles of faith, nor the conformity to any outward form of worship (as has been already said), can be available to the salvation of souls, unless the truth of the one, and the acceptableness of the other unto God, be thoroughly believed by those that so profess and practise. But penalties are no way capable to produce such belief. It is only light and evidence that can work a change in men's opinions; which light can in no manner proceed from corporal sufferings, or any other outward penalties.

In the third place, the care of the salvation of men's souls cannot belong to the magistrate; because, though the rigour of laws and the force of penalties were capable to convince and change men's minds, yet would not that help at all to the salvation of their souls. For there being but one truth, one way to heaven, what hope is there that more men would be led into it if they had no rule but the religion of the court, and were put under the necessity to quit the light of their own reason, and oppose the dictates of their own consciences, and blindly to resign themselves up to the will of their governors, and to the religion which either ignorance, ambition, or superstition had chanced to establish in the countries where they were born? In the variety and contradiction of opinions in religion, wherein the princes of the world are as much divided as in their secular interests, the narrow way would be much straitened; one country alone would be in the right, and all the rest of the world put under an obligation of following their princes in the ways that lead to destruction; and that which heightens the absurdity, and very ill suits the notion of a Deity, men would owe their eternal happiness or misery to the places of their nativity.

These considerations, to omit many others that might have been urged to the same purpose, seem unto me sufficient to conclude that all the power of civil government relates only to men's civil interests, is confined to the care of the things of this world, and hath nothing to do with the world to come.

Let us now consider what a church is. A church, then, I take to be a voluntary society of men, joining themselves together of their own accord in order to the public worshipping of God in such manner as they judge acceptable to him, and effectual to the salvation of their souls.

I say it is a free and voluntary society. Nobody is born a member of any church; otherwise the religion of parents would descend unto children by the same right of inheritance as their temporal estates, and every one would hold his faith by the same tenure he does his lands, than which nothing can be imagined more absurd. Thus, therefore, that matter stands. No man by nature is bound unto any particular church or sect, but every one joins himself voluntarily to that society in which he believes he has found that profession and worship which is truly acceptable to God. The hope of salvation, as it was the only cause of his entrance into that communion, so it can be the only reason of his stay there. For if afterwards he discover anything either erroneous in the doctrine or incongruous in the worship of that society to which he has joined himself, why should it not be as free for him to go out as it was to enter? No member of a religious society can be tied with any other bonds but what proceed from the certain expectation of eternal life. A church, then, is a society of members voluntarily uniting to that end.

It follows now that we consider what is the power of this church, and unto what laws it is subject.

Forasmuch as no society, how free soever, or upon whatsoever slight occasion instituted, whether of philosophers for learning, of merchants for commerce, or of men of leisure for mutual conversation and discourse, no church or company, I say, can in the least subsist and hold together, but will presently dissolve and break in pieces, unless it be regulated by some laws, and the members all consent to observe some order. Place and time of meeting must be agreed on; rules for admitting and excluding members must be established; distinction of officers, and putting things into a regular course, and such-like, cannot be omitted. But since the joining together of several members into this church-society, as has already been demonstrated, is absolutely free and spontaneous, it necessarily follows that the right of making its laws can belong to none but the society itself; or, at least (which is the same thing), to those whom the society by common consent has authorised thereunto. . . .

The end of a religious society (as has already been said) is the public worship of God, and, by means thereof, the acquisition of eternal life. All discipline ought therefore to tend to that end, and all ecclesiastical laws to be thereunto confined. Nothing ought nor can be transacted in this society relating to the possession of civil and worldly goods. No force is here to be made use of upon any occasion whatsoever. For force belongs wholly to the civil magistrate, and the possession of all outward goods is subject to his jurisdiction.

But, it may be asked, by what means then shall ecclesiastical laws be established, if they must be thus destitute of all compulsive power? I answer: They must be established by means suitable to the nature of such things, whereof the external profession and observation—if not proceeding from a thorough conviction and approbation of the mind—is altogether useless and unprofitable. The arms by which the members of this society are to be kept within their duty are exhortations, admonitions, and advices. If by these means the offenders will not be reclaimed, and the erroneous convinced, there remains nothing further to be done but that such stubborn and obstinate persons, who give no ground to hope for their reformation, should be cast out and separated from the society. This is the last and utmost force of ecclesiastical authority. No other punishment can thereby be inflicted than that, the relation ceasing between the body and the member which is cut off. The person so condemned ceases to be a part of that church.

These things being thus determined, let us inquire, in the next place: How far the duty of toleration extends, and what is required from every one by it?

And, first, I hold that no church is bound, by the duty of toleration, to retain any such person in her bosom as, after admonition, continues obstinately to offend against the laws of the society. For these being the condition of communion and the bond of the society, if the breach of them were permitted without any animadversion the society would immediately be thereby dissolved. . . .

Secondly, no private person has any right in any manner to prejudice another person in his civil enjoyments because he is of another church or religion. All the rights and franchises that belong to him as a man, or as a denizen, are inviolably to be preserved to him. These are not the business of religion. No violence nor injury is to be offered him, whether he be Christian or Pagan. Nay, we must not content ourselves with the narrow measures of bare justice; charity, bounty, and liberality must be added to it. This the Gospel enjoins, this reason directs, and this that natural fellowship we are born into requires of us. If any man err from the right way, it is his own misfortune, no injury to thee; nor therefore art thou to punish him in the things of this life because thou supposest he will be miserable in that which is to come.

What I say concerning the mutual toleration of private persons differing from one another in religion, I understand also of particular churches which stand, as it were, in the same relation to each other as private persons among themselves: nor has any one of them any manner of jurisdiction over any other; no, not even when the civil magistrate (as it sometimes happens) comes to be of this or the other communion. For the civil government can give no new right to the church, nor the church to the civil government. So that whether the magistrate join himself to any church, or separate from it, the church remains always as it was before—a free and voluntary society. It neither requires the power of the sword by the magistrate's coming to it, nor does it lose the right of instruction and excommunication by his going from it. This is the fundamental and immutable right of a spontaneous society—that it has power to remove any of its members who transgress the rules of its institution; but it cannot, by the accession of any new members, acquire any right of jurisdiction over those that are not joined with it. And therefore peace, equity, and friendship are always mutually to be observed by particular churches, in the same manner as by private persons, without any pretence of superiority or jurisdiction over one another.

. . .No peace and security, no, not so much as common friendship, can ever be established or preserved amongst men so long as this opinion prevails, that dominion is founded in grace and that religion is to be propagated by force of arms. . . .

Rights and the Entitlement Theory

Robert Nozick

Nozick begins with a strong commitment to pre-political, individual rights—rights that may not be transgressed by others, either as individuals or collectively as the state. Commonly called Lockean, or negative, these rights constitute "side constraints" on the actions of others, ensuring a person's freedom from interference in the pursuit of his or her own life. These rights are negative because they require only that others refrain from acting in certain ways, in particular, that they refrain from interfering with us. Beyond this, no one is obliged to do anything positive for us; we have no right, for example, to expect others to provide us with satisfying work or with any material goods we might need. Each individual is to be seen as autonomous and responsible, and should be left to fashion his or her own life free from the interference of others—as long as this is compatible with the right of others to do the same. Only the acknowledgment of this almost absolute right to be free from coercion, argues Nozick, fully respects the distinctiveness of persons, each with a unique life to lead.

This framework of individual rights and corresponding duties constitutes the basis of what power the government may legitimately have. In Nozick's view, the only morally legitimate state is the so-called night-watchman state, one whose functions are restricted to protecting the negative rights of citizens, that is, to protecting them against force, theft, fraud, and so on. In the selection which follows, Nozick is especially concerned with rejecting the claim that a larger state is necessary in order to achieve a just economic distribution.

In contrast to theories he calls end-state and patterned, Nozick proposes what he terms the entitlement theory of justice. According to this, a distribution is just if it arises from a prior just distribution by just means. For example, things may be acquired originally by one's taking something that belongs to no one else, and there are a number of ways of legitimately transferring justly acquired objects—gifts and voluntary exchange are among them, theft and blackmail are not. There is, however, no pattern to which a just distribution should conform. In the absence of force and fraud, people may do what they wish with their goods or holdings. They have a right to acquire and dispose of their property as they see fit, and individuals are entitled to their personal talents and characteristics and to whatever property they can obtain with them, as long as the negative rights of others are not violated in the process. In particular, Nozick claims that taxation is like forced labor and violates our individual rights.

Robert Nozick teaches philosophy at Harvard University. Besides the book from which this selection is taken, he has written *Philosophical Explanations* (1981) and *The Examined Life* (1989).

Individuals have rights, and there are things no person or group may do to them (without violating their rights). So strong and far-reaching are these rights that they raise the question of what, if anything, the state and its officials may do. How much room do individual rights leave for the state? The nature of the state, its legitimate functions and its justifications, if any, is the central concern of this book; a wide and diverse variety of topics intertwine in the course of our investigation.

Our main conclusions about the state are that a minimal state, limited to the narrow functions of protection against force, theft, fraud, enforcement of contracts, and so on, is justified; that any more extensive state will violate persons' rights not to be forced to do certain things, and is unjustified; and that the minimal state is inspiring as well as right. Two noteworthy implications are that the state may not use its coercive apparatus for the purpose of getting some citizens to aid others, or in order to prohibit activities to people for their *own* good or protection. . . .

WHY SIDE CONSTRAINTS?

. . .What is the rationale for placing the nonviolation of rights as a side constraint upon action?

Side constraints upon action reflect the underlying Kantian principle that individuals are ends and not merely means; they may not be sacrificed or used for the achieving of other ends without their consent. Individuals are inviolable. More should be said to illuminate this talk of ends and means. . . . In getting pleasure from seeing an attractive person go by, does one use the other solely as a means? Does someone so use an object of sexual fantasies? These and related questions raise very interesting issues for moral philosophy; but not, I think, for political philosophy.

Political philosophy is concerned only with *certain* ways that persons may not use others; primarily, physically aggressing against them. A specific side constraint upon action toward others expresses the fact that others may not be used in the specific ways the side constraint excludes. Side constraints express the inviolability of others, in the ways they specify. These modes of inviolability are expressed by the following injunction: "Don't use people in specified ways." An end-state view, on the other hand, would express the view that people are ends and not merely means (if it chooses to express this view at all), by a different injunction: "Minimize the use in specified ways of persons as means." Following this precept itself may involve using someone as a means in one of the ways specified. Had Kant held this view, he would have given the second formula of the categorical imperative as, "So act as to minimize the use of humanity simply as a means," rather than the one he actually used: "Act in such a way that you always treat humanity, whether in your own person or in the person of any other, never simply as a means, but always at the same time as an end."

Side constraints express the inviolability of other persons. But why may not one violate persons for the greater social good? Individually, we each sometimes choose to undergo some pain or sacrifice for a greater benefit or to avoid a greater harm: we go to the dentist to avoid worse suffering later; we do some unpleasant work for its results; some persons diet to improve their health or looks; some save money to support themselves when they are older. In each case, some cost is borne for the sake of the greater overall good. Why not, *similarly*, hold that some persons have to bear some costs that benefit other persons more, for the sake of the overall social good? But there is no *social entity* with a good that undergoes some sacrifice for its own good. There are only individual people, different individual people, with their own individual lives. Using one of these people for the benefit of others, uses him and benefits the others. Nothing more. What happens is that something is done to him for the sake of others. Talk of an overall social good covers this up. (Intentionally?) To use a person in this way does

not sufficiently respect and take account of the fact that he is a separate person, that his is the only life he has. *He* does not get some overbalancing good from his sacrifice, and no one is entitled to force this upon him— least of all a state or government that claims his allegiance (as other individuals do not) and that therefore scrupulously must be *neutral* between its citizens. . . .

DISTRIBUTIVE JUSTICE

The term "distributive justice" is not a neutral one. Hearing the term "distribution," most people presume that some thing or mechanism uses some principle or criterion to give out a supply of things. Into this process of distributing shares some error may have crept. So it is an open question, at least, whether *re*distribution should take place; whether we should do again what has already been done once, though poorly. However, we are not in the position of children who have been given portions of pie by someone who now makes last minute adjustments to rectify careless cutting. There is no *central* distribution, no person or group entitled to control all the resources, (jointly) deciding how they are to be doled out. What each person gets, he gets from others who give to him in exchange for something, or as a gift. In a free society, diverse persons control different resources, and new holdings arise out of the voluntary exchanges and actions of persons. There is no more a distributing or distribution of shares than there is a distributing of mates in a society in which persons choose whom they shall marry. The total result is the product of many individual decisions which the different individuals involved are entitled to make. Some uses of the term "distribution," it is true, do not imply a previous distributing appropriately judged by some criterion (e.g., "probability distribution"); nevertheless, despite the title of this essay, it would be best to use a terminology that clearly is neutral. We shall speak of people's holdings; a principle of justice in holdings describes (part of) what justice tells us (requires) about holdings. I shall state first what I take to be the correct view about justice in holdings, and then turn to the discussion of alternative views.

THE ENTITLEMENT THEORY

The subject of justice in holdings consists of three major topics. The first is the *original acquisition of holdings*, the appropriation of unheld things. This includes the issues of how unheld things may come to be held, the process(es) by which unheld things may come to be held, the things that may come to be held by these processes, the extent of what comes to be held by a particular process, and so on. We shall refer to the complicated truth about this topic, which we shall not formulate here, as the principle of justice in acquisition. The second topic concerns the *transfer of holdings* from one person to another. By what processes may a person transfer holdings to another? How may a person acquire a holding from another who holds it? Under this topic come general descriptions of voluntary exchange, and gift, and (on the other hand) fraud, as well as reference to particular conventional details fixed upon a given society. The complicated truth about this subject (with placeholders for conventional details) we shall call the principle of justice in transfer. (And we shall suppose it also includes principles governing how a person may divest himself of a holding, passing it into an unheld state.)

If the world were wholly just, the following inductive definition would exhaustively cover the subject of justice in holdings.

1. A person who acquires a holding in accordance with the principle of justice in acquisition is entitled to that holding.

2. A person who acquires a holding in accordance with the principle of justice in transfer, from someone else entitled to the holding, is entitled to the holding.

3. No one is entitled to a holding except by (repeated) applications of 1 and 2.

The complete principle of distributive justice would say simply that a distribution is just if everyone is entitled to the holdings they possess under the distribution.

A distribution is just if it arises from another (just) distribution by legitimate means. The legitimate means of moving from one distribution to another are specified by the principle of justice in transfer. The legitimate first "moves" are specified by the principle of justice in acquisition.[1] Whatever arises from a just situation by just steps is itself just. The means of change specified by the principle of justice in transfer, preserve justice. As correct rules of inference are truth preserving, and any conclusion deduced via repeated application of such rules from only true premises is itself true, so the means of transition from one situation to another specified by the principle of justice in transfer are justice preserving, and any situation actually arising from repeated transitions in accordance with the principle from a just situation is itself just. The parallel between justice-preserving transformations and truth-preserving transformations illuminates where it fails as well as where it holds. That a conclusion could have been deduced by truth-preserving means from premises that are true suffices to show its truth. That from a just situation a situation *could* have arisen via justice-preserving means does *not* suffice to show its justice. The fact that a thief's victims voluntarily *could* have presented him with gifts does not entitle the thief to his ill-gotten gains. Justice in holdings is historical; it depends upon what actually has happened. We shall return to this point later.

Not all actual situations are generated in accordance with the two principles of justice in holdings: the principle of justice in acquisition and the principle of justice in transfer. Some people steal from others, or defraud

---

[1] Applications of the principle of justice in acquisition may also occur as part of the move from one distribution to another. You may find an unheld thing now, and appropriate it. Acquisitions also are to be understood as included when, to simplify, I speak only of transitions by transfers.

them, or enslave them seizing their product and preventing them from living as they choose, or forcibly exclude others from competing in exchanges. None of these are permissible modes of transition from one situation to another. And some persons acquire holdings by means not sanctioned by the principle of justice in acquisition. The existence of past injustice (previous violations of the first two principles of justice in holdings) raises the third major topic under justice in holdings: the rectification of injustice in holdings. If past injustice has shaped present holdings in various ways, some identifiable and some not, what now, if anything, ought to be done to rectify these injustices? What obligations are the performers of injustice under to their victims? What obligations do the beneficiaries of injustice have to those whose position is worse than it would have been had the injustice not been done? Or, than it would have been had compensation been paid promptly? How, if at all, do things change if the beneficiaries and those made worse off are not the direct parties in the act of injustice, but, for example, their descendants? Is an injustice done to someone whose holding was itself based upon an unrectified injustice? How far back must one go in wiping clean the historical slate of injustices? What may victims of injustice permissibly do in order to rectify the injustices being done to them, including the many injustices done by persons acting through their government? I do not know of a thorough or theoretically sophisticated treatment of such issues. Idealizing greatly, let us suppose theoretical investigation will produce a principle of rectification. This principle uses historical information about previous situations and injustices done in them (as defined by the first two principles of justice, and rights against interference), and information about the actual course of events that flowed from these injustices, up until the present, and it yields a description (or descriptions) of holdings in the society. The principle of rectification presumably will make use of (its best estimate of) subjunctive information about what would have occurred (or a probability distribution over what might have occurred, using the expected value) if the injustice had not taken place. If the actual description of holdings turns out not to be one of the descriptions yielded by the principle, then one of the descriptions yielded must be realized.[2]

The general outlines of the theory of justice in holdings are that the holdings of a person are just if he is entitled to them by the principles of justice in acquisition and transfer, or by the principle of rectification of injustice (as specified by the first two principles). If each person's holdings are just then the total set (distribution) of holdings is just. To turn these general outlines into a specific theory we would have to specify the details of each of the three principles of justice in holdings: the principle of acquisition of holdings, the principle of transfer of holdings, and the principle of rectification of violations of the first two principles. I shall not attempt that task here. . . .

HISTORICAL PRINCIPLES AND END-RESULT PRINCIPLES

The general outlines of the entitlement theory illuminate the nature and defects of other conceptions of distributive justice. The entitlement theory of justice in distribution is *historical*; whether a distribution is just depends upon how it came about. In contrast, *current time-slice principles* of justice hold that the justice of a distribution is determined by how things are distributed (who has what) as judged by some *structural* principle(s) of just distribution. A utilitarian who judges be-

---

[2] If the principle of rectification of violations of the first two principles yields more than one description of holdings, then some choice must be made as to which of these is to be realized. Perhaps the sort of considerations about distributive justice and equality I argue against play a legitimate role in *this* subsidiary choice. Similarly, there may be room for such considerations in deciding which otherwise arbitrary features a statute will embody, when such features are unavoidable because other considerations do not specify a precise line, yet one must be drawn.

tween any two distributions by seeing which has the greater sum of utility and, if these tie, who applies some fixed equality criterion to choose the more equal distribution, would hold a current time-slice principle of justice. As would someone who had a fixed schedule of trade-offs between the sum of happiness and equality. All that needs to be looked at, in judging the justice of a distribution, according to a current time-slice principle, is who ends up with what; in comparing any two distributions one need look only at the matrix presenting the distributions. No further information need be fed into a principle of justice. It is a consequence of such principles of justice that any two structurally identical distributions are equally just. (Two distributions are structurally identical if they present the same profile, but (perhaps) have different persons occupying the particular slots. My having ten and your having five, and my having five and your having ten are structurally identical distributions.) Welfare economics is the theory of current time-slice principles of justice. The subject is conceived as operating on matrices representing only current information about distribution. This, as well as some of the usual conditions (e.g., the choice of distribution is invariant under relabeling of columns), guarantees that welfare economics will be a current time-slice theory, with all of its inadequacies.

Most persons do not accept current time-slice principles as constituting the whole story about distributive shares. They think it relevant in assessing the justice of a situation to consider not only the distribution it embodies, but also how that distribution came about. If some persons are in prison for murder or war crimes, we do not say that to assess the justice of the distribution in the society we must look only at what this person has, and that person has, and that person has . . . , at the current time. We think it relevant to ask whether someone did something so that he *deserved* to be punished, deserved to have a lower share. Most will agree to the relevance of further information with regard to punishments and penal-

ties. Consider also desired things. One traditional socialist view is that workers are entitled to the product and full fruits of their labor; they have earned it; a distribution is unjust if it does not give the workers what they are entitled to. Such entitlements are based upon some past history. No socialist holding this view would find it comforting to be told that because the actual distribution *A* happens to coincide structurally with the one he desires *D*, *A* therefore is no less just than *D*; it differs only in that the "parasitic" owners of capital receive under *A* what the workers are entitled to under *D*, and the workers receive under *A* what the owners are entitled to (under *D*), namely very little. Rightly in my view, this socialist holds onto the notions of earning, producing, entitlement, desert, etc. and he rejects (current time-slice) principles that look only to the structure of the resulting set of holdings. (The set of holdings resulting from what? Isn't it implausible that how holdings are produced and come to exist has no effect at all on who should hold what?) His mistake lies in his view of what entitlements arise out of what sorts of productive processes.

We construe the position we discuss too narrowly by speaking of *current* time-slice principles. Nothing is changed if structural principles operate upon a time sequence of current time-slice profiles and, for example, give someone more now to counterbalance the less he has had earlier. A utilitarian or an egalitarian or any mixture of the two over time will inherit the difficulties of his more myopic comrades. He is not helped by the fact that *some* of the information others consider relevant in assessing a distribution is reflected, unrecoverably, in past matrices. Henceforth, we shall refer to such unhistorical principles of distributive justice, including the current time-slice principles, as *end-result principles* or *end-state principles*.

In contrast to end-result principles of justice, *historical principles* of justice hold that past circumstances or actions of people can create differential entitlements or differential deserts to things. An injustice can be worked by moving from one distribution to another structurally identical one, for the second, in profile the same, may violate people's entitlements or deserts; it may not fit the actual history.

PATTERNING

The entitlement principles of justice in holdings that we have sketched are historical principles of justice. To better understand their precise character, we shall distinguish them from another subclass of the historical principles. Consider, as an example, the principle of distribution according to moral merit. This principle requires total distributive shares to vary directly with moral merit; no person should have a greater share than anyone whose moral merit is greater. (If moral merit could be not merely ordered but measured on an interval or ratio scale, stronger principles could be formulated.) Or consider the principle that results by substituting "usefulness to society" for "moral merit" in the previous principle. Or instead of "distribute according to moral merit," or "distribute according to usefulness to society," we might consider "distribute according to the weighted sum of moral merit, usefulness to society, and need," with the weights of the different dimensions equal. Let us call a principle of distribution *patterned* if it specifies that a distribution is to vary along with some natural dimension, weighted sum of natural dimensions, or lexicographic ordering of natural dimensions. And let us say a distribution is patterned if it accords with some patterned principle. (I speak of natural dimensions, admittedly without a general criterion for them, because for any set of holdings some artificial dimensions can be gimmicked up to vary along with the distribution of the set.) The principle of distribution in accordance with moral merit is a patterned historical principle, which specifies a patterned distribution. "Distribute according to I.Q." is a patterned principle that looks to information not contained in distributional matrices. It is not

historical, however, in that it does not look to any past actions creating differential entitlements to evaluate a distribution; it requires only distributional matrices whose columns are labeled by I.Q. scores. The distribution in a society, however, may be composed of such simple patterned distributions, without itself being simply patterned. Different sectors may operate different patterns, or some combination of patterns may operate in different proportions across a society. A distribution composed in this manner, from a small number of patterned distributions, we also shall term patterned. And we extend the use of "pattern" to include the overall designs put forth by combinations of end-state principles.

Almost every suggested principle of distributive justice is patterned: to each according to his moral merit, or needs, or marginal product, or how hard he tries, or the weighted sum of the foregoing, and so on. The principle of entitlement we have sketched is *not* patterned.[3] There is no one natural dimension or weighted sum or combination of (a small number of) natural dimensions that yields the distributions generated in accordance with the principle of entitlement. The set of holdings that results when some persons receive their marginal products, others win at gambling, others re-

---

[3] One might try to squeeze a patterned conception of distributive justice into the framework of the entitlement conception, by formulating a gimmicky obligatory 'principle of transfer' that would lead to the pattern. For example, the principle that if one has more than the mean income, one must transfer everything one holds above the mean to persons below the mean so as to bring them up (but not over) the mean. We can formulate a criterion for a 'principle of transfer' to rule out such obligatory transfers, or we can say that no correct principle of transfer, no principle of transfer in a free society will be like this. The former is probably the better course, though the latter also is true.

Alternatively, one might think to make the entitlement conception instantiate a pattern, by using matrix entries that express the relative strength of a person's entitlements as measured by some real-valued function. But even if the limitation to natural dimensions failed to exclude this function, the resulting edifice would *not* capture our system of entitlements to *particular* things.

ceive a share of their mate's income, others receive gifts from foundations, others receive interest on loans, others receive gifts from admirers, others receive returns on investment, others make for themselves much of what they have, others find things, and so on, will not be patterned. Heavy strands of patterns will run through it; significant portions of the variance in holdings will be accounted for by pattern variables. If most people most of the time choose to transfer some of their entitlements to others only in exchange for something from them, then a large part of what many people hold will vary with what they held that others wanted. More details are provided by the theory of marginal productivity. But gifts to relatives, charitable donations, bequests to children, and the like, are not best conceived, in the first instance, in this manner. Ignoring the strands of pattern, let us suppose for the moment that a distribution actually gotten by the operation of the principle of entitlement is random with respect to any pattern. Though the resulting set of holdings will be unpatterned, it will not be incomprehensible, for it can be seen as arising from the operation of a small number of principles. These principles specify how an initial distribution may arise (the principle of acquisition of holdings) and how distributions may be transformed into others (the principle of transfer of holdings). The process whereby the set of holdings is generated will be intelligible, though the set of holdings itself that results from this process will be unpatterned. . . .

HOW LIBERTY UPSETS PATTERNS

It is not clear how those holding alternative conceptions of distributive justice can reject the entitlement conception of justice in holdings. For suppose a distribution favored by one of these nonentitlement conceptions is realized. Let us suppose it is your favorite one and call this distribution D_1; perhaps everyone has an equal share, perhaps shares vary in accordance with some

dimension you treasure. Now suppose that Wilt Chamberlain is greatly in demand by basketball teams, being a great gate-attraction. (Also suppose contracts run only for a year, with players being free agents.) He signs the following sort of contract with a team: In each home game, twenty-five cents from the price of each ticket of admission goes to him. (We ignore the question of whether he is "gouging" the owners, letting them look out for themselves.) The season starts, and people cheerfully attend his team's games; they buy their tickets, each time dropping a separate twenty-five cents of their admission price into a special box with Chamberlain's name on it. They are excited about seeing him play; it is worth the total admission price to them. Let us suppose that in one season one million persons attend his home games, and Wilt Chamberlain winds up with $250,000, a much larger sum than the average income and larger even than anyone else has. Is he entitled to this income? Is this new distribution D_2 unjust? If so, why? There is *no* question about whether each of the people was entitled to the control over the resources they held, in D_1, because that was the distribution (your favorite) that (for the purposes of argument) we assumed was acceptable. Each of these persons *chose* to give twenty-five cents of their money to Chamberlain. They could have spent it on going to the movies, or on candy bars, or on copies of *Dissent* magazine, or of *Monthly Review*. But they all, at least one million of them, converged on giving it to Wilt Chamberlain in exchange for watching him play basketball. If D_1 was a just distribution, and people voluntarily moved from it to D_2, transferring parts of their shares they were given under D_1 (what was it for if not to do something with?), isn't D_2 also just? If the people were entitled to dispose of the resources to which they were entitled (under D_1), didn't this include their being entitled to give it to, or exchange it with, Wilt Chamberlain? Can anyone else complain on grounds of justice? Each other person already has his legitimate share under D_1. Under D_1 there is nothing that anyone has that anyone else has a claim of justice against. After someone transfers something to Wilt Chamberlain, third parties *still* have their legitimate shares; *their* shares are not changed. By what process could such a transfer among two persons give rise to a legitimate claim of distributive justice on a portion of what was transferred, by a third party who had no claim of justice on any holding of the others *before* the transfer?[4] To cut off objections irrelevant here, we might imagine the exchanges occurring in a socialist society, after hours. After playing whatever basketball he does in his daily work, or doing whatever other daily work he does, Wilt Chamberlain decides to put in *overtime* to earn additional money. (First his work quota is set; he works time over that.) Or imagine it is a skilled juggler people like to see, who puts on shows after hours.

Why might some people work overtime in a society in which it is assumed their needs are satisfied? Perhaps because they care about things other than needs. I like to write in books that I read, and to have easy access to books for browsing at odd hours. It would be very pleasant and convenient to have the resources of Widener Library in my back yard. No society, I assume, will provide such resources close to each person who would like them as part of his regular allotment (under D_1). Thus, persons either must do without some extra things that they want, or be allowed to do something extra to get (some of) these things. On what basis could the inequalities that would eventuate be forbidden? Notice also that small factories would spring up in a socialist society, unless forbidden. I melt down some of my personal possessions (under D_1) and build a machine out of the material. I offer you, and others, a philosophy lecture once a week in exchange for your cranking the handle on my machine, whose products I exchange for yet other things, and so on. (The raw materials used by the machine are given to me by others who possess them under D_1, in exchange for hearing lectures.) Each person might participate to gain things over and above their allotment under D_1. Some persons even might want to leave their job in socialist industry, and work full time in this private sector. I say something more about these issues elsewhere. Here I wish merely to note how private property, even in means of production, would occur in a socialist society that did not forbid people to use as they wished some of the resources they are given under the socialist distribution D_1. The socialist society would have to forbid capitalist acts between consenting adults.[5]

---

[4] Might not a transfer have instrumental effects on a third party, changing his feasible options? (But what if the two parties to the transfer independently had used their holdings in this fashion?) I discuss this question elsewhere, but note here that this question concedes the point for distributions of ultimate intrinsic non-instrumental goods (pure utility experiences, so to speak) that are transferrable. It also might be objected that the transfer might make a third party more envious because it worsens his position relative to someone else. I find it incomprehensible how it can be thought that this involves a claim of justice. On envy, see *Anarchy, State, and Utopia*, chap. 8.

Here and elsewhere in this essay, a theory which incorporates elements of pure procedural justice might find what I say acceptable, *if* kept in its proper place; that is, if background institutions exist to ensure the satisfaction of certain conditions on distributive shares. But if these institutions are not themselves the sum or invisible-hand result of people's voluntary (nonaggressive) actions, the constraints they impose require justification. At no point does *our* argument assume any background institutions more extensive than those of the minimal night-watchman state, limited to protecting persons against murder, assault, theft, fraud, etc.

[5] See the selection from John Henry MacKay's novel, *The Anarchists*, reprinted in Leonard Krimmerman and Lewis Perry, eds., *Patterns of Anarchy* (New York, 1966), pp. 16–33, in which an individualist anarchist presses upon a communist anarchist the question: "Would you, in the system of society which you call 'free Communism' prevent individuals from exchanging their labor among themselves by means of their own medium of exchange? And further: Would you prevent them from occupying land for the purpose of personal use?" The novel continues: "[the] question was not to be escaped. If he answered 'Yes!' he admitted that society had the right of control over the individual and threw overboard the autonomy of the individual which he had always zealously defended; if on the other hand, he answered 'No!' he admitted the right of private property which he had just denied so emphatically. . . . Then he answered 'In Anarchy any

The general point illustrated by the Wilt Chamberlain example and the example of the entrepreneur in a socialist society is that no end-state principle or distributional pattern principle of justice can be continuously realized without continuous interference into people's lives. Any favored pattern would be transformed into one unfavored by the principle, by people choosing to act in various ways; e.g., by people exchanging goods and services with other people, or giving things to other people, things the transferrers are entitled to under the favored distributional pattern. To maintain a pattern one must either continuously interfere to stop people from transferring resources as they wish to, or continually (or periodically) interfere to take from some persons resources that others for some reason chose to transfer to them. (But if some time limit is to be set on how long people may keep resources others voluntarily transfer to them, why let them keep these resources for *any* period of time? Why not have immediate confiscation?) It might be objected that all persons voluntarily will choose to refrain from actions which would upset the pattern. This presupposes unrealistically (a) that all will most want to maintain the pattern (are those who don't, to be "reeducated" or forced to undergo "self-criticism"?); (b) that each can gather enough information about his own actions and the ongoing activities of others to discover which of his actions will upset the pattern; and (c) that diverse and farflung persons can coordinate their actions to dovetail into

the pattern. Compare the manner in which the market is neutral among persons' desires, as it reflects and transmits widely scattered information via prices, and coordinates persons' activities. . . .

REDISTRIBUTION AND PROPERTY RIGHTS

Apparently patterned principles allow people to choose to expend upon themselves, but not upon others, those resources they are entitled to (or rather, receive) under some favored distributional pattern D_1. For if each of several persons chooses to expend some of his D_1 resources upon one other person, then that other person will receive more than his D_1 share, disturbing the favored distributional pattern. Maintaining a distributional pattern is individualism with a vengeance! Patterned distributional principles do not give people what entitlement principles do, only better distributed. For they do not give the right to choose what to do with what one has; they do not give the right to choose to pursue an end involving (intrinsically, or as a means) the enhancement of another's position. To such views, families are distributing; for within a family occur transfers that upset the favored distributional pattern. Either families themselves become units to which distribution takes place, the column occupiers (on what rationale?), or loving behavior is forbidden. We should note in passing the ambivalent position of radicals towards the family. Its loving relationships are seen as a model to be emulated and extended across the whole society, while it is denounced as a suffocating institution to be broken, and condemned as a focus of parochial concerns that interfere with achieving radical goals. Need we say that it is not appropriate to enforce across the wider society the relationships of love and care appropriate within family, relationships which are voluntarily undertaken? Incidentally, love is an interesting instance of another relationship that is historical, in that (like justice) it depends upon what actu-

---

number of men must have the right of forming a voluntary association, and so realizing their ideas in practice. Nor can I understand how any one could justly be driven from the land and house which he uses and occupies . . . every serious man must declare himself: for Socialism, and thereby for force and against liberty, or for Anarchism, and thereby for liberty and against force.' " In contrast, we find Noam Chomsky writing, "Any consistent anarchist must oppose private ownership of the means of production," and "the consistent anarchist then . . . will be a socialist . . . of a particular sort" (Introduction to Daniel Guerin, *Anarchism: From Theory to Practice* [New York, 1970], pp. xiii, xv).

ally occurred. An adult may come to love another because of the other's characteristics; but it is the other person, and not the characteristics, that is loved. The love is not transferable to someone else with the same characteristics, even to one who "scores" higher for these characteristics. And the love endures through changes of the characteristics that gave rise to it. One loves the particular person one actually encountered. Why love is historical, attaching to persons in this way and not to characteristics, is an interesting and puzzling question.

Proponents of patterned principles of distributive justice focus upon criteria for determining who is to receive holdings; they consider the reasons for which someone should have something, and also the total picture of holdings. Whether or not it is better to give than to receive, proponents of patterned principles ignore giving altogether. In considering the distribution of goods, income, etc., their theories are theories of recipient-justice; they completely ignore any right a person might have to give something to someone. Even in exchanges where each party is simultaneously giver and recipient, patterned principles of justice focus only upon the recipient role and its supposed rights. Thus discussions tend to focus on whether people (should) have a right to inherit, rather than on whether people (should) have a right to bequeath or on whether persons who have a right to hold also have a right to choose that others hold in their place. I lack a good explanation of why the usual theories of distributive justice are so recipient-oriented; ignoring givers and transferrers and their rights is of a piece with ignoring producers and their entitlements. But why is it *all* ignored?

Patterned principles of distributive justice necessitate *re*distributive activities. The likelihood is small that any actual freely arrived at set of holdings fits a given pattern; and the likelihood is nil that it will continue to fit the pattern as people exchange and give. From the point of view of an entitlement theory, redistribution is a serious matter indeed, involving, as it does, the viola-

tion of people's rights. (An exception is those takings that fall under the principle of the rectification of injustices.) From other points of view, also, it is serious.

Taxation of earnings from labor is on a par with forced labor.[6] Some persons find this claim obviously true: taking the earnings of *n* hours labor is like taking *n* hours from the person; it is like forcing the person to work *n* hours for another's purpose. Others find the claim absurd. But even these, *if* they object to forced labour, would oppose forcing unemployed hippies to work for the benefit of the needy. And they also would object to forcing each person to work five extra hours each week for the benefit of the needy. But a system that takes five hours' wages in taxes does not seem to them like one that forces someone to work five hours, since it offers the person forced a wider range of choice in activities than does taxation in kind with the particular labor specified. (But we can imagine a gradation of systems of forced labor, from one that specifies a particular activity, to one that gives a choice among two activities, to . . . ; and so on up.) Furthermore, people envisage a system with something like a proportional tax on everything above the amount necessary for basic needs. Some think this does not force someone to work extra hours, since there is no fixed number of extra hours he is forced to work, and since he can avoid the tax entirely by earning only enough to cover his basic needs. This is a very uncharacteristic view of forcing for those who *also* think people are forced to do something *whenever* the alternatives they face are considerably worse. However, *neither* view is correct. The fact that others intentionally intervene, in violation of a side-constraint against aggres-

---

[6] I am unsure as to whether the arguments I present below show that such taxation just *is* forced labor; so that "is on a par with" means "is one kind of." Or alternatively, whether the arguments emphasize the great similarities between such taxation and forced labor, to show it is plausible and illuminating to view such taxation in the light of forced labor. This latter approach would remind one of how John Wisdom conceives of the claims of metaphysicians.

sion, to threaten force to limit the alternatives, in this case to paying taxes or (presumably the worse alternative) bare subsistence, makes the taxation system one of forced labor, and distinguishes it from other cases of limited choices which are not forcings.[7]

The man who chooses to work longer to gain an income more than sufficient for his basic needs prefers some extra goods or services to the leisure and activities he could perform during the possible non-working hours; whereas the man who chooses not to work the extra time prefers the leisure activities to the extra goods or services he could acquire by working more. Given this, if it would be illegitimate for a tax system to seize some of a man's leisure (forced labor) for the purpose of serving the needy, how can it be legitimate for a tax system to seize some of a man's goods for that purpose? Why should we treat the man whose happiness requires certain material goods or services differently from the man whose preferences and desires make such goods unnecessary for his happiness? Why should the man who prefers seeing a movie (and who has to earn money for a ticket) be open to the required call to aid the needy, while the person who prefers looking at a sunset (and hence need earn no extra money) is not? Indeed, isn't it surprising that redistributionists choose to ignore the man whose pleasures are so easily attainable without extra labor, while adding yet another burden to the poor unfortunate who must work for his pleasures? If anything, one would have expected the reverse. Why is the person with the nonmaterial or nonconsumption desire allowed to proceed unimpeded to his most favored feasible alternative, whereas the man whose pleasures or desires involve material things and who must work for extra money (thereby serving whoever considers his activities valuable enough to pay him) is constrained in what

he can realize? Perhaps there is no difference in principle. And perhaps some think the answer concerns merely administrative convenience. (These questions and issues will not disturb those who think forced labor to serve the needy or realize some favored end-state pattern acceptable.) In a fuller discussion we would have (and want) to extend our argument to include interest, entrepreneurial profits, etc. Those who doubt that this extension can be carried through, and who draw the line here at taxation of income from labor, will have to state rather complicated patterned *historical* principles of distributive justice; since end-state principles would not distinguish *sources* of income in any way. It is enough for now to get away from end-state principles and to make clear how various patterned principles are dependent upon particular views about the sources or the illegitimacy or the lesser legitimacy of profits, interest, etc.; which particular views may well be mistaken.

What sort of right over others does a legally institutionalized end-state pattern give one? The central core of the notion of a property right in X, relative to which other parts of the notion are to be explained, is the right to determine what shall be done with X; the right to choose which of the constrained set of options concerning X shall be realized or attempted.[8] The constraints are set by other principles or laws operating in the society; in our theory by the Lockean rights people possess (under the minimal state). My property rights in my knife allow me to leave it where I will, but not in your chest. I may choose which of the acceptable options involving the knife is to be realized. This notion of property helps us to understand why earlier theorists spoke of people as having property in themselves and their labor. They viewed each person as having a right to decide what would become of himself and what he would do, and as having a right to reap the benefits of what he did.

---

[7] Further details that this statement should include are contained in my essay, "Coercion," in *Philosophy, Science, and Method*, ed. S. Morgenbesser, P. Suppes, and M. White (New York, 1969).

[8] On the themes in this and the next paragraph, see the writings of Armen Alchian.

This right of selecting the alternative to be realized from the constrained set of alternatives may be held by an *individual* or by a *group* with some procedure for reaching a joint decision; or the right may be passed back and forth, so that one year I decide what's to become of X, and the next year you do (with the alternative of destruction, perhaps, being excluded). Or, during the same time period, some types of decisions about X may be made by me, and others by you. And so on. We lack an adequate, fruitful, analytical apparatus for classifying the *types* of constraints on the set of options among which choices are to be made, and the *types* of ways decision powers can be held, divided, and amalgamated. A *theory* of property would, among other things, contain such a classification of constraints and decision modes, and from a small number of principles would follow a host of interesting statements about the *consequences* and effects of certain combinations of constraints and modes of decision.

When end-result principles of distributive justice are built into the legal structure of a society, they (as do most patterned principles) give each citizen an enforceable claim to some portion of the total social product; that is, to some portion of the sum total of the individually and jointly made products. This total product is produced by individuals laboring, using means of production others have saved to bring into existence, by people organizing production or creating means to produce new things or things in a new way. It is on this batch of individual activities that patterned distributional principles give each individual an enforceable claim. Each person has a claim to the activities and the products of other persons, independently of whether the other persons enter into particular relationships that give rise to these claims, and independently of whether they voluntarily take these claims upon themselves, in charity or in exchange for something.

Whether it is done through taxation on wages or on wages over a certain amount, or through seizure of profits, or through there

being a big *social pot* so that it's not clear what's coming from where and what's going where, patterned principles of distributive justice involve appropriating the actions of other persons. Seizing the results of someone's labor is equivalent to seizing hours from him and directing him to carry on various activities. If people force you to do certain work, or unrewarded work, for a certain period of time, they decide what you are to do and what purposes your work is to serve apart from your decisions. This process whereby they take this decision from you makes them a *part owner* of you; it gives them a property right in you. Just as having such partial control and power of decision, by right, over an animal or inanimate object would be to have a property right in it.

End-state and most patterned principles of distributive justice institute (partial) ownership by others of people and their actions and labor. These principles involve a shift from the classical liberals' notion of self-ownership to a notion of (partial) property rights in *other* people.

Considerations such as these confront end-state and other patterned conceptions of justice with the question of whether the actions necessary to achieve the selected pattern don't themselves violate moral side-constraints. Any view holding that there are moral side-constraints on actions, that not all moral considerations can be built into end-states that are to be achieved,[9] must face the possibility that some of its goals are not achievable by any morally permissible available means. An entitlement theorist will face such conflicts in a society that deviates from the principles of justice for the generation of holdings, if and only if the only actions available to realize the principles themselves violate some moral constraints. Since deviation from the first two principles of justice (in acquisition and transfer) will involve other persons' direct and aggressive intervention to violate rights, and since moral constraints will not exclude defensive or retributive action in such cases, the entitle-

---

[9] See *Anarchy, State, and Utopia*, chap. 3.

ment theorist's problem rarely will be pressing. And whatever difficulties he has in applying the principle of rectification to persons who did not themselves violate the first two principles, are difficulties in balancing the conflicting considerations so as correctly to formulate the complex principle of rectification itself; he will not violate moral side-constraints by applying the principle.

Proponents of patterned conceptions of justice, however, often will face head-on clashes (and poignant ones if they cherish each party to the clash) between moral side-constraints on how individuals may be treated on the one hand and, on the other, their patterned conception of justice that presents an end-state or other pattern that *must* be realized. . . .

Property and Hunger

Amartya Sen

After distinguishing three ways of understanding rights—as instruments, as constraints, and as goals—Professor Amartya Sen focuses on the right to hold, use, and bequeath property. He maintains that famines and starvation result not from absolute lack of food, but from failures of entitlements: Hunger is basically a matter of not owning enough food. This analysis of hunger and famine in terms of property rights rather than availability of food leads Sen to reject the view that property rights are morally inviolable regardless of their consequences. He goes on to discuss "the right not to be hungry," the general acceptance of which in India has, he contends, played a substantial role in preventing famines there. Throughout his essay, Sen stresses the relevance of empirical analysis of causes and effects for the assessment of claims of right.

Amartya Sen is Lamont University Professor at Harvard University. He has written extensively in ethics and in economics. Among his books are *Collective Choice and Social Welfare* (1970), *Poverty and Famines* (1981), and *The Standard of Living* (1987).

In an interesting letter to Anna George, the daughter of Henry George, Bernard Shaw wrote: "Your father found me a literary dilettante and militant rationalist in religion, and a barren rascal at that. By turning my

From *Economics and Philosophy*, Vol. 4, No. 1 (April 1988). Copyright © 1988 by Cambridge University Press. Reprinted with the permission of the author and Cambridge University Press.

mind to economics he made a man of me" (George, 1979, p. xiii). I am not able to determine what making a man of Bernard Shaw would exactly consist of, but it is clear that the kind of moral and social problems with which Shaw was deeply concerned could not be sensibly pursued without examining their economic aspects. For example, the claims of property rights, which some would defend and some (including Shaw) would dispute, are not just matters of basic moral belief that could not possibly be influenced one way or the other by any empirical arguments. They call for sensitive moral analysis responsive to empirical realities, including economic ones.

Moral claims based on intrinsically valuable rights are often used in political and social arguments. Rights related to ownership have been invoked for ages. But there are also other types of rights which have been seen as "inherent and inalienable,"[1] and the American Declaration of Independence refers to "certain unalienable rights," among which are "life, liberty and the pursuit of happiness." The Indian constitution talks even of "the right to an adequate means of livelihood."[2] The "right not to be hungry" has often been invoked in recent discussions on the obligation to help the famished.

RIGHTS: INSTRUMENTS, CONSTRAINTS, OR GOALS?

Rights can be taken to be morally important in three different ways. First, they can be considered to be valuable *instruments* to achieve other goals. This is the "instrumental view," and is well illustrated by the utilitarian approach to rights. Rights are, in that view, of no intrinsic importance. Violation of rights is not in itself a bad thing, nor fulfillment intrinsically good. But the acceptance of rights promotes, in this view, things that are ultimately important, to wit, utility. Jeremy Bentham rejected "natural rights" as "simple nonsense," and "natural and imprescriptible rights" as "rhetorical nonsense,

nonsense upon stilts."[3] But he attached great importance to rights as instruments valuable to the promotion of a good society, and devoted much energy to the attempt to reform appropriately the actual system of rights.

The second view may be called the "constraint view," and it takes the form of seeing rights as *constraints* on what others can or cannot do. In this view rights *are* intrinsically important. However, they don't figure in moral accounting as goals to be generally promoted, but only as constraints that others must obey. As Robert Nozick has put it in a powerful exposition of this "constraint view": "Individuals have rights, and there are things no person or group may do to them (without violating their rights)" (Nozick, 1974, p. xi). Rights "set the constraints within which a social choice is to be made, by excluding certain alternatives, fixing others, and so on" (Nozick, 1974, p. 166).

The third approach is to see fulfillments of rights as goals to be pursued. This "goal view" differs from the instrumental view in regarding rights to be intrinsically important, and it differs from the constraint view in seeing the fulfillment of rights as goals to be generally promoted, rather than taking them as demanding only (and exactly) that we refrain from violating the rights of others. In the "constraint view" there is no duty to help anyone with his or her rights (merely not to hinder), and also in the "instrumental view" there is no duty, in fact, to help unless the right fulfillment will also promote some other goal such as utility. The "goal view" integrates the valuation of rights—their fulfillment and violation—in overall moral accounting, and yields a wider sphere of influence of rights in morality.

I have argued elsewhere that the goal view has advantages that the other two approaches do not share, in particular, the

---

[1] The expression "inherent and unalienable" occurs in Thomas Jefferson's original draft of the Declaration of Independence.

[2] This is presented as a "Directive Principle of State Policy." It does not have a direct operational role in the working of the Indian legal system, but it has considerable political force.

[3] Ross Harrison (1983) provides an illuminating discussion of Bentham's treatment of rights, in *Bentham*, Chapter IV.

ability to accommodate integrated moral accounting including inter alia the intrinsic importance of a class of fundamental rights (Sen, 1982c; 1985b). I shall not repeat that argument here. But there is an interesting question of dual roles of rights in the sense that some rights may be *both* intrinsically important and instrumentally valuable. For example, the right to be free from hunger could—not implausibly—be regarded as being valuable in itself as well as serving as a good instrument to promote other goals such as security, longevity or utility. If so, both the goal view and the instrumental view would have to be simultaneously deployed to get a comprehensive assessment of such a right. This problem of comprehensiveness is a particularly important issue in the context of Henry George's discussion of rights, since he gave many rights significant dual roles.

The instrumental aspect is an inescapable feature of every right, since irrespective of whether a certain right is intrinsically valuable or not, its acceptance will certainly have other consequences as well, and these, too, have to be assessed along with the intrinsic value of rights (if any). A right that is regarded as quite valuable in itself may nevertheless be judged to be morally rejectable if its leads to disastrous consequences. This is a case of the rights playing a *negative* instrumental role. It is, of course, also possible that the instrumental argument will *bolster* the intrinsic claims of a right to be taken seriously. I shall presently argue that such is the case in George's analysis with the right of labor to its produce.

There are two general conclusions to draw, at this stage, from this very preliminary discussion. First, we must distinguish between (1) the intrinsic value of a right, and (2) the overall value of a right taking note inter alia of its intrinsic importance (if any). The acceptance of the intrinsic importance of any right is no guarantee that its overall moral valuation must be favorable.[4]

Second, no moral assessment of a right can be independent of its likely consequences. The need for empirical assessment of the effects of accepting any right cannot be escaped. Empirical arguments are quite central to moral philosophy.[5]

PROPERTY AND DEPRIVATION

The right to hold, use and bequeath property that one has legitimately acquired is often taken to be inherently valuable. In fact, however, many of its defenses seem to be actually of the instrumental type, e.g., arguing that property rights make people more free to choose one kind of a life rather than another (see, for example, Friedman and Friedman, 1980). Even the traditional attempt at founding "natural property rights" on the principles of "natural liberty" (with or without John Locke's proviso) has some instrumental features.[6] But even if we do accept that property rights may have some intrinsic value, this does not in any way amount to an overall justification of property rights, since property rights may have consequences which themselves will require assessment. Indeed, the causation of hunger as well as its prevention may materially depend on how property rights are structured. If a set of property rights leads, say, to starvation, as it well might, then the moral approval of these rights would certainly be compromised severely. In general, the need for consequential analysis of property rights is inescapable whether or not such rights are seen as having any intrinsic value.

Consider Henry George's formula of giv-

---

tures, so that moral goodness is not necessarily seen as a simple monotonic function of one homogeneous primitive quantity (e.g., utility, as it is supposed to be in "monist" utilitarian accounting). I have tried to discuss the issue of pluralism, among other things, in my "Well-being, Agency and Freedom: The Dewey Lectures 1984" (Sen, 1985a).

[5] On this see Sen, 1967; 1970, Chap. 5 and 6.

[6] Allan Gibbard (1976) has argued convincingly that these attempts at justification of natural property rights are not successful.

---

[4] The reasoning here (and in earlier arguments) is based on the permissibility of pluralist moral struc-

ing "the product to the producer" (George, 1981, p. 451; 1979). This is, of course, an ambiguous rule, since the division of the credits for production to different causal influences (e.g., according to "marginal productivities" in neoclassical theory, or according to human efforts in classical labor theory) is inevitably somewhat arbitrary, and full of problems involving internal tensions (on this see Sen, 1978). But no matter how the ambiguities are resolved, it is clear that this rule would give no part of the socially produced output to one who is unemployed since he or she is producing nothing. Also, a person whose productive contribution happens to be tiny, according to *whichever* procedure of such accounting we use, can expect to get very little based on this so-called "natural law." Thus, hunger and starvation are compatible with this system of rights. George thought that this would not occur, since the economic reforms he proposed (including the abolition of land rights) would eliminate unemployment, and provision for the disabled would be made through the sympathetic support of others. These are empirical matters. If these empirical generalizations do not hold, then the outlined system of rights would yield a serious conflict. The property rights to one's product (however defined) might be of some intrinsic moral importance, but we clearly must also take note of the moral disvalue of human misery (such as suffering due to hunger and nutrition-related diseases). The latter could very plausibly be seen as having more moral force than the former. A positive intrinsic value of the right to one's product can go with an overall negative value, taking everything into account.

This type of problem arises most powerfully in assessing the ethical force of some of the standard theories of rights. For example, neither a straightforward moral theory asserting inalienable property rights, nor an elaborate theory of an entitlement system of the kind outlined by Robert Nozick, can escape having to face the possibility that when applied to an actual society, the rights in

question may yield hunger, starvation, and even large-scale famine. I have tried to argue elsewhere—not in the context of disputing these moral theories but in trying to understand the causation of famines in the modern world—that famines are, in fact, best explained in terms of failures of entitlement systems.[7] The entitlements here refer, of course, to legal rights and to practical possibilities, rather than to moral status, but the laws and actual operation of private ownership economies have many features in common with the moral system of entitlements analyzed by Nozick and others.

The entitlement approach to famines need not, of course, be confined to private ownership economies, and entitlement failures of other systems can also be fruitfully studied to examine famines and hunger. In the specific context of private ownership economies, the entitlements are substantially analyzable in terms, respectively, of what may be called "endowments" and "exchange entitlements." A person's endowment refers to what he or she initially owns (including the person's own labor power), and the exchange entitlement mapping tells us what the person can obtain through exchanging what he or she owns, either by production (exchange with nature), or by trade (exchange with others), or a mixture of the two. A person has to starve if neither the endowments, nor what can be obtained through exchange, yields an adequate amount of food.

If starvation and hunger are seen in terms of failures of entitlements, then it becomes immediately clear that the total availability of food in a country is only one of several variables that are relevant. Many famines occur without any decline in the availability of food. For example, in the Great Bengal famine of 1943, the total food availability in Bengal was not particularly

---

[7] Sen, 1981. The motivation for that work was to understand the nature and causation of poverty and famines and to draw lessons for practical policy (based on a number of case studies). The question of its moral relevance was not posed there.

bad (considerably higher than two years earlier when there was no famine), and yet three million people died, in a famine mainly affecting the rural areas, through rather violent shifts in the relative purchasing powers of different groups, hitting the rural laborers the hardest (Sen, 1981, Chap. 6). The Ethiopian famine of 1973 took place in a year of average per capita food availability, but the cultivators and other occupation groups in the province of Wollo had lost their means of subsistence (through loss of crops and a decline of economic activity, related to a local drought) and had no means of commanding food from elsewhere in the country (Sen, 1981, Chap. 7). Indeed, some food moved *out* of Wollo to more prosperous people in other parts of Ethiopia, repeating a pattern of contrary movement of food that was widely observed during the Irish famines of the 1840s (with food moving out of famine-stricken Ireland to prosperous England which had greater power in the battle for entitlements) (Sen, 1981, Chap. 10). The Bangladesh famine of 1974 took place in a year of *peak* food availability, but several occupation groups had lost their entitlement to food through loss of employment and other economic changes (including inflationary pressures causing prices to outrun wages) (Sen, 1981, Chap. 9; see also Alamgir, 1980; Ravallion, 1987). Other examples of famines without significant (or any) decline in food availability can be found, and there is nothing particularly surprising about this fact once it is recognized that the availability of food is only one influence among many on the entitlement of each occupation group. Even when a famine *is* associated with a decline of food availability, the entitlement changes have to be studied to understand the particular nature of the famine, e.g., why one occupation group is hit but not another (Sen, 1981, Chaps. 8 and 10). The causation of starvation can be sensibly sought in failures of entitlements of the respective groups.

The causal analysis of famines in terms of entitlements also points to possible public policies of prevention. The main economic strategy would have to take the form of increasing the entitlements of the deprived groups, and in general, of guaranteeing minimum entitlements for everyone, paying particular attention to the vulnerable groups (Sen, 1981, Chap. 10; 1984a). This can, in the long run, be done in many different ways, involving both economic growth (including growth of food output) and distributional adjustments (see Sen, 1986). Some of these policies may, however, require that the property rights and the corresponding entitlements of the more prosperous groups be violated. The problem, in fact, is particularly acute in the short run, since it may not be possible to engineer rapid economic growth instantly. Then the burden of raising entitlements of the groups in distress would largely have to fall on reducing the entitlements of others more favorably placed. Transfers of income or commodities through various public policies may well be effective in quashing a famine (as the experience of famine relief in different countries has shown), but it may require substantial government intervention in the entitlements of the more prosperous groups.

There is, however, no great moral dilemma in this if property rights are treated as purely *instrumental*. If the goals of relief of hunger and poverty are sufficiently powerful, then it would be just right to violate whatever property rights come in the way, since—in this view—property rights have no intrinsic status. On the other hand, if property rights are taken to be morally inviolable irrespective of their consequences, then it will follow that these policies cannot be morally acceptable even though they might save thousands, or even millions, from dying. The inflexible moral "constraint" of respecting people's legitimately acquired entitlements would rule out such policies.[8]

---

[8] Even Robert Nozick keeps open the possibility of justly violating rights to avoid "catastrophic moral horrors." However, once consequential rejection of rights is admitted in a system that started off with a simple assertion of consequence-independent rights, it is not at all clear where and how lines are to be drawn. See Sen, 1985c.

In fact this type of problem presents a reductio ad absurdum of the moral validity of constraint-based entitlement systems. However, while the conclusions to be derived from that approach might well be "absurd," the situation postulated is not an imaginary one at all. It is based on studies of actual famines and the role of entitlement failures in the causation of mass starvation. If there is an embarrassment here, it belongs solidly to the consequence-independent way of seeing rights.

I should add that this dilemma does not arise from regarding property rights to be of intrinsic value, which can be criticized on other grounds, but not this one. Even if property rights *are* of intrinsic value, their violation may be justified on grounds of the favorable consequences of that violation. A right, as was mentioned earlier, may be intrinsically valuable and still be justly violated taking everything into account. The "absurdum" does not belong to attaching intrinsic value to property rights, but to regarding these rights as simply acceptable, regardless of their consequences. A moral system that values both property rights and other goals—such as avoiding famines and starvation, or fulfilling people's right not to be hungry—can, on the one hand, give property rights intrinsic importance, and on the other, recommend the violation of property rights when that leads to better overall consequences (*including* the disvalue of rights violation).[9]

The issue here is not the valuing of property rights, but their alleged inviolability. There is no dilemma here either for the purely instrumental view of property rights or for treating the fulfillment of property rights as one goal among many, but specifically for consequence-independent assertions of property rights and for the corresponding constraint-based approaches to moral entitlement of ownership.

That property and hunger are closely related cannot possibly come as a great surprise. Hunger is primarily associated with not owning enough food[10] and thus property rights over food are immediately and directly involved. Fights over that property right can be a major part of the reality of a poor country, and any system of moral assessment has to take note of that phenomenon. The tendency to see hunger in purely technocratic terms of food output and availability may help to hide the crucial role of entitlements in the genesis of hunger, but a fuller economic analysis cannot overlook that crucial role. Since property rights over food are derived from property rights over other goods and resources (through production and trade), the entire system of rights of acquisition and transfer is implicated in the emergence and survival of hunger and starvation.

THE RIGHT NOT TO BE HUNGRY

Property rights have been championed for a long time. In contrast, the assertion of "the right not to be hungry" is a comparatively recent phenomenon. While this right is much invoked in political debates, there is a good deal of skepticism about treating this

---

[9] This statement has more of a "consequentialist" ring than is necessary for making the point at issue. A consequence-sensitive system (even when not fully consequentialist) can recommend the violation of property rights in the light of consequential assessment (despite the intrinsic value of those property rights). There is the further issue of "agent-relativity" in dealing with this question, and while that adds to the complexity of the picture, the possibility of justly violating intrinsically valuable rights is not altered by that. I have tried to discuss the relationships among consequentialism, consequence-sensitivity, agent-relativity and goal-rights in Sen (1982c, 1985a, 1985b) and in my response (Sen, 1983b) to some interesting and important critical points made by Donald Regan (1983).

[10] This is, however, not the only causal link in the generation of hunger. There is the further problem of division of food *within* the family, which is not really a matter of ownership (since the food owned by the family is shared by all the members of it), but of intra-family distribution. In many of the poorer countries evidence of sex bias (against women) and of age bias (against children) are quite powerful, and this non-ownership issue is a matter of real practical importance. On this see Sen, 1984b, Chap. 15 and 16.

as truly a right in any substantial way. It is often asserted that this concept of "right not to be hungry" stands essentially for nothing at all ("simple nonsense," as Bentham called "natural rights" in general). That piece of sophisticated cynicism reveals not so much a penetrating insight into the practical affairs of the world, but a refusal to investigate what people mean when they assert the existence of rights that, for the bulk of humanity, are not in fact guaranteed by the existing institutional arrangements.

The right not to be hungry is not asserted as a recognition of an institutional right that already exists, as the right to property typically is. The assertion is primarily a moral claim as to what should be valued, and what institutional structure we should aim for, and try to guarantee if feasible. It can also be seen in terms of Ronald Dworkin's category of "background rights"—rights that provide a justification for political decisions by society in abstract" (Dworkin, 1977, p. 93). This interpretation serves as the basis for a reason to change the existing institutional structure and state policy.

It is broadly in this form that the right to "an adequate means of livelihood" is referred to in the Constitution of India: "The state shall, in particular, direct its policy towards securing . . . that the citizens, men and women equally, have the right to an adequate means of livelihood." This does not, of course, offer to each citizen a guaranteed right to an adequate livelihood, but the state is asked to take steps such that this right could become realizable for all.[11]

In fact, this right has often been invoked in political debates in India. The electoral politics of India does indeed give particular scope for such use of what are seen as background rights. It is, of course, not altogether clear whether the reference to this

right in the Indian constitution has in fact materially influenced the political debates. The constitutional statement is often cited, but very likely this issue would have figured in any case in these debates, given the nature of the moral and political concern. But whatever the constitutional contribution, it is interesting to ask whether the implicit acceptance of the value of the right to freedom from hunger makes any difference to actual policy.

It can be argued that the general acceptance of the right of freedom from acute hunger as a major goal has played quite a substantial role in preventing famines in India. The last real famine in India was in 1943, and while food availability per head in India has risen only rather slowly (even now the food availability per head is no higher than in many sub-Saharan countries stricken by recurrent famines), the country has not experienced any famine since independence in 1947. The main cause of that success is a policy of public intervention. Whenever a famine has threatened (e.g., in Bihar in 1967–68, in Maharashtra in 1971–73, in West Bengal in 1978–79), a public policy of intervention and relief has offered minimum entitlements to the potential famine victims, and thus have the threatening famines been averted. It can be argued that the quickness of the response of the respective governments (both state and central) reflects a political necessity, given the Indian electoral system and the importance attached by the public to the prevention of starvation.[12] Political pressures from opposi-

---

[11] In fact, strictly speaking this is a right to have a state policy that genuinely tries to achieve the right to adequate means for all. Elsewhere (Sen, 1982b), I have tried to analyse the right to a *policy p(x)* to achieve *x* as a "metaright" to *x*. The constitutional Directive Principle, thus, asserts a metaright to adequate means.

[12] In fact, the elimination of famine is one of the few major achievements of independent India. It is an achievement that deserves recognition, especially since famines have occurred in many other poor countries. A gigantic one took place even in China in 1958–61, in which excess mortality has been estimated to be "about 30 million" (Ashton et al., 1984), and this happened despite the fact that China's general record in improving nutritional standards and in reducing average morbidity and mortality rates is very impressive—far superior to India's. I have tried to discuss elsewhere the role of news media and opposition pressures in the prevention of famines in India (see Sen, 1982a, 1983a; see also Ram, 1986).

tion groups and the news media have kept the respective governments on their toes, and the right to be free from acute hunger and starvation has been achieved largely because it has been seen as a valuable right. Thus the recognition of the intrinsic moral importance of this right, which has been widely invoked in public discussions, has served as a powerful political instrument as well.[13]

On the other hand, this process has been far from effective in tackling pervasive and persistent undernourishment in India. There has been no famine in post-independence India, but perhaps a third of India's rural population is perennially undernourished. So long as hunger remains non-acute and starvation deaths are avoided (even though morbidity and mortality rates are enhanced by undernourishment), the need for a policy response is neither much discussed by the news media, nor forcefully demanded even by opposition parties. The elimination of famines coexists with the survival of widespread "regular hunger." The right to "adequate means" of *nourishment* does not at all seem to arouse political concern in a way that the right to "adequate means" to *avoid starvation* does.

The contrast can be due to one of several different reasons. It could, of course, simply be that the ability to avoid undernourishment is not socially accepted as very important. This could be so, though what is socially accepted and what is not is also partly a matter of how clearly the questions are posed. It is, in fact, quite possible that the freedom in question would be regarded as a morally important right if the question were posed in a transparent way, but this does not happen because of the nature of Indian electoral politics and that of news coverage. The issue is certainly not "dramatic" in the way in which starvation deaths and threatening famines are. Continued low-key misery may be too familiar a phenomenon to make it worthwhile for political leaders to get some mileage out of it in practical politics. The news media may also find little profit in emphasizing a non-spectacular phenomenon—the quiet survival of disciplined, non-acute hunger.[14]

If this is indeed the case, then the implications for action of the goal of eliminating hunger, or guaranteeing to all the means for achieving this, may be quite complex. The political case for making the quiet hunger less quiet and more troublesome for governments in power is certainly relevant. Aggressive political journalism might prove to have an instrumental moral value if it were able to go beyond reporting the horrors of visible starvation and to portray the pervasive, non-acute hunger in a more dramatic and telling way. This is obviously not the place to discuss the instrumentalities of practical politics, but the endorsement of the moral right to be free from hunger—both acute and non-acute—would in fact raise pointed questions about the means which might be used to pursue such a goal.

MORAL ASSESSMENT AND SOCIAL RELATIONS

Henry George's advice to Bernard Shaw to study economics may well be supplemented by advising the economist to study politics and sociology, and the "moral scientist," to use an old-fashioned term, to study them all. When fulfillments of such rights as freedom from hunger are accepted as goals (among other possible goals), the moral as-

---

[13] It is, in fact, hard to find an example of a substantial famine that has occurred in any country with electoral politics and a free press. However, much importance need not necessarily be attached to this empirical observation, since such countries are also typically rather rich. India, because of its poverty as well as its relatively free press, is thus one of the few test cases. There are also interesting contrasts within Africa, on which see Drèze and Sen, forthcoming.

[14] This is discussed in Sen, 1982a; 1983a. The nature of property rights in the news media is a further issue that requires examination in this context. While state-owned newspapers (and radio or T.V. services) tend very often to be a "wash out" in asserting people's rights (especially vis-à-vis the state), privately owned newspapers have their own biases as well.

sessment of actions and institutions will depend crucially on economic, social, and political analyses of how best to pursue these goals.

If there is one thing that emerges sharply from the discussion I have tried to present in this paper, it is the importance of factual analysis for moral assessment, including moral scrutiny of the acceptability and pursuit of specific rights. This is so even when the right in question is acknowledged to have intrinsic moral value, since valuing a right is not the same thing as accepting it. To affirm acceptability independently of consequences can be peculiarly untenable, as was discussed in analyzing entitlements and hunger. In assessing the claims of property rights, or the right not to be hungry, the examination cannot be confined to issues of basic valuation only, and much of the challenge of assessment lies in the empirical analysis of causes and effects. In the world in which we live—full of hunger as well as wealth—these empirical investigations can be both complex and quite extraordinarily important. The big moral questions are frequently also deeply economic, social, or political.

REFERENCES

ALAMGIR, M. 1980. *Famine in South Asia: Political Economy of Mass Starvation in Bangladesh.* Cambridge, Mass.: Oelgeschlager, Gunn, and Hain.

ASHTON, B., HILL, K., PIAZZA, A., and ZEITZ, R. 1984. "Famine in China, 1958–61." *Population and Development Review* 10:613–45.

DRÈZE, JEAN, and SEN, AMARTYA, editors. Forthcoming. *Hunger: Economics and Policy.* 4 vols. Oxford: Clarendon Press.

DWORKIN, RONALD. 1977. *Taking Rights Seriously.* London: Duckworth.

FRIEDMAN, MILTON, and FRIEDMAN, ROSE. 1980. *Free to Choose.* London: Secker and Warburg.

GEORGE, HENRY. 1979. *Poverty and Progress.* Centenary edition, with foreword by Agnes George de Mille. New York: Robert Schalkenbach Foundation.

————. 1981. *The Science of Political Economy.* New York: Robert Schalkenbach Foundation.

GIBBARD, ALLAN. 1976. "Natural Property Rights." *Nous* 10:77–88.

HARRISON, ROSS. 1983. *Bentham.* London: Routledge.

NOZICK, ROBERT. 1974. *Anarchy, State, and Utopia.* Oxford: Blackwell.

RAM, N. 1986. "An Independent Press and Anti-Hunger Strategies." WIDER Conference Paper. In *Hunger: Economics and Policy*, edited by J. Dreeze and A. Sen. Oxford: Clarendon. Forthcoming.

RAVALLION, MARTIN. 1987. *Markets and Famines.* Oxford: Clarendon Press.

REGAN, DONALD. 1983. "Against Evaluator Relativity: A Response to Sen." *Philosophy and Public Affairs* 12:93–112.

SEN, AMARTYA. 1967. "The Nature and Classes of Prescriptive Judgments." *Philosophical Quarterly* 17:46–62.

————. 1970. *Collective Choice and Social Welfare.* San Francisco: Holden Day. Reprint. Amsterdam: New Holland, 1979.

————. 1978. "On the Labour Theory of Value: Some Methodological Issues." *Cambridge Journal of Economics* 2:175–90.

————. 1981. *Poverty and Famines: An Essay on Entitlement and Deprivation.* Oxford: Clarendon Press; New York: Oxford University Press.

————. 1982a. "How is India Doing?" *New York Review of Books* 29, No. 20 (December 16):41–45. Reprinted in D. K. Basu and R. Sisson, eds., *Social and Economic Development in India* (Beverly Hills: Sage, 1986).

————. 1982b. "The Right Not to be Hungry." In *Contemporary Philosophy*, Vol. 2, edited by G. Fløistad, pp. 343–60. Boston: Martinus Nijhoff.

————. 1982c. "Rights and Agency." *Philosophy and Public Affairs* 11:3–39.

————. 1983a. "Development: Which Way Now?" *Economic Journal* 93:745–62. Reprinted in *Resources, Values and Development*.

————. 1983b. "Evaluator Relativity and Consequential Evaluation." *Philosophy and Public Affairs* 12:113–32.

————. 1984a. "Food Battles: Conflicts in the Access to Food." *Food and Nutrition*, FAP 10,

Tenth Anniversary Issue. (FAD, United Nations, Rome).

_____. 1984b. *Resources, Values, and Development.* Oxford: Blackwell and Cambridge: Harvard University Press.

_____. 1985a. "Well-being, Agency, and Freedom: The Dewey Lectures 1984." *Journal of Philosophy* 82:185–203.

_____. 1985b. "Rights as Goals." In *Equality and Discrimination: Essays in Freedom and Justice*, edited by S. Guest and A. Milne. Stuttgart: Franz Steiner.

_____. 1985c. "The Moral Standing of the Market." In *Ethics and Economics*, edited by E. F. Paul et al. Oxford: Blackwell.

_____. 1986. "Food, Economics, and Entitlements." *Lloyds Book Review*, No. 160, April.

Privacy and the Constitution

John Arthur

In recent years, many of the Supreme Court's most controversial decisions, including those concerning abortion and homosexuality, have turned on the meaning of the right to privacy. It is striking, then, that the word *privacy* never occurs in the U.S. Constitution, either in the original text or in the amendments. In this essay, John Arthur discusses the constitutional origins of the right to privacy. He then looks critically at two problems: (1) Is this right best understood as protecting liberty or information? (2) Does the right to privacy, as understood by the Court, protect citizens against government efforts to criminalize homosexual sodomy?

John Arthur is the editor of *Morality and Moral Controversies* (1988) and the author of *The Unfinished Constitution* (1989). Together with William H. Shaw, he has edited *Readings in Philosophy of Law* (1984) and *Justice and Economic Distribution* (1991). Professor Arthur teaches philosophy at the State University of New York at Binghamton where he is Director of the Program in Law and Society.

The poorest man may in his cottage bid defiance to the Crown. It may be frail; its roof may shake; the wind may enter; the rain may enter; but the King of England cannot enter; all his force dares not cross the threshold of the ruined tenement!

William Pitt[1]

Many Americans have come to regard privacy as among their basic rights, providing an important limitation on governmental intrusion into their personal lives. This, despite the fact that privacy is a largely judicial construction: the word never occurs in the U.S. Constitution. Courts have therefore relied on other provisions of the document in fashioning a legal basis for privacy, among them the search warrant requirement, the prohibition against self-incrimination, the First Amendment protections of

[1] Quoted in T. Cooley, *A Treatise on Constitutional Limitations*, 8th Ed. (Boston: Little Brown, 1927) at p. 611.

religion and speech, and even the guarantee against quartering troops in a house. But as Robert Bork and others have emphasized, the basis of the modern right to privacy, which goes well beyond such explicit constitutional language to limit governmental regulation of abortion, contraceptives, and education of children, is much in doubt.[2]

This essay explores some of the important issues underlying constitutional debate over privacy. Besides the origins and exact nature of privacy itself, and the problems of interpretation it raises, I also look carefully at a recent Supreme Court opinion which denied that privacy extends to homosexual relations between consenting adults. These disagreements illustrate well a central question of constitutional jurisprudence: may government legitimately impose a particular conception of the good or virtuous life on an unwilling minority? Clearly the free exercise of religion clause serves to protect minority *religious* values, but debate has raged over the degree to which the Constitution protects other individual values.[3]

The Bill of Rights was originally applied only to the national government, not to the states. Government support of a particular religion, though it would have been unconstitutional if undertaken by Congress, was common among the states. Some states, for example, required belief in God as a prerequisite for holding public office, and five states even had officially established, state-supported churches.

All this changed, of course, in the wake of the Civil War. The Fourteenth Amendment, in particular, commands that states not "abridge the privileges or immunities of citizens of the United States; nor shall any State deprive any person of life, liberty, or property, without due process of law; nor

deny to any person within its jurisdiction the equal protection of the laws." This Amendment was interpreted in this century to "incorporate" into the Constitution the important protections afforded by the Bill of Rights, so that states are now under the same limits as the national government. (Despite promising only that life, liberty, and property will not be taken *without due process*, it was the Fourteenth Amendment's due process clause rather than the privileges and immunities clause or the Ninth Amendment which was used to extend the Bill of Rights to state governments. This incorporation was not done wholesale, but instead occured gradually based on the Court's determination that a particular right was "fundamental.")

But the fact that the Fourteenth Amendment's protection of life, liberty, and property *includes* the Bill of Rights need not mean that constitutional protections are *limited* to those rights. A Court interested in protecting the right to privacy could have said simply that the "liberty" or "privileges or immunities of citizens" referred to in the Fourteenth Amendment includes privacy. That was not, however, the Court's approach. Instead, the Court has interpreted the Bill of Rights to include privacy and then applied the Bill of Rights to the states through the Fourteenth Amendment.

I. THE ORIGINS OF THE RIGHT TO PRIVACY

The use of informants and undercover surveillance is relatively new to the United States. Prior to World War I, such practices were rare not only in the United States but throughout the English-speaking world, although they had long been common on the continent of Europe. Fear of German espionage during the war brought on widespread use of political informers and surveillance, and they have been with us ever since. During the 1960s and 1970s the Federal Bureau of Investigation used a staggering number

---

[2] See for example Robert Bork, "Neutral Principles," reprinted above.

[3] For an extended account of modern constitutional debate arguing that this issue is central not only to privacy but across a range of topics, see John Arthur, *The Unfinished Constitution* (Belmont CA: Wadsworth Publishing Co., 1989).

of spies and informants: in 1967 it employed one informant for every 5.7 members of the Communist party of the United states.[4] It also had 316 regular informants in the Socialist Workers' Party—an organization whose membership never exceeded 2,500.[5] In the decade before 1976 it spent $2.5 million to hire 5,145 informants working the city of Chicago alone.[6]

Although English common law had protected the people from searches by private citizens—creditors or individuals looking for their stolen property, for example—it provided virtually no limitation on searches by agents of the Crown until the seventeenth century. During the reign of Elizabeth I, the infamous Star Chamber issued warrants granting officials nearly unlimited power to search virtually anywhere and bring whomever they chose before the Ecclesiastical Court for punishment. Opposition to these "general warrants" was fierce, contributing to Parliament's battles with the Crown in the mid-seventeenth century and eventually to the revolution of 1688.[7]

Despite the steady gains made against abuses by the Crown in England, those guarantees were not respected in the American Colonies. Writs of assistance were regularly issued to British customs officers, allowing them to conduct searches of any home or ship without probable cause in hopes of finding smugglers. The writs were valid for the life of the sovereign during whose reign they were issued. Colonial merchants bitterly opposed the writs of assistance, although they never succeeded in getting the British to stop using them. In the Declaration of Independence Jefferson's explicit criticism of the king for opposing the "rights of Englishmen" was based in part on the use of writs of assistance.

When the new Constitution failed to provide explicit protection of privacy, Patrick Henry attacked it in a bitter speech:

Excisemen may come in multitudes; for the limitations of their numbers no man knows. They may, unless the general government be restrained by a bill of rights, or some similar restriction, go into your cellars and rooms, and search, ransack, and measure, everything you eat, drink, and wear. They ought to be restrained within proper bounds.[8]

But perhaps the most eloquent statement of the dangers of police surveillance and seizure power was offered by an English historian, Thomas Erskine May:

Next in importance to personal freedom is immunity from suspicious and jealous observation. Men may be without restraints upon their liberty; they may pass to and fro at pleasure; but if their steps are tracked by spies and informers, their words noted down for crimination, their associates watched as conspirators, who shall say that they are free? Espionage haunts men like an evil genius, chills their gayety, restrains their wit, casts a shadow over their friendships, and blights their domestic hearth.[9]

The fourth Amendment envisions that courts will strike a balance between society's needs for an efficient system of criminal investigation and a healthy respect for individual privacy by requiring that a search warrant be issued only on probable cause and that it describe "the place to be searched and the persons or things to be seized." Additionally, the "right of the people to be secure in their persons, houses, papers, and effects, against unreasonable searches and seizures, shall not be violated." None of these terms is defined, however, nor is it clear if there can be exceptions to the rules.

---

[4] C. Marwick, "The Government Informer," *First Principles*, March 1977, at 3.

[5] *New York Times*, September 15, 1976, at 14.

[6] *Washington Post*, April 9, 1978, at A3.

[7] For a discussion of this historical background, see C. Pyle and J. Shattuck, *Privacy: Cases, Materials, and Questions* (unpublished; prepared for Seminar on Privacy, Harvard Law School, 1986).

[8] *Elliots Debates*, Vol. 3, at 448–449.

[9] Thomas Erskine May, *Constitutional History of England*, quoted in Pyle and Shattuck, *Privacy*, at 3–81.

What constitutes a "search," for example? If an officer happens to see a stolen radio in a car while issuing a ticket, did he "search" the car? And what if the incriminating evidence will be lost or destroyed if an officer takes time to get a warrant?

The basic requirement of a warrant based on probable cause is that police make written application to a judicial officer describing what they expect to find and where they intend to look for it. The judge issuing the warrant must then determine if there is "probable cause" to believe that a warrant is justified. Then, after the search has been completed, the warrant also requires the police officer to return a copy of the warrant to the judge along with a description of the material obtained. Officers are limited in their searches to the areas described in the warrant, and material not described in the warrant cannot be seized unless it is in "plain view."

There is a variety of exceptions to the general rule that police must have a warrant before undertaking a search: police can search without a warrant if the suspect has consented to be searched; if a search is necessary to protect an officer or prevent destruction or removal of evidence; or if police are in "hot pursuit"—for example, chasing a suspect into a building. In general, however, the idea is that a "reasonable" search is one pursuant to a warrant issued on probable cause.

Warrant or no, there is also controversy about whether certain types of search are "unreasonable." In one case, *Rochin* v. *California*[10] (1952), police forced a suspect to have his stomach pumped; in another they removed a container of heroin from a person's rectum.[11] In both cases the searches were held to be "reasonable."

However intrusive these techniques may seem, the most dangerous search practices from the perspective of the right to privacy are the electronic and other forms of surveillance made possible by modern technology. Spy satellites, for instance, can peer into people's back yards, and heat sensors can determine a person's location and activities through the walls of the home. Electronic computer messages and phone conversations are easily recorded. Applying the Fourth Amendment to these distinctly twentieth-century problems has demanded that judges weigh the underlying political and social purposes of the amendment, along with the demand that police officials be allowed to fight crime effectively.

Although it was eventually overturned, the case that prompted the most eloquent and thoughtful consideration of these problems arose out of federal police efforts to enforce prohibition. Roy Olmstead was convicted in federal court of importing and selling liquor. Evidence used at the trial was gathered by tapping the telephone line between Olmstead's home and office, and he was convicted despite his objection that the evidence was obtained in violation of his Fourth Amendment rights against unreasonable search and seizure and Fifth Amendment right against self-incrimination. In *Olmstead* v. *United States* (1928), a majority of the Supreme Court agreed that his rights had not been violated.[12] Justice Taft delivered the opinion of the Court:

The well-known historical purpose of the Fourth Amendment, directed against general warrants and writs of assistance, was to prevent the use of governmental force to search a man's house, his person, his papers, and his effects, and to prevent their seizure against his will.

The amendment itself shows that the search is to be of material things—the person, the house, his papers, or his effects. The description of the warrant necessary to make the proceeding lawful is that it must specify the place to be searched and the person or *things* to be seized. . . .

The amendment does not forbid what was done here. There was no searching. There was no seizure. The evidence was secured by the use

---

[10] 342 U.S. 165 (1952).

[11] *Blackford* v. *United States*, 247 F.2d 745 (9th Cir. 1975).

---

[12] 277 U.S. 438 (1928).

of the sense of hearing and that only. There was no entry of the houses or offices of the defendants.

From the majority's perspective, tapping a telephone is not a "search" within the meaning of the Fourth Amendment since the amendment's purpose is limited to the protection of "material things" such as one's house, papers, and "person." Since there was no entry into the house and nothing was seized, Justice Taft concludes that the Fourth Amendment was not violated.

Justice Brandeis wrote a vigorous dissent:

When the Fourth and Fifth Amendments were adopted, "the form that evil had theretofore taken" had been necessarily simple. Force and violence were then the only means known to man by which a government could directly effect self-incrimination. . . . But "time works changes, brings into existence new conditions and purposes." Subtler and more far-reaching means of invading privacy have become available to the government. Discovery and invention have made it possible for the government, by means far more effective than stretching upon the rack, to obtain disclosure in court of what is whispered in the closet. . . .

The makers of our Constitution undertook to secure conditions favorable to the pursuit of happiness. They recognized the significance of man's spiritual nature, of his feelings and of his intellect. They knew that only a part of the pain, pleasure and satisfactions of life are to be found in material things. They sought to protect Americans in their beliefs, their thoughts, their emotions and their sensations. They conferred, as against the government, the right to be let alone—the most comprehensive of rights and the right most valued by civilized men. To protect that right, every unjustifiable intrusion by the government upon the privacy of the individual, whatever the means employed, must be deemed a violation of the Fourth Amendment. And the use, as evidence in a criminal proceeding, of facts ascertained by such intrusion must be deemed a violation of the Fifth. . . .

As judges often do, Brandeis looks behind the amendment to its underlying purpose, rather than to the specific intentions of its authors. The Fourth Amendment not only forbids the specific abuses that eighteenth century governments might have imagined but enshrines a deeper value—the privacy of people's mental and emotional life—against the intrusions of government. It protects the "sanctities of a man's home and privacies of life"; its underlying purpose, he says, is to protect people's "beliefs, thoughts, emotions and sensations."

Almost forty years passed before the Court overturned *Olmstead*, but in doing so it provided a very different way of thinking about the scope of the Fourth Amendment than either Taft or Brandeis employed. Mr. Katz was convicted of using a public telephone to place bets at a racetrack, in violation of federal law. The evidence the government introduced was acquired with a recorder attached to the outside of the phone booth. In reversing the conviction in *Katz* v. *United States* (1967)[13], Justice Stewart wrote:

In the first place the correct solution of Fourth Amendment problems is not necessarily promoted by incantation of the phrase "constitutionally protected area." Secondly, the Fourth Amendment cannot be translated into a general constitutional "right to privacy." That Amendment protects individual privacy against certain kinds of governmental intrusion, but its protections go further, and often have nothing to do with privacy at all. Other provisions of the Constitution protect personal privacy from other forms of governmental invasion. But the protection of a person's *general* right to privacy—his right to be let alone by other people—is, like the protection of his property and of his very life, left largely to the law of the individual States.

Because of the misleading way the issues have been formulated . . . attention [has been deflected] from the problem presented by this case. For the Fourth Amendment protects people, not places. What a person knowingly exposes to the public, even in his own home or office, is not a subject of Fourth Amendment protection. . . .

---

[13] 389 U.S. 347 (1967).

But what he seeks to preserve as private, even in an area accessible to the public, may be constitutionally protected. . . .

The Government's activities in electronically listening to and recording the petitioner's words violated the privacy upon which he justifiably relied while using the telephone booth and thus constituted a "search and seizure" within the meaning of the Fourth Amendment. The fact that the electronic device employed to achieve that end did not happen to penetrate the wall of the booth can have no constitutional significance.

Katz explicitly overrules *Olmstead*, proclaiming that the Fourth Amendment protects people rather than places. The key is not whether the phone booth is a "protected area," as earlier decisions had emphasized, but rather whether the surveillance violated the privacy on which a person has "justifiably relied." Because Katz had a reasonable expectation that his phone conversation would not be overhead, the government violated his right against unreasonable search when it made its recording. A conversation in a public park, on the other hand, is not protected under the amendment.

While adopting part of Brandeis's view of an expanded right to privacy, the Court rejected the second, broader conception that he had articulated in *Olmstead*. Although privacy limits government observation even when there is no physical trespass, the Court rejected Brandeis's claim that the Fourth Amendment reflects a commitment that people should be left to make certain decisions for themselves. "The Fourth Amendment," wrote Justice Stewart, "cannot be translated into a general constitutional 'right to be let alone.'" The general question of individual liberty is left to the states, according to Stewart, along with the responsibilities to protect life and property. Nevertheless, both of Justice Brandeis's principles—the general right to be left alone and the sanctity of the home as a place for personal freedom and expression—soon became the focal point of constitutional argument.

2. THE BIRTH OF THE NEW PRIVACY

The right to privacy traditionally refers to the right to control information. Peeping into a window, opening mail, and bugging a telephone conversation are obvious violations. So although the word never appears in the Constitution, the Bill of Rights protects privacy through the Fourth Amendment's guarantee against unreasonable searches of "persons, houses, papers, and effects" and its requirement that officials get a warrant specifically describing the place to be searched and the persons or things to be seized.

Although there is much disagreement about how these features of the Fourth Amendment should be interpreted, by far the greatest controversy has arisen as the Court moved beyond this familiar conception of privacy to include rights not explicitly in the language of the Constitution, including the rights to use contraceptives and get an abortion.

An early example of the Court's willingness to expand its conception of "life, liberty and property" beyond the explicit language of the Bill of Rights occurred in the late nineteenth century as the Court undertook to block the rising tide of economic regulation. Liberty of contract was invoked over and over by the Court as it blocked minimum-wage laws, maximum-hour laws, and other forms of market regulation. Despite the fact that by the late 1930s those efforts were widely discredited, the Court has continued to protect many rights not explicitly mentioned anywhere in the Constitution. These include the right to travel, to vote, to send children to private school, to learn a foreign language, and to associate in groups. All of these rights were held to be implicit in the Bill of Rights, applied to states through the Fourteenth Amendment.

This new conception of privacy thus had its origin in the cases heard early in this century as the Court invalidated legislative enactments it deemed inconsistent with "fundamental" liberties. In *Meyer* v. *Nebraska* (1923), a decision the Court later used to defend the right to contraceptive devices and abortions, the Court overturned a Nebraska law prohibiting teaching a foreign language to young children. Justice McReynolds wrote in *Meyer*:

While this Court has not attempted to define with exactness the liberty guaranteed by the Fourteenth Amendment, the term has received much consideration and some of the included things have been definitely stated. Without doubt, it denotes not merely freedom from bodily restraint but also the right of the individual to contract, to engage in the common occupations of life, to acquire useful knowledge, to marry, establish a home and bring up children, to worship God according to the dictates of his own conscience, and generally to enjoy those privileges long recognized at common law as essential to the orderly pursuit of happiness by free men. The established doctrine is that this liberty may not be interfered with, under the guise of protecting the public interest, by legislative action which is arbitrary or without reasonable relation to some purpose within the competency of the State to effect.[14]

In 1925 the Court again relied on the Fourteenth Amendment's protection of liberty to overturn a state law requiring students to attend public rather than private school. And again Justice McReynolds emphasized the broad reach of the Fourteenth Amendment in personal privacy and family life, noting that the Constitution ensures that children cannot be made into "mere creatures of the state" by a government that attempts to "standardize" them.[15]

Four decades later these opinions resurfaced in a decision that expanded the Court's conception of liberty to include a broad notion of personal privacy. The executive director of the Planned Parenthood League of Connecticut and a Yale Medical School professor had been convicted of teaching married couples how to avoid pregnancy, in violation of state law, and had been fined $100. The two then brought suit, claiming that the Connecticut law was an unconstitutional violation of their rights under the Fourteenth Amendment. In fact, those with the money and the independence to travel outside the state had easy access to contraceptives. However, since the law prevented Planned Parenthood from operating in Connecticut, others did not. Justice Douglas wrote the opinion of the Court; the case was *Griswold* v. *Connecticut* (1965).[16]

. . . The . . . cases suggest that specific guarantees in the Bill of Rights have penumbras, formed by emanations from those guarantees that help give them life and substance. Various guarantees create zones of privacy. The right of association contained in the penumbra of the First Amendment is one, as we have seen. The Third Amendment in its prohibition against the quartering of soldiers "in any house" in time of peace without the consent of the owner is another facet of that privacy. The Fourth Amendment explicitly affirms the "right of the people to be secure in their persons, houses, papers, and effects, against unreasonable searches and seizures." The Fifth Amendment in its Self-Incrimination Clause enables the citizen to create a zone of privacy which government may not force him to surrender to his detriment. The Ninth Amendment provides: "The enumeration in the Constitution, of certain rights, shall not be construed to deny or disparage others retained by the people." . . .

The present case, then, concerns a relationship lying within the zone of privacy created by several fundamental constitutional guarantees. And it concerns a law which, in forbidding the *use* of contraceptives rather than regulating their manufacture or sale, seeks to achieve its goals by means having a maximum destructive impact upon that relationship. Such a law cannot stand in light of the familiar principle, so often applied by this Court, that a "governmental purpose to control or prevent activities constitutionally sub-

---

[14] 262 U.S. 390 (1923).

[15] *Pierce* v. *Society of Sisters*, 268 U.S. 510 (1925).

[16] 381 U.S. 479 (1965).

ject to state regulation may not be achieved by means which sweep unnecessarily broadly and thereby invade the area of protected freedoms." *NAACP v. Alabama.* Would we allow the police to search the sacred precincts of marital bedrooms for telltale signs of the use of contraceptives? The very idea is repulsive to the notions of privacy surrounding the marriage relationship. Marriage is intimate to the degree of being sacred. . . .

Justice Douglas's opinion is an excellent example of one form of legal argument. He begins by noting the well-entrenched principle in constitutional law that rights need not be mentioned explicitly in order to win protection. The Supreme Court, he emphasizes, has often held that the First Amendment extends beyond specifically enumerated rights of press and speech to protect freedom of association, the right to read and distribute material, and the right to believe what one wishes. Other amendments—the Third, Fourth, Fifth, and Ninth—have never been so narrowly construed as to prevent the Court from giving them "life and substance": constitutional provisions, in Douglas's famous phrase, have "penumbras."

The First Amendment's penumbra includes freedom of personal association, including freedom to belong to unpopular civil rights organizations, without fear of reprisal. Third and fourth Amendment guarantees against quartering soldiers and searching homes similarly safeguard personal privacy, as does the Fifth Amendment's protection against self-incrimination. Viewed as a whole, then, the Bill of Rights reflects a commitment to protect a "zone" of personal privacy.

But Douglas's opinion is misleading in one important respect. The objection raised against the Connecticut law was not that it made personal or private *information* public but that it prohibited an *act*—using contraceptives. What Douglas found objectionable was Connecticut's infringement on liberty, not on privacy in the narrow sense.[17]

[17] See, for example, W. A. Parent, "Privacy, Morality, and the Law," *Philosophy and Public Affairs*, 12:4 (Fall 1983).

Justice Black, in his dissent, accused Douglas of merely expressing his "personal and private notions" about the wisdom of Connecticut's law. "I like my privacy as much as the next one," he wrote, "but I am nevertheless compelled to admit that government has a right to invade it unless prohibited by some specific constitutional provision." Obviously the government must be free to regulate what goes on in the home, even the bedroom: murder cannot be protected merely because it is committed in a normally private place. But on what principle can some regulations be curtailed as violating the liberties protected in the Fourteenth Amendment while other regulations are condoned? Although Justice Douglas speaks of the sacred character of marriage, it is clear that he does not limit privacy to marriage. The constitutional principles he relies on—freedom of speech and association and the right to protection against unreasonable searches, seizures, and self-incrimination—suggest a vision of individual autonomy extending far beyond marriage. But such an approach, which identifies the liberties protected by the Fourteenth Amendment by determining the principles embedded in the Bill of Rights, leaves a great deal to discretion and the judgment of the justices.

Among those who share Justice Black's concern about Douglas's approach is Justice Harlan. Although he agrees with Justice Douglas's conclusion, Justice Harlan cannot accept the reasoning. Emphasizing the Connecticut law's incompatibility with traditional American values, he wrote:

[This] enactment involves what, by common understanding throughout the English-speaking world, must be granted to be a most fundamental aspect of "liberty," the privacy of the home in its most basic sense. . . .

It is clear, of course, that this Connecticut statute does not invade the privacy of the home in the usual sense, since the invasion involved here may [be] accomplished without any physical intrusion [into] the home. [But it] would surely be an extreme instance of sacrificing substance to form were it to be held that the Constitutional principle of privacy against arbitrary official intrusion comprehends only physical invasions by the police. [If] the physical curtilage of the home is protected, it is surely as a result of solicitude to protect the privacies of the life within. . . .

I would not suggest that adultery, homosexuality, fornication and incest are immune from criminal enquiry, however privately practiced. [But] not to discriminate between what is involved in this case and either the traditional offenses against good morals or crimes which, though they may be committed anywhere, happen to have been committed or concealed in the home, would entirely misconceive the argument that is being made.

[The] intimacy of husband and wife is necessarily an essential and accepted feature of the institution of marriage, an institution which the State not only must allow, but which always and in every age it has fostered and protected. It is one thing when the State exerts its power either to forbid extra-marital sexuality altogether, or to say who may marry, but it is quite another when, having acknowledged a marriage and the intimacies inherent in it, it undertakes to regulate by means of the criminal law the details of that intimacy. . . .

Harlan tries to avoid the expansive tendencies of Justice Douglas's analysis by stressing the importance of marriage and of its traditional role in American life. He emphasizes that the process of defining the "fundamental liberties" protected by the Fourteenth Amendment must be a rational one and that judges must not be allowed to "roam where unguided speculation might lead them." The fence that prevents such roaming is "respect for the teaching of history" and a "solid recognition of the basic values that underlie our society." Rather than imposing their *own* views, he says, judges must look to the common understanding throughout the "English-speaking world." Marital privacy is thought important by our historical tradition. Other activities that go on in the home—homosexuality and adultery, for example—are not among the "fundamental" liberties because they do not enjoy the same status in American history and tradition.

Douglas is willing to use philosophical argument to shape the constitutional right of privacy, tying it to the language of the Constitution at an abstract level. Like Justice Brandeis, he seeks to discover principles and values that lie behind the explicit guarantees of the Constitution. The Bill of Rights makes sense, he suggests, only if we ascribe to it a more general commitment to protect and respect individual autonomy and freedom of action. He thinks of the anticontraceptive law as an infringement of individual liberty, as an attempt to impose premarital chastity and parenthood on others, as well, perhaps, as an effort to embody certain religious views in law. Harlan, on the other hand, looks explicitly to the traditions and history of the people for guidance in defining constitutional rights, rights grounded on the sense of virtue and the good life that Americans share. It is perfectly legitimate, he says, for society to promote the "moral soundness of its people." Anticontraceptive laws, however, intrude into the intimate, protected relation between husband and wife; they attack the traditional family.

Although it provoked great interest among legal scholars, *Griswold* was largely ignored by the public. It was not until the Court confronted additional cases, sodomy and abortion in particular, that the public controversy surrounded privacy became evident. An important step between *Griswold* and these later opinions, however, was *Eisenstadt* v. *Baird*[18] (1972), which involved the denial of access to contraceptives to unmarried people. In *Eisenstadt* the Court considered and rejected Harlan's marriage-based interpretation of *Griswold* in favor of Douglas's. Justice Brennan wrote for a 6-to-1 majority:

Whatever the rights of the individual to access to contraceptives may be, the rights must be the same for unmarried and married alike. It is true that in *Griswold*, the right of privacy in question inhered in the marital relationship. Yet the mari-

---

[18] 405 U.S. 438 (1972).

tal couple is not an independent entity with a mind and heart of its own, but an association of two individuals each with a separate intellectual and emotional makeup. If the right of privacy means anything, it is the right of the *individual*, married or single, to be free from unwarranted governmental intrusion into matters so fundamentally affecting a person as the decision whether to bear or beget children.[19]

As we will see in the next section, there is room for considerable disagreement over just what privacy really means. One interpretation is that of Justice Brennan, who, perhaps echoing Brandeis's general idea of a right to be let alone, has characterized privacy as the right of the individual to be "free from unwarranted governmental intrusion." Marriage is one area of fundamental importance, to be sure, but the right to privacy on this view would concern far more than protecting and encouraging a particular institution. In *Eisenstadt* it appeared that the Court might be headed toward some more general principle of individual rights. There were many possibilities. One was for the Court to limit the right to privacy to contraception; another would be to extend protection to all areas of private sexual activity, including the choice of a partner and abortion; yet another even more expansive interpretation would allow the Court, still under the banner of privacy, to protect the right of individuals to do anything that does not harm others.

3. THE NATURE OF PRIVACY

The judicial protection of privacy prompted some of the most bitter criticism of the Court since the school desegregation and prayer cases. Some critics focused on the vagueness and lack of clear boundaries of the right to privacy; others have faulted the Court's logic. Former Supreme Court nominee Robert Bork put these points especially

sharply. [See his "Neutral Principles"[20] reprinted in this volume.] Yet the Court relied on *Griswold* to protect the rights of *unmarried* persons who wish to use contraceptives,[21] to overturn a Virginia statute prohibiting interracial marriage,[22] and eventually to reject a Texas statute prohibiting abortion. Some state courts have extended the right to privacy into still other areas. It was used to justify the right to die,[23] to use marijuana,[24] and to take laetrile to fight cancer.[25] All these privacy cases have their roots, says the Court, in earlier decisions protecting people's right to send children to private schools and to study the German language, as well as Fourth Amendment guarantees against unreasonable searches and seizures. How, then, should we understand "privacy"? Is it a single right of some sort, or should we interpret privacy as a family of rights that, though related in various respects, do not have a single feature in common?

It has seemed to many, including some who are sympathetic with the results of *Griswold* and its progeny, that the Court is confused when it uses the word *privacy* to describe those cases that actually involve liberty instead.[26] Contrary to the Court, *privacy*, according to this view, actually involves disclosure of personal *information* rather than restrictions on what we may *do*. Laws that prevent people from using contraceptives, sending children to private schools, or getting an abortion restrict *liberty* by denying them the opportunity to do what they want. The paradigm of a violation of privacy, in

---

[19] *Eisenstadt* v. *Baird*, 405 U.S. 438 (1972).

[20] R. Bork, "Neutral Principles and Some First Amendment Problems," 47 *Indiana Law Journal* (1971).

[21] *Eisenstadt* v. *Baird*, 405 U.S. 438 (1971).

[22] *Loving* v. *Virginia*, 388 U.S. 1 (1967).

[23] *The Matter of Quinlan*, 355 A. 2d. 647 (1976).

[24] *Ravin* v. *State*, 537 P.2d 494 (1975).

[25] *People* v. *Privitera*, 74 C.A. 3d. (1977). The California Supreme Court reversed this judgment, however, claiming that the right to privacy did not reach that broadly.

[26] See, for example, H. Gross, "Privacy and Autonomy", *Nomos XII: Privacy* (New York: Atherton, 1971).

contrast, is publication of embarrassing information or eavesdropping on an intimate phone conversation, not limiting freedom of action. Imagine, for example, somebody who allows publication of her personal secrets. Clearly she has given up her privacy, although because she consented she has not had her liberty infringed. Nor is the issue one of control over information: although privacy was lost, control over the information was maintained. So it has seemed to many that liberty and privacy are different.

If privacy consists in not having personal information about ourselves become known to others, then what is the *right* to privacy? The answer cannot be that the right is violated whenever personal information is made public; remember the woman who consented. There are other disclosures of private information that also do not violate the right to privacy: a wiretap on the phone of a suspected criminal might reveal personal information but would not necessarily be a violation of either a legal or moral right. Nor, to take another example, would it seem to be a violation of the *right* to privacy when a public figure's drinking habits are made public (assuming that the official's ability to perform is hampered), although that would be a disclosure of private information. Whether the moral right to privacy is violated will therefore depend on whether the personal information was *wrongfully* disclosed. That judgment—of the wrongfulness of the disclosure—will depend on many factors, including the importance of having the information made public, the way it was gathered, whether there was informed consent that it be made public, and what was done with the information after it was acquired. These will not make the acquisition of information any less an invasion of privacy; they can, however, make the invasion a legitimate one.

Are we then to conclude, coming back to the central issue, that the Court has simply confused liberty with privacy in *Griswold* and the other cases we have considered, treating violations of liberty as if they were wrongful

disclosures of information? I think not. For although the right to privacy clearly includes the right to prevent unjustified disclosure of personal information, it is not limited to that.

Suppose, for example, somebody repeatedly phoned you at your home despite requests to stop. Such an invasion of privacy, for surely it is that, could not be described as disclosure of personal information. Nonetheless, your privacy is violated: the caller has intruded into your personal, private life. She has violated your right to privacy. This example suggests that the Court is not off the mark when it includes certain liberties among the "right of privacy," especially ones that are associated with the home, family, and sexual intimacy. We do think of certain choices we want to make within the home as private ones with which others should not interfere in any way. It is not simply that others should not watch. Similarly, we often describe sexual and family decisions as private, again in the more inclusive sense that encompasses both freedom of action and lack of disclosure. The right to privacy thus has two aspects: one prevents unjustified disclosure of personal information, and the other protects certain types of liberty.

The two aspects are, however, connected. Notice, first, that not all disclosures of information about us could be an invasion of privacy. A photo of your car's left-rear tire, for example, would not qualify even if it appeared in the *New York Times*. Only if the information disclosed is personal would its disclosure constitute a violation of privacy. So both forms of privacy involve matters thought to be of a personal nature—sex, reproduction, family, and home, for example—and the Court has focused on just that feature in its privacy cases.

In fact, there is little suggestion in the opinions that the justices are confused about whether it is personal liberty or personal information that is being protected. In overturning laws preventing unmarried couples from using contraceptives, Justice Brennan wrote that the right to privacy prevents government from intruding into "matters so fundamentally affecting a person as the decision whether to bear or beget children." He was obviously aware that it is the *decision* to bear children that was at issue, not information about the person's private life. The Court is thus quite clear about what it wants to protect: privacy, in its view, can be invaded either by publication of intimate details of a person's life or by infringing on the person's liberty to pursue certain personal aspects of that life. So the right to privacy that grew out of *Griswold*, having roots in the Fourth Amendment's guarantees against unreasonable searches, has come to encompass more than information; it includes the right to make certain decisions.

The link between these two aspects of privacy seems to be that unlike other, relatively trivial decisions we make, ones involving home, children, sex, and reproduction play a role in defining who we are and what we shall become. They are personal in a literal sense: they are close to the identity of the *person*. Limiting access to personal information is important for our emotional development and well-being. We often find that being on public display makes reflection and relaxation impossible, and we are frequently embarrassed to have others know personal details about our lives. Informational privacy is also important if we are to develop the bonds of friendship and love that are an essential ingredient in the identities of most people. If everybody knew everything about our most intimate feelings and actions, our personal relationships would lose much of what makes them personal rather than public, and thus much of their meaning for us. So the right to limit access to information is crucial if we are to have and enjoy those relationships that are most important in shaping our identities—relationships of loved one, parent, child, friend. In that way, the liberties identified under the heading of "private" (involving decisions about family, contraception, and so on) serve the same function as the right to limit dispersal of personal information. Limiting such information, using contraceptives, passing on our religion and language to our children, and deciding to get an abortion are important aspects of personal integrity and identity.

Limiting the spread of personal information and exercising freedom to make personal decisions have something else in common. Just as sometimes personal information may be divulged without violating anybody's right, so too some personal decisions may be restricted without violating *that* aspect of the right to privacy. The mere fact that some desired action falls within the realm of intimate, personal choices or that some information is personal does not show that the government cannot prevent the action or must not acquire the information. We do not have a right to sexually abuse children, although doing so would certainly qualify as a "personal" decision, any more than we have an absolute right that government or others never discover or disclose facts of our personal lives.

It is a mistake, therefore, to suppose that the Court is confused about what's at stake in privacy. The liberties it has identified are connected with each other as well as with our need to limit dissemination of personal information because they all involve people's interest in shaping their personal identity. Protecting intimate, personal choices involving family and parenthood are important in that process of self-definition, as is the ability to control dissemination of personal information.

4. SEXUAL PREFERENCE

Georgia law defines *sodomy* as submitting to or committing "any act involving the sex organs of one person and the anus or mouth of another." Sodomy is a criminal act in Georgia, whatever the sexes of the actors; violators are subject to prison terms of one to ten years. Michael Hardwick had been at a bar where police, in an effort to harass gays, had arrested him for displaying an open beer bottle. Unaware that Hardwick had paid the fine, an officer went to his house to collect. A friend of Hardwick let him in, and the officer observed Hardwick in the bedroom having sex with another man. After about a minute the officer arrested Hardwick and took him to jail, where he spent one night. When the jailer locked Michael Hardwick up, he told the others in the cell that they would enjoy themselves, because Hardwick had been arrested for sodomy. Although the prosecutor chose not to present the case to a grand jury, Hardwick nonetheless challenged the constitutionality of the statute.

A federal appeals court held that the Fourteenth Amendment protected privacy, including sexual freedom. The Court did not, however, demand that the statute be overturned; it merely held that the state of Georgia must demonstrate before a federal judge that the law served a compelling state interest. It was only that decision—that Georgia would be required to defend its sodomy law—which the Supreme Court reviewed.

Immediately after hearing the case, Justice Powell indicated that he would join four others in requiring review of the statute. But he later changed his mind, and in a 5-to-4 opinion the court upheld the Georgia law. (Powell said in speech three years later, however, that he had again changed his mind and would now vote to overturn the law.)

Writing for the majority, Justice White writes that:

Respondent would have us announce, as the Court of Appeals did, a fundamental right to engage in homosexual sodomy. This we are quite unwilling to do. . . . In *Palko* v. *Connecticut*, it was said that fundamental liberties are "implicit in the concept of ordered liberty," such that "neither liberty nor justice would exist if [they] were sacrificed." A different description of fundamental liberties appeared in *Moore* v. *East Cleveland*, where they are characterized as those liberties that are "deeply rooted in this Nation's history and tradition." . . .

Proscriptions against that conduct have ancient roots. Sodomy was a criminal offense at common law and was forbidden by the laws of the original thirteen States when they ratified the Bill of Rights. In 1868, when the Fourteenth Amendment was ratified, all but 5 of the 37 States in the Union had criminal sodomy laws. In fact, until 1961, all States outlawed sodomy, and today, 24 States and the District of Columbia continue to provide criminal penalties for sodomy performed in private and between consenting adults. Against this background, to claim that a right to engage in such conduct is "deeply rooted in this Nation's history and tradition" or "implicit in the concept of ordered liberty" is, at best, facetious. . . .

Plainly enough, otherwise illegal conduct is not always immunized whenever it occurs in the home. Victimless crimes, such as the possession and use of illegal drugs do not escape the law where they are committed at home. . . . And if respondent's submission is limited to the voluntary sexual conduct between consenting adults, it would be difficult, except by fiat, to limit the claimed right to homosexual conduct while leaving exposed to prosecution adultery, incest, and other sexual crimes even though they are committed in the home. We are unwilling to start down that road.

Justice White argues that in previous cases the right to privacy revolved around marriage, family, and home, and that therefore homosexual sodomy does not fall within its scope. In short, Georgia's statute does not implicate any Fourteenth Amendment rights because only liberties that are fundamental or deeply rooted in our traditions are protected, and to make such a claim about sodomy is "at best facetious." Sodomy is not part of the traditional respect accorded the family, nor is it part of the basic liberties guaranteed by the Constitution.

Justice Blackmun, in dissent, argues that White has misunderstood the issue by focusing on the narrow question of sodomy instead of the principles that underlie the Court's earlier cases. In past privacy cases, he writes,

[T]he Court has proceeded along two somewhat distinct, albeit complementary, lines. First, it has recognized a privacy interest with reference to certain decisions that are properly for the individual to make. E.g., [*Roe* (right to abortion), *Pierce* (right to send children to private schools)]. Second, it has recognized a privacy interest with reference to certain places without regard for the particular activities in which the individuals who occupy them are engaged. The case before us implicates both the decisional and the spatial aspects of the right to privacy. . . .

[The] fact that individuals define themselves in a significant way through their intimate sexual relationships with others suggests, in a Nation as diverse as ours, that there may be many "right" ways of conducting those relationships, and that much of the richness of a relationship will come from the freedom an individual has to choose the form and nature of these intensely personal bonds. [The] Court claims that its decision today merely refuses to recognize a fundamental right to engage in homosexual sodomy; what the Court really has refused to recognize is the fundamental interest all individuals have in controlling the nature of their intimate associations with others.

The behavior for which Hardwick faces prosecution occurred in his own home, a place to which the Fourth Amendment attaches special significance. The Court's treatment of this aspect of the case is symptomatic of its overall refusal to consider the broad principles that have informed our treatment of privacy in specific cases. Just as the right to privacy is more than the mere aggregation of a number of entitlements to engage in specific behavior, so too, protecting the physical integrity of the home is more than merely a means of protecting specific activities that often take place there. . . .

I cannot agree that either the length of time a majority has held its convictions or the passions with which it defends them can withdraw legislation from this Court's scrutiny. [It] is precisely because the issue raised by this case touches the heart of what makes individuals what they are that we should be especially sensitive to the rights of those whose choices upset the majority. . . .

The mere knowledge that other individuals do not adhere to one's value system cannot be a legally cognizable interest, let alone an interest that can justify invading the houses, hearts, and minds of citizens who choose to live their lives differently.[27]

Justice Blackmun claims privacy has both a decisional and a spatial aspect. Some personal decisions are of such fundamental importance to the personal lives of individuals that they demand a compelling state interest before they can be restricted. The choice of a sexual partner is such a decision, Blackmun said, and is therefore included within the principles already enunciated by the Court. Privacy also has a spatial dimension: it matters where the law intrudes. Georgia's statute reaches into an area that the Constitution takes special care to shield from government: the home. *Bowers* therefore lies at the intersection of two important constitutional principles: protection of personal choices and protection of the sanctity of the home.

Justice Blackmun goes on to reject arguments advanced by Georgia to justify its restriction of Hardwick's liberty. There is no evidence, he says that the public health is protected by the law, nor can the law be defended on grounds of society's right to protect moral decency. Hardwick's behavior took place in private, out of sight of people who would find it offensive. In fact, he concludes, the statute is nothing more that an effort to dictate "private morality."

The disagreement between White and Blackmun turns in large measure on the same issues that divided Douglas and Harlan in *Griswold*. For White the majority is justified in enforcing its conception of the good life when, as in *Bowers*, it relies on the traditional values of family and marriage. Georgia's statute, however, does not present the conflict between tradition and the will of the legislature that Harlan saw in *Griswold*. Blackmun adopts the alternative view that government should aspire to neutrality and respect the rights of those who "choose to

---

[27] 106 S. Ct 2846 (1986).

live their lives differently," especially when the issue involves sexual identity and personality to the extent that this does. Neither traditional disapproval of the practice nor legislative enactments, even if they reflect majority will, can justify intrusion into this private decision.

Blackmun would not say, however, that any conception of the good should be protected merely because it involves personal, sexual decisions. Rape, even if done in privacy, must be criminalized. How, then, are we to assess the risks to society that homosexuality may pose? In his brief, Georgia Attorney General Michael Bowers gave two arguments in support of the claim that the legislature acted reasonably in banning sodomy. The first argument goes to support the contention, adopted by White, that privacy protects traditional values of family and marriage and therefore does not provide protection to homosexual conduct. The attorney general wrote that traditionally the Court has

recognized the right of individuals to be free from governmental intrusion in decisions relating to marriage and family life, and used as a guide the teachings of history and the basic values of society to conclude that the Constitution protects the sanctity of the family, even the extended family, "precisely because the institution of the family is deeply rooted in this nation's history and tradition. It is through the family that we inculcate and pass down many of our most cherished values, moral and cultural" [*Moore* v. *East Cleveland* (1977)]. . . . The statute most certainly does not interfere with personal decisions concerning marriage or family life.[28]

Not only is homosexuality beyond the bounds of the family, but it poses a danger to that institution. Georgia's law, he wrote, reflects the view that

Homosexual sodomy is the anathema of the basic units of our society—marriage and the family. To decriminalize or artificially withdraw the public's expression of its disdain for this conduct does not uplift sodomy, but rather demotes these sacred institutions to merely other alternative lifestyles. If the legal distinctions between the intimacies of marriage and homosexual sodomy are lost, it is certainly possible to make the assumption, perhaps unprovable at this time, that the order of society, our way of life, could be changed in a harmful way. The states have a legitimate and, it is argued, compelling interest in the protection of the organization of society.[29]

On what grounds might a legislator or judge believe that decriminalizing homosexuality would endanger the family, our society, and "our way of life"? The American Psychological Association and the American Public Health Association filed an amicus curiae ("friend of the court") brief that argued against Georgia.[30] In that brief they pointed out that from 70 to 80 percent of gay men and lesbian women live as couples, despite the lack of social and legal encouragement. Equally important,

Couplehood, either as a reality or an aspiration, is as strong among gay people as it is among heterosexuals. Principal concerns for all types of couples include equity, loyalty, stability, intimacy, and love. The nontraditional couples also often make substantial commitments to each other and in many cases stay together for decades.[31]

Many heterosexual couples marry and maintain a "family" despite the absence of children; why, then, are homosexual couples who wish to do the same a threat to "the order of society, our way of life"? It is not clear that Georgia's law is consistent with the

---

[28] Brief of Attorney General Michael Bowers, in *Bowers* v. *Georgia* (1985), at 30, 32.

[29] *Bowers* Brief, at 37–38.

[30] Brief of Amici Curiae American Psychological Association and American Public Health Association in Support of Respondents, *Bowers* v. *Hardwick* (1985), hereafter APA Brief.

[31] APA Brief (1985), at 14.

family values it purports to support. If the point of giving marriage special protection is to enable people to achieve bonds of love, intimacy, and commitment, then why should the fact that the partners are of different sexes be crucial? Oddly enough, Justice Powell, who provided the last-minute fifth vote in *Bowers*, had written an opinion just a few years earlier that indicated sympathy with people living in the "nontraditional" family. *Moore v. East Cleveland*[32] (1977) invalidated a Cleveland zoning law that limited occupancy within a dwelling to a single family. The ordinance defined "family" so narrowly that it prevented Mrs. Moore from living with her two grandsons. Powell wrote in *Moore*:

Whether or not such a family is established because of personal tragedy, the choice of relatives in this degree of kinship to live together may not lightly be denied by the State. [*Pierce*] The Constitution prevents East Cleveland from standardizing its children—and its adults—by forcing all to live in certain narrowly defined family patterns."[33]

Justice White, who wrote the *Bowers* opinion, dissented in *Moore*. So although there is no evidence that they even considered the fact of homosexual families, those on the Court who believed that laws should promote family values should also have considered the real meaning behind that ideal. If the point is to facilitate intimacy, stability, and family life, they should oppose sodomy laws making such values harder for homosexuals to realize. In fact, as we have seen, the evidence indicates that homosexuals seek relationships that are for all intents and purposes familial; the underlying purpose is identical to that of heterosexuals, and often even includes raising children. So besides Blackmun's objection to the majority in *Bowers*, there is also a potentially powerful conservative attack on Georgia's law that sees

the law as discouraging creation of stable families and undermining the same family values as Harlan invoked in *Griswold*.

Nor can it be maintained that homosexuality threatens the traditional family because it is contagious. Homosexuality is widely practiced in all societies, whether homosexuals are admired, ignored, or repressed.[34] And sexual preference, as opposed to sexual acts, is not something we choose. Estimates are that anywhere from 5 to 25 million Americans are homosexual in the sense that they are primarily or exclusively attracted to members of their own sex rather than of the opposite sex. Whether heterosexual or homosexual, we discover our sexual orientation rather as we discover that we are either right or left handed. Only a small fraction of those who find themselves attracted to people of the same sex could have their preference modified through therapy, perhaps no more than the percentage of heterosexuals whose preference would be changed.

The idea that sodomy laws protect heterosexual marriage is thus mistaken on two counts. Such laws do not reduce homosexual orientation of adults, and even if they did, normal contact with homosexual adults does not affect the sexual orientation of others.[35] Homosexuals pose no threat to the institution of marriage and family; and allowing them to create families would arguably promote rather than hinder those values.

Georgia made two additional arguments in its brief: that sodomy is "immoral" and that it is a reasonable response to the public health dangers posed by acquired immune deficiency syndrome (AIDS). I will look at each in turn.

Homosexual sodomy, the state claimed, is "purely an unnatural means of satisfying an unnatural lust, which has been declared by Georgia to be morally wrong."[36] Again, however, both the medical and psychological ev-

---

[32] 431 U.S. 494 (1977).
[33] *Moore v. East Cleveland*, 431 U.S. 494 (1977).

[34] APA Brief, at 7.
[35] APA Brief, at 28.
[36] *Bowers* Brief, at 27.

idence, as well as philosophical reflection, show this argument to be mistaken. Although the case was widely thought to involve only homosexuality, Georgia also criminalizes oral and anal intercourse between heterosexual couples. The law was passed at a time when such behavior was thought wrong regardless of the sex of those who do it. Today, however, sodomy is widely practiced among heterosexual as well as homosexual couples, and for exactly the same reasons. In a study cited in the American Psychological Association's brief, approximately 90 percent of heterosexual couples were found to engage in oral sex; another study found that 25 percent of all heterosexual married couples had engaged in anal intercourse within the past year.[37] Indeed, said the brief, such forms of intercourse are often recommended as a means to improve sexual function and health. Nor is there evidence that homosexuality causes mental illness or is associated with other emotional illnesses. Medical professionals are in wide agreement with the American Psychiatric Association's 1977 finding that "homosexuality per se implies no impairment in judgment, stability, reliability or general social or vocational capabilities . . . homosexuality does not constitute any form of mental disease."[38]

In what sense, then, is sodomy "unnatural" and therefore morally wrong? Is it unnatural only when done by people of the same sex? Certainly it is not unnatural in the sense that it is uncommon, nor does the mere fact that it is not the most common form of sexual practice—if indeed it isn't—have anything to do with its being moral. Lying is far more common than viola playing, though that hardly makes the former moral and the latter not. Perhaps the real point is that homosexuality and sodomy are contrary to the "natural" purpose of sexual organs. If the true purpose of sex is repro-

duction, which can only occur through sexual intercourse between people of the opposite sex, then sodomy is contrary to nature and thus wrong. Much traditionally condoned sexual activity, however, also has nothing to do with reproduction: kissing, hugging, sex done with contraceptives, and sexual intercourse when either partner is infertile. And the other purposes that these activities serve, including expression of love or commitment, are achieved by homosexuals and heterosexuals alike. There's also the question of why it should matter that people use sex for purposes other than the one biology seems to prescribe. Besides hearing, people use ears to support eyeglasses and earrings, though it seems a bit harsh to condemn them for it. The claim that sodomy is immoral cannot withstand scrutiny. It is not uncommon, and even if it were that is no ground for condemnation. Nor is it unnatural in any morally relevant sense.

Georgia might also have based its criminalization of homosexuality on religion, claiming for example that it is condemned in the Bible. One problem with this, of course, is that the First Amendment guarantees religious freedom, promising that government will neither establish religion nor prevent its free exercise. The fact that homosexuality is condemned by one religion, or even all, would not, standing alone, justify its criminalization. Another argument would appeal simply to the disgust and homophobia that many Americans feel. Indeed, it seems impossible to explain the justices' decision in *Bowers* without appreciating the extent of homophobia in this culture. But that argument—that society can express its irrational dislike of minorities—would also find few supporters on the Court, at least until it were dressed up in more acceptable terms.

Public health, and especially the threat of AIDS, is another matter. Here, finally, is an argument that does not obviously rest on antiquated medicine, special psychology, or bad philosophy: AIDS is a major health

---

[37] APA Brief, at 6.

[38] Resolution of the American Psychiatric Association, December 15, 1973, quoted in APA Brief, at 9.

problem. One of the two most common ways it is spread—anal intercourse—is a frequent practice of homosexual men. So perhaps Georgia's statute can be justified as a public health measure, though AIDS was clearly not what the legislature had in mind when the law was passed in 1816.

In fact, however, the evidence is overwhelming that sodomy laws not only are ineffective as a public health measure but are counterproductive. First, Georgia enforced its sodomy law only against homosexuals, making the statute doubly defective as a public health effort. It is too broad because it condemns oral sex, and there is no indication that people who practice oral sex, whatever the sexes of their partners, risk spreading AIDS. As it was actually enforced, the statute is also too narrow because it condemns anal intercourse only among homosexuals, despite the fact that the AIDS virus pays no attention to the sex of the person it infects. If the statute really were an attempt to prevent the spread of the disease then it would criminalize all and only anal intercourse, outlawing it between heterosexuals and homosexuals alike, without criminalizing other forms of homosexual conduct.

But even if it were meant as an attack on AIDS rather than homosexuals, health officials agree that criminalizing homosexuality makes the task of preventing the spread of AIDS much more difficult. There are many reasons for this. Antihomosexual statutes discourage accurate reporting and testing, requiring those who seek treatment to become prisoners. Sick people may not get treatment and are deterred from taking the tests that would tell them if they are likely to infect others.

Sodomy laws also frustrate researchers, making it more difficult for them to get the accurate information that is essential to fighting the disease effectively. Researchers initially found it difficult to explain why Haitians were a high-risk group, for example, because of the fears of those who were afflicted to report that they were either gay or intravenous drug users. Efforts at prevention are also hampered by sodomy laws. Condoms are extremely effective in limiting the spread of AIDS, yet government often finds it difficult to reconcile condemning sodomy through law with helping men practice it safely.

As a public health measure, Georgia's law is both badly drawn and counterproductive. This point is important because statutes limiting liberty must be closely tailored to meet their objectives. Even state laws that do not involve any fundamental right such as privacy must have at least a "rational basis" if the Supreme Court is to uphold them, although this test gives wide latitude to a legislature. Georgia's law not only fails the former test, of unduly infringing liberty, but is also arguably so irrational, counterproductive, and dangerous that it fails even the latter, "rational basis" test.

The *Bowers* decision did not meet with widespread approval, as the majority may have hoped. Many newspapers expressed surprise that the Court would allow Georgia to regulate consensual adult sexual activity in the bedroom. By ignoring the scientific and psychological evidence while adopting the state's homophobic moral arguments, the Court lost an opportunity to introduce a degree of thoughtful discussion to an important topic, contributed to the discrimination that homosexuals suffer, and added to the burdens facing responsible public health officials in trying to combat AIDS.

Wrong Rights

Elizabeth H. Wolgast

We are deeply committed to the concept of individual rights, but our concept of individual rights, argues professor Elizabeth H. Wolgast, rests on an atomistic view of persons, that is, on a view of human beings as fundamentally independent units, discrete and autonomous. Wolgast contends that this conception of independent individuals and their rights prevents us from addressing effectively certain injustices. In particular, our model of rights does not take sufficient account of the variety of relationships in which people take responsibility and care for one another. Rights have their place in social and political discourse, Wolgast argues, but their place is limited. The invocation of rights does not solve all the relevant moral and political problems that face us.

Elizabeth H. Wolgast is Professor of Philosophy at California State University, Hayward. She is the author of *Equality and the Rights of Women* (Cornell University Press, 1980) and *The Grammar of Justice* (Cornell University Press, 1987).

If the basic units of society are discrete and autonomous individuals, that fact must determine the way they should be treated. Thus it is a natural step from atomism to the concept of individual rights, rights that will attach to each individual regardless of his or her characteristics. As persons are independent, so their rights will be defined in a framework of independence. And as the indistinguishable atoms are equal, so their rights need to be equal. The concept of individual rights is a natural adjunct to atomism.

Reprinted from Elizabeth H. Wolgast, *The Grammar of Justice*. Copyright © 1987 by Cornell University. An earlier version of this essay appeared in *Hypatia*, Winter 1987. Used by permission of *Hypatia* and Cornell University Press.

The language of rights is also a way of looking at wrongs, a conceptual grid, a schema. It both gives us a sense of *how* wrongs are wrong and points to the way to address them, that is, by establishing a right. Although it is a powerful and useful tool, still the schema of rights is sometimes unfit for the uses we make of it. It can bind us to a senseless stance, stereotype our reasoning, and lead to remedies that are grotesque. Our commitment to this language is deep, however; even in the face of bizarre consequences we hold it fast and view the consequent problems as demands for further rights. Thus our reasoning often goes on in an enclosed framework of rights, a framework from which counterexamples are excluded a priori. What does this commitment to rights mean to us, and how can it be sensibly limited?

I

Rights are often spoken of in the language of possessions. They are, Richard Wasserstrom writes, "distinctive moral 'commodities,' "[1] H. L. A. Hart spells out the metaphor: "Rights are typically conceived of as *possessed* or *owned by* or *belonging to* individuals, and these expressions reflect the conception of moral rules as not only prescribing conduct but as forming a kind of moral property of individuals to which they are as individuals entitled; only when rules are conceived in this way can we speak of *rights* and *wrongs* as well as right and wrong actions."[2] The idea of rights as moral property, as belonging to individuals the way property does, is an important aspect of the concept of rights. It focuses attention on the person to whom something is due, just as property law focuses attention on the possessor of property. The individual person with his needs and desires is the central motif.

This perspective is in contrast with one that focuses on the misdeeds of the offender, that condemns the misdeeds and castigates the doer. Instead of condemning, our perspective asserts something positive, namely, that a certain kind of thing—a *right*—exists. But what kind of thing is this, and how can we prove its existence? The answers given in response to this question are often vague, and they commonly lead to talk of "natural" rights as necessary features of human existence.[3] In the end we have

something that sounds like a moral metaphysics. What is it that the possessor of a right holds? David Lyons explains:

> When *A* in particular, holds a certain right *against B*, *A* is a *claimant* against *B*. A "claimant" is one empowered to press or waive a claim against someone with a corresponding duty or obligation. He can, if he wishes, release the other from his obligation and cancel it, or he can insist upon its performance. . . . A claimant is thus one to whom the performance of a duty or obligation is *owed*—he is the one who holds the claim against the other and who is entitled to administer the claim as he chooses.[4]

Lyons describes an important feature of the language of rights: the power it puts in the hands of the owner to press his right against someone or some agency. Rights are there to be *claimed*—asserted, demanded, pressed—or, on the other hand, waived.[5] What the claimant is entitled to press for is no doubt a benefit; rights are generally associated with benefits, if only the benefit of being able to do something one doesn't want to do. But a right can be distinguished from a benefit in that a beneficiary often need not do anything; the role can be described as passive, you might say, while a rightholder can choose to claim his right or not; his right enables him to act in a certain way or to decline to do so.

Thus a right puts its possessor in an assertive position in which he may claim something, and to claim something is to claim it against another. So a right to a free education may be claimed by any child *against* the

---

[1] Richard Wasserstrom, "Rights, Human Rights, and Racial Discrimination," in *Rights*, ed. David Lyons (Belmont, Calif.: Wadsworth, 1979), p. 48.

[2] H. L. A. Hart, "Are There Any Natural Rights?" in *Rights*, ed. Lyons, p. 19.

[3] See Alasdair MacIntyre, *After Virtue* (Notre Dame: University of Notre Dame Press, 1981), pp. 68–70, for a good account of the relation between modern talk of rights and the ideas of the Enlightenment.

[4] David Lyons, "Rights, Claimants, and Beneficiaries," in *Rights*, ed. Lyons, p. 60.

[5] Joel Feinberg also emphasizes these options: if Nip has a claim against Tuck, he argues, then "Nip not only *has* a right, but he can choose whether or not to exercise it, whether to claim it, . . . even whether to release Tuck from his duty" ("The Nature and Value of Rights," in *Rights*, ed. Lyons, p. 85). For an interesting examination of the relation of rights and claims, see Alan White, "Rights and Claims," in *Law, Morality, and Rights*, ed. M. A. Stewart (Dordrecht: Reidel, 1983), pp. 139–60.

state, the right to vote may be asserted by any citizen *against* anyone who would interfere, the right of habeas corpus may be demanded *against* the court by anyone charged with a crime, and so on. But these rights differ quite a bit from benefits, since a gift generally doesn't need to be claimed, and the giver doesn't owe it if it is.

II

Rights put the rightholder in the driver's seat; a rightholder may be seen as active while the recipient of a benefit is passive. Joel Feinberg captures the difference by comparing a world with rights to a world without them. He imagines "Nowheresville," a world without rights, and asks "what precisely [such] a world is missing . . . and why that absence is morally important." The crucial thing absent, he argues, is the activity of claiming: "Nowheresvillians, even when they are discriminated against invidiously, or left without the things they need, or otherwise badly treated, do not think to leap to their feet and make righteous demands against one another. . . . They do not have a notion of what is their due." Claiming depends on a prior right to claim, and although a right may be waived, rights' "characteristic use, and that for which they are distinctively well suited, is to be claimed, demanded, affirmed, insisted upon."[6]

Why do rights have such crucial moral importance? Feinberg answers that it is precisely the feature of claiming that "gives rights their special moral significance." It is "connected . . . with the customary rhetoric about what it is to be a human being. Having rights enables us to 'stand up like men,' to look others in the eye, and to feel in some fundamental way the equal of anyone. To think of oneself as a holder of rights is not to be unduly but properly proud . . . and what

is called 'human dignity' may simply be the recognizable capacity to assert claims." People need to think of themselves as equal to others and thus able to claim their rights against others: that is a large part of what it is to be in the fullest sense a person. Nothing is more appropriate to a person than the possession of individual rights, rights that by their nature are given equally to everyone. In Feinberg's view the claiming of these possessions has a moral value of its own: "the activity of claiming . . . as much as any other thing, makes for self-respect and respect for others [and] gives a sense to the notion of personal dignity."[7]

The language in which Feinberg praises rights is recognizably atomistic. He thinks of individuals as independent units whose self-respect is of prime importance to them *as* separate entities. Further, their capacity to claim rights is an important part of their active pursuit of their own interests. In such ways the language of rights both confirms the main features of the atomistic model and relies on its implicit values.

My claim is that such a conception of individuals and their rights may not be an effective means of addressing some injustices.

III

Consider the issue of the maltreatment of patients by doctors and medical staff in hospitals. In a hospital a patient is entirely at the mercy of medical people, whose expertise and positions give them great power, and so they are vulnerable to abuses of that power. The patient who is weak and frightened is by definition dependent on the staff; and they, in virtue of their practical knowledge and ability, are in the position of his rescuers—can instruct him and help him to survive. Abuse of such power and authority is, in view of the patient's helplessness, a frightening possibility.

---

[6] Feinberg, "Nature and Value of Rights," p. 84.

[7] Ibid., pp. 87, 91.

Michel Foucault argues that with the development of clinics and the opportunities they offer to study disease, a new doctor-patient relationship develops. In this impersonal, scientific context the doctor becomes an expert in diseases, and "if one wishes to know the illness from which he is suffering, one must abstract the individual, with his particular qualities."[8] The doctor must look through the patient at the disease.

On the one side of the patient is the family, whose "gentle, spontaneous care, expressive of love and a common desire for a cure, assists nature in its struggle against the illness"; on the other side is the hospital doctor, who "sees only distorted, altered diseases, a whole teratology of the pathological." The traditional family doctor, in contrast, cannot have the clinical detachment of the hospital doctor, but in his practice "must necessarily be respectful" of the patient.[9] Foucault's account provides a plausible explanation of how the problem of disrespectful treatment of patients in a modern hospital comes about; it is a natural, logical development. Inevitably, too, the search for knowledge and the holding of power go hand in hand, and as the doctor seeks knowledge of a scientific kind, his patient becomes increasingly an object under his control, and less and less someone to be dealt with in personal terms.

Here's the problem, then. The patient is weak, frightened, helpless, but needs to be treated in many ways as a normal person—needs to be respected, even in his wishes regarding treatment, and ultimately perhaps in his wish to die or to be sent home uncured. The issue may be addressed in various ways, but the most common way of dealing with it is to say that the patient has a *right* to respectful and considerate treatment, a right to have his wishes in regard to his treatment respected, a right to be in-

formed about the character of his treatment, and so on. To force upon him decisions he might not accept if he weren't ill and dependent is then to subject him to a kind of domination. It is as if the patient could be mistreated *because he is ill,* and that thought recalls Samuel Butler's grotesque society Erewhon, where illness is a crime demanding punishment. There a judge trying a case of pulmonary congestion pronounces, "You may say that it is your misfortune to be criminal; I answer that it is your crime to be unfortunate."[10]

In the wake of protests over mistreatment of patients, the American Hospital Association instituted a code of patients' rights which has been widely adopted in this country. The first of these rights is "the right to considerate and respectful care," the fourth is the "right to refuse treatment to the extent permitted by law and to be informed of the medical consequences of his action," the eighth is the patient's "right to obtain information as to the existence of any professional relationships among individuals . . . who are treating him." Yet at the end we are told: "No catalog of rights can guarantee for the patient the kind of treatment he has a right to expect. . . . All [the hospital's various] activities must be conducted with an overriding concern for the patient, and above all, the recognition of his dignity as a human being."[11] Nonetheless, these rights are posted prominently in the hospital so that both patients and staff will be reminded of them as they go about their routines.

---

[8] Michel Foucault, *The Birth of the Clinic,* trans. A. M. Sheridan Smith (New York: Random House, 1975), p. 14.

[9] Ibid., p. 17.

[10] Samuel Butler, *Erewhon* (New York: Random House, 1927), p. 110.

[11] American Hospital Association, "Statement on a Patient's Bill of Rights," *Hospitals* 4 (February 16, 1973). This statement, which was affirmed by the Board of Trustees of the Association on November 17, 1972, is reprinted in *Contemporary Issues in Bioethics,* ed. Tom L. Beauchamp and LeRoy Walters (Belmont, Calif.: Wadsworth, 1982). See also *Patients' Rights Handbook,* printed and distributed by the State of California under the administration of Governor Edmund Brown, Jr., which also assures a patient of "the right to decent living conditions and uncensored mail" (p. 13).

Now what can be wrong with this way of dealing with patient care? First, these rights, like the right not to be beaten by your spouse, call to mind the abuses they were designed to mitigate. They imply that hospital personnel are commonly guilty of unethical or insensitive conduct; otherwise there would be no need to protect patients against abuse. Second, the institution of rights focuses on a patient as complainant. As we have seen, the language of rights gives the rightholder a license to protest under certain circumstances; that is part of the language and the reason it's connected with self-respect. But as we have also remarked, the patient is not in a good position to exercise such rights. In his weakened condition, under medication, who is he to complain? Giving him rights puts him in the role of an assertive and able individual, but this role is inconsistent with being ill.

Someone who presses a claim and demands respect for his rights does so from the stance of a peer vis-à-vis the one complained against, as Feinberg says; but the doctor–patient relationship is not one of peers.[12] As one writer observes, "strong statements of patient rights imply a parity between physician and patient not usually possible in the situations under which . . . physicians–patient relationships are developed." The patient needs the doctor; the doctor doesn't in the same way need him. Moreover, the patient "often enters into the arms of medicine as one might enter passionately into the arms of a lover—with great haste and need, but little forethought"; thus by definition a cool consideration of his situation is excluded.[13] Once recovered and out of the hospital, *then* the patient can exercise his rights—take the doctor and hospital administrator to court

and sue for damages. But this remedy is no remedy at all. What a sick and dependent person needs is responsible treatment from others *while he is unable to press claims against anyone.*

How then ought the problem to be addressed? The moral difficulty comes to roost in the doctor–patient or staff–patient relationship: something isn't right there. As the Patient's Bill of Rights asserts, a doctor has to treat his patients with respect and concern, for that is his responsibility and part of his professional role. If he fails to do so, he is not a good doctor, no matter how knowledgeable he is. Then why is a set of rights given to the patient? It's the doctor who needs to be reminded of his charge, and that's where the focus ought to be, logically—on the doctor and his or her responsibility.

The doctor who sees the disease as the object of his interest, and sees the patient's idiosyncrasies as distractions from the pure case he wants to understand, is surely dehumanizing the patient. Foucault speaks of this outlook as a botanical view of medicine, for it is similar to the view found in botany, as well as in mechanics and physics.[14] Moreover, if we regard medicine as a science, it is difficult to see why a doctor *should* take the patient seriously *as a person.* Such a view isn't *objective;* that isn't the way a physical scientist would view his subject. Humanity, sympathy, and sensitivity have no place in physical science. The problem of patient treatment, then, is connected with the way medicine is conceived, its claim to be a science, and its place in the community.

An obvious way to address the issue of disrespectful treatment of patients would be to approach the medical community with exactly this concern, a concern that pertains potentially to everyone. One can imagine penalties being imposed when an ethical code is violated. Medical practice might be monitored by people outside of the medical brotherhood. Various legal and institutional

---

[12] For a discussion of the relation of peers, see Elizabeth H. Wolgast, *Equality and the Rights of Woman* (Ithaca: Cornell University Press, 1980), chap. 3.

[13] H. Tristram Engelhardt, "Rights and Responsibilities of Patients and Physicians," in *Contemporary Issues in Bioethics,* ed. Beauchamp and Walters, p. 136.

[14] Foucault, *Birth of the Clinic,* p. 17.

ways could be devised to deal with the problem; we don't need to decide here which ones would be the most practical.

There are barriers to this approach, however. In the atomistic model, connections of responsibility and dependency don't appear; there aren't any. In the same way that molecular theory cannot allow that some molecules take care of others or defer to them, independent autonomous beings cannot be connected. The language of rights reflects this atomistic fact, that relations of individuals to one another are relations between entities who are peers. And as we saw, these peer relations give rise to contracts in which both parties pursue their self-interests. Looking at the doctor–patient relation in this light, we see that there's no room for—no representation of—the doctor's *responsibility for the patient*. There is similarly no room in the model for anyone's responsibility for another; everyone is responsible for himself and that's all. Thus we are blocked from dealing with the problem in terms of the medical professional's responsibility for patients. Atomism prefers to give the patient rights.

But it doesn't make sense to do what we do in this case, to put the burden of straightening out the problem of medical negligence and disrespect on the shoulders of those already unable to handle the practical details of life—to say to such people, "Here are your rights; now you may press a claim against the doctor in whose care you placed yourself or waive your right, just as you please." The relationship between doctor and patient is appropriately one of trust, while this remedy implies the absence of trust.

It is no solution to assume that a patient has a healthy person to speak for him and press his rights. For even when such a person exists, the patient's dependency may still prevent his taking action against those who are supposed to care for him. When he is well (if he recovers), he and his representative can then bring suit against the doctor or whoever. But here again the right he possesses is a right appropriate to a well person, not a sick one. I conclude that the conception of patients' rights is irrational and impractical. . . .

IV

Another class of wrong rights affects women and the connections between them and their children. Consider the "equal rights" guaranteed to women who have committed substantial parts of their lives to raising a family and managing a home, and who then need work. The theory says that they have equal rights to a job, an equal opportunity in a free, competitive labor market. The image operating here is that of similar units—men and women of all ages—similarly situated, and in that case fair treatment would be identical treatment of them all. A woman is discriminated against and pays a penalty for her sex only if she is denied a job *when other factors are equal*. But if we suppose her situation to be as I have described it, then other factors are not equal. The model and its assumptions beg the essential question, namely, how she should be treated given that her situation is not like a man's. Affirmative action programs and a ban on "age discrimination" are stopgap efforts that inherently conflict with the model and bow in apology for the offense. They rest on the factors that distinguish people from one another, while in the model any distinctions of treatment are discriminatory and thus unfair.[15] Thus there is no theoretical solution

---

[15] See Richard Wasserstrom, "Racism, Sexism, and Preferential Treatment: An Approach to the Topics," *UCLA Law Review*, July 1977, pp. 581–622, which argues for a model in which no sex differences are recognized, where both sexes are in detail treated alike. Wasserstrom's exercise shows how complex and deep the theoretical problem is; if we are determined to deal with it in terms of equal rights, we have to reconstruct our society so that equal rights *will be fair*. For a discussion of Wasserstrom's argument, see my *Equality and the Rights of Women*, chap. 1; also see my "Is Reverse Discrimination Fair?" in *Law, Morality, and Rights*, ed. Stewart, pp. 295–314.

to the problem. Measures that make reasonable moral sense are theoretically excluded.

Consider another issue, the debate over the constitutionality of mandated maternity leaves. The model requires this benefit to be couched in the language of equality; otherwise it appears as discriminatory against men. In order to avoid making a distinction between men and women, we assimilate maternity leaves to a disability or sickness leave, comparable to a leave one takes for the flu. When the benefit is thus clothed in sex-neutral terms, the question arises whether or not a right to maternity leave is an "equal right." The argument then turns on the importance of men's immunity to pregnancy. In such famous cases as *Miller-Wohl* and *California Federal Savings*,[16] the issue is exactly this: If a maternity leave is an equal right, it may be fair; otherwise it provides to women a benefit that is unavailable to men, and therefore it is unconstitutional under Title V of the Civil Rights Act. Thus the very document that was meant to ensure fairness in employment and education is used to frustrate a policy to accommodate the most fundamental process of human life, reproduction.

The reasoning that ensues from a concept of fairness defined as equality among autonomous agents is often strange. It is seriously asked, for instance, whether men have an equal maternity right because they could have such a leave *if they should become pregnant*. What a strange question—and how can a reasonable person answer? One legal writer discusses the Miller-Wohl case in these terms: "The equal treatment proponents . . . are thinking metaphysically. They approach the question [of the legality of maternity leave legislation] . . . by asking whether or not the statute conforms to a particular legal construct, i.e., the equal treatment principle. They focus the debate

on legal theoretical levels, rather than starting with an analysis of the concrete material problems of women in the workforce."[17]

Realistically, maternity leaves are needed because childbirth is exhausting and because a newborn baby and its mother need care. In part it is the child's needs that dictate that its mother shouldn't work full time just after its birth. But if we introduce the mother-child complex into the argument, we lose the framework of individual rights. And how else can we deal with the issue?

If we consider the central position of a baby in birth, we may decide that the baby has the principal right. But the issue is obscure: first we need to know if the baby is an individual who can possess rights, and then we have the harder question of whether that individual can have a right to its mother's maternity leave. On the face of it, that notion makes no sense. A right, as we have seen, attaches directly to a person; one person can't have a right *for* another. Moreover, involving the child in the maternal right won't work because it isn't born during the last weeks of pregnancy, when, just because its birth is imminent, the mother needs extra rest and leave from work.

The language of individual rights makes this issue into a puzzle in which by ingenious distortion we force something into a form that's essentially alien to it. How many people are involved in childbirth and do they each have a right, or together have a joint right, to maternity leave? And how does this complex of mother-and-baby compare with the less complicated case of a man? If both sexes are equal, which sex sets the standard? And if we are talking of disabilities, what

---

[16] Miller-Wohl Co. v. Commissioner of Labor and Industry, State of Montana, 575 F. Supp. 1264 (D. Mont. 1981); California Federal Savings & Loan v. Guerra, 55 U.S. Law Week 4077 (1987).

[17] Linda Krieger and Patricia Cooney, "The Miller-Wohl Controversy: Equal Treatment, Positive Action, and the Meaning of Women's Equality," *Golden Gate University Law Review* 13 (Summer 1983): 566. This article contains a good account of the theoretical problems presented by the maternity issue; however, the authors, like their opponents, couch the issue in terms of a *woman's* right, as if the problem involved no one else. For some suggestions about a different approach, see my *Equality and the Rights of Women*, chap. 4.

abilities, what kind of "disability" is it that leads to the birth of a child and a subsequent commitment to its care? The model gives no answers. Common sense would say that pregnancy isn't an illness but a strenuous productive period culminating in new responsibilities for a creature whose existence is fragile and who requires care to survive. But the model can't admit this description. The dignity of a rightholder brings no dignity to the condition of pregnancy or the occasion of childbirth.

The argument that a right to a maternity leave is a special and unfair right of women unless it is extended and adapted to men is a consequence of individualism and the language of equal rights. In this case it puts men in the position of jealous siblings, watching for any sign of partiality shown to others. They are in the position of competing with pregnant women for favorable treatment, and in this stance they show a blind disregard for the realities of childbirth.

The debate about abortion also shows the inadequacies of a theory of rights in regard to reproduction. It is a subject of serious debate whether the fetus is an autonomous individual with equal rights. If so, then it has all the rights of any person and should be able to claim its rights against its mother-to-be. But how can we imagine such a thing?[18]

The fetus's need for its mother is more total and unqualified than that of an infant for its parents. But if a fetus isn't a person, what else can it be? Some people have proposed to deal with it as a kind of property, as belonging to the mother as part of her body. To be sure, we sometimes speak this way of a foot or a kidney, and even of self-respect

and reputation. But a fetus *isn't* like a body part or reputation. It is a potential baby, which is to say a potential human being, and its birth is not like an amputation or organ removal but is the advent of a new member (albeit immature) into the community.

Either way of representing a fetus, as a person or as property, is fraught with difficulties. On the one hand we make too much of it, granting its rights that cannot apply to its case, and on the other we make too little of it, treating it as property whose owner can dispose of it any way she likes, for the point and virtue of ownership is one's right to do what one wants with one's property.

There are certainly two sides to the question of whether abortions should be restricted and what restrictions should be imposed; that's understandable. What is strange is the way we are forced to *present* the two sides, forced to caricature both the pregnant woman and the fetus. We are forced to caricature them by our commitment to fit the issue into a grid that has room only for individuals who are autonomous, have property, and make contracts. But the reasoning is bizarre.

Imagine a Martian who has come to study us and make sense of our society. He hears arguments about whether the fetus is a person (in the full and legal sense) or a bit of property (in the tort-law sense). Wouldn't he consider us morally undeveloped or mentally handicapped? A human fetus is not like anything except another fetus, conceptually more like a rabbit fetus or a racoon fetus or an elephant fetus than like a fully developed human. It is a stage in a process by which an infant comes into a community—a community of rabbits or racoons or elephants or humans. Apart from this framework it's indefinable. It would be best to say, then, that a fetus is sui generis, its own kind of thing, and so irreducible to something else.

What is wrong with us, the Martian wonders, that we don't see this and persist in arguing about fetal personhood and fetal rights? But basically what is wrong here is

---

[18] There is a wealth of a literature debating the question whether a fetus is a person. Mary Anne Warren, "On the Moral and Legal Status of Abortion," in *Philosophy and Women*, ed. Sharon Bishop and Marjorie Weinzweig (Belmont, Calif.: Wadsworth, 1979), pp. 216–26, works out a defense of the proposition that the fetus, while potentially human, lacks some necessary features of a human being, and thus cannot be considered a peer of its potential parent.

the grid we press upon the facts of reproduction.

V

One major problem with the model, as we have seen, is that it cannot show the variety of relationships in which people take responsibility and care for one another, some relationships of family, some of profession, some of simple concern. Its tendency to assimilate all relationships to that of independent, free, and self-interested persons also becomes a limitation in economic theory, as James Coleman observes. "Classical economic theory always assumes that the individual will act in his interest; but it never examines carefully the entity to which 'his' refers. Often, as when households are taken as the unit for income and consumption, it is implicitly assumed that 'the family' or 'the household' is this entity whose interest is being maximized. Yet this is without theoretical foundation, merely a convenient but slipshod device."[19] The "household" is a convenient device for preserving the outlines of atomism. But treating a family—which consists of more than one person—as a single individual "acting in its own interest" is at the same time at odds with the assumptions of atomism. The term *household* preserves the surface of atomism by making it a fictional person.

Rawls makes a similar adjustment, explaining that "the term 'person' is to be construed variously. . . . On some occasions it will mean human individuals, but in others it may refer to . . . business firms, churches, teams," and of course families. Each of these units is then regarded as a rational and self-interested entity.[20] How else can we conceive

of families? As a voluntary association of autonomous persons? That notion doesn't square with the facts.

When autonomous persons enter into an agreement, each party agrees to make some concessions in return for advantages to himself: mutual self-interest is the explanatory factor in all bonds. Milton Friedman emphasizes its exclusive power: "If an exchange between two parties is voluntary, it will not take place unless both believe they will benefit from it." Thus it is that "economic order can emerge as the unintended consequence of the actions of many people, each seeking his own interest."[21]

Apply this picture to the sick person, who needs help, and to the doctor, who has what Friedman calls his "personal capacity" to sell. According to Friedman, the doctor's only motive in helping the patient is his own interest, although he concedes that this interest can be defined as more than "myopic selfishness." "It is whatever it is that interests the participants, whatever they value, whatever goals they pursue. The scientist . . . the missionary . . . the philanthropist . . . are all pursuing their interests, as they see them, as they judge them by their own values."[22] The doctor may or may not be acting selfishly; he may have a personal interest in the patient's health. There's no room for a distinction, in Friedman's theory, between the good doctor and the clever mercenary one. None has any *responsibility* to concern himself with anyone else's health.

Plato thought the distinction between good and bad doctors was clear enough. In

---

[19] James Coleman, *Papers on Non-Marketing Decision-Making*, quoted in Howard Margolis, *Selfishness, Altruism, and Rationality: A Theory of Social Choice* (Cambridge: Cambridge University Press, 1982), p. 1.

[20] John Rawls, "Justice as Fairness," *Philosophical Review* 67 (April 1958): 166. One has to be careful here, as

Rawls also thinks of the group interest as consolidating but not merging the interests of individuals. An excellent criticism of this aspect of Rawls's argument may be found in Michael Sandel, *Liberalism and the Limits of Justice* (Cambridge: Cambridge University Press, 1982), esp. chaps. 1 and 4.

[21] Friedman, *Free to Choose*, pp. 13–14.

[22] Ibid., p. 27. Rawls also supposes that the interests of a person are sometimes benevolent and social, but they needn't be, and the moral justification of state policies is neutral on the question of whether it is these interests or purely selfish ones that are represented.

the *Republic* he has Socrates ask Thrasymachus, "But tell me, your physician in the precise sense . . . is he a money-maker, an earner of fees, or a healer of the sick? And remember to speak of the physician who is really such." Later he asks: "Then medicine . . . does not consider the advantage of medicine but of the body?" He concludes: "Can we deny, then . . . that neither does any physician in so far as he is a physician seek or enjoin the advantage of the physician but that of the patient? For we have agreed that the physician, 'precisely' speaking, is a ruler and governor of bodies and not a money-maker."[23]

Now if the doctor–patient relationship is a contract, and a sick person must approach a doctor who is motivated by his own gain, the contract is grossly unfair and susceptible to a multitude of exploitations, and therefore probably invalid. H. Tristram Engelhardt describes the initial approach like this: "The physician–patient relationship is likely to be assumed under circumstances that compromise the integrity of the patient. . . . At the very moments when much must be decided by the ill or dying person, he is often least able to decide with full competence. Disease not only places the patient at a general disadvantage . . . it also makes the patient dependent upon the physician."[24]

Here there is a relation governed by dependency, not autonomy, one in which most of the power and the clear options are on the side of the doctor. The patient is a poor example of the rational consumer. Given the doctor's motive and ability to get the best of him, it might be most rational in all self-interest for a patient not to approach him.

The best attitude of a sick person toward his doctor is trust, it is often remarked. The attitude intended is not trust that the doctor will fulfill a contract whose terms are unspecified, but trust in the doctor's concern. Without that sort of trust a doctor becomes a hired physiological consultant.

VI

A deeper question about the language of rights needs to be raised: Why, whenever we deal with a wrongful act or practice, do we feel impelled to refer to some right or other? Besides the influence of atomism, we think of a right as a justification for condemning something as wrong. Feinberg, for instance, says that claim rights are prior to and thus more basic than the duties with which they are correlated.[25] Thus they give a foundation for the demand that someone do or refrain from doing something and justify condemnation by showing the action as a violation of a (prior) right.

In practice the reasoning works like this. Burglary is wrong, everyone agrees; but what justifies us in calling it wrong? Some answer must exist, and one reasonable possibility is that it's wrong because a person has a right not to be burglarized, not to have his property invaded, abused, or stolen. Similarly we say that mugging is wrong, and then defend this judgment by arguing that it is wrong because a person has a right to walk down the street safely. Along these lines, murder is wrong because a person has a right to life; slander is wrong because a person has a right to be treated with respect; and so on. Rights proliferate as we seek justifications for every variety of things condemnable as wrong.

If justifications are needed, then the invocation of rights may make sense, but are such justifications necessary? Isn't murder simply wrong, wrong in itself? A common-

---

[23] Plato, *Republic*, trans. Paul Shorey, in *The Collected Dialogues of Plato*, ed. Edith Hamilton and Huntington Cairns (Princeton: Princeton University Press, 1961), V, 341c–342d.

[24] Engelhardt, "Rights and Responsibilities of Patients and Physicians," p. 133.

[25] Feinberg, "Nature and Value of Rights," p. 84. A. I. Melden also uses "rights" to mean moral rights, as ways to justify calling things morally wrong; see *Rights and Persons* (Berkeley: University of California Press, 1977), esp. chap. 4.

sense answer might be yes—why should one need to justify such an obvious judgment? And if we reflect on the logical path that brought us here, we see that it is our conviction that we are justified in calling murder wrong that makes us sure that something must *justify* our judgment.[26] We are of course justified; but does our justification imply that some separate justification lies behind it? What would happen if none did?

Murder's wrongness can be contrasted with the wrongness of something stipulated by a rule, such as moving a castle diagonally in chess. There a justification for the wrongness of the move clearly exists, that is, the rule that governs the way castles can move. And the wrongness of nonperformance of a contract has a justification, namely, that the contract specifies that one will do such-and-such. But in the case of some serious moral offenses it is less clear that analogous justifications exist. As Wittgenstein said of justifications of beliefs, "the chain of reasons has an end" and "at some point one has to pass from explanation to mere description."[27] Calling murder wrong is here like calling a certain color red, that is, what justifies us in using these terms is that the word means what it does. We are justified, but being justified is not the same as having a justification.

We have no particular reason to think that we need to invoke a right before we can call murder wrong. The "right to life" is unnecessary, and by eschewing it we avoid the curious consequence that death, which negates life, is wrong. We also acquire an important general benefit. When we leave rights aside, our view of murder takes on a different appearance, just as the mistreatment of patients looks different when we stop focusing on patients' rights. Saying that

Smith is wrong in murdering Jones because the murder violates Jones's right to life puts the focus on Jones and his rights, even makes it appear that there is something that Jones can do with this right after the fact, which is nonsense. What really concerns us in such a case is what Smith did; *his* action belongs in the center of our perspective, his culpability, not the violation of Jones's now-useless right. Seen this way, an emphasis on individual rights serves to obscure the focus of moral objection to killing rather than giving the objection a firm foundation.

Without doubt rights have an important place in our legal and political system and they often do give reasons for condemning actions that would be permissible without them. But since they are justifications in some instances—the right to vote, for example, justifies us in calling a poll tax wrong or unjust—we are led to think that they are always valuable, that without them our censure of wrongs is weakened and the substance of condemnation is in jeopardy. This conclusion is mistaken. Rights sometimes supply a justification, but sometimes they supply only the appearance or form of one. We should recognize that sometimes they are superfluous.

The corrective to the tendency to invoke rights as justifications is the realization that we know some things to be wrong more securely and fundamentally than we know what rights people have or ought to have. In discussing our demands for justifications for beliefs, Wittgenstein observed that "it is so difficult to find the *beginning*. Or, better: it is difficult to begin at the beginning. And not try to go further back."[28] We may distort our subject if we try always to find something deeper, look for another and another reason. There has to be an end to justifications, and with murder and lying and cheating we have hit bedrock.

This tendency to seek justifications has another, more unfortunate side. The notion

---

[26] For a discussion of the primacy of our recognition of wrong, see *The Grammar of Justice*, chap. 7.

[27] Ludwig Wittgenstein, *The Blue and Brown Books* (New York: Harper, 1958), p. 143, and *On Certainty*, ed. G. E. M. Anscombe and G. H. von Wright, trans. Denis Paul and Anscombe (New York: Harper & Row, 1969), 189.

---

[28] Wittgenstein, *On Certainty*, 471.

that one really needs a justification for the wrongness of murder implies that one isn't sure that murder is wrong, and that its wrongness depends on the adequacy of some further proof. But in that case, one's moral judgment in regard to murder is uncertain, and if it is uncertain about murder, then a great deal of moral understanding is missing. In that event, it's unclear how the demand could be satisfied. Uncertainty about something so basic may put the questioner beyond the framework in which moral justifications are meaningfully asked for and given, and beyond that framework is a no-man's-land often identified with skepticism. The demand for justification thus threatens to weaken rather than support the structure of moral thinking. The move cannot do any good here.

I conclude that rights and their invocation are often important and valuable. The right to performance of contract and the right to vote and the right to assemble are all embodied in protective legislation and certainly justify court action against anyone who would prevent exercise of them. But three kinds of problems can arise when rights are invoked too freely. The first concerns their application to people who are not in a position to exercise them. There the invocation of a right is often a means of avoiding placing responsibility on someone in a position of strength and control. In such a case our moral focus is wrong. The second problem has to do with people in situations and connections that vitiate assumptions in other ways, as the situations of women and fetuses do. The third has to do with justifying the condemnation of offenses whose moral wrongness is perfectly clear and unequivocal. The invocation of a right does not automatically fortify a conviction but may echo a doubt, and in some cases the doubt, once raised, cannot be put to rest, not by the invocation of a right or by any other means.[29]

Rights have their place, but their place is limited. They don't provide a moral panacea, a handy set of justifications to be called on when justification is desired. They need to be used with judgment and restraint, without a blanket commitment to the atomistic vision.

---

[29] For a parallel argument with regard to belief, see my *Paradoxes of Knowledge* (Ithaca: Cornell University Press, 1977), esp. chap. 4.

Wisconsin v. Yoder:
Free Exercise of Religion

Personal and religious freedom can sometimes conflict with larger social interests—society's need to educate the next generation of citizens, for example. The case of *Wisconsin v. Yoder* arose because Wisconsin law required all children to be sent to school until the age of 16. The Amish parents of two children, ages 14 and 15, refused to comply, arguing that compulsory school attendance beyond eighth grade violated their free exercise of religion as guaranteed by the First Amendment. The case went all the way to the Supreme Court, where Chief Justice Burger wrote the opinion of the court, upholding the right of the Amish parents to guide the religious future and education of their children. In his dissenting opinion, Justice Douglas worries about parents imposing their religious notions on children.

Mr. Chief Justice Burger: On complaint of the school district administrator for the public schools, respondents [Mr. and Mrs. Yoder] were charged, tried, and convicted of violating the compulsory-attendance law in Green County Court and were fined the sum of $5 each. Respondents defended on the ground that the application of the compulsory-attendance law violated their rights under the First and Fourteenth Amendments. The trial testimony showed that respondents believed, in accordance with the tenets of Old Order Amish communities generally, that their children's attendance at high school, public or private, was contrary to the Amish religion and way of life. . . . The State stipulated that respondents' religious beliefs were sincere.

In support of their position, respondents presented as expert witnesses scholars on

religion and education whose testimony is uncontradicted. They expressed their opinions on the relationship of the Amish belief concerning school attendance to the more general tenets of their religion, and described the impact that compulsory high school attendance could have on the continued survival of Amish communities as they exist in the United States today. . . .

Amish beliefs require members of the community to make their living by farming or closely related activities. Broadly speaking, the Old Order Amish religion pervades and determines the entire mode of life of its adherents. . . .

Amish objection to formal education beyond the eighth grade is firmly grounded in these central religious concepts. They object to the high school, and higher education generally, because the values they teach are in marked variance with Amish values and the Amish way of life; they view secondary school education as an impermissible expo-

406 U.S. 205 (1972).

sure of their children to a "worldly" influence in conflict with their beliefs. The high school tends to emphasize intellectual and scientific accomplishments, self-distinction, competitiveness, worldly success, and social life with other students. Amish society emphasizes informal learning-through-doing; a life of "goodness," rather than a life of intellect; wisdom, rather than technical knowledge; community welfare, rather than competition; and separation from, rather than integration with, contemporary worldly society.

Formal high school education . . . takes [Amish children] away from their community, physically and emotionally, during the crucial and formative adolescent period of life. During this period, the children must acquire Amish attitudes favoring manual work and self-reliance and the specific skills needed to perform the adult role of an Amish farmer or housewife. They must learn to enjoy physical labor. . . . And, at this time in life, the Amish child must also grow in his faith and his relationship to the Amish community if he is to be prepared to accept the heavy obligations imposed by adult baptism. . . .

The Amish do not object to elementary education through the first eight grades as a general proposition because they agree that their children must have basic skills in the "three R's" in order to read the Bible, to be good farmers and citizens, and to be able to deal with non-Amish people when necessary in the course of daily affairs. They view such a basic education as acceptable because it does not significantly expose their children to worldly values or interfere with their development in the Amish community during the crucial adolescent period. . . .

On the basis of such considerations, [an expert] testified that compulsory high school attendance could not only result in great psychological harm to Amish children, because of the conflicts it would produce, but would also, in his opinion, ultimately result in the destruction of the Old Order

Amish church community as it exists in the United States today. . . .

In order for Wisconsin to compel school attendance beyond the eighth grade against a claim that such attendance interferes with the practice of a legitimate religious belief, it must appear either that the State does not deny the free exercise of religious belief by its requirement, or that there is a state interest of sufficient magnitude to override the interest claiming protection under the Free Exercise Clause. . . .

A way of life, however virtuous and admirable, may not be interposed as a barrier to reasonable state regulation of education if it is based on purely secular considerations; to have the protection of the Religion Clauses, the claims must be rooted in religious belief. Although a determination of what is a "religious" belief or practice entitled to constitutional protection may present a most delicate question, the very concept of ordered liberty precludes allowing every person to make his own standards on matters of conduct in which society as a whole has important interests. Thus, if the Amish asserted their claims because of their subjective evaluation and rejection of the contemporary secular values accepted by the majority, much as Thoreau rejected the social values of his time and isolated himself at Walden Pond, their claims would not rest on a religious basis. Thoreau's choice was philosophical and personal rather than religious, and such belief does not rise to the demands of the Religion Clauses.

Giving no weight to such secular considerations, however, we see that the record in this case abundantly supports the claim that the traditional way of life of the Amish is not merely a matter of personal preference, but one of deep religious conviction, shared by an organized group, and intimately related to daily living. That the Old Order Amish daily life and religious practice stem from their faith is shown by the fact that it is in response to their literal interpretation of the Biblical injunction from the Epistle of Paul to the Romans, "be not conformed to this world. . . ." . . .

Their way of life in a church-oriented community, separated from the outside world and "worldly" influences, their attachment to nature and the soil, is a way inherently simple and uncomplicated, albeit difficult to preserve against the pressure to conform. Their rejection of telephones, automobiles, radios, and television, their mode of dress, of speech, their habits of manual work do indeed set them apart from much of contemporary society; these customs are both symbolic and practical. . . .

The State advances two primary arguments in support of its system of compulsory education. It notes, as Thomas Jefferson pointed out early in our history, that some degree of education is necessary to prepare citizens to participate effectively and intelligently in our open political system if we are to preserve freedom and independence. Further, education prepares individuals to be self-reliant and self-sufficient participants in society. We accept these propositions.

However, the evidence adduced by the Amish in this case is persuasively to the effect that an additional one or two years of formal high school for Amish children in place of their long-established program of informal vocational education would do little to serve those interests. . . . It is one thing to say that compulsory education for a year or two beyond the eighth grade may be necessary when its goal is the preparation of the child for life in modern society as the majority live, but it is quite another if the goal of education be viewed as the preparation of the child for life in the separated agrarian community that is the keystone of the Amish faith. . . .

Whatever their idiosyncrasies as seen by the majority, . . . the Amish community has been a highly successful social unit within our society, even if apart from the conventional "mainstream." Its members are productive and very law-abiding members of

society; they reject public welfare in any of its usual modern forms. . . .

This case involves the fundamental interest of parents, as contrasted with that of the State, to guide the religious future and education of their children. The history and culture of Western civilization reflect a strong tradition of parental concern for the nurture and upbringing of their children. This primary role of the parents in the upbringing of their children is now established beyond debate as an enduring American tradition. . . .

To be sure, the power of the parent, even when linked to a free exercise claim, may be subject to limitation . . . if it appears that parental decisions will jeopardize the health or safety of the child, or have a potential for significant social burdens. But in this case, the Amish have introduced persuasive evidence undermining the arguments the State has advanced to support its claims in terms of the welfare of the child and society as a whole.

Mr. Justice Douglas, dissenting in part: The Court's analysis assumes that the only interests at stake in the case are those of the Amish parents on the one hand, and those of the State on the other. The difficulty with this approach is that, despite the Court's claim, the parents are seeking to vindicate not only their own free exercise claims, but also those of their high-school-age children. . . .

No analysis of religious-liberty claims can take place in a vacuum. If the parents in this case are allowed a religious exemption, the inevitable effect is to impose the parents' notions of religious duty upon their children. Where the child is mature enough to express potentially conflicting desires, it would be an invasion of the child's rights to permit such an imposition without canvassing his views. . . . As the child has no other effective forum, it is in this litigation that his rights should be considered. And, if an Amish child desires to attend high school, and is mature enough to have that desire respected, the State may well be able to override the parents' religiously motivated objections.

This issue has never been squarely presented before today. Our opinions are full of talk about the power of the parents over the child's education. . . . And we have in the past analyzed similar conflicts between parent and State with little regard for the views of the child. . . . Recent cases, however, have clearly held that the children themselves have constitutionally protectible interests.

These children are "persons" within the meaning of the Bill of Rights. . . . While the parents, absent dissent, normally speak for the entire family, the education of the child is a matter on which the child will often have decided views. He may want to be a pianist or an astronaut or an oceanographer. To do so he will have to break from the Amish tradition. . . .

If a parent keeps his child out of school beyond the grade school, then the child will be forever barred from entry into the new and amazing world of diversity that we have today. . . .

[In the polygamy cases,] action which the Court deemed to be antisocial could be punished even though it was grounded on deeply held and sincere religious convictions.

What we do today, at least in this respect, opens the way to give organized religion a broader base than it has ever enjoyed.

In another way, however, the Court retreats when in reference to Henry Thoreau it says his "choice was philosophical and personal rather than religious, and such belief does not rise to the demands of the Religion Clauses." That is contrary to what we held in *United States* v. *Seeger,* where we were concerned with the meaning of the words "religious training and belief" in the Selective Service Act, which were the basis of many conscientious objector claims. We said: "Within that phrase would come all sincere religious beliefs which are based upon a power or being, or upon a faith, to which all else is subordinate or upon which all else is ultimately dependent. The test might be stated in these words: A sincere and meaningful belief which occupies in the life of its possessor a place parallel to that filled by the God of those admittedly qualifying for the exemption comes within the statutory definition. This construction avoids imputing to Congress an intent to classify different religious beliefs, exempting some and excluding others, and is in accord with the well-established congressional policy of equal treatment for those whose opposition to service is grounded in their religious tenets."

Smith v. Board of Education:
Secular Humanism and Religious Establishment

Besides guaranteeing citizens the right freely to exercise their religion, the First Amendment also prevents states from "establishing" a religion. In *Wisconsin v. Yoder* Justice Burger described the task of deciding which beliefs are to count as "religious" as a "most delicate question." The Amish qualify, he argued, because they have a deep conviction, they are an organized group, they are committed to the *Bible*, and their beliefs are intimately related to daily living. But if religion is broadly defined, then it is possible to argue that schools that teach "secular humanism" are establishing an official religion. U.S. District Court Judge Brevard Hand makes that argument in the case below, *Smith v. Board of Education of Mobile*.

The impetus for this case came in 1982 when the Supreme Court overruled an earlier decision by Judge Hand holding that a one-minute period of silent prayer in schools was not a violation of the establishment clause. Judge Hand did not let the issue die. He suggested in his original opinion that, should he be overruled (as he later was), he would then be willing to consider arguments that the school board had established another religion—secular humanism—in violation of the establishment clause. A group of religious conservatives took up the Judge's offer and filed another suit, *Smith v. Board of Education of Mobile*. After the trial, which included many expert witnesses on both sides, Judge Hand wrote a lengthy opinion contending that secular humanism is a religion and that the Mobile school board "established" it by requiring students to read certain textbooks. Although this decision was later overturned as well, Judge Hand's opinion in *Smith* raises important and difficult issues concerning the nature of religion, its connection with scientific theory, and the role of schools in teaching morality.

I. A First Amendment Definition of Religion

The Supreme Court has never stated an absolute definition of religion under the first amendment. . . .

---

655 F. Supp. 939 (S.D. Ala. 1987).

The court's focus has shifted over the years from monotheism to a broad and mayhap vague notion of ultimate concerns and equivalent beliefs. . . .

Out of these cases can be discerned several threads. First the requirement of neutrality affirmed in . . . the cases means that the Constitution protects every religious belief without regard to its theological foundations or idiosyncrasies. Second, what is religious is largely dependent on the way people in America currently think of religion, and this is a product of our past as a people. Third, the government cannot hinder or prohibit the growth of new beliefs by its definition of religion, since this growth is a product of the fundamental rights guaranteed by the first amendment. Fourth, the government is still obligated to perform its essential functions, thus reasonable boundaries may circumscribe acts performed in the name of religious freedom. . . .

These ideas revolve around an individualistic and subjective view of religion, as opposed to the objective test of the Mormon cases. Thus, in *Seeger* each claimant was found to have a sincere and meaningful belief that occupied "a place in the life of its possessor parallel to that filled by the orthodox belief in God." . . . In *Welsh* the petitioner held beliefs that were moral and ethical, and would not himself characterize them as religious, yet he was granted the exemption, the Court equating his beliefs with religious ones because they were held with equivalent strength.

The application of these principles to the question of what constitutes a religion under the first amendment indicates that the state may not decide the question by reference to the validity of the beliefs or practices involved. . . . The state must instead look to factors common to all religious movements to decide how to distinguish those ideologies worthy of the protection of the religious clauses from those which must seek refuge under other constitutional provisions.

Any definition of religion must not be limited, therefore, to traditional religions, but must encompass systems of belief that are equivalent to them for the believer. . . . The Supreme Court has focused on such factors as a person's "ultimate concern," organization and social structure, and on equivalency to belief in a Supreme Deity. All

of these are evidence of the type of belief a person holds. But all religious beliefs may be classified by the questions they raise and issues they address. Some of these matters overlap with non-religious governmental concerns. A religion, however, approaches them on the basis of certain fundamental assumptions with which governments are unconcerned. These assumptions may be grouped as about: (1) the existence of supernatural and/or transcendent reality; (2) the nature of man; (3) the ultimate end, or goal or purpose of man's existence, both individually and collectively; (4) the purpose and nature of the universe. . . .

Whenever a belief system deals with fundamental questions of the nature of reality and man's relationship to reality, it deals with essentially religious questions. A religion need not posit a belief *in* a deity, or a belief *in* supernatural existence. A religious person adheres to some position on whether supernatural and/or transcendent reality exists at all, and if so, how, and if not, why. A mere "comprehensive world-view" or "way of life" is not by itself enough to identify a belief system as religious. A world-view may be merely economic, or sociological, and a person might choose to follow a "way of life" that ignores ultimate issues addressed by religions. . . .

There are also a number of characteristics exhibited by most known religious groups to which courts can look when trying to determine if a set of theories or system of ideas is religious in nature. First would be the sincerity of the adherents' claims. . . . Another factor is group organization and hierarchical structure, which evidence the social characteristics of a movement, and show that the adherents sincerely follow a theory of human relationship. Literary manifestations of a movement may also be important, particularly if they take the form of an authoritative text. Ritual and worship also would be significant because they would be evidence of the religion's belief about supernatural or transcendent reality. . . .

II. Humanism a Religion?

In the present case, the plaintiffs contend that a particular belief system fits within the first amendment definition of religion. . . . All of the experts, and the class representatives, agreed that this belief system is a religion which: "makes a statement about supernatural existence a central pillar of its logic; defines the nature of man; and sets forth a goal or purpose for individual and collective human existence; and defines the nature of the universe, and thereby delimits its purpose." . . .

It purports to establish a closed definition of reality; not closed in that adherents know everything, but in that everything is knowable: can be recognized by human intellect aided only by the devices of that intellect's own creation or discovery. The most important belief of this religion is its denial of the transcendent and/or supernatural: there is no God, no creator, no divinity. By force of logic the universe is thus self-existing, completely physical and hence, essentially knowable. Man is the product of evolutionary, physical forces. He is purely biological and has no supernatural or transcendent spiritual component or quality. Man's individual purpose is to seek and obtain personal fulfillment by freely developing every talent and ability, especially his rational intellect, to the highest level. Man's collective purpose is to seek the good life by the increase of every person's freedom and potential for personal development.

In addition, humanism, as a belief system, erects a moral code and identifies the source of morality. This source is claimed to exist in humans and the social relationships of humans. Again, there is no spiritual or supernatural origin for morals: man is merely physical, and morals, the rules governing his private and social conduct, are founded only on man's actions, situation and environment. In addition to a moral code, certain attitudes and conduct are proscribed since they interfere with personal freedom and fulfillment. In particular any belief in a deity or adherence to a religious system that is theistic in any way is discouraged.

Secular humanism, or humanism in the sense of a religious belief system, (as opposed to humanism as just an interest in the humanities), has organizational characteristics. . . .

These organizations publish magazines, newsletters and other periodicals, including *Free Inquiry, The Humanist* and *Progressive World*. The entire body of thought has three key documents that furnish the text upon which the belief system rests as on a platform: *Humanist Manifesto I, Humanist Manifesto II*, and the *Secular Humanist Declaration*. . . . Secular humanism is religious for first amendment purposes because it makes statements based on faith-assumptions.

To say that science is only concerned with data collected by the five senses as enhanced by technological devices of man's creation is to define *science's* limits. These are the parameters within which scientists function. However, to claim that there is nothing real beyond observable data is to make an assumption based not on science, but on faith, faith that observable data is all that is real. A statement that there is no transcendent or supernatural reality is a *religious* statement. . . .

To demand that there be physical proof of the supernatural, and to claim that an apparent lack of proof means the supernatural cannot be accepted, is to create a religious creed. It is not scientific to say that because there is no physical proof of the supernatural, we must base moral theories on disbelief and skepticism. If there is no evidence, the theory, one way or the other, has nothing to do with science. Religious persons can and do conduct rational and systematic debate on matters of *faith*. The physical sciences do not preclude religion and religious faith. They examine other areas of inquiry, and are unconcerned, yet compatible with, religious inquiry. The

Court is holding that the promotion and advancement of a religious system occurs when one faith-theory is taught to the exclusion of others and this is prohibited by the first amendment religion clauses.

For purposes of the first amendment, secular humanism is a religious belief system, entitled to the protections of, and subject to the prohibitions of, the religion clauses. It is not a mere scientific methodology that may be promoted and advanced in the public schools.

III. Religious Promotion in Textbooks?

. . .[T]he Supreme Court has declared that teaching religious tenets in such a way as to promote or encourage a religion violates the religion clauses. This prohibition is not implicated by mere coincidence of ideas with religious tenets. Rather, there must be systematic, whether explicit or implicit, promotion of a belief system as a whole. The facts showed that the State of Alabama has on its state textbook list certain volumes that are being used by school systems in this state, which engage in such promotion. . . .

The virtually unanimous conclusion of the numerous witnesses, both expert and lay, party and non-party, was that textbooks in the fields examined were poor from an educational perspective. Mere rotten and inadequate textbooks, however, have not yet been determined to violate any constitutional provision, much less the religion clauses. . . . Their expert opinion was that religion was so deliberately underemphasized and ignored that theistic religions were effectively discriminated against and made to seem irrelevant and unimportant within the context of American history. . . . The religious influence on the abolitionist, women's suffrage, temperance, modern civil rights and peace movements is ignored or diminished to insignificance. The role of religion in the lives of immigrants and minorities, especially southern blacks, is rarely

mentioned. After the Civil War, religion is given almost no play.

Omissions, if sufficient, do affect a person's ability to develop religious beliefs and exercise that religious freedom guaranteed by the Constitution. Do the omissions in these history books cross that threshold? For some of them, yes. In addition to omitting particular historical events with religious significance, these books uniformly ignore the religious aspect of most American culture. The vast majority of Americans, for most of our history, have lived in a society in which religion was a part of daily life. . . . For many people, religion is still this important. One would never know it by reading these books. Religion, where treated at all, is generally represented as a private matter, only influencing American public life at some extraordinary moments. This view of religion is one humanists have been seeking to instill for fifty years. These books assist that effort by perpetuating an inaccurate historical picture. . . .

According to humanistic psychology, as with humanism generally, man is the center of the universe and all existence. Morals are a matter of taste, dependent upon whether the consequences of actions satisfy human "needs." These needs are always defined as purely temporal and nonsupernatural. . . .

The [social studies] books do not state that this is a *theory* of the way humans make choices, they teach the student that things *are* this way. . . . The books teach that the student must determine right and wrong based only on his own experience, feelings and "values." These "values" are described as originating from within. A description of the origin of morals must be based on a faith assumption: a religious dogma. The books are not simply claiming that a moral rule must be internally accepted before it becomes meaningful, because this is true of *all* facts *and* beliefs. . . . The books repeat, over and over, that the decision is "yours alone," or is "purely personal" or that "only you can decide." The emphasis and overall approach implies, and would cause any reasonable, thinking student to infer, that the book is teaching that moral choices are just a matter of preference, because, as the books say, "you are the most important person in your life." . . . This faith assumes that self-actualization is the goal of every human being, that man has no supernatural attributes or component, that there are only temporal and physical consequences for man's actions, and that these results, alone, determine the morality of an action. This belief strikes at the heart of many theistic religions' beliefs that certain actions are in and of themselves immoral, *whatever the consequences,* and that, in addition, actions will have extratemporal consequences. The Court is not holding that high school . . . books must not discuss various theories of human psychology. But it must not present faith based systems to the exclusion of other faith based systems, it must not present one as true and the other as false, and it *must* use a comparative approach to withstand constitutional scrutiny. . . .

With these [history and social studies] books, the State of Alabama has overstepped its mark, and must withdraw to perform its proper nonreligious functions. . . . The Court will enter an order to prohibit further use of the books.

Roe v. Wade:
The Right to Abortion

No issue has generated more controversy in recent years than the abortion issue, and no issue displays more sharply conflicting claims of rights. *Roe v. Wade* is the famous Supreme Court decision that guaranteed women the right to choose to abort their pregnancies. The case began in August 1969 when a young carnival worker named Norma McCorvey discovered she was pregnant. Too poor to travel from Texas to California, where abortions were legal, she sought legal help. A friend introduced her to two recent University of Texas Law School graduates, Sarah Weddington and Linda Coffee, and the three decided to challenge the constitutionality of Texas's law forbidding abortion.

Norma McCorvey never got her abortion and did not see her baby girl again after leaving the hospital. Hoping to remain anonymous, she became Jane Roe for purposes of the lawsuit against Henry Wade, District Attorney for Dallas County. Four years later, the Supreme Court took the controversial step of extending the right to privacy to include the right to get an abortion. Justice Blackmun wrote the majority opinion in this famous case; Justices White and Rehnquist wrote separate dissenting opinions.

Mr. Justice Blackmun: [We] forthwith acknowledge our awareness of the sensitive

_____
410 U.S. 113 (1973)

and emotional nature of the abortion controversy, of the vigorous opposing views, [and] of the deep and seemingly absolute convictions that the subject inspires. One's philosophy, one's experiences, one's exposure to the raw edges of human existence, one's religious training, one's attitudes toward life and family and their values and the moral standards one establishes and seeks to observe, are all likely to [influence] one's thinking [about] abortion. In addition, population growth, pollution, poverty, and racial overtones tend to complicate and not to simplify the problem. Our task, of course, is to resolve the issue by constitutional measurement, free of emotion and of predilection. We seek earnestly to do this, and, because we do, we have inquired into, and in this opinion place some emphasis upon, medical and medical-legal history and what that history reveals about man's attitudes toward the abortion procedure over the centuries.

Three reasons have been advanced to explain historically the enactment of criminal abortion laws in the 19th century and to justify their continued existence.

It has been argued occasionally that these laws were the product of a Victorian social concern to discourage illicit sexual conduct. Texas, however, does not advance this justification in the present case. . . .

A second reason is concerned with abortion as a medical procedure. When most criminal abortion laws were first enacted, the procedure was a hazardous one for the woman. . . .

Modern medical techniques have altered this situation. Appellants and various *amici* refer to medical data indicating that abortion in early pregnancy, that is, prior to the end of first trimester, although not without its risk, is now relatively safe. The prevalence of high mortality rates at illegal "abortion mills" strengthens, rather than weakens, the State's interest in regulating the conditions under which abortions are performed. Moreover, the risk to the woman increases as her pregnancy continues. Thus the State retains a definite interest in protecting the woman's own health and safety when an abortion is proposed at a late stage of pregnancy.

The third reason is the State's interest—some phrase it in terms of duty—in protecting prenatal life. Some of the argument for this justification rests on the theory that a new human life is present from the moment of conception. . . . Logically, of course, a legitimate state interest in this area need not stand or fall on acceptance of the belief that life begins at conception or at some other point prior to live birth. In assessing the State's interest, recognition may be given to the less rigid claim that as long as at least *potential* life is involved, the State may assert interests beyond the protection of the pregnant woman alone.

Parties challenging state abortion laws have sharply disputed in some courts the contention that a purpose of these laws, when enacted, was to protect prenatal life. . . . There is some scholarly support for this view of original purpose. The few state courts called upon to interpret their laws in the nineteenth and early twentieth centuries did focus on the State's interest in protecting the woman's health rather than in preserving the embryo and fetus. . . .

The Constitution does not explicitly mention any right of privacy. [However], the Court has recognized that a right of personal privacy, or a guarantee of certain areas or zones of privacy, does exist under the Constitution. In varying contexts, the Court or individual Justices have, indeed, found at least the roots of that right in the First Amendment [*Stanley* v. *Georgia*]; in the Fourth and Fifth Amendments; in the penumbras of the Bill of Rights [*Griswold*]. . . . These decisions make it clear that only personal rights that can be deemed "fundamental" or "implicit in the concept of ordered liberty" [*Palko*] are included in this guarantee of personal privacy. They also make it clear that the right has some extension to activities relating to marriage, procreation, contraception, family relationships, and child rearing and education.

This right of privacy, founded in the 14th Amendment's concept of personal liberty and restrictions upon state action, . . . is broad enough to encompass a woman's decision whether or not to terminate her pregnancy. The detriment that the State would impose upon the pregnant woman by denying this choice altogether is apparent. Specific and direct harm medically diagnosable even in early pregnancy may be involved. Maternity, or additional offspring, may force upon the woman a distressful life and future. Psychological harm may be imminent. Mental and physical health may be taxed by child care. There is also the distress, for all concerned, associated with the unwanted child, and there is the problem of bringing a child into a family already unable, psychologically and otherwise, to care for it. In other cases, as in this one, the additional difficulties and continuing stigma of unwed motherhood may be involved. All these are factors the woman and her responsible physician necessarily will consider in consultation.

On the basis of elements such as these, appellants and some *amici* argue that the woman's right is absolute and that she is entitled to terminate her pregnancy at whatever time, in whatever way, and for whatever reason she alone chooses. With this we do not agree. Appellants' arguments that Texas either has no valid interest at all in regulating the abortion decision, or no interest strong enough to support any limitation upon the woman's sole determination, is unpersuasive. The Court's decisions recognizing a right of privacy also acknowledge that some state regulation in areas protected by that right is appropriate. A state may properly assert important interests in safeguarding health, in maintaining medical standards, and in protecting potential life. At some point in pregnancy, these respective interests become sufficiently compelling to sustain regulation of the factors that govern the abortion decision. The privacy right involved, therefore, cannot be said to be absolute. In face, it is not clear to us that the claim asserted by some *amici* that one has an unlimited right to do with one's body as one pleases bears a close relationship to the right of privacy previously articulated in the Court's decisions. . . .

Where certain "fundamental rights" are involved, the Court has held that regulation limiting these rights may be justified only by a "compelling state interest," and that legislative enactments must be narrowly drawn to express only the legitimate state interests at stake. . . .

A. The appellee and certain *amici* argue that the fetus is a "person" within the language and meaning of the Fourteenth Amendment. In support of this they outline at length and in detail the well-known facts of fetal development. If this suggestion of personhood is established, the appellant's case, of course, collapses, for the fetus' right to life is then guaranteed specifically by the Amendment. . . . No case indicates with any assurance that it has any possible pre-natal application.

All this, together with our observation, *supra,* that throughout the major portion of the nineteenth century prevailing legal abortion practices were far freer than they are today, persuades us that the word "person," as used in the Fourteenth Amendment, does not include the unborn. . . .

This conclusion, however, does not of itself fully answer the contentions raised by Texas, and we pass on to other considerations.

B. The pregnant woman cannot be isolated in her privacy. She carries an embryo and, later, a fetus. . . .

Texas urges that, apart from the Fourteenth Amendment, life begins at conception and is present throughout pregnancy, and that, therefore, the State has a compelling interest in protecting that life from and after conception. We need not resolve the difficult question of when life begins. When those trained in the respective disciplines of medicine, philosophy, and theology are unable to arrive at any consensus, the judiciary, at this point in the development of man's knowledge, is not in a position to speculate as to the answer.

It should be sufficient to note briefly the

wide divergence of thinking on this most sensitive and difficult question. There has always been strong support for the view that life does not begin until live birth. This was the belief of the Stoics. It appears to be the predominant, though not the unanimous, attitude of the Jewish faith. . . . The Aristotelian theory of "mediate animation," that held sway throughout the Middle Ages and the Renaissance in Europe, continued to be official Roman Catholic dogma until the 19th century, despite opposition to this "ensoulment" theory from those in the Church who would recognize the existence of life from the moment of conception. The latter is now, of course, the official belief of the Catholic Church. As one of the briefs *amicus* discloses, this is a view strongly held by many non-Catholics as well.

In areas other than criminal abortion the law has been reluctant to endorse any theory that life, as we recognize it, begins before live birth or to accord legal rights to the unborn except in narrowly defined situations and except when the rights are contingent upon live birth. In most States recovery is said to be permitted only if the fetus was viable, or at least quick, when the injuries were sustained. . . .

In view of all this, we do not agree that, by adopting one theory of life, Texas may override the rights of the pregnant woman that are at stake. We repeat, however, that the State does have an important and legitimate interest in preserving and protecting the health of the pregnant woman, . . . and that is has still *another* important and legitimate interest in protecting the potentiality of human life. These interests are separate and distinct. Each grows in substantiality as the woman approaches term and, at a point during pregnancy, each becomes "compelling."

With respect to the State's important and legitimate interest in the health of the mother, the "compelling point, in the light of present medical knowledge, is at approximately the end of the first trimester. This is so because of the now established medical fact that until the end of the first trimester mortality in abortion is less than mortality in normal childbirth. It follows that, from and after this point, a State may regulate the abortion procedure to the extent that the regulation reasonably relates to the preservation and protection of maternal health. . . .

This means, on the other hand, that, for the period of pregnancy prior to this "compelling" point, the attending physician, in consultation with his patient, is free to determine, without regulation by the State, that in his medical judgment the patient's pregnancy should be terminated. If that decision is reached, the judgment may be effectuated by an abortion free of interference by the State.

With respect to the State's important and legitimate interest in potential life, the "compelling" point is at viability. This is so because the fetus then presumably has the capability of meaningful life outside the mother's womb. State regulation protective of fetal life after viability thus has both logical and biological justifications. If the State is interested in protecting fetal life after viability, it may go so far as to proscribe abortion during that period except when it is necessary to preserve the life or health of the mother.

Mr. Justice White, dissenting: At the heart of the controversy in these cases are those recurring pregnancies that pose no danger whatsoever to the life or health of the mother but are nevertheless unwanted for any one or more of a variety of reasons—convenience, family planning, economics, dislike of children, the embarrassment of illegitimacy, etc. The common claim before us is that for any one of such reasons, or for no reason at all, and without asserting or claiming any threat to life or health, any woman is entitled to an abortion at her request if she is able to find a medical advisor willing to undertake the procedure.

The Court for the most part sustains this position: During the period prior to the time the fetus becomes viable, the Constitution of the United States values the convenience, whim or caprice of the putative mother more than the life or potential life of the fetus; the Constitution, therefore, guarantees the right to an abortion as against any state law or policy seeking to protect the fetus from an abortion not prompted by more compelling reasons of the mother.

With all due respect, I dissent. I find nothing in the language or history of the Constitution to support the Court's judgment. The Court simply fashions and announces a new constitutional right for pregnant mothers and, with scarcely any reason or authority for its action, invests that right with sufficient substance to override most existing state abortion statutes. The upshot is that the people and the legislatures of the 50 States are constitutionally disentitled to weigh the relative importance of the continued existence and development of the fetus on the one hand against a spectrum of possible impacts on the mother on the other hand. As an exercise of raw judicial power, the Court perhaps has authority to do what it does today; but in my view its judgment is an improvident and extravagant exercise of the power of judicial review which the Constitution extends to this Court. . . .

In a sensitive area such as this, involving as it does issues over which reasonable men may easily and heatedly differ, I cannot accept the Court's exercise of its clear power of choice by interposing a constitutional barrier to state efforts to protect human life. . . .

Mr. Justice Rehnquist, dissenting: [I] have difficulty in concluding [that] the right of "privacy" is involved in this case. [Texas] bars the performance of a medical abortion by a licensed physician on a plaintiff such as *Roe*. A transaction resulting in an operation such as this is not "private" in the ordinary usage of the word. Nor is the "privacy" which the Court finds here even a distant relative of the [Fourth Amendment freedom from searches and seizures]. If the Court means by the term "privacy" no more than that the claim of a person to be free from unwanted state regulation of consensual transactions may be a form of "liberty" protected by the 14th Amendment, there is no doubt that similar claims have been upheld in our earlier decisions on the basis of that liberty. . . . But that liberty is not guaranteed absolutely against deprivation, but only against deprivation without due process of law. The test traditionally applied in the area of social and economic legislation is whether or not a law such as that challenged has a rational relation to a valid state objective. *[Lee Optical.]* [If] the Texas statute were to prohibit an abortion even where the mother's life is in jeopardy, I have little doubt that such a statute would lack a rational relation to a valid state objective under the test stated in *[Lee Optical].* But the Court's sweeping invalidation of any restrictions on abortion during the first trimester is impossible to justify under that [standard]. . . .

The fact that a majority of the [States] have had restrictions on abortions for at least a century is a strong indication, it seems to me, that the asserted right to an abortion is not "so rooted in the traditions and conscience of our people as to be ranked as fundamental." Even today, when society's views on abortion are changing, the very existence of the debate is evidence that the "right" to an abortion is not so universally accepted. . . .

Rust v. Sullivan:
Abortion Counselling

In the years since *Roe v. Wade* the Supreme Court has confronted a range of issues as states have sought, within the confines of that decision, to limit abortions. In *Webster v. Reproductive Services*, for example, the Court upheld a Missouri law prohibiting using public facilities or employees to perform abortions and requiring physicians to conduct viability tests prior to performing abortions after the fetus is twenty weeks old. In the following case, the Court considered another restriction, this time passed by the Department of Health and Human Services, prohibiting abortion counselling or promoting abortion as a method of family planning in any facilities receiving Title X funds. The regulations also required that such clinics remain physically and financially separate from abortion activities. The Department promulgated these new regulations as an interpretation of language in Title X stating that "none of the funds appropriated under this (act) shall be used in programs where abortion is a method of family planning." Many pregnant women, especially the poor, rely on such clinics for medical advice. Common practice in clinics had been to inform patients that their options were to pursue pre-natal care and either keep the baby or put it up for adoption or else to get an abortion at another clinic. Under the new guidelines, however, such advice would result in loss of federal funding.

Justice Rehnquist delivered the opinion of the Court: These cases concern a facial challenge to Department of Health and Human Services (H.H.I.S.) regulations which limit the ability of Title X fund recipients to engage in abortion-related activities. The United States Court of Appeals for the Second Circuit upheld the regulations, finding them to be a permissible construction of the statute as well as consistent with the First and Fifth Amendments of the Constitution. . . . We affirm.

89–1391 (1991).

In 1970 Congress enacted Title X of the Public Health Service Act (Act), which provides Federal funding for family-planning services. . . . Section 1008 of the Act, however, provides that "none of the funds appropriated under this subchapter shall be used in programs where abortion is a method of family planning." . . .

In 1988 the Secretary promulgated new regulations designed to provide " 'clear and operational guidance' to grantees about how to preserve the distinction between Title X programs and abortion as a method of family planning." . . .

The regulations attach three principal conditions on the grant of Federal funds for the Title X projects. First, the regulations specify that a "Title X project may not provide counseling concerning the use of abortion as a method of family planning or provide referral for abortion as a method of family planning." . . . Title X projects must refer every pregnant client "for appropriate prenatal and/or social services by furnishing a list of available providers that promote the welfare of the mother and the unborn child." . . . The Title X project is expressly prohibited from referring a pregnant woman to an abortion provider, even upon specific request. One permissible response to such an inquiry is that "the project does not consider abortion an appropriate method of family planning and therefore does not counsel of refer for abortion."

Second, the regulations broadly prohibit a Title X project from engaging in activities that "encourage, promote or advocate abortion as a method of family planning." Forbidden activities include lobbying for legislation that would increase the availability of abortion as a method of family planning, developing or disseminating materials advocating abortion as a method of family planning, providing speakers to promote abortion as a method of family planning, using legal action to make abortion available in any way as a method of family planning, and paying dues to any group that advocates abortion as a method of family planning as a substantial part of its activities.

Third, the regulations require that Title X projects be organized so that they are "physically and financially separate" from prohibited abortion activities. . . .

Petitioners are Title X grantees and doctors who supervise Title X funds suing on behalf of themselves and their patients. Respondent is the Secretary of the Department of Health and Human Services . . . Petitioners challenged the regulations on the grounds that they were not authorized by Title X and that they violate the First and Fifth Amendment rights of the Title X clients and the First Amendment rights of Title X health providers. . . .

We need not dwell on the plain language of the statute because we agree with every court to have addressed the issue that the language is ambiguous. The language of Sec. 1008—that "none of the funds appropriate under this subchapter shall be used in programs where abortion is a method of family planning"—does not speak directly to the issues of counseling, referral, advocacy, or program integrity. If a statute is "silent or ambiguous with respect to the specific issue, the question for the court is whether the agency's answer is based on a permissible construction of the statute." Chevron v. Natural Resources Defense Council (1984).

The Secretary's construction of Title X may not be disturbed as an abuse of discretion if it reflects a plausible construction of the plain language of the statute and does not otherwise conflict with Congress' expressed intent. . . . Substantial deference is accorded to the interpretation of the authorizing statute by the agency authorized with administering it.

The broad language of Title X plainly allows the Secretary's construction of the statute. By its own terms Sec. 1008 prohibits the use of Title X funds "in programs where abortion is a method of family planning." Title X does not define the term "method of family planning," nor does it enumerate what types of medical and counseling services are entitled to Title X funding. Based on the broad directives provided by Congress in Title X in general and Sec. 1008 in particular, we are unable to say that the Secretary's construction of the prohibition in Sec. 1008 to require a ban on counseling, referral, and advocacy within Title X project, is impermissible. . . .

When we find, as we do here, that the legislative history is ambiguous and unenlightening on the matters with respect to which the regulations deal, we customarily defer to the expertise of the agency. . . .

Congress forbade the use of appropriate

funds in programs where abortion is a method of family planning. It authorized the Secretary to promulgate regulations implementing this provision. The extensive litigation regarding governmental restrictions on abortion since our decision in Roe v. Wade, (1973), suggests that it was likely that any set of regulations promulgated by the Secretary—other than the ones in force prior to 1988 and found by him to be relatively toothless and ineffectual—would be challenged on constitutional grounds.

While we do not think that the constitutional arguments made by petitioners in this case are without some force, infra, we hold that they do not carry the day. Applying the canon of construction under discussion as best we can, we hold that the regulations promulgated by the Secretary do not raise the sort of grave and doubtful constitutional questions, that would lead us to assume Congress did not intend to authorize their issuance. Therefore, we need not invalidate the regulations in order to save the statute from unconstitutionality.

Petitioners contend that the regulations violate the First Amendment by impermissible discriminating based on viewpoint because they prohibit "all discussion about abortion as a lawful option—including counseling, referral, and the provision of neutral and accurate information about ending a pregnancy—while compelling the clinic or counselor to provide information that promotes continuing a pregnancy to term." They assert that the regulations violate the "free speech rights of private health care organizations that receive Title X funds, of their staff, and of their patients" by impermissibly imposing "viewpoint-discriminatory conditions on government subsidies" and thus penaliz[e] speech funded with non-Title X monies. . . .

The Court [earlier] rejected the claim that [state welfare regulation under which Medicaid recipients received payments for services related to childbirth, but not for non-therapeutic abortions] worked a violation of the Constitution. We held that the Government may "make a value judgment favoring childbirth over abortion, and . . . implement that judgment by the allocation of public funds." . . . The Government can, without violating the Constitution, selectively fund a program to encourage certain activities it believes to be in the public interest, without at the same time funding an alternate program which seeks to deal with the problem in another way. In so doing, the Government has not discriminated on the basis of viewpoint; it has merely chosen to fund one activity to the exclusion of the other. . . .

The challenged regulations implement the statutory prohibition by prohibiting counseling, referral and the provision of information regarding abortion as a method of family planning. They are designed to insure that the limits of the Federal program are observed. The Title X program is designed not for prenatal care, but to encourage family planning. A doctor who wished to offer prenatal care to a project patient who became pregnant could properly be prohibited from doing so because such service is outside the scope of the federally funded program. The regulations prohibiting abortion counseling and referral are of the same ilk; "no funds appropriated for the project may be used in programs where abortion is a method of family planning," and a doctor employed by the project may be prohibited in the course of his project duties from counseling abortion or referring for abortion. This is not a case of the Government "suppressing a dangerous idea," but of a prohibition on a project grantee or its employees from engaging in activities outside of its scope.

To hold that the Government unconstitutionally discriminates on the basis of viewpoint when it chooses to fund a program dedicated to advance certain permissible goals, because the program is advancing those goals necessarily discourages alternate goals, would render numerous government programs constitutionally suspect. When Congress established a National Endowment for Democracy to encourage other countries to adopt democratic principles, it was not constitutionally required to fund a program to encourage competing lines of political philosophy such as Communism and Fascism. Petitioners' assertions ultimately boil down to the position that if the Government chooses to subsidize one protected right, it must subsidize analogous counterpart rights. But the Court has soundly rejected that proposition. . . . Within far broader limits than petitioners are willing to concede, when the Government appropriates public funds to establish a program it is entitled to define the limits of that program. . . .

Petitioners rely heavily on their claim that the regulations would not, in the circumstance of a medical emergency, permit a Title X project to refer a woman whose pregnancy places her life in imminent peril to a provider of abortions or abortion-related services. This case, of course, involves only a facial challenge to the regulations, and we do not have before us any application by the Secretary to a specific fact situation. On their face, we do not read the regulations to bar abortion referral or counseling in such circumstances.

Abortion counseling as a "method of family planning" is prohibited, and it does not seem that a medically necessitated abortion in such circumstances would be the equivalent of its use as a "method of family planning." . . .

Petitioners also contend that the restrictions on the subsidization of abortion-related speech contained in the regulations are impermissible because they condition the receipt of a benefit, in this case Title X funding, on the relinquishment of a constitutional right, the right to engage in abortion advocacy and counseling. . . .

. . .Here the Government is not denying a benefit to anyone, but is instead simply insisting that public funds be spent for the purpose for which they were authorized. The Secretary's regulations do not force the Title X grantee to give up abortion-related speech; they merely require that the grantee keep such activities separate and distinct from Title X activities. . . .

The same principles apply to petitioners' claim that the regulations abridge the free speech rights of the grantee's staff.

We turn now to petitioners' argument that the regulations violate a woman's Fifth Amendment right to choose whether to terminate her pregnancy. . . . The Government has no constitutional duty to subsidize an activity merely because the activity is constitutionally protected and may validly choose to fund childbirth over abortion and " 'implement that judgment by the allocation of public funds' " for medical services relating to childbirth but not to those relating to abortion. Webster v. Reproductive Health Services (1989). The Government has no affirmative duty to "commit any resources to facilitating abortions." Webster.

Justice Blackmun, dissenting: Casting aside established principles of statutory construction and administrative jurisprudence, the majority in these cases today unnecessarily passes upon important questions of constitutional law. In so doing, the Court, for the first time, upholds viewpoint-based suppression of speech solely because it is imposed on those dependent upon the Government for economic support.

Under essentially the same rationale, the majority upholds direct regulation of dialogue between a pregnant woman and her physician when that regulation has both the purpose and the effect of manipulating her decision as to the continuance of her pregnancy. I conclude that the Secretary's regulation of referral, advocacy, and counseling activities exceeds his statutory authority, and also, that the regulations violate the First and Fifth Amendments of our Constitution. Accordingly, I dissent and would reverse the divided-vote judgment of the Court of Appeals. . . .

Until today the Court never has upheld viewpoint-based suppression of speech simply because that suppression was a condition upon the acceptance of public funds. Whatever may be the Government's power to condition the receipt of its largess upon the relinquishment of constitutional rights, it surely does not extend to a condition that suppresses the recipient's cherished freedom of speech based solely upon the content or viewpoint of that speech. . . .

It cannot seriously be disputed that the counseling and referral provisions at issue in the present cases constitute content-based regulation of speech. Title X grantees may provide counseling and referral regarding any of a wide range of family planning and other topics, save abortion. . . .

The regulations are also clearly viewpoint-based. While suppressing speech favorable to abortion with one hand, the Secretary compels anti-abortion speech with the other. . . .

Moreover, the regulations command that a project refer for prenatal care each woman diagnosed as pregnant, irrespective of the woman's expressed desire to continue or terminate her pregnancy. If a client asks directly about abortion, a Title X physician or counselor is required to say, in essence, that the project does not consider abortion to be an appropriate method of family planning. Both requirements are antithetical to the First Amendment. . . .

The Court concludes that the challenged regulations do not violate the First Amendment rights of Title X staff members because any limitation of the employees' freedom of expression . . . is simply a consequence of their decision to accept employment at a federally funded project. But it has never been sufficient to justify an otherwise unconstitutional condition upon public employment that the employee may escape the condition by relinquishing his or her job. It is beyond question "that a Government may not require an individual to relinquish rights guaranteed him by the First Amendment as a condition of public employment." Abood v. Detroit Board of Education. . . .

In the cases at bar, the speaker's interest in the communication is both clear and vital. In addressing the family-planning needs of their clients, the physicians and counselors who staff Title projects seek to provide them with the full range of information and options regarding their health and reproductive freedom. Indeed, the legitimate expectations of the patient and the ethical responsibilities of the medical profession demand no less. . . .

The Government's articulated interest in distorting the doctor/patient dialogue—insuring that Federal funds are not spent for a purpose outside the scope of the program—falls far short of that necessary to justify the suppression of truthful information and professional medical opinion regarding constitutionally protected conduct. . . .

By far the most disturbing aspect of today's ruling is the effect it will have on the Fifth Amendment rights of the women who, supposedly, are beneficiaries of Title X programs.

Contrary to the majority's characterization, this is not a case in which individuals seek government aid in exercising their fundamental rights. The Fifth Amendment right asserted by petitioners is the right of a pregnant woman to be free from affirmative governmental interference in her decision. Roe v. Wade, (1973), and its progeny are not so much about a medical procedure as they are about a woman's fundamental right to self-determination. . . .

It is crystal clear that the aim of the challenged provisions—an aim the majority cannot escape noticing—is not simply to insure that Federal funds are not used to perform abortions, but to "reduce the incidence of abortion."

The manipulation of the doctor/patient dialogue achieved through the Secretary's regulations is clearly an effort to deter a woman from making a decision that, with her physician, is hers to make. As such, it violates the Fifth Amendment.

PART IV Freedom and the Limits of Liberty

On Liberty

John Stuart Mill

In the following selection from his famous essay, *On Liberty*, John Stuart Mill examines a fundamental question of social and political philosophy: What are the proper limits to society's power over the individual? Mill's answer is that society may interfere with an individual's actions only on grounds of self-protection, that is, only to prevent the individual from harming other people. In line with this, Mill turns first to the realm of thought and expression, vigorously upholding freedom of opinion regardless of whether the viewpoint expressed is true or false. Although freedom of expression is a value cherished in our society, the critical reader must ask whether Mill is right in believing that there are no opinions that are so vile or potentially dangerous that society is justified in suppressing them.

In the final sections of the essay, Mill elaborates on his general principle that society may not compel the individual to do (or not do) something solely because society judges that it would be in the individual's own interest to do it. Although this principle sounds attractive, it has radical implications, and many social and political thinkers have rejected it. Accepting Mill's principle would require us to reconsider and perhaps repeal many laws now on the books whose only rationale appears to be that of protecting people from themselves (for example, laws against using certain drugs). Critics of Mill have also wondered whether one really can plausibly distinguish, as Mill attempts to do, between behavior that affects the individual only and behavior that affects others as well. In addition, they have questioned whether Mill can square his almost absolute commitment to individual liberty with his underlying utilitarianism. Might not utilitarianism sometimes require us to limit individual freedom in ways that *On Liberty* opposes in order to enhance total social welfare?

INTRODUCTORY

The subject of this essay is . . . civil, or social liberty: the nature and limits of power which can be legitimately exercised by society over the individual. A question seldom stated and hardly ever discussed in general terms, but which profoundly influences the practical controversies of the age by its latent presence, and is likely soon to make itself recognized as the vital question of the future. It is so far from being new, that, in a certain sense, it has divided mankind almost from the remotest ages; but in the stage of progress into which the more civilized portions of the species have now entered, it presents itself under new conditions, and

Reprinted from John Stuart Mill, *On Liberty* (1859).

requires a different and more fundamental treatment.

The struggle between liberty and authority is the most conspicuous feature in the portions of history with which we are earliest familiar, particularly in that of Greece, Rome, and England. But in old times this contest was between subjects, or some classes of subjects, and the government. By liberty, was meant protection against the tyranny of the political rulers. The rulers were conceived (except in some of the popular governments of Greece) as in a necessarily antagonistic position to the people whom they ruled. They consisted of a governing One, or a governing tribe or caste, who derived their authority from inheritance or conquest, who, at all events, did not hold it at the pleasure of the governed, and whose supremacy men did not venture, perhaps did not desire, to contest, whatever precautions might be taken against its oppressive exercise. Their power was regarded as necessary, but also as highly dangerous; as a weapon which they would attempt to use against their subjects, no less than against external enemies. To prevent the weaker members of the community from being preyed upon by innumerable vultures, it was needful that there should be an animal of prey stronger than the rest, commissioned to keep them down. But as the king of the vultures would be no less bent upon preying on the flock than any of the minor harpies, it was indispensable to be in a perpetual attitude of defense against his beak and claws. The aim, therefore, of patriots was to set limits to the power which the ruler should be suffered to exercise over the community; and this limitation was what they meant by liberty. It was attempted in two ways. First, by obtaining a recognition of certain immunities, called political liberties or rights, which it was to be regarded as a breach of duty in the ruler to infringe, and which if he did infringe, specific resistance, or general rebellion, was held to be justifiable. A second, and generally a later expedient, was the establishment of constitutional checks, by which the consent of the community, or of a body of some sort, supposed to represent its interests, was made a necessary condition to some of the more important acts of the governing power. To the first of these modes of limitation, the ruling power, in most European countries, was compelled, more or less, to submit. It was not so with the second; and, to attain this, or when already in some degree possessed, to attain it more completely, became everywhere the principal object of the lovers of liberty. And so long as mankind were content to combat one enemy by another, and to be ruled by a master, on condition of being guaranteed more or less efficaciously against his tyranny, they did not carry their aspirations beyond this point.

A time, however, came, in the progress of human affairs, when men ceased to think it a necessity of nature that their governors should be an independent power, opposed in interest to themselves. It appeared to them much better that the various magistrates of the State should be their tenants or delegates, revocable at their pleasure. In that way alone, it seemed, could they have complete security that the powers of government would never be abused to their disadvantage. By degrees this new demand for elective and temporary rulers became the prominent object of the exertions of the popular party, wherever any such party existed; and superseded, to a considerable extent, the previous efforts to limit the power of rulers. As the struggle proceeded for making the ruling power emanate from the periodical choice of the ruled, some persons began to think that too much importance had been attached to the limitation of the power itself. *That* (it might seem) was a resource against rulers whose interests were habitually opposed to those of the people. What was now wanted was, that the rulers should be identified with the people; that their interest and will should be the interest and will of the nation. The nation did not need to be protected against its own will. There was no fear of its tyrannizing over itself. Let the rulers be effectually responsible to it, promptly removably by it, and it could afford to trust them with power of which it could itself dictate the use to be made. Their power was but the nation's own power, concentrated, and in a form convenient for exercise. . . .

But in political and philosophical theories, as well as in persons, success discloses faults and infirmities which failure might have concealed from observation. . . . It was now perceived that such phrases as "self-government," and "the power of the people over themselves," do not express the true state of the case. The "people" who exercise the power are not always the same people with those over whom it is exercised; and the "self-government" spoken of is not the government of each by himself, but of each by all the rest. The will of the people, moreover, practically means the will of the most numerous or the most active *part* of the people—the majority, or those who succeed in making themselves accepted as the majority; the people, consequently, *may* desire to oppress a part of their number, and precautions are as much needed against this as against any other abuse of power. The limitation, therefore, of the power of government over individuals loses none of its importance when the holders of power are regularly accountable to the community, that is, to the strongest party therein. This view of things, recommending itself equally to the intelligence of thinkers and to the inclination of those important classes in European society to whose real or supposed interests democracy is adverse, has had no difficulty in establishing itself; and in political speculations "the tyranny of the majority" is now generally included among the evils against which society requires to be on its guard.

Like other tyrannies, the tyranny of the majority was at first, and is still vulgarly, held in dread, chiefly as operating through the acts of the public authorities. But reflecting persons perceived that when society is itself the tyrant—society collectively over the separate individuals who compose it—its means of tyrannizing are not restricted to the acts which it may do by the hands of its

political functionaries. Society can and does execute its own mandates; and if it issues wrong mandates instead of right, or any mandates at all in things with which it ought not to meddle, it practises a social tyranny more formidable than many kinds of political oppression, since, though not usually upheld by such extreme penalties, it leaves fewer means of escape, penetrating much more deeply into the details of life, and enslaving the soul itself. Protection, therefore, against the tyranny of the magistrate is not enough; there needs protection also against the tyranny of the prevailing opinion and feeling, against the tendency of society to impose, by other means than civil penalties, its own ideas and practices as rules of conduct on those who dissent from them; to fetter the development and, if possible, prevent the formation of any individuality not in harmony with its ways, and compels all characters to fashion themselves upon the model of its own. There is a limit to the legitimate interference of collective opinion with individual independence; and to find that limit, and maintain it against encroachment, is as indispensable to a good condition of human affairs as protection against political despotism.

But though this proposition is not likely to be contested in general terms, the practical question, where to place the limit—how to make the fitting adjustment between individual independence and social control—is a subject on which nearly everything remains to be done. . . .

The object of this essay is to assert one very simple principle, as entitled to govern absolutely the dealings of society with the individual in the way of compulsion and control, whether the means used be physical force in the form of legal penalties or the moral coercion of public opinion. That principle is, that the sole end for which mankind are warranted, individually or collectively, in interfering with the liberty of action of any of their number, is self-protection. That the only purpose for which power can be rightfully exercised over any member of a civilized community, against his will, is to prevent harm to others. His own good, either physical or moral, is not a sufficient warrant. He cannot rightfully be compelled to do or forbear because it will be better for him to do so, because it will make him happier, because, in the opinions of others, to do so would be wise or even right. These are good reasons for remonstrating with him, or reasoning with him, or persuading him, or entreating him, but not for compelling him or visiting him with any evil in case he do otherwise. To justify that, the conduct from which it is desired to deter him must be calculated to produce evil to someone else. The only part of the conduct of anyone, for which he is amenable to society, is that which concerns others. In the part which merely concerns himself, his independence is, of right, absolute. Over himself, over his own body and mind, the individual is sovereign.

It is, perhaps, hardly necessary to say that this doctrine is meant to apply only to human beings in the maturity of their faculties. We are not speaking of children, or of young persons below the age which the law may fix as that of manhood or womanhood. Those who are still in a state to require being taken care of by others, must be protected against their own actions as well as against external injury. For the same reason, we may leave out of consideration those backward states of society in which the race itself may be considered as in its nonage. The early difficulties in the way of spontaneous progress are so great, and there is seldom any choice of means for overcoming them; and a ruler full of the spirit of improvement is warranted in the use of any expedients that will attain an end, perhaps otherwise unattainable. Despotism is a legitimate mode of government in dealing with barbarians, provided the end be their improvement, and the means justified by actually effecting that end. Liberty, as a principle, has no application to any state of things anterior to the time when mankind have become capable of being improved by free and equal discussion. Until then, there is nothing for them but implicit obedience to

an Akbar or a Charlemagne, if they are so fortunate as to find one. But as soon as mankind have attained the capacity of being guided to their own improvement by conviction or persuasion (a period long since reached in all nations with whom we need here concern ourselves), compulsion, either in the direct form or in that of pains and penalties for noncompliance, is no longer admissible as a means to their own good, and justifiable only for the security of others.

It is proper to state that I forego any advantage which could be derived to my argument from the idea of abstract right, as a thing independent of utility. I regard utility as the ultimate appeal on all ethical questions; but it must be utility in the largest sense, grounded on the permanent interests of a man as a progressive being. These interests, I contend, authorized the subjection of individual spontaneity to external control, only in respect to those actions of each which concern the interest of other people. If anyone does an act hurtful to others, there is a *prima facie* case for punishing him, by law, or, where legal penalties are not safely applicable, by general disapprobation. There are also many positive acts for the benefit of others, which he may rightfully be compelled to perform: such as to give evidence in a court of justice; to bear his fair share in the common defense, or in any other joint work necessary to the interest of the society of which he enjoys the protection; and to perform certain acts of individual beneficence, such as saving a fellow-creature's life, or interposing to protect the defenseless against ill-usage, things which whenever it is obviously a man's duty to do, he may rightfully be made responsible to society for not doing. A person may cause evil to others not only by his actions but by his inaction, and in either case he is justly accountable to them for the injury. The latter case, it is true, requires a much more cautious exercise of compulsion than the former. To make anyone answerable for doing evil to others is the rule; to make him answerable for not preventing evil is, comparatively speaking, the exception. Yet there are many cases clear enough and grave enough to justify that exception. . . .

But there is a sphere of action in which society, as distinguished from the individual, has, if any, only an indirect interest; comprehending all that portion of a person's life and conduct which affects only himself, or if it also affects others, only with their free, voluntary, and undeceived consent and participation. When I say only himself, I mean directly, and in the first instance; for whatever affects himself, may affect others through himself; and the objection which may be grounded on this contingency, will receive consideration in the sequel. This, then is the appropriate region of human liberty. It comprises, *first,* the inward domain of consciousness; demanding liberty of conscience in the most comprehensive sense; liberty of thought and feeling; absolute freedom of opinion and sentiment on all subjects, practical or speculative, scientific, moral or theological. The liberty of expressing and publishing opinions may seem to fall under a different principle, since it belongs to that part of the conduct of an individual which concerns other people; but, being almost of as much importance as the liberty of thought itself, and resting in great part on the same reasons, is practically inseparable from it. *Secondly,* the principle requires liberty of tastes and pursuits; of framing the plan of our life to suit our own character; of doing as we like, subject to such consequences as may follow: without impediment from our fellow-creatures, so long as what we do does not harm them, even though they should think our conduct foolish, perverse, or wrong. *Thirdly,* from this liberty of each individual, follows the liberty, within the same limits, of combinations among individuals; freedom to unite, for any purpose not involving harm to others: the persons combining being supposed to be of full age, and not forced or deceived.

No society in which these liberties are not, on the whole, respected, is free, whatever may be its form of government; and none is completely free in which they do not exist absolute and unqualified. The only freedom which deserves the name, is that of pursuing our own good in our own way, as long as we do not attempt to deprive others of theirs, or impede their efforts to obtain it. Each is the proper guardian of his own health, whether bodily, or mental and spiritual. Mankind are greater gainers by suffering each other to live as seems good to themselves, than by compelling each to live as seems good to the rest. . . .

OF THE LIBERTY OF THOUGHT AND DISCUSSION

The time, it is to be hoped, is gone by, when any defense would be necessary of the "liberty of the press" as one of the securities against corrupt or tyrannical government. No argument, we may suppose, can now be needed against permitting a legislature or an executive, not identified in interest with the people, to prescribe opinions to them, and determine what doctrines or what arguments they shall be allowed to hear. . . . Let us suppose . . . that government is entirely at one with the people, and never thinks of exerting any power of coercion unless in agreement with what it conceives to be their voice. But I deny the right of the people to exercise such coercion, either by themselves or by their government. The power itself is illegitimate. The best government has no more title to it than the worst. It is as noxious, or more noxious, when exerted in accordance with public opinion than when in opposition to it. If all mankind minus one were of one opinion, mankind would be no more justified in silencing that one person than he, if he had the power, would be justified in silencing mankind. Were an opinion a personal possession of no value except to the owner, if to be obstructed in the enjoyment of it were simply a private injury, it would make some difference whether the injury was inflicted only on a few persons or on many. But the peculiar evil of silencing the expression of an opinion is that it is robbing the human race, posterity as well as the existing generation—those who dissent from the opinion, still more than those who hold it. If the opinion is right, they are deprived of the opportunity of exchanging error for truth; if wrong, they lose, what is almost as great a benefit, the clearer perception and livelier impression of truth produced by its collision with error.

It is necessary to consider separately these two hypotheses, each of which has a distinct branch of the argument corresponding to it. We can never be sure that the opinion we are endeavoring to stifle is a false opinion; and if we were sure, stifling it would be an evil still.

First, the opinion which it is attempted to suppress by authority may possibly be true. Those who desire to suppress it, of course, deny its truth; but they are not infallible. They have no authority to decide the question for all mankind and exclude every other person from the means of judging. To refuse a hearing to an opinion because they are sure that it is false to assume that *their* certainty is the same thing as *absolute* certainty. All silencing of discussion is an assumption of infallibility. Its condemnation may be allowed to rest on this common argument, not the worse for being common.

Unfortunately for the good sense of mankind, the fact of their fallibility is far from carrying the weight in their practical judgment which is always allowed to it in theory; for while everyone well knows himself to be fallible, few think it necessary to take any precautions against their own fallibility, or admit the supposition that any opinion of which they feel very certain may be one of the examples of the error to which they acknowledge themselves to be liable. . . .

The objection likely to be made to this argument would probably take some such form as the following. There is no greater assumption of infallibility in forbidding the propagation of error than in any other thing which is done by public authority on its own judgment and responsibility. . . . It is the duty of governments, and of individuals, to form the truest opinions they can; to form them carefully, and never impose them upon others unless they are quite sure

of being right. But when they are sure (such reasoners may say), it is not conscientiousness but cowardice to shrink from acting on their opinions and allow doctrines which they honestly think dangerous to the welfare of mankind, either in this life or in another, to be scattered abroad without restraint, because other people, in less enlightened times, have persecuted opinions now believed to be true. . . . There is no such thing as absolute certainty, but there is assurance sufficient for the purposes of human life. We may, and must, assume our opinion to be true for the guidance of our own conduct; and it is assuming no more when we forbid bad men to pervert society by the propagation of opinions which we regard as false and pernicious.

I answer, that it is assuming very much more. There is the greatest difference between presuming an opinion to be true because, with every opportunity for contesting it, it has not been refuted, and assuming its truth for the purpose of not permitting its refutation. Complete liberty of contradicting and disproving our opinion is the very condition which justifies us in assuming its truth for purposes of action; and on no other terms can a being with human faculties have any rational assurance of being right. . . .

In the present age—which has been described as "destitute of faith, but terrified at skepticism"—in which people feel sure, not so much that their opinions are true as that they should not know what to do without them—the claims of an opinion to be protected from public attack are rested not so much on its truth as on its importance to society. There are, it is alleged, certain beliefs so useful, not to say indispensable, to well-being that it is as much the duty of governments to uphold those beliefs as to protect any other of the interests of society. In a case of such necessity, and so directly in the line of their duty, something less than infallibility may, it is maintained, warrant, and even bind, governments to act on their own opinion confirmed by the general opinion of mankind. It is also often argued, and still oftener thought, that none but bad men would desire to weaken these salutary beliefs; and there can be nothing wrong, it is thought, in restraining bad men and prohibiting what only such men would wish to practice. This mode of thinking makes the justification of restraints on discussion not a question of the truth of doctrines but of their usefulness, and flatters itself by that means to escape the responsibility of claiming to be an infallible judge of opinions. But those who thus satisfy themselves do not perceive that the assumption of infallibility is merely shifted from one point to another. The usefulness of an opinion is itself a matter of opinion—as disputable, as open to discussion, and requiring discussion as much as the opinion itself. There is the same need of an infallible judge of opinions to decide an opinion to be noxious as to decide it to be false, unless the opinion condemned has full opportunity of defending itself. And it will not do to say that the heretic may be allowed to maintain the utility or harmlessness of his opinion, though forbidden to maintain its truth. The truth of an opinion is part of its utility. If we would know whether or not it is desirable that a proposition should be believed, is it possible to exclude the consideration of whether or not it is true? In the opinion, not of bad men, but of the best men, no belief which is contrary to truth can be really useful. . . .

The dictum that truth always triumphs over persecution is one of those pleasant falsehoods which men repeat after one another till they pass into commonplaces, but which all experience refutes. History teems with instances of truth put down by persecution. If not suppressed forever, it may be thrown back for centuries. To speak only of religious opinions: the Reformation broke out at least twenty times before Luther, and was put down. . . . Even after the era of Luther, wherever persecution was persisted in, it was successful. . . .

Let us now pass to the second division of the argument, and dismissing the supposition that any of the received opinions may be false, let us assume them to be true and examine into the worth of the manner in which they are likely to be held when their truth is not freely and openly canvassed. However unwillingly a person who has a strong opinion may admit the possibility that his opinion may be false, he ought to be moved by the consideration that, however true it may be, if it is not fully, frequently, and fearlessly discussed, it will be held as a dead dogma, not a living truth. . . .

If the cultivation of the understanding consists in one thing more than in another, it is surely in learning the grounds of one's own opinions. Whatever people believe, on subjects on which it is of the first importance to believe rightly, they ought to be able to defend against at least the common objections. . . . On every subject on which difference of opinion is possible, the truth depends on a balance to be struck between two sets of conflicting reasons. Even in natural philosophy, there is always some other explanation possible of the same facts; some geocentric theory instead of heliocentric, some phlogiston instead of oxygen; and it has to be shown why that other theory cannot be the true one; and until this is shown, and until we know how it is shown, we do not understand the grounds of our opinion. But when we turn to subjects infinitely more complicated, to morals, religion, politics, social relations, and the business of life, three-fourths of the arguments for every disputed opinion consist in dispelling the appearances which favor some opinion different from it. The greatest orator, save one, of antiquity, has left it on record that he always studied his adversary's case with as great, if not still greater, intensity than even his own. What Cicero practiced as the means of forensic success requires to be imitated by all who study any subject in order to arrive at the truth. He who knows only his own side of the case knows little of that. His reasons may be good, and no one may have been able to refute them. But if he is equally unable to refute the reasons on the opposite side, if he does not so much as know what they are, he has no ground for preferring either opinion. The rational position for him would be suspension of judgment, and unless he contents himself with that, he is either led by authority or adopts, like the generality of the world, the side to which he feels most inclination. Nor is it enough that he should hear the arguments of adversaries from his own teachers, presented as they state them, and accompanied by what they offer as refutations. That is not the way to do justice to the arguments or bring them into real contact with his own mind. He must be able to hear them from persons who actually believe them, who defend them in earnest and do their very utmost for them. He must know them in their most plausible and persuasive form; he must feel the whole force of the difficulty which the true view of the subject has to encounter and dispose of, else he will never really possess himself of the portion of truth which meets and removes that difficulty. . . .

The fact . . . is that not only the grounds of the opinion are forgotten in the absence of discussion, but too often the meaning of the opinion itself. The words which convey it cease to suggest ideas, or suggest only a small portion of those they were originally employed to communicate. Instead of a vivid conception and a living belief, there remain only a few phrases retained by rote; or, if any part, the shell and husk only of the meanings is retained, the finer essence being lost. The great chapter in human history which this fact occupies and fills cannot be too earnestly studied and meditated on.

It is illustrated in the experience of almost all ethical doctrines and religious creeds. They are all full of meaning and vitality to those who originate them, and to the direct disciples of the originators. Their meaning continues to be felt in undiminished strength, and is perhaps brought out into even fuller consciousness, so long as the struggle lasts to give the doctrine or creed an ascendancy over other creeds. At last it either prevails and becomes the general opinion, or its progress stops; it keeps possession of the ground it has gained, but ceases to spread further. When either of these results has become apparent, controversy on the subject flags, and gradually dies away. The doctrine has taken its place, if not as a received opinion, as one of the admitted sects of divisions of opinion; those who hold it have generally inherited, not adopted it; and conversion from one of these doctrines to another, being now an exceptional fact, occupies little place in the thoughts of their professors. Instead of being, as at first, constantly on the alert either to defend themselves against the world or to bring the world over to them, they have subsided into acquiescence and neither listen, when they can help it, to arguments against their creed, nor trouble dissentients (if there be such) with arguments in its favor. From this time may usually be dated the decline in the living power of the doctrine. . . .

We have hitherto considered only two possibilities: that the received opinion may be false, and some other opinion, consequently, true; or that, the received opinion being true, a conflict with the opposite error is essential to a clear apprehension and deep feeling of its truth. But there is a commoner case than either of these: when the conflicting doctrines, instead of being one true and the other false, share the truth between them, and the nonconforming opinion is needed to supply the remainder of the truth of which the received doctrine embodies only a part. Popular opinions, on subjects not palpable to sense, are often true, but seldom or never the whole truth. They are a part of the truth, sometimes a greater, sometimes a smaller part, but exaggerated, distorted, and disjointed from the truths by which they ought to be accompanied and limited. Heretical opinions, on the other hand, are generally some of these suppressed and neglected truths, bursting the bonds which kept them down, and either seeking reconciliation with the truth contained in the common opinion, or fronting it as enemies, and setting themselves up, with similar exclusiveness, as the whole truth. The latter case is hitherto the most frequent, as, in the human mind, one-sidedness has always been the rule, and many-sidedness the exception. Hence, even in revolutions of opinion, one part of the truth usually sets while another rises. Even progress, which ought to superadd, for the most part only substitutes one partial and incomplete truth for another; improvement consisting chiefly in this, that the new fragment of truth is more wanted, more adapted to the needs of the time than that which it displaces. Such being the partial character of prevailing opinions, even when resting on a true foundation, every opinion which embodies somewhat of the portion of truth which the common opinion omits ought to be considered precious, with whatever amount of error and confusion that truth may be blended. . . .

We have now recognized the necessity to the mental well-being of mankind (on which all their other well-being depends) of freedom of opinion, and freedom of the expression of opinion, on four distinct grounds, which we will now briefly recapitulate:

First, if any opinion is compelled to silence, that opinion may, for aught we can certainly know, be true. To deny this is to assume our own infallibility.

Secondly, although the silenced opinion be an error, it may, and very commonly does, contain a portion of truth; and since the general or prevailing opinion on any subject is rarely or never the whole truth, it is only by the collision of adverse opinions that the remainder of the truth has any chance of being supplied.

Thirdly, even if the received opinion be not only true, but the whole truth; unless it is suffered to be, and actually is, vigorously and earnestly contested, it will, by most of those who receive it, be held in the manner of a prejudice, with little comprehension or feeling of its rational grounds. And not only this, but fourthly, the meaning of the doctrine itself will be in danger of being lost or enfeebled, and deprived of its vital effect on the character and conduct: the dogma becoming a mere formal profession, inefficacious for good, but cumbering the ground and preventing the growth of any real and heartfelt conviction from reason or personal experience. . . .

Before quitting the subject of freedom of opinion, it is fit to take some notice of those who say that the free expression of all opinions should be permitted on condition that the manner be temperate, and do not pass the bounds of fair discussion. Much might be said on the impossibility of fixing where these supposed bounds are to be placed; for if the test be offense to those whose opinions are attacked, I think experience testifies that this offense is given whenever the attack is telling and powerful, and that every opponent who pushes them hard, and whom they find it difficult to answer, appears to them, if he shows any strong feeling on the subject, an intemperate opponent. . . . With regard to what is commonly meant by intemperate discussion, namely invective, sarcasm, personality, and the like, the denunciation of these weapons would deserve more sympathy if it were ever proposed to interdict them equally to both sides; but it is only desired to restrain the employment of them against the prevailing opinion; against the unprevailing they may not only be used without general disapproval, but will be likely to obtain for him who uses them the praise of honest zeal and righteous indignation. Yet whatever mischief arises from their use is greatest when they are employed against the comparatively defenseless; and whatever unfair advantage can be derived by any opinion from this mode of asserting it accrues almost exclusively to received opinions. . . . In general, opinions contrary to these commonly received can only obtain a hearing by studied moderation of language, and the most cautious avoidance of unnecessary offense, from which they hardly every deviate even in a slight degree without losing ground; while unmeasured vituperation employed on the side of the prevailing opinion really does deter people from professing contrary opinions, and from listening to those who profess them.

For the interest, therefore, of truth and justice, it is far more important to restrain this employment of vituperative language than the other; and, for example, if it were necessary to choose, there would be much more need to discourage offensive attacks on infidelity than on religion. It is, however, obvious that law and authority have no business restraining either, while opinion ought, in every instance, to determine its verdict by the circumstances of the individual case; condemning everyone, on whichever side of the argument he places himself, in whose mode of advocacy either want of candor, or malignity, bigotry, or intolerance of feeling manifest themselves; but not inferring these vices from the side which a person takes, though it be the contrary side of the question of our own; and giving merited honor to everyone, whatever opinion he may hold, who has calmness to see and honesty to state what his opponents and their opinions really are, exaggerating nothing to their discredit, keeping nothing back which tells or can be supposed to tell, in their favor. This is the real morality of public discussion; and if often violated, I am happy to think that there are many controversialists who to a great extent observe it, and a still greater number who conscientiously strive towards it.

OF INDIVIDUALITY, AS ONE OF THE ELEMENTS OF WELL-BEING

Such being the reasons which make it imperative that human beings should be free to form opinions, and to express their opinions without reserve; and such the baneful consequences to the intellectual, and through that to the moral nature of man, unless this liberty is either conceded, or asserted in spite of prohibition; let us next examine whether the same reasons do not require that men should be free to act upon their opinions—to carry these out in their lives, without hindrance, either physical or moral, from their fellow-men, so long as it is

at their own risk and peril. This last provision is of course indispensable. No one pretends that actions should be as free as opinions. On the contrary, even opinions lose their immunity when the circumstances in which they are expressed are such as to constitute their expression a positive instigation to some mischievous act. An opinion that corn-dealers are starvers of the poor, or that private property is robbery, ought to be unmolested when simply circulated through the press, but may justly incur punishment when delivered orally to an excited mob assembled before the house of a corn-dealer, or when handed about among the same mob in the form of a placard. Acts, of whatever kind, which without justifiable cause do harm to others, may be, and in the more important cases absolutely require to be, controlled by the unfavorable sentiments, and, when needful, by the active interference of mankind. The liberty of the individual must be thus far limited; he must not make himself a nuisance to other people. But if he refrains from molesting others in what concerns them, and merely acts according to his own inclination and judgment in things which concern himself, the same reasons which show that opinion should be free, prove also that he should be allowed, without molestation, to carry his opinions into practice at his own cost. That mankind are not infallible; that their truths, for the most part, are only half-truths; that unity of opinion, unless resulting from the fullest and freest comparison of opposite opinions, is not desirable, and diversity not an evil, but a good, until mankind are much more capable than at present of recognizing all sides of the truth, are principles applicable to men's modes of action, not less than to their opinions. As it is useful that while mankind are imperfect there should be different opinions, so it is that there should be different experiments of living; that free scope should be given to varieties of character, short of injury to others; and that the worth of different modes of life should be proved practically, when anyone thinks fit to try them. It is desirable, in short, that in things which do not primarily concern others, individuality should assert itself. Where not the person's own character, but the traditions or customs of other people are the rule of conduct, there is wanting one of the principal ingredients of human happiness, and quite the chief ingredient of individual and social progress.

In maintaining this principle, the greatest difficulty to be encountered does not lie in the appreciation of means towards an acknowledged end, but in the indifference of persons in general to the end itself. If it were felt that the free development of individuality is one of the leading essentials of well-being; that it is not only a co-ordinate element with all that is designated by the terms civilization, instruction, education, culture, but is itself a necessary part and condition of all those things; there would be no danger that liberty should be undervalued, and the adjustment of the boundaries between it and social control would present no extraordinary difficulty. But the evil is, that individual spontaneity is hardly recognized by the common modes of thinking as having any intrinsic worth, or deserving any regard on its own account. The majority, being satisfied with the ways of mankind as they now are (for it is they who make them what they are), cannot comprehend why those ways should not be good enough for everybody; and what is more, spontaneity forms no part of the ideal of the majority of moral and social reformers, but is rather looked on with jealousy, as a troublesome and perhaps rebellious obstruction to the general acceptance of what these reformers, in their own judgment, think would be best for mankind. Few persons, out of Germany, even comprehend the meaning of the doctrine which Wilhelm von Humboldt, so eminent both as a *savant* and as a politician, made the text of a treatise— that "the end of man, or that which is prescribed by the eternal or immutable dictates of reason, and not suggested by vague and transient desires, is the highest and most harmonious development of his powers to a complete and consistent whole," that, therefore, the object "towards which every human being must ceaselessly direct his efforts, and on which especially those who design to influence their fellow-men must ever keep their eyes, is the individuality of power and development;" that for this there are two requisites, "freedom, and variety of situations;" and that from the union of these arise "individual vigor and manifold diversity," which combine themselves in "originality." . . .

He who lets the world, or his own portion of it, choose his plan of life for him, has no need of any other faculty than the ape-like one of imitation. He who chooses his plan for himself, employs all his faculties. He must use observation to see, reasoning and judgments to foresee, activity to gather materials for decision, discrimination to decide, and when he has decided, firmness and self-control to hold to his deliberate decision. And these qualities he requires and exercises exactly in proportion as the part of his conduct which he determines according to his own judgment and feelings is a large one. It is possible that he might be guided in some good path, and kept out of harm's way, without any of these things. But what will be his comparative worth as a human being? It really is of importance, not only what men do, but also what manner of men they are that do it. Among the works of man which human life is rightly employed in perfecting and beautifying, the first in importance surely is man himself. Supposing it were possible to get houses built, corn grown, battles fought, causes tried, and even churches erected and prayers said, by machinery—by automatons in human form—it would be a considerable loss to exchange for these automatons even the men and women who at present inhabit the more civilized parts of the world, and who assuredly are but starved specimens of what nature can and will produce. Human nature is not a machine to be built after a model, and set to do exactly the work prescribed for it, but a tree, which requires to grow and develop itself on all sides, according to the tendency of the inward forces which make it a living thing. . . .

But society has now fairly got the better of individuality; and the danger which threatens human nature is not the excess, but the deficiency, of personal impulses and preferences. Things are vastly changed since the passions of those who were strong by station or by personal endowment were in a state of habitual rebellion against laws and ordinances, and required to be rigorously chained up to enable the persons within their reach to enjoy any particle of security. In our times, from the highest class of society down to the lowest, everyone lives as under the eye of a hostile and dreaded censorship. Not only in what concerns others, but in what concerns only themselves, the individual or the family do not ask themselves—what do I prefer? or, what would suit my character and disposition? or, what would allow the best and highest in me to have fair play, and enable it to grow and thrive? They ask themselves, what is suitable to my position? what is usually done by persons of my station and pecuniary circumstances? or (worse still) what is usually done by persons of a station and circumstances superior to mine? I do not mean that they choose what is customary in preference to what suits their own inclination. It does not occur to them to have any inclination, except for what is customary. Thus the mind itself is bowed to the yoke: even in what people do for pleasure, conformity is the first thing thought of; they like crowds; they exercise choice only among things commonly done: peculiarity of taste, eccentricity of conduct, are shunned equally with crimes: until by dint of not following their own nature they have no nature to follow: their human capacities are withered and starved: they become incapable of any strong wishes or native pleasures, and are generally without either opinions or feelings of home growth, or properly their own. Now is this, or is it not, the desirable condition of human nature? . . .

OF THE LIMITS TO THE AUTHORITY OF SOCIETY OVER THE INDIVIDUAL

What, then, is the rightful limit to the sovereignty of the individual over himself? Where does the authority of society begin? How much of human life should be assigned to individuality, and how much to society?

Each will receive its proper share, if each has that which more particularly concerns it. To individuality should belong the part of life in which it is chiefly the individual that is interested; to society, the part which chiefly interests society.

Though society is not founded on a contract, and though no good purpose is answered by inventing a contract in order to deduce social obligations from it, everyone who receives the protection of society owes a return for the benefit, and the fact of living in society renders it indispensable that each should be bound to observe a certain line of conduct towards the rest. This conduct consists, *first,* in not injuring the interests of one another; or rather certain interests, which either by express legal provision or by tacit understanding, ought to be considered as rights; and *secondly,* in each person's bearing his share (to be fixed on some equitable principle) of the labors and sacrifices incurred for defending the society or its members from injury and molestation. These conditions society is justified in enforcing, at all costs to those who endeavor to withhold fulfillment. Nor is this all that society may do. The acts of an individual may be hurtful to others, or wanting in due consideration for their welfare, without going to the length of violating any of their constituted rights. The offender may then be justly punished by opinion, though not by law. As soon as any part of a person's conduct affects prejudicially the interests of others, society has jurisdiction over it, and the question whether the general welfare will or will not be promoted by interfering with it, becomes open to discussion. But there is no room for entertaining any such question when a person's conduct affects the interests of no persons besides himself, or need not affect them unless they like (all the persons concerned being of full age, and the ordinary amount of understanding). In all such cases, there should be perfect freedom, legal and social, to do the action and stand the consequences.

It would be a great misunderstanding of this doctrine to suppose that it is one of selfish indifference, which pretends that human beings have no business with each other's conduct in life, and that they should not concern themselves about the well-doing or well-being of one another, unless their own interest is involved. Instead of any diminution, there is need of a great increase of disinterested exertion to promote the good of others. But disinterested benevolence can find other instruments to persuade people to their good than whips and scourges, either of the literal or the metaphorical sort. I am the last person to undervalue the self-regarding virtues: they are only second in importance, if even second, to the social. It is equally the business of education to cultivate both. But even education works by conviction and persuasion as well as by compulsion, and it is by the former only that, when the period of education is passed, the self-regarding virtues should be inculcated. Human beings owe to each other help to distinguish the better from the worse, and encouragement to choose the former and avoid the latter. They should be forever stimulating each other to increased exercise of their higher faculties, and increased direction of their feelings and aims towards wise instead of foolish, elevating instead of degrading, objects and contemplations. But neither one person, nor any number of persons, is warranted in saying to another human creature of ripe years, that he shall not do with his life for his own benefit what he chooses to do with it. He is the person most interested in his own well-being: the interest which any other person, except in cases of strong personal attachment, can have in it, is trifling, compared with that which he himself has; the interest which society has in him individually (except as to conduct to others) is fractional, and altogether indirect; while with respect to his own feelings and circumstances, the most ordinary man or woman has means of knowledge immeasurably surpassing those that can be possessed by anyone else. The interference of society to overrule his judgment and purposes in what only regards himself must be grounded on general presumptions; which may be altogether wrong, and even if right, are as likely as not to be misapplied to individual cases, by persons no better acquainted with the circumstances of such cases than those are who look at them merely from without. In this department, therefore, of human affairs, individuality has its proper field of action. In the conduct of human beings towards one another it is necessary that general rules should for the most part be observed, in order that people may know what they have to expect; but in each person's own concerns his individual spontaneity is entitled to free exercise. Considerations to aid his judgment, exhortations to strengthen his will, may be offered to him, even obtruded on him, by others: but he himself is the final judge. All errors which he is likely to commit against advice and warning are far outweighed by the evil of allowing others to constrain him to what they deem his good. . . .

Though doing no wrong to anyone, a person may so act as to compel us to judge him, and feel to him, as a fool, or as a being of an inferior order; and since this judgment and feeling are a fact which he would prefer to avoid, it is doing him a service to warn him of it beforehand, as of any other disagreeable consequence to which he exposes himself. . . . We have a right, also, in various ways, to act upon our unfavorable opinion of anyone, not to the oppression of his individuality, but in the exercise of ours. We are not bound, for example, to seek his society; we have a right to avoid it (though not to parade the avoidance), for we have a right to choose the society most acceptable to us. We have a right, and it may be our duty, to caution others against him, if we think his example or conversation likely to have a pernicious effect on those with whom he associates. We may give others a preference over him in optional good offices, except those which tend to his improvement. In these various modes a person may suffer very severe penalties at the hands of others for faults which directly concern only himself; but he suffers these penalties only in so far as they are the natural and, as it were, the spontaneous consequences of the faults themselves, not because they are purposely inflicted on him for the sake of punishment. . . .

What I contend for is, that the inconveniences which are strictly inseparable from the unfavorable judgment of others, are the only ones to which a person should ever be subjected for that portion of his conduct and character which concerns his own good, but which does not affect the interest of others in their relations with him. Acts injurious to others require a totally different treatment. Encroachment on their rights; infliction on them of any loss or damage not justified by his own rights; falsehood or duplicity in dealing with them; unfair or ungenerous use of advantages over them; even selfish abstinence from defending them against injury—these are fit objects of moral reprobation, and, in grave cases, of moral retribution and punishment. And not only these acts, but the dispositions which lead to them, are properly immoral, and fit subjects of disapprobation which may rise to abhorrence. . . .

The distinction here pointed out between the part of a person's life which concerns only himself, and that which concerns others, many persons will refuse to admit. How (it may be asked) can any part of the conduct of a member of society be a matter of indifference to the other members? No person is an entirely isolated being; it is impossible for a person to do anything seriously or permanently hurtful to himself, without mischief reaching at least to his near connections, and often far beyond them. If he injures his property, he does harm to those who directly or indirectly derived support from it, and usually diminishes, by a greater

or less amount, the general resources of the community. If he deteriorates his bodily or mental faculties, he not only brings evil upon all who depended on him for any portion of their happiness, but disqualifies himself for rendering the services which he owes to his fellow-creatures generally; perhaps becomes a burden on their affection or benevolence; and if such conduct were very frequent, hardly an offense that is committed would detract more from the general sum of good. Finally, if by his vices or follies a person does no direct harm to others, he is nevertheless (it may be said) injurious by his example; and ought to be compelled to control himself, for the sake of those whom the sight or knowledge of his conduct might corrupt or mislead.

And even (it will be added) if the consequences of misconduct could be confined to the vicious or thoughtless individual, ought society to abandon to their own guidance those who are manifestly unfit for it? If protection against themselves is confessedly due to children and persons under age, is not society equally bound to afford it to persons of mature years who are equally incapable of self-government? If gambling, or drunkenness, or incontinence, or idleness, or uncleanliness, are as injurious to happiness, and as great a hindrance to improvement, as many or most of the acts prohibited by law, why (it may be asked) should not law, so far as is consistent with practicability and social convenience, endeavor to repress these also? And as a supplement to the unavoidable imperfections of law, ought not opinion at least to organize a powerful police against these vices, and visit rigidly with social penalties those who are known to practice them? There is no question here (it may be said) about restricting individuality, or impeding the trial of new and original experiments in living. The only things it is sought to prevent are things which have been tried and condemned from the beginning of the world until now; things which experience has shown not to be useful or suitable to any person's individuality. There must be some length of time and amount of experience after which a moral or prudential truth may be regarded as established: and it is merely desired to prevent generation after generation from falling over the same precipice which has been fatal to their predecessors.

I fully admit that the mischief which a person does to himself may seriously affect, both through their sympathies and their interests, those nearly connected with him and, in a minor degree, society at large. When, by conduct of this sort, a person is led to violate a distinct and assignable obligation to any other person or persons, the case is taken out of the self-regarding class and becomes amenable to moral disapprobation in the proper sense of the term. If, for example, a man, through intemperance or extravagance, becomes unable to pay his debts, or, having undertaken the moral responsibility of a family, becomes from the same cause incapable of supporting or educating them, he is deservedly reprobated, and might be justly punished; but it is for the breach of duty to his family or creditors, not for the extravagance. If the resources which ought to have been devoted to them, had been diverted from them for the most prudent investment, the moral culpability would have been the same. George Barnwell murdered his uncle to get money for his mistress, but if he had done it to set himself up in business he would equally have been hanged. Again, in the frequent case of a man who causes grief to his family by addiction to bad habits, he deserves reproach for his unkindness or ingratitude; but so he may for cultivating habits not in themselves vicious, if they are painful to those with whom he passes his life, or who from personal ties are dependent on him for their comfort. Whoever fails in the consideration generally due to the interests and feelings of others, not being compelled by some more imperative duty, or justified by allowable self-preference, is a subject of moral disapprobation for that failure, but not for the cause of it, nor for the errors, merely personal to himself, which may have remotely led to it. In like manner, when a person disables himself, by conduct purely self-regarding, from the performance of some definite duty incumbent on him to the public, he is guilty of a social offense. No person ought to be punished simply for being drunk; but a soldier or policeman should be punished for being drunk on duty. Whenever, in short, there is a definite damage, or a definite risk of damage, either to an individual or to the public, the case is taken out of the province of liberty and placed in that of morality or law.

But with regard to the merely contingent or, as it may be called, constructive injury which a person causes to society by conduct which neither violates any specific duty to the public, nor occasions perceptible hurt to any assignable individual except himself, the inconvenience is one which society can afford to bear, for the sake of the greater good of human freedom. If grown persons are to be punished for not taking proper care of themselves, I would rather it were for their own sake than under pretense of preventing them from impairing their capacity or rendering to society benefits which society does not pretend it has a right to exact. But I cannot consent to argue the point as if society had no means of bringing its weaker members up to its ordinary standard of rational conduct, except waiting till they do something irrational, and then punishing them, legally or morally, for it. Society has had absolute power over them during all the early portion of their existence; it has had the whole period of childhood and nonage in which to try whether it could make them capable of rational conduct in life. The existing generation is master both of the training and the entire circumstances of the generation to come; it cannot indeed make them perfectly wise and good, because it is itself so lamentably deficient in goodness and wisdom; and its best efforts are not always, in individual cases, its most successful ones; but it is perfectly well able to make the rising generation, as a whole, as good as, and a little better than, itself. If society lets any considerable number of its members grow up mere children, incapable of being acted on by rational consideration of distant motives, society has itself to blame for the consequences. Armed not only with all the powers of education, but with the ascendency which the authority of a received opinion always exercises over the minds who are least fitted to judge for themselves, and aided by the *natural* penalties which cannot be prevented from falling on those who incur the distaste or the contempt of those who know them—let not society pretend that it needs, besides all this, the power to issue commands and enforce obedience in the personal concerns of individuals in which, on all principles of justice and policy, the decision ought to rest with those who are to abide the consequences. Nor is there anything which tends more to discredit and frustrate the better means of influencing conduct than a resort to the worse. If there be among those whom it is attempted to coerce into prudence or temperance any of the material of which vigorous and independent characters are made, they will infallibly rebel against the yoke. No such person will ever feel that others have a right to control him in his concerns, such as they have to prevent him from injuring them in theirs; and it easily comes to be considered a mark of spirit and courage to fly in the face of such usurped authority and do with ostentation the exact opposite of what it enjoins, as in the fashion of grossness which succeeded, in the time of Charles II, to the fanatical moral intolerance of the Puritans. With respect to what is said of the necessity of protecting society from the bad example set to others by the vicious or the self-indulgent, it is true that bad example may have a pernicious effect, especially the example of doing wrong to others with impunity to the wrongdoer. But we are now speaking of conduct which, while it does no wrong to others, is supposed to do great harm to the agent himself; and I do not see how those who believe this can think otherwise than that the example, on the whole, must be more salutary than hurtful, since, if it displays the misconduct, it displays also the painful or degrading consequences which, if the conduct is justly censured, must be sup-

posed to be in all or most cases attendant on it.

But the strongest of all the arguments against the interference of the public with purely personal conduct is that, when it does interfere, the odds are that it interferes wrongly and in the wrong place. On questions of social morality, of duty to others, the opinion of the public, that is, of an overruling majority, though often wrong, is likely to be still oftener right, because on such questions they are only required to judge of their own interests, of the manner in which some mode of conduct, if allowed to be practiced, would affect themselves. But the opinion of a similar majority, imposed as a law on the minority, on questions of self-regarding conduct is quite as likely to be wrong as right, for in these cases public opinion means, at the best, some people's opinion of what is good or bad for other people, while very often it does not even mean that—the public, with the most perfect indifference, passing over the pleasure or convenience of those whose conduct they censure and considering only their own preference. There are many who consider as an injury to themselves any conduct which they have a distaste for, and resent it as an outrage to their feelings; as a religious bigot, when charged with disregarding the religious feelings of others, has been known to retort that they disregard his feelings by persisting in their abominable worship or creed. But there is no parity between the feeling of a person for his own opinion and the feeling of another who is offended at his holding it, no more than between the desire of a thief to take a purse and the desire of the right owner to keep it. And a person's taste is as much his own peculiar concern as his opinion or his purse. It is easy for anyone to imagine an ideal public which leaves the freedom and choice of individuals in all uncertain matters undisturbed and only requires them to abstain from modes of conduct which universal experience has condemned. But where has there been seen a public which set any such limit to its censorship? Or when does the public trouble itself about universal experience? In its interferences with personal conduct it is seldom thinking of anything but the enormity of acting or feeling differently from itself. . . .

APPLICATIONS

The principles asserted in these pages must be more generally admitted as the basis for discussion of details before a consistent application of them to all the various departments of government and morals can be attempted with any prospect of advantage. The few observations I propose to make on questions of detail are designed to illustrate the principles rather than to follow them out to their consequences. I offer not so much applications as specimens of application, which may serve to bring into greater clearness the meaning and limits of the two maxims which together form the entire doctrine of this essay, and to assist the judgment in holding the balance between them in the cases where it appears doubtful which of them is applicable to the case.

The maxims are, first, that the individual is not accountable to society for his actions in so far as these concern the interests of no person but himself. Advice, instruction, persuasion, and avoidance by other people, if thought necessary by them for their own good, are the only measures by which society can justifiably express its dislike or disapprobation of his conduct. Secondly, that for such actions as are prejudicial to the interests of others, the individual is accountable and may be subjected either to social or to legal punishment if society is of opinion that the one or the other is requisite for its protection.

In the first place, it must by no means be supposed, because damage, or probability of damage, to the interests of others can alone justify the interference of society, that therefore it always does justify such interference. In many cases an individual, in pursuing a legitimate object, necessarily and therefore legitimately causes pain or loss to others, or intercepts a good which they had

a reasonable hope of obtaining. Such oppositions of interest between individuals often arise from bad social institutions, but are unavoidable while those institutions last; and some would be unavoidable under any institutions. Whoever succeeds in an overcrowded profession or in a competitive examination, whoever is preferred to another in any contest for an object which both desire, reaps benefit from the loss of others, from their wasted exertion and their disappointment. But it is, by common admission, better for the general interest of mankind that persons should pursue their objects undeterred by this sort of consequences. In other words, society admits no right, either legal or moral, in the disappointed competitors to immunity from this kind of suffering, and feels called on to interfere only when means of success have been employed which it is contrary to the general interest to permit—namely, fraud or treachery, and force.

Again, trade is a social act. Whoever undertakes to sell any description of goods to the public does what affects the interest of other persons, and of society in general; and thus his conduct, in principle, comes within the jurisdiction of society; accordingly, it was once held to be the duty of governments, in all cases which were considered of importance, to fix prices and regulate the process of manufacture. But it is now recognized, though not till after a long struggle, that both the cheapness and the good quality of commodities are most effectually provided for by leaving the producers and sellers perfectly free, under the sole check of equal freedom to the buyers for supplying themselves elsewhere. This is the so-called doctrine of "free trade," which rests on grounds different from, though equally solid with, the principle of individual liberty asserted in this essay. Restrictions on trade, or on production for purposes of trade, are indeed restraints; and all restraint, *qua* restraint, is an evil; but the restraints in question affect only that part of conduct which society is competent to restrain, and are wrong solely because they do not really produce the results which it is desired to produce by them. As the principle of individual liberty is not involved in the doctrine of free trade, so neither is it in most of the questions which arise respecting the limits of that doctrine, as, for example, what amount of public control is admissible for the prevention of fraud by adulteration; how far sanitary precautions, or arrangements to protect workpeople employed in dangerous occupations, should be enforced on employers. Such questions involve considerations of liberty only in so far as leaving people to themselves is always better, *caeteris paribus*, than controlling them; but that they may be legitimately controlled for these ends is in principle undeniable. On the other hand, there are questions relating to interference with trade which are essentially questions of liberty, such as the Maine Law*, already touched upon; the prohibition of the importation of opium into China; the restriction of the sale of poisons—all cases, in short, where the object of the interference is to make it impossible or difficult to obtain a particular commodity. These interferences are objectionable, not as infringements on the liberty of the producer or seller, but on that of the buyer. . . .

It is a proper office of public authority to guard against accidents. If either a public officer or anyone else saw a person attempting to cross a bridge which had been ascertained to be unsafe, and there were no time to warn him of his danger, they might seize him and turn him back, without any real infringement of his liberty; for liberty consists in doing what one desires, and he does not desire to fall into the river. Nevertheless, when there is not a certainly, but only a danger of mischief, no one but the person himself can judge of the sufficiency of the motive which may prompt him to incur the risk; in this case, therefore (unless he is a child, or delirious, or in some state of excitement or absorption incompatible with the

full use of the reflecting faculty), he ought, I conceive, to be only warned of the danger; not forcibly prevented from exposing himself to it. Similar considerations, applied to such a question as the sale of poisons, may enable us to decide which among the possible modes of regulation are or are not contrary to principle. Such a precaution, for example, as that of labeling the drug with some word expressive of its dangerous character may be enforced without violation of liberty: the buyer cannot wish not to know that the thing he possesses has poisonous qualities. But to require in all cases the certificate of a medical practitioner would make it sometimes impossible, always expensive, to obtain the article for legitimate uses. . . .

A further question is whether the State, while it permits, should nevertheless indirectly discourage conduct which it deems contrary to the best interests of the agent; whether, for example, it should take measures to render the means of drunkenness more costly, or add to the difficulty of procuring them by limiting the number of the places of sale. On this, as on most other practical questions, many distinctions require to be made. To tax stimulants for the sole purpose of making them more difficult to be obtained is a measure differing only in degree from their entire prohibition, and would be justifiable only if that were justifiable. Every increase of cost is a prohibition to those whose means do not come up to the augmented price; and to those who do, it is a penalty laid on them for gratifying a particular taste. Their choice of pleasures and their mode of expending their income, after satisfying their legal and moral obligations to the State and to individuals, are their own concern and must rest with their own judgment. These considerations may seem at first sight to condemn the selection of stimulants as special subjects of taxation for purposes of revenue. But it must be remembered that taxation for fiscal purposes is absolutely inevitable; that in most countries it is necessary that a considerable part of that taxation should be indirect; that the

---

* Mill is referring to laws that prohibit the sale of alcohol—eds.

State, therefore, cannot help imposing penalties, which to some persons may be prohibitory, on the use of some articles of consumption. It is hence the duty of the State to consider, in the imposition of taxes, what commodities the consumers can best spare; and *a fortiori,* to select in preference those of which it deems the use, beyond a very moderate quantity, to be positively injurious. Taxation, therefore, of stimulants up to the point which produces the largest amount of revenue (supposing that the State needs all the revenue which it yields) is not only admissible, but to be approved of. . . .

It was pointed out in an early part of this essay, that the liberty of the individual, in things wherein the individual is alone concerned, implies a corresponding liberty in any number of individuals to regulate by mutual agreement such things as regard them jointly, and regard no persons but themselves. This question presents no difficulty, so long as the will of all the persons implicated remains unaltered; but since that will may change, it is often necessary, even in things in which they alone are concerned that they should enter into engagements with one another; and when they do, it is fit, as a general rule, that those engagements should be kept. Yet, in the laws, probably, of every country, this general rule has some exceptions. Not only persons are not held to engagements which violate the rights of third parties, but it is sometimes considered a sufficient reason for releasing them from an engagement, that it is injurious to themselves. In this and most other civilized countries, for example, an engagement by which a person should sell himself, or allow himself to be sold, as a slave, would be null and void; neither enforced by law nor by opinion. The ground for thus limiting his power of voluntarily disposing of his own lot in life, is apparent, and is very clearly seen in this extreme case. The reason for not interfering unless for the sake of others, with a person's voluntary acts, is consideration for his liberty. His voluntary choice is evidence that what he so chooses is desirable, or at least endurable, to him, and his good is on the whole best provided for by allowing him to take his own means of pursuing it. But by selling himself for a slave, he abdicates his liberty; he foregoes any future use of it beyond that single act. He therefore defeats, in his own case, the very purpose which is the justification of allowing him to dispose of himself. He is no longer free; but is thenceforth in a position which has no longer the presumption in its favor, that would be afforded by his voluntarily remaining in it. The principle of freedom cannot require that he should be free not to be free. It is not freedom to be allowed to alienate his freedom. These reasons, the force of which is so conspicuous in this peculiar case, are evidently of far wider application; yet a limit is everywhere set to them by the necessities of life, which continually require, not indeed that we should resign our freedom, but that we should consent to this and the other limitation of it. The principle, however, which demands uncontrolled freedom of action in all that concerns only the agents themselves, requires that those who have become bound to one another, in things which concern no third party, should be able to release one another from the engagement: and even without such voluntary release there are perhaps no contracts or engagements, except those that relate to money or money's worth, of which one can venture to say that there ought to be no liberty whatever of retraction.

Two Concepts of Liberty

Isaiah Berlin

In this famous essay, Isaiah Berlin distinguishes between two different concepts of freedom—negative and positive—that run through the history of political thought. Negative freedom is the freedom to do what one wants, unobstructed by others. This is the notion of freedom that Mill employed in the previous selection. Hobbes, Locke, Jefferson, and many other writers use the word "freedom" in this same sense although they differ in the amount of freedom they are prepared to grant to the individual. After bringing out some of the distinctive aspects of Mill's position, Berlin turns to a discussion of positive freedom, which, as he sees it, essentially consists in being one's own master: I am free to the extent that my life is the product of conscious and rational choice rather than subject to external forces or irrational passions. Conceptions of positive freedom typically presuppose a dualistic theory of the person, Berlin argues, in which self-mastery involves controlling our lower selves. For this reason, Berlin is wary of the notion of positive freedom, contending that it can too easily be used to justify ignoring people's actual wishes on behalf of their "real" selves.

Sir Isaiah Berlin, President of Wolfson College, Oxford, from 1966 to 1975 and Professor of Social and Political Theory at Oxford from 1957 to 1967, is a Fellow of All Souls College, Oxford. His most important essays are collected in his four-volume *Selected Works*, edited by Henry Hardy. He is also the author of *Karl Marx* and *Four Essays on Liberty*, among other works.

I

To coerce a man is to deprive him of freedom—freedom from what? Almost every moralist in human history has praised freedom. Like happiness and goodness, like nature and reality, the meaning of this term is so porous that there is little interpretation that it seems able to resist. I do not propose to discuss either the history or the more than two hundred senses of this protean word, recorded by historians of ideas. I propose to examine no more than two of these senses—but those central ones, with a great deal of human history behind them, and, I dare say, still to come. The first of these political senses of freedom or liberty (I shall use both words to mean the same), which (following much precedent) I shall call the "negative" sense, is involved in the answer to the question "What is the area within which the subject—a person or group of persons—is or should be left to do or be what he is able to do or be, without interference by other persons?" The second, which I shall call the positive sense, is involved in the answer to the question "What, or who, is the source of control or interference, that can determine someone to do, or be, one thing rather than another?" The two questions are clearly different, even though the answers to them may overlap.

The Notion of "Negative" Freedom

I am normally said to be free to the degree to which no human being interferes with my activity. Political liberty in this sense is simply the area within which a man can act unobstructed by others. If I am prevented by other persons from doing what I could otherwise do, I am to that degree unfree; and if this area is contracted by other men beyond a certain minimum, I can be described as being coerced, or, it may be, enslaved. Coercion is not, however, a term that covers every form of inability. If I say that I am unable to jump more than 10 feet in the air, or cannot read because I am blind, or cannot understand the darker pages of Hegel, it would be eccentric to say that I am to that degree enslaved or coerced. Coercion implies the deliberate interference of other human beings within the area in which I could otherwise act. You lack political liberty or freedom only if you are prevented from attaining a goal by human beings.[1] Mere incapacity to attain a goal is not lack of political freedom.[2] This is brought out by the use of such modern expressions as "economic freedom" and its counterpart, "economic slavery". It is argued, very plausibly, that if a man is too poor to afford something on which there is no legal ban—a loaf of bread, a journey round the world, recourse to the law courts—he is as little free to have it as he would be if it were forbidden him by law. If my poverty were a kind of disease, which prevented me from buying bread or paying for the journey round the world, or getting my case heard, as lameness prevents me from running, this inability would not naturally be described as a lack of freedom, least of all political freedom. It is only because I believe that my inability to get a given thing is due to the fact that other human beings have made arrangements whereby I am, whereas others are not, prevented from having enough money with which to pay for it, that I think myself a victim of coercion or slavery. In other words, this use of the term depends on a particular social and economic theory about the causes of my poverty or weakness. If my lack of material means is due to my lack of mental or physical capacity, then I begin to speak of being deprived of freedom (and not simply of poverty) only if I accept the theory.[3] If, in addition, I believe that I am being kept in want by a specific arrangement which I consider unjust or unfair, I speak of economic slavery or oppression. "The nature of things does not madden us, only ill will does," said Rousseau. The criterion of oppression is the part that I believe to be played by other human beings, directly or indirectly, with or without the intention of doing so, in frustrating my wishes. By being free in this sense I mean not being interfered with by others. The wider the area of non-interference the wider my freedom.

This is what the classical English political philosophers meant when they used this

---

[1] I do not, of course, mean to imply the truth of the converse.

[2] Helvétius made this point very clearly: "The free man is the man who is not in irons, nor imprisoned in a gaol, nor terrorized like a slave by the fear of punishment . . . it is not lack of freedom not to fly like an eagle or swim like a whale."

[3] The Marxist conception of social laws is, of course, the best-known version of this theory, but it forms a large element in some Christian and utilitarian, and all socialist, doctrines.

word.[4] They disagreed about how wide the area could or should be. They supposed that it could not, as things were, be unlimited, because if it were, it would entail a state in which all men could boundlessly interfere with all other men; and this kind of "natural" freedom would lead to social chaos in which men's minimum needs would not be satisfied; or else the liberties of the weak would be suppressed by the strong. Because they perceived that human purposes and activities do not automatically harmonize with one another; and, because (whatever their official doctrines) they put high value on other goals, such as justice, or happiness, or culture, or security, or varying degrees of equality, they were prepared to curtail freedom in the interests of other values and, indeed, of freedom itself. For, without this, it was impossible to create the kind of association that they thought desirable. Consequently, it is assumed by these thinkers that the area of men's free action must be limited by law. But equally it is assumed, especially by such libertarians as Locke and Mill in England, and Constant and Tocqueville in France, that there ought to exist a certain minimum area of personal freedom which must on no account be violated; for if it is overstepped, the individual will find himself in an area too narrow for even that minimum development of his natural faculties which alone makes it possible to pursue, and even to conceive, the various ends which men hold good or right or sacred. It follows that a frontier must be drawn between the area of private life and that of public authority. Where it is to be drawn is a matter of argument, indeed of haggling. Men are largely interdependent, and no man's activity is so completely private as never to obstruct the lives of others in any way. . . .

Philosophers with an optimistic view of human nature, and a belief in the possibility of harmonizing human interests, such as Locke or Adam Smith and, in some moods, Mill, believed that social harmony and progress were compatible with reserving a large area for private life over which neither the state nor any other authority must be allowed to trespass. Hobbes, and those who agreed with him, especially conservative or reactionary thinkers, argued that if men were to be prevented from destroying one another, and making social life a jungle or a wilderness, greater safeguards must be instituted to keep them in their places, and wished correspondingly to increase the area of centralized control, and decrease that of the individual. But both sides agreed that some portion of human existence must remain independent of the sphere of social control. To invade that preserve, however small, would be despotism. The most eloquent of all defenders of freedom and privacy, Benjamin Constant, who had not forgotten the Jacobin dictatorship, declared that at the very least the liberty of religion, opinion, expression, property, must be guaranteed against arbitrary invasion. Jefferson, Burke, Paine, Mill, compiled different catalogues of individual liberties, but the argument for keeping authority at bay is always substantially the same. We must preserve a minimum area of personal freedom if we are not to "degrade or deny our nature." We cannot remain absolutely free, and must give up some of our liberty to preserve the rest. But total self-surrender is self-defeating. What then must the minimum be? That which a man cannot give up without offending against the essence of his human nature. What is this essence? What are the standards which it entails? This has been, and perhaps always will be, a matter of infinite debate. But whatever the principle in terms of which the area of non-interference is to be drawn, whether it is that of natural law or natural rights, or of utility or the pronouncements of a categorical imperative, or the sanctity of the social contract, or any other concept with which men have sought to clarify and justify their convictions, liberty in this sense means liber-

---

[4] "A free man", said Hobbes, "is he that . . . is not hindered to do what he hath the will to do." Law is always a "fetter," even if it protects you from being bound in chains that are heavier than those of the law, say, arbitrary despotism or chaos. Bentham says much the same.

ty *from;* absence of interference beyond the shifting, but always recognizable, frontier. "The only freedom which deserves the name is that of pursuing our own good in our own way," said the most celebrated of its champions. If this is so, is compulsion ever justified? Mill had no doubt that it was. Since justice demands that all individuals be entitled to a minimum of freedom, all other individuals were of necessity to be restrained, if need be by force, from depriving anyone of it. Indeed, the whole function of law was the prevention of just such collisions: the state was reduced to what Lassalle contemptuously described as the functions of a night-watchman or traffic policeman.

What made the protection of individual liberty so sacred to Mill? In his famous essay he declares that unless men are left to live as they wish "in the path which merely concerns themselves," civilization cannot advance; the truth will not, for lack of a free market in ideas, come to light; there will be no scope for spontaneity, originality, genius, for mental energy, for moral courage. Society will be crushed by the weight of "collective mediocrity." Whatever is rich and diversified will be crushed by the weight of custom, by men's constant tendency to conformity, which breeds only "withered capacities," "pinched and hidebound," "cramped and warped" human beings. "Pagan self-assertion is as worthy as Christian self-denial." "All the errors which a man is likely to commit against advice and warning are far outweighed by the evil of allowing others to constrain him to what they deem is good." The defence of liberty consists in the "negative" goal of warding off interference. To threaten a man with persecution unless he submits to a life in which he exercises no choices of his goals; to block before him every door but one, no matter how noble the prospect upon which it opens, or how benevolent the motives of those who arrange this, is to sin against the truth that he is a man, a being with a life of his own to live. This is liberty as it has been conceived by liberals in the modern world from the days of Erasmus (some would say of Occam)

to our own. Every plea for civil liberties and individual rights, every protest against exploitation and humiliation, against the encroachment of public authority, or the mass hypnosis of custom or organized propaganda, springs from this individualistic, and much disputed, conception of man.

Three facts about this position may be noted. In the first place Mill confuses two distinct notions. One is that all coercion is, in so far as it frustrates human desires, bad as such, although it may have to be applied to prevent other, greater evils; while non-interference, which is the opposite of coercion, is good as such, although it is not the only good. This is the negative conception of liberty in its classical form. The other is that men should seek to discover the truth or to develop a certain type of character of which Mill approved—fearless, original, imaginative, independent, non-conforming to the point of eccentricity, and so on—and that truth can be found, and such character can be bred, only in conditions of freedom. Both these are liberal views, but they are not identical, and the connexion between them is, at best, empirical. No one would argue that truth or freedom of self-expression could flourish where dogma crushes all thought. But the evidence of history tends to show (as, indeed, was argued by James Stephen in his formidable attack on Mill in his *Liberty, Equality, Fraternity*) that integrity, love of truth and fiery individualism grow at least as often in severely disciplined communities, among, for example, the puritan Calvinists of Scotland or New England, or under military discipline, as in more tolerant or indifferent societies; and if this is so Mill's argument for liberty as a necessary condition for the growth of human genius falls to the ground. If his two goals proved incompatible, Mill would be faced with a cruel dilemma, quite apart from the further difficulties created by the inconsistency of his doctrines with strict utilitarianism, even in his own humane version of it.[5]

---

[5] This is but another illustration of the natural tendency of all but a very few thinkers to believe that all

In the second place, the doctrine is comparatively modern. There seems to be scarcely any discussion of individual liberty as a conscious political ideal (as opposed to its actual existence) in the ancient world. Condorcet has already remarked that the notion of individual rights is absent from the legal conceptions of the Romans and Greeks; this seems to hold equally of the Jewish, Chinese, and all other ancient civilizations that have since come to light. The domination of this idea has been the exception rather than the rule, even in the recent history of the West. Nor has liberty in this sense often formed a rallying cry for the great masses of mankind. The desire not to be impinged upon, to be left to oneself, has been a mark of high civilization both on the part of individuals and communities. The sense of privacy itself, of the area of personal relationships is something sacred in its own right, derives from a conception of freedom which, for all its religious roots, is scarcely older, in its developed state, than the Renaissance or the Reformation.[6] Yet its decline would mark the death of a civilization, of an entire moral outlook.

The third characteristic of this notion of liberty is of greater importance. It is that liberty in this sense is not incompatible with some kinds of autocracy, or at any rate with the absence of self-government. Liberty in this sense is principally concerned with the area of control, not with its source. Just as a democracy may, in fact, deprive the individual citizen of a great many liberties which he might have in some other form of society, so it is perfectly conceivable that a liberal-minded despot would allow his subjects a large measure of personal freedom. The despot who leaves his subjects a wide area of liberty may be unjust, or encourage the wildest inequalities, care little for order, or virtue, or knowledge; but provided he does not curb their liberty, or at least curbs it less than many other régimes, he meets with Mill's specification.[7] Freedom in this sense is not, at any rate logically, connected with democracy or self-government. Self-government may, on the whole, provide a better guarantee of the preservation of civil liberties than other régimes, and has been defended as such by libertarians. But there is no necessary connexion between individual liberty and democratic rule. The answer to the question "Who governs me?" is logically distinct from the question "How far does government interfere with me?" It is in this difference that the great contrast between the concepts of negative and positive liberty, in the end, consists.[8] For the "positive" sense

---

[7] Indeed, it is arguable that in the Prussia of Frederick the Great or in the Austria of Josef II, men of imagination, originality, and creative genius, and, indeed, minorities of all kinds, were less persecuted and felt the pressure, both of institutions and custom, less heavy upon them than in many an earlier or later democracy.

[8] "Negative liberty" is something the extent of which, in a given case, it is difficult to estimate. It might, prima facie, seem to depend simply on the power to choose between at any rate two alternatives. Nevertheless, not all choices are equally free, or free at all. If in a totalitarian state I betray my friend under threat of torture, perhaps even if I act from fear of losing my job, I can reasonably say that I did not act freely. Nevertheless, I did, of course, make a choice, and could, at any rate in theory, have chosen to be killed or tortured or imprisoned. The mere existence of alternatives is not, therefore, enough to make my action free (although it may be voluntary) in the normal sense of the word. The extent of my freedom seems to depend on (a) how many possibilities are open to me (although the method of counting these can never be more than impressionistic. Possibilities of action are not discrete entities like apples, which can be exhaustively enumerated); (b) how easy or difficult each of these possibilities is to actualize; (c) how important in my plan of life, given my character and circumstances, these possibilities are when compared with each other; (d) how far they are closed and opened by deliberate human acts; (e) what value not merely the agent, but the general sentiment of the society in which he lives, puts on the

---

the things they hold good must be intimately connected, or at least compatible, with one another. The history of thought, like the history of nations, is strewn with examples of inconsistent, or at least disparate, elements artificially yoked together in a despotic system, or held together by the danger of some common enemy. In due course the danger passes, and conflicts between the allies arise, which often disrupt the system, sometimes to the great benefit of mankind.

[6] Christian (and Jewish or Moslem) belief in the absolute authority of divine or natural laws, or in the equality of all men in the sight of God, is very different from belief in freedom to live as one prefers.

of liberty comes to light if we try to answer the question, not "What am I free to do or be?", but "By whom am I ruled?" or "Who is to say what I am, and what I am not, to be or do?" The connexion between democracy and individual liberty is a good deal more tenuous than it seemed to many advocates of both. The desire to be governed by myself, or at any rate to participate in the process by which my life is to be controlled, may be as deep a wish as that of a free area for action, and perhaps historically older. But it is not a desire for the same thing. So different is it, indeed, as to have led in the end to the great clash of ideologies that dominates our world. For it is this—the 'positive' conception of liberty: not freedom from, but freedom to—which the adherents of the 'negative' notion represent as being, at times, not better than a specious disguise for brutal tyranny.

II

The Notion of "Positive" Freedom

The "positive" sense of the word "liberty" derives from the wish on the part of the individual to be his own master. I wish my

---

various possibilities. All these magnitudes must be "integrated", and a conclusion, necessarily never precise, or indisputable, drawn from this process. It may well be that there are many incommensurable degrees of freedom, and that they cannot be drawn up on a single scale of magnitude, however conceived. Moreover, in the case of societies, we are faced by such (logically absurd) questions as "Would arrangement X increase the liberty of Mr. A more than it would that of Messrs. B, C, and D between them, added together?" The same difficulties arise in applying utilitarian criteria. Nevertheless, provided we do not demand precise measurement, we can give valid reasons for saying that the average subject of the King of Sweden is, on the whole, a good deal freer today than the average citizen of the Republic of Rumania. Total patterns of life must be compared directly as wholes, although the method by which we make the comparison, and the truth of the conclusions, are difficult or impossible to demonstrate. But the vagueness of the concepts, and the multiplicity of the criteria involved, is an attribute of the subject-matter itself, not of our imperfect methods of measurement, or incapacity for precise thought.

life and decisions to depend on myself, not on external forces of whatever kind. I wish to be the instrument of my own, not of other men's, acts of will. I wish to be a subject, not an object; to be moved by reasons, by conscious purposes which are my own, not by causes which affect me, as it were, from outside. I wish to be somebody, not nobody; a doer—deciding, not being decided for, self-directed and not acted upon by external nature or by other men as if I were a thing, or an animal, or a slave incapable of playing a human role, that is, of conceiving goals and policies of my own and realizing them. This is at least part of what I mean when I say that I am rational, and that it is my reason that distinguishes me as a human being from the rest of the world. I wish, above all, to be conscious of myself as a thinking, willing, active being, bearing responsibility for his choices and able to explain them by reference to his own ideas and purposes. I feel free to the degree that I believe this to be true, and enslaved to the degree that I am made to realize that it is not.

The freedom which consists in being one's own master, and the freedom which consists in not being prevented from choosing as I do by other men, may, on the face of it, seem concepts at no great logical distance from each other—no more than negative and positive ways of saying the same thing. Yet the "positive" and "negative" notions of freedom historically developed in divergent directions not always by logically reputable steps, until, in the end, they came into direct conflict with each other.

One way of making this clear is in terms of the independent momentum which the, initially perhaps quite harmless, metaphor of self-mastery acquired. "I am my own master"; "I am slave to no man"; but may I not (as, for instance, T. H. Green is always saying) be a slave to nature? Or to my own "unbridled" passions? Are these not so many species of the identical genus "slave"—some political or legal, others moral or spiritual? Have not men had the experience of liberating themselves from spiritual slavery, or slavery to nature, and do they not in the course of it become aware, on the one hand, of a self which dominates, and, on the other, of something in them which is brought to heel? The dominant self is then variously identified with reason, with my "higher nature", with the self which calculates and aims at what will satisfy it in the long run, with my "real", or "ideal", or "autonomous" self, or with myself "at its best"; which is then contrasted with irrational impulse, uncontrolled desires, my "lower" nature, the pursuit of immediate pleasures, my "empirical" or "heteronomous" self, swept by every gust of desire and passion, needing to be rigidly disciplined if it is ever to rise to the full height of its "real" nature. Presently the two selves may be represented as divided by an even larger gap: the real self may be conceived as something wider than the individual (as the term is normally understood), as a social "whole" of which the individual is an element or aspect: a tribe, a race, a church, a state, the great society of the living and the dead and the yet unborn. This entity is then identified as being the "true" self which, by imposing its collective, or "organic", single will upon its recalcitrant "members", achieves its own, and, therefore, their, "higher" freedom. The perils of using organic metaphors to justify the coercion of some men by others in order to raise them to a "higher" level of freedom have often been pointed out. But what gives such plausibility as it has to this kind of language is that we recognize that it is possible, and at times justifiable, to coerce men in the name of some goal (let us say, justice or public health) which they would, if they were more enlightened, themselves pursue, but do not, because they are blind or ignorant or corrupt. This renders it easy for me to conceive of myself as coercing others for their own sake, in their, not my, interest. I am then claiming that I know what they truly need better than they know it themselves. What, at most, this entails is that they would not resist me if they were rational, and as wise as I, and understood their interests as I do. But I may go on to

claim a good deal more than this. I may declare that they are actually aiming at what in their benighted state they consciously resist, because there exists within them an occult entity—their latent rational will, or their "true" purpose—and that this entity, although it is belied by all that they overtly feel and do and say, is their "real" self, of which the poor empirical self in space and time may know nothing or little; and that this inner spirit is the only self that deserves to have its wishes taken into account.[9] Once I take this view, I am in a position to ignore the actual wishes of men or societies, to bully, oppress, torture them in the name, and on behalf, of their "real" selves, in the secure knowledge that whatever is the true goal of man (happiness, fulfillment of duty, wisdom, a just society, self-fulfillment) must be identical with his freedom—the free choice of his "true", albeit submerged and inarticulate, self.

This paradox has been often exposed. It is one thing to say that I know what is good for X, while he himself does not; and even to ignore his wishes for its—and his—sake; and a very different one to say that he has *eo ipso* chosen it, not indeed consciously, not as he seems in everyday life, but in his role as a rational self which his empirical self may not know—the "real" self which discerns the good, and cannot help choosing it once it is revealed. This monstrous impersonation, which consists in equating what X would choose if he were something he is not, or at least not yet, with what X actually seeks and chooses, is at the heart of all political theories of self-realization. It is one thing to say that I may be coerced for my own good which I am too blind to see: this may, on

---

[9] "The ideal of true freedom is the maximum of power for all the members of human society alive to make the best of themselves," said T. H. Green in 1881. Apart from the confusion of freedom with equality, this entails that if a man chose some immediate pleasure—which (in whose view?) would not enable him to make the best of himself (what self?) what he is exercising is not "true" freedom: and, if deprived of it, he would not lose anything that mattered. Green was a genuine liberal: but many a tyrant could use this formula to justify his worst oppression.

occasion, be for my benefit; indeed it may enlarge the scope of my liberty; it is another to say that if it is my good, then I am not being coerced, for I have willed it, whether I know this or not, and am free—or "truly" free—even while my poor earthly body and foolish mind bitterly reject it, and struggle against those who seek however benevolently to impose it, with the greatest desperation.

This magical transformation, or sleight of hand (for which William James so justly mocked the Hegelians), can no doubt be perpetrated just as easily with the "negative" concept of freedom, where the self that should not be interfered with is no longer the individual with his actual wishes and needs as they are normally conceived, but the "real" man within, identified with the pursuit of some ideal purpose not dreamed of by his empirical self. And, as in the case of the "positively" free self, this entity may be inflated into some superpersonal entity— a state, a class, a nation, or the march of history itself, regarded as a more "real" subject of attributes than the empirical self. But the "positive" conception of freedom as self-mastery, with its suggestion of a man divided against himself, has in fact, and as a matter of the history of doctrines and of practice, lent itself more easily to this splitting of personality into two: the transcendent, dominant controller, and the empirical bundle of desires and passions to be disciplined and brought to heel. This demonstrates (if demonstration of so obvious a truth is needed) that the conception of freedom directly derives from the view that is taken of what constitutes a self, a person, a man. Enough manipulation with the definition of man, and freedom can be made to mean whatever the manipulator wishes. Recent history has made it only too clear that the issue is not merely academic.

Freedom and Society

Frithjof Bergmann

Writers like Mill and Berlin understand freedom in a negative sense, and they value it as providing a kind of moat around each individual, a barrier that keeps others, including the government, at a proper distance. In this imaginative selection from his book *On Being Free,* Professor Frithjof Bergmann of the University of Michigan challenges some of our most common ways of thinking about freedom, in particular the notion that curtailing the activities of the state invariably enhances our freedom. Slogans like "the government that governs least governs best" suppose that people would somehow be free without a state. Such slogans single out only one obstacle to liberty—the state—while overlooking how the state can also increase freedom. Instead of talking of freedom in the abstract, Bergmann argues, we should look more concretely at the real obstacles that face people in their lives and the ways in which government can increase or reduce those obstacles.

Reprinted by permission of the publisher from Frithjof Bergmann, *On Being Free* (Notre Dame, IN: University of Notre Dame Press, 1977).

Imagine that late at night you are walking through the deserted streets of a small town, and suddenly a man, dressed somewhat like a peddler, accosts you and waves you on to follow. In the spirit of one who has only recently arrived and wants to explore, you turn after him into an alley, climb up a staircase, and moments later you are in a large, bare and whitewalled room. A yoga class seems to be in progress. A number of young people lie on the floor, their bodies in a pose of relaxation. Their teacher, wearing a black leotard, appears to be in the middle of an explanation. You notice that everybody's eyes are not closed but extraordinarily wide open and alive; then you begin to listen:

"So you see," the yoga teacher says, "that there are situations, in which all this is obvious and evident and easy. You can walk around in it as if you were at home, in your own living room, in socks. You need not even look, it all goes without saying. And yet there are other contexts in which without any warning certain pictures capture our minds. It is strange, almost as if we had been hypnotized, for these images are crude and clumsy, but nonetheless possess great power. And they enthrall us not when we stay close to the ground, but when we rise up to the heights on which we theorize. The paradox is thus twofold: one layer of it is the sheer compartmentalization of our usual intelligence—that we should see so clearly from one angle and yet be so benumbed when we look from another. The second layer consists in the inversion: that we are stupider and much more mesmerized in our subtle theories, and for once (and perhaps not just for once) far more intelligent in our ordinary habits. So the pictures we discuss are childish; it is embarrassing to look at them; yet they are all the same deeper than the rest of our thinking.

"Take, for example, the most common saying, that under a democracy the people are naturally free, while this is not true under other dispensations, and ask yourself: What image seems to make this so self-evident? Is it not more than anything the notion that we are protected, that there are limits beyond which our government is not allowed to go; that it does not cover the whole ground like an inundation, but that there are checks, like dams, which hold it back? And does this not mean that we think freedom and the state exclude each other, that where one begins the other ends? And is it not true that this mythic or children's imagery lies only just below all kinds of axioms and philosophical appearing propositions? Man is born free, we say together with Rousseau, and conjure up the story of a cunning barter: this much, but no more of an original inheritance, a birthright, we surrender, in exchange for security, for protection, but some of that original endowment we hold back. We draw a line; the freedom on the far side of it we pay as a price, but the inner circle we would like to keep. And how do we think of rights? Are they, too, not like a moat around each individual keeping us at a proper distance from each other; and do they not enclose a plot of ground that is immune, a sanctuary in which we have license? But take this to its extreme. Where does it lead? Must it not reach its culmination in the idea that the government which governs least is best? Is this not the logical conclusion, the obviously most advantageous trade? Will that not leave intact the largest quantity of freedom, and give away a minimum of that immensely precious good? Is it not clear that the famous Jeffersonian dictum presupposes the images we just described? Could one come to this conclusion and experience it as evident if one had not been raised in a nursery in which these pictures hung?

"So let us take this sentence—the government that governs least is best—and look at it up close. What does it say? Imagine you told it to someone who never heard it, who had grown up in a completely different culture. What would be his reaction? Is it not likely that a traveler from far off might stare at you with bafflement and consternation; that he might blink and then burst into the response: 'What an unheard-of and weird thing to say! You would not say this of a doctor, would you? You would not think that a doctor who cured least was the best? Or that a gardener who gardened very little was the one to hire? Or that a worker who hardly worked was better than all others? So why do you hold such bizarre opinions when it comes to government? Maybe if a government barely governs, it only means that it does not perform its function, that it is a failure, a mistake?'

"And such a stranger might continue: 'If you really believe in this inverse proportion, why do you have any government at all? Surely, if the state marks the borderline of freedom, you would have still more freedom if there were no government whatever? Only the absence of government would be really least, and consequently best of all. So why do you not draw the logical conclusion and get rid of the state—or at least make sure it withers away gradually?'

"How would we reply," the yoga teacher asks, "if someone said this? Would we not respond that the results of such an abolition would be very different; that some few ruthless men perhaps would be still freer than under the most minimal of governments, but that the vast majority would be under the oppression of those few? But then, would you or I, mild as we are, not be among the latter? Would we not end up nearer to the bottom, with a much harsher life? Might not our existence be very like that of a dog, complete with bones from the table and a chain around our necks? So we owe a great deal to the interference of the state. Many of us would fall to a much lower level if it did not intercede.

"And this acknowledgment is important, for it implies that much of our picture-thinking has to be revised. Not all of us would be completely free in the 'natural condition' prior to the state. Some of us might be far more constrained than we are now, and the story that we have traded in some part of our freedom for security is therefore just a myth. But if this is true, if we never possessed this incommensurately precious good to barter it away, then our resisting and begrudging attitude also is not so obviously justified. Then at least some

kinds of government—though certainly not all—give us not just material safety for a spiritual sacrifice, but do much more and should get their reward.

"Of course we know this. To our concrete thinking all this is very evident. If you work as a nurse's aide, you understand that your paycheck would be less if it were not for the minimum wage guarantees enforced by the state. The point is that from the clouds of our theoretical opinions our feet no longer touch this obvious ground. On that level a Pavlovian reflex jerks us back: authority, the state, makes us less free.

"Yet our traveler, recovered from his initial shock, might speak to us a second time. 'Why do you say that limiting the state makes people free? That word has such a grand and bell-like ring. But what real purpose does it serve when the facts are so very plain? A state imposes penalties and fines, and these are obstacles that hinder you in certain actions. But there are other obstacles besides those represented by the state—they surround you on all sides. Limiting the state reduces only some very few of all the obstacles you face. What of the remnant? How can the lowering of one kind of obstacle make you free? Why do you think of yourself in an open space when only one wall of your cage has been moved backwards by three feet?

" 'But in reality not even this occurred. You did not simply gain more space, for that ignores another and still more crucial fact: you cannot remove one obstacle in isolation. There is no fixed and stable sum from which you can subtract. A change in one place makes a difference in all others. The elements of the system interact. If you diminish hindrances in one sphere, those in other areas will go up. So your weakening of the state changed only one weight in a complicated clockwork mechanism. And what were the effects of this in other places?

" 'Consider the hindrances of poverty for instance. Go through a supermarket: not the asparagus because it costs too much. Not fresh bread but a loaf that is four days old. Where is the basket with the damaged cans?

That's when the obstacles close in on you, and every step is up against a wall. Or take the barriers linked to work. You may not have the license to do the one thing which you could do best, and that can stop you cold—for then you cannot be insured; and there is the continuous control imposed on you within the work you do. Is it not as if your hands were strapped to a machine? Now put this block on top of the other, and now, like it or not, the next. Does not this grind you down more than all other pressures? Again, are you not impeded by ill health that could have been avoided; by a schooling that covers spontaneity with gravel, perhaps most of all by an indifference that spreads like a gas? But is it not likely that many of these obstacles grew larger as the direct result of the diminishment of others? You took the rocks that had pinned down someone's legs and lifted them from off his feet. But you piled them back on—and this time on his head!

" 'The one force in your culture on which most people have some influence you weakened. The state whose leaders are at least selected by elections you limited till it did least. But all the other powers you allowed to grow. Yet in their affairs you do not have a vote, and who their leaders are you hardly know. Is this not downright mad? To tie down and hold back the one force which in spite of all its flaws is somewhat open and accountable to you, and to give the advantage of this debility to elements which are inaccessible and closed? Is it not evident that this is upside-down; that you should have strengthened the one force over which you have some hold, so that through it you might have kept the rest in check? But this still misses the main point; for your state in actuality is not weak or limited at all! Your dictum that "least is best" must be a kind of game, like that with scissors, paper and a rock. For you accept compulsory education, do you not? But that allows the state to meddle with the raising of your children. And you apply for a license to get married. And it is the state that grants you a divorce; and there are even laws against homosexuality

and fornication. So how large is your private territory? You can be arrested for having a too noisy party—that disturbs the peace, even if the country is at war. Sitting on a park bench can be a criminal offense. The government can tell you how big your bathroom has to be if you are building your own home. You even need a permit to bring your garbage to the dump! Just how far back have you pushed the state?

" 'Think of the slogan: the means of violence belong to the government. Spelled out this means that if your government betrays you, you can only sign petitions and write letters to your congressman. If you break a single window it is still a crime. But if the state decides that you were traitorous to it, then it can execute you. So whose hands are still tied, and who still throws the switches?

" 'Or take the measure of your deference to the law. From the time you watch Western movies: "He took the law into his own hands" is made to sound as if divinity has been defiled. The film cannot end, the sunset has to wait, till the law has been restored to the state. Your own beliefs count here for very little: if you disagree on a specific issue—on school busing or integrated housing, for example—you are wrong if you act on your own convictions. It is the law that has to be obeyed. You are more submissive than a child, for even parents say to their growing children: "These are my reasons. Weigh my arguments and then make your decision," but relative to laws your culture does just the reverse: this is right, because it is the law; no further questions—but laws are the voice of the state!

" 'No, you did not build a fence against the government so you could grow your own small garden. Your story has a very different plot. On the whole you were a very humble servant, but you did choose a single place—there you dug in your heels and drew a line: trade you made free; the economic you marked off; property became inviolable. The foundations for this predilection, for this one barricade against the state, were laid right from the start. They can be found in Hobbes and in Rousseau, and most especially in

Locke. Their theories prepared the ground on which your institutions were erected. And that is still the single enclave you defend: What do you call it when the government stands helpless and has no control? In any area except for the economic this is Anarchy, and you associate it with pandemonium and slaughter. But in the economic the same condition has a different name: there it is Free Enterprise. And vice versa: if the state is vigilant in any other area, then that is Law and Order, but in the economic area the word for that is Socialism.

" 'Your double standard stretches one's imagination. On one side you protest a total tax on incomes in excess of 80,000 dollars. That is an abridgement of your rights. You think the state has no claim on that money, and no prerogative to redistribute it. Here you forget that no one produces the value represented by 80,000 dollars quite by himself, that others must have lent a hand, and that all kinds of chance conventions and arbitrary social customs need to be observed for such a paycheck to materialize. You isolate a single fact: that someone has possession of that money, that it is his property, and then you wonder how anyone but him could have a right to it.

" 'Yet, on the other side, you hardly question the right of governments to declare wars. Most of you condone the institution of conscription, and even the selection by lottery—a bingo game—of those the government will send to war. You refuse the government the right to property which is not even unambiguously yours. But to stake your life on the turning up of the right number on a throw of dice, to that you give the state the right!

" 'And with that we come to the real issue. The hindrances of poverty, of mindless labor and disease you did not choose to fight. You only wanted to curtail the state, and that by no means generally but only in one segment, that of the economic, of Free Enterprise—on that short front you took your stand. But this one spot which you finally selected was the worst and most calamitous place you could possibly have

picked. How great a toll in sacrifices would have been exacted if the state had intervened more in the sphere of property or business? What real loss in freedom—in genuine self-expression—would be imposed by regulating mergers and other similar transactions? How many actions vital to the self would that stop? Would the affected notice it in their own personal lives, or would the difference be known only to their accountants? So how much freedom is gained? But what a price is paid! For by putting that very small restraint on a mere handful (who could still have had their private yachts—just slightly shorter ones) you could turn around the lives of millions. A minimal increase in some obstacles faced by a very few would empower you to take down hindrances which daunt the great majority far more than abstract governmental regulations—obstacles so insurmountable and close that their will to be themselves capitulates in desperation.

" 'Do not imagine therefore that your culture has granted you a high degree of freedom. The question of genuine freedom, of self-expression, has so far hardly ever been raised. That was not the measure by which your politics were judged. Your failures and successes, your long-range strategies and daily tactics can be assessed in the much plainer language of obstacles that either were removed or left to mount. Seen in that way, and coldly, your advances up to date are unimpressive and your retreats are very great. You have reduced some few hindrances, but only in that one most unintelligently chosen place, and other barriers grew higher than they were before. It is the waste of it, the crevasse between what you might have done and what you did, that seems most baffling and appalling. For no fundamental change, no total construction was required. Minor adjustments might have sufficed. But you balked. You did not end that terrible imbalance. You watched its tilt grow steeper, but stood by and did not move.' "

After bringing the traveler's speech to this conclusion, the yoga teacher paced across the floor. Then he began anew: "This is the impression a visitor might form. That it is in some ways much too simple should be obvious. The lines are not that neat and sharp. Not only trade and finance were blocked off against incursions from the state. Speech, too, was protected, and so was religion and much else. And conversely: not the whole of the economic was off limits for the state. Far from it! The switch from resisting interference to inviting and submitting to all manner of controls—the double standard—occurred not only between the economic and the rest. It was also invoked inside the economic. Think of its blatant use in the relationship between the so-called mother countries and their colonies. In their dealings with each other the industrialized nations asked the state for the most nurturing protection. As long as their own plants were weak, a veritable greenhouse of differential customs, tariffs, and currency exchanges was put up. It was only when they were strong and ready, and 'open doors' to their advantage, that the ideology of Free Trade was hoisted to the mast. And the same shuttling between government control and laissez-faire was naturally also practiced inside each country's own domestic sphere, and often in exactly the same way: the powerful received the benefits of governmental interference, and the weak were told that freedom had to be preserved.

"So the borderline between the territory which one protected against intrusions from the state and the other areas in which the state was welcomed with red carpets was not fixed and drawn with a straight edge. It meandered and zigzagged and was continuously moved from place to place. The geometric picture in which only the economic was exempted is therefore certainly too crude. But we need not study the pressures which bent this line now this way and then back. Its exact location, and even that it sometimes disappeared is not to our purpose. We can admit that our traveler was mistaken on this score. That still leaves intact the lessons we can learn from him, and some of these we might compress into a list.

"The first comes to the fundamental irrationality of our prejudice against the state. Consider this in a psychological perspective: it seems a fact that we associate the establishment of rules, and especially the increase of government and regulations, with the idea that there will be more situations in which someone can tell us 'what to do,' and that we therefore will be less free. But this is actually an astonishing naiveté, and one should ask: What mistake delivers us into the arms of this conclusion? The answer is that it happens when we monopolize the stage. We slip into the fantasy that we are quite alone—like Robinson Crusoe on his small island—and we imagine that the only pertinent relationship is that between ourselves and these rules. If this were indeed the case, then our apprehension would be justified; then there really might be a proportionality between the increase of rules and our being hindered by them. But this would be true only if we were alone. As soon as this pretense is dropped and a genuinely social context is imagined, the absurdity of our fears becomes apparent: for with a multitude of others present most rules will far more often prevent them from infringing on me than they will impinge on me directly. The red traffic light which I have to obey keeps fifty others out of my way for every time it forces me to stop.

"So this mistake—this egocentric fallacy—is an arresting specimen, for in effect it constitutes a contradiction: precisely at the point at which we assess an instrument which is in its very essence social, i.e., a social rule or a government—and where a social thinking is mandatory, we relapse into a private, an asocial or even anti-social mode of thought.

"In the second place we can advance a summary critique of Anarchism. That word, too, has many meanings. Much of what it stands for inspires admiration and respect, but on one understanding of it freedom is to be achieved through the abolition or the gradual dismantling of the state. If this is taken literally and is not a hyperbole for a drastic decentralization and democratization of the state (a transformation with an outcome that many would no longer call a 'state'), then it is open to the following objections: (1) It singles out one obstacle—that of the state—and expects freedom from leveling this one to the ground, forgetting all the other obstacles which would still hem us in. (2) It overlooks that the various sets of obstacles interact with each other and that the abolition of the state would probably increase other barriers which might be even more debilitating than the state. (3) It commits the 'egocentric fallacy' for it thinks of the state as principally an obstacle or a limit on my freedom. But in a social context the right kind of state may increase my freedom rather than diminish it. In essence it is thus guilty of the very errors inherent in the 'least is best' conception, with the difference that Anarchism is consistent and carries them to their extreme.

"The third and most crucial lesson implicit in our traveler's reactions subsumes the two we have just detailed under a more comprehensive claim: in essence it constitutes a rejection of the framework in which these issues have been often posed.

"The pillars of this structure of assumptions were the notions that man as such was free before the state, that some of that primordial freedom was surrendered through the act of contracting into society or the state, and arising from this basis, the conception that freedom and the state exclude each other, that the territory given over to the state marks the borderlines of the preserved and to-be-defended sphere of our privacy.

"Our reasons for breaking with this mode of thought will stand out most clearly if we see it against the backdrop of the shift by now familiar, from the elusive and deceptive thought of freedom, to firmer and more incisive categories. As soon as we substitute the conception of facing obstacles for the idea of freedom, the discussion of man's condition prior to the state loses much of its mysteriousness. We can move away from postulating arbitrary myths that legitimate prearranged conclusions: from the story of

a universal war in which life was nasty, brutish and short, which justifies gratitude and submission to the state, but also from its opposite, from the fable of the noble savage, which turns the whole of culture and society into a malady. If we ask not about freedom, but about the obstacles men faced, we can see at once that all men certainly faced some, and from there a discussion which compares societies that did not yet have a state to later ones that were so organized, can start.

"And the same holds for the rest. Once we think in terms of obstacles it becomes apparent that our joining of the state entailed not only a forfeiture of freedom, but that some barriers were lowered as others rose; and with that the picture of the two territories, where the state encroaches upon freedom, and freedom reigns only in the remnant, is brought to its collapse. For we are not free in the sphere from which government has been banished, since other barriers still remain and are apt to increase, and we are not unfree in areas over which the government has some control, for its interference might reduce the obstacles we otherwise would face.

"In essence this dispenses with a merely quantitative thinking that attempts only to measure the more or less of government, and makes room for a thinking that is qualitative in two different ways: government is for us only one of several modalities through which we and others act or can be influenced and hindered. It must be held up against other forces which may be less accessible to us, and which may have greater power over our lives. In addition it is the quality, the nature of government, that for us becomes all important: the material question is not whether it governs more or less or least, but how it governs: closed off from us or under our eyes, intelligently or with stupidity, a weapon in the hands of others, or a tool we all can use.

"Our fourth and last conclusion is that the identification of the absence of government interference with freedom is an ideological device whose function is very like the big brass gong in a certain ancient village. When a minimum of government was in the interest of some group, then they pronounced this to be freedom, and many others—deafened—acquiesced and fell into line. When a strong state was wanted, then Anarchy threatened at the gates, and many could again be herded in the opposite direction. The muffling of that gong was part of our aim.

"We began from the idea that crude and childish pictures sometimes mesmerize a part of our minds. Three separate charges have now been laid against the mode of thought which conjures up the one most hypnotizing image: (1) It talks as if the state were one undifferentiated force, and fails to recognize that the quality and nature of the state is far more important than its magnitude or strength. (2) It forgets that there are other obstacles besides those represented by the state. (3) It overlooks that the diversity of obstacles affect each other in a systematic way. To have recognized the threesome of these errors should break the spell this metaphor has cast. We can now take the picture which makes of the state the borderline of our freedom and turn it to the wall."

With these words the yoga teacher stopped.

Enquiries for Liberators

Janet Radcliffe Richards

Because feminists want to liberate women, they value freedom. But the meaning of freedom is unclear, and discussions of its value and implications are sometimes confused. In this selection from her book, *The Sceptical Feminist*, Janet Radcliffe Richards argues that we are free to the extent that we control our own destinies and can do as we like and that freedom so understood is good as an end in itself. Some feminists, however, seem to doubt this. Contending that women have been conditioned by male society, some would-be liberators of women believe that a liberated woman is not one who is free to choose without restraints but, rather, a woman who makes certain kinds of choices. In response, Richards argues that the fact that women are as they are because of social influences does not show that their choices are not their own. She explores carefully the relation between freedom and conditioning and discusses the ways in which conditioning ought properly to be attacked.

Janet Radcliffe Richards is Lecturer in Philosophy at the Open University in England.

Freedom is a central issue in feminism, since even in those parts of the movement which

Reprinted by permission from Janet Radcliffe Richards, *The Sceptical Feminist* (Harmondsworth, England: Penguin, 1982).

do not actually call themselves 'Women's Liberation' it is generally agreed that freedom for women is one of the things which must be achieved. That, however, is probably as far as the consensus goes. The area is

full of confusions and talk at cross purposes. . . .

KINDS OF FREEDOM

The first thing to do is to point out that
there is one part of the ordinary English use
of the word 'free' which is a very clear dis-
traction from the main issue, and a good
deal of confusion will be avoided if it is
removed from the path at the outset. This
concerns the distinction between being free
(*simpliciter*), and being free *from* something.

Whenever something calling itself a liberation movement appears on the political
scene, as happens not infrequently, it is natural to presume that it is trying to get for the
people it wants to liberate an increase in
something rather like a possession: they are
to be given more liberty rather as they might
be given more money, or more health care,
or more holidays. However, this is not necessarily so, and we have to move cautiously.
To liberate people is usually to free them
from something or other, and in order to say
with perfect linguistic propriety that you
want to free people from something, nothing more is necessary than your intending to
get rid of something which you take to be
bad for them. It does not matter whether
they agree with you about the badness of the
thing you want to remove. Feminists may
talk of liberating women from wifehood,
even though a woman so liberated against
her will might put the matter very differently and say that she had been *deprived* of
the possibility of being supported by a husband. In principle you could claim to liberate people from absolutely anything as long
as you disapproved of whatever it was, and
any reforming movement can with only the
slightest ingenuity formulate its aims so as to
present itself as a liberation movement. If
we had no more than the name to go by, we
could not tell whether something calling itself Women's Liberation was trying to free
women from the power of men, or conventional stereotypes, or political responsibility,
or the lure of the unfeminine, or even the
blandishments of the feminist movement.
Unexplained, it could be anything whatever.

What is quite certain is that there is no
necessary connection whatever between a
movement's wanting to free people *from*
something and its being concerned to give
them an increase in some commodity which
could legitimately be described as freedom.
It is *possible* for the two intentions to be combined: if you free people from something
which restricts their freedom, such as a tyrannical government, you certainly increase
their freedom in doing so. However, there
are all kinds of cases where you might want
to free people *from* something without wanting to increase their freedom (*simpliciter*) at
all. . . .

The discussion of liberty in this chapter is
not concerned with the matter of freeing
people *from* various evils, because whether
liberation from something is good depends
on the logically prior question of whether
the thing they are to be liberated from is
really bad. The problem here is to define,
and consider the value of, freedom as a possession.

FREEDOM AS A POSSESSION

Obviously the first thing to do is to establish
what freedom in this sense of the word actually is. However, there is some danger in
putting it that way, since it gives the impression that there already is something determinate whose nature is waiting to be discovered by the careful enquirer. This is not the
right way to look at it at all. 'Free' is a word
which often has a precise meaning to be
discovered *in particular contexts*, but take it
out of context, give it a capital letter and try
to establish what Freedom in general is, and
the matter is quite different. In fact the connotations of 'free' seem to vary so much
from one context to another, to the extent
even of conflicting with each other, that it is
probably quite hopeless to try to find any

general meaning of the word which will not be obviously inadequate or even wrong in some ordinary contexts. This is no doubt why over the years philosophers have produced so many different accounts of the nature of freedom.

If the language actually contains no determinate answer to the question of what 'freedom', independently of particular contexts, really means, then the question of *what freedom really is* is one which has no answer. Nevertheless the idea of freedom in general, as a kind of thing which people can gain or lose, is very commonly used. Furthermore, 'freedom' is like 'natural' in having such good connotations that people are only too delighted to take advantage of any confusion to juggle with half a dozen meanings of the word at once in order to confuse their opponents and win political points. The only thing to do, therefore, is to be determined to keep whatever definition is being used clear at all times, never presuming that it must be clear because everybody knows what freedom is.

There are various possible acceptable definitions of freedom, all reflecting various aspects of the context-dependent use of 'free' (and all ignoring some of them). It is necessary here to fix on what seems to be the best of them, defend it, and then decide on the value of freedom *as explained in that particular way*, bearing in mind that if a different explanation is taken, the assessment of the value of freedom may have to change.

The best account seems to be this. Roughly speaking, freedom can be explained by saying that *people are free to the extent that they are in control of their own destinies, and not controlled by other people or other alien forces.* This definition, it should be stressed, makes freedom not a thing which you either have or have not, but something of which you have more or less. Feminists think that men have too much, at the expense of women, who have correspondingly little. . . .

The reason for some people's objection to explaining freedom as the ability to control one's own destiny is that it seems to draw no distinction between freedom and power, and to our ordinary way of thinking, as the philosopher Thomas Hobbes pointed out, there is a considerable difference between the two. Our inability to do various things we should like to do may come from lack of freedom, but equally it may not. A bird in a cage is not free to fly, but in our case the inability to fly has nothing to do with an absence of *freedom*. No one is stopping us from flying, it is just that we can't do it.

If the way feminists use the word 'freedom' does not take account of this, it means the feminist position is open to attack. For instance, it is a common feminist complaint that women are not (or at least have not been through most of history) free to control their own reproduction, partly because there has never been enough research into contraception, and partly because even when contraceptives have been in existence they have often been expensive or difficult to get. Someone like Hobbes, however, would presumably argue that it was quite misleading to say that because of these things women were not *free* to control their reproduction. Even if women are justified in asking for more contraceptives, he would be likely to say, feminists are cheating in describing their demand as a demand for freedom. They are not asking for the removal of a constraint which prevents their doing what they otherwise could have done, but assistance to make them capable of doing what they otherwise could not do. And as Isaiah Berlin said, 'Everything is what it is: liberty is liberty, not equality or fairness or justice or culture. . . . Nothing is gained by a confusion of terms.'[1] That is quite right, of course, and if we want to talk about freedom in contexts like this one, where it seems more natural to talk about ability or power, we must justify doing so.

---

[1] Berlin, 'Two Concepts of Liberty' in Berlin, *Four Essays on Liberty*, p. 125.

In general when people complain about limitations on freedom the complaints arise, as has been suggested already, within particular contexts. The complaint is that other people[2] are coming between them and *what they otherwise could have done*. Now what anyone 'otherwise could have done' is clearly a thing which is heavily context dependent, because what you can do at any time depends not only on your own intrinsic abilities, but also on the situation you are in. . . . Whether a particular interference does restrict your freedom to do something depends on whether you could have done whatever it was *but for that interference*. Complaints of infringements of freedom, occurring as they usually do within specific contexts, always refer to what could otherwise have been done *within that context*.

. . . There is no way of saying in general, out of context, what people could or could not have done but for a particular interference. Once again, what people can do depends not only on their intrinsic abilities but also on environment, and even intrinsic ability depends on earlier, formative environment. But if we have no general standard for what someone can do uninterfered with, there is no general criterion either for what is to count as interference. If we are to have a *general* account of what it is to increase or lessen freedom, the criterion of active interference, which does well enough in particular contexts, is one which has to go.

However, this is not too serious as long as it is clear. We cannot expect to carry all the connotations of a context-dependent word over into a context-free use. And anyway, another problem about trying to keep the idea that you infringe someone's freedom only when you actively hinder and not when you fail to help is that it takes no account of another thing which is certainly an important ingredient in the concept of freedom: the idea that *your freedom is diminished when other people's desires come between you and your desires*. The effects other people can have on your desires are not limited to direct prohibitions and forcible interventions, but extend to the whole man-made environment in which we live. If when we complain of lack of freedom we are objecting to the fact that someone else's will is getting between us and our desires, we are not trying to say that people are preventing us from doing what we could have done in a state of nature. We can say that our freedom is curtailed if the social background, against which we are working, is arranged to their benefit rather than ours. To quote Berlin again:[3]

It is argued, very plausibly, that if a man is too poor to afford something on which there is no legal ban—a loaf of bread, a journey round the world, recourse to the law courts—he is as little free to have it as he would be if it were forbidden him by law. . . . It is . . . because I believe that my inability to get a given thing is due to the fact that other human beings have made arrangements whereby I am, whereas others are not, prevented from having enough money with which to pay for it, that I think myself a victim of coercion or slavery.

If we are going to have a general idea of freedom as a state in which other people's desires do not interfere with our own, it has to take account of the fact that we could have had things more to our liking if other people had made different social arrangements. To the extent that these arrangements have been made to the advantage of one group rather than another the second's freedom is curtailed, because its members can do less of what they want to do than they could have done if things had been different. In the case of contraceptives, for instance, we can argue that although in a

---

[2] Almost invariably other people, rather than things, because complaints about limitations on freedom are the subject of moral indignation, and blame is a thing which can be levelled only at morally responsible beings. That is why we complain about lack of freedom, but not generally about lack of power. As Rousseau said, 'The nature of things does not madden us; only ill-will does' (quoted ibid., p. 123).

[3] Ibid., p. 122.

sense women were free to get contraceptives as long as there were no laws preventing their manufacture or distribution, men as effectively prevented women's getting them by making sure that science was entirely in the control of men as they would have done by making laws. If laws which make contraceptives inaccessible can be said to restrict women's freedom to get them, it would be silly to argue that general social arrangements whose consequences were the same did not restrict in the same way.

The conclusion of this is that the only reasonable way to talk about freedom in general in a social context is this: *your freedom is restricted by society to the extent that different social arrangements might have made it possible to do more of what you wanted.* If society could have made it possible for you to do something but has not, it has to that extent restricted your freedom. This means that *within a social context freedom and power are virtually the same;* the only powers whose lack does not count as a lack of freedom are those which could not have been given by any possible social arrangement. . . .

A DEFENCE OF LIBERTY

Here, then, is an acceptable account of freedom as a possession: you are free to the extent that other people's desires do not come between you and your own. Another, apparently rival, account will appear later in the chapter, but for now we shall concentrate on this one. If this is freedom, what is its value?

One obvious and common defence of freedom is that it is a means to happiness. People who approve of freedom say that it leads to happiness because we are made unhappy if we know that other people control what we do, or because we know better than anyone else what we want and will be made happiest by being left to decide for ourselves, or because freedom leads to strength and self-reliance which in turn lead to happiness. Other people are doubtful about

these arguments, and say that, on the contrary, too much freedom makes people unhappy. People do not really know what is best for them, it is argued, so they may be happier if other people make the decisions. Midge Decter, for instance, in her arguments against Women's Liberation, says that what is making women dissatisfied is not a lack of freedom but a surfeit of it.[4]

All these arguments are of course important, but here they are beside the point. Here the issue is not whether freedom is an effective means to some *other* end like happiness, but whether it is good *as an end in itself.* Can we argue that freedom is good irrespective of whether it leads to happiness or anything else we value? And if so, how valuable is it in comparison with these other things?

In some sense there can be very little argument on subjects like this one, because with questions of ultimate values there does not seem to be any common ground for discussion between people who disagree. If people really, in the last analysis, value different things, there is nothing more to be said. However it is possible to do something not unlike arguing. It does seem possible to make it clear by illustration that a great many people, whether they realize it or not, do in fact value freedom as an end in itself, and that many value it even more than happiness. . . .

Suppose, for instance, you were an outstandingly gifted but miserably neurotic artist or musician, and someone offered you a drug which would make you happy, but would result in your losing all your ability. There are already drugs along these lines, but we are to think of one so entirely effective that once having taken it the patient would not even regret having lost the desire or ability to compose or paint. Suppose also that you had complete faith in its efficacy, and in the intentions of the person who offered it. Would you take it? Some people would no doubt be very happy to, but there

---

[4] Decter, *The New Chastity*, p. 51.

must be many who in such a situation would rather remain unhappy than achieve happiness at the cost of losing a skill they valued far more than any prospect of happiness.

Suppose, again, you lived in a country with a political régime you disliked intensely, with no way of escaping and not much hope of making things more to your liking. Suppose also that the government had a programme of 're-education' which you believed would be completely effective, and which would make you entirely happy with the political situation afterwards. Would you be willing to undergo this programme? Many people would certainly not. They would rather remain unhappy than be so radically changed. Or suppose that you were very dissatisfied with your life as it was. Would you welcome the opportunity (to take a classic example) to become a satisfied pig? Again, probably not.

Of course these thought experiments are all rather artificial. They presuppose impossibilities, and anyway are not specific enough: whether we should be willing to become satisfied pigs would probably depend a good deal on the degree of our unhappiness as human beings. Nevertheless, the arguments are useful because they do suggest that to many people there are things which are more important than happiness.

So far, of course, this does not prove that anyone prefers *freedom* to happiness because the discussion has only been about which of two things we should take if we were in a position to choose, and as long as there is a question of choice some freedom is built into the example. All this shows is that there are occasions where people would choose to cling to what might be called their identities, rather than lose them for the sake of happiness. No doubt they would like happiness as well, but given the necessity of choice, happiness might well be abandoned first. However, it is possible to look at the question of freedom by considering similar cases which involve other people.

Why is it, for instance, that so many people object to Soviet dissidents' being put in psychiatric hospitals? Of course there are several reasons. We may not think the 'treatment' will work, and we may not like the system the patients' minds are being changed to fit. However, even supposing we did approve of the political system, and supposing we did believe that after treatment the dissidents would fit happily into Russian society and regard their former activities and attitudes as absurd, would we then approve of the practice? Probably not. We might be happy for people to be offered such treatment if they wanted it, but still think that they should be allowed to choose for themselves whether they would rather be altered and made happy, or remain unhappy but still themselves. And if we think that it is more important to give people this choice than to force happiness on them, it means we are in favour of freedom, and regard it as more important than happiness.

There are many other examples of this sort of attitude. For instance, most of us would be shocked by this advertisement described by Sheila Rowbotham:[5] 'There was a picture of a young mother with a pram in front of a big block of flats and the heading "She can't change her environment but you can change her mood with Serenid-D".' There are all kinds of reasons for being upset about putting people on happiness drugs, including being afraid of side effects and long-term consequences. Nevertheless, part of the objection is to the idea of making women happy *without fulfilling their desires*. If we were concerned only with happiness for people we should not worry about putting them on effective happiness drugs. If happiness is all that matters there is nothing intrinsically wrong with brainwashing, or forcible medication, or giving people sedatives and tranquilizers instead of coping with their emotional problems. Most of us do care about allowing people to determine the course of their own lives, rather than having other people make them happy in

---

[5] Rowbotham, *Woman's Consciousness, Man's World*, pp. 75–6.

ways they do not want. Since there can hardly be a feminist in existence who would regard it as an acceptable solution to women's problems that someone should invent some kind of medication or special process of re-education which would make women happy in their present lot, but had to be administered against their wills, we must think that most feminists value freedom more than happiness for women. The firm feminist rejection of male paternalism comes not only through the recognition that men's apparent concern for women's well-being is by some curious coincidence remarkably well adapted to the interests of men. Even if men's dominance were wholly good for women, we should still reject its being forced on them. As Kant said, 'paternalism is the worst despotism imaginable'. And as Mill said, 'the only purpose for which power can be rightfully exercised over any member of a civilized community, against his will, is to prevent harm to others. His own good, either physical or moral, is not a sufficient warrant.'[6]

There is probably no way of arguing with any feminist who disagrees with all this, as doubtless some must. However, the principle of freedom will be taken as fundamental to feminism throughout this book, and where it produces statements with which feminists disagree, at least it will be obvious where the disagreement stems from. Freedom is being taken as a fundamental good in its own right, and a thing of which we should, therefore, all have as much as possible. How much each individual should have when the claims of other people are taken into consideration is a question of distributive justice, the subject of the next chapter.

INNER FREEDOM

Two main propositions have been argued for in the previous two sections. One is that

we are free to the extent that we can do as we like (which means that we are not properly described as free or not-free, only as more or less free). The other is that freedom, understood in this way, is good in itself. We should all have as much of it as possible, and if our freedom is to be curtailed it is to be for the sake only of other people, not ourselves.

However, we now have to look at the question of whether feminists do indeed think that freedom is a good thing, and want it for women. If freedom is the ability to fulfil one's desires, and if feminists do want it for women, they should surely be trying to make the world as much as possible as women would like it to be. However, it is a most conspicuous fact about some feminists that they seem to include among their aims things which not only *men* find objectionable, but which women do too. There are all kinds of things which women seem to want and have no wish to change, and yet which many feminists apparently want to abolish. Traditional marriage and division of labour seem to be happily chosen by many women; many enjoy making themselves attractive to men, and giving men certain kinds of service in return for being protected by them. Many would rather look after a home and family than do anything else. And many, with the appearance of total freedom, choose to enter beauty competitions (which are watched as willingly by millions more women), or to become striptease artists, 'hostesses' of various sorts, and prostitutes.

Of course, you can argue here that some of these apparently free choices are not very free at all, because choosing the best of a bad lot does not give women what they really want. They probably would not choose to become housewives or prostitutes if better things were readily available to them. There is much truth in that, no doubt, but it does not provide the slightest reason for taking away the best there is and leaving these women with something which must, in their eyes, be still worse. The true liberator can always be recognized by her wanting to *in-*

---

[6] Mill, 'On Liberty', in *The Essential Works of John Stuart Mill*, ed. Lerner, p. 263.

crease the options open to the people who are to be liberated, and there is never any justification for taking a choice away from a group you want to liberate unless it is demonstrable beyond all reasonable doubt that removing it will bring other, more important, options into existence. To give women freedom we must give them more choice, and then if they really do not want the things they are choosing now, like homes and families, those things will just die out without our having to push them.

Of course there are many feminists who do want to increase the options open to women. Consider, for instance, the programme for the picketing of a Miss America Pageant, which stated 'There will be . . . Lobbying Visits to the contestants urging our sisters to reject the Pageant Farce and join us . . . we do not plan heavy disruptive tactics. . . .'[7] That was genuinely liberating. The women entering the competition might not have thought of other routes to success, or they might not have realized that there were groups of people where different things were valued. However that is, or at least seems (it is not always easy to know how literally things are to be taken) a very different matter from the demonstrations at the Miss World competition in London where feminist protestors would apparently have liked to disrupt the whole proceedings. To prevent women from doing what they have chosen to do is not to be concerned with their freedom. Nevertheless, that does seem to be the aim of some feminists.

But that is not the end of the matter. This kind of feminist need not accept yet the accusation that she is not really offering women freedom. In general, when the liberators of women or anyone else take the view that they know better than the beneficiaries of their efforts what should be done for them, they will argue that these people are *conditioned,* and therefore not in a state of mind to be able to choose freely no matter

how many alternatives are open to them. *That* is why the liberators sometimes have to make choices on their behalf.

This kind of view certainly has intuitive plausibility about it. However, it does present many problems, and in particular the immediate one of seeming to call for (at least) a modification of the account of freedom so far given. It has been argued so far that an individual's freedom is a function mainly of how many choices there are available. If we are to accept, however, that it may sometimes be acceptable to *restrict* such choices in the name of freedom, on the grounds that the person to be liberated is conditioned and therefore unable to choose, a new element seems to have entered into the idea of liberty. It seems that to be free it is not enough to have a wide range of options open. As well as, or perhaps even instead of, having such options, the free individual must be in a certain state of mind. Freedom must be at least in part an internal thing.

There certainly is no doubt that some such view is widespread in feminism. Perhaps the most striking indication of it is the use of the word 'liberated' when applied to women. To the outsider as well as to the feminist a liberated woman is not one who is free to choose among a great many options, but one who makes *certain kinds of choice;* she is not a woman with a tolerant and helpful husband who encourages her to achieve all her ambitions, but one who would not stand any nonsense from her husband if he tried any.

Now there is indeed a long philosophical tradition of saying that true freedom does not consist in being in an environment which permits you to do as you please, but consists (at least partly, depending on the theory) in being in a particular state of mind. Theories like these still do keep to the basic idea of freedom as the satisfaction of desire, but it is differently interpreted and analyzed. There are innumerable variants on the theme, but we need consider only two, and without too much detail.

---

[7] 'No More Miss America!' in *Sisterhood is Powerful,* ed. Morgan, p. 584.

The first, and more extreme, is the idea that freedom is contained *entirely* within the mind of the free person, with outside circumstances irrelevant. According to this view you are truly free when your desires have been so adjusted that you desire nothing you cannot get. According to the Stoic idea, for instance, if the slave reaches total tranquility of mind while the master is in the grips of unrealized desire, the slave is the freer of the two. And in Christianity, the reason for saying that perfect freedom is to be found in the service of God is that once the Christian has achieved a state of mind in which nothing is desired but to do the will of God, that desire need never be unfulfilled: the will of God can be done in any circumstances whatever. This extreme idea of freedom is not much found in feminism, although there are traces of it. The woman who determines that she will no longer care about things which previously obsessed her, like the approval of men, may be looking for freedom in this way. If she ceases to care about what men think she can act to please herself rather than men, and so lessen the extent of her unfulfilled desire.

The second, more moderate, view of internal freedom is one more commonly found in feminism. This idea is that being in the right state of mind is not enough on its own to make you free: to be free you *also* need the kind of freedom we have been discussing in this chapter, which involves being able to do as you like. However, that is not enough on its own, and a necessary condition of your choosing freely is that you should be in the right state of mind before deciding among the options which are open to you. There are all kinds of variants on this idea, but common to them all is something like the view that each individual has a *true self* which should be doing the choosing, but that its activities are obstructed by various contaminants which have got into the person in some way, and which prevent real choice as effectively as obstructions in the environment do. Plato, for instance, thought that there were parts of the soul,

and that the lower parts were always trying to pull the highest part from its chosen path. A common idea in religion is that the uncontaminated soul would choose what was good, but that evil powers may take possession of it and force evil choices. More recently, there is the psychoanalytic idea that you cannot be truly free without getting rid of the neuroses which come between yourself and your real desires. Of course, an idea along these lines is very common in feminism. The domination of men has been so complete that the male has entered women's souls, making them choose on behalf of men and against their own interests. That they think themselves free is beside the point: all that shows is how well the work of conditioning has been done.

Now it is quite clear that however difficult all this may be to work out in detail, there is something in it. It is also true that (risky as it may sound) it is *sometimes* reasonable to override people's immediate wishes in the cause of their greater freedom, even when the earlier definition of freedom is taken and we say that people are free to the extent that they can do as they like. For instance, if a friend wanted to achieve something which was very important to her, and we knew beyond any doubt that she was setting about it the wrong way but could not persuade her to change, we might override her immediate wishes because we wanted her to get something which we knew she wanted more. Or again, since freedom is not simply a matter of how many immediate choices there are, but also of *scope* of choice, we might override some trivial choice to make sure that there was a greater range of choices later on. This is always being done in the case of children. Parents are not (necessarily) working against their children's freedom if, for instance, they do not let the children decide which schools they should go to. If a school is so much better than another that it will allow the children far more important choices later on in life, it is in the interests of the children's freedom that they should not be allowed to choose now.

Nevertheless, it is obvious that if we are going to take this sort of line, we have to take *great care*. If women's wishes are to be ignored in the name of their freedom, on the grounds that they are conditioned, it is essential to know exactly what is meant by conditioning, why it is supposed to impair freedom, to what extent it is legitimate to ignore what people want if they are conditioned, and how to distinguish women who are conditioned from the ones who are not. If we do not take care, we run the risk of planning a scheme in which the only freedom women get is the freedom to do what their liberators want them to do.

That is a tempting line anyway. As an early feminist Margaret Rhondda said, 'the passion to decide to look after your fellow-men, to do good to them in your way, is far more common than the desire to put into everyone's hand the power to look after themselves.'[8] The danger becomes intensified a thousand times when you can do this but still be able to convince yourself that you are offering freedom because the whole issue has been obscured under more or less indiscriminate accusations of conditioning. If the idea of conditioning is to be used to enhance freedom, and not as a general device by which a liberation movement can do as it likes in the name of freedom, it must be pinned down more precisely.

CONDITIONING AND THE REAL WOMAN

There is one point which must be made quite clear before going any further. The conditioning which was referred to in the previous section is supposed to be a sort of thing which is *actually a constraint* on a woman; something which comes between herself and her true desires. Now the word 'conditioning' is one which is extremely commonly used in feminism, in all kinds of circum-

stances, and what must on no account be presumed is that *whenever* the word is used the so-called conditioned desires, attitudes and responses are things which actually do prevent the real woman from fulfilling her real desires.

In feminist contexts the usual ground for making an accusation of conditioning is to point to the social root of the habit of mind in question (which is, of course, always one which is disapproved of). Women want to make themselves beautiful only because society has made them want to; they think that their mission in life is to be mothers because everyone has been drumming it into them since the age of two; they lack ambition because they have been brought up from birth to think that the female is the natural servant of the male and on no account to compete with him. This may all be true. However, to establish that a woman is conditioned in *that* sense of the word is nothing like enough to show that she is conditioned in the very different sense of having something in her personality which gets between herself and the fulfillment of her real desires, and therefore that these environmentally produced characteristics limit her freedom.

The reason why conditioning in the sense of 'coming from a (disapproved of) social influence' cannot be the same as conditioning in the sense of 'getting in the way of the true woman's desires' is obvious from the discussion of the nature of woman in the last chapter. You cannot distinguish between the woman as she now is and what is supposed to be the 'true' woman by pointing to the way society has shaped her. It is absolutely inevitable that the adult woman should be as she is partly as a result of social influence, and it is a thing we cannot possibly object to unless we are to suggest that people should be sent to grow up among wolves (and anyway there are social pressures even among wolves). We cannot say of social pressures *in general* that they turn the woman into something which is not her true self; on the contrary, they cannot be any-

---

[8] Quoted Firestone, *The Dialectic of Sex*, p. 20.

thing other than a contribution to what she actually is.

Of course we may not *like* the way women are at present, and if we do not we can argue that their upbringing ought to be changed. Very obviously, for instance, feminists are bound to disapprove of any upbringing which is so much at odds with women's intrinsic natures that they are bound to be unhappy. They can also reasonably object to women's being brought up to depend on men in the achievement of what they want, because that is unreliable and their success in life should be more firmly based. They can disapprove of women's being encouraged to see their main aim in life as relationships with men, and all their ambitions directed towards pleasing men in one way or another, because it is undignified and they want women to be dignified. They can say that women ought not to be brought up to confine their interests and activities to domestic matters and concentrate their energies on trivia, because they would prefer them to be well-educated, ambitious and serious-minded. Since there is no neutral way to bring children up (they must be surrounded by influences of one kind or another) we have a good deal of choice about how adults eventually turn out. We certainly could make women other than they are now, and it is not surprising that feminists would like to see a good many changes.

On the other hand, none of this provides any reason at all for saying that women as they are now, with the desires they have now, are not *free*. We may think it a good thing that women should be brought up to be happy, dignified, independent, serious and useful, but, once again, everything is what it is. Happiness is happiness, dignity is dignity, independence is independence: none of these things is freedom. Even though there may be some difficulty about finding a definitive account of freedom there are limits to what we can reasonably decide to adopt, and it really would be travesty of the language (as well as potentially

treacherous) to say that people were not free just because we did not like the way they were, or that in making them into something we liked better we should be giving them freedom. We may argue with perfect justice that women are as they are because of social influences, but that is not enough to show that the choices they are making are not their own real choices. And if by 'conditioned' we want to mean 'not in a state to make free choices' we must mean something more than 'influenced by social pressures we disapprove of'.

Of course we can still, if we want to, say that 'conditioned' does just refer to socially induced characteristics in women, rather than aspects of a woman's character which somehow do get in the way of her real desires. However, this is dangerous. The word has now such deeply entrenched connotations of interference with freedom that if we take a definition which does not include those connotations we open the floodgates to mistakes and double dealing. I shall therefore take it that 'conditioning' is properly used only when it does refer to a real restriction on freedom. The problem is, now that we have decided that a woman brought up one way is no less her real self than a woman brought up any other way, to work out what form conditioning might take.

FREEDOM AND CONDITIONING

Since we are trying to distinguish the social pressures which condition a woman from the ones which simply form her character, one obvious starting point is the fact that from the point of view of each individual there is a great difference between different kinds of social pressure. Whereas some are congenial and easily conformed to, others are not: some social pressures push people towards doing things for which they have an intrinsic dislike.

Nevertheless, people often go along even with these, because doing so is less unpleasant than suffering the social consequences of resistance. So a woman who has no natural interest in beauty may make herself as beautiful as she can; or one who is not interested in children may do her best to absorb herself in the concerns of a family; or a woman by nature apt to explore jungles may become a secretary, because that is the feminine thing to do and that way she will get social approval. None of this shows conditioning. The environment is constricting, but nevertheless a woman who makes the best choice among the limited set available to her is behaving perfectly rationally and choosing in her own interest, and as long as she is doing that the only restrictions on her freedom are external, not internal.

However, what happens to these women who go along with uncongenial social pressures when liberators appear on the scene, and suggest to them that the world would be a better place if women did not spend so much time on their appearance, or that children are not necessarily the ideal object of every woman's devotion? Or what happens if they find themselves in a situation where the uncongenial social pressures are beginning to lessen, and following their natural inclinations would bring down less social censure?

If they thoroughly understand the situation in which they have grown up there may be no difficulty. They may instantly join in the campaign to change the things which are alien to their natures, or at least take advantage of any changes which come about. But this may well not happen. Usually when children are subjected to pressures in growing up they do not think separately about what they would like to do and what adult pressures and encouragements compel them to do; they just get into habits of doing what produces the least unacceptable consequences. The result is that when the situation changes, or when there is some prospect of its changing, they may not rush to embrace the new but cling to the habits they have grown up with. Probably they do not understand that their present prefer-

ences came about by the forcible suppression of their natural (that is, inherent) inclinations, but even if they do they may well have difficulty in ridding themselves of the habits they have gathered. These habits may then come between the adults and their real desires.

A simple analogy can be drawn from an entirely different context. When you learn to drive you rapidly pick up the skills of braking and steering, and your responses to various situations become so automatic that you can usually do the right thing without thinking. But you may well learn these habits without knowing much about how braking and steering work, and the result is that the first time you skid you react in the way you always have reacted when the car moves too fast in the wrong direction, by braking as hard as possible and hauling the steering wheel round. The consequences are exactly the opposite of what you want. In order to avoid the situation in future you have to do two things. The first is to understand the theory, so that you know under what conditions the usual methods will and will not work, and the second is to free yourself of your habitual actions.

As a motorist you have very definite desires (to move in particular directions), but you yourself may interfere with their fulfilment through ignorance, or bad habits, or both. Much the same may happen with women. Their failure to understand the situation they are in, and the persistence of deeply entrenched habits, may get in the way of what they want to do. And where this happens we can say that a woman's state of mind is obstructing her desires, *without having to resort to dubious theories about hidden desires in the core of her imaginary real self.*

Failure to understand the nature of the world and the structure of possibilities within it acts against women in all kinds of ways. For instance, many women (if not all) are by nature as inclined as men to seek fame and fortune, but the traditional restricted upbringing of a woman means that in most cases there is only a limited number of forms in which she is capable of casting this ambition: she may think as a matter of course that success for a woman must take the form of being pursued by men, envied by women and renowned for beauty. But if that is the only way in which she can imagine making an impact on the world she is likely to have condemned herself to failure before even setting out. Few women succeed in being renowned for beauty, and anyway beauty does not last. Or she may have more specific ambitions, and look for political power, but may automatically presume that political success for a woman must take the form of being the wife of a politician, and in that case her potential for success is restricted from the start by the casting of her ambitions in a form which sets a low upper limit on possible success. If women squeeze their desires into a conventionally feminine mould they are likely to be doomed to failure from the first. But even if they succeed in it, may still fail because of habits of mind which interfere: perhaps she cannot avoid feeling that she ought to take care with her dress, or feeling guilty if she lets her husband do his fair share of the housework, however clearly she may understand the unreasonableness of such feelings. Her ingrained habits of mind prevent the fulfilment of her strongest desires.

This analysis seems to provide a very good account of what it is to be conditioned, and there is no difficulty at all about seeing it as an internal lack of freedom: something about the woman which prevents her from doing as she really wants. One aspect of conditioning is *ignorance;* probably the greatest curtailer of freedom there is, because if someone does not know or fully grasp that the world contains certain possibilities, as far as that person is concerned they might just as well not exist. The other aspect is the inability to change unwelcome aspects of oneself, which is as much a restriction on the fulfilment of desire as the inability to change anything in the outside world. If you want to be more beautiful, or run faster, or be stronger, or be able to charm people, but cannot do whatever it is, you are as curtailed in your desires as you would be through not having money, or influence, or a car, or tools for a trade.

The upshot of all this is that feminists are indeed right in thinking that lack of freedom can be internal: a woman may be in a state where her own mind prevents her from achieving what she really wants (a matter which must not be confused with her mind preventing what she would have wanted if she had been someone else). However, although the comparisons drawn in the last paragraph between internal and external restrictions on freedom do show that freedom can be limited by aspects of the mind, what they also show at the same time is that there is no intrinsic difference between external and internal lack of freedom; they are essentially the same sort of thing. Internal lack of freedom does not consist in being in a special state of mind or having a particular set of desires, only in having within oneself (rather than in surrounding circumstances) the things which prevent fulfilment of desire. This means that, in fact, there is no problem about reconciling the concept of internal freedom with the first account of freedom given in this chapter. The only acceptable interpretation of 'internal freedom' (the only account of it which does not involve calling something quite different by the name of freedom, or presuming that the real woman is something uninfluenced by society) is one which makes it essentially a matter of being unimpeded in one's desires by one's own ignorance and habits. This is important. Once it is clear people will be less likely to be confused by the vague way in which 'conditioned' is often used, or lured into thinking that if women have socially induced desires which the liberators disapprove of, they are necessarily not free.

THE ATTACK ON CONDITIONING

When women are really conditioned, their preconceptions and immediate desires do get in the way of what, in some perfectly obvious way, they really want. If they are conditioned, therefore, it does seem that other people may be justified in overriding their immediate desires in order to produce not what the liberators think they should want, but what they actually do want.

However, there is an obvious danger in taking this attitude, because the only case in which it would be reasonable to override a woman's wishes in the name of her freedom would be where it was absolutely certain that she was conditioned, and equally certain what she really wanted and how it could be brought about. And the simple fact of the matter is that it is virtually impossible even to approach certainty in cases like this, let alone reach it. It is very hard to tell when, and to what extent, people are conditioned.

The main reason why this must be so is probably obvious from what has gone before. The point is that it is quite impossible to tell conditioned women from unconditioned ones[9] by their preferences. The pressures on women to be beautiful and maternal and domestic and deferential to men have no doubt left in many women habits of mind which will prevent their ever achieving what they really want to achieve, but we are not entitled to presume that the pressures which produced these mental blocks in some women did the same for all. For the women to whom these pressures were congenial, as they must have been for some, the desires produced became their own most basic desires, and not obstacles to the fulfilment of others. If a woman is interested mainly in dress or nursery design it is no doubt true to say that it can be attributed to her background to some extent: if she had been brought up differently she would have had different interests. However, these may be genuinely hers, and ideally suited to her nature. The 'conditioned' responses may be

genuinely her own. It is therefore impossible to tell whether or not a woman is conditioned just by knowing about her likes and dislikes, or about her formative influences.

What that means is that the only attack which can be safely mounted against conditioning must be directed to its source. It is too dangerous to try to 'free' women who are regarded as conditioned by forcing them to do what the prevailing feminist ideology presumes they must want, because with that method there is always the danger of ignoring women's real wishes. They may not be conditioned at all. The only thing to do is start from the beginning and try, even at this late stage, to remove the cause of the trouble, and give conditioned women a chance to become unconditioned in a way which runs no risk of damaging those who are not, because it still leaves women to make their own choices.

There are two stages to this process, corresponding to the two aspects of conditioning. The first is to increase understanding of how the present state of things came about and how it works, so that women who have been doing what does not suit them can understand why, and at the same time what alternatives are possible. The second is to make help available to women who decide as a result of this that they do want to change their habits.

There are all kinds of ways in which advances could be made on these two fronts. The key to the first is *diversity*. Women must be exposed to all kinds of new influences and information (in addition to the old, of course, not instead of them) to make them fully aware of the possibilities the world contains. Some people, no doubt, will try to turn the freedom argument against this procedure by saying that if people have new alternatives thrust before them they are *forced to choose*, and that in itself is an infringement of liberty because people ought to have the freedom not to choose if that is what they would prefer. However, that argument cannot possibly work. This is because it is true as a matter of *logic* that peo-

---

[9] More accurately, of course, *more* or *less* conditioned, and in certain ways rather than just in general. Throughout arguments of this sort it must not be forgotten that freedom is a matter of degree.

ple cannot be the ultimate determiners of their own degree of freedom. Whatever anyone chooses to do, that choice comes from among alternatives which already exist, and those alternatives were not themselves chosen. Since, therefore, the ultimate degree of freedom is always out of the hands of the individual we are right to insist that the choice given should always be as great as possible. We cannot, in the name of liberty for women, force them to do anything against their wills or bring about states of society they do not like, but we are bound to give them more knowledge of possibilities.

The second part of the attack on conditioning is to reinforce this for women who do decide that they would like to change their lives by giving them every help in overcoming unwelcome habits of mind: help ranging from the support of other women who understand the position to full-scale psychotherapy. As long as this was directed to bringing about what women themselves wanted, and not to persuading them into something they did not want, it would be genuinely liberating.

Still, however energetically we pursued such a programme, we should have to be hopelessly optimistic to think that we should actually eliminate all existing conditioning as a result of it, and perhaps this seems to justify the wish of some feminists to make a firm attack on the symptoms of conditioning, rather than going in this gently way for its cause. However much we may want freedom for women, they could argue, even the freedom to stay conditioned, can we allow them this freedom if the price of it is to trap other women in the same bonds? Can we allow a conditioned mother to bring up her daughter in the same way? Surely for the sake of the daughters we ought to be willing to run the risk of attacking directly what we believe to be the mothers' conditioned desires, even though we may run some risk of going against their real wishes? Surely we should work directly against bad influences, and deliberately get rid of (for instance)

beauty competitions, sexist literature in schools, and anything else we think objectionable, whatever the conditioned mothers may think of the matter?

However, even though conditioned mothers will certainly tend to bring up conditioned daughters, and although we certainly cannot allow that, this conclusion is not the proper one to draw. The way to prevent the daughters from becoming conditioned is not to keep them out of the range of influence of the things which are believed to have conditioned their mothers, because it was not *being in the range of those influences* which did the harm, but *being out of the range of others*. If we bring the daughters up on a diet of so-called non-sexist literature (much of what is around at present is actually *female* sexist) to think that there should be no sex roles, that does not free them from conditioning: it only brings them up with a different sort. If to get feminist approval a little girl is forced to sneer at the idea of beauty competitions, she is as much coerced as her mother was by parents who expected her to look pleased when she was given dolls and pretty party frocks. Once again, whether or not a girl is conditioned cannot be judged by which slogans she grows up chanting, because in theory she could be conditioned into chanting any.

The solution to the problem, as always with questions of freedom, is once again diversity. We can perhaps summarize the claims of conditioned mothers and those of daughters who are to be rescued from conditioning by proposing a solution to the widely debated problem of how free a parent should be to determine a child's education. We can put it this way. Within practicable limits, the parent should be allowed to say that the child *must* learn certain things, and have lessons from people of particular political, moral or religious views. On the other hand, no parent should have the right to *prevent* the child's learning anything (going to scripture classes in the wrong religion or having sex education) or being exposed to other people's views. The education authorities should have a positive duty to diversify influences, since in that way the parents' wishes are respected but the child's freedom is not impaired. That should be what feminists want. As Germaine Greer said of a similar problem, 'censorship is the weapon of the opposition, not ours'.[10]

CONCLUDING NOTE

This chapter has been about the nature of freedom, its importance, and how to achieve it. What it has not dealt with in much detail is the relationship between freedom and other valuable things, such as the absence of suffering.

This is a complicated question, but in conclusion let me give a quick outline of the position I think acceptable. That is that freedom is the most important thing, and from their own points of view all people should be given as much freedom as possible. It is only when they are not in a position to choose, and we do not know what they would have chosen if they had been, that the questions

of happiness and suffering arise separately. As long as they can choose they should decide their own priorities, restricted only by considerations of other people's freedom. But when we have to decide for someone else, we should make the decision on the basis of minimizing suffering. That is controversial, since many people would say that we ought rather to concentrate on maximizing happiness.[11] I hope, however, the difference between the two will not be important for too many of the discussions which are to follow, and during the rest of this book it will be presumed that our first consideration for any individual should be to maximize freedom, and our second to minimize suffering.

---

[10] Greer, *The Female Eunuch*, p. 309.

[11] One situation in which disagreement would arise would be, for instance, on the subject of whether it would be worthwhile to bring new people into the world or not. Someone who wanted freedom and the absence of suffering would say that it was worthwhile to bring new people into the world only because they were wanted by people who already existed. Someone who wanted to maximize happiness would say that it was worthwhile to bring new people into the world, as long as they would be happy, without depending on the wishes of people already in existence. See, e.g., Glover, *Causing Death and Saving Lives*, p. 69.

Grounds for Coercion

Joel Feinberg

Proving that freedom is good for its own sake, like demonstrating the worth of any basic value, may be impossible. But Joel Feinberg argues that there is a basic presumption in favor of freedom. Coercion may prevent great evils and be wholly warranted, but it always has its price. After rejecting as too simple two accounts of when social and political coercion are justified, Feinberg goes on to examine the harm-to-others principle that Mills defends in *On Liberty* and to consider some possible objections to that principle. After distinguishing various other grounds for limiting liberty besides the harm principle, Feinberg discusses the use of state coercion to protect individuals from self-inflicted harm (the doctrine of legal paternalism). He maintains that the state has the right to prevent self-regarding harmful conduct only when it is substantially non-voluntary or when temporary intervention is necessary to establish whether it is voluntary or not. He concludes by considering the use of state coercion to promote the achievement of collective goods.

THE PRESUMPTIVE CASE FOR LIBERTY

Whatever else we believe about freedom, most of us believe it is something to be praised, or so luminously a Thing of Value that is beyond praise. What is it that makes freedom a good thing? Some say that freedom is good in itself quite apart from its consequences. On the other hand, James Fitzjames Stephen wrote that ". . . the question whether liberty is a good or a bad thing appears as irrational as the question whether fire is a good or a bad thing."[1] Freedom,

according to Stephen, is good (when it is good) only because of what it does, not because of what it is.

It would be impossible to demonstrate that freedom is good for its own sake, and indeed, this proposition is far from self-evident. Still, Stephen's analogy to fire seems an injustice to freedom. Fire has no constant and virtually invariant effects that tend to make it, on balance, a good thing whenever and wherever it occurs, and bad only when its subsequent remoter effects are so evil as to counterbalance its direct and immediate ones. Thus, a fire in one's bed while one is sleeping is dreadful because its effects are evil, but a fire under the pot on the stove is splendid because it makes possible a hot cup of coffee when one wants it. The direct effect of fire in these and all

Reprinted from Joel Feinberg, *Social Philosophy* (Englewood Cliffs, N.J.: Prentice-Hall, 1973).

[1] James Fitzjames Stephen, *Liberty, Equality, Fraternity* (London: 1873), p. 48.

other cases is to oxidize material objects and raise the temperature in its immediate environment; but *these* effects, from the point of view of human interests, and considered just in themselves, are neither good nor bad.

Freedom has seemed to most writers quite different in this respect. When a free man violates his neighbor's interests, then his freedom, having been put to bad use, was, on balance, a bad thing, but unlike the fire in the bed, it was not an unalloyed evil. Whatever the harmful consequences of freedom in a given case, there is always a direct effect on the person of its possessor which must be counted a positive good. Coercion may prevent great evils, and be wholly justified on that account, but it always has its price. Coercion may be on balance a great gain, but its direct effects always, or nearly always, constitute a definite loss. If this is true, there is always a *presumption* in favor of freedom, even though it can in some cases be overridden by more powerful reasons on the other side.

The presumption in favor of freedom is usually said to rest on freedom's essential role in the development of traits of intellect and character which constitute the good of individuals and are centrally important means to the progress of societies. One consensus argument, attributable with minor variations to Von Humboldt, Mill, Hobhouse, and many others, goes roughly as follows. The highest good for man is neither enjoyment nor passive contentment, but rather a dynamic process of growth and self-realization. This can be called "happiness" if we mean by that term what the Greeks did, namely, "The exercise of vital powers along lines of excellence in a life affording them scope."[2] The highest social good is then the greatest possible amount of individual self-realization and (assuming that different persons are inclined by their natures in different ways) the resultant diversity and fullness of life. Self-realization consists in the actualization of certain uniquely human potentialities, the bringing to full development of certain uniquely human potentialities, the bringing to full development of certain powers and abilities. This in turn requires constant practice in making difficult choices among alternative hypotheses, policies, and actions—and the more difficult the better. John Stuart Mill explained why:

The human faculties of perception, judgment, discriminative feeling, mental activity, and even moral preference are exercised only in making a choice. He who does anything because it is the custom makes no choice. He gains no practice either in discerning or in desiring what is best. The mental and moral, like the muscular, powers are improved only by being used.[3]

In short, one does not realize what is best in oneself when social pressures to conform to custom lead one mindlessly along. Even more clearly, one's growth will be stunted when one is given no choice in the first place, either because of being kept in ignorance or because one is terrorized by the wielders of bayonets.

Freedom to decide on one's own while fully informed of the facts thus tends to promote the good of the person who exercises it, even if it permits him to make foolish or dangerous mistakes. Mill added to this argument the citation of numerous social benefits that redound indirectly but uniformly to those who grant freedom as well as those who exercise it. We all profit from the fruits of genius, he maintained, and genius, since it often involves doggedness and eccentricity, is likely to flourish only where coercive pressures toward conformity are absent. Moreover, social progress is more likely to occur where there is free criticism of prevailing ways and adventurous experiments in living. Finally, true understanding of human nature requires freedom, since without liberty there will be little diversity,

[2] See Edith Hamilton, *The Greek Way* (New York: W. W. Norton & Company, Inc., 1942), pp. 35 ff.

[3] John Stuart Mill, *On Liberty* (New York: Liberal Arts Press, 1956), p. 71.

and without diversity *all* aspects of the human condition will be ascribed to fixed nature rather than to the workings of a particular culture.

Such are the grounds for holding that there is always a presumption in favor of freedom, that whenever we are faced with an option between forcing a person to do something and letting him decide on his own whether or not to do it, other things being equal, we should always opt for the latter. If a strong general presumption for freedom has been established, the burden of proof rests on the shoulders of the advocate of coercion, and the philosopher's task will be to state the conditions under which the presumption can be overridden.

THE ANARCHISTIC PRINCIPLE

It will be instructive to see why certain very simple statements of the conditions for justified social and political coercion are unsatisfactory. The first of these, which might with propriety be called "anarchistic," insists that society and the state should grant to every citizen "complete liberty to do whatever he wishes." In this view, no coercive power exercised by state or society is ever justified. What then of the coercion imposed by one individual or group on another? If every man is free to do whatever he wishes, it follows that all men are free to inflict blows on John Doe, to hold noisy parties under his window every night, and to help themselves to his possessions. How can it then be true that John Doe is free at the same time to come and go as he pleases, to sleep at night, and to enjoy exclusive use of his possessions? . . .

Given that the important desires of men can and usually do conflict, one person will be free to act on a desire only to the extent that others are unfree to act on conflicting desires; if the state is to guarantee to all men the freedom to do one certain kind of thing, then, in all likelihood, it must make all men unfree to prevent others from doing that sort of thing. "As against the coercion applicable by individual to individual," wrote Bentham, "no liberty can be given to one man but in proportion as it is taken away from another. All coercive laws, therefore, and in particular all laws creative of liberty, are as far as they go abrogative of liberty."[4] But if prohibitive laws destroy a liberty for every liberty they confer or protect, while the anarchistic principle would neither add nor subtract liberties from the natural situation of men, don't they yield precisely the same net totals of liberty and constraint, differing merely in the manner of distribution? This conclusion is yet another trap we can fall into by interpreting usefully loose talk about "amounts" of freedom in a precise quantitative way.

Most civilized societies have prohibitive laws or other social devices to prevent individuals from inflicting blows on the faces of other individuals. There is sometimes a great deal of pleasure to be derived from bopping someone in the nose, but most of us think that this pleasure is worth sacrificing for the greater good of security from physical attack by others. Suppose, however, that some rugged individualist complains that our law infringes on his freedom, making it virtually impossible for him to enjoy the thrill of smashing noses, and just because of the scruples of a lot of weak-kneed, lily-livered sissies. "Since the days of the frontier," he might say, "there hasn't been any real freedom in this country." We should no doubt try to explain to him that the interest people have in the physical integrity of their noses is *more important* than their aggressive interests, and therefore more worthy of protection.

Now suppose that we had quite different rules, and that more people were free to hit others in the nose, and correspondingly fewer were free to enjoy the full beauty and utility of their own unbloodied proboscises.

---

[4] Jeremy Bentham, "Anarchical Fallacies," in *The Works of Jeremy Bentham*, Vol. 2, ed. John Bowring (Edinburgh, 1843).

Would this new arrangement have a greater or smaller "amount" of freedom in it, on balance? Perhaps it is least misleading to say that there would be not "less" freedom but freedom of a morally inferior kind. Most societies have recognized that there are some relatively permanent desires present in all men that must be singled out, given precedence, and made legally sacrosanct. When these interests are so recognized and protected by law, they come to be called *rights*. . . . Selection of those interests important enough to be protected in this way is made in accordance with the settled value judgments of the community by application of some standard other than that of "simple freedom" itself, which is quite insufficient. To receive "complete liberty" from society and its government would be to incur other constraints from private individuals, and almost all who have thought about this exchange consider it a bad trade.

THE FORMALISTIC PRINCIPLE

The second unsatisfactory principle of freedom distribution does not have such obvious failings. In fact, many have spoken as if it were a self-evident truth. Society, it says, should grant to every person "full liberty to do what he pleases providing only that he does not interfere with the like liberty of another."[5] This principle is the right answer to the wrong question. It insists that liberty should be distributed impartially, and that no individual take exception to the general prohibitive laws. But if it is taken as an answer to our question—when is political or social coercion justified?—it is entirely formal and empty, and consistent with any system of legal constraints that is not arbitrary. A general rule permitting nose-bopping would satisfy it just as well as one prohibit-

ing it; the anarchistic principle conforms to it, as well as a principle prohibiting all aggressive behavior. The principle employs a sound maxim of justice, insisting as it does on nondiscriminatory legislation and impartial enforcement, but it provides no guide to the proper *content* of the law. Its inadequacy as a substantive principle of freedom distribution was well appreciated by L. T. Hobhouse, who wrote, "My right to keep my neighbor awake by playing the piano all night is not satisfactorily counterbalanced by his right to keep a dog which howls all the time the piano is being played."[6] Each party in this example would use his freedom to the detriment of the other under a law which recognizes a "like liberty" for the other party to do the same if he can. That the law is nondiscriminatory would be small consolation to either party if it permitted his interests to be seriously harmed.

THE CONCEPT OF HARM

If social and political coercion is a harm-causing evil, then one way to justify it is to show that it is necessary for the prevention of even greater evils. That is the generating insight of the "harm to others principle" (henceforth called simply "the harm principle") which permits society to restrict the liberty of some persons in order to prevent harm to others. Two versions of this principle can be distinguished. The first would justify restriction of one person's liberty to prevent injury to other specific individuals, and can therefore be called "the private harm principle." The second can be invoked to justify coercion on the distinct ground that it is necessary to prevent impairment of institutional practices and regulatory systems that are in the public interest; thus it can be called "the public harm principle." That the private harm principle (whose chief advocate was J. S. Mill) states at least

[5] L. T. Hobhouse, *The Elements of Social Justice* (London: George Allen & Unwin Ltd., 1922), p. 60. Hobhouse rejects this formula, and I have adapted his argument against it in the text.

[6] L. T. Hobhouse, *Liberalism* (New York: Holt, Rinehart and Winston, Inc., 1911), pp. 63–64.

one of the acceptable grounds for coercion is virtually beyond controversy. Hardly anyone would deny the state the right to make criminal such directly injurious conduct as willful homicide, assault and battery, and robbery. Mill often wrote as if prevention of private harm is the *sole* valid ground for state coercion, but this must not have been his considered intention. He would not have wiped from the books such crimes as tax evasion, smuggling, and contempt of court, which need not injure any specific individuals, except insofar as they weaken public institutions in whose health we all have a stake. I shall assume that Mill held both the public and private versions of the harm principle.

In its simplest formulations, the harm principle is still a long way from being a precise guide to the ideal legislator, especially in those difficult cases where harms of different orders, magnitudes, and probabilities must be balanced against one another. . . .

LINES OF ATTACK ON MILL

Arguments against Mill's unsupplemented harm principle (his claim that the private and public harm principles state the *only* grounds for justified interference with liberty) have been mainly of two different kinds.[7] Many have argued that the harm principle justifies too much social and political interference in the affairs of individuals. Others allow that the prevention of individual and social harm is always a ground for interference, but insist that it is by no means the only ground.

(i) "No Man Is An Island"

Mill maintained in *On Liberty* that social interference is never justified in those of a man's affairs that concern himself only. But

no man's affairs have effects on himself alone. There are a thousand subtle and indirect ways in which every individual act, no matter how private and solitary, affects others. It would therefore seem that society has a right, on Mill's own principles, to interfere in every department of human life. Mill anticipated this objection and took certain steps to disarm it. Let it be allowed that no human conduct is entirely, exclusively, and to the last degree self-regarding. Still, Mill insisted, we can distinguish between actions that are plainly other-regarding and those that are "directly," "chiefly," or "primarily" self-regarding. There will be a twilight area of cases difficult to classify, but that is true of many other workable distinctions, including that between night and day.

It is essential to Mill's theory that we make a distinction between two different kinds of consequences of human actions: the consequences *directly* affecting the interests of others, and those of primarily self-regarding behavior which only *indirectly* or *remotely* affect the interests of others. "No person ought to be punished simply for being drunk," Mill wrote, "but a soldier or policeman should be punished for being drunk on duty."[8] A drunk policeman directly harms the interests of others. His conduct gives opportunities to criminals and thus creates grave risk of harm to other citizens. It brings the police into disrepute, and makes the work of his colleagues more dangerous. Finally, it may lead to loss of the policeman's job, with serious consequences for his wife and children.

Consider, on the other hand, a hard working bachelor who habitually spends his evening hours drinking himself into a stupor, which he then sleeps off, rising fresh in the morning to put in another hard day's work. His drinking does not *directly* affect others in any of the ways of the drunk policeman's conduct. He has no family; he drinks alone and sets no direct example; he is not prevented from discharging any of his

---

[7] Cf. H. L. A. Hart, *Law, Liberty, and Morality* (Stanford: Stanford University Press, 1963), p. 5.

[8] Mill, *On Liberty*, pp. 99–100.

public duties; he creates no substantial risk of harm to the interests of other individuals. Although even his private conduct will have some effects on the interests of others, these are precisely the sorts of effects Mill would call "indirect" and "remote." First, in spending his evenings the way he does, our solitary tippler is *not* doing any number of other things that might be of greater utility to others. In not earning and spending more money, he is failing to stimulate the economy (except for the liquor industry) as much as he might. Second, he fails to spend his evening time improving his talents and making himself a better person. Perhaps he has a considerable native talent for painting or poetry, and his wastefulness is depriving the world of some valuable art. Third, he may make those of his colleagues who like him sad on his behalf. Finally, to those who know of his habits, he is a "bad example."[9] All of these "indirect harms" together, Mill maintained, do not outweigh the direct and serious harm that would result from social or legal coercion.

Mill's critics have never been entirely satisfied by this. Many have pointed out that Mill is concerned not only with political coercion and legal punishment but also with purely social coercion—moral pressure, social avoidance, ostracism. No responsible critic would wish the state to punish the solitary tippler, but social coercion is another matter. We can't prevent people from disapproving of an individual for his self-regarding faults or from expressing that disapproval to others, without undue restriction on *their* freedom. Such expressions, in Mill's view, are inevitably coercive, constituting a "milder form of punishment." Hence "social punishment" of individuals for conduct that directly concerns only themselves—the argument concludes—is

both inevitable and, according to Mill's own principles, proper.

Mill anticipated this objection, too, and tried to cope with it by making a distinction between types of social responses. We cannot help but lower in our estimation a person with serious self-regarding faults. We will think ill of him, judge him to be at fault, and make him the inevitable and proper object of our disapproval, distaste, even contempt. We may warn others about him, avoid his company, and withhold gratuitous benefits from him—"not to the oppression of his individuality but in the exercise of ours."[10] Mill concedes that all of these social responses can function as "penalties"—but they are suffered "only in so far as they are the natural and, as it were, the spontaneous consequences of the faults themselves, not because they are purposely inflicted on him for the sake of punishment."[11] Other responses, on the other hand, add something to the "natural penalties"—pointed snubbing, economic reprisals, gossip campaigns, and so on. The added penalties, according to Mill, are precisely the ones that are never justified as responses to merely self-regarding flaws— "if he displeases us, we may express our distaste; and we may stand aloof from a person as well as from a thing that displeases us, but we shall not therefore feel called on to make his life uncomfortable."[12]

(ii) Other Proposed Grounds for Coercion

The distinction between self-regarding and other-regarding behavior, as Mill intended it to be understood, does seem at least roughly serviceable, and unlikely to invite massive social interference in private affairs. I think most critics of Mill would grant that, but reject the harm principle on the opposite ground that it doesn't permit

---

[9] Mill has a ready rejoinder to this last point: If the conduct in question is supposed to be greatly harmful to the actor himself, "the example, on the whole must be more salutary" than harmful socially, since it is a warning lesson, rather than an alluring model, to others. See Mill, *On Liberty*, p. 101.

[10] Mill, *On Liberty*, p. 94.

[11] Mill, *On Liberty*, p. 95.

[12] Mill, *On Liberty*, p. 96.

enough interference. These writers would allow at least one, and as many as five or more, additional valid grounds for coercion. Each of these proposed grounds is stated in a principle listed below. One might hold that restriction of one person's liberty can be justified:

1. To prevent harm to others, either
   a. injury to individual persons *(The Private Harm Principle)*, or
   b. impairment of institutional practices that are in the public interest *(The Public Harm Principle)*;
2. To prevent offense to others *(The Offense Principle)*;
3. To prevent harm to self *(Legal Paternalism)*;
4. To prevent or punish sin, i.e., to "enforce morality as such" *(Legal Moralism)*;
5. To benefit the self *(Extreme Paternalism)*;
6. To benefit others *(The Welfare Principle)*.

The liberty-limiting principles on this list are best understood as stating neither necessary nor sufficient conditions for justified coercion, but rather specifications of the *kinds* of reasons that are always relevant or acceptable in support of proposed coercion, even though in a given case they may not be conclusive.[13] Each principle states that interference might be permissible *if* (but not *only if*) a certain condition is satisfied. Hence the principles are not mutually exclusive; it is possible to hold two or more of them at once, even all of them together, and it is possible to deny all of them. Moreover, the principles cannot be construed as stating sufficient conditions for legitimate interference with liberty, for even though the principle is satisfied in a given case, the general presumption against coercion might not be outweighed. The harm principle, for example, does not justify state interference to prevent a tiny bit of inconsequential

harm. Prevention of minor harm always counts in favor of proposals (as in a legislature) to restrict liberty, but in a given instance it might not count *enough* to outweigh the general presumption against interference, or it might be outweighed by the prospect of practical difficulties in enforcing the law, excessive costs, and forfeitures of privacy. A liberty-limiting principle states considerations that are always good reasons for coercion, though neither exclusively nor, in every case, decisively good reasons.

It will not be possible to examine each principle in detail here, and offer "proofs" and "refutations." The best way to defend one's selection of principles is to show to which positions they commit one on such issues as censorship of literature, "morals offenses," and compulsory social security programs. General principles arise in the course of deliberations over particular problems, especially in the efforts to defend one's judgments by showing that they are consistent with what has gone before. If a principle commits one to an antecedently unacceptable judgment, then one has to modify or supplement the principle in a way that does the least damage to the harmony of one's particular and general opinions taken as a group. On the other hand, when a solid, well-entrenched principle entails a change in a particular judgment, the overriding claims of consistency may require that the judgment be adjusted. This sort of dialectic is similar to the reasonings that are prevalent in law courts. When similar cases are decided in opposite ways, it is incumbent on the court to distinguish them in some respect that will reconcile the separate decisions with each other and with the common rule applied to each. Every effort is made to render current decisions consistent with past ones unless the precedents seem so disruptive of the overall internal harmony of the law that they must, reluctantly, be revised or abandoned. In social and political philosophy every person is on his own, and the counterparts to "past decisions" are the most confident judgments one makes in or-

---

[13] I owe this point to Professor Michael Bayles. See his contribution to *Issues in Law and Morality*, ed. Norman Care and Thomas Trelogan (Cleveland: The Press of Case Western Reserve University, 1973).

dinary normative discourse. The philosophical task is to extract from these "given" judgments the principles that render them consistent, adjusting and modifying where necessary in order to convert the whole body of opinions into an intelligible, coherent system. There is no a priori way of refuting another's political opinions, but if our opponents are rational men committed to the idea of consistency, we can always hope to show them that a given judgment is inconsistent with one of their own acknowledged principles. Then something will have to give. . . .

LEGAL PATERNALISM

The liberty-limiting principle called legal paternalism justifies state coercion to protect individuals from self-inflicted harm, or, in its extreme version, to guide them, whether they like it or not, toward their own good. Parents can be expected to justify interference in the lives of their children (e.g., telling them what they must eat and when they must sleep) on the ground that "daddy knows best." Legal paternalism seems to imply that, since the state often perceives the interests of individual citizens better than do the citizens themselves, it stands as a permanent guardian of those interests *in loco parentis*. Put this bluntly, paternalism seems a preposterous doctrine. If adults are treated as children they will come in time to be like children. Deprived of the right to choose for themselves, they will soon lose the power of rational judgment and decision. Even children, after a certain point, had better not be "treated as children," or they will never acquire the outlook and capability of responsible adults.

Yet if we reject paternalism entirely, and deny that a person's own good is ever a valid ground for coercing him, we seem to fly in the face both of common sense and long-established customs and laws. In the criminal law, for example, a prospective victim's freely granted consent is no defense to the charge of mayhem or homicide. The state simply refuses to permit anyone to agree to his own disablement or killing. The law of contracts similarly refuses to recognize as valid contracts to sell oneself into slavery, or to become a mistress, or a second wife. Any ordinary citizen is legally justified in using reasonable force to prevent another from mutilating himself or committing suicide. No one is allowed to purchase certain drugs even for therapeutic purposes without a physician's prescription (doctor knows best). The use of other drugs, such as heroin, for mere pleasure is not permitted under any circumstances. It is hard to find any convincing rationale for all such restrictions apart from the argument that beatings, mutilations, death, concubinage, slavery, and bigamy are always bad for a person whether he or she knows it or not, and that antibiotics are too dangerous for any nonexpert, and narcotics for anyone at all, to take on his own initiative.

The trick is stopping short once one undertakes this path, unless we wish to ban whiskey, cigarettes, and fried foods, which tend to be bad for people, too. We must somehow reconcile our general repugnance for paternalism with the apparent necessity, or at least reasonableness, of some paternalistic regulations. The way to do this is to find mediating maxims or standards of application for the paternalistic principle which restrict its use in a way analogous to that in which the universality and reasonable avoidance tests delimit the offense principle. Let us begin by rejecting the views that the protection of a person from himself is *always* a valid ground for interference and that it is *never* a valid ground. It follows that it is a valid ground only under certain conditions, which we must now try to state.

It will be useful to make some preliminary distinctions. The first is between those cases in which a person directly produces harm to himself (where the harm is the certain and desired end of his conduct), and those cases in which a person simply creates a *risk* of harm to himself in the course of activities directed toward other ends. The man who knowingly swallows a lethal dose of arsenic will certainly die, and death must be imputed as his goal. Another man is offended by the sight of his left hand, so he grasps an ax in his right hand and chops his left hand off. He does not thereby "endanger" his interest in the physical integrity of his limbs, or "risk" the loss of his hand; he brings about the loss directly and deliberately. On the other hand, to smoke cigarettes or to drive at excessive speeds is not to harm oneself directly and deliberately. On the other hand, to smoke cigarettes or to drive at excessive speeds is not to harm oneself directly, but rather to increase beyond a normal level the probability that harm to oneself will result.

The second distinction is that between reasonable and unreasonable risks. There is no form of activity (or inactivity, for that matter) that does not involve some risks. On some occasions we have a choice between more and less risky actions, and prudence dictates that we take the less risky course. However, what is called "prudence" is not always reasonable. Sometimes it is more reasonable to assume a great risk for a great gain than to play it safe and forfeit a unique opportunity. Thus, it is not necessarily more reasonable for a coronary patient to increase his life expectancy by living a life of quiet inactivity than to continue working hard at his career in the hope of achieving something important, even at the risk of a sudden fatal heart attack. Although there is no simple mathematical formula to guide one in making such decisions or for judging them "reasonable" or "unreasonable," there are some decisions that are manifestly unreasonable. It is unreasonable to drive at sixty miles an hour through a twenty mile an hour zone in order to arrive at a party on time, but it may be reasonable to drive fifty miles an hour to get a pregnant wife to the maternity ward. It is foolish to resist an armed robber in an effort to protect one's wallet, but it may be worth a desperate lunge to protect one's very life.

All of these cases involve a number of distinct considerations. If there is time to deliberate one should consider: (1) the degree of probability that harm to oneself will result from a given course of action, (2) the seriousness of the harm being risked, i.e., "the value or importance of that which is exposed to the risk," (3) the degree of probability that the goal inclining one to shoulder the risk will in fact result from the course of action, (4) the value or importance of achieving that goal, that is, just how worthwhile it is to one (this is the intimately personal factor, requiring a decision about one's own preferences, that makes it so difficult for the outsider to judge the reasonableness of a risk), and (5) the necessity of the risk, that is, the availability or absence of alternative, less risky, means to the desired goal.

Certain judgments about the reasonableness of risk assumptions are quite uncontroversial. We can say, for example, that the greater are considerations 1 and 2, the less reasonable the risk, and the greater are considerations 3, 4, and 5, the more reasonable the risk. But in a given difficult case, even where questions of "probability" are meaningful and beyond dispute, and where all the relevant facts are known, the risk decision may defy objective assessment because of its component personal value judgments. In any case, if the state is to be given the right to prevent a person from risking harm to himself (and only himself), it must not be on the ground that the prohibited action is risky, or even extremely risky, but rather that the risk is extreme and, in respect to its objectively assessable components, manifestly unreasonable. There are sometimes very good reasons for regarding even a person's judgment of personal worthwhileness (consideration 4) to be "manifestly unreasonable," but it remains to be seen whether (or when) that kind of unreasonableness can be sufficient grounds for interference.[14]

---

14 The distinctions in this paragraph have been borrowed from Henry T. Terry, "Negligence," *Harvard Law Review*, XXIX (1915), pp. 40–50.

The third and final distinction is between fully voluntary and not fully voluntary assumptions of a risk. One assumes a risk in a fully voluntary way when one shoulders it while informed of all relevant facts and contingencies, and in the absence of all coercive pressure or compulsion. To whatever extent there is neurotic compulsion, misinformation, excitement or impetuousness, clouded judgment (as, e.g., from alcohol), or immature or defective faculties of reasoning, the choice falls short of perfect voluntariness.[15] Voluntariness, then, is a matter of degree. One's "choice" is *completely involuntary* when it is no choice at all, properly speaking—when one lacks all muscular control of one's movements, or is knocked down or sent reeling by a blow or an explosion—or when, through ignorance, one chooses something other than what one means to choose, as when one thinks the arsenic powder is table salt and sprinkles it on one's scrambled eggs. Most harmful choices, as most choices generally, fall somewhere between the extremes of perfect voluntariness and complete involuntariness.

The central thesis of Mill and other individualists about paternalism is that the fully voluntary choice or consent (to another's doing) of a mature and rational human being concerning matters that directly affect only his own interests is so precious that no one else (especially the state) has a right to interfere with it simply for the person's "own good." No doubt this thesis was also meant to apply to almost-but-not-quite fully voluntary choices as well, and probably even to some substantially nonvoluntary ones (e.g., a neurotic person's choice of a wife who will satisfy his neurotic needs, but only at the price of great unhappiness, eventual divorce, and exacerbated guilt). However, it is not probable that the individualist thesis was meant to apply to choices near the bottom of the voluntariness scale, and Mill himself left no doubt that he did not intend it to apply to completely involuntary "choices." Neither should we expect antipaternalistic individualism to deny protection to a person from his own nonvoluntary choices, for insofar as the choices are not voluntary they are just as alien to him as the choices of someone else.

Thus Mill would permit the state to protect a man from his own ignorance, at least in circumstances that create a strong presumption that his uninformed or misinformed choice would not correspond to his eventual enlightened one.

If either a public officer or anyone else saw a person attempting to cross a bridge which had been ascertained to be unsafe, and there were no time to warn him of his danger, they might seize him and turn him back, without any real infringement of his liberty; for liberty consists in doing what one desires, and he does not desire to fall into the river.[16]

Of course, for all the public officer may know, the man on the bridge does desire to fall into the river, or to take the risk of falling for other purposes. Then, Mill argues, if the person is fully warned of the danger and wishes to proceed anyway, that is his business alone, despite the advance presumption that most people do not wish to run such risks. Hence the officer was justified, Mill would argue, in his original interference.

On other occasions a person may need to be protected from some other condition that may render his informed choice substantially less than voluntary. He may be "a child, or delirious, or in some state of excitement or absorption incompatible with the full use of the reflecting faculty."[17] Mill would not permit any such person to cross an objectively unsafe bridge. On the other hand, there is no reason why a child, or an excited person, or a drunkard, or a mentally ill person should not be allowed to proceed

---

[15] My usage of the term "voluntary" differs from that of Aristotle in his famous analysis in Book III of the *Nicomachean Ethics*, but corresponds closely to what Aristotle called "deliberate choice."

[16] Mill, *On Liberty*, p. 117.

[17] Mill, *On Liberty*, p. 117.

on his way home across a perfectly safe thoroughfare. Even substantially nonvoluntary choices deserve protection unless there is good reason to judge them dangerous.

For all we can know, the behavior of a drunk or an emotionally upset person would be exactly the same even if he were sober and calm. But when the behavior seems patently self-damaging and is of a sort in which most calm and normal persons would not engage, then there are strong grounds, if only of a statistical sort, for inferring the opposite; these grounds, on Mill's principle, would justify interference. It may be that there is no kind of action of which it can be said, "No mentally competent adult in a calm, attentive mood, fully informed, and so on, would ever choose (or consent to) that." Nevertheless, there are some actions that create a powerful presumption that an actor in his right mind would not choose them. The point of calling this hypothesis a "presumption" is to require that it be completely overridden before legal permission be given to a person who has already been interfered with to go on as before. For example, if a policeman (or anyone else) sees John Doe about to chop off his hand with an ax, he is perfectly justified in using force to prevent him, because of the presumption that no one could voluntarily choose to do such a thing. The presumption, however, should always be taken as rebuttable in principle; it will be up to Doe to prove before an official tribunal that he is calm, competent, and free, and still wishes to chop off his hand. Perhaps this is too great a burden to expect Doe himself to "prove," but the tribunal should require that the presumption against voluntariness be overturned by evidence from some source or other. The existence of the presumption should require that an objective determination be made, whether by the usual adversary procedures of law courts, or simply by a collective investigation by the tribunal into the available facts. The greater the presumption to be overridden, the more elaborate and fastidious should be the legal paraphernalia required, and the stricter the standards of evidence. The point of the procedure would not be to evaluate the wisdom or worthiness of a person's choice, but rather to determine whether the choice really is his.

This seems to lead us to a form of paternalism so weak and innocuous that it could be accepted even by Mill, namely, that the state has the right to prevent self-regarding harmful conduct only when it is substantially nonvoluntary, or when temporary intervention is necessary to establish whether it is voluntary or not. A strong presumption that no normal person would voluntarily choose or consent to the kind of conduct in question should be a proper ground for detaining the person until the voluntary character of his choice can be established. We can use the phrase "the standard of voluntariness" as a label for considerations that mediate application of the principle that a person can be protected from his own folly.

Consider some typical hard cases for the application of the voluntariness standard. First take the problem of harmful drugs. Suppose that Richard Roe requests a prescription of drug X from Dr. Doe, and the following discussion ensues:

DR. DOE: I cannot prescribe drug X to you because it will do you physical harm.
MR. ROE: But you are mistaken. It will not cause me physical harm.

In a case like this, the state, of course, backs the doctor, since it deems medical questions to be technical matters subject to expert opinions. If a layman disagrees with a physician on a question of medical fact, the layman is presumed wrong, and if he nevertheless chooses to act on his factually mistaken belief, his action will be substantially less than fully voluntary. That is, the action of *ingesting a substance which will in fact harm him* is not the action he voluntarily chooses to do (because he does not believe that it is harmful). Hence the state intervenes to protect him not from his own free and voluntary choices, but from his own ignorance.

Suppose however that the exchange goes as follows:

DR. DOE: I cannot prescribe drug X to you because it will do you physical harm.

MR. ROE: Exactly. That's just what I want. I want to harm myself.

In this case Roe is properly apprised of the facts; he suffers from no delusions or misconceptions. Yet his choice is so odd that there exists a reasonable presumption that he has been deprived of the "full use of his reflecting faculty." It is because we know that the overwhelming majority of choices to inflict injury for its own sake on oneself are not fully voluntary that we are entitled to presume that the present choice is not fully voluntary. If no further evidence of derangement, illness, severe depression, or unsettling excitation can be discovered, however, and the patient can convince an objective panel that his choice is voluntary (unlikely event!), then our "voluntariness standard" would permit no further state constraint.

Now consider the third possibility:

DR. DOE: I cannot prescribe drug X to you because it is very likely to do you physical harm.

MR. ROE: I don't care if it causes me physical harm. I'll get a lot of pleasure first, so much pleasure, in fact, that it is well worth running the risk of physical harm. If I must pay a price for my pleasure I am willing to do so.

This is perhaps the most troublesome case. Roe's choice is not patently irrational on its face. A well thought-out philosophical hedonism may be one of his profoundest convictions, involving a fundamental decision of principle to commit himself to the intensely pleasurable, even if brief, life. If no

third party interests are directly involved, the state can hardly be permitted to declare his philosophical convictions unsound or "sick" and prevent him from practicing them, without assuming powers that it will inevitably misuse.

On the other hand, this case may be quite similar to the preceding one, depending on what the exact facts are. If the drug is known to give only an hour's mild euphoria and then cause an immediate, violently painful death, then the risks appear so unreasonable as to create a powerful presumption of nonvoluntariness. The desire to commit suicide must always be presumed to be both nonvoluntary and harmful to others until shown otherwise. (Of course, in some cases it can be shown otherwise.) Alternatively, drug X may be harmful in the way nicotine is now known to be harmful; twenty or thirty years of heavy use may create a grave risk of lung cancer or heart disease. Using the drug for pleasure when the risks are of this kind may be to run unreasonable risks, but that is no strong evidence of nonvoluntariness. Many perfectly normal, rational persons voluntarily choose to run precisely these risks for whatever pleasures they find in smoking. To assure itself that such practices are truly voluntary, the state should continually confront smokers with the ugly medical facts so that there is no escaping the knowledge of the exact medical risks to health. Constant reminders of the hazards should be at every hand, with no softening of the gory details. The state might even be justified in using its taxing, regulatory, and persuasive powers to make smoking (and similar drug usage) more difficult or less attractive; but to prohibit it outright would be to tell the voluntary risk-taker that his informed judgments of what is worthwhile are less reasonable than those of the state, and therefore he may not act on them. This is paternalism of the strong kind, unmediated by the voluntariness standard. As a principle of public policy it has an acrid moral flavor, and creates serious risks of governmental tyranny.

COLLECTIVE GOODS
AND COLLECTIVE ACTION

Despite the presumptive case for liberty, there seem to be numerous examples in which the modern state has no choice but to force (usually by compulsory taxation) both willing and unwilling citizens to support public projects that are clearly in the public interest. In many of these cases those who do not benefit directly from a public service are made to pay as much in its support as those who do, or even more. Thus nondrivers are taxed to support highways and nonparents to support schools. This has the appearance of injustice, and the justification of unhappy necessity. Often the alternative to mandatory taxation—a system of purely voluntary support requiring only users to pay fees—is subject to a fatal defect that forces us to choose between universal compulsory support for the public facility or no facility at all.

Consider, for example, public municipal parks. Suppose the town of Metropolis decides to create a large public park with gardens, woods, trails, and playgrounds. John Doe appreciates living in an attractive community but has no direct personal need for such a park, since he already has a ten acre yard with gardens, picnic tables, tennis courts, and the like. Why, he asks, should he be forced to support something he doesn't need and doesn't want strongly enough to pay for? Suppose, however, that the city charges only those who wish to use the park, and that this group constitutes 90 percent of the population. The richest 10 percent opt out, thus raising the average costs to the remainder. That rise, in turn, forces some of the 90 percent to withdraw, thus raising the cost to the others, forcing still more to drop out, and so on. This process will continue until either a very expensive equilibrium is reached, or, what is more likely, the whole project collapses (as in the case of some voluntary public medical and insurance plans).

It is avoidance of this characteristic escalation effect, rather than paternalism, that provides the rationale for compulsory social security and medicare programs. Here it is important to apply the various principles of liberty distribution not to individual cases, such as the compulsory taxation of John Doe, but to rules and general financing schemes. Compulsory rather than voluntary schemes are justified when the social good in question cannot be secured in any other way. Whether compulsion on this ground accords with the harm principle depends on whether loss of the good would be classified as a social harm or the mere withholding of a benefit. . . . Where the good is security, medical care, or education, there is little doubt that its loss would properly be called a "harm" to those who incur it.

In cases of the sort we have been considering, some people who don't want a given public service are forced to pay for it because there is no other practical way of supporting it, and its loss would be a harm to those who do want it. In a more interesting and troublesome kind of case, *all* of the members of a community or group want some good which is in fact in the interests of each individual equally, and yet it is in no individual's interest to contribute toward the goal unless all are *made* to do so. This paradoxical state of affairs has attracted considerable attention from economists who have noticed its similarity to the condition of a company in an industry that enjoys "perfect competition." So long as the price of a manufactured product on the free market exceeds the marginal cost of production, it will be in the interest of each company to increase its output and thus maximize its profit. But the consequence of increased output will be lower prices, so in the end all companies will be worse off for "maximizing profits" than they might otherwise have been. If any single firm, anticipating this unhappy result, were to restrict its own output unilaterally, it would be in still more trouble, for its restriction of output in a large industry would not prevent the fall of prices, and it would suffer lower sales in addition to lower prices. It is in the interest of each firm that *all the others* restrict output, but, in a purely competitive situation, none of the others dare do that. Where there is no coercion, we have the paradoxical result that it is "rational" for each firm to pursue policies that will destroy its interests in the end. It is more rational still to prefer general coercion.

Problems like that raised by "perfect competition" tend to occur wherever large organizations have come into existence to advance the interests of their members. A great many such organizations, from consumer societies and labor unions to (as many have claimed) the political state itself, exist primarily to advance some common interest in virtue of which the members can be supposed to have banded together in the first place. Now, some of the collective aims to which large organizations are devoted have a very special character. They are directed at goods which, if they are made available to any one member of the group, cannot feasibly be withheld from any other member. Examples of such generalized and indivisible goods are supported prices for companies in the same industry in a not-so-competitive market, the power of collective bargaining for members of a union, and certain goods provided for its citizens by the state, such as police protection, courts of law, armies, navies, and public health agencies. Perhaps it would be technically possible to "sell" these goods only to those willing to pay for them, but it would hardly be "feasible." It is not clear, for example, how an organization, private or public, could eliminate air pollution only for those willing to pay. Nonpayers would breathe the expensively purified air, and there would be no way of preventing this "freeloading" short of banishment or capital punishment. In such cases, it is in each member's interest to let the others pay the bill and then share in consumption of the indivisible benefit; since each member knows that every member knows this as well as he, each has reason to think that he may be taken advantage of if he voluntarily pays his share. Yet if each member, following his own self-interest, refuses to pay, the collective good for which they are united cannot be achieved. Voluntarily submitting to a coercion understood by each to apply to all seems the only way out.

It is in virtue of such considerations that compulsory taxation, at least in support of collective goods and indivisible services of an essential kind, can be justified by the harm principle. That principle would not justify compulsory taxation in support of benefits to private groups, or even of public benefits of the sort whose loss would not constitute a serious harm, but that does not mean that the friends of public libraries, museums, and parks need be driven to embrace the welfare principle. . . . When persons and groups are deprived of what they *need*, they are harmed; it may not be implausible to insist that the country as a whole, in this and future generations (including people who have no present desire for culture, history, nature, or beauty), *needs* large national parks, wilderness areas, enormous libraries, museums, atomic accelerators for physical research, huge telescopes, and so on. To argue that we need these things is to claim that we cannot in the end get along very well without them. That is the kind of case that must be made if we are to justify compulsion, on liberal principles, to the reluctant taxpayer.

Pornography and the Tyranny of the Majority

Elizabeth H. Wolgast

Many people who reject social control of pornography rely on Mill's arguments on behalf of freedom of expression, while critics of pornography frequently appeal to Mill's harm-to-others principle. Elizabeth H. Wolgast argues that censorship of pornography can be justified on a different basis—because women find it degrading and demeaning. Drawing an analogy with race discrimination, she defends her position against various objections and maintains that Mill himself would have viewed it sympathetically.

I

"If all mankind minus one were of one opinion," John Stuart Mill wrote, "mankind would be no more justified in silencing that one person than he, if he had the power, would be justified in silencing mankind." No matter how great the majority, the very power to control opinion and expression is illegitimate, he argued. Worse, such power "is robbing the human race" of the chance to hear different sides of a question whether right or wrong, and thus does injury to the whole community.[1]

Society has no right to demand conformity to a set of beliefs, to "maim by compression, like a Chinese lady's foot, every part of human nature which stands out prominently, and tends to make the person markedly dissimilar in outline to commonplace humanity." A person needs opportunity to live as he chooses, to take up causes passionately, make mistakes, change his or her mind. Only in this way can anyone develop to the fullest potential. "Human nature is not a machine to be built after a model, and set to do exactly the work prescribed for it, but a tree, which requires to grow and develop itself on all sides, according to the tendency of the inward forces which make it a living thing."[2] Society will itself benefit when people have liberty to experiment in ideas and ways of living, Mill believed, for it is innovators, not conformists, who advance culture.

Truth also is advanced when people are allowed to express all opinions and to debate every question. And who is it argues against a popular view but a minority of dissenters? They are the ones, then, who need the most protection: "On any of the great open questions . . . if either of the two opinions has a better claim than the other, not merely to be tolerated but to be encouraged . . . it is the one which happens at the

[1] John Stuart Mill, *On Liberty* (Bungay: Penguin, 1980), p. 76.

[2] Ibid., p. 135.

particular time and place to be in a minority. That is the one which for the time being represents the neglected interests, the side of human well-being which is in danger of obtaining less than its share."[3]

Even in the gentler form of custom, majority tyranny is as much to be feared as political tyranny, Mill believes, and maybe more. His criterion for interference is that only if harm or injury to someone results should people be restrained from acting and living as they please. There is a presumption that in the absence of proof of injury, individuals should be left alone.

I quote extensively from Mill because his language is echoed in modern discussions of free speech, particularly those related to control of pornography. Control is seen as a simple case of the majority forcing others into conformity with their (puritanical) moral standard without argument. It appears a clear case of social compression, what Mill would call a "Calvinistic" demand for "Christian self-denial," aimed at stifling the virtue of "Pagan self-assertion." Similarly Joel Feinberg refers to control as "moralistic paternalism." Other writers echo Mill's attitude.

For Americans this is a powerful and seductive argument against restrictions on any published material, including pornography. All the libertarian or the nonconformist minority asks of the majority is tolerance of its curious ways. What problem is there in that? Others don't have to look or buy; one person should be free to enjoy pornography even though others prefer not to, just as they are free to accept or reject escargots or dandelion wine. Passionate tastes are not a bad thing, Mill argued; they are the very "raw material of human nature," capable of both more good and more evil than ordinary feelings. "Strong impulses are but another name for energy. A person whose desires and impulses are his own—are the expression of his own nature—. . . is said to have a character."[4] And society needs peo-

ple of strong character: that is the romantic message.

To understand the role of Mill's argument, it is important to recognize that he wrote long after the Bill of Rights became law, and that his view of freedom was not the one that prompted the First Amendment, or even one shared by the early Americans. The idea that truth depends on a "marketplace of ideas," that freedom of expression advances the universal search for truth, that self-expression is an essential part of a person's self-development, that— most important—the only restriction rightly placed on a person's freedom is the injunction not to injure others—such ideas are those of Mill's time, not of Jefferson's. They originated with romantic philosophers of the nineteenth century, not with the political and moral thinkers of seventeenth-century England and eighteenth-century America, who stressed individual responsibility, restraint, and self-governance. Such virtues Mill would probably find much too straitlaced. It is therefore a wild anachronism to use Mill's *On Liberty* as a gloss on the First Amendment. But my argument does not turn on this point. I will argue that one kind of moral issue raised by pornography overshadows and requires us to reevaluate the free-speech issue. Further, once the argument against protecting pornography is spelled out, I believe Mill can be rallied to its support instead of to the libertarian side.

Two points about "harm" should be made. First, the language of injury and harm are no part of the First Amendment. The framers of that amendment did not suggest that if someone's practice of religion, for example, were to cause injury in some vague sense, the right of religious practice is restrictable. One might conclude from their terse statement that on the contrary, the right to practice religion should be very difficult to restrict. The "injury" proviso, which may originate with utilitarians, is therefore a gauntlet I do not propose to pick up. Second, Mill's single proviso that a person's exercise of freedom should not harm others places a heavy burden of proof

---

[3] Ibid., p. 123.
[4] Mill, *On Liberty*, pp. 124–25.

on anyone defending pornography's restriction, and sets the presumption that freedom should prevail. How can injury be shown? How can it even be understood here? Who is injured when pornography is aimed at adult customers, free to decide whether they are interested in it?

To answer these questions we appear to need both a specific conception of harm and persuasive evidence of a causal connection, both of which various critics have shown to be problematic. I will argue, on the contrary, that to accept this burden of proof—that harm or injury to an individual has been caused—is an error of strategy. It is to accept a difficult or even impossible challenge when a more direct and powerful moral argument is available.

II

Freedom of speech and press are commonly connected with democratic government and seen as essential to it. Tocqueville, for instance, wrote: "In the countries in which the doctrine of the sovereignty of the people ostensibly prevails, the censorship of the press is not only dangerous, but it is absurd.[5] It was a connection not lost on the framers of the Constitution, who were on their guard against the danger that government might seek to impose its will on reluctant citizens. We don't need to doubt the connection here. The question is: Does protection of free expression legitimately protect pornography?

A reasonable statement on this point is made by Ronald Dworkin, who argues that the right to have an equal voice in the political process is not denied when a person "is forbidden to circulate photographs of genitals to the public at large, or denied his right to listen to argument when he is forbidden to consider these photographs at his lei-

sure."[6] Some other basis for protection is needed, according to him.

The Supreme Court argued along similar lines in *Roth v. United States*. What the amendment protects, it says, is the "unfettered interchange of ideas for the bringing about of political and social changes desired by the people." And pornography is "no essential part of any exposition of ideas."[7]

In my view the distinction set forth in *Roth* is important and should have been developed. But instead of developing it, the Court went on to give another reason not to protect pornography, namely that a "social interest in order and mortality" clearly "outweighed" pornography's right to protection. Such a move was plainly hazardous: if other "social interests" can "outweigh" the right to free expression, then the protection of the First Amendment has been greatly diluted. The better argument would follow along the original lines, saying that pornography isn't in the category of "expression" meant to be protected.

A knotty problem arises, however, when pornography is excluded from protection: the amendment speaks of freedom of the *press*. So from one angle it looks as if the amendment was meant to protect not citizens who want to read but publishers in the business of selling printed matter of whatever kind. And pornography certainly belongs in this large domain.[8]

Were the framers trying to protect one kind of business while refusing to protect

---

[5] Alexis de Tocqueville, *Democracy in America*, trans. George Lawrence, ed. J. P. Mayer (Garden City, N.Y.: Doubleday, 1969), 1:10, 118.

[6] Ronald Dworkin, "Do We have a Right to Pornography?" in *A Matter of Principle* (Cambridge: Harvard University Press, 1985), p. 336. Dworkin goes on to argue that we can value free expression and "accept a presumption against censorship" and still allow that presumption to be overcome, for example, "by some showing that the harm the activity threatens is grave, probable, and uncontroversial" (pp. 337–38). This is basically the strategy of the report of the Committee on Pornography and Obscenity.

[7] Roth v. United States, 354 U.S. 481.

[8] I include films in this argument, since they, like the press, deal with fiction and pornographic materials as well as with information.

others? We are helped here by remembering that the First Amendment also dealt with freedom of worship and the right to congregate. The rights to worship and congregate in public rest on the respect of one's need to commune with God on the one hand and with one's fellow citizens on the other. The latter right has something to do with the role citizens play in the whole process of government, their sense that the government is there to serve them and it is their job to monitor it. None of this suggests why publishers should be protected by a fundamental constitutional right, rather than cobblers or hotelkeepers. The more plausible connection is that between protecting the press and protecting citizens from oppression through censorship. The citizens have a need to know and hear printed opinions, just as they have a need to get together and talk, if they are to do their civic duty and live by their consciences. However, this ambiguity in the language of the First Amendment, this way of speaking of the press as if publishers per se are protected and not the free exchange of opinion, seems never to have been cogently dealt with by the courts, and it perennially causes problems, as it does in the present case.

The main point here is that if the amendment is understood to protect publishers as a special form of business protection, then it has no particular moral weight; business protections and trade restrictions may change with the times and do, and a business may seek protection for some political reason or other without invoking the First Amendment or any basic constitutional values.

Another problem with the *Roth* argument is that it invites the comparison of pornography with art, thereby suggesting that good art is more entitled to protection than bad. Good art presumably should survive lack of social value; bad art shouldn't. But what validity is there in this idea? It invites the comment that the degree of badness is relative and may well be a matter of taste, that history has shown . . . and so on. A more important point is that bad literature—bad essays on politics, appealing to weak and unworthy motives of a reader—*are* surely protected by the First Amendment. And bad political art too. Then why not the poor-quality stuff called pornography? The case made in *Roth* for restricting pornography is worse than unconvincing: it provides ground for a kind of moral repression that both the Constitution's framers and Mill would abhor. We still have to explain what is bad about pornography that is not bad about bad literature and bad art in general.

III

Joel Feinberg's use of "pornography," he says, is "purely descriptive"; he uses the term to refer to "sexually explicit writing and pictures designed entirely and plausibly to induce sexual excitement in the reader or observer."[9] According to this definition, pornography is a genre of materials of an erotic sort, some of which may be objectionable while the rest is not. Some Japanese prints or Indian murals could be described as pornographic and still appreciated as art by this characterization, for "pornography" is used in a morally neutral way. But since we are not concerned at the moment with erotic materials that are not offensive, I propose to use "pornography" as a pejorative term, which is to say in the way Feinberg would speak of *offensive* pornography. In response to the objection that the word is (most) commonly used in a descriptive and neutral way, I suggest that many ordinary people, including many feminists, commonly use it in a pejorative way, and that in much ordinary speech to call something

---

[9] Feinberg, "Pornography and the Criminal Law," p. 110. Ann Garry writes that couples might watch pornographic films as they watch "old romantic movies on TV" ("Pornography and Respect for Women," *Social Theory and Practice* 4 [Summer 1978]: 395–421; reprinted in *Applying Ethics*, ed. Vincent Barry [Belmont, Calif.: Wadsworth, 1985], p. 110).

pornographic is to say that it is offensive.[10] That is sufficient justification for using the term in this way.

It needs to be pointed out that to say that pornography is objectionable is not to demonstrate that it should be controlled. Many things that people do and say are acknowledged to be bad, including being unfaithful to one's spouse, misusing and deceiving friends, neglecting elderly parents, and lying. But we don't have laws against these things. As Feinberg says, in many respects "the Court has interpreted [the Constitution] . . . to permit responsible adults to go to Hell morally in their own way provided only they don't drag others unwillingly along with them."[11] Such interpretations constitute a formidable defense against controls.

Though pornography may be objectionable in various dimensions (and I believe it is), I will focus on only one kind of objection that I claim to have moral weight. I will substantiate the claim that there *is* such an objection by citing expressions of it. Then I will defend the claim that this kind of objection should carry enough legal weight to justify the control of the objectionable materials. Last, I will argue that such control is quite compatible with the Constitution and the First Amendment and, finally, John Stuart Mill.

The objections I focus on are those expressed by women against certain representations of women in sexual situations: objections against representations of women "being raped, beaten or killed for sexual stimulation," and women enjoying brutal sexual treatment, usually at the hands of men. One pornography model demands censorship of "all pornography which portrays torture, murder, and bondage for erotic stimulation and pleasure."[12] What is objectionable is not just the representations but the lack of a context in which they are understood to be reprehensible and condemnable. Without some such context, the representations carry the message that such treatment of women is all right. This is one kind of objection.

Another model protests against the circulation of any representation "that reduces women to passive objects to be abused, degraded, and used in violence against women, because now every woman is for sale to the lowest bidder and to all men." She adds that a government that protects this kind of image making expresses "an ideology of women as sexual objects and nothing else."[13] A related criticism was made by Gloria Steinem: "[Pornography's] message is violence, dominance, and conquest. . . . If we are to feel anything, we must identify with conqueror or victim." It is a poor choice for women: "we can only experience pleasure through the adoption of some degree of sadism or masochism. . . . We may feel diminished by the role of conqueror, or enraged, humiliated, and vengeful by sharing identity with the victim."[14]

---

[10] There is a problem with using "obscenity" to do the work of "objectionable pornography." First, there is no more a generally accepted definition of obscenity than there is of pornography. But also an invocation of the broader category doesn't clarify anything and can be a positive hindrance, widening the discussion to matters that are not offensive in the same dimension and deflecting the effort to clarify the issue of why we should control pornography.

[11] Feinberg, "Pornography and the Criminal Law," p. 133.

[12] Diana Russell with Laura Lederer, "Questions We Get Asked Most Often," in *Take Back the Night*, ed. Lederer, p. 25. Russell adds that "pornography is detrimental to all women" (p. 29). A similar complaint from another pornography model includes this observation: "The misogyny I see today is so blatant and so accepted as a matter of fact that when we challenge it, we're seen as irrational or bad sports. . . . We're training little girls and boys to view sadomasochistic behavior as normal. . . . To me the acceptability of pornography is the clearest statement about the acceptability of women-hating and of women's real place in society" ("Then and Now: An Interview with a Former Pornography Model," in ibid., p. 70).

[13] "Testimony against Pornography: Witness from Denmark," ed. Diana E. H. Russell, in *Take Back the Night*, ed. Lederer, pp. 84–85.

[14] Gloria Steinem, "Erotica and Pornography: A Clear and Present Difference," in *Take Back the Night*, ed. Lederer, pp. 37–38. A similar voice is Andrea Dworkin's: in pornography, she says, "a woman's sex is

These quotations illustrate one general kind of objection made to pornography. That it is objectionable in these respects is an inference I make from the facts that (1) people do make vehement objections to it and (2) they see the offense as a moral one, concerning the respect due any individual.

I emphasize that although I take it for granted that pornography deals with human sexuality, I am not defining it, although many writers consider a definition crucial for a coherent argument. There is a variety of erotic material that could be called pornographic, and whether we call something pornographic or not will depend in part on whether people find it seriously objectionable. But my argument isn't meant to fit all varieties of such material. I am testing only one dimension of objectionability against the First Amendment defense with the claim that it has moral weight.

My partial characterization is this: some pornography is objectionable because it is perceived as seriously degrading and demeaning to women as a group. This characterization draws on the fact that the materials are perceived by women as representing them as inferior or less-than-human beings to be used by others in sexual and sadistic ways. . . .

IV

Granted that there is a prima facie reason to think women are demeaned by pornographic materials, how does censorship become justified? Isn't some other means to deal with it available and wouldn't that be preferable? The answer is that of course it's possible and other means may be preferable, for there certainly are dangers in permitting one group to control what others may read or see. It is not my thesis that censorship of pornography is the only answer to the moral complaint or that it should

be invoked lightly. In fact, it might be invoked as a last resort when such moral protests are raised. But censorship is one answer, and my aim is to show that the justification for using it is not rebutted by an appeal to the First Amendment. Whatever answer is given, that answer needs to address the moral objection to the way treatment of women is represented. The establishment of guidelines for sexual representations might be a solution. Must we decide in general which kind of response is best? I propose rather that there is no theoretical and final answer, but that an acceptable response will take serious account of the perceptions of the objecting group.

One has to ask, however, whether there isn't a danger in appealing to the moral standards of any one group when laws are formulated. As Mill suggests, shouldn't anyone have the right to live anyway he wishes? Isn't experimentation generally a good and not a bad thing?

. . .Why shouldn't Mill's argument for freedom apply here? Why shouldn't the objection still hold that if women don't want to look at pornographic pictures or film, they shouldn't look? So long as there is "reasonable avoidability" and people can avoid pornography if they want to, where, as Feinberg argues, is the offense? "When the 'obscene' book sits on a shelf, who is there to be offended?" If pornography lies between "decorous covers," no one need look at it who doesn't want to. It is only when pornography produces an offense on a par with "shame, or disgust, or noisome stenches" (however they would translate in this case) that the law may justifiably interfere. That is to say, pornography should be restricted only when it becomes a nuisance difficult to avoid.[15] To restrict it on other grounds would be to engage in moral paternalism. It would be to set standards for those who enjoy pornography in order to save them from themselves.

---

appropriated, her body is possessed, she is used and she is despised: the pornography does it and the pornography proves it" (*Pornography: Men Possessing Women* [New York: Putnam, 1979], p. 223).

[15] Joel Feinberg, *Rights, Justice, and the Bounds of Liberty* (Princeton: Princeton University Press, 1980), pp. 87, 89.

This protest, however, misses the point. The felt insult and indignity that women protest is not like a noise or bad odor, for these are group-neutral and may offend anyone, while pornography is felt to single women out as objects of insulting attention. There is a clear division in the community here, unlike the division between people who mind an odor very much and others who can ignore it. The question of how the rest of the community should respond to the perceived debasement that women feel is not analogous to the way the community should treat people particularly sensitive to and offended by certain smells. There is a democracy with respect to smells but with pornography there is a felt hostile discrimination.

V

. . .Pornographic materials may be seen differently by one group than by another. They may be felt as insulting by one group but inoffensive to another, as seriously demeaning by one and silly by another. An analogy can be drawn with the different perceptions of blacks and whites, or of Jews and Gentiles, regarding certain materials: blacks may find demeaning an image that others think innocuous. It is crucial for my argument that such differences in perception be acknowledged as a social reality, and that our understanding of what it is to treat everyone with respect allow for such differences in the *perception* of respect. It is important, in short, that we do not assume that there is one Everyman view, with the only question being which view that is. Only by respecting different perceptions about what is demeaning will we see that there may be a reason to limit materials that some group— even the largest—finds unobjectionable. . . .

VI

Feinberg questions Justice William Brennan's argument in *Roth* by asking, "What is the alleged 'state interest' that makes the unobtrusive and willing enjoyment of pornographic materials the state's business to control and prevent?"[16] What is the positive ground for interference?

This demand is legitimate and it needs to be answered in full. Even if a moral argument such as I have outlined can be made for control of pornography, how can the moral argument be translated into constitutional terms? If controls are justified, their justification should answer Feinberg's question. The need to protect respect may be clear but the means for protecting it are not. Is there an analogy or a precedent to guide us?

I will argue at a common-sense level, not meaning to interpret the notion of "state interest" in its technical legal sense. Given that respect for persons is an important constitutional value, I propose to show a strategy that connects respect with controls on pornography, to show that the means, the logical path, is there already and has no need to be newly cut. The connection between respect and constitutional action has been made already.

What we need here is reasoning somewhat like that in *Brown* v. *Board of Education*. There the Court decided that educational facilities—equal "with respect to buildings, curricula . . . and other 'tangible' factors"— might nevertheless be unequal in an important sense. And one of the reasons they might be counted unequal was (as one summary puts it) that "to separate [children] from others . . . solely because of their race generates a feeling of inferiority as to their status in the community that may affect their hearts and minds in a way unlikely ever to be undone."[17] Such an institution

---

[16] Feinberg, "Pornography and the Criminal Law," pp. 132–33.

[17] This paraphrase is Gerald Gunther's, in *Constitutional Law: Cases and Materials*, 9th ed. (Mineola, N.Y.: Foundation Press, 1975), p. 715. Gunther goes on to quote an earlier decision in the Brown case which referred to the effect of segregation on a child's motivation and its "tendency to [retard] the educational and mental development of negro children." In this connection also see Edmund Cahn, "Jurisprudence," 30

with the "sanction of law" which thus produces the sense of inferiority of one race is unconstitutional. Respect is not to be measured in the specifics of equipment or curriculum but in the felt implication of inferiority.

In rejecting the justice of "separate but equal" facilities, the Court specifically rejected the protest that any "badge of inferiority" supposed to be implied by segregation exists "not by reason of anything found in the act, but solely because the colored race chooses to put that construction upon it."[18] The insult perceived by blacks has priority over protests of innocence by those charged with offending. It is not crucial that *they* see the offense in the same way. Thus the Court answered by analogy the parallel argument in the pornography issue, that women shouldn't be so sensitive about pornography, for, since no one intends to demean them by it, there is nothing demeaning in it. The parallel answer is that whether there was intent to demean or not is irrelevant.

The argument in *Brown* exemplifies the general form of reasoning we need: an institution that perceptibly demeans some group and represents its members as inferior impugns the claim to equality of those members; in doing so it violates the Constitution's provisions; thus it shouldn't be protected by the federal government. There is no reference here to interpretations of other provisions of the Constitution. Of course the production of pornography isn't an institution; yet insofar as pornography is felt to demean women, its protection by the government under the First Amendment cannot be easily argued.

A caveat is needed here. This argument does not imply that if some group feels demeaned—say, by advertising or institutional arrangements—then censorship is automatically justified. Considerations other than the offense taken are often relevant, some of which may also be moral, and these considerations may overbalance the initial concern for respect. Nonetheless, if what is needed is a line of reasoning that can be used to support control of pornographic materials in the face of First Amendment protections, then such a line is clearly available.

In its general conception this approach accords with Ronald Dworkin's view that absolute principles are not what is needed in much legal reasoning. Instead we often need to balance one kind of claim or principle against others. That's the case here. The First Amendment is terribly important to us as a democracy; there's no dispute about that. But it doesn't give the last word on the question "What may a printer print and what may a store sell?" While this approach shows a way to defeat the absolutist claim of the First Amendment and open the possibility of censorship, I have no desire to insist that this course be taken. Other solutions may be preferable.

A number of features of the pornography issue are illuminated by its analogy with race discrimination.[19] For one thing, it would be irrelevant to argue that the demeaning of blacks causes no "injury" and therefore is harmless. What it causes is not the issue: the harm and the offense lie in the practices themselves, and the felt implications for people's status, the light cast upon them as citizens, and the like. Second, just as it would be bizarre to appeal to a group of whites to determine whether racial inferiority is part of the message of segregation, it is curious to consult only men about the offense of pornography. Third, the protest that not all blacks were offended would be taken as specious. Even if many blacks denied that they felt offended, we might still

---

N.Y.U. Law Review 15 (1955); he justifies the Brown decision by speaking of the humiliating treatment of any group as "morally evil."

[18] Plessy v. Ferguson, 163 U.S. 537 (1896); Gunther, *Constitutional Law*, p. 709.

[19] Ronald Dworkin also finds the analogy between expressions of racial hatred and pornography instructive, and remarks that while British law supports the control of incitements to racial hatred, the First Amendment prevents such laws in America ("Do We Have a Right to Pornography?" p. 335).

acknowledge the vigorous complaints of others. The same holds for women; if some are not offended by pornography, it remains true that many are, and that they see the offense as one against women as a group.

But imagine that the Commission on Obscenity were to make the following argument: If we do nothing in the way of controls, we shall at least be doing nothing wrong.[20] And in such a doubtful matter, with something as important as First Amendment protection at issue, it is better to do nothing. The answer to this argument contains a point often overlooked. When a powerful plea for respectful treatment is addressed by some group to the government, no "neutral" or safe response is possible. Inaction is a kind of action; it signifies toleration of the practice and thus condones it, and in condoning endorses it. Thus to respond to discrimination by arguing that the rights of states and communities are sacred matters, and that one risks a slide down a "slippery slope" if one interferes with them, would be hollow and disingenuous and recognized as such. Similarly I propose that there is also no "neutral" and safe response against pornography's demeaning of women. The issue demands to be addressed by a government that wants *not* to give sanction to the message carried by the images. A state that wants to ensure an atmosphere of respect for all persons has to face the issue in more decisive terms than protection of the First Amendment.

The Constitution does not lead us to believe that our first duty is to protect the First Amendment, as if its application needed no justification, as if it stood above other values, including that of respect for all persons. On the contrary, the rights of free speech, religion, and assembly are protected *because* of the respect due to citizens and their consequent need to be free of government control in certain ways. Freedom of speech is not a fundamental right of a certain kind of enterprise—namely, the press—but stems from a view of humans as morally autonomous.

Therefore it is curious that the Court and libertarian writers show such dedication to freedom of the press as an abstraction, as a principle taken by itself. They deal with it, so it seems to me, as with an ikon of a faith whose main tenets they have forgotten. In this respect theirs is less than a high moral stand. Remarking the irony of this liberal position, one writer comments that "women may rightly ask why the Constitution must be read to value the pornographer's first amendment claim to individual dignity and choice over women's equal rights claim to their own dignity and choice."[21] It is a curious turn of thinking that asks citizens to lay down their claim to respect at the feet of this idol.

Mill warned us about the threat presented by people who think they have the "right" moral perspective and therefore the only "right" answers to serious questions. I agree; we need to beware of all sorts of tyranny, however righteous, well-meaning, and scholarly. For on its side the protection of pornography also may represent a kind of tyranny of opinion, a libertarian tyranny that treats would-be censors as neurotic, misguided zealots and dismisses the moral complaint altogether.

Looked at from the perspective of women, the tolerance of pornography is hard to understand. Equally hard to understand is a point of view that sees the offense of pornography only in terms of its impact on and significance to men, as if the women of the society were irrelevant or invisible.[22] And a

---

[20] In a recent federal court decision (American Booksellers Association v. Hudnut) the court took the attitude that the "state interest [in protecting women from degrading depictions that may contribute to discrimination] . . . though important and valid . . . in other contexts, is not so fundamental an interest as to warrant a broad intrusion into otherwise free expression" (quoted in "Anti-Pornography Laws and First Amendment Values," *Harvard Law Review* 98 [December 1984]: 481).

[21] "Anti-Pornography Laws and First Amendment Values," p. 46.

[22] The invisibility of women in much of our thinking and its connection with atomism are discussed in my

more political point can be added. In the light of women's increasing protests against pornography and the proliferation of defenses of it, the issue carries the hazard of generating conflict between two definable groups, roughly between libertarian men on the one hand and outraged women on the other. Given these dimensions, it seems imperative to straighten the arguments and the issue out.

VII

I wish to say something more about the claim that a definition of pornography is needed for the present argument. My argument has followed the tactic of considering certain objections to pornography without a definition of pornography or a criterion as to what objections are valid. While it focuses on objections of a certain kind, those imputing a demeaning character to pornography, it doesn't specify what kinds of things are legitimately objected to or what is really objectionable.

Where could we get a definition of pornography suitable to the role I give it, the role of materials to which a certain vague kind of objection is made? Who should define it authoritatively? Common sense does not endorse the view that legal authorities should set standards for the rest of the community, should decide about the inherent rightness or wrongness of certain pictures,

for example; for there might be no strong moral objection to pictures the community calls pornographic, and in the absence of such objection the pictures are not, on my view, pornographic at all. My argument says only that the law *might* justifiably restrict materials that are found insulting in a sexual way, as some materials are by women.

Because the argument is so vague, however, it arouses concern. How will pornographic pictures be distinguished from sexy art, and pornography distinguished from sexy literature—Lawrence's portrayal of Constance Chatterly, for instance? The answer is that the lack of a sharp line is precisely what I allow for, as I allow for changing attitudes. If a public work of art is found insulting by some part of the community that has to look at it, then that is a reason—though only one—for restricting it in some way. If no one objects, then a definition that makes it objectionable would be superfluous and really beside the point.

The terms of the issue as I frame it require only the value of individual respect, which is part of our moral heritage, and the perceptions by members of the community about how they are respected. They therefore allow for changes in customs and tastes, allow that what is demeaning in one time may not be found so in another. When pornography is defined in terms of what is *perceptibly* demeaning, not what is permanently and abstractly so, there is no force to the protest that since "Grandpa was excited even by bare ankles, dad by flesh above the knee, grandson only by flimsy bikinis," no standards can be set.[23] As fashions change, their moral implications change too. So if what was found demeaning once is not found so any longer, any problem regarding it has vanished. It is better not to define pornography for all time, or to define it at all.

Equality and the Rights of Women, chap. 6. Anthony Woozley argues that a law that made "publishers liable for prosecution for the publication of material which intentionally exploits sex by insulting it, and by degrading the parties to it," would have his support ("The Tendency to Deprave and Corrupt," in *Law, Morality, and Rights*, ed. M. A. Stewart [Dordrecht: Reidel, 1983], p. 221). By talking of "insulting sex" and of the genderless "parties to it," however, he defuses the impact of the feminists' complaint, namely, that it is demeaning of *them* in particular. That is to say, someone who argued, as Fred Berger does in "Pornography, Sex, and Censorship," that it isn't demeaning of sex or of the male participants would still not have dealt with the main objection.

---

[23] Feinberg, "Pornography and the Criminal Law," p. 122.

VIII

One important problem involving the First Amendment still needs to be considered. Suppose we are considering a work that asserts and argues that women are inferior to men, more animal than men, and that they enjoy brutal and sadistic treatment. Imagine such a work: it *asserts* that there is evidence to show that women enjoy a subservient, animal, victimized role, and that this is a correct and proper way to treat women, particularly with regard to sex. Some evidence or other is cited, and it is argued that "equality" is simply inappropriate for beings of this kind, belonging to an inferior level of sensibility or whatever.[24] To be sure, these ideas run directly against the moral idea that an individual, qua individual, has worth; nonetheless, we believe in free pursuit of all manner of debate, moral, scientific, and political, without government interference. So would such a work, purporting to be a scientific study, come under the protections of the First Amendment, or may it be treated like pornography and restricted on the same grounds? Does it differ from the case of hard pornographic pictures and films, and if so how?

On this question I side with the libertarians, for the difference between pornographic pictures and such a report is a signal one for us and for the First Amendment. Mill also would recognize the difference, for he based the freedom of circulation of opinion on the possibility of refuting an opinion that is false and criticizing one that's poorly founded. In his vision an opinion or argument is at continual risk of being refuted, and so it cannot endanger a community where reason and truth are valued. We can draw the distinction by saying that the materials that say nothing are beyond this risk of refutation, and therefore by protecting

them we give them an immunity to criticism that expressions of opinion do not enjoy. The argument of a work may be objectionable but, like all arguments, it is vulnerable to criticism, while pornography lacks such vulnerability.

This distinction is one I believe the framers of the Constitution would also have recognized. The need for opinions to be circulated freely is part of the respect for citizens which prompted the Bill of Rights. But protection of opinion could be distinguished then as well as now from protection of the press to print what it likes, including offensive pictures.

Defenses of pornography have often turned on leaving this distinction obscure, arguing, for example, "that pornography is intended not as a statement of fact, but as an opinion or fantasy about male and female sexuality." Taken this way, it cannot be prohibited on the ground of being false. At the same time, however, one hears that "correction of opinion depends . . . 'on the competition of other ideas.' " It is a catch-22. Critics of pornography who are told that they should "compete in the marketplace of ideas with their own views of sexuality" while pornography doesn't *present* ideas are placed in an impossible situation.[25] The pictures don't argue for a demeaning attitude toward women in regard to sex or present a view of sexuality; at the same time they *are* demeaning. They don't argue that women enjoy being brutally handled; they show brutality and insinuate the victims' pleasure. While an author would be correct in saying that pornography carries an *implied* message that brutal treatment of women is acceptable, the fact that it is implied rather than explicit is important.

With this argument I believe Mill would concur, for he consistently maintained the need for respect of differences, including different points of view, and here the difference is one relating to the two sex groups. Respect for persons in all their variety was at

---

[24] Works that assert women's genetic inferiority include Aristotle's *Politics*, Schopenhauer's essay "On Women," and Otto Weininger's Sex and Character (Geschlecht und Charakter); none, however, goes so far as my fictional author.

[25] "Anti-Pornography Laws and First Amendment Values," p. 471.

the heart of both his libertarianism and his ethical philosophy. However difficult they may be to understand in terms of one's own principles, people are worthy of respect: that was his repeated theme. "Man is not a machine," he wrote, and he surely did not think women are machines for sex.[26] To demean women in the way pornography is felt to do is to treat them as possessions or as servants. So in the end I think that Mill, who argued passionately for women's rights and

equal worth and dignity, would find it intolerable to have his views invoked to protect pornography, as they have been.

Although the libertarian case against controls seemed clear-cut and irrefutable, appeal to atomistic ideas cannot solve such a powerfully felt moral issue. If respect for people really exists, it will appear in the way complaints of insult are handled and not only in the propositions used to rebut them. What is needed is not a vision of justice, a simple doctrinaire solution, but a carefully plotted middle way between broad and oppressive controls and reckless liberty. Such an approach will go beyond atomism and deal with injustice in a different and less theoretical way.

---

[26] One needs only to read Mill's essay *The Subjection of Women* (Cambridge: Harvard University Press, 1970) to see a heavy irony in using his arguments to defend pornography from controls. See particularly pp. 42–44, 59.

JFK Memorial Hospital v. Heston: Paternalism

As Joel Feinberg explained, legal paternalism is the liberty-limiting principle that justifies state coercion to protect individuals from self-inflicted harm. Legal paternalism implies that sometimes the state knows the interests of individual citizens better than they themselves do. The case below, argued before the New Jersey Supreme Court, concerns a young woman who for religious reasons tried to refuse a blood transfusion deemed medically necessary to save her life.

The opinion of the Court was delivered by Weintraub, C. J.: Delores Heston, age 22 and unmarried, was severely injured in an automobile accident. She was taken to the plaintiff's hospital where it was determined that she would expire unless operated upon for a ruptured spleen and that if operated upon she would expire unless whole blood was administered. Miss Heston and her parents are Jehovah's Witnesses and a tenet of their faith forbids blood transfusions. Miss

Heston insists she expressed her refusal to accept blood, but the evidence indicates she was in shock on admittance to the hospital and in the judgment of the attending physicians and nurses was then or soon became disoriented and incoherent. Her mother remained adamant in her opposition to a transfusion, and signed a release of liability for the hospital and medical personnel. Miss Heston did not execute a release; presumably she could not. Her father could not be located.

Death being imminent, plaintiff on notice to the mother made application at 1:30 A.M.

---

58 N.J. 576 (1971).

to a judge of the Superior Court for the appointment of a guardian for Miss Heston with directions to consent to transfusions as needed to save her life. At the hearing, the mother and her friends thought a certain doctor would pursue surgery without a transfusion, but the doctor, in response to the judge's telephone call, declined the case. The court appointed a guardian with authority to consent to blood transfusions "for the preservation of the life of Delores Heston." Surgery was performed at 4:00 A.M. the same morning. Blood was administered. Miss Heston survived.

Defendants then moved to vacate the order. Affidavits were submitted by both sides. The trial court declined to vacate the order. This appeal followed. We certified it before argument in the Appellate Division.

The controversy is moot. Miss Heston is well and no longer in plaintiff's hospital. The prospect of her return at some future day in like circumstances is too remote to warrant a declaratory judgment as between the parties. Nonetheless, the public interest warrants a resolution of the cause, and for that reason we accept the issue. (See *State v. Perricone*, N.J. 1962).

In *Perricone*, we sustained an order for compulsory blood transfusion for an infant despite the objection of the parents who were Jehovah's Witnesses. In *Raleigh Fitkin-Paul Morgan Memorial Hospital v. Anderson*, N.J. (1964), it appeared that both the mother, a Jehovah's Witness, and the child she was bearing would die if blood were not transfused should she hemorrhage. We held that a blood transfusion could be ordered if necessary to save the lives of the mother and the unborn child. We said:

We have no difficulty in so deciding with respect to the infant child. The more difficult question is whether an adult may be compelled to submit to such medical procedures when necessary to save his life. Here we think it is unnecessary to decide that question in broad terms because the welfare of the child and the mother are so intertwined and inseparable that it would be impracticable to attempt to distinguish between them with respect to the sundry factual patterns which may develop. The blood transfusions (including transfusions made necessary by the delivery) may be administered if necessary to save her life or the life of her child, as the physician in charge at the time may determine.

The case at hand presents the question we thus reserved in *Raleigh Fitkin-Paul Morgan Memorial Hospital.*

It seems correct to say there is no constitutional right to choose to die. Attempted suicide was a crime at common law and was held to be a crime under N.J.S.A. 2A:85–1. It is now denounced as a disorderly persons offense. N.J.S.A. 2A:170–25.6. Ordinarily nothing would be gained by a prosecution, and hence the offense is rarely charged. Nonetheless the Constitution does not deny the State an interest in the subject. It is commonplace for the police and other citizens, often at great risk to themselves, to use force or stratagem to defeat efforts at suicide, and it could hardly be said that thus to save someone from himself violated a right of his under the Constitution subjecting the rescuer to civil or penal consequences.

Nor is constitutional right established by adding that one's religious faith ordains his death. Religious beliefs are absolute, but conduct in pursuance of religious beliefs is not wholly immune from governmental restraint. *Mountain Lakes Bd. of Educ. v. Maas*, N.J. (1960) (vaccination of children); *Bunn v. North Carolina*, (1949) (the use of snakes in a religious ritual); *Baer v. City of Bend, Or.* (1956) (fluoridation of drinking water). Of immediate interest is *Reynolds v. United States*, (1878), in which it was held that Congress could punish polygamy in a territory notwithstanding that polygamy was permitted or demanded by religious tenet, and in which the Court said:

Laws are made for the government of actions, and while they cannot interfere with mere religious belief and opinions, they may with practices. Suppose one believed that human sacrifices were a necessary part of religious worship, would it be seriously contended that the civil government under which he lived could not interfere to prevent a sacrifice? Or if a wife religiously believed it was her duty to burn herself upon the funeral pile of her dead husband, would it be beyond the power of the civil government to prevent her carrying her belief into practice?

Complicating the subject of suicide is the difficulty of knowing whether a decision to die is firmly held. Psychiatrists may find that beneath it all a person bent on self-destruction is hoping to be rescued, and most who are rescued do not repeat the attempt, at least not at once. Then, too, there is the question whether in any event the person was and continues to be competent (a difficult concept in this area) to choose to die. And of course there is no opportunity for a trial of these questions in advance of intervention by the State or a citizen.

Appellant suggests there is a difference between passively submitting to death and actively seeking it. The distinction may be merely verbal, as it would be if an adult sought death by starvation instead of a drug. If the State may interrupt one mode of self-destruction, it may with equal authority interfere with the other. It is arguably different when an individual, overtaken by illness, decides to let it run a fatal course. But unless the medical option itself is laden with the risk of death or of serious infirmity, the State's interest in sustaining life in such circumstances is hardly distinguishable from its interest in the case of suicide.

Here we are not dealing with deadly options. The risk of death or permanent injury because of a transfusion is not a serious factor. Indeed, Miss Heston did not resist a transfusion on that basis. Nor did she wish to die. She wanted to live, but her faith demanded that she refuse blood even at the price of her life. The question is not whether the State could punish her for refusing a transfusion. It may be granted that it would serve no State interest to deal criminally with one who resisted a transfusion on the basis of religious faith. The question is whether the State may authorize force to prevent death or may tolerate the use of force by others to that end. Indeed, the issue is not solely between the State and Miss Heston, for the controversy is also between Miss Heston and a hospital and staff who did not seek her out and upon whom the dictates of her faith will fall as a burden.

Hospitals exist to aid the sick and the injured. The medical and nursing professions are consecrated to preserving life. That is their professional creed. To them, a failure to use a simple, established procedure in the circumstances of this case would be malpractice, however the law may characterize that failure because of the patient's private convictions. A surgeon should not be asked to operate under the strain of knowing that a transfusion may not be administered even though medically required to save his patient. The hospital and its staff should not be required to decide whether the patient is or continues to be competent to make a judgment upon the subject, or whether the release tendered by the patient or a member of his family will protect them from civil responsibility. The hospital could hardly avoid the problem by compelling the removal of a dying patient, and Miss Heston's family made no effort to take her elsewhere.

When the hospital and staff are thus involuntary hosts and their interests are pitted against the belief of the patient, we think it reasonable to resolve the problem by permitting the hospital and its staff to pursue their functions according to their professional standards. The solution sides with life, the conservation of which is, we think, a matter of State interest. A prior application to a court is appropriate if time permits it, although in the nature of the emergency the only question that can be explored satisfactorily is whether death will probably ensue if medical procedures are not followed. If a court finds, as the trial court did, that death will likely follow unless a transfusion is administered, the hospital and the physician should be permitted to follow that medical procedure.

For the reasons already given, we find that the interest of the hospital and its staff, as well as the State's interest in life, warranted the transfusion of blood under the circumstances of this case. The judgment is accordingly affirmed.

Paris Adult Theatre v. Slaton:
Obscenity

Pornography poses a challenge to the principle of unbridled freedom of expression. The case of *Paris Adult Theatre v. Slaton* arose when police prevented two Atlanta movie theaters from showing sexually explicit movies. No sexually explicit material was displayed outside the theater, and a sign at the entrance said "Adult Theatre—You must be 21 and able to prove it. If viewing the nude body offends you, Please Do Not Enter." The local district attorney tried to get two of the films declared obscene because of their graphic depiction of sexual acts. The lower court agreed that the films were obscene but also held that because there was "requisite notice" to the public of their nature and reasonable protection against admittance of minors, the showing of the films was constitutionally protected. The U.S. Supreme Court, however, disagreed.

Chief Justice Burger, speaking for a majority of the justices, delivered the Supreme Court's verdict that the state is permitted to ban the public exhibition of obscene material in order to maintain a decent society. In a dissenting opinion, Justice Brennan argues that it is impossible to define "obscenity" satisfactorily.

Mr. Chief Justice Burger: It should be clear from the outset that we do not undertake to tell the States what they must do, but rather to define the area in which they may chart their own course in dealing with obscene material. This Court has consistently held that obscene material is not protected by the First Amendment as a limitation on the state police power by virtue of the Fourteenth Amendment. . . .

We categorically disapprove the theory, apparently adopted by the trial judge, that

obscene, pornographic films acquire constitutional immunity from state regulation simply because they are exhibited for consenting adults only. . . .

In particular, we hold that there are legitimate state interests at stake in stemming the tide of commercialized obscenity, even assuming it is feasible to enforce effective safeguards against exposure to juveniles and to passersby. Rights and interests "other than those of the advocates are involved." These include the interest of the public in the quality of life and the total community environment; the tone of commerce in the

413 U.S. 49 (1973).

great city centers, and, possibly, the public safety itself. The Hill-Lind Minority Report of the Commission on Obscenity and Pornography indicates that there is at least an arguable correlation between obscene material and crime. Quite apart from sex crimes, however, there remains one problem of large proportions aptly described by Professor Bickel: "It concerns the tone of the society, the mode, or to use terms that have perhaps greater currency, the style and quality of life, now and in the future. A man may be entitled to read an obscene book in his room, or expose himself indecently there. . . . We should protect his privacy. But if he demands a right to obtain the books and pictures he wants in the market, and to foregather in public places—discreet, if you will, but accessible to all—with others who share his tastes, *then to grant him his right is to affect the world about the rest of us, and to impinge on other privacies.* Even supposing that each of us can, if he wishes, effectively avert the eye and stop the ear (which, in truth, we cannot), what is commonly read and seen and heard and done intrudes upon us all, want it or not." 22 The Public Interest 25–26 (Winter 1971). (Emphasis added.)

As Mr. Chief Justice Warren stated, there is a "right of the Nation and of the States to maintain a decent society . . . ," *Jacobellis* v. *Ohio.*

But, it is argued, there are no scientific data which conclusively demonstrate that exposure to obscene material adversely affects men and women or their society. It is urged on behalf of the petitioners that, absent such a demonstration, any kind of state regulation is "impermissible." We reject this argument. It is not for us to resolve empirical uncertainties underlying state legislation, save in the exceptional case where that legislation plainly impinges upon rights protected by the Constitution itself. . . .

The sum of experience, including that of the past two decades, affords an ample basis for legislatures to conclude that a sensitive, key relationship of human existence, central to family life, community welfare, and the development of human personality, can be debased and distorted by crass commercial exploitation of sex. Nothing in the Constitution prohibits a State from reaching such a conclusion and acting on it legislatively. . . .

It is also argued that the State has no legitimate interest in "control [of] the moral content of a person's thoughts," and we need not quarrel with this. But we reject the claim that the State of Georgia is here attempting to control the minds or thoughts of those who patronize theaters. Preventing unlimited display or distribution of obscene material, which by definition lacks any serious literary, artistic, political, or scientific value as communication, is distinct from a control of reason and the intellect. . . . Where communication of ideas, protected by the First Amendment, is not involved, or the particular privacy of the home protected by *Stanley* or any of the other "areas or zones" of constitutionally protected privacy, the mere fact that, as a consequence, some human "utterances" or "thoughts" may be incidentally affected does not bar the State from acting to protect legitimate state interests. . . .

The issue in this context goes beyond whether someone, or even the majority, considers the conduct depicted as "wrong" or "sinful." The States have the power to make a morally neutral judgment that public exhibition of obscene material, or commerce in such material, has a tendency to injure the community as a whole, to endanger the public safety, or to jeopardize, in Mr. Chief Justice Warren's words, the States' "right . . . to maintain a decent society." *Jacobellis* v. *Ohio.* . . .

Mr. Justice Brennan, dissenting: . . . I am convinced that the approach initiated 16 years ago in *Roth* v. *United States*, 354 U.S. 476 (1957), and culminating in the Court's decision today, cannot bring stability to this area of the law without jeopardizing fundamental First Amendment values, and I have concluded that the time has come to make a significant departure from that approach. . . .

The essence of our problem in the obscenity area is that we have been unable to provide "sensitive tools" to separate obscenity from other sexually oriented but constitutionally protected speech, so that efforts to suppress the former do not spill over into the suppression of the latter. . . .

To be sure, five members of the Court did agree in *Roth* that obscenity could be determined by asking "whether to the average person, applying contemporary community standards, the dominant theme of the material taken as a whole appeals to prurient interest." 354 U.S., at 489. But agreement on that test—achieved in the abstract and without reference to the particular material before the Court—was, to say the least, short lived. . . .

Today a majority of the Court offers a slightly altered formulation of the basic *Roth* test, while leaving entirely unchanged the underlying approach.

Our experience with the *Roth* approach has certainly taught us that the outright suppression of obscenity cannot be reconciled with the fundamental principles of the First and Fourteenth Amendments. For we have failed to formulate a standard that sharply distinguishes protected from unprotected speech. . . . By disposing of cases through summary reversal or denial of certiorari we have deliberately and effectively obscured the rationale underlying the decisions. It comes as no surprise that judicial attempts to follow our lead conscientiously have often ended in hopeless confusion. . . .

The vagueness of the standards in the obscenity area produces a number of separate problems, and any improvement must rest on an understanding that the problems are to some extent distinct. First, a vague statute fails to provide adequate notice to persons who are engaged in the type of conduct that the statute could be thought to proscribe. The Due Process Clause of the Fourteenth Amendment requires that all criminal laws provide fair notice of "what the State commands or forbids." *Lanzetta* v. *New Jersey*. . . .

In addition to problems that arise when any criminal statute fails to afford fair notice of what it forbids, a vague statute in the areas of speech and press creates a second level of difficulty. . . .

[R]ecognizing the inherent vagueness of any definition of obscenity, we have held that the definition of obscenity must be drawn as narrowly as possible so as to minimize the interference with protected expression. . . .

The problems of fair notice and chilling protected speech are very grave standing alone. But it does not detract from their importance to recognize that a vague statute in this area creates a third, although admittedly more subtle, set of problems. These problems concern the institutional stress that inevitably results where the line separating protected from unprotected speech is excessively vague. In *Roth* we conceded that "there may be marginal cases in which it is difficult to determine the side of the line on which a particular fact situation falls. . . ." Our subsequent experience demonstrates that almost every case is "marginal." And since the "margin" marks the point of separation between protected and unprotected speech, we are left with a system in which almost every obscenity case presents a constitutional question of exceptional difficulty. . . .

Our experience since *Roth* requires us not only to abandon the effort to pick out obscene materials on a case-by-case basis, but also to reconsider a fundamental postulate of *Roth*: that there exists a definable class of sexually oriented expression that may be totally suppressed by the Federal and State Governments. Assuming that such a class of expression does in fact exist, I am forced to conclude that the concept of "obscenity" cannot be defined with sufficient specificity and clarity to provide fair notice to persons who create and distribute sexually oriented materials, to prevent substantial erosion of protected speech as a byproduct of the attempt to suppress unprotected speech, and to avoid very costly institutional harms.

American Booksellers v. Hudnut: Pornography

This case arose when the Indianapolis City Council passed an ordinance outlawing the production, sale, exhibition, and distribution of pornography. The ordinance defined pornography as any "graphic sexually explicit subordination of women" that also presented women as sexual objects "who enjoy rape, pain, or humiliation; enjoy being penetrated by objects or animals; in scenarios of degradation, injury, debasement, torture, shown as filthy or inferior; or presented as sexual objects for domination, conquest, violation, exploitation, possession, or use." The ordinance also allowed women who have been injured as a direct result of pornography to seek damages from the person who produced, sold, exhibited, or distributed it. The district court held the ordinance unconstitutional, and in the selection below, Judge Easterbrook, of the court of appeals, affirmed that decision.

Judge Easterbrook: We do not try to balance the arguments for and against an ordinance such as this. The ordinance discriminates on the ground of the content of the speech. Speech treating women in the approved way—in sexual encounters "premised on equality" is lawful no matter how sexually explicit. Speech treating women in the disapproved way—as submissive in matters sexual or as enjoying humiliation—is unlawful no matter how significant the literary, artistic, or political qualities of the work taken as a whole. The state may not ordain preferred viewpoints in this way. The Constitution forbids the state to declare one perspective right and silence opponents. . . .

"If there is any fixed star in our constitutional constellation, it is that no official, high or petty, can prescribe what shall be orthodox in politics, nationalism, religion, or other matters of opinion or force citizens to

771 F.2d 323 (1985).

confess by word or act their faith therein." *West Virginia State Board of Education* v. *Barnette,* 319 U.S. 624, 642 (1943). Under the First Amendment the government must leave to the people the evaluation of ideas. Bald or subtle, an idea is as powerful as the audience allows it to be. . . . A belief may be pernicious—the beliefs of Nazis led to the death of millions, those of the Klan to the repression of millions. A pernicious belief may prevail. Totalitarian governments today rule much of the planet, practicing suppression of billions and spreading dogma that may enslave others. One of the things that separates our society from theirs is our absolute right to propagate opinions that the government finds wrong or even hateful. . . .

Under the ordinance graphic sexually explicit speech is "pornography" or not depending on the perspective the author adopts. Speech that "subordinates" women and also, for example, presents women as

359

enjoying pain, humiliation, or rape, or even simply presents women in "positions of servility or submission or display" is forbidden, no matter how great the literary or political value of the work taken as a whole. Speech that portrays women in positions of equality is lawful, no matter how graphic the sexual content. This is thought control. It establishes an "approved" view of women, of how they may react to sexual encounters, of how the sexes may relate to each other. Those who espouse the approved view may use sexual images; those who do not, may not.

Indianapolis justifies the ordinance on the ground that pornography affects thoughts. Men who see women depicted as subordinate are more likely to treat them so. Pornography is an aspect of dominance. It does not persuade people so much as change them. It works by socializing, by establishing the expected and the permissible. In this view pornography is not an idea; pornography is the injury.

There is much to this perspective. Beliefs are also facts. People often act in accordance with the images and patterns they find around them. People raised in a religion tend to accept the tenets of that religion, often without independent examination. People taught from birth that black people are fit only for slavery rarely rebelled against that creed; beliefs coupled with the self-interest of the masters established a social structure that inflicted great harm while enduring for centuries. Words and images act at the level of the subconscious before they persuade at the level of the conscious. Even the truth has little chance unless a statement fits within the framework of beliefs that may never have been subjected to rational study.

Therefore we accept the premises of this legislation. Depictions of subordination tend to perpetuate subordination. The subordinate status of women in turn leads to affront and lower pay at work, insult and injury at home, battery and rape on the streets. . . .

Yet this simply demonstrates the power of pornography as speech. All of these un-happy effects depend on mental intermediation. Pornography affects how people see the world, their fellows, and social relations. If pornography is what pornography does, so is other speech. Hitler's orations affected how some Germans saw Jews. Communism is a world view, not simply a *Manifesto* by Marx and Engels or a set of speeches. Efforts to suppress communist speech in the United States were based on the belief that the public acceptability of such ideas would increase the likelihood of totalitarian government. Religions affect socialization in the most pervasive way. The opinion in *Wisconsin* v. *Yoder* shows how a religion can dominate an entire approach to life, governing much more than the relation between the sexes. . . .

Racial bigotry, anti-semitism, violence on television, reporters' biases—these and many more influence the culture and shape our socialization. None is directly answerable by more speech, unless that speech too finds its place in the popular culture. Yet all is protected as speech, however insidious. Any other answer leaves the government in control of all of the institutions of culture, the great censor and director of which thoughts are good for us.

Sexual responses often are unthinking responses, and the association of sexual arousal with the subordination of women therefore may have a substantial effect. But almost all cultural stimuli provoke unconscious responses. Religious ceremonies condition their participants. Teachers convey messages by selecting what not to cover; the implicit message about what is off limits or unthinkable may be more powerful than the messages for which they present rational argument. Television scripts contain unarticulated assumptions. People may be conditioned in subtle ways. If the fact that speech plays a role in a process of conditioning were enough to permit governmental regulation, that would be the end of freedom of speech. . . .

Much of Indianapolis's argument rests on the belief that when speech is "unanswerable," and the metaphor that there is a "marketplace of ideas" does not apply, the First Amendment does not apply either. The metaphor is honored; Milton's *Areopagitica* and John Stewart Mill's *On Liberty* defend freedom of speech on the ground that the truth will prevail, and many of the most important cases under the First Amendment recite this position. The Framers undoubtedly believed it. As a general matter it is true. But the Constitution does not make the dominance of truth a necessary condition of freedom of speech. To say that it does would be to confuse an outcome of free speech with a necessary condition for the application of the amendment.

A power to limit speech on the ground that truth has not yet prevailed and is not likely to prevail implies the power to declare truth. At some point the government must be able to say (as Indianapolis has said): "We know what the truth is, yet a free exchange of speech has not driven out falsity, so that we must now prohibit falsity." If the government may declare the truth, why wait for the failure of speech? Under the First Amendment, however, there is no such thing as a false idea. . . . The government may not restrict speech on the ground that in a free exchange truth is not yet dominant. . . .

We come, finally, to the argument that pornography is "low value" speech, that it is enough like obscenity that Indianapolis may prohibit it. Some cases hold that speech far removed from politics and other subjects at the core of the Framers' concerns may be subjected to special regulation. . . .

In *Pacifica* the FCC sought to keep vile language off the air during certain times. The Court held that it may; but the Court would not have sustained a regulation prohibiting scatological descriptions of Republicans but not scatological descriptions of Democrats, or any other form of selection among viewpoints. . . .

At all events, "pornography" is not low value speech within the meaning of these cases. . . . True, pornography and obscenity have sex in common. But Indianapolis left out of its definition any reference to literary, artistic, political, or scientific value. . . .

Texas v. Johnson: ## Flag Burning

After burning the U.S. flag as an act of political protest, Gregory Lee Johnson was convicted of desecrating a flag in violation of Texas law. The case was appealed to the U.S. Supreme Court, which had to decide whether his conviction was consistent with the First Amendment's protection of freedom of speech. By a narrow 5 to 4 vote, the Court held that the Texas law was unconstitutional. Delivering the opinion of the Court, Justice Brennan argues that the state cannot "prescribe what shall be orthodox" by punishing symbolic actions like flag burning. The way to preserve the flag's special role in our national life, he argues, is not to punish those who feel differently about this symbol but to persuade them that they are wrong. In their separate dissents, Justice Rehnquist and Justice Stevens reject the idea that the flag is just another symbol, towards which it would be unconstitutional to require minimal respect.

57 L. W. 4770 (1989).

Justice Brennan: As in *Spence* [*v. Washington*, a 1974 case on expressive conduct], "[w]e are confronted with a case of prosecution for the expression of an idea through activity," and "[a]ccordingly, we must examine with particular care the interests advanced by [petitioner] to support its prosecution." . . . Johnson was not, we add, prosecuted for the expression of just any idea; he was prosecuted for his expression of dissatisfaction with the policies of this country, expression situated at the core of our First Amendment values.

Moreover, Johnson was prosecuted because he knew that his politically charged expression would cause "serious offense." If he had burned the flag as a means of disposing of it because it was dirty or torn, he would not have been convicted of flag desecration under this Texas law: federal law designates burning as the preferred means of disposing of a flag "when it is in such condition that it is no longer a fitting emblem for display." . . .

If we are to hold that a state may forbid flag-burning wherever it is likely to endanger the flag's symbolic role, but allow it wherever burning a flag promotes that role—as where, for example, a person ceremoniously burns a dirty flag—we would be saying that when it comes to impairing the flag's physical integrity, the flag itself may be used as a symbol—as a substitute for the written or spoken work or a "short cut from mind to mind"—only in one direction. We would be permitting a state to "prescribe what shall be orthodox" by saying that one may burn the flag to convey one's attitude toward it and its referents only if one does not endanger the flag's representation of nationhood and national unity.

We never before have held that the government may ensure that a symbol he used to express only one view of that symbol or its referents. . . .

We are fortified in today's conclusion by our conviction that forbidding criminal punishment for conduct such as Johnson's will not endanger the special role played by our flag or the feelings it inspires. To paraphrase Justice [Oliver Wendell] Holmes, we submit that nobody can suppose that this one gesture of an unknown man will change our nation's attitude towards its flag. . . . Indeed, Texas's argument that the burning of an American flag " 'is an act having a high likelihood to cause a breach of peace,' " . . . and its statute's implicit assumption that physical mistreatment of the flag will lead to "serious offense," tend to confirm that the flag's special role is not in danger; if it were, no one would riot or take offense because a flag had been burned.

We are tempted to say, in fact, that the flag's deservedly cherished place in our community will be strengthened, not weakened, by our holding today. Our decision is a reaffirmation of the principles of freedom and inclusiveness that the flag best reflects, and of the conviction that our toleration of criticism such as Johnson's is a sign and source of our strength. Indeed, one of the proudest images of our flag, the one immortalized in our own national anthem, is of the bombardment it survived at Fort McHenry. It is the nation's resilience, not its rigidity, that Texas sees reflected in the flag—and it is that resilience that we reassert today.

The way to preserve the flag's special role is not to punish those who feel differently about these matters. It is to persuade them that they are wrong. "To courageous, self-reliant men, with confidence in the power of free and fearless reasoning applied through the processes of popular government, no danger flowing from speech can be deemed clear and present, unless the incidence of the evil apprehended is so imminent that it may befall before there is opportunity for full discussion. If there be time to expose through discussion the falsehood and fallacies, to avert the evil by the processes of education, the remedy to be applied is more speech, not enforced silence." . . . And, precisely because it is our flag that is involved, one's response to the flag-burner may exploit the uniquely persuasive power of the flag itself. We can imagine no more appropriate response to burning a flag than waving one's own, no better way to counter a flag-burner's message than by saluting the flag that burns, no surer means of preserving the dignity even of the flag that burned than by—as one witness here did—according its remains a respectful burial. We do not consecrate the flag by punishing its desecration, for in doing so we dilute the freedom that this cherished emblem represents.

Johnson was convicted for engaging in expressive conduct. The state's interest in preventing breaches of the peace does not support his conviction because Johnson's conduct did not threaten to disturb the peace. Nor does the state's interest in preserving the flag as a symbol of nationhood and national unity justify his criminal conviction for engaging in political expression. The judgment of the Texas Court of Criminal Appeals is therefore affirmed.

Justice Rehnquist, dissenting: In holding this Texas statute unconstitutional, the court ignores Justice Holmes's familiar aphorism that "a page of history is worth a volume of logic." . . . For more than 200 years, the American flag has occupied a unique position as the symbol of our nation, a uniqueness that justifies a governmental prohibition against flag burning in the way respondent Johnson did here. . . .

In the First and Second World Wars, thousands of our countrymen died on foreign soil fighting for the American cause. At Iwo Jima in the Second World War, United States Marines fought hand-to-hand against thousands of Japanese. By the time the Marines reached the top of Mount Suribachi, they raised a piece of pipe upright and from one end fluttered a flag. That ascent had cost nearly 6,000 American lives. . . .

During the Korean War, the successful amphibious landing of American troops at Inchon was marked by the raising of an American flag within an hour of the event. . . .

The government is simply recognizing as a fact the profound regard for the American flag created by that history when it enacts statutes prohibiting the disrespectful public burning of the flag.

The court concludes its opinion with a regrettably patronizing civics lecture, presumably addressed to members of both houses of Congress, the members of the 48 state legislatures that enacted prohibitions against flag burning and the troops fighting under that flag in Vietnam who objected to its being burned: "The way to preserve the flag's special role is not to punish those who feel differently about these matters. It is to persuade them that they are wrong." . . .

The court's role as the final expositor of the Constitution is well established, but its role as a platonic guardian admonishing those responsible to public opinion as if they were truant school children has no similar place in our system of government. The cry of "no taxation without representation" animated those who revolted against the English crown to found our nation—the idea that those who submitted to government should have some say as to what kind of laws would be passed. Surely one of the high purposes of a democratic society is to legislate against conduct that is regarded as evil and profoundly offensive to the majority of people—whether it be murder, embezzlement, pollution or flag burning.

Our Constitution wisely places limits on powers of legislative majorities to act, but the declaration of such limits by this court "is, at all times, a question of much delicacy, which ought seldom, if ever, to be decided in the affirmative, in a doubtful case." . . . Uncritical extension of constitutional protection to the burning of the flag risks the frustration of the very purpose for which organized governments are instituted. The court decides that the American flag is just another symbol, about which not only must opinions pro and con be tolerated, but for which the most minimal public respect may not be enjoined. The government may conscript men into the armed forces where they must fight and perhaps die for the flag, but the government may not prohibit the public burning of the banner under which they fight. I would uphold the Texas statute as applied in this case.

Justice Stevens, dissenting: As the court analyzes this case, it presents the question whether the state of Texas, or indeed the federal government, has the power to prohibit the public desecration of the American flag. The question is unique. In my judgment, rules that apply to a host of other symbols, such as state flags, armbands or various privately promoted emblems of political or commercial identity, are not necessarily controlling. Even if flag burning could be considered just another species of symbolic speech under the logical application of the rules that the court has developed in its interpretation of the First Amendment in other contexts, this case has an intangible dimension that makes those rules inapplicable.

A country's flag is a symbol of more than "nationhood and national unity." . . . It also signifies the ideas that characterize the society that has chosen that emblem as well as the special history that has animated the growth and power of those ideas. The fleurs-de-lis and the tricolor both symbolized "nationhood and national unity," but they had vastly different meanings. The message conveyed by some flags—the swastika, for example—may survive long after it has outlived its usefulness as a symbol of regimented unity in a particular nation.

So it is with the American flag. It is more than a proud symbol of the courage, the determination and the gifts of nature that transformed 13 fledgling colonies into a world power. It is a symbol of freedom, of equal opportunity, of religious tolerance and of goodwill for other peoples who share our aspirations. The symbol carries its message to dissidents both at home and abroad who may have no interest at all in our national unity or survival.

The value of the flag as a symbol cannot be measured. Even so, I have no doubt that the interest in preserving that value for the future is both significant and legitimate. Conceivably that value will be enhanced by the court's conclusion that our national commitment to free expression is so strong that even the United States as ultimate guarantor of that freedom is without power to prohibit the desecration of its unique symbol. But I am unpersuaded. . . .

The case has nothing to do with "disagreeable ideas." . . . it involves disagreeable conduct that, in my opinion, diminishes the value of an important national asset.

The court is therefore quite wrong in blandly asserting that respondent "was prosecuted for his expression of dissatisfaction with the policies of this country, expression situated at the core of our First Amendment values." . . . Respondent was prosecuted because of the method he chose to express his dissatisfaction with those policies. Had he chosen to spray paint—or perhaps convey with a motion picture projector—his message of dissatisfaction on the facade of the Lincoln Memorial, there would be no question about the power of the government to prohibit his means of expression. The prohibition would be supported by the legitimate interest in preserving the quality of an important national asset. Though the asset at stake in this case is intangible, given its unique value, the same interest supports a prohibition on the desecration of the American flag.

The ideas of liberty and equality have been an irresistible force in motivating leaders like Patrick Henry, Susan B. Anthony and Abraham Lincoln, schoolteachers like Nathan Hale and Booker T. Washington, the Philippine Scouts who fought at Bataan, and the soldiers who scaled the bluff at Omaha Beach. If those ideas are worth fighting for—and our history demonstrates that they are—it cannot be true that the flag that uniquely symbolizes their power is not itself worthy of protection from unnecessary desecration.

I respectfully dissent.

PART V   Problems of Equality

Equality and Its Implications

Peter Singer

Our society is firmly wedded to the principle that all human beings are equal. But what exactly does this mean and what are its social and political implications? In this selection from his book *Practical Ethics*, Peter Singer discusses the principle of equality. Given the fact that human beings differ greatly in their characteristics and abilities, Singer argues, the only way to understand equality is as a principle requiring equal consideration of interests. Although equal consideration of interests does not entail equal treatment, it is more than a purely formal principle. Singer elaborates on the meaning of equal consideration and illustrates the principle's substantive implications with regard to racial and sexual differences, equality of opportunity, and reverse discrimination.

THE BASIS OF EQUALITY

. . .When we say that all humans are equal, irrespective of race or sex, what exactly are we claiming? Racists, sexists and other opponents of equality have often pointed out that, by whatever test we choose, it simply is not true that all humans are equal. Some are tall, some are short; some are good at mathematics, other are poor at it; some can run 100 metres in ten seconds, some take fifteen or twenty; some would never intentionally hurt another being, others would kill a stranger for $100 if they could get away with it; some have emotional lives which touch the heights of ecstasy and the depths of despair, while others live on a more even plane, relatively untouched by what goes on around them . . . and so we could go on.

The plain fact is that humans differ, and the differences apply to so many characteristics that the search for a factual basis on which to erect the principle of equality seems hopeless.

John Rawls has suggested, in his influential book *A Theory of Justice*, that equality can be founded on the natural characteristics of human beings, provided we select what he calls a 'range property.' Suppose we draw a circle on a piece of paper. Then all points within the circle—this is the 'range'—have the property of being within the circle, and they have this property equally. Some points may be closer to the centre and others nearer the edge, but all are, equally, points inside the circle. Similarly, Rawls suggests, the property of 'moral personality' is a property which virtually all humans possess, and all humans who possess this property possess it equally. By 'moral personality' Rawls does not mean 'morally good personality'; he is using 'moral' in contrast to 'amoral'. A moral person, Rawls says, must have a sense of justice. More broadly, one might say that to be a moral person is to be the kind of person to whom one can make moral appeals, with some prospect that the appeal will be heeded.

Rawls maintains that moral personality is the basis of human equality, a view which derives from his 'contract' approach to justice. The contract tradition sees ethics as a kind of mutually beneficial agreement—roughly, 'Don't hit me and I won't hit you.' Hence only those capable of appreciating that they are not being hit, and of restraining their own hitting accordingly, are within the sphere of ethics.

There are problems with using moral personality as the basis of equality. One objection is that moral personality is, unlike being inside a circle, a matter of degree. Some people are highly sensitive to issues of justice and ethics generally; others, for a variety of reasons, have only a very limited awareness of such principles. The suggestion that being a moral person is the minimum necessary for coming within the scope of the principle of equality still leaves it open just where this minimal line is to be drawn. Nor is it intuitively obvious why, if moral personality is so important, we should not have grades of moral status, with rights and duties corresponding to the degree of refinement of one's sense of justice.

Still more serious is the objection that it is not true that all humans are moral persons, even in the most minimal sense. Infants and small children, along with some mentally defective humans, lack the required sense of justice. Shall we then say that all humans are equal, except for very young or mentally defective ones? This is certainly not what we ordinarily understand by the principle of equality. If this revised principle implies that we may disregard the interests of very young or mentally defective humans in ways that would be wrong if they were older or more intelligent, we would need far stronger arguments to induce us to accept it. (Rawls deals with infants and children by including *potential* moral persons along with actual ones within the scope of the principle of equality. But this is an *ad hoc* device, confessedly designed to square his theory with our ordinary moral intuitions, rather than something for which independent arguments can be produced. Moreover although Rawls admits that those with irreparable mental defects 'may present a difficulty' he offers no suggestions towards the solution of this difficulty.)

So the possession of 'moral personality' does not provide a satisfactory basis for the principle that all humans are equal. I doubt that any natural characteristic, whether a 'range property' or not, can fulfil this function, for I doubt that there is any morally significant property which all humans possess equally.

There is another possible line of defence for the belief that there is a factual basis for a principle of equality which prohibits racism and sexism. We can admit that humans differ as individuals, and yet insist that there are no morally significant differences between the races and sexes. Knowing that someone is black or white, female or male, does not enable us to draw conclusions about her or his intelligence, sense of justice, depth of feelings, or anything else that would entitle us to treat her or him as less than equal. The racist claim that whites are superior to blacks in these capacities is in this sense false. The differences between individuals do not adhere to racial lines, and some blacks are superior to some whites in all these respects. The same is true of the parallel sexist stereotype which sees women as more emotional, less rational, less aggressive and less enterprising than men. Obviously this is not true of women as a whole. Some women are less emotional, more rational, more aggressive and more enterprising than some men.

The fact that humans differ as individuals, not as races or sexes, is important and we shall return to it when we come to discuss the implications of the claims made by Jensen, Eysenck and others; yet it provides neither a satisfactory principle of equality, nor an adequate defence against a more sophisticated opponent of equality than the blatant racist or sexist. Suppose that someone proposes that people should be given intelligence tests and then classified into higher or lower status categories on the basis of the results. Perhaps those who scored above 125 would be a slave-owning class; those scoring between 100 and 125 would be free citizens but lack the right to own slaves; while those scoring below 100 would be made the slaves of those who had scored above 125. A hierarchical society of this sort seems as abhorrent as one based on race or sex; but if we base our support for equality on the factual claim that differences between individuals cut across racial and sexual boundaries, we have no grounds for opposing this kind of inegalitarianism. For this hierarchical society would be based on real differences between people.

We can reject this 'hierarchy of intelligence' and similar fantastic schemes only if we are clear that the claim to equality does not rest on intelligence, moral personality, rationality or similar matters of fact. There is no logically compelling reason for assuming that a difference in ability between two people justifies any difference in the amount of consideration we give to their interests. Equality is a basic ethical principle, not an assertion of fact. We can see this if we return to our earlier discussion of the universal aspect of ethical judgments.

We saw in [a] previous chapter that when I make an ethical judgment I must go beyond a personal or sectional point of view and take into account the interests of all those affected. This means that we weigh up interests, considered simply as interests and not as my interests, or the interests of Australians, or of whites. This provides us with a basic principle of equality: the principle of equal consideration of interests.

The essence of the principle of equal consideration of interests is that we give equal weight in our moral deliberations to the like interests of all those affected by our actions. This means that if only X and Y would be affected by a possible act, and if X stands to lose more than Y stands to gain, it is better not to do the act. We cannot, if we accept the principle of equal consideration of interests, say that doing the act is better, despite the facts described, because we are more concerned about Y than we are about X. What the principle really amounts to is: an interest is an interest, whoever's interest it may be.

We can make this more concrete by considering a particular interest, say the interest we have in the relief of pain. Then the principle says that the ultimate moral reason for relieving pain is simply the undesirability of pain as such, and not the undesirability of X's pain, which might be different from the undesirability of Y's pain. Of course, X's pain might be more undesirable than Y's pain because it is more painful, and then the principle of equal consideration would give greater weight to the relief of X's pain. Again, even where the pains are equal, other factors might be relevant, especially if others are affected. If there has been an earthquake we might give priority to the relief of a doctor's pain so she can treat other victims. But the doctor's pain itself counts only once, and with no added weighting. The principle of equal consideration of interests acts like a pair of scales, weighing interests impartially. True scales favour the side where the interest is stronger or where several interests combine to outweigh a smaller number of similar interests; but they take no account of whose interests they are weighing.

From this point of view race is irrelevant to the consideration of interests; for all that counts are the interests themselves. To give less consideration to a specified amount of pain because that pain was experienced by a black would be to make an arbitrary distinction. Why pick on race? Why not on whether a person was born in a leap year? Or whether there is more than one vowel in her surname? All these characteristics are equally irrelevant to the undesirability of pain from the universal point of view. Hence the principle of equal consideration of interests shows straightforwardly why the most blatant forms of racism, like that of the Nazis, are wrong. For the Nazis were concerned only for the welfare of members of the 'Aryan' race, and the sufferings of Jews, Gypsies and Slavs were of no concern to them.

The principle of equal consideration of interests is sometimes thought to be a purely formal principle, lacking in substance and too weak to exclude any inegalitarian practice. We have already seen, however, that it does exclude racism and sexism, at least in their most blatant forms. If we look at the impact of the principle on the imaginary hierarchical society based on intelligence tests we can see that it is strong enough to provide a basis for rejecting this more sophisticated form of inegalitarianism too.

The principle of equal consideration of interests prohibits making our readiness to consider the interests of others depend on their abilities or other characteristics, apart from the characteristic of having interests. It is true that we cannot know where equal consideration of interests will lead us until we know what interests people have, and this may vary according to their abilities or other characteristics. Consideration of the interests of mathematically gifted children may lead us to teach them advanced mathematics at an early age, which for different children might be entirely pointless or positively harmful. But the basic element, the taking into account of the person's interests, whatever they may be, must apply to everyone, irrespective of race, sex or scores on an intelligence test. Enslaving those who score below a certain line on an intelligence test would not—barring extraordinary and implausible beliefs about human nature—be compatible with equal consideration. Intelligence has nothing to do with many important interests that humans have, like the interest in avoiding pain, in developing one's abilities, in satisfying basic needs for food and shelter, in enjoying friendly and loving relations with others, and in being free to

pursue one's projects without unnecessary interference from others. Slavery prevents the slaves from satisfying these interests as they would want to; and the benefits it confers on the slaveowners are hardly comparable in importance to the harm it does to the slaves.

So the principle of equal consideration of interests is strong enough to rule out an intelligence-based slave society as well as cruder forms of racism and sexism. It looks as if it may be a defensible form of the principle that all humans are equal, a form which we can use in discussing more controversial issues about equality. Before we go on to these topics, however, it will be useful to say a little more about the nature of the principle.

Equal consideration of interests is a minimal principle of equality in the sense that it does not dictate equal treatment. Take a relatively straightforward example of an interest, the interest in having physical pain relieved. Imagine that after an earthquake I come across two victims, one with a crushed leg, in agony, and one with a gashed thigh, in slight pain. I have only two shots of morphine left. Equal treatment would suggest that I give one to each injured person, but one shot would not do much to relieve the pain of the person with the crushed leg. She would still be in much more pain than the other victim, and even after I have given her one shot, giving her the second shot would bring greater relief than giving a shot to the person in slight pain. Hence equal consideration of interests in this situation leads to what some may consider an inegalitarian result: two shots of morphine for one person, and none for the other.

There is a still more controversial inegalitarian implication of the principle of equal consideration of interests. In the case above, although equal consideration of interests leads to unequal treatment, this unequal treatment is an attempt to produce a more egalitarian result. By giving the double dose to the more seriously injured person, we bring about a situation in which there is less difference in the degree of suffering felt by the two victims than there would be if we gave one dose to each. Instead of ending up with one person in considerable pain and one in no pain, we end up with two people in slight pain. This is in line with the principle of declining marginal utility, a principle well-known to economists, which states that for a given individual, a set amount of something is more useful when the individual has little of it than when he has a lot. If I am struggling to survive on 200 grammes of rice a day, and you provide me with an extra fifty grammes per day, you have improved my position significantly; but if I already have a kilo of rice per day, I probably couldn't care less about the extra fifty grammes. When marginal utility is taken into account the principle of equal consideration of interests inclines us towards an equal distribution of income, and to that extent the egalitarian will endorse its conclusions. What is likely to trouble the egalitarian about the principle of equal consideration of interests is that there are circumstances in which the principle of declining marginal utility does not hold or is overridden by countervailing factors.

We can vary the example of the earthquake victims to illustrate this. Let us say, again, that there are two victims, one more severely injured than the other, but this time we shall say that the more severely injured victim, A, has lost a leg and is in danger of losing a toe from her remaining leg; while the less severely injured victim, B, has an injury to her leg, but the limb can be saved. We have medical supplies for only one person. If we use them on the more severely injured victim the most we can do is save her toe, whereas if we use them on the less severely injured victim we can save her leg. In other words, we assume that the situation is: without medical treatment, A loses a leg and a toe, while B loses only a leg; if we give the treatment to A, A loses a leg and B loses a leg; if we give the treatment to B, A loses a leg and a toe, while B loses nothing.

Assuming that it is worse to lose a leg than it is to lose a toe (even when that toe is on one's sole remaining foot) the principle of declining marginal utility does not hold in this situation. We will do more to further the interests, impartially considered, of those affected by our actions if we use our limited resources on the less seriously injured victim than on the more seriously injured one. Therefore this is what the principle of equal consideration of interests leads us to do. Thus equal consideration of interests can, in special cases, widen rather than narrow the gap between two people at different levels of welfare. It is for this reason that the principle is a minimal principle of equality, rather than a thorough-going egalitarian principle. A more thorough-going form of egalitarianism would, however, be difficult to justify, both in general terms and in its application to special cases of the kind just described. . . .

EQUALITY AND GENETIC DIVERSITY

In 1969 Arthur Jensen published a long article in the *Harvard Educational Review* entitled 'How Much Can We Boost IQ and Scholastic Achievement?' One short section of the article discussed the probable causes of the undisputed fact that—on average—American blacks do not score as well as American whites in standard IQ tests. Jensen summarized the upshot of this section as follows:

all we are left with are various lines of evidence, no one of which is definitive alone, but which, viewed altogether, make it a not unreasonable hypothesis that genetic factors are strongly implicated in the average negro-white intelligence difference. The preponderance of evidence is, in my opinion, less consistent with a strictly environmental hypothesis than with a genetic hypothesis, which, of course, does not exclude the influence of environment or its interaction with genetic factors.

This heavily qualified statement comes in the midst of a detailed review of a complex scientific subject, published in a scholarly journal. It would hardly have been surprising if it passed unnoticed by anyone but scientists working in the area of psychology or genetics. Instead it was widely reported in the popular press as an attempt to defend racism on scientific grounds. Jensen was accused of spreading racist propaganda, and likened to Hitler. His lectures were shouted down. Students demanded that he be dismissed from his university post, which was a relatively mild fate compared to other suggestions that appeared on the walls of university buildings. H. J. Eysenck and others who support Jensen's theories have received similar treatment, in Britain and Australia as well as in the USA.

The opposition to genetic explanations of alleged racial differences in intelligence is only one manifestation of a more general opposition to genetic explanations in other socially sensitive areas. It closely parallels, for instance, feminist hostility to the idea that there are biological factors behind male dominance; and it has obvious links with the intensity of feeling aroused by the new approach to the study of behaviour known as 'sociobiology'.

It would be inappropriate for me to attempt to assess the scientific merits of biological explanations of human behaviour in general, or of racial or sexual differences in particular. My concern is rather with the implications of these theories for the ideal of equality. For this purpose it is not necessary for us to establish whether the theories are right. All we have to ask is: suppose that Jensen is right. Does this mean that racism is defensible, and we have to reject the principle of equality? A similar question can be asked about the impact of theories of biological differences between the sexes. In neither case does the question assume that the theories are sound. It would be most unfortunate if our scepticism about such things led us to neglect these questions and then unexpected evidence turned up confirming the theories, with the result that a confused and unprepared public took them to have implications for the ideal of equality which they do not have.

I shall begin by considering the implications of the view that there is a difference in the average IQ of blacks and whites, and that genetic factors are responsible for at least a part of this difference. I shall then consider the impact of alleged differences in temperament and ability between the sexes.

Racial Differences and Racial Equality

To date, almost all the discussion of alleged genetic differences in ability between the races has focused on differences in intelligence, particularly between American whites and American blacks. I shall follow this emphasis. But first a word of caution. When someone like Jensen talks of 'the average negro–white intelligence difference' what he really means is the average negro–white difference in scores on standard IQ tests. Now 'IQ' stands for 'Intelligence Quotient' but this does not mean that an IQ test really measures what we mean by 'intelligence' in ordinary contexts. Obviously there is some correlation between the two: if schoolchildren regarded by their teachers as highly intelligent did not generally score better on IQ tests than schoolchildren regarded as below normal intelligence, the tests would have to be changed—as indeed they were changed in the past. But this does not show how close the correlation is, and since our ordinary concept of intelligence is vague, there is no way of telling. Some psychologists have attempted to overcome this difficulty by simply defining 'intelligence' as 'what intelligence tests measure' but this merely introduces a new concept of 'intelligence', which is easier to measure than our ordinary notion, but may be quite different in meaning. Since 'intelligence' is a word in everyday use, to use the same word in a different sense is a sure path to confusion. What we should talk about, then, is 'the average negro–white IQ difference' since this is all that the available evidence can possibly support.

The distinction between intelligence and scores on IQ tests has led some to conclude that IQ is of no importance; this is the opposite, but equally erroneous, extreme to the view that IQ is identical with intelligence. IQ is important in our society. One's IQ is a factor in one's prospects of improving one's occupational status, income or social class. If there are genetic factors in racial differences in IQ, there will be genetic factors in racial differences in occupational status, income and social class. So if we are interested in equality we cannot ignore IQ.

When whites and blacks are given IQ tests, whites tend to get higher scores than blacks. The average white score is 100, the average black score around 85. These findings, although limited to comparisons of American blacks and whites, are not seriously disputed. What is hotly disputed is whether the difference is primarily to be explained by heredity or by environment—in other words, whether it reflects an innate difference between whites and blacks, or whether it is due to the deprived social and educational situation in which many blacks find themselves. (We should note that Jensen and others arguing for the genetic hypothesis accept that environmental factors do influence the difference in scores, although they believe this influence to be a minor one, not accounting for more than a third of the 15 point gap.)

Let us suppose that the genetic hypothesis turns out to be correct (making this supposition, as I have said, not because we believe it is correct but in order to explore its implications); what would be the implications of a genetically based difference of 10–15 points in the average IQs of whites and blacks? I believe that the implications of this supposition are less drastic than they are often supposed to be, and give no comfort to genuine racists. I have three reasons for this view.

First, the genetic hypothesis does not imply that we should reduce our efforts to overcome the environmental disadvantage which black children have in their homes and their schools. Admittedly, if the genetic hypothesis is correct, these efforts will not bring about a situation in which whites and blacks have equal IQs. Even if it were possible to eliminate all environmental disadvantages, the average white IQ would be about 10 points higher than the average black IQ. But this is no reason for accepting a gap of 15 points, or a situation in which blacks are hindered by their environment from doing as well as they can. Indeed, one could well argue for the opposite conclusion: that if IQ is important, blacks should have a superior environment in order to compensate for the position of disadvantage from which they start.

Second, the fact that the average IQ of whites is 15 points higher than that of blacks does not allow anyone to say that all whites have higher IQs than blacks—this is clearly false—or that any particular individual white has a higher IQ than a particular individual black—this will often be false. The point is that these figures are averages and say nothing about individuals. Many blacks score higher than the average white and many whites score below the average black. So whatever the cause of the difference in average IQs, it provides no justification for racial segregation in education or any other field. It remains true that individual blacks and whites must be treated as individuals, irrespective of their race.

The third reason why the genetic hypothesis gives no support for racism is the most fundamental of the three. It is simply that, as we saw earlier, the principle of equality is not based on any actual equality which all people share. I have argued that the only defensible basis for the principle of equality is equal consideration of interests, and I have also suggested that the most important human interests—like the interest in avoiding pain, in developing one's abilities, in satisfying basic needs for food and shelter, in enjoying warm personal relationships, in being free to pursue one's projects without interference, and many others—are not affected by differences in intelligence. We can be even more confident that they are not affected by differences in IQ. Thomas Jefferson, who drafted the ringing assertion of equality with which the American Declaration of Independence begins, knew this. In reply to an author who had endeavoured to refute the then common view that negroes lack intelligence, he wrote:

Be assured that no person living wishes more sincerely than I do, to see a complete refutation of the doubts I have myself entertained and expressed on the grade of understanding allotted to them by nature, and to find that they are on a par with ourselves . . . but whatever be their degree of talent, it is no measure of their rights. Because Sir Isaac Newton was superior to others in understanding, he was not therefore lord of the property or person of others.

Jefferson was right. Equal status does not depend on intelligence. Racists who maintain the contrary are in peril of being forced to kneel before the next genius they encounter.

These three reasons suffice to show that claims that for genetic reasons blacks are not as good as whites at IQ tests do not provide grounds for denying the moral principle that all humans are equal. The third reason, however, has further ramifications which we shall follow up after discussing differences between the sexes.

Sexual Differences and Sexual Equality

Recent discussions of alleged psychological differences between blacks and whites have focused on IQ. IQ has not been an issue in debates over psychological differences between females and males. On general IQ tests there are no consistent differences in the average score of females and males. But IQ tests measure a range of different abilities, and when we break the results down according to the type of ability measured, we do find significant differences between the sexes. There is solid evidence to show that females have greater verbal ability than males. This involves not merely living up to the popular female stereotype of being more talkative, but also being better able to understand complex pieces of writing and being more creative with words. Males, on the other hand, appear to have greater mathematical ability, and also do better on tests involving what is known as 'visual–spatial' ability. An example of a task requiring visual–spatial ability is one in which the subject is asked to find a shape, say a square, which is embedded or hidden in a more complex design.

We shall discuss the significance of these relatively minor differences in intellectual abilities shortly. There is also one major non-intellectual characteristic in respect of which there is a marked difference between the sexes: aggression. Studies conducted on children in several different cultures have borne out what parents have long suspected: boys are more likely to play roughly, attack each other and fight back when attacked, than girls. Males are readier to hurt others than females; a tendency reflected in the fact that almost all violent criminals are male. It has been suggested that aggression is associated with competitiveness, and the drive to dominate others and get to the top of whatever pyramid one is a part of.

These are the major psychological differences which have been observed between females and males. What is the origin of these differences? Once again the rival explanations are environmental versus biological, nurture versus nature. Although this question of origin is important in some special contexts I shall suggest that it is often given *too* much importance by feminists who assume that the case for women's liberation rests on acceptance of the environmental side of the controversy. What is true of racial discrimination holds here too: discrimination can be shown to be wrong whatever the origin of the known psychological differences. But first let us look briefly at the rival explanations.

Anyone who has had anything to do with

children will know that in all sorts of ways children learn that the sexes have different roles. Boys get trucks or guns for their birthday presents: girls get dolls or brush and comb sets. Girls are put into frilly pink dresses and told how nice they look: boys are dressed in jeans and praised for their physical strength. Children's books portray fathers going out to work while mothers clean the house and cook the dinner. It is surprising how little influence the feminist movement of the last ten years has had on all this.

Social conditioning exists, certainly, but does it explain the existence of differences between the sexes? It is, at best, an incomplete explanation. We still need to know *why* our society—and not just ours, but practically every human society—should shape children in this way. The usual feminist answer is that in earlier, simpler societies, the sexes had different roles because women had to breast-feed their children during the long period before weaning. This meant that the women stayed put while the men went out to get food. As a result females evolved a more social and emotional character, while males became tougher and more aggressive. Because physical strength and aggression were the ultimate forms of power in these simple societies, males became dominant. The sex roles that exist today are, feminists contend, an inheritance from these simpler circumstances, an inheritance which became obsolete once technology made it possible for the weakest person to operate a crane which lifts fifty tons, or fire a missile which kills millions. Nor do women have to be tied to home and children in the way they used to be, since, except for a short period around the birth of her children, a woman can combine motherhood and a career.

The alternative view is that while social conditioning plays some role in determining psychological differences between the sexes, biological factors are also at work. The evidence for this view is particularly strong in respect of aggression. Eleanor Emmons Maccoby and Carol Nagy Jacklin, whose book *The Psychology of Sex Differences* is the most thorough review of the field yet published, give four grounds for their belief that the greater aggression of males has a biological component: (1) Males are more aggressive than females in all human societies in which the difference has been studied. (2) Similar differences are found in humans and in apes and other closely related animals. (3) The differences are found in very young children, at an age when there is no evidence of any social conditioning in this direction (indeed Maccoby and Jacklin found some evidence that boys are *more* severely punished for showing aggression than girls). (4) Aggression has been shown to vary according to the level of sex hormones and females become more aggressive if they receive male hormones.

The evidence for a biological basis of the differences in visual-spatial ability is a little more complicated, but it consists largely of genetic studies which suggest that this ability is influenced by a recessive sex-linked gene. As a result, it is estimated, approximately 50% of males have a genetic advantage in situations demanding visual-spatial ability, but only 25% of females have this advantage.

Evidence for and against a biological factor in the superior verbal ability of females and the superior mathematical ability of males is, at present, too weak to suggest a conclusion one way or the other.

Adopting the strategy we used before in discussing race and IQ, I shall not go further into the evidence for and against these biological explanations of differences between males and females. Instead I shall ask what the implications of the biological hypotheses would be.

The differences in the intellectual strengths and weaknesses of the sexes cannot explain more than a minute proportion of the difference in positions that males and females hold in our society. It might explain why, for example, there should be *more* males than females in professions like architecture and engineering, professions which, perhaps, require visual–spatial ability; but even in these professions, the magnitude of the differences in numbers cannot be explained by the genetic theory of visual–spatial ability. This theory suggests that half as many females are as genetically advantaged in this area as males, which would account for the lower average scores of females in tests of visual–spatial ability, but cannot account for the fact that there are not merely twice as many males as females in architecture and engineering, but at least ten times as many, and in most countries, even more. Moreover, if superior visual–spatial ability explains the male dominance of architecture and engineering, why isn't there a corresponding female dominance of professions requiring high verbal ability? It is true that there are more women journalists than engineers, and probably more women have achieved lasting fame as novelists than in any other area of life; yet female journalists and television commentators are heavily outnumbered by males, outside specifically 'women's subjects' like cookery and child care. So even if one accepts biological explanations for the patterning of these abilities, one can still argue that women do not have the same opportunities as men to make the most of the abilities they have.

What of differences in aggression? One's first reaction might be that feminists should be delighted with the evidence on this point—what better way could there be of showing the superiority of females than their greater reluctance to hurt others? But the fact that most violent criminals are male may be only one side of greater male aggression. The other side could be greater male competitiveness, ambition, and drive to achieve power. This would have different, and for feminists less welcome, implications. An American sociologist, Steven Goldberg, has built a provocatively entitled book, *The Inevitability of Patriarchy*, around the thesis that the biological basis of greater male aggression will always make it impossible to bring about a society in which women have

as much political power as men. From this claim it is easy to move to the view that women should accept their inferior position in society and not strive to compete with males, or to bring up their daughters to compete with males in these respects; instead women should return to their traditional sphere of looking after the home and children. It is these conclusions which have aroused the hostility of some feminists to biological explanations of male dominance.

As in the case of race and IQ, the moral conclusions alleged to follow from the biological theories do not really follow from them at all. Similar arguments apply.

First, whatever the origin of psychological differences between the sexes, social conditioning can emphasize or soften these differences. As Maccoby and Jacklin stress, the biological bias towards, say, male visual–spatial superiority is really a greater natural readiness to learn these skills. Where women are brought up to be independent their visual–spatial ability is much higher than when they are kept at home and dependent on males. This is no doubt true of other differences as well. Hence feminists may well be right to attack the way in which we encourage girls and boys to develop in distinct directions, even if this encouragement is not itself responsible for creating psychological differences between the sexes, but only reinforces innate predispositions.

Second, whatever the origin of psychological differences between the sexes, they exist only when averages are taken, and some females are more aggressive and have better visual–spatial ability than some males. We have seen that the genetic hypothesis offered in explanation of male visual–spatial superiority itself suggests that a quarter of all females will have greater natural visual–spatial ability than half of all males. Our own observations should convince us that there are females who are also more aggressive than some males. So, biological explanations or not, we are never in a position to say: 'You're a woman, so you can't become an engineer', or 'Because you are female, you will not have the drive and ambition needed to succeed in politics.' Nor should we assume that no male can possibly have sufficient gentleness and warmth to stay at home with the children while their mother goes out to work. We must assess people as individuals, not merely lump them into 'female' and 'male' if we are to find out what they are really like; and we must keep the roles occupied by females and males flexible if people are to be able to do what they are best suited for.

The third reason is, like the previous two, parallel to the reasons I have given for believing that a biological explanation of racial differences in IQ would not justify racism. The most important human interests are no more affected by differences in aggression than they are by differences in intelligence. Less aggressive people have the same interest in avoiding pain, developing their abilities, having adequate food and shelter, enjoying good personal relationships, and so on, as more aggressive people. There is no reason why more aggressive people ought to be rewarded for their aggression with higher salaries and the ability to provide better for these interests.

Since aggression, unlike intelligence, is not generally regarded as a desirable trait, the male chauvinist is hardly likely to deny that greater aggression in itself provides no ethical justification of male supremacy. He may, however, offer it as an explanation, rather than a justification, of the fact that males hold most of the leading positions in politics, business, the universities and other areas in which people of both sexes compete for power and status. He may then go on to suggest that this shows that the status quo is merely the result of competition between males and females under conditions of equal opportunity. Hence, it is not, he may say, unfair. This suggestion raises the further ramifications of biological differences between people which, as I said at the close of our discussion of the race and IQ issue, need to be followed up in more depth.

FROM EQUALITY OF OPPORTUNITY TO EQUALITY OF CONSIDERATION

In our society large differences in income and social status are commonly thought to be all right, so long as they were brought into being under conditions of equal opportunity. The idea is that there is no injustice in Jill earning $100,000 and Jack earning $10,000, as long as Jack had his chance to be where Jill is today. Suppose that the difference in income is due to the fact that Jill is a doctor whereas Jack is a farm worker. This would be acceptable if Jack had the same opportunity as Jill to be a doctor, and this is taken to mean that Jack was not kept out of medical school because of his race, or religion or something similar—in effect, if Jack's school results had been as good as Jill's, he would have been able to study medicine, become a doctor and earn $100,000 a year. Life, on this view, is a kind of race in which it is fitting that the winners should get the prizes, so long as all get an equal start. The equal start represents equality of opportunity and this, some say, is as far as equality should go.

To say that Jack and Jill had equal opportunities to become a doctor, because Jack would have got into medical school if his results had been as good as Jill's, is to take a superficial view of equal opportunity which will not stand up to further probing. We need to ask *why* Jack's results were not as good as Jill's. Perhaps his education up to that point had been inferior—bigger classes, less qualified teachers, inadequate resources and so on. If so he was not competing on equal terms with Jill after all. Genuine equality of opportunity requires us to ensure that schools give the same advantages to everyone.

Making schools equal would be difficult enough, but it is the easiest of the tasks that await a thorough-going proponent of equal opportunity. Even if schools are the same, some children will be favoured by the kind of home they come from. A quiet room to study, plenty of books, and parents who encourage their child to do well at school could explain why Jill succeeds where Jack, forced to share a room with two younger brothers and put up with his father's complaints that he is wasting his time with books instead of getting out and earning his keep, does not. But how does one equalize a home? Or parents? Unless we are prepared to abandon the traditional family setting and bring up our children in communal nurseries, we can't.

This might be enough to show the inadequacy of equal opportunity as an ideal of equality, but the ultimate objection—the one which connects with our previous discussion of equality—is still to come. Even if we did rear our children communally, as on a *kibbutz* in Israel, they would inherit different abilities and character traits, including different levels of aggression and different IQs. Eliminating differences in the child's environment would not affect differences in genetic endowment. True, it might reduce the disparity between, say, IQ scores, since it is likely that, at present, social differences accentuate genetic differences; but the genetic differences would remain and on most estimates they are a major component of the existing differences in IQ. (Remember that we are now talking of *individuals*. We do not know if race affects IQ, but there is little doubt that differences in IQ between individuals of the same race are, in part, genetically determined.)

So equality of opportunity is not an attractive ideal. It rewards the lucky, who inherit those abilities that allow them to pursue interesting and lucrative careers. It penalizes the unlucky, whose genes make it very hard for them to achieve similar success.

We can now fit our earlier discussion of race and sex differences into a broader picture. Whatever the facts about the social or genetic basis of racial differences in IQ, removing social disadvantages will not suffice to bring about an equal or a just distribution of income—not an equal distribution, be-

cause those who inherit the abilities associated with high IQ will continue to earn more than those who do not; and not a just distribution because distribution according to the abilities one inherits is based on an arbitrary form of selection which has nothing to do with what people deserve or need. The same is true of visual–spatial ability and aggression, if these do lead to higher incomes or status. If, as I have argued, the basis of equality is equal consideration of interests, and the most important human interests have little or nothing to do with these factors, there is something questionable about a society in which income and social status correlate to a significant degree with them.

When we pay people high salaries for programming computers and low salaries for cleaning offices we are, in effect, paying people for having a high IQ, and this means that we are paying people for something largely determined before they are born and almost wholly determined before they reach an age at which they are responsible for their actions. From the point of view of justice and utility there is something wrong here. Both would be better served by a society which adopted the famous Marxist slogan: 'From each according to his ability, to each according to his needs.' If this could be achieved the differences between the races and sexes would lose their social significance. Only then would we have a society truly based on the principle of equal consideration of interests.

Is it realistic to aim at a society which rewards people according to their needs rather than their IQ, aggression or other inherited abilities? Don't we have to pay people more to be doctors or lawyers or university professors, to do the intellectually demanding work which is essential for our well-being?

There are difficulties in paying people according to their needs rather than their inherited abilities. If one country attempts to introduce such a scheme while others do not, the result is likely to be some kind of 'brain drain'. We can already see this, on a small scale, in the number of scientists and doctors emigrating from Britain to the United States, Canada and Australia—which is not because Britain does pay people according to need rather than inherited abilities, but because these sections of the community, though relatively well-paid by British standards, would be much better paid in some other countries. If Britain were to make a serious attempt to equalize the salaries of doctors and manual workers, there can be no doubt that the number of doctors emigrating would greatly increase. This is part of the problem of 'socialism in one country'. Marx expected the socialist revolution to be a worldwide one. When the Russian Marxists found that their revolution had not sparked off the anticipated world revolution, they had to adapt Marxist ideas to this new situation. They did so by harshly restricting freedom, including the freedom to emigrate. These restrictions still exist, in the Soviet Union and other communist states. Without them, and despite the considerable pay differentials which still exist in these nations,* there would very likely be an enormous outflow of skilled people to the capitalist nations, which reward skill more highly. But if 'socialism in one country' requires making the country an armed camp, with border guards keeping watch on the citizens within as well as the enemy without, socialism may not be worth the price.

To allow these difficulties to lead us to the conclusion that we can do nothing to improve the distribution of income that now exists in capitalist countries would, however, be too pessimistic. For one thing, the Western world now has, to a large extent, a common culture. If a trend towards a more equal distribution of income exists in some Western nations, it is very likely to spread to others, thus reducing the incentive for migration. For another, there is, in the more affluent Western nations, a good deal of scope for reducing pay differentials before the point is reached at which people begin to think of emigrating. This is, of course, especially true of those countries, like the United States, where pay differentials are presently very great. It is here that pressure for a more equitable distribution can best be applied.

What of the problems of redistribution within a single nation? There is a popular belief that if we did not pay people a lot of money to be doctors or university professors, they would not undertake the studies required to achieve these positions. I do not know what evidence there is in support of this assumption, but it seems to me highly dubious. My own salary is considerably higher than the salaries of the people employed by the university to mow the lawns and keep the grounds clean, but if our salaries were identical I would still not want to swap positions with them—although their jobs are a lot more pleasant than some lowly-paid work. Nor do I believe that my doctor would jump at a chance to change places with his receptionist if their salaries did not differ. It is true that my doctor and I have had to study for several years to get where we are, but I at least look back on my student years as one of the most enjoyable periods of my life.

Although I do not think it is because of the money that people choose to become doctors rather than receptionists, there is one qualification to be made to the suggestion that payment should be based on need rather than ability. It must be admitted that the prospect of earning more money sometimes leads people to make greater efforts to use the abilities they have, and these greater efforts can benefit patients, customers, students, or the public as a whole. It might therefore be worth trying to reward *effort*, which would mean paying people more if they worked near the upper limits of their

---

* According to one observer, salary differentials in China are quite steep, in some areas steeper than in Western nations. For instance, a full professor gets almost seven times as much as a junior lecturer, whereas in Britain, Australia or the US the ratio is more like three to one. See Simon Leys, *Chinese Shadows* (New York, 1977).

abilities, whatever those abilities might be. This, however, is quite different from paying people for the level of ability they happen to have, which is something they cannot themselves control. As Jeffrey Gray, a psychologist at Oxford University, has written, the evidence for genetic control of IQ suggests that to pay people differently for 'upper class' and 'lower class' jobs is 'a wasteful use of resources in the guise of "incentives" which either tempt people to do what is beyond their powers or reward them more for what they would do anyway'.

We have, up to now, been thinking of people like university professors, who are paid by the government, and doctors, whose incomes are determined either by government bodies, where there is some kind of national health service, or by the government protection given to professional associations like a medical association, which enables the profession to exclude anyone who might seek to advertise his services at a lower cost. These incomes are therefore already subject to government control, and could be altered without drastically changing the powers of government. The private business sector of the economy is a different matter. Business people who are quick to seize an opportunity will, under any private enterprise system, make more money than their rivals or, if they are employed by a large corporation, may be promoted faster. Taxation can help to redistribute some of this income, but there are limits to how effective a steeply progressive tax system can be—there almost seems to be a law to the effect that the higher the rate of tax, the greater the amount of tax avoidance.

So do we have to abolish private enterprise if we are to eliminate undeserved wealth? That suggestion raises issues too large to be discussed here; but it can be said that private enterprise has a habit of reasserting itself under the most inhospitable conditions. Communist societies still have their black markets, and if you want your plumbing fixed swiftly it can be advisable to pay a bit extra on the side. Only a radical

change in human nature—a decline in acquisitive and self-centred desires—could overcome the tendency for people to find a way around any system which suppresses private enterprise. Since no such change in human nature is in sight we shall probably continue to pay most to those with inherited abilities, rather than those who have the greatest needs. To hope for something entirely different is unrealistic. On the other hand to work for wider recognition of the principle of payment according to needs and effort rather than inherited ability is both realistic and, I believe, right.

REVERSE DISCRIMINATION

The preceding section suggested that moving to a more egalitarian society in which differences of income are reduced is ethically desirable but likely to prove difficult. Short of bringing about general equality, we might at least attempt to ensure that where there are important differences in income, status and power, women and racial minorities should not be on the worse end in numbers disproportionate to their numbers in the community as a whole. Inequalities between whites may be no more justifiable than those between blacks and whites, or males and females, but when these inequalities coincide with an obvious difference between people like the differences between blacks and whites or males and females, they do more to produce a divided society with a sense of superiority on the one side and a sense of inferiority on the other. Racial and sexual inequality may therefore have a more divisive effect than other forms of inequality. It may also do more to create a feeling of hopelessness among the inferior group, since their sex or their race is not the product of their own actions and there is nothing they can do to change it.

How are racial and sexual equality to be achieved within an inegalitarian society? We have seen that equality of opportunity is practically unrealizable, and if it could be realized might allow innate differences in aggression or IQ unfairly to determine membership of the upper strata. One way of overcoming these obstacles is to go beyond equality of opportunity and give preferential treatment to members of disadvantaged groups. This is reverse discrimination. It may be the best hope of reducing long-standing inequalities; yet it appears to offend against the principle of equality itself. Hence it is controversial.

Reverse discrimination is most often used in education and employment. Education is a particularly important area, since it has an important influence on one's prospects of earning a high income, holding a satisfying job, and achieving power and status in the community. Moreover in the United States education has been at the centre of the dispute over reverse discrimination because of Supreme Court cases over university admission procedures involving reverse discrimination. These cases have arisen because white males were denied admission to courses although their academic records and admission test scores were better than those of some black students admitted. The universities did not deny this; they sought to justify it by explaining that they operated admission schemes intended to help disadvantaged students.

The leading case, so far as United States law is concerned, is *Regents of the University of California vs. Bakke*. Alan Bakke applied for admission to the medical school of the University of California at Davis. In an attempt to increase the number of members of minority groups who attended medical school, the university reserved 16 out of every 100 places for students belonging to a disadvantaged minority. Since these students would not have won so many places in open competition, fewer white students were admitted than there would have been without this reservation. Some white students denied places would certainly have been offered them if, scoring as they did on the admission tests, they had been black. Bakke was among these white students and on being rejected

he sued the university. Let us take this case as a standard case of reverse discrimination. Is it defensible?

I shall start by putting aside one argument sometimes used to justify reverse discrimination. It is sometimes said that if, say, 16% of the population is black, and yet only 2% of doctors are black, this is sufficient evidence that, somewhere along the line, our community discriminates against blacks. (Similar arguments have been mounted in support of claims of sexual discrimination.) Our discussion of the genetics versus environment debate indicates why this argument is inconclusive. It *may* be the case that blacks are, *on average*, less gifted for the kind of study one must do to become a doctor. I am not saying that this is true, or even probable, but it cannot be ruled out at this stage. So a disproportionately small number of black doctors is not in itself proof of discrimination against blacks. (Just as the disproportionately large number of black athletes in the US Olympic team is not in itself proof of discrimination against whites.) There might, of course, be other evidence suggesting that the small number of black doctors really is the result of discrimination; but this would need to be shown. In the absence of positive evidence of discrimination against blacks, it is not possible to justify reverse discrimination on the grounds that it merely redresses the balance of discrimination existing in the community.

Another way of defending a decision to accept a black student in preference to a white student who scored higher in admission tests would be to argue that standard tests do not give an accurate indication of ability when one student has been severely disadvantaged. This is in line with the point made in the last section about the impossibility of achieving equal opportunity. Education and home background presumably influence test scores. A student with a background of deprivation who scores 55% in an admission test may have better prospects of graduating in minimum time than another student who scores 70%. Adjusting test scores on this basis would not mean admitting black students in preference to better-qualified white students. It would reflect a decision that the disadvantaged students really were better qualified than the whites. This is not racial discrimination.

The University of California could not attempt this defence, for its medical school at Davis had simply reserved 16% of places for minority students. The quota did not vary according to the ability displayed by minority applicants. This may be in the interests of ultimate equality, but it is undeniably racial discrimination.

In this chapter we have seen that the only possible basis for the claim that all humans are equal is the principle of equal consideration of interests. That principle outlaws forms of racial and sexual discrimination which give less weight to the interests of those discriminated against. Could Bakke claim that in rejecting his application the medical school gave less weight to his interests that to those of black students?

We have only to ask this question to appreciate that university admission is not normally a result of consideration of the interests of each applicant. It depends rather on matching the applicants against standards which the university draws up with certain policies in mind. Take the most straightforward case: admission rigidly governed by scores on an intelligence test. Suppose those rejected by this procedure complained that their interests had been given less consideration than the interests of applicants of higher intelligence. The university would reply that its procedure did not take the applicants' interests into account at all, and so could hardly give less consideration to the interests of one applicant than it gave to others. We could then ask the university why it used intelligence as the criterion of admission. It might say, first, that to pass the examinations required for graduation takes a high level of intelligence. There is no point in admitting students unable to pass, for they will not be able to graduate. They will waste their own time and the univer-

sity's resources. Secondly, the university may say, the higher the intelligence of our graduates, the more useful they are likely to be to the community. The more intelligent our doctors, the better they will be at preventing and curing disease. Hence the more intelligent the students a medical school selects, the better value the community gets for its outlay on medical education.

This particular admission procedure is of course one-sided; a good doctor must have other qualities in addition to a degree of intelligence. It is only an example, however, and that objection is not relevant to the point I am using the example to make. This point is that no one objects to intelligence as a criterion for selection in the way that they object to race as a criterion; yet those of higher intelligence admitted under an intelligence-based scheme have no more of an intrinsic right to admission than those admitted by reverse discrimination. Higher intelligence, I have argued before, carries with it no right or justifiable claim to more of the good things our society offers. If a university admits students of higher intelligence it does so not in consideration of their greater interest in being admitted, nor in recognition of their right to be admitted, but because it favours goals which it believes will be advanced by this admission procedure. So if this same university should adopt new goals and use reverse discrimination to promote them, applicants who would have been admitted under the old procedure cannot claim that the new procedure violates their right to be admitted, or treats them with less respect than others. They had no special claim to be admitted in the first place; they were the fortunate beneficiaries of the old university policy. Now that this policy has changed others benefit, not they. If this seems unfair, it is only because we had become accustomed to the old policy.

So reverse discrimination cannot be justifiably condemned on the grounds that it violates the rights of university applicants, or treats them with less than equal consideration. There is no inherent right to admission, and equal consideration of the interests of applicants is not involved in normal admission tests. If reverse discrimination is open to objection it must be because the goals it seeks to advance are bad, or because it will not really promote these goals.

The principle of equality might be a ground for condemning the goals of a racially discriminatory admissions procedure. When universities discriminate against already disadvantaged minorities we suspect that the discrimination really does result from less concern for the interests of the minority. Almost certainly this was why universities in the American South excluded blacks until segregation was held to be unconstitutional. Here, in contrast to the reverse discrimination situation, those rejected could justifiably claim that their interests were not being weighed equally with the interests of whites who were admitted. Other explanations may have been offered, but they were surely specious.

Opponents of reverse discrimination have not objected to the goals of social equality and greater minority representation in the professions. They would be hard put to do so. Equal consideration of interests supports moves towards equality because of the principle of diminishing marginal utility, because it relieves the feeling of hopeless inferiority that can exist when members of one race or sex are always worse off than members of another race or the other sex, and because severe inequality between races means a divided community with consequent racial tension.

Within the overall goal of social equality, greater minority representation in professions like law and medicine is desirable for several reasons. Members of minority groups are more likely to work among their own people than whites, and this may help to overcome the scarcity of doctors and lawyers in poor neighbourhoods where most members of disadvantaged minorities live. They may also have a better understanding of the problems disadvantaged people face than any outsider would have. Black and female doctors and lawyers can serve as role models to other blacks and females, breaking down the unconscious mental barriers against aspiring to such positions. Finally, white male students may themselves learn more about the attitudes of blacks and women, and thus become better doctors and lawyers, if their fellow students include members of these groups.

Opponents of reverse discrimination are on stronger ground when they claim that reverse discrimination will not promote equality. As Justice Powell said, in the *Bakke* case, 'Preferential programs may only reinforce common stereotypes holding that certain groups are unable to achieve success without special protection.' To achieve real equality, it might be said, blacks and women must win their places on their merits. As long as blacks get into law school more easily than whites, black law graduates will be regarded as inferior—including those who would have got in under open competition.

There is also a long-term objection to reverse discrimination as a means to equality. In the present social climate we may be confident that race will be taken into account only to benefit disadvantaged minorities; but will this climate last? Should old-fashioned racism return, won't our approval of racial quotas now make it easier to turn them against minority groups? Can we really expect the introduction of racial distinctions to advance the goal of the elimination of racial distinctions?

These practical objections raise difficult factual issues. Though they were referred to in the *Bakke* case, they have not been central in the American legal battles over reverse discrimination. Judges are properly reluctant to decide cases on factual grounds on which they have no special expertise. Alan Bakke won his case chiefly on the grounds that the US Civil Rights Act of 1964 provides that no person shall, on the grounds of colour, race or national origin, be excluded from any activity receiving Federal financial assistance. A bare majority of the judges held that this excluded all discrimination, benign or not. They added, however, that there would be no objection to a university including race as one among a number of factors, like athletic or artistic ability, work experience, demonstrated compassion, a history of overcoming disadvantage, or leadership potential. The court thus effectively allowed universities to choose their student body in accord with their own goals, so long as they did not use quotas.

That is now the law in the United States. From an ethical, rather than a legal, point of view the distinction between quotas and other ways of giving preference to disadvantaged groups may be less significant. The important point is that reverse discrimination, whether by quotas or some other method, is not contrary to any sound principle of equality and does not violate any rights of those excluded by it. Properly applied, it is in keeping with equal consideration of interests, in its aspirations at least. The only real doubt is whether it will work. We cannot yet tell. In the absence of more promising alternatives it seems worth a try.

Before concluding this chapter I should mention a minor instance of reverse discrimination to be found in this book. Feminists often object to the use of the pronoun 'he' to include both males and females in sentences like: 'If someone were to deny this, he would have to argue . . .' Grammarians have replied that the use of the masculine in this instance is a matter of gender, rather than sex—a subtle distinction more easily observed in French or German where tables and chairs can be masculine or feminine, than in English where all males are masculine, females feminine and the rest, barring ships perhaps, neuter. Whatever its origin, however, the use of 'he' does bring to mind males rather than females, so serving to perpetuate the unconscious idea that most writing is about males. And it is surely not just a coincidence that in a male-dominated society we use the male term to include the female, rather than the other way around. I propose a simple remedy. Let us for a time use 'she' to include both females and males. It may jar at first, but we will soon get used to it—and it is much more elegant than the cumbersome 'she or he' or 'she/he' some people have adopted in a valiant effort to avoid sexism. Once 'she' is as naturally read to include the male as 'he' is now read to include the female, we can start using whichever pronoun we please. That is a piece of reverse discrimination that violates no rights, ethical or legal.

Why Liberals Should Care About Equality

Ronald Dworkin

As a political theory, liberalism seems firmly committed to social and political equality, but Ronald Dworkin argues that one can distinguish two versions of liberalism, which differ in the value they place on equality. One version is based on neutrality; it takes as fundamental the idea that government must not take sides on moral issues, and it supports equality only as a derivative value. The other version is based on equality; it takes as fundamental the idea that government treat its citizens as equals, and it insists on moral neutrality only to the extent that equality requires it. Dworkin sets out the main principles of liberalism based on equality, explaining how it justifies both the traditional liberal principle that government should not enforce private morality and a complex theory of economic justice which permits markets but adjusts their allocations. He then considers whether liberal insistence on equality of resources should be tempered in light of the argument of conservative economists that redistributive welfare programs damage the economy and hurt the interests of future generations.

Though liberalism is often discussed as a single political theory, there are in fact two basic forms of liberalism and the distinction between them is of great importance. Both argue against the legal enforcement of private morality—both argue against the Moral Majority's views of homosexuality and abortion, for example—and both argue for greater sexual, political, and economic equality. But they disagree about which of these two traditional liberal values is fundamental and which derivative. Liberalism based on neutrality takes as fundamental the idea that government must not take sides on moral issues, and it supports only

such egalitarian measures as can be shown to be the result of that principle. Liberalism based on equality takes as fundamental that government treat its citizens as equals, and insists on moral neutrality only to the degree that equality requires it.

The difference between these two versions of liberalism is crucial because both the content and appeal of liberal theory depends on which of these two values is understood to be its proper ground. Liberalism based on neutrality finds its most natural defense in some form of moral skepticism, and this makes it vulnerable to the charge that liberalism is a negative theory for uncommitted people. Moreover it offers no effective argument against utilitarian and other contemporary justifications for economic inequality, and therefore provides no philosophical support for those who are appalled at the Reagan administration's economic program. Liberalism based on equality suffers from neither of these defects. It rests on a positive commitment to an egalitarian morality and provides, in that morality, a firm contrast to the economics of privilege.

In this essay I shall set out what I believe are the main principles of liberalism based on equality. This form of liberalism insists that government must treat people as equals in the following sense. It must impose no sacrifice or constraint on any citizen in virtue of an argument that the citizen could not accept without abandoning his sense of his equal worth. This abstract principle requires liberals to oppose the moralism of the New Right, because no self-respecting person who believes that a particular way to live is most valuable for him can accept that this way of life is base or degrading. No self-respecting atheist can agree that a community in which religion is mandatory is for that reason finer, and no one who is homosexual that the eradication of homosexuality makes the community purer.

So liberalism as based on equality justifies the traditional liberal principle that government should not enforce private morality of this sort. But it has an economic as well as a social dimension. It insists on an economic system in which no citizen has less than an equal share of the community's resources just in order that others may have more of what he lacks. I do not mean that liberalism insists on what is often called "equality of result," that is, that citizens must each have the same wealth at every moment of their lives. A government bent on the latter ideal must constantly redistribute wealth, eliminating whatever inequalities in wealth are produced by market transactions. But this would be to devote *unequal* resources to different lives. Suppose that two people have very different bank accounts, in the middle of their careers, because one decided not to work, or not to work at the most lucrative job he could have found, while the other

single-mindedly worked for gain. Or because one was willing to assume especially demanding or responsible work, for example, which the other declined. Or because one took larger risks which might have been disastrous but which were in fact successful, while the other invested conservatively. The principle that people must be treated as equals provides no good reason for distribution in these circumstances; on the contrary, it provides a good reason *against* it.

For treating people as equals requires that each be permitted to use, for the projects to which he devotes his life, no more than an equal share of the resources available for all, and we cannot compute how much any person has consumed, on balance, without taking into account the resources he has contributed as well as those he has taken from the economy. The choices people make about work and leisure and investment have an impact on the resources of the community as a whole, and this impact must be reflected in the calculation equality demands. If one person chooses work that contributes less to other people's lives than different work he might have chosen, then, although this might well have been the right choice for him, given his personal goals, he has nevertheless added less to the resources available for others, and this must be taken into account in the egalitarian calculation. If one person chooses to invest in a productive enterprise rather than spend his funds at once, and if his investment is successful because it increases the stock of goods or services other people actually want, without coercing anyone, his choice has added more to social resources than the choice of someone who did not invest, and this, too, must be reflected in any calculation of whether he has, on balance, taken more than his share.

This explains, I think, why liberals have in the past been drawn to the idea of a market as a method of allocating resources. An efficient market for investment, labor, and goods works as a kind of auction in which the cost to someone of what he consumes, by way of goods and leisure, and the value of what he adds, through his productive labor or decisions, is fixed by the amount his use of some resource costs others, or his contributions benefit them, in each case measured by their willingness to pay for it. Indeed, if the world were very different from what it is, a liberal could accept the results of an efficient market as *defining* equal shares of community resources. If people start with equal amounts of wealth, and have roughly equal levels of raw skill, then a market allocation would ensure that no one could properly complain that he had less than others, over his whole life. He could have had the same as they if he had made the decisions to consume, save, or work that they did.

But in the real world people do not start their lives on equal terms; some begin with marked advantages of family wealth or of formal and informal education. Others suffer because their race is despised. Luck plays a further and sometimes devastating part in deciding who gains or keeps jobs everyone wants. Quite apart from these plain inequities, people are not equal in raw skill or intelligence or other native capacities; on the contrary, they differ greatly, through no choice of their own, in the various capacities that the market tends to reward. So some people who are perfectly willing, even anxious, to make exactly the choices about work and consumption and savings that other people make end up with fewer resources, and no plausible theory of equality can accept this as fair. This is the defect of the ideal fraudulently called "equality of opportunity": fraudulent because in a market economy people do not have equal opportunity who are less able to produce what others want.

So a liberal cannot, after all, accept the market results as defining equal shares. His theory of economic justice must be complex, because he accepts two principles which are difficult to hold in the administration of a dynamic economy. The first requires that people have, at any point in their lives, different amounts of wealth insofar as the genuine choices they have made have been more or less expensive or beneficial to the community, measured by what other people want for their lives. The market seems indispensable to this principle. The second requires that people not have different amounts of wealth just because they have different inherent capacities to produce what others want, or are differently favored by chance. This means that market allocations must be corrected in order to bring some people closer to the share of resources they would have had but for these various differences of initial advantage, luck, and inherent capacity.

Obviously any practical program claiming to respect both these principles will work imperfectly and will inevitably involve speculation, compromise, and arbitrary lines in the face of ignorance. For it is impossible to discover, even in principle, exactly which aspects of any person's economic position flow from his choices and which from advantages or disadvantages that were not matters of choice; and even if we could make this determination for particular people, one by one, it would be impossible to develop a tax system for the nation as a whole that would leave the first in place and repair only the second. There is therefore no such thing as the perfectly just program of redistribution. We must be content to choose whatever programs we believe bring us closer to the complex and unattainable ideal of equality, all things considered, than the available alternatives, and be ready constantly to reexamine that conclusion when new evidence or new programs are proposed.

Nevertheless, in spite of the complexity of that ideal, it may sometimes be apparent that a society falls far short of any plausible interpretation of its requirements. It is, I think, apparent that the United States falls far short now. A substantial minority of Americans are chronically unemployed or earn wages below any realistic "poverty line" or are handicapped in various ways or burdened with special needs; and most of these people would do the work necessary to earn a decent living if they had the opportunity and capacity. Equality of resources would require more rather than less redistribution than we now offer.

This does not mean, of course, that we should continue past liberal programs, however inefficient these have proved to be, or even that we should insist on "targeted" programs of the sort some liberals have favored—that is, programs that aim to provide a particular opportunity or resource, like education or medicine, to those who need it. Perhaps a more general form of transfer, like a negative income tax, would prove on balance more efficient and fairer, in spite of the difficulties in such schemes. And whatever devices are chosen for bringing distribution closer to equality of resources, some aid undoubtedly goes to those who have avoided rather than sought jobs. This is to be regretted, because it offends one of the two principles that together make up equality of resources. But we come closer to that ideal by tolerating this inequity than by denying aid to the far greater number who would work if they could. If equality of resources were our only goal, therefore, we could hardly justify the present retreat from redistributive welfare programs.

We must therefore consider a further and more difficult question. Must liberals insist on equality of resources no matter what the cost to the national economy as a whole? It is far from obvious that treating people as equals forbids any deviation from equality of resources for any reason whatsoever. On the contrary, people with a lively sense of their own equal worth, and pride in their own convictions, can nevertheless accept certain grounds for carrying special burdens for the sake of the community as a whole. In a defensive war, for example, we expect those who are capable of military service to assume a vastly greater share of danger than others. Nor is inequality permissible only in emergencies when the survival of the community is at stake. We

might think it proper, for example, for the government to devote special resources to the training of exceptionally talented artists or musicians, beyond what the market would pay for the services these artists produce, even though this reduces the share others have. We accept this not because we think that the life of an artist is inherently more valuable than other lives, but because a community with a lively cultural tradition provides an environment within which citizens may live more imaginatively, and in which they might take pride. Liberalism need not be insensitive to these and similar virtues of community. The question becomes not whether any deviation is permitted, but what reasons for deviation are consistent with equal concern and respect.

That question is now pressing for this reason. Many economists believe that reducing economic inequality through redistribution is damaging to the general economy and, in the long run, self-defeating. Welfare programs, it is said, are inflationary, and the tax system necessary to support them depresses incentive and therefore production. The economy, it is claimed, can be restimulated only by reducing taxes and adopting other programs that will, in the short run, produce high unemployment and otherwise cause special damage to those already at the bottom of the economy. But this damage will only be temporary. For a more dynamic economy will produce prosperity, and this will in the end provide more jobs and more money for the handicapped and others truly needy.

Each of these propositions is doubtful, and they may well all be wrong. But suppose we were to accept them. Do they make a case for ignoring those in the economic cellar now? The argument would be unanswerable, of course, if *everyone* who lost because of stringent policies now would actually be better off in the long run. But though this is often suggested in careless supply-side rhetoric, it is absurd. People laid off for several years, with no effective retraining, are very unlikely to recoup their losses later, particularly if their psychological losses are counted. Children denied adequate nutrition or any effective chance of higher education will suffer permanent loss even if the economy follows the most optimistic path of recovery. Some of those who are denied jobs and welfare now, particularly the elderly, will in any case not live long enough to share in that recovery, however general it turns out to be.

So the currently popular argument, that we must reduce benefits now in order to achieve general prosperity later, is simply a piece of utilitarianism, which attempts to justify irreversible losses to a minority in order to achieve gains for the large majority. (One report of Reagan's Council of Economic Advisers was quite explicit in embracing that utilitarian claim: it argued that his economic policies were required in order to avoid treating the very poor, who will permanently lose, as a special interest!) But this denies the principle fundamental to liberalism based on equality, the principle that people must be treated with equal concern. It asks some people to accept lives of great poverty and despair, with no prospect of a useful future, just in order that the great bulk of the community may have a more ample measure of what they are forever denied. Perhaps people can be forced into this position. But they cannot accept it consistently with a full recognition of their independence, and their right to equal concern on the part of their government.

But suppose the case for the administration's policies is put differently, by calling attention to the distinct social dangers of continuing or expanding past programs of redistribution. We might imagine two arguments of this sort. The first calls attention to the damage inflation does, not simply to the spending power, savings, and prospects of the majority, as individuals, but also to the public environment in which all citizens must live and in which all might take either pride or shame. As society becomes poorer, because production falls and wealth decays, it loses a variety of features we cherish. Its

culture fails, its order declines, its system of criminal and civil justice becomes less accurate and less fair; in these and other ways it steadily recedes from our conception of a good society. The decline cannot be arrested by further taxation to support these public goods, for that will only shrink production further and accelerate the decline. According to this argument, those who lose by programs designed to halt inflation and reinvigorate the economy are called upon to make a sacrifice, not just in order to benefit others privately, but out of a sense of loyalty to the public institutions of their own society.

The second argument is different because it calls attention to the interests of future generations. It asks us to suppose that if we are zealous for equality now, we will so depress the wealth of the community that future Americans will be even less well off than the very poor are now. Future Americans will have no more, perhaps, than the citizens of economically depressed third world countries in the present world. The second argument comes to this: the present poor are asked to sacrifice in favor of their fellow citizens now, in order to prevent a much greater injustice, to many more citizens, later.

Neither of these two arguments plainly violates the liberal's axiomatic principle of equal concern and respect. Each can be offered to people who take pride in their equal worth and in the value of their convictions. But only in certain circumstances. Both arguments, though in different ways, appeal to the idea that each citizen is a member of a community, and that he can find, in the fate of that community, a reason for special burdens he can accept with honor rather than degradation. This is appropriate only when that community offers him, at a minimum, the opportunity to develop and lead a life he can regard as valuable both to himself and to it.

We must distinguish, that is, between passive and active membership in a community. Totalitarian regimes suppose that anyone who is present in their community, and so is amenable to its political force, is a member of the community from whom sacrifice might fairly be asked in the name of that community's greatness and future. Treating people as equals requires a more active conception of membership. If people are asked to sacrifice for their community, they must be offered some reason why the community which benefits from that sacrifice is their community; there must be some reason why, for example, the unemployed blacks of Detroit should take more interest in either the public virtue or the future generations of Michigan than they do in those of Mali.

We must ask in what circumstances someone with the proper sense of his own independence and equal worth can take pride in a community as being his community, and two conditions, at least, seem necessary to this. He can take pride in its present attractiveness—in the richness of its culture, the justice of its institutions, the imagination of its education—only if his life is one that in some way draws on and contributes to these public virtues. He can identify himself with the future of the community and accept present deprivation as sacrifice rather than tyranny, only if he has some power to help determine the shape of that future, and only if the promised prosperity will provide at least equal benefit to the smaller, more immediate communities for which he feels special responsibilities, for example, his family, his descendants, and, if the society is one that has made this important to him, his race.

These seem minimal conditions, but they are nevertheless exigent. Together they impose serious restraints on any policy that denies any group of citizens, however small or political negligible, the equal resources that equal concern would otherwise grant them. Of course no feasible program can provide every citizen with a life valuable in his own eyes. But these constraints set a limit to what a government that respects equality may deliberately choose when other choices are available. People must not be con-

demned, unless this is unavoidable, to lives in which they are effectively denied any active part in the political, economic, and cultural life of the community. So if economic policy contemplates an increase in unemployment, it must also contemplate generous public provision for retraining or public employment. The children of the poor must not be stinted of education or otherwise locked into positions at the bottom of society. Otherwise their parents' loyalty to them acts not as a bridge but as a bar to any identification with the future these parents are meant to cherish.

If this is right, then it suggests an order of priorities which any retrenchment in welfare programs should follow. Programs like food stamps, Aid to Families with Dependent Children, and those using federal funds to make higher education available for the poor are the last programs that should be curtailed, or (what amounts to the same thing) remitted to the states through some "new federalism." If "targeted" programs like these are thought to be too expensive, or too inefficient, then government must show how alternative plans or programs will restore the promise of participation in the future that these programs offered. In any case, cutbacks in the overall level of welfare provided to the poor should be accompanied by efforts to improve the social integration and political participation of blacks and other minorities who suffer most, in order to assure them a more prominent role in the community for which they sacrifice. Reductions in welfare should not be joined to any general retreat from affirmative action and other civil rights programs, or to any effort to repeal or resist improvements in the Voting Rights Act. That is why the economic and social programs so far proposed or enacted by the present administration seem so mean-spirited and cynical. Taken together, they would reduce rather than enlarge the political participation and social mobility of the class from which they demand the greatest sacrifice.

These observations offer only rough guidelines to the necessary conditions for asking people to sacrifice equal resources for the sake of their community. Different people will interpret these guidelines differently, and disagree about when they have been violated. But they may nevertheless serve as the beginning of an overdue development of liberal theory. During the long period of liberal ascendancy, from the New Deal through the 1960s, liberals felt confident that the immediate reduction of poverty was in every way good for the larger community. Social justice would, in Lyndon Johnson's phrase, make the society great. Liberals thus avoided the question of what liberalism requires when prosperity is threatened rather than enhanced by justice. They offered no coherent and feasible account of what might be called economic rights for hard times: the floor beneath which people cannot be allowed to drop for the greater good.

If liberals remember the counsel of equal concern, they will construct such a theory now, by pointing to the minimal grounds on which people with self-respect can be expected to regard a community as their community, and to regard its future as in any sense their future. If government pushes people below the level at which they can help shape the community and draw value from it for their own lives, or if it holds out a bright future in which their own children are promised only second-class lives, then it forfeits the only premise on which its conduct might be justified.

We need not accept the gloomy predictions of the New Right economists that our future will be jeopardized if we try to provide everyone with the means to lead a life with choice and value, or if we continue to accept mobility as an absolute priority and try to provide appropriate higher education for everyone qualified. But if these gloomy predictions were sound, we should simply have to tailor our ambitions for the future accordingly. For society's obligation runs first to its living citizens. If our government can provide an attractive future only through present injustice—only by forcing some citizens to sacrifice in the name of a community from which they are in every sense excluded—then the rest of us should disown that future, however attractive, because we should not regard it as our future either.

Human Worth and Moral Merit

John Kekes

The egalitarian belief that all human beings have equal worth independent of their moral merit and, therefore, certain fundamental rights dominates our age, and many social programs in liberal democracies presuppose it. John Kekes challenges this belief. He argues that it rests on the following three assumptions, each of which he rejects:

1. that selves are distinct from, and to be valued independently of, their qualities;
2. that human worth attaches to universal qualities of humanity, while moral merit is due to individual qualities that people have but do not deserve; and
3. that because human nature is basically good, an individual's potentialities have a moral value independent of moral merit.

Accordingly, Kekes rejects the claim that we are required to treat human beings as if they had equal worth and, consequently, equal rights to freedom and well-being.

Professor Kekes teaches at the State University of New York at Albany. He has written numerous articles in ethics and is, most recently, the author of *Facing Evil* (Princeton University Press, 1990).

I

It is a depressingly common phenomenon in human history that a false belief pervades the sensibility of an age and exerts a deep influence on the prevailing moral, political, and legal practices. The divine right of kings to rule, the barbarity of people who do not share some favored form of life, the sinfulness of sex outside of marriage, the influence of evil spirits on human affairs, and the wickedness or backwardness of peo-

Reprinted by permission from *Public Affairs Quarterly*, Vol. 2, No. 1 (January 1988).

ple who fail to worship a particular god are all examples of the kind of belief I have in mind. I think that we, in our age, are also threatened with being engulfed by such a belief. It is the egalitarian one that all human beings have equal worth independently of their moral merit. The implication of this belief is that because of their equal worth all human beings have rights to certain benefits, and further, that one fundamental purpose of our moral, political, and legal institutions ought to be to maintain a system of justice to safeguard these rights. People have rights, it is believed, simply because they are human. Differences in moral merit are acknowledged, but they are supposed to be irrelevant to human worth and to the possession of the concomitant rights.

Although this egalitarian belief is presupposed by many social programs proposed, and often implemented, in liberal democracies, we have to turn to philosophers for explicit statements of it. Thus Rawls writes: "There is a tendency for common sense to suppose that . . . the good things in life . . . should be distributed according to moral desert. . . . Now justice as fairness rejects this assumption." Dworkin, arguing in support of Rawls, agrees: "Justice as fairness rests on the assumption of a natural right of men and women to equality of concern and respect, a right they possess not by virtue of birth or characteristic or merit or excellence but simply as human beings." Vlastos thinks that "the human worth of all persons is equal, however unequal may be their merit."[1]

The practical implication of this egalitarianism is that the vicious and the kind, the cruel and the benevolent, the just and the unjust should be granted equal rights to other people's support of their freedom and welfare. Justice, according to egalitarians, requires that we should ignore the use to which people have and are likely in the future to put their freedom and well-being. Lifelong patterns of moral or immoral conduct are supposed to be irrelevant to what we think of the respective worth of people whose conduct forms these patterns. The decent and the despicable have the same human worth and are entitled to the same share of whatever contribution others can make toward their freedom and well-being.

Defenders of egalitarianism attempt to mitigate the implausibility of this belief by the qualification that the attribution of equal human worth is not absolute but prima facie. There is a presumption in favor of all people possessing it, and thus having equal rights to freedom and well-being, but the presumption can be justifiably overruled, provided the resulting inequality strengthens the protection of overall freedom and well-being. Thus criminals, for instance, are properly deprived of their freedom, because they have violated the rights of others. But the justification of unequal distribution is, and can only be, that it is required by equal distribution. As Vlastos puts it: "an equalitarian concept of justice may admit inequalities without inconsistency if, and only if, it provides grounds for equal human rights."[2]

This is a step in the right direction, but taking it has two fundamentally damaging consequences for the prima facie case for egalitarianism. The first is that the reasons which can justifiably lead to the defeat of the prima facie case for human worth being independent of moral merit are nothing but appeals to moral merit. We can violate the rights of right-violators, if they habitually and intentionally harm others. And since, on any view, morality is centrally concerned with the benefit and harm people cause each other, those who habitually and intentionally harm others are deficient in moral merit, and this is what justifies depriving them of their rights. So if the case for equal human worth is prima facie, not absolute, then human worth is not independent of moral merit.

The response to this may be that the prima facie case rests not only on the presumption of equal human worth but also on that of moral merit. People are assumed not to have harmed others, unless there are overriding reasons to believe otherwise. Safeguarding people's rights to freedom and well-being should not be made to depend on the favorable outcome of an investigation into their moral merit. This claim leads to

[1] John Rawls, *A Theory of Justice* (Cambridge, Mass: Harvard, 1971), p. 310; R. Dworkin, *Taking Rights Seriously* (Cambridge, Mass: Harvard, 1977), p. 182; Gregory Vlastos, "Justice and Equality," *Social Justice*, ed. by R. B. Brandt (Englewood Cliffs: Prentice-Hall, 1962), p. 43.

[2] Vlastos, ibid., p. 40.

the second of the damaging consequences mentioned above.

The presumption in favor of the possession of moral merit may or may not be reasonable; whether it is depends, among other things, on the general level of morality prevailing in a social context. Consider, therefore, the following social context:

Wherever you looked, in all our institutions, in all our homes, *skloka* was brewing. *Skloka* is a phenomenon born of our social order, an entirely new term and concept, not to be translated into any language of the civilized world. It is hard to define. It stands for base, trivial hostility, unconscionable spite breeding petty intrigues, the vicious pitting of one clique against another. It thrives on calumny, informing, spying, slander, the igniting of base passions. Taut nerves and weakening morals allow one individual or group rabidly to hate another individual or group. *Skloka* is natural for people who have been incited to attack one another, who have been made bestial by desperation, who have been driven to the wall.[3]

In a social context where *skloka* dominates, the presumption of moral merit is unreasonable, because people habitually and intentionally harm others. Some individuals, of course, may still escape corruption, but *skloka* shows that most people do not. The implication is that in such societies the prima facie case is systematically defeated. Consequently, we cannot reasonably attribute human worth to people simply in virtue of their humanity, because their moral merit and their social context exerting a strong influence on their moral merit are also relevant.

Thus the egalitarian belief that people have equal human worth independently of their moral merit ought to fizzle out. The rights to freedom and well-being should be seen as partly dependent on the morality of agents and on the prevailing social conditions. But what should happen does not happen. This extraordinary belief continues

to be strongly held in spite of its implausibility and the existence of such obvious criticisms of it as I have just adduced. At least part of the reason for this is that underlying egalitarianism, there are three deep and basic assumptions, and they lend support to it. I shall, therefore, proceed to state and criticize these assumptions.

II

The first assumption rests on a distinction between two aspects of being a person.[4] One is the self, and the other is various qualities. The self is the subject who possesses these qualities. Some of these qualities may exist as potentialities at birth, others are acquired by conditioning, accident, education, or choice. The self is at least relatively enduring and continuous; it is the bearer of one's name; the referent of "I"; the guarantor of some minimal personal identity. By contrast, qualities are changeable; they can be developed and lost. In some sense, persons necessarily possess their selves, but the possession of qualities is contingent. It is, of course, very difficult to specify the appropriate senses of necessity and contingency, continuity and change, or the nature of personal identity. But I do not think that the use egalitarians make of this distinction depends on having precise logical answers to these complicated questions.

The heart of the egalitarian case is that human worth attaches to selves, while moral merit depends on qualities. One reason why human worth is thought to be independent of moral merit, according to egalitarians, is that selves are distinct from their qualities. Since people possess selves necessarily and universally and qualities only contingently, people also have human worth necessarily and universally, and moral merit only contingently.

The proper interpretation of equal human rights to freedom and well-being, ac-

---

[3] *The Correspondence of Boris Pasternak and Olga Friedenberg, 1910–1954*, ed. & tr. by E. Mossman (New York: Harcourt, 1982), pp. 303–304.

[4] My discussion of this assumption is indebted to M. J. Sandel's *Liberalism and the Limits of Justice* (Cambridge: Cambridge University Press, 1982).

cording to egalitarians, is not that people are rewarded by these rights for their morally good qualities, but that human rights are necessary conditions for people developing morally good qualities. Thus human rights protect selves and make their development possible; and rights are equal because all human beings possess selves simply in virtue of being human. Human worth is prior to moral merit, because the possession of selves is prior to their development. Justice consists in social arrangements guaranteeing equal protection for all people so that they may develop their selves. This is why justice, equality, and human rights attach to people per se, rather than only to those who have morally merited them. To express this in terms of human worth is to indicate that one belongs to the party of humanity, that one thinks that there is a prima facie case in favor of people's development of their selves.

This assumption is behind Vlastos's claim that:

if there is a value attaching to the person himself as an integral and unique individual, *this* value will not fall under merit or be reducible to it. For it is the essence of merit . . . to be a grading concept; and there is no way of grading individuals as such.[5]

And this is part of the rationale for Rawls's placing prospective agents in the original position where, behind the veil of ignorance, they know, as it were, only their selves, but not their qualities. They are to legislate so as to enable people to develop their selves. "The self," Rawls writes, "is prior to the ends which are affirmed by it."[6] "The parties' aim in the original position is to establish just and favorable conditions for each to fashion his own [plan of life]."[7]

So the first assumption upon which the supposed independence of human worth from moral merit rests is that these two no-

tions should not be seen as competing grounds for the ascription of rights. When they are properly understood, it becomes apparent that human worth is logically and morally prior to moral merit, because the self is prior to its qualities, and while human worth is a necessary and universal feature of all human beings, moral merit is merely a contingent one.

III

The initial problem with the supposed priority of the self to its qualities is that if this were true, then there could not be a reason for attributing human worth to the self. The problem is logical. For if the self were regarded merely as the logical subject of which qualities were predicated, then there could be no reason for thinking that the self was a human self. Animals, plants, and material objects also possess logical subjects in this pure sense. But if we go beyond pure logical subjects, so that the kind of logical subjects human beings have could be distinguished from other kinds of logical subjects, then the distinction must be made in terms of some quality or another. In that case, however, the identification of a logical subject as a human self necessarily involves reference to some quality. Consequently, if a logical subject were prior to its qualities, then the attribution of moral worth to it would be illegitimate, since the logical subject may not be a human self. On the other hand, if human worth were justifiably assigned to a self, then there would have to be some quality present justifying the ascription, and then the self would not be prior to *that* quality.

Now, whatever that quality is, it would have to be one that distinguishes human subjects from non-human ones. Rationality, altruism, the good will, self-direction, conscience, and self-consciousness are some of the frequently proposed candidates. However, regardless of what the quality is, critics of egalitarianism would reasonably claim that its possession is the minimal ground of

[5] Vlastos, op. cit., p. 43.
[6] Rawls, op. cit., p. 560.
[7] Ibid., p. 563.

moral merit. And, then, human worth would go hand in hand with moral merit. For if people lost the relevant quality, they would ipso facto be deprived of both human worth and moral merit. The former, because the subject of human worth would not have been shown to be human, and the latter, because moral merit would lose its minimal ground. Contrariwise, if the relevant quality were present, then the ascription of human worth and minimal moral merit would be equally justified and be justified on the same grounds. So the first assumption upon which the supposed independence of human worth from moral merit rests is vitiated by a logical error.

One of Vlastos' arguments illustrates this error. He writes:

If *A* is valued for some meritorious quality, *m*, his individuality does not enter into the valuation. As an individual he is then dispensable; his place could be taken without loss of value by any other individual with as good an *m*-rating. Nor would matters change by multiplying and diversifying the meritorious qualities with which *A* is endowed. No matter how enviable a package of well-rounded excellence *A* may represent, it would still follow that, if he is valued only for his merit, he is not being valued as an individual.[8]

The implication is clear: if *A* is to be valued as an individual, then he must be valued independently of his qualities. Hence *A* could be a ping pong ball or a cobweb.

To make clear what he means by the above quote, Vlastos gives as an example a parent (*P*) valuing his son (*A*) in the right way:

P prizes [*A*'s] . . . conjunct of qualities (*M*), [and] he values *A* also as an individual. . . . If so, his affection will be for *A*, not for *M*-qualities. The latter, *P* approves, admires, takes pride in, and the like. But his affection and good will are for *A*, and *not only because* or *insofar as A* has the *M*-qualities.[9]

Thus *P*'s affection and good will ought not to depend on *A*'s qualities. So if *A* turned out not to be *P*'s son, if *P* had not watched *A*'s growth and development, if *A* did not have a long intimate relationship with *P*, then, and only then, would *P*'s affection and good will be directed at *A* as an individual. Vlastos fails to see that if *A*'s qualities are removed, then *A* ceases to be an individual whom *P* can reasonably value, or that if *P* is reasonable in valuing *A*, then the valuing must be based on some quality or qualities of *A*.

Suppose this logical point is conceded by egalitarians. They may attempt to defend the independence of human worth from moral merit by arguing that the identification of logical subjects as human beings does rest on some qualities, and these are sufficient to justify the ascription of human worth, but the qualities are morally neutral, and hence insufficient for the ascription of moral merit. Some of Rawls's arguments can be cited in support of this approach. He writes, for instance, that:

[T]he natural distribution [of qualities] is neither just not unjust; nor is it unjust that persons are born into society at some particular position. These are simply natural facts. What is just an unjust is the way institutions deal with these facts.[10]

The suggestion is that some non-moral qualities are prior to the establishment of institutions, while moral merit is contingent on institutions, since institutions define what a particular society counts as morally meritorious qualities:

A good person . . . is someone who has in a higher degree than the average the broadly based features of moral character that it is rational for persons in the original position to want in one another. Since the principles of justice have been chosen . . . each knows that in society he will want the others to have the moral sentiments that support adherence to these standards.[11]

---

[8] Vlastos, op. cit., p. 44.
[9] Ibid., p. 44.

[10] Rawls, op. cit., p. 104.
[11] Ibid., p. 437.

But while the principles of justice may be regarded as establishing what counts as moral merit in *some* cases, they cannot establish it in *all* cases. For Rawls himself insists that some moral considerations are appropriate prior to the choice of the principles of justice:

[I]t is characteristic of natural duties that they apply to us without regard to our voluntary acts. Moreover, they have no necessary connection with institutions or social practices; their content is not, in general, defined by the rules of these arrangement. Thus we have a natural duty not to be cruel, and a duty to help another, whether or not we have committed ourselves to these actions.[12]

If we suppose what is obvious, namely, that there are both people who habitually and intentionally violate their natural duties and people who habitually and intentionally honor them, then we have clear instances of the presence and absence of moral merit prior to institutions or to people's commitment to them. Consequently, the attempt to separate morally neutral pre-institutional qualities from morally evaluative institutional qualities fails. And so also fails the attempted rescue of the independence of human worth from moral merit. For we cannot reasonably connect human worth with pre-institutional qualities and moral merit with institutional ones. I conclude that the logical error involved in trying to distinguish the self from its qualities is not avoided by the distinction between pre-institutional and institutional qualities. If the self is a pure logical subject, then the ascription of neither human worth nor moral merit is justified; and if the self is allowed to have some qualities, then the ascription of both human worth and moral merit is contingent on the possession of these qualities. In neither case can the independence of human worth from moral merit be reasonably maintained. And so egalitarians have given no good reason yet for rejecting the obvious point that

people who are habitually and intentionally immoral, and thus lack moral merit, have less human worth and are entitled to less protection of their freedom and well-being than people who show a lifelong pattern of moral conduct, and thus have moral merit.

IV

The second assumption underlying the supposed independence of human worth from moral merit is that human worth attaches to universal qualities of humanity, while moral merit is partly due to individual qualities people have but do not deserve. The universal qualities upon which human worth depends are common human potentialities, such as rationality, altruism, self-direction, and so on. Justice, equality, and the rights to freedom and well-being protect the conditions in which these potentialities may be realized. By contrast, moral merit depends on character. But character, in turn, depends, to a considerable extent, on natural endowments and social circumstances. Morally good character requires some intelligence, the capacity for self-control, a mental equilibrium that makes it possible to pay attention to others, the absence of brutalizing influences, and victimization by extreme poverty, discrimination, or exploitation. People with morally good character have been lucky in the genetic lottery and in being raised in a hospitable setting. Luck, however, is an arbitrary ground for moral merit. Therefore, it would be unjust to distribute rights to freedom and well-being unequally, according to moral merit. It is far more reasonable to distribute them according to human worth and human potentialities so that the arbitrariness of natural endowments and the conditions of birth and upbringing are minimized. As Rawls puts it:

It seems to be one of the fixed points of our considered judgments that no one deserves his place in the distribution of native endowments, any more than one deserves one's initial starting

---

[12] Ibid., p. 114–115.

place in society. The assertion that a man deserves the superior character that enables him to cultivate his abilities is equally problematic; for his character depends in large part upon fortunate family and social circumstances for which he can claim no credit. The notion of desert seems not to apply to these cases.[13]

V

The immediate consequence of this argument is that human worth has exactly the same status as moral merit, so that if one is arbitrary, and hence an unjust ground for the unequal distribution of rights, then so is the other. If desert does not apply to moral merit, then it does not apply to human worth either, for whether people possess the potentialities justice, equality, and rights are meant to protect is just as much a matter of luck in the genetic lottery as the possession of a morally good character is said to be.

Now Rawls is prepared to accept this. He writes:

A just scheme . . . answers to what men are entitled to; it satisfies their legitimate expectations as founded upon social institutions. But what they are entitled to is not proportional to nor dependent upon their intrinsic worth. The principles of justice . . . do not mention . . . desert, and there is no tendency for distributive shares to correspond to it.[14]

Sandel's comment on this passage seems to me to be absolutely correct:

The principles of justice do not mention . . . desert because, strictly speaking, no one can be said to deserve anything. Similarly, the reason people's entitlements are not proportional to nor dependent upon their intrinsic worth is that, on Rawls's view, *people have no intrinsic worth*, no worth that is intrinsic in the sense that it is theirs prior to or independent of or apart from what institutions attribute to them.[15]

And there is no doubt that this is what Rawls means, for he explicitly says:

The essential point is that the concept of moral worth [i.e., a combination of what I mean by human worth *and* moral merit] does not provide a first principle of distributive justice. This is because it cannot be introduced until after the principles of justice and of natural duty and obligation have been acknowledged . . . [T]he concept of moral worth is secondary to those of right and justice, and it plays no role in the substantive definition of distributive shares.[16]

So the price we have to pay for giving up the idea that desert ought to be proportional to moral merit is that we also have to give up the idea that desert ought to be based on human worth.

Why, then, should we treat people whose conduct systematically harms others in the same way as we do those whose conduct systematically benefits them? The answer with which we began, and whose underlying assumptions we are now examining, appealed to universal and necessary human worth as a ground for desert to override differences in individual moral merit. But since this appeal can no longer be made, the question stands.

VI

This brings us to the third assumption underlying the supposed independence of human worth from moral merit. It may be said that although no one deserves anything in pre-institutional settings, there is still a deep sense in which we are committed to the idea that it is good if people can develop their potentialities. We are human, and it is natural for us to wish well for humanity. Justice, equality, and the rights to freedom and well-being protect the conditions in which human potentialities can be developed, and this is the fundamental reason for defending them. The idea of human worth is

---

[13] Ibid., p. 104.
[14] Ibid., p. 311.
[15] Sandel, op. cit., p. 88.

[16] Rawls, op. cit., p. 312–313.

meant to capture this commitment we have, or ought to have, to the welfare of humanity collectively. The presumption in favor of the human worth of individuals is a distributive consequence of the general idea.

The obvious difficulty with this is that human potentialities are mixed; they are benign and aggressive, altruistic and selfish, generous and envious, gentle and cruel. If the commitment to human welfare calls for the development of morally good human potentialities, it also calls for the suppression of morally bad potentialities. If human worth licensed the indiscriminate fostering of human potentialities, it would not support human welfare. But the appeal to moral merit allows us to distinguish between morally good and bad potentialities, and it provides a ground for encouraging the first and discouraging the second. So human welfare is better served by fostering or suppressing human potentialities proportionally to their likely contribution to moral merit than by the egalitarian indiscriminateness that follows from human worth.

Now it seems to me that the only way to resist this argument is by denying that morally good and bad human potentialities have an equal status in human nature. To put it bluntly, the defence of the egalitarian belief presupposes that human nature is primarily, predominantly, or chiefly good. If this were so, then there would indeed be a reason for fostering the development of human potentialities. I think that it is widely presupposed that human nature is like this. But I cannot offer textual support from current literature as evidence. Although the presupposition is unstated, it is in the background, the egalitarian belief requires it, and it is a pervasive influence upon contemporary moral sensibility. It is part of our inheritance from the Enlightenment beliefs in the possibility of progress, the rationality of humanity, and the ascription of evil to the corruption caused by badly designed institutions. Its patron saint is Rousseau.

In reaction to it, I cannot improve on James Fitzjames Stephen's trenchant words:

It is one of the commonest beliefs of the day that the human race collectively has before it splendid destinies of various kinds, and that the road to them is found . . . in the recognition of a substantial equality between all human creatures. . . . These doctrines . . . are regarded not merely as truths, but as truths for which those who believe in them are ready to do battle. . . . Such, stated of course in the most general terms, is the religion of which I take "Liberty, Equality, Fraternity" to be the creed. I do not believe it.

I believe that many men are bad, a vast majority of men indifferent, and many good, and that the great mass of indifferent people sway this way or that according to circumstances, one of the most important of which circumstances is the predominance for the time being of the bad or good.[17]

Let us now consider how the assumption that human nature is predominantly good translates into a support for the egalitarian belief. The usual strategy for supporting human worth against moral merit is to contrast people who have greater or lesser moral merit. It is then argued that the ones with less moral merit do not get written out of morality; they are still moral agents and they have a claim on our moral regard. The reason for this is that although they have misused their potentialities, they still possess them. Therefore, there is hope for reform and improvement. Human worth attaches to potentialities which cannot be lost, but only misused. Since potentialities are prior to their use or misuse, human worth is prior to moral merit.

There goes with this thinking a particular metaphor for morality. Morality is like language, and becoming a moral agent is like learning one's mother tongue. Both are skills, both are possessed by just about everybody, both are acquired as a matter of course and it is not their possession but rather their lack that requires explanation. Both allow for grading agents according to their performance, both are necessary for the

---

[17] J. F. Stephen, *Liberty, Equality, Fraternity*, ed. by R. J. White (Cambridge: Cambridge University Press, 1967), pp. 52–53 and 226.

well-being of individuals as well as of society, both require conformity to rules, both can tolerate some violations of the rules, and the rules of both can be changed either deliberately or by gradual evolution. Thinking of morality as a skill, of course, has a long history going back at least to Plato.[18]

The suggestion implicit in this way of thinking, and the significant one for our present purposes, is that *vis-à-vis* the skill, we all start, as it were, at zero, and go on from there. We become more or less good at it, our performances have various merits, but it cannot happen, no matter how poor our performances are, that we fall below zero. In this realm, there cannot be negative merit. As with language-learning, so with moral development, we cannot deteriorate in the opposite direction. The zero where we start is absolute zero. The important implication is that immorality is not the opposite of morality, but is merely poor moral performance. Immorality is due to the inadequate development of our moral potentialities; it is not the development, if that is the word, of another countervailing potentiality. The worst that can happen is that we fail to develop the moral potentialities at all. And the corollary is that what needs explanation is why it is that we fail to develop or perform poorly. Since everybody has the potentialities, the explanation must be some interference with the development of potentialities. This is behind the egalitarian idea that human worth supports inalienable, imprescriptible, indefeasible rights to the conditions in which the potentialities can be developed without interference.

VII

The trouble with the language metaphor is that it cannot accommodate central features of morality. It is true that one form of immorality is to fail to do what would be beneficial, but another form is to do harm. And,

often, to do harm is not to fail to act according to the dictates of our morally good potentialities, but to act according to our morally bad potentialties. Immorality is not just a form of omission, due to ignorance or weakness, but also a form of active malevolence. Selfishness, cruelty, aggression, greed, hostility, and malice are also human potentialities; they are regular performers in the repertoire of human motivation.

Immoral actions are often done by people who know that they are doing harm, who mean to do it, and whose intention is not to prevent even greater harm. Such people know that morality prohibits what they are doing, they are familiar with the relevant facts, and yet they coolly and deliberately choose the immoral actions without feeling remorse or regret afterwards. Confidence men who defraud the elderly of their savings, powerful people who exploit those dependent on them, street gangs who maim people for fun, false friends who abuse trust for private advantage, manufacturers who knowingly sell spoiled products are some of the many examples of this kind of immorality. Let us call it *malevolent immorality*.[19]

The significance of malevolent immorality is that it shows the inadequacy of the metaphor suggested by egalitarianism. For people whose actions show a lifelong pattern of malevolent immorality do not merely have unrealized morally good potentialities; they have realized morally bad potentialities. They do not just lack moral merit, they have moral demerit. It is not that they have risen only a very little above the absolute zero point at which morality, according to the egalitarian metaphor, starts. Rather, they have sunk more than a little in the opposite direction, in the direction of immorality. Consequently, the mere existence of malevolent immorality, quite independently of its frequency, shows that it is a mistake to think of morality as a skill, like

----

[18] For the use Plato made of it, see Terence Irwin, *Plato's Moral Theory* (Oxford: Clarendon Press, 1977).

[19] R. D. Milo in *Immorality* (Princeton: Princeton University Press, 1984) distinguishes among different forms of immorality in much greater detail than I have been able to do here.

language, in whose acquisition we can only improve.

If we must have a metaphor for morality, it should be one that allows for both improvement and deterioration, gain and loss, perfectibility and corruptibility. One metaphor that suggests itself is that morality is like health, while immorality is like sickness. Normal human beings are born with potentialities of both, and as they live their lives, so they may develop one or the other, and often a mixture of both. Just as people can be healthy or sick, so they can be moral or immoral. Human life is a continuum between the extremes of perfect health and fatal illness, and different people are situated at different points on it. Moral life is similarly a continuum between total corruption and saintly perfection.

If we think about morality and immorality on this model, then the inappropriateness of regarding human worth as necessary becomes apparent. Human worth can be lost, because people may accumulate so much moral demerit as to reach a position on the moral continuum well below the point at which moral goodness and malevolent immorality are equally balance (or at which the potentialities to go in one or the other of these opposite directions are equally unrealized). Kant, the great defender of human worth to whom egalitarians often turn for support, is quite clear about this. Human worth can be lost through moral demerit: "Lying is the . . . obliteration of one's dignity as a human being. A man who does not himself believe what he says to another . . . has even less worth than if he were a mere thing."[20]

Critics of egalitarianism need not peg their case on Kant being right about the seriousness of lying. But, as I have been arguing, Kant's general point is correct. Human worth is proportional to moral merit,

partly because the egalitarian attempt does not succeed in tying universal and necessary human worth to morally good potentialities which can never be lost. The problem is not that morally good potentialities can be lost, but rather that they can be overwhelmed by morally bad potentialities. As morally bad potentialities may dominate morally good ones, so human worth may be replaced by its opposite. And its opposite is not less worth, but the virulent growth of baseness, or whatever it is that we would want to call the domination of a life by malevolent immorality.

VIII

My conclusion is that egalitarians do not provide an acceptable reason for rejecting the obvious and commonsensical conviction that human worth is proportional to moral merit. It is rationally and morally justified to recognize the inequality between people who habitually and intentionally harm others and those who systematically benefit them. Correspondingly, it is likewise justified to distribute benefits, vouchsafed by the rights to freedom and well-being, according to people's different moral merits.

The practical implication of the rejection of egalitarianism is not that we are free to declare open season on people with lifelong patterns of immorality; of course we should not harm them indiscriminately. But it does seem to me that it is both reasonable and morally right that people who habitually and intentionally harm others should be appropriately punished. The nature of this punishment varies; it may be imprisonment, if the offences are criminal, but it may take such other forms as moral contempt, social ostracism, or public dishonor.

Now I do not think that egalitarians would disagree about this. My point is that they cannot both agree and continue to hold that human worth is independent of moral merit. For the moral demerit of such people undermines the claim that they have the same human worth as benefactors of hu-

---

[20] I. Kant, *The Metaphysical Principles of Virtue*, being Part II of *The Metaphysics of Morals*, tr. by J. W. Ellington (Indianapolis: Hacket, 1983), pp. 90–91; the quoted passage is in the Second Chapter, I, "Concerning Lying," par. 9.

manity. Since egalitarians are committed to such absurd consequences of their position as, for instance, that Stalin or Hitler and Einstein or Hume have equal human worth, they should give up their position.

Furthermore, it also seems to be reasonable and morally right that in prevailing circumstances people with lifelong patterns of immorality should be discriminated against in respect to the protection they receive of their rights to freedom and well-being. The prevailing circumstances I have in mind are established by the scarcity of resources. How could it be other than just that mafiosi should not get the same police protection as do the district attorneys who prosecute them, or that school lunches should be more nutritious than prison lunches, or that we should care more about the welfare of hostages than about the welfare of terrorists? And the same goes for freedom-rights. How could it be seriously advocated that people who have shown themselves to be vicious and corrupt should have the same rights to be elected to public office, teach the young, or administer the criminal law as those who are fair and kind?

My argument has been that egalitarians cannot give the obvious answers to these questions and hold, as Rawls does, that it is wrong for "common sense to suppose that . . . the good things in life . . . should be distributed according to moral desert," or

say, with Vlastos, that "the worth of all persons is equal, however unequal may be their merit."[21] It is rationally and morally justified that common sense should prevail against the ill-advised social program of egalitarianism.

To avoid misunderstanding, let me emphasize that the merit to which I believe human worth is proportional is moral, not merit based on birth, talents, membership in some social group, or inheritance. Nor do I think that we should get rid of the ideals of equality and rights. On the contrary, properly interpreted, these ideals are important moral forces. But their proper interpretation excludes the claim that morality requires treating human beings as if they had equal human worth and consequently equal rights to freedom and well-being.

I am keenly aware of the abuse to which arguments based on moral merit are prone. We learn from history about the horrible things that have been perpetrated in its name. However, it seems to me that this is a danger all ideals face. The remedy is not to deny the obvious rational and moral credentials of the ideal, but to prevent its abuse.[22]

---

[21] See note 1 above.

[22] I am grateful to Josiah Gould, Jean Y. Kekes, and Bonnie Steinbock for their helpful comments on this paper.

Why Should We Care About Group Inequality?

Glenn C. Loury

Many social and political theorists take for granted the need to equalize disparities among ethnic, racial, and sexual groups. But there is little evidence to suggest that, in the absence of oppression based on group membership, all groups of people would receive the same economic rewards. Moreover, why do we reject inequalities between groups but accept inequalities within groups? Glenn C. Loury argues that social discrimination can perpetuate indefinitely group inequalities caused by past economic discrimination. In order to remedy this (rather than to make reparations for past mistreatment), group-conscious public action is justified. Loury, however, is alert to the possible dangers of affirmative action, in particular, the ways in which it can work to the disadvantage of its intended beneficiaries. Accordingly, he recommends caution when undertaking efforts to increase "out-group" participation.

Glenn C. Loury teaches at the Kennedy School of Government, Harvard University, and has written on a variety of topics in economic theory. Professor Loury's most recent research focuses on the politics and economics of racial inequality in the United States.

I. THE PROBLEM OF GROUP INEQUALITY

This essay is about the ethical propriety and practical efficacy of a range of policy undertakings which, in the last twenty years, has come to be referred to as "affirmative action." These policies have been contentious and problematic, and a variety of arguments have been advanced in their support. Here I try to close a gap, as I see it, in this "literature of justification" which has grown up around the practice of preferential treatment. My principal argument along these lines is offered in the next section. I then consider how some forms of argument in support of preferential treatment, distinctly different from that offered here, not only fail to justify the practice but, even worse, work to undermine the basis for cooperation among different ethnic groups in the American democracy. Finally, I observe that as a practical matter the use of group preference can, under circumstances detailed in the sequel, produce results far different from the egalitarian objectives which most often motivate their adoption.

It may seem fatuous in the extreme to

Reprinted from *Social Philosophy and Policy*, Vol. 5, No. 1 (Autumn 1987). Copyright © 1987 by *Social Philosophy and Policy*.

raise as a serious matter, in the contemporary United States, the question "Why should we care about group inequality?" Is not the historical and moral imperative of such concern self-evident? Must not those who value the pursuit of justice be intensely concerned about economic disparities among groups of persons? The most obvious answer to the title question would seem, then, to be: "We should care because such inequality is the external manifestation of the oppression of individuals on the basis of their group identity."

Yet, this response, upon examination, is not entirely adequate. Why should the mere existence of group disparities evidence the oppressive treatment of individuals? There is little support in the historical record for the notion that, in the absence of oppression based upon group membership, all socially relevant aggregates of persons would achieve roughly the same distribution of economic rewards.[1] Indeed, to hold this view is to deny the economic relevance of historically determined and culturally reinforced beliefs, values, interests, and attitudes which constitute the defining features of distinct ethnicities. Distinct cultures will necessarily produce distinct patterns of interest and work among their adherents. And while this need not be an argument against egalitarianism, since distinct interests and different work need not receive different remuneration, it does serve to shift our focus from disparities among groups *per se* to disparities in the rewards of the different types of activities toward which various groups' members incline.

In fact, there is a subtle logical problem

---

[1] See e.g., Thomas Sowell, *The Economics and Politics of Race: An International Perspective* (New York: William Morrow and Co., 1983). Sowell chronicles numerous instances around the world in which group differences in economic status do not correspond to the presence or absence of oppression. Often, as with the Chinese in Southeast Asian countries, or Indians in East Africa, or Jews in Western Europe, those subject to oppression have done better economically than those in the role of oppressor.

which haunts the idea of equality among groups. To the extent that the arguments for equal group results presuppose the continued existence of general inequality, they end up (merely) demanding an equality *between groups* of a given amount of inequality *within groups*. They leave us with the question: Why is inequality among individuals of the same group acceptable when inequality between the groups is not? Indeed, there is "group inequality" whenever there is inequality—one need only take those at the bottom to constitute a "group." This is precisely what a radical, class analysis of society does. The unanswered question here is why the ethnic-racial-sexual identification of "group" should take precedence over all others. It is a question usually avoided in popular discussions of the need to equalize group disparities. . . .

In contemporary American society such disparities are often taken to constitute a moral problem, and occasion a public policy response. The use of racial preferences in education, employment, or even politics is a frequent policy response. This has been controversial; courts and philosophers have sought to define the circumstances under which such preferences might legitimately be employed. Recently, both in the courts and in public discourse, questions have been raised about the legitimacy of government efforts on behalf of women, blacks, and other racial minorities. Some of these questions strike deeply at the philosophical foundation of preferential policies.

It is a tenet of long standing in American liberalism that the use by the state of ascriptive personal characteristics as a basis for discriminating among individuals, whether that discrimination be in their favor or to their disadvantage, is wrong. Such practice stigmatizes the individuals involved and reinforces private inclinations to make invidious distinctions based upon the same ascriptive characteristics. The antidiscrimination principle, codified in so many statutes and court rulings of recent decades, is founded upon such a world view. Martin

King put it well when he said: "I have a dream that my four little children will one day live in a nation where they will not be judged by the color of their skin, but by the content of their character."[2] Plaintiffs' attorneys in the landmark *Brown* cases, in oral argument before the Supreme Court, made similar representations when urging the Court to overturn the "separate but equal" doctrine. Civil rights advocates in the legislature, when working for the passage of the Civil Rights Act of 1964, offered extensive assurances that they sought only to enforce on the private sector such restrictions in their business practices as were consistent with assuring colorblind hiring and promotion standards.[3] Throughout this early history of the civil rights revolution, the classical liberal principle of aversion to the use of racial (or religious or sexual) classification was adhered to by the advocates of change. And this antidiscrimination principle has a noble intellectual pedigree, harking back to the Enlightenment-era challenge to hereditary authority, and reflected in the "anonymity axiom" of modern social choice theory.[4]

Yet, in a historically remarkable transformation this position of the liberal political community in our country has dramatically changed.[5] Today, King's dream that race might one day become an insignificant category in American civic life seems naively utopian. It is no small irony that, a mere two decades after King's moving oration, the passionate evocation in public debate of his "colorblind" ideal is for many an indication of a limited commitment to the goal of racial justice. The recalcitrant persistence of group disparity in the face of formal equality of opportunity has forced many liberals to look to race-conscious public action as the only viable remedy. . . .

II. A MINIMALIST'S ARGUMENT FOR DEPARTING FROM THE COLORBLIND STANDARD

I want to make here what might be called a "minimalist's" argument for departure from the colorblind standard. My purpose will be, in the first instance, to establish that a plausible specification of how multi-ethnic societies actually function will lead to the conclusions that *social justice is not consistent with a blanket prohibition on the use of group categories as a basis for state action*. In making this argument I will rely on an intellectual tradition long familiar to economics—one which justifies departures from *laissez faire* when, due to some sort of market failure, the outcomes of private actions are socially undesirable. The market failure to which I refer, it will be seen, rests upon the very social behavior which induces there to exist, as a permanent, structural matter, distinct racial and ethnic groups among which inequality might arise in the first place.[6]

My approach to this problem will be to inquire whether, in theory, we should ex-

---

[2] Martin Luther King, Jr., "I Have A Dream," speech reprinted in F. Broderick and A. Meier, *Negro Protest Thought in the Twentieth Century* (Bobbs-Merrill: Indianapolis, 1965).

[3] Hubert Humphrey's speech to the Senate during the floor debate on the Civil Rights Act of 1964 is often cited in this regard.

[4] E.g., see Amartya Sen, *Collective Choice and Social Welfare* (Amsterdam: North Holland Publishing Co., 1979), p. 68. The anonymity axiom requires a social decision maker to be indifferent as between two distributions of economic advantage which differ only in terms of who gets what reward, but which have the same overall pattern of reward.

[5] See, for discussion of this transformation, William Bennett and Terry Eastland, *Counting by Race* (Ithaca, NY: Cornell Univ. Press, 1976); and, with particular focus on the area of school desegregation, Raymond Wolters, *The Burden of Brown* (Knoxville: Univ. of Tennessee Press, 1984).

[6] The following argument draws on my previous work. See *Essays in the Theory of Income Distribution*, PhD. Thesis, Dept. of Economics, M.I.T., 1976, Ch. 1; "A Dynamic Theory of Racial Income Differences," P. A. Wallace and A. LaMond, eds., *Women, Minorities and Employment Discrimination* (Lexington, MA: Lexington Books, 1977); "Is Equal Opportunity Enough?" *Am. Econ. Rev. Proc.*, 5 May 1981, pp. 122–126; and "Beyond Civil Rights," *The New Republic*, October 5, 1985.

pect the continued application of racially neutral procedures to lead eventually to an outcome no longer reflective of our history of discrimination. If the answer to this query were negative, then adherence to a policy of equal opportunity alone would condemn those whose rights had historically been violated (and their progeny) to suffer indefinitely from what most would regard as ethically illegitimate acts. Since, presumably, this would be an ethically unacceptable state of affairs, a (weak) case for intervention would thereby be made. My point is that there are reasons to believe that the consequences of apparently innocuous and ubiquitous social behaviors are such as to systematically and intrinsically pass on from one generation to the next that group inequality originally engendered by historical discrimination. . . .

Imagine an economic model in which persons compete for jobs on competitive labor markets, where job assignments are made under conditions of equal opportunity, based solely on an individual's productive characteristics, and in which the markets for jobs operate without regard to individuals' ascriptive characteristics. Suppose, however, that the individual's acquisition of productive characteristics is favorably influenced by the economic success of the individual's parents. That is, and this is key, the notion of equal opportunity does not extend to the realm of social backgrounds, and differences in background are permitted to affect a person's access to training resources.[7] This is much like the world in which we live. Persons begin life with endowments of what might be called "social capital," nontransferable advantages of

birth which are conveyed by parental behaviors bearing on later-life productivity. In such a world, the deleterious consequences of past discrimination for (say) a racial minority are reflected in the fact that minority young people have, on the average, less favorable parental influences on their skill-acquisition processes.

Further, imagine that families group themselves together into social clusters, or local "communities," and that certain "local public goods" important to subsequent individual productivity are provided uniformly to young people of the same community. These "local public goods" may be very general in nature. One thinks naturally of public education, but also important might be peer influences which shape the development of personal character, contacts which generate information about the world of work, and friendship networks which evolve among persons situated in the same or closely related "communities." What is critical is that these community "goods" (or, possibly, "bads") be provided *internally* to the social clusters in question, and that outsiders be excluded from the consumption of such goods. What I am calling here "communities" are to represent the private, voluntary associational behaviors common to all societies, in which persons choose their companions, often on the basis of common ethnicity, religion, or economic class. Since access to these "communities" could depend on parents' social status, this provides another avenue by which parental background influences offsprings' achievement—another source of social capital.

In order to pose the question most sharply, I assume that all individuals have identical preferences with respect to economic choices, and that an identical distribution of innate aptitudes characterizes each generation of majority and minority workers.[8]

---

[7] James Fishkin has recently discussed the philosophical implications of what he calls "background inequalities" for a liberal theory of status disparities. His notion of the "trilemma of equal opportunity"—an unresolvable tension between the ideals of equal opportunity, reward according to desert, and the autonomy of the family—is closely related to the argument offered below. See Fishkin, *Justice, Equal Opportunity, and the Family* (New Haven: Yale Univ. Press, 1983).

[8] In keeping with my earlier discussion, it would be possible to treat such differences in tastes that have economic consequences (e.g., occupational preferences, entrepreneurial inclinations) as a part of what is conveyed through parents' social capital.

Thus, in the absence of any historical economic discrimination, and notwithstanding the tendency for persons to cluster socially, we should expect that the economic status of minority and majority group members would be equal, on average. I want now to inquire whether, in this idealized world, the competitive labor market would function in such a way as eventually to eliminate any initial differences in the average status of the two groups which historical discrimination might have produced.

One can investigate this question by writing down a mathematical representation of this idealized world. It can be shown that the results obtained depend upon whether only family income, or both family income and race, influence the set of social clusters—i.e., "communities"—to which a family may belong. When persons in society discriminate in their choice of associates on the basis of economic class, but not ethnic group, one can show (with a few additional, technical assumptions) that equal opportunity as defined here always leads (eventually) to an equal distribution of outcomes between the groups.[9] However, when there is social segregation in associational behavior along group as well as class lines, then it is not generally true that historically generated differences between the groups attenuate in the face of racially neutral procedures. Examples may be constructed in which group inequality persists indefinitely, even though no underlying group differences in tastes or abilities exist.

This happens because, when there is some racial segregation among communities—that is, when race operates as a basis of social discrimination, though not economic discrimination—the process by which status is transfered across generations does not work in the same way for minority and majority families. *The inequality of family circum-*

stances generated by historical economic discrimination is exacerbated by differential access to the benefits of those quasi-public resources available only in the affiliational clusters which I have called communities. A kind of negative intragroup "externality" is exerted, through local public goods provision, by the (relatively more numerous) lower income minority families on higher income minority families of the same communities. (Or, if you prefer, a positive intragroup externality is exerted by the relatively more numerous higher income majority families on the lower income majority families of the same communities.) And, because in a world of some social segregation the group composition of one's community depends in part on the choices of one's neighbors, this effect cannot be completely avoided by an individual's actions.[10] As a consequence, the ability of equal opportunity to bring about equal results is impaired by the desire of majority and minority families to share communities with their own kind. This social clustering of the groups is, of course, an essential feature of a multi-ethnic society such as ours. Indeed, in its absence, there would not be selective mating by racial groups, and in short order (2–3 generations) the "problem" of group inequality would be submerged by wholesale miscegenation.

This discussion suggests that, as a general matter, we cannot expect *laissez faire* to produce equality of result between equally endowed social groups if these groups have experienced differential treatment in the past, and if among the channels through which parents pass on status to their children are included the social clustering of

---

[9] See Loury, "A Dynamic Theory of Racial Income Differences"; for a rigorous mathematical treatment of this question, see Loury, *Essays in the Theory of Income Distribution.*

[10] See, e.g., Thomas Schelling, *Micromotives and Macrobehaviors* (New York: W.W. Norton, 1978), Ch. 4, for an analysis of how even a very mild individual preference for association with one's own kind can lead, in the aggregate, to a highly segregated outcome. For instance, Schelling notes that if everyone would merely prefer to live in a neighborhood in which their group is in the majority, then only complete separation will satisfy the preferences of all members of both groups.

individuals along group-exclusive lines. On this argument, state action which is cognizant of groups is *legitimated* by the claim that, in its absence, the consequences of historical wrongs could be with us for the ages. It is *necessitated* by the fact that individuals, in the course of their private social intercourse, engage in racial distinctions which have material consequences. These distinctions are reflected in this model by what I referred to as the "choice of community"—with whom to spend one's time, in what neighborhoods to live, among which children to encourage one's offspring to play, to what set of clubs and friendship networks to belong, and with what sort of person to encourage one's children to mate. Such decisions, in our law and in our ethics, lie beyond the reach of the antidiscrimination mandate. They are private matters which, though susceptible to influence and moral suasion about the tolerance of diversity and the like, are not thought to constitute the proper subject of judicial or legislative decree. Freedom to act on the prejudices and discriminations which induce each of us to seek our identities with and to make our lives among a specific, restricted set of our fellows, are for many if not most Americans among those inalienable rights to life, liberty, and the pursuit of happiness enshrined in our Declaration of Independence.

There are two points I wish to stress about this "minimalist's" argument. First, it rests quite specifically on a conception of group differences in the transmission of status across generations, and thus points to those state interventions which are intended to neutralize such disparities. That is, racial preference is not defended here in the abstract, as a generalized remedy for racial inequality or repayment for past wrong. Rather, a specific mechanism which passes on from past to present to future the consequences of wrongful acts has been explicated. It is to neutralize *that* mechanism that "taking color into account" is legitimated. And, I would argue, any alternative justification for racial preference should be sim-

ilarly grounded on an explicit delineation of the "fine structure" of social life which causes the need for such extraordinary state action to arise. The simple evocation of "two hundred years of slavery" or of "past discrimination against minorities and women" does not begin to meet this standard. For the question remains: what specifically have been the consequences of past deeds which require for their reversal the employment of racial classification? The attainment of equal educational opportunities through race-conscious public policy provides a good example. Racial criteria used in the siting or allocation of public housing units would be another. But those racial preferences which confer benefits upon minority group members who do not suffer background related impediments to their mobility (e.g., minority business set-asides) could only be rationalized in this way if it could be demonstrated that the recipients' connection to their less fortunate fellows was such as to insure a sufficiently large beneficial spillover effect on the social mobility of the poor. This is a difficult empirical test for many current practices to meet.

Moreover, other remedies, not dependent on race-conscious action, but intended severely to reduce for all citizens the differential advantages due to poor social background (such as early childhood education, employment programs for disadvantaged urban youths, or publicly financed assistance in the acquisition of higher education) might also be sufficient to avoid the perpetuation of past racial wrongs.[11] In other

---

[11] This, in essence, is what sociologist William Julius Wilson has been arguing with respect to the inner-city poor. He notes that the primary problems facing poor blacks derive from their economic plight, and afflict poor whites as well. Moreover, he argues that political support for dramatic efforts to reverse these problems will be more readily had if those efforts are couched in racially universal terms. See, generally, his *The Declining Significance of Race* (Chicago: Univ. of Chicago Press, 1978), and more specifically his recent article "Race-Specific Policies and the Truly Disadvantaged," *Yale Law and Policy Review*, vol. II, no. 2 (Spring 1984), pp. 272–290.

words, the type of argument which the late Justice William O. Douglas made in his *De-Funis* dissent, which acknowledges the legitimacy of taking social background into account when making admissions decisions at a public law school, but nonetheless rejects explicit racial considerations, might well suffice to meet the concerns raised here. Again, it becomes an empirical question, resolved by inquiry into the explicit mechanisms of social mobility, on which the legitimacy of explicitly racial intervention would turn.

The second, perhaps more important point is that, in addition to providing a rationale for extraordinary state action intended to limit the degree of group inequality, the underlying behavioral premises of this model suggest that there are *limits* on what one can hope to achieve through the use of racial classification by the state. As noted above, our political and philosophical traditions are such that the reach of civil rights laws will be insufficient to eliminate all socially and economically relevant discriminatory behavior. That is, we are evidently not willing to undertake the degree of intrusion into the intimate associational choices of individuals which an equalizing redistribution of social capital would require[12]. . . .

Moreover, it seems likely that the state's use of racial classification will generally be insufficient to overcome the economic consequences of this private discriminatory practice. For the fact that such exclusive social "clubs" do form along group lines has important economic consequences. There is an extensive literature in economics and sociology which documents the importance of family and community background as factors influencing a child's later success. Much evidence suggests that the social and economic benefits deriving from privileged access to the "right" communities cannot be

___

[12] The Supreme Court's decision in the Detroit cross-district busing case, *Milliken v. Bradley*, 418 U.S. 717 (1974), limiting the use of metropolitan busing to solve the "white flight" problem, gives a classic illustration of this point.

easily offset through the state's use of racial classification.

III. CARING ABOUT GROUP INEQUALITY FOR THE WRONG REASONS

Having offered a rationale for departure from the "colorblind" standard, one could ask at this point whether there are not unsound rationales for worrying about group inequality which have been offered in our public debates. I think this is decidedly so. As political theorists have long recognized, more is required in the achievement and maintenance of a just society than the writing of a philosophical treatise or a constitution which upholds essential principles of liberty and equality. It is also necessary to secure, as a practical matter, the means through which such principles might be lived by and followed in the everyday life of the policy. In a pluralist society such as ours, where distinctions of race and religion are deep and widespread, this is not a trivial matter. I would venture that at this historical juncture, a sincere commitment in our government to reducing racial inequality is a necessary element of what is needed to establish a just political community in the United States. But this concern is not, by itself, sufficient to that task.

Indeed, certain features of our public discourse over the legitimacy of racial preferences undermine the maintenance of this kind of community. For example, affirmative action represents to many blacks not merely needed public action in the face of past wrong, but rather a just recompense for that wrong. The distinction is vital. For many, affirmative action finds its essential rationale in an interpretation of history—i.e., in an ideology: that blacks have been wronged by American society in such a way that justice now demands they receive special consideration as a matter of right. This is to be contrasted with the means-end calculus which I have offered above as justification for the practice. This reparations argument, however, immediately raises the question: Why do the wrongs of this particular group and not those of others deserve recompense? This can be a poisonous question for the politics of a pluralistic democracy.

There is, of course, a favored answer to this question: slavery. But this answer does not really satisfy anyone—black or white. For no amount of recounting the unique sufferings attendant to the slave experience makes plain why a middle-class black should be offered an educational opportunity which is being denied to a lower-class white. It is manifestly the case that many Americans are descended from forebearers who had, indeed, suffered discrimination and mistreatment at the hands of hostile majorities both here and in their native lands. Yet, and here is the crucial point, these Americans on the whole have no claim to the public acknowledgement and ratification of their past suffering as do blacks under affirmative action. The institution of this policy, rationalized in this specific way, therefore implicitly confers special *public* status on the historic injustices faced by its beneficiary groups, and hence devalues, implicitly, the injustices endured by others.

The public character of this process of acknowledgement and ratification is central to my argument. We are a democratic, ethnically heterogeneous polity. Racial preferences become issues in local, state, and national elections; they are the topic of debate in corporate board rooms and university faculty meetings; their adoption and maintenance requires public consensus, notwithstanding the role that judicial decree has played in their propagation. Therefore, the public consensus requisite to the broad use of such preferences results, *de facto*, in the complicity of every American in a symbolic recognition of extraordinary societal guilt and culpability regarding the plight of a particular group of citizens. Failure to embrace the consensus in favor of such practice invites the charge of insensitivity to the

wrongs of the past or, indeed, the accusation of racism.[13]

But perhaps most important, the public discourse around racial preference inevitably leads to comparisons among the sufferings of different groups—an exercise in what one might call "comparative victimology." Was the anti-Asian sentiment in the western states culminating in the Japanese interments during World War II "worse" than the discrimination against blacks? Were the restrictions and attendant poverty faced by Irish immigrants to Northeast cities a century ago "worse" than those confronting black migrants to those same cities some decades later? And ultimately, was the Holocaust a more profound evil than chattel slavery?

Such questions are, of course, unanswerable, if for no other reason than that they require us to compare degrees of suffering and extents of moral outrage as experienced internally, subjectively, privately, by different peoples. There is no neutral vantage, no Archimedian point, from which to take up such a comparison. We cannot expect that the normal means of argument and persuasion will reconcile divergent perceptions among ethnic groups about the relative moral affront which history has forced upon them. We must not, therefore, permit such disputes to arise, if we are to maintain an environment of comity among groups in this ethnically diverse society. . . .

IV. UNINTENDED NEGATIVE CONSEQUENCE OF THE USE OF RACIAL PREFERENCE

In the final section of this essay I would like to explore some of the deleterious side-effects which can issue from the use of color-conscious methods in the public or private sectors. There is the danger that re-

---

[13] I have made this argument in somewhat more detail in my essay "Behind the Black–Jewish Split," *Commentary*, January 1986.

liance on affirmative action to achieve minority or female representation in highly prestigious positions can have a decidedly negative impact on the esteem of the groups, because it can lead to the general presumption that members of the beneficiary groups would not be able to qualify for such positions without the help of special preference.

If, in an employment situation, say, it is known that racial classification is in use, so that differential selection criteria are employed for the hiring of different racial groups, and if it is known that the quality of performance on the job depends on how one did on the criteria of selection, then it is a rational statistical inference, absent further information, to impute a lower expected quality of job performance to persons of the race which was preferentially favored in selection. Using racial classification in selection for employment creates objective incentives for customers, co-workers, and so forth, to take race into account after the employment decision has been made. Selection by race makes race "informative" in the post-selection environment.

In what kind of environments is such an "informational externality" likely to be important? Precisely when it is difficult to obtain objective and accurate readings on a person's productivity, and when that unknown productivity is of significance to those sharing the employment environment with the preferentially selected employee. For example in a "team production" situation (like a professional partnership, or among students forming study groups), where output is the result of the effort of several individuals, though each individual's contribution cannot be separately identified, the willingness of workers to participate in "teams" containing those suspected of having been preferentially selected will be less than it would have been if the same criteria of selection had been used for all employees.[14]

Also, when the employment carries prestige and honor, because it represents an unusual accomplishment of which very few individuals are capable (an appointment to a top university faculty, for example), the use of preferential selection will undermine the ability of those preferred to garner for themselves the honorary, as distinct from pecuniary, benefits associated with the employment. (And this is true even for individuals who do not themselves require the preference.) If, for example, Nobel prizes in physics were awarded with the idea in mind that each continent should be periodically represented, it would be widely suspected (by those insufficiently informed to make independent judgements in such matters, and that includes nearly everyone) that a physicist from Africa who won the award had not made as significant a contribution to the science as one from Europe, even if the objective scientific merit of the African's contribution were as great. If Law Review appointments at a prestigious law school were made to insure appropriate group balance, it could become impossible for students belonging to the preferred groups to earn honor available to others, no matter how great their individual talents.

An interesting example of the phenomenon I am discussing here can be found in the U.S. military. Recently, sociologist Charles Moskos published an article in *The Atlantic* describing the results of his investigation of the status of blacks in the U.S. Army.[15] He noted that roughly 7 percent of all Army generals are now black, as is nearly 10 percent of the Army's officer corps. Moskos reports that among the black officers he interviewed the view was widely held that in the Army blacks "(s)till . . . have to be better

---

[14] Recently, lawsuits have been brought by mid-level minority employees working in large bureaucracies, at

IBM and the U.S. State Department, for example, alleging that they are not treated the same by supervisors and co-workers. Yet, if they were hired under different criteria than the co-workers, they in fact, on the average, *are not* the same! Differential treatment, though regrettable, should come therefore as no surprise.

[15] Charles Moskos, "Success Story: Blacks in the Army," *The Atlantic Monthly*, May 1986, p. 64.

qualified than whites in order to advance." That is, racial discrimination still exists here. One senior black officer was "worried about some of the younger guys. They don't understand that a black still has to do more than a white to get promoted. . . . If they think equal effort will get equal reward, they've got a big surprise coming." Yet, despite this awareness of racial discrimination, these officers were dubious about the value of racially preferential treatment in the military. Black commanders tended to be tougher in their fitness evaluation of black subordinates than were white commanders of their white subordinates. Even those officers who thought affirmative action necessary in civilian life disapproved of its use in the military. According to Moskos: "They draw manifest self-esteem from the fact that they themselves have not been beneficiaries of such [preferential] treatment—rather the reverse. Black officers distrust black leaders in civilian life who would seek advancement through racial politics or as supplicants of benevolent whites."[16]

Further illustration of the kind of unintended consequence which should be taken much more seriously by proponents of affirmative action, combining both the "team

production" and the "honor" effects, comes from the world of corporate management. Many of those charged with the responsibility of managing large companies in the U.S. economy today are quite concerned with the state of their minority hiring efforts. The advent of affirmative action masks some serious, continuing disparities in the rates at which blacks, Hispanics, and women are penetrating the very highest ranks of power and control within these institutions. While equal opportunity could be said to be working tolerably well at the entry and middle level positions, it has proven exceedingly difficult for these "newcomers" to advance to the upper echelons of their organizations. The problem is so widespread that a name has been invented for it—the "plateau-ing phenomenon."

Increasingly, able and ambitious young women and blacks talk of taking the entrepreneurial route to business success, feeling stymied by their inability to get on the "fast track" of rapid promotion to positions of genuine power within their companies. Wall Street brokerage and law firms, though increasing the number of young black associates in their ranks, still have very few black partners and virtually no senior or managing partners.[17] Though many large companies now have their complement of minority vice-presidents and staff personnel (especially in the governmental relations and equal opportunity areas), they remain with very few minorities at the rank of senior vice-president or higher, and with a paucity of non-whites in those authoritative line positions where the companies' profits and future leaders are made.

The failure of women and minorities to penetrate the highest levels of the organization involves factors beyond the raw competence of the individuals involved. While people differ in their abilities, no one today suggests that there do not exist blacks or

---

[16] Indeed, in order to defend such programs in the private sector, it becomes necessary for advocates to argue that almost no blacks could reach the positions in question without special favors. When there is internal disagreement among black intellectuals, for example, about the merits of affirmative action, critics of the policy are attacked as being disingenuous, since (it is said) they clearly owe their own prominence to the very policy they criticize. (See, e.g., Cornel West, "Unmasking the Black Conservatives," *The Christian Century*, July 16–23, p. 645). The specific circumstances of the individual do not matter in this, for it is presumed that *all* blacks are indebted to civil rights activity for their achievements. The consequence is a kind of "socialization" of the individual's success. The individual's effort to claim achievement for himself (and thus to secure the autonomy and legitimacy needed to deviate from group consensus) is perceived as a kind of betrayal. From the reasonable observation that all blacks are indebted to those who fought and beat Jim Crow, these intellectuals draw the conclusion that the group's most accomplished persons, by celebrating their personal achievements as being due to their ability and not to racial preferences, have betrayed their fellows!

[17] Frank Raines, black partner in Lazard Freres, reported in an interview that there are only three black partners in Wall Street investment firms, two of whom handle public finance issues (local, black governments being primary among their clients).

women with the aptitude and dedication to succeed at the highest levels in the corporate world. The fact that so very few of them do succeed suggests that, in addition to old-fashioned racism, the problem may well stem from subtle aspects of interpersonal relations within companies. When a company determines to increase the numbers of women and minorities in its management ranks, the normal way of proceeding is to make the recruitment and retention of such persons an organizational goal, and to evaluate the performance of those with authority to hire, in part, by the extent to which they succeed in advancing this goal. That is, the company encourages its personnel decision makers to use racial (or gender) classification in addition to other employment screens. This practice of goal setting is done with an explicitness and seriousness which, of course, varies from company to company. Yet the inevitable result is to confer some advantage upon minority and women employees in the competition for entry and mid-level positions in the company. Even when such preferential treatment is avoided by management, the perception among white male employees, in this era of constant focus on the need to increase minority and female participation, is likely to be that the "newcomers" are getting some kind of break which is not available to them.

In addition, minority or female employees may be hired or promoted into jobs for which they are not ready; better qualified nonminority personnel may, from time to time, be passed over for promotion. Here too, nonfavored employees will often *perceive* that mistakes of this sort are being made, even when in fact they are not. Resentments and jealousies are likely to arise. Charges of "reverse discrimination" will, in all probability, be mumbled more or less quietly among white men who sense themselves disadvantaged. It only takes one or two "disasters," in terms of minority appointments which do not work out, to reinforce already existing prejudices and convince many in the organization that all minority managers are suspect. *The use of racial or sexual employment goals is therefore likely to alter the way in which minority or women managers are viewed by their white male subordinates and superiors.*

And even though most minority employees may measure up to, or even exceed, the standards of performance which others in the firm must meet, the presence of just a few who do not casts an aura of suspicion over the others. Such uncertainty about so-called "affirmative action hires"—those who, it is suspected, would not have their jobs if they were not minority or female—may only reflect the prejudice or bigotry of their co-workers. But, and this is crucial, to the extent that the suspicion is widely held, it can work to undermine the objective effectiveness of the minority manager.

Given that competition for advancement from the lower rungs of the corporate ladder is sure to be keen, there is a natural tendency for those not benefiting from the organization's equal opportunity goals to see the progress of minorities or women as due in great part to affirmative action. If, to illustrate, four white men and one woman are competing for a position which ultimately is awarded to the woman, all four male employees may harbor the suspicion that *they* were unfairly passed over in the interest of meeting diversity goals, when in fact this supposition must be false for at least three of them who would not have been promoted in any case.[18] When, as happens in many companies, the attainment of equal opportunity goals is seen as something which occurs only at the expense of productivity—as a price to be paid for doing business in the inner city, or to "keep the feds off our backs"—then these suspicions are given tacit confirmation by the organization's very approach to the problem of diversity.

---

[18] Psychological "incentives" exist for people to use this excuse even when it is not true. This gives them a good rationale for their own failure. As one colleague cleverly observed, "Affirmative Action is a boon to mediocre whites—by giving them reason to think better of themselves than they otherwise could."

Thus, the use of racial classification can entail serious costs. It can, if not properly and clearly administered, create or promote a general perception that those minorities or women who benefit from the firm's interest in increasing diversity are somehow less qualified than others competing for the same positions. And this general perception, when widely held, whether well-founded or merely a reflection of prejudice, can work to limit the degree of success and long-term career prospects of minority and female managers. For it is plausible to hold that in such a managerial environment, the productivity of an individual is not merely determined by the individual's knowledge, business judgment, industry, or vision. It depends as well on the ability of the manager to induce the cooperation, motivation, trust, and confidence of those whom he or she must lead. It depends, in other words, on the extent to which the manager can command the *respect* of his or her colleagues and subordinates.

This observation illustrates the fact that general suspicion of the competence of minority or female managerial personnel can become a self-fulfilling prophecy. When the bottom-line performance of a manager depends on his or her ability to motivate others, and when those who are to be motivated begin with a lack of confidence in the ability of the manager, then even the most technically competent, hard-working individual may fail to induce top performance in his or her people. And the fact that top performance is not achieved only serves to confirm the belief of those who doubted the manager's competence in the first place.[19]

This self-reinforcing cycle of negative expectations is likely to be a particularly significant problem in the higher-level and line, as distinct from lower-level and staff, positions in an organization. Here an individual's contribution to company profitability depends heavily upon leadership and interpersonal qualities, securing the confidence and trust of peers, motivating subordinates to achieve up to their potential. Managerial performance at this level depends rather less on individual, technical skills. That is, whether or not one becomes really "good" at these jobs is determined, in part, by how "good" others believe one can be.

Another critical factor at this level of an organization is self-confidence. This, too, may be undermined by the use of racial classification. Among the questions most frequently asked by minority personnel about to assume a post of unusual responsibility is: "Would I have been offered this position if I had not been a black (or woman, or . . .)?" Most people in such a situation want to be reassured that their achievement has been earned and is not based simply on the organizational requirement of diversity. And not only that, they want their prospective associates and subordinates to be assured of this as well. When appointments are being made partly on a racial or sexual basis, the inevitable result is to weaken the extent to which the recipients can confidently assert, if only to themselves, that they are as good as their achievements would seem to suggest. A genuinely outstanding person who rises quickly to the mid-level of an organization without ever knowing for sure whether or not this career advance would have taken place in the absence of affirmative action may not approach the job with the same degree of self-assurance as other-

---

[19] Consider the position of a female commander of troops in a combat situation. This person will be ineffective if, when issuing critical orders under duress, she is unable to inspire the obedience and confidence of her troops. Her troops' belief in her capacities is thus an objective determinant of her capacities. It would seem particularly unwise, in the face of widespread male suspicion of the performance capabilities of female commanders, to promote a woman into such a position who did not exhibit absolutely unimpeachable

qualifications. That is, until the ability of women to function under combat conditions had been amply demonstrated, it would seem to be unwise to employ *preferential* criteria for the selection of women to such positions. To do so encourages precisely those beliefs which could undermine the effectiveness of the new commander.

wise would be the case.[20] And this absence of the full measure of confidence which the person's abilities would have otherwise produced can make the difference between success and failure in the upper managerial ranks.

All of these potentially detrimental effects which I associate with the use of preferential treatment of non-white and female employees within an enterprise are reinforced by the general discussion of racial and sexual inequality in our society. The constant attention to numerical imbalances in the numbers of blacks vs. whites, or women vs. men, who have achieved a particular rank in the corporate sector, in addition to placing what may be entirely warranted pressure on individual companies, serves to remind people—black and white, male and female—of the fact that such preferences are a part of their work environment. In order to defend affirmative action in the political arena, its advocates often seem to argue that almost no blacks or women could reach the highest levels of achievement without the aid of special pressures. Yet, this tactic runs the risk of establishing the presumption that all blacks or women, whether directly or indirectly, are indebted to civil rights activity for their achievements. And this presumption may reinforce general suspicion about minority or female competence which already exists.

None of this should be construed as an expression of doubt about the desirability of vigorously promoting diversity in corporate management, or elsewhere in American society. What seems crucial is that, in light of the pitfalls discussed above, the process of achieving diversity be *managed* with care, mindful of the dangers inherent in the situation. What is involved with affirmative action is not simply the *rights* of individuals, as many lawyers are given to argue, but also the *prudence* of particular means used to advance their interests. The "plateau" phenomenon, where able young minority or female managers find themselves unable to advance to the top ranks of their companies, undoubtedly reflects factors beyond those I have discussed. But it is the consensus judgment of personnel managers with whom I have talked that these factors are involved in many cases. In particular, it seems quite probable that general distrust of the capabilities of minority and female managers will accompany and reinforce old-fashioned racist or sexist aversion to having "outsiders" join the "old boys network" of those holding real power within the organization. Such suspicions can, where occasionally validated by experience, provide the perfect excuse for preexisting prejudices. These prejudices are not merely "bad" behaviors which should be sanctioned. They are a part of the environment in which these policies operate and may determine their success or failure.

V. CONCLUSION

In this essay I have suggested the need for a more rigorous justification than has been offered of the departure from the simple "color-blind" interpretation of the antidiscrimination principle which the contemporary practice of preferential treatment represents. I have sought, in Section II, to provide such a justification. My argument turns on the extent to which social discrimination among today's citizens can perpetuate indefinitely the group inequality engendered by *economic* discrimination which may have occurred in the past. Because the antidiscrimination principle does not extend into the most intimate of private, associational choices, it is compatible with the continued practice of racial discrimination in such choices. Yet this practice, together with a history of racial discrimination in the public sphere, can insure that the consequences of past bigotry become a permanent part of

---

[20] Moreover, if you push too fast, good people may fail and be marked for life by that failure. Consider the case of the graduate student who would have done just fine at State U., but who ends up at the bottom of his class at Harvard.

the social landscape. To avoid this possibility, I argue, the use of group-conscious public action is justified.

Yet, I have recognized that such preferential policies may not be the only, or the best, response to persistent group inequality. And I have suggested that some of the arguments used to justify racial preference seem likely to exacerbate, rather than diminish, the problems of racial conflict which continue to afflict our society. I have been particularly critical of the "reparations" argument, which justifies special treatment of today's blacks on the basis of the mistreatment of blacks in the past. I have noted that such public practice implicitly elevates the past suffering of blacks to a privileged position over the mistreatments endured by other ethnic Americans, and does so in a way likely to be particularly controversial. This problem seems especially severe when the preferential practices in question benefit blacks of comfortable economic circumstances at the expense of ethnic whites who may be more poorly situated.

Finally, I have noted that, even where justified, the use of racial preference need not be wise. This is a prudential argument which is meant to have only restricted applicability. There are certain types of environments where the danger of the negative unintended consequences of racial preference which I identify seems particularly acute. I try to characterize these in Section IV. In these environments I urge that much greater caution be employed when efforts to increase "out-group" participation are undertaken. For under the conditions outlined, the use of differential standards for members of different groups can work to undermine the capacity of the intended beneficiaries to garner for themselves the full benefits of their achievements, and can even objectively impede their functioning.

The debate over affirmative action has been too much left to lawyers and philosophers, and has too little engaged the interests of economists, sociologists, political scientists, and psychologists. It is as if for this policy, unlike all others, we could determine *a priori* the wisdom of its application in all instances—as if its practice were either "right" or "wrong," never simply "prudent" or "unwise." If I accomplish anything here, I hope it is to impress upon the reader the ambiguity and complexity of this issue, to make him see that there is in this area the opportunity to do much good, but also the risk of doing much harm. The impassioned pursuit of justice, untempered by respect for a reasoned evaluation of the consequences of our efforts, is not obviously an advance over indifference.

Sexual Equality and Discrimination

Will Kymlicka

Anti-discrimination statutes have not brought about sexual equality. Why is this? According to Will Kymlicka, sex discrimination is commonly interpreted as the arbitrary or irrational use of gender in the awarding of benefits or positions. That is, sex discrimination is unequal treatment that cannot be justified by reference to some sexual difference. This "difference approach" to discrimination perceives sexual equality in terms of the ability of women to compete under general-neutral rules for various roles and positions. The problem, Kymlicka argues, is that these roles and positions may be defined in such a way as to make men more suited to them, even under gender-neutral competition.

Will Kymlicka is a policy analyst with the Canadian Royal Commission on New Productive Technologies. He has taught philosophy at the University of Toronto, Princeton University, and Queen's University in Kingston, Ontario, and is the author of *Liberalism, Community, and Culture* (1989) and *Contemporary Political Philosophy* (1990).

Until well into this century, most male theorists on all points of the political spectrum accepted the belief that there was a 'foundation in nature' for the confinement of women to the family, and for the 'legal and customary subjection of women to their husbands' within the family (Okin 1979:200).[1] Restrictions on women's civil and political rights were said to be justified by the fact that women are, by nature, unsuited for political and economic activities outside the home. Contemporary theorists have progressively abandoned this assumption of women's natural inferiority. They have ac-

[1] In accepting this prevailing view that there is 'a Foundation in Nature' for the rule of the husband 'as the abler and the stronger' (Locke, in Okin 1979:200), classical liberals created a serious contradiction for themselves. For they also argued that all humans are by nature equal, that nature provides no grounds for an inequality of rights. This, we have seen, was the point of their state-of-nature theories (ch. 3, s. 3 above). Why should the supposed fact that men are 'abler and stron-ger' justify unequal rights for women when, as Locke himself says, 'differences in excellence of parts or ability' do not justify unequal rights? One cannot both maintain equality amongst men as a class, on the grounds that differences in ability do not justify different rights, and also exclude women as a class, on the grounds that they are less able. If women are excluded on the grounds that the average woman is less able than the average man, then all men who are less able than the average man must also be excluded. As Okin puts it, 'If the basis of his individualism was to be firm, he needed to argue that individual women were equal with individual men, just as weaker men were with stronger ones' (Okin 1979:199).

cepted that women, like men, should be viewed as 'free and equal beings', capable of self-determination and a sense of justice, and hence free to enter the public realm. And liberal democracies have progressively adopted anti-discrimination statutes intended to ensure that women have equal access to education, employment, political office, etc.

But these anti-discrimination statutes have not brought about sexual equality. In the United States and Canada, the extent of job segregation in the lowest-paying occupations is increasing. Indeed, if present trends continue, all of the people below the poverty line in America in the year 2000 will be women or children (Wietzman 1985: 350). Moreover, domestic violence and sexual assault are increasing, as are other forms of violence and degradation aimed at women. Catherine Mackinnon summarizes her survey of the effects of equal rights in the United States by saying that 'sex equality law has been utterly ineffective at getting women what we need and are socially prevented from having on the basis of a condition of birth: a chance at productive lives of reasonable physical security, self-expression, individuation, and minimal respect and dignity' (Mackinnon, 1987:32).

Why is this? Sex discrimination, as commonly interpreted, involves the arbitrary or irrational use of gender in the awarding of benefits or positions. On this view, the most blatant forms of sex discrimination are those where, for example, someone refuses to hire a woman for a job even though gender has no rational relationship to the task being performed. Mackinnon calls this the 'difference approach' to sexual discrimination, for it views as discriminatory unequal treatment that cannot be justified by reference to some sexual difference.

Sex discrimination law of this sort was modelled on race discrimination law. And just as race equality legislation aims at a 'colour-blind' society, so sex equality law aims at a sex-blind society. A society would be non-discriminatory if race or gender never entered into the awarding of benefits. Of course, while it is conceivable that political and economic decisions could entirely disregard race, it is difficult to see how a society could be entirely sex-blind. A society which provides for pregnancy benefits, or for sexually segregated sports, is taking sex into account, but this does not seem unjust. And while racially segregated washrooms are clearly discriminatory, most people do not feel that way about sex-segregated washrooms. So the 'difference approach' accepts that there are legitimate instances of differential treatment of the sexes. These are not discriminatory, however, so long as there is a genuine sexual difference which explains and justifies the differential treatment. Opponents of equal rights for women often invoked the spectre of sexually integrated sports (or washrooms) as evidence that sex equality is misguided. But defenders of the difference approach respond that the cases of legitimate differentiation are sufficiently rare, and the cases of arbitrary differentiation so common, that the burden of proof rests on those who claim that sex is a relevant ground for assigning benefits or positions.

This difference approach, as the standard interpretation of sex equality law in most Western countries, has had some successes. Its 'moral thrust' is to 'grant women access to what men have access to', and it has indeed 'gotten women some access to employment and education, the public pursuits, including academic, professional, and blue-collar work, the military, and more than nominal access to athletics' (Mackinnon 1987: 33, 35). The difference approach has helped create gender-neutral access to, or competition for, existing social benefits and positions.

But its successes are limited, for it ignores the gender inequalities which are built into the very definition of these positions. The difference approach sees sex equality in terms of the ability of women to compete under gender-neutral rules for the roles that men have defined. But equality cannot be achieved by allowing men to build social institutions according to their interests, and then ignoring the gender of the candidates when deciding who fills the roles in these institutions. The problem is that the roles may be defined in such a way as to make men more suited to them, even under gender-neutral competition.

Consider that fact that most jobs 'require that the person, gender neutral, who is qualified for them will be someone who is not the primary caretaker of a preschool child' (Mackinnon 1987: 37). Given that women are still expected to take care of children in our society, men will tend to do better than women in competing for such jobs. This is not because women applicants are discriminated against. Employers may pay no attention to the gender of the applicants, or may in fact wish to hire more women. The problem is that many women lack a relevant qualification for the job—i.e. being free from child-care responsibilities. There is gender-neutrality, in that employers do not attend to the gender of applicants, but there is no sexual equality, for the job was defined under the assumption that it would be filled by men who had wives at home taking care of the children. The difference approach insists that gender should not be taken into account in deciding who should have a job, but it ignores the fact 'that day one of taking gender into account was the day the job was structured with the expectation that its occupant would have no child care responsibilities' (Mackinnon 1987:37).

Whether or not gender-neutrality yields sexual equality depends on whether and how gender was taken into account earlier. As Janet Radcliffe Richards says,

If a group is kept out of something for long enough, it is overwhelmingly likely that activities of that sort will develop in a way unsuited to the excluded group. We know for certain that women have been kept out of many kinds of work, and this means that the work is quite likely to be unsuited to them. The most obvious example of this is the incompatibility of most work with the bearing and raising of children; I am firmly convinced that if women had been fully involved in the running of society from the start they would have *found* a way of arranging work and children

to fit each other. Men have had no such motivation, and we can see the results. (Radcliffe Richards 1980: 113–14)

This incompatibility that men have created between child-rearing and paid labour has profoundly unequal results for women. The result is not only that the most valued positions in society are filled by men, while women are disproportionately concentrated into lower-paying part-time work, but also that many women become economically dependent on men. Where most of the 'household income' comes from the man's paid work, the woman who does the unpaid domestic work is rendered dependent on him for access to resources. The consequences of this dependence have become more apparent with the rising divorce rate. While married couples may share the same standard of living during marriage, regardless of who earns the income, the effects of divorce are catastrophically unequal. In California, men's average standard of living goes up 42 per cent after divorce, women's goes down 73 per cent, and similar results have been found in other states (Okin 1989*b*: 161). However, none of these unequal consequences of the incompatibility of child care and paid work are discriminatory, according to the difference approach, for they do not involve arbitrary discrimination. The fact is that freedom from child-care responsibilities is relevant to most existing jobs, and employers are not being arbitrary in insisting on it. Because it is a relevant qualification, the difference approach says that it is not discriminatory to insist upon it, regardless of the disadvantages it creates for women. Indeed, the difference approach sees the concern with child-care responsibilities, rather than irrelevant criteria like gender, as evidence that sex discrimination has been eliminated. It cannot see that the relevance of child-care responsibilities is itself a profound source of sexual inequality, one that has arisen from the way men have historically structured the economy to suit their interests.

So before we decide whether gender

should be taken into account, we need to know how it has already been taken into account. And the fact is that almost all important roles and positions have been structured in gender-biased ways:

virtually every quality that distinguishes men from women is already affirmatively compensated in this society. Men's physiology defines most sports, their needs define auto and health insurance coverage, their socially-designed biographies define workplace expectations and successful career patterns, their perspectives and concerns define quality in scholarship, their experiences and obsessions define merit, their objectification of life defines art, their military service defines citizenship, their presence defines family, their inability to get along with each other—their wars and rulerships—defines history, their image defines god, and their genitals define sex. For each of their differences from women, what amounts to an affirmative action plan is in effect, otherwise known as the structure and values of American society. (Mackinnon 1987: 36)

All of this is 'gender-neutral', in the sense that women are not arbitrarily excluded from pursuing the things society defines as valuable. But it is sexist, because the things being pursued in a gender-neutral way are based on men's interests and values. Women are disadvantaged, not because chauvinists arbitrarily favour men in the awarding of jobs, but because the entire society systematically favours men in the defining of jobs, merits, etc.

Indeed, the more society defines positions in a gendered way, the less the difference approach is able to detect an inequality. Consider a society which restricts access to contraception and abortion, which defines paying jobs in such a way as to make them incompatible with child-bearing and child-rearing, and which does not provide economic compensation for domestic labour. Every woman who faces an unplanned pregnancy, and who cannot both raise children and work for wages, is rendered economically dependent on someone who is a stable income-earner (i.e. a man).

In order to ensure that she acquires this support, she must become sexually attractive to men. Knowing that this is their likely fate, many girls do not try as hard as boys to acquire employment skills which can only be exercised by those who avoid pregnancy. Where boys pursue personal security by increasing their employment skills, girls pursue security by increasing their attractiveness to men. This, in turn, results in a system of cultural identifications in which masculinity is associated with income-earning, and femininity is defined in terms of sexual and domestic service for men, and the nurturing of children. So men and women enter marriage with different income-earning potential, and this disparity widens during marriage, as the man acquires valuable job experience. Since the woman faces greater difficulty supporting herself outside of the marriage, she is more dependent on maintaining the marriage, which allows the man to exercise greater control within it.

In such a society, men as a group exercise control over women's general life-chances (through political decisions about abortion, and economic decisions concerning job requirements), and individual men exercise control over economically vulnerable women within marriages. Yet there need be no arbitrary discrimination. All of this is gender-neutral, in that one's gender does not necessarily affect how one is treated by those in charge of distributing contraception, jobs, or domestic pay. By whereas the difference approach takes the absence of arbitrary discrimination as evidence of the absence of sexual inequality, it may in fact be evidence of its pervasiveness. It is precisely because women are dominated in this society that there is no need for them to be discriminated against. Arbitrary discrimination in employment is not only unnecessary for the maintenance of male privilege, it is unlikely to occur, for most women will never be in a position to be arbitrarily discriminated against in employment. Perhaps the occasional woman can overcome the social pressures supporting traditional sex-roles. But the greater the domination, the less the likelihood that any women will be in a position to compete for employment, and hence the less room for arbitrary discrimination. The more sexual inequality there is in society, the more that social institutions reflect male interests, the less arbitrary discrimination there will be.

None of the contemporary Western democracies correspond exactly to his model of a patriarchal society, but they all share some of its essential features. And if we are to confront these forms of injustice, we need to reconceptualize sexual inequality as a problem, not of arbitrary discrimination, but of domination. As Mackinnon puts it,

> to require that one be the same as those who set the standard—those which one is already socially defined as different from—simply means that sex equality is conceptually designed never to be achieved. Those who most need equal treatment will be the least similar, socially, to those whose situation sets the standard as against which one's entitlement to be equally treated is measured. Doctrinally speaking, the deepest problems of sex inequality will not find women 'similarly situated' to men. Far less will practices of sex inequality require that acts be intentionally discriminatory. (Mackinnon 1987:44; cf. Taub and Schneider 1982:134)

The subordination of women is not fundamentally a matter of irrational differentiation on the basis of sex, but of male supremacy, under which gender differences are made relevant to the distribution of benefits, to the systematic disadvantage of women (Mackinnon 1987:42; Frye 1983:38).

Since the problem is domination, the solution is not only the absence of discrimination, but the presence of power. Equality requires not only equal opportunity to pursue male-defined roles, but also equal power to create female-defined roles, or to create androgynous roles men and women have an equal interest in filling. The result of such empowerment could be very different from our society, or from the equal-opportunity-to-enter-male-institutions that is favoured by contemporary sex-discrimination theory. From a position of equal power, we would not have created a system of social roles that defines 'male' jobs as superior to 'female' jobs. For example, the roles of male and female health practitioners were redefined by men against the will of women in the field. With the professionalization of medicine, women were squeezed out of their traditional health care roles as midwives and healers, and relegated to the role of nurse—a position which is subservient to, and financially less rewarding than, the role of doctor. That redefinition would not have happened had women been in a position of equality, and will have to be rethought now if women are to achieve equality.

Facial Discrimination

Editors, Harvard Law Review

Unattractive people regularly face discrimination and are poorly treated in such diverse areas as employment decisions, criminal sentencing, and apartment renting. This essay from the *Harvard Law Review* argues that decisions based on appearance frequently rest on personal dislike or prejudice rather than merit and it maintains that existing legislation to protect the handicapped should be interpreted to protect people against employment discrimination on the basis of immutable aspects of their physical appearance.

"He had but one eye, and the popular prejudice runs in favour of two."

—Charles Dickens, *Nicholas Nickleby*

The most physically unattractive members of our society face severe discrimination. People who are regarded as unattractive are, for example, perhaps the only noncriminal, noncontagious group in America ever to have been barred by law from appearing in public.[1] The unattractive are poorly treated in such diverse contexts as employment decisions, criminal sentenc-

ing, and apartment renting. Although appearance discrimination can have a devastating economic, psychological, and social impact on individuals, its victims have not yet found a legal recourse.

This Note will argue that appearance, like race and gender, is almost always an illegitimate employment criterion, and that it is frequently used to make decisions based on personal dislike or prejudicial assumptions rather than actual merit. It will suggest that existing legislation—in particular, the Rehabilitation Act of 1973, prohibiting discrimination on the basis of physical handicaps—should be construed to protect people against employment discrimination on the basis of largely immutable aspects of bodily and facial appearance. Thus, mutable aspects of personal grooming such as hair length, cleanliness, or nontraditional dress are outside of the discussion of this Note, whereas shortness, obesity, and unattractive facial characteristics are the sort of criteria considered.[2] Rather than attempting

[1] Until recently, a number of major American cities had so-called "ugly laws," generally part of their vagrancy laws, which imposed fines on "unsightly" people who were seen in public places. For an example of such a statute, see CHICAGO, ILL. MUN. CODE § 36-34 (1966) (repealed 1974) (imposing fines on persons who appear in public who are "diseased, maimed, mutilated or in any way deformed so as to be an unsightly or disgusting object") . . . As recently as 1974, the city of Omaha, Nebraska arrested a man under a similar city ordinance.

[2] Some argue that appearance is under the control of the individual, and that individuals who do not pre-

to delineate specific categories of physical appearance to be protected, this Note proposes that administrative agencies and courts accord handicap status to appearance discrimination victims using the same case-by-case analysis of the individual's impairment and employment situation that is generally used in handicap law.

Part I of the note describes the problem of appearance discrimination in a number of contexts, with particular reference to employment. . . . Part II explores how the employment process can be restructured to alleviate appearance discrimination.

I. THE PHENOMENON OF APPEARANCE DISCRIMINATION

To be human is to discriminate. Humans constantly evaluate people, places, and things and choose some over others. The premise of antidiscrimination law is that in some areas, such as employment and housing, certain criteria are not permissible bases of selection. Antidiscrimination law has yet to state a general model of discrimination that describes precisely which criteria are "illegitimate." Despite the difficulty of developing such criteria, some inner and outer bounds are clear. In the domain of employment, for example, members of racial and religious minority groups are legally protected from discrimination. Those who

---

sent a more appealing physical appearance are themselves at fault. This argument is frequently made in the case of the obese. In many instances, however, this simply is not true. Recent evidence suggests that many obese persons are overweight for biological reasons largely beyond their own control. *See* Brody, *Research Lifts Blame From Many Obese*, N. Y. Times, March 24, 1987, at C1 col. 3 (stating that "[o]ne by one, obesity experts are concluding that many, if not most, people with serious weight problems can hardly be blamed for their rotund shape"). Furthermore, many other aspects of physical appearance are immutable characteristics that "good grooming" would not affect. *See* G. PATZER. THE PHYSICAL ATTRACTIVENESS PHENOMENA 154 (1985) (listing some immutable aspects of a person's face that have been found to be important components of physical attractiveness).

score poorly on employment aptitude tests found to bear a legitimate relation to the job generally are not.

One approach to antidiscrimination law would protect any member of a minority group who faces discrimination because of membership in that group. This approach is consistent with Louis Wirth's influential definition of a minority: "a group of people who, because of their physical or cultural characteristics, are singled out from the others in the society in which they live for differential and unequal treatment and who therefore regard themselves as objects of collective discrimination." Physically unattractive people do not fall precisely within Wirth's formulation. First, the physically unattractive do not constitute a cohesive group; a thin person with an unattractive face, for example, may feel little kinship with an obese person. In addition, physical attractiveness is a continuum, and neat determinations of who is "unattractive" are impossible. Nevertheless, the physically unattractive share many of the burdens of Wirth's minority groups. Although our society professes a commitment to judge people by their inner worth, physically unattractive people often face differential and unequal treatment in situations in which their appearance is unrelated to their qualifications or abilities. In the employment context, appearance often functions as an illegitimate basis on which to deny people jobs for which they are otherwise qualified.

A. Appearance Discrimination Generally

People in our society often have a visceral dislike for individuals whom they find unattractive. The bias is so strong that it is not deemed inappropriate to express this dislike; the physically unattractive are a frequent subject of derisive humor. People frequently believe, either consciously or unconsciously, that people with unattractive exteriors were either born with equally unattractive interiors or gradually developed them. By contrast, people tend to think, often with very little basis, that people they find physically attractive are generally worthy and appealing or that, as the title of one study has it, "What Is Beautiful Is Good."

Social science studies have shown that people attribute a wide range of positive characteristics to those whom they find physically attractive. These studies also indicate that when less attractive people are compared to more attractive people, the less attractive men and women are accorded worse treatment simply because of their appearance. This less-favored treatment apparently begins as early as the first few months of life. Throughout childhood, unattractive children face parents who have lower expectations for their success than for more attractive children, teachers who have lower expectations for their academic success, and contemporaries who prefer more attractive children as friends. This less generous treatment of unattractive people continues through adulthood. For example, studies of "helping behavior"—the willingness of subjects to do small favors for a stranger—show that such behavior varies directly with the stranger's attractiveness. Likewise, simulation studies of court proceedings have found that unattractive people receive higher sentences in criminal cases and lower damage awards in civil lawsuits.

Physical appearance can also warp the functioning of ordinarily "objective" evaluations of individuals' work. This distortion has been shown in studies in which subjects were asked to evaluate a written essay that was accompanied by a photograph of the purported author. When copies of the same essay were evaluated with a photograph of an attractive or an unattractive person attached, the essays with the more attractive purported author were judged to have better ideas, better style, and more creativity. Moreover, studies have shown that in general, attractive people are disproportionately likely to receive credit for good outcomes, whereas the good outcomes of unattractive

people are more likely to be attributed to external factors, such as luck. Such biases might easily lead an employer to underrate the talents of an unattractive job applicant.

Empirical research on the real-world effects of appearance discrimination supports the results of these simulation exercises. Considerable empirical research has been done in the area of obesity. One study showed that obese high school students were significantly less likely than non-obese students to be admitted to selective colleges, when academic achievement, motivation, and economic class were held constant; another found that obese adults were discriminated against in the renting of apartments.

Appearance discrimination thus seems to occur in a wide variety of situations. Clearly, the law cannot intervene directly to prevent all such discrimination; no law, for example, can itself make a teacher have more faith in an unattractive child's academic success. The law can, however, address discrimination in discrete areas. One such area is employment selection, in which appearance discrimination is widespread.

B. Appearance Discrimination in Employee Selection

Physical appearance is a significant factor in employee selection, regardless of the nature of the job or the relevance of appearance to the task at hand. One of the primary methods of assessing applicants for all levels of jobs is the personal interview, in which the applicant's appearance is a central criterion. One survey found that appearance was the single most important factor in determining candidate acceptability for a wide variety of jobs, regardless of the level of training of the interviewers. Another study asked 2804 employment interviewers throughout the United States to give "favorability" scores to a variety of characteristics of applicants for various positions. Interviewers considered as important positive characteristics such factors as "Has a good complexion" and rated as important negative characteristics factors such as "Is markedly overweight," and, for men, "Physique appears feminine." Interview manuals written for employers make clear the importance of physical appearance in the selection process. One general employment handbook places "Appearance" first on its list of "hire appeal" factors.

Research in specific areas of physical difference reinforces the claim that appearance discrimination pervades the job market. The National Association to Aid Fat Americans found that fifty-one percent of its members who responded to a survey reported instances of employment discrimination. A report of the State of Maryland's Commission on Human Relations concluded that it may well be easier to place a thin black person on a job than a fat white person. Extremely short people also experience severe employment discrimination.

There have as yet been no direct challenges to appearance discrimination, although appearance issues have been raised in other lawsuits. Hiring practices based on explicit evaluations of applicants' physical appearance were challenged in the courts for the first time in the 1960s and early 1970s in lawsuits charging airlines with sex and race discrimination in the hiring of flight attendants. One Equal Employment Opportunity Commission hearing of a race discrimination claim revealed that an interview form contained the written comment that a black applicant had "unattractive, large lips." The Commission found that this negative evaluation of a race-related aspect of the applicant's appearance provided reasonable cause to believe that unlawful racial discrimination had taken place. More recently, a computer programmer successfully sued under New York State law a company that failed to hire her because she was obese. The challenge alleged, however, that obesity was a medical handicap, and did not raise the broader issue of appearance discrimination. . . .

C. Deciding Which Jobs Are Covered

Even if physical unattractiveness can at times be a handicap, difficult questions emerge concerning which jobs should be covered under the Act. In many cases, employers will likely argue that an attractive appearance is "necessary" for a job. Courts will have to decide, when, if ever, an employer should be permitted to reject an applicant on the basis of appearance.

Under the Act, the question would be phrased in terms of when an applicant is "otherwise qualified" for the job at issue. Courts have been unclear in their interpretations of this concept. It may be argued that certain jobs—for example, modeling and acting—require people who look a certain way. Nevertheless, courts have defined job "requirements" narrowly. "The test," said the Fifth Circuit in *Prewett v. United States Postal Service*, "is whether a handicapped individual who meets all employment criteria except for the challenged discriminatory criterion 'can perform the essential functions of the position in question without endangering the health and safety of the individuals or others.' "

No doubt employers would urge exceptions to appearance discrimination rules not only for persons, such as models and actors, who perform clearly appearance-related work, but also for receptionists, flight attendants, salespeople, and many other jobs in which physical attractiveness might be an important asset. Courts should grant such exceptions sparingly. If they follow the lead of *Prewett*, they will take a narrow view of the "essence" of a job and will in most cases decide that appearance is not relevant. The flight attendant litigation under title VII of the Civil Rights Act of 1964 provides a good model for courts in defining jobs narrowly. Those cases held that appearance was not part of the essence of the job of flight attendant. As the Fifth Circuit stated in holding that men were just as capable as women of being flight attendants, "[w]hile a pleasant environment, enhanced by the obvious cosmetic effect that female stewardesses provide . . . [may] be important, [it is] tangential to the essence of the business involved." By similar logic, it should be determined that physical attractiveness is not essential to most jobs. . . .

II. REFORMING EMPLOYMENT SELECTION TO PREVENT APPEARANCE DISCRIMINATION

In addition to the deterrent effect of individual complaints, restructuring the employment selection process can also prevent appearance discrimination. Employers may be reluctant at first to embark on new approaches to selecting employees. But the Rehabilitation Act and its accompanying regulations are written in aspirational terms. The regulations state that "[t]he Federal Government shall become a model employer of handicapped individuals." This Part will suggest several ways to restructure the system to make the federal government and its contractors such a model. In addition, it will discuss some of the tensions and broader issues raised by efforts to minimize appearance discrimination.

A. Restructuring Employment Selection To Reduce Appearance Discrimination

Even if employers agreed in principle that considerations of physical appearance should ideally be eliminated from the hiring process, this ideal would be difficult to achieve in practice. As long as hiring is based on face-to-face interviews, physical appearance will inevitably have an impact on impressions. This problem can be avoided, however, by restructuring the hiring process to eliminate or reduce information about applicants' appearance when applicants are evaluated and hiring decisions are made.

The regulations promulgated by the HHS bar "preemployment inquiries" concerning a job applicant's handicapped status, unless the inquires specifically concern the applicant's ability to do the job. To meet this requirement, employers could publicly announce a policy of not soliciting information about an applicant's appearance, other than grooming and neatness, and of not considering appearance as a factor in employee selection. The standard face-to-face interview, in which the applicant's appearance is highly salient, in many ways resembles just such a statutorily forbidden preemployment inquiry into appearance handicaps. To conform with the ban on preemployment inquiries, employers should reevaluate their commitment to the standard employment interview.

To be sure, interviews undoubtedly have some informational value beyond permitting illegitimate appearance evaluations. An employer may justifiably be concerned, for example, with an applicant's interpersonal skills. But this information can be obtained in ways that avoid the prejudicial process of face-to-face interviews. One possible method is the expanded use of telephone interviews. Another possibility, which could work well for many kinds of jobs, is the adoption of the practice used by virtually every American symphony orchestra to avoid discrimination and favoritism in hiring: auditions conducted behind screens. Such an interview process would provide employers with useful information about an applicant, revealing factors such as a "pleasant personality," without prejudicing the selection process by injecting appearance into the calculus.

Employers could also reduce or eliminate appearance discrimination through less dramatic modifications in the selection process. They could, for example, set a rigid dividing line between the person who meets and interviews job applicants and the person who makes the decision about whom to hire. The interviewer could pass along a form to the decisionmaker that includes only job-related information and impressions. Although the applicant's appearance might still influence the interviewer's perceptions of other subjective qualities, it would nevertheless be a considerable reform.

Objections that employment decisions will be difficult or "random" under such a new regime are misplaced. Workable selection procedures and criteria can be maintained without permitting appearance discrimination. Employers could continue to use the battery of legitimate, work-related criteria: they could ask about education, prior work experience, and success in school and at previous jobs. And they could administer bona fide, work-related, nondiscriminatory tests. Indeed, to the extent that these reforms eliminate irrelevant criteria, they should lead to a greater weighting of job-relevant criteria and hence a fairer overall process.

B. Moving From "Efficiency" to Equality

Efforts to eliminate appearance discrimination would significantly restructure employment practices. Inevitably, such proposed reforms raise questions about the sort of criteria on which our society should permit employment decisions to be based. One objection to eliminating physical appearance as a criterion for hiring is an argument about economic efficiency. If an employer can show that an applicant's appearance makes him or her more profitable, why should this not be a valid criterion for employment? The response to this objection is that "efficiency" is not always an acceptable basis on which to make distinctions in the employment process.

In fact, many sorts of discrimination may be "economically efficient." For example, a restaurant owner in a racist neighborhood might enlarge his or her clientele—and thus increase profits—by refusing to hire black waiters and waitresses. Yet in all forms of antidiscrimination law we proclaim that our society has some principles of equality that it holds more dear than efficiency.

Michael M. v. Sonoma County Superior Court: Sex Discrimination

This case concerns equality between the sexes. A 17-year-old man was convicted under California law for the statutory rape of a 16-year-old female. Men, but not women, are liable under the statute, which makes it illegal to have sex with a female under 18, whether or not she consents. Justice Rehnquist, writing for a plurality of the Supreme Court, upheld the California law, maintaining that it does not discriminate against men or women. In a dissenting opinion, Justice Brennan argues that California has not shown that this law will reduce pregnancies more effectively than one that does not make any distinction based on sex.

Mr. Justice Rehnquist: [We] have not held that gender-based classifications are

---

450 U. S. 464 (1981).

"inherently suspect" and thus we do not apply so-called "strict scrutiny" to those classifications. Our cases have held, however, that the traditional minimum rationality test takes on a somewhat "sharper focus" when gender-based classifications are challenged. In *Reed v. Reed,* for example, the Court stated that a gender-based classification will be upheld if it bears a "fair and substantial relationship" to legitimate state ends, while in *Craig v. Boren,* the Court restated the test to require the classification to bear a "substantial relationship" to "important governmental objectives."

Underlying these decisions is the principle that a legislature may not "make overbroad generalizations based on sex which are entirely unrelated to any differences between men and women or which demean the ability or social status of the affected class." But because the Equal Protection Clause does not "demand that a statute necessarily apply equally to all persons" or require "things which are different in fact to be treated in law as though they were the same," this Court has consistently upheld statutes where the gender classification is not invidious, but rather realistically reflects the fact that the sexes are not similarly situated in certain circumstances. . . .

Applying those principles to this case, the fact that the California Legislature criminalized the act of illicit sexual intercourse with a minor female is a sure indication of its intent or purpose to discourage that conduct. Precisely why the legislature desired that result is of course somewhat less clear. . . .

The justification for the statute offered by the State, and accepted by the Supreme Court of California, is that the legislature sought to prevent illegitimate teenage pregnancies. . . .

We are satisfied not only that the prevention of illegitimate pregnancy is at least one of the "purposes" of the statute, but also that the State has a strong interest in preventing such pregnancy. . . .

We need not be medical doctors to discern that young men and young women are not similarly situated with respect to the problems and the risks of sexual intercourse. Only women may become pregnant, and they suffer disproportionately the profound physical, emotional, and psychological consequences of sexual activity. The statute at issue here protects women from sexual intercourse at an age when those consequences are particularly severe.

[Although petitioner concedes that the State has a "compelling" interest in preventing teenage pregnancy, he contends that the "true" purpose of [the statute] is to protect the virtue and chastity of young women. As such, the statute is unjustifiable because it rests on archaic stereotypes. What we have said above is enough to dispose of that contention. The question for us—and the only question under the Federal Constitution—is whether the legislation violates the Equal Protection Clause of the Fourteenth Amendment, not whether its supporters may have endorsed it for reasons no longer generally accepted.]

The question thus boils down to whether a State may attack the problem of sexual intercourse and teenage pregnancy directly by prohibiting a male from having sexual intercourse with a minor female. We hold that such a statute is sufficiently related to the State's objectives to pass constitutional muster.

Because virtually all of the significant harmful and inescapably identifiable consequences of teenage pregnancy fall on the young female, a legislature acts well within its authority when it elects to punish only the participant who, by nature, suffers few of the consequences of his conduct. It is hardly unreasonable for a legislature acting to protect minor females to exclude them from punishment. Moreover, the risk of pregnancy itself constitutes a substantial deterrence to young females. No similar natural sanctions deter males. A criminal sanction imposed solely on males thus serves to roughly "equalize" the deterrents on the sexes. . . .

[We] cannot say that a gender-neutral statute would be as effective as the statute California has chosen to enact. The State persuasively contends that a gender-neutral statute would frustrate its interest in effective enforcement. Its view is that a female is surely less likely to report violations of the statute if she herself would be subject to criminal prosecution. . . .

There remains only petitioner's contention that the statute is unconstitutional as it is applied to him because he, like [his partner], was under 18 at the time of sexual intercourse. Petitioner argues that the statute is flawed because it presumes that as between two persons under 18, the male is the culpable aggressor. We find petitioner's contentions unpersuasive. Contrary to his assertions, the statute does not rest on the assumption that males are generally the aggressors. It is instead an attempt by a legislature to prevent illegitimate teenage pregnancy by providing an additional deterrent for men. The age of the man is irrelevant since young men are as capable as older men of inflicting the harm sought to be prevented. . . .

Justice Brennan, dissenting: The State of California vigorously asserts that the "important governmental objective" to be served by [the statute] is the prevention of teenage pregnancy. It claims that its statute furthers this goal by deterring sexual activity by males—the class of persons it considers more responsible for causing those pregnancies. [In a remarkable display of sexual stereotyping, the California Supreme Court stated: "The Legislature is well within its power in imposing criminal sanctions against males, alone, because they are the *only* persons who may physiologically cause the result which the law properly seeks to avoid."] But even assuming that prevention of teenage pregnancy is an important governmental objective and that it is in fact an objective of [the statute], California still has the burden of proving that there are fewer teenage pregnancies under its gender-based statutory rape law than there would be if the law were gender neutral. To meet this burden, the State must show that because its statutory rape law punishes only males, and

not females, it more effectively deters minor females from having sexual intercourse. . . .

A State's bare assertion that its gender-based statutory classification substantially furthers an important governmental interest is not enough to meet its burden of proof. . . . Rather, the State must produce evidence that will persuade the Court that its assertion is true. [Even] assuming that a gender-neutral statute would be more difficult to enforce, the State has still not shown that those enforcement problems would make such a statute less effective than a gender-based statute in deterring minor females from engaging in sexual intercourse. Common sense, however, suggests that a gender-neutral statutory rape law is potentially a *greater* deterrent of sexual activity than a gender-based law, for the simple reason that a gender-neutral law subjects both men and women to criminal sanctions and thus arguably has a deterrent effect on twice as many potential violators. Even if fewer persons were prosecuted under the gender-neutral law, as the State suggests, it would still be true that twice as many persons would be *subject* to arrest.

Until very recently, no California court or commentator had suggested that the purpose of California's statutory rape law was to protect young women from the risk of pregnancy. Indeed, the historical development of [the statute] demonstrates that the law was initially enacted on the premise that young women, in contrast to young men, were to be deemed legally incapable of consenting to an act of sexual intercourse. Because their chastity was considered particularly precious, those young women were felt to be uniquely in need of the State's protection. In contrast, young men were assumed to be capable of making such decisions for themselves; the law therefore did not offer them any special protection. . . .

I would hold that [the statute] violates the Equal Protection Clause of the Fourteenth Amendment. . . .

Dothard v. Rawlinson:
BFOQ and Sex Discrimination

At a prior hearing, Dianne Rawlinson had established that the refusal of Alabama's Board of Corrections to consider her application for employment as a prison guard based on its height and weight requirements violated her rights under provisions of Title VII of the Civil Rights Act of 1964 preventing discrimination based on sex. While that case was still pending, however, the Corrections Board adopted Administrative Regulation 204, which explicitly established gender as a basis for assigning guards (which Alabama called "correctional counselors"). According to the new regulation, no women were to serve in maximum security institutions requiring continuous close contact with inmates. Alabama (appellants) justified the regulation based on the bona fide occupational qualification (BFOQ) exception in the Civil Rights Act.

Mr. Justice Stewart delivered the opinion of the Court: Unlike the statutory height and weight requirements, Regulation 204 explicitly discriminates against women on the basis of their sex. In defense of this overt discrimination, the appellants rely on § 703(e) of Title VII, which permits sex-based discrimination "in those certain instances where . . . sex . . . is a bona fide occupational qualification reasonably necessary to the normal operation of that particular business or enterprise."

The District Court rejected the bona fide occupational qualification (bfoq) defense, relying on the virtually uniform view of the federal courts that § 703(e) provides only the narrowest of exceptions to the general rule requiring equality of employment opportunities. This view has been variously

433 U. S. 321 (1977).

formulated. In Diaz v. Pan American World Airways, 442 F.2d 385, 388, the Court of Appeals for the Fifth Circuit held that "discrimination based on sex is valid only when the *essence* of the business operation would be undermined by not hiring members of one sex exclusively." (Emphasis in original.) [Discrimination] on the basis of stereotyped characterizations of the sexes [is invalid], and the District Court in the present case held in effect that Regulation 204 is based on just such stereotypical assumptions.

We are persuaded—by the restrictive language of § 703(e), the relevant legislative history, and the consistent interpretation of the Equal Employment Opportunity Commission—that the bfoq exception was in fact meant to be an extremely narrow exception to the general prohibition of discrimination on the basis of sex. In the particular factual circumstances of this case, however, we conclude that the District Court erred in rejecting the State's contention that Regulation 204 falls within the narrow ambit of the bfoq exception.

The environment in Alabama's penitentiaries is a peculiarly inhospitable one for human beings of whatever sex. Indeed, a federal district court has held that the conditions of confinement in the prisons of the State, characterized by "rampant violence" and a "jungle atmosphere," are constitutionally intolerable. James v. Wallace, 406 F. Supp. 318, 325 (MD Ala). The record in the present case shows that because of inadequate staff and facilities, no attempt is made in the four maximum security male penitentiaries to classify or segregate inmates according to their offense or level of dangerousness—a procedure that, according to expert testimony, is essential to effective penalogical administration. Consequently, the estimated 20% of the male prisoners who are sex offenders are scattered throughout the penitentiaries' dormitory facilities.

In this environment of violence and disorganization, it would be an oversimplification to characterize Regulation 204 as an exercise in "romantic paternalism." Cf. Frontiero v. Richardson, 411 U. S. 677, 684. In the usual case, the argument that a particular job is too dangerous for women may appropriately be met by the rejoinder that it is the purpose of Title VII to allow the individual woman to make that choice for herself. More is at stake in this case, however, than an individual woman's decision to weigh and accept the risks of employment in a "contact" position in a maximum security male prison.

The essence of a correctional counselor's job is to maintain prison security. A woman's relative ability to maintain order in a male, maximum security, unclassified penitentiary of the type Alabama now runs could be directly reduced by her womanhood. There is a basis in fact for expecting that sex offenders who have criminally assaulted women in the past would be moved to do so again if, access to women were established within the prison. There would

also be a real risk that other inmates, deprived of a normal heterosexual environment, would assault women guards because they were women. In a prison system where violence is the order of the day, where inmate access to guards is facilitated by dormitory living arrangements, where every institution is understaffed, and where a substantial portion of the inmate population is composed of sex offenders mixed at random with other prisoners, there are few visible deterrents to inmate assaults on women custodians.

The plaintiffs' own expert testified that dormitory housing for aggressive inmates poses a greater security problem than single-cell lockups, and further testified that it would be unwise to use women as guards in a prison where even 10% of the inmates had been convicted of sex crimes and were not segregated from the other prisoners. The likelihood that inmates would assault a woman because she was a woman would pose a real threat not only to the victim of the assault but also to the basic control of the penitentiary and protection of its inmates and the other security personnel. The employee's very womanhood would thus directly undermine her capacity to provide the security that is the essence of a correctional counselor's responsibility.

There was substantial testimony from experts on both sides of this litigation that the use of women as guards in "contact" positions under the existing conditions in Alabama maximum security male penitentiaries would pose a substantial security problem, directly linked to the sex of the prison guard. On the basis of that evidence, we conclude that the District Court was in error in ruling that being male is not a bona fide occupational qualification for the job of correctional counselor in a "contact" position in an Alabama male maximum security penitentiary.

The judgment is accordingly affirmed in part and reversed in part, and the case is remanded to the District Court for further proceedings consistent with this opinion.

Mr. Justice Marshall, with whom Mr. Justice Brennan joins, concurring in part and dissenting in part: The Court properly rejects two proffered justifications for denying women jobs as prison guards. It is simply irrelevant here that a guard's occupation is dangerous and that some women might be unable to protect themselves adequately. Those themes permeate the testimony of the state officials below, but as the Court holds, "the argument that a particular job is too dangerous for women" is refuted by the "purpose of Title VII to allow the individual women to make that choice for herself." Some women, like some men, undoubtedly are not qualified and do not wish to serve as prison guards, but that does not justify the exclusion of all women from this employment opportunity. Thus, "[i]n the usual case," ibid., the Court's interpretation of the bfoq exception would mandate hiring qualified women for guard jobs in maximum security institutions. The highly successful experiences of other States allowing such job opportunities, see Briefs *amicus curiae* of the States of California and Washington, confirm that absolute disqualification of women is not, in the words of Title VII, "reasonably necessary to the normal operation" of a maximum security prison.

What would otherwise be considered unlawful discrimination against women is justified by the Court, however, on the basis of the "barbaric and inhumane" conditions in Alabama prisons, conditions so bad that state officials have conceded that they violate the Constitution. See James v. Wallace, 406 F. Supp. 318, 329, 331 (MD Ala. 1976). To me, this analysis sounds distressingly like saying two wrongs make a right. It is refuted by the plain words of § 703(e). The statute requires that a bfoq be "reasonably necessary to the normal operation of that particular business or enterprise." But no governmental "business" may operate "normally" in violation of the Constitution. Every action of government is constrained by constitutional limitations. While those limits may be violated more frequently than we would

wish, no one disputes that the "normal operation" of all government functions takes place within them. A prison system operating in blatant violation of the Eighth Amendment is an exception that should be remedied with all possible speed, as Judge Johnson's comprehensive order in James v. Wallace, supra, is designed to do. In the meantime, the existence of such violations should not be legitimized by calling them "normal." Nor should the Court accept them as justifying conduct that would otherwise violate a statute intended to remedy age-old discrimination.

The Court's error in statutory construction is less objectionable, however, than the attitude it displays toward women. Though the Court recognizes that possible harm to women guards is an unacceptable reason for disqualifying women, it relies instead on an equally speculative threat to prison discipline supposedly generated by the sexuality of female guards. There is simply no evidence in the record to show that women guards would create any danger to security in Alabama prisons significantly greater than already exists. All of the dangers—with one exception discussed below—are inherent in a prison setting whatever the gender of the guards.

The Court first sees women guards as a threat to security because "there are few visible deterrents to inmate assaults on women custodians." In fact, any prison guard is constantly subject to the threat of attack by inmates and "invisible" deterrents are the guard's only real protection. No prison guard relies primarily on his or her ability to ward off an inmate attack to maintain order. Guards are typically unarmed and sheer numbers of inmates could overcome the normal complement. Rather, like all other law enforcement officers, prison guards must rely primarily on the moral authority of their office and the threat of future punishment for miscreants. As one expert testified below, common sense, fairness, and mental and emotional stability are the qualities a guard needs to cope with the dangers of the job. Well qualified and properly trained women, no less than men, have these psychological weapons at their disposal.

The particular severity of discipline problems in the Alabama maximum security prisons is also no justification for the discrimination sanctioned by the Court. The District Court found in James v. Wallace, supra, that guards "must spend all their time attempting to maintain control or to protect themselves." 406 F. Supp., at 325. If male guards face an impossible situation, it is difficult to see how women could make the problem worse, unless one relies on precisely the type of generalized bias against women that the Court agrees Title VII was intended to outlaw. For example, much of the testimony of appellants' witnesses ignores individual differences among members of each sex and reads like "ancient canards about the proper role of women." Phillips v. Martin Marietta Corp., supra, 400 U. S. at 545. The witnesses claimed that women guards are not strict disciplinarians; that they are physically less capable of protecting themselves and subduing unruly inmates; that inmates take advantage of them as they did their mothers, while male guards are strong father figures who easily maintain discipline, and so on.[1] Yet the record shows that the presence of women guards has not led to a single incident amounting to a serious breach of security in any Alabama institution.[2] And in any event, "Guards rarely enter the cell blocks and dormitories," James v. Wallace, supra, 406 F. Supp., at 325, where the danger of inmate attacks is the greatest.

It appears that the real disqualifying factor in the Court's view is "[t]he employee's very womanhood." The Court refers to the large number of sex offenders in Alabama prisons, and to "the likelihood that inmates would assault a woman because she was a woman." In short, the fundamental justification for the decision is that women as guards will generate sexual assaults. With all respect, this rationale regrettably perpetuates one of the most insidious of the old myths about women—that women, wittingly or not, are seductive sexual objects. The effect of the decision, made I am sure with the best of intentions, is to punish women because their very presence might provoke sexual assaults. It is women who are made to pay the price in lost job opportunities for the threat of depraved conduct by prison inmates. Once again, "[t]he pedestal upon which women have been placed has . . ., upon closer inspection, been revealed as a cage." Sail'er Inn, Inc. v. Kirby, 5 Cal.3d 1, 20 (1971). It is particularly ironic that the cage is erected here in response to feared misbehavior by imprisoned criminals.[3]

The Court points to no evidence in the record to support the asserted "likelihood that inmates would assault a woman because she was a woman." Perhaps the court relies upon common sense, or "innate recogni-

---

[1] The State Commissioner of Corrections summed up these prejudices in his testimony:

"Q Would a male that is 5′6″, 140 lbs., be able to perform the job of Correctional Counselor in an all male institution?

"A Well, if he qualifies otherwise, yes.

"Q But a female 5′6″, 140 lbs., would not be able to perform all the duties?

"A No.

"Q What do you use as a basis for that opinion?

"A The innate intention between a male and a female. The physical capabilities, the emotions that go into the psychic make-up of a female vs. the psychic make-up of a male. The attitude of the rural type inmate we have vs. that of a woman. The superior feeling that a man has, historically, over that of a female." App. 153.

[2] The Court refers to two incidents involving potentially dangerous attacks on women in prisons. Ante, at n. 22. But these did not involve trained corrections officers; one victim was a clerical worker and the other a student visiting on a tour.

[3] The irony is multiplied by the fact that enormous staff increases are required by the District Court's order in James v. Wallace, supra. This necessary hiring would be a perfect opportunity for appellants to remedy their past discrimination against women, but instead the Court's decision permits that policy to continue. Moreover, once conditions are improved in accordance with the *James* order, the problems that the Court perceives with women guards will be substantially alleviated.

tion." Brief for Appellants, at 51. But the danger in this emotionally laden context is that common sense will be used to mask the "romantic paternalism" and persisting discriminatory attitudes that the Court properly eschews. To me, the only matter of innate recognition is that the incidence of sexually motivated attacks on guards will be minute compared to the "likelihood that inmates will assault" a *guard* because he or she is a *guard*.

The proper response to inevitable attacks on both female and male guards is not to limit the employment opportunities of law-abiding women who wish to contribute to their community, but to take swift and sure punitive action against the inmate offenders. Presumably, one of the goals of the Alabama prison system is the eradication of inmates' antisocial behavior patterns so that prisoners will be able to live one day in free society. Sex offenders can begin this process by learning to relate to women guards in a socially acceptable manner. To deprive women of job opportunities because of the threatened behavior of convicted criminals is to turn our social priorities upside down. . . .

San Antonio School District v. Rodriquez: Equal Opportunity and Public Education

Because education represents the major route by which individuals and groups can improve their social and economic standing, both liberals and conservatives value it highly. But educational opportunity is far from equal in this country, as the case of *San Antonio School District v. Rodriquez* makes clear. This case grew out of a challenge to the method used by Texas to finance public education. Like many other states, Texas relies on local property taxes to pay a large portion of the cost of running schools. In Texas, the effect of this has been that far less is spent to educate children living in poorer districts that in wealthier districts. For example, one Texas school district was able to raise only $26 per student while another raised $333, even though that district's tax rate was lower. Despite extra help provided by the state, students in the wealthier district still had more than twice as much spent on them as on children from poorer areas. A federal district court, applying the "strict scrutiny" that is normally used in race cases, held that the Texas scheme violated the "equal protection" clause of the Fourteenth Amendment. The Supreme Court, however, reversed this decision.

Mr. Justice Powell delivered the opinion of the Court: This suit attacking the Texas system of financing public education was initiated by Mexican-American parents whose children attend the elementary and second-ary schools in the Edgewood Independent School District, an urban school district in San Antonio, Texas. They brought a class action on behalf of schoolchildren throughout the State who are members of minority groups or who are poor and reside in school districts having a low property tax base. . . .

411 U. S. 1 (1973).

In December 1971 the panel rendered its judgment in a *per curiam* opinion holding the Texas school finance system unconstitutional under the Equal Protection Clause of the Fourteenth Amendment. The State appealed, and we noted probable jurisdiction to consider the far-reaching constitutional questions presented. . . . For the reasons stated in this opinion, we reverse the decision of the District Court. . . .

. . . Disparities, largely attributable to differences in the amounts of money collected through local property taxation . . . led the District Court to conclude that Texas' dual system of public school financing violated the Equal Protection Clause. The District Court held that the Texas system discriminates on the basis of wealth in the manner in which education is provided for its people. . . . Finding that *wealth* is a *"suspect"* classification and that *education* is a *"fundamental"* interest, the District Court held that the Texas system could be sustained only if the State could show that it was premised upon some compelling state interest. On this issue the court concluded that "[n]ot only are defendants unable to demonstrate compelling state interests . . . they fail even to establish a reasonable basis for these classifications." . . .

. . . We must decide, first, whether the Texas system of financing public education operates to the disadvantage of some suspect class or impinges upon a fundamental right explicitly or implicitly protected by the Constitution, thereby requiring strict judicial scrutiny. If so, the judgment of the District Court should be affirmed. If not, the Texas scheme must still be examined to determine whether it rationally furthers some legitimate, articulated state purpose and therefore does not constitute an invidious discrimination in violation of the Equal Protection Clause of the Fourteenth Amendment.

The District Court's opinion does not reflect the novelty and complexity of the constitutional questions posed by appellees' challenge to Texas' system of school financing. In concluding that strict judicial scrutiny was required, that court relied on decisions dealing with the rights of indigents to equal treatment in the criminal trial and appellate processes, and on cases disapproving wealth restrictions on the right to vote. Those cases, the District Court concluded, established wealth as a suspect classification. . . .

The wealth discrimination discovered by the District Court in this case, and by several other courts that have recently struck down school-financing laws in other States, is quite unlike any of the forms of wealth discrimination heretofore reviewed by this Court. . . . The individuals, or groups of individuals, who constituted the class discriminated against in our prior cases shared two distinguishing characteristics: because of their impecunity they were completely unable to pay for some desired benefit, and as a consequence, they sustained an absolute deprivation of a meaningful opportunity to enjoy that benefit. . . .

. . . [N]either appellees nor the District Court addressed the fact that, unlike the foregoing cases, lack of personal resources has not occasioned an absolute deprivation of the desired benefit. The argument here is not that the children in districts having relatively low assessable property values are receiving no public education; rather, it is that they are receiving a poorer quality education than that available to children in districts having more assessable wealth. Apart from the unsettled and disputed question whether the quality of education may be determined by the amount of money expended for it, a sufficient answer to appellees' argument is that, at least where wealth is involved, the Equal Protection Clause does not require absolute equality or precisely equal advantages. . . .

. . . [I]n recognition of the fact that this Court has never heretofore held that wealth discrimination alone provides an adequate basis for invoking strict scrutiny, appellees have not relied solely on this contention. They also assert that the State's system impermissibly interferes with the exercise of a "fundamental" right and that accordingly the prior decisions of this Court require the application of the strict standard of judicial review. . . . It is this question—whether education is a fundamental right, in the sense that it is among the rights and liberties protected by the Constitution—which has so consumed the attention of courts and commentators in recent years.

In *Brown v. Board of Education*, . . . a unanimous Court recognized that "education is perhaps the most important function of state and local governments." What was said there in the context of racial discrimination has lost none of its vitality with the passage of time. . . .

". . . In these days, it is doubtful that any child may reasonably be expected to succeed in life if he is denied the opportunity of an education. Such an opportunity, where the state has undertaken to provide it, is a right which must be made available to all on equal terms."

. . . But the importance of a service performed by the State does not determine whether it must be regarded as fundamental for purposes of examination under the Equal Protection Clause. . . .

. . . It is not the province of this Court to create substantive constitutional rights in the name of guaranteeing equal protection of the laws. Thus, the key to discovering whether education is "fundamental" is not to be found in comparisons of the relative societal significance of education as opposed to subsistence or housing. Nor is it to be found by weighing whether education is as important as the right to travel. Rather, the answer lies in assessing whether there is a right to education explicitly or implicitly guaranteed by the Constitution. . . .

Education, of course, is not among the rights afforded explicit protection under our Federal Constitution. Nor do we find any basis for saying it is implicitly so protected. . . . It is appellees' contention, however, that education is distinguishable from other services and benefits provided by the

State because it bears a peculiarly close relationship to other rights and liberties accorded protection under the Constitution. Specifically, they insist that education is itself a fundamental personal right because it is essential to the effective exercise of First Amendment freedoms and to intelligent utilization of the right to vote. In asserting a nexus between speech and education, appellees urge that the right to speak is meaningless unless the speaker is capable of articulating his thoughts intelligently and persuasively. The "marketplace of ideas" is an empty forum for those lacking basic communicative tools. Likewise, they argue that the corollary right to receive information becomes little more than a hollow privilege when the recipient has not been taught to read, assimilate, and utilize available knowledge.

A similar line of reasoning is pursued with respect to the right to vote. Exercise of the franchise, it is contended, cannot be divorced from the educational foundation of the voter. The electoral process, if reality is to conform to the democratic ideal, depends on a informed electorate: a voter cannot cast his ballot intelligently unless his reading skills and thought processes have been adequately developed.

We need not dispute any of these propositions. The Court has long afforded zealous protection against unjustifiable governmental interference with the individual's rights to speak and to vote. Yet we have never presumed to possess either the ability or the authority to guarantee to the citizenry the most *effective* speech or the most *informed* electoral choice. That these may be desirable goals of a system of freedom of expression and of a representative form of government is not to be doubted. These are indeed goals to be pursued by a people whose thoughts and beliefs are freed from governmental interference. But they are not values to be implemented by judicial intrusion into otherwise legitimate state activities.

. . . Whatever merit appellees' argument might have if a State's financing system occasioned an absolute denial of educational opportunities to any of its children, that argument provides no basis for finding an interference with fundamental rights where only relative differences in spending levels are involved and where—as is true in the present case—no charge fairly could be made that the system fails to provide each child with an opportunity to acquire the basic minimal skills necessary for the enjoyment of the rights of speech and of full participation in the political process.

. . . [T]he logical limitations on appellees' nexus theory are difficult to perceive. How, for instance, is education to be distinguished from the significant personal interests in the basics of decent food and shelter? Empirical examination might well buttress an assumption that the ill-fed, ill-clothed, and ill-housed are among the most ineffective participants in the political process, and that they derive the least enjoyment from the benefits of the First Amendment. . . .

We have carefully considered each of the arguments supportive of the District Court's finding that education is a fundamental right or liberty and have found those arguments unpersuasive. . . .

Mr. Justice Marshall, with whom Mr. Justice Douglas concurs, dissenting: The Court today decides, in effect, that a State may constitutionally vary the quality of education which it offers its children in accordance with the amount of taxable wealth located in the school districts within which they reside. . . .

In my judgment, the right of every American to an equal start in life, so far as the provision of a state service as important as education is concerned, is far too vital to permit state discrimination on grounds as tenuous as those presented by this record. Nor can I accept the notion that it is sufficient to remit these appellees to the vagaries of the political process which, contrary to the majority's suggestion, has proved singularly unsuited to the task of providing a remedy for this discrimination. I, for one, am unsatisfied with the hope of an ultimate "political" solution sometime in the indefi-

nite future while, in the meantime, countless children unjustifiably receive inferior educations that "may affect their hearts and minds in a way unlikely ever to be undone." *Brown v. Board of Education*, 347 U. S. 483, 494 (1954). I must therefore respectfully dissent. . . .

Even if the Equal Protection Clause encompassed some theory of constitutional adequacy, discrimination in the provision of educational opportunity would certainly seem to be a poor candidate for its application. Neither the majority nor appellants inform us how judicially manageable standards are to be derived for determining how much education is "enough" to excuse constitutional discrimination. One would think that the majority would heed its own fervent affirmation of judicial self-restraint before undertaking the complex task of determining at large what level of education is constitutionally sufficient. . . .

In my view, then, it is inequality—not some notion of gross inadequacy—of educational opportunity that raises a question of denial of equal protection of the laws.

. . . A principled reading of what this Court has done reveals that it has applied a spectrum of standards in reviewing discrimination allegedly violative of the Equal Protection Clause. This spectrum clearly comprehends variations in the degree of care with which the Court will scrutinize particular classifications, depending, I believe, on the constitutional and societal importance of the interest adversely affected and the recognized invidiousness of the basis upon which the particular classification is drawn. . . .

I therefore cannot accept the majority's labored efforts to demonstrate that fundamental interests, which call for strict scrutiny of the challenged classification, encompass only established rights which we are somehow bound to recognize from the text of the Constitution itself. To be sure, some interests which the Court has deemed to be fundamental for purposes of equal protection analysis are themselves constitutionally protected rights. Thus, discrimination against the guaranteed right of freedom of speech has called for strict judicial scrutiny. . . . But it will not do to suggest that the "answer" to whether an interest is fundamental for purposes of equal protection analysis is *always* determined by whether that interest "is a right . . . explicitly or implicitly guaranteed by the Constitution." . . .

I would like to know where the Constitution guarantees the right to procreate . . . or the right to vote in state elections, . . . or the right to an appeal from a criminal conviction. . . . These are instances in which, due to the importance of the interests at stake, the Court has displayed a strong concern with the existence of discriminatory state treatment. But the Court has never said or indicated that these are interests which independently enjoy full-blown constitutional protection. . . .

While ultimately disputing little of this, the majority seeks refuge in the fact that the Court has "never presumed to possess either the ability or the authority to guarantee to the citizenry the most *effective* speech or the most *informed* electoral choice." This serves only to blur what is in fact at stake. With due respect, the issue is neither provision of the most *effective* speech nor of the most *informed* vote. Appellees do not seek the best education Texas might provide. They do seek, however, an end to state discrimination resulting from the unequal distribution of taxable district property wealth that directly impairs the ability of some districts to provide the same educational opportunity that other districts can provide with the same or even substantially less tax effort. The issue is, in other words, one of discrimination that affects the quality of the education which Texas has chosen to provide its children; and, the precise question here is what importance should attach to education for purposes of equal protection analysis of that discrimination. . . .

We are told that in every prior case involving a wealth classification, the members of the disadvantaged class have "shared two distinguishing characteristics: because of their impecunity they were completely unable to pay for some desired benefit, and as a consequence, they sustained an absolute deprivation of a meaningful opportunity to enjoy that benefit." . . . I cannot agree.

In *Harper,* the Court struck down as violative of the Equal Protection Clause an annual Virginia poll tax of $1.50, payment of which by persons over the age of 21 was a prerequisite to voting in Virginia elections. . . . [T]he Court struck down the poll tax *in toto;* it did not order merely that those too poor to pay the tax be exempted; complete impecunity clearly was not determinative of the limits of the disadvantaged class, nor was it essential to make an equal protection claim.

Similarly, *Griffin* and *Douglas* refute the majority's contention that we have in the past required an absolute deprivation before subjecting wealth classifications to strict scrutiny. . . .

The right of appeal itself was not absolutely denied to those too poor to pay; but because of the cost of a transcript and of counsel, the appeal was a substantially less meaningful right for the poor than for the rich. It was on these terms that the Court found a denial of equal protection, and those terms clearly encompassed degrees of discrimination on the basis of wealth which do not amount to outright denial of the affected right or interest. . . .

Nor can we ignore the extent to which, in contrast to our prior decisions, the State is responsible for the wealth discrimination in this instance. . . .

The means for financing public education in Texas are selected and specified by the State. It is the State that has created local school districts, and tied educational funding to the local property tax and thereby to local district wealth.

Regents of the University of California v. Bakke: Affirmative Action

Affirmative action programs are intended to help rectify the racial, sexual, and socioeconomic inequalities in our society. Yet critics of affirmative action contend that it violates the principle of equality by showing preference to members of certain groups. The controversy over affirmative action came to a head in the famous Supreme Court case, *Regents of the University of California v. Bakke.*

Allan Bakke is a white man who applied for admission to the medical school at the University of California at Davis. Only a tiny percentage of doctors are not white. In order to help remedy this situation, Davis had an affirmative action program that set aside sixteen out of its hundred entrance places for minority students. If qualified minority students could not be found, those places were not to be filled. In addition to the special admission process, minority students were free to compete through the regular admission process for one of the unrestricted eighty-four positions. Bakke was refused admission, but he sued the University of California, contending that he had been discriminated against in violation of both the 1964 Civil Rights Act and the equal protection clause of the Constitution. He argued that he would have won admission if those sixteen places had not been withdrawn from open competition and reserved for minority students. The University of California did not deny this, but contended that its program was legally permissible and socially necessary.

A badly divided Supreme Court reached a compromise. Although striking down rigid quotas for minority applicants, it also held that universities need not be color-blind in their admissions policies but may instead consider racial diversity as a goal in selecting students. Justice Powell delivered the opinion of the court, while Justice Brennan dissented in part.

Mr. Justice Powell: Although many of the Framers of the Fourteenth Amendment conceived of its primary function as bridging the vast distance between members of the Negro race and the white "majority," the

438 U. S. 265 (1978).

Amendment itself was framed in universal terms, without reference to color, ethnic origin, or condition of prior [servitude.] . . .

Over the past 30 years, this Court has embarked upon the crucial mission of interpreting the Equal Protection Clause with the view of assuring to all persons "the protection of equal laws" in a Nation confronting a legacy of slavery and racial discrimination. . . .

Petitioner [U. C. Davis] urges us to adopt for the first time a more restrictive view [and] hold that discrimination against members of the white "majority" cannot be suspect if its purpose can be characterized as "benign." [But it] is far too late to argue that the guarantee of equal protection to *all* persons permits the recognition of special wards entitled to a degree of protection greater than that accorded others. . . .

The concepts of "majority" and "minority" necessarily reflect temporary arrangements and political judgments. The white "majority" itself is composed of various minority groups, most of which can lay claim to a history of prior discrimination at the hands of the state and private individuals. Not all of these groups can receive preferential treatment and corresponding judicial tolerance of distinctions drawn in terms of race and nationality, for then the only "majority" left would be a new minority of White Anglo-Saxon Protestants. There is no principled basis for deciding which groups would merit "heightened judicial solicitude" and which would not. . . .

Moreover, there are serious problems of justice connected with the idea of preference itself. . . . Preferential programs may only reinforce common stereotypes holding that certain groups are unable to achieve success without special protection based on a factor having no relationship to individual worth. . . . There is [also] a measure of inequity in forcing innocent persons in respondent's position to bear the burdens of redressing grievances not of their making.

In this case, [there] has been no determination by the legislature or a responsible administrative agency that the University engaged in a discriminatory practice requiring remedial efforts. . . . [When] a classification denies an individual opportunities or benefits enjoyed by others solely because of his race or ethnic background, it must be regarded as suspect.

[The] special admissions program purports to serve the purposes of: (i) "reducing the historic deficit of traditionally disfavored minorities in medical schools and the medical profession"; (ii) countering the effects of societal discrimination; (iii) increasing the number of physicians who will practice in communities currently underserved; and (iv) obtaining the educational benefits that flow from an ethnically diverse student body. It is necessary to decide which, if any, of these purposes is substantial enough to support the use of a suspect classification.

A. If petitioner's purpose is to assure within its student body some specified percentage of a particular group merely because of its race or ethnic origin, such preferential purpose must be rejected not as insubstantial but as facially invalid. Preferring members of any one group for no reason other than race or ethnic origin is discrimination for its own sake. This the Constitution forbids.

B. The State certainly has a legitimate and substantial interest in ameliorating, or eliminating where feasible, the disabling effects of identified discrimination. . . . We have never approved a classification that aids persons perceived as members of relatively victimized groups at the expense of other innocent individuals in the absence of judicial, legislative, or administrative findings of constitutional or statutory violations. . . . Petitioner does not purport to have made, and is in no position to make, such findings. . . .

Hence, the purpose of helping certain groups whom the faculty of the Davis Medical School perceived as victims of "societal discrimination" does not justify a classification that imposes disadvantages upon persons like respondent, who bear no responsibility for whatever harm the beneficiaries of the special admissions program are thought to have suffered. . . .

C. Petitioner identifies, as another purpose of its program, improving the delivery of health care services to communities currently underserved. . . . It may be correct to assume that some of them will carry out this intention, and that it is more likely they will practice in minority communities than the average white doctor. . . . An applicant of whatever race who has demonstrated his concern for disadvantaged minorities in the past and who declares that practice in such a community is his primary professional goal would be more likely to contribute to alleviation of the medical shortage than one who is chosen entirely on the basis of race and disadvantage. . . .

D. The fourth goal asserted by petitioner is the attainment of a diverse student body. . . . Physicians serve a heterogeneous population. An otherwise qualified medical student with a particular background—whether it be ethnic, geographic, culturally advantaged or disadvantaged—may bring to a professional school of medicine experiences, outlooks and ideas that enrich the training of its student body and better equip its graduates to render with understanding their vital service to humanity.

Ethnic diversity, however, is only one element in a range of factors a university properly may consider in attaining the goal of a heterogeneous student body. . . . [The] diversity that furthers a compelling state interest encompasses a far broader array of qualifications and characteristics of which racial or ethnic origin is but a single though important element. Petitioner's special admissions program, focused *solely* on ethnic diversity, would hinder rather than further attainment of genuine diversity. . . .

The experience of other university admissions programs, which take race into account in achieving the educational diversity valued by the First Amendment, demonstrates that the assignment of a fixed number of places to a minority group is not a necessary means toward that end. An illuminating example is found in the Harvard College program.

In such an admissions program, race or ethnic background may be deemed a "plus" in a particular applicant's file, yet it does not insulate the individual from comparison with all [others]. . . . This kind of program treats each applicant as an individual in the admissions process. The applicant who loses out [to] another candidate receiving a "plus" on the basis of ethnic background will not have been foreclosed from all consideration [simply] because he was not the right color or had the wrong surname. . . .

It has been suggested that an admissions program which considers race only as one factor is simply a subtle and more sophisticated—but no less effective—means of according racial preference than the Davis program. A facial intent to discriminate, however, is evident [in] this case. No such facial infirmity exists in an admissions program where race or ethnic background is simply one element—to be weighed fairly against other elements—in the selection process. . . .

[W]hen a State's distribution of benefits or imposition of burden hinges on the color of a person's skin or ancestry, that individual is entitled to a demonstration that the challenged classification is necessary to promote a substantial state interest. Petitioner has failed to carry this burden. . . .

In enjoining petitioner from ever considering the race of any applicant, however, the courts below failed to recognize that the State has a substantial interest that legitimately may be served by a properly devised admissions program involving the competitive consideration of race and ethnic origin. For this reason, so much of the California court's judgment as enjoins petitioner from any consideration of the race of any applicant must be reversed.

Mr. Justice Brennan, concurring in the judgment and dissenting in part: Since we conclude that the [program] is constitutional, we would reverse the judgment below in all respects. Mr. Justice Powell agrees that some uses of race in university admissions are permissible and, therefore, he joins with us to make five votes reversing the judgment below insofar as it prohibits the University from establishing race-conscious programs in the future. . . .

[E]ven today officially sanctioned discrimination is not a thing of the past. Against this background, claims that law must be "color-blind" or that the datum of race is no longer relevant to public policy must be seen as aspiration rather than as description of reality. This is not to denigrate aspiration; for reality rebukes us that race has too often been used by those who would stigmatize and oppress minorities. Yet we cannot [let] color blindness become myopia which masks the reality that many "created equal" have been treated within our lifetimes as inferior both by the law and by their fellow citizens. . . .

[A] government practice or statute which restricts "fundamental rights" or which contain "suspect classifications" is to be subjected to "strict scrutiny." . . . But no fundamental right is involved here. . . . Nor do whites as a class have any of the "traditional indicia of suspectness: the class is not saddled with such disabilities, or subjected to such a history of purposeful unequal treatment, or relegated to such a position of political powerlessness as to command extraordinary protection from the majoritarian political process." . . .

Moreover, [this] is not a case where racial classifications are "irrelevant and therefore prohibited." Nor has anyone suggested that the University's purposes contravene the cardinal principle that racial classifications that stigmatize—because they are drawn on the presumption that one race is inferior to another or because they put the weight of government behind racial hatred and separatism—are invalid without more. . . .

Davis had a sound basis for believing that the problem of underrepresentation of minorities was substantial and chronic and that the problem was attributable to handicaps imposed on minority applicants by past and present racial discrimination. Until at least 1973, the practice of medicine in this country [was] largely the prerogative of whites. . . .

Davis clearly could conclude that the serious and persistent underrepresentation [is] the result of handicaps under which minority applicants labor as a consequence of a background of deliberate, purposeful discrimination against minorities in education and in society generally, as well as in the medical profession. . . .

The habit of discrimination and the cultural tradition of race prejudice [were] not immediately dissipated [by *Brown I*]. Rather, massive official and private resistance prevented, and to a lesser extent still prevents, attainment of equal opportunity in education at all levels and in the professions. The generation of minority students applying to Davis Medical School since it opened in 1968—most of whom were born before or about the time *Brown I* was decided—clearly have been victims of this discrimination. Judicial decrees recognizing discrimination in public education in California testify to the fact of widespread discrimination suffered by California-born minority applicants; many minority group members living in California, moreover, were born and reared in school districts in southern States segregated by law. [T]he conclusion is inescapable that applicants to medical school must be few indeed who endured the effects of de jure segregation, the resistance to *Brown I*, or the equally debilitating pervasive private discrimination fostered by our long history of official discrimination, and yet come to the starting line with an education equal to whites.

It is not even claimed that Davis' program in any way operates to stigmatize or single out any discrete and insular, or even any identifiable, nonminority group. Nor will harm comparable to that imposed upon racial minorities by exclusion or separation on grounds of race be the likely result of the program. It does not, for example, establish an exclusive preserve for minority [students]. Rather, its purpose is to overcome the effects of segregation by bringing the races together. True, whites are excluded from participation in the special admissions program, but this fact only operates to reduce the number of whites to be admitted in the regular admissions program in order to permit admission of a reasonable percentage—less than their proportion of the California population—of otherwise underrepresented qualified minority applicants.

Nor was Bakke in any sense stamped as inferior by [rejection].

Unlike discrimination against racial minorities, the use of racial preferences for remedial purposes does not inflict a pervasive injury upon individual whites in the sense that wherever they go or whatever they do there is a significant likelihood that they will be treated as second-class citizens because of their color. This distinction does not mean that the exclusion of a white resulting from the preferential use of race is not sufficiently serious to require justification; but it does mean that the injury inflicted by such a policy is not distinguishable from disadvantages caused by a wide range of government actions, none of which has ever been thought impermissible for that reason alone.

In addition, there is simply no evidence that the Davis program discriminates intentionally or unintentionally against any minority group which it purports to benefit. The program does not establish a quota in the invidious sense of a ceiling on the number of minority applicants to be admitted. Nor can the program reasonably be regarded as stigmatizing the program's beneficiaries or their race as inferior. The Davis program does not simply advance less qualified applicants; rather, it compensates applicants, whom it is uncontested are fully qualified to study medicine, for educational disadvantage which it was reasonable to conclude was a product of state-fostered discrimination. Once admitted, these students must satisfy the same degree [requirements]; they are taught by the same faculty in the same classes; and their performance is evaluated by the same standards by which regularly admitted students are judged. . . . We disagree with the lower courts' conclusion that the Davis program's use of race was unreasonable in light of its objectives. First, as petitioner argues, there are no practical means by which it could achieve its ends in the foreseeable future without the use of race-conscious measures. . . .

Second, [the] program does not simply equate minority status with disadvantage. Rather, Davis considers [each] applicant's personal history to determine whether he or she has likely been disadvantaged by racial discrimination. The record makes clear that only minority applicants likely to have been isolated from the mainstream of American life are considered in the special [program].

Finally, Davis' special admissions program cannot be said to violate the Constitution simply because it has set aside a predetermined number of places for qualified minority applicants rather than using minority status as a positive factor to be considered in evaluating the applications of disadvantaged minority applicants. For purposes of constitutional adjudication, there is no difference between the two approaches.

PART VI Justice, Community, and Gender

Republic

Plato

Plato wrote the *Republic* about twenty years after Socrates' death. It presents a conversation taking place twenty-five or thirty years earlier between Socrates and several other discussants, including Plato's brothers Glaucon and Adeimantus. The most widely accepted scholarly view is that the *Republic* uses the character of Socrates as a literary device for expounding Plato's own views, which were not necessarily those of the historical Socrates. An exploration of the nature of justice both in the individual and in the city, the *Republic* is Plato's masterpiece and generally considered a classic of both philosophy and literature. (See Section I for more information on Plato's life and works.)

BOOK III

The Guardians

[Socrates has begun his discussion of the ideal city and turns now to the question of who the rulers of the city shall be. He has already mentioned the class of guardians who are to protect and defend the city. From this group, the rulers of the city are to be selected, while the remaining guardians will be their helpers or auxiliaries.—eds.]

. . .Very well, I said. Shall we choose as our text topic of discussion which of these same men shall rule, and which be ruled?—Why not?

Now it is obvious that the rulers must be older men and that the younger must be ruled.—Obviously.

And that the rulers must be the best of them?—That too.

Translated by G. M. A. Grube. Reprinted from *Plato's Republic* (Indianapolis: Hackett Publishing Co., 1974) by permission of the publisher.

The best farmers are those who have to the highest degree the qualities required for farming?—Yes.

Now as the rulers must be the best among the guardians, they must have to the highest degree the qualities required to guard the city?—Yes.

And for this they must be intelligent, able, and also care for the city?—That is so.

Now one cares most for that which one loves.—Necessarily.

And one loves something most when one believes that what is good for it is good for oneself, and that when it is doing well the same is true of oneself, and so with the opposite.—Quite so, he said.

We must therefore select from among our guardians those who, as we test them, hold throughout their lives to the belief that it is right to pursue eagerly what they believe to be to the advantage of the city, and who are in no way willing to do what is not.—Yes, for they are good men.

I think we must observe them at all ages to see whether they are guardians of this principle, and make sure that they cannot be tempted or forced to discard or forget the belief that they must do what is best for the city.—What, he said, do you mean by discarding?

I will tell you, I said. I think the discarding of a belief is either voluntary or involuntary; voluntary when the belief is false, and as a result of learning one changes one's mind, involuntary when the belief is true.— I understand the voluntary discarding, but not the involuntary.

Really? Do you think that men are unwilling to be deprived of good things, but willingly deprived of bad things? Is not untruth and missing the truth a bad thing, while to be truthful is good? And is not to have a true opinion to be truthful?—You are right, he said, and people are unwilling to be deprived of a true opinion.

But they can be so deprived by theft, or compulsion, or under a spell?—I do not understand even now.

I fear I must be talking like a tragic poet! I apply the word "theft" to those who change their mind or those who forget, not realizing that time or argument has robbed them of their belief. Do you understand now?—Yes.

By compulsion I mean those whom pain or suffering causes to change their mind.— That too I understand and you are right.

Those under a spell I think you would agree are those who change their mind because they are bewitched by pleasure or fear.—It seems to me, he said, that anything which deceives bewitches.

As I said just now, we must find out who are the best guardians of their belief that they must always do whatever they think to be in the best interest of the city. We must keep them under observation from childhood and set them tasks which would most easily lead one to forget this belief, or to be deceived. We must select the one who keeps on remembering and is not easily deceived, the other we will reject. Do you agree?— Yes.

We must also subject them to labours, sufferings, and contests in which to observe this.—Right.

Then, I said, for the third kind we must observe how they face bewitchment. Like those who lead colts into noise and tumult to see if they are fearful, so we must expose our young to fears and pleasures to test them, much more thoroughly than one tests gold in fire, and see whether a guardian is hard to bewitch and behaves well in all circumstances as a good guardian of himself and of the cultural education he has received, always showing himself a gracious and harmonious personality, the best man for himself and for the city. The one who is thus tested as a child, as a youth, and as an adult, and comes out of it untainted, is to be made a ruler as well as a guardian. He is to be honoured both in life and after death and receive the most esteemed rewards in the form of tombs and memorials. The one who does not prove himself in this way is to be rejected. It seems to me, Glaucon, I said, that rulers and guardians must be selected and established in some such way as this, to speak in a general way and not in exact detail.—I also think it must be done in some such way.

These are the men whom it is most correct to call proper guardians, so that the enemies without shall not have the power, and their friends within shall not have the desire, to harm the city. Those young men whom we have called guardians hitherto we shall call auxiliaries to help the rulers in their decisions.—I agree.

What device could we find to make our rulers, or at any rate the rest of the city, believe us if we told them a noble fiction, one of those necessary untruths of which we have spoken?—What kind of fiction?

Nothing new, I said, but a Phoenician story which the poets say has happened in many places and made people believe them; it has not happened among us, though it might, and it will take a great deal of persuasion to have it believed.

You seem hesitant to tell your story, he said.

When you hear it you will realize that I have every reason to hesitate.

Speak without fear.

This is the story—yet I don't know that I am bold enough to tell it or what words I shall use. I shall first try to persuade the rulers and the soldiers, and then the rest of the city, that the upbringing and the education we gave them, and the experience that went with them, were a dream as it were, that in fact they were then being fashioned and nurtured inside the earth, themselves and their weapons and their apparel. Then, when they were quite finished, the earth, being their mother, brought them out into the world. So even now they must take counsel for, and defend, the land in which they live as their mother and nurse, if someone attacks it, and they must think of their fellow-citizens as their earth-born brothers.

It is not for nothing that you were shy, he said, of telling your story.

Yes, I said, I had very good reason. Nevertheless, hear the rest of the tale. "All of you in the city are brothers" we shall tell him as we tell our story, "but the god who fashioned you mixed some gold in the nature of those capable of ruling because they are to be honoured most. In those who are auxiliaries he has put silver, and iron and bronze in those who are farmers and other workers. You will for the most part produce children like yourselves, but, as you are all related, a silver child will occasionally be born from a golden parent, and vice versa, and all the others from each other. So the first and most important command of the god to the rulers is that there is nothing they must guard better or watch more carefully than the mixture in the souls of the next generation. If their own offspring should be found to have iron or bronze in his nature, they must not pity him in any way, but give him the esteem appropriate to his nature; they must drive him out to join the workers and farmers. Then again, if an offspring of these is found to have gold or silver in his nature they will honour him and bring him up to join the rulers or guardians, for there is an oracle that the city will be ruined if ever it has an iron or bronze guardian." Can you suggest any device which will make our citizens believe this story?

I cannot see any way, he said, to make them believe it themselves, but the sons and later generations might, both theirs and those of other men.

Even that, I said, would help to make them care more for their city and each other, for I do understand what you mean. But let us leave this matter to later tradition. Let us now arm our earthborn and lead them forth with their rulers in charge. And as they march let them look for the best place in the city to have their camp, a site from which they could most easily control those within, if anyone is unwilling to obey the laws, and ward off any outside enemy who came like a wolf upon the flock. When they had established their camp and made the right sacrifices, let them see to their sleeping quarters, or what do you suggest?—I agree.

These must protect them adequately both in winter and summer.

Of course, he said, you mean their dwellings.

Yes, I said, dwellings for soldiers, not for money-makers.

What would you say is the difference? he asked.

I will try to tell you, I said. The most terrible and shameful thing for a shepherd is to train his dogs, who should help the flocks, in such a way that, through lack of discipline or hunger or bad habits, those very dogs maltreat the animals and behave like wolves rather than dogs.—Quite true.

We must therefore take every precaution to see that our auxiliaries, since they are the stronger, do not behave like that toward the citizens, and became cruel masters instead of kindly allies.—We must watch this.

And a really good education would endow them with the greatest caution in this regard?—But surely they have had that.

And I said: Perhaps we should not assert this dogmatically, my dear Glaucon. What we can assert is what we were saying just now, that they must have the correct education, whatever that is, in order to attain the greatest degree of gentleness toward each other and toward those whom they are protecting.—Right.

Besides this education, an intelligent man might say that they must have the amount of housing and of other property which would not prevent them from being the best guardians and would not encourage them to maltreat the other citizens.—That would be true.

Consider then, said I, whether they should live in some way as this if they are to be the kind of men we described: First, not one of them must possess any private property beyond what is essential. Further, none of them should have a house or a storeroom which anyone who wishes is not permitted to enter. Whatever moderate and courageous warrior-athletes require will be provided by taxation upon the other citizens as a salary for their guardianship, no more and no less than they need over the year. They will have common messes and live together as soldiers in a camp. We shall tell them that the gold and silver they always have in their nature as a gift from the gods makes the possession of human gold unnecessary, indeed that it is impious for them to defile this divine possession by any admixture of the human kind of gold, because many an impious deed is committed in connection with the currency of the majority, and their own must remain pure. For them alone among the city's population it is unlawful to touch or handle gold or silver; they must not be under the same roof with it, or wear any, or drink from gold or silver goblets; in this way they may preserve themselves and the city. If they themselves acquire private land and houses and currency, they will be household managers and farmers instead of guardians, hostile masters of the other citizens instead of their allies; they will spend their whole life hating and being hated, plotting and being plotted against; they will be much more afraid of internal than of external enemies, and they will rush themselves and their city very close to ruin. For all these

reasons, I said, let us say that the guardians must be provided with housing and other matters in this way, and these are the laws we shall establish.

Certainly, said Glaucon.

BOOK IV

The Guardians and Happiness

Adeimantus took up the argument and said: What defence, Socrates, would you offer against the charge that you are not making your guardians very happy, and that through their own fault? The city is really in their power, yet they derive no good from this. Others own land, build grand and beautiful houses, acquire furnishings appropriate to them, make their own private sacrifices to the gods, entertain, also, as you mentioned just now, have gold and silver and all the possessions which are thought to belong to people who will be happy. One might well say that your guardians are simply settled in the city like paid mercenaries, with nothing to do but to watch over it.

Yes, said I. Moreover, they work for their keep and get no extra wages as the others do, so that if they want to leave the city privately they cannot do so; they have nothing to give their mistresses, nothing to spend in whatever other way they wish, as men do who are considered happy. You have omitted these and other such things from the charge.—Let these accusations be added, he said.

Now you ask what defence we shall offer?—Yes.

I think we shall discover what to say if we follow the same path as before, I said. We shall say that it would not be at all surprising if these men too were very happy. In any case, in establishing our city, we are not aiming to make any one group outstandingly happy, but to make the whole city so, as far as possible. We thought that in such a city we would most easily find justice, find injustice in a badly governed one, and then decide what we have been looking for all the same. Now we think we are fashioning the happy city not by separating a few people in it and making them happy, but by making the whole city so. We shall look at the opposite kind of city presently. If someone came to us while we were painting a statue* and objected because we did not apply the finest colours to the finest parts of the body, for the eyes are the most beautiful part, and they are not made purple but black, we should appear to offer a reasonable defence if we said: "My good sir, do not think that we must make the eyes so beautiful that they no longer appear to be eyes at all, and so with the other parts, but look to see whether by dealing with each part appropriately we are making the whole statue beautiful." And so now, do not force us to give our guardians the kind of happiness which would make them anything but guardians.

We know how to clothe our farmers too in purple robes, surround them with gold and tell them to work the land at their pleasure, and how to settle our potters on couches by the fire, feasting and passing the wine, put their wheel by them and tell them to make pots as much as they want; we know how to make all the others also happy in the same way, so that the whole city is happy. Do not exhort us to do this, however. If we do, the farmer will not be a farmer, nor the potter a potter; nor would anyone else fulfill any of the functions which make up the state. For the others this is less important: if shoemakers become inferior and corrupt, and claim to be what they are not, the state is not in peril, but, if the guardians of our laws and city only appear to be guardians and are not, you surely see that they destroy the city utterly, as they alone have the opportunity to govern it well and to make it happy.

If then we are making true guardians who are least likely to work wickedness upon the city, whereas our accuser makes some farmers into banqueters, happy as at some festival but not in a city, he would be talking about something else than a city. We should examine then, with this in mind, whether our aim in establishing our guardians should be to give them the greatest happiness, or whether we should in this matter look to the whole city and see how its greatest happiness can be secured. We must compel and persuade the auxiliaries and the guardians to be excellent performers of their own task, and so with all the others. As the whole city grows and is well governed, we must leave it to nature to provide each group with its share of happiness. . . .

Justice

[Socrates now turns to the question of what makes the city just. After distinguishing justice from wisdom (which resides in the guardian class), from bravery (which is characteristic of the auxiliaries), and from moderation (which is the acceptance of all classes of the rule of the guardians), Socrates offers his definition of justice in the city and in the individual.—eds.]

Well, son of Ariston, I said, your city might now be said to be established. The next step is for you to look inside it with what light you can procure, to call upon your brother and Polemarchus and the others, if we can somehow see where justice resides in it, and where injustice, what the difference is between them, and which of the two the man who intends to be happy should possess, whether gods and men recognize it or not.

Nonsense, said Glaucon. You promised to look for them yourself because you said it was impious for you not to come to the rescue of justice in every way you could.

True, I said, as you remind me; I must do so, but you must help.—We will, he said.

I hope to find it, I said, in this way. I think our city, if it is rightly founded, is completely good.—Necessarily so, he said.

Clearly then it is wise, brave, moderate, and just.*—Clearly.

---

*There is no doubt that the Greeks painted their statues, at times only certain parts of them—G. M. A. Grube.

---

*The doctrine of the four cardinal virtues is often met with in Plato. It seems to be referred to here as well

Therefore whichever of these we find in the city, the rest will be what we have not found?—You mean?

As with any four things, if we were looking for any one of them in anything, if we first recognize it, that would be enough, but if we recognize the other three first, then by that very fact we recognize what we are looking for. For clearly it can be no other than what is left.—Correct, he said. . . .

Very well, I said. We have now found three of the four in the city, as far as our present discussion takes us. What would the remaining kind be which still makes the city share in virtue? Or is it clear that this is justice?—Quite clear.

So now we must concentrate our attention like hunters surrounding a coppice, lest justice escape us and vanish without our seeing it, for obviously it is somewhere around here. Look eagerly, now, in case you see it before I do, and tell me. . . .

Well, I said, listen whether I am talking sense. I think that justice is the very thing, or some form of the thing which, when we were beginning to found our city, we said had to be established throughout. We stated, and often repeated, if you remember, that everyone must pursue one occupation of those in the city, that for which his nature best fitted him.—Yes, we kept saying that.

Further, we have heard many people say, and have often said ourselves, that justice is to perform one's own task and not to meddle with that of others.—We have said that.

This then, my friend, I said, when it happens, is in some way justice, to do one's own job. And do you know what I take to be a proof of this?—No, tell me.

I think what is left over of those things we have been investigating, after moderation and courage and wisdom have been found, was that which made it possible for those three qualities to appear in the city and to continue as long as it is present. We also said that what remained after we found the other three was justice.—It had to be.

And surely, I said, if we had to decide which of the four will make the city good by its presence, it would be hard to judge whether it is a common belief among the rulers and the ruled, or the preservation among the soldiers of a law-inspired belief as to the nature of what is, and what is not, to be feared, or the knowledge and guardianship of the rulers, or whether it is, above all, the presence of this fourth in child and woman, slave and free, artisan, ruler and subject, namely that each man, a unity in himself, performed his own task and was not meddling with that of others.—How could this not be hard to judge?

It seems then that the capacity for each in the city to perform his own task rivals wisdom, moderation, and courage as a source of excellence for the city.—It certainly does.

You would then describe justice as a rival to them for excellence in the city?—Most certainly.

Look at it this way and see whether you agree: you will order your rulers to act as judges in the courts of the city?—Surely.

And will their exclusive aim in delivering judgment not be that no citizen should have what belongs to another or be deprived of what is his own?—That would be their aim.

That being just?—Yes.

In some way then possession of one's own and the performance of one's own task could be agreed to be justice.*—That is so.

Consider then whether you agree with me in this: if a carpenter attempts to do the work of a cobbler, or a cobbler that of a carpenter, and they exchange their tools and the esteem that goes with the job, or the same man tries to do both, and all the other exchanges are made, do you think that this does any great harm to the city?—No.

But I think that when one who is by na-

---

known. *Hosiotês* or piety is often a candidate for a place in the list.—G. M. A. Grube.

*The difference between moderation and justice seems clear in the Greek. The city is moderate if each group is satisfied with its position in the state, and they all agree as to who should rule. Justice is more positive, it implies that each group actually performs its function in the state. Moreover, those who are dissatisfied with their own are likely to interfere with the work which properly belongs to others.—G. M. A. Grube.

ture a worker or some other kind of money-maker is puffed up by wealth, or by the mob, or by his own strength, or some other such thing, and attempts to enter the warrior class, or one of the soldiers tries to enter the group of counsellors and guardians, though he is unworthy of it, and these exchange their tools and the public esteem, or when the same man tries to perform all these jobs together, then I think you will agree that these exchanges and this meddling bring the city to ruin.—They certainly do.

The meddling and exchange between the three established orders does very great harm to the city and would most correctly be called wickedness.—Very definitely.

And you would call the greatest wickedness worked against one's own city injustice?—Of course.

That then is injustice. And let us repeat that the doing of one's own job by the moneymaking, auxiliary, and guardian groups, when each group is performing its own task in the city, is the opposite, it is justice and makes the city just.—I agree with you that this is so.

Do not let us, I said, take this as quite final yet. If we find that this quality, when existing in each individual man, is agreed there too to be justice, then we can assent to this—for what can we say?—but if not, we must look for something else. For the present, let us complete that examination which we thought we should make, that if we tried to observe justice in something larger which contains it, this would make it easier to observe it in the individual. We thought that this larger thing was a city, and so we established the best city we could, knowing well that justice would be present in the good city. It has now appeared to us there, so let us now transfer it to the individual and, if it corresponds, all will be well. But if it is seen to be something different in the individual, then we must go back to the city and examine this new notion of justice. By thus comparing and testing the two, we might make justice light up like fire from the rubbing of firesticks, and when it has become clear, we

shall fix it firmly in our own minds.—You are following the path we set, and we must do so.

Well now, when you apply the same name to a thing whether it is big or small, are these two instances of it like or unlike with regard to that to which the same name applies?—They are alike in that, he said.

So the just man and the just city will be no different but alike as regards the very form of justice.—Yes, they will be.

Now the city was thought to be just when the three kinds of men within it each performed their own task, and it was moderate and brave and wise because of some other qualities and attitudes of the same groups.—True.

And we shall therefore deem it right, my friend, that the individual have the same parts in his own soul, and through the same qualities in those parts will correctly be given the same names.—That must be so. . . .

We have now made our difficult way through a sea of argument to reach this point, and we have fairly agreed that the same kinds of parts, and the same number of parts, exist in the soul of each individual as in our city.—That is so.

It necessarily follows that the individual is wise in the same way, and in the same part of himself, as the city.—Quite so.

And the part which makes the individual brave is the same as that which makes the city brave, and in the same manner, and everything which makes for virtue* is the same in both?—That necessarily follows.

Moreover, Glaucon, I think we shall say that a man is just in the same way as the city is just.—That too is inevitable.

We have surely not forgotten that the city

---

*Plato uses the word *aretê* in two somewhat different senses. It can refer to *the* quality, or combination of qualities, which makes a person, an animal, or even an object good at doing something which nothing else can do, or at least do as well and it is then best translated by excellence. Each of the virtues, however, is also an *aretê*, and it is then best translated "virtue." Of course, the two senses merge at times; we may note, however, that in this discussion Plato does not use the term to describe the individual virtues.—G. M. A. Grube.

was just because each of the three classes in it was fulfilling its own task.—I do not think, he said, that we have forgotten that.

We must remember then that each one of us within whom each part is fulfilling its own task will himself be just and do his own work.—We must certainly remember this.

Therefore it is fitting that the reasonable part should rule, it being wise and exercising foresight on behalf of the whole soul, and for the spirited part to obey it and be its ally.—Quite so. . . .

We have then completely realized the dream we had when we suspected that, by the grace of god, we came upon a principle and mould of justice right at the beginning of the founding of our city.—Very definitely.

Indeed, Glaucon—and this is why it is useful—it was a sort of image of justice, namely that it was right for one who is by nature a cobbler to cobble and to do nothing else, and for the carpenter to carpenter, and so with the others.—Apparently.

And justice was in truth, it appears, something like this. It does not lie in a man's external actions, but in the way he acts within himself, really concerned with himself and his inner parts. He does not allow each part of himself to perform the work of another, or the sections of his soul to meddle with one another. He orders what are in the true sense of the word his own affairs well; he is master of himself, puts things in order, is his own friend, harmonizes the three parts like the limiting notes of a musical scale, the high, the low, and the middle, and any others there may be between. He binds them all together, and himself from a plurality becomes a unity. Being thus moderate and harmonious, he now performs any action, be it about the acquisition of wealth, the care of his body, some public actions, or private contract. In all these fields he thinks the just and beautiful action, which he names as such, to be that which preserves this inner harmony and indeed helps to achieve it, wisdom to be the knowledge which oversees this action, an unjust action to be that which always destroys it, and igno-

rance the belief which oversees that.—Socrates you are altogether right.

Very well, I said, we would then not be thought to be lying if we claim that we have found the just man, the just city, and the justice that is in them.—No by Zeus, we would not. . . .

BOOK V

Sexual Equality Among the Guardians

[Socrates now argues that differences between the sexes are not relevant to politics and that women in the guardian class should have the same education, share in the same duties, and partake equally in war.—eds.]

Do we think that the wives of our guardian watchdogs should join in whatever guardian duties the men fulfill, join them in the hunt, and do everything else in common, or should we keep the women at home as unable to do so because they must bear and rear their young, and leave to the men the labour and the whole care of the flock?

All things, he said, should be done in common, except that the women are physically weaker and the men stronger.

And is it possible, I asked, to make use of living creatures for the same purposes unless you give them the same upbringing and education?—It is not possible.

So if we use the women for the same tasks as the men, they must be taught the same things.—Yes.

Now we gave the men artistic and physical culture.—Yes.

So we must give both also to the women, as well as training in war, and use them for the same tasks.—That seems to follow from what you say.

Perhaps, I said, many of the things we are saying, being contrary to custom, would stir up ridicule, if carried out in practice in the way we are telling them.—They certainly would, he said.

What, I asked, is the most ridiculous feature you see in this? Or is it obviously that women should exercise naked in the palaestra along with the men, not only the young women but the older women too, as the old men do in the gymnasia when their bodies are wrinkled and not pleasant to look at and yet they are fond of physical exercise?—Yes, by Zeus, he said, it would appear ridiculous as things stand now.

Surely, I said, now that we have started on this argument, we must not be afraid of all the jokes of the kind that the wits will make about such a change in physical and artistic culture, and not least about the women carrying arms and riding horses.—You are right, he said.

As we have begun this discussion we must go on to the tougher part of the law and beg these people not to practise their own trade of comedy at our expense but to be serious and to remember that it is not very long since the Greeks thought it ugly and ridiculous, as the majority of barbarians still do, for men to be seen naked. When first the Cretans and then the Lacedaemonians started their physical training, the wits of those days could have ridiculed it all, or do you not think so?—I do.

But I think that after it was found in practice to be better to strip than to cover up all those parts, then the spectacle ceased to be looked on as ridiculous because reasonable argument had shown that it was best. This showed that it is foolish to think anything ridiculous except what is bad, or to try to raise a laugh at any other spectacle than that of ignorance and evil as being ridiculous, as it is foolish to be in earnest about any other standard of beauty than that of the good.—Most certainly.

Must we not first agree whether our proposals are possible or not? And we must grant an opportunity for discussion to anyone who, in jest or seriously, wishes to argue the point whether female human nature can share all the tasks of the male sex, or none at all, or some but not others, and to which of the two waging war belongs. Would this not be the best beginning and likely to lead to the best conclusion?—Certainly.

Do you then want us to dispute among ourselves on behalf of those others, lest the other side of the argument fall by default?—There is nothing to stop us.

Let us then speak on their behalf: "Socrates and Glaucon, there is no need for others to argue with you. You yourselves, when you began to found your city, agreed that each person must pursue the one task for which he is fitted by nature." I think we did agree to this, of course.—"Can you deny that a woman is by nature very different from a man?"—Of course not. "And is it not proper to assign a different task to each according to their nature?"—Certainly. "How then are you not wrong and contradicting yourselves when you say that men and women must do the same things, when they have quite separate natures?" Do you have any defence against that argument, my good friend?

That is not very easy offhand, he said, but I ask and beg you to explain the argument on our side, whatever it is. . . .

We are bravely, but in a disputatious and verbal fashion, pursuing the principle that a nature which is not the same must not engage in the same pursuits, but when we assigned different tasks to a different nature and the same to the same nature, we did not examine at all what kind of difference and sameness of nature we had in mind and in what regard we were distinguishing them.—No, we did not look into that.

We might therefore just as well, it seems, ask ourselves whether the nature of bald men and long-haired men is the same and not opposite, and then, agreeing that they are opposite, if we allow bald men to be cobblers, not allow long-haired men to be, or again if long-haired men are cobblers, not allow the others to be.—That would indeed be ridiculous.

Is it ridiculous for any other reason than because we did not fully consider their same or different natures in every respect but we were only watching the kind of difference and sameness which applied to those particular pursuits? For example, a male and a female physician, we said, have the same nature of soul, or do you not think so?—I do.

But a physician and a carpenter have a different nature?—Surely.

Therefore, I said, if the male and the female are seen to be different as regards a particular craft or other pursuit we shall say this must be assigned to one or the other. But if they seem to differ in this particular only, that the female bears children while the male begets them, we shall say that there has been no kind of proof that a woman is different from a man as regards the duties we are talking about, and we shall still believe that our guardians and their wives should follow the same pursuits.—And rightly so.

Next we shall bid anyone who holds the contrary view to instruct us in this: with regard to what craft or pursuit concerned with the establishment of the city is the nature of man and woman not the same but different?—That is right.

Someone else might very well say what you said a short time ago, that it is not easy to give an immediate reply, but that it would not be at all difficult after considering the question.—He might say that.

Do you then want us to beg the one who raises these objections to follow us to see whether we can show him that no pursuit connected with the management of the city belongs in particular to a woman?—Certainly.

Come now, we shall say to him, give us an answer: did you mean that one person had a natural ability for a certain pursuit, while another had not, when the first learned it easily, the latter with difficulty? The one, after a brief period of instruction, was able to find things out for himself form what he had learned, while the other, after much instruction, could not even remember what he had learned; the former's body adequately served his mind, while the other's physical reactions opposed his. Are there any other ways in which you distinguished the naturally gifted in each case from those who were not?—No one will say anything else.

Do you know of any occupation practised by mankind in which the male sex is not superior to the female in all these respects? Or shall we pursue the argument at length by mentioning weaving, baking cakes, cooking vegetables, tasks in which the female sex certainly seems to distinguish itself, and in which it is most laughable of all for women to be inferior to men?

What you say is true, he said, namely that one sex is much superior to the other in almost everything, yet many women are better than many men in many things, but on the whole it is as you say.

There is therefore no pursuit connected with city management which belongs to woman because she is a woman, or to a man because he is a man, but various natures are scattered in the same way among both kinds of persons. Woman by nature shares all pursuits, and so does man, but in all of them woman is a physically weaker creature than man.—Certainly.

Shall we then assign them all to men, and none to a woman?—How can we?

One woman, we shall say, is a physician, another is not, one is by nature artistic, another is not.—Quite so.

One may be athletic or warlike, while another is not warlike and has no love of athletics.—I think so.

Further, may not one woman love wisdom, another hate it, or one may be high-spirited, another be without spirit?—That too.

So one woman may have a guardian nature, the other not. Was it not a nature with these qualities which we selected among men for our male guardians too?—We did.

Therefore the nature of man and woman is the same as regards guarding the city, except in so far as she is physically weaker, and the man's nature stronger.—So it seems.

Such women must then be chosen along with such men to live with them and share their guardianship, since they are qualified and akin to them by nature.—Certainly.

Must we not assign the same pursuits to the same natures?—The same.

We have come round then to what we said before, and we agree that it is not aga ˙ ˙ nature to give to the wives of the guardians an education in the arts and physical culture.—Definitely not.

We are not legislating against nature or indulging in mere wishful thinking since the law we established is in accord with nature. It is rather the contrary present practice which is against nature as it seems.—It appears so.

Now we were to examine whether our proposals were possible and the best.—We were.

That they are possible is now agreed?—Yes.

After this we must seek agreement whether they are the best.—Clearly.

With a view to having women guardians, we should not have one kind of education to fashion the men, and another for the women, especially as they have the same nature to begin with.—No, not another.

What is your opinion of this kind of thing?—Of what?

About thinking to yourself that one man is better and another worse, or do you think that they are all alike?—Certainly not.

In the city we were establishing, do you think the guardians are made better men by the education they have received, or the cobblers who were educated for their craft?—Your question is ridiculous.

I know, said I. Well, are these guardians not the best of all the citizens?—By far.

Will then these women guardians not be the best of women?—That too by far.

Is there anything better for a city than to have the best possible men and women?—Nothing.

And it is the arts and physical culture, as we have described them, which will achieve this?—Of course.

So the institution we have established is not only possible but also the best.—That is so.

The women then must strip for their physical training, since they will be clothed in excellence. They must share in war and the other duties of the guardians about the city, and have no other occupation; the lighter duties will be assigned to them be-

cause of the weakness of their sex. The man who laughs at the sight of naked women exercising for the best of reasons is "plucking the unripe fruit of laughter", he understands nothing of what he is laughing at, it seems, nor what he is doing. For it is and always will be a fine saying that what is beneficial is beautiful, what is harmful is ugly.—Very definitely.

Let us say then that we have escaped from one wave of criticism in our discussion of the law about women, and we have not been altogether swamped when we laid it down that male and female guardians must share all their duties in common, and our argument is consistent when it states that this is both possible and beneficial. . . .

Philosophers as Kings

[The subsequent discussion turns to Socrates's position that among the guardians there should be "common ownership of wives and children." More specifically, Socrates advocates that marriages among the guardians be purely temporary and that parents not know their own children, who are to be raised communally. These measures, he believes, will create ties of family affection throughout the guardian class as a whole, thus strengthening its commonality of purpose and preventing private concerns from disrupting its unity. Although marriages are supposed to be determined by lot, in fact the rulers in Socrates's scheme secretly manipulate the system so that the most desirable parents are married more often. Socrates now addresses the question of whether his ideal city is possible.—eds.]

. . . I think, Socrates, that if one lets you talk on these subjects, you will never remember the subject you postponed before you said all this, namely, that it is possible for this city to exist and how it can be brought about. I agree that, if it existed, all the things we have mentioned would be good for the city in which they occurred, including things you are leaving out: they would be excellent fighters against an enemy because they would be least likely to desert each other, since they know each other as, and call each other by the name of, brothers, fathers, sons. Moreover, if their women joined their campaigns, whether in the same ranks or drawn up behind as reserves, either to frighten the enemy or as reinforcements, should they ever be needed, I know that this would make them quite unbeatable. I also see that a number of good things would ensue for them at home which have not been mentioned. Take it that I agree that all these things would happen as well as innumerable others, if this kind of government were to exist. Say no more on this subject but let us now try to convince ourselves of this, namely that it is possible and how it is possible. Let the rest go.

This is a sudden attack you have made upon my argument, I said, and you show no leniency towards my loitering. You may not realize that I have barely escaped from the first two waves of objections as you bring the third upon me, the biggest and most difficult to deal with. When you hear and see it you will surely be more lenient towards my natural hesitation and fear to state, and attempt thoroughly to examine, such a paradox.

The more you speak like this, he said, the less we shall let you off from telling us how this city is possible. So speak and do not waste time.

Well then, I said, we must first remember that we have come to this point while we were searching for the natures of justice and injustice.—We must, but what of it?

Nothing, but if we find out what justice is, shall we require that the just man be in no way different from that justice itself, and be like justice in every respect, or shall we be satisfied if he comes as close to it as possible, and share in it far more than others?—That will satisfy us.

It was then to have a model, I said, that we were seeking the nature of justice itself, and of the completely just man, if he should exist, and what kind of man he would be if he did, and so with injustice and the most

unjust man. Our purpose was, with these models before us, to see how they turned out as regards happiness and its opposite. Thus we would be forced to come to an agreement about ourselves, that he who was as like them as possible would also have a life most like theirs. It was not our purpose to prove that these could exist.—What you say is true.

Do you think a man is any less a good painter if, having painted a model of what the most beautiful man would be, and having rendered all the details satisfactorily in his picture, he could not prove that such a man can come into being?—By Zeus, I do not.

Well then, do we not also say that we were making a model of a good city in our argument?—Certainly.

Do you think our discussion less worthwhile if we cannot prove that it is possible to found a city such as we described?—Not at all.

And indeed, I said, that is the truth. But if we must, to please you, exert ourselves to pursue this topic, namely to show how and in what respect this might best be possible, then you in turn should agree that the same thing applies to this demonstration.—What thing?

Is it possible to realize anything in practice as it can be formulated in words or is it natural for practice to have a lesser grip on truth than theory,* even if some people do not think so? Will you first agree to this or not?—I agree.

Then do not compel me to show that the things we have described in theory can exist precisely in practice. If we are able to discover how the administration of a city can come closest to our theories, shall we say that we have found that those things are possible

---

* This sounds strange to us because we regard the practical and material world as more "true" and more real than theory; but to Plato, the unchanging Platonic Forms and such things as mathematical realities were not only more exact, but also more real and true than the world of phenomena. As these are always changing no real knowledge of them is possible, but only opinion or belief—G.M.A. Grube.

which you told us to prove so? Or will you not be satisfied with that measure of success? For I would be satisfied.—So would I.

Next, it seems, we should try to find out and to show what is now badly done in the cities which prevents them from being governed in this way, and what is the smallest change which would enable a city to reach our type of government—one change if possible, or, if not one, then two, or at any rate as few changes as insignificant in their effects as possible.—By all means.

There is one change to which I think we could point which would accomplish this. It is certainly neither small nor easy, but it is possible.—What is it?

I have now come, I said, to what we likened to the greatest wave. However, it shall be said even if, like a wave of laughter, it will simply drown me in ridicule and contempt.—Say on.

And I said: Cities will have no respite from evil, my dear Glaucon, nor will the human race, I think, unless philosophers* rule as kings in the cities, or those whom we now call kings and rulers genuinely and adequately study philosophy, until, that is, political power and philosophy coalesce, and the various natures of those who now pursue the one to the exclusion of the other are forcibly debarred from doing so. Otherwise the city we have been describing will never grow into a possibility or see the light of day. It is because I saw how very paradoxical this statement would be that I have for some time hesitated to make it. It is hard to realize that there can be no happiness, public or private, in any other city. . . .

---

* It is important to remember in this context that the word *philosophos*, which was not in common use before this time, retained its etymological meaning as a lover of truth and wisdom rather than a philosopher in our more restricted sense. Plato does not mean that the world should be ruled by pale metaphysicians from the remoteness of their studies; he is maintaining that a statesman needs to be a thinker, a lover of truth, beauty, and the Good, with a highly developed sense of values. The rest of this book and the next two are largely devoted to explaining the character and necessary training of the Platonic *philosophos*, and this includes practical experience.—G.M.A. Grube.

BOOK VII

The Allegory of the Cave

[Socrates defines the philosopher as one who has knowledge of the eternal Forms that underlie the changing objects of everyday experience. For example, the philosopher knows Beauty itself, its eternal and unchanging Form, while others can perceive only beautiful things. The highest of the Forms, knowledge of which philosophers seek, is the Form of the Good. Socrates says that he cannot describe the Good, but he compares it to the sun, the role of which in the physical world is analogous to that of the Good in the realm of the Forms. Now in Book VII, Socrates explains his view with the famous allegory of the cave.]

Next, I said, compare the effect of education and the lack of it upon our human nature to a situation like this: imagine men to be living in an underground cave-like dwelling place, which has a way up to the light along its whole width, but the entrance is a long way up. The men have been there from childhood, with their neck and legs in fetters, so that they remain in the same place and can only see ahead of them, as their bonds prevent them turning their heads. Light is provided by a fire burning some way behind and above them. Between the fire and the prisoners, some way behind them and on a higher ground, there is a path across the cave and along this a low wall has been built, like the screen at a puppet show in front of the performers who show their puppets above it.—I see it.

See then also men carrying along that wall, so that they overtop it, all kinds of artifacts, statues of men, reproductions of other animals in stone or wood fashioned in all sorts of ways, and, as is likely, some of the carriers are talking while others are silent.—This a strange picture, and strange prisoners.

They are like us, I said. So you think, in the first place, that such men could see anything of themselves and each other* except the shadows which the fire casts upon the wall of the cave in front of them?—How could they, if they have to keep their heads still throughout life?

And is not the same true of the objects carried along the wall?—Quite.

If they could converse with one another, do you not think that they would consider these shadows to be the real things?—Necessarily.

What if their prison had an echo which reached them from in front of them? Whenever one of the carriers passing behind the wall spoke, would they not think that it was the shadow passing in front of them which was talking? Do you agree?—By Zeus I do.

Altogether then I said such men would believe the truth to be nothing else than the shadows of the artifacts?—They must believe that.

Consider then what deliverance from their bonds and the curing of their ignorance would be if something like this naturally happened to them. Whenever one of them was freed, had to stand up suddenly, turn his head, walk, and look up toward the light, doing all that would give him pain, the flash of the fire would make it impossible for him to see the objects of which he had earlier seen the shadows. What do you think he would say if he was told that what he saw then was foolishness, that he was now somewhat closer to reality and turned to things that existed more fully, that he saw more correctly? If one then pointed to each of the objects passing by, asked him what each was, and forced him to answer, do you not think he would be at a loss and believe that the things which he saw earlier were truer than the things now pointed out to him?—Much truer.

If one then compelled him to look at the

fire itself, his eyes would hurt, he world turn round and flee toward those things which he could see, and think that they were in fact clearer than those now shown to him.—Quite so.

And if one were to drag him thence by force up the rough and steep path, and did not let him go before he was dragged into the sunlight, would he not be in physical pain and angry as he was dragged along? When he came into the light, with the sunlight filling his eyes, he would not be able to see a single one of the things which are now said to be true.—Not at once, certainly.

I think he would need time to get adjusted before he could see things in the world above; at first he would see shadows most easily, then reflections of men and other things in water, then the things themselves. After this he would see objects in the sky and the sky itself more easily at night, the light of the stars and the moon more easily than the sun and the light of the sun during the day.—Of course.

Then, at last, he would be able to see the sun, not images of it in water or in some alien place, but the sun itself in its own place, and be able to contemplate it.—That must be so.

After this he would reflect that it is the sun which provides the seasons and the years, which governs everything in the visible world, and is also in some way the cause of those other things which he used to see.—Clearly that would be the next stage.

What then? As he reminds himself of his first dwelling place, of the wisdom there and of his fellow prisoners, would he not reckon himself happy for the change, and pity them?—Surely.

And if the men below had praise and honours from each other, and prizes for the man who saw most clearly the shadows that passed before them, and who could best remember which usually came earlier and which later, and which came together and thus could most ably prophesy the future, do you think our man would desire those rewards and envy those who were honoured and held power among the prisoners, or

---

* These shadows of themselves and each other are never mentioned again. A Platonic myth or parable, like a Homeric simile, is often elaborated in considerable detail. These contribute to the vividness of the picture but often have no other function, and it is a mistake to look for any symbolic meaning in them. It is the general picture that matters.—G.M.A. Grube.

would he feel, as Homer put it, that he certainly wished to be "serf to another man without possessions upon the earth"* and go through any suffering, rather than share their opinions and live as they do?—Quite so, he said, I think he would rather suffer anything.

Reflect on this too, I said. If this man went down into the cave again and sat down in the same seat, would his eyes not be filled with darkness, coming suddenly out of the sunlight?—They certainly would.

And if he had to contend again with those who had remained prisoners in recognizing those shadows while his sight was affected and his eyes had not settled down—and the time for this adjustment would not be short—would he not be ridiculed? Would it not be said that he had returned from his upward journey with his eyesight spoiled, and that it was not worthwhile even to attempt to travel upward? As for the man who tried to free them and lead them upward, if they could somehow lay their hands on him and kill him, they would do so.—They certainly would.

This whole image, my dear Glaucon, I said, must be related to what we said before. The realm of the visible should be compared to the prison dwelling, and the fire inside it to the power of the sun. If you interpret the upward journey and the contemplation of things above as the upward journey of the soul to the intelligible realm, you will grasp what I surmise since you were keen to hear it. Whether it is true or not only the god knows, but this is how I see it, namely that in the intelligible world the Form of the Good is the last to be seen, and with difficulty; when seen it must be reckoned to be for all the cause of all that is right and beautiful, to have produced in the visible world both light and the fount of light, while in the intelligible world it is itself that which produces and controls truth and intelligence, and he who is to act intelligently

in public or in private must see it.—I share your thought as far as I am able.

Come then, share with me this thought also: do not be surprised that those who have reached this point are unwilling to occupy themselves with human affairs, and that their souls are always pressing upward to spend their time there, for this is natural if things are as our parable indicates.—That is very likely.

Further, I said, do you think it at all surprising that anyone coming to the evils of human life from the contemplation of the divine behaves awkwardly and appears very ridiculous while his eyes are still dazzled and before he is sufficiently adjusted to the darkness around him, if he is compelled to contend in court or some other place about the shadows of justice or the objects of which they are shadows, and to carry through the contest about these in the way these things are understood by those who have never seen Justice itself?—That is not surprising at all.

Anyone with intelligence, I said, would remember that the eyes may be confused in two ways and from two causes, coming from light into darkness as well as from darkness into light. Realizing that the same applies to the soul, whenever he sees a soul disturbed and unable to see something, he will not laugh mindlessly but will consider whether it has come from a brighter life and is dimmed because unadjusted, or has come from greater ignorance into greater light and is filled with a brighter dazzlement. The former he would declare happy in its life and experience, the latter he would pity, and if he should wish to laugh at it, his laughter would be less ridiculous than if he laughed at a soul that has come from the light above.—What you say is very reasonable.

We must then, I said, if these things are true, think something like this about them, namely that education is not what some declare it to be; they say that knowledge is not present in the soul and that they put it in, like putting sight into blind eyes.—They surely say that.

---

* *Odyssey* 11, 489–90, where Achilles says to Odysseus, on the latter's visit to the underworld, that he would rather be a servant to a poor man on earth than king among the dead.—G.M.A. Grube.

Our present argument shows, I said, that the capacity to learn and the organ with which to do so are present in every person's soul. It is as if it were not possible to turn the eye from darkness to light without turning the whole body; so one must turn one's whole soul from the world of becoming until it can endure to contemplate reality, and the brightest of realities, which we say is the Good.—Yes.

Education then is the art of doing this very thing, this turning around, the knowledge of how the soul can most easily and most effectively be turned around; it is not the art of putting the capacity of sight into the soul; the soul possesses that already but it is not turned the right way or looking where it should. This is what education has to deal with.—That seems likely.

Now the other so-called virtues of the soul seem to be very close to those of the body—they really do not exist before and are added later by habit and practice—but the virtue of intelligence belongs above all to something more divine, it seems, which never loses its capacity but, according to which way it is turned, becomes useful and beneficial or useless and harmful. Have you never noticed in men who are said to be wicked but clever, how sharply their little soul looks into things to which it turns its attention? Its capacity for sight is not inferior, but it is compelled to serve evil ends, so that the more sharply it looks the more evils it works.—Quite so.

Yet if a soul of this kind had been hammered at from childhood and those excrescences had been knocked off it which belong to the world of becoming and have been fastened upon it by feasting, gluttony, and similar pleasures, and which like leaden weights draw the soul to look downward—if, being rid of these, it turned to look at things that are true, then the same soul of the same man would see these just as sharply as it now sees the things towards which it is directed.—That seems likely.

Further, is it not likely, I said, indeed it follows inevitably from what was said before, that the uneducated who have no experience of truth would never govern a city satisfactorily, nor would those who are allowed to spend their whole life in the process of educating themselves; the former would fail because they do not have a single goal at which all their actions, public and private, must aim; the latter because they would refuse to act, thinking that they have settled, while still alive, in the faraway islands of the blessed.—True.

It is then our task as founders, I said, to compel the best natures to reach the study which we have previously said to be the most important, to see the Good and to follow that upward journey. When they have accomplished their journey and seen it sufficiently, we must not allow them to do what they are allowed to do today.—What is that?

To stay there, I said, and to refuse to go down again to the prisoners in the cave, there to share both their labours and their honours, whether these be of little or of greater worth.*

Are we then, he said, to do them an injustice by making them live a worse life when they could live a better one?

You are again forgetting, my friend, I said, that it is not the law's concern to make some one group in the city outstandingly happy but to contrive to spread happiness throughout the city, by bringing the citizens into harmony with each other by persuasion or compulsion, and to make them share with each other the benefits which each group can confer upon the community. The law has not made men of this kind in the city in order to allow each to turn in any direction they wish but to make use of them to bind the city together.—You are right, I had forgotten.

Consider then, Glaucon, I said, that we shall not be doing an injustice to those who have become philosophers in our city, and that what we shall say to them, when we

---

* Plato does indeed require his philosopher to go back into the cave to help those less fortunate than himself, but only as a duty, not because he loves his neighbour or gets any emotional satisfaction from helping him.—G.M.A. Grube.

compel them to care for and to guard the others, is just. For we shall say: "Those who become philosophers in other cities are justified in not sharing the city's labours, for the have grown into philosophy of their own accord, against the will of the government in each of those cities, and it is right that what grows of its own accord, as it owes no debt to anyone for its upbringing, should not be keen to pay it to anyone. But we have made you in our city kings and leaders of the swarm, as it were, both to your own advantage and to that of the rest of the city; you are better and more completely educated than those others, and you are better able to share in both kinds of life. Therefore you must each in turn go down to live with other men and grow accustomed to seeing in the dark. When you are used to it you will see infinitely better than the dwellers below; you will know what each image is and of what it is an image, because you have seen the truth of things beautiful and just and good, and so, for you as for us, the city will be governed as a waking reality and not as in a dream, as the majority of cities are now governed by men who are fighting shadows and striving against each other in order to rule as if this were a great good." For this is the truth: a city in which the prospective rulers are least keen to rule must of necessity be governed best and be most free from civil strife, whereas a city with the opposite kind of rulers is governed in the opposite way.—Quite so.

Do you think that those we have nurtured will disobey us and refuse to share the labours of the city, each group in turn, though they may spend the greater part of their time dwelling with each other in a pure atmosphere?

They cannot, he said, for we shall be giving just orders to just men, but each of them will certainly go to rule as to something that must be done, the opposite attitude from that of the present rulers in every city.

That is how it is, my friend, I said. If you can find a way of life which is better than governing for the prospective governors, then a well-governed city can exist for you.

Only in that city will the truly rich rule, not rich in gold but in the wealth which the happy man must have, a life with goodness and intelligence. If beggars hungry for private goods go into public life, thinking that they must snatch their good from it, the well-governed city cannot exist, for then office is fought for, and such a war at home inside the city destroys them and the city as well.—Very true. . . .

Education of the Guardians

Let us not forget that in our earlier selection we chose older men, but this is not possible this time, for we shall not believe Solon that as a man grows old he can learn many things. He can do that even less than he can run, and all great and numerous labours belong to the young.—Necessarily.

Calculation and geometry and the whole of the preliminary studies which must precede dialectic must be offered to them in boyhood, but our method of teaching must not be by compulsion.—How so?

Because, I said, no free man must learn anything under compulsion like a slave. Physical labour performed under duress does no harm to the body, but nothing learned under compulsion stays in the mind.—True.

Do not, therefore, my excellent friend, I said, instruct the boys in these studies by force, but in play, so that you will also see better what each of them is by nature fitted for.—That seems reasonable.

You remember, I said, that we stated the boys were to be led even into war, as observers on horseback and, wherever it is safe to do so, they should be brought close and taste blood, like puppies.—I remember.

In all these things, I said, in physical labours, in studies, in circumstances provoking fear, whoever is seen to be always very skillful is to be inscribed on a list.—At what age?

When they give up compulsory physical training, I said. For during that period whether it be two or three years, youth is unable to do anything else. Physical labour and sleep are the enemies of study. At the same time this physical training is itself one of the tests, and not the least important, as to how each of them performs in physical exercises.—Of course.

After that time, that is, from the age of twenty, those who are chosen will also receive more honours than the others. The studies which have been indiscriminately taught in the education of the boys must now be brought together for them in order to give them a synoptic view of their kinship with each other and with the nature of reality.—Indeed, only the kind of instruction in which this place will remain with them.

It is also, I said, the best test of the dialectical nature, for that man who sees things as a whole is a dialectician; the man who does not, is not.—I think so too.

You will have to oversee these things to discover those among them who show these qualities and who remain steadfast in their studies, steadfast in war and other lawful activities. These, after they complete their thirtieth year, you will in turn choose from among the chosen group and award them greater honours and then find out, testing them by the power of dialectic, who can relinquish the eyes and the other senses and take the way of truth to reality itself, a task which requires great care, my friend.—Why mostly?

Do you not realize, I said, the great evil which has now come upon dialectic?—What is that?

Those who practice it are filled with lawlessness, I said.—They surely are.

Do you think that what is happening to them is surprising, and do you not forgive them?—In what way particularly?

It is, I said, as if some child were brought up among great wealth, in a numerous and great family with many flatterers, and when he had grown to manhood he discovered that he was not the child of his professed parents, but he did not find out who his real parents were. Do you think you can foretell his attitude toward the flatterers and his

supposed parents both at the time he did not know about his parentage, and again at the time when he did know, or do you want to hear what I surmise?—I do indeed.

I expect that, during the time when he did not know the truth, he would honour his father and mother and his other supposed relations more than the flatterers, that he would pay greater attention to their needs, that he would be less likely to treat them lawlessly in word or deed, more likely to be persuaded by them than by flatterers in any matters of importance.—That is likely.

When he learned the truth, however, he would honour and care for them less, while his relations with the flatterers would become more intense, he would be persuaded by them far more than before, he would now live in the way they did and keep company with them openly, and, unless he had a very fine nature indeed, he would not care at all for that father of his and his other supposed relatives.

All this, he said, might well happen as you say, but what relevance has this image to those who concern themselves with reasoned discourse?

The following: we hold from childhood certain beliefs about just and beautiful things; we are brought up in these beliefs as by parents, we obey and honour them.—That is so.

However, there are other pursuits contrary to these which give pleasure, flatter our soul, and attract it toward themselves, but they do not persuade those who are at all moderate. These honour the principles of their fathers which we mentioned and obey them.—That is so.

And then, I said, a questioner comes along and asks a man in those circumstances what is the beautiful, and, when he answers what he has heard from the lawgiver, the argument refutes him, and does this often and in many places. This reduces him to the belief that this thing is no more beautiful than it is ugly, and the same with what is just and good and the things he honoured most. What do you think his attitude would be about honouring and obeying his early beliefs?—Of necessity, he said, he will not honour and obey them as much.

Then, I said, when he no longer believes these principles to be his own nor to be obeyed, as he did before, and he does not discover true ones, is he likely to adopt any other kind of life than the flattering kind?—Not likely.

An so from law abiding he becomes lawless.—Inevitably.

That is why the experience of those who come to reasoned discourse in this way is, as I said just now, both probable and deserving much forgiveness.—And pity too.

It is also why, in order not to feel pity for your thirty-year-olds, you must be extremely careful how you introduce them to dialectic.—Yes indeed.

Is not one lasting precaution not to let them have a taste of it while young? I do not think it has escaped your notice that when youths get their first taste of reasoned discourse they take it as a game and always use it to contradict. They imitate those who cross-examined them and themselves cross-examine others, rejoicing like puppies to drag along and tear to bits in argument whoever is near them.—Yes, to excess.

And when they have themselves cross-examined many people and been cross-examined by many, they fall vehemently and quickly into disbelieving what they believed before. As a result, they themselves and the whole of philosophy are discredited in the eyes of other men.—Very true.

An older man, I said, would not want to take part in such folly; he will imitate one who is willing to converse in order to discover the truth rather than one who is merely playing and contradicting for play; he will himself be more measured and will bring honour rather than discredit to the pursuit of philosophy.—Quite right.

Indeed, all that we said before this was said for the sake of caution, that those whom one allows to partake in reasoned discourse should by nature be orderly and steady, not as now when anyone engages in

it, even if he is quite unfit.—Quite so.

It will be enough to stay with the study of dialectic continuously and intensely, doing nothing else, in a similar way to the time spent in physical training, but for twice the number of years.—Do you mean four or six?

No matter, I said make it five, for after that they must go down into that cave for you, and they must be compelled to rule on matters of war and the government of youth, so that they shall not be inferior to others in experience. And even in those years they must be tested as to whether they will remain steadfast as they are pulled this way and that, or whether they will change anything.—And how long do you fix that period? He asked.

Fifteen years, I said. Then, at the age of fifty, those who have survived the tests and have been successful both in action and in the scientific studies must be led to the goal and must be compelled to lift up the eyes of their soul to what itself provides light to all and, as they look upon the Good itself and taking it as their model, they must put in order the city and its citizens as well as themselves for the remainder of their life, each in turn. They will spend much of their time with philosophy, but, when their turn comes, they must each labour and rule in public affairs, and they will do this not as something splendid but as a duty. Thus, having educated others to be men of their kind, and leaving other guardians to take their place, they will depart to the islands of the blessed and dwell there. The city will publicly establish memorials and sacrifices for them as for divine spirits, if the Pythian agrees, or if not, then for happy and divinely inspired men.

Like a sculptor, Socrates, he said, you fashioned these rulers as magnificent statues of men.

And of women too, Glaucon, I said, for you must not think that what I have said applies to men any more than it applies to women, those that may be born sufficiently able by nature.

You are right, he said, if they share equally, as we said they should, all the activities of men.

You agree then that what we have said about the city and its constitution is not altogether wishful thinking, that these things are difficult, but somehow possible, though only in the way we indicated, whenever true philosophers, be it one or more, become rulers in a city. They will despise the present honours as mean and worthless; they will attach the greatest importance to doing what is right and to the honours deriving from that; they will regard justice as the greatest and most essential thing; they will serve it and increase it as they set their city in order.—How will they do that?

All in the city, I said, over ten years of age they will send into the country. Then they will take the children in hand, away from their parents' way of life, and bring them up in their own ways and by their own laws which will be such as we have described. This is the quickest and the easiest way to establish the city and constitution we have discussed, for it to be happy and to confer the greatest benefits upon the people among whom it may be established.

Much the easiest way, he said, and you seem to me, Socrates, to have described very well how it should arise, if it ever does.

Have we now said enough about the city and about the man who resembles it? It is surely clear what kind of man we shall declare he must be.

Quite clear, he said. As for your question, I think we have come to the end of this topic.

Politics

Aristotle

Aristotle (384–322 B.C.) was born in Stagira, a town near Macedonia. He went to Athens when he was seventeen-years old and studied with Plato at the Academy for twenty years. When Plato died, Aristotle left Athens and traveled to Macedonia, where he tutored the young heir to the throne—who was later to become known as "Alexander the Great." In 334 B.C., Aristotle returned to Athens and founded his own school, the Lyceum. When Alexander died in 323, there was strong, anti-Macedonian feeling in Athens, and Aristotle left for Chalcis, where he died the next year at sixty-two.

Aristotle studied and wrote about an astonishing range of subjects. His knowledge was encyclopedic and deep. No one person has ever founded and advanced so many fields of learning. He wrote separate treatises on physics, biology, logic, psychology, ethics, metaphysics, aesthetics, literary criticism, and political science. In the middle ages, he was simply known as "The Philosopher."

Aristotle's Politics is a classic of Western political thought, combining—what we would call today—political philosophy with the first scientific study of comparative politics. Aristotle was not an elegant literary stylist like Plato. His writing tends to be terse, and his *Politics* was probably written as a series of lectures for students.

BOOK I

Chapter 1
The State as an Association

Observation tells us that every state is an association, and that every association is formed with a view to some good purpose. I say 'good', because in all their actions all men do in fact aim at what they think good. Clearly then, as all associations aim at some good, that association which is the most sov-

ereign among them all and embraces all others will aim highest, i.e. at the most sovereign of all goods. This is the association which we call the state, the association which is 'political'.

It is an error to suppose, as some do, that the roles of a statesman, of a king, of a household-manager and of a master of slaves are the same, on the ground that they differ not in kind but only in point of numbers of persons—that a master of slaves, for example, has to do with a few people, a household-manager with more, and a statesman or king with more still, as if there were no differences between a large household and a small state. They also reckon that

Translated by T.A. Sinclair, as revised by Trevor J. Saunders. Reprinted form Aristotle, *The Politics* (Harmondsworth, England: Penguin Books, 1981) by permission of the publisher.

463

when one person is in personal control over the rest he has the role of a king, whereas when he takes his turn at ruling and at being ruled according to the principles of the science concerned, he is a statesman. But these assertions are false.

This will be quite evident if we examine the matter according to our established method. We have to analyze other composite things till they can be subdivided no further, because we have reached the smallest parts of the wholes; so let us in the same way examine the component parts of the state and we shall see better how these too differ from each other, and whether we can acquire any systematic knowledge about the several roles mentioned.

Chapter 2
The State Exists by Nature

We shall, I think, in this as in other subjects, get the best view of the matter if we look at the natural growth of thing from the beginning. The first point is that those which are incapable of existing without each other must be united as a pair. For example, (a) the union of male and female is essential for reproduction; and this is not a matter of *choice*, but is due to the *natural* urge, which exists in the other animals too and in plants, to propagate one's kind. Equally essential is (b) the combination of the natural ruler and ruled, for the purpose of preservation. For the element that can use its intelligence to look ahead is by nature ruler and by nature master, while that which has the bodily strength to do the actual work is by nature a slave, one of those who are ruled. Thus there is a common interest uniting master and slave.

Formation of the Household. Nature, then, has distinguished between female and slave: she recognizes different functions and lavishly provides different tools, not an all-purpose tool like the Delphic knife; for every instrument will be made best if it serves not many purposes but one. But non-Greeks assign to female and slave exactly the same status. This is because they have

nothing which is by nature fitted to rule; their association consists of a male slave and a female slave. So, as the poets say, 'It is proper that Greeks should rule non-Greeks', the implication being that non-Greek and slave are by nature identical.

Thus it was out of the association formed by men with these two, women and slaves, that a household was first formed; and the poet Hesiod was right when he wrote, 'Get first a house and a wife and an ox to draw the plough.' (The ox is the poor man's slave.) This association of persons, established according to nature for the satisfaction of daily needs, is the household, the members of which Charondas calls 'bread-fellows', and Epimenides the Cretan 'stable-companions'.

Formation of the Village. The next stage is the village, the first association of a number of houses for the satisfaction of something *more* than daily needs. It comes into being through the processes of nature in the fullest sense, as offshoots of a household are set up by sons and grandsons. The members of such a village are therefore called by some 'homogalactic'. This is why states were at first ruled by kings, as are foreign nations to this day: they were formed from constituents which were themselves under kingly rule. For every household is ruled by its senior member, as by a king, and the offshoots too, because of their blood relationship, are ruled in the same way. This kind of rule is mentioned in Homer: 'Each man has power of law over children and wives.' He is referring to scattered settlements, which were common in primitive times. For this reason the gods too are said to be governed by a king—namely because men themselves were originally ruled by kings and some are so still. Just as men imagine gods in human shape, so they imagine their way of life to be like that of men.

Formation of the State. The final association, formed of several villages, is the state. For all practical purposes the process is now complete; self-sufficiency has been reached, and while the state came about as a means of securing life itself, it continues in being to secure the *good* life. Therefore every state exists by nature, as the earlier associations too were natural. This association is the end of those others, and nature is itself an end; for whatever is the end-product of the coming into existence of any object, that is what we call its nature—of a man, for instance, or a horse or a household. Moreover the aim and the end is perfection; and self-sufficiency is both end and perfection.

The State and the Individual. It follows that the state belongs to the class of objects which exist by nature, and that man is by nature a political animal. Any one who by his nature and not simply by ill-luck has no state is either too bad or too good, either subhuman or superhuman—he is like the war-mad man condemned in Homer's words as 'having no family, no law, no home'; for he who is such by nature is mad on war: he is a non-cooperator like an isolated piece in a game of draughts.

But obviously man is a political animal in a sense in which a bee is not, or any other gregarious animal. Nature, as we say, does nothing without some purpose; and she has endowed man alone among the animals with the power of speech. Speech is something different from voice, which is possessed by other animals also and used by them to express pain or pleasure; for their nature does indeed enable them not only to feel pleasure and pain but to communicate these feelings to each other. Speech, on the other hand serves to indicate what is useful and what is harmful, and so also what is just and what is unjust. For the real difference between man and other animals is that humans alone have perception of good and evil, just and unjust, etc. It is the sharing of a common view in *these* matters that makes a household and a state.

Furthermore, the state has a natural priority over the household and over any individual among us. For the whole must be prior to the part. Separate hand or foot from the whole body, and they will no longer be hand or foot except in name, as one might speak of a 'hand' or 'foot' sculptured in stone. That will be the condition of the spoilt hand, which no longer has the capacity and the function which define it. So, though we may say they have the same names, we cannot say that they are, in that condition, the same things. It is clear then that the state is both natural and prior to the individual. For if an individual is not fully self-sufficient after separation, he will stand in the same relationship to the whole as the parts in the other case do. Whatever is incapable of participating in the association which we call the state, a dumb animal for example, and equally whatever is perfectly self-sufficient and has no need to (e.g. a god), is not a part of the state at all.

Among all men, then, there is a natural impulse towards this kind of association; and the first man to construct a state deserves credit for conferring very great benefits. For as man is the best of all animals when he has reached his full development, so he is worst of all when divorced from law and justice. Injustice armed is hardest to deal with; and though man is born with weapons which he can use in the service of practical wisdom and virtue, it is all too easy for him to use them for the opposite purposes. Hence man without virtue is the most savage, the most unrighteous, and the worst in regard to sexual licence and gluttony. The virtue of justice is a feature of a state; for justice is the arrangement of the political association, and a sense of justice decides what is just.

Chapter 3
The Household

Now that I have explained what the component parts of a state are, and since every state consists of households, it is essential to begin with household-management. This topic can be subdivided so as to correspond to the parts of which a complete household is made up, namely, the free and the slaves; but our method requires us to examine everything when it has been reduced to its smallest parts, and the first and smallest division of a household into parts gives three pairs—master and slave, husband and wife, father and children. And so we must ask ourselves what each one of these three relationships is, and what sort of thing it ought to be. The word 'mastership' is used to describe the first, and we may use 'matrimonial' (in the case of the union of man and woman) and 'paternal' to describe the other two, as there is no more specific term for either. We may accept these three; but we find that there is a fourth element, which some people regard as covering the whole of household-management, others as its most important part; and our task is to consider its position. I refer to what is called 'the acquisition of wealth.'

First let us discuss master and slave, in order to see (a) how they bear on the provision of essential services, (b) whether we can find a better way towards understanding this topic than if we started from the suppositions usually made. For example, some people suppose that being a master requires a certain kind of knowledge, and that this is the same knowledge as is required to manage a household or to be a statesman or a king—an error which we discussed at the beginning. Others say that it is contrary to nature to rule as master over slave, because the distinction between slave and free is one of convention only, and in nature there is no difference, so that this form of rule is based on force and is therefore not just.

Chapter 4
Slavery

Now property is part of a household, and the acquisition of property part of household-management; for neither life itself nor the good life is possible without a certain minimum supply of the necessities. Again, in any special skill the availability of the proper tools will be essential for the performance of the task; and the household-manager must have his likewise. Tools may be animate as well as inanimate; for instance, a ship's captain uses a lifeless rudder, but a living man for watch; for a servant is,

from the point of view of his craft, categorized as one of its tools. So any piece of property can be regarded as a tool enabling a man to live, and his property is an assemblage of such tools; a slave is a sort of living piece of property; and like any other servant is a tool in charge of other tools. For suppose that every tool we had could perform its task, either at our bidding or itself perceiving the need, and if—like the statues made by Daedalus or the tripods of Hephaestus, of which the poet says that 'self-moved they enter the assembly of the gods'—shuttles in a loom could fly to and fro and a plucker play a lyre of their own accord, then mastercraftsmen would have no need of servants nor masters of slaves.

Tools in the ordinary sense are productive tools, whereas a piece of property is meant for action. I mean, for example, a shuttle produces something other than its own use, a bed or a garment does not. Moreover, since production and action differ in kind and both require tools, the difference between their tools too must be of the same kind. Now life is action and not production; therefore the slave, a servant, is one of the tools that minister to action.

A piece of property is spoken of in the same way as a part is; for a part is not only part of something but belongs to it *tout court;* and so too does a piece of property. So a slave is not only his master's slave but belongs to him *tout court,* while the master is his slave's master but does not belong to him. These considerations will have shown what the nature and functions of the slave are: any human being that by nature belongs not to himself but to another is by nature a slave; and a human being belongs to another whenever, in spite of being a *man*, he is a piece of property, i.e., a tool having a separate existence and meant for action.

Chapter 5
Slavery As Part of a Universal Natural Pattern

But whether anyone does in fact by nature answer to this description, and whether or not it is a just and a better thing for one man to be a slave to another, or whether all slavery is contrary to nature—these are the questions which must be considered next. Neither theoretical discussion nor empirical observations presents any difficulty. That one should command and another obey is both necessary and expedient. Indeed some things are so divided right from birth, some to rule, some to be ruled. There are many different forms of this ruler-ruled relationship, and the quality of the rule depends primarily on the quality of the subjects, rule over man being better than rule over animals; for that which is produced by better men is a better piece of work; and the ruler–ruled relationship is itself a product created by the men involved in it.

For wherever there is a combination of elements, continuous or discontinuous, and a common unity is the result, in all such cases the ruler–ruled relationship appears. It appears notably in living creatures as a consequence of their whole nature (and it can exist also where there is no life, as dominance in a musical scale, but that is hardly relevant here). The living creature consists in the first place of mind and body, and of these the former is ruler by nature, the latter ruled. Now we must always look for nature's own norm in things whose condition is according to nature, and not base our observations on degenerate forms. We must therefore in this connexion consider the man who is in good condition mentally and physically, one in whom the rule of mind over body is conspicuous—because the bad and unnatural condition of a permanently or temporarily depraved person will often give the impression that his body is ruling over his soul.

However that may be, it is, as I say, within living creatures that we first find it possible to see both the rule of a master and that of a statesman. The rule of soul over body is like a master's rule, while the rule of intelligence over desire is like a statesman's or a king's. In these relationships it is clear that it is both natural and expedient for the body to be ruled by the soul, and for the emotional part of our natures to be ruled by the mind, the part which possesses reason. The reverse, or even parity, would be fatal all around. This is also true as between man and the other animals; for tame animals are by nature better than wild, and it is better for them all to be ruled by men, because it secures their safety. Again, as between male and female the former is by nature superior and ruler, the latter inferior and subject. And this must hold good of mankind in general.

Therefore whenever there is the same wide discrepancy between human beings as there is between soul and body or between man and beast, then those whose condition is such that their function is the use of their bodies and nothing better can be expected of them, those, I say, are slaves by nature. It is better for them, just as in the cases mentioned, to be ruled thus. For the 'slave by nature' is he that can and therefore does belong to another, and he that participates in reason so far as to recognize it but not so as to possess it (whereas the other animals obey not reason but emotions). The use made of slaves hardly differs at all from that of tame animals: they both help with their bodies to supply our essential needs. It is, then, nature's purpose to make the bodies of free men to differ from those of slaves, the latter strong enough to be used for necessary tasks, the former erect and useless for that kind of work, but well suited for the life of a citizen of a state, a life which is in turn divided between the requirements of war and peace.

But the opposite often occurs: people who have the right kind of bodily physique for free men, but not the soul, others who have the right soul but not the body. This much is clear: suppose that there were men whose mere bodily physique showed the same superiority as is shown by the statues of gods, then all would agree that the rest of mankind would deserve to be their slaves. And if this is true in relation to physical superiority, the distinction would be even more justly made in respect of superiority of soul; but it is much more difficult to see beauty of soul than it is to see beauty of body. It is clear then that by nature some are free, others slaves, and that for these it is both just and expedient that they should serve as slaves.

Chapter 6
The Relation Between Legal and Natural Slavery

On the other hand it is not hard to see that those who take opposing views are also right up to a point. The expressions 'state of slavery' and 'slave' have a double connotation: there exists also a *legal* slave and state of slavery. The law in question is a kind of agreement, which provides that all that is conquered in war is termed the property of the conquerors. Against this right many of those versed in law bring a charge analogous to that of 'illegality' brought against an orator: they hold it to be indefensible that a man who has been overpowered by the violence and superior might of another should become his property. Others see no harm in this; and both views are held by experts.

The reason for this difference of opinion, and for the overlap in the arguments used, lies in the fact that in a way it is virtue, when it acquires resources, that is best able actually to use force; and in the fact that anything which conquers does so because it excels in some good. It seems therefore that force is not without virtue, and that the only dispute is about what is just. Consequently some think that 'just' in this connection is a nonsense, others that it means precisely this, that 'the stronger shall rule'. But when these propositions are disentangled, the other arguments have no validity or power to show that the superior in virtue ought not to rule and be master.

Some take a firm stand (as they conceive it) on 'justice' in the sense of 'law,' and claim that enslavement in war is just, simply as being legal; but they simultaneously deny it, since it is quite possible that undertaking the war may have been unjust in the first place. Also one cannot use the term 'slave' properly of one who is undeserving of being a slave; otherwise we should find among slaves and descendants of slaves even men who seem to be of the noblest birth, should any of them be captured and sold. For this reason they will not apply the term slave to such people but use it only for non-Greeks. But in so doing they are really seeking to define the slave by nature, which was our starting point; for one has to admit that there are some who are slaves everywhere, others who are slaves nowhere. And the same is true of noble birth: nobles regard themselves as of noble birth not only among their own people but everywhere, and they allow nobility of birth of non-Greeks to be valid only in non-Greek lands. This involves making two grades of free status and noble birth, one absolute, the other conditional. (In a play by Theodectes, Helen is made to say 'Who would think it proper to call me a slave, who am sprung of divine lineage on both sides?') But in introducing this point they are really basing the distinction between slave and free, noble-born and base-born, upon virtue and vice. For they maintain that as man is born of man, and beast of beast, so good is born of good. But frequently, though this may be nature's intention, she is unable to realize it.

It is clear then that there is justification for the difference of opinion: while it is not invariably true that slaves are slaves by nature and others free, yet this distinction does in some cases actually prevail—cases where it is expedient for the one to be master, the other to be the slave. Whereas the one must be ruled, the other should exercise the rule for which he is fitted by nature, thus being the master. For, if the work of being a master is badly done, that is contrary to the interest of both parties; for the part and the whole, the soul and the body, have identical interests; and the slave is in a sense a part of his master, a living but separate part of his body. For this reason there is an interest in common and a feeling of friendship between master and slave, wherever they are by nature fitted for this relationship; but not when the relationship arises out of the use of force and by the law which we have been discussing.

Chapter 12
Brief Analysis of the Authority of Husband and Father

There are, as we saw, three parts of household-management, one being the rule of a master, which has already been dealt with, next the rule of a father, and a third which arises out of the marriage relationship. This is included because rule is exercised over wife and children—over both of them as free persons, but in other respects differently: over a wife, rule is as by a statesman; over children, as by a king. For the male is more fitted to rule than the female, unless conditions are quite contrary to nature; and the elder and fully grown is more fitted than the younger and undeveloped. It is true that in most cases of rule by statesmen there is an interchange of the role of ruler and ruled, which aims to preserve natural equality and non-differentiation; nevertheless, so long as one is ruling and the other is being ruled, the ruler seeks to mark distinctions in outward dignity, in style of address, and in honours paid. (Witness what Amasis said about his foot-basin.) As between male and female this kind of relationship is permanent. Rule over children is royal, for the begetter is ruler by virtue both of affection and of age, and this type of rule is royal. Homer therefore was right in calling Zeus 'father of gods and men', as he was king over them all. For a king ought to have a natural superiority, but to be no different in birth; and this is just the condition of elder in relation to younger and of father to son.

BOOK III

Chapter 1
Citizenship

. . .Who is a citizen? and, Whom should we call one? Here too there is no unanimity, no agreement as to what constitutes a citizen; it often happens that one who is a citizen in a democracy is not a citizen in any oligarchy. (I think we may leave out of account those who merely acquire the title indirectly, e.g.,the 'made' citizens.) Nor does mere residence in a place confer citizenship: resident foreigners and slaves are not citizens, but do share domicile in the country. Another definition is 'those who have access to legal processes, who may prosecute or be prosecuted'. But this access is open to any person who is covered by a commercial treaty. . . .

What effectively distinguishes the citizen proper from all others is his participation in giving judgment and in holding office. Some offices are distinguished in respect of length of tenure, some not being tenable by the same person twice under any circumstances, or only after an interval of time. Others, such as membership of a jury or of an assembly, have no such limitation. It might be objected that such persons are not really officials, and that these functions do not amount to participation in office. But they have the fullest sovereign power, and it would be ridiculous to deny their participation in office. In any case nomenclature ought not to make any difference; it is just that there is no name covering that which is common to a juryman and to a member of an assembly, which ought to be used of both. For the sake of a definition I suggest that we say 'unlimited office'. We therefore define citizens as those who participate in this. Such a definition seems to cover, as nearly as may be, those to whom the term citizen is in fact applied.

On the other hand we must remember that in the case of things in which the substrata differ in kind, one being primary, another secondary, and so on, there is nothing, or scarcely anything, which is common to all those things, in so far as they are the kind of thing they are. Thus we see the various constitutions differing from each other in kind, some being prior to others—since those that have gone wrong or deviated must be posterior to those which are free from error. I will explain later what I mean by 'deviated'. A citizen, therefore, will necessarily vary according to the constitution in each case. . . .

Chapter 4
The Good Man and the Good Citizen

Connected with the matters just discussed is the question whether we ought to regard the virtue of a good man and that of a sound citizen as the same virtue, or not. If this is a point to be investigated, we really must try to form some rough conception of the virtue of a citizen.

So then: we say a citizen is a member of an association, just as a sailor is; and each member of the crew has his different function and a name to fit it—rower, helmsman, look-out, and the rest. Clearly the most exact description of each individual will be a special description of this virtue; but equally there will also be a general description that will fit them all, because there is a task in which they all play a part—the safe conduct of the voyage; for each member of the crew aims at securing that. Similarly the task of all the citizens, however different they may be, is the stability of the association, that is, the constitution. Therefore the virtue of the citizen must be in relation to the constitution; and as there are more kinds of constitution than one, there cannot be just one single *and perfect* virtue of the sound citizen. On the other hand we do say that the good *man* is good because of one single virtue which *is* perfect virtue. Clearly then it is possible to be a sound citizen without having that virtue which makes a sound man. . . .

Chapter 5
Should Workers Be Citizens?

There remains still a question about the citizen. Is a citizen really 'one who has the chance to participate in offices', or are we to count mechanics too as citizens? If we do the latter, i.e. given them the title citizen though they do not share in government, then the virtue of the citizen ceases to be that of every citizen, since the mechanic too is a citizen. On the other hand, if he is not a citizen, where *does* he belong, since he is not a foreign resident or a visitor either? But perhaps this kind of reasoning does not really result in any absurdity. After all, slaves do not belong to any of the above-mentioned categories, nor do freed slaves: true it is that we must not give the name citizen to all persons whose presence is necessary for the existence of the state. (Nor yet are children citizens in an unqualified sense, like grown men; children can be called citizens only in a hypothetical sense: they *are* citizens, but incomplete ones.) Indeed, in ancient times in certain countries the mechanics *were* slaves or foreigners, and therefore mostly still are. But the best state will not make the mechanic a citizen. But if even he is to be a citizen, then at any rate what we have called the virtue of a citizen cannot be ascribed to everyone, nor yet to free men alone, but simply to those who are in fact relieved of necessary tasks. Some tasks of this kind are discharged by services to an individual, by slaves, others by mechanics and hired labourers, who serve the public at large.

A little further examination will show how it stands with these people, and our earlier statement of the position will itself suffice to make matters clear: as there are several constitutions, so there must be several kinds of citizen, particularly of citizen under a ruler. Thus in one constitution it will be necessary, in another impossible, for the mechanic and the hired labourer to be a citizen. It would, for example, be impossible in any constitution called aristocratic or any other in which honours depend on merit and virtue; for it is quite impossible, while living the life of mechanic or hireling, to occupy oneself as virtue demands. In oligarchies it is not possible for a hireling to be a citizen, because of the high property-qualifications required for participating in office; but it may be possible for a mechanic, since in fact most skilled workers become rich. In Thebes, however, there was a law requiring an interval of ten years to elapse between giving up trade and participating in office.

In many constitutions the law admits to citizenship a certain number even of foreigners; in some democracies the son of a citizen mother is a citizen, and in many places the same applies to illegitimate children. Lack of population is the usual reason for resorting to laws such as these. But when, after making such persons citizens because of a dearth of legitimate citizens, the state has filled up its numbers, it gradually reduces them, dropping first the sons of slave father or slave mother, then sons of citizen mother but not father, and finally they confine citizenship to those of citizen birth on both sides.

From all this two points emerge clearly: first, that there are several kinds of citizen, but second, that a citizen in the fullest sense is one who has a share in honours. We are reminded of Homer's 'Like some immigrant settler, without honour'. For he who has no share in honours is no better than a resident alien. (Sometimes such efforts are concealed, so that the fellow-inhabitants may be deceived.)

We have now answered the question whether it is the same or a different virtue that makes a good man and a sound citizen, and have shown that in one state they will be the same person, and in another different; and that where they are the same, not every sound citizen will be a good man, but only the statesman, that is one who is in sovereign control, or capable of being in control, either alone or in conjunction with others, of the administration of public affairs.

Chapter 7
Rule by the One, Few, or Many

Having drawn these distinctions we must next consider what constitutions there are and how many. We begin with those that are correct, since when these have been defined it will be easy to see the deviations. As we have seen, 'constitution' and 'citizen-body' mean the same thing, and the citizen-body is the sovereign power in states. Sovereignty necessarily resides either in one man, or in a few, or in the many. Whenever the one, the few, or the many rule with a view to the common good, these constitutions must be correct; but if they look to the private advantage, be it of the one or the few or the mass, they are deviations. For either, we

must say that those who do not participate are not citizens, or they must share in the benefit.

The usual names for right constitutions are as follows: (a) Monarchy aiming at the common interest: kingship. (b) Rule of more than one man but only a few: aristocracy (so called either because the *best* men rule or because it aims at what is *best* for the state and all its members). (c) Political control exercised by the mass of the populace in the common interest: polity. This is the name common to all constitutions. It is reasonable to use this term, because, while it is possible for one man or a few to be outstanding in point of virtue, it is difficult for a larger number to reach a high standard in all forms of virtue—with the conspicuous exception of military virtue, which is found in a great many people. And that is why in this constitution the defensive element is the most sovereign body, and those who share in the constitution are those who bear arms.

The corresponding deviations are: from kingship, tyranny; from aristocracy, oligarchy; from polity, democracy. For tyranny is monarchy for the benefit of the monarch, oligarchy for the benefit of the men of means, democracy for the benefit of the men without means. None of the three aims to be of profit to the common interest.

Chapter 8
An Economic Classification of Constitutions

We must however go into a little more detail about what each of these constitutions is. Certain difficulties are involved, which one whose aim is strictly practical might be allowed to pass over; but a man who examines each subject from a philosophical standpoint cannot neglect them: he has to omit nothing, and state the truth about each topic.

Tyranny, as has been said, is a monarchy which is exercised like a mastership over the association which is the state; oligarchy occurs when the sovereign power of the constitution is in the hands of those with possessions, democracy when it is in the hands of those who have no stock of possessions and are without means. The first difficulty concerns definitions. Suppose the majority to be well-off, and to be sovereign in the state; then we have a democracy, since the mass of the people is sovereign. So too, if it is somewhere the case that those who do not own property, while fewer in number than those who do, are more powerful and in sovereign control of the constitution, then that is called an oligarchy, since the few are sovereign. It looks therefore as if there were something wrong with our way of defining constitutions.

Even if we try to include both criteria of nomenclature, combining wealth with fewness of numbers in the one case (calling it oligarchy when those who are both wealthy and few hold office), lack of wealth with large numbers in the other (calling it democracy when those who are both poor and numerous hold office)—even then we are only raising a fresh difficulty. For if there is not in fact any other constitution than those with which we have been dealing, what names can we give to the two just mentioned, one in which the wealthy are more numerous, and one in which the poor are less numerous, each category being in its own case in sovereign control of the constitution? The argument seems to show that it is a matter of accident whether those who are sovereign be few or many (few in oligarchies, many in democracies): it just happens that way because everywhere the rich are few and the poor are many. So in fact the grounds of difference have been given wrongly: what really differentiates oligarchy and democracy is wealth or the lack of it. It inevitably follows that where men rule because of the possession of wealth, whether their number be large or small, that is oligarchy, and when the poor rule, that is democracy. But, as we have said, in actual fact the former are few, the latter many. Few are wealthy, but all share freedom alike: and these are the grounds of their respective claims to the constitution.

BOOK IV

Chapter 11
The Best Constitution

What is the best constitution and what is the best life for the majority of states and the majority of men? We have in mind men whose virtue does not rise above that of ordinary people, and whose education does not depend on the luck either of their natural ability or of their resources; and who have not an ideally perfect constitution, but first, a way of living in which as many as possible can join and, second, a constitution within the compass of the greatest number of states. The 'aristocracies', as they are called, that we have just been discussing do not fall within the competence of most states, but some of them do approximate closely to what we call polity (hence we ought to speak of both constitutions as though they were one and the same).

The decision on all these points rests on the same set of elementary principles. If we were right when in our *Ethics* we stated that virtue is a mean, and that the happy life is a life without hindrance in its accordance with virtue, then the best life must be the middle life, consisting in a mean which is open to men of every kind to attain. And the same principles must be applicable to the virtue or badness of constitutions and states. For the constitution of a state is in a sense the way it lives.

In all states there are three state-sections: the very well-off, the very badly off, and thirdly those in between. Since therefore it is agreed that moderation and a middle position are best, it is clear that, in the matter of the goods of fortune also, to own a middling amount is best of all. This condition is most easily obedient to reason, and following reason is just what is difficult both for the exceedingly rich, handsome, strong and well-born, and for their opposites, the extremely poor, the weak, and those grossly deprived of honour. The former incline more to arrogance and crime on a large scale, the latter are more than averagely prone to wicked ways and petty crime. The unjust deeds of the one class are due to an arrogant spirit, the unjust deeds of the other to wickedness. Add the fact that it is among the members of the middle section that you find least reluctance to hold office as well as least eagerness to do so; and both these attitudes, eagerness and reluctance, are detrimental to states.

There are other drawbacks about the two extremes. Those who have a superabundance of good fortune, strength, riches, friends, and so forth, neither wish to submit to rule nor understand how to do so; and this is engrained in them from childhood at home: even at school they are so full of *la dolce vita* that they have never grown used to being ruled. Those on the other hand who are greatly deficient in these qualities are too subservient. So they do not know how to rule, but only how to be ruled as a slave is; while the others do not know how to be ruled in any way at all, and can command only like a master ruling over slaves. The result is a state not of free men but of slaves and masters, the former full of envy, the latter of contempt. Nothing could be farther removed from friendship or from partnership in a state. Sharing is a token of friendship; one does not want to share even a journey with one's enemies. The state aims to consist as far as possible of those who are like and equal, a condition found chiefly among the middle people. And so the best run constitution is certain to be found in this state, whose composition is, we maintain, the natural one for a state to have.

It is the middle citizens in a state who are the most secure: they neither covet, like the poor, the possessions of others, nor do others covet theirs as the poor covet those of the rich. So they live without risk, not scheming and not being schemed against. Phocylides' prayer was therefore justified when he wrote, 'Those in the middle have many advantages; that is where I wish to be in the state.'

It is clear then both that the best partnership in a state is one which operates through the middle people, and also that those states in which the middle element is large, and stronger if possible than the other two together, or at any rate stronger than either of them alone, have every chance of having a well-run constitution. For the addition of its weight to either side will turn the balance and prevent excess at the opposing extremes. For this reason it is a most happy state of affairs when those who take part in the constitution have a middling, adequate amount of property; since where one set of people possess a great deal and the other nothing, the result is either extreme democracy or unmixed oligarchy, or a tyranny due to the excesses of either. For tyranny often emerges from an over-enthusiastic democracy or from an oligarchy, but much more rarely from intermediate constitutions or from those close to them. The reason for this we will speak of later when we deal with changes in constitutions.

The superiority of the middle constitution is clear also from the fact that it alone is free from factions. Where the middle element is large, there least of all arise factions and divisions among the citizens. And big states are freer from faction, for this same reason, namely that their middle element is large. In small states it is easy for the whole body of citizens to become divided into two, which leaves no middle at all, and nearly everybody either rich or poor. Democracies too are safer than oligarchies in this respect and longer-lasting thanks to their middle people, who are more numerous and take a larger share of honours in democracies than in oligarchies. For when in their absence the unpropertied preponderate in numbers, trouble arises and they soon come to grief. An indication of the truth of what we have been saying is to be found in the fact that the best lawgivers have come from the middle citizens—Solon, for example, whose middle position is revealed in his poems, and Lycurgus, who was not a king, and Charondas and most of the rest.

Leviathan

Thomas Hobbes

Thomas Hobbes was born in 1588 when the approach of the Spanish Armada was threatening Britain. "Fear and I were born twins," he would later say, emphasizing his conviction that the need for security was the foundation of society and the basis of political obligation. Hobbes lived until 91, having enjoyed a life of travel, study, polemical controversy, and literary and philosophical activity. He wrote on a variety of subjects, but his most famous work by far is *Leviathan*, published in 1691 and thought by many to be the greatest masterpiece of political philosophy in English.

Hobbes was influenced by the new, Galilean scientific method, and thought that physical laws could account for human behavior, just as they do all other phenomena. In *Leviathan*, he explains how our desires determine our actions, and he argues that reason and nature induce us to leave a "state of nature" and agree to be ruled by a common power strong enough to enforce our contracts and ensure peace.

THE FIRST PART: OF MAN

Chapter 6
Of the Interior Beginnings of Voluntary Motions, Commonly Called the Passions; and the Speeches by Which They are Expressed

Motion, vital and animal. Endeavour. There be in animals, two sorts of *motions* peculiar to them: one called *vital*; begun in generation, and continued without interruption through their whole life; such as are the *course* of the *blood*, the *pulse*, the *breathing*, the *concoction, nutrition, excretion*, &c., to which motions there needs no help of imagination: the other is *animal motion*, otherwise called *voluntary motion*; as to *go*, to *speak*, to *move* any of our limbs, in such manner as is first fancied in our minds. That sense is motion in the organs and interior parts of man's body, caused by the action of the things we see, hear, &c.; and that fancy is but the relics of the same motion, remaining after sense, has been already said in the first and second chapters. And because *going, speaking*, and the like voluntary motions, depend always upon a precedent thought of *whither, which way*, and *what*; it is evident, that the imagination is the first internal beginning of all voluntary motion. And although unstudied men do not conceive any motion at all to be there, where the thing moved is invisible; or the space it is moved in is, for the shortness of it, insensible; yet that doth not hinder, but that such motions are. For let a space be never so little, that which is moved over a greater space, whereof that little one is part, must first be moved over that. These small beginnings of motion, within the body of man, before they appear in walking, speaking, striking, and other visible actions, are commonly called ENDEAVOUR.

Appetite. Desire. Hunger. Thirst. Aversion. This endeavour, when it is toward something which causes it, is called APPETITE, or DESIRE; the latter, being the general name; and the other oftentimes restrained to signify the desire of food, namely *hunger* and *thirst*. And when the endeavour is fromward something, it is generally called AVERSION. These words, *appetite* and *aversion*, we have from the Latins; and they both of them signify the motions, one of approaching, the other of retiring. So also do the Greek words for the same. . . . For nature itself does often press upon men those truths, which afterwards, when they look for somewhat beyond nature, they stumble at. For the Schools find in mere appetite to go, or move, no actual motion at all: but because some motion they must acknowledge, they call it metaphorical motion; which is but an absurd speech: for though words may be called metaphorical; bodies and motions can not.

Love. Hate. That which men desire, they are also said to LOVE: and to HATE those things for which they have aversion. So that desire and love are the same thing; save that by desire, we always signify the absence of the object; by love, most commonly the presence of the same. So also by aversion, we signify the absence; and by hate, the presence of the object.

Contempt. Of appetites and aversions, some are born with men; as appetite of food, appetite of excretion, and exoneration, which may also and more properly be called aversions, from somewhat they feel in their bodies; and some other appetites, not many. The rest which are appetites of particular things, proceed from experience, and trial of their effects upon themselves or other men. For of things we know not at all, or believe not to be, we can have no further desire, than to taste and try. But aversion we

have for things, not only which we know have hurt us, but also that we do not know whether they will hurt us, or not.

Those things which we neither desire, nor hate, we are said to *contemn*: CONTEMPT being nothing else but an immobility, or contumacy of the heart, in resisting the action of certain things; and proceeding from that the heart is already moved otherwise, by other more potent objects; or from want of experience of them.

And because the constitution of a man's body is in continual mutation, it is impossible that all the same things should always cause in him the same appetites, and aversions: much less can men consent, in the desire of almost any one and the same object.

Good. Evil. But whatsoever is the object of any man's appetite or desire, that is it which he for his part calleth *good*: and the object of his hate and aversion, *evil*; and of his contempt, *vile* and *inconsiderable*. For these words of good, evil, and contemptible, are ever used with relation to the person that useth them: there being nothing simply and absolutely so; nor any common rule of good and evil, to be taken from the nature of the objects themselves; but from the person of the man, where there is no commonwealth; or, in a commonwealth, from the person that representeth it; or from an arbitrator or judge, whom men disagreeing shall by consent set up, and make his sentence the rule thereof. . . .

These simple passions called *appetite, desire, love, aversion, hate, joy*, and *grief*, have their names for divers considerations diversified. As first, when they one succeed another, they are diversely called from the opinion men have of the likelihood of attaining what they desire. Secondly, from the object loved or hated. Thirdly, from the consideration of many of them together. Fourthly, from the alteration or succession itself. . . .

Deliberation. When in the mind of man, appetites, and aversions, hopes, and fears, concerning one and the same thing, arise alternately; and divers good and evil consequences of the doing, or omitting the thing propounded, come successively into our thoughts; so that sometimes we have an appetite to it; sometimes an aversion from it; sometimes hope to be able to do it; sometimes despair, or fear to attempt it; the whole sum of desires, aversions, hopes and fears continued till the thing be either done, or thought impossible, is that we call DELIBERATION.

Therefore of things past, there is no *deliberation*; because manifestly impossible to be changed: nor of things known to be impossible, or thought so; because men know, or think such deliberation vain. But of things impossible, which we think possible, we may deliberate; not knowing it is in vain. And it is called *deliberation*; because it is a putting an end to the *liberty* we had of doing, or omitting, according to our own appetite, or aversion.

This alternate succession of appetites, aversions, hopes and fears, is no less in other living creatures than in man: and therefore beasts also deliberate.

Every *deliberation* is then said to *end*, when that whereof they deliberate, is either done, or thought impossible; because till then we retain the liberty of doing, or omitting; according to our appetite, or aversion.

The will. In *deliberation*, the last appetite, or aversion, immediately adhering to the action, or to the omission thereof, is that we call the WILL; the act, not the faculty, of *willing.* And beasts that have *deliberation*, must necessarily also have *will.* The definition of the *will*, given commonly by the Schools, that it is a *rational appetite*, is not good. For if it were, then could there be no voluntary act against reason. For a *voluntary act* is that, which proceedeth from the *will*, and no other. But if instead of a rational appetite, we shall say an appetite resulting from a precedent deliberation, then the definition is the same that I have given here. *Will* therefore *is the last appetite in deliberating.* And though we say in common discourse, a man had a will once to do a thing, that

nevertheless he forbore to do; yet that is properly but an inclination, which makes no action voluntary; because the action depends not of it, but of the last inclination, or appetite. For if the intervenient appetites, make any action voluntary; then by the same reason all intervenient aversions, should make the same action involuntary; and so one and the same action, should be both voluntary and involuntary.

By this it is manifest, that not only actions that have their beginning from covetousness, ambition, lust, or other appetites to the thing propounded; but also those that have their beginning from aversion, or fear of those consequences that follow the omission, are *voluntary actions.* . . .

Felicity. Continual *success* in obtaining those things which a man from time to time desireth, that is to say, continual prospering, is that men call FELICITY; I mean the felicity of this life. For there is no such thing as perpetual tranquillity of mind, while we live here; because life itself is but motion, and can never be without desire, nor without fear, no more than without sense. What kind of felicity God hath ordained to them that devoutly honour Him, a man shall no sooner know, than enjoy; being joys, that now are as incomprehensible, as the word of Schoolmen *beatifical vision* is unintelligible. . . .

Chapter 10
Of Power, Worth, Dignity, Honour, and Worthiness

Power. The POWER *of a man*, to take it universally, is his present means, to obtain some future apparent good; and is either *original* or *instrumental.*

Natural power, is the eminence of the faculties of body, or mind: as extraordinary strength, form, prudence, arts, eloquence, liberality, nobility. *Instrumental* are those powers, which acquired by these, or by fortune, are means and instruments to acquire more: as riches, reputation, friends, and the secret working of God, which men call good luck. For the nature of power, is in this point, like to fame, increasing as it proceeds; or like the motion of heavy bodies, which the further they go, make still the more haste.

The greatest of human powers, is that which is compounded of the powers of most men, united by consent, in one person, natural, or civil, that has the use of all their powers depending on his will; such as is the power of a commonwealth: or depending on the wills of each particular; such as is the power of a faction or of divers factions leagued. Therefore to have servants, is power; to have friends, is power: for they are strengths united.

Also riches joined with liberality, is power; because it procureth friends, and servants: without liberality, not so; because in this case they defend not; but expose men to envy, as a prey.

Reputation of power, is power; because it draweth with it the adherence of those that need protection.

So is reputation of love of a man's country, called popularity, for the same reason.

Also, what quality soever maketh a man beloved, or feared of many; or the reputation of such quality, is power; because it is a means to have the assistance, and service of many.

Good success is power; because it maketh reputation of wisdom, or good fortune; which makes men either fear him, or rely on him.

Affability of men already in power, is increase of power; because it gaineth love.

Reputation of prudence in the conduct of peace or war, is power; because to prudent men, we commit the government of ourselves, more willingly than to others.

Nobility is power, not in all places, but only in those commonwealths, where it has privileges: for in such privileges, consisteth the power.

Eloquence is power, because it is seeming prudence.

Form is power; because being a promise of good, it recommendeth men to the favour of women and strangers.

The sciences, are small power; because not eminent; and therefore, not acknowledged in any man; nor are at all, but in a few, and in them, but of a few things. For science is of that nature, as none can understand it to be, but such as in a good measure have attained it.

Arts of public use, as fortification, making of engines, and other instruments of war; because they confer to defence, and victory, are power: and though the true mother of them, be science, namely the mathematics; yet, because they are brought into the light, by the hand of the artificer, they be esteemed, the midwife passing with the vulgar for the mother, as his issue.

Worth. The *value*, or WORTH of a man, is as of all other things, his price; that is to say, so much as would be given for the use of his power: and therefore is not absolute; but a thing dependant on the need and judgment of another. An able conductor of soldiers, is of great price in time of war present, or imminent; but in peace not so. A learned and uncorrupt judge, is much worth in time of peace; but not so much in war. And as in other things, so in men, not the seller, but the buyer determines the price. For let a man, as most men do, rate themselves at the highest value they can; yet their true value is no more than it is esteemed by others.

The manifestation of the value we set on one another, is that which is commonly called honouring, and dishonouring. To value a man at a high rate, is to *honour* him; at a low rate, is to *dishonour* him. But high, and low, in this case, is to be understood by comparison to the rate that each man setteth on himself. . . .

Chapter 11
Of the Difference of Manners

What is here meant by manners. By MANNERS, I mean not here, decency of behaviour; as how one should salute another, or how a man should wash his mouth, or pick his teeth before company, and such other points of the *small morals*; but those qualities of mankind, that concern their living together in peace, and unity. To which end we are to consider, that the felicity of this life, consisteth not in the repose of a mind satisfied. For there is no such *finis ultimus*, utmost aim, nor *summum bonum*, greatest good, as is spoken of in the books of the old moral philosophers. Nor can a man any more live, whose desires are at an end, than he, whose senses and imaginations are at a stand. Felicity is a continual progress of the desire, from one object to another; the attaining of the former, being still but the way to the latter. The cause whereof is, that the object of man's desire, is not to enjoy once only, and for one instant of time; but to assure for ever, the way of his future desire. And therefore the voluntary actions, and inclinations of all men, tend, not only to the procuring, but also to the assuring of a contented life; and differ only in the way: which ariseth partly from the diversity of passions, in divers men; and partly from the difference of the knowledge, or opinion each one has of the causes, which produce the effect desired.

A restless desire of power in all men. So that in the first place, I put for a general inclination of all mankind, a perpetual and restless desire of power after power, that ceaseth only in death. And the cause of this, is not always that a man hopes for a more intensive delight, than he has already attained to; or that he cannot be content with a moderate power: but because he cannot assure the power and means to live well, which he hath present, without the acquisition of more. And from hence it is, that kings, whose power is greatest, turn their endeavours to the assuring it at home by laws, or abroad by wars: and when that is done, there succeedeth a new desire; in some, of fame from new conquest; in others, of ease and sensual pleasure; in others, of admiration, or being flattered for excellence in some art, or other ability of the mind.

Love of contention from competition. Competition of riches, honour, command, or other power, inclineth to contention, enmity, and war: because the way of one competitor, to the attaining of his desire, is to kill, subdue, supplant, or repel the other. Particularly, competition of praise, inclineth to a reverence of antiquity. For men contend with the living, not with the dead; to these ascribing more than due, that they may obscure the glory of the other.

Civil obedience from love of ease. From fear of death, or wounds. Desire of ease, and sensual delight, disposeth men to obey a common power: because by such desires, a man doth abandon the protection that might be hoped for from his own industry, and labour. Fear of death, and wounds, disposeth to the same; and for the same reason. On the contrary, needy men, and hardy, not contented with their present condition; as also, all men that are ambitious of military command, are inclined to continue the causes of war; and to stir up trouble and sedition: for there is no honour military but by war; not any such hope to mend an ill game, as by causing a new shuffle. . . .

Chapter 13
Of the Natural Condition of Mankind as Concerning Their Felicity and Misery

Men by nature equal. Nature hath made men so equal, in the faculties of the body, and mind; as that though there be found one man sometimes manifestly stronger in body, or of quicker mind than another; yet when all is reckoned together, the difference between man, and man, is not so considerable, as that one man can thereupon claim to himself any benefit, to which another may not pretend, as well as he. For as to the strength of body, the weakest has strength enough to kill the strongest, either by secret machination, or by confederacy with others, that are in the same danger with himself.

And as to the faculties of the mind, setting aside the arts grounded upon words, and especially that skill of proceeding upon general, and infallible rules, called science; which very few have, and but in few things; as being not a native faculty, born with us: nor attained, as prudence, while we look after somewhat else, I find yet a greater equality amongst men, than that of strength. For prudence, is but experience; which equal time, equally bestows on all men, in those things they equally apply themselves unto. That which may perhaps make such equality incredible, is but a vain conceit of one's own wisdom, which almost all men think they have in a greater degree, than the vulgar; that is, than all men but themselves, and a few others, whom by fame, or for concurring with themselves, they approve. For such is the nature of men, that howsoever they may acknowledge many others to be more witty, or more eloquent, or more learned; yet they will hardly believe there be many so wise as themselves; for they see their own wit at hand, and other men's at a distance. But this proveth rather that men are in that point equal, than unequal. For there is not ordinarily a greater sign of the equal distribution of any thing, than that every man is contented with his share.

From equality proceeds diffidence. From this equality of ability, ariseth equality of hope in the attaining of our ends. And therefore if any two men desire the same thing, which nevertheless they cannot both enjoy, they become enemies; and in the way to their end, which is principally their own conservation, and sometimes their delectation only, endeavour to destroy, or subdue one another. And from hence it comes to pass, that where an invader hath no more to fear, than another man's single power; if one plant, sow, build, or possess a convenient seat, others may probably be expected to come prepared with forces united, to dispossess, and deprive him, not only of the fruit of his labour, but also of his life, or liberty. And the invader again is in the like danger of another.

From diffidence war. And from this diffidence of one another, there is no way for any man to secure himself, so reasonable, as anticipation; that is, by force, or wiles, to master the persons of all men he can, so long, till he see no other power great enough to endanger him: and this is no more than his own conservation requireth, and is generally allowed. Also because there be some, that taking pleasure in contemplating their own power in the acts of conquest, which they pursue farther than their security requires; if others, that otherwise would be glad to be at ease within modest bounds, should not by invasion increase their power, they would not be able, long time, by standing only on their defence, to subsist. And by consequence, such augmentation of dominion over men being necessary to a man's conservation, it ought to be allowed him.

Again, men have no pleasure, but on the contrary a great deal of grief, in keeping company, where there is no power able to over-awe them all. For every man looketh that his companion should value him, at the same rate he sets upon himself: and upon all signs of contempt, or undervaluing, naturally endeavours, as far as he dares, (which amongst them that have no common power to keep them in quiet, is far enough to make them destroy each other), to extort a greater value from his contemners, by damage; and from others, by the example.

So that in the nature of man, we find three principal causes of quarrel. First, competition; secondly, diffidence; thirdly, glory.

The first, maketh men invade for gain; the second, for safety; and the third, for reputation. The first use violence, to make themselves masters of other men's persons, wives, children, and cattle; the second, to defend them; the third, for trifles, as a word, a smile, a different opinion, and any other sign of undervalue, either direct in their persons, or by reflection in their kindred, their friends, their nation, their profession, or their name.

Out of civil states, there is always war of every one against every one. Hereby it is manifest, that during the time men live without a common power to keep them all in awe, they are in that condition which is called war; and such a war, as is of every man, against every man. For WAR, consisteth not in battle only, or the act of fighting; but in a tract of time, wherein the will to contend by battle is sufficiently known: and therefore the notion of *time*, is to be considered in the nature of war; as it is in the nature of weather. For as the nature of foul weather, lieth not in a shower or two of rain; but in an inclination thereto of many days together: so the nature of war, consisteth not in actual fighting; but in the known disposition thereto, during all the time there is no assurance to the contrary. All other time is PEACE.

The incommodities of such a war. Whatsoever therefore is consequent to a time of war, where every man is enemy to every man; the same is consequent to the time, wherein men live without other security, than what their own strength, and their own invention shall furnish them withal. In such condition, there is no place for industry; because the fruit thereof is uncertain: and consequently no culture of the earth; no navigation, nor use of the commodities that may be imported by sea; no commodious building; no instruments of moving, and removing, such things as require much force; no knowledge of the face of the earth; no account of time; no arts; no letters; no society; and which is worst of all, continual fear, and danger of violent death; and the life of man, solitary, poor, nasty, brutish, and short.

It may seem strange to some man, that has not well weighed these things; that nature should thus dissociate, and render men apt to invade, and destroy one another: and he may therefore, not trusting to this inference, made from the passions, desire perhaps to have the same confirmed by experience. Let him therefore consider with himself, when taking a journey, he arms himself, and seeks to go well accompanied; when going to sleep, he locks his doors; when even in his house he locks his chests; and this when he knows there be laws, and public officers, armed, to revenge all injuries shall be done him; what opinion he has of his fellow-subjects, when he rides armed; of his fellow citizens, when he locks his doors; and of his children, and servants, when he locks his chests. Does he not there as much accuse mankind by his actions, as I do by my words? But neither of us accuse man's nature in it. The desires, and other passions of man, are in themselves no sin. No more are the actions, that proceed from those passions, till they know a law that forbids them: which till laws be made they cannot know: nor can any law be made, till they have agreed upon the person that shall make it.

It may peradventure be thought, there was never such a time, nor condition of war as this; and I believe it was never generally so, over all the world: but there are many places, where they live so now. For the savage people in many places of America, except the government of small families, the concord whereof dependeth on natural lust, have no government at all; and live at this day in that brutish manner, as I said before. Howsoever, it may be perceived what manner of life there would be, where there were no common power to fear, by the manner of life, which men that have formerly lived under a peaceful government, use to degenerate into, in a civil war.

But though there had never been any time, wherein particular men were in a condition of war one against another; yet in all times, kings, and persons of sovereign authority, because of their independency, are in continual jealousies, and in the state and posture of gladiators; having their weapons pointing, and their eyes fixed on one another; that is, their forts, garrisons, and guns upon the frontiers of their kingdoms; and continual spies upon their neighbours; which is a posture of war. But because they uphold thereby, the industry of their subjects; there does not follow from it, that misery, which accompanies the liberty of particular men.

In such a war nothing is unjust. To this war of every man, against every man, this also is consequent; that nothing can be unjust. The notions of right and wrong, justice and injustice have there no place. Where there is no common power, there is no law: where no law, no injustice. Force, and fraud, are in war the two cardinal virtues. Justice, and injustice are none of the faculties neither of the body, nor mind. If they were, they might be in a man that were alone in the world, as well as his senses, and passions. They are qualities, that relate to men in society, not in solitude. It is consequent also to the same condition, that there be no propriety, no dominion, no *mine* and *thine* distinct; but only that to be every man's, that he can get: and for so long, as he can keep it. And thus much for the ill condition, which man by mere nature is actually placed in; though with a possibility to come out of it, consisting partly in the passions, partly in his reason.

The passions that incline men to peace. The passions that incline men to peace, are fear of death; desire of such things as are necessary to commodious living; and a hope by their industry to obtain them. And reason suggesteth convenient articles of peace, upon which men may be drawn to agreement. These articles, are they, which otherwise are called the Laws of Nature: whereof I shall speak more particularly, in the two following chapters.

Chapter 14
Of the First and Second Natural Laws, and of Contracts

Right of nature what. The RIGHT OF NATURE, which writers commonly call *jus naturale*, is the liberty each man hath, to use his own power, as he will himself, for the preservation of his own nature; that is to say, of his own life; and consequently, of doing any thing, which in his own judgment, and reason, he shall conceive to be the aptest means thereunto.

Liberty what. By LIBERTY, is understood, according to the proper signification of the word, the absence of external impediments: which impediments, may oft take away part of a man's power to do what he would; but cannot hinder him from using the power left him, according as his judgment, and reason shall dictate to him.

A law of nature what. Difference of right and law. A LAW OF NATURE, *lex naturalis*, is a precept or general rule, found out by reason, by which a man is forbidden to do that, which is destructive of his life, or taketh away the means of preserving the same; and to omit that, by which he thinketh it may be best preserved. For though they that speak of this subject, use to confound *jus*, and *lex, right* and *law*: yet they ought to be distinguished; because RIGHT, consisteth in liberty to do, or to forbear: whereas LAW, determineth, and bindeth to one of them: so that law, and right, differ as much, as obligation, and liberty; which in one and the same matter are inconsistent.

Naturally every man has right to every thing. The fundamental law of nature. And because the condition of man, as hath been declared in the precedent chapter, is a condition of war of every one against every one; in which case every one is governed by his own reason; and there is nothing he can make use of, that may not be a help unto him, in preserving his life against his enemies; it followeth, that in such a condition, every man has a right to every thing; even to one another's body. And therefore, as long as this natural right of every man to every thing endureth, there can be no security to any man, how strong or wise soever he be, of living out the time, which nature ordinarily alloweth men to live. And consequently it is a precept, or general rule of reason, *that every man, ought to endeavour peace, as far as he has hope of obtaining it; and when he cannot obtain it, that he may seek, and use, all helps, and advantages of war.* The first branch of which rule, containeth the first, and fundamental law of nature; which is, *to seek peace, and follow it.* The second, the sum of the right of nature; which is, *by all means we can, to defend ourselves.*

The second law of nature. From this fundamental law of nature, by which men are commanded to endeavour peace, is derived this second law; *that a man be willing, when others are so too, as far-forth, as for peace, and defence of himself he shall think it necessary, to lay down this right to all things; and be contented with so much liberty against other men, as he would allow other men against himself.* For as long as every man holdeth this right, of doing any thing he liketh; so long are all men in the condition of war. But if other men will not lay down their right, as well as he; then there is no reason for any one to divest himself of his: for that were to expose himself to prey, which no man is bound to, rather than to dispose himself to peace. This is that law of the Gospel; *whatsoever you require that others should do to you, that do ye to them.* And that law of all men, *quod tibi fieri non vis, alteri ne feceris. . . .*

Not all rights are alienable. Whensoever a man transferreth his right, or renounceth it; it is either in consideration of some right reciprocally transferred to himself; or for some other good he hopeth for thereby. For it is a voluntary act: and of the voluntary acts of every man, the object is some *good to himself.* And therefore there be some rights, which no man can be understood by any words, or other signs, to have abandoned, or transferred. As first a man cannot lay down the right of resisting them, that assault him by force, to take away his life; because he cannot be understood to aim thereby, at any good to himself. The same may be said of wounds, and chains, and imprisonment; both because there is no benefit consequent to such patience; as there is to the patience of suffering another to be wounded, or imprisoned: as also because a man cannot tell, when he seeth men proceed against him by violence whether they intend his death or not. And lastly the motive, and end for which this renouncing, and transferring of right is introduced, is nothing else but the security of a man's person, in his life, and in the means of so preserving life, as not to be weary of it. And therefore if a man by words, or other signs, seem to despoil himself of the end, for which those signs were intended; he is not to be understood as if he meant it, or that it was his will; but that he was ignorant of how such words and actions were to be interpreted.

Contract what. The mutual transferring of right, is that which men call CONTRACT. . . .

Covenants of mutual trust, when invalid. If a covenant be made, wherein neither of the parties perform presently, but trust one another; in the condition of mere nature, which is a condition of war of every man against every man, upon any reasonable suspicion, it is void; but if there be a common power set over them both, with right and force sufficient to compel performance, it is not void. For he that performeth first, has no assurance the other will perform after; because the bonds of words are too weak to bridle men's ambition, avarice, anger, and other passions, without the fear of some coercive power; which in the condition of mere nature, where all men are equal, and judges of the justness of their own fears, cannot possibly be supposed. And therefore he which performeth first does but betray himself to his enemy; contrary to the right, he can never abandon, of defending his life, and means of living.

But in a civil estate, where there is a power set up to constrain those that would otherwise violate their faith, that fear is no more reasonable; and for that cause, he which by the covenant is to perform first, is obliged so to do. . . .

Covenants extorted by fear are valid. Covenants entered into by fear, in the condition of mere nature, are obligatory. For example, if I covenant to pay a ransom, or service for my life, to an enemy; I am bound by it: for it is a contract, wherein one receiveth the benefit of life; the other is to receive money, or service for it; and consequently, where no other law, as in the condition of mere nature, forbiddeth the performance, the covenant is valid. Therefore prisoners of war, if trusted with the payment of their ransom, are obliged to pay it: and if a weaker prince, make a disadvantageous peace with a stronger, for fear; he is bound to keep it; unless, as hath been said before, there ariseth some new, and just cause of fear, to renew the war. And even in commonwealths, if I be forced to redeem myself from a thief by promising him money, I am bound to pay it, till the civil law discharge me. For whatsoever I may lawfully do without obligation, the same I may lawfully covenant to do through fear; and what I lawfully covenant, I cannot lawfully break. . . .

A man's covenant not to defend himself is void. A covenant not to defend myself from force, by force, is always void. For, as I have showed before, no man can transfer, or lay down his right to save himself from death, wounds, and imprisonment, the avoiding whereof is the only end of laying down any right; and therefore the promise of not resisting force, in no covenant transferreth any right; nor is obliging. For though a man may covenant thus, *unless I do so, or so, kill me*; he cannot covenant thus, *unless I do so, or so, I will not resist you, when you come to kill me*. For man by nature chooseth the lesser evil, which is danger of death in resisting; rather than the greater, which is certain and present death in not resisting. And this is granted to be true by all men, in that they lead criminals to execution, and prison, with armed men, notwithstanding that such criminals have consented to the law, by which they are condemned. . . .

The end of an oath. The form of an oath. The force of words, being, as I have formerly noted, too weak to hold men to the performance of their covenants; there are in man's nature, but two imaginable helps to strengthen it. And those are either a fear of the consequence of breaking their word; or a glory, or pride in appearing not to need to break it. This latter is a generosity too rarely found to be presumed on, especially in the pursuers of wealth, command, or sensual pleasure; which are the greatest part of mankind. The passion to be reckoned upon, is fear; whereof there be two very general objects: one, the power of spirits invisible; the other, the power of those men they shall therein offend. Of these two, though the former be the greater power, yet the fear of the latter is commonly the greater fear. . . .

Chapter 15
Of Other Laws of Nature

The third law of nature, justice. From that law of nature, by which we are obliged to transfer to another, such rights, as being retained, hinder the peace of mankind, there followeth a third; which is this, *that men perform their covenants made*: without which, covenants are in vain, and but empty words; and the right of all men to all things remaining, we are still in the condition of war.

Justice and injustice what. And in this law of nature, consisteth the fountain and original of JUSTICE. For where no covenant hath preceded, there hath no right been transferred, and every man has right to every thing; and consequently, no action can be unjust. But when a covenant is made, then to break it is *unjust*: and the definition of INJUSTICE, is no other than *the not performance of covenant*. And whatsoever is not unjust, is *just*.

Justice and propriety begin with the constitution of commonwealth. But because covenants of mutual trust, where there is a fear of not performance on either part, as hath been said in the former chapter, are invalid; though the original of justice be the making of covenants; yet injustice actually there can be none, till the cause of such fear be taken away; which while men are in the natural condition of war, cannot be done. Therefore before the names of just, and unjust can have place, there must be some coercive power, to compel men equally to the performance of their covenants, by the terror of some punishment, greater than the benefit they expect by the breach of their covenant; and to make good that propriety, which by mutual contract men acquire, in recompense of the universal right they abandon: and such power there is none before the erection of a commonwealth. And this is also to be gathered out of the ordinary definition of justice in the Schools: for they say, that *justice is the constant will of giving to every man his own.* And therefore where there is no *own,* that is no propriety, there is no injustice; and where there is no coercive power erected, that is, where there is no commonwealth, there is no propriety; all men having right to all things: therefore where there is no commonwealth, there nothing is unjust. So that the nature of justice, consisteth in keeping of valid covenants: but the validity of covenants begins not but with the constitution of a civil power, sufficient to compel men to keep them: and then it is also that propriety begins.

Justice not contrary to reason. The fool hath said in his heart, there is no such thing as justice; and sometimes also with his tongue: seriously alleging, that every man's conservation, and contentment, being committed to his own care, there could be no reason, why every man might not do what he thought conduced thereunto: and therefore also to make, or not make; keep, or not keep covenants, was not against reason, when it conduced to one's benefit. He does not therein deny, that there be covenants; and that they are sometimes broken, sometimes kept; and that such breach of them may be called injustice, and the observance of them justice: but he questioneth, whether injustice, taking away the fear of God, for the same fool hath said in his heart there is no God, may not sometimes stand with that reason, which dictateth to every man his own good; and particularly then, when it conduceth to such a benefit, as shall put a man in a condition, to neglect not only the dispraise, and revilings, but also the power of other men. The kingdom of God is gotten by violence: but what if it could be gotten by unjust violence? were it against reason so to get it, when it is impossible to receive hurt by it? and if it be not against reason, it is not against justice; or else justice is not to be approved for good. From such reasoning as this, successful wickedness hath obtained the name of virtue: and some that in all other things have disallowed the violation of faith; yet have allowed it, when it is for the getting of a kingdom. And the heathen that believed, that Saturn was deposed by his son Jupiter, believed nevertheless the same Jupiter to be the avenger of injustice: somewhat like to a piece of law in Coke's *Commentaries on Littleton*; where he says, if the right heir of the crown be attainted of treason; yet the crown shall descend to him, and *eo instante* the attainder be void: from which instances a man will be very prone to infer; that when the heir apparent of a kingdom, shall kill him that is in possession, though his father; you may call it injustice, or by what other name you will; yet it can never be against reason, seeing all the voluntary actions of men tend to the benefit of themselves; and those actions are most reasonable, that conduce most to their ends. This specious reasoning is nevertheless false.

For the question is not of promises mutual, where there is no security of performance on either side; as when there is no civil power erected over the parties promising; for such promises are no covenants: but either where one of the parties has performed already; or where there is a power to make him perform; there is the question whether it be against reason, that is, against the benefit of the other to perform, or not. And I say it is not against reason. For the manifestation whereof, we are to consider; first, that when a man doth a thing, which notwithstanding any thing can be foreseen, and reckoned on, tendeth to his own destruction, howsoever some accident which he could not expect, arriving may turn it to his benefit; yet such events do not make it reasonably or wisely done. Secondly, that in a condition of war, wherein every man to every man, for want of a common power to keep them all in awe, is an enemy, there is no man who can hope by his own strength, or wit, to defend himself from destruction, without the help of confederates; where every one expects the same defence by the confederation, that any one else does: and therefore he which declares he thinks it reason to deceive those that help him, can in reason expect no other means of safety, than what can be had from his own single power. He therefore that breaketh his covenant, and consequently declareth that he thinks he may with reason do so, cannot be received into any society, that unite themselves for peace and defence, but by the error of them that receive him; nor when he is received, be retained in it, without seeing the danger of their error; which errors a man cannot reasonably reckon upon as the means of his security: and therefore if he be left, or cast out of society, he perisheth; and if he live in society, it is by the errors of other men, which he could not foresee, nor reckon upon; and consequently against the reason of his preservation; and so, as all men that contribute not to his destruction, forbear him only out of ignorance of what is good for themselves.

As for the instance of gaining the secure and perpetual felicity of heaven, by any way; it is frivolous: there being but one way imaginable; and that is not breaking, but keeping of covenant.

And for the other instance of attaining sovereignty by rebellion: it is manifest, that though the event follow, yet because it cannot reasonably be expected, but rather the contrary; and because by gaining it so, others are taught to gain the same in like manner, the attempt thereof is against reason. Justice therefore, that is to say, keeping of covenant, is a rule of reason, by which we are forbidden to do any thing destructive to our life; and consequently a law of nature.

There be some that proceed further; and will not have the law of nature, to be those rules which conduce to the preservation of man's life on earth; but to the attaining of an eternal felicity after death; to which they think the breach of covenant may conduce; and consequently be just and reasonable; such are they that think it a work of merit to kill, or depose, or rebel against, the sovereign power constituted over them by their own consent. But because there is no natural knowledge of man's estate after death; much less of the reward that is then to be given to breach of faith; but only a belief grounded upon other men's saying, that they know it supernaturally, or that they know those, that knew them, that knew others, that knew it supernaturally; breach of faith cannot be called a precept of reason, or nature....

THE SECOND PART: OF COMMONWEALTH

Chapter 17
Of the Causes, Generation, and Definition of a Commonwealth

The end of commonwealth, particular security. The final cause, end, or design of men, who naturally love liberty, and dominion over others, in the introduction of that restraint upon themselves, in which we see them live in commonwealths, is the foresight of their own preservation, and of a more contented life thereby; that is to say, of getting themselves out from that miserable condition of war, which is necessarily consequent, as hath been shown (chapter 13), to the natural passions of men, when there is no visible power to keep them in awe, and tie them by fear of punishment to the performance of their covenants, and observation of those laws of nature set down in the fourteenth and fifteenth chapters.

Which is not to be had from the law of nature. For the laws of nature, as *justice, equality, modesty, mercy,* and, in sum, *doing to others, as we would be done to,* of themselves, without the terror of some power, to cause them to be observed, are contrary to our natural passions, that carry us to partiality, pride, revenge, and the like. And covenants, without the sword, are but words, and of no strength to secure a man at all. Therefore notwithstanding the laws of nature (which every one hath then kept, when he has the will to keep them, when he can do it safely) if there be no power erected or not great enough for our security; every man will, and may lawfully rely on his own strength and art, for caution against all other men. . . . For if we could suppose a great multitude of men to consent in the observation of justice, and other laws of nature, without a common power to keep them all in awe; we might as well suppose all mankind to do the same; and then there neither would be, nor need to be any civil government, or commonwealth at all; because there would be peace without subjection.

And that continually. Nor is it enough for the security, which men desire should last all the time of their life, that they be governed, and directed by one judgment, for a limited time; as in one battle, or one war. For though they obtain a victory by the unanimous endeavour against a foreign enemy; yet afterwards, when they have no common enemy, or he that by one part is held for an enemy, is by another part held for a friend, they must needs by the difference of their interests dissolve, and fall again into a war amongst themselves. . . .

The generation of a commonwealth. The definition of a commonwealth. The only way to erect such a common power, as may be able to defend them from the invasion of foreigners, and the injuries of one another, and thereby to secure them in such sort, as that by their own industry, and by the fruits of the earth, they may nourish themselves and live contentedly; is, to confer all their power and strength upon one man, or upon one assembly of men, that may reduce all their wills, by plurality of voices, unto one will: which is as much as to say, to appoint one man, or assembly of men, to bear their person; and every one to own, and acknowledge himself to be author of whatsoever he that so beareth their person, shall act, or cause to be acted, in those things which con-

cern the common peace and safety; and therein to submit their wills, every one to his will, and their judgments, to his judgment. This is more than consent, or concord; it is a real unity of them all, in one and the same person, made by covenant of every man with every man, in such manner, as if every man should say to every man, *I authorize and give up my right of governing myself, to this man, or to this assembly of men, on this condition, that thou give up thy right to him, and authorize all his actions in like manner.* This done, the multitude so united in one person, is called a COMMONWEALTH, in Latin CIVITAS. This is the generation of that great LEVIATHAN, or rather, to speak more reverently, of that *mortal god*, to which we owe under the *immortal God*, our peace and defence. For by this authority, given him by every particular man in the commonwealth, he hath the use of so much power and strength conferred on him, that by terror thereof, he is enabled to form the wills of them all, to peace at home, and mutual aid against their enemies abroad. And in him consisteth the essence of the commonwealth; which, to define it, is *one person, of whose acts a great multitude, by mutual covenants one with another, have made themselves every one the author, to the end he may use the strength and means of them all, as he shall think expedient, for their peace and common defence.*

Sovereign, and subject, what. And he that carrieth this person, is called SOVEREIGN, and said to have *sovereign power*; and every one besides, his SUBJECT.

The attaining to this sovereign power, is by two ways. One, by natural force; as when a man maketh his children, to submit themselves, and their children to his government, as being able to destroy them if they refuse; or by war subdueth his enemies to his will, giving them their lives on that condition. The other, is when men agree amongst themselves, to submit to some man, or assembly of men, voluntarily, on confidence to be protected by him against all others. This latter, may be called a political commonwealth, or commonwealth by *institution*; and the former, a commonwealth by acquisition. And first, I shall speak of a commonwealth by institution.

Chapter 18
Of the Rights of Sovereigns
by Institution

The act of instituting a commonwealth, what. A *commonwealth* is said to be *instituted*, when a *multitude* of men do agree, and *covenant, every one, with every one*, that to whatsoever *man*, or *assembly of men*, shall be given by the major part, the *right* to *present* the person of them all, that is to say, to be their *representative*; every one, as well he that *voted for it*, as he that *voted against it*, shall *authorize* all the actions and judgments, of that man, or assembly of men, in the same manner, as if they were his own, to the end, to live peaceably amongst themselves, and be protected against other men.

The consequences to such institutions, are: From this institution of a commonwealth are derived all the *rights*, and *faculties* of him, or them, on whom the sovereign power is conferred by the consent of the people assembled.

1. The subjects cannot change the form of government. First, because they covenant, it is to be understood, they are not obliged by former covenant to any thing repugnant hereunto. And consequently they that have already instituted a commonwealth, being thereby bound by covenant, to own the actions, and judgments of one, cannot lawfully make a new covenant, amongst themselves, to be obedient to any other, in any thing whatsoever, without his permission. And therefore, they that are subjects to a monarch, cannot without his leave cast off monarchy, and return to the confusion of a disunited multitude; nor transfer their person from him that beareth it, to another man, or other assembly of men: for they are bound, every man to every man, to own, and be reputed author of all, that he that already is their sovereign, shall do, and judge fit to be done: so that any one man dissenting, all the

rest should break their covenant made to that man, which is injustice: and they have also every man given the sovereignty to him that beareth their person; and therefore if they depose him, they take from him that which is his own, and so again it is injustice. Besides, if he that attempteth to depose his sovereign, be killed, or punished by him for such attempt, he is author of his own punishment, as being by the institution, author of all his sovereign shall do: and because it is injustice for a man to do any thing, for which he may be punished by his own authority, he is also upon that title, unjust. . . .

2. Sovereign power cannot be forfeited. Secondly, because the right of bearing the person of them all, is given to him they make sovereign, by covenant only of one to another, and not of him to any of them; there can happen no breach of covenant on the part of the sovereign; and consequently none of his subjects, by any pretence of forfeiture, can be freed from his subjection. . . . Besides, if any one, or more of them, pretend a breach of the covenant made by the sovereign as his institution; and others, or one other of his subjects, or himself alone, pretend there was no such breach, there is in this case, no judge to decide the controversy; it returns therefore to the sword again; and every man recovereth the right of protecting himself by his own strength, contrary to the design they had in the institution. It is therefore in vain to grant sovereignty by way of precedent covenant. The opinion that any monarch receiveth his power by covenant, that is to say, on condition, proceedeth from want of understanding this easy truth, that covenants being but words and breath, have no force to oblige, contain, constrain, or protect any man, but what it has from the public sword; that is, from the untied hands of that man, or assembly of men that hath the sovereignty, and whose actions are avouched by them all, and performed by the strength of them all, in him united. . . .

3. No man can without injustice protest against the institution of the sovereign de-

clared by the major part. Thirdly, because the major part hath by consenting voices declared a sovereign; he that dissented must now consent with the rest; that is, be contented to avow all the actions he shall do, or else justly be destroyed by the rest. For if he voluntarily entered into the congregation of them that were assembled, he sufficiently declared thereby his will, and therefore tacitly covenanted, to stand to what the major part should ordain: and therefore if he refuse to stand thereto, or make protestation against any of their decrees, he does contrary to his covenant, and therefore unjustly. And whether he be of the congregation, or not; and whether his consent be asked, or not, he must either submit to their decrees, or be left in the condition of war he was in before; wherein he might without injustice be destroyed by any man whatsoever.

4. The sovereign's actions cannot be justly accused by the subject. Fourthly, because every subject is by this institution author of all the actions, and judgments of the sovereign instituted; it follows, that whatsoever he doth, it can be no injury to any of his subjects; nor ought he to be by any of them accused of injustice. For he that doth anything by authority from another, doth therein no injury to him by whose authority he acteth: but by this institution of a commonwealth, every particular man is author of all the sovereign doth: and consequently he that complaineth of injury from his sovereign, complaineth of that whereof he himself is author; and therefore ought not to accuse any man but himself, no nor himself of injury; because to do injury to one's self, is impossible. It is true that they that have sovereign power may commit iniquity; but not injustice, or injury in the proper signification.

5. Whatsoever the sovereign doth is unpunishable by the subject. Fifthly, and consequently to that which was said last, no man that hath sovereign power can justly be put to death, or otherwise in any manner by his subjects punished. For seeing every subject is author of the actions of his sovereign; he punisheth another for the actions committed by himself.

6. The sovereign is judge of what is necessary for the peace and defence of his subjects. And because the end of this institution, is the peace and defence of them all; and whosoever has right to the end, has right to the means; it belongeth of right, to whatsoever man, or assembly that hath the sovereignty, to be judge both of the means of peace and defence, and also of the hindrances, and disturbances of the same; and to do whatsoever he shall think necessary to be done, both beforehand, for the preserving of peace and security, by prevention of discord at home, and hostility from abroad; and, when peace and security are lost, for the recovery of the same. And therefore,

And judge of what doctrines are fit to be taught them. Sixthly, it is annexed to the sovereignty, to be judge of what opinions and doctrines are averse, and what conducing to peace; and consequently, on what occasions, how far, and what men are to be trusted withal, in speaking to multitudes of people; and who shall examine the doctrines of all books before they be published. For the actions of men proceed from their opinions; and in the well-governing of opinions, consisteth the well-governing of men's actions, in order to their peace, and concord. And though in matter of doctrine, nothing ought to be regarded but the truth; yet this is not repugnant to regulating the same by peace. For doctrine repugnant to peace, can no more be true, than peace and concord can be against the law of nature. It is true, that in a commonwealth, where by the negligence, or unskilfulness of governors, and teachers, false doctrines are by time generally received; the contrary truths may be generally offensive. Yet the most sudden, and rough busling in of a new truth, that can be, does never break the peace, but only sometimes awake the war. For those men that are so remissly governed, that they dare take up arms to defend, or introduce an opinion, are still in war; and their condition not peace, but only a cessation of arms for fear of one another; and they live, as it were, in the precincts of battle continually. It belongeth therefore to him that hath the sovereign power, to be judge, or constitute all judges of opinions and doctrines, as a thing necessary to peace; thereby to prevent discord and civil war.

7. The right of making rules; whereby the subjects may every man know what is so his own, as no other subject can without injustice take it from him. Seventhly, is annexed to the sovereignty, the whole power of prescribing the rules, whereby every man may know, what goods he may enjoy, and what actions he may do, without being molested by any of his fellow-subjects; and this is it men call *propriety*. For before constitution of sovereign power, as hath already been shown, all men had right to all things; which necessarily causeth war: and therefore this propriety, being necessary to peace, and depending on sovereign power, is the act of that power, in order to the public peace. These rules of propriety, or *meum* and *tuum*, and of *good, evil, lawful*, and *unlawful* in the actions of subjects, are the civil laws; that is to say, the laws of each commonwealth in particular: though the name of civil law be now restrained to the ancient civil laws of the city of Rome; which being the head of a great part of the world, her laws at that time were in these parts the civil law.

8. To him also belongeth the right of judicature and decision of controversy. Eightly, is annexed to the sovereignty, the right of judicature; that is to say, of hearing and deciding all controversies, which may arise concerning law, either civil, or natural; or concerning fact. For without the decision of controversies, there is no protection of one subject, against the injuries of another; the laws concerning *meum* and *tuum* are in vain; and to every man remaineth, from the natural and necessary appetite of his own conservation, the right of protecting himself by his private strength, which is the condition of war, and contrary to the end for which every commonwealth is instituted. . . .

Sovereign power not so hurtful as the want of it, and the hurt proceeds for the greatest part from not submitting readily to a less. But a man may here object, that the condition of subjects is very miserable; as being obnoxious to the lusts, and other irregular passions of him, or them that have so unlimited a power in their hands. And commonly they that live under a monarch, think it the fault of monarchy; and they that live under the government of democracy, or other sovereign assembly, attribute all the, inconvenience to that form of commonwealth; whereas the power in all forms, if they be perfect enough to protect them, is the same: not considering that the state of man can never be without some incommodity or other; and that the greatest, that in any form of government can possibly happen to the people in general, is scarce sensible in respect of the miseries, and horrible calamities, that accompany a civil war, or that dissolute condition of masterless men, without subjection to laws, and a coercive power to tie their hands from rapine and revenge: nor considering that the greatest pressure of sovereign governors, proceedeth not from any delight, or profit they can expect in the damage or weakening of their subjects, in whose vigour, consisteth their own strength and glory; but in the restiveness of themselves, that unwillingly contributing to their own defence, make it necessary for their governors to draw from them what they can in time of peace, that they may have means on any emergent occasion, or sudden need, to resist, or take advantage on their enemies. For all men are by nature provided of notable multiplying glasses, that is their passions and self-love, through which, every little payment appeareth a great grievance; but are destitute of those prospective glasses, namely moral and civil science, to see afar off the miseries that hang over them, and cannot without such payments be avoided.

Chapter 21
Of the Liberty of Subjects

Liberty, what. LIBERTY, or FREEDOM, signifieth, properly, the absence of opposition; by opposition, I mean external impediments of motion; and may be applied no less to irrational, and inanimate creatures, than to rational. For whatsoever is so tied, or environed, as it cannot move but within a certain space, which space is determined by the opposition of some external body, we say it hath not liberty to go further. And so of all living creatures, whilst they are imprisoned, or restrained, with walls, or chains; and of the water whilst it is kept in by banks, or vessels, that otherwise would spread itself into a larger space, we use to say, they are not at liberty, to move in such manner, as without those external impediments they would. But when the impediment of motion, is in the constitution of the thing itself, we use not to say; it wants the liberty; but the power to move; as when a stone lieth still, or a man is fastened to his bed by sickness.

What it is to be free. And according to this proper, and generally received meaning of the word, a FREEMAN, *is he that in those things, which by his strength and wit he is able to do, is not hindered to do what he has a will to.* But when the words *FREE*, and *liberty*, are applied to any thing but *bodies*, they are abused; for that which is not subject to motion, is not subject to impediment: and therefore, when it is said, for example, the way is free, no liberty of the way is signified, but of those that walk in it without stop. And when we say a gift is free, there is not meant any liberty of the gift, but of the giver, that was not bound by any law or covenant to give it. So when we *speak freely*, it is not the liberty of voice, or pronunciation, but of the man, whom no law hath obliged to speak otherwise than he did. Lastly, from the use of the word *free-will*, no liberty can be inferred of the will, desire, or inclination, but the liberty of the man; which consisteth in this, that he finds no stop, in doing what he has the will, desire, or inclination to do.

Fear and liberty consistent. Fear and liberty are consistent; as when a man throweth his goods into the sea for *fear* the ship should sink, he doth it nevertheless very willingly, and may refuse to do it if he will: it is therefore the action of one that was *free*: so a man sometimes pays his debt, only for *fear* of imprisonment, which because nobody hindered him from detaining, was the action of a man at *liberty*. And generally all actions which men do in commonwealths, for *fear* of the law, are actions, which the doers had *liberty* to omit.

Liberty and necessity consistent. Liberty, and *necessity* are consistent: as in the water, that hath not only *liberty*, but a *necessity* of descending by the channel; so likewise in the actions which men voluntarily do: which, because they proceed from their will, proceed from *liberty*; and yet, because every act of man's will, and every desire, and inclination proceedeth from some cause, and that from another cause, in a continual chain, whose first link is in the hand of God the first of all causes, proceed from *necessity*. So that to him that could see the connexion of those causes, the *necessity* of all men's voluntary actions, would appear manifest. And therefore God, that seeth, and disposeth all things, seeth also that the *liberty* of man in doing what he will, is accompanied with the *necessity* of doing that which God will, and no more, nor less. For though men may do many things, which God does not command, nor is therefore author of them; yet they can have no passion, nor appetite to any thing, of which appetite God's will is not the cause. And did not his will assure the *necessity* of man's will, and consequently of all that on man's will dependeth, the *liberty* of men would be a contradiction, and impediment to the omnipotence and *liberty* of God. And this shall suffice, as to the matter in hand, of that natural *liberty*; which only is properly called *liberty*. . . .

Liberty of subjects how to be measured. To come now to the particulars of the true liberty of a subject; that is to say, what are the things, which though commanded by the sovereign, he may nevertheless, without injustice, refuse to do; we are to consider, what rights we pass away, when we make a commonwealth; or, which is all one, what liberty we deny ourselves, by owning all the actions, without exception, of the man, or assembly we make our sovereign. For in the act of our *submission*, consisteth both our *obligation*, and our *liberty*; which must therefore be inferred by arguments taken from thence; there being no obligation on any man, which ariseth not from some act of his own; for all men equally, are by nature free. And because such arguments, must either be drawn from the express words, I *authorize all his actions*, or from the intention of him that submitteth himself to his power, which intention is to be understood by the end for which he so submitteth; the obligation, and liberty of the subject, is to be derived, either from those words, or others equivalent; or else from the end of the institution of sovereignty, namely, the peace of the subjects within themselves, and their defence against a common enemy.

Subjects have liberty to defend their own bodies, even against them that lawfully invade them. First therefore, seeing sovereignty by institution, is by covenant of every one to every one; and sovereignty by acquisition, by covenants of the vanquished to the victor, or child to the parent; it is manifest, that every subject has liberty in all those things, the right whereof cannot by covenant be transferred. I have shewn before in the 14th chapter, that covenants, not to defend a man's own body, are void. Therefore,

Are not bound to hurt themselves. If the sovereign command a man, though justly condemned, to kill, wound, or maim himself; or not to resist those that assault him; or to abstain from the use of food, air, medicine, or any other thing, without which he cannot live; yet hath that man the liberty to disobey.

If a man be interrogated by the sovereign, or his authority, concerning a crime done by himself, he is not bound, without assurance of pardon, to confess it; because no man, as I have shown in the same chapter, can be obliged by covenant to accuse himself.

Again, the consent of a subject to sovereign power, is contained in these words, *I authorize, or take upon me, all his actions*; in which there is no restriction at all, of his own former natural liberty: for by allowing him to *kill me*, I am not bound to kill myself when he commands me. It is one thing to say, *kill me, or my fellow, if you please*; another thing to say, *I will kill myself, or my fellow*. It followeth therefore, that

No man is bound by these words themselves, either to kill himself, or any other man; and consequently, that the obligation a man may sometimes have, upon the command of the sovereign to execute any dangerous, or dishonourable office, dependeth not on the words of our submission; but on the intention, which is to be understood by the end thereof. When therefore our refusal to obey, frustrates the end for which the sovereignty was ordained; then there is no liberty to refuse: otherwise there is.

Nor to warfare, unless they voluntarily undertake it. Upon this ground, a man that is commanded as a soldier to fight against the enemy, though his sovereign have right enough to punish his refusal with death, may nevertheless in many cases refuse, without injustice; as when he substituteth a sufficient soldier in his place: for in this case he deserteth not the service of the commonwealth. And there is allowance to be made for natural timorousness; not only to women, of whom no such dangerous duty is expected, but also to men of feminine courage. When armies fight, there is on one side, or both, a running away; yet when they do it not out of treachery, but fear, they are not esteemed to do it unjustly, but dishonourably. For the same reason, to avoid battle, is not injustice, but cowardice. But he that enrolleth himself a soldier, or taketh imprest money, taketh away the excuse of a timorous nature; and is obliged, not only to go to the battle, but also not to run from it, without his captain's leave. And when the defence of the commonwealth, requireth at once the help of all that are able to bear arms, every one is obliged; because otherwise the institution of the commonwealth, which they have not the purpose, or courage to preserve, was in vain.

To resist the sword of the commonwealth, in defence of another man, guilty, or innocent, no man hath liberty; because such liberty takes away from the sovereign, the means of protecting us; and is therefore destructive of the very essence of government. But in case a great many men together, have already resisted the sovereign power unjustly, or committed some capital crime, for which every one of them expecteth death, whether have they not the liberty then to join together, and assist, and defend one another? Certainly they have: for they but defend their lives, which the guilty man may as well do, as the innocent. There was indeed injustice in the first breach of their duty; their bearing of arms subsequent to it, though it be to maintain what they have done, is no new unjust act. And if it be only to defend their persons, it is not unjust at all. But the offer of pardon taketh from them, to whom it is offered, the plea of self-defence, and maketh their perseverance in assisting, or defending the rest, unlawful.

The greatest liberty of subjects, dependeth on the silence of the law. As for other liberties, they depend on the silence of the law. In cases where the sovereign has prescribed no rule, there the subject hath the liberty to do, or forbear, according to his own discretion. And therefore such liberty is in some places more, and in some less; and in some times more, in other times less, according as they that have the sovereignty shall think most convenient. As for example, there was a time, when in England a man might enter into his own land, and dispossess such as wrongfully possessed it, by force. But in aftertimes, that liberty of forcible entry, was taken away by a statute made, by the king, in parliament. And in some places of the world, men have the liberty of many wives: in other places, such liberty is not allowed. . . .

In what cases subjects are absolved of their obedience to their sovereign. The obligation of subjects to the sovereign, is understood to last as long, and no longer, than the power lasteth, by which he is able to protect them. For the right men have by nature to protect themselves, when none else can protect them, can by no covenant be relinquished. The sovereignty is the soul of the commonwealth; which once departed from the body, the members do no more receive their motion from it. The end of obedience is protection; which, wheresoever a man seeth it, either in his own, or in another's sword, nature applieth his obedience to it, and his endeavour to maintain it. And though sovereignty, in the intention of them that make it, be immortal; yet is it in its own nature, not only subject to violent death, by foreign war; but also through the ignorance, and passions of men, it hath in it, from the very institution, many seeds of a natural mortality, by intestine discord. . . .

Second Treatise of Government

John Locke

Locke's *Two Treatises of Government* was published anonymously in 1689 (although apparently written some years earlier) and was widely acclaimed. The second of these treatises presents Locke's social contract theory and his defense of the right of a people to change governments, which have had an enduring impact on political thought. (See Section III for more information on Locke's life and work.)

Chapter II
Of the State of Nature

4. To understand political power right, and derive it from its original, we must consider what state all men are naturally in, and that is, a state of perfect freedom to order their actions, and dispose of their possessions, and persons as they think fit, within the bounds of the law of Nature, without asking leave, or depending upon the will of any other man.

A state also of equality, wherein all the power and jurisdiction is reciprocal, no one having more than another: there being nothing more evident, than that creatures of the same species and rank promiscuously born to all the same advantages of Nature, and the use of the same faculties, should also be equal one amongst another without subordination or subjection, unless the Lord and Master of them all, should by any manifest declaration of his will set one above another, and confer on him by an evident and clear appointment an undoubted right to dominion and sovereignty.

6. But though this be a state of liberty, yet it is not a state of licence, though man in that state have an uncontrollable liberty, to dispose of his person or possessions, yet he has not liberty to destroy himself, or so much as any creature in his possession, but where some nobler use, than its bare preservation calls for it. The state of Nature has a law of Nature to govern it, which obliges every one: and reason, which is that law, teaches all mankind, who will but consult it, that being all equal and independent, no one ought to harm another in his life, health, liberty, or possessions. For men being all the workmanship of one Omnipotent, and infinitely wise Maker; all the servants of one Sovereign Master, sent into the world by his order and about his business; they are his property, whose workmanship they are, made to last during his, not one another's pleasure. And being furnished with like faculties, sharing all in one community of Nature, there cannot be supposed any such subordination among us, that may authorize us to destroy one another, as if we were made for one another's uses, as the inferior ranks of creatures are for ours. Every one as he is bound to preserve himself, and not to quit his station willfully; so by the like reason when his own preservation comes not in competition, ought he, as much as he can, to preserve the rest of mankind, and may not unless it be to do justice on an offender, take away, or impair the life, or what tends to the

preservation of the life, liberty, health, limb or goods of another.

7. And that all men may be restrained from invading others' rights, and from doing hurt to one another, and the law of Nature be observed, which wills the peace and preservation of all mankind, the execution of the law of Nature is in that state, put into every man's hands, whereby every one has a right to punish the transgressors of that law to such a degree, as may hinder its violation. For the law of Nature would, as all other laws that concern men in this world, be in vain, if there were no body that in the state of Nature, had a power to execute that law, and thereby preserve the innocent and restrain offenders, and if any one in the state of Nature may punish another, for any evil he has done, every one may do so. For in that state of perfect equality, where naturally there is no superiority or jurisdiction of one, over another, what any may do in prosecution of that law, every one must needs have a right to do.

8. And thus in the state of Nature, one man comes by a power over another; but yet no absolute or arbitrary power, to use a criminal when he has got him in his hands, according to the passionate heats, or boundless extravagancy of his own will, but only to retribute to him, so far as calm reason and conscience dictates, what is proportionate to his transgression, which is so much as may serve for reparation and restraint. For these two are the only reasons, why one man may lawfully do harm to another, which is that we call punishment. In transgressing the law of Nature, the offender declares himself to live by another rule, than that of reason and common equity, which is that measure God has set to the actions of men, for their mutual security: and so he becomes dangerous to mankind, the tie, which is to secure them from injury and violence, being slighted and broken by him. Which being a trespass against the whole species, and the peace and safety of it, provided for by the law of Nature, every man upon this score, by the right he has to preserve mankind in general, may restrain, or where it is necessary, destroy things noxious to them, and so may bring such evil on any one, who has transgressed that law, as may make him repent the doing of it, and thereby deter him, and by his example others, from doing the like mischief. And in this case, and upon this ground, every man has a right to punish the offender, and be executioner of the law of Nature.

14. It is often asked as a mighty objection, Where are, or ever were, there any men in such a state of Nature? To which it may suffice as an answer at present; that since all princes and rulers of independent governments all through the world, are in a state of Nature, it is plain the world never was, nor ever will be, without numbers of men in that state. I have named all governors of independent communities, whether they are, or are not, in league with others: for it is not every compact that puts an end to the state of Nature between men, but only this one of agreeing together mutually to enter into one community, and make one body politic; other promises and compacts, men may make one with another, and yet still be in the state of Nature. The promises and bargains for truck, & c. between the two men in the desert island, mentioned by Garcilasso de la Vega, in his history of Peru, or between a Swiss and an Indian, in the woods of America, are binding to them, though they are perfectly in a state of Nature, in reference to one another. For truth and keeping of faith belongs to men, as men, and not as members of society.

Chapter V
Of Property

25. Whether we consider natural reason, which tells us, that men, being once born, have a right to their preservation, and consequently to meat and drink, and such other things, as Nature affords for their subsistence: or revelation, which gives us an account of those grants God made of the world to Adam, and to Noah, and his sons, it is very clear, that God, as King David says, *Psal.* CXV, xvi. has given the Earth to the

children of men, given it to mankind in common. But this being supposed, it seems to some a very great difficulty, how any one should ever come to have a property in anything: I will not content myself to answer, that if it be difficult to make out property, upon a supposition, that God gave the world to Adam and his posterity in common; it is impossible that any man, but one universal monarch, should have any property, upon a supposition, that God gave the world to Adam, and his heirs in succession, exclusive of all the rest of his posterity. But I shall endeavour to show how men might come to have a property in several parts of that which God gave to mankind in common, and that without any express compact of all the commoners.

26. God, who has given the world to men in common, has also given them reason to make use of it, to the best advantage of life, and convenience. The Earth, and all that is therein, is given to men for the support and comfort of their being. And though all the fruits it naturally produces, and beasts it feeds, belong to mankind in common, as they are produced by the spontaneous hand of Nature; and nobody has originally a private dominion, exclusive of the rest of mankind, in any of them, as they are thus in their natural state: yet being given for the use of men, there must of necessity be a means to appropriate them some way or other before they can be of any use, or at all beneficial to any particular man. The fruit, or venison, which nourishes the wild Indian, who knows no inclosure, and is still a tenant in common, must be his, and so his, i.e. a part of him, that another can no longer have any right to it, before it can do him any good for the support of his life.

27. Though the Earth, and all inferior creatures be common to all men, yet every man has a property in his own person. This nobody has any right to but himself. The labour of his body, and the work of his hands, we may say, are properly his. Whatsoever then he removes out of the state that Nature has provided, and left it in, he has mixed his labour with, and joined to it some-

thing that is his own, and thereby makes it his property. It being by him removed from the common state Nature placed it in, has by his labour something annexed to it, that excludes the common right of other men. For this labour being the unquestionable property of the labourer, no man but he can have a right to what that is once joined to, at least where there is enough, and as good left in common for others.

28. He that is nourished by the acorns he picked up under an oak, or the apples he gathered from the trees in the wood, has certainly appropriated them to himself. Nobody can deny but the nourishment is his. I ask then, When did they begin to be his? When he digested? Or when he eat? Or when he boiled? Or when he brought them home? Or when he picked them up? And it is plain, if the first gathering made them not his, nothing else could. That labour put a distinction between them and common. That added something to them more than Nature, the common mother of all, had done; and so they became his private right. And will any one say he had no right to those acorns or apples he thus appropriated, because he had not the consent of all mankind to make them his? Was it a robbery thus to assume to himself what belonged to all in common? If such a consent as that was necessary, man had starved, notwithstanding the plenty God had given him. We see in commons, which remain so by compact, that it is the taking any part of what is common, and removing it out of the state Nature leaves it in, which begins the property; without which the common is of no use. And the taking of this or that part does not depend on the express consent of all the commoners. Thus the grass my horse has bit; the turfs my servant has cut; and the ore I have dug in any place where I have a right to them in common with others, become my property, without the assignation or consent of any body. The labour that was mine, removing them out of the common state they were in, has fixed my property in them.

31. It will perhaps be objected to this, that if gathering the acorns, or other fruits of the earth, &c. makes a right to them, then any one may ingross as much as he will. To which I answer, not so. The same law of Nature, that does by this means give us property, does also bound that property too. "God has given us all things richly" (*1 Tim.* vi. 17) is the voice of reason confirmed by inspiration. But how far has he given it us? To enjoy. As much as any one can make use of to any advantage of life before it spoils; so much he may by his labour fix a property in. Whatever is beyond this, is more than his share, and belongs to others. Nothing was made by God for man to spoil or destroy. And thus considering the plenty of natural provisions there was a long time in the world, and the few spenders, and to how small a part of that provision the industry of one man could extend itself, and ingross it to the prejudice of others; especially keeping within the bounds, set by reason of what might serve for his use; there could be then little room for quarrels or contentions about property so established.

32. But the chief matter of property being now not the fruits of the Earth, and the beasts that subsist on it, but the Earth itself; as that which takes in and carries with it all the rest: I think it is plain, that property in that too is acquired as the former. As much land as a man tills, plants, improves, cultivates, and can use the product of, so much is his property. He by his labour does, as it were, inclose it from the common. Nor will it invalidate his right to say, everybody else has an equal title to it; and therefore he cannot appropriate, he cannot inclose, without the consent of all his fellow commoners, all mankind. God, when he gave the world in common to all mankind, commanded man also to labour, and the penury of his condition required it of him. God and his reason commanded him to subdue the Earth, i.e. improve it for the benefit of life, and therein lay out something upon it that was his own, his labour. He that in obedience to this command of God, subdued, tilled and sowed any part of it, thereby annexed to it something that was his property,

which another had no title to, nor could without injury take from him.

33. Nor was this appropriation of any parcel of land, by improving it, any prejudice to any other man, since there was still enough, and as good left; and more than the yet unprovided could use. So that in effect, there was never the less left for others because of his enclosure for himself. For he that leaves as much as another can make use of, does as good as take nothing at all. Nobody could think himself injured by the drinking of another man, though he took a good draught, who had a whole river of the same water left him to quench his thirst. And the case of land and water, where there is enough of both, is perfectly the same.

Chapter VI
Of Paternal Power

52. It may perhaps be censured as an impertinent criticism, in a discourse of this nature, to find fault with words and names that have obtained in the world; and yet possibly it may not be amiss to offer new ones when the old are apt to lead men into mistakes, as this of "paternal power" probably has done, which seems so to place the power of parents over their children wholly in the father, as if the mother had no share in it; whereas, if we consult reason or revelation, we shall find she has an equal title. This may give one reason to ask whether this might not be more properly called "parental power," for whatever obligation nature and the right of generation lays on children, it must certainly bind them equally to both concurrent causes of it. And accordingly we see the positive law of God everywhere joins them together without distinction when it commands the obedience of children: "Honour thy father and thy mother" (Exod. xx. 12); "Whosoever curseth his father or his mother" (Lev. xx. 9); "Ye shall fear every man his mother and his father" (Lev. xix. 5); "Children, obey your parents," etc. (Eph. vi. I), is the style of the Old and New Testament.

53. Had but this one thing been well considered, without looking any deeper into the matter, it might perhaps have kept men from running into those gross mistakes they have made about this power of parents, which, however it might without any great harshness bear the name of absolute dominion and regal authority, when under the title of "paternal power" it seemed appropriated to the father, would yet have sounded but oddly and in the very name shown the absurdity if this supposed absolute power over children had been called "parental," and thereby have discovered that it belonged to the mother, too; for it will but very ill serve the turn of those men who contend so much for the absolute power and authority of the fatherhood, as they call it, that the mother should have any share in it; and it would have but ill supported the monarchy they contend for, when by the very name it appeared that that fundamental authority from whence they would derive their government of a single person only was not placed in one but two persons jointly. But to let this of names pass.

54. Though I have said above (Chap. II) that all men by nature are equal, I cannot be supposed to understand all sorts of equality. Age or virtue may give men a just precedence; excellence of parts and merit may place others above the common level; birth may subject some, and alliance or benefits others, to pay an observance to those whom nature, gratitude, or other respects may have made it due; and yet all this consists with the equality which all men are in, in respect of jurisdiction or dominion one over another, which was the equality I there spoke of as proper to the business in hand, being that equal right that every man has to his natural freedom, without being subjected to the will or authority of any other man.

55. Children, I confess, are not born in this state of equality, though they are born to it. Their parents have a sort of rule and jurisdiction over them when they come into the world, and for some time after, but it is

but a temporary one. The bonds of this subjection are like the swaddling clothes they are wrapped up in and supported by in the weakness of their infancy; age and reason, as they grow up, loosen them, till at length they drop quite off and leave a man at his own free disposal.

57. The law that was to govern Adam was the same that was to govern all his posterity—the law of reason. But his offspring having another way of entrance into the world, different from him, by a natural birth that produced them ignorant and without the use of reason, they were not presently under the law; for nobody can be under a law which is not promulgated to him; and this law being promulgated or made known by reason only, he that is not come to the use of his reason cannot be said to be under this law; and Adam's children, being not presently as soon as born under this law of reason, were not presently free; for law, in its true notion, is not so much the limitation as the direction of a free and intelligent agent to his proper interest, and prescribes no further than is for the general good of those under that law. Could they be happier without it, the law, as a useless thing, would of itself vanish; and that ill deserves the name of confinement which hedges us in only from bogs and precipices. So that, however it may be mistaken, the end of law is not to abolish or restrain but to preserve and enlarge freedom; for in all the states of created beings capable of laws, where there is no law, there is no freedom. For liberty is to be free from restraint and violence from others, which cannot be where there is not law; but freedom is not, as we are told: a liberty for every man to do what he lists—for who could be free, when every other man's humor might domineer over him?—but a liberty to dispose and order as he lists his person, actions, possessions, and his whole property, within the allowance of those laws under which he is, and therein not to be subject to the arbitrary will of another, but freely follow his own.

58. The power, then, that parents have

over their children arises from that duty which is incumbent on them—to take care of their offspring during the imperfect state of childhood. To inform the mind and govern the actions of their yet ignorant nonage till reason shall take its place and ease them of that trouble is what the children want and the parents are bound to; for God, having given man an understanding to direct his actions, has allowed him a freedom of will and liberty of acting as properly belonging thereunto, within the bounds of that law he is under. But while he is in an estate wherein he has not understanding of his own to direct his will, he is not to have any will of his own to follow; he that understands for him must will for him, too; he must prescribe to his will and regulate his actions; but when he comes to the estate that made his father a freeman, the son is a freeman, too.

Chapter VII
Of Political or Civil Society

77. God, having made man such a creature that in his own judgment it was not good for him to be alone, put him under strong obligations of necessity, convenience, and inclination to drive him into society, as well as fitted him with understanding and language to continue and enjoy it. The first society was between man and wife, which gave beginning to that between parents and children; to which, in time, that between master and servant came to be added; and though all these might, and commonly did, meet together and make up but one family wherein the master or mistress of it had some sort of rule proper to a family—each of these, or all together, came short of political society, as well shall see if we consider the different ends, ties, and bounds of each of these.

78. Conjugal society is made by a voluntary compact between man and woman; and though it consist chiefly in such a communion and right in one another's bodies as is necessary to its chief end, procreation, yet it draws with it mutual support and assistance,

and a communion of interests, too, as necessary not only to unite their care and affection, but also necessary to their common offspring, who have a right to be nourished and maintained by them till they are able to provide for themselves.

79. For the end of conjunction between male and female being not barely procreation but the continuation of the species, this conjunction betwixt male and female ought to last, even after procreation, so long as is necessary to the nourishment and support of the young ones who are to be sustained by those that got them till they are able to shift and provide for themselves. This rule, which the infinite wise Maker has set to the works of his hands, we find the inferior creatures steadily obey. In those viviparous animals which feed on grass, the conjunction between male and female lasts no longer than the very act of copulation, because the teat of the dam being sufficient to nourish the young till it be able to feed on grass, the male only begets, but concerns not himself for the female or young to whose sustenance he can contribute nothing. But in beasts of prey the conjunction lasts longer because, the dam not being able well to subsist herself and nourish her numerous offspring by her own prey alone, a more laborious as well as more dangerous way of living than by feeding on grass, the assistance of the male is necessary to the maintenance of their common family, which cannot subsist till they are able to prey for themselves but by the joint care of male and female. The same is to be observed in all birds—except some domestic ones, where plenty of food excuses the cock from feeding and taking care of the young brood—whose young needing food in the nest, the cock and hen continue mates till the young are able to use their wing and provide for themselves.

80. And herein, I think, lies the chief, if not the only, reason why the male and female in mankind are tied to a longer conjunction than other creatures, viz., because the female is capable of conceiving, and *de* *facto* is commonly with child again and brings forth, too, a new birth long before the former is out of a dependency for support on his parents' help and able to shift for himself and has all the assistance that is due to him from his parents; whereby the father, who is bound to take care for those he has begot, is under an obligation to continue in conjugal society with the same woman longer than other creatures whose young being able to subsist of themselves before the time of procreation returns again, the conjugal bond dissolves of itself, and they are at liberty, till Hymen at his usual anniversary season summons them again to choose new mates. Wherein one cannot but admire the wisdom of the great Creator, who, having given to man foresight and an ability to lay up for the future as well as to supply the present necessity, has made it necessary that society of man and wife should be more lasting than of male and female amongst other creatures, that so their industry might be encouraged and their interest better united to make provision and lay up goods for their common issue, which uncertain mixture or easy and frequent solutions of conjugal society would mightily disturb.

81. But though these are ties upon mankind which make the conjugal bonds more firm and lasting in man than the other species of animals, yet it would give one reason to inquire why this compact, where procreation and education are secured and inheritance taken care for, may not be made determinable, either by consent, or at a certain time, or upon certain conditions, as well as any other voluntary compacts, there being no necessity in the nature of the thing nor to the ends of it that it should always be for life; I mean, to such as are under no restraint of any positive law which ordains all such contracts to be perpetual.

82. But the husband and wife, though they have but one common concern, yet having different understandings, will unavoidably sometimes have different wills, too; it therefore being necessary that the last determination—i.e., the rule—should be placed somewhere, it naturally falls to the man's share, as the abler and the stronger. But this, reaching but to the things of their common interest and property, leaves the wife in the full and free possession of what by contract is her peculiar right, and gives the husband no more power over her life than she has over his; the power of the husband being so far from that of an absolute monarch that the wife has in many cases a liberty to separate from him where natural right or their contract allows it, whether that contract be made by themselves in the state of nature, or by the customs or laws of the country they live in; and the children upon such separation fall to the father's or mother's lot, as such contract does determine.

83. For all the ends of marriage being to be obtained under politic government as well as in the state of nature, the civil magistrate does not abridge the right or power of either naturally necessary to those ends, viz., procreation and mutual support and assistance while they are together, but only decides any controversy that may arise between man and wife about them. If it were otherwise, and that absolute sovereignty and power of life and death naturally belonged to the husband and were necessary to the society between man and wife, there could be no matrimony in any of those countries where the husband is allowed no such absolute authority. But the ends of matrimony requiring no such power in the husband, the condition of conjugal society put it not in him, it being not at all necessary to that state. Conjugal society could subsist and attain its ends without it; nay, community of goods and the power over them, mutual assistance and maintenance, and other things belonging to conjugal society, might be varied and regulated by that contract which unites man and wife in that society as far as may consist with procreation and the bringing up of children till they could shift for themselves, nothing being necessary to any society that is not necessary to the ends for which it is made.

86. Let us therefore consider a master of a family with all these subordinate relations of wife, children, servants, and slaves, united under the domestic rule of a family; which, what resemblance soever it may have in its order, offices, and number, too, with a little commonwealth, yet is very far from it, both in its constitution, power, and end; or, if it must be thought a monarchy, and the paterfamilias the absolute monarch in it, absolute monarchy will have but a very shattered and short power when it is plain, by what has been said before, that the master of the family has a very distinct and differently limited power both as to time and extent over those several persons that are in it; for excepting the slave—and the family is as much a family, and his power as paterfamilias as great, whether there be any slaves in his family or no—he has no legislative power of life and death over any of them, and none, too, but what a mistress of a family may have as well as he. And he certainly can have no absolute power over the whole family who has but a very limited one over every individual in it. But how a family or any other society of men differ from that which is properly political society, we shall best see by considering wherein political society itself consists.

87. Man being born, as has been proved, with a title to perfect freedom, and an uncontrolled enjoyment of all the rights and privileges of the law of Nature, equally with any other man, or number of men in the world, has by nature a power, not only to preserve his property, that is, his life, liberty and estate, against the injuries and attempts of other men; but to judge of, and punish the breaches of that law in others, as he is persuaded the offence deserves, even with death itself, in crimes where the heinousness of the fact, in his opinion, requires it. But because no political society can be, nor subsist without having in itself the power to preserve the property, and in order thereunto punish the offences of all those of that society; there, and there only is political society, where every one of the members has

quitted this natural power, resigned it up into the hands of the community in all cases that exclude him not from appealing for protection to the law established by it. And thus all private judgment of every particular member being excluded, the community comes to be umpire, by settled standing rules, indifferent, and the same to all parties; and by men having authority from the community, for the execution of those rules, decides all the differences that may happen between any members of that society, concerning any matter of right; and punishes those offences, which any member has committed against the society, with such penalties as the law has established: whereby it is easier to discern who are, and who are not, in political society together. Those who are united into one body, and have a common established law and judicature to appeal to, with authority to decide controversies between them, and punish offenders, are in civil society one with another: but those who have no such common appeal, I mean on Earth, are still in the state of Nature, each being, where there is no other, judge for himself, and executioner; which is, as I have before shown it, the perfect state of Nature.

88. And thus the commonwealth comes by a power to set down, what punishment shall belong to the several transgressions which they think worthy of it, committed amongst the members of that society—which is the power of making laws—as well as it has the power to punish any injury done unto any of its members, by any one that is not of it—which is the power of war and peace—and all this for the preservation of the property of all the members of that society, as far as is possible. But though every man who has entered into civil society, and is become a member of any commonwealth, has thereby quitted his power to punish offences against the law of Nature, in prosecution of his own private judgment; yet with the judgment of offences which he has given up to the legislative in all cases, where he can appeal to the magistrate, he has given a right to the commonwealth to employ his force, for the execution of the judgments of the commonwealth, whenever he shall be called to it; which indeed are his own judgments, they being made by himself, or his representative. And herein we have the original of the legislative and executive power of civil society, which is to judge by standing laws how far offences are to be punished, when committed within the commonwealth; and also to determine by occasional judgments founded on the present circumstances of the fact, how far injuries from without are to be vindicated, and in both these to employ all the force of all the members when there shall be need.

89. Wherever therefore any number of men are so united into one society, as to quit everyone his executive power of the law of Nature, and to resign it to the public, there and there only is a political, or civil society. And this is done wherever any number of men, in the state of Nature, enter into society to make one people, one body politic under one supreme government, or else when anyone joins himself to, and incorporates with any government already made. For hereby he authorizes the society, or which is all one, the legislative thereof to make laws for him as the public good of the society shall require; to the execution whereof, his own assistance (as to his own decrees) is due. And this puts men out of a state of Nature into that of a commonwealth, by setting up a judge on Earth, with authority to determine all the controversies, and redress the injuries, that may happen to any member of the commonwealth; which judge is the legislative, or magistrates appointed by it. And wherever there are any number of men, however associated, that have no such decisive power to appeal to, there they are still in the state of Nature.

90. Hence it is evident, that absolute monarchy, which by some men is counted the only government in the world, is indeed inconsistent with civil society, and so can be no form of civil government at all. For the end of civil society, being to avoid, and remedy those inconveniencies of the state of Nature, which necessarily follow from every man's being judge in his own case, by setting up a known authority, to which everyone of that society may appeal upon any injury received, or controversy that may arise, and which everyone of the society ought to obey; wherever any persons are, who have not such an authority to appeal to, for the decision of any difference between them, there those persons are still in the state of Nature. And so is every absolute prince in respect of those who are under his dominion.

Chapter VIII
Of the Beginning of Political Societies

95. Men being, as has been said, by Nature, all free, equal and independent, no one can be put out of this estate, and subjected to the political power of another, without his own consent. The only way whereby any one divests himself of his natural liberty, and puts on the bonds of civil society is by agreeing with other men to join and unite into a community, for their comfortable, safe, and peaceable living one amongst another, in a secure enjoyment of their properties, and a greater security against any that are not of it. This any number of men may do, because it injures not the freedom of the rest; they are left as they were in the liberty of the state of Nature. When any number of men have so consented to make one community or government, they are thereby presently incorporated, and make one body politic, wherein the majority have a right to act and conclude the rest.

96. For when any number of men have, by the consent of every individual, made a community, they have thereby made that community one body, with a power to act as one body, which is only by the will and determination of the majority. For that which acts any community, being only the consent of the individuals of it, and it being necessary to that which is one body to move one way; it is necessary the body should move that way whither the greater force carries it, which is the consent of the majority: or else it is impossible it should act or continue one body, one community, which the consent of every individual that united into it, agreed that it should; and so every one is bound by that consent to be concluded by the majority. And therefore we see that in assemblies empowered to act by positive laws where no number is set by that positive law which empowers them, the act of the majority passes for the act of the whole, and of course determines, as having by the law of Nature and reason, the power of the whole.

97. And thus every man, by consenting with others to make one body politic under one government, puts himself under an obligation to every one of that society, to submit to the determination of the majority, and to be concluded by it; or else this original compact, whereby he with others incorporates into one society, would signify nothing, and be no compact, if he be left free, and under no other ties, than he was in before in the state of Nature. For what appearance would there be of any compact? What new engagement if he were no farther tied by any decrees of the society, than he himself thought fit, and did actually consent to? This would be still as great a liberty, as he himself had before his compact, or any one else in the state of Nature has, who may submit himself and consent to any acts of it if he thinks fit.

98. For if the consent of the majority shall not in reason, be received, as the act of the whole, and conclude every individual; nothing but the consent of every individual can make any thing to be the act of the whole: but such a consent is next impossible ever to be had, if we consider the infirmities of health, and avocations of business, which in a number, though much less than that of a commonwealth, will necessarily keep many away from the public assembly. To which if we add the variety of opinions, and contrariety of interests, which unavoidably happen in all collections of men, the coming into society upon such terms, would be only like Cato's coming into the theatre, only to go out again. Such a constitution as this would make the mighty *Leviathan* of a shorter duration, than the feeblest creatures; and not let it outlast the day it was born in: which cannot be supposed till we can think, that rational creatures should desire and constitute societies only to be dissolved. For where the majority cannot conclude the rest, there they cannot act as one body, and consequently will be immediately dissolved again.

99. Whosoever therefore out of a state of Nature unite into a community, must be understood to give up all the power, necessary to the ends for which they unite into society, to the majority of the community, unless they expressly agreed in any number greater than the majority. And this is done by barely agreeing to unite into one political society, which is all the compact that is, or needs be, between the individuals, that enter into, or make up a commonwealth. And thus that, which begins and actually constitutes any political society, is nothing but the consent of any number of freemen capable of a majority to unite and incorporate into such a society. And this is that, and that only, which did, or could give beginning to any lawful government in the world.

119. Every man being, as has been shown, naturally free, and nothing being able to put him into subjection to any earthly power, but only his own consent; it is to be considered, what shall be understood to be a sufficient declaration of a man's consent, to make him subject to the laws of any government. There is a common distinction of an express and a tacit consent, which will concern our present case. Nobody doubts that an express consent, of any man, entering into any society, makes him a perfect member of that society, a subject of that government. The difficulty is, what ought to be looked upon as a tacit consent, and how far it binds, i.e. how far anyone shall be looked on to have consented, and thereby submitted to any government, where he has made no expressions of it at all. And to this I say, that every Man, that has any possession, or enjoyment, of any part of the dominions of any government, does thereby give his tacit consent, and is as far forth obliged to obedience to the laws of that government, during such enjoyment, as any one under it; whether this his possession be of land, to him and his heirs for ever, or a lodging only for a week; or whether it be barely travelling freely on the highway; and in effect, it reaches as far as the very being, of any one within the territories of that government.

Chapter IX
Of the Ends of Political Society and Government

123. If man in the state of Nature be so free, as has been said; if he be absolute lord of his own person and possessions, equal to the greatest and subject to nobody, why will he part with his freedom? Why will he give up this empire, and subject himself to the dominion and control of any other power? To which it is obvious to answer, that though in the state of Nature he has such a right, yet the enjoyment of it is very uncertain, and constantly exposed to the invasion of others. For all being kings as much as he, every man his equal, and the greater part no strict observers of equity and justice, the enjoyment of the property he has in this state is very unsafe, very insecure. This makes him willing to quit a condition, which however free, is full of fears and continual dangers: and it is not without reason, that he seeks out, and is willing to join in society with others who are already united, or have a mind to unite for the mutual preservation of their lives, liberties and estates, which I call by the general name, property.

124. The great and chief end therefore, of men's uniting into commonwealths, and putting themselves under government, is the preservation of their property. To which in the state of Nature there are many things wanting.

First, there wants an established, settled, known law, received and allowed by common consent to be the standard of right and wrong, and the common measure to decide all controversies between them. For though the law of Nature be plain and intelligible to

all rational creatures; yet men being biassed by their interest, as well as ignorant for want of study of it, are not apt to allow it as a law binding to them in the application of it to their particular cases.

125. Secondly, in the state of Nature there wants a known and indifferent judge, with authority to determine all differences according to the established law. For everyone in that state being both judge and executioner of the law of Nature, men being partial to themselves, passion and revenge is very apt to carry them too far, and with too much heat, in their own cases; as well as negligence, and unconcernedness, to make them too remiss, in other men's.

126. Thirdly, in the state of Nature there often wants power to back and support the sentence when right, and to give it due execution. They who by any injustice offended, will seldom fail, where they are able, by force to make good their injustice: such resistance many times makes the punishment dangerous, and frequently destructive, to those who attempt it.

127. Thus mankind, notwithstanding all the privileges of the state of Nature, being but in an ill condition, while they remain in it, are quickly driven into society. Hence it comes to pass, that we seldom find any number of men live any time together in this state. The inconveniencies, that they are therein exposed to, by the irregular and uncertain exercise of the power every man has of punishing the transgressions of others, make them take sanctuary under the established law of government, and therein seek the preservation of their property. It is this makes them so willingly give up every one his single power of punishing to be exercised by such alone as shall be appointed to it amongst them; and by such rules as the community, or those authorised by them to that purpose, shall agree on. And in this we have the original right and rise of both the legislative and executive power, as well as of the governments and societies themselves.

131. But though men when they enter into society, give up the equality, liberty, and executive power they had in the state of

Nature, into the hands of the society, to be so far disposed of by the legislative, as the good of the society shall require; yet it being only with an intention in every one the better to preserve himself his liberty and property; (for no rational creature can be supposed to change his condition with an intention to be worse) the power of the society, or legislative constituted by them, can never be supposed to extend farther than the common good; but is obliged to secure every one's property by providing against those three defects above-mentioned, that made the state of Nature so unsafe and uneasy. And so whoever has the legislative or supreme power of any commonwealth, is bound to govern by established standing laws, promulgated and known to the people, and not by extemporary decrees; by indifferent and upright judges, who are to decide controversies by those laws; and to employ the force of the community at home, only in the execution of such laws, or abroad to prevent or redress foreign injuries, and secure the community from inroads and invasion. And all this to be directed to no other end, but the peace, safety, and public good of the people.

Chapter XI
Of the Extent of Legislative Power

137. Absolute arbitrary power, or governing without settled standing laws, can neither of them consist with the ends of society and government, which men would not quit the freedom of the state of Nature for, and tie themselves up under, were it not to preserve their lives, liberties and fortunes, and by stated rules of right and property to secure their peace and quiet. It cannot be supposed that they should intend, had they a power so to do, to give to any one, or more, an absolute arbitrary power over their persons and estates, and put a force into the magistrate's hand to execute his unlimited will arbitrarily upon them. This were to put themselves into a worse condition than the state of Nature, wherein they had a liberty to defend their right

against the injuries of others, and were upon equal terms of force to maintain it, whether invaded by a single man, or many in combination.

139. But government, into whatsoever hands it is put, being, as I have before shewed, intrusted with this condition, and for this end, that men might have and secure their properties; the prince, or senate, however it may have power to make laws, for the regulating of property between the subjects one amongst another, yet can never have a power to take to themselves the whole, or any part of the subjects, property, without their own consent: for this would be in effect to leave them no property at all.

140. It is true, governments cannot be supported without great charge, and it is fit every one who enjoys his share of the protection, should pay out of his estate his proportion for the maintenance of it. But still it must be with his own consent, i.e. the consent of the majority, giving it either by themselves, or their representatives chosen by them: for if any one shall claim a power to lay and levy taxes on the people, by his own authority, and without such consent of the people, he thereby invades the fundamental law of property, and subverts the end of government: for what property have I in that, which another may by right take, when he pleases, to himself?

142. These are the bounds which the trust, that is put in them by the society, and the law of God and nature, have set to the legislative power of every commonwealth, in all forms of government.

First, They are to govern by promulgated established laws, not to be varied in particular cases, but to have one rule for rich and poor, for the favourite at court, and the country man at plough.

Secondly, These laws also ought to be designed for no other end ultimately, but the good of the people.

Thirdly, They must not raise taxes on the property of the people, without the consent of the people, given by themselves, or their deputies. And this properly concerns only such governments where the legislative is always in being, or at least where the people have not reserved any part of the legislative to deputies, to be from time to time chosen by themselves.

Fourthly, The legislative neither must nor can transfer the power of making laws to any body else, or place it any where, but where the people have.

Chapter XIX
Of the Dissolution of Government

222. The reason why men enter into society, is the preservation of their property; and the end why they choose and authorize a legislative, is, that there may be laws made, and rules set as guards and fences to the properties of all the members of the society, to limit the power, and moderate the dominion of every part and member of the society. For since it can never be supposed to be the will of the society, that the legislative should have a power to destroy that, which every one designs to secure, by entering into society, and for which the people submitted themselves to the legislators of their own making; whenever the legislators endeavour to take away, and destroy the property of the people, or to reduce them to slavery under arbitrary power, they put themselves into a state of war with the people, who are thereupon absolved from any further obedience, and are left to the common refuge, which God has provided for all men, against force and violence. Whensoever therefore the legislative shall transgress this fundamental rule of society; and either by ambition, fear, folly or corruption, endeavour to grasp themselves, or put into the hands of any other an absolute power over the lives, liberties, and estates of the people; by this breach of trust they forfeit the power, the people had put into their hands, for quite contrary ends, and it devolves to the people, who have a right to resume their original liberty, and, by the establishment of a new legislative (such as they shall think fit) provide for their own safety and security, which is the end for which they are in society.

240. Here, it is like, the common question will be made, who shall be judge whether the prince or legislative act contrary to their trust? This, perhaps, ill affected and factious men may spread amongst the people, when the prince only makes use of his due prerogative. To this I reply, the people shall be judge; for who shall be judge whether his trustee or deputy acts well, and according to the trust reposed in him, but he who deputes him, and must, by having deputed him have still a power to discard him, when he fails in his trust? If this be reasonable in particular cases of private men, why should it be otherwise in that of the greatest moment; where the welfare of millions is concerned, and also where the evil, if not prevented, is greater, and the redress very difficult, dear, and dangerous?

243. To conclude, the power that every individual gave the society, when he entered into it, can never revert to the individuals again, as long as the society lasts, but will always remain in the community; because without this, there can be no community, no commonwealth, which is contrary to the original agreement: so also when the society has placed the legislative in any assembly of men, to continue in them and their successors, with direction and authority for providing such successors, the legislative can never revert to the people whilst that government lasts: because having provided a legislative with power to continue for ever, they have given up their political power to the legislative, and cannot resume it. But if they have set limits to the duration of their legislative, and made this supreme power in any person, or assembly, only temporary: or else when by the miscarriages of those in authority, it is forfeited; upon the forfeiture of their rulers, or at the determination of the time set, it reverts to the society, and the people have a right to act as supreme, and continue the legislative in themselves, or erect a new form, or under the old form place it in new hands, as they think good.

The Communist Manifesto

Karl Marx and Frederick Engels

Karl Marx was born into a middle-class family in Trier, Germany in 1818. After receiving a doctorate in philosophy and marrying his childhood sweetheart, he moved to Paris. In September of 1844, Marx met Engels, the son of a prosperous manufacturer. A lifelong friendship and intellectual collaboration began.

In 1848, they wrote *The Communist Manifesto* for a small workers' organization to which they belonged, the Communist League. *The Communist Manifesto* was a polemical political pamphlet, written when Marx and Engels were relatively young. But because it expresses in succinct form their understanding of history and their vision of politics, they allowed it to be republished many times and to be translated into many different languages during their lives—even though they went on to elaborate the ideas it contains with greater sophistication in their later work.

Marx and Engels were active in Germany during the upheavals of 1848, but when the revolutionary movement collapsed, they settled in England, Engels in Manchester working at the family firm, and Marx in London studying at the British Museum and writing *Capital*, his masterpiece. Marx died in 1883, but Engels lived for another twelve years, doing scholarly research, editing his friend's unfinished work, and popularizing their political views.

The Communist Manifesto portrays history as the history of struggle between classes—in the modern era, between the capitalist or bourgeois class and the class of workers or proletarians. Although Marx and Engels credit the bourgeoisie with having broken the bonds of feudalism and with having developed modern industry to extraordinary heights of productivity, they believed that capitalism was plagued by internal contradictions, which would provoke the working class to overthrow it and replace it by a socialist or communist system that would better serve human needs. In *The Communist Manifesto*, Marx and Engels lay down a challenge to any philosophical theory of justice and community that ignores the importance of socioeconomic development and class divisions in understanding human society.

I. Bourgeois and Proletarians[1]

The history of all hitherto existing society[2] is the history of class struggles.

Free man and slave, patrician and plebian, lord and serf, guild master and journeyman, in a word, oppressor and oppressed, stood in constant opposition to one another, carried on an uninterrupted, now hidden, now open fight, a fight that each time ended either in a revolutionary reconstitution of society at large or in the common ruin of the contending classes.

In the earlier epochs of history we find almost everywhere a complicated arrangement of society into various orders, a manifold gradation of social rank. In ancient Rome we have patricians, knights, plebians, slaves; in the Middle Ages, feudal lords, vassals, guild masters, journeymen, apprentices, serfs; in almost all of these classes, again, subordinate gradations.

The modern bourgeois society that has sprouted from the ruins of feudal society has not done away with class antagonisms. It has but established new classes, new conditions of oppression, new forms of struggle in place of the old ones.

Our epoch, the epoch of the bourgeoisie, possesses, however, this distinctive feature: it has simplified the class antagonisms. Society as a whole is more and more splitting up into two great hostile camps, into two great classes directly facing each other: bourgeoisie and proletariat.

From the serfs of the Middle Ages sprang the chartered burghers of the earliest towns. From these burgesses the first elements of the bourgeoisie were developed.

The discovery of America, the rounding of the Cape opened up fresh ground for the rising bourgeoisie. The East Indian and Chinese markets, the colonization of America, trade with the colonies, the increase in the means of exchange and in commodities generally, gave to commerce, to navigation, to industry an impulse never before known, and thereby, to the revolutionary element in the tottering feudal society, a rapid development.

The feudal system of industry, under which industrial production was monopolized by closed guilds, now no longer sufficed for the growing wants of the new markets. The manufacturing system took its place. The guild-masters were pushed on one side by the manufacturing middle class; division of labor between the different corporate guilds vanished in the face of division of labor in each single workshop.

Meantime the markets kept ever growing, the demand ever rising. Even manufacturers no longer sufficed. Thereupon steam and machinery revolutionized industrial production. The place of manufacture was taken by the giant, modern industry, the place of the industrial middle class by industrial millionaires, the leaders of whole industrial armies, the modern bourgeois.

Modern industry has established the world market, for which the discovery of America paved the way. This market has given an immense development to commerce, to navigation, to communication by land. This development has, in its turn, reacted on the extension of industry; and in proportion as industry, commerce, navigation, railways extended, in the same proportion the bourgeoisie developed, increased its capital, and pushed into the background every class handed down from the Middle Ages.

---

[1] By bourgeoisie is meant the class of modern capitalists, owners of the means of social production and employers of wage-labour. By proletariat, the class of modern wage-labourers who, having no means of production of their own, are reduced to selling their labor-power in order to live. (Note by Engels in English edition of 1888.)

[2] That is, all *written* history. In 1847, the pre-history of society, the social organization existing previous to recorded history, was all but unknown. Since then . . . village communities were found to be, or to have been the primitive form of society everywhere from India to Ireland. . . . With the dissolution of these primeval communities society begins to be differentiated into separate and finally antagonistic classes. . . . (Note by Engels in the English edition of 1888.)

We see, therefore, how the modern bourgeoisie is itself the product of a long course of development, of a series of revolutions in the modes of production and of exchange.

Each step in the development of the bourgeoisie was accompanied by a corresponding political advance of that class. An oppressed class under the sway of the feudal nobility, an armed and self-governing association in the medieval commune; here independent urban republic (as in Italy and Germany), there taxable "third estate" of the monarchy (as in France), afterwards, in the period of manufacture proper, serving either the semi-feudal or the absolute monarchy as a counterpoise against the nobility, and, in fact, cornerstone of the great monarchies in general, the bourgeoisie has at last, since the establishment of modern industry and of the world market, conquered for itself, in the modern representative state, exclusive political sway. The executive of the modern state is but a committee for managing the common affairs of the whole bourgeoisie.

The bourgeoisie, historically, has played a most revolutionary part.

The bourgeoisie, wherever it has got the upper hand, has put an end to all feudal, patriarchal, idyllic relations. It has pitilessly torn asunder the motley feudal ties that bound man to his "natural superiors," and has left remaining no other nexus between man and man than naked self-interest, than callous "cash payment." It has drowned the most heavenly ecstasies of religious fervor, of chivalrous enthusiasm, of Philistine sentimentalism in the icy water of egotistical calculation. It has resolved personal worth into exchange value and, in place of the numberless indefeasible chartered freedoms, has set up that single, unconscionable freedom—free trade. In one word, for exploitation, veiled by religious and political illusions, it has substituted naked, shameless, direct, brutal exploitation.

The bourgeoisie has stripped of its halo every occupation hitherto honored and looked up to with reverent awe. It has converted the physician, the lawyer, the priest, the poet, the man of science into its paid wage laborers.

The bourgeoisie has torn away from the family its sentimental veil, and has reduced the family relation to a mere money relation.

The bourgeoisie has disclosed how it came to pass that the brutal display of vigor in the Middle Ages, which reactionists so much admire, found its fitting complement in the most slothful indolence. It has been the first to show what man's activity can bring about. It has accomplished wonders far surpassing Egyptian pyramids, Roman aqueducts, and Gothic cathedrals; it has conducted expeditions that put in the shade all former exoduses of nations and crusades.

The bourgeoisie cannot exist without constantly revolutionizing the instruments of production, and thereby the relations of production, and with them the whole relations of society. Conservation of the old modes of production in unaltered form was, on the contrary, the first condition of existence for all earlier industrial classes. Constant revolutionizing of production, uninterrupted disturbance of all social conditions, everlasting uncertainty and agitation distinguish the bourgeois epoch from all earlier ones. All fixed, fast-frozen relations, with their train of ancient and venerable prejudices and opinions, are swept away, all new-formed ones become antiquated before they can ossify. All that is solid melts into air, all that is holy is profaned, and man is at last compelled to face with sober senses his real conditions of life and his relations with his kind.

The need of a constantly expanding market for its products chases the bourgeoisie over the whole surface of the globe. It must nestle everywhere, settle everywhere, establish connections everywhere.

The bourgeoisie has through its exploitation of the world market given a cosmopolitan character to production and consumption in every country. To the great chagrin of reactionists, it has drawn from under the feet of industry the national ground on which it stood. All old-established national industries have been destroyed or are daily being destroyed. They are dislodged by new industries, whose introduction becomes a life and death question for all civilized nations, by industries that no longer work up indigenous raw material, but raw material drawn from the remotest zones; industries whose products are consumed not only at home, but in every quarter of the globe. In place of the old wants, satisfied by the productions of the country, we find new wants, requiring for their satisfaction the products of distant lands and climes. In place of the old local and national seclusion and self-sufficiency we have intercourse in every direction, universal interdependence of nations. And as in material, so also in intellectual production. The intellectual creations of individual nations become common property. National one-sidedness and narrow-mindedness become more and more impossible, and from the numerous national and local literatures there arises a world literature.

The bourgeoisie, by the rapid improvement of all instruments of production, by the immensely facilitated means of communication, draws all, even the most barbarian, nations into civilization. The cheap prices of its commodities are the heavy artillery with which it batters down all Chinese walls, with which it forces the barbarians' intensely obstinate hatred of foreigners to capitulate. It compels all nations, on pain of extinction, to adopt the bourgeois mode of production; it compels them to introduce what it calls civilization into their midst, i.e., to become bourgeois themselves. In one word, it creates a world after its own image.

The bourgeoisie has subjected the country to the rule of the towns. It has created enormous cities, has greatly increased the urban population as compared with the rural, and has thus rescued a considerable part of the population from the idiocy of rural life. Just as it has made the country dependent on the towns, so it has made barbarian and semi-barbarian countries dependent on the civilized ones, nations of peasants on nations of bourgeois, the East on the West.

The bourgeoisie keeps more and more doing away with the scattered state of the population, of the means of production, and of property. It has agglomerated population, centralized means of production, and has concentrated property in a few hands. The necessary consequence of this was political centralization. Independent, or but loosely connected provinces, with separate interests, laws, governments and systems of taxation, became lumped together into one nation, with one government, one code of laws, one national class interest, one frontier, and one customs tariff.

The bourgeoisie, during its rule of scarce one hundred years, has created more massive and more colossal productive forces than have all preceding generations together. Subjection of nature's forces to man, machinery, application of chemistry to industry and agriculture, steam navigation, railways, electric telegraphs, clearing of whole continents for cultivation, canalization of rivers, whole populations conjured out of the ground—what earlier century had even a presentiment that such productive forces slumbered in the lap of social labor?

We see then: the means of production and of exchange, on whose foundation the bourgeoisie built itself up, were generated in feudal society. At a certain stage in the development of these means of production and of exchange, the conditions under which feudal society produced and exchanged, the feudal organization of agriculture and manufacturing industry, in one word, the feudal relations of property, became no longer compatible with the already developed productive forces; they became so many fetters. They had to be burst asunder; they were burst asunder.

Into their place stepped free competition, accompanied by a social and political constitution adapted to it, and by the economic and political sway of the bourgeois class.

A similar movement is going on before our own eyes. Modern bourgeois society with its relations of production, of exchange, and of property, a society that has conjured up such gigantic means of production and of exchange, is like the sorcerer who is no longer able to control the powers of the nether world whom he has called up by his spells. For many a decade past, the history of industry and commerce is but the history of the revolt of modern productive forces against modern conditions of production, against the property relations that are the conditions for the existence of the bourgeoisie and of its rule. It is enough to mention the commercial crises that by their periodic return put on its trial, each time more threateningly, the existence of the entire bourgeois society. In these crises a great part not only of the existing products but also of the previously created productive forces are periodically destroyed. In these crises there breaks out an epidemic that in all earlier epochs would have seemed an absurdity—the epidemic of over-production. Society suddenly finds itself put back into a state of momentary barbarism; it appears as if a famine, a universal war of devastation had cut off the supply of every means of subsistence; industry and commerce seem to be destroyed; and why? Because there is too much civilization, too much means of subsistence, too much industry, too much commerce. The productive forces at the disposal of society no longer tend to further the development of the conditions of bourgeois property; on the contrary, they have become too powerful for these conditions, by which they are fettered, and as soon as they overcome these fetters they bring disorder into the whole of bourgeois society, endanger the existence of bourgeois property. The conditions of bourgeois society are too narrow to comprise the wealth created by them. And how does the bourgeoisie get over these crises? On the one hand, by enforced destruction of a mass of productive forces; on the other, by the conquest of new markets, and by the more thorough exploitation of the old ones. That is to say, by paving the way for more extensive and more destructive crises, and

by diminishing the means whereby crises are prevented.

The weapons with which the bourgeoisie felled feudalism to the ground are now turned against the bourgeoisie itself.

But not only has the bourgeoisie forged the weapons that bring death to itself; it has also called into existence the men who are to wield those weapons—the modern working class—the proletarians.

In proportion as the bourgeoisie, i.e., capital, is developed, in the same proportion is the proletariat, the modern working class, developed—a class of laborers, who live only so long as they find work, and who find work only so long as their labor increases capital. These laborers, who must sell themselves piecemeal, are a commodity, like every other article of commerce, and are consequently exposed to all the vicissitudes of competition, to all the fluctuations of the market.

Owing to the extensive use of machinery and to division of labor, the work of the proletarians has lost all individual character and, consequently, all charm for the workman. He becomes an appendage of the machine, and it is only the simplest, most monotonous, and most easily acquired knack that is required of him. Hence the cost of production of a workman is restricted, almost entirely, to the means of subsistence that he requires for his maintenance and for the propagation of his race. But the price of a commodity, and therefore also of labor, is equal to its cost of production. In proportion, therefore, as the repulsiveness of the work increases, the wage decreases. Nay, more, in proportion as the use of machinery and division of labor increases, in the same proportion the burden of toil also increases, whether by prolongation of the working hours, by increase of the work exacted in a given time, or by increased speed of the machinery, etc.

Modern industry has converted the little workshop of the patriarchal master into the great factory of the industrial capitalist. Masses of laborers, crowded into the factory, are organized like soldiers. As privates of the industrial army they are placed under a command of a perfect hierarchy of officers and sergeants. Not only are they slaves of the bourgeois class, and of the bourgeois state; they are daily and hourly enslaved by the machine, by the overlooker, and, above all, by the individual bourgeois manufacturer himself. The more openly this despotism proclaims gain to be its end and aim, the more petty, the more hateful, and the more embittering it is.

The less the skill and exertion of strength implied in manual labor, in other words, the more modern industry becomes developed, the more is the labor of men superseded by that of women. Differences of age and sex have no longer any distinctive social validity for the working class. All are instruments of labor, more or less expensive to use, according to their age and sex.

No sooner is the exploitation of the laborer by the manufacturer over, to the extent that he receives his wages in cash, than he is set upon by the other portions of the bourgeoisie, the landlord, the shopkeeper, the pawnbroker, etc.

The lower strata of the middle class—the small tradespeople, shopkeepers, and retired tradesmen generally, the handicraftsmen and peasants—all these sink gradually into the proletariat, partly because their diminutive capital does not suffice for the scale on which modern industry is carried on, and is swamped in the competition with the large capitalists, partly because their specialized skill is rendered worthless by new methods of production. Thus the proletariat is recruited from all classes of the population.

The proletariat goes through various stages of development. With its birth begins its struggle with the bourgeoisie. At first the contest is carried on by individual laborers, then by the workpeople of a factory, then by the operatives of one trade, in one locality, against the individual bourgeois who directly exploits them. They direct their attacks not against the bourgeois conditions of production, but against the instruments of production themselves; they destroy imported wares that compete with their labor, they smash to pieces machinery, they set factories ablaze, they seek to restore by force the vanished status of the workman of the Middle Ages.

At this stage the laborers still form an incoherent mass scattered over the whole country and broken up by their mutual competition. If anywhere they unite to form more compact bodies, this is not yet the consequence of their own active union, but of the union of the bourgeoisie, which class, in order to attain its own political ends, is compelled to set the whole proletariat in motion, and is moreover yet, for a time, able to do so. At this stage, therefore, the proletarians do not fight their enemies, but the enemies of their enemies, the remnants of absolute monarchy, the landowners, the non-industrial bourgeois, the petty bourgeoisie. Thus the whole historical movement is concentrated in the hands of the bourgeoisie; every victory so obtained is a victory for the bourgeoisie.

But with the development of industry the proletariat not only increases in number; it becomes concentrated in greater masses, its strength grows, and it feels that strength more. The various interests and conditions of life within the ranks of the proletariat are more and more equalized, in proportion as machinery obliterates all distinctions of labor and nearly everywhere reduces wages to the same low level. The growing competition among the bourgeois and the resulting commercial crises make the wages of the workers ever more fluctuating. The unceasing improvement of machinery, ever more rapidly developing, makes their livelihood more and more precarious; the collisions between individual workmen and individual bourgeois take more and more the character of collisions between two classes. Thereupon the workers begin to form combinations (trade unions) against the bourgeois; they club together in order to keep up the rate of wages; they found permanent associations in order to make provision beforehand for these occasional revolts. Here and there the contest breaks out into riots.

Now and then the workers are victorious, but only for a time. The real fruit of their battles lies not in the immediate result, but in the ever expanding union of the workers. This union is helped on by the improved means of communication that are created by modern industry and that place the workers of different localities in contact with one another. It was just this contact that was needed to centralize the numerous local struggles, all of the same character, into one national struggle between classes. But every class struggle is a political struggle. And that union, to attain which the burghers of the Middle Ages, with their miserable highways, required centuries, the modern proletarians, thanks to railways, achieve in a few years.

This organization of the proletarians into a class, and consequently into a political party, is continually being upset again by the competition between the workers themselves. But it ever rises up again, stronger, firmer, mightier. It compels legislative recognition of particular interests of the workers by taking advantage of the divisions among the bourgeoisie itself. . . .

Finally, in times when the class struggle nears the decisive hour, the process of dissolution going on within the ruling class, in fact within the whole range of old society, assumes such a violent, glaring character that a small section of the ruling class cuts itself adrift and joins the revolutionary class, the class that holds the future in its hands. Just as, therefore, at an earlier period, a section of the nobility went over to the bourgeoisie, so now a portion of the bourgeoisie goes over to the proletariat, and in particular, a portion of the bourgeois ideologists, who have raised themselves to the level of comprehending theoretically the historical movement as a whole.

Of all the classes that stand face to face with the bourgeoisie today, the proletariat alone is a really revolutionary class. The other classes decay and finally disappear in the face of modern industry; the proletariat is its special and essential product. . . .

All previous historical movements were movements of minorities, or in the interest of minorities. The proletarian movement is the self-conscious, independent movement of the immense majority, in the interests of the immense majority. The proletariat, the lowest stratum of our present society, cannot stir, cannot raise itself up, without the whole super-incumbent strata of official society being sprung into the air.

Though not in substance, yet in form, the struggle of the proletariat with the bourgeoisie is at first a national struggle. The proletariat of each country must, of course, first of all settle matters with its own bourgeoisie.

In depicting the most general phases of the development of the proletariat, we traced the more or less veiled civil war, raging within existing society, up to the point where that war breaks out into open revolution, and where the violent overthrow of the bourgeoisie lays the foundation for the sway of the proletariat.

Hitherto every form of society has been based, as we have already seen, on the antagonism of oppression and oppressed classes. But in order to oppress a class certain conditions must be assured to it under which it can, at least, continue its slavish existence. The serf, in the period of serfdom, raised himself to membership in the commune, just as the petty bourgeois, under the yoke of feudal absolutism, managed to develop into a bourgeois. The modern laborer, on the contrary, instead of rising with the progress of industry, sinks deeper and deeper below the conditions of existence of his own class. He becomes a pauper, and pauperism develops more rapidly than population and wealth. And here it becomes evident that the bourgeoisie is unfit any longer to be the ruling class in society, and to impose its conditions of existence upon society as an overriding law. It is unfit to rule because it is incompetent to assure an existence to its slave within his slavery, because it cannot help letting him sink into such a state that it has to feed him instead of being fed by him. Society can no longer live under this bourgeoisie: in other words, its existence is no longer compatible with society.

The essential condition for the existence, and for the sway of the bourgeois class, is the formation and augmentation of capital; the condition for capital is wage labor. Wage labor rests exclusively on competition between the laborers. The advance of industry, whose involuntary promoter is the bourgeoisie, replaces the isolation of the laborers, due to competition, by their revolutionary combination, due to association. The development of modern industry, therefore, cuts from under its feet the very foundation on which the bourgeoisie produces and appropriates products. What the bourgeoisie, therefore, produces, above all, is its own gravediggers. Its fall and the victory of the proletariat are equally inevitable.

II. PROLETARIANS AND COMMUNISTS

In what relation do the communists stand to the proletarians as a whole?

The communists do not form a separate party opposed to other working-class parties.

They have no interests separate and apart from those of the proletariat as a whole.

They do not set up any sectarian principles of their own, by which to shape and mold the proletarian movement.

The communists are distinguished from the other working-class parties by this only: 1. In the national struggles of the proletarians of the different countries they point out and bring to the front the common interests of the entire proletariat, independent of all nationality. 2. In the various stages of development which the struggle of the working class against the bourgeoisie has to pass through, they always and everywhere represent the interests of the movement as a whole.

The communists, therefore, are on the one hand, practically, the most advanced and resolute section of the working-class parties of every country, that section which pushes forward all others; on the other hand, theoretically, they have over the great mass of the proletariat the advantage of clearly understanding the line of march, the conditions, and the ultimate general results of the proletarian movement.

The immediate aim of the communists is the same as that of all the other proletarian parties: formation of the proletariat into a class, overthrow of the bourgeois supremacy, conquest of political power by the proletariat.

The theoretical conclusions of the communists are in no way based on ideas or principles that have been invented, or discovered, by this or that would-be universal reformer.

They merely express, in general terms, actual relations springing from an existing class struggle, from a historical movement going on under our very eyes. The abolition of existing property relations is not at all a distinctive feature of communism.

All property relations in the past have continually been subject to historical change consequent upon the change in historical conditions.

The French Revolution, for example, abolished feudal property in favor of bourgeois property.

The distinguishing feature of communism is not the abolition of property generally, but the abolition of bourgeois property. But modern bourgeois private property is the final and most complete expression of the system of producing and appropriating products that is based on class antagonisms, on the exploitation of the many by the few.

In this sense the theory of the communists may be summed up in the single sentence: Abolition of private property.

We communists have been reproached with the desire of abolishing the right of personally acquiring property as the fruit of man's own labor, which property is alleged to be the groundwork of all personal freedom, activity, and independence.

Hard-won, self-acquired, self-earned property! Do you mean the property of the petty artisan and of the small peasant, a form of property that preceded the bourgeois form? There is no need to abolish that; the development of industry has to a great extent already destroyed it, and is still destroying it daily.

Or do you mean modern bourgeois private property?

But does wage labor create any property for the laborer? Not a bit. It creates capital, i.e., that kind of property which exploits wage labor, and which cannot increase except upon condition of begetting a new supply of wage labor for fresh exploitation. Property, in its present form, is based on the antagonism of capital and wage labor. Let us examine both sides of this antagonism.

To be a capitalist is to have not only a purely personal but a social *status* in production. Capital is a collective product, and only by the united action of many members, nay, in the last resort only by the united action of all members of society, can it be set in motion.

Capital is, therefore, not a personal, it is a social power.

When, therefore, capital is converted into common property, into the property of all members of society, personal property is not thereby transformed into social property. It is only the social character of the property that is changed. It loses its class character.

Let us now take wage labor.

The average price of wage labor is the minimum wage, i.e., that quantum of the means of subsistence which is absolutely requisite to keep the laborer in bare existence as a laborer. What, therefore, the wage laborer appropriates by means of his labor merely suffices to prolong and reproduce a bare existence. We by no means intend to abolish this personal appropriation of the products of labor, an appropriation that is made for the maintenance and reproduction of human life, and that leaves no surplus wherewith to command the labor of others. All that we want to do away with is the miserable character of this appropriation, under which the laborer lives merely to increase capital, and is allowed to live only in so far as the interest of the ruling class requires it.

In bourgeois society, living labor is but a means to increase accumulated labor. In communist society accumulated labor is but a means to widen, to enrich, to promote the existence of the laborer.

In bourgeois society, therefore, the past dominates the present; in communist society the present dominates the past. In bourgeois society capital is independent and has individuality, while the living person is dependent and has no individuality.

And the abolition of this state of things is called by the bourgeois, abolition of individuality and freedom! And rightly so. The abolition of bourgeois individuality, bourgeois independence, and bourgeois freedom is undoubtedly aimed at.

By freedom is meant, under the present bourgeois conditions of production, free trade, free selling and buying.

But if selling and buying disappear, free selling and buying disappear also. This talk about free selling and buying, and all the other "brave words" of our bourgeoisie about free in general, have a meaning, if any, only in contrast with restricted selling and buying, with the fettered traders of the Middle Ages, but have no meaning when opposed to the communistic abolition of buying and selling, of the bourgeois conditions of production, and of the bourgeoisie itself.

You are horrified at our intending to do away with private property. But in your existing society private property is already done away with for nine tenths of the population; its existence for the few is solely due to its non-existence in the hands of those nine tenths. You reproach us, therefore, with intending to do away with a form of property the necessary condition for whose existence is the non-existence of any property for the immense majority of society.

In one word, you reproach us with intending to do away with your property. Precisely so; that is just what we intend.

From the moment when labor can no longer be converted into capital, money, or rent, into a social power capable of being monopolized, i.e., from the moment when individual property can no longer be transformed into bourgeois property, into capital, from that moment, you say, individuality vanishes.

You must, therefore, confess that by "individual" you mean no other person than the bourgeois, than the middle-class owner of property. This person must, indeed, be swept out of the way and made impossible.

Communism deprives no man of the power to appropriate the products of society; all that it does is to deprive him of the power to subjugate the labor of others by means of such appropriation.

It has been objected that upon the abolition of private property all work will cease and universal laziness will overtake us.

According to this, bourgeois society ought long ago have gone to the dogs through sheer idleness, for those of its members who work acquire nothing and those who acquire anything do not work. The whole of this objection is but another expression of the tautology that there can no longer be any wage labor when there is no longer any capital.

All objections urged against the communistic mode of producing and appropriating material products have, in the same way, been urged against the communistic modes of producing and appropriating intellectual products. Just as, to the bourgeois, the disappearance of class property is the disappearance of production itself, so the disappearance of class culture is to him identical with the disappearance of all culture.

That culture, the loss of which he laments, is, for the enormous majority, a mere training to act as a machine.

But don't wrangle with us so long as you apply, to our intended abolition of bourgeois property, the standard of your bourgeois notions of freedom, culture, law, etc. Your very ideas are but the outgrowth of the conditions of your bourgeois production and bourgeois property, just as your jurisprudence is but the will of your class made into a law for all, a will whose essential character and direction are determined by the economic conditions of existence of your class.

The selfish misconception that induces you to transform into eternal laws of nature and of reason the social forms springing from your present mode of production and form of property—historical relations that rise and disappear in the progress of production—this misconception you share with every ruling class that has preceded you. What you see clearly in the case of ancient property, what you admit in the case of feudal property, you are of course forbidden to admit in the case of your own bourgeois form of property.

Abolition of the family! Even the most radical flare up at this infamous proposal of the communists.

On what foundation is the present family, the bourgeois family based? On capital, on private gain. In its completely developed form this family exists only among the bourgeoisie. But this state of things finds its complement in the practical absence of the family among the proletarians, and in public prostitution.

The bourgeois family will vanish as a matter of course when its complement vanishes, and both will vanish with the vanishing of capital.

Do you charge us with wanting to stop the exploitation of children by their parents? To this crime we plead guilty.

But you will say, we destroy the most hallowed of relations when we replace home education by social.

And your education! Is not that also social, and determined by the social conditions under which you educate, by the intervention, direct or indirect, of society, by means of schools, etc.? The communists have not invented the intervention of society in education; they do but seek to alter the character of that intervention, and to rescue education from the influence of the ruling class.

The bourgeois claptrap about the family and education, about the hallowed co-relation of parent and child, becomes all the more disgusting, the more, by the action of modern industry, all family ties among the proletarians are torn asunder and their children transformed into simple articles of commerce and instruments of labor. . . .

The communists are further reproached with desiring to abolish countries and nationality.

The workingmen have no country. We cannot take from them what they have not got. Since the proletariat must first of all acquire political supremacy, must rise to be the leading class of the nation, must constitute itself *the* nation, it is, so far, itself national, though not in the bourgeois sense of the word.

National differences and antagonisms between peoples are daily more and more vanishing, owing to the development of the bourgeoisie, to freedom of commerce, to the world market, to uniformity in the mode of production and in the conditions of life corresponding thereto.

The supremacy of the proletariat will cause them to vanish still faster. United action, of the leading civilized countries at least, is one of the first conditions for the emancipation of the proletariat.

In proportion as the exploitation of one individual by another is put to an end, the exploitation of one nation by another will also be put to an end. In proportion as the antagonism between classes within the nation vanishes, the hostility of one nation to another will come to an end.

The charges against communism made from a religious, a philosophical, and, generally, from an ideological standpoint are not deserving of serious examination.

Does it require deep intuition to comprehend that man's ideas, views, and conceptions, in one word, man's consciousness, change with every change in the conditions of his material existence, in his social relations, and in his social life?

What else does the history of ideas prove than that intellectual production changes its character in proportion as material production is changed? The ruling ideas of each age have been the ideas of its ruling class.

When people speak of ideas that revolutionize society they do not express the fact that within the old society the elements of a new one have been created, and that the dissolution of the old ideas keeps even pace with the dissolution of the old conditions of existence.

. . .The history of all past society has consisted in the development of class antagonisms, antagonisms that assumed different forms at different epochs.

But whatever form they may have taken, one fact is common to all past ages, viz., the exploitation of one part of society by the other. No wonder then that the social consciousness of past ages, despite all the multiplicity and variety it displays, moves within certain common forms, or general ideas, which cannot completely vanish except with the total disappearance of class antagonisms.

The communist revolution is the most radical rupture with traditional property relations; no wonder that its development involves the most radical rupture with traditional ideas.

But let us have done with the bourgeois objections to communism.

We have seen above that the first step in the revolution by the working class is to raise the proletariat to the position of ruling class, to win the battle of democracy.

The proletariat will use its political supremacy to wrest, by degrees, all capital from the bourgeoisie, to centralize all instruments of production in the hands of the state, i.e., of the proletariat organized as the ruling class, and to increase the total of productive forces as rapidly as possible.

Of course, in the beginning this cannot be effected except by means of despotic inroads on the rights of property and on the conditions of bourgeois production; by means of measures, therefore, which appear economically insufficient and untenable, but which, in the course of the movement, outstrip themselves, necessitate further inroads upon the old social order, and are unavoidable as a means of entirely revolutionizing the mode of production.

These measures will of course be different in different countries.

Nevertheless, in the most advanced countries the following will be pretty generally applicable:

1. Abolition of property in land and application of all rents of land to public purposes.
2. A heavy progressive or graduated income tax.
3. Abolition of all right of inheritance.
4. Confiscation of the property of all emigrants and rebels.
5. Centralization of credit in the hands of the state, by means of a national bank with state capital and an exclusive monopoly.
6. Centralization of the means of communication and transport in the hands of the state.
7. Extension of factories and instruments of production owned by the state; the bringing into cultivation of wastelands, and the improvement of the soil generally in accordance with a common plan.
8. Equal liability of all to labor. Establishment of industrial armies, especially for agriculture.
9. Combination of agriculture with manufacturing industries; gradual abolition of the distinction between town and country, by a more equable distribution of the population over the country.
10. Free education for all children in public schools. Abolition of children's factory labor in its present form. Combination of education with industrial production, etc.

When, in the course of development, class distinctions have disappeared and all production has been concentrated in the hands of a vast association of the whole nation, the public power will lose its political character. Political power, properly so called, is merely the organized power of one class for oppressing another. If the proletariat during its contest with the bourgeoisie is compelled, by the force of circumstances, to organize itself as a class, if, by means of a revolution, it makes itself the ruling class and, as such, sweeps away by force the old conditions of production, then it will, along with these conditions, have swept away the conditions for the existence of class antagonisms and of classes generally, and will thereby have abolished its own supremacy as a class.

In place of the old bourgeois society, with its classes and class antagonisms, we shall have an association in which the free development of each is the condition for the free development of all.

Anarchism

Peter Kropotkin

Born of an aristocratic family in 1842, Peter Kropotkin seemed destined to follow his father into the military. But while in the Mounted Cossacks, he studied the Russian prison system and became involved in politics. He then trained as a geographer and naturalist, but his thinking again turned increasingly to politics and social activism. His imprisonment by the French for membership in the International Workingmen's Association aroused widespread international protest and, in 1886, he went to England, where he had won a large following. There Kropotkin undertook to base his political theories not on speculation but instead on the firm scientific footing of evolution. People are naturally social, he argued, although the injustice and repression of government obscures humankind's true cooperative and ethical nature. Late in life, he returned to communist Russia and later denounced the Soviet state for its repression and totalitarianism. When he died in 1921, his funeral turned into a major anti-Soviet demonstration.

I. LAW AND AUTHORITY

. . . In existing States a fresh law is looked upon as a remedy for evil. Instead of themselves altering what is bad, people begin by demanding a *law* to alter it. If the road between two villages is impassable, the peasant says:—"There should be a law about parish roads." If a park-keeper takes advantage of the want of spirit in those who follow him with servile observance and insults one of them, the insulted man says "There should be a law to enjoin more politeness upon park keepers." If there is stagnation in agriculture or commerce, the husbandman, cattle-breeder, or corn speculator argues, "It is protective legislation that we require." Down to the old clothesman there is not one who does not demand a law to protect his own little trade. If the employer lowers wages or increases the hours of labour, the politician in embryo exclaims, "We must have a law to put all that to rights," instead of telling the workers that there are other, and much more effectual means of settling these things straight; namely, recovering from the employer the wealth of which he has been despoiling the workmen for generations. In short, a law everywhere and for everything! A law about fashions, a law about mad dogs, a law about virtue, a law to put a stop to all the vices and all the evils which result from human indolence and cowardice.

From *Law and Authority* (Moscow: International Publishing Co., 1886) and "Anarchist Communism" in *Kropotkin's Revolutionary Pamphlets*, 1927 edition.

We are so perverted by an education which from infancy seeks to kill in us the spirit of revolt, and to develop that of submission to authority; we are so perverted by this existence under the ferule of a law, which regulates every event in life—our birth, our education, our development, our love, our friendship—that, if this state of things continues, we shall lose all initiative, all habit of thinking for ourselves. Our society seems no longer able to understand that it is possible to exist otherwise than under the reign of Law, elaborated by a representative government and administered by a handful of rulers. . . .

[However] rebels are everywhere to be found, who no longer wish to obey the law without knowing whence it comes, what are its uses, and whither arises the obligation to submit to it, and the reverence with which it is encompassed. The rebels of our day are criticising the very foundations of Society, which have hitherto been held sacred, and first and foremost amongst them that fetish, law. Just for this reason, the upheaval which is at hand, is no mere insurrection, it is a *Revolution*.

The critics analise the sources of law, and find there, either a god, product of the terrors of the savage, and stupid, paltry and malicious as the priests who vouch for its supernatural origin, or else, bloodshed, conquest by fire and sword. They study the characteristics of law, and instead of perpetual growth corresponding to that of the human race, they find its distinctive trait to be immobility, a tendency to crystalise what should be modified and developed day by day. They ask how law has been maintained, and in its service they see the atrocities of Byzantinism, the cruelties of the Inquisition, the tortures of the Middle Ages, living flesh torn by the lash of the executioner, chains, clubs, axes, the gloomy dungeons of prisons, agony, curses and tears. In our own days they see, as before, the axe, the cord, the rifle, the prison; on the one hand, the brutalised prisoner, reduced to the condition of a caged beast by the debasement of his whole moral being, and on the other, the judge, stripped of every feeling which does honor to human nature, living like a visionary in a world of legal fictions, revelling in the infliction of imprisonment and death, without even suspecting, in the cold malignity of his madness, the abyss of degradation into which he has himself fallen before the eyes of those whom he condemns.

They see a race of law-makers legislating without knowing what their laws are about; to-day voting a law on the sanitation of towns, without the faintest notion of hygiene, tomorrow making regulations for the armament of troops, without so much as understanding a gun; making laws about teaching and education without ever having given a lesson of any sort, or even an honest education to their own children; legislating at random in all directions, but never forgetting the penalties to be meted out to ragamuffins, the prison and the galleys, which are to be the portion of men a thousand times less immoral than these legislators themselves.

Finally, they see the gaoler on the way to lose all human feeling, the detective trained as a bloodhound, the police spy despising himself; "informing," metamorphosed into a virtue; corruption, erected into a system; all the vices, all the evil qualities of mankind countenanced and cultivated to insure the triumph of law.

All this we see, and therefore, instead of inanely repeating the old formula, "Respect the law," we say, "Despise law and all its attributes!" In place of the cowardly phrase "Obey the law," our cry is "Revolt against all laws!"

Only compare the misdeeds accomplished in the name of each law, with the good it has been able to effect, and weigh carefully both good and evil, and you will see if we are right.

The millions of laws which exist for the regulation of humanity, appear upon investigation to be divided into three principal categories—protection of property, protection of persons, protection of government. And by analysing each of these three categories, we arrive at the same logical and necessary conclusion: *the uselessness and hurtfulness of law.*

Socialists know what is meant by protection of property. Laws on property are not made to guarantee either to the individual or to society the enjoyment of the produce of their own labor. On the contrary, they are made to rob the producer of a part of what he has created, and to secure to certain other people that portion of the produce which they have stolen either from the producer or from society as a whole. When, for example, the law establishes Mr. So-and-So's right to a house, it is not establishing his right to a cottage he has built for himself, or to a house he has erected with the help of some of his friends. In that case no one would have disputed his right. On the contrary, the law is establishing his right to a house which is *not* the product of his labor; first of all, because he has had it built for him by others, to whom he has not paid the full value of their work; and next, because that house represents a social value, which he could not have produced for himself. The law is establishing his right to what belongs to everybody in general and to nobody in particular. The same house built in the midst of Siberia would not have the value it possesses in a large town, and, as we know, that value arises from the labor of something like fifty generations of men who have built the town, beautified it, supplied it with water and gas, fine promenades, colleges, theatres, shops, railways, and roads leading in all directions. Thus, by recognising the right of Mr. So-and-So to a particular house in Paris, London, or Rouen, the law is unjustly appropriating to him a certain portion of the produce of the labour of mankind in general. And it is precisely because this appropriation and all other forms of property bearing the same character, are a crying injustice, that a whole arsenal of laws, and a whole army of soldiers, policemen, and judges are needed to maintain it against the good sense and just feeling inherent in humanity.

Well, half our laws, the civil code in each country, serves no other purpose than to maintain this appropriation, this monopoly for the benefit of certain individuals against the whole of mankind. Three-fourths of the causes decided by the tribunals are nothing but quarrels between monopolists—two robbers disputing over their booty. And a great many of our criminal laws have the same object in view, their end being to keep the workman in a subordinate position towards his employer, and thus afford security to exploitation.

As for guaranteeing the product of his labour to the producer, there are no laws which even attempt such a thing. It is so simple and natural, so much a part of the manners and customs of mankind, that law has not given it so much as a thought. Open brigandage, sword in hand, is no feature of our age. Neither does one workman ever come and dispute the produce of his labour with another. If they have a misunderstanding they settle it by calling in a third person, without having recourse to law. The only person who exacts from another what that other has produced, is the proprietor, who comes in and deducts the lion's share. As for humanity in general, it everywhere respects the right of each to what he has created, without the interposition of any special laws.

As all the laws about property, which make up thick volumes of codes, and are the delight of our lawyers, have no other object than to protect the unjust appropriation of human labour by certain monopolists, there is no reason for their existence, and, on the day of the Revolution, social revolutionists are thoroughly determined to put an end to them. Indeed, a bonfire might be made with perfect justice of all laws bearing upon the so-called "rights of property," all title-deeds, all registers, in a word, of all that is in any way connected with an institution which will soon be looked upon as a blot in the history of humanity, as humiliating as the slavery and serfdom of past ages.

The remarks just made upon laws concerning property are quite as applicable to the second category of laws; those for the maintenance of government *i.e.* Constitutional Law.

It again is a complete arsenal of laws, decrees, ordinances, orders in council, and what not, all serving to protect the diverse forms of representative government, delegated or usurped, beneath which humanity is writhing. We know very well—Anarchists have often enough pointed out in their perpetual criticism of the various forms of government—that the mission of all governments, monarchical, constitutional, or republican, is to protect and maintain by force the privileges of the classes in possession, the aristocracy, clergy, and traders. A good third of our laws—and each country possesses some tens of thousands of them—the fundamental laws on taxes, excise duties, the organization of ministerial departments and their offices, of the army, the police, the Church, &c., have no other end than to maintain, patch up, and develop the administrative machine. And this machine in its turn serves almost entirely to protect the privileges of the possessing classes. Analyse all these laws, observe them in action day by day, and you will discover that not one is worth preserving.

About such laws there can be no two opinions. Not only Anarchists, but more or less revolutionary radicals also, are agreed that the only use to be made of laws concerning the organization of government is to fling them into the fire.

The third category of law still remains to be considered, that relating to the protection of the person and the detection and prevention of "crime." This is the most important, because most prejudices attach to it; because, if law enjoys a certain amount of consideration, it is in consequence of the belief that this species of law is absolutely indispensable to the maintenance of security in our societies. These are laws developed from the nucleus of customs useful to human communities, which have been turned to account by rulers to sanctify their own domination. The authority of the chiefs of tribes, of rich families in towns, and of the king, depended upon their judicial functions, and even down to the present day, whenever the necessity of government is spoken of, its function as supreme judge is the thing implied. "Without a government men would tear one another to pieces," argues the village orator. "The ultimate end of all government is to secure twelve honest jurymen to every accused person," said Burke.

Well, in spite of all the prejudices existing on this subject, it is quite time that Anarchists should boldly declare this category of laws as useless and injurious as the preceding ones.

First of all, as to so-called "crimes"—assaults upon persons—it is well-known that two-thirds, and often as many as three-fourths, of such "crimes" are instigated by the desire to obtain possession of someone's wealth. This immense class of so-called "crimes and misdemeanours" will disappear on the day on which private property ceases to exist. "But," it will be said, "there will always be brutes who will attempt the lives of their fellow-citizens, who will lay their hands to a knife in every quarrel, and revenge the slightest offence by murder, if there are no laws to restrain and punishments to withhold them." This refrain is repeated every time the right of society *to punish* is called in question.

Yet there is one fact upon this head which at the present time is thoroughly established; the severity of punishment does not diminish the amount of crime. Hang, and, if you like, quarter murderers, and the number of murders will not decrease by one. On the other hand, abolish the penalty of death and there will not be one murder more; there will be fewer. Statistics prove it. But if the harvest is good, and bread cheap, and the weather fine, the number of murders immediately decreases. This again is proved by statistics. The amount of crime always augments and diminishes in proportion to the price of provisions and the state of the weather. Not that all murderers are actuated by hunger. That is not the case. But when the harvest is good and provisions are at an obtainable price, and when the sun shines, men, lighter hearted and less miserable than usual, do not give way to gloomy passions, do not from trivial motives, plunge a knife into the bosom of a fellow creature.

Moreover, it is also a well-known fact that the fear of punishment has never stopped a single murderer. He who kills his neighbour from revenge or misery does not reason much about consequences; and there have been few murderers who were not firmly convinced that they should escape prosecution.

Without speaking of a society in which a man will receive a better education, in which the development of all his faculties, and the possibility of exercising them, will procure him so many enjoyments that he will not seek to poison them by remorse—without speaking of the society of the future—even in our society, even with those sad products of misery, whom we see today in the public-houses of great cities—on the day when no punishment is inflicted upon murderers, the number of murders will not augment by a single case; and it is extremely probable that it will be, on the contrary, diminished by all those cases which are due at present to habitual criminals, who have been brutalised in prisons.

We are continually being told of the benefits conferred by law, and the beneficial effect of penalties, but have the speakers ever attempted to strike a balance between the benefits attributed to laws and penalties, and the degrading effect of these penalties upon humanity? Only calculate all the evil passions awakened in mankind by the atrocious punishments formerly inflicted in our streets! Man is the cruellest animal upon earth; and who has pampered and developed the cruel instincts unknown, even amongst monkeys, if it is not the king, the judge, and the priest, armed with law, who caused flesh to be torn off in strips, boiling pitch to be poured into wounds, limbs to be dislocated, bones to be crushed, men to be sawn asunder to maintain their authority? Only estimate the torrent of depravity let loose in human society by the "informing," which is countenanced by judges, and paid in hard cash by governments, under pretext of assisting in the discovery of "crime." Only go into the gaols and study what man becomes when he is deprived of freedom and shut up with other depraved beings, steeped in the vice and corruption which oozes from the very walls of our existing prisons. Only remember that the more these prisons are reformed, the more detestable they become; our model modern penitentiaries are a hundred-fold more abominable than the dungeons of the middle ages. Finally, consider what corruption, what depravity of mind, is kept up amongst men by the idea of obedience, the very essence of law; of chastisement; of authority have the right to punish, to judge irrespective of our conscience and the esteem of our friends; of the necessity for executioners, gaolers, and informers—in a word, by all the attributes of law and authority. Consider all this, and you will assuredly agree with us in saying that a law inflicting penalties is an abomination which should cease to exist.

Peoples without political organization, and therefore less depraved than ourselves, have perfectly understood that the man who is called "criminal" is simply unfortunate; that the remedy is not to flog him, to chain him up, or to kill him on the scaffold or in prison, but to relieve him by the most brotherly care, by treatment based on equality, by the usages of life amongst honest men. In the next revolution we hope that this cry will go forth:

"Burn the guillotines; demolish the prisons; drive away the judges, policemen, and informers—the impurest race upon the face of the earth; treat as a brother the man who has been led by passion to do ill to his fellow; above all, take from the ignoble products of middle-class idleness the possibility of displaying their vices in attractive colours; and be sure that but few crimes will mar our society."

The main supports of crime are idleness, law and authority; laws about property, laws about government, laws about penalties and misdemeanours; and authority, which takes upon itself to manufacture these laws and to apply them.

No more laws! No more judges! Liberty, equality, and practical human sympathy are the only effectual barriers we can oppose to the anti-social instincts of certain amongst us.

2. ANARCHIST COMMUNISM: ITS BASIS AND PRINCIPLES

ANARCHISM, the no-government system of socialism, has a double origin. It is an outgrowth of the two great movements of thought in the economic and the political fields which characterize the nineteenth century, and especially its second part. In common with all socialists, the anarchists hold that the private ownership of land, capital, and machinery has had its time; that it is condemned to disappear; and that all requisites for production must, and will, become the common property of society, and be managed in common by the producers of wealth. And in common with the most advanced representatives of political radicalism, they maintain that the ideal of the political organization of society is a condition of things where the functions of government are reduced to a minimum, and the individual recovers his full liberty of initiative and action for satisfying, by means of free groups and federations—freely constituted—all the infinitely varied needs of the human being.

As regards socialism, most of the anarchists arrive at its ultimate conclusion, that is, at a complete negation of the wage-system and at communism. And with reference to political organization, by giving a further development to the above-mentioned part of the radical program, they arrive at the conclusion that the ultimate aim of society is the reduction of the functions of government to *nil*—that is, to a society without government, to an-archy. . . .

In arriving at these conclusions anarchism proves to be in accordance with the conclusions arrived at by the philosophy of evolution. By bringing to light the plasticity of organization, the philosophy of evolution has shown the admirable adaptability of organisms to their conditions of life, and the ensuing development of such faculties as render more complete both the adaptations of the aggregates to their surroundings and those of each of the constituent parts of the aggregate to the needs of free cooperation. It has familiarized us with the circumstances that throughout organic nature the capacities for life in common grow in proportion as the integration of organisms into compound aggregates becomes more and more complete; and it has enforced thus the opinion already expressed by social moralists as to the perfectibility of human nature. It has shown us that, in the long run of the struggle for existence, "the fittest" will prove to be those who combine intellectual knowledge with the knowledge necessary for the production of wealth, and not those who are now the richest because they, or their ancestors, have been momentarily the strongest.

By showing that the "struggle for existence" must be conceived not merely in its restricted sense of a struggle between individuals for the means of subsistence but in its wider sense of adaptation of all individuals of the species to the best conditions for the survival of the species, as well as for the greatest possible sum of life and happiness for each and all, it has permitted us to deduce the laws of moral science from the social needs and habits of mankind. It has shown us the infinitesimal part played by positive law in moral evolution, and the immense part played by the natural growth of altruistic feelings, which develop as soon as the conditions of life favor their growth. It has thus enforced the opinion of social reformers as to the necessity of modifying the conditions of life for improving man, instead of trying to improve human nature by moral teachings while life works in an opposite direction. Finally, by studying human society from the biological point of view, it has come to the conclusions arrived at by anarchists from the study of history and present tendencies as to further progress being in the line of socialization of wealth and integrated labor combined with the fullest possible freedom of the individual.

It has happened in the long run of ages that everything which permits men to increase their production, or even to continue it, has been appropriated by the few. The land, which derives its value precisely from its being necessary for an ever-increasing population, belongs to the few, who may prevent the community from cultivating it. The coalpits, which represent the labor of generations, and which also derive their value from the wants of the manufacturers and railroads, from the immense trade carried on and the density of population, belong again to the few, who have even the right of stopping the extraction of coal if they choose to give another use to their capital. . . .

Who is the sophist who will dare to say that such an organization is just? But what is unjust cannot be beneficial to mankind; and *it is not.* In consequence of this monstrous organization, the son of a workman, when he is able to work, finds no acre to till, no machine to set in motion, unless he agrees to sell his labor for a sum inferior to its real value. His father and grandfather have contributed to drain the field, or erect the factory, to If our productive powers were fully applied to increasing the stock of the staple necessities for life; if a modification of the present conditions of property increased the number of producers by all those who are not producers of wealth now; and if manual labor reconquered its place of honor in society, the communist tendencies already existing would immediately enlarge their sphere of application.

Taking all this into account, and still more the practical aspects of the question as to how private property *might* become common property, most of the anarchists maintain that the very next step to be made by society, as soon as the present regime of property undergoes a modification, will be

in a communist sense. We are communists. But our communism is not that of the authoritarian school: it is anarchist communism, communism without government, free communism. It is a synthesis of the two chief aims pursued by humanity since the dawn of its history—economic freedom and political freedom.

I have already said that anarchism means no-government. We know well that the word "anarchy" is also used in current phraseology as synonymous with disorder. But that meaning of "anarchy," being a derived one, implies at least two suppositions. It implies, first, that wherever there is no government there is disorder; and it implies, moreover, that order, due to a strong government and a strong police, is always beneficial. Both implications, however, are anything but proved. There is plenty of order—we should say, of harmony—in many branches of human activity where the government, happily, does not interfere. As to the beneficial effects of order, the kind of order that reigned at Naples under the Bourbons surely was not preferable to some disorder started by Garibaldi; while the Protestants of this country will probably say that the good deal of disorder made by Luther was preferable, at any rate, to the order which reigned under the Pope. While all agree that harmony is always desirable, there is no such unanimity about order, and still less about the "order" which is supposed to reign in our modern societies. So that we have no objection whatever to the use of the word "anarchy" as a negation of what has been often described as order.

By taking for our watchword anarchy in its sense of no-government, we intend to express a pronounced tendency of human society. In history we see that precisely those epochs when small parts of humanity broke down the power of their rules and reassumed their freedom were epochs of the greatest progress, economic and intellectual. Be it the growth of the free cities, whose unrivalled monuments—free work of free associations of workers—still testify to the revival of mind and of the well-being of the citizen; be it the great movement which gave birth to the Reformation—those epochs when the individual recovered some part of his freedom witnessed the greatest progress. And if we carefully watch the present development of civilized nations, we cannot fail to discover in it a marked and ever-growing movement towards limiting more and more the sphere of action of government, so as to leave more and more liberty to the initiative of the individual. After having tried all kinds of government, and endeavored to solve the insoluble problem of having a government "which might compel the individual to obedience, without escaping itself from obedience to collectivity," humanity is trying now to free itself from the bonds of any government whatever, and to respond to its needs of organization by the free understanding between individuals pursuing the same common aims.

Home Rule, even for the smallest territorial unit or group, becomes a growing need. Free agreement is becoming a substitute for law. And free cooperation a substitute for governmental guardianship. One after the other those activities which were considered as the functions of government during the last two centuries are disputed; society moves better the less it is governed. And the more we study the advance made in this direction, as well as the inadequacy of governments to fulfill the expectations placed in them, the more we are bound to conclude that humanity, by steadily limiting the functions of government, is marching towards reducing them finally to *nil*. We already foresee a state of society where the liberty of the individual will be limited by no laws, no bonds—by nothing else but his own social habits and the necessity, which everyone feels, of finding cooperation, support, and sympathy among his neighbors.

Every day millions of transactions are made without the slightest interference of government; and those who enter into agreements have not the slightest intention of breaking bargains. Nay, those agreements which are not protected by government (those of the exchange, or card debts) are perhaps better kept than any others. The simple habit of keeping one's word, the desire of not losing confidence, are quite sufficient in an overwhelming majority of cases to enforce the keeping of agreements. Of course it may be said that there is still the government which might enforce them if necessary. But without speaking of the numberless cases which could not even be brought before a court, everyone who has the slightest acquaintance with trade will undoubtedly confirm the assertion that, if there were not so strong a feeling of honor in keeping agreements, trade itself would become utterly impossible. Even those merchants and manufacturers who feel not the slightest remorse when poisoning their customers with all kinds of abominable drugs, duly labelled, even they also keep their commercial agreements. But if such a relative morality as commercial honesty exists now under the present conditions, when enrichment is the chief motive, the same feeling will further develop very quickly as soon as robbing someone of the fruits of his labor is no longer the economic basis of our life.

Another striking feature of our century tells in favor of the same no-government tendency. It is the steady enlargement of the field covered by private initiative, and the recent growth of large organizations resulting merely and simply from free agreement. The railway net of Europe—a confederation of so many scores of separate societies—and the direct transport of passengers and merchandise over so many lines which were built independently and federated together, without even so much as a Central Board of European Railways, is a most striking instance of what is already done by mere agreement. If fifty years ago somebody had predicted that railways built by so many separate companies finally would constitute so perfect a net as they do today, he surely would have been treated as a fool. It would have been urged that so many companies, prosecuting their own interests, would never agree without an International Board of Railways, supported by an International Convention of the European States, and endowed with governmental powers. But no such board was resorted to, and the agreement came nevertheless. The Dutch associations of ship and boat owners are now extending their organizations over the rivers of Germany and even to the shipping trade of the Baltic. The numberless amalgamated manufacturers' associations, and the *syndicates* of France, are so many instances in point. If it be argued that many of these organizations are organizations for exploitation, that proves nothing, because, if men pursuing their own egotistic, often very narrow, interests can agree together, better inspired men, compelled to be more closely connected with other groups, will necessarily agree still more easily and still better.

Utilitarianism and The Subjection of Women

John Stuart Mill

In his book *Utilitarianism,* John Stuart Mill first undertakes to explain the utilitarian theory and to defend it against its critics. Then, in the concluding chapter, Mill responds to the oft-heard charge that utilitarian theory cannot provide an acceptable account of social justice. Many have thought, for example, that any utilitarian who holds that the ultimate test of moral and political practices is their consequences for everyone's happiness will of necessity be committed to sacrificing the rights of some to the larger social good. Mill, however, rejects that charge. He begins by noting the various contexts where notions of justice and injustice apply. This analysis shows, according to Mill, that justice is simply the name for certain classes of moral rules which are especially important to human well-being. So rather than being contrary to justice, the utility principle supports it and explains why we give special weight to the specific moral rules grouped under the heading of justice.

The second selection is from another of Mill's works, *The Subjection of Women.* In the history of political philosophy, this is the only work devoted to the topic written by a man. When Mill wrote this, in 1869, women were not only barred by law from various occupations, they were even required to turn over their property and earnings to their new husbands.

I. UTILITARIANISM

What Utilitarianism Is

. . . The creed which accepts as the foundation of morals *utility* or the *greatest happiness principle* holds that actions are right in proportion as they tend to promote happiness, wrong as they tend to produce the reverse of happiness. By "happiness" is intended pleasure, and the absence of pain; by "unhappiness," pain, and the privation of pleasure. To give a clear view of the moral standard set up by the theory, much more requires to be said; in particular, what things it includes in the ideas of pain and pleasure, and to what extent this is left an open question. But these supplementary explanations do not affect the theory of life on which this theory of mortality is grounded—namely, that pleasure, and freedom from pain, are the only things desirable as ends;

From John Stuart Mill, *Utilitarianism* (1861) and *The Subjection of Women* (1869).

and that all desirable things (which are as numerous in the utilitarian as in any other scheme) are desirable either for the pleasure inherent in themselves, or as means to the promotion of pleasure and the prevention of pain.

Now such a theory of life excites in many minds, and among them in some of the most estimable in feeling and purpose, inveterate dislike. To suppose that life has (as they express it) no higher end than pleasure—no better and nobler object of desire and pursuit—they designate as utterly mean and groveling; as a doctrine worthy only of swine. . . .

[But it] is quite compatible with the principle of utility to recognize the fact, that some *kinds* of pleasure are more desirable and more valuable than others. It would be absurd that while, in estimating all other things, quality is considered as well as quantity, the estimation of pleasures should be supposed to depend on quantity alone.

If I am asked what I mean by difference of quality in pleasures, or what makes one pleasure more valuable than another merely as a pleasure, except its being greater in amount, there is but one possible answer. Of two pleasures, if there be one to which all or almost all who have experience of both give a decided preference, irrespective of any feeling of moral obligation to prefer it, that is the more desirable pleasure. If one of the two is, by those who are competently acquainted with both, placed so far above the other that they prefer it, even though knowing it to be attended with a greater amount of discontent, and would not resign it for any quantity of the other pleasure which their nature is capable of, we are justified in ascribing to the preferred enjoyment a superiority in quality, so far outweighing quantity as to render it, in comparison, of small account.

Now it is an unquestionable fact that those who are equally acquainted with, and equally capable of appreciating and enjoying, both, do give a most marked preference to the manner of existence which employs their higher faculties. Few human creatures would consent to be changed into any of the lower animals, for a promise of the fullest allowance of a beast's pleasures; no intelligent human being would consent to be a fool; no instructed person would be an ignoramus, no person of feeling and conscience would be selfish and base, even though they should be persuaded that the fool, the dunce, or the rascal is better satisfied with his lot than they are with theirs. They would not resign what they possess more than he for the most complete satisfaction of all the desires which they have in common with him. If they ever fancy they would, it is only in cases of unhappiness so extreme, that to escape from it they would exchange their lot for almost any other, however undesirable in their own eyes. A being of higher faculties requires more to make him happy, is capable probably of more acute suffering, and certainly accessible to it at more points, than one of an inferior type; but in spite of these liabilities, he can never really wish to sink into what he feels to be a lower grade of existence. We may give what explanation we please of this unwillingness; we may attribute it to pride, a name which is given indiscriminately to some of the most and to some of the least estimable feelings of which mankind are capable; we may refer it to the love of liberty and personal independence, an appeal to which was with the Stoics one of the most effective means for the inculcation of it; to the love of power, or to the love of excitement, both of which do really enter into and contribute to it: but its most appropriate appellation is a sense of dignity, which all human beings possess in one form or other, and in some, though by no means in exact, proportion to their higher faculties, and which is so essential a part of the happiness of those in whom it is strong, that nothing which conflicts with it could be, otherwise than momentarily, an object of desire to them. . . .

From this verdict of the only competent judges I apprehend there can be no appeal. On a question which is the best worth having of two pleasures, or which of two modes of existence is the most grateful to the feelings, apart from its moral attributes and from its consequences, the judgment of those who are qualified by knowledge of both, or, if they differ, that of the majority among them, must be admitted as final. And there need be the less hesitation to accept this judgment respecting the quality of pleasures, since there is no other tribunal to be referred to even on the question of quantity. What means are there of determining which is the acutest of two pains, or the intensest of two pleasurable sensations, except the general suffrage of those who are familiar with both? Neither pains nor pleasures are homogeneous, and pain is always heterogeneous with pleasure. What is there to decide whether a particular pleasure is worth purchasing at the cost of a particular pain, except the feelings and judgment of the experienced? When, therefore, those feelings and judgment declare the pleasures derived from the higher faculties to be preferable *in kind,* apart from the question of intensity, to those of which the animal nature, disjoined from the higher faculties, is suspectible, they are entitled on this subject to the same regard.

I have dwelt on this point, as being a necessary part of a perfectly just conception of utility, or happiness, considered as the directive role of human conduct. But it is by no means an indispensable condition to the acceptance of the utilitarian standard; for that standard is not the agent's own greatest happiness, but the greatest amount of happiness altogether; and if it may possibly be doubted whether a noble character is always the happier for its nobleness, there can be no doubt that it makes other people happier, and that the world in general is immensely a gainer by it. Utilitarianism, therefore, could only attain its end by the general cultivation of nobleness of character, even if each individual were only benefited by the nobleness of others, and his own, so far as happiness is concerned, were a sheer deduction from the benefit. But the bare enunciation of such an absurdity as this last renders refutation superfluous.

According to the "greatest happiness principle," as above explained, the ultimate end, with reference to and for the sake of which all other things are desirable (whether we are considering our own good or that of other people), is an existence exempt as far as possible from pain, and as rich as possible in enjoyments, both in point of quantity and quality; the test of quality, and the rule for measuring it against quantity, being the preference felt by those who in their opportunities of experience, to which must be added their habits of self-consciousness and self-observation, are best furnished with the means of comparison. This, being, according to the utilitarian opinion, the end of human action, is necessarily also the standard of morality, which may accordingly be defined 'the rules and precepts for human conduct,' by the observance of which an existence such as has been described might be, to the greatest extent possible, secured to all mankind; and not to them only, but, so far as the nature of things admits, to the whole sentient creation. . . .

Though it is only in a very imperfect state of the world's arrangements that anyone can best serve the happiness of others by the absolute sacrifice of his own, yet so long as the world is in that imperfect state, I fully acknowledge that the readiness to make such a sacrifice is the highest virtue which can be found in man. I will add that in this condition of the world, paradoxical as the assertion may be, the conscious ability to do without happiness gives the best prospect of realizing such happiness as is attainable. For nothing except that consciousness can raise a person above the chances of life, by making him feel that, let fate and fortune do their worst, they have not power to subdue him. . . .

The utilitarian morality does recognize in human beings the power of sacrificing their own greatest good for the good of others. It only refuses to admit that the sacrifice is itself a good. A sacrifice which does not increase, or tend to increase, the sum total of happiness, it considers as wasted. . . .

On the Connection Between Justice and Utility

In all ages of speculation, one of the strongest obstacles to the reception of the doctrine that Utility or Happiness is the criterion of right and wrong, has been drawn from the idea of Justice. The powerful sentiment and apparently clear perception which that word recalls, with a rapidity and certainty resembling an instinct, have seemed to the majority of thinkers to point to an inherent quality in things, to show that the Just must have an existence in nature as something absolute, generically distinct from every variety of the Expedient and, in idea, opposed to it, though (as is commonly acknowledged) never, in the long run, disjoined from it in fact. . . .

Mankind are always predisposed to believe that any subjective feeling not otherwise accounted for, is a revelation of some objective reality. Our present object is to determine whether the reality to which the feeling of justice corresponds, is one which needs any such special revelation, whether the justice or injustice of an action is a thing intrinsically peculiar, and distinct from all its other qualities, or only a combination of certain of those qualities, presented under a peculiar aspect. . . .

To throw light upon this question, it is necessary to attempt to ascertain what is the distinguishing character of justice or of injustice; what is the quality, or whether there is any quality, attributed in common to all modes of conduct designated as unjust (for justice, like many other moral attributes, is best defined by its opposite), and distinguishing them from such modes of conduct as are disapproved, but without having that particular epithet of disapprobation applied to them. If, in everything which men are accustomed to characterize as just or unjust, some one common attribute or collection of attributes is always present, we may judge whether this particular attribute, or combination of attributes, would be capable of gathering round it a sentiment of that peculiar character and intensity by virtue of the general laws of our emotional constitution, or whether the sentiment is inexplicable and requires to be regarded as a special provision of nature. If we find the former to be the case, we shall, in resolving this question, have resolved also the main problem; if the latter, we shall have to seek for some other mode of investigating it. To find the common attributes of a variety of objects, it is necessary to begin by surveying the objects themselves in the concrete. Let us therefore avert successively to the various modes of action, and arrangements of human affairs, which are classed, by universal or widely spread opinion, as Just or Unjust. The things well known to excite the sentiments associated with those names are of a very multifarious character. I shall pass them rapidly in review, without studying any particular arrangement.

In the first place, it is mostly considered unjust to deprive any one of his personal liberty, his property, or any other thing which belongs to him by law. Here, therefore, is one instance of the application of the terms Just and Unjust in a perfectly definite sense, namely, that it is just to respect, unjust to violate, the *legal rights* of any one. But this judgment admits of several exceptions, arising from the other forms in which the notions of justice and injustice present themselves. For example: The person who suffers the deprivation may (as the phrase is) have *forfeited* the rights which he is so deprived of; a case to which we shall return presently. . . .

Secondly, The legal rights of which he is deprived may be rights which *ought* not to have belonged to him; in other words, the law which confers on him these rights may be a bad law. When it is so, or when (which is the same thing for our purpose) it is supposed to be so, opinions will differ as to the justice or injustice of infringing it. Some maintain that no law, however bad, ought to be disobeyed by an individual citizen, that his opposition to it, if shown at all, should only be shown in endeavoring to get it altered by competent authority. This opinion (which condemns many of the most illustrious benefactors of mankind, and would often protect pernicious institutions against the only weapons which, in the state of things existing at the time, have any chance of succeeding against them) is defended, by those who hold it, on grounds of expediency, principally on that of the importance, to the common interest of mankind, of maintaining inviolate the sentiment of submission to law. Other persons, again, hold the directly contrary opinion that any law judged to be bad may blamelessly be disobeyed, even though it be not judged to be unjust, but only inexpedient, while others would confine the license of disobedience to the case of unjust laws. But, again, some say that all laws which are inexpedient are unjust, since every law imposes some restriction on the natural liberty of mankind, which restriction is an injustice, unless legitimated by tending to their good. Among these diversities of opinion, it seems to be universally admitted that there may be unjust laws, and that law, consequently, is not the ultimate criterion of justice, but may give to one person a benefit, or impose on another an evil, which justice condemns. When, however, a law is thought to be unjust, it seems always to be regarded as being so in the same way in which a breach of law is unjust—namely, by infringing somebody's right; which, as it cannot in this case be a legal right, receives a different appellation and is called a *moral right*. We may say, therefore, that a second case of injustice consists in taking or withholding from any person that to which he has a *moral right*.

Thirdly, It is universally considered just that each person should obtain that (whether good or evil) which he *deserves*, and unjust, that he should obtain a good, or be made to undergo an evil, which he does not deserve. This is, perhaps, the clearest and most emphatic form in which the idea of justice is conceived by the general mind. As it involves the notion of desert, the question arises, What constitutes desert? Speaking in a general way, a person is understood to

deserve good if he does right, evil, if he does wrong; and, in a more particular sense, to deserve good from those to whom he does or has done good, and evil from those to whom he does or has done evil. The precept of returning good for evil has never been regarded as a case of the fulfillment of justice, but as one in which the claims of justice are waived, in obedience to other considerations.

Fourthly, It is confessedly unjust to *break faith* with any one, to violate an engagement, either express or implied, or disappoint expectations raised by our own conduct, at least if we have raised those expectations knowingly and voluntarily. . . .

Fifthly, It is, by universal admission, inconsistent with justice to be *partial*, to show favor or preference to one person over another in matters to which favor and preference do not properly apply. Impartiality, however, does not seem to be regarded as a duty in itself, but rather as instrumental to some other duty, for it is admitted that favor and preference are not always censurable, and indeed the cases in which they are condemned are rather the exception than the rule. A person would be more likely to be blamed than applauded for giving his family or friends no superiority in good offices over strangers, when he could do so without violating any other duty, and no one thinks it unjust to seek one person in preference to another as a friend, connection, or companion. . . .

Impartiality, in short, as an obligation of justice, may be said to mean being exclusively influenced by the considerations which it is supposed ought to influence the particular case in hand, and resisting the solicitation of any motives which prompt to conduct different from what those considerations would dictate.

Nearly allied to the idea of impartiality is that of *equality*, which often enters as a component part both into the conception of justice and into the practice of it and, in the eyes of many persons, constitutes its essence. But, in this still more than in any other case, the notion of justice varies in different persons, and always conforms in its variations to their notion of utility. Each person maintains that equality is the dictate of justice, except where he thinks that expediency requires inequality. The justice of giving equal protection to the rights of all is maintained by those who support the most outrageous inequality in the rights themselves. Even in slave countries, it is theoretically admitted that the rights of the slave, such as they are, ought to be as sacred as those of the master, and that a tribunal which fails to enforce them with equal strictness is wanting in justice, while, at the same time, institutions which leave to the slave scarcely any rights to enforce are not deemed unjust, because they are not deemed inexpedient. Those who think that utility requires distinctions of rank do not consider it unjust that riches and social privileges should be unequally dispensed, but those who think this inequality inexpedient think it unjust also. Whoever thinks that government is necessary sees no injustice in as much inequality as is constituted by giving to the magistrate powers not granted to other people. Even among those who hold leveling doctrines, there are as many questions of justice as there are differences of opinion about expediency. Some Communists consider it unjust that the produce of the labor of the community should be shared on any other principle than that of exact equality, others think it just that those should receive most whose wants are greatest, while others hold that those who work harder, or who produce more, or whose services are more valuable to the community, may justly claim a larger quota in the division of the produce. And the sense of natural justice may be plausibly appealed to in behalf of every one of these opinions.

Among so many diverse applications of the term Justice, which yet is not regarded as ambiguous, it is a matter of some difficulty to seize the mental link which holds them together, and on which the moral sentiment adhering to the term essentially depends. . . .

Now, it is known that ethical writers divide moral duties into two classes, denoted by the ill-chosen expressions, duties of perfect and of imperfect obligation; the latter being those in which, though the act is obligatory, the particular occasions of performing it are left to our choice, as in the case of charity or beneficence, which we are indeed bound to practice, but not towards any definite person, nor at any prescribed time. In the more precise language of philosophic jurists, duties of perfect obligation are those duties in virtue of which a correlative *right* resides in some person or persons; duties of imperfect obligation are those moral obligations which do not give birth to any right. I think it will be found that this distinction exactly coincides with that which exists between justice and the other obligations of morality. . . . It seems to me that this feature in the case—a right in some person, correlative to the moral obligation—constitutes the specific difference between justice and generosity or beneficence. Justice implies something which it is not only right to do and wrong not to do, but which some individual person can claim from us as his moral right. No one has a moral right to our generosity or beneficence, because we are not morally bound to practice those virtues towards any given individual. . . . Wherever there is a right, the case is one of justice, and not of the virtue of beneficence, and whoever does not place the distinction between justice and morality in general where we have now placed it will be found to make no distinction between them at all, but to merge all morality in justice. . . .

We have seen that the two essential ingredients in the sentiment of justice are the desire to punish a person who has done harm, and the knowledge or belief that there is some definite individual or individuals to whom harm has been done.

Now, it appears to me that the desire to punish a person who has done harm to some individual is a spontaneous outgrowth from two sentiments, both in the highest degree natural, and which either are or resemble instincts—the impulse of self-defense, and the feeling of sympathy.

It is natural to resent, and to repel or retaliate, any harm done or attempted against ourselves or against those with whom we sympathize. . . . By virtue of his superior intelligence, even apart from his superior range of sympathy, a human being is capable of apprehending a community of interest between himself and the human society of which he forms a part, such that any conduct which threatens the security of the society generally is threatening to his own, and calls forth his instinct (if instinct it be) of self-defense. The same superiority of intelligence, joined to the power of sympathizing with human beings generally, enables him to attach himself to the collective idea of his tribe, his country, or mankind, in such a manner that any act hurtful to them raises his instinct of sympathy, and urges him to resistance.

The sentiment of justice, in that one of its elements which consists of the desire to punish, is thus, I conceive, the natural feeling of retaliation or vengeance, rendered by intellect and sympathy applicable to those injuries—that is, to those hurts—which wound us through, or in common with, society at large. This sentiment in itself has nothing moral in it; what is moral is the exclusive subordination of it to the social sympathies, so as to wait on and obey their call. For the natural feeling would make us resent indiscriminately whatever any one does that is disagreeable to us, but, when moralized by the social feeling, it only acts in the directions conformable to the general good: just persons resenting a hurt to society, though not otherwise a hurt to themselves, and not resenting a hurt to themselves, however painful, unless it be of the kind which society has a common interest with them in the repression of. . . .

To recapitulate: The idea of justice supposes two things—a rule of conduct and a sentiment which sanctions the rule. The first must be supposed common to all mankind, and intended for their good; the other (the sentiment) is a desire that punishment may be suffered by those who infringe the rule. There is involved, in addition, the conception of some definite person who suffers by the infringement, whose rights (to use the expression appropriated to the case) are violated by it. And the sentiment of justice appears to me to be the animal desire to repel or retaliate a hurt or damage to one's self or to those with whom one sympathizes, widened so as to include all persons, by the human capacity of enlarged sympathy, and the human conception of intelligent self-interest. From the latter elements, the feeling derives its morality; from the former, its peculiar impressiveness and energy of self-assertion.

I have throughout treated the idea of a *right* residing in the injured person, and violated by the injury, not as a separate element in the composition of the idea and sentiment, but as one of the forms in which the other two elements clothe themselves. These elements are a hurt to some assignable person or persons on the one hand, and a demand for punishment on the other. An examination of our own minds, I think, will show that these two things include all that we mean when we speak of violation of a right. When we call any thing a person's right, we mean that he has a valid claim on society to protect him in the possession of it, either by the force of law, or by that of education and opinion. If he has what we consider a sufficient claim, or whatever account, to have something guaranteed to him by society, we say that he has a right to it. If we desire to prove that anything does not belong to him by right, we think this done as soon as it is admitted that society ought not to take measures for securing it to him, but should leave him to chance or to his own exertions. Thus a person is said to have a right to what he can earn in fair professional competition, because society ought not to allow any other person to hinder him from endeavoring to earn in that manner as much as he can. But he has not a right to three hundred a year, though he may happen to be earning it, because society is not called on to provide that he shall earn that sum. On the contrary, if he owns ten thousand pounds three-per-cent stock, he *has* a right to three hundred a year, because society has come under an obligation to provide him with an income of that amount.

To have a right then is, I conceive, to have something which society ought to defend me in the possession of. If the objector goes on to ask why it ought, I can give him no other reason than general utility. . . .

If the preceding analysis, or something resembling it, be not the correct account of the notion of justice, if justice be totally independent of utility, and be a standard *per se*, which the mind can recognize by simple introspection of itself—it is hard to understand why that internal oracle is so ambiguous, and why so many things appear either just or unjust, according to the light in which they are regarded. . . .

We are continually informed that Utility is an uncertain standard, which every different person interprets differently, and that there is no safety but in the immutable, ineffaceable, and unmistakable dictates of Justice, which carry their evidence in themselves and are independent of the fluctuations of opinion. . . .

For instance: There are some who say that it is unjust to punish any one for the sake of example to others, that punishment is just, only when intended for the good of the sufferer himself. Others maintain the extreme reverse, contending that to punish persons who have attained years of discretion, for their own benefit, is despotism and injustice, since, if the matter at issue is solely their own good, no one has a right to control their own judgment of it, but that they may justly be punished to prevent evil to others, this being the exercise of the legitimate right of self-defense. Mr. Owen, again, affirms that it is unjust to punish at all, for the criminal did not make his own character; his education, and the circumstances which surrounded him, have made him a criminal, and for these he is not responsible. . . .

To take another example from a subject already once referred to. In a co-operative industrial association, it is just or not that talent or skill should give a title to superior remuneration? On the negative side of the question it is argued, that whoever does the best he can, deserves equally well, and ought not in justice to be put in a position of inferiority for no fault of his own; that superior abilities have already advantages more than enough, in the admiration they excite, the personal influence they command, and the internal sources of satisfaction attending them, without adding to these a superior share of the world's goods; and that society is bound in justice rather to make compensation to the less favoured, for this unmerited inequality of advantages, than to aggravate it. On the contrary side it is contended, that society receives more from the more efficient labourer; that his services being more useful, society owes him a larger return for them; that a greater share of the joint result is actually his work, and not to allow his claim to it is a kind of robbery; that if he is only to receive as much as others, he can only be justly required to produce as much, and to give a smaller amount of time and exertion, proportioned to his superior efficiency. Who shall decide between these appeals to conflicting principles of justice? Justice has in this case two sides to it, which it is impossible to bring into harmony, and the two disputants have chosen opposite sides; the one looks to what it is just that the individual should receive, the other to what it is just that the community should give. Each, from his own point of view, is unanswerable; and any choice between them, on grounds of justice, must be perfectly arbitrary. Social utility alone can decide the preference.

How many, again, and how irreconcilable, are the standards of justice to which reference is made in discussing the repartition of taxation. One opinion is that payment to the State should be in numerical proportion to pecuniary means. Others think that justice dictates what they term graduated taxation; taking a higher percentage from those who have more to spare. . . .

From these confusions there is no other mode of extrication than the ultilitarian.

Is, then, the difference between the Just

and the Expedient a merely imaginary distinction? Have mankind been under a delusion in thinking that justice is a more sacred thing than policy, and that the latter ought only to be listened to after the former has been satisfied? By no means. The exposition we have given of the nature and origin of the sentiment recognizes a real distinction, and no one of those who profess the most sublime contempt for the consequences of actions as an element in their morality attaches more importance to the distinction than I do. While I dispute the pretensions of any theory which sets up an imaginary standard of justice not grounded on utility, I account the justice which is grounded on utility to be the chief part, and incomparably the most sacred and binding part, of all morality. Justice is a name for certain classes of moral rules which concern the essentials of human well-being more nearly, and are therefore of more absolute obligation, than any other rules for the guidance of life, and the notion which we have found to be of the essence of the idea of justice, that of a right residing in an individual, implies and testifies to this more binding obligation.

The moral rules which forbid mankind to hurt one another (in which we must never forget to include wrongful interference with each other's freedom) are more vital to human well-being than any maxims, however important, which only point out the best mode of managing some department of human affairs. They have also the peculiarity that they are the main element in determining the whole of the social feelings of mankind. It is their observance which alone preserves peace among human beings; if obedience to them were not the rule, and disobedience the exception, everyone would see in every one else an enemy, against whom he must be perpetually guarding himself. What is hardly less important, these are the precepts which mankind have the strongest and the most direct inducements for impressing upon one another. . . . The most marked cases of injustice, and those which give the tone to the feeling of repugnance which characterizes the sentiment,

are acts of wrongful aggression, or wrongful exercise of power over some one; the next are those which consist in wrongfully withholding from him something which is his due; in both cases, inflicting on him a positive hurt, either in the form of direct suffering, or of the privation of some good which he had reasonable ground either of a physical or of a social kind, for counting upon.

The same powerful motives which command the observance of these primary moralities, enjoin the punishment of those who violate them; and as the impulses of self-defence, of defence of others, and of vengeance, are all called forth against such persons, retribution, or evil for evil, becomes closely connected with the sentiment of justice, and is universally included in the idea. Good for good is also one of the dictates of justice; and this, though its social utility is evident, and though it carries with it a natural human feeling, has not at first sight that obvious connexion with hurt or injury, which, existing in the most elementary cases of just and unjust, and is the source of the characteristic intensity of the sentiment. But the connexion, though less obvious, is not less real. He who accepts benefits, and denies a return of them when needed, inflicts a real hurt, by disappointing one of the most natural and reasonable of expectations, and one which he must at least tacitly have encouraged, otherwise the benefits would seldom have been conferred. . . .

The principle, therefore, of giving to each what they deserve—that is, good for good, as well as evil for evil—is not only included within the idea of Justice as we have defined it, but is a proper object of that intensity of sentiment which places the Just, in human estimation, above the simply Expedient. . . .

II. THE SUBJECTION OF WOMEN

Chapter 1. The object of this Essay is to explain as clearly as I am able, the grounds of an opinion which I have held from the very earliest period when I had formed any opinions at all on social or political matters, and which, instead of being weakened or modified, has been constantly growing stronger by the progress of reflection and the experience of life: That the principle which regulates the existing social relations between the two sexes—the legal subordination of one sex to the other—is wrong in itself, and now one of the chief hindrances to human improvement; and that it ought to be replaced by a principle of perfect equality, admitting no power or privilege on the one side, no disability on the other. . . .

The generality of a practice is in some cases a strong presumption that it is, or at all events once was, conducive to laudable ends. This is the case, when the practice was first adopted, or afterwards kept up, as a means to such ends, and was grounded on experience of the mode in which they could be most effectually attained. If the authority of men over women, when first established, had been the result of a conscientious comparison between different modes of constituting the government of society; if, after trying various other modes of social organization—the government of women over men, equality between the two, and such mixed and divided modes of government as might be invented—it had been decided, on the testimony of experience, that the mode in which women are wholly under the rule of men, having no share at all in public concerns, and each in private being under the legal obligation of obedience to the man with whom she has associated her destiny, was the arrangement most conducive to the happiness and well being of both; its general adoption might then be fairly thought to be some evidence that, at the time when it was adopted, it was the best: though even then the considerations which recommended it may, like so many other primeval social facts of the greatest importance, have subsequently, in the course of ages, ceased to exist. But the state of the case is in every respect the reverse of this. In the first place, the opinion in favour of the present system, which entirely subordinates the weaker sex to the stronger, rests upon theory only; for there never has been trial made

of any other: so that experience, in the sense in which it is vulgarly opposed to theory, cannot be pretended to have pronounced any verdict. And in the second place, the adoption of this system of inequality never was the result of deliberation, or forethought, or any social ideas, or any notion whatever of what conduced to the benefit of humanity or the good order of society. It arose simply from the fact that from the very earliest twilight of human society, every woman (owing to the value attached to her by men, combined with her inferiority in muscular strength) was found in a state of bondage to some man. Laws and systems of polity always begin by recognising the relations they find already existing between individuals. They convert what was a mere physical fact into a legal right, give it the sanction of society, and principally aim at the substitution of public and organized means of asserting and protecting these rights, instead of the irregular and lawless conflict of physical strength. Those who had already been compelled to obedience became in this manner legally bound to it. . . . But this dependence, as it exists at present, is not an original institution, taking a fresh start from considerations of justice and social expediency—it is the primitive state of slavery lasting on, through successive mitigations and modifications occasioned by the same causes which have softened the general manners, and brought all human relations more under the control of justice and the influence of humanity. It has not lost the taint of its brutal origin. No presumption in its favour, therefore, can be drawn from the fact of its existence. . . . The inequality of rights between men and women has no other source than the law of the strongest.

But, it will be said, the rule of men over women differs from all these others in not being a rule of force: it is accepted voluntarily; women make no complaint, and are consenting parties to it. In the first place, a great number of women do not accept it. Ever since there have been women able to make their sentiments known by their writings (the only mode of publicity which society permits to them), an increasing number of them have recorded protests against their present social condition. . . .

All causes, social and natural, combine to make it unlikely that women should be collectively rebellious to the power of men. They are so far in a position different from all other subject classes, that their masters require something more from them than actual service. Men do not want solely the obedience of women, they want their sentiments. All men, except the most brutish, desire to have, in the woman most nearly connected with them, not a forced slave but a willing one, not a slave merely, but a favourite. They have therefore put everything in practice to enslave their minds. The masters of all other slaves rely, for maintaining obedience, on fear; either fear of themselves, or religious fears. The masters of women wanted more than simple obedience, and they turned the whole force of education to effect their purpose. All women are brought up from the very earliest years in the belief that their ideal of character is the very opposite to that of men; not self-will, and government by self-control, but submission, and yielding to the control of others. All the moralities tell them that it is the duty of women, and all the current sentimentalities that it is their nature, to live for others; to make complete abnegation of themselves, and to have no life but in their affections. And by their affections are meant the only ones they are allowed to have—those to the men with whom they are connected, or to the children who constitute an additional and indefeasible tie between them and a man. When we put together three things—first, the natural attraction between opposite sexes; secondly, the wife's entire dependence on the husband, every privilege or pleasure she has being either his gift, or depending entirely on his will; and lastly, that the principal object of human pursuit, consideration, and all objects of social ambition, can in general be sought or obtained by her only through him, it would be a miracle if the object of being attractive to men had not become the polar star of feminine education and formation of character. And, this great means of influence over the minds of women having been acquired, an instinct of selfishness made men avail themselves of it to the upmost as a means of holding women in subjection, by representing to them meekness, submissiveness, and resignation of all individual will into the hands of a man, as an essential part of sexual attractiveness. Can it be doubted that any of the other yokes which mankind have succeeded in breaking, would have subsisted till now if the same means had existed, and had been as sedulously used, to bow down their minds to it? . . .

Neither does it avail anything to say that the *nature* of the two sexes adapts them to their present functions and position, and renders these appropriate to them. Standing on the ground of common sense and the constitution of the human mind, I deny that any one knows, or can know, the nature of the two sexes, as long as they have only been seen in their present relation to one another. . . .

One thing we may be certain of—that what is contrary to women's nature to do, they never will be made to do by simply giving their nature free play. The anxiety of mankind to interfere in behalf of nature, for fear lest nature should not succeed in effecting its purpose, is an altogether unnecessary solicitude. . . .

Chapter 2. . . . Marriage being the destination appointed by society for women, the prospect they are brought up to, and the object which it is intended should be sought by all of them, except those who are too little attractive to be chosen by any man as his companion; one might have supposed that everything would have been done to make this condition as eligible to them as possible, that they might have no cause to regret being denied the option of any other. Society, however, both in this, and, at first, in all other cases, has preferred to attain its object by foul rather than fair means: but this is the only case in which it has substantially persisted in them even to the present day.

Originally women were taken by force, or regularly sold by their father to the husband. . . .

[Today] the wife is the actual bond-servant of her husband: no less so, as far as legal obligation goes, than slaves commonly so called. She vows a life-long obedience to him at the altar, and is held to it all through her life by law. Casuists may say that the obligation of obedience stops short of participation in crime, but it certainly extends to everything else. She can do no act whatever but by his permission, at least tacit. She can acquire no property but for him; the instant it becomes hers, even if by inheritance, it becomes *ipso facto* his. In this respect the wife's position under the common law of England is worse than that of slaves in the laws of many countries. . . . The two are called "one person in law," for the purpose of inferring that whatever is hers is his, but the parallel inference is never drawn that whatever is his is hers; the maxim is not applied against the man, except to make him responsible to third parties for her acts, as a master is for the acts of his slaves or of his cattle. I am far from pretending that wives are in general no better treated than slaves; but no slave is a slave to the same lengths, and in so full a sense of the word, as a wife is. Hardly any slave, except one immediately attached to the master's person, is a slave at all hours and all minutes; in general he has, like a soldier, his fixed task, and when it is done, or when he is off duty, he disposes, within certain limits, of his own time, and has a family life into which the master rarely intrudes. "Uncle Tom" under his first master had his own life in his "cabin," almost as much as any man whose work takes him away from home, is able to have in his own family. But it cannot be so with the wife. Above all, a female slave has (in Christian countries) an admitted right, and is considered under a moral obligation, to refuse to her master the last familiarity. Not so the wife: however brutal a tyrant she may unfortunately be chained to—though she may know that he hates her, though it may be his daily pleasure to torture her, and though she may feel it impossible not to loathe him—he can claim from her and enforce the lowest degradation of a human being, that of being made the instrument of an animal function contrary to her inclinations. While she is held in this worst description of slavery as to her own person, what is her position in regard to the children in whom she and her master have a joint interest? They are by law *his* children. He alone has any legal rights over them. Not one act can she do towards or in relation to them, except by delegation from him. Even after he is dead she is not their legal guardian, unless he by will has made her so. He could even send them away from her, and deprive her of the means of seeing or corresponding with them, until this power was in some degree restricted by Serjeant Talfourd's Act. This is her legal state. And from this state she has no means of withdrawing herself. If she leaves her husband, she can take nothing with her, neither her children nor anything which is rightfully her own. If he chooses, he can compel her to return, by law, or by physical force; or he may content himself with seizing for his own use anything which she may earn, or which may be given to her by her relations. . . .

When we consider how vast is the number of men, in any great country, who are little higher than brutes, and that this never prevents them from being able, through the law of marriage, to obtain a victim, the breadth and depth of human misery caused in this shape alone by the abuse of the institution swells to something appalling. . . . I grant that the wife, if she cannot effectually resist, can at least retaliate; she, too, can make the man's life extremely uncomfortable, and by that power is able to carry many points which she ought, and many which she ought not, to prevail in. But this instrument of self-protection—which may be called the power of the scold, or the shrewish sanction—has the fatal defect, that it avails most against the least tyrannical superiors, and in favour of the least deserving dependents. It is the weapon of irritable and self-willed women; of those who would make the worst use of power if they themselves had it, and who generally turn this power to a bad use. . . .

But how, it will be asked, can any society exist without government? In a family, as in a state, some one person must be the ultimate ruler. Who shall decide when married people differ in opinion? Both cannot have their way, yet a decision one way or the other must be come to.

It is not true that in all voluntary association between two people, one of them must be absolute master: still less that the law must determine which of them it shall be. . . .

It is quite true that things which have to be decided every day, and cannot adjust themselves gradually, or wait for a compromise, ought to depend on one will: one person must have their sole control. But it does not follow that this should always be the same person. The natural arrangement is a division of powers between the two; each being absolute in the executive branch of their own department, and any change of system and principle requiring the consent of both. . . .

The real practical decision of affairs, to whichever may be given the legal authority, will greatly depend, as it even now does, upon comparative qualifications. The mere fact that he is usually the eldest, will in most cases give the preponderance to the man; at least until they both attain a time of life at which the difference in their years is of no importance. There will naturally also be a more potential voice on the side, whichever it is, that brings the means of support. . . .

After what has been said respecting the obligation of obedience, it is almost superfluous to say anything concerning the more special point included in the general one—a woman's right to her own property; for I need not hope that this treatise can make any impression upon those who need anything to convince them that a woman's inheritance or gains ought to be as much her own after marriage as before. The rule is simple: whatever would be the husband's or wife's if they were not married, should be under their exclusive control during marriage. . . .

When the support of the family depends, not on property, but on earnings, the common arrangement, by which the man earns the income and the wife superintends the domestic expenditure, seems to me in general the most suitable division of labour between the two persons. If, in addition to the physical suffering of bearing children, and the whole responsibility of their care and education in early years, the wife undertakes the careful and economical application of the husband's earnings to the general comfort of the family; she takes not only her fair share, but usually the larger share, of the bodily and mental exertion required by their joint existence. If she undertakes any additional portion, it seldom relieves her from this, but only prevents her from performing it properly. The care which she is herself disabled from taking of the children and the household, nobody else takes; those of the children who do not die, grow up as they best can, and the management of the household is likely to be so bad, as even in point of economy to be a great drawback from the value of the wife's earnings. In an otherwise just state of things, it is not, therefore, I think, a desirable custom, that the wife should contribute by her labour to the income of the family. In an unjust state of things, her doing so may be useful to her, by making her of more value in the eyes of the man who is legally her master; but, on the other hand, it enables him still farther to abuse his power, by forcing her to work, and leaving the support of the family to her exertions, while he spends most of his time in drinking and idleness. The *power* of earning is essential to the dignity of a woman, if she has not independent property. But if marriage were an equal contract, not implying the obligation of obedience; if the connexion were no longer enforced to the oppression of those to whom it is purely a mischief, but a separation, on just terms (I do not now speak of a divorce), could be obtained by any woman who was morally entitled to it; and if she would then find all honourable employments as freely open to her as to men; it would not be necessary for her protection, that during marriage she should make this particular use of her faculties. Like a man when he chooses a profession, so, when a woman marries, it may in general be understood that she makes choice of the management of a household, and the bringing up of a family, as the first call upon her exertions, during as many years of her life as may be required for the purpose; and that she renounces, not all other objects and occupations, but all which are not consistent with the requirements of this. The actual exercise, in a habitual or systematic manner, of outdoor occupations, or such as cannot be carried on at home, would by this principle be practically interdicted to the greater number of married women. But the utmost latitude ought to exist for the adaptation of general rules to individual suitabilities; and there ought to be nothing to prevent faculties exceptionally adapted to any other pursuit, from obeying their vocation notwithstanding marriage: due provision being made for supplying otherwise any falling-short which might become inevitable, in her full performance of the ordinary functions of mistress of a family. These things, if once opinion were rightly directed on the subject, might with perfect safety be left to be regulated by opinion, without any interference of law.

Chapter 3. On the other point which is involved in the just equality of women, their admissibility to all the functions and occupations hitherto retained as the monopoly of the stronger sex, I should anticipate no difficulty in convincing any one who has gone with me on the subject of the equality of women in the family. I believe that their disabilities elsewhere are only clung to in order to maintain their subordination in domestic life. . . . It is not sufficient to maintain that women on the average are less gifted than men on the average, with certain of the higher mental faculties, or that a smaller number of women than of men are fit for occupations and functions of the highest in-

tellectual character. It is necessary to maintain that no women at all are fit for them, and that the most eminent women are inferior in mental faculties to the most mediocre of the men on whom those functions at present devolve. . . . Is there so great a superfluity of men fit for high duties, that society can afford to reject the service of any competent person? Are we so certain of always finding a man made to our hands for any duty or function of social importance which falls vacant, that we lose nothing by putting a ban upon one-half of mankind, and refusing beforehand to make their faculties available, however distinguished they may be? And even if we could do without them, would it be consistent with justice to refuse to them their fair share of honour and distinction, or to deny to them the equal moral right of all human beings to choose their occupation (short of injury to others) according to their own preferences, at their own risk? Nor is the injustice confined to them: it is shared by those who are in a position to benefit by their services. . . .

But (it is said) there is anatomical evidence of the superior mental capacity of men compared with women: they have a larger brain. I reply, that in the first place the fact itself is doubtful. It is by no means established that the brain of a woman is smaller than that of a man. . . . Next, I must observe that the precise relation which exists between the brain and the intellectual powers is not yet well understood, but is a subject of great dispute. . . . It would not be surprising—it is indeed an hypothesis which accords well with the differences actually observed between the mental operations of the two sexes—if men on the average should have the advantage in the size of the brain, and women in activity of cerebral circulation. The results which conjecture, founded on analogy, would lead us to expect from this difference of organization, would correspond to some of those which we most commonly see. In the first place, the mental operations of men might be expected to be slower. They would neither be so prompt as women in thinking, nor so quick to feel.

Large bodies take more time to get into full action. On the other hand, when once got thoroughly into play, men's brains would bear more work. It would be more persistent in the line first taken; it would have more difficulty in changing from one mode of action to another, but, in the one thing it was doing, it could go on longer without loss of power or sense of fatigue. And do we not find that the things in which men most excel women are those which require most plodding and long hammering at a single thought, while women do best what must be done rapidly? A woman's brain is sooner fatigued, sooner exhausted; but given the degree of exhaustion, we should expect to find that it would recover itself sooner. I repeat that this speculation is entirely hypothetical. . . .

Let us take, then, the only marked case which observation affords, of apparent inferiority of women to men, if we except the merely physical one of bodily strength. No production in philosophy, science, or art, entitled to the first rank, has been the work of a woman. Is there any mode of accounting for this, without supposing that women are naturally incapable of producing them?

In the first place, we may fairly question whether experience has afforded sufficient grounds for an induction. It is scarcely three generations since women, saving very rare exceptions, have begun to try their capacity in philosophy, science, or art. It is only in the present generation that their attempts have been at all numerous; and they are even now extremely few, everywhere but in England and France. It is a relevant question, whether a mind possessing the requisites of first-rate eminence in speculation or creative art could have been expected, on the mere calculation of chances, to turn up during that lapse of time, among the women whose tastes and personal position admitted of their devoting themselves to these pursuits. . . .

Chapter 4. There remains a question, not of less importance than those already discussed, and which will be asked the most importunately by those opponents whose conviction is somewhat shaken on the main point. What good are we to expect from the changes proposed in our customs and institutions? Would mankind be at all better off if women were free? If not, why disturb their minds, and attempt to make a social revolution in the name of an abstract right? . . .

To which let me first answer, [there is] the advantage of having the most universal and pervading of all human relations regulated by justice instead of injustice. The vast amount of this gain to human nature, it is hardly possible, by any explanation or illustration, to place in a stronger light than it is placed by the bare statement, to any one who attaches a moral meaning to words. All the selfish propensities, the self-worship, the unjust self-preference, which exist among mankind, have their source and root in, and derive their principal nourishment from, the present constitution of the relation between men and women. Think what it is to a boy, to grow up to manhood in the belief that without any merit or any exertion of his own, though he may be the most frivolous and empty or the most ignorant and stolid of mankind, by the mere fact of being born a male he is by right the superior of all and every one of an entire half of the human race. . . . What must be the effect on his character, of this lesson? And men of the cultivated classes are often not aware how deeply it sinks into the immense majority of male minds. For, among right-feeling and well-bred people, the inequality is kept as much as possible out of sight; above all, out of sight of the children. As much obedience is required from boys to their mother as to their father: they are not permitted to domineer over their sisters, nor are they accustomed to see these postponed to them, but the contrary; the compensations of the chivalrous feeling being made prominent, while the servitude which requires them is kept in the background. . . .

The second benefit to be expected from giving to women the free use of their faculties, by leaving them the free choice of their employments, and opening to them the same field of occupation and the same prizes and encouragements as to other human beings, would be that of doubling the mass of mental faculties available for the higher service of humanity. . . . This great accession to the intellectual power of the species, and to the amount of intellect available for the good management of its affairs, would be obtained, partly, through the better and more complete intellectual education of women. . . .

The opinion of women would then possess a more beneficial, rather than a greater, influence upon the general mass of human belief and sentiment. I say a more beneficial, rather than a greater influence; for the influence of women over the general tone of opinion has always, or at least from the earliest known period, been very considerable. . . .

. . . The wife's influence tends, as far as it goes, to prevent the husband from falling below the common standard of approbation of the country. It tends quite as strongly to hinder him from rising above it. The wife is the auxiliary of the common public opinion. A man who is married to a woman his inferior in intelligence, finds her a perpetual dead weight, or, worse than a dead weight, a drag, upon every aspiration of his to be better than public opinion requires him to be. It is hardly possible for one who is in these bonds, to attain exalted virtue. . . .

Though it may stimulate the amatory propensities of men, it does not conduce to married happiness, to exaggerate by differences of education whatever may be the native differences of the sexes. If the married pair are well-bred and well-behaved people, they tolerate each other's tastes; but is mutual toleration what people look forward to, when they enter into marriage? . . .

What marriage may be in the case of two persons of cultivated faculties, identical in opinions and purposes, between whom there exists that best kind of equality, similarity of powers and capacities with reciprocal superiority in them—so that each can enjoy the luxury of looking up to the other, and can have alternately the pleasure of leading and of being led in the path of development—I will not attempt to describe. To those who can conceive it, there is no need; to those who cannot, it would appear the dream of an enthusiast. But I maintain, with the profoundest conviction, that this, and this only, is the ideal of marriage; and that all opinions, customs, and institutions which favour any other notion of it, or turn the conceptions and aspirations connected with it into any other direction, by whatever pretences they may be coloured, are relics of primitive barbarism. The moral regeneration of mankind will only really commence, when the most fundamental of the social relations is placed under the rule of equal justice, and when human beings learn to cultivate their strongest sympathy with an equal in rights and in cultivation.

A Theory of Justice

John Rawls

Political philosophy has experienced a renaissance in recent years, in part due to the work of John Rawls. In his book, *A Theory of Justice*, Rawls revives the social contract tradition. The focus of social justice, he stresses, is society's basic structure—its constitution and its economic system—not the justice or injustice of individual acts. Rawls's social contract is hypothetical rather than historical: correct principles of justice are ones which would be chosen in a fair position of equality. That, in turn, requires us to imagine ourselves in an "original position" behind a "veil of ignorance" which prevents us from relying on such morally irrelevant factors as race, gender, social class, or even our particular talents. Situated in such a position, he argues, people would choose to construct their government according to principles that (1) respect basic liberties and (2) allow social and economic inequalities only if they benefit everybody, in particular society's least advantaged, and assure that everyone is given genuine (fair) equality of opportunity to seek various positions.

THE SUBJECT OF JUSTICE

Many different kinds of things are said to be just and unjust: not only laws, institutions, and social systems, but also particular actions of many kinds, including decisions, judgments, and imputations. We also call the attitudes and dispositions of persons, and persons themselves, just and unjust. Our topic, however, is that of social justice. For us the primary subject of justice is the basic structure of society, or more exactly, the way in which the major social institutions distribute fundamental rights and duties and determine the division of advantages from social cooperation. By major institutions I understand the political constitution and the principal economic and social arrangements. Thus the legal protection of freedom of thought and liberty of conscience, competitive markets, private property in the means of production, and the monogamous family are examples of major social institutions. Taken together as one scheme, the major institutions define men's rights and duties and influence their life-prospects, what they can expect to be and how well they can hope to do. The basic structure is the primary subject of justice because its effects are so profound and present from the start. The intuitive notion here is that this structure contains various social positions and that men born into different positions have different expectations of life determined, in part, by the political system as well as by economic and social circumstances. In this way the institutions of society favor certain starting places over others. These are especially deep inequalities. Not only are they pervasive, but they affect men's initial chances in life; yet they cannot possibly be justified by an appeal to the notions of merit or desert. It is these inequalities, presumably inevitable in the basic structure of any society, to which the principles of social justice must in the first instance apply. These principles, then, regulate the choice of a political constitution and the main elements of the economic and social system. The justice of a social scheme depends essentially on how fundamental rights and duties are assigned and on the economic opportunities and social conditions in the various sectors of society. . . .

THE MAIN IDEA OF
THE THEORY OF JUSTICE

My aim is to present a conception of justice which generalizes and carries to a higher level of abstraction the familiar theory of the social contract as found, say, in Locke, Rousseau, and Kant.[1] In order to do this we are not to think of the original contract as one to enter a particular society or to set up a particular form of government. Rather, the guiding idea is that the principles of justice for the basic structure of society are the object of the original agreement. They are the principles that free and rational persons concerned to further their own interests would accept in an initial position of equality as defining the fundamental terms of their association. These principles are to regulate all further agreements: they specify the kinds of social cooperation that can be entered into and the forms of government that can be established. This way of regarding the principles of justice I shall call justice as fairness.

Thus we are to imagine that those who engage in social cooperation choose together, in one joint act, the principles which are to assign basic rights and duties and to determine the division of social benefits. Men are to decide in advance how they are to regulate their claims against one another and what is to be the foundation charter of their society. Just as each person must decide by rational reflection what constitutes his good, that is, the system of ends which it is rational for him to pursue, so a group of persons must decide once and for all what is to count among them as just and unjust. The choice which rational men would make in this hypothetical situation of equal liberty, assuming for the present that this choice

---

[1] As the text suggests, I shall regard Locke's *Second Treatise of Government*, Rousseau's *The Social Contract*, and Kant's ethical works beginning with *The Foundations of the Metaphysics of Morals* as definitive of the contract tradition. For all of its greatness, Hobbes's *Leviathan* raises special problems. A general historical survey is provided by J. W. Gough, *The Social Contract*, 2nd ed. (Oxford, The Clarendon Press, 1957), and Otto Gierke, *Natural Law and the Theory of Society*, trans. with an introduction by Ernest Barker (Cambridge, The University Press, 1934). A presentation of the contract view as primarily an ethical theory is to be found in G. R. Grice, *The Grounds of Moral Judgment* (Cambridge, The University Press, 1967).

problem has a solution, determines the principles of justice.

In justice as fairness the original position of equality corresponds to the state of nature in the traditional theory of the social contract. This original position is not, of course, thought of as an actual historical state of affairs, much less as a primitive condition of culture. It is understood as a purely hypothetical situation characterized so as to lead to a certain conception of justice. Among the essential features of this situation is that no one knows his place in society, his class position or social status, nor does any one know his fortune in the distribution of natural assets and abilities, his intelligence, strength, and the like. I shall even assume that the parties do not know their conceptions of the good or their special psychological propensities. The principles of justice are chosen behind a veil of ignorance. This ensures that no one is advantaged or disadvantaged in the choice of principles by the outcome of natural chance or the contingency of social circumstances. Since all are similarly situated and no one is able to design principles to favor his particular condition, the principles of justice are the result of a fair agreement or bargain. For given the circumstances of the original position, the symmetry of everyone's relations to each other, this initial situation is fair between individuals as moral persons, that is, as rational beings with their own ends and capable, I shall assume, of a sense of justice. The original position is, one might say, the appropriate initial status quo, and thus the fundamental agreements reached in it are fair. This explains the propriety of the name "justice as fairness": it conveys the idea that the principles of justice are agreed to in an initial situation that is fair. The name does not mean that the concepts of justice and fairness are the same, any more than the phrase "poetry as metaphor" means that the concepts of poetry and metaphor are the same.

Justice as fairness begins, as I have said, with one of the most general of all choices which persons might make together, namely, with the choice of the first principles of a conception of justice which is to regulate all subsequent criticism and reform of institutions. Then, having chosen a conception of justice, we can suppose that they are to choose a constitution and a legislature to enact laws, and so on, all in accordance with the principles of justice initially agreed upon. Our social situation is just if it is such that by this sequence of hypothetical agreements we would have contracted into the general system of rules which defines it. Moreover, assuming that the original position does determine a set of principles (that is, that a particular conception of justice would be chosen), it will then be true that whenever social institutions satisfy these principles those engaged in them can say to one another that they are cooperating on terms to which they would agree if they were free and equal persons whose relations with respect to one another were fair. They could all view their arrangements as meeting the stipulations which they would acknowledge in an initial situation that embodies widely accepted and reasonable constraints on the choice of principles. The general recognition of this fact would provide the basis for a public acceptance of the corresponding principles of justice. No society can, of course, be a scheme of cooperation which men enter voluntarily in a literal sense; each person finds himself placed at birth in some particular position in some particular society, and the nature of this position materially affects his life prospects. Yet a society satisfying the principles of justice as fairness comes as close as a society can to being a voluntary scheme, for it meets the principles which free and equal persons would assent to under circumstances that are fair. In this sense its members are autonomous and the obligations they recognize self-imposed.

One feature of justice as fairness is to think of the parties in the initial situation as rational and mutually disinterested. This does not mean that the parties are egoists, that is, individuals with only certain kinds of interests, say in wealth, prestige, and domination. But they are conceived as not taking an interest in one another's interests. They are to presume that even their spiritual aims may be opposed, in the way that the aims of those of different religions may be opposed. Moreover, the concept of rationality must be interpreted as far as possible in the narrow sense, standard in economic theory, of taking the most effective means to given ends. I shall modify this concept to some extent, as explained later, but one must try to avoid introducing into it any controversial ethical elements. The initial situation must be characterized by stipulations that are widely accepted.

In working out the conception of justice as fairness one main task clearly is to determine which principles of justice would be chosen in the original position. To do this we must describe this situation in some detail and formulate with care the problem of choice which it presents. These matters I shall take up in the immediately succeeding chapters. It may be observed, however, that once the principles of justice are thought of as arising from an original agreement in a situation of equality, it is an open question whether the principle of utility would be acknowledged. Offhand it hardly seems likely that persons who view themselves as equals, entitled to press their claims upon one another, would agree to a principle which may require lesser life prospects for some simply for the sake of a greater sum of advantages enjoyed by others. Since each desires to protect his interests, his capacity to advance his conception of the good, no one has a reason to acquiesce in an enduring loss for himself in order to bring about a greater net balance of satisfaction. In the absence of strong and lasting benevolent impulses, a rational man would not accept a basic structure merely because it maximized the algebraic sum of advantages irrespective of its permanent effects on his own basic rights and interests. Thus it seems that the principle of utility is incompatible with the conception of social cooperation among equals for mutual advantage. It appears to be inconsistent with the idea of reciprocity implicit in the notion of a well-ordered society. Or, at any rate, so I shall argue.

I shall maintain instead that the persons in the initial situation would choose two rather different principles: the first requires equality in the assignment of basic rights and duties, while the second holds that social and economic inequalities, for example inequalities of wealth and authority, are just only if they result in compensating benefits for everyone, and in particular for the least advantaged members of society. These principles rule out justifying institutions on the grounds that the hardships of some are offset by a greater good in the aggregate. It may be expedient but it is not just that some should have less in order that others may prosper. But there is no injustice in the greater benefits earned by a few provided that the situation of persons not so fortunate is thereby improved. The intuitive idea is that since everyone's well-being depends upon a scheme of cooperation without which no one could have a satisfactory life, the division of advantages should be such as to draw forth the willing cooperation of everyone taking part in it, including those less well situated. Yet this can be expected only if reasonable terms are proposed. The two principles mentioned seem to be a fair agreement on the basis of which those better endowed, or more fortunate in their social position, neither of which we can be said to deserve, could expect the willing cooperation of others when some workable scheme is a necessary condition of the welfare of all. Once we decide to look for a conception of justice that nullifies the accidents of natural endowment and the contingencies of social circumstance as counters in quest for political and economic advantage, we are led to these principles. They express the result of leaving aside those aspects of the social world that seem arbitrary from a moral point of view.

The problem of the choice of principles, however, is extremely difficult. I do not expect the answer I shall suggest to be convincing to everyone. It is, therefore, worth noting from the outset that justice as fairness, like other contract views, consists of two parts: (1) an interpretation of the initial situation and of the problem of choice posed there, and (2) a set of principles which, it is argued, would be agreed to. One may accept the first part of the theory (or some variant thereof), but not the other, and conversely. The concept of the initial contractual situation may seem reasonable although the particular principles proposed are rejected. To be sure, I want to maintain that the most appropriate conception of this situation does lead to principles of justice contrary to utilitarianism and perfectionism, and therefore that the contract doctrine provides an alternative to these views. Still, one may dispute this contention even though one grants that the contractarian method is a useful way of studying ethical theories and of setting forth their underlying assumptions.

Justice as fairness is an example of what I have called a contract theory. Now there may be an objection to the term "contract" and related expressions, but I think it will serve reasonably well. Many words have misleading connotations which at first are likely to confuse. The terms "utility" and "utilitarianism" are surely no exception. They too have unfortunate suggestions which hostile critics have been willing to exploit; yet they are clear enough for those prepared to study utilitarian doctrine. The same should be true of the term "contract" applied to moral theories. As I have mentioned, to understand it one has to keep in mind that it implies a certain level of abstraction. In particular, the content of the relevant agreement is not to enter a given society or to adopt a given form of government, but to accept certain moral principles. Moreover, the undertakings referred to are purely hypothetical: a contract view holds that certain principles would be accepted in a well-defined initial situation.

The merit of the contract terminology is that it conveys the idea that principles of justice may be conceived as principles that would be chosen by rational persons, and that in this way conceptions of justice may

be explained and justified. The theory of justice is a part, perhaps the most significant part, of the theory of rational choice. Furthermore, principles of justice deal with conflicting claims upon the advantages won by social cooperation; they apply to the relations among several persons or groups. The word "contract" suggests this plurality as well as the condition that the appropriate division of advantages must be in accordance with principles acceptable to all parties. The condition of publicity for principles of justice is also connoted by the contract phraseology. Thus, if these principles are the outcome of an agreement, citizens have a knowledge of the principles that others follow. It is characteristic of contract theories to stress the public nature of political principles. Finally there is the long tradition of the contract doctrine. Expressing the tie with this line of thought helps to define ideas and accords with natural piety. There are then several advantages in the use of the term "contract." With due precautions taken, it should not be misleading. . . .

THE ORIGINAL POSITION AND JUSTIFICATION

I have said that the original position is the appropriate initial status quo which insures that the fundamental agreements reached in it are fair. This fact yields the name "justice as fairness." It is clear, then, that I want to say that one conception of justice is more reasonable than another, or justifiable with respect to it, if rational persons in the initial situation would choose its principles over those of the other for the role of justice. Conceptions of justice are to be ranked by their acceptability to persons so circumstanced. Understood in this way the question of justification is settled by working out a problem of deliberation: we have to ascertain which principles it would be rational to adopt given the contractual situation. This connects the theory of justice with the theory of rational choice.

If this view of the problem of justification

is to succeed, we must, of course, describe in some detail the nature of this choice problem. A problem of rational decision has a definite answer only if we know the beliefs and interests of the parties, their relations with respect to one another, the alternatives between which they are to choose, the procedure whereby they make up their minds, and so on. As the circumstances are presented in different ways, correspondingly different principles are accepted. The concept of the original position, as I shall refer to it, is that of the most philosophically favored interpretation of this initial choice situation for the purposes of a theory of justice.

But how are we to decide what is the most favored interpretation? I assume, for one thing, that there is a broad measure of agreement that principles of justice should be chosen under certain conditions. To justify a particular description of the initial situation one shows that it incorporates these commonly shared presumptions. One argues from widely accepted but weak premises to more specific conclusions. Each of the presumptions should by itself be natural and plausible; some of them may seem innocuous or even trivial. The aim of the contract approach is to establish that taken together they impose significant bounds on acceptable principles of justice. The ideal outcome would be that these conditions determine a unique set of principles; but I shall be satisfied if they suffice to rank the main traditional conceptions of social justice.

One should not be misled, then, by the somewhat unusual conditions which characterize the original position. The idea here is simply to make vivid to ourselves the restrictions that it seems reasonable to impose on arguments for principles of justice, and therefore on these principles themselves. Thus it seems reasonable and generally acceptable that no one should be advantaged or disadvantaged by natural fortune or social circumstances in the choice of principles. It also seems widely agreed that it should be impossible to tailor principles to

the circumstances of one's own case. We should insure further that particular inclinations and aspirations, and persons' conceptions of their good do not affect the principles adopted. The aim is to rule out those principles that it would be rational to propose for acceptance, however little the chance of success, only if one knew certain things that are irrelevant from the standpoint of justice. For example, if a man knew that he was wealthy, he might find it rational to advance the principle that various taxes for welfare measures be counted unjust; if he knew that he was poor, he would most likely propose the contrary principle. To represent the desired restrictions one imagines a situation in which everyone is deprived of this sort of information. One excludes the knowledge of those contingencies which sets men at odds and allows them to be guided by their prejudices. In this manner the veil of ignorance is arrived at in a natural way. This concept should cause no difficulty if we keep in mind the constraints on arguments that it is meant to express. At any time we can enter the original position, so to speak, simply by following a certain procedure, namely, by arguing for principles of justice in accordance with these restrictions.

It seems reasonable to suppose that the parties in the original position are equal. That is, all have the same rights in the procedure for choosing principles; each can make proposals, submit reasons for their acceptance, and so on. Obviously the purpose of these conditions is to represent equality between human beings as moral persons, as creatures having a conception of their good and capable of a sense of justice. The basis of equality is taken to be similarity in these two respects. Systems of ends are not ranked in value; and each man is presumed to have the requisite ability to understand and to act upon whatever principles are adopted. Together with the veil of ignorance, these conditions define the principles of justice as those which rational persons concerned to advance their interests would consent to as equals when none are known to be advantaged or disadvantaged by social and natural contingencies.

There is, however, another side to justifying a particular description of the original position. This is to see if the principles which would be chosen match our considered convictions of justice or extend them in an acceptable way. We can note whether applying these principles would lead us to make the same judgments about the basic structure of society which we now make intuitively and in which we have the greatest confidence; or whether, in cases where our present judgments are in doubt and given with hesitation, these principles offer a resolution which we can affirm on reflection. There are questions which we feel sure must be answered in a certain way. For example, we are confident that religious intolerance and racial discrimination are unjust. We think that we have examined these things with care and have reached what we believe is an impartial judgment not likely to be distorted by an excessive attention to our own interests. These convictions are provisional fixed points which we presume any conception of justice must fit. But we have much less assurance as to what is the correct distribution of wealth and authority. Here we may be looking for a way to remove our doubts. We can check an interpretation of the initial situation, then, by the capacity of its principles to accommodate our firmest convictions and to provide guidance where guidance is needed.

In searching for the most favored description of this situation we work from both ends. We begin by describing it so that it represents generally shared and preferably weak conditions. We then see if these conditions are strong enough to yield a significant set of principles. If not, we look for further premises equally reasonable. But if so, and these principles match our considered convictions of justice, then so far well and good. But presumably there will be discrepancies. In this case we have a choice. We can either modify the account of the initial situation or we can revise our existing judgments, for even the judgments we take provisionally as fixed points are liable to revision. By going back and forth, sometimes altering the conditions of the contractual circumstances, at others withdrawing our judgments and conforming them to principle, I assume that eventually we shall find a description of the initial situation that both expresses reasonable conditions and yields principles which match our considered judgments duly pruned and adjusted. This state of affairs I refer to as reflective equilibrium[2]. It is an equilibrium because at last our principles and judgments coincide; and it is reflective since we know to what principles our judgments conform and the premises of their derivation. At the moment everything is in order. But this equilibrium is not necessarily stable. It is liable to be upset by further examination of the conditions which should be imposed on the contractual situation and by particular cases which may lead us to revise our judgments. Yet for the time being we have done what we can to render coherent and to justify our convictions of social justice. We have reached a conception of the original position.

I shall not, of course, actually work through this process. Still, we may think of the interpretation of the original position that I shall present as the result of such a hypothetical course of reflection. It represents the attempt to accommodate within one scheme both reasonable philosophical conditions on principles as well as our considered judgments of justice. In arriving at the favored interpretation of the initial situation there is no point at which an appeal is made to self-evidence in the traditional sense either of general conceptions or particular convictions. I do not claim for the principles of justice proposed that they are necessary truths or derivable from such truths. A conception of justice cannot be

---

[2] The process of mutual adjustment of principles and considered judgments is not peculiar to moral philosophy. See Nelson Goodman, *Fact, Fiction, and Forecast* (Cambridge, Mass., Harvard University Press, 1955), pp. 65–68, for parallel remarks concerning the justification of the principles of deductive and inductive inference.

deduced from self-evident premises or conditions on principles; instead, its justification is a matter of the mutual support of many considerations, of everything fitting together into one coherent view.

A final comment. We shall want to say that certain principles of justice are justified because they would be agreed to in an initial situation of equality. I have emphasized that this original position is purely hypothetical. It is natural to ask why, if this agreement is never actually entered into, we should take any interest in these principles, moral or otherwise. The answer is that the conditions embodied in the description of the original position are ones that we do in fact accept. Or if we do not, then perhaps we can be persuaded to do so by philosophical reflection. Each aspect of the contractual situation can be given supporting grounds. Thus what we shall do is to collect together into one conception a number of conditions on principles that we are ready upon due consideration to recognize as reasonable. These constraints express what we are prepared to regard as limits on fair terms of social cooperation. One way to look at the idea of the original position, therefore, is to see it as an expository device which sums up the meaning of these conditions and helps us to extract their consequences. On the other hand, this conception is also an intuitive notion that suggests its own elaboration, so that led on by it we are drawn to define more clearly the standpoint from which we can best interpret moral relationships. We need a conception that enables us to envision our objective from afar: the intuitive notion of the original position is to do this for us. . . .

THE VEIL OF IGNORANCE

The idea of the original position is to set up a fair procedure so that any principles agreed to will be just. . . . Somehow we must nullify the effects of specific contingencies which put men at odds and tempt them to exploit social and natural circumstances to their own advantage. Now in order to do this I assume that the parties are situated behind a veil of ignorance. They do not know how the various alternatives will affect their own particular case and they are obliged to evaluate principles solely on the basis of general considerations.

It is assumed, then, that the parties do not know certain kinds of particular facts. First of all, no one knows his place in society, his class position or social status; nor does he know his fortune in the distribution of natural assets and abilities, his intelligence and strength, and the like. Nor, again, does anyone know his conception of the good, the particulars of his rational plan of life, or even the special features of his psychology such as his aversion to risk or liability to optimism or pessimism. More than this, I assume that the parties do not know the particular circumstances of their own society. That is, they do not know its economic or political situation, or the level of civilization and culture it has been able to achieve. The persons in the original position have no information as to which generation they belong. These broader restrictions on knowledge are appropriate in part because questions of social justice arise between generations as well as within them, for example, the question of the appropriate rate of capital saving and of the conservation of natural resources and the environment of nature. There is also, theoretically anyway, the question of a reasonable genetic policy. In these cases too, in order to carry through the idea of the original position, the parties must not know the contingencies that set them in opposition. They must choose principles the consequences of which they are prepared to live with whatever generation they turn out to belong to.

As far as possible, then, the only particular facts which the parties know is that their society is subject to the circumstances of justice and whatever this implies. It is taken for granted, however, that they know the general facts about human society. They understand political affairs and the principles of economic theory; they know the basis of social organization and the laws of human psychology. Indeed, the parties are presumed to know whatever general facts affect the choice of the principles of justice. There are no limitations on general information, that is, on general laws and theories, since conceptions of justice must be adjusted to the characteristics of the systems of social cooperation which they are to regulate, and there is no reason to rule out these facts. It is, for example, a consideration against a conception of justice that in view of the laws of moral psychology, men would not acquire a desire to act upon it even when the institutions of their society satisfied it. For in this case there would be difficulty in securing the stability of social operation. It is an important feature of a conception of justice that it should generate its own support. That is, its principles should be such that when they are embodied in the basic structure of society men tend to acquire the corresponding sense of justice. Given the principles of moral learning, men develop a desire to act in accordance with its principles. In this case a conception of justice is stable. This kind of general information is admissible in the original position.

The notion of the veil of ignorance raises several difficulties. Some may object that the exclusion of nearly all particular information makes it difficult to grasp what is meant by the original position. Thus it may be helpful to observe that one or more persons can at any time enter this position, or perhaps, better, stimulate the deliberations of this hypothetical situation, simply by reasoning in accordance with the appropriate restrictions. In arguing for a conception of justice we must be sure that it is among the permitted alternatives and satisfies the stipulated formal constraints. No considerations can be advanced in its favor unless they would be rational ones for us to urge were we to lack the kind of knowledge that is excluded. The evaluation of principles must proceed in terms of the general consequences of their public recognition and universal application, it being assumed that they will be complied with by everyone. To say that a certain conception of justice would be chosen in the original position is equivalent to saying that rational deliberation satisfying certain conditions and restrictions would reach a certain conclusion. If necessary, the argument to this result could be set out more formally. I shall, however, speak throughout in terms of the notion of the original position. It is more economical and suggestive, and brings out certain essential features that otherwise one might easily overlook. . . .

Thus there follows the very important consequence that the parties have no basis for bargaining in the usual sense. No one knows his situation in society nor his natural assets, and therefore no one is in a position to tailor principles to his advantage. We might imagine that one of the contractees threatens to hold out unless the others agree to principles favorable to him. But how does he know which principles are especially in his interests? The same holds for the formation of coalitions: if a group were to decide to band together to the disadvantage of the others, they would not know how to favor themselves in the choice of principles. Even if they could get everyone to agree to their proposal, they would have no assurance that it was to their advantage, since they cannot identify themselves either by name or description. . . .

The restrictions on particular information in the original position are, then, of fundamental importance. Without them we would not be able to work out any definite theory of justice at all. We would have to be content with a vague formula stating that justice is what would be agreed to without being able to say much, if anything, about the substance of the agreement itself. . . . The veil of ignorance makes possible a unanimous choice of a particular conception of justice. Without these limitations on knowledge the bargaining problem of the original position would be hopelessly complicated. Even if theoretically a solution were to exist, we would not, at present anyway, be able to determine it. . . .

THE TWO PRINCIPLES OF JUSTICE

I shall now state in a provisional form the two principles of justice that I believe would be chosen in the original position. In this section I wish to make only the most general comments, and therefore the first formulation of these principles is tentative. As we go on I shall run through several formulations and approximate step by step the final statement to be given much later. I believe that doing this allows the exposition to proceed in a natural way.

The first statement of the two principles reads as follows.

First: each person is to have an equal right to the most extensive basic liberty compatible with a similar liberty for others.

Second: social and economic inequalities are to be arranged so that they are both (a) reasonably expected to be to everyone's advantage, and (b) attached to positions and offices open to all.

There are two ambiguous phrases in the second principle, namely "everyone's advantage" and "equally open to all." Determining their sense more exactly will lead to a second formulation of the principle. . . .

By way of general comment, these principles primarily apply, as I have said, to the basic structure of society. They are to govern the assignment of rights and duties and to regulate the distribution of social and economic advantages. As their formulation suggests, these principles presuppose that the social structure can be divided into two more or less distinct parts, the first principle applying to the one, the second to the other. They distinguish between those aspects of the social system that define and secure the equal liberties of citizenship and those that specify and establish social and economic inequalities. The basic liberties of citizens are, roughly speaking, political liberty (the right to vote and to be eligible for public office) together with freedom of speech and assembly; liberty of conscience and freedom of thought; freedom of the person along with the right to hold (personal) property;

and freedom from arbitrary arrest and seizure as defined by the concept of the rule of law. These liberties are all required to be equal by the first principle, since citizens of a just society are to have the same basic rights.

The second principle applies, in the first approximation, to the distribution of income and wealth and to the design of organizations that make use of differences in authority and responsibility, or chains of command. While the distribution of wealth and income need not be equal, it must be to everyone's advantage, and at the same time, positions of authority and offices of command must be accessible to all. One applies the second principle by holding positions open, and then, subject to this constraint, arranges social and economic inequalities so that everyone benefits.

These principles are to be arranged in a serial order with the first principle prior to the second. This ordering means that a departure from the institutions of equal liberty required by the first principle cannot be justified by, or compensated for, by greater social and economic advantages. The distribution of wealth and income, and the hierarchies of authority, must be consistent with both the liberties of equal citizenship and equality of opportunity.

It is clear that these principles are rather specific in their content, and their acceptance rests on certain assumptions that I must eventually try to explain and justify. A theory of justice depends upon a theory of society in ways that will become evident as we proceed. For the present, it should be observed that the two principles (and this holds for all formulations) are a special case of a more general conception of justice that can be expressed as follows.

All social values—liberty and opportunity, income and wealth, and the bases of self-respect—are to be distributed equally unless an unequal distribution of any, or all, of these values is to everyone's advantage.

Injustice, then, is simply inequalities that are not to the benefit of all. Of course, this conception is extremely vague and requires interpretation.

As a first step, suppose that the basic structure of society distributes certain primary goods, that is, things that every rational man is presumed to want. These goods normally have a use whatever a person's rational plan of life. For simplicity, assume that the chief primary goods at the disposition of society are rights and liberties, powers and opportunities, income and wealth. (Later on . . . the primary good of self-respect has a central place.) These are the social primary goods. Other primary goods such as health and vigor, intelligence and imagination, are natural goods; although their possession is influenced by the basic structure, they are not so directly under its control. Imagine, then, a hypothetical initial arrangement in which all the social primary goods are equally distributed: everyone has similar rights and duties, and income and wealth are evenly shared. This state of affairs provides a benchmark for judging improvements. If certain inequalities of wealth and organizational powers would make everyone better off than in this hypothetical starting situation, then they accord with the general conception.

Now it is possible, at least theoretically, that by giving up some of their fundamental liberties men are sufficiently compensated by the resulting social and economic gains. The general conception of justice imposes no restrictions on what sort of inequalities are permissible; it only requires that everyone's position be improved. We need not suppose anything so drastic as consenting to a condition of slavery. Imagine instead that men forego certain political rights when the economic returns are significant and their capacity to influence the course of policy by the exercise of these rights would be marginal in any case. It is this kind of exchange which the two principles as stated rule out; being arranged in serial order they do not permit exchanges between basic liberties and economic and social gains. The serial ordering of principles expresses an underlying preference among primary social goods.

When this preference is rational so likewise is the choice of these principles in this order. . . .

The fact that the two principles apply to institutions has certain consequences. Several points illustrate this. First of all, the rights and liberties referred to by these principles are those which are defined by the public rules of the basic structure. Whether men are free is determined by the rights and duties established by the major institutions of society. Liberty is a certain pattern of social forms. The first principle simply requires that certain sorts of rules, those defining basic liberties, apply to everyone equally and that they allow the most extensive liberty compatible with a like liberty for all. The only reason for circumscribing the rights defining liberty and making men's freedom less extensive than it might otherwise be is that these equal rights as institutionally defined would interfere with one another.

Another thing to bear in mind is that when principles mention persons, or require that everyone gain from an inequality, the reference is to representative persons holding the various social positions, or offices, or whatever, established by the basic structure. Thus in applying the second principle I assume that it is possible to assign an expectation of well-being to representative individuals holding these positions. This expectation indicates their life prospects as viewed from their social station. In general, the expectations of representative persons depend upon the distribution of rights and duties throughout the basic structure. When this changes, expectations change. I assume, then, that expectations are connected: by raising the prospects of the representative man in one position we presumably increase or decrease the prospects of representative men in other positions. Since it applies to institutional forms, the second principle (or rather the first part of it) refers to the expectations of representative individuals. As I shall discuss below, neither principle applies to distributions of particular goods to particular individuals who may be identified by their proper names. The situation where someone is considering how to allocate certain commodities to needy persons who are known to him is not within the scope of the principles. They are meant to regulate basic institutional arrangements. We must not assume that there is much similarity from the standpoint of justice between an administrative allotment of goods to specific persons and the appropriate design of society.

Now the second principle insists that each person benefit from permissible inequalities in the basic structure. This means that it must be reasonable for each relevant representative man defined by this structure, when he views it as a going concern, to prefer his prospects with the inequality to his prospects without it. One is not allowed to justify differences in income or organizational powers on the ground that the disadvantages of those in one position are outweighed by the greater advantages of those in another. Much less can infringements of liberty be counterbalanced in this way.

[Eds. note: Rawls next considers different interpretations of the second principle. He argues that since people do not deserve their socio-economic class, "open to all" should express not just FORMAL equality of opportunity (all have an equal right to pursue positions) but also FAIR equality of opportunity (those with similar natural talents should have similar life chances.) But, Rawls contents, talents are also undeserved, and even willingness to put forth effort depends on family circumstances and opportunities, so "everyone's advantage" is best interpreted as expressing the "difference principle" i.e. inequalities must be justifiable from the perspective of the least advantaged.]

The difference principle . . . removes the indeterminateness . . . by singling out a particular position from which the social and economic inequalities of the basic structure are to be judged. Assuming the framework of institutions required by equal liberty and fair equality of opportunity, the higher expectations of those better situated are just if and only if they work as part of a scheme which improves the expectations of the least advantaged members of society. The intuitive idea is that the social order is not to establish and secure the more attractive prospects of those better off unless doing so is to the advantage of those less fortunate. . . .

To illustrate the difference principle, consider the distribution of income among social classes. Let us suppose that the various income groups correlate with representative individuals by reference to whose expectations we can judge the distribution. Now those starting out as members of the entrepreneurial class in a property-owning democracy, say, have a better prospect than those who begin in the class of unskilled laborers. It seems likely that this will be true even when the social injustices which now exist are removed. What, then, can possibly justify this kind of initial inequality in life prospects? According to the difference principle, it is justifiable only if the difference in expectation is to the advantage of the representative man who is worse off, in this case the representative unskilled worker. The inequality in expectation is permissible only if lowering it would make the working class even more worse off. Supposedly, given the rider in the second principle concerning open positions, and the principle of liberty generally, the greater expectations allowed to entrepreneurs encourages them to do things which raise the long-term prospects of the laboring class. Their better prospects act as incentives so that the economic process is more efficient, innovation proceeds at a faster pace, and so on. Eventually the resulting material benefits spread throughout the system and to the least advantaged. I shall not consider how far these things are true. The point is that something of this kind must be argued if these inequalities are to be just by the difference principle. . . .

. . . And therefore, as the outcome of the last several sections, the second principle is to read as follows.

Social and economic inequalities are to be arranged so that they are both (a) to the greatest benefit of the least advantaged and (b) attached to offices and positions open to all under conditions of fair equality of opportunity.

Finally, it should be observed that the difference principle, or the idea expressed by it, can easily be accommodated to the general conception of justice. In fact, the general conception is simply the difference principle applied to all primary goods including liberty and opportunity and so no longer constrained by other parts of the special conception. This is evident from the earlier brief discussion of the principles of justice. These principles in serial order are, as I shall indicate from time to time, the form that the general conception finally assumes as social conditions improve. This question ties up with that of the priority of liberty which I shall discuss later on. For the moment it suffices to remark that in one form or another the difference principle is basic throughout. . . .

THE REASONING LEADING TO THE TWO PRINCIPLES

It seems clear from these remarks that the two principles are at least a plausible conception of justice. The question, though, is how one is to argue for them more systematically. Now there are several things to do. One can work out their consequences for institutions and note their implications for fundamental social policy. In this way they are tested by a comparison with our considered judgments of justice. . . . But one can also try to find arguments in their favor that are decisive from the standpoint of the original position. In order to see how this might be done, it is useful as a heuristic device to think of the two principles as the maximum solution to the problem of social justice. There is an analogy between the two principles and the maximum rule for choice under certainty. This is evident from the fact that the two principles are those a person would choose for the design of a society in which his enemy is to assign him his place.

The maximum rule tells us to rank alternatives by their worst possible outcomes: we are to adopt the alternative the worst outcome of which is superior to the worst outcomes of the others. The persons in the original position do not, of course, assume that their initial place in society is decided by a malevolent opponent. As I note below, they should not reason from false premises. The veil of ignorance does not violate this idea, since an absence of information is not misinformation. But that the two principles of justice would be chosen if the parties were forced to protect themselves against such a contingency explains the sense in which this conception is the maximum solution. And this analogy suggests that if the original position has been described so that it is rational for the parties to adopt the conservative attitude expressed by this rule, a conclusive argument can indeed be constructed for these principles. Clearly the maximum rule is not, in general, a suitable guide for choices under uncertainty. But it is attractive in situations marked by certain special features. My aim, then, is to show that a good case can be made for the two principles based on the fact that the original position manifests these features to the fullest possible degree, carrying them to the limit, so to speak.

Consider the gain-and-loss table below. It represents the gains and losses for a situation which is not a game of strategy. There is no one playing against the person making the decision; instead he is faced with several possible circumstances which may or may not obtain. Which circumstances happen to exist does not depend upon what the person choosing decides or whether he announces his moves in advance. The numbers in the table are monetary values (in hundreds of dollars) in comparison with some initial situation. The gain (g) depends upon the individual's decision (d) and the circumstances (c). Thus $g = f(d, c)$. Assuming that there are three possible decisions and three possible circumstances, we might have this gain-and-loss table.

Decisions	Circumstances		
	C_1	C_2	C_3
d_1	−7	8	12
d_2	−8	7	14
d_3	5	6	8

The maximum rule requires that we make the third decision. For in this case the worst that can happen is that one gains five hundred dollars, which is better than the worst for the other actions. If we adopt one of these we may lose either eight or seven hundred dollars. Thus, the choice of d_3 maximizes f (d,c) for that value of c, which for a given d, minimizes f. The term "maximin" means the *maximum minimorum*; and the rule directs our attention to the worst that can happen under any proposed course of action, and to decide in the light of that.

Now there appear to be three chief features of situations that give plausibility to this unusual rule.[9] First, since the rule takes no account of the likelihoods of the possible circumstances, there must be some reason for sharply discounting estimates of these probabilities. Offhand, the most natural rule of choice would seem to be to compute the expectation of monetary gain for each decision and then to adopt the course of action with the highest prospect. . . . Thus it must be, for example, that the situation is one in which a knowledge of likelihoods is impossible, or at best extremely insecure. In this case it is unreasonable not to be skeptical of probabilistic calculations unless there is no other way out, particularly if the decision is a fundamental one that needs to be justified to others.

The second feature that suggests the maximin rule is the following: the person choosing has a conception of the good such that he cares very little, if anything, for what he might gain above the minimum stipend that he can, in fact, be sure of by following the maximin rule. It is not worthwhile for him to take a chance for the sake of a further advantage, especially when it may turn out that he loses much that is important to him. This last provision brings in the third

feature, namely, that the rejected alternatives have outcomes that one can hardly accept. The situation involves grave risks. Of course these features work most effectively in combination. The paradigm situation for following the maximin rule is when all three features are realized to the highest degree. This rule does not, then, generally apply, nor of course is it self-evident. Rather, it is a maxim, a rule of thumb, that comes into its own in special circumstances. Its application depends upon the qualitative structure of the possible gains and losses in relation to one's conception of the good, all this against a background in which it is reasonable to discount conjectural estimates of likelihoods.

It should be noted, as the comments on the gain-and-loss table say, that the entries in the table represent monetary values and not utilities. This difference is significant since for one thing computing expectations on the basis of such objective values is not the same thing as computing expected utility and may lead to different results. The essential point though is that in justice as fairness the parties do not know their conception of the good and cannot estimate their utility in the ordinary sense. In any case, we want to go behind de facto preferences generated by given conditions. Therefore expectations are based upon an index of primary goods and the parties make their choice accordingly. The entries in the example are in terms of money and not utility to indicate this aspect of the contract doctrine.

Now, as I have suggested, the original position has been defined so that it is a situation in which the maximin rule applies. In order to see this, let us review briefly the nature of this situation with these three special features in mind. To begin with, the veil of ignorance excludes all but the vaguest knowledge of likelihoods. The parties have no basis for determining the probable nature of their society, or their place in it. Thus they have strong reasons for being wary of probability calculations if any other course is open to them. They must also take in account the fact that their choice of principles should seem reasonable to others, in particular their descendants, whose rights will be deeply affected by it. There are further grounds for discounting that I shall mention as we go along. For the present it suffices to note that these considerations are strengthened by the fact that the parties know very little about the gain-and-loss table. Not only are they unable to conjecture the likelihoods of the various possible circumstances, they cannot say much about what the possible circumstances are, much less enumerate them and foresee the outcome of each alternative available. Those deciding are much more in the dark than the illustration by a numerical table suggests. It is for this reason that I have spoken of an analogy with the maximin rule.

Several kinds of arguments for the two principles of justice illustrate the second feature. Thus, if we can maintain that these principles provide a workable theory of social justice, and that they are compatible with reasonable demands of efficiency, then this conception guarantees a satisfactory minimum. There may be, on reflection, little reason for trying to do better. Thus much of the argument . . . is to show, by their application to the main questions of social justice, that the two principles are a satisfactory conception. These details have a philosophical purpose. Moreover, this line of thought is practically decisive if we can establish the priority of liberty, the lexical ordering of the two principles. For this priority implies that the persons in the original position have no desire to try for greater gains at the expense of the equal liberties. The minimum assured by the two principles in lexical order is not one that the parties wish to jeopardize for the sake of greater economic and social advantages. . . . I present the case for this ordering [elsewhere].

Finally, the third feature holds if we can assume that other conceptions of justice may lead to institutions that the parties would find intolerable. For example, it has sometimes been held that under some conditions the utility principle (in either form)

justifies, if not slavery or serfdom, at any rate serious infractions of liberty for the sake of greater social benefits. We need not consider here the truth of this claim, or the likelihood that the requisite conditions obtain. For the moment, this contention is only to illustrate the way in which conceptions of justice may allow for outcomes which the parties may not be able to accept. And having the ready alternative of the two principles of justice which secure a satisfactory minimum, it seems unwise, if not irrational, for them to take a chance that these outcomes are not realized.

So much, then, for a brief sketch of the features of situations in which the maximin rule comes into its own and of the way in which the arguments for the two principles of justice can be subsumed under them. . . . These principles would be selected by the rule. The original position clearly exhibits these special features to a very high degree in view of the fundamental character of the choice of a conception of justice. These remarks about the maximin rule are intended only to clarify the structure of the choice problem in the original position. They depict its qualitative anatomy. The arguments for the two principles will be presented more fully as we proceed. . . .

SOME MAIN GROUNDS FOR THE TWO PRINCIPLES OF JUSTICE

In this section my aim is to use the conditions of publicity and finality to give some of the main arguments for the two principles of justice. I shall rely upon the fact that for an agreement to be valid, the parties must be able to honor it under all relevant and foreseeable circumstances. There must be a rational assurance that one can carry through. The arguments I shall adduce fit under the heuristic schema suggested by the reasons for following the maximin rule. That is, they help to show that the two principles are an adequate minimum conception of justice in a situation of great uncertainty. Any further advantages that might be won by the principle of utility, or whatever, are highly problematical, whereas the hardships if things turn out badly are intolerable. It is at this point that the concept of a contract has a definite role: it suggests the condition of publicity and sets limits upon what can be agreed to. Thus justice as fairness uses the concept of contract to a greater extent than the discussion so far might suggest.

The first confirming ground for the two principles can be explained in terms of . . . the strains of commitment. I said that the parties have a capacity for justice in the sense that they can be assured that their undertaking is not in vain. Assuming that they have taken everything into account, including the general facts of moral psychology, they can rely on one another to adhere to the principles adopted. Thus they consider the strains of commitment. They cannot enter into agreements that may have consequences they cannot accept. They will avoid those that they can adhere to only with great difficulty. Since the original agreement is final and made in perpetuity, there is no second chance. In view of the serious nature of the possible consequences, the question of the burden of commitment is especially acute. A person is choosing once and for all the standards which are to govern his life prospects. Moreover, when we enter an agreement we must be able to honor it even should the worst possibilities prove to be the case. Otherwise we have not acted in good faith. Thus the parties must weigh with care whether they will be able to stick by their commitment in all circumstances. Of course, in answering this question they have only a general knowledge of human psychology to go on. But this information is enough to tell which conception of justice involves the greater stress.

In this respect the two principles of justice have a definite advantage. Not only do the parties protect their basic rights but they insure themselves against the worst eventualities. They run no chance of having to acquiesce in a loss of freedom over the course of their life for the sake of a greater good enjoyed by others, an undertaking that in actual circumstances they might not be able to keep. Indeed, we might wonder whether such an agreement can be made in good faith at all. Compacts of this sort exceed the capacity of human nature. How can the parties possibly know or be sufficiently sure, that they can keep such an agreement? Certainly they cannot base their confidence on a general knowledge of moral psychology. To be sure, any principle chosen in the original position may require a large sacrifice for some. The beneficiaries of clearly unjust institutions (those founded on principles which have no claim to acceptance) may find it hard to reconcile themselves to the changes that will have to be made. But in this case they will know that they could not have maintained their position anyway. Yet should a person gamble with his liberties and substantive interests hoping that the application of the principle of utility might secure him a greater well-being, he may have difficulty abiding by his undertaking. He is bound to remind himself that he had the two principles of justice as an alternative. If the only possible candidates all involved similar risks, the problem of the strains of commitment would have to be waived. This is not the case, and judged in this light the two principles seem distinctly superior.

A second consideration invokes the condition of publicity as well as that of the constraints on agreements. I shall present the argument in terms of the question of psychological stability. Earlier I stated that a strong point in favor of a conception of justice is that it generates its own support. When the basic structure of society is publicly known to satisfy its principles for an extended period of time, those subject to these arrangements tend to develop a desire to act in accordance with these principles and to do their part in institutions which exemplify them. A conception of justice is stable when the public recognition of its realization by the social system tends to bring about the corresponding sense of justice. Now whether this happens depends, of course, on the laws of moral psychology and the availability of human motives. I shall discuss these matters later on. At the moment we may observe that the principle of utility seems to require a greater identification is difficult to achieve. When the two principles are satisfied, each person's liberties are secured and there is a sense defined by the difference principle in which everyone is benefited by social cooperation. Therefore we can explain the acceptance of the social system and the principles it satisfies by the psychological law that persons tend to love, cherish, and support whatever affirms their own good. Since everyone's good is affirmed, all acquire inclinations to uphold the scheme.

When the principle of utility is satisfied, however, there is no such assurance that everyone benefits. Allegiance to the social system may demand that some should forgo advantages for the sake of the greater good of the whole. Thus the scheme will not be stable unless those who must make sacrifices strongly identify with interests broader than their own. But this is not easy to bring about. The sacrifices in question are not those asked in times of social emergency when all or some must pitch in for the common good. The principles of justice apply to the basic structure of the social system and to the determination of life prospects. What the principle of utility asks is precisely a sacrifice of these prospects. We are to accept the greater advantages of others as a sufficient reason for lower expectations over the whole course of our life. This is surely an extreme demand. In fact, when society is conceived as a system of cooperation designed to advance the good of its members, it seems quite incredible that some citizens should be expected, on the basis of political principles, to accept lower prospects of life for the sake of others. It is evident then why utilitarians should stress the role of sympathy in moral learning and the central place of benevolence among the moral virtues. Their conception of justice is threatened with instability unless sympathy and benevolence can be widely and intensely cultivated. Looking at the question from the standpoint of the original position, the parties recog-

nize that it would be highly unwise if not irrational to choose principles which may have consequences so extreme that they could not accept them in practice. They would reject the principle of utility and adopt the more realistic idea of designing the social order on a principle of reciprocal advantage. We need not suppose, of course, that persons never make substantial sacrifices for one another, since moved by affection and ties of sentiment they often do. But such actions are not demanded as a matter of justice by the basic structure of society.

Furthermore, the public recognition of the two principles gives greater support to men's self-respect and this in turn increases the effectiveness of social cooperation. Both effects are reasons for choosing these principles. It is clearly rational for men to secure their self-respect. A sense of their own worth is necessary if they are to pursue their conception of the good with zest and to delight in its fulfillment. Self-respect is not so much a part of any rational plan of life as the sense that one's plan is worth carrying out. Now our self-respect normally depends upon the respect of others. Unless we feel that our endeavors are honored by them, it is difficult if not impossible for us to maintain the conviction that our ends are worth advancing. Hence for this reason the parties would accept the natural duty of mutual respect which asks them to treat one another civilly and to be willing to explain the grounds of their actions, especially when the claims of others are overruled. Moreover, one may assume that those who respect themselves are more likely to respect each other and conversely. Self-contempt leads to contempt of others and threatens their good as much as envy does. Self-respect is reciprocally self-supporting.

Thus a desirable feature of a conception of justice is that it should publicly express mens' respect for one another. In this way they insure a sense of their own value. Now the two principles achieve this end. For when society follows these principles, everyone's good is included in a scheme of mutual benefit and this public affirmation in institutions of each man's endeavors supports men's self-esteem. The establishment of equal liberty and the operation of the difference principle are bound to have this effect. The two principles are equivalent, as I have remarked, to an undertaking to regard the distribution of natural abilities as a collective asset so that the more fortunate are to benefit only in ways that help those who have lost out. I do not say that the parties are moved by the ethical propriety of this idea. But there are reasons for them to accept this principle. For by arranging inequalities for reciprocal advantage and by abstaining from the exploitation of the contingencies of nature and social circumstance within a framework of equal liberty, persons express their respect for one another in the very constitution of their society. In this way they insure their self-esteem as it is rational for them to do.

Another way of putting this is to say that the principles of justice manifest in the basic structure of society men's desire to treat one another not as means only but as ends in themselves. I cannot examine Kant's view here. Instead I shall freely interpret it in the light of the contract doctrine. The notion of treating men as ends in themselves and never as only a means obviously needs an explanation. There is even a question whether it is possible to realize. How can we always treat everyone as an end and never as a means only? Certainly we cannot say that it comes to treating everyone by the same general principles, since this interpretation makes the concept equivalent to formal justice. On the contract interpretation treating men as ends in themselves implies at the very lest treating them in accordance with the principles to which they would consent in an original position of equality. For in this situation men have equal representation as moral persons who regard themselves as ends and the principles they accept will be rationally designed to protect the claims of their person. The contract view as such defines a sense in which men are to be treated as ends and not as means only.

But the question arises whether there are substantive principles which convey this idea. If the parties wish to express this notion visibly in the basic structure of their society in order to secure each man's rational interest in his self-respect, which principles should they choose? Now it seems that the two principles of justice achieve this aim: for all have an equal liberty and the difference principle explicates the distinction between treating men as a means only and treating them also as ends in themselves. To regard persons as ends in themselves in the basic design of society is to agree to forgo those gains which do not contribute to their representative expectations. By contrast, to regard persons as means is to be prepared to impose upon them lower prospects of life for the sake of the higher expectations of others. Thus we see that the difference principle, which at first appears rather extreme, has a reasonable interpretation. If we further suppose that social cooperation among those who respect each other and themselves as manifest in their institutions is likely to be more effective and harmonious, the general level of expectations, assuming we could estimate it, may be higher when the two principles of justice are satisfied than one might otherwise have thought. The advantage of the principle of utility in this respect is no longer so clear.

The principle of utility presumably requires some to forgo greater life prospects for the sake of others. . . .

FAIR EQUALITY OF OPPORTUNITY AND PURE PROCEDURAL JUSTICE

. . . Now I have said that the basic structure is the primary subject of justice. This means, as we have seen, that the first distributive problem is the assignment of fundamental rights and duties and the regulation of social and economic inequalities and of the legitimate expectations founded on these. Of course, any ethical theory recognizes the importance of the basic structure as a subject of justice, but not all theories regard its importance in the same way. In justice as fairness society is interpreted as a cooperative venture for mutual advantage. The basic structure is a public system of rules defining a scheme of activities that leads men to act together so as to produce a greater sum of benefits and assigns to each certain recognized claims to a share in the proceeds. What a person does depends upon what the public rules say he will be entitled to, and what a person is entitled to depends on what he does. The distribution which results is arrived at by honoring the claims determined by what persons undertake to do in the light of these legitimate expectations.

These considerations suggest the idea of treating the question of distributive shares as a matter of pure procedural justice. The intuitive idea is to design the social system so that the outcome is just whatever it happens to be, at least so long as it is within a certain range. The notion of pure procedural justice is best understood by a comparison with perfect and imperfect procedural justice. To illustrate the former, consider the simplest case of fair division. A number of men are to divide a cake: assuming that the fair division is an equal one, which procedure, if any, will give this outcome? Technicalities aside, the obvious solution is to have one man divide the cake and get the last piece, the others being allowed their pick before him. He will divide the cake equally, since in this way he assures for himself the largest share possible. This example illustrates the two characteristic features of perfect procedural justice. First, there is an independent criterion for what is a fair division, a criterion defined separately from and prior to the procedure which is to be followed. And second, it is possible to devise a procedure that is sure to give the desired outcome. Of course, certain assumptions are made here, such as that the man selected can divide the cake equally, wants as large a piece as he can get, and so on. But we can ignore these details. The essential thing is that there is an independent standard for deciding which outcome is just and a procedure guaranteed to lead to it. Pretty clearly, perfect procedural justice is rare, if not

impossible, in cases of much practical interest.

Imperfect procedural justice is exemplified by a criminal trial. The desired outcome is that the defendant should be declared guilty if and only if he has committed the offense with which he is charged. . . . Even though the law is carefully followed, and the proceedings fairly and properly conducted, [the trial] may reach the wrong outcome. An innocent man may be found guilty, a guilty man may be set free. In such cases we speak of a miscarriage of justice: the injustice springs from no human fault but from a fortuitous combination of circumstances which defeats the purpose of the legal rules. The characteristic mark of imperfect procedural justice is that while there is an independent criterion for the correct outcome, there is no feasible procedure which is sure to lead to it.

By contrast, pure procedural justice obtains when there is no independent criterion for the right result: instead there is a correct or fair procedure such that the outcome is likewise correct or fair, whatever it is, provided that the procedure has been properly followed. This situation is illustrated by gambling. If a number of persons engage in a series of fair bets, the distribution of cash after the last bet is fair, or at least not unfair, whatever this distribution is. . . . What makes the final outcome of betting fair, or not unfair, is that it is the one which has arisen after a series of fair gambles. A fair procedure translates its fairness to the outcome only when it is actually carried out.

In order, therefore, to apply the notion of pure procedural justice to distributive shares it is necessary to set up and to administer impartially a just system of institutions. Only against the background of a just basic structure, including a just political constitution and a just arrangement of economic and social institutions, can one say that the requisite just procedure exists. . . . The intuitive idea is familiar. Suppose that law and government act effectively to keep markets competitive, resources fully employed, property and wealth (especially if private ownership of the means of production is allowed) widely distributed by the appropriate forms of taxation, or whatever, and to guarantee a reasonable social minimum. Assume also that there is fair equality of opportunity underwritten by education for all; and that the other equal liberties are secured. Then it would appear that the resulting distribution of income and the pattern of expectations will tend to satisfy the difference principle. In this complex of institutions, which we think of as establishing social justice in the modern state, the advantages of the better situated improve the condition of the least favored. Or when they do not, they can be adjusted to do so, for example, by setting the social minimum at the appropriate level. As these institutions presently exist they are riddled with grave injustices. But there presumably are ways of running them compatible with their basic design and intention so that the difference principle is satisfied consistent with the demands of liberty and fair equality of opportunity. It is this fact which underlies our assurance that these arrangements can be made just.

It is evident that the role of the principle of fair opportunity is to insure that the system of cooperation is one of pure procedural justice. Unless it is satisfied, distributive justice could not be left to take care of itself, even within a restricted range. Now the great practical advantage of pure procedural justice is that it is no longer necessary in meeting the demands of justice to keep track of the endless variety of circumstances and the changing relative positions of particular persons. . . .

THE FOUR-STAGE SEQUENCE

. . . We may think of the political process as a machine which makes social decisions when the views of representatives and their constituents are fed into it. A citizen will regard some ways of designing this machine as more just than others. So a complete conception of justice is not only able to assess laws and policies but it can also rank procedures for selecting which political opinion is to be enacted into law. . . . The citizen accepts a certain constitution as just, and he thinks that certain traditional procedures are appropriate, for example, the procedure of majority rule duly circumscribed. Yet since the political process is at best one of imperfect procedural justice, he must ascertain when the enactments of the majority are to be complied with and when they can be rejected as no longer binding. In short, he must be able to determine the grounds and limits of political duty and obligation. Thus a theory of justice has to deal with [several] types of questions, and this indicates that it may be useful to think of the principles as applied in a several-stage sequence.

At this point, then, I introduce an elaboration of the original position. So far I have supposed that once the principles of justice are chosen the parties return to their place in society and henceforth judge their claims on the social system by these principles. But if several intermediate stages are imagined to take place in a definite sequence, this sequence may give us a schema for sorting out the complications that must be faced. Each stage is to represent an appropriate point of view from which certain kinds of questions are considered. (The idea of a four-stage sequence is suggested by the United States Constitution and its history.) Thus I suppose that after the parties have adopted the principles of justice in the original position, they move to a constitutional convention. Here they are to decide upon the justice of political forms and choose a constitution: they are delegates, so to speak, to such a convention. Subject to the constraints of the principles of justice already chosen, they are to design a system for the constitutional powers of government and the basic rights of citizens. It is at this stage that they weigh the justice of procedures for coping with diverse political views. Since the appropriate conception of justice has been agreed upon, the veil of ignorance is partially lifted. The persons in the convention have, of course, no information about particular individuals: they do not know their own social position, their place in the distribution of natural attributes, or their conception of the good. But in addition to an understanding of the principles of social theory, they now know the relevant general facts about their society, that is, its natural circumstances and resources, its level of economic advance and political culture, and so on. . . . Given their theoretical knowledge and the appropriate general facts about their society, they are to choose the most effective just constitution, the constitution that satisfies the principles of justice and is best calculated to lead to just and effective legislation.

At this point we need to distinguish two problems. Ideally a just constitution would be a just procedure arranged to insure a just outcome. The procedure would be the political process governed by the constitution, the outcome the body of enacted legislation, while the principles of justice would define an independent criterion for both procedure and outcome. In pursuit of this ideal of perfect procedural justice, the first problem is to design a just procedure. To do this the liberties of equal citizenship must be incorporated into and protected by the constitution. These liberties include those of liberty of conscience and freedom of thought, liberty of the person, and equal political rights. The political system, which I assume to be some form of constitutional democracy, would not be a just procedure if it did not embody these liberties.

Clearly any feasible political procedure may yield an unjust outcome. In fact, there is no scheme of procedural political rules which guarantees that unjust legislation will not be enacted. In the case of a constitutional regime, or indeed of any political form, the ideal of perfect procedural justice cannot be realized. The best attainable scheme is one of imperfect procedural justice. Nevertheless some schemes have a greater tendency than others to result in unjust laws. The second problem, then, is to select from among the procedural arrangements that are both just and feasible those which are most likely to lead to a just and effective legal order. . . . [T]his is Bentham's problem of the artificial identification of interests, only here the rules (just procedure) are to be framed to give legislation (just outcome) likely to accord with the principles of justice rather than the principle of utility. To solve this problem intelligently requires a knowledge of the beliefs and interests that men in the system are liable to have and of the political tactics that they will find it rational to use given their circumstances. The delegates are assumed, then, to know these things. Provided they have no information about particular individuals including themselves, the idea of the original position is not affected.

In framing a just constitution I assume that the two principles of justice already chosen define an independent standard of the desired outcome. If there is no such standard, the problem of constitutional design is not well posed, for this decision is made by running through the feasible just constitutions (given, say, by enumeration on the basis of social theory) looking for the one that in the existing circumstances will most probably result in effective and just social arrangements. Now at this point we come to the legislative stage, to take the next step in the sequence. The justice of laws and policies is to be assessed from this perspective. Proposed bills are judged from the position of a representative legislator who, as always, does not know the particulars about himself. Statutes must satisfy not only the principles of justice but whatever limits are laid down in the constitution. By moving back and forth between the stages of the constitutional convention and the legislature, the best constitution is found.

Now the question whether legislation is just or unjust, especially in connection with economic and social policies, is commonly subject to reasonable differences of opinion. In these cases judgment frequently depends upon speculative political and economic doctrines and upon social theory generally. Often the best that we can say of a law or policy is that it is at least not clearly unjust.

The application of the difference principle in a precise way normally requires more information than we can expect to have and, in any case, more than the application of the first principle. It is often perfectly plain and evident when the equal liberties are violated. These violations are not only unjust but can be clearly seen to be unjust: the injustice is manifest in the public structure of institutions. But this stage of affairs is comparatively rare with social and economic policies regulated by the difference principle.

I imagine then a division of labor between stages in which each deals with different questions of social justice. This division roughly corresponds to the two parts of the basic structure. The first principle of equal liberty is the primary standard for the constitutional convention. Its main requirements are that the fundamental liberties of the person and liberty of conscience and freedom of thought be protected and that the political process as a whole be a just procedure. Thus the constitution establishes a secure common status of equal citizenship and realizes political justice. The second principle comes into play at the stage of the legislature. It dictates that social and economic policies be aimed at maximizing the long-term expectations of the least advantaged under conditions of fair equality of opportunity, subject to the equal liberties being maintained. At this point the full range of general economic and social facts is brought to bear. The second part of the basic structure contains the distinctions and hierarchies of political, economic, and social forms which are necessary for efficient and mutually beneficial social cooperation. Thus the priority of the first principle of justice to the second is reflected in the priority of the constitutional convention to the legislative stage.

The last stage is that of the application of rules to particular cases by judges and administrators, and the following of rules by citizens generally. At this stage everyone has complete access to all the facts. No limits on knowledge remain since the full system of rules has now been adopted and applies to persons in virtue of their characteristics and circumstances. . . .

Morality and the Liberal Ideal

Michael J. Sandel

One of the most important trends in contemporary political philosophy is often labeled "communitarianism." The communitarian perspective cuts across traditional political categories, and the themes and emphases of communitarian writers vary. But they are united in their opposition to what they see as the dominant political philosophy of our times, namely, *liberalism.* In the following essay, Michael Sandel explores the differences among three political philosophies: utilitarianism, the rights-based (or Kantian) liberalism of John Rawls and Robert Nozick, and Sandel's own communitarianism. While agreeing that utilitarianism must be rejected, he argues against rights-based liberalism, claiming it rests on a mistaken conception of the self as existing prior to its ends and roles, as independent of the aims and attachments that make us who we are. He then considers some of the political disagreements that divide liberals from communitarians.

Michael Sandel is Professor of Government at Harvard University and author of *Liberalism and the Limits of Justice* (1982).

Liberals often take pride in defending what they oppose—pornography, for example, or unpopular views. They say the state should not impose on its citizens a preferred way of life, but should leave them as free as possible to choose their own values and ends, consistent with a similar liberty for others. This commitment to freedom of choice requires liberals constantly to distinguish between permission and praise, between allowing a practice and endorsing it. It is one thing to allow pornography, they argue, something else to affirm it.

Conservatives sometimes exploit this distinction by ignoring it. They charge that those who would allow abortions favor abortion, that opponents of school prayer oppose prayer, that those who defend the rights of Communists sympathize with their cause. And in a pattern of argument familiar in our politics, liberals reply by invoking higher principles; it is not that they dislike pornography less, but rather that they value toleration, or freedom of choice, or fair procedures more.

But in contemporary debate, the liberal rejoinder seems increasingly fragile, its moral basis increasingly unclear. Why should toleration and freedom of choice prevail when other important values are also at stake? Too often the answer implies some version of moral relativism, the idea that it is wrong to "legislate morality" because all morality is merely subjective. "Who is to say what is literature and what is filth? That is a value judgment, and whose values should decide?"

Relativism usually appears less as a claim than as a question. "Who is to judge?" But it is a question that can also be asked of the values that liberals defend. Toleration and freedom and fairness are values too, and they can hardly be defended by the claim that no values can be defended. So it is a mistake to affirm liberal values by arguing that all values are merely subjective. The relativist defense of liberalism is no defense at all.

What, then, can be the moral basis of the higher principles the liberal invokes? Recent political philosophy has offered two main alternatives—one utilitarian, the other Kantian. The utilitarian view, following John Stuart Mill, defends liberal principles in the name of maximizing the general welfare. The state should not impose on its citizens a preferred way of life, even for their own good, because doing so will reduce the sum of human happiness, at least in the long run; better that people choose for themselves, even if, on occasion, they get it wrong. "The only freedom which deserves the name," writes Mill in *On Liberty*, "is that of pursuing our own good in our own way, so long as we do not attempt to deprive others of theirs, or impede their efforts to obtain it." He adds that his argument does not depend on any notion of abstract right, only on the principle of the greatest good for the greatest number. "I regard utility as the ultimate appeal on all ethical questions; but it must be utility in the largest sense, grounded on the permanent interests of man as a progressive being."

Many objections have been raised against utilitarianism as a general doctrine of moral philosophy. Some have questioned the concept of utility, and the assumption that all human goods are in principle commensurable. Others have objected that by reducing all values to preferences and desires, utilitarians are unable to admit qualitative distinctions of worth, unable to distinguish noble desires from base ones. But most recent

debate has focused on whether utilitarianism offers a convincing basis for liberal principles, including respect for individual rights.

In one respect, utilitarianism would seem well suited to liberal purposes. Seeking to maximize overall happiness does not require judging people's values, only aggregating them. And the willingness to aggregate preferences without judging them suggests a tolerant spirit, even a democratic one. When people go to the polls we count their votes, whatever they are.

But the utilitarian calculus is not always as liberal as it first appears. If enough cheering Romans pack the Coliseum to watch the lion devour the Christian, the collective pleasure of the Romans will surely outweigh the pain of the Christian, intense though it be. Or if a big majority abhors a small religion and wants it banned, the balance of preferences will favor suppression, not toleration. Utilitarians sometimes defend individual rights on the grounds that respecting them now will serve utility in the long run. But this calculation is precarious and contingent. It hardly secures the liberal promise not to impose on some the values of others. As the majority will is an inadequate instrument of liberal politics—by itself it fails to secure individual rights—so the utilitarian philosophy is an inadequate foundation for liberal principles.

The case against utilitarianism was made most powerfully by Immanuel Kant. He argued that empirical principles, such as utility, were unfit to serve as basis for the moral law. A wholly instrumental defense of freedom and rights not only leaves rights vulnerable, but fails to respect the inherent dignity of persons. The utilitarian calculus treats people as means to the happiness of others, not as ends in themselves, worthy of respect.

Contemporary liberals extend Kant's argument with the claim that utilitarianism fails to take seriously the distinction between persons. In seeking above all to maximize the general welfare, the utilitarian treats society as a whole as if it were a single person;

it conflates our many, diverse desires into a single system of desires. It is indifferent to the distribution of satisfactions among persons, except insofar as this may affect the overall sum. But this fails to respect our plurality and distinctness. It uses some as means to the happiness of all, and so fails to respect each as an end in himself.

In the view of modern-day Kantians, certain rights are so fundamental that even the general welfare cannot override them. As John Rawls writes in his important work, *A Theory of Justice*, "Each person possesses an inviolability founded on justice that even the welfare of society as a whole cannot override. . . . The rights secured by justice are not subject to political bargaining or to the calculus of social interests."

So Kantian liberals need an account of rights that does not depend on utilitarian considerations. More than this, they need an account that does not depend on any particular conception of the good, that does not presuppose the superiority of one way of life over others. Only a justification neutral about ends could preserve the liberal resolve not to favor any particular ends, or to impose on its citizens a preferred way of life. But what sort of justification could this be? How is it possible to affirm certain liberties and rights as fundamental without embracing some vision of the good life, without endorsing some ends over others? It would seem we are back to the relativist predicament—to affirm liberal principles without embracing any particular ends.

The solution proposed by Kantian liberals is to draw a distinction between the "right" and the "good"—between a framework of basic rights and liberties, and the conceptions of the good that people may choose to pursue within the framework. It is one thing for the state to support a fair framework, they argue, something else to affirm some particular ends. For example, it is one thing to defend the right to free speech so that people may be free to form their own opinions and choose their own ends, but something else to support it on the

grounds that a life of political discussion is inherently worthier than a life unconcerned with public affairs, or on the grounds that free speech will increase the general welfare. Only the first defense is available in the Kantian view, resting as it does on the ideal of a neutral framework.

Now, the commitment to a framework neutral with respect to ends can be seen as a kind of value—in this sense the Kantian liberal is no relativist—but its value consists precisely in its refusal to affirm a preferred way of life or conception of the good. For Kantian liberals, then, the right is prior to the good, and in two senses. First, individual rights cannot be sacrificed for the sake of the general good; and second, the principles of justice that specify these rights cannot be premised on any particular vision of the good life. What justifies the rights is not that they maximize the general welfare or otherwise promote the good, but rather that they comprise a fair framework within which individuals and groups can choose their own values and ends, consistent with a similar liberty for others.

Of course, proponents of the rights-based ethic notoriously disagree about what rights are fundamental, and about what political arrangements the ideal of the neutral framework requires. Egalitarian liberals support the welfare state, and favor a scheme of civil liberties together with certain social and economic rights—rights to welfare, education, health care, and so on. Libertarian liberals defend the market economy, and claim that redistributive policies violate peoples' rights; they favor a scheme of civil liberties combined with a strict regime of private property rights. But whether egalitarian or libertarian, rights-based liberalism begins with the claim that we are separate, individual persons, each with our own aims, interests, and conceptions of the good; it seeks a framework of rights that will enable us to realize our capacity as free moral agents, consistent with a similar liberty for others.

Within academic philosophy, the last decade or so has seen the ascendance of the rights-based ethic over the utilitarian one, due in large part to the influence of Rawls's *A Theory of Justice*. The legal philosopher H. L. A. Hart recently described the shift from "the old faith that some form of utilitarianism must capture the essence of political morality" to the new faith that "the truth must lie with a doctrine of basic human rights, protecting specific basic liberties and interests of individuals. . . . Whereas not so long ago great energy and much ingenuity of many philosophers were devoted to making some form of utilitarianism work, latterly such energies and ingenuity have been devoted to the articulation of theories of basic rights."

But in philosophy as in life, the new faith becomes the old orthodoxy before long. Even as it has come to prevail over its utilitarian rival, the rights-based ethic has recently faced a growing challenge from a different direction, from a view that gives fuller expression to the claims of citizenship and community than the liberal vision allows. The communitarian critics, unlike modern liberals, make the case for a politics of the common good. Recalling the arguments of Hegel against Kant, they question the liberal claim for the priority of the right over the good, and the picture of the freely choosing individual it embodies. Following Aristotle, they argue that we cannot justify political arrangements without reference to common purposes and ends, and that we cannot conceive of ourselves without reference to our role as citizens, as participants in a common life.

This debate reflects two contrasting pictures of the self. The rights-based ethic, and the conception of the person it embodies, were shaped in large part in the encounter with utilitarianism. Where utilitarians conflate our many desires into a single system of desire, Kantians insist on the separateness of persons. Where the utilitarian self is simply defined as the sum of its desires, the Kantian self is a choosing self, independent of the desires and ends it may have at any

moment. As Rawls writes, "The self is prior to the ends which are affirmed by it; even a dominant end must be chosen from among numerous possibilities."

The priority of the self over its ends means I am never defined by my aims and attachments, but always capable of standing back to survey and assess and possibly to revise them. This is what it means to be a free and independent self, capable of choice. And this is the vision of the self that finds expression in the ideal of the state as a neutral framework. On the rights-based ethic, it is precisely because we are essentially separate, independent selves that we need a neutral framework, a framework of rights that refuses to choose among competing purposes and ends. If the self is prior to its ends, then the right must be prior to the good.

Communitarian critics of rights-based liberalism say we cannot conceive ourselves as independent in this way, as bearers of selves wholly detached from our aims and attachments. They say that certain of our roles are partly constitutive of the persons we are—as citizens of a country, or members of a movement, or partisans of a cause. But if we are partly defined by the communities we inhabit, then we must also be implicated in the purposes and ends characteristic of those communities. As Alasdair MacIntyre writes in his book, *After Virtue*, "What is good for me has to be the good for one who inhabits these roles." Open-ended though it be, the story of my life is always embedded in the story of those communities from which I derive my identity—whether family or city, tribe or nation, party or cause. In the communitarian view, these stories make a moral difference, not only a psychological one. They situate us in the world and give our lives their moral particularity.

What is at stake for politics in the debate between unencumbered selves and situated ones? What are the practical differences between a politics of rights and a politics of the common good? On some issues, the two theories may produce different arguments for similar policies. For example, the civil rights movement of the 1960s might be justified by liberals in the name of human dignity and respect for persons, and by communitarians in the name of recognizing the full membership of fellow citizens wrongly excluded from the common life of the nation. And where liberals might support public education in hopes of equipping students to become autonomous individuals, capable of choosing their own ends and pursuing them effectively, communitarians might support public education in hopes of equipping students to become good citizens, capable of contributing meaningfully to public deliberations and pursuits.

On other issues, the two ethics might lead to different policies. Communitarians would be more likely than liberals to allow a town to ban pornographic bookstores, on the grounds that pornography offends its way of life and the values that sustain it. But a politics of civic virtue does not always part company with liberalism in favor of conservative policies. For example, communitarians would be more willing than some rights-oriented liberals to see states enact laws regulating plant closings, to protect their communities from the disruptive effects of capital mobility and sudden industrial change. More generally, where the liberal regards the expansion of individual rights and entitlements as unqualified moral and political progress, the communitarian is troubled by the tendency of liberal programs to displace politics from smaller forms of association to more comprehensive ones. Where libertarian liberals defend the private economy and egalitarian liberals defend the welfare state, communitarians worry about the concentration of power in both the corporate economy and the bureaucratic state, and the erosion of those intermediate forms of community that have at times sustained a more vital public life.

Liberals often argue that a politics of the common good, drawing as it must on particular loyalties, obligations, and traditions, opens the way to prejudice and intolerance. The modern nation-state is not the Athenian polls, they point out; the scale and diversity of modern life have rendered the Aristotelian political ethic nostalgic at best and dangerous at worst. Any attempt to govern by a vision of the good is likely to lead to a slippery slope of totalitarian temptations.

Communitarians reply, rightly in my view, that intolerance flourishes most where forms of life are dislocated, roots unsettled, traditions undone. In our day, the totalitarian impulse has sprung less from the convictions of confidently situated selves than from the confusions of atomized, dislocated, frustrated selves, at sea in a world where common meanings have lost their force. As Hannah Arendt has written, "What makes mass society so difficult to bear is not the number of people involved, or at least not primarily, but the fact that the world between them has lost its power to gather them together, to relate and to separate them." Insofar as our public life has withered, our sense of common involvement diminished, we lie vulnerable to the mass politics of totalitarian solutions. So responds the party of the common good to the party of rights. If the party of the common good is right, our most pressing moral and political project is to revitalize those civic republican possibilities implicit in our tradition but fading in our time.

Political Theory and Gender

Robin West

Western political thought has been dominated by men, as the readings in this or any political philosophy text shows. Robin West argues that this introduces a deep, pervasive bias into the debate: the fundamental experiences and stories males use to understand politics are radically different from women's experience and the stories they would have told had they influenced political theory and law.

West distinguishes what she terms *liberal legalism*—a view she traces to Hobbes, Dworkin, and Rawls—from critical legal studies or "CLS." CLS *legal* scholarship emphasizes the role political ideology plays in law's development, particularly the ideological and political contradictions found in legal doctrine and theory. Legal debate cannot, claims CLS, be separated from political conflict. CLS is also critical of much traditional political theory, which it sees as overly individualistic at the expense of the values of community. Michael Sandel is among the contemporary political thinkers with whom many critical legal theorists identify. West's focus, however, is on the conflict between these two male political approaches, liberal legalism and critical legal studies, on the one hand, and the two approaches to politics taken by feminists, namely, cultural feminism and radical feminism, on the other.

The references to jurisprudence in the article should not mislead; West is concerned with the political realities lying behind and within the law, not on the specifics of the law. Jurisprudence, for her, includes all the basic issues of political philosophy and more.

Robin West is professor of law at the University of Maryland School of Law.

What is a human being? Legal theorists must, perforce, answer this question: jurisprudence, after all, is about human beings.

From Robin West, "Jurisprudence and Gender," *The University of Chicago Law Review*, Vol. 55, No. 1 (Winter 1988). ©1988 by The University of Chicago. Reprinted by permission.

The task has not proven to be divisive. In fact, virtually all modern American legal theorists, like most modern moral and political philosophers, either explicitly or implicitly embrace what I will call the "separation thesis" about what it means to be a human being: a "human being," whatever else he is, is physically separate from all other human beings. I am one human being and you are another, and that distinction between you and me is central to the meaning of the phrase "human being." . . . We are each physically "boundaried"—this is the trivially true meaning of the claim that we are all individuals. In Robert Nozick's telling phrase, the "root idea" of any acceptable moral or political philosophy is that "there are individuals with separate lives."[1] Although Nozick goes on to derive from this insight an argument for the minimal state, the separation thesis is hardly confined to the libertarian right. According to Roberto Unger, premiere spokesperson for the communitarian left, "[t]o be conscious is to have the experience of being *cut off* from that about which one reflects: it is to be a subject that stands over against its objects . . . . *The subjective awareness of separation . . . defines consciousness.*" . . .[2]

The first purpose of this essay is to put forward the global and critical claim that by virtue of their shared embrace of the separation thesis, all of our modern legal theory—by which I mean "liberal legalism" and "critical legal theory" collectively—is essentially and irretrievably masculine. My use of "I" above was inauthentic, just as the modern, increasing use of the female pronoun in liberal and critical legal theory, although well-intended, is empirically and experientially false. For the cluster of claims that jointly constitute the "separation thesis"—the claim that human beings are, definitionally, distinct from one another, the claim that the referent of "I" is singular and unambiguous, the claim that the word "individual" has an uncontested biological meaning, namely that we are each physically individuated from every other, the claim that we are individuals "first," and the claim that what separates us is epistemologically and morally prior to what connects us— while "trivially true" of men, are patently untrue of women. Women are not essen-

tially, necessarily, inevitably, invariably, always, and forever separate from other human beings: women, distinctively, are quite clearly "connected" to another human life when pregnant. In fact, women are in some ,sense "connected" to life and to other human beings during at least four recurrent and critical material experiences: the experience of pregnancy itself; the invasive and "connecting" experience of heterosexual penetration, which may lead to pregnancy; the monthly experience of menstruation, which represents the potential for pregnancy; and the post-pregnancy experience of breast-feeding. Indeed, perhaps the central insight of feminist theory of the last decade has been that women are "essentially connected," not "essentially separate," from the rest of human life, both materially, through pregnancy, intercourse, and breast-feeding, and existentially, through the moral and practical life. If by "human beings" legal theorists mean women as well as men, then the "separation thesis" is clearly false. If, alternatively, by "human beings" they mean those for whom the separation thesis is true, then women are not human beings. It's not hard to guess which is meant.

. . .[T]his Article will contrast the "human being" constructed and described by (non-legal) feminist theory, with the "human being" constructed, described, or simply assumed by masculine jurisprudence. I will try to show that the "human being" sometimes explicated, and most often simply assumed by our modern legal theory contrasts in every particular with the "woman" sometimes assumed but more often carefully constructed by modern feminist theory. That contrast, however, is not a simple one. Neither masculine jurisprudence nor feminist theory is internally hegemonic. First, masculine jurisprudence is presently divided into two camps: "liberal legalism" on the one hand, and "critical legal theory" on the other. While both liberal legal theorists and critical legal theorists subscribe to the "separation thesis" described above, each group presents radically divergent accounts of what I will call the "subjective ex-

---

[1] Robert Nozick, *Anarchy, State, and Utopia* 33 (1974).

[2] Roberto Mangabeira Unger, *Knowledge and Politics* 200 (1975) (citation omitted) (emphasis added).

perience" of the state of separation. Similarly, "feminist theory" is sharply divided between "cultural feminism" on the one hand and "radical feminism" on the other. And, in a parallel sense, while both cultural and radical feminists subscribe to the "connection thesis" described above, they present divergent accounts of the subjective experience of the state of connection. Therefore, . . . this article will present what is ultimately a four-way contrast between the complex and possibly conflicted human being constructed by masculine jurisprudence on the one hand, and the complex and possibly conflicted woman constructed by feminist theory on the other. . . .

The by now very well publicized split in masculine jurisprudence between legal liberalism and critical legal theory can be described in any number of ways. The now standard way to describe the split is in terms of politics: "liberal legal theorists" align themselves with a liberal political philosophy which entails, among other things, allegiance to the Rule of Law and the Rule of Law virtues, while "critical legal theorists," typically left wing and radical, are skeptical of the Rule of Law and the split between law and politics which the Rule of Law purportedly delineates. Critical legal theorists are potentially far more sensitive to the political underpinnings of purportedly neutral legalistic constructs than are liberal legalists. I think this traditional characterization is wrong for a number of reasons: liberal theorists are not necessarily politically naive, and critical theorists are not necessarily radical. However, my purpose is not to critique it. Instead, I want to suggest another way to understand the divisions in modern legal theory.

An alternative description of the difference (surely not the only one) is that liberal legal theory and critical legal theory provide two radically divergent phenomenological descriptions of the pardigmatically male experience of the inevitability of separation of the self from the rest of the species, and indeed from the rest of the natural world. Both schools, as we shall see, accept the sep-

aration thesis; they both view human beings as materially (or physically) separate from each other, and both view this fact as fundamental to the origin of law. But their accounts of the subjective experience of physical separation from the other—an individual other, the natural world, and society—are in nearly diametrical opposition. Liberal legalists, in short, describe an inner life enlivened by freedom and autonomy from he separate other, and threatened by the danger of annihilation by him. Critical legal theorists, by contrast, tell a story of inner lives dominated by feelings of alienation and isolation from the separate other, and enlivened by the possibility of association and community with him. These differing accounts of the subjective experience of being separate from others, I believe, are at the root of at least some of the divisions between critical and liberal legal theorists. I want to review each of these experiential descriptions of separation in some detail, for I will ultimately argue that they are not as contradictory as they first appear. Each story, I will suggest, constitutes a legitimate and true part of the total subjective experience of masculinity.

. . . I will start with the liberal description of separation, because it is the most familiar, and surely the most dominant. According to liberal legalism, the inevitability of the individual's material separation from the "other," entails, first and foremost, an existential state of highly desirable and much valued freedom: because the individual is *separate* from the other, he is *free* of the other. Because I am separate from you, *my* ends, *my* life, *my* path, *my* goals are necessarily my own. Because I am separate, I am "autonomous." Because I am separate, I am existentially free (whether or not I am politically free). And, of course, this is true not just of me, but of everyone: it is the universal human condition. We are each separate and we are all separate, so we are each free and we are all free. We are, that is, equally free.

This existential condition of freedom in turn entails the liberal's conception of value. Because we are all free and we are each equally free, we should be treated by our government as free, and as equally free. The individual must be treated by his government (and by others) in a way that respects his equality and his freedom. The government must honor at the level of politics the existential claim made above: that my ends are *my* ends; that I cannot be forced to embrace your ends as my own. Our separation entails our freedom which in turn entails our right to establish and pursue our own concept of value, independent of the concept of value pursued or favored by others. Ronald Dworkin puts the point in this way:

What does it mean for the government to treat its citizens as equals? *That is . . . the same question as the question of what it means for the government to treat all its citizens as free, or as independent,* or with equal dignity . . . . [To accord with this demand, a government must] be neutral on what might be called the question of the good life. . . . [P]olitical decisions must be, so far as is possible, independent of any particular conception of the good life, or of what gives value to life. Since the citizens of a society differ in their conceptions, the government does not treat them as equals if it prefers one conception to another, either because the officials believe that one is intrinsically superior, or because one is held by the more numerous or more powerful group.[3]

Because of the dominance of liberalism in this culture, we might think of autonomy as the "official" liberal value entailed by the physical, material condition of inevitable separation from the other: separation from the other entails my freedom from him, and that in turn entails my political right to autonomy. I can form my own conception of the good life, and pursue it. Indeed, any conception of the good which *I* form, will necessarily by *my* conception of the good life. That freedom must be respected. Because I am free, I value and have a right to autonomy. You must value it as well. The

state must protect it. This in turn implies other (more contested) values, the most important of which is (or may be) equality. Dworkin continues:

I now define a liberal as someone who holds. . . . [a] liberal . . . theory of what equality requires. Suppose that a liberal is asked to found a new state. He is required to dictate its constitution and fundamental institutions. He must propose a general theory of political distribution . . . . He will arrive initially at something like this principal of rough equality: resources and opportunities should be distributed, so far as possible, equally, so that roughly the same share of whatever is available is devoted to satisfying the ambitions of each. Any other general aim of distribution will assume either that the fate of some people should be of greater concern than that of others, or that the ambitions or talents of some are more worthy, and should be supported more generously on that account.[4]

Autonomy, freedom and equality collectively constitute what might be called the "up side" of the subjective experience of separation. Autonomy and freedom are both entailed by the separation thesis, and autonomy and freedom both feel very good. However, there's a "down side" to the subjective experience of separation as well. Physical separation from the other entails not just my freedom; it also entails my vulnerability. Every other discrete, separate individual—because he is the "other"—is a source of danger to me and a threat to my autonomy. I have reason to fear you solely by virtue of the fact that I am me and you are you. You are not me, so by definition *my* ends are not your ends. Our ends might conflict. You might try to frustrate my pursuit of my ends. In an extreme case, you might even try to kill me—you might cause my annihilation.

Annihilation by the other, we might say, is the official *harm* of liberal theory, just as autonomy is its official value. Hobbes, of course, gave the classic statement of the ter-

---

[3] Ronald Dworkin, *A Matter of Principle* 191 (1985) (capitalization omitted) (emphasis added).

[4] Id. at 192–3 (capitalization omitted).

rifying vulnerability that stems from our separateness from the other:

Nature hath made men so equall, in the faculties of body, and mind; as that though there bee found one man sometimes manifestly stronger in body, or of quicker mind then [*sic*] another; yet when all is reckoned together, the difference between man, and man, is not so considerable, as that one man can thereupon claim to himselfe any benefit, to which another may not pretend, as well as he. For as to the strength of body, the weakest has strength enough to kill the strongest, either by secret machination, or by confederacy with others, that are in the same danger with himselfe . . . . From this equality of ability, ariseth equality of hope in the attaining of our Ends. And therefore if any two men desire the same thing, which neverthelesse they cannot both enjoy, they become enemies; and in the way to their End, (which is principally their own conservation, . . .) endeavour to destroy, or subdue one another. And from hence it comes to passe, that where an Invader hath no more to feare, than another mans single power; if one plant, sow, build, or possesse a convenient Seat, others may probably be expected to come prepared with forces united, to dispossesse, and deprive him, not only of the fruit of his labour, but also of his life, or liberty. And the Invader again is in the like danger of another.[5] . . .

. . . Thus, according to liberal legalism, the subjective experience of physical separation from the other determines both what we value (autonomy) and what we fear (annihilation). We value, and seek societal protection, of our autonomy: the liberal insists on my right to define and pursue my own life, my own path, my own identity, and my own conception of the good life free of interference from others. Because I am me and you are you, I value what I value, and you value what you value. The only value we truly share, then, is our joint investment in autonomy from each other: we both value our right to pursue our lives relatively free of outside control. We can jointly insist that our government grant us this protection. We also share the same fears. I fear the possibility—indeed the likelihood—that our ends will conflict, and you will frustrate my ends and is an extreme case cause my annihilation, and you fear the same thing about me. I want the right and the power to pursue my own chosen ends free of the fear that you will try to prevent me from doing so. You, of course, want the same.

We can call this liberal legalist phenomenological narrative the "official story" of the subjectivity of separation. According to the official story, we value the freedom that our separateness entails, while we seek to minimize the threat that it poses. We do so, of course, through creating and then respecting the state. Whether or not Robert Nozick is right that the minimal state achieves the liberal's ideal, he has nevertheless stated that liberal ideal well in the following passage:

The minimal state treats us is inviolate individuals . . .; it treats us as persons having individual rights with the dignity this constitutes. . . . [This treatment] allows us, individually or with whom we choose, to choose our life and to realize our ends and our conception of ourselves, insofar as we can, aided by the voluntary cooperation of other individuals possessing the same dignity. How *dare* any state or group of individuals do more. Or less. . . . [T]here is no *social entity* with a good that undergoes some sacrifice for its own good. There are only individual people, different individual people, with their own individual lives. Using one of these people for the benefit of the others, uses him and benefits others. Nothing more.[6]

Now, Critical Legal Theory diverges from liberal legalism on many points, but one striking contrast is this: critical theorists provide a starkly divergent phenomenological description of the subjective experience of separation. According to our critical legal

---

[5] Thomas Hobbes, *Leviathan* 183–84 (C. B. Macpherson, ed. 1968).

[6] Nozick, *Anarchy, State, and Utopia* at 333–34, 32–33 (emphasis in original) (cited in note 2).

theorists, what that material state of separation existentially entails is not a perpetual celebration of autonomy, but rather, a perpetual longing for community, or attachment, or unification, or *connection*. The separate individual strives to connect with the "other" from whom he is separate. The separate individual lives in a state of perpetual dread not of annihilation by the other, but of the alienation, loneliness, and existential isolation that his material separation from the other imposes upon him. The individual strives through love, work, and government to achieve a unification with the other, the natural world, and the society from which he was originally and continues to be existentially separated. The separate individual seeks *community*—not autonomy—and dreads isolation and alienation from the other—not annihilation by him. If we think of liberalism's depiction of the subjectivity of separation as the official story, then, we might think of this alternative description of the subjectivity of separation as the unofficial story. It is the subterranean, unofficial story of the unrecognized and—at least by liberals—slightly detested subjective craving of lost individuals.

Thus, there is a vast gap, according to critical theory, between the "official value" of liberal legalism—autonomy—and what the individual *truly* subjectively desires, which is to establish a true connection with the other. Similarly, there is a vast gap between the "official harm" of liberal legalism—annihilation by the other—and what the individual *truly* subjectively dreads, which is not annihilation by him, but isolation and alienation from him. According to the critical theorist, while the dominant liberal culture insists we value autonomy and fear the other, what the individual truly desires, craves, and longs to establish is some sort of connection with the other, and what the individual truly dreads is alienation from him. . . .

In another sense, though, the longing for connection persists not so much "in spite of" the dominant culture's valuation of autonomy, but *because* of that value. The value we

place on autonomy, according to some critical legal theorists, aggravates our alienation, isolation and loneliness. Duncan Kennedy describes the feeling:

> The "freedom" of individualism is negative, alienated and arbitrary. It consists in the absence of restraint on the individual's choice of ends, and has no moral content whatever. When the group creates an order consisting of spheres of autonomy separated by (property) and linked by (contract) rules, each member declares her indifference to her neighbor's salvation—washes her hands of him the better to "deal" with him. The altruist asserts that the staccato alternation of mechanical control and obliviousness is destructive of every value that makes freedom a thing to be desired. We can achieve real freedom only collectively, through group self-determination. We are simply too weak to realize ourselves in isolation. . . . The problem is the conversion of force into moral force, in the fact of the experience of moral indeterminacy. A definition of freedom that ignores this problem is no more than a rationalization of indifference, or the velvet glove for the hand of domination through rules.[7]

The longing for connection with the other, and the dread of alienation from him, according to the critical theorists, is in a state of constant "contradiction" with the official value and official harm that flow from separation—autonomy from the other and annihilation by him. Nevertheless, in spite of that tension, both the dread of alienation and the desire for connection are constantly *there*. The dominant culture insists we value autonomy from the other and fear annihilation by him. But subjectively, the individual lives with a more or less unrealized desire to connect with the other, and a constant dread or fear, of becoming permanently alienated, isolated—lost—from the other.

To summarize: according to liberal legalism, each of us is physically separate from every other, and because of that separation, we value our autonomy from the other and fear our annihilation by him. I have called

---

[7] Duncan Kennedy, "Form and Substance in Private Law Adjudication," 89 *Harv.L. Rev.* 1685, 1774 (1976).

these our "officially" recognized values and harms. Critical legal theory tells the unofficial story. According to critical legal theory, we are indeed physically separate from the other, but what that existentially entails is that we dread the alienation and isolation from the separate other, and long for connection with him. While liberal culture officially and publicly claims that we love our autonomy and fear the other, subjective life belies this claim. Subjectively, and in spite of the dominant culture's insistence to the contrary, we long to establish some sort of human connection with the other in order to overcome the pain of isolation and alienation which our separateness engenders. These two contrasting stories of the subjective experience of perpetual separation from the rest of human life might be schematized in this way:

	(The Official Story) Liberal Legalism	*(The Unofficial Story)* Critical Legalism
VALUE (or Longing):	Autonomy	Connection; Community
HARM (or Dread):	Annihilation; Frustration	Alienation; Isolation

Let me now turn to feminist theory. Although the legal academy is for the most part unaware of it, modern feminist theory is as fundamentally divided as legal theory. One way to characterize the conflict—the increasingly standard way to characterize the conflict—is that while most modern feminists agree that women are different from men and agree on the importance of the difference, feminists differ over which differences between men and women are most vital. According to one group of feminists, sometimes called "cultural feminists," the important difference between men and women is that women raise children and men don't. According to a second group of feminists, now called "radical feminists," the important difference between men and women is that women get fucked and men fuck: "women," definitionally, are "those from whom sex is taken," just as workers,

definitionally, are those from whom labor is taken. Another way to put the difference is in political terms. Cultural feminists appear somewhat more "moderate" when compared with the traditional culture: from a mainstream non-feminist perspective, cultural feminists appear to celebrate many of the same feminine traits that the traditional culture has stereotypically celebrated. Radical feminists, again from a mainstream perspective, appear more separatist, and, in contrast with standard political debate, more alarming. They also appear to be more "political" in a sense which perfectly parallels the critical theory-liberal theory split described above: radical feminists appear to be more attuned to power disparities between men and women than are cultural feminists.

I think this traditional characterization is wrong on two counts. First, cultural feminists no less than radical feminists are well aware of women's powerlessness vis-à-vis men, and second, radical feminism, as I will later argue, is as centrally concerned with pregnancy as it is with intercourse. But again, instead of arguing against this traditional characterization of the divide between radical and cultural feminism, I want to provide an alternative. My alternative characterization structurally (although not substantively) parallels the characterization of the difference between liberal and critical legalism. Underlying both radical and cultural feminism is a conception of women's existential state that is grounded in women's potential for physical, material connection to human life, just as underlying both liberal and critical legalism is a conception of men's existential state that is grounded in the inevitability of men's physical separation from the species. I will call the shared conception of women's existential lives the "connection thesis." The divisions between radical and cultural feminism stem from the divergent accounts of the subjectivity of the potential for connection, just as what divides liberal from critical legal theory are divergent accounts of the subjectivity of the inevitability of separation.

The "connection thesis" is simply this: Women are actually or potentially materially connected to other human life. Men aren't. This material fact has existential consequences. While it may be true *for men* that the individual is "epistemologically and morally prior to the collectivity," it is not true for women. The potential for material connection with the other defines women's subjective, phenomenological and existential state, just as surely as the inevitability of material separation from the other defines men's existential state. Our potential for material connection engenders pleasures and pains, values and dangers, and attractions and fears, which are entirely different from those which follow, for men, from the necessity of separation. Indeed, it is the rediscovery of the multitude of implications from this material difference between men and women which has enlivened (and divided) both cultural and radical feminism in this decade (and it is those discoveries which have distinguished both radical and cultural feminism from liberal feminism). As Carol Gilligan notes, this development is somewhat paradoxical: during the same decade that liberal feminist political activists and lawyers pressed for equal (meaning same) treatment by the law, feminist theorists in non-legal disciplines rediscovered women's differences from men.[8] Thus, what unifies radical and cultural feminist theory (and what distinguishes both from liberal feminism) is the discovery, or rediscovery, of the importance of women's fundamental material difference from men. As we shall see, neither radical feminists nor cultural feminists are entirely explicit in their embrace of the connection thesis. But both groups, implicitly if not explicitly, adhere to some version of it.

If both cultural and radical feminists hold some version of the connection thesis, then one way of understanding the issues that divide radical and cultural feminists, different from the standard account given

above, is that while radical and cultural feminists agree that women's lives are distinctive in their potential for material connection to others, they provide sharply contrasting accounts of the subjective experience of the material and existential state of connection. According to cultural feminist accounts of women's subjectivity, women value intimacy, develop a capacity for nurturance, and an ethic of care for the "other" with which we are connected, just as we learn to dread and fear separation from the other. Radical feminists tell a very different story. According to radical feminism, women's connection with the "other" is above all else invasive and intrusive: women's potential for material "connection" invites invasion into the physical integrity of our bodies, and intrusion into the existential integrity of our lives. Although women my "officially" value the intimacy of connection, we "unofficially" dread the intrusion it inevitably entails, and long for the individuation and independence that deliverance from that state of connection would permit. Paralleling the structure above, I will call these two descriptions feminism's official and unofficial stories of women's subjective experience of physical connection.

In large part due to the phenomenal success of Carol Gilligan's book *In a Different Voice*, cultural feminism may be the most familiar of these two feminist strands, and for that reason *alone*, I call it feminism's "official story." "Cultural feminism" (in this country and among academics) is in large part defined by Gilligan's book. Defined as such, cultural feminism begins not with a commitment to the "material" version of the connection thesis (as outlined above), but rather, with a commitment to its more observable existential and psychological consequences. Thus limited, we can put the cultural feminist point this way: women have a "sense" of existential "connection" to other human life which men do not. That sense of connection in turn entails a way of learning, a path of moral development, an aesthetic sense, and a view of the world and of one's place within it which sharply contrasts with

---

[8] Carol Gilligan, *In a Different Voice* 6–8 (1982).

men's. To reverse Sandel's formulation, for women, connection is "prior," both epistemologically and, therefore, morally, to the individual. One cultural feminist—Suzanna Sherry—calls this women's view of the world a "feminine" rather than "feminist" perspective. She summarizes the "feminine perspective" in this way:

[T]he feminine perspective views individuals primarily as interconnected members of a community. Nancy Chodorow and Carol Gilligan, in groundbreaking studies on the development of self and morality, have concluded that women tend to have a more intersubjective sense of self than men and that the feminine perspective is therefore more other-directed . . . . *The essential difference between the male and female perspectives [is that] . . . "the basic feminine sense of self is connected to the world, the basic masculine sense of self is separate." Women thus tend to see others as extensions of themselves rather than as outsiders or competitors.*[9]

Why are men and women different in this essential way? The cultural feminist explanation for women's heightened sense of connection is that women are more "connected" to life than are men because it is women who are the primary caretakers of young children. A female child develops her sense of identity as "continuous" with her caretaker's, while a young boy develops a sense of identity that is distinguished from his caretaker's. Because of the gender alignment of mothers and female children, young girls "fuse" their growing sense of identity with a sense of sameness with and attachment to the other, while because of the gender distinction between mothers and male children, young boys "fuse" their growing sense of identity with a sense of difference and separation from the other. This turns out to have truly extraordinary and far reaching consequences, for both cognitive and moral development. Nancy Chodorow explains:

[This means that] [g]irls emerge from this period with a basis for "empathy" built into their primary definition of self in a way that boys do not . . . . [G]irls come to experience themselves as less differentiated than boys, as more continuous with and related to the external object-world and as differently oriented to their inner object-world as well.[10]

Women are therefore capable of a degree of physical as well as psychic *intimacy* with the other which greatly exceeds men's capacity. Carol Gilligan finds that:

The fusion of identity and intimacy . . . [is] clearly articulated . . . in [women's] . . . self-descriptions. In response to the request to describe themselves, . . . women describe a relationship, depicting their identity *in* the connection of future mother, present wife, adopted child, or past lover. Similarly, the standard of moral judgment that informs their assessment of self is a standard of relationship, an ethic of nurturance, responsibility, and care . . . [In] women's descriptions, identity is defined in a context of relationship and judged by a standard of responsibility and care. Similarly, morality is seen by these women as arising from the experience of connection and conceived as a problem of inclusion rather than one of balancing claims.[11]

One of Gilligan's subjects, Claire, eloquently expresses her subjective sense of epistemological, moral, and psychological connection:

By yourself, there is little sense to things. It is like the sound of one hand clapping, the sound of one man or one woman, there is something lacking. It is the collective that is important to me, and that collective is based on certain guiding principles, one of which is that everybody belongs to it and that you all come from it. You have to love someone else, because while you may not like them, you are inseparable from them. In a way, it is like loving your right hand. *They are part of you;* that other person is part of that giant collection of people that you are connected to.[12]

---

[9] Suzanna Sherry, "Civic Virtue and the Feminine Voice in Constitutional Adjudication," 72 *Va.L.Rev.* 543, 584–85 (1986) (citations omitted) (emphasis added).

[10] Nancy Chodorow, *The Reproduction of Mothering* 167 (1978).

[11] Gilligan, *In a Different Voice* at 159–60 (cited in note 13).

[12] Id. at 160.

Thus, according to Gilligan (and her subjects), women view themselves as fundamentally connected to, not separate from, the rest of life. This difference permeates virtually every aspect of our lives. According to the vast literature on difference now being developed by cultural feminists, women's cognitive development, literary sensibility, aesthetic taste, and psychological development, no less than our anatomy, are all fundamentally different from men's, and are different in the same way: unlike men, we view ourselves as connected to, not separate from, the other. As a consequence, women's ways of knowing are more "integrative" than men's; women's aesthetic and critical sense is "embroidered" rather than "laddered;" women's psychological development remains within the sphere of "attachment" rather than "individuation."

The most significant aspect of our difference, though, is surely the moral difference. According to cultural feminism, women are more nurturant, caring, loving and responsible to others than are men. This capacity for nurturance and care dictates the moral terms in which women, distinctively, construct social relations: women view the morality of actions against a standard of responsibility to others, rather than against a standard of rights and autonomy from others. As Gilligan puts it:

The moral imperative . . . [for] women is an injunction to care, a responsibility to discern and alleviate the "real and recognizable trouble" of this world. For men, the moral imperative appears rather as an injunction to respect the rights of others and thus to protect from interference the rights to life and self-fulfillment.[13]

Cultural feminists, to their credit, have reidentified these differences as women's strengths, rather than women's weaknesses. Cultural feminism does not simply *identify* women's differences—patriarchy too insists on women's differences—it celebrates them. Women's art, women's craft, women's nar-

rative capacity, women's critical eye, women's ways of knowing, and women's heart, are all, for the cultural feminist, redefined as things to celebrate. Quilting, cultural feminism insists, is not just something women do; it is art, and should be recognized as such. Integrative knowledge is not a confused and failed attempt to come to grips with the elementary rules of deductive logic; it is a way of knowledge and should be recognized as such. Women's distinctive aesthetic sense is as valid as men's. Most vital, however, for cultural feminism is the claim that intimacy is not just something women *do*, it is something human beings *ought* to do. Intimacy is a source of value, not a private hobby. It is morality, not habit.

To pursue my structural analogy to masculine legal theory, then, intimacy and the ethic of care constitute the entailed *values* of the existential state of connection with others, just as autonomy and freedom constitute the entailed values of the existential state of separation from others for men. Because women are fundamentally connected to other human life, women value and enjoy intimacy with others (just as because men are fundamentally separate from other human life men value and enjoy autonomy). Because women are connected with the rest of human life, intimacy with the "other" comes naturally. Caring, nurturance, and an ethic of love and responsibility for life is second nature. Autonomy, or freedom from the other constitutes a value for men because it reflects an existential state of being: separate. Intimacy is a value for women because it reflects an existentially connected state of being.

Intimacy, the capacity for nurturance and the ethic of care constitute what we might call the "up side" of the subjective experience of connection. It's all good. Intimacy feels good, nurturance is good, and caring for others morally is good. But there's a "down side" to the subjective experience of connection. There's danger, harm, and fear entailed by the state of connection as well as value. Whereas men fear annihilation from the separate other (and conse-

---

[13] Id. at 100.

quently have trouble achieving intimacy), women fear separation from the connected other (and consequently have trouble achieving independence). Gilligan makes the point succinctly: "Since masculinity is defined through separation while femininity is defined through attachment, male gender identity is threatened by intimacy while female gender identity is threatened by separation."[11] Separation, then, might be regarded as the official harm of cultural feminism. When a separate self must be asserted, women have trouble asserting it. Women's separation from the other in adult life, and the tension between that separation and our fundamental state of connection, is felt most acutely when a woman must make choices, and when she must speak the truth. It is at those times that separation and individuation are at a premium. Gilligan explains:

Since women, however, define their identity through relationships of intimacy and care, the moral problems that they encounter pertain to issues of a different sort. *When relationships are secured by masking desire and conflict is avoided by equivocation, then confusion arises about the locus of responsibility and truth.* [Mary] McCarthy, describing her 'representation' to her grandparents, explains: "Whatever I told them was usually so blurred and glossed, in the effort to meet their approval . . . that except when answering a direct question, I hardly knew whether what I was saying was true or false. I really tried, or so I thought, to avoid lying, but it seemed to me that they forced it on me by the difference in their vision of things, so that I was always transposing reality for them into the terms they could understand. To keep matters straight with my conscience, I shrank, whenever possible from the lie absolute, just as, from a sense of precaution, I shrank from the plain truth.

The critical experience then becomes not intimacy but choice, creating an encounter with self that clarifies the understanding of responsibility and truth.[15]"

Separation, and the fear of separation, can lead to real harm, especially in later life. In her final chapter, Gilligan elaborates:

[B]ecause women's sense of integrity appears to be entwined with an ethic of care, so that to see themselves as women is to see themselves in a relationship of connection, the major transitions in women's lives would seem to involve changes in the understanding and activities of care. Certainly the shift from childhood to adulthood witnesses a major redefinition of care. . . .

In the same vein, however, the events of midlife—the menopause and changes in family and work—can alter a woman's activities of care in ways that affect her sense of herself. If mid-life brings an end to relationships, to the sense of connection on which she relies, as well as to the activities of care through which she judges her worth, then the mourning that accompanies all life transitions can give way to the melancholia of self-deprecation and despair.[16]

Now, while Gilligan is undoubtedly explaining a real experiential phenomenon—I don't know of any woman who hasn't recognized herself somewhere in this book—her material explanation of that phenomenon is incomplete. Which is not to say it isn't *true*: It seems quite plausible that women are more psychically connected to others in just the way Gilligan describes and for just the reason she expounds. Mothers raise children, and as a consequence girls, and not boys, think of themselves as continuous with, rather than separate from, that first all-important "other"—the mother. But this psychological and developmental explanation just raises—it does not answer—the background material question: why do women, rather than men, raise, nurture, and cook for children? What is the cause of *this* difference?

Although Gilligan doesn't address the issue, other cultural feminists have, and their explanations converge, I believe, implicitly if not explicitly, on a material, or mixed material-cultural, and not just a cultural answer: women *raise* children—and hence raise girls who are more connected and nurturant, and therefore more likely to be nur-

---

[11] Id. at 8.

[15] Id. at 164 (emphasis added).

[16] Id. at 171.

turant caretakers themselves—because it is women who bear children. Women are not inclined to abandon an infant they've carried for nine months and then delivered. If so, then women are ultimately more "connected"—psychically, emotionally, and morally—to other human beings because women, as children were raised by women and women raise children because women, uniquely, are physically and materially "connected" to those human beings when the human beings are fetuses and then infants. Women are more empathic to the lives of others because women are physically tied to the lives of others in a way which men are not. Women's moral voice is one of responsibility, duty and care for others because women's material circumstance is one of responsibility, duty and care for those who are first physically attached, then physically dependent, and then emotionally interdependent. Women think in terms of the needs of others rather than the rights of others because women materially, and then physically, and then psychically, provide for the needs of others. Lastly, women fear separation from the other rather than annihilation by him, and "count" it as a harm, because women experience the "separating" pain of childbirth and more deeply feel the pain of the maturation and departure of adult children. . . .

The response to this "central reality" among American liberal feminists and American feminist lawyers has been to deny or minimize the importance of the pregnancy difference, thus making men and women more "alike," so as to force the legal system to treat men and women similarly.

Although a review of the history of liberal feminism is well beyond the scope of this essay, suffice it to say that there is a growing awareness amongst even liberal feminist legal theorists that this strategy has to some extent backfired. It has become increasingly clear that feminists must attack the burdens of pregnancy and its attendant differences, rather than denying the uniqueness of pregnancy. . . .

Whether we embrace a material or a purely developmental explanation of women's heightened connection with the other, however, the "story" of women's relationship with the other as told by cultural feminists contrast in virtually every particular with the story of men's relationship to the other as told by liberals. First, men, according to the Hobbesian account, are by nature equal. "Nature hath made men so equall, in the faculties of body, and mind; as that though there bee found one man sometimes manifestly stronger in body . . . ; yet when all is reckoned together, the difference between man, and man, is not so considerable, as that one man can thereupon claim to himself any benefit. . . . [T]he weakest has strength enough to kill the strongest. . . ."[17] Women, by contrast, are not "equal" in strength to the most important "other" they encounter: the fetus and then the newborn child. Rather, the fetus and the woman and later the infant and the mother occupy what might be called a natural, hierarchical web of inequality, not a natural state of equality: whereas men may be "by nature equal" women are "by nature stronger" than those who are most important to them and most dependent upon them. The natural physical equality between self and other on which Hobbes insists is simply untrue of women's natural state. Second, according to Hobbes, "men" are naturally inclined to aggress against those they perceive as the vulnerable other. Again, women are not: infants are dependent upon mothers and vulnerable to them, yet the natural mother does not aggress against her child, she breastfeeds her. And lastly, men respond to the vulnerability of natural equality by developing morality and a civil state that demand respect for the equality, rights and freedom of the other. Women do not. Women respond to their natural state of inequality by developing a morality of nurturance that is responsible for the well-being of the dependent, and an ethic of care that responds to the greater needs of the weak. Men respond to the natural state of equality with an ethic of auton-

---

[17] Hobbes, *Leviathan* at 183.

omy and rights. Women respond to the natural state of inequality with an ethic of responsibility and care.

We might summarize cultural feminism in this way: women's potential for a material connection to life entails (either directly, as I have argued, or indirectly, through the reproduction of mothering) an experiential and psychological sense of connection with other human life, which in turn entails both women's concept of value, and women's concept of harm. Women's concept of value revolves not around the axis of autonomy, individuality, justice and rights, as does men's, but instead around the axis of intimacy, nurturance, community, responsibility and care. For women, the creation of value, and the living of a good life, therefore depend upon relational, contextual, nurturant and affective responses to the needs of those who are dependent and weak, while for men the creation of value, and the living of the good life, depend upon the ability to respect the rights of independent co-equals, and the deductive, cognitive ability to infer from those rights rules for safe living. Women's concept of harm revolves not around a fear of annihilation by the other but around a fear of separation and isolation from the human community on which she depends, and which is dependent upon her. If, as I have suggested, cultural feminism is our dominant feminist dogma, then this account of the nature of women's lives constitutes the "official text" of feminism, just as liberal legalism constitutes the official text of legalism.

These two "official stories" sharply contrast. Whereas according to liberal legalism, men value autonomy from the other and fear annihilation by him, women, according to cultural feminism, value intimacy with the other and fear separation from her. Women's sense of connection with others determines our special competencies and special vulnerabilities, just as men's sense of separation from others determines theirs. Women value and have special competency for intimacy, nurturance, and relational thinking, and a special vulnerability to and

fear of isolation, separation from the other, and abandonment, just as men value and have a special competency for autonomy, and a special vulnerability to and fear of annihilation.

Against the cultural feminist backdrop, the story that radical feminists tell of women's invaded, violated lives is "subterranean" in the same sense that, against the backdrop of liberal legalism, the story critical legal theorists tell of men's alienation and isolation from others is subterranean. According to radical feminism, women's connection to others is the source of women's misery, not a source of value worth celebrating. For cultural feminists, women's connectedness to the other (whether material or cultural) is the source, the heart, the root, and the cause of women's different morality, different voice, different "ways of knowing," different genius, different capacity for care, and different ability to nurture. For radical feminists, that same potential for connection—experienced materially in intercourse and pregnancy, but experienced existentially in all spheres of life—is the source of women's debasement, powerlessness, subjugation, and misery. It is the cause of our pain, and the reason for our stunted lives. Invasion and intrusion, rather than intimacy, nurturance and care, is the "unofficial" story of women's subjective experience of connection.

Thus, modern radical feminism is unified among other things by its insistence on the invasive, oppressive, destructive implications of women's material and existential connection to the other. So defined, radical feminism (of modern times) begins not with the eighties critique of heterosexuality, but rather in the late sixties, with Shulamith Firestone's angry and eloquent denunciation of the oppressive consequences for women of the physical condition of pregnancy. Firestone's assessment of the importance and distinctiveness of women's reproductive role parallels Marilyn French's. Both view women's physical connection with nature and with the other as in some sense the "cause" of patriarchy. But their analyses of the chain of causation sharply contrast. For French, women's reproductive role—the paradigmatic experience of physical connection to nature, to life and to the other, and thus the core of women's moral difference—is also the cause of patriarchy, primarily because of men's fear of and contempt for nature. Firestone has a radically different view. Pregnancy is indeed the paradigmatic experience of physical connection, and it is indeed the core of women's difference, but according to Firestone, it is for that reason *alone* the cause of women's oppression. Male contempt has nothing (at first) to do with it. *Pregnancy itself*, independent of male contempt, is invasive, dangerous and oppressive; it is an assault on the physical integrity and privacy of the body. For Firestone, the strategic implication of this is both clear and clearly material. The technological separation of reproduction from the female body is the necessary condition for women's liberation.[18]

In a moment, I will turn to heterosexual intercourse, for it is intercourse, rather than pregnancy, which consumes the attention of the modern radical feminism of our decade. But before doing so it's worth recognizing that the original radical feminist case for reproductive freedom did not turn on rights of "privacy" (either of the doctor-patient relationship, or of the marriage, or of the family), or rights to "equal protection," or rights to be free of "discrimination." it did not turn on rights at all. Rather, the original feminist argument for reproductive freedom turned on the definitive radical feminist insight that pregnancy—the invasion of the body by the other to which women are distinctively vulnerable—is an injury and ought to be treated as such. Pregnancy connects us with life, as the cultural feminist insists, but that connection is not something to celebrate; it is that very connection that hurts us. This argument, as I will argue later, is radically incommensurate with liberal legal ideology. There's no legal category that fits it. But it is nevertheless the

radical argument—that pregnancy is a dangerous, psychically consuming, existentially intrusive, and physically invasive assault upon the body which in turn leads to a dangerous, consuming, intrusive, invasive assault on the mother's self-identity—that best captures women's own sense of the injury and danger of pregnancy, whether or not it captures the law's sense of what an unwanted pregnancy involves, or why women should have the right to terminate it.

The radical feminist argument for reproductive freedom appears in legal argument only inadvertently or surreptitiously, but it does on occasion appear. It appeared most recently in the phenomenological descriptions of unwanted pregnancies collated in the *Thornburgh* amicus brief recently filed by the National Abortion Rights Action League ("NARAL").[19] The descriptions of pregnancy collated in that peculiarly non-legal legal document are filled with metaphors of invasion—metaphors, of course, because we lack the vocabulary to name these harms precisely. Those descriptions contrast sharply with the "joy" that cultural feminists celebrate in pregnancy, childbirth and child-raising. The invasion of the self by the other emerges as a source of oppression, not a source of moral value.

"During my pregnancy," one woman explains, "I was treated *like a baby machine—an incubator without feelings*."[20] "Then I got pregnant again," another woman writes,

This one would be only 13 months younger than the third child. I was faced with the unpleasant fact that I could not stop the babies from coming no matter what I did . . . . *You cannot possibly know what it is like to be the helpless pawn of nature*. I am a 71 year old widow.[21]

---

[18] Shulamith Firestone, *The Dialectic of Sex* (1970).

[19] Amicus Brief for the National Abortion Rights Action League, et. al., Thornburgh v. American College of Obstetricians and Gynecologists, Nos. 84–495 and 84–1379 ("NARAL Amicus Brief") (on file at The University of Chicago Law Review). For the Supreme Court opinion, see 476 U.S. 747 (1986).

[20] NARL Amicus Brief at 13 (emphasis added).

[21] Id. at 19 (emphasis added).

"Almost exactly a decade ago," writes another, "I learned I was pregnant. . . . I was sick in my heart and I thought I would kill myself. *It was as if I had been told my body had been invaded with cancer.* It seemed that very wrong."[22]

One woman speaks directly, without metaphor: "On the ride home from the clinic, the relief was enormous. I felt happy for the first time in weeks. I had a future again. *I had my body back.*"[23]

According to these women's self-descriptions, when the unwanted baby arrives, the injury is again one of invasion, intrusion and limitation. The *harm* of an unwanted pregnancy is that the baby will elicit a *surrender* (not an end) of the mother's life. The *fear* of unwanted pregnancy is that one will lose control of one's individuated being (not that one will die). Thus, one woman writes, "I was like any other woman who had an unintended pregnancy, I was terrified and felt as though my life was out of my control."[24]

This danger, and the fear of it, is gender-specific. It is a fear which grips women, distinctively, and it is a fear about which men, apparently, know practically nothing. Another woman writes:

I was furiously angry, dismayed, dismal, by turns. I could not justify an abortion on economic grounds, on grounds of insufficient competence or on any other of a multitude of what might be perceived as "legitimate" reasons. But I kept being struck by the ultimate unfairness of it all. I could not conceive of any event which would so profoundly impact upon any man. Surely my husband would experience some additional financial burden, and additional "fatherly" chores, but his whole future plan was not hostage to this unchosen, undesired event. Basically his life would remain the same progression of ordered events as before.[25]

And another:

Being a mother is hard at any age but being a teenager makes it harder. . . . Things I may have wanted to do before getting pregnant, like college and a career are different now. Before I think about my dreams, I have to think about taking care of a baby. . . . I could be making plans for my future, but instead I'm making plans for my baby's future.[26]

Conversely, women who had abortions felt able to form their own destiny. One woman wrote: "Personally legal abortion allowed me the choice as a teenager living on a very poor Indian Reservation to finish growing up and make something of my life."[27] And another:

I was not glad that I was faced with an unwanted, unplanned pregnancy, however I am glad that I made the decision to have an abortion. The experience was a very positive one for me. It helped me learn that I am a person and I can make independent decisions. Had I not had the abortion I would have probably ended up a single mother struggling for survival and dealing with a child that I was not ready for.[28]

As noted above, radical feminism of the eighties has focused more on intercourse than on pregnancy. But this may represent less of a divergence than it first appears. From the point of view of the "connection thesis," what the radical feminists of the eighties find objectionable, invasive, and oppressive about heterosexual intercourse, is precisely what the radical feminists of the sixties found objectionable, invasive, and oppressive about pregnancy and motherhood. According to the eighties radical critique, intercourse, like pregnancy, blurs the physical boundary between self and other, and that blurring of boundaries between self and other constitutes a profound invasion of the self's physical integrity. That invasion—the "dissolving of boundaries"—is something to condemn, not celebrate. Andrea Dworkin explains:

---

[22] Id. at 28 (emphasis added).
[23] Id. at 29 (emphasis added).
[24] Id. at 29.
[25] Id. at 29.

[26] Id. at 24.
[27] Id. at 29.
[28] Id.

Sexual intercourse is not intrinsically banal, though pop-culture magazines like *Esquire* and *Cosmopolitan* would suggest that it is. It is intense, often desperate. The internal landscape is violent upheaval, a wild and ultimately cruel disregard of human individuality, . . . no respecter of boundaries. . . .

Sometimes, the skin comes off in sex. *The people merge, skinless. The body loses its boundaries. . . .* There is no physical distance, no self-consciousness, nothing withdrawn or private or alienated, no existence outside physical touch. The skin collapses as a boundary—it has no meaning . . . . Instead, there is necessity, nothing else—being driven, physical immersion in "each other" but with no experience of "each other" as separate entities coming together. . . .

The skin is a line of demarcation, a periphery, the fence, the form, the shape, the first clue to identity in a society . . ., and, in purely physical terms, the formal precondition for being human. It is a thin veil of matter separating the outside from the inside. . . . The skin is separation, individuality, the basis for corporeal privacy, ...[29]

Women, distinctively, lose this "formal precondition for being human" and they lose it in intercourse:

A human being has a body that is inviolate; and when it is violated, it is abused. A woman has a body that is penetrated in intercourse: permeable, its corporeal solidness a lie. The discourse of male truth—literature, science, philosophy, pornography—calls that penetration *violation.* This it does with some consistency and some confidence. *Violation* is a synonym for intercourse. At the same time, the penetration is taken to be a use, not an abuse; a normal use; it is appropriate to enter her, to push into ("violate") the boundaries of her body. She is human, of course, but by a standard that does not include physical privacy. She is, in fact, human by a standard that precludes physical privacy, since to keep a man out altogether and for a lifetime is deviant in the extreme, a psychopathology, a repudiation of the way in which she is expected to manifest her humanity.[30]

Like pregnancy, then, intercourse is inva-

sive, intrusive and violative, and like pregnancy it is therefore the cause of women's oppressed, invaded, intruded, violated, and debased lives. Dworkin concludes:

This is nihilism; or this is truth. He has to push in past boundaries. There is the outline of a body, distinct, separate, its integrity an illusion, a tragic deception, because unseen there is a slit between the legs, and he has to push into it. There is never a real privacy of the body that can co-exist with intercourse: with being entered. The vagina itself is muscled and the muscles have to be pushed apart. The thrusting is persistent invasion. She is opened up, split down the center. She is occupied—physically, internally, in her privacy . . . .

She, a human being, is supposed to have a privacy that is absolute; except that she, a woman, has a hole between her legs that men can, must, do enter. This hole, her hole, is synonymous with entry. A man has an anus that can be entered, but his anus is not synonymous with entry. A woman has an anus that can be entered, but her anus is not synonymous with entry. The slit between her legs, so simple, so hidden—frankly, so innocent—for instance, to the child who looks with a mirror to see if it *could* be true—is there an entrance to her body down there? . . .—that slit which means entry into her—intercourse—appears to be the key to women's lower human status. By definition, . . she is intended to have a lesser privacy, a lesser integrity of the body, a lesser sense of self, . . . [and] this lesser privacy, this lesser integrity, this lesser self, establishes her lesser significance. . . . She is defined by how she is made, that hole, which is synonymous with entry; *and intercourse, the act fundamental to existence, has consequences to her being that may be intrinsic, not socially imposed.*[31]

Although Dworkin herself does not draw the parallel, for both Dworkin and Firestone, women's potential for material connection with the other—whether through intercourse or pregnancy—constitutes an invasion upon our physical bodies, an intrusion upon our lives, and consequently an assault upon our existential freedom, whether or not it is also the root of our

---

[29] Andrea Dworkin, *Intercourse* 21–22 (1987) (emphasis added).

[30] Id. at 122.

[31] Id. at 122–23 (emphasis added on the words "and intercourse, the act," otherwise emphasis in original).

moral distinctiveness (the claim cultural feminism makes on behalf of pregnancy), or the hope of our liberation (the claim sexual liberationists make on behalf of sex). Both intercourse and pregnancy are literal, physical, material invasions and occupations of the body. The fetus, like the penis, literally occupies my body. In their extremes, of course, both unwanted heterosexual intercourse and unwanted pregnancy can be life threatening experiences of physical invasion. An unwanted fetus, no less than an unwanted penis, invades my body, violates my physical boundaries, occupies my body and can potentially destroy my sense of self. Although the culture does not recognize them as such, the physical and existential invasions occasioned by unwanted pregnancy and intercourse are real harms. They are events we should fear. They are events which any sane person should protect herself against. What unifies the radical feminism of the sixties and eighties is the argument that women's potential for material, physical connection with the other constitutes an invasion which is a very real harm causing very real damage, and which society ought to recognize as such.

The material, sporadic violation of a woman's body occasioned by pregnancy and intercourse implies an existential and pervasive violation of her privacy, integrity and life projects. According to radical feminists, women's longings for individuation, physical privacy, and independence go well beyond the desire to avoid the dangers of rape or unwanted pregnancy. Women also long for liberation from the oppression of intimacy (and its attendant values) which both cultural feminism and most women officially, and wrongly, overvalue. Intimacy, in short, is *intrusive*, even when it isn't life threatening (perhaps *especially* when it isn't life threatening). An unwanted pregnancy is disastrous, but even a *wanted* pregnancy and motherhood are intrusive. The child *intrudes*, just as the fetus invades.

Similarly, while unwanted heterosexual intercourse is disastrous, even wanted heterosexual intercourse is intrusive. The penis

occupies the body and "divides the woman" internally, to use Andrea Dworkin's language, in consensual intercourse no less than in rape. It preempts, challenges, negates, and *renders impossible* the maintenance of physical integrity and the formation of a unified self. The deepest unofficial story of radical feminism may be that intimacy—the official value of cultural feminism—is itself oppressive. Women secretly, unofficially, and surreptitiously long for the very individuation that cultural feminism insists women fear: the freedom, the independence, the individuality, the sense of wholeness, the confidence, the self-esteem, and the security of identity which can only come from a life, a history, a path, a voice, a sexuality, a womb, and a body of one's own. Dworkin explains:

In the experience of intercourse, she loses the capacity for integrity because her body—the basis of privacy and freedom in the material world for all human beings—is entered and occupied; the boundaries of her physical body are—neutrally speaking—violated. What is taken from her in that act is not recoverable, and she spends her life—wanting, after all to have something— pretending that pleasure is in being reduced through intercourse to insignificance . . . . She learns to eroticize powerlessness and self-annihilation. The very boundaries of her own body become meaningless to her, and even worse, useless to her. The transgression of those boundaries comes to signify a sexually charged degradation into which she throws herself, having been told, convinced, that identity, for a female, is there—somewhere beyond privacy and self-respect.[32]

Radical feminism, then, is unified by a particular description of the subjectivity of the material state of connection. According to that description, women dread intrusion and invasion, and long for an independent, individualized, *separate* identity. While women may indeed "officially" value intimacy, what women unofficially crave is physical privacy, physical integrity, and sexual

---

[32] Id. at 137–38.

celibacy—in a word, physical exclusivity. In the moral realm, women officially value contextual, relational, caring, moral thinking, but secretly wish that everyone would get the hell out of our lives so that we could pursue our own projects—we loathe the intrusion that intimacy entails. In the epistemological and moral realms, while women officially value community, the web, the spinning wheel, and the weave, we privately crave solitude, self-regard, self-esteem, linear thinking, legal rights, and principled thought.

The contrasting accounts of women's subjective lives that emerge from modern feminist theory's rediscovery of women's difference might be schematized in this way:

	Cultural Feminism	*Radical Feminism*
VALUE (or Longing):	Intimacy	Individuation Integrity
HARM (or Dread):	Separation	Invasion; Intrusion

Finally, then, we can schematize the contrast between the description of the "human being" that emerges from modern legal theory, and the description of women that emerges from modern feminism:

	The Official Story (Liberal legalism and cultural feminism)		The Unofficial Story (Critical legalism and radical feminism)	
	Value	Harm	Longing	Dread
LEGAL THEORY (human beings)	Autonomy	Annihilation; Frustration	Attachment; Connection	Alienation
FEMINIST THEORY (women)	Intimacy	Separation	Individuation	Invasion; Intrusion

As the diagram reveals, the descriptions of the subjectivity of human existence told by feminist theory and legal theory contrast at every point. There is no overlap. First, and most obviously, the "official" descriptions of human beings' subjectivity and women's ~biectivity contrast rather than compare. ~ding to liberal theory; human beings ~gressively to their natural state of ~cal equality. In response to the

great dangers posed by their natural aggression, they abide by a sharply anti-naturalist morality of autonomy, rights, and individual spheres of freedom, which is intended to and to some extent does curb their natural aggression. They respect a civil state that enforces those rights against the most egregious breaches. The description of women's subjectivity told by cultural feminism is much the opposite. According to cultural feminism, women inhabit a realm of natural *inequality*. They are physically stronger than the fetus and the infant. Women respond to their natural inequality over the fetus and infant not with aggression, but with nurturance and care. That natural and nurturant response evolves into naturalist moral ethic of care which is consistent with women's natural response. The substantive moralities consequent to these two stories, then, unsurprisingly, are also diametrically opposed. The autonomy that human beings value and the rights they need as a restriction on their natural hostility to the equal and separate other are in sharp contrast to the intimacy that women value, and the ethic of care that represents not a limitation upon, but an extension of, women's natural nurturant response to the dependent, connected other.

The subterranean descriptions of subjectivity that emerge from the unofficial stories of radical feminism and critical legalism also contrast rather than compare. According to the critical legalists, human beings respond to their natural state of physical separateness not with aggression, fear and mutual suspicion, as liberalism holds, but with longing. Men suffer from a perpetual dread of isolation and alienation and a fear of rejection, and harbor a craving for community, connection, and association. Women, by contrast, according to radical feminism, respond to their natural state of material connection to the other with a craving for individuation and a loathing for invasion. Just as clearly, the subterranean dread men have of alienation (according to critical legalism) contrasts sharply with the subterranean dread that women have of invasion and intrusion (according to radical feminism).

The *responses* of human beings and women to these subterranean desires also contrast in substance, although, interestingly, the responses are structurally similar. According to both critical legalism and radical feminism, human beings and women, respectively, for the most part deny the subterranean desires that permeate their lives. Instead, they collaborate, to some degree, in the official culture's elaborate attempt to deny while partially accommodating the intensity of those felt needs. Both do so for the same reason: both human beings and women deny their subterranean desires because of a fear legitimately grounded—that the subterranean need, if asserted, will be met by either violence or rejection by the dominant culture. The dominant male culture condemns as aberrant the man who needs others, just as the dominant female culture condemns the woman who wants to exist apart from others. Thus, men deny their need for attachment and women deny their need for individuation. The mechanisms by which the two groups effect the denial are fundamentally opposed in substance, albeit structurally parallel. According to critical theory, human beings deny their need for attachment primarily through the distancing and individuating assertion of individual rights. It is the purpose and content of those rights to largely deny the human need for attachment and communion with the other. According to radical feminism, women deny their need for individuation through the "intimating" mechanisms of romance, sentiment, familial ideology, the mystique of motherhood, and commitment to the false claims of affective attachment. It is the purpose and content of romance and familial ideology to largely deny women's need for individuation, separation, and individual identity.

Somewhat less obviously, the "unofficial" description of subjectivity provided by each side is not simply the equivalent of the "official" description of the other, although they are often mistaken as such. The mistaken belief that they are is responsible, I think, for the widespread and confused claim that

critical legal studies already *is* feminist because the critical scholars' description of subjectivity converges with the cultural feminists' description of subjectivity, and the less widespread but equally confused claim that radical feminism is "just" liberalism, for the parallel reason.

First, the subjectivity depicted by critical legalism—the craving for connection and the dread of alienation—is not the subjectivity depicted by cultural feminism—the capacity for intimacy, the ethic of care, and the fear of separation. It is not hard to see the basis for the confused claim that cultural feminism's depiction of feminine subjectivity mirrors critical conceptions of the subjective experience of masculinity, though. There are two reasons for this confused identification. First, as Duncan Kennedy correctly notes, liberalism is indeed the rhetoric of the status quo. The description of subjectivity upon which critical legalists insist—"withdrawn selves" who cringe from autonomy and secretly crave community—contrasts sharply with the description of subjectivity endorsed by dominant, mainstream liberal ideology. The critics' description of subjective life is not well regarded by people in power, to put the point lightly. Indeed, it is somewhat despised. Vis-à-vis liberal ideology, it is truly radical. It is underground. Similarly, women and women's values, to put the point lightly, are underground, despised, opposed, or at best undervalued by people in power. Vis-à-vis *feminism*, cultural feminism may be "dominant," but vis-à-vis *liberalism*, cultural feminism is at least as deeply underground and disapproved as critical legalism, if not more so. Cultural feminism and critical legalism share the outsider's status.

Further, the potential for connection which women naturally have and which cultural feminism celebrates, is in a sense the *goal* of critical legalism's alienated hero. For that reason, perhaps, the critical description of subjectivity may be confusedly identified as feminist. Nevertheless, the identification is over-stated. . . .

[W]omen value love and intimacy because they express the unity of self and nature within our own selves. More generally, women do not struggle toward connection with others, against what turnout to be insurmountable obstacles. Intimacy is not something which women fight to become capable of. We just do it. It is ridiculously easy. It is also, I suspect, qualitatively beyond the pale of male effort. The difference might be put pictorially: the intimacy women value is a sharing of intersubjective territory that preexists the effort made to identify it. The connection that I suspect men strive for does not preexist the effort, and it is not a sharing of space; at best it is an adjacency. Gilligan inadvertently sums the difference between the community critical legal studies insists that men surreptitiously seek, and the intimacy that cultural feminism insists that women value: "The discovery now being celebrated by men in mid-life of the importance of intimacy, relationships, and care is something that women have known from the beginning."[33]

Similarly, the dread of alienation that (according to critical legal studies) permeates men's lives is not the same as the fear of isolation and separation from the other that characterizes women's lives. The fear of separation, for women, is fundamental, physical, economic, empathic, and psychological, as well as psychic. Separation from one's infant will kill the infant to whom the mother has been physically and then psychically connected, and therefore a part of the mother will die as well; separation from one's community may have similarly life threatening consequences. The alienation men dread is not the fear that oneself or the one with whom one is in symbiosis will be threatened. The alienation that men dread is not a sorrow over fundamental, basic, "first" existential state of being. The longing to overcome alienation is a socially constructed reaction against the natural fact of individuation. More bluntly—love, for men, is an acquired skill; separation (and therefore autonomy) is what comes naturally.

The separation that endangers women, by contrast, is what is socially constructed—attachment is natural. Separation, and the dread of it, is the response to the natural (and pleasant) state of connection.

Second, the description of women's subjective nature, aspirations, and fears drawn by radical feminism is not the same as the description of "human nature" employed by liberalism. It is not hard, however, to see the basis for this confusion. Both radical feminism and liberalism view the other as a danger to the self: liberalism identifies the other as a threat to autonomy and to life itself; radical feminism identifies the other as a threat to individuation and to physical integrity. It is hardly surprising, then, that radical feminists borrow heavily from liberalism's protective armor of rights and distance. From the radical feminist point of view, "liberal rights-talk," so disparaged by critical legalists, is just fine, and it would be even better if it protected women against the dangers that characterize their lives, as well as protecting men against the dangers that characterize their lives.

The structural similarity ends there, though. The *invasion* and *intrusion* that women dread from the penetrating and impregnating potential of the connected other is not the same as the annihilation and frustration by the separate other that men fear. Men's greatest fear is that of being wiped out—of being killed. The fear of sexual and fetal invasion and intrusion that permeates women's lives is not the fear of annihilation or frustration. The fear of sexual and fetal invasion is the fear of being occupied *from within*, not annihilated from without; of having one's self overcome, not ended; of having one's own physical and material life taken over by the pressing physical urgency of another, not ended by the conflicting interests of another; of being, in short, overtaken, occupied, displaced, and invaded, not killed. Furthermore, the intrusiveness of less damaging forms of intimacy—"wanted" intimacy—is not equivalent to the lesser form of annihilation liberalism recognizes: having one's ends frustrated by the

---

[33] Gilligan, *In a Different Voice* at 17.

conflicting ends of the other. I do not fear having my "ends" frustrated; I fear having my ends "displaced" before I even formulate them. I fear that I will be refused the right to be an "I" who fears. I fear that my ends will not be my own. I fear that the phrase "my ends" will prove to be (or already is) oxymoronic. I fear I will never feel the freedom, or have the space, to become an ends-making creature.

Similarly, the individuation prized by radical feminism is not the same as the autonomy liberalism heralds, although it may be a precondition of it. The "autonomy" praised by liberalism is one's right to pursue one's own ends. "Individuation," as understood by radical feminism, is the right *to be* the sort of creature who might have and then pursue one's "own" ends. Women's longing for individuation is a longing for a transcendent state of individuated being against that which is internally contrary, given, fundamental, and first. Autonomy is something which is natural to men's existential state and which the state might protect. Individuation, by contrast, is the material pre-condition of autonomy. Individuation is what you need to be before you can even begin to think about what you need to be free.

These, then, are the differences between the "human beings" assumed by legal theory and women, as their lives are now being articulated by feminist theory. The human being, according to legal theory, values autonomy and fears annihilation, while at the same time he subjectively dreads the alienation that his love of autonomy inevitably entails. Women, according to feminist theory, value intimacy and fear separation, while at the same time longing for the individuation which our fear of separation precludes, and dreading the invasion which our love of intimacy entails. The human being assumed or constituted by legal theory precludes the woman described by feminism.

. . .Women often, and perhaps increasingly, experience heterosexual intercourse as freely chosen intimacy, not invasive bondage. A radicalism that flatly denies the reality of such a lived experience runs the risk of making itself unintelligible and irrelevant to all people, not to mention the audience that matters most: namely, those women for whom intercourse is not free, not chosen, and anything but intimate, and who have no idea that it either could be or should be both.

This "critique of the intimacy critique" can easily be misconstrued. . . .I am not denying that heterosexuality is compulsory in this culture or that women as a consequence of that compulsion become alienated from their desire for freedom. It is indeed true that both heterosexuality and heterosexual intercourse are compulsory. But heterosexuality is compulsory because of the institutions that render it compulsory, not because of the nature of the act. The same is true of motherhood and pregnancy. Because they are compulsory, motherhood and heterosexuality are tremendously constraining, damaging, and oppressive. It is indeed true that the institutions which render them such need to be, ought to be, and will be destroyed. But it does not follow from any of this that either motherhood or intercourse themselves will be, need to be, or ought to be destroyed. . . .

Now, it is also true—emphatically true—that neither motherhood nor intercourse have been "released" from patriarchy. Until they are, there is no project more vital to our understanding of women's present oppression than the description of the subjective experience of motherhood, and of intercourse, within the patriarchal institutions that render those activities compulsory. This is the importance of Rich's multi-textured work on compulsory motherhood and heterosexuality, and of Dworkin's passionate but disappointingly unidimensional work on intercourse. We need to be aware—to be made aware—of those institutions *as institutions* that constrain as they define the act. But, as Rich clearly saw with respect to mothering, that is not all we need to understand. Feminists also need to understand what it means to mother and to enjoy intercourse with aspirational conditions of freedom, for it is those conditions which potentially and increasingly, for many of us, define the nature of those events. When we reach this understanding, or at least strive for it, we will have a better understanding of what non-institutional and non-patriarchal intercourse and motherhood might be and might ultimately become.

Of course, to again borrow from Rich, to catch even a glimpse of mothering or intercourse within a non-patriarchal culture requires a "quantum leap" of imagination. It requires, most of all, the ability to imagine ourselves in a society in which women are in full possession of our bodies:

> [T]he "quantum leap" [of imagination] implies that even as we try to deal with backlash and emergency, we are imagining the new: a future in which women are powerful, full of our own power, not the old patriarchal power-over but the power-to-create, power-to-think, power-to-articulate and concretize our visions and transform our lives and those of our children. I believe . . . that this power will begin to speak in us more and more as we repossess our own bodies, including the decision to mother or not to mother, and how, and with whom, and when. For the struggle of women to become self-determining is rooted in our bodies, and it is an indication of this that the token women artist or intellectual or professional has so often been constrained to deny her female physicality in order to enter realms designated as male domain.[37]

Yet we make small versions of these "quantum leaps" every day. We continue to mother and to want to mother in spite of the compulsory nature of institutional motherhood. We also make small versions of the same "quantum leap" with respect to intercourse. Women do, increasingly, freely engage in heterosexual intercourse in spite of the compulsory nature of the institution of intercourse. Increasingly, we have a sense of what intercourse feels like when "released"

from compulsory heterosexuality. Explanations that rest on denial of the possibility that equality and freedom can define intercourse and motherhood fail to incorporate real glimpses that we increasingly have of a world without the present oppressive institutions. They consequently endanger the seriousness and the truth of the radical feminist insight that many women, indeed most women, define their intimate relationships within the confines of necessity rather than possibility, and within the dictates of compulsion, rather than choice. . . .

Minimally, I want to suggest that feminists should think about the possibility that the notion of a "fundamental" experienced contradiction, [expressed in the differences between cultural and radical feminists] might help us explain women's subjective lives, as well as close the broadening gap between cultural and radical feminist theory. The presence of such a contradiction, for example, explains why some women see the possibility of intimacy in pornographic depictions of females sexual submission while others see the threat of invasion (and it would explain why many women see both). The presence of a contradiction underlying women's subjective lives also clarifies the existential basis of many of the apparent tensions in feminist legal reforms. It explains why women insist upon and embrace an ethic of care and the right to have children without economic hardship, while at the same time fighting for rights of individuation, physical privacy, and freedom. Finally, it explains the complex relationship between the emerging feminist legal theory and dominant legal theory: it explains, for example, why legal feminists are both attracted to liberal rights of individuation, physical privacy, and individual security, and at the same time are threatened by them. The contradiction explains why feminists understand, and even sympathize with, critical legal theory's rights critique, but will never endorse it.

That women live with a fundamental contradiction between invasion and intimacy is much harder to test than the parallel

---

[37] Adrienne Rich, On Lies, Secrets and Silence (1979) at 271–72.

claim that men live in a fundamental contradiction between autonomy and alienation for this simple reason: the fundamental contradiction that characterizes men's lives is manifested absolutely all over the place in public life. As Kennedy correctly claims, once we are sensitized to it, we see the "fundamental contradiction" in art, literature, music, and, perhaps most emphatically, in virtually every field of law. The fundamental contradiction that characterizes women's lives (if it does), by contrast, has no outlet. Women are silent, particularly with respect to the injuries we suffer. This is, of course, changing: Women speak, write books, compose music, produce art, drama and dance, and increasingly even legislate, advocate and adjudicate law. But nevertheless, women express their subjectivity with nowhere near the voice of authority with which men express theirs. Women's subjectivity, unlike men's subjectivity, is not expressed in the objective world. Women's silence, more than any other single factor, inhibits the study of women's subjective lives.

We can, though, test the sense of this contradiction against the evidence of our own experienced lives, if not the evidence of art, literature and legal doctrine. When I read Carol Gilligan's book for the first time several years ago, I had an unequivocal shock of recognition. What she is saying, I thought then and still think, is important, transformative, empowering, exciting, enlivening, and, most fundamentally, it is simply *true*. It is true of me, and was true of my mother, and is true of my sisters. She has described the way I think, what I value, what I fear, how I have grown, and how I hope to grow. And she has described the moral lives of the women I know as well. Her book captures what I know and have always known but have never been able to claim as my own moral vision, and what parts of that vision I share with women generally. When I read Andrea Dworkin's book, I had the same unequivocal shock of recognition. What Dworkin is saying about intercourse is important, transformative, empowering, exciting, liberating, enliven-

ing, and most fundamentally, it is simply true. It is true of me, was true of my mother, and is true of my sisters. She is describing how I have been debased, victimized, intruded, invaded, harmed, damaged, injured, and *violated* by intercourse. Yet it also seems undeniably true to me that these two feminist visions of my subjective life rest on flatly contradictory premises. . . .

Of course, there is a major difference between the presence of contradiction in legal theory and the presence of contradiction in feminist theory. Even if it is true that women, like men, live within the parameters of a contradiction, women live within the parameters of this fundamental contradiction *within the oppressive conditions of patriarchy*. Men don't (although men do live within the parameters of the oppressive conditions of capitalism). Therefore, feminists need to develop not just an examination of the experience of the contradiction between invasion and intimacy to which our potential for connection gives rise, but also a description of how patriarchy effects, twists, perverts, and surely to some extent causes that contradiction. We also need, however, to imagine how the contradiction would be felt outside of patriarchy, and we need to reflect on our own experiences of non-patriarchal mothering, intercourse, and intimacy to generate such imaginings. For while women's bodies may continue to be "materially connected" to others as long as they are women's bodies, they need not forever be *possessed* by others. Our connection to the other is a function of our material condition; our possession by the other, however, is a function of patriarchy. We need to imagine both having power over our bodies and power over our contradictory material state. We need to imagine how this fundamental contradiction would feel outside of the context of the dangers and fears that patriarchy requires. Adrienne Rich asks, of non-constrained, non-compulsory, truly chosen motherhood in a world free of patriarchy:

What would it mean to mother in a society where women were deeply valued and respected, in a culture which was woman-affirming? What would it mean to bear and raise children in the fullness of our power to care for them, provide for them, in dignity and pride?. . . What would it mean to mother in a society which was making full use of the spiritual, intellectual, emotional, physical gifts of women, in all our difference and diversity? What would it mean to mother in a society which laid no stigma upon lesbians, so that women grew up with real emotional and erotic options in the choice of life companions and lovers? What would it mean to live and die in a culture which affirmed both life and death, in which both the living world and the bodies of women were released at last from centuries of violation and control? This is the quantum leap of the radical feminist vision.[38]

We need to ask these questions of intercourse as well. What would intercourse feel like, or *be*, in a world in which it was freely chosen? What would it mean to have intercourse in a world in which women's pleasures were honored, and women's injuries were cared for, and women's labor was compensated? And finally we need to ask these questions of intimacy generally. How would the "contradiction" between invasion and intimacy feel in a world free of the fear of male sexual aggression? Would intimacy be entirely non-threatening where there was no reason to fear rape? Would individuation be as enticing where intercourse and motherhood were not mandatory? Would separation be as harmful where familial association was not the assumed form of women's lives? How would the contradiction between intimacy and intrusion feel, if we had no reason to fear the more life threatening forms of invasion? We need to ask these questions, but we also need to *answer* them.

We need to show what the exclusion of women from law's protection has meant to both women and law, and we need to show what it means for the Rule of Law to exclude women and women's values.

The way to do this—the only way to do this—is to tell true stories of women's lives. The Hobbesian "story" of deliverance from the state of nature to the Rule of Law, as both liberal and radical legal scholars are fond of pointing out, does not purport to be history. But that doesn't make it fantasy. The Hobbesian story of the state of nature (and the critical story of alienation as well) is a synthesis of umpteen thousands of personal, subjective, everyday, male experiences. *Images* are generated from that synthesis, and those images, sometimes articulate, sometimes not, of what it means to be a human being then become the starting point of legal theory. Thus, for example, the Hobbesian, liberal picture of the "human being" as someone who treasures autonomy and fears annihilation from the other comes from men's primary experiences, presumably, of school yard fights, armed combat, sports, games, work, big brothers, and fathers. Similarly, the critical picture of the human being as someone who longs for attachment and dreads alienation comes from the male child's memory of his mother, from rejection experiences painfully culled from his adolescence, and from the adult male's continuing inability to introspect, converse, or commune with the natural world, including the natural world of others.

The "separation thesis," I have argued, is drastically untrue of women. What's worth noting by way of conclusion is that it is not entirely true of man either. First, it is not true materially. Men are connected to another human life prior to the cutting of the umbilical cord. Furthermore, men are somewhat connected to women during intercourse, and men have openings that can be sexually penetrated. Nor is the separation thesis necessarily true of men existentially. As Suzanna Sherry has shown, the existence of the entire classical republican tradition belies the claim that masculine biology mandates liberal values.[39] More generally, . . . material biology does not *mandate*

---

[38] Ibid at 272–73.

[39] Suzanna Sherry, 72 Ua.L. Rev. (cited above) at 584.

existential value: men *can* connect to other human life. Men can nurture life. Men can mother. Obviously, men can care, and love, and support, and affirm life. Just as obviously, however, most men don't. One reason that they don't, of course, is male privilege. Another reason, though, may be the blinders of our masculinist utopian visionary. Surely one of the most important insights of feminism has been that biology is indeed destiny when we are unaware of the extent to which biology is narrowing our fate, but that *biology is destiny only to the extent of our ignorance*. As we become increasingly aware, we become increasingly free. As we become increasingly free, we, rather than biology, become the authors of our fate. Surely this is true both of men and women.

On the flip side, the "connection thesis" is also not entirely true of women, either materially or existentially. Not all women become pregnant, and not all women are sexually penetrated. Women can go through life unconnected to other human life. Women can also go through life fundamentally unconcerned with other human life. Obviously, as the liberal feminist movement firmly established, many women can and do individuate, speak the truth, develop integrity, pursue personal projects, embody freedom, and attain an atomistic liberal individuality. Just as obviously, most women don't. Most women are indeed forced into motherhood and heterosexuality. One reason for this is utopian blinders: women's lack of awareness of existential choice in the face of what are felt to be biological imperatives. But that is surely not the main reason. The primary reason for the stunted nature of women's lives is male power.

The Idea of an Overlapping Consensus

John Rawls

In this concluding essay, John Rawls weighs the limits and potentialities of political philosophy. In particular, he is concerned with the difficult, important question of how diverse, pluralistic societies such as western democracies can achieve political stability without betraying their commitment to individual rights and democratic values.

In answering that question, Rawls develops what he terms a "political conception of justice." Such a conception, he argues, has three features: it is a moral conception applied to society's basic structure; it is *not* a comprehensive moral vision meant to apply to the full range of moral problems, such as Kant and Mill offered; and it is formulated in the common terms of public reason rather than any particular religious, moral or philosophical doctrine.

In the final sections of the paper, Rawls discusses four possible objec-

John Rawls, "The Idea of an Overlapping Consensus" *Oxford Journal of Legal Studies* Vol. 7 No. 1 Spring 1987.
© Oxford University Press. Reprinted by permission. Some footnotes omitted.

tions against the idea of political theory understood in terms of such an overlapping consensus. The first is that his account is nothing more than a *modus vivendi* like that proposed by Hobbes—a treaty adhered to merely because each party regards it in its interest rather than for moral reasons. Next is the claim that to view political philosophy as seeking a political conception suggests skepticism or indifference to the possible truth of the political theory. Third, he considers whether it is possible to resolve the various political conflicts over rights and economic justice using only a political conception or if a comprehensive theory might be needed. The final objection is that his political conception is utopian in the sense that it would be unable to win the wide support necessary for a stable political regime. Here Rawls is led to consider how liberalism as a political conception can meet the three prerequisites for stability. Liberalism, so understood, is committed to liberty of conscience and speech, the rule of law, equal political rights, fair equality of opportunity and economic justice. Though it is a moral conception, such a political theory is not comprehensive.

Rawls's claim, then, is that liberal theory, viewed as a political conception rather than a full moral theory, can avoid many controversial political and philosophical disputes and win the support of citizens with widely differing religious and cultural perspectives. Throughout the essay, Rawls is concerned to stress the theory's practical side—liberalism (such as his own social contract theory, which is in the background of much of this essay) seeks reasonable agreements that can provide the basis of a common political culture and provide the framework for reasonable, peaceful resolution of what often seems intractable conflicts.

Implicit in this argument is a response to the communitarian criticisms leveled against liberalism by Michael Sandel. Rawls's use of the original position and veil of ignorance is not meant as a philosophical statement about the nature of persons but instead as a means of elaborating the idea of society as a fair system of cooperation among equal citizens. We do well, he claims, to view *citizens* as autonomous, "unencumbered" selves, but that in no way rules out other conceptions of the self that might be adopted by people holding a particular comprehensive moral or philosophical doctrine. Liberalism seeks an overlapping consensus on a political conception of justice, not a full moral theory.

The aims of political philosophy depend on the society it addresses. In a constitutional democracy one of its most important aims is presenting a political conception of justice that can not only provide a shared public basis for the justification of political and social institutions but also helps ensure stability from one generation to the next. Now a basis of justification that rests on self- or group-interests alone cannot be stable; such a basis must be, I think, even when moderated by skillful constitutional design, a mere *modus vivendi*, dependent on a fortuitous conjunction of contingencies. What is needed is a regulative political conception of justice that can articulate and order in a principled way the political ideals and values of a democratic regime, thereby specifying the aims the constitution is to achieve and the limits it must respect. In addition, this political conception needs to be such that there is some hope of its gaining the support of an overlapping consensus, that is, a consensus in which it is affirmed by the opposing religious, philosophical and moral doctrines likely to thrive over generations in a more or less just constitutional democracy, where the criterion of justice is that political conception itself.

In the first part of my discussion (Secs I–II) I review three features of a political conception of justice and note why a conception with these features is appropriate given the historical and social conditions of a modern democratic society, and in particular, the condition I shall refer to as the fact of pluralism. The second part (Secs III–VII) takes up four illustrative—but I think misplaced—objections we are likely to have to the idea of an overlapping consensus, and to its corollary that social unity in a democracy cannot rest on a shared conception of the meaning, value and purpose of human life. This corollary does not imply, as one might think, that therefore social unity must rest solely on a convergence of self- and group-interests, or on the fortunate outcome of political bargaining. It allows for the possibility of stable social unity secured by an overlapping consensus on a reasonable political conception of justice. It is this conception of social unity for a democratic society I want to explain and defend.

By way of background, several comments. When Hobbes addressed the contentious divisions of his day between religious sects, and between the Crown, aristocracy and middle-classes, the basis of his appeal was self-interest: men's fear of death and their desire for the means of a commodious life. On this basis he sought to justify obedience to an existing effective (even if need be absolute) sovereign. Hobbes did not think this form of psychological egoism was true; but he thought it was accurate enough for his purposes. The assumption was a political one, adopted to give his views practical effect. In a society fragmented by sectarian divisions and warring interests, he saw no other common foothold for political argument.

How far Hobbes's perception of the situation was accurate we need not consider, for in our case matters are different. We are the beneficiaries of three centuries of democratic thought and developing constitutional practice; and we can presume not only some public understanding of, but also some allegiance to, democratic ideals and values as realized in existing political institutions. This opens the way to elaborate the idea of an overlapping consensus on a political conception of justice: such a consensus, as we shall see, is moral both in its object and grounds, and so is distinct from a consensus, inevitably fragile, founded solely on self- or group-interest, even when ordered by a well-framed constitution. The idea of an overlapping consensus enables us to understand how a constitutional regime characterized by the fact of pluralism might, despite its deep divisions, achieve stability and social unity by the public recognition of a reasonable political conception of justice.

I

The thesis of the first part of my discussion is that the historical and social conditions of a modern democratic society require us to regard a conception of justice for its political institutions in a certain way. Or rather, they require us to do so, if such a conception is to be both practicable and consistent with the limits of democratic politics. What these conditions are, and how they affect the features of a practicable conception, I note in connection with three features of a political conception of justice, two of which I now describe, leaving the third for the next section.

The first feature of a political conception of justice is that, while such a conception is, of course, a moral conception, it is a moral conception worked out for a specific kind of subject, namely, for political, social and economic institutions.[1] In particular, it is worked out to apply to what we may call the 'basic structure' of a modern constitutional democracy. (I shall use 'constitutional democracy', and 'democratic regime', and similar phrases interchangeably.) By this structure I mean a society's main political, social and economic institutions, and how they fit together into one unified scheme of social cooperation. The focus of a political conception of justice is the framework of basic institutions and the principles, standards and precepts that apply to them, as well as how those norms are expressed in the character and attitudes of the members of society who realize its ideals. One might suppose that this first feature is already implied by the meaning of a political conception of justice: for if a conception does not apply to the basic structure of society, it would not be a political conception at all. But I mean more than this, for I think of a political conception of justice as a conception framed in the first instance solely for the special case of the basic structure.

The second feature complements the first: a political conception is not to be understood as a general and comprehensive moral conception that applies to the political order, as if this order was only another subject, another kind of case, falling under that conception. Thus, a political conception of justice is different from many familiar moral doctrines, for these are widely understood as general and comprehensive views. Perfectionism and utilitarianism are clear examples, since the principles of perfection and utility are thought to apply to all kinds of subjects ranging from the conduct of individuals and personal relations to the organization of society as a whole, and even to the law of nations. Their content as political doctrines is specified by their application to political institutions and questions of social policy. Idealism and Marxism in their various forms are also general and comprehensive. By contrast, a political conception of justice involves, so far as possible, no prior commitment to any wider doctrine. It looks initially to the basic structure and tries to elaborate a reasonable conception for that structure alone.

Now one reason for focusing directly on a political conception for the basic structure is that, as a practical political matter, no general and comprehensive view can provide a publicly acceptable basis for a political conception of justice.[2] The social and historical conditions of modern democratic regimes have their origins in the Wars of Religion following the Reformation and the subsequent development of the principle of toleration, and in the growth of constitutional government and of large industrial market economies. These conditions profoundly affect the requirements of a workable conception of justice: among other things, such a conception must allow for a diversity of general and comprehensive doctrines, and for the plurality of conflicting, and indeed incommensurable, conceptions of the meaning, value and purpose of human life (or what I shall call for short 'conceptions of the good') affirmed by the citizens of democratic societies.

This diversity of doctrines—the fact of pluralism—is not a mere historical condition that will soon pass away; it is, I believe, a permanent feature of the public culture of modern democracies. Under the political and social conditions secured by the basic rights and liberties historically associated with these regimes, the diversity of views will persist and may increase. A public and workable agreement on a single general and comprehensive conception could be maintained only by the oppressive use of state

---

[1] In saying that a conception is moral I mean, among other things, that its content is given by certain ideals, principles and standards; and that these norms articulate certain values, in this case political values.

[2] By a publicly acceptable basis I mean a basis that includes ideals, principles and standards that all members of society can not only affirm but also mutually recognize before one another. A public basis involves, then, the public recognition of certain principles as regulative of political institutions, and as expressing political values that the constitution is to be framed to realize.

power.[3] Since we are concerned with securing the stability of a constitutional regime, and wish to achieve free and willing agreement on a political conception of justice that establishes at least the constitutional essentials, we must find another basis of agreement than that of a general and comprehensive doctrine. And so, as this alternative basis, we look for a political conception of justice that might be supported by an overlapping consensus.

We do not, of course, assume that an overlapping consensus is always possible, given the doctrines currently existing in any democratic society. It is often obvious that it is not, not at least until firmly held beliefs change in fundamental ways. But the point of the idea of an overlapping consensus on a political conception is to show how, despite a diversity of doctrines, convergence on a political conception of justice may be achieved and social unity sustained in long-run equilibrium, that is, over time from one generation to the next.

II

So far I have noted two features of a political conception of justice: first, that it is expressly framed to apply to the basic structure of society: and second, that it is not to be seen as derived from any general and comprehensive doctrine.

Perhaps the consequences of these features are clear. Yet it may be useful to survey them. For while no one any longer supposes that a practicable political conception for a constitutional regime can rest on a shared devotion to the Catholic or the Protestant Faith, or to any other religious view, it may still be thought that general and comprehensive philosophical and moral doctrines might serve in this role. The second feature denies this not only for Hegel's idealism and Marxism, and for teleological moral views, as I have said, but also for many forms of liberalism as well. While I believe that in fact any workable conception of political justice for a democratic regime must indeed be in an appropriate sense liberal—I come back to this question later—its liberalism will not be the liberalism of Kant or of J. S. Mill, to take two prominent examples.

Consider why: the public role of a mutually recognized political conception of justice is to specify a point of view from which all citizens can examine before one another whether or not their political institutions are just. It enables them to do this by citing what are recognized among them as valid and sufficient reasons singled out by that conception itself. Questions of political justice can be discussed on the same basis by all citizens, whatever their social position, or more particular aims and interests, or their religious, philosophical or moral views. Justification in matters of political justice is addressed to others who disagree with us, and therefore it proceeds from some consensus: from premises that we and others recognize

---

[3] For convenience, I give a fuller list of these social and historical conditions, beginning with the three already mentioned above: (1) the fact of pluralism; (2) the fact of the permanence of pluralism, given democratic institutions; (3) the fact that agreement on a single comprehensive doctrine presupposes the oppressive use of state power. Four additional ones are: (4) the fact that an enduring and stable democratic regime, one not divided into contending factions and hostile classes, must be willingly and freely supported by a substantial majority of at least its politically active citizens; (5) the fact that a comprehensive doctrine, whenever widely, if not universally, shared in society, tends to become oppressive and stifling; (6) the fact that reasonably favourable conditions (administrative, economic, technological and the like), which make democracy possible, exist; and finally, (7) the fact that the political culture of a society with a democratic tradition implicitly contains certain fundamental intuitive ideas from which it is possible to work up a political conception of justice suitable for a constitutional regime. (This last is important when we characterize a political conception of justice in the next section.) We may think of the first six of these seven conditions as known by common sense, that is, as known from our shared history and the evident features and aspects of our political culture and present circumstances. They belong to what we might refer to as the common sense political sociology of democratic societies. When elaborating a political conception of justice, we must bear in mind that it must be workable and practicable in a society in which the first six conditions obtain.

as true, or as reasonable for the purpose of reaching a working agreement on the fundamentals of political justice. Given the fact of pluralism, and given that justification begins from some consensus, no general and comprehensive doctrine can assume the role of a publicly acceptable basis of political justice.

From this conclusion it is clear what is problematic with the liberalisms of Kant and Mill. They are both general and comprehensive moral doctrines: general in that they apply to a wide range of subjects, and comprehensive in that they include conceptions of what is of value in human life, ideals of personal virtue and character that are to inform our thought and conduct as a whole. Here I have in mind Kant's ideal of autonomy and his connecting it with the values of the Enlightenment, and Mill's ideal of individuality and his connecting it with the values of modernity. These two liberalisms both comprehend far more than the political. Their doctrines of free institutions rest in large part on ideals and values that are not generally, or perhaps even widely, shared in a democratic society. They are not a practicable public basis of a political conception of justice, and I suspect the same is true of many liberalisms besides those of Kant and Mill.

Thus we come to a third feature of a political conception of justice, namely, it is not formulated in terms of a general and comprehensive religious, philosophical or moral doctrine but rather in terms of certain fundamental intuitive ideas viewed as latent in the public political culture of a democratic society. These ideas are used to articulate and order in a principled way its basic political values. We assume that in any such society there exists a tradition of democratic thought, the content of which is at least intuitively familiar to citizens generally. Society's main institutions, together with the accepted forms of their interpretation, are seen as a fund of implicitly shared fundamental ideas and principles. We suppose that these ideas and principles can be elaborated into a political conception of justice, which we hope can gain the support of an overlapping consensus. Of course, that this can be done can be verified only by actually elaborating a political conception of justice and exhibiting the way in which it could be thus supported. It's also likely that more than one political conception may be worked up from the fund of shared political ideas; indeed, this is desirable, as these rival conceptions will then compete for citizens' allegiance and be gradually modified and deepened by the contest between them.

Here I cannot, of course, even sketch the development of a political conception. But in order to convey what is meant, I might say that the conception I have elsewhere called 'justice as fairness' is a political conception of this kind. It can be seen as starting with the fundamental intuitive idea of political society as a fair system of social cooperation between citizens regarded as free and equal persons, and as born into the society in which they are assumed to lead a complete life. Citizens are further described as having certain moral powers that would enable them to take part in social cooperation. The problem of justice is then understood as that of specifying the fair terms of social cooperation between citizens so conceived. The conjecture is that by working out such ideas, which I view as implicit in the public political culture, we can in due course arrive at widely acceptable principles of political justice.

The details are not important here. What is important is that, so far as possible, these fundamental intuitive ideas are not taken for religious, philosophical or metaphysical ideas. For example, when it is said that citizens are regarded as free and equal persons, their freedom and equality are to be understood in ways congenial to the public political culture and explicable in terms of the design and requirements of its basic institutions. The conception of citizens as free and equal is, therefore, a political conception, the content of which is specified in connection with such things as the basic rights and liberties of democratic citizens. The hope is that the conception of justice to which this conception of citizens belongs will be acceptable to a wide range of comprehensive doctrines and hence supported by an overlapping consensus.

But, as I have indicated and should emphasize, success in achieving consensus requires that political philosophy try to be, so far as possible, independent and autonomous from other parts of philosophy, especially from philosophy's long-standing problems and controversies. For given the aim of consensus, to proceed otherwise would be self-defeating. But as we shall see (in Sec IV) we may not be able to do this entirely when we attempt to answer the objection that claims that aiming for consensus implies scepticism or indifference to religious, philosophical or moral truth. Nevertheless, the reason for avoiding deeper questions remains. For as I have said above, we can present a political view either by starting explicitly from within a general and comprehensive doctrine, or we can start from fundamental intuitive ideas regarded as latent in the public political culture. These two ways of proceeding are very different, and this difference is significant even though we may sometimes be forced to assert certain aspects of our own comprehensive doctrine. So while we may not be able to avoid comprehensive doctrines entirely, we do what we can to reduce relying on their more specific details, or their more disputed features. The question is: what is the least that must be asserted; and if it must be asserted, what is its least controversial form?

Finally, connected with a political conception of justice is an essential companion conception of free public reason. This conception involves various elements. A crucial one is this: just as a political conception of justice needs certain principles of justice for the basic structure to specify its content, it also needs certain guidelines to enquiry and publicly recognized rules of assessing evidence to govern its application. Otherwise, there is no agreed way for determining whether those principles are satisfied, and for settling what they require of particular institutions, or in particular situations.

Agreement on a conception of justice is worthless—not an effective agreement at all—without agreement on these further matters. And given the fact of pluralism, there is, I think, no better practicable alternative than to limit ourselves to the shared methods of, and the public knowledge available to, common sense, and the procedures and conclusions of science when these are not controversial. It is these shared methods and this common knowledge that allows us to speak of *public* reason. As I shall stress later on, the acceptance of this limit is not motivated by scepticism or indifference to the claims of comprehensive doctrines; rather, it springs from the fact of pluralism, for this fact means that in a pluralist society free public reason can be effectively established in no other way.[1]

III

I now turn to the second part of my discussion (Secs III–VII) and take up four objections likely to be raised against the idea of social unity founded on an overlapping consensus on a political conception of justice. These objections I want to rebut, for they can prevent our accepting what I believe is the most reasonable basis of social unity available to us. I begin with perhaps the most obvious objection, namely, that an overlapping consensus is a mere *modus vivendi*. But first several explanatory comments.

Earlier I noted what it means to say that a conception of justice is supported by an

---

[1] Two other elements of the idea of free public reason in justice as fairness are these: the first is a publicly recognized conception of everyone's (rational) advantage, or good, to be used as an agreed basis of interpersonal comparisons in matters of political justice. This leads to an account of primary goods. . . . The second further element is the idea of publicity, which requires that the principles of political justice and their justification (in their own terms) be publicly available to all citizens, along with the knowledge of whether their political institutions are just or unjust. . . .

overlapping consensus. It means that it is supported by a consensus including the opposing religious, philosophical and moral doctrines likely to thrive over generations in the society effectively regulated by that conception of justice. These opposing doctrines we assume to involve conflicting and indeed incommensurable comprehensive conceptions of the meaning, value and purpose of human life (or conceptions of the good), and there are no resources within the political view to judge those conflicting conceptions. They are equally permissible provided they respect the limits imposed by the principles of political justice. Yet despite the fact that there are opposing comprehensive conceptions affirmed in society, there is no difficulty as to how an overlapping consensus may exist. Since different premises may lead to the same conclusions, we simply suppose that the essential elements of the political conception, its principles, standards and ideals, are theorems, as it were, at which the comprehensive doctrines in the consensus intersect or converge.

To fix ideas I shall use a model case of an overlapping consensus to indicate what is meant; and I shall return to this example from time to time. It contains three views: one view affirms the political conception because its religious doctrine and account of faith lead to a principle of toleration and underwrite the fundamental liberties of a constitutional regime; the second view affirms the political conception on the basis of a comprehensive liberal moral doctrine such as those of Kant and Mill; while the third supports the political conception not as founded on any wider doctrine but rather as in itself sufficient to express political values that, under the reasonably favourable conditions that make a more or less just constitutional democracy possible, normally outweigh whatever other values may oppose them. Observe about this example that only the first two views—the religious doctrine and the liberalism of Kant or Mill—are general and comprehensive. The political conception of justice itself is not; although it does hold that under reasonably favourable

conditions, it is normally adequate for questions of political justice. Observe also that the example assumes that the two comprehensive views agree with the judgments of the political conception in this respect.

To begin with the objection: some will think that even if an overlapping consensus should be sufficiently stable, the idea of political unity founded on an overlapping consensus must still be rejected, since it abandons the hope of political community and settles instead for a public understanding that is at bottom a mere *modus vivendi*. To this objection, we say that the hope of political community must indeed by abandoned, if by such a community we mean a political society united in affirming a general and comprehensive doctrine. This possibility is excluded by the fact of pluralism together with the rejection of the oppressive use of state power to overcome it. I believe there is no practicable alternative superior to the stable political unity secured by an overlapping consensus on a reasonable political conception of justice. Hence the substantive question concerns the significant features of such a consensus and how these features affect social concord and the moral quality of public life. I turn to why an overlapping consensus is not a mere *modus vivendi*.[5]

---

[5] Note that what is impracticable is not *all* values of community (recall that a community is understood as an association or society whose unity rests on a comprehensive conception of the good) but only *political* community and its values. Justice as fairness assumes, as other liberal political views do also, that the values of community are not only essential but realizable, first in the various associations that carry on their life within the framework of the basic structure, and second in those associations that extend across the boundaries of nation-states, such as churches and scientific societies. Liberalism rejects the state as a community because, among other things, it leads to the systematic denial of basic liberties and to the oppressive use of the state's monopoly of (legal) force. I should add that in the well-ordered society of justice as fairness citizens share a common aim, and one that has high priority: namely, the aim of political justice, that is, the aim of ensuring that political and social institutions are just, and of giving justice to persons generally, as what citizens need for themselves and want for one another. It is not true, then, that on a liberal view citizens have no fundamental common aims. Nor is it true that the aim of

A typical use of the phrase *'modus vivendi'* is to characterize a treaty between two states whose national aims and interests put them at odds. In negotiating a treaty each state would be wise and prudent to make sure that the agreement proposed represents an equilibrium point: that is, that the terms and conditions of the treaty are drawn up in such a way that it is public knowledge that it is not advantageous for either state to violate it. The treaty will then be adhered to because doing so is regarded by each as in its national interest, including its interest in its reputation as a state that honours treaties. But in general both states are ready to pursue their goals at the expense of the other, and should conditions change they may do so. This background highlights the way in which a treaty is a mere *modus vivendi*. A similar background is present when we think of social consensus founded on self- or group-interests, or on the outcome of political bargaining: social unity is only apparent as its stability is contingent on circumstances remaining such as not to upset the fortunate convergence of interests.

Now, that an overlapping consensus is quite different from a *modus vivendi* is clear from our model case. In that example, note two aspects: first, the object of consensus, the political conception of justice, is itself a moral conception. And second, it is affirmed on moral grounds, that is, it includes conceptions of society and of citizens as persons, as well as principles of justice, and an account of the cooperative virtues through which those principles are embodied in human character and expressed in public life. An overlapping consensus, therefore, is not merely a consensus on accepting certain authorities, or in complying with certain institutional arrangements, founded on a convergence of self- or group-interests. All

three views in the example affirm the political conception: as I have said, each recognizes its concepts, principles and virtues as the shared content at which their several views coincide. The fact that those who affirm the political conception start from within their own comprehensive view, and hence begin from different premises and grounds, does not make their affirmation any less religious, philosophical or moral, as the case may be. . . .

IV

I turn to the second objection to the idea of an overlapping consensus on a political conception of justice: namely, that the avoidance of general and comprehensive doctrines implies indifference or scepticism as to whether a political conception of justice is true. This avoidance may appear to suggest that such a conception might be the most reasonable one for us even when it is known not to be true, as if truth were simply beside the point. In reply, it would be fatal to the point of a political conception to see it as sceptical about, or indifferent to, truth, much less as in conflict with it. Such scepticism or indifference would put political philosophy in conflict with numerous comprehensive doctrines, and thus defeat from the outset its aim of achieving an overlapping consensus. In following the method of avoidance, as we may call it, we try, so far as we can, neither to assert nor to deny any religious, philosophical or moral views, or their associated philosophical accounts of truth and the status of values. Since we assume each citizen to affirm some such view or other, we hope to make it possible for all to accept the political conception as true, or as reasonable, from the standpoint of their own comprehensive view, whatever it may be.[6]

---

political justice is not an important part of their identity (using the term 'identity', as is now often done, to include the basic aims and projects by reference to which we characterize the kind of person we very much want to be). But this common aim of political justice must not be mistaken for (what I have called) a conception of the good. . . .

---

[6] It is important to see that the view that philosophy in the classical sense as the search for truth about a prior and independent moral order cannot provide the shared basis for a political conception of justice . . .

Properly understood, then, a political conception of justice need be no more indifferent, say, to truth in morals than the principle of toleration, suitably understood, need to be indifferent to truth in religion. We simply apply the principle of toleration to philosophy itself. In this way we hope to avoid philosophy's long-standing controversies, among them controversies about the nature of truth and the status of values as expressed by realism and subjectivism. Since we seek an agreed basis of public justification in matters of justice, and since no political agreement on those disputed questions can reasonably be expected, we turn instead to the fundamental intuitive ideas we seem to share through the public political culture. We try to develop from these ideas a political conception of justice congruent with our considered convictions on due reflection. Just as with religion, citizens situated in thought and belief within their comprehensive doctrines, regard the political conception of justice as true, or as reasonable, whatever the case may be.

Some may not be satisfied with this: they may reply that, despite these protests, a political conception of justice must express indifference or scepticism. Otherwise it could not lay aside fundamental religious, philosophical and moral questions because they are politically difficult to settle, or may prove intractable. Certain truths, it may be said, concern things so important that differences about them have to be fought out, even should this mean civil war. To this we say first, that questions are not removed from the political agenda, so to speak, solely because they are a source of conflict. Rather, we appeal to a political conception of justice to distinguish between those questions that can be reasonably removed from the political agenda and those that cannot, all the while aiming for an overlapping consensus. Some questions still on the agenda will be controversial, at least to some degree; this is normal with political issues.

To illustrate: from within a political conception of justice let's suppose we can account both for equal liberty of conscience, which takes the truths of religion off the political agenda, and the equal political and civil liberties, which by ruling out serfdom and slavery takes the possibility of those institutions off the agenda.[7] But controversial issues inevitably remain: for example, how more exactly to draw the boundaries of the basic liberties when they conflict (where to set 'the wall between church and state'); how to interpret the requirements of distributive justice even when there is considerable agreement on general principles for the basic structure; and finally, questions of policy such as the use of nuclear weapons. These cannot be removed from politics. But by avoiding comprehensive doctrines we try to bypass religion and philosophy's profound-

---

does not presuppose the controversial metaphysical claim that there is no such order. The above paragraph makes clear why it does not. The reasons I give for that view are historical and sociological, and have nothing to do with metaphysical doctrines about the status of values. What I hold is that we must draw the obvious lessons of our political history since the Reformation and the Wars of Religion, and the development of modern constitutional democracies. As I say in Sec I above, it is no longer reasonable to expect us to reach *political* agreement on a general and comprehensive doctrine as a way of reaching political agreement on constitutional essentials, unless, of course, we are prepared to use the apparatus of the state as an instrument of oppression. If we are not prepared to do that, we must, as a practical matter, look for what I have called a political conception of justice.

[7] To explain: when certain matters are taken off the political agenda, they are no longer regarded as proper subjects for political decision by majority or other plurality voting. In regard to equal liberty of conscience and rejection of slavery and serfdom, this means that the equal basic liberties in the constitution that cover these matters are taken as fixed, settled once and for all. They are part of the public charter of a constitutional regime and not a suitable topic for on-going public debate and legislation, as if they can be changed at any time, one way or the other. Moreover, the more established political parties likewise acknowledge these matters as settled. Of course, that certain matters are taken off the political agenda does not mean that a political conception of justice should not explain why this is done. Indeed, as I note above, a political conception should do precisely this. For thinking of basic rights and liberties as taking certain questions off the political agenda I am indebted to Stephen Holmes.

est controversies so as to have some hope of uncovering a basis of a stable overlapping consensus.

Nevertheless in affirming a political conception of justice we may eventually have to assert at least certain aspects of our own comprehensive (by no means necessarily fully comprehensive) religious or philosophical doctrine. This happens whenever someone insists, for example, that certain questions are so fundamental that to ensure their being rightly settled justifies civil strife. The religious salvation of those holding a particular religion, or indeed the salvation of a whole people, may be said to depend on it. At this point we may have no alternative but to deny this, and to assert the kind of thing we had hoped to avoid. But the aspects of our view that we assert should not go beyond what is necessary for the political aim of consensus. Thus, for example, we may assert in some form the doctrine of free religious faith that supports equal liberty of conscience; and given the existence of a just constitutional regime, we deny that the concern for salvation requires anything incompatible with that liberty. We do not state more of our comprehensive view than we think would advance the quest for consensus. . . .

V

A third objection is the following: even if we grant that an overlapping consensus is not a *modus vivendi*, it may be said that a workable political conception must be general and comprehensive. Without such a doctrine on hand, there is no way to order the many conflicts of justice that arise in public life. The idea is that the deeper the conceptual and philosophical bases of those conflicts, the more general and comprehensive the level of philosophical reflection must be if their roots are to be laid bare and an appropriate ordering found. It is useless, the objection concludes, to try to work out a political conception of justice expressly for the basic structure apart from any comprehen-

sive doctrine. And as we have just seen, we may be forced to refer, at least in some way, to such a view.[8]

This objection is perfectly natural: we are indeed tempted to ask how else could these conflicting claims be adjudicated. Yet part of the answer is found in the third view of our model case: namely, a political conception of justice regarded not as a consequence of a comprehensive doctrine but as in itself sufficient to express values that normally outweigh whatever other values oppose them, at least under the reasonably favourable conditions that make a constitutional democracy possible. Here the criterion of a just regime is specified by that political conception; and the values in question are seen from its principles and standards, and from its account of the cooperative virtues of political justice, and the like. Those who hold this conception have, of course, other views as well, views that specify values and virtues belonging to other parts of life; they differ from citizens holding the two other views in our example of an overlapping consensus in having no fully (as opposed to partially) comprehensive doctrine within which they see all values and virtues as being ordered. They don't say such a doctrine is impossible, but rather practically speaking unnecessary. Their conviction is that, within the scope allowed by the basic liberties and the other provi-

---

[8] It is essential to distinguish between general and comprehensive views and views we think of as abstract. Thus, when justice as fairness begins from the fundamental intuitive idea of society as a fair system of cooperation and proceeds to elaborate that idea, the resulting conception of political justice may be said to be abstract. It is abstract in the same way that the conception of a perfectly competitive market, or of general economic equilibrium, is abstract: that is, it singles out, or focuses on, certain aspects of society as especially significant from the standpoint of political justice and leaves others aside. But whether the conception that results itself is general and comprehensive, as I have used those terms, is a separate question. I believe the conflicts implicit in the fact of pluralism force political philosophy to present conceptions of justice that are abstract, if it is to achieve its aims; but the same conflicts prevent those conceptions from being general and comprehensive.

sions of a just constitution, all citizens can pursue their way of life on fair terms and properly respect its (non-public) values. So long as those constitutional guarantees are secure, they think no conflict of values is likely to arise that would justify their opposing the political conception as a whole, or on such fundamental matters as liberty of conscience, or equal political liberties, or basic civil rights, and the like.

Those holding this partially comprehensive view might explain it as follows. We should not assume that there exist reasonable and generally acceptable answers for all or even for many questions of political justice that might be asked. Rather, we must be prepared to accept the fact that only a few such questions can be satisfactorily resolved. Political wisdom consists in identifying those few, and among them the most urgent. That done, we must frame the institutions of the basic structure so that intractable conflicts are unlikely to arise; we must also accept the need for clear and simple principles, the general form and content of which we hope can be publicly understood. A political conception is at best but a guiding framework of deliberation and reflection which helps us reach political agreement on at least the constitutional essentials. If it seems to have cleared our view and made our considered convictions more coherent; if it has narrowed the gap between the conscientious convictions of those who accept the basic ideas of a constitutional regime, then it has served its practical political purpose. And this remains true even though we can't fully explain our agreement: we know only that citizens who affirm the political conception, and who have been raised in and are familiar with the fundamental ideas of the public political culture, find that, when they adopt its framework of deliberation, their judgments converge sufficiently so that political cooperation on the basis of mutual respect can be maintained. They view the political conception as itself normally sufficient and may not expect, or think they need, greater political understanding than that.

But here we are bound to ask: how can a political conception of justice express values that, under the reasonably favourable conditions that make democracy possible, normally outweigh whatever other values conflict with them? One way is this. As I have said, the most reasonable political conception of justice for a democratic regime will be, broadly speaking, liberal. But this means, as I will explain in the next section, that it protects the familiar basic rights and assigns them a special priority; it also includes measures to ensure that all persons in society have sufficient material means to make effective use of those basic rights. Faced with the fact of pluralism, a liberal view removes from the political agenda the most divisive issues, pervasive uncertainty and serious contention about which must undermine the bases of social cooperation.

The virtues of political cooperation that make a constitutional regime possible are, then, *very great* virtues. I mean, for example, the virtues of tolerance and being ready to meet others halfway, and the virtue of reasonableness and the sense of fairness. When these virtues (together with the modes of thought and sentiments they involve) are widespread in society and sustain its political conception of justice, they constitute a very great public good, part of society's political capital.[9] Thus, the values that conflict with the political conception of justice and its sustaining virtues may be normally outweighed because they come into conflict with the very conditions that make fair social cooperation possible on a footing of mutual respect.

Moreover, conflicts with political values are much reduced when the political conception is supported by an overlapping consensus, the more so the more inclusive the consensus. For in this case the political conception is not viewed as incompatible with

---

[9] The term 'capital' is appropriate and familiar in this connection because these virtues are built up slowly over time and depend not only on existing political and social institutions (themselves slowly built up), but also on citizens' experience as a whole and their knowledge of the past. Again, like capital, these virtues depreciate, as it were, and must be constantly renewed by being reaffirmed and acted from in the present.

basic religious, philosophical and moral values. We avoid having to consider the claims of the political conception of justice against those of this or that comprehensive view; nor need we say that political values are intrinsically more important than other values and that's why the latter are overridden. Indeed, saying that is the kind of thing we hope to avoid, and achieving an overlapping consensus enables us to avoid it.

To conclude: given the fact of pluralism, what does the work of reconciliation by free public reason, and thus enables us to avoid reliance on general and comprehensive doctrines, is two things: first, identifying the fundamental role of political values in expressing the terms of fair social cooperation consistent with mutual respect between citizens regarded as free and equal; and second, uncovering a sufficiently inclusive concordant fit among political and other values as displayed in an overlapping consensus.

VI

The last difficulty I shall consider is that the idea of an overlapping consensus is utopian; that is, there are not sufficient political, social, or psychological forces either to bring about an overlapping consensus (when one does not exist), or to render one stable (should one exist). . . .

Now let's suppose that at a certain time, as a result of various historical events and contingencies, the principles of a liberal conception have come to be accepted as a mere *modus vivendi,* and that existing political institutions meet their requirements. This acceptance has come about, we may assume, in much the same way as the acceptance of the principle of toleration as a *modus vivendi* came about following the Reformation: at first reluctantly, but nevertheless, as providing the only alternative to endless and destructive civil strife. Our question, then, is this: how might it happen that over generations the initial acquiescence in a liberal conception of justice as a *modus vivendi* develops into a stable and en-

during overlapping consensus? In this connection I think a certain looseness in our comprehensive views, as well as their not being fully comprehensive, may be particularly significant. To see this, let's return to our model case.

One way in which that example is atypical is that two of the three doctrines were described as fully general and comprehensive, a religious doctrine of free faith and the comprehensive liberalism of Kant or Mill. In these cases the acceptance of the political conception was said to be derived from and to depend solely on the comprehensive doctrine. But how far in practice does the allegiance to a political conception actually depend on its derivation from a comprehensive view? There are several possibilities. For simplicity distinguish three cases: the political conception is derived from the comprehensive doctrine; it is not derived from but is compatible with that doctrine; and last, the political conception is incompatible with it. In everyday life we have not usually decided, or even thought much about, which of these cases hold. To decide among them would raise highly complicated issues; and it is not clear that we need to decide among them. Most people's religious, philosophical and moral doctrines are not seen by them as fully general and comprehensive, and these aspects admit of variations of degree. There is lots of slippage, so to speak, many ways for the political conception to cohere loosely with those (partially) comprehensive views, and many ways within the limits of a political conception of justice to allow for the pursuit of different (partially) comprehensive doctrines. This suggests that many if not most citizens come to affirm their common political conception without seeing any particular connection, one way or the other, between it and their other views. Hence it is possible for them first to affirm the political conception and to appreciate the public good it accomplishes in a democratic society. Should an incompatibility later be recognized between the political conception and their wider doctrines, then they might very well adjust or revise these doctrines rather than reject the political conception.

At this point we ask: in virtue of what political values might a liberal conception of justice gain an allegiance to itself? An allegiance to institutions and to the conception that regulates them may, of course, be based in part on long-term self- and group-interests, custom and traditional attitudes, or simply on the desire to conform to what is expected and normally done. . . .

Now when a liberal conception effectively regulates basic political institutions, it meets three essential requirements of a stable constitutional regime. First, given the fact of pluralism—the fact that necessitates a liberal regime as a *modus vivendi* in the first place—a liberal conception meets the urgent political requirement to fix, once and for all, the content of basic rights and liberties, and to assign them special priority. Doing this takes those guarantees off the political agenda and puts them beyond the calculus of social interests, thereby establishing clearly and firmly the terms of social cooperation on a footing of mutual respect. To regard that calculus as relevant in these matters leaves the status and content of those rights and liberties still unsettled; it subjects them to the shifting circumstances of time and place, and by greatly raising the stakes of political controversy, dangerously increases the insecurity and hostility of public life. Thus, the unwillingness to take these matters off the agenda perpetuates the deep divisions latent in society; it betrays a readiness to revive those antagonisms in the hope of gaining a more favourable position should later circumstances prove propitious. So, by contrast, securing the basic liberties and recognizing their priority achieves the work of reconciliation and seals mutual acceptance on a footing of equality.

The second requirement is connected with a liberal conception's idea of free public reason. It is highly desirable that the form of reasoning a conception specifies should be, and can publicly be seen to be, correct and reasonably reliable in its own terms.[10] A liberal conception tries to meet these desiderata in several ways. As we have seen, in working out a political conception of justice it starts from fundamental intuitive ideas latent in the shared public culture; it detaches political values from any particular comprehensive and sectarian (non-public) doctrine; and it tires to limit that conception's scope to matters of political justice (the basic structure and its social policies). Further, (as we saw in Sec II) it recognizes that an agreement on a political conception of justice is to no effect without a companion agreement on guidelines of public enquiry and rules for assessing evidence. Given the fact of pluralism, these guidelines and rules must be specified by reference to the forms of reasoning available to common sense, and by the procedures and conclusions of science when not controversial. The role of these shared methods and this common knowledge in applying the political conception makes reason *public;* the protection given to freedom of speech and thought makes it *free.* The claims of religion and philosophy (as previously emphasized) are not excluded out of scepticism or indifference, but as a condition of establishing a shared basis for free public reason.

A liberal conception's idea of public reason also has a certain simplicity. To illustrate: even if general and comprehensive teleological conceptions were acceptable as political conceptions of justice, the form of public reasoning they specify would be politically unworkable. For if the elaborate theoretical calculations involved in applying their principles are publicly admitted in questions of political justice (consider, for example, what is involved in applying the principle of utility to the basic structure),

---

[10] Here the phrase 'in its own terms' means that we are not at present concerned with whether the conception in question is true, or reasonable (as the case may be), but with how easily its principles and standards can be correctly understood and reliably applied in public discussion.

the highly speculative nature and enormous complexity of these calculations are bound to make citizens with conflicting interests highly suspicious of one another's arguments. The information they presuppose is very hard if not impossible to obtain, and often there are insuperable problems in reaching an objective and agreed assessment. Moreover, even though we think our arguments sincere and not self-serving when we present them, we must consider what it is reasonable to expect others to think who stand to lose when our reasoning prevails. Arguments supporting political judgments should, if possible, not only be sound but such that they can be publicly seen to be sound The maxim that justice must not only be done, but be seen to be done, holds good not only in law but in free public reason.

The third requirement met by a liberal conception is related to the preceding ones. The basic institutions enjoined by such a conception, and its conception of free public reason—when effectively working over time—encourage the cooperative virtues of political life: the virtue of reasonableness and a sense of fairness, a spirit of compromise and a readiness to meet others halfway, all of which are connected with the willingness if not the desire to cooperate with others on political terms that everyone can publicly accept consistent with mutual respect. Political liberalism tests principles and orders institutions with an eye to their influence on the moral quality of public life, on the civic virtues and habits of mind their public recognition tends to foster, and which are needed to sustain a stable constitutional regime. This requirement is related to the preceding two in this way. when the terms of social cooperation are settled on a footing of mutual respect by fixing once and for all the basic liberties and opportunities with their priority, and when this fact itself is publicly recognized, there is a tendency for the essential cooperative virtues to develop. And this tendency is further strengthened by successful conduct of free public reason in arriving at what are regarded as just policies and fair understandings.

The three requirements met by a liberal conception are evident in the fundamental structural features of the public world it realizes, and in its effects on citizens' political character, a character that takes the basic rights and liberties for granted and disciplines its deliberations in accordance with the guidelines of free public reason. A political conception of justice (liberal or otherwise) specifies the form of a social world—a background framework within which the life of associations, groups and individual citizens proceeds. Inside that framework a working consensus may often be secured by a convergence of self- or group-interests; but to secure stability that framework must be honoured and seen as fixed by the political conception, itself affirmed on moral grounds.

The conjecture, then, is that as citizens come to appreciate what a liberal conception does, they acquire an allegiance to it, an allegiance that becomes stronger over time. They come to think it both reasonable and wise for them to confirm their allegiance to its principles of justice as expressing values that, under the reasonably favourable conditions that make democracy possible, normally counterbalance whatever values may oppose them. With this an overlapping consensus is achieved. . . .

VII

I conclude by commenting briefly on what I have called political liberalism. We have seen that this view steers a course between the Hobbesian strand in liberalism—liberalism as a *modus vivendi* secured by a convergence of self- and group-interests as coordinated and balanced by well-designed constitutional arrangements—and a liberalism founded on a comprehensive moral doctrine such as that of Kant or Mill. By itself, the former cannot secure an enduring social unity, the latter cannot gain sufficient agreement. Political liberalism is represented in our model case of an overlapping consensus by the third view once we take the political conception in question as liberal. So understood political liberalism is the view that under the reasonably favourable conditions that make constitutional democracy possible, political institutions satisfying the principles of a liberal conception of justice realize political values and ideals that normally outweigh whatever other values oppose them.

Political liberalism must deal with two basic objections: one is the charge of scepticism and indifference, the other that it cannot gain sufficient support to assure compliance with its principles of justice. Both of these objections are answered by finding a reasonable liberal conception of justice that can be supported by an overlapping consensus. For such a consensus achieves compliance by a concordant fit between the political conception and general and comprehensive doctrines together with the public recognition of the very great value of the political virtues. But as we saw, success in finding an overlapping consensus forces political philosophy to be, so far as possible, independent of and autonomous from other parts of philosophy, especially from philosophy's long-standing problems and controversies. And this in turn gives rise to the objection that political liberalism is sceptical of religious and philosophical truth, or indifferent to their values. But if we relate the nature of a political conception to the fact of pluralism and with what is essential for a shared basis of free public reason, this objection is seen to be mistaken. We can also note (see the end of Sec IV) how political philosophy's independence and autonomy from other parts of philosophy connects with the freedom and autonomy of democratic citizenship.

Some may think that to secure stable social unity in a constitutional regime by looking for an overlapping consensus detaches political philosophy from philosophy and makes it into politics. Yes and no: the politician, we say, looks to the next election, the statesman to the next generation, and philosophy to the indefinite future. Philosophy sees the political world as an on-going system of cooperation over time, in perpetuity practically speaking. Political philosophy is related to politics because it must be concerned, as moral philosophy need not be, with practical political possibilities. This has led us to outline, for example, how it is possible for the deep divisions present in a pluralistic society to be reconciled through a political conception of justice that gradually over generations becomes the focus of an overlapping consensus. Moreover, this concern with practical possibility compels political philosophy to consider fundamental institutional questions and the assumptions of a reasonable moral psychology.

Thus political philosophy is not mere politics: in addressing the public culture it takes the longest view, looks to society's permanent historical and social conditions, and tries to mediate society's deepest conflicts. It hopes to uncover, and to help to articulate, a shared basis of consensus on a political conception of justice drawing upon citizens' fundamental intuitive ideas about their society and their place in it. In exhibiting the possibility of an overlapping consensus in a society with a democratic tradition confronted by the fact of pluralism, political philosophy assumes the role Kant gave to philosophy generally: the defence of reasonable faith. In our case this becomes the defence of reasonable faith in the real possibility of a just constitutional regime.